Pete)

To a good Friend and

great co-worker! enjoy the

Book,

Todd Jones

2/2/05

Publisher	John Wait
Editor-in-Chief	John Kane
Executive Editor	Jim Schachterle
Cisco Representative	Anthony Wolfenden
Cisco Press Program Manager	Nannette M. Noble
Acquisitions Editor	Amy Moss
Production Manager	Patrick Kanouse
Senior Development Editor	Christopher Cleveland
Development Editor	Jennifer Foster
Project Editor	Ginny Bess Munroe
Copy Editors	Krista Hansing,
	Laura Williams
Technical Editors	Jody Carbone,
	Christopher Gulley,
	Jeff Schlesser,
	Markus Schneider
Team Coordinator	Tammi Barnett
Cover Designer	Louisa Adair
Composition	Octal Publishing, Inc.
Indexer	Julie Bess

CISCO SYSTEMS

Corporate Headquarters
Cisco Systems, Inc.
170 West Tasman Drive
San Jose, CA 95134-1706
USA
www.cisco.com
Tel: 408 526-4000
 800 553-NETS (6387)
Fax: 408 526-4100

European Headquarters
Cisco Systems International BV
Haarlerbergpark
Haarlerbergweg 13-19
1101 CH Amsterdam
The Netherlands
www-europe.cisco.com
Tel: 31 0 20 357 1000
Fax: 31 0 20 357 1100

Americas Headquarters
Cisco Systems, Inc.
170 West Tasman Drive
San Jose, CA 95134-1706
USA
www.cisco.com
Tel: 408 526-7660
Fax: 408 527-0883

Asia Pacific Headquarters
Cisco Systems, Inc.
Capital Tower
168 Robinson Road
#22-01 to #29-01
Singapore 068912
www.cisco.com
Tel: +65 6317 7777
Fax: +65 6317 7799

Cisco Systems has more than 200 offices in the following countries and regions. Addresses, phone numbers, and fax numbers are listed on the
Cisco.com Web site at www.cisco.com/go/offices.

Argentina • Australia • Austria • Belgium • Brazil • Bulgaria • Canada • Chile • China PRC • Colombia • Costa Rica • Croatia • Czech Republic
Denmark • Dubai, UAE • Finland • France • Germany • Greece • Hong Kong SAR • Hungary • India • Indonesia • Ireland • Israel • Italy
Japan • Korea • Luxembourg • Malaysia • Mexico • The Netherlands • New Zealand • Norway • Peru • Philippines • Poland • Portugal
Puerto Rico • Romania • Russia • Saudi Arabia • Scotland • Singapore • Slovakia • Slovenia • South Africa • Spain • Sweden
Switzerland • Taiwan • Thailand • Turkey • Ukraine • United Kingdom • United States • Venezuela • Vietnam • Zimbabwe

About the Authors

Todd Stone is a technical marketing engineer at the ECS business unit of Cisco, the makers of Unity. Todd's career spans more than 17 years in the computer industry, including an initial stint in the U.S. Army as a tech controller at a fixed communications station near Washington, D.C. Todd attended Northern Kentucky University and holds various technical certifications. His background includes telecommunications, voice systems, and data communications management and design; large-scale server and infrastructure-deployment projects; and administration and management with various directories and messaging systems. Todd also has been heavily engaged in various other design- and deployment-oriented activities.

Todd was hired by Active Voice as a network engineer in its QA department just before the release of Unity 1.0 (limited release); he joined Cisco when it acquired Active Voice in 2001. He recently became a technical marketing engineer for the same business unit after spending five years in QA and Development. Todd and his wife Michelle have three children: Brandyn, Sarah, and Colin. They live in a small town located on the Kitsap Peninsula on the western side of Puget Sound in Washington.

Dustin Grant, CCIE No. 5803, is a senior escalation engineer in the Technical Assistance Center. Dustin has been with Cisco for five years, during which time he has acquired three CCIEs (Routing and Switching, ISP-Dial, and Voice). He is also a coauthor of the CCIE Voice written and lab exams. Dustin enjoys learning, traveling, and driving fast.

Jeff Lindborg received his bachelor of science in computer science from the University of Washington in 1991. He then worked for Active Voice for more than ten years as a QA engineer, team lead, program manager, and technical lead and developer in the engineering group that designed and built the first versions of Unity. Jeff continues to work in and around the Unity product line in the ESC business unit at Cisco as a technical leader for the Customer Applications Team. When he is not injuring himself in amusing home-improvement accidents, he can be found monitoring the Unified Communications forum and maintaining the www.ciscounitytools.com website. Jeff and his wife Heidi live in Seattle, Washington.

Steve Olivier entered the software industry after an illustrious five-year stint in the coffee industry. He is currently a software engineer and the team lead for the CPR (Critical Problem Resolution) team at the ECS business unit of Cisco. Steve joined Active Voice in 1998 as a technical support engineer and transitioned into the Development group as a PBX integration engineer. Steve holds a few Cisco and Microsoft certifications. When Steve is not looking at memory dumps or debugging Unity code, he and his wife Uli usually chase after their two children, Evan and Ivy. Steve and his family live in Seattle, Washington, not too far from Mr. Lindborg.

About the Contributing Authors

Joseph (Jody) Carbone is a network consulting engineer who works for the World Wide Voice Practice in Cisco Advanced Services. Jody's Cisco experience began five years ago. In that time, he has worked in several roles, supporting voice and messaging solutions with field implementations, technical support, and enablement activities for Cisco partners. One of his roles in the WWVP consists of identifying and creating leading practices for enterprise voice products and solutions, contributing to the partner portal Steps to Success. Jody has been in information technology for more than 20 years and has several Cisco and Microsoft certifications.

Keith Chambers is a senior escalation engineer in the Technical Assistance Center in Seattle, Washington. He has been with Cisco for four years. Before that, Keith was a network engineer for Saltmine, the first customer to have Cisco CallManager and Active Voice Unity integrated. He has a passion for technology and customer success, which drives him to improve Unity. Outside of work, Keith is a progressive trance DJ. He also enjoys volunteering and contributing to the Leukemia & Lymphoma Society. All proceeds that Keith earns from this book will be donated to the Leukemia & Lymphoma Society.

Shane Lisenbea is a technical marketing engineer in the Enterprise Communication Software Business Unit. Shane has been with Cisco for three years. Before coming to Cisco, he was with Active Voice, which originally developed the Unity product. Shane also has more than 14 years of experience in the telephony and voice messaging industry. When he is not traveling and spreading the love of Unity, Shane loves spending quality time with his son, "Little Shane," and dancing.

Michael McCann is a quality assurance engineer in the Enterprise Communications Software Business Unit at Cisco. He has been with Cisco for three years. He previously worked for Active Voice Corporation, starting in 1998. Mike has been working with Unity since the early days, before its first release, so he has had the opportunity to work with most areas of the product. Mike graduated from the University of Notre Dame with a degree in physics in 1997 and then spent a year volunteering as a teacher in Chicago through the Capuchin Franciscan Volunteer Corp. An avid baseball fan, Mike also enjoys skiing and playing soccer and tennis.

Toby Young is a test engineer for Cisco Systems in the Enterprise Communications Business Unit, the business unit responsible for developing the Unity product. He spent just over one year with Active Voice Corporation testing the Unity product before Cisco Systems acquired Active Voice. He has been with Cisco System for three years and still tests Unity. Toby holds a Ph.D. in analytical chemistry from the University of Washington, where he learned the proper methodology for conducting research and designing experiments. After graduate school, his focus changed from conducting experiments on chemicals to conducting experiments on software. Outside of testing, Toby is an avid climber and active member of the Washington Alpine Club. He lives in Seattle, Washington, and spends his weekends climbing in the Cascade Mountains.

About the Technical Reviewers

Christopher Gulley works as a software engineer at Cisco Systems, Inc. He contributed to the earliest versions of Unity as a software quality assurance engineer. Later, as a software engineer, he was responsible for software that integrates Unity with Microsoft Active Directory and Microsoft Exchange. Christopher currently works on Cisco Unity Express. He holds a bachelor of science in computer science from the University of Texas at Dallas.

Jeff Schlesser is a customer support engineer with Cisco TAC, where he serves as a technical lead for the San Jose–based team. His responsibilities include training TAC engineers and serving as a worldwide escalation. He assisted with creating the Unity Bootcamp, used to train Cisco partners and customers worldwide. Jeff works closely with the Unity development team to provide feedback on serviceability and troubleshooting tools. He has been at Cisco for more than three years and has worked in the networking/telecom industry for more than seven years. He holds numerous certifications from Microsoft and Cisco.

Markus Schneider, CCIE No. 2863, is a diagnostic engineer for the Cisco Advanced Engineering Services in Research Triangle Park, North Carolina. He is responsible for helping Cisco customers design, implement, and troubleshoot IP Telephony solutions in their environment. He works closely with the Cisco development and TAC support teams to provide support for a variety of products and technologies. He has workied for Cisco as a network engineer for more than seven years.

Dedications

Todd Stone: To my wife, Michelle, for her patience and unending support: Michelle, I couldn't have done this without you. And for my kids, who have had to learn patience during this whole process and who have continuously reminded me how important it is for me to finish this book. And yes, now that we are done, we can go fishing. I know we also have a ton of little projects waiting to be worked! I dedicate this book to all of you: Michelle, Brandyn, Sarah, and Colin. You are my life, and you are the greatest!

Dustin Grant: To my parents, for making me into the person I am today, trusting my instincts and abilities, and being great parents who are actually fun to spend time with. To my Princess, for giving me someone to love. To the greatest group of friends: Tron, Nikko, BDA, Bull, Matty, Rusty, and Krafty—thanks for all the adventures. And last but not least, to my brothers and sisters: Holly, Paul, Laura, Stephanie, and Travis, as well as Otis and Peaches.

Jeff Lindborg: I'd first like to thank my parents for not having me institutionalized or sent to military school during my youth, even when it was apparent to everyone that this was the appropriate course of action. Thanks for always being supportive, Mom and Dad. I'd also like to thank my wife Heidi. From her steady hand on the compound miter saw to being able to explain biology and chemistry to me in small words, she continues to improve the quality of my life in many ways. I love you.

Steve Olivier: To all of my family (Uli, Evan, Ivy, Mom, Dad, Kevin, Sybille, Klaus, and Susi) for the encouragement and support while writing of this book. We can finally say, "Yes, we're done now." You all have always been supportive of me throughout my career, and to you all, I dedicate my work in this book.

Acknowledgments

Todd Stone: Working for more than 17 years in the high-tech computer industry has made me feel like I've been on a long-lost journey just to get back home. (But am I home yet?) Throughout my travels, and even from the start, I've had the privilege to meet some of the most effective and knowledgeable people in the various jobs I've held—people who have encouraged me and supported me and taught me how to make technology work, not how it was supposed to, but how we needed it to. The most influential people to me are Sgt. (ret.) Thomas Wilson and Carl Bishop from the Army days; Dan Goetz and John Meditz from the airline days and, afterward, from the computer reseller days and public sector days; and, most important, Dave Hickey (first as my customer and then as my manager), who not only influenced me by teaching me the business, but who also inspired me to strive for excellence like no one else. I won't say that Dave made me who I am because I don't think he would stop laughing at me if I did, but he has been a positive influence in my career and an absolutely wonderful person to work for. Dave, thank you for teaching me and being such a positive influence on me—and thank you also for your friendship over the years.

Since I've been with Active Voice and Cisco, there are several people I'd like to thank, starting with Vibhavaree Gargeya, who hired me and supports me even to this day. I would also like to thank Joe Burton, Mark Jancola, Ed Masters, Kevin Chestnut, Cleo Raulerson, Dan Albaum, Tom Wesselman, John Elder, Anil Verma, Sridhar Gaddipati, Tim Fujita-Yuhas, and Ty Thorsen for their help and support during my stay.

For those who have helped out in some way with this book, large or small: Thanks to the main authors, Jeff Lindborg, Dustin Grant, Steve Olivier: There is simply no way that I could have done this without you guys being there and taking on a significant part of the effort—especially Jeff Lindborg). Thanks also to the contributing authors: Mike McCann, Toby Young, Shane Lisenbea, Keith Chambers, and Jody Carbone: Thanks, guys, for bailing me out. And thanks to the technical reviewers, Chris Gulley, Markus Schnieder, Jeff Schlesser, and Jody again: You guys are hard-core, and it was great to have you review what we wrote and help us focus what we attempted to convey in our writings. I would also like to thank Pete Hansen, who helped out with Chapter 10, and Lin Chang; we modified a few of her original Unity diagrams for Chapter 13. Then Murray Mar and Deepayan Acharjya helped square me away on Chapter 4, which was sorely needed.

To Sandra Cole and Dave Cronberger, who both helped me in ways they don't even know about (pertaining to Unity, of course—they inspired me to write this book). And finally, a special thanks to my current manager, Dave Oss. Dave, your support in this project has been beyond expectation, and I truly thank you for being there and helping me out along the way. Thanks for letting me work for you, too! And last but not least, I'd like to thank my fellow TMEs, Frank Nobili (we are always arguably agreeable), Pete Hansen (no, Pete, I don't have "softie" phone yet), Shane Lisenbea (my "bro"), and Michael Lewandowski—you guys rock!

Dustin Grant: I would like to thank Paul Lukan and Marty Martinez for giving me the time to work on this book; Raja Sundaram, for giving a kid off the street a chance; Andrew Maximow, Keith Stewart, and Marla Chikhani, for always being there to give advice; and all of my co-workers over the years for helping me learn and build the skill sets that I have today.

Jeff Lindborg: I've worked with some fantastic people in the last 13 years in this business, and there are many more people to acknowledge here than would fit on a page. However, I'd specifically like to thank my manager Ty Thorsen for giving me all the latitude an employee could ever hope for, and for protecting me from myself, when necessary. I'd also like to thank Brad Degrazia, the best skunk works developer on the West Coast, who has pulled off some fantastic saves on this project over the years. Of course, I'd like to thank my fellow Customer Applications Team developers, Sean Milligan and Ken Wiebe, for doing such a great job on the wide variety of weird things that get tossed their way and doing all those ugly tasks for me that make my brain hurt. Finally, I'd like to thank my long-suffering QA lead, Kelley Rogers, who quietly does an outstanding job laboring to protect the innocent masses from my less polished efforts.

Steve Olivier: I'd like to thank Todd Stone and Jeff Lindborg for the opportunity to participate in the writing of this book. I'd like to thank the folks at Active Voice for hiring a coffee jerk. I've had the chance to work with some outstanding engineers and managers throughout my days at Active Voice and Cisco, and the thank you list could go on and on. For some of the engineers I've been blessed to work with, I'd like to thank Murray Mar, not only for being the nicest guy I know, but also for knowing so much and teaching me so much about Unity code. I'd also like to thank Chris Gulley for his assistance with this book and all of the help he gave me on the job (I remember Chris patiently showing me how to set up the debugger). I thank Erich Von Normann and Aaron Belcher (two positively incredible engineers) for not cringing every time I stopped by to ask questions. For all of the other members of the Unity CPR (Critical Problem Resolution) team for all their hard work and dedication, I thank you. Oh yeah, and those managers. . . . I'd like to thank Jami Stewart for excellent leadership during my days in Tech Support. I'd like to also thank Darren Massey and Sridhar Gaddipati for the encouragement and development support they provided for me and other CPR team members.

Contents at a Glance

Foreword   xxxvi

Introduction   xxxviii

Part I   **Concepts and Architecture   3**

Chapter 1   About Unified Messaging   5

Chapter 2   Unity Architecture Overview   31

Chapter 3   Components and Subsystems: Object Model   83

Chapter 4   Components and Subsystems: Directory   135

Chapter 5   Components and Subsystems: Messaging/Unity Message Repository   173

Chapter 6   Components and Subsystems: Telephony Services   205

Chapter 7   Components and Subsystems: Features   225

Part II   **Deployment   271**

Chapter 8   Deployment Methodology   273

Chapter 9   Planning   283

Chapter 10 Typical Configurations and Deployment Models   311

Chapter 11 Designing a Unity Solution   377

Chapter 12 Unity Networking   413

Chapter 13 Unity with Microsoft Exchange   461

Chapter 14 Unity with Lotus Domino   527

Chapter 15 Upgrades and Migrations   567

Chapter 16 Installation   585

Chapter 17 Unity Telephony Integration   601

Part III   **Solutions, Systems Management, and Administration** **663**

Chapter 18   Audio-Text Applications 665

Chapter 19   Administering Multiple Unity Servers 755

Chapter 20   Subscriber Administration 769

Chapter 21   Administering Unity Programmatically 817

Chapter 22   Third-Party Tools and Applications 909

Chapter 23   The Future of Unity 915

Appendix A   Switch File Settings 917

Index 927

Table of Contents

Foreword   xxxvi

Introduction   xxxviii

Part I   Concepts and Architecture   3

Chapter 1   About Unified Messaging   5

The Evolution of Unified Messaging   5

Unity as a Pure UM Product   7
  Unity Messaging Repository   9
  Comparison of Unified and Integrated Messaging   10

Challenges with Unified Messaging in an Organization   11
  Who Manages the Messaging Topology?   12
  Managing Perception Issues When Combining Voice Mail with E-mail   14
  Usage and New Security Issues   17
    Privacy and Confidentiality in Voice Messaging Across an E-mail
    Enterprise   17
    Privacy and Confidentiality in Text to Speech of E-mail Through the
    Telephone   18
    Encrypted Messages, Encrypted Calls   19
  Storing Voice Messages   19
    Remote Users, End Users, and Accessibility   20
    Voice Mail and UM Coexistence   22
    Integrating Fax   23
  Solutions and Deployment   23
    Cross-Departmental Participation   23
  Adapting the User Community to Unified Messaging   24
    Training   24
    Easing in Features Over Time   24
    Changes in End-User Behavior (the Turnpike Effect)   25
  Administrative, Management, and Help Desk Considerations   26

Messaging Technologies   27
  Unity's Messaging Technology   27
  The MAPI Profile and System Mailbox   27

Integration Technologies   27

Summary   28

Chapter 2   Unity Architecture Overview   31

System Architecture   32

AVCsGateway   34

AVCsMgr   34
Data Object Hierarchy   35
Resource Manager   36
Arbiter   36
Ruler   37
Unity Messaging Repository   37
TUI Applications   38
Log Manager   40
Media Interface Unit   42
Telephone Application Programming Interface   42
Integration   43
Session Initiation Protocol   43
UnityAVWAVE   44
Virtual Queue   44
RDBSvr   44
Telephone Record and Playback Connection Server   44
DOHMMSvr   45
AVWM   45

AVNotificationMgr   46
Notifier   46
Notification Queue   47

AVMsgStoreMonitorSvr   47

Directory Monitor   49
Exchange 5.5   50
Exchange 2000/2003   51
Domino   52

AVDirChangeWriter   52

AVSQLSynchSvr   53

AVLic   53

AVRepDirSvrSvc   54

CSEMSSvc   55

AVMMProxySvr   55

AVTTSSvc   56

CSBridgeConnector   56

AVCsNodeMgr   57

TomCat   58

Component Walkthroughs   59
　Outside Caller Leaves a Message   59
　Change to Mail User in Directory   72
　Administrator Updates Subscriber in SA   77

Summary   80

Chapter 3   Components and Subsystems: Object Model   83

Applications   85

Call Handlers   85
　AVP_CONTACT_RULES   87
　AVP_MENU_ENTRIES   87
　AVP_MESSAGING_RULES   87
　AVP_ADMINISTRATOR_OBJECT_ID   89
　AVP_RECIPIENT_OBJECT_ID   90
　AVP_LOCATION_OBJECT_ID   91
　AVP_AFTER_MESSAGE_ACTION,
　AVP_AFTERMESSAGE_CONVERSATION, and
　AVP_AFTER_MESSAGE_OBJECT_ID   92
　AVP_SCHEDULE_OBJECT_NAME   92
　AVP_ALTERNATE_DTMF_IDS   93

COS Objects   93

Distribution Lists   94

FaxLibrary Handlers   95

FaxMail Handler   95

Interview Handlers   96

Locations   96

Mail Users   97
　AVP_NOTIFICATION_DEVICE   97
　AVP_NOTIFICATION_RULE   98
　AVP_NOTIFICATION_MWI   98
　AVP_PERSONAL_DLS   99
　AVP_CALL_HANDLER_OBJECT_ID   99
　AVP_COS_OBJECT_ID   99
　AVP_LOCATION_OBJECT_ID   100
　Alternate Extensions   100

Mail User Templates   100

Name Lookup Handlers   101
  AVP_EXIT_OBJECT_ID, AVP_EXIT_ACTION, and
  AVP_EXIT_CONVERSATION   102
  AVP_NO_SELECTION_OBJECT_ID, AVP_NO_SELECTION_ACTION, and
  AVP_NO_SELECTION_CONVERSATION   102
  AVP_NO_INPUT_OBJECT_ID, AVP_NO_INPUT_ACTION, and
  AVP_NO_INPUT_CONVERSATION   103
  AVP_ZERO_OBJECT_ID, AVP_ZERO_ACTION, and
  AVP_ZERO_CONVERSATION   103

Primary Domain Accounts   103

Primary Domain Groups   103

PW Policies   104

Restriction Tables   104
  AVP_NUMBER_PATTERNS   104

Trusted Domains   104

Data Storage   105
  SQL   105
    UnityDB   107
    ReportDB   121
  Registry   122
  Directory   130
  Local Files   131

Summary   133

Chapter 4   Components and Subsystems: Directory   135

Message Store and Directory Monitor Used   136

Protocols Used   137

Scope   138
  Exchange 5.5   138
  Exchange 2000/2003   141
  Domino   143

Synchronization Queries   143

Full Synchronization   146

Extensibility of the Directory   149

Default Unity Objects   153

Exchange 5.5 Directory Monitor: AvDSEx55   154
    Objects and Their Attributes   154
    Distribution List   159
    Global Data   160

Exchange 2000 or Exchange 20003 Directory Monitors: AvDSAD and
AvDSGlobalCatalog   161
    Objects and Their Attributes   162

Domino Directory Monitor: AvDSDomino   166
    Objects and Their Attributes   167

Summary   170

Chapter 5   Components and Subsystems: Messaging/Unity Message Repository   173

Messaging Actions in Unity   173
    Message Creation, Delivery, and Retrieval   174
    Notification/MWI   176

Messaging Components   176
    Messaging Abstraction Layer   176
    Windows Monitor   177
    Unity Messaging Repository   178
    Message Store Monitor   180
        AvMsgStoreMonitorSvr   180

MAPI   181
    Startup and Initialization   182
    Conversation Use of Messaging Components   183
        Outside Caller Messages   183
        Subscriber-to-Subscriber Messages   189
        The Notification Process   196
        TUI Message Retrieval   200

Summary   203

Chapter 6   Components and Subsystems: Telephony Services   205

Media Interface Unit   205
    A Few Words About TAPI   207
    Telephony Subsystem Initialization   209
    Extracting Call Information   211
    Responding to Client Telephony Requests   212
    Responding to Telephone System Events   213
    Playing, Recording, and Processing Audio   213

MIU Architecture 213

    MIU Server 213

    MIU Call (Call Object) 215

    Integration Object 216

    Switch Configuration 216

    MIU Line Servers 217

    MIU Line (Line Object) 217

    Media Object 218

    TTS Object 218

    UnityAvWav 218

    Fitting it Together 219

Summary 223

Chapter 7 Components and Subsystems: Features 225

Unity Subscriber Features 226

    Subscriber TUI Features 226

        Message Sending over the TUI 226

        Message Playback over TUI 227

        Message Management over TUI 227

        Personal Administration over TUI 228

    Subscriber Features Through Mail Clients 229

        Message Sending from Mail Clients 230

        Message Playback from Mail Clients 231

        Message Management from Mail Clients 231

    Subscriber Features Through the Cisco PCA 232

        Cisco Unity Inbox 232

        Cisco Unity Assistant 234

    Other Subscriber Features 235

        Message Waiting Indicator 235

        Message Notification 236

        Alternate Extensions 238

Unity Administrative Features 239

    Cisco Unity Administrator 239

        Subscriber Templates 240

        Class of Service 240

        Media Master Control 241

        Online Help and Field Help 241

    Cisco Unity Greetings Administrator 241

Tools Depot Applications   242
   Bulk Edit   242
   Cisco Unity Bulk Import Wizard   243
   Global Subscriber Manager   244
   Audio Text Manager   245
   Advanced Settings Tool   246

Unity Maintenance Features   246
   Reports   247
   Port Usage Analyzer   247
   HTML Status Monitor   248
   Unity Performance Counters   249
   Tools Depot Applications   250
      Message Store Manager   250
      Event Monitoring Service   251
      Disaster-Recovery Tools   251
      Database Walker   252

Unity Security Features   252
   Unity TUI Security   253
   Administrative Interface Security   253
   Unity System Security   254

Unity System Features   255
   Unity Failover   255
   License Pooling and Demo Licenses   256
   Languages and Multilingual Capabilities   257
   Schedules, Holidays, and Time Zones   259
   Accessibility Features   260
   Fax   260
   TTS   261
   Hospitality   262
   AGC and Message Storage Audio Format   263
   Networking   264
      Digital Networking   264
      SMTP Networking   265
      Networking with Other Vendors' Voice-Messaging Systems   265
   Telephony Features   266
      Integration Features   266
      Integrating with Multiple Phone Systems   267
      Unity Telephony Integration Manager   268
   Feature Parity Between Unity for Exchange and Unity for Domino   269

Summary   269

Part II   Deployment   271

Chapter 8   Deployment Methodology   273

Presales or Decision Making   273
Unified Messaging   275
Voice Messaging-Only   276

Planning   277

Design   278

Implementation   278

Installation   279

Operations   279
Administration   280
Systems Management   280
Performance   281

Optimization   281

Summary   281

Chapter 9   Planning   283

Testing Unity's Features and Functionality   283
Test or Pilot Unity   284
Perform an End-User Feature/Function Analysis   285
Customization Instructions   287

Determining Migration Tasks   288
Migrating to Unified Messaging   290
Migrating to Voice Messaging Only   291
Extracting User Data from Legacy Voice-Messaging Systems   291
Dial Plans   292

Installation Requirements or Dependencies   292

Determining Unity Installation Dependencies   292
Switch Connectivity   293
PBXs Supported   293
Verify That Unity Can Support Your Switch   293
Understand the Integration to Use Between Unity and Your Switch   293
Ensure That Your Switch Can Support Unity   294
Address Any Programming Necessary to Support the Unity Server   294
CallManager Versions   294
SIP Proxy   295

Messaging System Connectivity   295
   Single Messaging System   295
   With Exchange   295
   With Domino   296
   Directory Connectivity   297
   Single Infrastructure   297
   Directory Capacity Planning   298
Messaging Infrastructure Readiness   298
   Survey Your Messaging Servers for Capacity and Performance   299
   Survey Your Domain Controllers for Proximity and Performance   300
   Survey Your Name-Resolution Hosts for Proximity and Performance   301
   Survey Your Domain for Proper Configuration   301
   Survey Your Network to Ensure That it Is Well Connected and Is Highly
   Available   302

Mailbox Store for Voice Messaging   302

The Correlation Point: How to Size and Place a Server   303
   Server Sizing   304
   Ports or Sessions   305

Subscriber Access   305

Performing Site Surveys   306

Gathering Design Criteria   307

Summary   307

Chapter 10   Typical Configurations and Deployment Models   311

Typical Configurations   312
   Voice Messaging   313
      Single-Server Configuration   313
      Multiserver Configuration   314
      Allocating the Proper Number of Domain Controllers for Exchange 2000 and
      Unity 4.0   317
   Unified Messaging   318
      Partner Server   319
      Unity with Exchange 5.5   319
      Exchange 5.5 Site Boundaries   320
      Exchange 5.5 Site Where Unity Should Not Be Deployed   320
      Exchange 5.5 Sites Where Unity Is Deployable   322
      Domain Boundaries   325
      Exchange 5.5 Server Configurations   326
      Unity with Exchange 2000/2003   327
      Exchange 2000   331

        Unity with Domino R5   334
        Windows 2000 Domain Requirements   335
    Failover   336
        Unity with Exchange 5.5   337
        Unity with Exchange 2000   337

Deployment Models   339
    Cisco IP Telephony Deployment Models   340
    Cisco Messaging Deployment Models   340
    Messaging Boundaries   343
    Combining Deployment Models   344
    Single-Site Call Processing/Single-Site Messaging   345
        Single-Server Voice Messaging-Only Configuration   346
        Multiserver Voice Messaging-Only   348
        Voice Messaging-Only with GUI/Web Client Access, Single Site   351
        Unified Messaging for a Single Site   353
    Multisite WAN with Centralized Messaging/Multisite WAN with Centralized Call Processing   359
        Unity with Exchange 5.5 Unified Messaging   363
        Unity with Exchange 2000 Unified Messaging or Voice Messaging-Only with Client Web Access   364
        Unity with Exchange 2000 Voice Messaging-Only with No Client Web Access   364
        Unity with Domino R5 Unified Messaging-Only   365
    Multisite IP WAN with Centralized Call Processing/Multisite IP WAN with Distributed Messaging   366
    Multisite IP WAN with Distributed Call Processing/Multisite IP WAN with Centralized Messaging   366
    Multisite WAN with Distributed Messaging/Multisite WAN Model with Distributed Call Processing   366
        Unity with Exchange 5.5 Unified Messaging   368
        Unity with Exchange 2000 Unified Messaging or Voice Messaging-Only with Client Web Access   369
        Unity with Exchange 2000 Voice Messaging-Only with No Client Web Access   370
        Unity with Domino R5 or R6 Unified Messaging Only   370
    Failover Deployment Models Clustering Over the IP WAN/Disaster Recovery-System Redundancy Sites   371
        Unity with Exchange 5.5 Unified Messaging   373
        Unity with Exchange 2000 Unified Messaging or Voice Messaging Only with Client Web Access   373
        Unity with Exchange 2000 Voice Messaging-Only with No Client Web Access   373
        Unity with Domino R5   374

Summary   374

Chapter 11   Designing a Unity Solution   377

Design Process   377

The Decision-Making or Presales Phase   382
Requirements Development   382
Acceptance Criteria   382
Matching Requirements to Capability   383
Finalizing the Decision   383
Preliminary Design Proposal   384
Survey   384
Verification of Interoperability   386
Developing Preliminary Design Options   387
Finalizing the Preliminary Design   388
Budgetary Analysis   388
Estimating Hardware and Software Costs   388
Estimating Services Costs   389
Bill of Materials   389

Planning Phase   389
Feature/Functionality Evaluation of Unity   390
Traditional Voice-Mail Functionality   390
Dependency Assessment   390
Impact Analysis   391
Capacity Planning   391
Legacy Voice-Messaging System End-User Usage Analysis   391
Developing Questionnaires   391
Surveying Different End-User Groups/Usage Observation   392
Focus Groups   392
Special-Case Usage Requirements   392
Feature/Functional Usage Gaps   392
System Configuration Analysis   392
Traffic Patterns   393
Support Analysis   393
Training Criteria   393
Lab Trials and Proofing Your Concept   394
Configuration Options   394
Executing Test Plans   394
Mockup of Production Network and Installing Unity   394
Assessing Installation into the Mockup   395

Piloting in Production   395
    Pilot Installation Plan   395
    Selection of Pilot Members   395
    Implementing the Pilot   396
    Monitoring and Documenting the Experience   396
    Surveying Pilot Members of Experience   396
    Analyzing Results   397
Site Surveys   397
    Messaging Infrastructure   397
    Switching Infrastructure   398
    Physical Placement   398
    User Density   398
Compiling Data   399
    Finalizing Feature/Functional Analysis   399
    Usage Analysis Results   399

Design Phase   399
High-Level Design   400
    High-Level Design Description   400
    High-Level Design Diagram   401
Low-Level Design   401
    Low-Level Design Description   402
    Unity System Description   402
    Unity Switch Integration Detail   404
    Unity Messaging Infrastructure Detail   404
    Administration and Management   408
Criteria for Implementation   410

Summary   410

Chapter 12   Unity Networking   413

Digital Networking Architecture   414
    Protocol Introduction   414
    The Origins of Digital Networking   414
    Shared Messaging   415
    Networking Data Replication Model   416
    Logical Data Structure   417
    Synchronization Process   418

Digital Networking Features   419
Dial Plans   419
    Dialing Domain   420
    Alternate Extensions   424
    Extension Length   425

Core Digital Networking Features 425
Distribution Lists 425
Message Addressing 426
Subscriber Settings 428
License Pooling 428

Assessing the Environment 430
Step 1: Assessing the Messaging Environment 431
Step 2: Define the Physical Structure 431
Step 3: Define Each Phone Switch 432
Step 4: Define the Dial Plan 432
Step 5: Define Each Legacy Voice-Messaging Node 434
Step 6: Define Legacy Voice-Messaging Extension Length 435
Step 7: Define Legacy Message Addressing Scheme 436
Step 8: Define Each Unity Node 438
Step 9: Define Unity Node Extension Length 440
Step 10: Define Legacy Distribution Lists 443

Designing the Digital Network 443
Documenting the Design 444
Define Extension Length 444
Define the Dialing Domains 445
Message Addressing 446
Addressing Scope 446
Addressing by Extension 446
Addressing by Name 449
Preferred Addressing Method 450
Automated Attendant 451
Transfer by Extension 451
Directory Handler 452
Pooled Licensing 454
Public Distribution Lists 455
Public Distribution List Extensions 455
Populating Public Distribution Lists 456
Controlling Access 457

Summary 458

Chapter 13 Unity with Microsoft Exchange 461

The Characteristics of MS Exchange 461
Exchange 5.5 462
Exchange 2000/2003 469
Exchange in a Mixed-Messaging Configuration: Mixed-Mode Messaging and
Native-Mode Messaging 476

Unity's Perspective and Requirements   480
    Exchange 5.5   480
        How Unity Sees Exchange 5.5   480
    Exchange 2000/2003   485
    Exchange in a Mixed-Messaging Configuration   489
    The Unity Exchange 5.5 Directory Monitor-Exchange 5.5 Mailboxes Only   489
    The Unity Exchange 2000/2003 Directory Monitor-Exchange 5.5 Mailboxes
    and Exchange 2000/2003   491

Planning a Unity Installation   492
    Installing Unity to Service Exchange   493
    Assessing Exchange For UM Readiness   493
    Capacity Planning   496
    Trending   497
    How Unity Can Affect Exchange   499
    How Unity Is Affected by Exchange   501

Planning to Administer Unity with Exchange   501

Designing for Sustainable Operations   502

How to Deploy Unity with Exchange   503
    Exchange 5.5   503
        Server Placement   506
        Unity Networking   510
        Selecting a Partner Server   512
    Exchange 2000/2003   514
    Exchange in a Mixed-Messaging Configuration   520

Maximizing Unity's Servicing Capabilities   524

Summary   524

Chapter 14   Unity with Lotus Domino   527

The Characteristics of Lotus Domino and Notes   527
    Server Component: Lotus Domino   528
    Client Component: Notes, Administrator, Designer   529
    Databases and Database Design   531
        Views   532
        Forms   533
        Database Templates   533
        Database Replicas   534
        Server Tasks   535
    The Domino Domain   535
    The Directory   536
    Naming in Domino Is Hierarchical   537

Scaling Servers Within a Domain   539
Server Documents   540
Mail Routing   541
Database Replication   544

Security and Domino/Notes   548
Note ID File   548
Access Control Lists   549

Unity's Perspective of Lotus Domino   550
Database Permissions   551
Domino Directory: Editor + Delete Documents Rights   551
Administration Process: Editor Rights   552
Mail Files   552
Delivery and Retrieval of Voice Messages   553
Message Waiting Indicator Light   553
New Message Arrival   554
Profile Documents   556

Planning a Unity for Domino Installation   558
Trending   558
Placement of Unity Within a Domino Domain   560
Deployment of Domino Unified Communications Services (DUCS)   563

Summary   565

Chapter 15   Upgrades and Migrations   567

Upgrades   567
Managing Unity Upgrades   567
Planning Upgrades   568
Evaluating the Unity Version You Plan to Upgrade To   569
Performing an Upgrade Lab Trial   569
Performing a Fallback Lab Trial   570
Cleaning Up and Preparing Your Production Servers   570
Performing a Project Walkthrough and Fallback Readiness Evaluation   571
Conducting a Site Survey of Each Unity Server to Be Upgraded   572
Handling Scheduling and Notification of Downtime Messages   572
Performing the Upgrade   573
Verifying Operations After the Upgrade   573
Falling Back   574

Reconfiguring Unity   574

Migrations   575
   Migrating from a Legacy Voice-Messaging System to Unity   575
      AMIS   576
      VPIM   577
      Unity Bridge   578
   Migrating from a Unity Voice Messaging-Only Configuration to a Unity Unified
   Messaging Configuration   578
   Migrating the Messaging System That Unity Services   579
      Exchange 5.5 to Exchange 2000 or 2003   580
      Mixed-Mode Exchange   580
   Migrating Unity Between Different Active Directory Forests   581
   Migrations with Unity and Domino   582

Summary   582

Chapter 16   Installation   585

Implementation Plan Development   586

Preinstallation Tasks   586
   Administrative Console   587
   Monitoring Facility   588
   Account Creation and Permissions Verification   588
   Schema Extension   588

Installation   589

Precutover Tasks   590
   Configuration Testing   590
   Conversations Test Plan   591
   Integration Test Plan   591
   Simulated Load Testing   592
      Performing the Simulated Test   592
   Go/No Go Decision Making   594
   Precutover Subscriber Enrollment   595

Cutover   595

Fallback Readiness   597
   Performing Fallback   597

Operations Acceptance Criteria   597
   Post-Installation Server Tuning   598
   Post-Cutover Hand-Off to Operations   598
   Post-Implementation Assessment   599

Summary   599

Chapter 17   Unity Telephony Integration   601

   The TDM World of PBXs and Unity   602
      Switch Files and Integration Files   603
      Call Information Extraction (Analog DTMF Integration)   604
      Call Information Extraction (Serial Integrations)   612
      Call Control   630
         Call Control Settings: Incoming Ring Voltage   631
         Tone Definitions   634
         Disconnect Supervision   637

   Cisco Unity CallManager Telephone Service Provider   638
      Call Control   640
      Call Information   642
      Audio Control   643
      Startup and Initialization   645
      MWI Functionality   646
      Multiple CallManager Cluster Support   646

   SIP   649
      Overview of Unity SIP Component   650
      SIP Methods Unity Uses   650
      Call Information with SIP Integration   655
      Media Format Negotiation   655
      Digit Detection and Generation   657
      Unity SIP Failover   657
      PIMG Integration   658

   Summary   660

Part III   **Solutions, Systems Management, and Administration   663**

Chapter 18   Audio-Text Applications   665

   Call Handlers   666
      Profile   666
      Call Transfer   669
      Greetings   674
      Caller Input   676
      Messages   678
      Call Handler Flow   679
      Transfer Rules   682
      Greeting Rules   683
      After-Greeting Action   684
      After-Message Action   684

Subscribers   685

Interview Handlers   685

Directory Handlers   688

Routing Rules   695
   Checking Your Sources   695
   Understanding Rule Order   698

Extension Remapping   701

Languages, Prompts, and Greetings   702

Default Configuration of Unity   703
   Common Problems   705

Scenario Examples   706
   Audio Text Manager   706
   Basic Audio-Text Application   707
      Tiny Audio Text Application Call Handler   708
      Product Information Call Handler   709
      Technical Support Call Handler   709
      All Seattle Employees Name-Lookup Handler   710
      All Chicago Employees Name-Lookup Handler   710
   Transferring to External Numbers in Unity 4.0(4) and Later   712
   Transferring to External Numbers in Unity 4.0(3) and Earlier   713
   Locking Down Handlers and Subscribers   715
      Error Greetings   715
      Restricting Dial Options   717
   Changing Greetings for Call Handlers over the Phone   719
   Multiple-Language Applications   720
   Group Mailboxes   722
   Find First Available Extension (Simple Hunt Group)   724
   Holiday Greetings   726
   Separate Caller-Input Options for Day and Off-Hours Schedules   728
   Separate Transfer Rules for Subscribers   729
   Working Around Forwarding Transfer Rule Override   730
   Send Directly to Greeting from the Operator Console   731
   Tenant Services   732
   Customizing Unity Prompts   735
      Finding Your Prompt   736
      "Please Hold While I Transfer Your Call"   736
      "You May Record Your Message After the Tone; Stay on the Line for More Options"   737
      Directory Handler Name-Spelling Options   738

Building Applications for TTY/TDD Users   738
Call Traffic Reports   741

Damage Control   742
Backups   742
Reconstruct Default Objects   743
Reconstructing the Default Routing Rules   745
Reconstructing the Default Schedules   746
Rebuilding the Default Subscriber Templates   746

Troubleshooting   746
Event Log   746
Call Viewer   747
Port Status Monitor   748
Call-Routing Rules Diagnostic Traces   750

Summary   753

Chapter 19   Administering Multiple Unity Servers   755

Unity Administrator Accounts and Access   755
Using Class of Service for Administrative Access   755
Administering Multiple Unity Servers with a Single Account   757
The GrantUnityAccess Tool   760

Global Subscriber Management   764
Using the GSM to Import Users from Active Directory   765
Using the GSM to Delete Subscribers   765
Using the GSM to Move Subscribers Between Unity Servers   766
Using the GSM Off-Box   766

Summary   767

Chapter 20   Subscriber Administration   769

Subscriber Templates   769

Bulk Import Utility   770
Importing User Data from a CSV File   770
Required Column Headers for a CSV File   773
Optional Column Headers for a CSV File   776
Importing User Data Directly from a Message Store Directory   776
Correcting Import Errors   777
Correct Errors That Occurred When Importing Data from the
Message Store   778
Correct Errors That Occurred When Importing Data from a CSV File   778
Modifying Existing Cisco Unity Subscriber Accounts   779

Bulk Subscriber Delete   780

Bulk Edit   782
   Main Form   783
   Select Subscribers   784
      CSV Format   785
   Select Subscriber Changes   786
      Profile   786
      Account   787
      Passwords   788
      Conversation   788
      Transfer   790
      Greetings   792
      Caller Input   794
      Messages   796
      Notification   798
      Extension   798
      Alternate Extensions   799
      Exit Destination   799
   Apply Subscriber Changes   800
   Select Call Handlers   800
      CSV Format   802
   Select Call Handler Changes   802
      Profile   803
      Transfer   803
      Greetings   805
      Caller Input   808
      Messages   809
      Alternate Extensions   811
   Apply Call Handler Changes   811

Migrate Subscriber Data Tool   811
   How to Migrate Subscriber Data   812
   Requirements/Special Notes   813
   Configuring Permissions for MSD   813
      Exchange 5.5   814
      Exchange 2000/2003 or Mixed 2000/2003/55   814

Summary   814

Chapter 21   Administering Unity Programmatically   817

   APIs and Support   819

   Rights Needed in SQL   820

SQL Rules of the Road   822

Exercises   823
    Finding and Connecting to a Unity Server on the Network   823
        Retrieve a List of All Servers Running SQL on a Domain   823
        Deciding on a Connection Method   825
        Learning to Share   829
        Making the Connection   831
        Getting Version and License Information   833
    Find All Unity Servers in the Enterprise   838
    Listing and Finding Subscribers Anywhere in the Enterprise   838
    Find an Extension Anywhere in the Dialing Domain with Unity 4.0(3) or
    Later Versions   841
    Find an Extension Anywhere in the Dialing Domain with Unity 4.0(1)
    or 4.0(2)   842
    Open an SA Web Page Directly to Any Object   847
    Call Handler Information Dump   848
    Subscriber Information Dump   853
    Create New Subscribers   856
    Import Subscriber   865
    Edit Subscriber   868
        Add an Alternate Extension to a Subscriber, Unity 4.0(4) and Earlier   872
        Add an Alternate Extension to a Subscriber, Unity 4.0(4) and Later   875
        Updating One Key Rules to Go Directly to the Opening Greeting   876
        Updating Passwords   878
        Updating the Behavior of an Error Greeting in Unity 4.0(3) and Earlier   879
    Batch Subscriber Operations   881
    Delete Subscriber   884
    Remove Unity Properties from an Active Directory Object   893
    Adding a New Public Distribution List   896
    Removing an Existing Public Distribution List   900
    Adding a Member to a Public Distribution List   903

Summary   907

Chapter 22   Third-Party Tools and Applications   909

Supported Backup Software   909

Supported Fax Server Software   909

Supported Monitoring Software   910

Supported Virus-Scanning Software   910

Additional Supported Software   911

Unsupported Third-Party Software   912

Chapter 23   The Future of Unity   915

Appendix A   Switch File Settings   917

Index   927

Icons Used in This Book

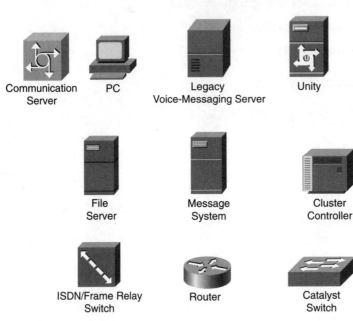

Communication Server

PC

Legacy Voice-Messaging Server

Unity

Directory

File Server

Message System

Cluster Controller

ISDN/Frame Relay Switch

Router

Catalyst Switch

Network Cloud

Line: Ethernet

Line: Serial

Line: Switched Serial

Command Syntax Conventions

The conventions used to present command syntax in this book are the same conventions used in the Microsoft Windows command line to run utilities and executables or to launch DOS-based or Windows GUI-based applications.

In addition, the file system directory format consists of <drive letter + ":">\directory name\.

An executable is run from the command line as shown in the following example:

```
"Run the setup by selecting <drive>\commserver\configurationsetup\setup.exe"
```

Any additional parameters used by the executable is typically denoted via a "/" or "-" as in the following example:

```
"Run the setup by selecting <drive>\commserver\configurationsetup\setup.exe /sync"
```

Keypress steps are also denoted between "<" and ">", as shown in the following:

```
<enter>
```

Foreword

When it comes to business communication, some people prefer the phone, whereas others prefer e-mail. Most of us end up using both at some point, but we often favor one over the other. With me, it's e-mail. For others, it's voice (often salespeople or executive management conduct business over the phone). And if you can't reach someone live, there's always voice mail, which controls the red message lamp on your phone.

But what if the distinction between voice mail and e-mail was blurred? Would it make the communication experience at work more effective? More productive? Could different message types be handled in a consistent way over the phone or from an e-mail client application? This is what unified messaging is all about—and is why Active Voice started to build Unity eight years ago. It is also why Cisco acquired Unity, expanding its IP Telephony product portfolio.

Simply put, if it is deployed and supported correctly, unified messaging—more specifically, Unity—has the potential to change the way organizations communicate. For example, when working in my office or from home (over a broadband connection), I check both e-mail and voice mail from my e-mail client application—no need to use the phone to check voice messages. It is fast and convenient. Voice messages can be sorted and stored like e-mail messages, and Unity lets me create mixed-media messages (respond by e-mail to a voice-mail message). When traveling, I listen to e-mail using Text-to-Speech on my mobile phone, and I can respond to an e-mail message using voice. Unified messaging provides flexibility that has changed the way I communicate at work.

Although unified messaging is conceptually straightforward, its initial success depends on a well-planned and effective deployment. To better understand this, consider the current environment Unified Messaging exists within.

For starters, unified messaging from Cisco's perspective includes voice and e-mail (optionally, fax and in the future, video) stored in a common message database with shared directory services. Typically, the Unity message store is a Microsoft Exchange Server or Lotus Domino Server. Both groupware environments provide directory services and a client application for message access. In addition, Unified messaging systems must integrate with other business systems. In the case of Unity, these can include the Cisco CallManager phone system, a legacy PBX phone system, other legacy voice-mail systems, and administrative applications.

Of note are the two distinct types of interoperability that unified messaging requires: telecom connectivity to the phone system(s) and optional legacy voice-mail systems; and datacom connectivity to the message store, directory services, and client and optional administrative applications. Although telecom and datacom have some common characteristics, they are different in many respects. These differences are important in the context of unified messaging.

As a brief review, the telecom industry was established in the early part of the 20th century, and customers have come to expect a "five nines" level of service. Equipment upgrades are typically evolutionary, often with extensive backward compatibility, and the primary user interface has been more or less the same for the last century. In contrast, the datacom industry picked up momentum in the latter part of the 20th century and has a less stringent service-level expectation. New products and technologies are introduced frequently, often accompanied by significant change, and there are various (nonstandard) approaches to user interface, given the flexibility with client applications. Clearly, telecom and datacom are different animals, with different customer and distribution channel expectations.

And it is here that unified messaging is situated squarely: between telecom and datacom. This central position makes Unity a valuable business solution. This position also can create challenges if the deployment is not planned properly or is implemented poorly. If Unity is deployed successfully, the customer will realize the intended business benefits from unified messaging and never will look back at the previous voice-messaging solution.

So what is required to realize a successful Unity deployment and avoid potential issues? First is a thorough technical understanding of Unity. This includes both the product architecture and the appropriate component details. Next is knowledge of Unity networking and integration with other business systems. Unity depends on interoperability with other products, so it is critical for these integrations to be implemented properly. Last, but certainly not least, is a solid understanding of Unity design practices and planning methods. You need to know where you are headed and how you are going to get there.

Having worked with Todd Stone for many years, I know that his passion for unified messaging and knowledge of Unity are best characterized as "extreme." He has been involved with the largest Unity design and deployment efforts, has spent countless hours with customers and distribution partners working on Unity-related projects, and has led a variety of Unity technical initiatives. Todd's accumulated knowledge of unified messaging and Unity is well represented in this book.

In addition to Todd's work on this project, Jeff Lindborg, Steve Olivier, Dustin Grant, Keith Chambers, Mike McCann, Toby Young, and Shane Lisenbea each authored specific chapter(s). Chris Gulley, Jeff Schlesser, Markus Schneider, and Jody Carbone also reviewed the technical content. Each of these contributors is highly qualified in the field of unified messaging; many have more than ten years of experience in their respective area of expertise.

If you are involved with the deployment or support of Unity, this book is an excellent resource that provides high-level product concepts with in-depth technical details. Whether you intend to read the entire book from start to finish or need a refresher in a specific area of Unity, you will find this a valuable source of product information.

Unity has evolved from the inspiration, dedication, and hard work of many talented people. The vision of unified messaging is as relevant today as it was when Unity development began—perhaps more so, given the increasing number of messages that many of us handle each day. It is my hope this book will become more than a valuable technical resource and that you will be inspired to become an advocate of Unity and all the benefits unified messaging can provide.

Ed Masters
Director of Product Development
Cisco Systems, Enterprise Communications Software Business Unit

Introduction

Cisco Unity is one of the best examples of an IP Telephony convergence application, and in this book you read about how and why it is one of the best examples. An important trait of Unity is its seemingly endless features and functionality, which can provide a unique solution for anyone who buys and uses the product.

Throughout this book, main themes are repeated to give you an idea of what Unity is about. Unity is a unified messaging product, for sure, but it is more than that. It is an enabler, an open door to a different way of communicating with co-workers and outside callers. It changes the way you work. When you begin to see these changes, you will not want to go back to your old way of sending messages to one another.

Enough with the fluff: This book is technical, although it could be even more technical than what it is. It is not for the beginner, although the beginner can learn a great deal more about Unity after reading this book. It can be used in many ways: as a reference, a guide, and even a learning tool. Regardless, although a considerable amount of information is presented in this book, more can be added. Whether more information is presented this way in the future is up to you. Let us know.

Goals and Methods

The purpose of this book is to provide an in-depth look at Unity's architecture, how to design a Unity solution, and how to administer it after it has been deployed. To make it easier, we share not only the underworkings of the product, but we also give you a very good idea of the product's features and how they function.

After presenting the architecture and features, it is important to present how to deploy Unity with the goal of designing a sustainable solution. The last section of the book is intended to show you how to administer Cisco Unity in different ways.

This book also acts as a reference point to the upcoming "Cisco Unity Design and Networking" course, which conveys the design process used in this book, as well as the deployment models, configurations, and other concepts presented in Part II.

One important goal of this book is to convey how Unity sees things: its perspective and why it has that perspective. The intention is to show the reader how to look at Unity the same way and make it easier to design a solution or to administer the product.

This book is not a step-by-step book for the beginner. In fact, it is anything but that. Steps are mentioned throughout, but that is merely the side effect of clarification.

If anything can be gleaned from this book, it is that a deeper level of understanding can be transferred from the authors to the readers to help clarify any preconceptions, real or false, and also to help guide the reader down the same path that the authors would take to apply a Unity solution in their own organization.

Who Should Read This Book?

If you want to deploy Unity and manage it afterward, this book will serve as a useful guide. In fact, it might be considered the ultimate resource. If you want to design a solution using Unity or write a customer administrative interface, this book is for you. If you want to get a deeper understanding of the way that Unity uses the various messaging systems that it services, this book is definitely for you.

Part of this book is geared toward the solutions designer or the systems architect who evaluates Unity, and who determines how to best design a solution using the design process described in this book and how to use the technical building blocks described throughout to put it all together.

If you currently use or administer Unity and would like to better understand the architecture or the specific functionality within Unity, this book will serve as a useful resource for you.

If you work as a systems engineer or a consultant for a solutions provider, this book will be an important resource for understanding the architecture and for designing a Unity solution using a repeatable deployment methodology.

How This Book Is Organized

This book is divided into three different parts. To understand how to deploy and develop a Unity solution, it is essential that you read and understand Part I, which covers the system architecture and concepts associated with the use of that architecture. Part II focuses on deployment and includes planning, design, and implementation phases of the Unity design process. Finally, Part III focuses on solutions and the management of Unity.

The beginning of each section provides an introduction to the section and includes a chapter summary. The parts of the book can be summarized as follows:

- **Part I, "Concepts and Architecture"**—The concepts and architecture chapters focus on the Unity systems underlying architecture and discuss the key components of the architecture in detail. All the architecture and its capability are explained detail; you certainly will not lack information when you are finished reading it. This part of the book also includes a detailed description of Unity features that is not found anywhere else.

- **Part II, "Deployment"**—The deployment section gives you the information you need to deploy just about any Unity solution. It identifies the most important issues and tells you how to address them. It concentrates on the Unity design process used to put your Unity design together. When you have your design in place, this section also explains how you can plan your installation. It covers important deployment topics, such as capacity planning. Unity digital networking, migrations, and switch integrations, to name a few.

- **Part III: "Solutions, Systems Management, and Administration"**—This part focuses on capabilities in Unity that can provide sustainable solutions for your implementation of the product. It includes an in-depth overview of Unity tools, such as the Audio Text Application manager. It also provides in-depth coverage on administering Unity programmatically and focuses on administration throughout the entire section.

PART I

Concepts and Architecture

Chapter 1   About Unified Messaging

Chapter 2   Unity Architecture Overview

Chapter 3   Components and Subsystems: Object Model

Chapter 4   Components and Subsystems: Directory

Chapter 5   Components and Subsystems: Messaging/Unity Message Repository

Chapter 6   Components and Subsystems: Telephony Services

Chapter 7   Components and Subsystems: Features

About Unified Messaging

The essence of communication is breaking down barriers. The telephone, for instance, breaks distance and time barriers so that people can communicate in real time or near–real time when they are not in the same place. But as communications evolve, there are new barriers to be overcome. New forms of communication emerge, such as e-mail, voice mail, fax machines, and pagers, and people use different devices for each of these. Unified messaging (UM) is designed to overcome these barriers. It breaks down the terminal and media barriers so that people using different technologies, different media, and different terminals can still communicate with anyone, anywhere, at any time. Unified messaging is the integration of several different communications media so that users can retrieve and send voice, fax, and e-mail messages from a single interface, whether that is a wireline phone, a wireless phone, a PC, or an Internet-enabled PC.

This chapter introduces the concept of unified messaging and discusses how the technology, along with Unity, has evolved. The topics covered in this chapter are ones that mostly concern organizations, including who manages unified messaging and why, organizational perceptions, and security issues related to converging voice messages with e-mail. Some attention is given to different ways that a user community might adapt unified messaging, as well as what the implementer and manager of unified messaging should expect. Finally, messaging technologies are covered along with legacy switching technologies and Cisco IP Telephony call-processing systems, such as Cisco CallManager.

The Evolution of Unified Messaging

When the concept of unified messaging first was introduced, it appeared to be a grand idea. However, as the technology was implemented, the original idea behind unified messaging was lost. Some vendors developed products that were so purely unified messaging (meaning that they were totally dependent upon the third-party messaging system they were servicing; without this dependency, it couldn't stand on its own) that their very existence was dependent on the messaging system they were installed to service, including the mailbox store and directory. Cisco Unity was one of these pure UM products. Thus, although Unity realized early success, there was a lot to be desired. Reliability and the capability to sustain voice messaging (VM) when the messaging system was unavailable were serious challenges to the early implementations of the product.

Some of Unity's competitors went to the opposite end of the UM spectrum and came out with what the industry calls integrated messaging solutions instead of unified messaging. With integrated messaging, a client deployed at the end user's desktop unifies the messages from the two disparate systems (e-mail and voice). Many companies thought it made sense to deploy these types of solutions. However, if you add fax to this, you mainly have a confused mix of implementations that can vary as much as the features that a given vendor provides in a product. The problem with integrated messaging highlights the fact that, with the current developments in communication, standards are important. Products that offer interoperability are needed. These products might not be from the same vendor, but they must operate together to form powerful solutions for customers.

One thing is certain: The whole idea of unified messaging stirred the messaging industry. Although many options existed, pure e-mail-only systems left less than suitable solutions for companies of any size. The addition of fax vendor support and other multimedia applications integrated into legacy e-mail systems made any notion of useful, easily implemented standards nearly impossible. For the most part, some of these systems have very strong and capable implementations (Microsoft Exchange, Lotus Domino, and Novell Groupwise, to name a few), but this disparity in implemented standards essentially makes it necessary to write code using the proprietary application programming interfaces (APIs) of these messaging vendors. A good example of this is the way in which IMAP is implemented among these applications. Many similarities exist, but there are enough differences to make it challenging to write one solution for all. Thus, for integrated solutions, useful technologies, such as drag-and-drop, would make you think there is more interoperability than there really is.

For unified messaging, the opposite issue is true. Unified messaging solutions such as Unity use the APIs provided by the messaging vendors in lieu of using proprietary ones (to access mail and directory resources). The challenge of using third-party messaging APIs (such as Microsoft's MAPI or the Lotus Notes API) is that, although it is possible to write very functional and capable unified messaging solutions, these messaging APIs lack real voice-messaging support. Instead of treating Unity like a voice-messaging interface into the messaging environment — in other words, like a voice-messaging client — Unity is relegated to acting just like an e-mail client. Unity must compensate for this by accounting for the differences in behavior between an e-mail client and what a voice-mail client should be when accessing these messaging systems.

If the notion of a voice-mail client actually existed within a given messaging system, it would have a different set of characteristics than a legacy e-mail client. These characteristics include giving unified messaging clients — more basically, voice-messaging clients — higher priority when accessing the system than e-mail or other types of clients. This is because the key to voice messaging is the capability to provide a real-time voice interface (such as the Unity Telephone User Interface, or TUI) into the subscriber's messaging store, or voice mailbox. In addition to higher client type prioritization for voice messaging (which can be considered much like application-level QoS), a voice-mail client has other needs that should be exploited through the TUI interface but supported through the voice-messaging client interface in a given messaging system *if* they were to exist. These needs include fast retrieval of addresses when addressing messages and fast retrieval of spoken names for message addressing. Without these, subscribers experience slow response times in the TUI.

So, back to the present, it is necessary to provide a typical and (after a few years' maturation) simple definition of unified messaging: Using a single message store for voice, e-mail, and fax messages, a unified messaging solution can provide subscriber access to messages with the TUI or GUI in a consistent fashion.

This means moving voice messaging and all the functionality that subscribers are traditionally accustomed to essentially on top of a legacy e-mail system. Add fax on top of that, and you have a perfect solution. Achievable? Without a doubt. A realistic unified messaging solution certainly is viable and obtainable now.

So what does this mean? In essence, unified messaging is the convergence of voice, video, and data at the application layer, pure and simple. Saying this is probably too "worn" or repeated; nevertheless, the implications of unified messaging simply will not go away just because it sounds like an old idea. From this book's standpoint, this also means that Cisco Unity is a convergence product because it fully bridges the gap between legacy voice messaging and electronic messaging. To narrow or eliminate the gap between legacy voice technologies and data technologies is the whole idea behind Unity as a convergence product.

Unity as a Pure UM Product

In its original form, Unity was too pure of a UM product. Its original implementation was with Exchange 5.5. It used the Exchange 5.5 directory to store all its data and save a few pieces, and it used the Exchange 5.5 information store to store all messages. It did not store any data other than messages in the Exchange 5.5 store. The data that it stored on the local server consisted of the system prompts and default greetings, the call routing, rules, and the system schedule. Unity was installed with Exchange 5.5 on-box and was installed either as a self-contained system (which meant that it also had to be a domain controller) or as a member server in an existing Windows NT domain.

Some fundamental problems arose with this approach. The whole notion of using the Exchange 5.5 directory to store the UM-specific data required for the system to operate and for e-mail–enabled end users to act as Unity subscribers was not effective: The LDAP-enabled Exchange 5.5 directory was not fast enough to provide the real-time searching capabilities that Unity needed, and it often became unresponsive (the DAPI access was not any better). It was also very problematic for administrators, who had to worry about the impact of adding a large amount of data into the directory, challenging its directory size. Finally, the Exchange 5.5 directory forced replication for the entire object each time an attribute belonging to that object was modified. This meant that Unity caused directory replication to increase anywhere from marginal levels to very high levels, depending upon the actual subscriber traffic on the system.

Unity's use of the Exchange 5.5 information store represented a complete dependency on the capability of Exchange 5.5 to maintain a stable and operational store for e-mail clients and Unity alike. This dependency caused problems because it subjected Unity to frequent interruptions as the information store became impaired or unavailable.

To make things worse, Unity used the directory poorly, without regard for the response time from the directory and the way it depended upon message retrieval delays from the message store by playing back what it experienced into the subscriber's or outside caller's ear. As a result, the subscriber or caller heard all delays that Unity was experiencing—sometimes the delays were so bad that the system simply was not serviceable.

The challenge was to find ways to eliminate the response time issues. The directory was tackled first, so a proprietary cache was created in Unity that would cache the directory data. This made Unity capable of accessing the cache quicker than it could access the directory, making it faster and less susceptible to the inherent delays in accessing the directory directly. The information store came next: Continuous modifications and improvements were made in Unity's use of MAPI to compensate for the constant timeouts and loss of access resulting from the frequently unavailable or impaired information store.

As Unity matured as a product, and as Microsoft released Exchange 2000, more work was done to enable Unity to maintain sustainable operations. Thus, its pure UM implementation evolved to make it more reliable and to relieve its dependencies on the message store if it became unresponsive. The Unity cache, internally called the Dohcache (see Chapter 3, "Components and Subsystems: Object Model") was eliminated and replaced by MS SQL Server 2000. Using SQL was fully justified when it was determined that Exchange 2000's directory, Active Directory, was no faster than the Exchange 5.5 directory for the type of real-time directory access that Unity required. Thus, the SQL server implementation within Unity made the product more stable and more readily capable of providing a consistent end-user experience.

A part of this SQL server effort also included the notion of taking the information store off the Unity server, thus eliminating Unity's dependency on an on-box message store that could get bogged down by its connectivity to the other servers it communicated with. Thus, the standard implementation of Unity came with an off-box message store. This was perfect and desirable for unified messaging.

As a replacement product for a legacy voice-messaging system, Unity comes with a separation of account/directory functionality and message store functionality. Figure 1-1 shows the difference between a legacy voice-messaging system and Unity. In the figure, the main difference is that a legacy voice-messaging system contains its own mail store and some type of address book or directory. With Unity, those components are found in the customer's environment. Unity uses either MS Exchange or Lotus Domino. For specific versions, see Part II, "Deployment."

Figure 1-1   *A Legacy Voice-Messaging System Compared to a Unified Messaging Solution*

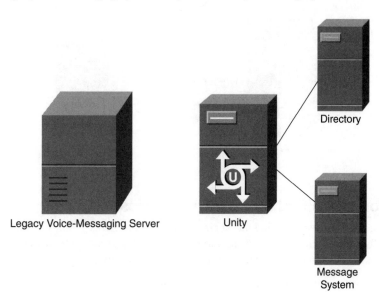

Legacy Voice-Messaging Server   Unity

Directory

Message
System

Unity Messaging Repository

The Unity Messaging Repository (UMR) was put in place because of the prevailing risk of losing access to the information store. The premise was that with the repository, voice messages would go into a holding place prior being delivered to the off-box Exchange server and stored there if the Exchange server or servers were offline. When a user's Exchange server is unavailable, the messages in the UMR are available to the user through the TUI, but not through the GUI interfaces. As soon as the messaging store comes back online, the messages are delivered and sent to the subscriber's mailbox. For more information, see Chapter 5, "Components and Subsystems: Messaging/Unity Message Repository."

Figure 1-2 shows Unity with the UMR in place. If it loses access to the messaging system that it services, it will continue to take messages from outside callers.

Figure 1-2   *The Unity Messaging Repository*

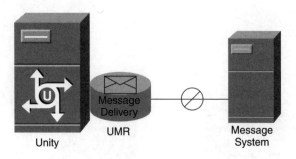

Comparison of Unified and Integrated Messaging

So, why stick with unified messaging if all these problems occur with the directory and the information store? Two very important reasons exist. First, you have just as many—although different—problems with integrated messaging.

With integrated messaging, you have the following:

- Separate directories
- Separate message stores
- Client connection to both e-mail and voice mail (VM) systems
- Required VM address book when composing VM for an e-mail client
- No shared distribution lists

With unified messaging, you have the following:

- Same directory
- Same message store
- Client connected to the e-mail system only, but it can connect to Unity to use the Telephone Record and Playback (TRaP) feature for recording and playing back messages
- E-mail address book available when composing a voice messages for an e-mail client
- Shared distribution lists

Figure 1-3 shows the difference between unified messaging and integrated messaging. With unified messaging, the unified messaging server provides services to subscribers by becoming a part of the messaging environment where the subscribers reside. With integrated messaging, the integrated messaging servers become a second messaging infrastructure on top of the existing messaging infrastructure. The client then must connect to both messaging infrastructures to experience "unified" messaging.

Figure 1-3   *Unified Messaging Versus Integrated Messaging*

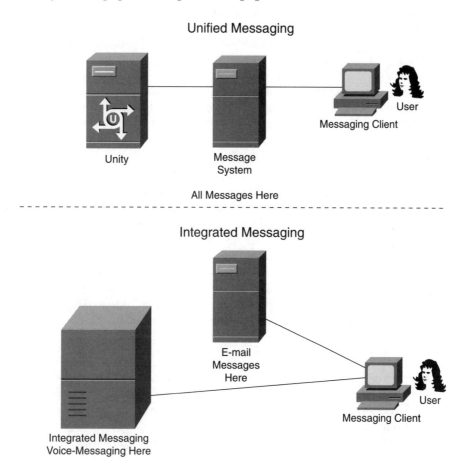

With integrated messaging, the focus moves off the messaging store onto the client, to unify the different types of messages. As a result, integrated messaging systems typically have a challenge in providing reliable notification services, such as lighting message waiting indicators, on a timely basis.

Challenges with Unified Messaging in an Organization

As with IP telephony, most businesses, especially Fortune 500 businesses, strongly desire unified messaging. For most organizations, moving toward unified messaging requires a lot of effort. This is of particular concern because of the legacy structure of most IS organizations and their prevalent separation of voice and data (for both technology and the responsibility of managing it). For this reason, UM may not only be *challenging* to deploy, but it also could be entirely *impossible* to deploy. One interesting thing about this issue is that it has nothing to do with technical challenges or limitations of the product. Instead, it is mostly organizational. Many organizational issues arise in preparing a given company for unified messaging (although some technical challenges might exist for the organization's network and messaging infrastructure, such as readiness requirements and capacity planning needs). So, without understanding that a given organization's IS structure might prevent the deployment of unified messaging, little progress will be made in trying to deploy a unified messaging solution such as Unity within some companies.

NOTE   Lack of organizational alignment toward UM is often a primary reason that larger companies choose to deploy Unity in a large-scale, voice mail-only configuration first and then deploy UM later: They want time to take advantage of Unity's technology and features, as well as the time to align organizationally to manage UM. This is fine and doable, but it also incurs a lot of extra work. A lot more work is involved because you must design a dedicated solution for Unity and then also take into consideration how you will migrate to UM. Occasionally, a migration to UM means moving data (subscriber information and possibly messages as well) off the voice messaging-only messaging systems to a newer version of the messaging system (such as migrating from Ex55 to E2K, or from Exchange to Domino). For more information, see the chapters in Part II.

After the organizational challenges are addressed, the technical challenges can be addressed. The organizational challenges actually might take considerably more effort than the technical challenges; it is very important to understand the issues surrounding organizational alignment—or the lack thereof. The following sections discuss the organizational issues that you should address before you deploy a unified messaging solution.

Who Manages the Messaging Topology?

Organizations that want to deploy unified messaging must start with determining who internally manages the messaging topology. The messaging topology includes everything necessary for managing the messaging systems including dependencies. From the perspective of legacy voice messaging, the first response is that the voice team owns the voice-messaging solution. Is this still true with unified messaging? Absolutely. However, because UM focuses on centralizing different types of messages into the same messaging store, the voice team must actively be a part of the group managing the messaging topology.

Having the voice team join the e-mail team is a good start, although this is not perfect. An ideal scenario is one in which voice and electronic messaging skills, roles, and responsibilities are given to both teams as they join together. This might be considered just a certain way to look at the situation, but the emphasis is important. Bringing both groups together or making both groups messaging-centric moves the emphasis from e-mail services and voice-mail services to messaging services.

Figure 1-4 shows a centralized messaging team with the responsibility for all aspects of messaging within a given organization. This includes voice messaging, fax, and e-mail—all parts of unified messaging.

Figure 1-4   *Organizing a Centralized Messaging Team*

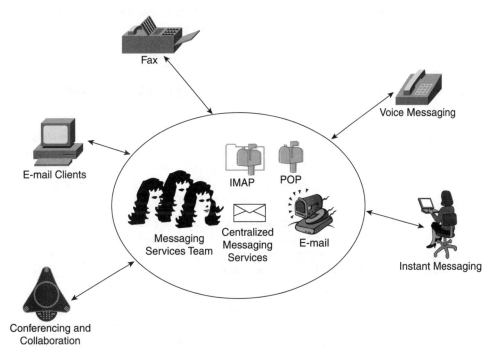

So, why is merging the voice-messaging team and the e-mail team so important? It comes down to placing the emphasis on the core expertise required to maintain unified messaging, and it de-emphasizes the core competencies of separate e-mail and voice-mail teams. It is important to note that unified messaging puts new burdens on the e-mail infrastructure that require attention from the e-mail team. Unified messaging also builds a dependency between the voice-mail system and the e-mail system that the voice-messaging team needs to understand and manage. The benefits of merging both teams into one are numerous: Their joint expertise enables the effective support of unified messaging as a convergence technology. Many times, all team members must have IP telephony skills because when IP telephony is part of the deployment, the changes required can fuel changes to the voice-messaging legacy deployment and support team as well. Another benefit is that merging the two teams' expertise prepares this same team for other types of messaging services in the near future, such as video messaging.

This is just one way that a cross-functional organization can be put together to properly support unified messaging. To maintain Unity as an application, the team must understand more than voice messaging: It also needs a core knowledge of the telephony integration methods that Unity uses. Within an organization that emphasizes messaging services— where voice messaging is just as crucial as electronic messaging—it is easier to manage the core competencies of the separate groups and allows them to share commonalities in their areas of responsibility. These common areas include second-tier end-user support, administration, and the common use of the messaging backbone and its directory service by all these different types of messaging.

Managing Perception Issues When Combining Voice Mail with E-mail

Another interesting paradigm to understand is how Unity and unified messaging affect organizations' typical perceptions of the differences between legacy voice mail and e-mail. It is often surprising to note that some companies expect and account for e-mail–based service interruptions on a regular basis. It might be scary to think that regular unscheduled e-mail outages are expected, but they are in some organizations.

In contrast, legacy voice messaging is perceived to always be available and isn't necessarily mission-critical. This seems to be a contradiction, but it might be the result of conditioning: A legacy e-mail system is typically liable to suffer service interruptions, and a legacy voice-messaging system never seems to have them.

One the one hand, for Unity to provide reliable voice messaging for subscribers and outside callers, it must always be available, even though it is not considered mission-critical. On the other hand, when Unity is installed in a messaging environment that is considered mission-critical yet unreliable, just knowing that Unity's service (normal operations) can be disturbed by an occasionally unavailable e-mail server can be enough to prompt the given company to uninstall the system before it even has a chance to provide unified messaging services to subscribers and before the company can realize its benefits.

If this is the case, what is the answer? How can Unity be deployed as a unified messaging solution if the messaging system that it connects to is occasionally unavailable? The answer is twofold. First, the perception must be changed. Reliability for any corporate messaging system (voice or e-mail) is essential to a successful and highly productive organization. So, if there is a concern about whether an electronic-messaging system can support unified messaging because the electronic-messaging system is unreliable, you must address those unreliability issues first. You must achieve the goal of reliability before you introduce Unity and unified messaging. Second, if achieving reliability in your messaging environment requires a redesign, include unified messaging requirements from the start. If it requires just a correction of server hardware or OS, or the resolution of messaging application issues, make sure that Unity can operate reliably in this environment. Part II discusses in detail ways to assess and evaluate whether Unity can achieve normal operations with your messaging environment. Naturally, the emphasis on reliability with Unity includes two points:

- Ensuring adherence to deployment and design requirements found throughout this book—especially in the deployment section in Part II

- Focusing on a sustainable Unity solution, one where the loss of access to Unity's dependencies are minimized and Unity servers are placed in failover configurations

The messaging environment can and should be readied for Unity and should be maintained at that same high state of readiness, even after the product is deployed. In this case, a high state of readiness implies Unity's capability to maintain normal operations in an ongoing, persistent fashion. When the messaging infrastructure is readied, the next step is to understand Unity's relationship with and dependencies on this messaging infrastructure. In addition, it is important to understand how service interruptions, planned or unplanned, can affect Unity's capability to provide acceptable voice-messaging services in the same way as a legacy voice-messaging system that never goes down, as well as to voice-enable e-mail playback over the telephone. Ensuring this ongoing state of readiness is the primary way to prevent or minimize the chances of misperceptions of the product's reliability.

Back to organizational alignment to support unified messaging: Another very important argument for organizational alignment (aside from the need for centralized technical expertise) is that, without it, you are guaranteed to experience service interruptions with Unity. Of course, this creates undue perception problems about Unity's capability to provide reliable services to end users. It is easy enough to ignore Unity's messaging requirements for subscribers when it is trying to service their voice-messaging requests. Without properly aligning your messaging services, you are guaranteed to face serviceability issues between Unity and the messaging system that it is trying to service. This is another paradigm shift and is a prime justification for establishing a centralized messaging team that has both voice and e-mail expertise. One might say that this is the same paradigm shift, but so many technical and organizational issues are driven by these perceptions of unified messaging—and, in most cases, misperceptions—that they must be identified individually instead of being considered one in the same paradigm shift. So, because these paradigms are all interrelated, they must all be known, understood, and planned for if unified messaging is to be successful.

As an example, if your IS or IT organization is not aligned as previously discussed, it may not have all the information that it needs to work efficiently. If the e-mail teamtakes the messaging system out of service without telling the voice-messaging team to prepare for the same outage, you end up with a scheduled e-mail outage and an unscheduled voice-messaging outage. Both outages will affect the same end users, but in different ways. The users will know that the e-mail system will be unavailable during a certain period of time, but they will still expect to retrieve and leave voice messages and will be disappointed when they cannot. So, without the organizational alignment, the end-user community suffers, propagating the perception that unified messaging is not suitable for its needs.

Another perception issue regarding unified messaging products in general is the expectation that features and functionality found in some legacy voice-messaging systems will transfer to unified messaging without any change in the behavior of those features or alteration of their functionality. This might or might not be the case. To address this concern and overcome the perception that this traditional functionality is lost, you absolutely must identify the functionality that is most critical for migrating to unified messaging. You do this by performing a usage analysis of your existing legacy voice-messaging systems and surveying your end users. In fact, end-user involvement is at the heart of a usage analysis: This analysis cannot be considered valid without end-user input and active participation in the migration to unified messaging. This usage analysis yields a considerable amount of data on everything you need to do to prepare for your migration. This includes what features of your legacy voice-messaging systems are most important to your end users, as well as a gap analysis between the legacy system and Unity. For more information on performing an end-user usage analysis, see Part II, especially Chapter 8, "Deployment Methodology;" Chapter 9, "Planning;" and Chapter 11, "Designing a Unity Solution."

An example of legacy voice-messaging functionality that is "lost" when moving to UM is deleting voice messages automatically that are reserved for a short period of time. Some of the most popular legacy voice-messaging systems offer a feature that enables users to store messages for a certain number of days before they are deleted. Subscribers depend upon this feature and use the system with an eye toward the eventual deletion of their stored messages. They know that the messages will be deleted and do not have to worry about maintaining their messages; thus, they do not have to worry about managing the size of the mailbox. This can be considered a nice convenience, but it is sorely lacking in unified messaging. For example, Unity uses a messaging system, such as Exchange or Domino, as its off-box store; it does not have the type of control necessary to delete old messages that have been left in a subscriber's e-mail box after a matter of days. Could it have that type of control programmatically through code? Absolutely.

Often an organization puts out an RFP stating that the UM system must delete voice messages after 12 or 14 or 16 days. At the same time, however, the organization does not want a product such as Unity to have that type of automated control over the messaging environment. So, it is possible to automate the management of voice messages in Exchange, for instance, but it is certainly considered too risky to enable Unity or any other unified messaging product to do this safely and without error. Most e-mail administrators are reluctant to enable any application to sit on top of their e-mail system and manage specific activities in this way, especially activities that include deleting messages periodically. So, even though it is desirable to have Unity delete messages after a certain number of days—and it would be useful to adhere to it—in the end, it is not practical for Unity have this type of capability within a messaging system, even if it is programmatically possible. Doing so gives Unity the liability for managing its subscribers' voice messages stored in the e-mail system.

Ease of installation and use are often differentiators between a legacy VM system and a UM system such as Unity. This major difference is the result of two primary reasons. First, most companies do not install their own legacy voice-mail systems. They typically have the maker of the product or one of their service's partners do the installation. With Unity, you must install it or have a Cisco partner install it. The second difference is that, during the installation operations, uncertainty arises concerning how the product actually should be installed. Unity has the same familiar, seemingly easy-to-use installation interfaces as other software-based products that use Microsoft technologies and APIs. However, you cannot just sit down and install it without having some knowledge of what the product is doing (or, in some cases, significant knowledge and access rights to the corporate directory and mail store). Thus, learning about what Unity does or is supposed to do is a key step in the installation process—and it is too often ignored. Do you want to stay out of trouble when installing Unity? Make sure that you know what it is supposed to do. Also do a few dry runs (in a lab) before you actually install it into your environment, regardless of the size of your environment.

Usage and New Security Issues

When voice messaging is introduced to the data environment, a whole set of new security issues arises. Understanding these issues and how to address them is crucial to a successful transition from legacy voice messaging to unified messaging. Ignoring these security issues and others like them will prevent you from realizing the finer benefits of unified messaging. It should be considered a best practice to address these issues during the planning and design process for any given Unity deployment:

- Privacy and confidentiality in voice messaging across an e-mail enterprise.

- Privacy and confidentiality in text to the speech of electronic mail through the telephone.

- Encrypted messages for the end user regardless if they're using their GUI e-mail client or the Unity TUI.

- Encrypted calls from Unity to CallManager and then from Unity to the messaging system it services.

These issues are presented in the following sections so that the awareness of them is raised from the start.

Privacy and Confidentiality in Voice Messaging Across an E-mail Enterprise

In a legacy voice-messaging system, messages do not have the freedom to travel in such an "out-of-control" way as what you might see with an e-mail message. Thus, a confidential voice message left for a voice-mail subscriber is heard only by that person—no one else. Not many options are available for forwarding confidential messages to just anyone, and users do not have the freedom to edit the contents of the confidential voice message and resend it as if it came from the same original sender.

When voice messaging is introduced to a legacy e-mail environment, such as Exchange or Domino, confidentiality parameters must be addressed in the legacy e-mail or messaging environment. To prevent messages marked as confidential from being sent to just anyone, these confidentiality flags (marking a message confidential) must be used and maintained in your messaging environment. Without the support of and use of such confidentiality flags, voice messages can be sent to a wide number of people rapidly, without any capability to control who can receive the messages.

Privacy and Confidentiality in Text to Speech of E-mail Through the Telephone

With unified messaging, new functionality is present that does not exist in a legacy voice-messaging environment. Unified messaging has the capability to "voice-enable" a legacy e-mail environment, enabling the subscriber to play back voice messages *and* e-mail messages over the telephone. To play back e-mail messages over the telephone, text-to-speech (TTS) technology is used. This certainly sounds like a good idea, but what happens now that an outside caller can dial into a unified messaging system, log in as someone else—say, the CEO—and play back that person's confidential e-mail messages over the telephone? What happens is a very unhappy CEO.

Fortunately for Unity, it can support two-factor authentication that can then be tied to a class of service that supports TTS for subscribers. This means that subscribers who have the capability to play back their messages can do so only if they authenticate over the telephone using two-factor authentication. In Unity's case, this is the subscriber's extension and SecureID pass code entered from the subscriber's token or FOB. Without a pass code, Unity denies access into the system and prevents unwanted intrusion into mailboxes that have the capability to play back TTS. For more information about Unity's support for two-factor authentication, see the Unity Administration Guide on the Cisco website at www.cisco.com.

So, here is another paradigm shift. In a legacy voice-messaging environment, an intruder can call into the system and access the CEO's voice mail if that person can figure out his or her password. This has been an ongoing issue that seems to have been ignored or "played down" in its level of criticality to a business's daily operations. However, if you have a unified messaging solution and the same intruder accesses the CEO's voice mail, the issue is considered quite critical because the intruder also has a chance to listen to e-mail messages over the phone (if this feature is enabled). Both issues should be considered critical and they merit equal attention and care. In essence, by adding two-factor authentication capabilities to your unified messaging system, you alleviate both problems equally. As a subscriber, you must use your subscriber ID and SecureID pass code to access the system, whether you are checking voice mail or playing back e-mail. From an authentication standpoint, both are now more secure. This means that, when it is applied, Unity's support of two-factor authentication for unified messaging is a far more suitable solution for playing back any type of message over the phone. If you will not use two-factor security, you can best keep your e-mail secure by not using TTS for subscribers to check their e-mail messages over the TUI.

Encrypted Messages, Encrypted Calls

If you resolve the issue of e-mail playback using TTS by implementing two-factor authentication, you take care of limiting security issues surrounding authentication. However, there are other forms of access, such as eavesdropping on the over-the-wire phone session. Thus, phones are not secure if the call between the phone and the switch that it is connected to is not encrypted. If all phone calls were encrypted, you would not have to worry about any eavesdropping: If eavesdroppers accessed the audio portion of the call, they would hear only the noise of encrypted audio.

Encrypted calls are out of the scope of Unity's capability. Nevertheless, they are always brought up as an issue when discussing message playback. Surprisingly, some organizations mention this issue during product evaluation more with message playback than with over-the-phone conversations.

Storing Voice Messages

The next question asked with any UM system such as Unity is, "Okay, so where are the voice messages stored, really?" The answer, of course, is that they are stored in the e-mail message store. This is actually a hard concept for people to accept. Are the voice messages stored somewhere on Unity? The answer is no. The voice messages are deposited in the Unity Messaging Repository (UMR); as long as the messaging system that Unity services is still online when the message is left there, it is delivered right away. A message stays on the Unity server only if the message system is unavailable. Should voice messages be stored on Unity or in both places, just in case? Possibly. They likely will be in the future—but not because Unity has to have any control over them. Unity eventually will need to consider its dependency on the messaging store to be essential but also behave in a benign way (that is, to minimize the impact the loss of this dependency on its normal operations) so that subscribers who simply want to dial in and check for new messages or manage old voice messages can do so, even if the message store is unavailable to them.

The important thing to note here is that Unity 3.1*x* and 4.0*x* can temporarily store messages (in the UMR) left by a subscriber or outside caller *if* the message cannot be delivered to an unavailable message store.

Another concern arises about storing voice messages with e-mail centers on the size of voice messages. Voice messages are created essentially as wave file attachments to an e-mail message. To play back the message, subscribers must use either the telephone or the

VMO snap-in for Exchange or DUC client for Domino in the e-mail client. These snap-ins for the e-mail client recognize the voice message and enable subscribers to interface with the voice-messaging system so that they can record voice messages from their e-mail client (GUI) and send to others.

If voice messages are just wave file attachments to e-mail messages, then how big are the messages? That depends on two things: the codec or codecs used to encode the voice messages, and the average size of the message. Does this mean that voice messages have an impact on an e-mail system? Absolutely! You cannot migrate your entire legacy voice-messaging system onto your e-mail system without affecting it in at least three ways:

- An increase in the number of messages
- An increase in the average size of a message
- An increase in the overall disk storage

Any unified messaging system also affects the load of your messaging systems—some worse than others. Unity's load on an existing messaging system varies, depending upon feature/function usage, the number of subscribers, and the number of messages submitted and retrieved. Be prepared to understand the effects that Unity has on your messaging systems. These effects are not a bad thing, but it is important to be realistic about the potential impact. They *can* become a bad thing if you are unprepared for them or don't manage them.

To learn more about Unity's use of codecs, see Chapter 7, "Components and Subsystems: Features;" Chapter 13, "Unity with Microsoft Exchange;" and Chapter 14, "Unity with Lotus Domino." To learn about capacity planning for your message store, see Chapter 9.

Remote Users, End Users, and Accessibility

Unified messaging represents a change for your end users. It represents a change in the way they communicate and interact with fellow coworkers or outside callers. With unified messaging, the end user now has the capability to review a voice message—say, from an outside caller—and then forward the message to that outside caller's e-mail address and respond to it using text (see Figure 1-5).

Having the capability to respond to voice messages using text or text messages using voice seem trivial and of no consequence. However, it is a means for end users to enhance or even improve upon their productivity, especially if it saves them time in communicating with one another.

Figure 1-5 *Responding to a Voice Message with Text*

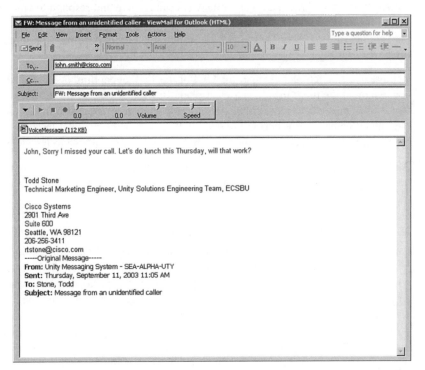

With unified messaging, there is a contrast in conveniences for the different types of end users. End users who work in a corporate office every day will appreciate the convenience of unified messaging in their GUI interface. They can maintain a high level of productivity by staying at the computer and not being bothered with changing from computer to telephone to check for different types of messages. Telephone Record and Playback (TRaP) is the capability to use a media control in your messaging GUI client to record and play back your messages by having the control call your phone to use as a microphone or speaker. With this technology, a subscriber will still use a phone, but the phone is a part of the GUI experience. Of course, this means that users spend less time on the phone walking through conversations (listening to and responding to prompts played to them over the phone) and checking and responding to messages. In addition, end users can set their special phone settings, such as greetings and notification devices, through the Cisco Personal Communications Assistant (CPCA).

For mobile users, access to and use of the phone is essential, especially while they are in transit. With unified messaging, mobile users can receive and respond to voice messages, e-mail messages, and fax messages, and can maintain a higher level of productivity while they are out of the office. This benefit of unified messaging becomes important as usage increases over time.

Remote users benefit using either the GUI or the TUI, depending upon what is more convenient at the time. In some cases, especially with remote locations that have lower bandwidth, it might be more convenient for end users to use the TUI for accessing both e-mail and voice mail. When ample bandwidth is available, the GUI might be the only preferred method of access. In this case, both options are available to the end user.

All three examples show how different types of workers—office, mobile, and remote—can benefit from the use of unified messaging to improve their daily productivity.

Voice Mail and UM Coexistence

Another reasonable request is to integrate unified messaging with voice messaging. This just means that often it is desirable to have some subscribers use unified messaging and other subscribers use voice messaging only. So how is this performed? Because Unity uses an existing messaging system, it is necessary to configure the Unity unified messaging servers and the Unity voice-messaging servers to use the same e-mail organization instead of separate ones. For Exchange, this means the same organization name; for Domino, it means the same domain name. In this case, a messaging organization is the topmost messaging boundary established by the respective messaging systems when you first install them. The organizational boundary typically means the same address book and shared directory information.

With Cisco Unity, it is possible to have subscribers in one Unity server address messages to subscribers on other Unity servers. This is traditionally called digital networking; it is also called Unity networking.

This creates a challenge because now you have voice mail-only subscribers in your global address list. To keep unified messaging subscribers from sending e-mail to voice mail-only subscribers, it is necessary to hide their address in the global address book. Otherwise, they will receive e-mail messages that they cannot read.

NOTE   Subscribers can play back e-mail over the phone by using text-to-speech. However, this is not considered a voice-mail feature and, therefore, is not available with a voice mail-only license. It is only available with a UM license.

So, although it is possible to mix voice mail-only subscribers and unified messaging subscribers within the same organization, the users must be separated on different servers because of licensing. To keep unified messaging subscribers from sending e-mail messages to voice mail-only subscribers, the voice mail-only subscribers must be hidden in the global address list.

Integrating Fax

Earlier versions of Unity contained a fax solution called Active Fax that was built into the Unity product offering as a separate server. Active Fax offered unified administration, and that was the biggest advantage of using it. Since Unity 3.0, Active Fax is no longer offered as a fax solution. However, Unity does have the capability to integrate with different fax vendors, depending upon the following:

- The offering is currently available on Exchange only.
- The fax vendor must use an Exchange message class to identify the message as a fax.

Solutions and Deployment

When you understand the paradigm shifts associated with unified messaging, you can begin to work on your solution and deployment. To develop your solution, you must understand how to define and execute the tasks necessary to transition or shift your organization to unified messaging. Then you must address the technical issues described throughout this book. When developing your solution, it is important to have an excellent understanding of Unity's capabilities. See the end of this chapter for a brief walkthrough of the different sections in the book, to make sure you understand the importance of each one. Play close attention to the Part II and Part III, "Solutions, Systems Management, and Administration," so that you can understand how to deploy Unity and also how to manage both it and your subscribers as you move to unified messaging.

Part II provides you with an in-depth look at how to plan for, design, and implement a Unity solution, regardless of the size of your deployment. Initially, it might seem complicated, but this will be easier when you understand how to identify the tasks associated with deploying Unity under various configurations.

Cross-Departmental Participation

One of the things you can do to address the seemingly large set of complicated issues is to give yourself an opportunity to openly identify the issues and features that are most important to your end users, regardless of where they are in the organizational structure. Some might frown upon this idea, but you simply cannot expect your end users to easily accept something as different as unified messaging without involving them in the process. In a nutshell, it is easier for end users to accept the change that any new product brings with it, especially one as capable as Unity, if they can participate in the process.

It is possible to enable end users to participate and still allow them to be productive with their normal duties. Participation does not mean that they should be required to spend every working hour on the project. Aside from being directly involved, end users can participate by attending presentations and demonstrations of the product, by having access to the product in their area so they have a chance to understand what it does and how it does it, or by asking them to fill out surveys or questionnaires on the product's features and functionality. Other options include creating focus groups or working groups from different departments or divisions that can provide direct input into the product and how it might be used.

Adapting the User Community to Unified Messaging

So, how do you adapt the user community to unified messaging? when you involve users in the process, it is easier. You can do a few things to ensure that the end-user community has a chance to adapt to the technology:

- Offering training
- Easing in features over time
- Being aware of the changes in end-user behavior that might affect the system's performance (also known as the turnpike effect)

Training

Without a doubt, Unity's TUI conversation is different than others in the industry—no two conversations are exactly alike. Many of the key presses and conversation statements might be exactly the same or similar, but without including training in your deployment effort, you certainly will have significant support overhead. It might not be worth deploying a technology such as unified messaging if you cannot train your end users on how to be Unity subscribers. Make sure that you provide the necessary training for the end users.

Easing in Features Over Time

It is not necessary to turn on every feature or make every feature available to all end users at the time of deployment. As a matter of fact, you might find that doing so overwhelms the end users so much that they will not want to even use the product. Instead, limit the number of features and functionality. For instance, it is not necessary to grant every subscriber TTS access. This can be managed by planning your class of service settings and making sure that some of your class of service groups do not have TTS access available. Another example is the web interface. Although it is functional, it might seem like too much to remember right from the start. Instead, give the subscribers some time to learn how to use the Unity TUI, and then phase in additional features over time. Doing so ensures a more pleasant end-user experience and makes your job easier in the long run. Your help desk will appreciate it as well.

Changes in End-User Behavior (the Turnpike Effect)

When trying to determine how to map features and functionality from your legacy voice-messaging system to unified messaging, consider a few important facts. First, to ease the transition, it is a good idea to attempt to closely match functionality between your legacy voice-messaging system and Unity. When you do, you can identify the gaps or differences in Unity's functionality with that of your legacy system. The gaps are areas where you will identify key training points for all end users.

In addition, end users might not be familiar with new features and functionality. These new features and functionality are the strict UM characteristics; they include technologies such as TRaP, TTS, and the capability to access personal settings (including settings such as notification devices and greetings) over the web. When subscribers begin using some or all of these features frequently, you will see a change in the performance of your solution. Thus, it is important to be aware of this up front so that you can plan for it. You can end up with a turnpike effect: End users might access the system more than they used to. So, at the beginning you might see the subscribers using the phone more often, or using the phone to record and play back messages using TRaP because controlling the phone from the computer is an exciting and new opportunity to use old technology. In this scenario, it is important to monitor port usage and call volume so that you can adjust accordingly. Again, as with all the critical issues listed in this chapter, do not ignore the possibility of the turnpike affect. Doing so can spell disaster for your new deployment.

Of course, you might find a complete change of habit over time. It is possible that phone usage will drop off drastically as subscribers become familiar with using the GUI interface to manage all their messages (see Figure 1-6).

Does this means that the subscribers will stop using the phone altogether? No, but it might mean that they will stop using the phone in the same way they used it previously, when the legacy voice-messaging system was in place. Figure 1-7 shows the difference between TRaP usage and legacy phone usage.

Figure 1-6   *Phone Usage Over Time*

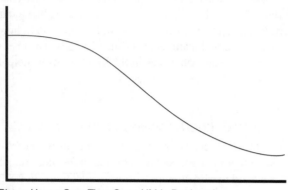

Phone Usage Over Time Once UM Is Deployed

Figure 1-7   *Different Types of Phone Usage Over Time*

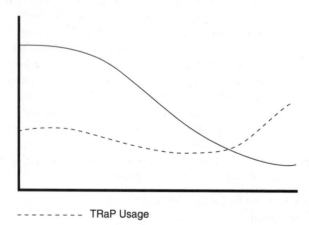

- - - - - - - - TRaP Usage

Administrative, Management, and Help Desk Considerations

Part II discusses how to plan for supporting your end users. The process that accompanies this planning is called an end-user feature/function analysis, and it includes identifying the feature differences between the legacy voice-messaging systems and Unity. This becomes the basis for support along with the new functionality that is provided to the subscribers over time.

On top of determining how to put a support structure in place, there are other considerations for administration and management of the unified messaging infrastructure. Most of these considerations are addressed in Part III, "Solutions, System Management and Administration," and include how to administrate multiple Unity servers and also how to do so programmatically. Take a look at the chapters in Part III to understand how you might build your support and administration structure around a new Unity deployment.

Messaging Technologies

Other chapters in this book discuss the messaging technologies that Unity uses; specifically, see Chapter 5. To give you a good idea of how Unity uses these different technologies, they are presented here briefly.

Unity's Messaging Technology

Unity's use of Exchange is based on the Messaging Application Programming Interface (MAPI). The MAPI implementation focuses on accessing subscriber mailboxes to retrieve messages on their behalf, sending messages on their behalf, and notifying subscribers when they receive messages.

The MAPI Profile and System Mailbox

With Exchange, Unity's key to servicing subscribers is through MAPI. That includes its use of a MAPI profile and system mailbox that is used to address messages from outside callers to subscribers of the system. The system mailbox also provides notification services for subscribers by monitoring their mailboxes for new messages and filtering on new voice messages. It basically monitors the state of all messages in a subscriber's mailbox so that it can act upon the state appropriately.

Unity's use of Domino is based on the Notes API; it uses the Lotus Notes client to access the Domino directory and messaging system. Through the Notes client, Unity provides unified messaging services to all subscribers. The implementation is a little different than in the Exchange version. This is largely the result of DUCS, which is in place to provide end-user proxy services for outside callers and to deliver messages to subscribers. The DUCS client provides a media master control for playing back and recording messages.

Integration Technologies

Unity was an early adapter of Telephony Application Programming Interface (TAPI) and made use of it for both its original voice board interface and its interface into CallManager. It uses TAPI through the telephony service provider (TSP), which is the interface connected to the voice board or CallManager. The early voice board manufacturer used by Unity was Dialogic and is still in use today.

Unity's implementation into CallManager became more scalable and capable when it began using the Skinny Station Protocol in its TSP to connect to CallManager.

Along with Unity's support of multiple integration types, the Unity 4.0 offering includes a TAPI-independent implementation of the Session Initiation Protocol (SIP). In the future, the next-generation replacement of legacy voice boards used by Dialogic includes SIP as its primary interface. Unity will integrate with this interface for Dialogic. In addition, Unity can support third-party SIP proxy servers from different vendors.

A couple of very important chapters focus on these integration technologies: Chapter 6, "Components and Subsystems: Telephony Services," and "Chapter 17, "Unity Telephony Integration." In addition, you will find switch file settings in the appendix.

Summary

This chapter discusses the challenges associated with unified messaging as a part of the voice data convergence paradigm for the messaging application layer. It recommends that you pay equal attention to organizational alignment as to the technical aspects of migrating to a unified messaging system. It highlights several ways to address the different issues that the unified messaging paradigms present to organizations that are interested in adapting unified messaging as their strategic direction. It also discusses other important issues, such as how to prepare for unified messaging both technically and organizationally. Finally, it covers topics that end users might be concerned about as well, such as privacy and security.

CHAPTER 2

Unity Architecture Overview

This chapter provides an overview of the Unity 4.*x* architecture, including several "walk-throughs" that cover typical system-usage scenarios and how individual services and components work within those scenarios. The reader should take away an understanding of what the various services and components are responsible for in the Unity system, how Unity interacts with the directory and message stores, and how the client interfaces into Unity work at a high level.

This document assumes that the reader has a basic knowledge of the Unity administration interfaces. If you are unfamiliar with terms such as *call handlers*, *call routing rules*, and *Media Master control*, or if you do not know your way around the web-based system administration (SA) interface, you will want to first review the Unity System Administration Guide and Unity User Guides. Documentation for all versions of Unity can be found here:

http://www.cisco.com/univercd/cc/td/doc/product/voice/c_unity/

The Cisco Unity server is a complex and powerful application that is made up of numerous individual components and services installed both on the local Unity server itself and, in some cases, on other servers in the network. Furthermore, Cisco Unity interacts with a number of other external applications including Microsoft SQL 2000 or Microsoft MSDE, Microsoft Exchange 2000 or 2003, Microsoft Exchange 5.5, Active Directory, Microsoft Internet Information Services, and Lotus Domino. It also integrates with various phone switches including Cisco CallManager, SIP phone systems, and a number of legacy PBX phone systems on the market today.

On a typical Unity 4.0 installation, you will see more than 10 separate services added by the setup process in the Windows Service Control Manager. Understanding all the components in each of these services and how they interact with each other and all the external components that Unity integrates with can seem like a daunting task. At the end of this chapter, you will have a solid understanding of how the Unity product works, and much of the rest of this book will make a lot more sense. Terms, such as *DOH*, *MIU*, and *directory monitor,* are used elsewhere in this book with the assumption that you know what we are talking about. If you follow this chapter and the next carefully, you will.

This chapter takes a high-level look at the system architecture, reviews the major components, and discusses what function they serve. The subsequent sections provide walkthroughs and discuss the role of each component in the following tasks:

- The caller leaves a message.
- The MWI is turned on for that message.
- An administrator makes a change to a subscriber's record through the system administration console.
- A change takes place for a subscriber in the directory.

System Architecture

Figure 2-1 provides an overview of all the services and primary components installed on a Unity 4.x server. In the figure, all of the rounded rectangles represent a service or set of services. The ones with a dark background represent items that the Unity install did not add to the system but that are required for Unity to operate properly.

The following sections introduce the services and discuss their role in the Unity system. You will notice that most of the Unity-related services start with AV. This is because Cisco purchased Active Voice for the Unity product line in 2000; such designations in the services, Registry keys, message classes, and other places not directly visible to end users were left as is. Although Figure 2-1 shows Unity connected to a CallManager, remember that Unity can also hook up to legacy PBX switches, SIP gateways, or combinations of all three—just the CallManager interface is shown here for simplicity. More details on the switch-integration capabilities of Unity are covered in Chapter 17, "Unity Telephony Integration."

Figure 2-1   *High-Level Diagram of the Unity Architecture*

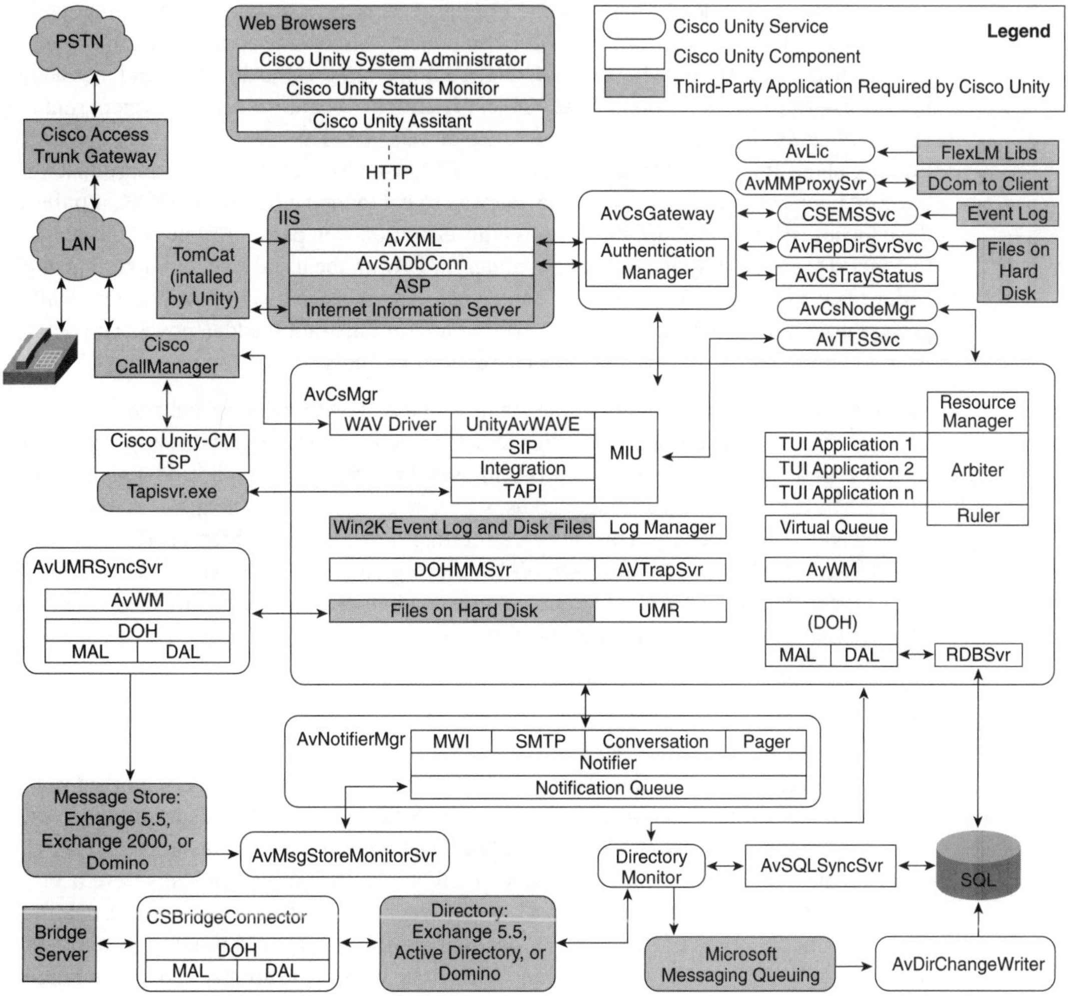

AVCsGateway

The gateway service does what its name implies: It acts as a gateway into the main Unity components that run under the AVCsMgr component. All outside applications that want to connect to the Data Object Hierarchy (DOH, a wrapper around the directory and messaging interfaces—see the later section "Data Object Hierarchy") or any other component running under AVCsMgr must authenticate with the gateway first. The AVSADBConn component running under Internet Information Services (IIS), used by the ASP pages to produce the SA web interface, must go through the gateway to get to the DOH. At the DOH, it pulls all the data necessary to produce the various administration web pages. Although it is possible to connect to most components running under AVCsMgr, the usual target for external applications is the DOH. As discussed in Chapter 21, "Administering Unity Programmatically," going through the proprietary DOH interfaces for administration adds, moves, and deletes is no longer required, as it was for earlier versions of Unity.

The gateway service also monitors the status of the AVCsMgr service and can report whether it is in-service or out-of-service to external clients. The tray status application, for instance, polls the gateway periodically and uses this information to decide which icon it shows. The tray status application also uses interfaces exposed on the gateway service for starting and stopping Unity. This involves shutting down the AVCsMgr, AVRepDirSvr, AVTTSSvr, AVMsgStoreMonitorSvr, AVNotifierMgr, and AVUMRSyncSvr services. The rest of the services—most notably, the directory monitors and, of course, the gateway service itself—stay up and running, even if Unity is offline.

AVCsMgr

The Active Voice CommServer Manager (AVCsMgr) is the main Unity component in the system. In older Unity versions, in fact, only the AVCsMgr and AVCsGateway services were present on a new installation. Literally everything ran under the single AVCsMgr component. As Unity has scaled up and added features, various components have been taken "out of process" into their own services. Eventually, as Unity moves toward a true clustering model, some of these services actually will be capable of running on another server entirely. At some point, for instance, it will be possible to simply add another media server to provide more text-to-speech (TTS) or voice port capacity to a Unity installation.

Although this is the direction Unity is headed, it is not there now; everything runs on a single Windows 2000/2003 server at this point. Sites that need to scale beyond the capacity of a single Unity server for ports or subscriber resources must leverage Unity's digital networking capabilities and use separate Unity servers to balance the load. See Chapter 12, "Unity Networking," for more on that.

A number of important components run under the AVCsMgr service. The following sections discuss the most important components.

Data Object Hierarchy

The DOH is the abstraction layer over the directory and messaging back ends supported by Unity. A back end is the system that is being used as the message repository and directory backbone that the Unity server is installed into—either Exchange 5.5, Exchange 2000, Exchange 2003, or Domino. With the DOH, the idea is simple: Provide a common interface for all client applications, such as phone conversations, administration interface, reports, and the like for accessing directory and messaging information from Exchange 5.5, Exchange 2000, Exchange 2003, Active Directory, and Domino.

The DOH has two main subcomponents: the Directory Access Layer (DAL) and the Message Access Layer (MAL). The original idea was to provide different MAL and DAL "plug-ins" for each back end Unity supported. Clients would be unaware of the wildly different access protocols going on underneath the DOH. The first incarnation of the DOH was an abstraction layer over the Exchange 5.5 directory and mailbox data for Unity 2.x, in which all Unity directory information and messages were stored in Exchange. The LDAP and MAPI interfaces used to get at this data in Exchange 5.5 is more of an art than a science; having a fully functional wrapper around this complexity was an absolute must.

When Unity 3.0 introduced SQL as the primary directory repository, the need to have the DOH wrapper around database access was not nearly as critical. Unity now employs directory monitors to pull in data from the directory to a local SQL database and to write necessary changes back to the directory. This enables clients simply to use standard SQL access mechanisms to retrieve and update data instead of using the proprietary DOH interfaces. However, time to market considerations made it necessary to leave the client interfaces into the DOH alone and simply reprogram the DOH back ends to talk to both the directory monitors and the SQL database.

Although the DOH is still in use in Unity 4.x, its days as the primary back-end wrapper for the directory are numbered. As discussed in Chapter 21, in Unity 4.x, it is possible to interface directly with SQL for all your basic Unity administration needs and never talk to the DOH at all. The long-term model is to have all clients use interfaces right into the Unity SQL database (through XML, SOAP, ADO, ODBC, JDBC, and other interfaces) and rely on the directory monitors to do the heavy lifting for the various back ends supported. See the "Directory Monitor" section later in this chapter for more information.

Although the DAL component under the DOH is being phased out, the MAL wrapper around the messaging tasks likely will be available in some form for a while at least. In the case of Exchange, the MAL uses MAPI client access methods very similar to what an Outlook client does to gain access to a mailbox. During configuration setup, a special mailbox named Unity_(server name) is created on the Exchange server selected as the partner server for Unity (which could be on the same server with Unity). This mailbox is referred to as the Unity system mailbox in the Unity administration documentation. A MAPI profile is created on the local Unity server that "points" to that mailbox. This message profile is very similar to a profile you would create for your Outlook client that points back to the Exchange home server that your mailbox is stored on. The Unity system mailbox profile, however, is optimized in a couple of ways so that it can support many hundreds of simultaneous MAPI connections, which is not possible with a standard profile. In short, this profile is Unity's gateway into the Exchange messaging back end through MAPI, and you use it to gain access to all mailboxes for subscribers serviced on the local Unity server. This profile and the Unity system mailbox account are critical to the proper functioning of the system; if they are not found, the DOH creates them automatically. In earlier versions of Unity, these items were checked for at startup, and the profile and account were created as soon as Unity came online. In 4.0(3), however, this check was moved to the first time a mailbox was accessed. The automatic creation logic turned out to be necessary because so many folks gave in to the natural human instinct to destroy that which they do not understand and deleted one or both of these items when they encountered them without realizing what they were doing. If something goes wrong with the account or the profile, it is as easy to delete them and restart Unity as it is to fix it.

In the case of Domino, the DOH uses the Notes client interface (which you must install on each Unity server) to retrieve messages for subscribers and send messages of its own. The Domino Server sees Unity as a client, but the user ID that you use to log in has rights to the server's address book and the administrative request database. This allows the Unity system to log in to subscribers' mailboxes and get at the directory (address book) information. See Chapter 14, "Unity with Lotus Domino," for details on deploying Unity in a Domino environment.

Resource Manager

The resource manager is used to help avoid contention for limited resources on the server. For instance, the notification MWI device manager (see the "Notifier" section, later in this chapter) asks the resource manager whether a port is available for Message Waiting Indicator (MWI) dialout. If one is, the resource manager reserves that port for the device manager, which then can ask the Arbiter to initiate the dialout. Similarly, if a conversation used for playing messages back to subscribers over the phone wants to use the Text-to-Speech (TTS) engine to play the body of an e-mail to a subscriber, it reserves a TTS session from the resource manager. If a session is available, things proceed as normal; if not, the conversation tells the subscriber to try again later. In this way, no more than the licensed number of TTS sessions ever can be active at the same time.

Arbiter

The Arbiter is the "traffic cop" of the Unity system. All components that need access to a voice port first must go through the Arbiter to get one. The Arbiter component reads the port capability settings configured on the Ports page in the SA and enforces them. The Arbiter also uses the ruler (see the next section) to process the routing rules configured on the Call Routing page in the SA. These rules are used in deciding where new inbound calls go in the system. The processing and debugging of these rules are covered in Chapter 18, "Audio Text Applications."

Ruler

The Arbiter uses the ruler component to evaluate the routing rules when deciding where a new inbound call goes in the system. The ruler pulls the call-routing rules from a SQL table in versions 3.1(3) and later. In earlier versions of Unity, these rules were stored in the Routing.RUL flat file in the Commserver\Support directory. The Arbiter passes in the call information (calling number, forwarding number, dialed number, whether it is a direct or forwarded call), and the ruler evaluates all the rules in order until it finds one that matches. Then the ruler passes the rule back to the Arbiter so that it can take action. As mentioned earlier, this process is covered later in Chapter 18.

Later, the "Component Walkthroughs" section in this chapter includes a call flow walk-through and details more about how this process works, including taking a look at some trace output from the various components.

Unity Messaging Repository

The interface is part of the mechanism that helps insulate Unity from volatility in the external network. Because Unity uses the Exchange or Domino message stores directly instead of using a proprietary message store and synchronizing, the availability of those mail stores affects user access to messages over the phone interface. The UMR is used to enable callers to continue to leave messages and retrieve some voice-mail messages when access to remote Exchange servers is interrupted.

Outside caller messages are delivered through the UMR component. When the message is recorded by one of the phone conversations (or Telephone User Interface [TUI] applications in Figure 2-2), the UMR component under AVCsMgr deposits the message as a pair of files (the message itself and a routing file indicating where it needs to go) in a directory on the local hard drive. The AVUMRSyncSvr service (see the "Unity Messaging Repository" section) picks up and delivers these messages to the mail store's back end through the MAL interface of the DOH. If the message hand-off to the Exchange or Domino back ends is interrupted, the messages remain on the local hard drive until they can be delivered. While messages wait on the hard drive for delivery, the subscriber conversation can access them and let users retrieve messages left when connectivity to the mail store is interrupted using a limited UMR conversation.

TUI Applications

Telephone User Interface applications (or simply "conversations") make up the user experience when interacting with Unity over the telephone. Not every conversation consists of a traditional recorded prompt, voice names, and greetings played to a caller. Dozens of separate conversations are used for doing everything from finding subscribers in the directory to recording messages, to logging subscribers into their mailboxes. Chapter 18 covers some of the traces and diagnostic tools that show which conversations are invoked and what inputs are passed into them.

The most visible conversations are the top-level routable conversations that show up as options in the SA and other administration applications, such as the Audio Text Manager. For instance, when you select an after-greeting action that sends the caller to the operator call handler and tell it to "send to greeting," you are actually telling Unity to invoke the PHGreeting conversation with the operator call handler as a parameter. As a call moves through Unity, it carries with it a handle back to the Media Interface Unit (MIU—see the section "Media Interface Unit"). Conversations get user inputs (touch tones pressed or a call hang-up) and can request the MIU play greetings, voice names, and prompts that make up the Unity phone conversation. Conversations also have access to the call information through this handle, including the calling number and forwarding number that the MIU got from the phone system when the call first arrived.

The following is a list of the routable conversations externally visible in Unity:

- **PHGreeting**. The Phone Handler Greeting conversation needs a call handler as an input. This conversation processes the greeting rules on a call handler. Based on which rules are active, which schedule the handler is associated with, the origin of the call, and the reason the call came to Unity, it selects and executes a greeting rule. Every subscriber is associated with a special, hidden call handler known as a primary call handler. This same conversation is used to send callers to a subscriber or an audio text application call handler. See the "Data Object Model" section in Chapter 3, for more on call handlers and subscriber structures in Unity.

- **PHTransfer**. The Phone Handler Transfer conversation also expects a call handler, but this conversation processes the transfer or contact rules on the handler. Depending on which transfer rules are active and the schedule the call handler is associated with, this conversation executes a transfer rule. If the transfer rule is set to not transfer at all, but to go straight to the greeting for the call handler, the PHTransfer conversation invokes the PHGreeting conversation for the same call handler. One of the most common things folks stumble on is the "entry point" into the call handler: They expect it to try to ring the phone, but instead it goes to the greeting. We cover this and some of the techniques for debugging problems with incoming calls in Chapter 18.

- **SubSignIn**. The Subscriber Sign In conversation collects the ID and the password (if configured) of a subscriber who wants to log into the mailbox and check messages. This conversation is similar to, but not the same as the AttemptSignIn conversation, later in this list. When the user is authenticated, the call is passed to the subscriber inbox conversation, which enables users to access their inbox and other options configurable over the phone.

- **PHInterview**. The Phone Handler Interview conversation expects an interview handler to be passed to it. It then plays all the questions recorded for an interview handler and records the caller's responses.

- **Alpha Directory (AD)**. The AD conversation expects a reference to a directory handler to be passed to it. This conversation has been around since the first version of Unity. However, in versions earlier than 4.x, there has always been a single hard-coded directory handler. In version 4.0(1) and later, administrators can create any number of directory handlers, with different sets of users associated with each.

- **AttemptSignIn**. The Attempt Sign In conversation is referenced by the default routing rules for processing new incoming direct calls. This conversation searches for the calling number in the database. If a match is found for a subscriber, it prompts the caller to enter a password, if one has been configured. If no match is found, the conversation releases the call to the Arbiter, which continues down the list of routing rules looking for a match. We talk about how routing rules work in detail in Chapter 18.

- **AttemptForwardToGreeting**. The Attempt Forward To Greeting conversation also is used by the default routing rules for handling new incoming calls. However, this rule is used for calls that forward into Unity. The forwarding number is searched in the directory for a subscriber or call handler that matches. If a match is found, the call is handed to the PHGreeting conversation, with the matching call handler as a parameter. Note that the PHTransfer rule specifically is not used here, to prevent a looping call scenario in which Unity transfers to a number that forwards to Unity, and Unity transfers to that number again, and so on. Sometimes you want Unity to transfer to another number when a call forwards in, however; techniques for dealing with that problem are covered in Chapter 18.

- **GreetingsAdministrator**. This is a new routable conversation that was added in Unity 4.0. It enables administrators to set up one key map so that they can enter a special conversation that allows them to record the greetings for call handlers over the phone interface. They must log in as a subscriber in this conversation. GreetingsAdministrator checks that a subscriber is the owner (or a member of the distribution list that is the owner) of the call handler before allowing the administrator to change the greetings for a handler.

- **Hospitality Checked Out**. This is a new routable conversation added in Unity 4.0(3). It is used in conjunction with the Property Management System (PMS) integration feature called Bellhop. This conversation enables the front desk staff to access the mailbox of a hotel guest that already has checked out of the hotel within the number of archive days set on the system. This way, if a guest realizes after checkout that he needs to access a message, he can do so by calling the front desk.

- **CVM Mailbox Reset**. This is a new routable conversation added in Unity 4.0(3) for the Community Voice Mail project. This project updates Unity for organizations that specialize in providing voice mail to folks who do not have regular access to a phone and need messaging services.

Log Manager

The log manager is responsible for all diagnostic and data (for reports) logging to flat files on the local Unity server. It also handles information bound for the event logs. It is important to note that each Unity service initiates its own instance of the log manager, not just the AVCsMgr service. If only one instance of the log manager were running under AVCsMgr, all other services would have to authenticate against the gateway to gain access to it and use it. This would be very inefficient. Instead, each service has its own log manager. For simplicity, Figure 2-1 shows only a single log manager under the AVCsMgr service. When you troubleshoot a Unity server or perhaps try to pull information to generate a report, it is important to realize that each service logs into its own files under Commserver\ Logs. If you look in this directory, you will see a series of files named data_AVCsMgr_ YYYYMMDD_HHMMSS.txt, data_AVDirChangeWriter_YYYYMMDD_ HHMMSS.txt, data_AVTTSSvr_YYYYMMDD_HHMMSS.txt, and so on. Each service that generates report-related information that is represented in Figure 2-1 has a data file associated with it in the logs directory. Not all services, such as the directory monitors, generate report information, so you will not see DATA files for all of them. You also will see diag_*.txt files in the same name format: the service name, the date in [year][month][day] format, and the time in [hour][minute][second] format to ensure uniqueness. However, if you do not have diagnostics on for any component running under that service, the diagnostic file itself will contain basic startup information and not much else. As a side note, other applications that use the log manager will open their own log files. For instance, if you open DOHPropTest.exe, it creates its own diagnostic file based on DOH diagnostic settings that are turned on.

This puts the onus on technicians to know, for instance, that when they turn on an MIU trace, that information will show up in the diag_AVCsMgr*.txt file because that is the service it runs under. On the other hand, the TTS traces, which are closely related to the MIU, actually show up in the diag_AVTTSSvr*.txt file. To put it mildly, this can be a bit frustrating to someone new to Unity who wants to figure out what he is looking at. The Unity Diagnostic Tool found under the Tools Depot on the desktop is designed to help pull the information you need from the various log files for you; however, it is helpful if you understand the process.

One of the goals of this chapter is to help you understand what each component does and which service it runs under. If you take a quick look at the micro traces section of the Unity Diagnostic Tool (found in the Tools Depot on the desktop), you will find that most of the high-level sections offered are represented as either a service or a component running under a service in Figure 2-1. Although this book is not a troubleshooting guide, in several sections we will be turning on traces and reviewing their output to help you better understand how the services work.

One last note must be made about the log manager. The keen observer will note that some components show up under more than one service. For example, the DOH runs under AVCsMgr, CSBridgeConnector, and AVUMRSyncScr. So what happens when you enable DOH traces in the Unity Diagnostic Tool? Output from these DOH traces shows up in each of the diagnostic logs for each separate service. That is a little tricky, but it makes sense if you consider that each service also has its own instance of the log manager. Every component that runs under it will log to the file opened by that service using the log manager.

TIP

The raw Diag*.txt file stamps its entries with a time from the local Unity server, as you would expect. However, the Data*.txt file stamps its entries with the system time, which is Greenwich Mean Time (GMT). Windows API calls can convert these times to the local time, which is necessary when generating reports from these files. It was done this way to facilitate, at some point, the capability to merge report data from multiple Unity servers into single reports.

When Unity runs reports, it pulls information from the ReportDB database (see the "Unity Data Object Model" in Chapter 3 for more on this). The curious observer might ask how information gets from the DATA log files generated by the log manager into the ReportDB database. A process called the scavenger kicks off every 30 minutes. It pulls relevant report data from the DATA files and stuffs it into the ReportDB tables, where the report's modules can get at them. This is one of the reasons why, when you make some test calls and then immediately run a report, your data does not show up. I have taken a number of questions on the forums along these lines in the past. There is no way to force the scavenger to run immediately—you just have to wait until it does its job.

NOTE   When viewing diagnostic files, it is best to use the Unity Diagnostic Tool to gather the logs instead of viewing them raw off the hard drive. The UDT tool formats the logs and makes them more readable by adding insertion strings for hex codes that produce more human-understandable output. This tool also has some handy functions to show you information associated only with the specific traces you are interested in seeing. This can help narrow nicely what you are looking at. For more information on the Unity Diagnostic Tool and its companion, the Unity Diagnostic Viewer (as well as a brief training video), see its home page at http://www.ciscounitytools.com/App_UDV.htm.

Media Interface Unit

The MIU is responsible for interacting with the telephone switch(es) Unity is connected to. All audio, integration information, digit presses, dialouts, and so on go through this component. The MIU is a sophisticated component that can communicate with numerous phone systems using many different integration methods. It can also talk to two different phone systems at the same time on a single Unity server, which is a unique capability in the industry.

Chapter 17 includes detailed discussions on the MIU architecture; this is just a high-level overview so that you know what the component is responsible for in the bigger Unity picture.

Telephone Application Programming Interface

Before Unity 4.0(1), all the switch integrations that Unity supported went through the TAPI interface in some way. Moving ahead, Unity will shift to alternative interface mechanisms, such as SIP, that allow more robust and scalable solutions for switch interaction.

Integrations with traditional PBXs use Dialogic voice cards, which come with a TAPI service provider that sends information to and from the MIU through the Microsoft Telephony service. Unfortunately, the TAPI protocol does not natively support serial data and inband Dual Tone Multi Frequency (DTMF) information for call integrations with many PBXs. As a result, the MIU has to do a little extra work to get this information, when necessary. This is the "integration" block under the MIU in Figure 2-1. Part of the dream of TAPI was that Unity could support any number of phone systems and voice cards, with minimal development effort on our end. Unity did, in fact, also support Natural MicroSystems and, briefly, Brootrout voice cards, which provided their own TSPs. However, that equipment is no longer supported.

Even though CallManager supports a native TAPI interface, Unity does not use it. Instead, Cisco Systems created a TAPI Service Provider (TSP) that talks directly to the Skinny interface into CallManager. In turn, the Skinny interface communicates through Microsoft's telephony service to and from the MIU. Cisco programmers created this because the Skinny interface is considerably lighter and faster than the direct TAPI interface into CallManager; it supports only a subset of the full TAPI functionality that Unity needs.

Support for TAPI declines as new, more flexible, faster, and more interesting interfaces, such as SIP, become available. TAPI support in Unity will continue for a while, but work with Dialogic on a SIP-based interface to its equipment is already well underway. For more information on the TAPI interfaces and the Microsoft telephony model that it is a part of, visit the MSDN Telephony Overview site at http://msdn.microsoft.com/library/default.asp?url=/library/en-us/tapi/intro_2khj.asp.

Integration

For legacy PBXs that require serial or analog integration information, the MIU must go around TAPI because the specification does not account for much in the way of custom integration information. Unity has flexible switch-definition and integration instruction files that allow fairly easy and robust integrations with numerous switch types and models. Cisco Technical Assistance Center (TAC) supports only a limited subset of the larger PBXs on the market, but remember that Unity was built on top of an integration engine that was designed to attach to just about any phone system. Chapter 17 discusses the creation and customization of the switch-definition and integration protocol files and covers how to troubleshoot various integration problems with legacy PBXs.

Session Initiation Protocol

As of version 4.0(1) Unity supports the Session Initiation Protocol (SIP) for communicating with phone systems. SIP is a multimedia control protocol that was designed to initiate, modify, and tear down IP sessions. Standards-based, it is defined by the IETF in RFC 3261, ratified in 1999.

In short, SIP is a peer-to-peer protocol that utilizes the architecture of the WWW. This means that end devices, called SIP User-Agents (UA), can have various levels of intelligence as well as utilize the services available within the network. SIP UAs can take various formats including SIP Phones, SIP-based PC clients, SIP VoIP (Voice over Internet Protocol) gateways, or any other device that might be contacted for a SIP session. SIP services might include device registration, call routing, call redirection, feature invocation, device notification, or various other aspects that affect a session. These services might be provided by a SIP proxy server, a SIP redirect server, a SIP registration server, or other SIP UAs. This means that a phone system based on SIP can scale reasonably well: The central switch duties are limited to just initiating, routing, and tearing down calls. The UAs are smart enough to talk directly to one another when they find each other.

The Unity SIP component talks to SIP natively via a SIP Stack that was developed within Cisco, based on the original SIP RFC254bis-04. It does *not* go through TAPI for call control. The Unity SIP component requires a SIP proxy for registration and call routing/forwarding calls into voice mail. Currently, we are using SIP only for traditional voice-mail services but are pursuing other interesting applications, such as presence and video messaging and a lot of other things that make sales folks' toes curl. Stay tuned.

UnityAVWAVE

This component sits over the WAV drivers supplied by the Dialogic, CallManager, or the SIP interchange folks. It provides extended services that are not handled by standard WAV drivers. Automatic Gain Control (AGC) is handled here for systems that do not use Dialogic cards (the Dialogic drivers have their own AGC capabilities built in). Other features, such as speed control and codec conversion (that is, switching from 711 to 729a or back), are also included here.

The capabilities and flexibility of the MIU's switch-integration capability are covered in more detail in Chapter 17.

Virtual Queue

The virtual queue is used for call-holding functionality within Unity. The queue contains all calls currently on hold while waiting for an extension to become available.

RDBSvr

The Relational Database Server (RDBSvr) component is a thin layer over the SQL data access. In short, this is just a set of libraries that make finding, adding, and updating information to the SQL tables easier.

Telephone Record and Playback Connection Server

The TRaP connection server is used to satisfy connection requests from clients that want to use their phone to play back and record messages, greetings, and voice names. The Media Master control tries to make a direct connection to both the AVTRAPConnectionServer and the DOHMMSvr components to play back the requested WAV file at the client desktop.

The clients, including the System Administration (SA), Personal Communications Assistant (PCA), Voice Messaging Interface (VMI) web pages, and View Mail for Outlook (VMO) e-mail forms, use the Media Master ActiveX control to attach directly to the TRaP connection server to establish a phone connection to the client's desktop. The TRaP Connection server then takes care of talking to the resource manager and the Arbiter components, to see if a port is available to do a Media Master dialout. If no ports are available to handle this request, the client is sent an error message; the user is told at the desktop that no ports are available and to try again later. If a port is available, the MIU is instructed to dial out to the extension number specified in the Media Master configuration at the desktop. When the user picks up the phone, a media connection is established, and all playback and recording of WAV files takes place over that phone connection.

One thing to keep in mind, however, is that the Media Master ActiveX control on the clients uses the Distributed Component Object Model (DCOM) to connect directly back to the Unity server from the desktop. Because DCOM does not work properly through firewalls or proxy servers without jumping through a number of hoops, it is difficult to establish a Media Master connection (either using TRaP or just your speakers and sound card on the local client) from outside the local intranet. Furthermore, when using NT LAN management (NTLM) authentication for the SA, the ActiveX control must authenticate a second time when the client and the Unity server are in separate domains. Because it cannot piggyback on the NTLM challenge and response authentication that the user had to supply when first accessing the page, it needs its own security token. Unity 4.0 offers an alternative to NTLM to help with sites that do not use NT as their primary network authentication mechanism or that want to work around the firewall/proxy server/domain boundary issues. This is covered in detail in the chapters of Part II, "Deployment."

DOHMMSvr

The DOH Media Master Server is used with the Media Master on the web client pages and the VMO form in Outlook to stream voice files. If the subscriber uses TRaP or just local speakers and sound cards to play back or record greetings, voice names, and messages through VMO or the SA, the client needs to make a connection back to the DOH Media Master server to establish a stream for the WAV file in question. The client passes in the identifier of the WAV file that it has been asked to play back or record to the Media Master server. The server establishes a stream handle and passes it back to the client, which then can play or record the WAV file.

If the client wants to use TRaP to play back a greeting, for instance, the Media Master control on the SA connects to both the AVTRAPSvr and DOHMMSvr components directly via DCOM. When a port has established a connection to the local phone, the Media Master server is asked to establish a stream connection to the WAV file desired over the phone connection. At this point, the message is streamed over the network to the client machine and is played there.

AVWM

The Windows Monitor (or "wedgie manager," as it affectionately is known in-house) is responsible for determining the up or down status of all Exchange servers that the local

Unity system cares about. In short, Unity cares about any Exchange server that houses one or more subscribers on it. These Exchange servers are added to the list of systems that the windows manager pings every 15 seconds (in versions 3.1[3] and earlier, this was every 30 seconds). If the server is offline or the Exchange directory (in the case of Exchange 5.5) or mail store services (for both Exchange 55 and 2000) are not responsive, or if the Service Control Manager (SCM) itself is not responsive, this server is marked internally as being down. When a subscriber signs into the Unity server over the phone to gain access to messages, the conversation first checks to see whether that Exchange server is up or down before attempting to log into that user's mailbox. If it is down, subscribers are not allowed to attempt the login to their mailboxes over the phone because this can result in very long MAPI timeouts and can end with a call being stuck or "wedged" for a long period of time. If the Exchange server that you selected during the configuration setup (the partner Exchange server, as it is called in the documentation) is offline, Unity goes into full UMR mode and stores voice messages locally until connectivity can be re-established.

In the case of Domino, the monitoring service cannot assume that the server is running on top of a Windows platform, so things get a little trickier. The service simply pings the server by name and checks for a response to make sure it is up. It does not, however, know whether the Domino services on that server function properly.

Whenever the avWM component marks a server as being down or back up again, an event log message is written through to the application event log. The Event Monitoring Service (EMS) Exchange Monitor Tool introduced for Unity 4.0(2) resides in the Tools Depot. It is designed to give the administrator the capability to be notified in a variety of ways when specific errors or classes of errors are written to the event log. For sites that have trouble with their external Exchange servers or that experience severe network latency issues, this can be helpful in staying on top of such problems.

AVNotificationMgr

For the Unity 4.0(3) release, the notification processes that are responsible for lighting MWIs, sending out notification e-mails, sending pages, and so on based on inbox activity have been pulled out of the AVCsMgr group into their own process here.

Notifier

What is referred to generally as "the notifier" is actually a set of three separate components. The AVMsgStoreMonitorSvr (see the upcoming section with this name) watches all inboxes of subscribers on the local Unity server for changes and then pushes that information onto the notification queue. The notifier engine in the AVNotificationMgr process watches the queue for items that it needs to react to and hands off the request to one of four device managers for MWIs, SMTP (text pagers), conversations (phone notification device), or pagers (tone pagers). Each of these device managers is responsible for sending the e-mails, lighting the message lamps, or making the phone calls to satisfy the delivery requirements for the subscriber in question. The notifier is also responsible for kicking off the AMIS message delivery process, covered in Chapter 12.

The MWI, conversations, and pager device managers all work with the resource manager and the Arbiter components in the AVCsMgr process to initiate the dialout/MWI requests. The SMTP device manager talks directly to the DOH component to send the e-mails for text pagers and the VMI notification devices. When they fail or succeed to carry out their notification duties, they push a message to this effect onto the notification queue to let the notifier know that the request is complete one way or the other. Each notification device maintains a local queue of tasks and is responsible for handling the retries configured for that device. For instance, deliveries to the home phone can be set to retry up to four times if the line is busy, or MWIs can be configured to retry several times in the case of a serial integration. A notification attempt is marked as failed only after exhausting all the retries configured for that device.

Later in this chapter, when we do a call flow walkthrough, we discuss a little more how this process works and take a look at some trace output from the various components to show what goes on under the covers.

Notification Queue

As its name implies, the notification queue is a simple queue of events that the notification engine watches. The AVMsgStoreMonitorSvr service (see the next section) is responsible for watching subscriber mailboxes for events that require the services of the notification engine and pushing those events onto the queue. The individual notification device managers mentioned earlier also push events onto this queue, to let the notifier know whether it was successful in satisfying the notification request.

AVMsgStoreMonitorSvr

The message monitor server service is responsible for watching the mailboxes of all the subscribers on the local Unity server. Whenever a change of any kind happens in an inbox that it monitors, it pushes the event and the mailbox identifier on the notification queue in the AVNotificationMgr service. The notifier, in turn, pulls that information off the queue and filters the inbox to get a message count; it then decides whether a notification action, such as an MWI on/off or an e-mail page or the like, needs to happen.

In the case of Exchange 5.5 or Exchange 2000, the message store monitor logs into the mailbox for all subscribers homed on the local Unity server. If this mailbox is off the Unity box (that is, the Exchange server is not installed on the same box), a security warning (more specifically, a success audit) is logged in the application event log. This is because Unity logs in using the account associated with AVMsgStoreMonitorSvr. Exchange logs this whenever another account logs into a mailbox that is not its own, even if it has rights to do so. Thus, this is not a message to be concerned about:

> Windows 2000 User LINDBORGLABS\Administrator logged on to
> EAdmin@lindborglabs.thinkpad.com mailbox, and is not the primary
> Windows 2000 account on this mailbox.

Note that when Exchange is busy or too many changes take place on an inbox in too little time (for instance, the user deletes many messages at once), Exchange can return an event indicating that you simply need to resynch the entire mailbox. In this case, the notifier must fetch the inbox and sort it to know what to do. In most cases, however, it is not necessary to filter the entire inbox; the notifier can determine what needs to be done specifically from the change notice that the message store monitor pushes onto the queue. This makes it a little difficult to look at the diagnostics kicked out by the notifier and message store monitor components because there is no hard and fast rule for when Exchange decides that it is too busy to issue a specific change request or a general resynch notice for an inbox.

In the case of Domino, the message store monitor actually registers for changes on any inboxes that it is interested in through the Domino Unified Communications Service (DUCS) interface on each Domino server that houses one or more Unity subscribers. When any message is added, removed, or modified, the message store monitor is notified of this change and pushes the appropriate event onto the notification queue in the same way the Exchange message store monitor does. At startup, Unity logs into each user's mailbox and synchs; after that, it is simply a matter of adjusting as necessary based on change events for each user's mailbox.

It is important to note that the message store monitor itself does not determine whether something needs to happen; it indicates only that a change has occurred on a mailbox that it is watching. It knows what type of action happened—a new message was added, or a message was modified (for example, marked as read) or deleted—but it does not know what needs to be done for the subscriber when action takes place. The notifier running under AVNotifierMgr must do the work to determine whether anything needs to be done, such as lighting an MWI light or initiating a pager dialout.

When the directory monitor has found an object in the directory that has been updated, it pulls information about that object into SQL again. When a change or an add comes along in the directory, the monitor pushes that information into the Microsoft Messaging Queue (MSMQ), which is watched by the AVDirChangeWriter service. AVDirChangeWriter then writes the change through to the local SQL tables as necessary. Later, in the "Component Walkthroughs" section of this chapter, we walk through what happens when an administrator makes a change in the SA. In that section, we look at some of the directory monitor, directory change writer, and MSMQ traces for a system using Active Directory (Exchange 2000/2003).

Directory Monitor

The directory monitor actually goes under different names, depending on which back end Unity is configured for, but the functionality is the same. The directory monitor is responsible for all adds, moves, and changes for all objects Unity writes to in the directory. This includes mail users (subscribers), public distribution lists, contacts (custom recipients in Exchange 5.5), and location objects. The discussion of the directory in Chapter 4, "Components and Subsystems: Directory," goes into more detail about which properties are updated on each object for the different back ends.

The monitor is also responsible for finding users in the directory that are not yet subscribers. The SA import and standalone import tools in Unity use this interface provided by the monitor, called the Import Directory Connector (IDC), to allow administrators to make standing mail users in the directory subscribers. The IDC also provides support for importing contacts (Internet subscribers) and distribution lists. In addition, the directory monitor is responsible for finding all subscribers and location objects added to the directory by other Unity servers on the network. These objects are added to the global subscriber and global locations tables in the local SQL database, and are used for digital networking functionality. The Unity Networking discussion in Chapter 12 talks about these tables in SQL and how they are used.

Changes or deletions of subscribers and distribution lists in the directory are noted by the directory monitor, and their local representations in SQL are updated by the directory change writer. The actual process of determining which objects in the directory are new, deleted, or updated is not as obvious as you would think. ChangeObjectID in SQL (which corresponds to the USN in AD) is used for all subscribers and distribution lists, but the directory monitors do not poll each object to see whether its change ID is less than or greater than the one in the directory (which would be the intuitive thing to assume here). That process would be much too slow, particularly on a large directory. Instead, Unity queries the directory (or, more specifically, the domain controller for the domain in question) for a list of all objects that have a changed ID that is greater than the greatest change ID in the last synch cycle. It then iterates through that list and checks to see if any subscribers or distribution lists it monitors are in that list. If objects monitored by the local Unity server are in that list, it checks the change ID against the one for that object in SQL. If the one in SQL is smaller, it pulls in the values from the directory for that object into SQL. That check is really not strictly necessary because not very many scenarios exist in which the change ID on an object in SQL will be greater; it is one of those "just in case" checks. The directory monitor then notes the largest change ID in the list, saves it to the Registry, and sleeps until the next synchronization cycle.

When the directory monitor wakes up again in a few minutes, it uses that updated maximum change ID in a query to get new updated objects since the last time we queried, and so on. This works because change IDs on a particular object do not roll by just one number when you change that object. Each domain controller keeps a running number for all changes for all objects it sees. When an object changes, it gets assigned this value and then the value increments by 1. As such, if 100 objects change in a domain, the last object gets a changed ID that is 100 greater than the first object to be changed. This is pretty simple, but the catch is that each domain controller keeps its own count. As a result, different domain controllers can have a different change ID value for the same object in the directory. Normally, this does not cause a problem; however, if you must change the domain controller that Unity points at for a particular domain, you should keep in this in mind. The Total Resync button in the AD Monitor section of DOHPropTest is designed to help with this by forcing Unity to search all objects in the directory, reset all change ID counters, and update the maximum change ID value in the Registry accordingly.

After the directory monitor finds an object in the directory that has been updated, it pulls information about that object into SQL again. When a change or an add comes along in the directory, the monitor pushes that information into the Microsoft Messaging Queue (MSMQ), which the AVDirChangeWriter service watches. AVDirChangeWriter then writes the change through to the local SQL tables as necessary. Later in this chapter, the "Component Walkthroughs" section explores what happens when an administrator makes a change in the SA and looks at some of the directory monitor, directory change writer, and MSMQ traces for a system using Active Directory (Exchange 2000/2003).

It is important to note that the directory monitor is not responsible for knowing when an item in SQL is updated and then propagated that to the directory. Currently, clients that use the DOH do not have to worry about this because the DOH writes changes through to the directory by way of the monitor and then updates SQL after the directory update has completed successfully. For client applications that want to update SQL directly and have those changes propagate through to the directory without dealing with the DOH or updating the directory manually, you need to use the SQLSynchSvr service discussed later. Updated stored procedures in later versions of Unity 4.0(x) include flags to do this for you automatically, greatly reducing the complexity for developers.

The directory monitor is actually one or two services named differently, depending on which directory back end Unity is connected to. The next sections explore the service name(s) for the different back ends.

Exchange 5.5

The directory monitor service is called AVDSEx55. By default, the AVDSEx55 service watches all containers from the site or organization level down in the Exchange 5.5 site it is installed in, based on what you select during installation. However, this scope can be changed, if necessary, by editing the Registry or by going through the DOHPropTest application. The Unity digital networking documentation covers the details of how to do this.

Exchange 2000/2003

For Exchange 2000, two services make up the directory monitor functionality: AVDSAD and AVDSGlobalCatalog.

The AVDSAD service watches for updates to subscribers that are homed on the local Unity server. It monitors only domains and containers that it absolutely has to because it polls for changes in objects in those containers. Yes, you can get AD to notify you of changes to objects, but you can request notification for a single object or the immediate children of a container. Applications that must monitor multiple containers or unrelated objects can register up to five notification requests. So, believe it or not, the short story is that this has proven to be considerably less reliable and far slower than simply polling. By default, the polling process is done every 2 minutes, but it is adjustable in the Registry, if necessary. It is not a good idea to change this polling time, however, unless you have a good reason for doing so (for example, the Cisco TAC has asked you to). This has to do with how long it takes for a mailbox to be created for a new user added to AD. The mailbox actually is created by the Remote Update Service (RUS), and it can lag the creation of the user in AD by a bit, depending on where the network topology at the site. Until RUS finishes running, the AD record has no SMTP address that Unity requires before you can log into your mailbox or take messages for a user. So, if you update the AVDSAD to check for changes only every hour, it can take up to an hour before new users can access the mailbox. Keeping the process at 2 minutes keeps this potential window to a minimum.

If a subscriber is imported by an administrator that is in a new domain that the service is not watching already, that domain is added to the list the directory monitor is keeping an eye on. You can see a list of the domains it looks at in the Registry under HKLM\Software\ Active Voice\Directory Connectors\DirSynchAD\1.00\Domains\. Each domain has a top-level container (or "search root," in Microsoft-speak) for subscriber and distribution lists that the directory monitor watches. This container and all its subcontainers are polled for changes to mail user or distribution list objects. It is possible for this root container to be the domain root itself. In the Registry, the container is referenced by an object GUID (referred to in our SQL tables as a directory ID). This object GUID will not tell you much, but you also can see this information in DOHPropTest under the AD Monitor button; it lists all the domains visible on the network. For each domain, it shows a list of properties on the right, including human-readable container names that are the top-level search roots when looking for mail users, distribution lists, and locations. More details on this are found in Chapter 4.

The AVDSGlobalCatalog service, on the other hand, watches for subscribers, distribution lists, and location objects added to the directory by other Unity servers in the forest. It pulls in this information and writes it to MSMQ, where the Directory Change Writer updates the global subscriber, global locations, and the distribution list tables in the local SQL database. Because it cannot know which containers or domains those Unity servers are installed in, it has to watch the entire forest. Again, it must poll the directory for adds, moves, and deletes, but because this information is much less critical than updates to local subscribers, this polling interval defaults to 15 minutes. The AVDSGlobalCatalog service always watches all containers in all domains in the entire forest; there is no way to limit its scope to a smaller subset. This service also provides the IDC interface mentioned earlier, which is used by the import utilities to find mail users in AD that can be imported by administrators as a subscriber.

Domino

In the case of Domino, the directory service name is AVDSDomino, and it works in much the same way as the other directory monitors for Exchange. In Domino, however, the directory is actually the address book that contains user information. Each Domino server has an address book; administrators can configure a Unity server to watch one or more address books for changes and to allow imports of users in those address books. If a Unity server handles more than one Domino server, the administrator must include each and every address book containing users that they want to service with that Unity installation in the SA.

Every minute or so, the monitor checks for changes made to the address books that Unity is configured to watch. Updates to users who are subscribers on a Unity server on the network then are pulled into SQL using the same mechanism. Again, any changes to a user in the address book result in a "bulk write" of all the properties in the address book for that user into the local SQL subscribers table.

AVDirChangeWriter

The AVDirChangeWriter service is the same, regardless of which back end Unity is connected to. All the directory monitor services write the adds, moves, and deletes that need to be updated in the local SQL database to the MSMQ queue, which the directory change writer watches. When updates are pushed by the directory monitors onto the MSMQ queue, the directory change writer pulls them off and executes the update in SQL.

Blocks of properties for subscribers are written to SQL even if you change only a single property on the user or distribution list in the directory. As such, if you change the display name of a subscriber in AD, all properties that Unity cares about for that mail user in the directory, including the display name, are pushed into SQL again. Because each object in the directory has only a single change ID value, the directory monitors cannot know what property changed on an object; they know only that it has been updated. This also means, of course, that if you change a property that Unity does not care about, such as the manager of a mail user, the directory monitors still note that the object has changed and pull in all the properties for that user into the MSMQ queue; the change writer then updates SQL.

Later in this chapter, the "Component Walkthroughs" section, walks through what happens for SA and directory changes and covers in more detail some of the directory change writer, directory monitor, and MSMQ traces to show how this process works.

AVSQLSynchSvr

The SQL Synchronization Server service (or just the "syncher," as it is referred to internally) is new to Unity 4.0. This service walks through the mail user, locations, and distribution list tables in SQL and asks the directory monitors to update the directory, if necessary.

This service's primary job is to handle the bulk import utilities, including the CSV import, the FullDB Import/Export tools used to migrate from 2.x to 3.x/4.x systems, and the Disaster Recovery Tools (DiRT). It is also used by the configuration setup to add the default objects to the directory (Example administrator, example subscriber, and so on). This allows client applications to add users and distribution lists to SQL and then to kick off the syncher either to find the corresponding user/DL in the directory and bind to it, or to create a new subscriber/DL in the directory as necessary.

Client applications also can use AVSQLSynchSvr to update subscriber properties in SQL directly and then have the syncher talk to the directory monitor to "push" the changes for that subscriber into the directory. This allows applications to talk directly to SQL for doing the vast majority of their Unity administration tasks, and then ask the syncher to make sure that the directory is up-to-date. As such, it is no longer strictly necessary to interface with the DOH components or update the various directories supported by Unity when writing administration applications for Unity.

The SQLSynchServer DLL has been available since Unity 3.0(1), but it has not been possible to call it from an off-box application. To use the SQLSyncher in 3.x, it was necessary for the administration application using it to run on the same server as Unity and to create an instance of the SQLSynchServer to use it. This is why applications such as DiRT, Audio Text Manager (ATM), the Import tools, and others ran only on-box in 3.x. In 4.0, the SQL-SynchSvr service can be safely initiated remotely by using an SQL stored procedure; this stored procedure then talks to the SQLSynchSvr service, which, in turn, fires up an instance of the syncher itself to execute the updates to the directory through the directory monitors. This is an advantage if you want to develop your own applications for Unity administration using standard SQL connectivity. This process is covered in more detail in Chapter 21, where we show you how to use the service, which optional parameters can be passed in, and what the trace output for this component looks like.

AVLic

The Licensing service has two primary roles. The SA uses it to determine whether there are enough licenses to allow it to be activated on a class-of-service object (such as TTS users). When users are added to the system or moved between classes of service, the totals for all the licensed features are updated. If there is not enough of a particular license to accommodate the add/move, the SA rejects the action. The AVLic service is also responsible for keeping the license counts up-to-date for the new pooled licensing feature in 4.x. Multiple Unity servers can share a pool of licenses instead of each one requiring its own set. This is handy for large sites that require multiple Unity servers to handle the number of subscribers they need. A specific Unity server can opt out of the license pool, if necessary, and not contribute to or pull from the shared pool of licenses.

The AVLic service writes these changes into the primary location object, which has fields to keep track of the total number of subscribers, ports, and feature license counts for each Unity server. It writes these changes into SQL directly and then uses the SQLSynchSvr service discussed earlier to have those changes written through to the directory. Other Unity servers in the directory pick up the changes to the location object and pull the updated license information into their local SQL databases. If the Unity server participates in the pooled licenses with the Unity server that made the change, it updates its local license counts accordingly.

AVRepDirSvrSvc

The Report Director Server service is responsible for launching all the reports requested through the SA and providing status updates for queued, running, and completed reports that the status monitor web pages display.

The first step in the reports process actually has nothing to do with the AVRepDirSvrSvc. A "scavenger" service running under AVCsMgr kicks off every 30 minutes and "scrapes" report-related information from the data files in the \commserver\logs directory. Then this service stuffs it into appropriate tables in the ReportDB database. The reports engine pulls its data from here, not directly from the DATA files, as it did in earlier versions of Unity.

Each report offered in the SA is actually a set of DLLs that generate the report in three steps. First, a DLL called the report pump extracts the raw information from the tables in the ReportDB database or from the UnityDB database, as appropriate. Another DLL called the report crunch is then responsible for transforming that raw data into a temporary MDB database file that the crystal reports engine can use to generate the final report. Finally, a third DLL uses the Crystal Reports engine to generate an HTML or CSV report from that database table, depending on what the administrator requested when launching the report. The Report Directory Server launches the appropriate set of DLLs for each report queued up one at a time. While the report is running, the Report Directory Server keeps track of its progress, which is displayed in the status monitor web page. Only one report can run at any given time; all other reports wait in line to be serviced.

The report director service runs at the lowest possible priority, to avoid cutting into the main AVCsMgr service's capability to process calls in real time. This means that reports sometimes can take a while to complete, even if Unity is not particularly busy. To help with this problem, when the report is completed, the report director server sends an e-mail to the administrator who requested the report. The e-mail contains a link to the final report under the \commserver\reports share. This is handy because administrators can queue up numerous reports to run, and the output waits for them in their inbox when they come in the next day.

It is important to note that any of the pump report DLLs that need access to the directory information, such as the subscriber report that shows the mailbox size of each mail user, goes through the gateway service, and "talks" to the DOH running under AVCsMgr to get at this information. Even though reports are hard-coded to the lowest possible processing priority, if a subscriber report is run during heavy call traffic, it adds to the load on the DOH component under AVCsMgr, which is, of course, also busy processing calls on the system. The obvious solution to this is to provide a mechanism to schedule a report to run in the off hours, but Unity currently does not offer this. The reports engine is slated for a major overhaul, and this scheduling function will be revisited then.

CSEMSSvc

The Event Monitoring Service is new for 4.0(3). It replaces the old, much beleaguered AVGAENSvc service used for notifying administrators of event log activity.

The Cisco Systems Event Monitoring Service (CSEMSSvc) monitors the event logs for specified entries and then executes the notification rule set up by the administrators. The administrators can instruct it to leave a voice mail or e-mail in a specified subscriber's inbox or directly e-mailing out an SMTP port to an external e-mail server in the case Unity no longer can properly communicate with the mail back end it is connected to. The updated EMS tool can trigger notification events on specific events, entire classes of events, or any Unity-related event. This differs from the old AVGAEN service, which can trigger only on a list of specific events entered into its database.

Unity ships with the CSEMSSvc service not installed. When you run the administration tool for the EMS (found in the Tools Depot), it automatically installs and activates the CSEMSSvc service on-the-fly.

If the set action when a watched event shows up in the event log is to send a voice mail or an e-mail to a subscriber or a public distribution list, the CSEMSSvc uses the DOH to drop the selected message into the appropriate mailbox. To get at the DOH, it authenticates with the gateway service and uses the running DOH in AVCsMgr.

AVMMProxySvr

The Active Voice Media Master Proxy Server (AVMMProxyServer) service is used in conjunction with a new authentication method offered in Unity 4.0. This method allows for Media Master connections across domains without requiring a second authentication from the client.

As noted previously in the discussion about the AVTRAPSvr and DOHMMSvr components running under AVCsMgr, clients that want to use the Media Master to play back or
record a greeting or voice name through a web client use the Media Master ActiveX control
to connect back to the Unity server to do this. When NTLM authentication is used, the
ActiveX control can connect directly to the DOHMMSvr component and, if using the
phone for a media device through TRaP, also to the AVTRAPSvr component. If the user
comes from a different domain than the one Unity runs in, another authentication dialog
box pops up, even though the user already might have authenticated upon first launching
the SA.

Unity 4.0 offers administrators the choice of using the Unity authentication mechanism or
sticking with the NTLM security. However, this presents a problem because the Media
Master controls on the client side use DCOM, which requires a security token from NT
before it allows a connection to the client. To get around this problem, after Unity has
authenticated the user, it uses the AVMMProxSvr service to act as a proxy. This service
establishes a DCOM connection to the client and, in turn, gets TRaP and WAV stream
handles from the DOH running under AVCsMgr, which then is passed through to the client.
In this way, the client has to authenticate only once and does not need to be logged into an
NT domain at all (for example, Domino users) to use the SA or the new Cisco Unity
Personal Assistant pages in 4.0.

AVTTSSvc

Before Unity 4.0(1), the AVTTSSvc service interfaced with two TTS engines: TTS3000
and the Real Speak products offered by L&H. As of the release of Unity 4.0(1), only
RealSpeak is supported.

When conversations request a TTS session to play back the text of an e-mail to a caller over
the phone, the conversation passes the MIU a text file to play. The MIU then passes it
through to the TTS service. Finally, the TTS service uses the third-party TTS vendor APIs
to convert that into a WAV stream and play it out the voice port that the conversation uses.

As other TTS vendors and engines are tested and qualified, it should only be necessary to
install their engines and update the TTS service to accommodate them. At the time of this
writing, other TTS engines are being investigated, but none is slated to be released in the
Unity 4.0 line.

CSBridgeConnector

The CSBridgeConnector service is installed in Unity 3.1(3) and later. However, it is used
only if the system uses the Cisco Unity bridge server to talk to other foreign voice mail
servers by way of the analog OctelNet protocol. It also should be noted that this service

works only with Exchange 2000/2003 in AD; it does not work with Domino or Exchange 5.5 as the back end, at the time of this writing.

CSBridgeConnector is responsible for updating mail user information on the bridge server itself for both the local Unity server that this service runs on and other Unity servers in the directory. Similarly, it gets user information about subscribers residing on the foreign voice-mail servers using OctelNet. In this way, Unity subscribers can address messages to remote users through OctelNet by name or ID, and get voice name confirmation back just as if they were addressing another Unity subscriber on the network.

The CSBridgeConnector gets information about adds, moves, or changes to Unity subscriber by monitoring the global subscriber table in SQL. When it notices a change, it pushes a small subset of information about this user (including the voice name) to the bridge server by sending an e-mail through the DOH's MAL interface. All communication between the bridge server and the CSBridgeConnector service is done with SMTP messages like this. When the bridge server sends an SMTP message indicating an add, move, or change, the CSBridgeConnector service uses the DOH to create new mail-enabled contacts representing the subscribers on the foreign voice-mail server or update existing ones. Going through the DOH to do this ensures that both SQL and Active Directory records are created and updated automatically. However, because the DOH does not provide an interface for deleting objects in the directory (only adding or modifying is allowed for security reasons), it has to go right to Active Directory to delete contacts when a user is removed. These are only contacts that cannot have message stores, so the risk for deleting objects in this case is low; as a result, this workaround is allowed.

The reference to Active Directory is deliberate in this case. The bridge server works only with Unity servers running with Exchange 2000/2003, or mixed Exchange 2000/2003 and Exchange 5.5 systems that use Active Directory. This currently is not supported for pure Exchange 5.5 or Domino systems.

The Cisco Unity bridge server functionality is covered in some more detail in Chapter 12.

AVCsNodeMgr

The Node Manager service is responsible for keeping primary and secondary Unity servers up-to-date with one another for failover configurations. In a failover configuration, the secondary Unity server is dormant but on "hot standby," ready to take over call processing and notification duties, if necessary. For more information on the failover configuration and administration process, see the Failover Guide in the Unity documentation.

The node manager services on both the primary and the secondary Unity servers in this configuration send each other messages about the states of their services and components on their respective local servers. When the primary server fails (because of loss of connectivity) to the secondary Unity, services or components becoming unresponsive, calls overflowing to the secondary server, an administrator manually forcing a failover for maintenance reasons, or some other reason), the secondary server takes over handling calls and notification duties until the primary comes back online and a "fail back" event is executed by the administrator.

Besides communicating service and component status back and forth between the primary and secondary servers, the node manager is responsible for keeping selected data in the Registry and for keeping the greetings and voice name WAV files synchronized between the two servers. When a new greeting is recorded for a call handler on the primary Unity server, for instance, it is important that the updated greeting for that handler also be copied over to the secondary Unity server as quickly as possible. This ensures that the systems are not out of sequence if the primary fails. SQL synchronization is configured between the two servers during the failover setup process, to keep the Unity databases identical between the boxes as well. However, the node manager is not involved in this process directly.

TomCat

The TomCat service is responsible for generating the HTML pages for the new Cisco Unity Personal Communication Assistant (CPCA) pages offered in Unity 4.0. The TomCat service uses JSP and Java scriptlets to produce web pages based on information pulled from the directory and mail store via the DOH.

Currently, only the Cisco Unity Personal Communication Assistant pages use this service. The SA and status monitor pages still use ASP code to generate the HTML pages, as they have in previous versions of Unity. However, the processes used for the SA/SM and the CPCA page generation from a high level are fairly similar, even if they do use different code to generate the final HTML sent back to the client.

When a client requests a CPCA page from the desktop, the request hits IIS and, based on the URL requested, redirects it to the TomCat server. The TomCat server connects to the DOH by going through the AVXML component running under IIS and authenticating through the gateway service, much like the SA uses the SADbConn component to do the same thing. It uses the DOH to retrieve both directory information about the requesting subscribers' account and the messages in their mailbox. Using this information, it constructs the HTML page and sends it back to IIS which, in turn, feeds it to the requesting client's browser.

One big difference between the CPCA and the SA, however, is that the CPCA currently does not support NTLM—it supports only the new Unity authentication offered in Unity 4.0. The SA, on the other hand, optionally can support either NTML or the new Unity authentication mechanism, depending on what the customer is more comfortable with.

Component Walkthroughs

So far, this chapter has examined the services that Unity adds to the server and the basic components running under those services. The following sections describe scenarios that show how the components work together.

Outside Caller Leaves a Message

As mentioned in the previous chapter, Unity uses the selected mail store (Exchange 5.5, Exchange 2000, or Domino) as its message repository instead of storing messages in a local database and pushing/pulling updates in and out by polling the remote store. In this section, we walk through the details of what happens when an outside caller forwards into Unity after dialing the extension of a subscriber's phone and leaves a voice-mail message for a subscriber, triggering a new MWI event.

For this walkthrough, we will have an outside caller at 206-555-5555 call the subscriber at extension 1234 using Direct Inward Dial (DID). We will assume that the extension rang four times and then forwarded ring-no-answer into Unity.

Figure 2-2 shows the first step in a new inbound call. The call forwards ring-no-answer from extension 1234 to a hunt group of lines that includes the voice ports assigned to Unity. The CallManager sends information about the call by way of the Skinny to the AVSkinnyTSP, which talks to the MIU via TAPI. The MIU establishes an audio channel through the VoIP WAV driver provided by the CallManager folks.

The MIU now has all the information about the call, including the calling number, the forwarding number, the dialed number, which Unity port ID was used to handle the incoming call, and the fact that the call forwarded RNA to Unity. This all is associated with the call object that clients further upstream have access to, including conversations (TUI applications). For some switch integrations, at this point the call has been answered already (gone off-hook on the call) and an audio channel is established. For analog (or DTMF) integrations, the MIU does not get details about the call until it goes off-hook and receives a stream of DTMF digits indicating the same data that the CallManager sends through its Skinny interface. As such, it is not possible for Unity now to decide based on the call information that it will not take the call and will redirect, or deflect, the call to another number. As they say, the cow is out of the barn and we have to handle the incoming call. In the case of CallManager integration, however, all the data arrives through the TSP.

Figure 2-2 *A New Inbound Call Arrives on a Unity Port*

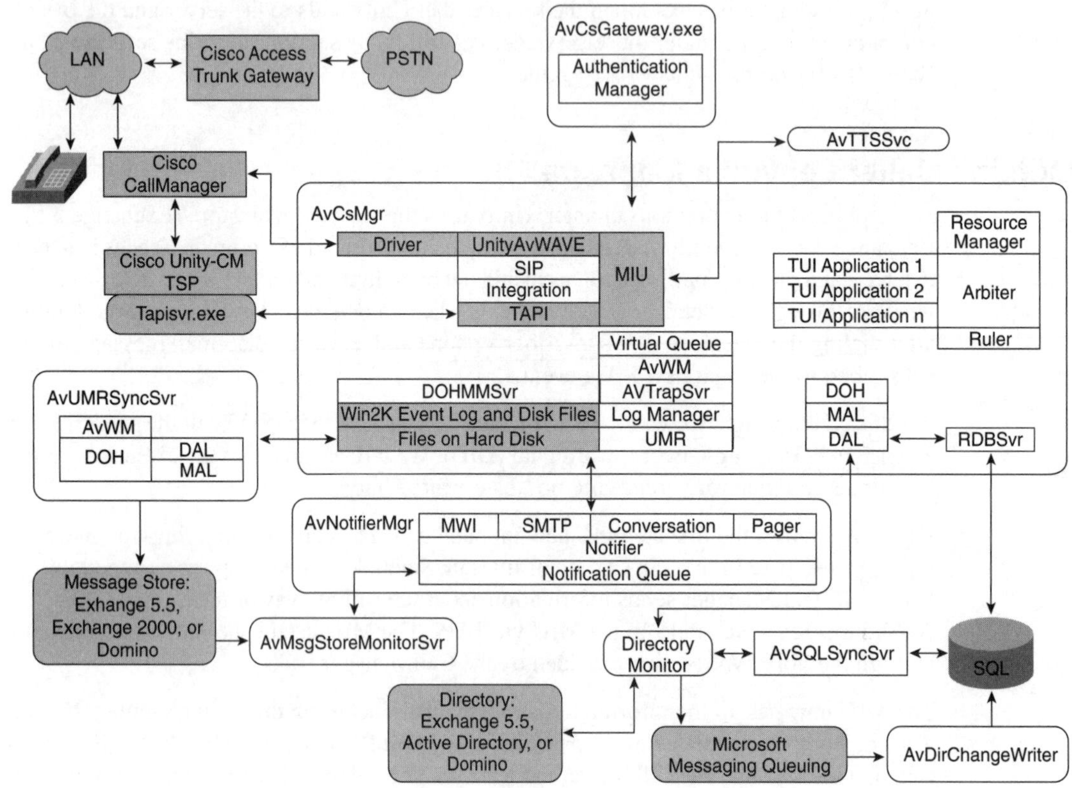

This might seem like a strange detail, but it can cause you trouble if you are not careful. For instance, if you are using an analog integration (or a dual switch with CallManager and an analog switch) and you have all subscriber phones forwarding to a hunt group that includes all the Unity ports, but some of those ports are not set to allow incoming calls, you can easily get into a difficult situation: An inbound call is answered but cannot be handled, and the user simply gets hung up on. For this reason, if you are going to dedicate some ports to MWI or notification dialouts only, for instance, be sure that those ports are not included in the hunt group that subscriber phones are forwarded to. This also helps avoid collisions, in which Unity attempts to go off-hook to do a dialout at the same time an incoming call is trying to use that same port.

You can turn on a very large number of MIU-related traces that show a huge array of information coming from the switch, the WAV driver, TAPI, and so on, far beyond the scope of this chapter or this book. If you are interested in getting more details about how MIU works, however, a highly detailed MIU troubleshooting document discusses the various traces that you can turn on and tells how to read their output. You can get a copy of this at http://www.ciscounitytools.com/Applications/DiagnosingMiu.doc.

In the next step shown in Figure 2-3, the MIU hands off the new call to the Arbiter component for initial processing. The Arbiter, in turn, uses the ruler component to process the routing rules configured for the system to decide where this call should go. In this case, we will assume default settings here: The attemptForwardToGreeting conversation gets called with the forwarding number of 1234 passed in. This conversation searches for a match on the extension in the SQL database in the call handler table. The extension corresponds to a subscriber (a match is found for that subscriber's primary call handler, in other words), so the PHGreeting conversation is evoked with the call handler for the subscriber 1234.

Figure 2-3   *A New Call Is Processed and Routed By the Arbiter Component*

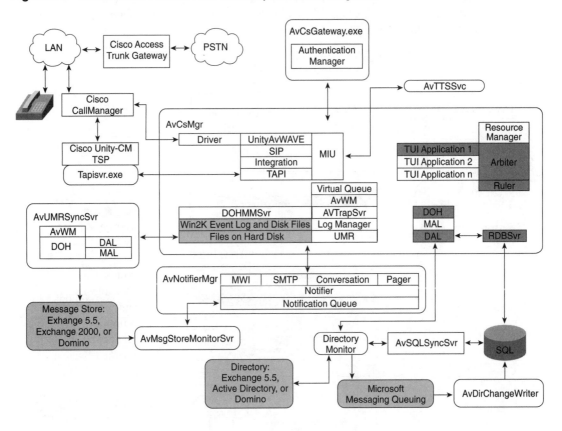

In Chapter 18, we take a look at the Arbiter traces that show which routing rules are evaluated and how the inbound calls are routed. We also take a look at the CallViewer output for troubleshooting where calls are ending up in the system and why; this is a common challenge in the field, especially for sites that create numerous complex routing rules. We also discuss why the PHGreeting transfer is used here instead of the PHTransfer conversation. In short, all calls that come into Unity forwarded from an extension explicitly skip the transfer rules when routed to a call handler or a subscriber, to avoid a potential transfer loop scenario. In rare situations when you want to override this, there are methods for doing so; we discuss those as well.

Figure 2-4 shows the call being handed to the PHGreeting conversation with the call handler for the subscriber at extension 1234. When this happens, the PHGreeting conversation evaluates the greeting rules for that handler to determine what to do with the call. In this case, we assume that the subscriber has a standard greeting recorded and that the after greeting action is set to take a message, which is the default behavior. The Data Object Model discussion in Chapter 3 goes into more detail on all the parts of a subscriber, call handlers, and other objects the make up the Unity directory, including greeting rules and contact rules, mentioned throughout this chapter.

Figure 2-4   *A Call Is Handed to the PHGreeting Conversation*

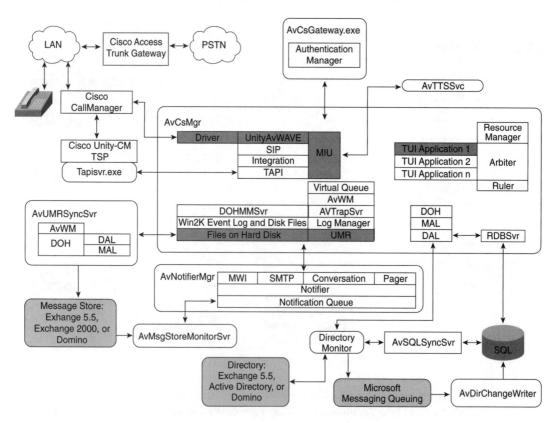

The PHGreeting conversation works through the MIU to play out the appropriate greeting WAV file stored under the \Commserver\Stream Files directory. Assuming that the user enters no digits during this process, the conversation proceeds to the after message action, which is set to take a message.

A quick note about full mailboxes with Exchange and the Unity messaging process is needed here. In Unity 3.1(5) and later, the PHGreeting conversation can be configured to make a quick check to ensure that the subscriber whom the message is sent to does not have a full inbox before taking a message for that user. Running out and checking the status of a mailbox across the network is sometimes a slow process, so this check is off by default; it can be enabled with a Registry edit (see the Advanced Settings tool for this). If Unity takes a message from an outside caller for a subscriber who has a full mailbox, the UMR ends up delivering it to the mail store. Of course, the mail store will end up rejecting its delivery to that server and will bounce the mail back to the Unity Messaging System account. The message ends up getting forwarded to the Unaddressed Messages public distribution list for handling in that case.

NOTE   The check for a full mailbox is done *only* when an outside caller leaves messages for individual subscribers. Subscriber-to-subscriber messages always are sent by the mail store back end. For instance, if you log in as a subscriber and send a message to another subscriber who has a full mailbox, it will be sent just as if you had delivered it by an e-mail client. The mail server then sends it back to you nondelivery receipt (NDR), indicating that the user's mailbox is full.

When Unity is connected to a Domino mail system, the full mailbox check is not made because Domino does not enforce full mailboxes in the same way Exchange does. When a subscriber's mailbox is past its set limit, the message still is delivered to the user, but an error is added to the Misc Events view in the Log.NSF file.

NOTE   You might want to look at the Message Store Manager tool, available for download at www.ciscounitytools.com. This tool can help you manage your users' message storage usage, run reports, and delete messages based on various rules, such as the read status, age, urgency, and so on. You can read the help file and check out the training videos for the tool on its home page for more details.

Assuming that the subscriber at extension 1234 has kept the inbox to a reasonable level, the PHGreeting conversation sends the record request to the MIU, and the caller records a message. If the recording is at least 1 second long, it is considered a valid message. The

MIU takes care of trimming leading and trailing silence so that if the caller said nothing, the silence is trimmed and the resulting recording is discarded. In some cases with PBX integrations, if a user hangs up instead of recording a message and the disconnect event does not come down right away, some clicking noise gets recorded as a message and left for the subscriber. To help with this scenario, it is possible to edit this minimum recording time on the SA under the Configuration\Recordings page; however, you should exercise extreme caution if you opt to bump this value up from 1 second because it is entirely possible for people to leave legitimate messages that are 2 or 3 seconds long.

When the MIU has completed recording the message by timing out on silence or the user enters a DTMF to terminate the record session, the handle to the resulting file is passed back to the conversation. In this case, because the message is from an unidentified caller, the PHGreeting conversation goes through the UMR component to leave the message for the target user. If instead the caller either first signed into Unity as a subscriber and then left a message, or the calling number corresponded to a subscriber on the local Unity server, the PHGreeting conversation would submit the message to the DOH. The DOH then would deliver it from the sender's mailbox directly. In this way, the message is from the sender, so the person getting the message, either over the phone or through an in inbox client, simply can reply to it directly.

When the UMR component running under AVCsMgr gets the message, it writes two files out to the \Commserver\UnityMTA directory. One file is the WAV file for the recorded message itself. The other file is the "routing" file that indicates to the AVUMRSyncSvr service where it should ask the mail store to deliver the message when it picks it up. We cover this in the next step of our call flow example.

By default, the after-message action for a call handler is to go to the "say goodbye" call handler, which plays a greeting ending the call and then hangs up. Assuming that this is the case here, the call then terminates, and the line is freed up and is ready to take another call.

The message is not yet in the mailbox of the target subscriber at this point; it sits as a pair of files in the UnityMTA directory, which is, by default, at \Commserver\UnityMTA. As noted earlier, you can set this directory during installation or change it after install using the Advanced Settings Tool. Figure 2-5 shows what happens when the conversation deposits the message in the UnityMTA directory.

The conversation sets an event that the AVUMRSyncSvr watches to check for messages in that folder right away. If the AVUMRSyncSvr does not get such an event within 60 seconds, it "wakes up" and checks the folder anyway to look for messages that might have synched over from a failover server, for instance. The AVUMRSyncSvr process uses its own instance of the DOH to deliver the message to the mailbox of the target subscriber using the MAL interface. In the case of Exchange, the message is sent from the Unity Messaging System account that resides on the Exchange server selected during the configuration setup.

Figure 2-5 *The UMR Delivers the Message to the Target Subscriber*

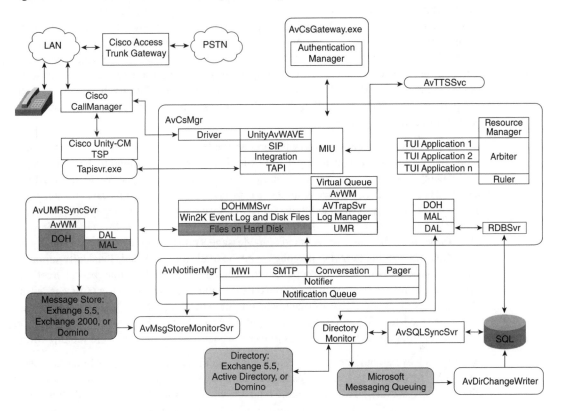

Notice in the architecture diagrams throughout this chapter that the AVUMRSyncSvr has an instance of the AVWM component running as well. It uses this component specifically to find out whether the Exchange server that the Unity Messaging System account resides on (that is, the partner Exchange server) is currently available. If not, it does not attempt to deliver the messages in the UnityMTA directory. Instead, Unity switches into UMR mode and allows subscribers to get at voice-mail messages residing in the UnityMTA directory until connectivity is restored. Note that if the Windows Monitoring service (see the "AVWM Service" section) considers the recipient subscriber's home Exchange server to be off-line, that message stays in the local UMR directory until that server is back online and functioning properly. In versions of Unity before 3.1(5), as long as the partner Exchange server was up and running, the message was handed off to Exchange; in this case, it sat in the Exchange Message Transfer Agent (MTA) queue until the target Exchange server came back online.

By default, the MTA attempted to deliver the message every 10 minutes for 24 hours. If after that time it still could not deliver the message, it returned it to the sending party NDR; in this case, it is the Unity Messaging System account that we send all outside caller message from. These messages then got forwarded to the Unaddressed Messages public distribution list for handling by an administrator. Because it is not easy to see what messages currently are stacked up in the MTA, these messages would appear to end users to be "lost." As such, in Unity 3.1(5) and later, the message is not handed off to Exchange unless both the partner Exchange server and the home Exchange server of the target subscriber both are known to be up and functioning.

To see the outside message-delivery process a little better, it is instructive to take a look at some diagnostics. Go ahead and open the Unity Diagnostic Tool, found in the Tools Depot or the Unity program group. Select Configure Micro Traces. Then go down to the UMR section and expand it. You will see a number of trace options there. In this case, we just want to see when messages are added to the UnityMTA directory and when they are picked up and delivered. Turn on traces 10, General UMR Sync Thread Messages, and 12, MTA Walkthrough. In this case, MTA stands for Message Transfer Agent; this is technically an Exchange 5.5-specific term, but it applies to all the mail store back ends that Unity supports. Trace 12 is actually the UMR component that runs under AVCsMgr that the PHGreeting conversation talks to when submitting the outside caller message. Because it runs under the AVCsMgr component, it logs its diagnostic output to the diag_AVCsMgrxxx.txt file. When you finish the Micro Trace Wizard, you might want to select the Start New Log Files option to cycle the diagnostic trace logs; this makes it easier to see what you were looking for.

When you leave an outside caller message, you can open the diag_AVCsMgrxxx.txt and diag_AVUMRSyncSvr_xxx.txt files in the \Commserver\Logs directory directly and view the output. However, the traces are more readable when they are formatted. To do this, again use the UDT and select the Gather Traces option to collect the files noted earlier and save them in formatted output. After formatting, the files are appended with a _fmtd.txt extension. All trace output shown in this document is formatted.

The AVCSMgr trace file should contain the messages in Example 2-1.

Example 2-1 *AVCSMgr Trace File Messages*

```
08:14:17:375 (AVUMR_MC,152,UMR,12) MTA Directory: =C:\CommServer\unityMta\ on line
   330 of e:\views\Unity3.1.3.23\un_Conv3\UnityUMR\UnityMTA\AVMtaSession.cpp
08:14:17:376 (AVUMR_MC,152,UMR,12) New MTA Message file Name=C:\CommServer\
   unityMta\JLindborg_20020728_081417375_cbe96ed3-5245-47d0-b1ea-f67da7279c2c on
   line 101 of e:\views\Unity3.1.3.23\un_Conv3\UnityUMR\UnityMTA\AVMtaSession.cpp
08:14:17:375 (AVUMR_MC,153,UMR,12) CAVMtaMessage::GetAudioStream() : New Message
   Stream on line 343 of e:\views\Unity3.1.3.23\un_Conv3\UnityUMR\UnityMTA\
   AVMtaMessage.cpp
```

The lines of code noted by components always reference drive letters, as in e:\..., although the Unity server might not have an E drive. This is actually the drive configuration of the server that stores and builds the Unity code; it has nothing to do with the local Unity installation. This information is useful only to development people who are tracking down a problem. The first column always contains the time/date stamp, and the fourth and fifth columns contain the trace category (AVUMR, in this case) and the trace number that generated the output (12, in this case). This holds true for all diagnostic trace output and can be useful if you want to extract information for a specific trace from, say, the diag_ AVCsMgrxxx.txt file (which can contain a very large amount of output if you have any number of traces turned on).

In this case, you can see the new message that arrived resulted in the creation of a file in the C:\Commserver\UnityMTA\ directory named JLindborg_20020728_081417375_ cbe96ed3-5245-47d0-b1ea-f67da7279c2c. Two files with that name will exist in the directory: one with a .WAV file extension, which is the voice message itself, and one with a .TXT extension, which is the routing file that the AVUMRSyncSvr service uses when addressing the message. If you want to see this, you can simply stop the AVUMRSyncSvr service and leave an outside caller message. This does not prevent Unity from running normally, other than the fact that outside caller messages are not delivered while it is offline. If you do this and pop open the .TXT file, it will look something like Example 2-2.

Example 2-2 *AVUMRSyncSvr Service Message Routing File*

```
RecipientAlias:JLindborg
To:
Subject:Message from an unidentified caller
Priority:1
Sensitivity:0
Date:1026351166
X-AVMailHandlerId:=?unicode?b?AQAHADAAMwA6AHsANgAxAEIAMAA2ADMANwBFAC0AQQAyADQAN
  wAtADQAQQBFAEUALQBCADkANQAyAC0ANgAzADAAOABEADkARgA1AEIAQQA1ADUAfQAAAA==?=
```

AVUMRSyncSvr uses the AVMailHandlerID field to address the message. If the calling number was collected from the switch and passed on, the subject field would contain that information. In this case, the calling number did not come through in the integration, so the generic "Message from an unidentified caller" is used by default. Currently, this is not con-figurable. The priority and sensitivity fields are the same ones you have access to when sending an e-mail using the desktop client. AVMailHandlerID is the base 64 format for the ObjectID of the primary call handler for the subscriber (if you are confused, hang tight until we cover the Data Object Model section in the next chapter). When the UMR goes to send the message, it actually uses this ID to find the primary call handler. It then finds the mail user associated with it and grabs the data from there to fill in the message send information that it passes to Exchange. You can copy and paste this string into DOHPropTest's Find By ObjectID dialog box; it translates it into a regular object ID and finds the call handler for you, which can be useful for troubleshooting.

If you launch the AVUMRSyncSvr service again (or if you left it alone to begin with), it picks up the pair of files and delivers the message to the mail store back end. As noted in Figure 2-5, it does this by creating its own instance of the DOH and delivering the message from the Unity Messaging System Account created by Unity setup. If you take a look at the diag_AVUMRSyncSvrxxx.txt file, it will look something like Example 2-3.

Example 2-3 *The diag_AVUMRSyncSvrxxx.txt File*

```
08:14:26:953 (AVUMR_MC,150,UMR,10) [Thread 0x00000E28] Proceeding to deliver
  messages from UMR on line 413 of e:\views\Unity3.1.3.23\un_Conv3\UnityUMR\
  AVUMRSyncSvr\UMRThread.cpp
08:14:27:031 (AVUMR_MC,150,UMR,10) [Thread 0x00000E28] Message for [JLindborg] in
  the UMR on line 995 of e:\views\Unity3.1.3.23\un_Conv3\UnityUMR\AVUMRSyncSvr\
  UMRThread.cpp
08:14:27:125 (AVUMR_MC,150,UMR,10) [Thread 0x00000E28] Message delivered on line
  514 of e:\views\Unity3.1.3.23\un_Conv3\UnityUMR\AVUMRSyncSvr\UMRThread.cpp
08:14:27:126 (AVUMR_MC,150,UMR,10) [Thread 0x00000E28] No more messages in the UMR
  on line 615 of e:\views\Unity3.1.3.23\un_Conv3\UnityUMR\AVUMRSyncSvr\UMRThread.cpp
08:14:27:125 (AVUMR_MC,150,UMR,10) [Thread 0x00000E28] No messages in the UMR wait
  till we have more messages on line 339 of e:\views\Unity3.1.3.23\un_Conv3\
  UnityUMR\AVUMRSyncSvr\UMRThread.cpp
```

You can see that it picked up the message bound for the subscriber with the alias of Jlindborg, noted that it delivered it, and then noted that there are no more messages in the UnityMTA directory to be delivered. The last line there is just a note that it will wait until more files arrive in the UnityMTA directory.

If the AVUMRSyncSvr service gets an error back from the mail server (for instance, the RecipientAlias does not exist in its directory) when it attempts to deliver the message, the pair of files will be moved to the failed delivery folder. By default, this is located at \Commserver\UnityMTA\Failed\. It attempts to deliver these failed messages periodically and logs errors to the event log to let you know there is a problem. In earlier versions of Unity, a failed message delivery backed up the UnityMTA directory, and nothing behind the bad message got through. Starting in 3.1(4), the failed directory is used as a mechanism to get around this. The first step in troubleshooting such a problem is to open the routing .TXT file to see where it attempts to send the message and to make sure that the destination exists and is accessible. As noted earlier, Exchange does not issue an error if the target mailbox is full; it simply sends the message back as nondelivery receipt (NDR) to the sender. The conversations can be set to check the full mailbox condition for outside callers wanting to leave messages, to help prevent problems here.

In the case of Domino, the messaging back end does not enforce the full mailbox state as it is in Exchange. As such, Unity does not specifically warn users or prevent the sending or receiving of messages based on specific mailbox size restrictions. With Exchange, there is no choice because the mail store enforces it. Later versions of Domino might include stricter mailbox quota enforcement; at that point, Unity will need to check those limits and act accordingly.

Assuming that the message is handed off to the mail store properly in the last step and that it then delivers the message to the mailbox of the target subscriber, this is where the notifier component begins. Figure 2-6 shows which components are involved in the process of turning on an MWI light.

Figure 2-6   *The Notifier Component Turns on the MWI Light for the Message Recipient*

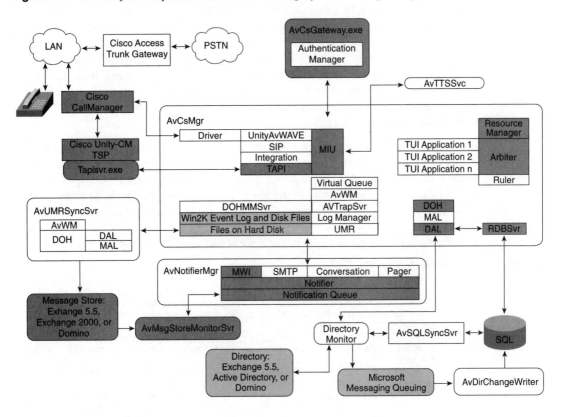

First, the underlying mail server (Exchange 5.5/2000/2003/Domino) notifies the AVMsg-StoreMonitorSvr service as soon as the message arrives with a New Message event and a message ID. It pushes this information onto the notification queue, which runs in the AVNotifierMgr service. The notifier then picks this information out of the queue and decides what to do with it. In this case, we will assume that subscriber 1234's lamp is not on and no notification devices other than the MWI device itself are active. As such, the notifier adds the MWI on request to the MWI device manager. The MWI device manager then asks the resource manager running in the AVCsMgr service if a port is available to do an MWI request; it makes this same request even if the MWIs are done through the serial port or a voice port. Assuming that a port is available, the resource manager reserves it for the MWI device manager and passes the reserved port ID back. The MWI device manager then sends this ID to the Arbiter when it requests the actual dialout to turn on the lamp. The MWI device manager waits until the Arbiter returns success or failure for the MWI request; if it fails, the MWI device manager takes care of requeuing the request to try again at a specified interval for a set number of tries. It considers the MWI attempt failed only after the total number of retries has been exhausted. When the MWI request has either succeeded or failed, it pushes this result back onto the notification queue to let the notifier know that it has been completed. The MWI device manager also takes care of updating the subscriber's record in the database to indicate Unity thinks the MWI lamp is currently turned on; this shows up on the messages page in the SA for the subscriber as the current Indicator Lamps status. The message store monitor uses the DOH to write this through to the local SQL record; the lamp status of the subscriber is not written through to the directory, so the directory monitor is not involved here.

Let us again turn on some traces for the components in question and walk through the output you would see from the previous example scenario. In this case, you want to turn on traces for the notifier and the MWI device manager running under the AVCsMgr service. In the Unity Diagnostic Tool, return to the Micro Traces section and, in the Notifier section, turn on traces 12, MWI Device, and 21, NotifyQ. Both these traces, of course, write out into the AVNotifierMgr diagnostic file because these components run under that service. Popping open that diagnostic file, you will see something like Example 2-4.

Example 2-4 *AVNotifierMgr Diagnostic File*

```
08:14:27:937 (AVNotifier_MC,1146,Notifier,21) [Thread 0x00000DA8] NotifyQ popped
  eNOTIFYQ_ACTION_MSG_NEW [2], mailbox='cn=JLindborg cn=Recipients ou=First
  Administrative Group o=E2KDomain', arg1=2, arg2=3, arg3=1, varMessageData=
  (UnexpectedVariantType:8209!!).
08:14:27:938 (AVNotifier_MC,1158,Notifier,12) [Thread 0x00000DA8] Jeff
  Lindborg:MWI-1(1189), 1 messages (message just Added), current status Off, current
  attempt None
08:14:27:937 (AVNotifier_MC,1113,Notifier,12) [Thread 0x00000DA8] Queued MWI task
  for mailuser=Jeff Lindborg, extension=1189, status=On
08:14:27:984 (AVNotifier_MC,1108,Notifier,12) [Thread 0x00000D7C] MWI Device - MWI
  Entry AV_MWI_ON Received: Task Jeff Lindborg 1189 timestamp 1027869267, Port 4
08:14:30:812 (AVNotifier_MC,1146,Notifier,21) [Thread 0x00000DA8] NotifyQ popped
  eNOTIFYQ_ACTION_MWION_COMPLETE [7], mailbox='cn=JLindborg cn=Recipients ou=First
  Administrative Group o=E2KDomain', arg1=4, arg2=0, arg3=0, varMessageData='MWI-
  1' (VT_BSTR).
08:14:30:843 (AVNotifier_MC,1113,Notifier,12) [Thread 0x00000D7C] Completed MWI
  task for mailuser=Jeff Lindborg, extension=1189, status=On
```

The first entry is the notifier component picking up the message that the AVMsgStore-Monitor service wrote to the notifier queue when the new voice-mail message arrived in the mailbox. The notifier then takes action on that message by adding an item to the MWI device manager's queue (the second message in the trace). The MWI Device manager then issues an MWI ON event, which completes it and then pushes an event back onto the notifier queue to that effect (the eNOTIFYQ_ACTION_MWION_COMPLETE message). What is not shown in the traces is the notifier acting on the MWI ON complete message and using the DOH to update the subscriber's record to indicate that the lamp is now on (at least, as far as Unity knows).

One thing to note is that you will not always get the specific mail store event from the message store monitor (the eNOTIFYQ_ACTION_MSG_NEW event in the first line of the diagnostic output). If Exchange is busy or several events happen at once (multiple messages are deleted or marked read at the same time), sometimes a simple event indicating that "something changed" comes across and that the notifier needs to filter the entire inbox instead of acting specifically on the message state change received. Under normal circumstances, however, the message store monitor gets a specific new, updated, or deleted message notification that includes the message type.

If the previous message were left on a Domino system, the notifier traces would look reasonably similar to those from an Exchange server, shown earlier. Let us look at the message-monitoring traces for a Domino system in this case. The traces in Example 2-5 are pulled from a Unity server connected to a Domino back end with the Domino Monitor trace 12, Mailbox Login, turned on. They show a new message arriving and then being read 10 minutes later.

Example 2-5 *Message Monitor Traces for a Domino System*

```
15:45:50:094 (AVDominoMonitor_MC,1093,DominoMonitor,12) [Thread 1756] [Thread
   0x000006DC] Received Notification packet from dna-test1: <notification>
   <handlerid>unitynotifier</handlerid><applicationdata></applicationdata><user>
   </user><database>bQBhAGkAbABcAGYAbABkADEALgBuAHMAZgA=</database>
    <event>NewMessage</event><newmessagedata><type>V</type><priority>N
   </priority><sender>ZgAyAF8AbAAyAC8ARABuAGEAZABvAG0AJQBjAG8AbQAlAGMAbwBtAAA=
   </sender><subject>TQBlAHMAcwBhAGcAZQAgAEYAcgBvAG0AIABVAG4AaQB0AHkA</
   subject><id>2330</id></newmessagedata></notification>
15:45:50:093 (AVDominoMonitor_MC,1096,DominoMonitor,12) [Thread 1756] [Thread
   0x000006DC] Received NewMessage Notification packet: Type:V; Prio:N; From:f2_l2/
   Dnadom%com%com; Subj:Message From Unity; ID:2330
15:45:52:562 (AVDominoMonitor_MC,1093,DominoMonitor,12) [Thread 1756] [Thread
   0x000006DC] Received Notification packet from dna-test1: <notification>
   <handlerid>unitynotifier</handlerid><applicationdata></applicationdata>
   <user></user><database>bQBhAGkAbABcAGYAbABkADEALgBuAHMAZgA=</database>
   <event>CountChange</event><countchangedata><count>2</count></countchangedata>
   <id>2330</id><priority>N</priority><type>V</type><eventtype>1
   </eventtype></notification>
15:45:52:563 (AVDominoMonitor_MC,1094,DominoMonitor,12) [Thread 1756] [Thread
   0x000006DC] Received CountChange Notification packet: Cnt:2; ID:2330; Prio:N;
   Type:V; EType:1;
16:10:18:074 (AVDominoMonitor_MC,1093,DominoMonitor,12) [Thread 1756] [Thread
   0x000006DC] Received Notification packet from dna-test1: <notification>
   <handlerid>unitynotifier</handlerid><applicationdata></applicationdata>
   <user></user><database>bQBhAGkAbABcAGYAbABkADEALgBuAHMAZgA=</database>
   <event>CountChange</event><countchangedata><count>1</count></countchangedata>
   <id>2330</id><priority>2</priority><type>V</type><eventtype>6
   </eventtype></notification>
16:10:18:075 (AVDominoMonitor_MC,1094,DominoMonitor,12) [Thread 1756] [Thread
   0x000006DC] Received CountChange Notification packet: Cnt:1; ID:2330; Prio:2;
   Type:V; EType:6;
```

Messages come in pairs—one showing the raw XML message coming in, and a second showing what that message means to Unity. You can read through the first four messages there and reasonably easily tell that a new message has arrived for the user f2_l2 (yes, those are bulk-created usernames and are not really creative). You can see the type of V there, which stands for voice, of course. You can also see F, E, I, R, O, for fax, e-mail, invitation, report, and other, in this field. The message count noted in the third and fourth entry comes after the new arrival and simply notes that there are now two unread voice message counts.

The deletion event (the last two entries) simply is noted as a message count state change. You can see that the count for voice-mail messages is now 1. As such, the notifier knows to leave the MWI on; it turns it off when that count gets to 0. The count returned in the packet indicates the number of unread messages for the specified type. If the type had been E, that would have indicated the number of unread e-mail messages, of interest perhaps for notification triggers set up to deliver a page, for instance, based on e-mail messages in the inbox.

Change to Mail User in Directory

If an administrator changes—for instance, the display name of a subscriber in the directory (through Active Directory Users and Computers)—how does Unity update the local SQL database to reflect that change? This is where the directory monitor services come into play. The directory monitors watch objects in the directory for updates, additions, and deletions. They push that information into the MSMQ queue, where the avDirChangeWriter service pulls from to update SQL. Let us run through a quick example.

Imagine that an administrator changes the display name of Jeff Lindborg, who also happens to be a subscriber on the local Unity server. Figure 2-7 shows what happens when a scenario like this takes place and the directory monitor pulls that information into the database.

Let us turn on some traces and take a look at what the process looks like. In the case of Active Directory (Exchange 2000/2003), we want to watch the AVDSAD service and the AVDirChangeWriter service to see what changes are noted in the directory and what the AVDirChangeWriter is pushing into SQL. Again, in the Unity Diagnostic Tool, go to the Micro Traces section; in the Directory Change Writer section, turn on trace 16, All Change Requests, and in the DSAD section, turn on trace 11, Changes Queued. Go ahead and make a change to the display name of a subscriber, and wait 2 minutes. Remember, the synch time for the avDSAD service is 2 minutes; for the AVDSGlobalCatalog service, it is 15 minutes. You can force the sync to take place immediately using the DOHPropTest tool.

What you will see in the AVDSAD diagnostics is simple:

```
12:24:40:953,AVDirSynch_MC,1127,3652,-1,DSAD,11,AVOBJECTTYPE_MAILUSER,CN=JLindborg
    CN=Users DC=LindborgLabs DC=com
```

Figure 2-7   *The Directory Monitors Replicate Updated Information from AD into SQL*

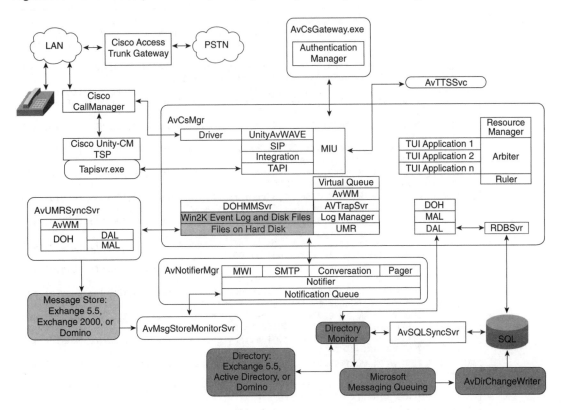

This is just a notation that the record for Jlindborg has changed since the last time you did a synch. This means that the information in the directory is probably newer than what you have locally in SQL. This is determined through a change ID stored in the directory, which you also keep track of locally. Whenever any change is made to an object in the directory, this number is incremented. If the AVDSAD service, in this case, notes that it is newer than the number you have stored, it pushes all the information for that user that Unity cares about into the MSMQ store so that it is written through to SQL. You can see the details of which values are pulled from the directory in the AVDirChangeWriter diagnostic output in Example 2-6.

Example 2-6 *AVDirChangeWriter Diagnostic Output*

```
12:24:41:265,AVDcw_MC,1049,3748,-1,Directory Change Writer,16,CHANGEREQ: [LogId]
392 [ReqType] AV_DIRCHANGE_MODIFY | AV_DIRCHANGE_DOMAIN_CONTROLLER [ObjType]
AVOBJECTTYPE_MAILUSER [DirLogId] 423 [LocLogId] 424 [PropIdsId] 425 [PropValsId]
426
12:24:41:266,AVDcw_MC,1049,3748,-1,Directory Change Writer,16,VARIANT: [LogId] 423
[vt] VT_BSTR [Data] 4DF880B4E68A4F4B96394F4D97B49698
12:24:41:265,AVDcw_MC,1049,3748,-1,Directory Change Writer,16,OBJID: [LogId] 424
[Hdr] 0x00070001 [ObjType] AVOBJECTTYPE_LOCATION [ID] {FEC3952E-3119-4FAF-82E2-
A6534E193635}
12:24:41:266,AVDcw_MC,1049,3748,-1,Directory Change Writer,16,IDLIST: [LogId] 425
[NumElems] 27
12:24:41:265,AVDcw_MC,1049,3748,-1,Directory Change Writer,16,IDLIST: [LogId] 425
[PropId] AVP_ADDRTYPE [ExpType] VT_BSTR
12:24:41:266,AVDcw_MC,1049,3748,-1,Directory Change Writer,16,IDLIST: [LogId] 425
[PropId] AVP_ALIAS [ExpType] VT_BSTR
12:24:41:265,AVDcw_MC,1049,3748,-1,Directory Change Writer,16,IDLIST: [LogId] 425
[PropId] AVP_ALTERNATE_DTMF_IDS [ExpType] VT_ARRAY | VT_VARIANT
12:24:41:266,AVDcw_MC,1049,3748,-1,Directory Change Writer,16,IDLIST: [LogId] 425
[PropId] AVP_AMIS_DISABLE_OUTBOUND [ExpType] VT_BOOL
12:24:41:265,AVDcw_MC,1049,3748,-1,Directory Change Writer,16,IDLIST: [LogId] 425
[PropId] AVP_DIRECTORY_ID [ExpType] VT_BSTR
12:24:41:266,AVDcw_MC,1049,3748,-1,Directory Change Writer,16,IDLIST: [LogId] 425
[PropId] AVP_DISPLAY_NAME [ExpType] VT_BSTR
12:24:41:265,AVDcw_MC,1049,3748,-1,Directory Change Writer,16,IDLIST: [LogId] 425
[PropId] AVP_DTMF_ACCESS_ID [ExpType] VT_BSTR
12:24:41:266,AVDcw_MC,1049,3748,-1,Directory Change Writer,16,IDLIST: [LogId] 425
[PropId] AVP_RECIPIENT_EMAIL_ADDRESS [ExpType] VT_BSTR
12:24:41:265,AVDcw_MC,1049,3748,-1,Directory Change Writer,16,IDLIST: [LogId] 425
[PropId] AVP_FIRST_NAME [ExpType] VT_BSTR
12:24:41:266,AVDcw_MC,1049,3748,-1,Directory Change Writer,16,IDLIST: [LogId] 425
[PropId] AVP_LAST_NAME [ExpType] VT_BSTR
12:24:41:265,AVDcw_MC,1049,3748,-1,Directory Change Writer,16,IDLIST: [LogId] 425
[PropId] AVP_LIST_IN_DIRECTORY [ExpType] VT_BOOL
12:24:41:266,AVDcw_MC,1049,3748,-1,Directory Change Writer,16,IDLIST: [LogId] 425
[PropId] AVP_LOCATION_OBJECT_ID [ExpType] VT_ARRAY | VT_UI1
12:24:41:265,AVDcw_MC,1049,3748,-1,Directory Change Writer,16,IDLIST: [LogId] 425
[PropId] AVP_MAIL_DATABASE [ExpType] VT_BSTR
12:24:41:266,AVDcw_MC,1049,3748,-1,Directory Change Writer,16,IDLIST: [LogId] 425
[PropId] AVP_MAIL_SERVER [ExpType] VT_BSTR
12:24:41:265,AVDcw_MC,1049,3748,-1,Directory Change Writer,16,IDLIST: [LogId] 425
[PropId] AVP_MAILBOX_ID [ExpType] VT_BSTR
12:24:41:266,AVDcw_MC,1049,3748,-1,Directory Change Writer,16,IDLIST: [LogId] 425
[PropId] AVP_MAILBOX_SEND_LIMIT [ExpType] VT_I4
12:24:41:265,AVDcw_MC,1049,3748,-1,Directory Change Writer,16,IDLIST: [LogId] 425
[PropId] AVP_MAILBOX_SEND_RECEIVE_LIMIT [ExpType] VT_I4
12:24:41:266,AVDcw_MC,1049,3748,-1,Directory Change Writer,16,IDLIST: [LogId] 425
[PropId] AVP_MAILBOX_USE_DEFAULT_LIMITS [ExpType] VT_BOOL
12:24:41:265,AVDcw_MC,1049,3748,-1,Directory Change Writer,16,IDLIST: [LogId] 425
[PropId] AVP_MAILBOX_WARNING_LIMIT [ExpType] VT_I4
12:24:41:266,AVDcw_MC,1049,3748,-1,Directory Change Writer,16,IDLIST: [LogId] 425
[PropId] AVP_OBJECT_CHANGED_ID [ExpType] VT_BSTR
12:24:41:265,AVDcw_MC,1049,3748,-1,Directory Change Writer,16,IDLIST: [LogId] 425
[PropId] AVP_PRIMARY_FAX_NUMBER [ExpType] VT_BSTR
12:24:41:266,AVDcw_MC,1049,3748,-1,Directory Change Writer,16,IDLIST: [LogId] 425
[PropId] AVP_REMOTE_ADDRESS [ExpType] VT_BSTR
```

Example 2-6 *AVDirChangeWriter Diagnostic Output (Continued)*

```
12:24:41:265,AVDcw_MC,1049,3748,-1,Directory Change Writer,16,IDLIST: [LogId] 425
  [PropId] AVP_SID [ExpType] VT_ARRAY | VT_UI1
12:24:41:266,AVDcw_MC,1049,3748,-1,Directory Change Writer,16,IDLIST: [LogId] 425
  [PropId] AVP_SID_HISTORY [ExpType] VT_ARRAY | VT_VARIANT
12:24:41:265,AVDcw_MC,1049,3748,-1,Directory Change Writer,16,IDLIST: [LogId] 425
  [PropId] AVP_SMTP_ADDRESS [ExpType] VT_BSTR
12:24:41:266,AVDcw_MC,1049,3748,-1,Directory Change Writer,16,IDLIST: [LogId] 425
  [PropId] AVP_VOICE_NAME_DATA [ExpType] VT_ARRAY | VT_UI1
12:24:41:265,AVDcw_MC,1049,3748,-1,Directory Change Writer,16,IDLIST: [LogId] 425
  [PropId] AVP_XFER_STRING [ExpType] VT_BSTR
12:24:41:266,AVDcw_MC,1049,3748,-1,Directory Change Writer,16,VARIANT: [LogId] 426
  [vt] VT_ARRAY | VT_VARIANT [Dim] 1 [ElemSize] 16 [NumElems] 27 [LBound] 0
  [Data(first 32 bytes)] 08 00 00 00 00 00 00 00 84 A9 16 00 00 00 00 00 08 00 00
  00 00 00 00 00 B4 3E 18 00 00 00 00 00
12:24:41:265,AVDcw_MC,1049,3748,-1,Directory Change Writer,16,VARIANT: [LogId] 426
  [vt] VT_BSTR [Data] EX
12:24:41:266,AVDcw_MC,1049,3748,-1,Directory Change Writer,16,VARIANT: [LogId] 426
  [vt] VT_BSTR [Data] JLindborg
12:24:41:265,AVDcw_MC,1049,3748,-1,Directory Change Writer,16,VARIANT: [LogId] 426
  [vt] VT_NULL [Data(entire union)] 00 00 00 00 00 00 00 00
12:24:41:266,AVDcw_MC,1049,3748,-1,Directory Change Writer,16,VARIANT: [LogId] 426
  [vt] VT_NULL [Data(entire union)] 00 00 00 00 00 00 00 00
12:24:41:265,AVDcw_MC,1049,3748,-1,Directory Change Writer,16,VARIANT: [LogId] 426
  [vt] VT_BSTR [Data] 4df880b4e68a4f4b96394f4d97b49698
12:24:41:266,AVDcw_MC,1049,3748,-1,Directory Change Writer,16,VARIANT: [LogId] 426
  [vt] VT_BSTR [Data] Jeff Lindborg
12:24:41:265,AVDcw_MC,1049,3748,-1,Directory Change Writer,16,VARIANT: [LogId] 426
  [vt] VT_BSTR [Data] 1189
12:24:41:266,AVDcw_MC,1049,3748,-1,Directory Change Writer,16,VARIANT: [LogId] 426
  [vt] VT_BSTR [Data] cn=JLindborg cn=Recipients ou=First Administrative Group
  o=Lindborg Labs
12:24:41:265,AVDcw_MC,1049,3748,-1,Directory Change Writer,16,VARIANT: [LogId] 426
  [vt] VT_BSTR [Data] Jeff
12:24:41:266,AVDcw_MC,1049,3748,-1,Directory Change Writer,16,VARIANT: [LogId] 426
  [vt] VT_BSTR [Data] Lindborg
12:24:41:265,AVDcw_MC,1049,3748,-1,Directory Change Writer,16,VARIANT: [LogId] 426
  [vt] VT_BOOL [Data(entire union)] FF FF 00 00 00 00 00 00
12:24:41:266,AVDcw_MC,1049,3748,-1,Directory Change Writer,16,VARIANT: [LogId] 426
  [vt] VT_ARRAY | VT_UI1 [Dim] 1 [ElemSize] 1 [NumElems] 88 [LBound] 0 [Data(first
  32 bytes)] 01 00 07 00 30 00 39 00 3A 00 7B 00 46 00 45 00 43 00 33 00 39 00 35
  00 32 00 45 00 2D 00 33 00
12:24:41:265,AVDcw_MC,1049,3748,-1,Directory Change Writer,16,VARIANT: [LogId] 426
  [vt] VT_BSTR [Data(first 128 chars)] CN=Mailbox Store (BIGBOY) CN=First Storage
  Group CN=InformationStore CN=BIGBOY CN=Servers CN=First Administrative Group
  CN=Admin
12:24:41:266,AVDcw_MC,1049,3748,-1,Directory Change Writer,16,VARIANT: [LogId] 426
  [vt] VT_BSTR [Data] BIGBOY
12:24:41:265,AVDcw_MC,1049,3748,-1,Directory Change Writer,16,VARIANT: [LogId] 426
  [vt] VT_BSTR [Data] cn=JLindborg cn=Recipients ou=First Administrative Group
  o=Lindborg Labs
12:24:41:266,AVDcw_MC,1049,3748,-1,Directory Change Writer,16,VARIANT: [LogId] 426
  [vt] VT_NULL [Data(entire union)] 00 00 00 00 00 00 00 00
12:24:41:265,AVDcw_MC,1049,3748,-1,Directory Change Writer,16,VARIANT: [LogId] 426
  [vt] VT_NULL [Data(entire union)] 00 00 00 00 00 00 00 00
12:24:41:266,AVDcw_MC,1049,3748,-1,Directory Change Writer,16,VARIANT: [LogId] 426
  [vt] VT_BOOL [Data(entire union)] FF FF 00 00 00 00 00 00
```

continues

Example 2-6 *AVDirChangeWriter Diagnostic Output (Continued)*

```
12:24:41:265,AVDcw_MC,1049,3748,-1,Directory Change Writer,16,VARIANT: [LogId] 426
  [vt] VT_NULL [Data(entire union)] 00 00 00 00 00 00 00 00
12:24:41:266,AVDcw_MC,1049,3748,-1,Directory Change Writer,16,VARIANT: [LogId] 426
  [vt] VT_BSTR [Data] ?
12:24:41:265,AVDcw_MC,1049,3748,-1,Directory Change Writer,16,VARIANT: [LogId] 426
  [vt] VT_NULL [Data(entire union)] 00 00 00 00 00 00 00 00
12:24:41:266,AVDcw_MC,1049,3748,-1,Directory Change Writer,16,VARIANT: [LogId] 426
  [vt] VT_NULL [Data(entire union)] 00 00 00 00 00 00 00 00
12:24:41:265,AVDcw_MC,1049,3748,-1,Directory Change Writer,16,VARIANT: [LogId] 426
  [vt] VT_ARRAY | VT_UI1 [Dim] 1 [ElemSize] 1 [NumElems] 28 [LBound] 0 [Data] 01 05
  00 00 00 00 00 05 15 00 00 00 57 29 02 4C E7 CB DD 7D 23 5F 63 6B 5A 0E 00 00
12:24:41:266,AVDcw_MC,1049,3748,-1,Directory Change Writer,16,VARIANT: [LogId] 426
  [vt] VT_NULL [Data(entire union)] 00 00 00 00 00 00 00 00
12:24:41:265,AVDcw_MC,1049,3748,-1,Directory Change Writer,16,VARIANT: [LogId] 426
  [vt] VT_BSTR [Data] JLindborg@LindborgLabs.com
12:24:41:266,AVDcw_MC,1049,3748,-1,Directory Change Writer,16,VARIANT: [LogId] 426
  [vt] VT_NULL [Data(entire union)] 00 00 00 00 00 00 00 00
12:24:41:265,AVDcw_MC,1049,3748,-1,Directory Change Writer,16,VARIANT: [LogId] 426
  [vt] VT_BSTR [Data] 1189
```

This is a rather long section of diagnostic to include here, but it is instructive to see it in its entirety. You see a list of 27 properties that are pulled in from the directory by the directory monitor (AVDSAD, in this case) on the object that changed in the directory. They are listed twice: once with the [propID] tag, which indicates which property name in the Unity object model the value maps through to, and again in the same order with the [vt] tag, which shows the actual value pulled from the directory. For instance, to find the display name value, you must look at the propID tag, which is the six item listed (in bold). Then go to the seventh item in the vt tags, and notice that the actual value is Jeff Lindborg (also in bold). We skip the first item with a vt tag, so the first PropID corresponds to the second vt entry, and so on. The values, meanings, and locations of the constants in the propID tag list (AVP_DISPLAY_ NAME) are covered more in the data object model discussion in Chapter 3.

Although 27 properties are pulled from the directory, only a small handful of them are visible using normal administrative tools for viewing the directory. The first name, last name, display name, and alias round out the list of obvious ones. Most of the information, however, is specific to Unity and is written through hidden values in the directory. You can see this with tools, such as the ADSI editor, but normally they do not show up. Also notice that all 27 values are updated even though, in this case, only the display name was changed. The directory monitor has no way of knowing which property was changed in the directory— only that the object has changed in some way. It is possible that none of the values Unity cares about was updated; because the change ID has rolled, the monitor pushes the values through anyway.

What happens if a user is deleted in the directory entirely? In previous versions of Unity, this presented a problem because some subscriber data still hung around unless the administrator first removed the person as a subscriber in Unity before removing the associated record in the directory. Of course, this did not always happen. In Unity 3.1(*x*) and later, however, the directory monitor handles this. In this case, if you went ahead and deleted the Jlindborg account out of AD, you would see this line in the AVDSAD trace output:

```
12:30:42:671,AVDirSynch_MC,1127,3652,-1,DSAD,11,AVOBJECTTYPE_
MAILUSER,CN=JLindborg\ DEL:b480f84d-8ae6-4b4f-9639-4f4d97b49698 CN=Deleted Objects
DC=LindborgLabs DC=com
```

The DEL: xxx notation indicates that this is a deletion request. The AVDSAD then pushes the information onto the MSMQ queue, and the AVDirChangeWriter deletes the appropriate record from the subscriber table in the UnityDB SQL database. Triggers in SQL take care of cleaning the rest of the tables in the database of information related to that subscriber, such as their call handlers, transfer rules, and greeting rules. These structures all are covered in Chapter 3.

Before moving on, it is important to note that the monitors also pull in information about subscribers, location objects, and distribution lists that are added, changed, or deleted on other Unity servers in the directory. In the case of Active Directory, this is done by the AVDSGlobalCatalog service, which watches the entire forest for objects of interest. For instance, when a mail user is found who is tagged as a subscriber, it pushes a similar-looking information push request onto the MSMQ queue for the AVDirChangeWriter service to pick up and push into the GlobalSubscriber table in the UnityDB database in SQL. This information is used to provide the digital networking functionality described in Chapter 12.

Administrator Updates Subscriber in SA

This flow walks through an administrator logging in through the SA and making a change to a subscriber that then gets pushed to the directory. The first step of the process is shown in Figure 2-8 in which the administrator launches the Unity SA URL from the Internet Explorer client at the desktop.

The SA URL includes the server name of the Unity server the administrator wants to connect to. This is subtle but important. This requires DNS to be functioning properly: Even if you resort to using the IP address of the server, subsequent URLs generated by links from within the SA will insert the server name. As such, the SA will not function properly.

Figure 2-8 *Administrator Accesses the SA Web Interface*

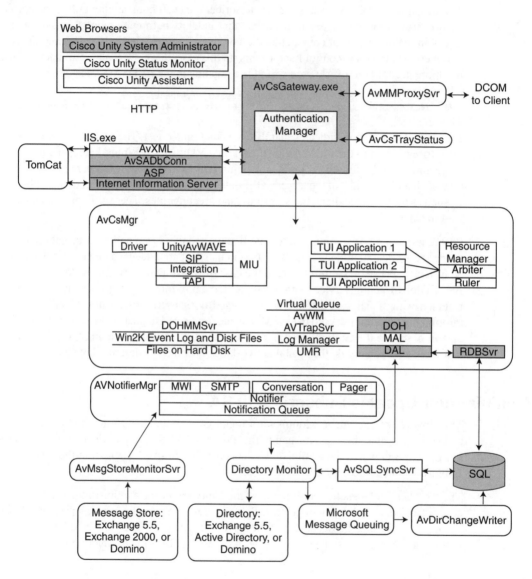

Unity setup registers pages for the SA, Status Monitor, and the new Cisco Unity Personal Configuration Assistant (CPCA) web pages with IIS on the local server. In this case, the administrator launches the SA, which is http://servername/saweb. If Unity is configured to use NT security (the only option for systems earlier than Unity 4.0), IIS first ensures that the user is authenticated. If the user is logged into the local domain or is logged into a domain that the local domain trusts, the process proceeds. If the user is not logged into a trusted domain, that user gets a challenge and response login dialog box before being allowed to proceed. It is important to note that Unity is not involved in the process up to this point. When the Unity web pages are added to IIS during the setup process, they are configured so that only authenticated users can access them—no anonymous or clear-text authentication is allowed. If the system is configured for the new Unity authentication method, the user gets a web page requiring a login name and password stored on the local Unity server before proceeding. It is possible to allow clients to store a login name or password for defined periods of time on their client machines, but, by default, this is disabled. This authentication model allows sites that are not using Windows NT or that are using multiple domains that do not trust each other to more easily gain Unity client access. More details on the authentication mechanisms available for Unity 4.0 are in the Unity documentation at http://www.cisco.com/univercd/cc/td/doc/product/voice/c_unity/unity40/index.htm. If that is too much for you to type, you can find this link and numerous other useful Unity related links on www.ciscounitytools.com.

After the user is authenticated, the SA uses the AVSADbConn.DLL from the IIS process to connect to the DOH in the AVCsMgr component, to see if the user has Unity administration rights on the local Unity server. If the user resolves to a subscriber that has a Class of Service setting that allows SA access, or if the user is mapped to a local user who has such rights, that user is allowed to proceed. The mapping process is a simple matter of adding the SID of a domain account to a table in SQL indicating that the user has the admin rights of a local subscriber (usually the built-in installer account created by Unity during setup). This mechanism is in place so that administrators responsible for maintaining multiple Unity servers on a network easily can gain SA access on all the boxes, without having to create separate accounts added as subscribers to each to do it. The tool for adding such mappings is the GrantUnityAccess application, which you can find in the Tools Depot applet on the Unity desktop.

Assuming that the user is a subscriber who has administration access, the Unity SA screen pops up, and the user can how go about his business. In this case, the subscriber changes the display name and then saves it. The SA pages again go through the SADBConn.dll to talk to the DOH to request that the subscriber's changes be written through to both the local database and the directory, if appropriate. The DOH writes the changes first through to the directory by way of the directory monitor service. After that, it writes the changes to the local SQL database. If the update to the directory fails (for instance, because of a permissions problem), the changes are not propagated to SQL and the SA is passed back an error.

It is important to note here that when the SA requests the subscriber's information be updated, it means all the data on the page(s) that are marked "dirty" (in other words, every page on which one or more properties was updated) for that user, not just the individual property (display name, in this case) that the administrator might have updated. The SA is not granular enough to keep track of which individual properties have been updated for a user—it knows only which pages contain updated values. In much the same way that the directory monitor pulls in all data for a user in the directory that has been updated because it does not know which specific property has changed, changes in the SA result in a similar block-write going back out to the directory.

Summary

We covered a lot of material in some depth in this chapter. It is certainly not expected that you will be able to now turn on traces and debug a Unity system in the field. However, you should have a reasonably good understanding of what all the Unity services you see in the Service Control Manager are responsible for—at least, in general terms. You also should have a basic grasp of how the directory monitors, message store monitors, and notifier components work together to integrate with Exchange 5.5, 2000, 2003, Domino directory, and messaging back ends. Finally, you should understand how the different client applications, such as the SA and PCA, connect to the Unity server and update data to both the local database and the directory Unity is connected to. Armed with this information, you are ready to move on to the next chapter, which covers in more detail how the Unity database is structured and how the various objects relate to one another in the system.

CHAPTER 3

Components and Subsystems: Object Model

Before getting too far into the inner workings of Unity, it is important to get an understanding of the basic Unity object model. It is difficult to grasp the administration structure, how calls flow through Unity, and how various conversations work without understanding how all the objects that make up the Unity database work together. The terminology and objects discussed here will come up again often as we discuss administration topics, audio text applications, and digital networking, among other things. It is important to make sure you understand the relationships among all these objects moving forward, or many of the topics covered later might not make sense. This chapter assumes that you have a fairly good understanding of the Unity web-based system administration console (SA), as well as a basic understanding of the objects that you can create and use with the SA and how they work.

NOTE	This chapter covers the high-level object model; the next section gives a quick overview of the SQL tables in the Unity database. Chapter 21, "Administering Unity Programmatically," takes a more detailed look at the tables and columns that make up the SQL back end for Unity.

We look at the object model by using the DOH Property Tester (DPT) tool. In the early days of Unity development, this utility was the only administration interface into Unity because the web-based system administration console was one of the last items to be completed in the first production release. It continues to ship with the product as a mechanism for support staff to use for troubleshooting reasons.

Although it is possible to go directly to the SQL database that Unity uses to store its information, using DPT is usually easier and faster for exploring the object model because it groups everything into proper collections and enables you easily to jump around between related objects automatically. We cover the SQL tables themselves and discuss the mappings between individual properties in DPT and their respective counterparts in SQL later in this chapter. For now, we walk through the object collections and their relationships. If you have a running version of Unity 3.0(1) or later handy, I highly encourage you to open DPT and explore as we go through this chapter.

You will find the DPT tool in the Tools Depot in Unity 3.1(3) or later, or you can run it directly off the hard drive from \Commserver\TechTools\DohPropTest.exe. You will be prompted for a password, which you can leave blank and then select Ignore on the subsequent password-check dialog box. The tool opens in read-only mode without the password, which is just fine for the exploring we want to do here.

Figure 3-1 shows the DPT interface when opened without the password. Notice that the Set, Delete, Create, and Remove buttons are not active. The main collections of objects are in the far-left column, the members of that collection are in the middle column, and the properties of the selected object are in the far-right column. Fun fact: The AVP_ prefix on all the property names stands for Active Voice Property, which is what our company was called before joining Cisco.

Figure 3-1 *DOHPropTest Interface in Read-Only Mode*

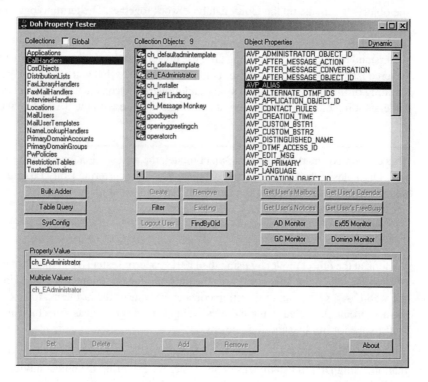

Although the back-end storage scheme for Unity data has changed dramatically between the 2.x and 3.x lines, the basic object model for Unity has not changed significantly since 2.0 was released in 1997. New properties have been added to objects, and collections have been expanded to include more items and the like. Still, if you fire up DPT on Unity 2.2, 2.3, 2.4, 3.0, 3.1, or 4.0, they look remarkably similar to Figure 3-1.

The following sections briefly describe each of the primary objects in the system and discuss some of their more important properties. A more complete list of each property, what its value means, and which columns in which SQL tables each property maps to are covered in Chapter 21.

Applications

The applications object currently is not exposed in the Unity administration tools and is not used for anything. All call handlers, interview handlers, and name lookup handlers are associated with the one default application object in this collection, by convention. The original idea behind this was to use it as a way to tie together objects into separate application groups for providing tenant services type of applications, but work for this was never done. Future versions of Unity might press this collection into service for tenanting applications.

Call Handlers

Call handlers are the essential building blocks for constructing audio-text applications within Unity and are the primary mechanism for both routing calls within Unity and sending callers to internal and external phones. The call handler plays custom-recorded greetings to callers, responds to input from users, and rings phones. In short, it is the most fundamentally important object in the system.

Each subscriber is associated with a call handler, which is referred to as the primary call handler for that user. If you look on the Unity SA and compare the call handler's administration pages with the subscribers pages, you will notice that a subscriber is an almost perfect superset of a call handler. The information that you see on the subscriber pages includes almost all the information on the call handlers pages, plus additional subscriber-specific items. The only important limitation that a primary call handler has that a standalone call handler does not is that the subscriber administration interface allows only one transfer rule to be enabled (the alternate). A standalone call handler has three transfer rules (alternate, standard, and off-hours). This limitation was imposed early on, to simplify the subscriber administration phone conversation. Subscribers can simply enable or disable transfers to their phones because dealing with lists of devices that can each be enabled or disabled through a phone interface can be somewhat daunting.

In Figure 3-1, the call handlers that have a prefix of ch_ are primary call handlers that are associated with a subscriber. The alias of the primary call handler contains the alias of the subscriber that it is associated with. For example, ch_jsmith is the primary call handler for the mail user with the alias jsmith. The cht_test template call handler seen in Figure 3-1 is a primary call handler for a subscriber template. Oddly, the two built-in subscriber templates are associated with primary call handlers ch_DefaltTemplate and ch_DefaultAdminTemplate. New templates that you create will be prefaced with cht_, however. The call handlers that have no prefix are standalone call handlers, and they appear in the Unity administration interface under the call handlers page. The other call handlers listed in the collection do not appear on their own in the SA; their properties are exposed on the subscriber and the subscriber templates pages instead.

All call handlers also have three subcollections of objects: contact rules, menu entries, and messaging rules. If you click on any of these properties in DPT, a pop-up window appears on top of the main DPT interface to show the objects in the collection. Figure 3-2 shows the AVP_CONTACT_RULES collection.

Figure 3-2   *The Contact (Transfer) Rules Collection Opened for the Example Administrator in DOHPropTest*

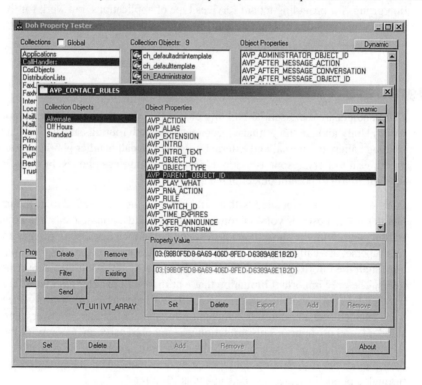

AVP_CONTACT_RULES

Contact rules is the internal term for what the Unity SA calls transfer rules. Three transfer rules are present on each call handler, although, as noted earlier, primary call handlers associated with subscribers use only one: the alternate. The values for most of these properties are exposed on the Call Transfer page for call handlers, subscribers, and subscriber template pages in the SA.

In short, a contact rule is designed to optionally allow you to ring a phone when a call is passed to that call handler. By default, the first thing a call handler does when a call is passed into it is to process its contact rules and act on them. We cover this in more detail in Chapter 18, "Audio-Text Applications."

The three rules in the collection are alternate, standard, and off-hours. Which rule is evaluated depends on which is enabled and what time of day it is. If the alternate rule is active, it is always the one evaluated; it overrides the other two in all cases. If the off-hours rule is enabled in the SA and the schedule that the call handler/subscriber is associated with indicates that it is after hours, this rule is evaluated. If neither the alternate nor the off-hours rules trigger, the standard rule is evaluated. The standard rule never can be disabled in the SA; if it is disabled programmatically or by fiddling directly with SQL or DTP, callers can end up being sent to the failsafe phone conversation and will hear, "I am sorry, I cannot talk to you now. . . " The standard rule always is supposed to be enabled so that it can act as a backstop and prevent calls from falling through all three rules like that.

AVP_MENU_ENTRIES

The menu entries collection corresponds to the data visible on the Caller Input pages on the call handler and the subscriber pages in the Unity SA. A total of 12 objects in this collection represent the programmable actions for the 0–9, *, and # keys.

Each key can be set up to perform an action when pressed during the greeting for a call handler or subscriber. You can opt to hang up the call, take a message, send the caller to a different handler, route the call to the subscriber sign-in conversation, and so on.

The same set of menu entries is active and takes action for any of the five greetings that can play for a handler. This means that you cannot have different key actions active during the day than during after-hours; this can present difficulties in some audio-text applications. We cover ways to work around this in Chapter 18.

AVP_MESSAGING_RULES

The messaging rules correspond to the greetings on the call handler and subscriber pages in the SA. You will see six messaging rules in this collection, but the astute observer will note that only five greetings are visible in the SA. By default, the Error greeting is hidden in the SA, but it can be exposed by making a Registry edit available in the Advanced Settings tool. You also can edit the Error greeting using the Bulk Edit utility. The Error greeting is a special greeting that dictates what happens when a user attempts to dial an extension that does not exist in the system during a greeting. This is hidden on the SA by default: We got so many calls and questions about how it worked in early versions, and the need to customize it is reasonably rare in the field.

When a call is handed off to a call handler (either standalone or a primary call handler associated with a subscriber), the transfer rules are processed first by default. Then the call proceeds to the messaging rules if the transfer rules allow for it (in other words, if we did not do a successful transfer to a phone and release the call). You can change this to skip the transfer rules entirely by sending the caller to the greetings entry point in the call handler directly, which is discussed in detail in Chapter 18. The schedule that the handler is associated with and the source of the call and how it was routed to Unity determine which greeting gets played. The greetings are processed in the following order:

1 **Alternate**. If the alternate greeting is enabled, it always plays. It overrides all other greetings when active.

2 **Internal**. If the internal greeting is enabled and the calling extension corresponds to a subscriber in the database, the internal greeting plays.

3 **Busy**. If the busy greeting is enabled and the forwarding reason is busy, this greeting plays.

4 **After Hours**. If the after-hours greeting is active and the schedule associated with the call handler indicates that it is after hours, this greeting plays.

5 **Standard**. If none of the other greetings kicks in, the standard greeting always plays. It cannot be disabled in the SA and is always active.

6 **Error**. The Error greeting is always active and enabled by default, and is the one that gets played only when a caller enters an extension that cannot be found in the database while another greeting for the call handler or subscriber plays. By default, it tells the user, "I am sorry, I did not hear that entry. . ." and routes the caller back to the opening greeting call handler created by setup. This can cause headaches for folks trying to do a simple tenant services type of application because there could be multiple opening greeting handlers for multiple incoming numbers. Ways for dealing with basic tenant services types of scenarios are covered in Chapter 18.

Aside from the subcollections noted, a call handler has several important properties that link it to other objects in the system:

- AVP_ADMINISTRATOR_OBJECT_ID
- AVP_RECIPIENT_OBJECT_ID
- AVP_LOCATION_OBJECT_ID

- AVP_AFTER_MESSAGE_ACTION, AVP_AFTERMESSAGE_ CONVERSATION, and AVP_AFTER_MESSAGE_OBJECT_ID
- AVP_SCHEDULE_OBJECT_NAME

AVP_ADMINISTRATOR_OBJECT_ID

The Administrator object ID corresponds to the owner property on the profile page of a call handler or an interview handler. Anything that has the object ID tag on it indicates a unique identifier for an object in a collection. In most cases, when you click on any AVP_xxx property that ends in OBJECT_ID in the DPT application, you get a pop-up dialog box similar to Figure 3-3.

Figure 3-3   *An ObjectID Jump Dialog Box in DOHPropTest*

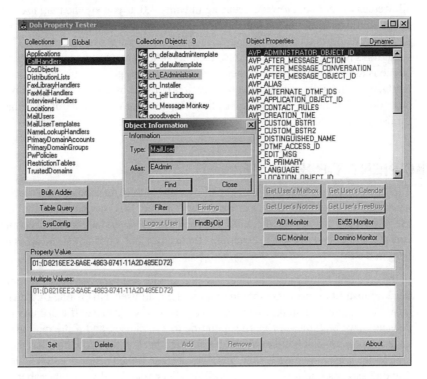

If you click on the Find button, DPT automatically takes you to the appropriate object collection and shows you that object. This is handy for jumping around to follow various links off an object because the object ID values themselves are not human-readable in Unity

3.x. In versions of Unity 2.4.x and earlier, the object ID values were LDAP-distinguished names that referenced the container and alias of the object; this made it reasonably easy to figure out which one it was pointing at. In 3.x and later, they are GUID strings, which would require tedious manual filtering to run down on your own. The fine folks in the DOH group added this functionality to make our lives a bit easier.

The Administrator object ID can point to either a mail user or a distribution list. It is found on call handlers, public distribution lists, interview handlers, and name lookup handlers. Although the Administrator object ID value has been in the schema since day one, it has not been used for anything of significance until the release of Unity 4.0. This value origi-nally was intended to allow owners of objects to administer them over the phone or through the SA interface. For instance, the capability to record the greeting on a call handler over the phone would be limited to the owner(s) of that handler. This was another one of those things that originally was slated to go in early on, but the resources and time just never allowed us to get to it. However, starting in Unity 4.0, if you are the mail user or a member of the public distribution list noted as the administrator (or owner in the SA) for a call han-dler, you are allowed to record the greetings for that handler over the phone. This will make some folks happy in the field because the only other way to change the greeting over the phone is to use a dummy subscriber — of course, this requires a subscriber license. Cur-rently, that is the only use for this property; it is not yet possible to change properties on any other objects in the directory over the phone. It should be noted that this value has no impact for user access to objects via the web-based SA interface.

AVP_RECIPIENT_OBJECT_ID

The Recipient object ID points to a mail user or a public distribution list object that gets messages left for a call handler or interview handler. This is exposed on the SA on the Messages page for call handlers. For subscribers, however, the message recipient is, of course, hard-coded to be the subscribers themselves and does not show up as a separate field in the SA.

In the case of a primary call handler associated with a subscriber, both the recipient and the administrator object IDs should point to the mail user. This is one of the checks the dbWalker application makes while crawling the Unity database. If a primary call handler does not have both these properties pointing to a mail user, and if the mail user does not have the primary call handler object ID pointing back at the same handler, there is a prob-lem. When a user-creation action fails, such a cross-linked primary call handler can result. The one exception to this is primary call handlers associated with subscriber templates. Templates are special because the owner and recipients are assigned when the subscriber is created using the templates.

The first thing Unity does when a call is sent to a call handler is to fetch handles to both the recipient and the administrator objects. Even though the call handler might not be set up to take messages, both of these objects must be valid and found, or the caller will go to the failsafe conversation. This is where Unity sends calls that it does not know what to do with. The caller hears, "I am sorry, I cannot talk to you now. Please try your call again later." Then Unity logs one or more errors in the application event log to help in diagnosing the situation. We decided to do this instead of risk the possibility of taking a message that we could not deliver.

For instance, if you have a customer feedback call handler set up to leave a message for Bill, and you delete Bill as a subscriber (or delete Bill's mail account entirely), that call handler has a broken link and will not work properly. The dbWalker utility is designed to quickly run down and help administrators fix such broken links. It is important to understand that Unity currently does not dynamically fix up these types of links when objects are removed, however, because it is very difficult to do this on-the-fly. For instance, deciding what to do with broken owner and recipient links requires some sort of user feedback from the administrator. In Chapter 21, we cover an example of how to do a clean removal of a user from the system without breaking any links programmatically.

AVP_LOCATION_OBJECT_ID

The location object ID points to the location that this call handler is associated with. All objects in the Unity database are associated with a location object, but only special types of subscribers can be associated with anything other than the default location object created by the Unity setup. Eventually, this design might allow for full tenant applications in Unity by allowing entire groups of objects (call handlers, interview handlers, subscribers, directory handlers, COS objects, and so on) to be associated with different locations on the same Unity server. Currently, however, only one primary location object exists per Unity box.

Administrators can create additional location objects for various networking schemes using AMIS, SMTP, the Cisco Unity Bridge, and VPIM transport mechanisms to other Unity servers or other foreign voice-mail systems. This is covered in detail in Chapter 12, "Unity Networking."

The location object also serves an important role for identifying other Unity servers on the network and finding out which Unity server a subscriber in the directory is associated with. When you install a Unity server onto your network, the setup creates a uniquely named primary location object, and a corresponding object is created in the directory. All Unity servers in the directory, then, can identify one another through information in these location objects and their subscribers, which are also in the directory. The details of how this works are covered in Chapter 12. Chapter 21 also includes an example that shows how to find and attach to a remote Unity server's database to update the properties on a subscriber found in the directory.

AVP_AFTER_MESSAGE_ACTION, AVP_AFTERMESSAGE_CONVERSATION, and AVP_AFTER_MESSAGE_OBJECT_ID

These three properties work together to define where a caller is sent after leaving a message for a call handler or subscriber. The values for these are exposed on the Messages page for call handlers and subscribers under the After Message Action section in the SA.

You will see a very similar trilogy of properties for action, conversation, and destination object IDs in the Messaging Rules collection objects as well. They all work in much the same way. The action determines whether a call is to be hung up or sent to another object. The conversation indicates which type of object this is and how it is to be used if the action is set to send the caller to another object. The destination object ID indicates which object will get the call.

For instance, if an administrator sets the after-message action in the SA to go to the greeting for the Operator Call handler, the AVP_AFTER_MESSAGE_ACTION would be 2, the AVP_AFTER_MESSAGE_CONVERSATION would be phGreeting, and the AFTER_MESSAGE_OBJECT_ID would be the object ID for the Operator Call Handler object in the call handlers collection. The 2 there is a generic "goto" value that is the most common setting for action properties. Do not worry—in Chapter 21, we cover how to check what the values for the action and conversations fields mean and what legal values you have to choose from.

TIP　　The conversation phGreeting actually stands for Phone Handler Greeting. Early in the development of Unity, we called things phone handlers until it dawned on us that we were not handling phones—we were handling calls. In the user interface, things were renamed to call handlers, but the underlying conversation code was already in place with the *ph* prefix; it remains there today.

AVP_SCHEDULE_OBJECT_NAME

Schedules do not appear in the DOH Property Tester tool, but call handlers have an AVP_SCHEDULE_OBJECT_NAME reference. This schedule defines what times of the day are considered standard and what times are considered off-hours, in 30 minute increments for each of the 7 days of the week. The phone conversations use this to determine which greeting and transfer rules are triggered for the call handler when processing calls. In Unity 3.1(3) and later, schedule definitions appear in the Schedule table in the UnityDB database in SQL. For earlier versions of Unity, they appear as separate keys in the Registry under HKLM\Software\Active Voice\Schedule.

The unique identifier for schedules in all versions is simply their name (for example, Day Shift). You define different schedules in the SA on the Schedules page. There is no limit to the number of schedules that you can create.

TIP	Although the SA exposed only 30-minute increments in its interface for constructing schedules, the schedules are actually stored in 15-minute segments in the database. If you need more granularity in your schedules, you can use the Schedules option in the Audio Text Manager (ATM) application to expose schedules in 15-minute increments. You will find the ATM application in your Tools Depot on the Unity desktop or at www.ciscounitytools.com.

AVP_ALTERNATE_DTMF_IDS

This is a collection of extensions that administrators can assign to subscribers. Athough this appears on all call handlers, of course, it applies only to primary call handlers that are associated with subscribers. Up to nine alternate extensions can be associated with each subscriber, and they are listed here.

COS Objects

Administrators use the class of serviceobject to dictate which features a subscriber has access to over the phone; which administration functions a subscriber is allowed to perform through the web administration interface, if any; and which numbers a subscriber is allowed to dial. This is how the administration interfaces enforce licensing and administration restrictions, and how dialing restrictions are imposed throughout the system. Every subscriber is associated with only one COS object when it is created, and this association can be viewed and edited on the profile page for subscribers in the Unity SA. No other objects are associated with COS objects other than subscribers.

When you delete a class of service object via the SA interface, the interface does provide you with a mechanism for replacing references to the deleted COS object with a link to a valid one. You are not left with just a broken link, as is the case with most other objects that you can remove through the SA. If you break this link by editing SQL or DPT directly, you can cause many problems at the phone conversation and administration end of things.

The COS object contains no subcollections, but it does include links to three external objects that are of interest. AVP_FAX_RESTRICTION_OBJECT_ID, AVP_OUTCALL_ RESTRICTION_OBJECT_ID, and AVP_XFER_RESTRICTION_OBJECT_ID all point to objects found under the restriction tables collection. The restriction tables limit which numbers can be entered into the fax delivery number, outgoing dial delivery numbers, and transfer numbers, respectively. It is important to note that these restrictions are enforced at the time they are changed, not at the time they are dialed. This was done so that administrators can change fax, delivery, and transfer numbers for subscribers using their own COS privileges. After a number is accepted into a field, Unity always dials it, with no questions asked. This approach to dial-restriction enforcement causes a lot of folks in the field to stumble; we cover this concept in more detail in Chapter 18.

Unity does not use a number of properties on the COS object. Most of the administration-access properties (such as AVP_ACCESS_CALL_HANDLER_CUD) end in _CUD and _RO, which originally was going to provide read-only and change/update/delete rights on a per-access flag basis. This never was implemented, and only the _CUD flags actually have any affect. You will notice that the COS objects created by setup might have the _RO flags set to 1, but any COS that you create yourself will never change any of those values from 0, no matter what you do in the SA.

In Unity 3.1, a more granular SA access scheme was added to the COS object. Access to subscribers, public distribution lists, and the COS administration pages in the SA was expanded to include read, edit, add, and delete flags for each. This gives customers more specific limitations for these areas for help-desk type applications in which full administration access is not desired. You will see these as sets of four flags for each of those objects (AVP_PDL_ADD_ACCESS, AVP_PDL_DELETE_ACCESS, AVP_PDL_MODIFY_ ACCESS, and AVP_PDL_READ_ACCESS). Earlier versions of Unity do not contain these properties.

Distribution Lists

Public distribution lists (DLs) are unique in the Unity object model, in that they are shared objects across all Unity servers in a directory. No other objects in the scheme are shared across multiple systems like this. For instance, a subscriber is a mail user in Exchange/ Domino, but it can be a Unity subscriber in only one Unity system. Attempting to import that same subscriber into another Unity server will fail. Public DLs in Unity are actually just regular distribution lists in Exchange or Domino. When you "import" a distribution list through the SA, it simply writes a few properties through to the list object, indicating to Unity that it is a distribution list that we know about. The properties we write through to the directory itself are covered in the Directory discussion in chapter 4. If you have configured Unity to be capable of creating new distribution lists through the SA, if you add a new list, it will show up in Exchange 5.5/AD/Domino as a normal distribution list. There is nothing special or proprietary about these lists. In DPT, you see only distribution lists in this collection that have been imported into Unity using the SA.

A public distribution list (DL) is available for addressing over the phone directly only if it has an extension number or a voice name recorded on it. However, you can import a distribution list and make it the recipient of a call handler's messages, for instance, as a way to get messages to a group of users without having them address the distribution list by name or by ID. This is also a way to let unidentified callers leave messages for groups of users. It is not necessary to associate an extension with a distribution list or to record a voice name for it to use a distribution list in this way.

Up through Unity 4.0, any properties changed on a distribution list through the SA simply write through to the distribution list object itself in the directory. For instance, if two Unity servers use the same public distribution list in Active Directory and an administrator changes the extension number on it through the SA, this change also happens on the other Unity server. This can cause problems in large organizations in which some distribution lists will be shared across numerous Unity servers. Unity eventually might move to a model in which each Unity server can dictate its own values for extension and voice names on each distribution list instead of having to share those values. However, currently this is not the case. You will want to plan carefully when choosing to assign extensions to distribution lists.

The public distribution list object has one subcollection, AVP_MEMBERS, that contains a list of all the top-level mail users and distribution lists contained in the public DL. It does not provide a full, flattened list of all members of all sublists (and subsublists, and so on) contained in the distribution list. DOHPropTest does not show the new scope distribution lists that do have tables that include all members of all sublists contained within them. These scope distribution lists are used to provide a limited search scope when finding users by name using the name lookup handlers in Unity 4.0(1) and later. This is discussed in more detail in Chapter 18.

NOTE   When Unity sends a message to a public distribution list, it simply addresses the message to the DL itself and lets Exchange or Domino flatten the list of addresses for. You do not populate the To line with the members of the DL on your own. It is much faster and easier to let the messaging back end handle it for you.

FaxLibrary Handlers

FaxLibrary handlers are not used in Unity at this point. Early on, Cisco intended to implement the capability to have large collections of faxes bundled into libraries that callers could browse over the phone and have sent to their fax machines. For instance, a library of specifications for various hardware platforms could be on file, and customers could call in and select the document(s) they wanted from the library by ID or document name instead of having to call a support person to have the document faxed to them.

FaxMail Handler

Along with FaxLibrary handlers, the FaxMail handler has not been implemented in Unity.

A FaxMail handler was envisioned as a mechanism to switch dynamically from voice to fax services within Unity for handling "one-number fax" functionality. For instance, if a call came into a subscriber's mailbox and a fax tone was detected, the call would be routed to the fax mail handler for that user. The fax mail handler then would accept the fax and make sure that it got delivered to the user's mailbox.

This feature depends on, among other things, dynamic fax tone-detection capabilities and the capability to switch from voice services to fax on the fly. A number of items external to Unity need to change to make this a reality, so, again, I am uncertain of when or if this feature will be implemented.

Interview Handlers

Interview handlers are a special type of call handler that has specific and limited functionality. You can configure an interview handler to ask a series of questions and get answers for each. It appends all the answers, separated by beeps, and sends the resulting message to the selected recipient. The recipient can be either a single subscriber or a public distribution list.

An interview handler has no greetings collection, no transfer capabilities, and no user input capabilities or anything else. Its sole purpose in life is to ask callers a series of questions and collect the answers. These typically are used for support-type applications in which it is important for the caller to leave his or her name, number, version number, customer ID, and so on when requesting a callback.

Although the interviewers have fewer properties than call handlers, you will notice that most of the properties on interview handlers are also seen on call handlers. These properties serve the same purpose for interviewers as they do for call handlers. For instance, the administrator and recipient object ID values and the after-message action/conversation/ destination object ID work the same as they do on call handlers. The one item in the property collection for interviewers that you will not find on call handlers is the AVP_QUESTIONS sub collection. This is the list of questions that you can add to the interviewer—up to 20. The questions are played in the order of the alias names (1–20), even though DOHPropTest does not display them in order—it sorts them alphabetically instead.

Locations

All objects in the Unity database are associated with a location object, but the administrator can associate only special types of subscribers with anything other than the default location object created by Unity setup. Eventually, this design might allow for full tenant applications in Unity by allowing entire groups of objects (call handlers, interview handlers, subscribers, directory handlers, COS objects, and so on) to be associated with different location on the same Unity server. Currently, however, only one primary location object exists per Unity box, which is created by setup.

Additional location objects can be created for various networking schemes using AMIS, SMTP, the Cisco Unity Bridge, and VPIM transport mechanisms to other Unity servers and other foreign voice-mail systems. This is covered in detail in Chapter 12.

The location object also serves an important role for identifying other Unity servers on the network and finding out which Unity server a subscriber in the directory is associated with. When you install a Unity server onto your network, the setup creates a uniquely named primary location object, which is also replicated into the directory. All Unity servers in the directory then can identify one another by information in these location objects and their subscribers also in the directory. The details of how this works are covered in Chapter 12. An example of a simple application that finds and attaches to a remote Unity server's database to update the properties on a subscriber found in the directory also are covered in Chapter 21.

Mail Users

The mail users collection includes all the subscribers on the local Unity server. As noted in Chapter 1, "About Unified Messaging," subscribers in Unity are simply regular mail users in Exchange or Domino that have some additional properties written through to them in the directory. Chapter 4, "Components and Subsystems: Directory," covers the details of which properties are added to the directory schema for mail users.

Several types of subscribers are contained in the mail users collection. The value for the AVP_SUBSCRIBER_TYPE dictates which one you are looking at. The basic distinction is between a full or regular subscriber (type 1), and an Internet subscriber (types 2, 4, 6, and 8). A regular subscriber is built on top of a full mail user in Exchange/Domino and has a mail store; this subscriber can call in to check messages and do all the things you would expect a voice-mail subscriber to do. An Internet subscriber is basically a routing mechanism for getting messages to a remote store by way of SMTP, AMIS, OctelNet, or VPIM transport mechanisms. These subscribers appear to callers as any other subscriber, but they do not have a message store associated with them; as such, they cannot call into Unity and sign in as an Internet subscriber. The various subscriber types are covered in more detail in Chapter 12.

The Mail User object contains four subcollections:

- AVP_NOTIFICATION_DEVICE
- AVP_NOTIFICATION_RULE
- AVP_NOTIFICATION_MWI
- AVP_PERSONAL_DLS

AVP_NOTIFICATION_DEVICE

The notification device collection contains all the definitions for the devices that Unity can use to notify subscribers that they have messages of a specific type and urgency. In Unity 4.0, these include 13 devices for phones, text pagers (e-mail addresses), and DTMF pagers that a subscriber can configure to contact them based on a simple set of rules. Information about the devices shows up for subscribers in the SA on the Message Notification page.

The notification device object can include the numbers to be dialed (in the case of a phone or tone pager), the e-mail address to use (in the case of a text pager), what to dial (if anything) after connecting, how many times to retry if the number is RNA/busy, and the like. It works in conjunction with the AVP_NOTIFICATON_RULES collection.

NOTE	Earlier versions of Unity have fewer notification objects. Additional notification devices were added in versions 2.3.6, 2.4.5, and 3.1. It is not possible to simply add new objects into this collection to increase the number of delivery devices in Unity. The notifier component that actually triggers the delivery action references these objects by alias, and it will not simply use any object that it finds in the collection.

AVP_NOTIFICATION_RULE

The notification rule collection contains the same 13 object aliases that the notification device collection does. The rules collection defines the types of messages that the device should trigger on (that is, urgent voice messages), what schedule the notification device should use (for example, so you do not get paged at 3 A.M.), what to do if the device fails to connect, how many times to trigger the device, and the like. The notification rules and the notification devices collection together contain all the settings you see on the Message Notification page for subscribers in the SA.

The rule and the device information are stored separately because originally the idea was that folks might have a device, such as a cell phone, with multiple sets of rules and schedules associated with it. This concept proved to be more confusing than helpful, though, so the idea was dropped; the work to merge the tables into one was never done, however.

AVP_NOTIFICATION_MWI

The notification MWI collection contains information about activating message-waiting indicators when a voice-mail message arrives for a subscriber. Normally, this collection contains one object named MWI-1, which is the default MWI extension found on the Messages page for subscribers in the SA. However, you can add up to 10 alternate MWI strings for a single subscriber, which show up as additional items in this collection. When a voice message arrives for a subscriber, all active MWI objects for that user have their lamp activated. This can be useful for phone systems that support multiple message-waiting lamps per phone or for doing simple shared-mailbox scenarios.

Customers often ask if they can turn on MWIs for other types of messages than voice-mail messages. This cannot be done. The Notifier component that triggers the dialouts is hard-coded to look specifically for messages in the inbox that are considered voice mails for triggering the MWI devices.

Unity simultaneously can support lighting lamps on multiple switches using multiple methods, such as dialing DTMF codes on analog lines and sending serial packets across RS-232 connections. See Chapter 17, "Unity Telephony Integration," for more details on how this is configured.

AVP_PERSONAL_DLS

The personal distribution list collection contains up to 20 lists of objects for each subscriber that can be used to address messages to groups of subscribers or public distribution lists. Private lists are visible only to the subscriber they belong to; they cannot be shared across users and do not appear in the directory for Exchange or Domino. The personal DLs can contain references to subscribers or public distribution lists, not other private distribution lists.

In Unity 3.x and later, each private list can contain any number of mail users and public distribution list references. In earlier versions, each private list had a limited number of entries allowed because they had to be crammed into existing fields in the Exchange 5.5 schema.

By default, the personal DLs collection is empty for new subscribers. Users can create and edit personal distribution lists using the SA or the personal assistant web interface.

The Mail User object has three important references to other external objects:

- AVP_CALL_HANDLER_OBJECT_ID
- AVP_COS_OBJECT_ID
- AVP_LOCATION_OBJECT_ID

AVP_CALL_HANDLER_OBJECT_ID

This references an object in the call handler collection that is the primary call handler for this subscriber. As noted earlier, the call handler controls greetings rules, transfer rules, and user-input mappings that are exposed on the subscriber pages in the SA.

AVP_COS_OBJECT_ID

This references which class of service object the subscriber is associated with. As noted earlier, this dictates which features the user has access to, what numbers the user is allowed to set for dialout, fax delivery or message-notification delivery, and user access, if any, to the web-based administration consoles.

AVP_LOCATION_OBJECT_ID

This points to the location object that the mail user is associated with. As noted earlier, for normal subscribers, this is not editable and points to the primary call handler created by Unity setup. For Internet subscribers, this value can point to other location objects used to connect to remote voice-mail systems using AMIS, OctelNet, VPIM, or SMTP transport mechanisms. This is covered in Chapter 12.

Alternate Extensions

The keen observer might have noticed one very big hole in the mail user's collection: What about alternate extensions? If you add more extensions for a subscriber in the SA (Unity allows for up to nine of these) and then go looking in DPT for where those extensions show up, you will not find them on the subscriber. You have to jump over to the primary call handler for the subscriber and look at the AVP_ALTERNATE_DTMF_IDS collection. All alternate extensions are written to the DTMFAccessID table in the UnityDB database in SQL. This table holds all information about all extensions for call handlers, subscribers, interviewers, public distribution lists, location objects, and name lookup handlers in the Unity database, as of Unity 4.0(3). Earlier versions had primary extensions for subscribers stored in their primary call handler and extensions for all other objects stored on their respective tables. We cover how to deal with alternate extensions and check for ID uniqueness using this table in Chapter 21.

Mail User Templates

Mail user templates are similar to mail users, with just a few exceptions. The mail user templates are used to define a set of default data that is copied onto a new mail user when they are created or imported by an administrator. By default, Unity setup creates a Default Subscriber and a Default Administrator mail user template. You can add other templates from the Subscriber Template page in the SA. As noted earlier, mail user templates are associated with a primary call handler just like mail users are. New templates created after setup get a call handler that has a prefix of CHT_ for an alias, instead of a prefix of CH_ for mail users.

The primary difference between mail user templates and mail users is that templates do not have properties that must be defined on a per-user basis (including extensions, alternate extensions, and private distribution lists). The subscriber template includes a few properties that are not found on the normal mail user:

- AVP_ADD_TO_DLS is a collection of public distribution lists that a new subscriber is added to when created or imported using this template. Although it is a collection, DPT does not pop up the usual collection dialog box that it does for most other collections in the system. Public distribution lists simply are referenced in a table at the bottom by their object ID.

- AVP_DEFAULT_PW_XXX is a set of four properties that dictate default Telephone User Interface (TUI) and NT passwords. The phone password defaults are applied to all new or imported users. The NT passwords are used only when creating a new user in the directory; imported users do not use this value.

It is important to note that changes made to the subscriber templates affect only new users created after that change. This question comes up in the field from time to time. Changes made to a COS object affect users associated with that COS immediately because mail users reference that COS object directly via the AVP_COS_OBJECT_ID property noted earlier. Values in the mail user template, however, simply are copied over when the user is created. There is no reference back to the template used to create a new user.

Name Lookup Handlers

The Name Lookup Handler corresponds to the Directory Handler page in the SA. This is the object that handles outside callers searching for subscribers by spelling their name if they do not know the user's extension number. In versions earlier than Unity 4.0, there was only one system-wide name lookup handler per Unity install. In 4.0 and later, multiple name lookup handlers are possible, and each can be configured to allow users to search a different group of users across the directory.

The name lookup handler in 4.0 has a couple of properties added to handle the new search scope options. The AVP_SEARCH_SCOPE and AVP_SEARCH_SCOPE_OBJECT_ID values work together to determine which subscribers the caller's spelled name search includes for this particular name lookup handler. You can refer to the data dictionary build into the Cisco Unity Data Link Explorer (CUDLE) application to get details on what values in these two fields mean. The use of this tool is covered in Chapter 21.

The Name Lookup handler has the usual links to external objects that include the location object ID, the administrator object ID (not used for anything yet), and the application object ID (also not used) that show up on other objects in the system. However, you should notice four important sets of links to external objects in the name lookup handler:

- AVP_EXIT_OBJECT_ID, AVP_EXIT_ACTION, AVP_EXIT_CONVERSATION
- AVP_NO_SELECTION_OBJECT_ID, AVP_NO_SELECTION_ACTION, AVP_NO_SELECTION_CONVERSATION
- AVP_NO_INPUT_OBJECT_ID, AVP_NO_INPUT_ACTION, AVP_NO_INPUT_CONVERSATION
- AVP_ZERO_OBJECT_ID, AVP_ZERO_ACTION, AVP_ZERO_CONVERSATION

AVP_EXIT_OBJECT_ID, AVP_EXIT_ACTION, and AVP_EXIT_ CONVERSATION

These three properties work together to determine what Unity does with a call when the subscriber exits the name lookup handler by pressing * (the Exit key). Obviously, if a user selects a subscriber by name, Unity sends the caller to that mail user. However, if the user backs out by hitting *, that is considered an exit action, and the values for these three properties determine what Unity does with the call. You have the option of hanging up on the call; sending the caller to another object; sending the caller to a specific conversation, such as the subscriber sign-in conversation; and the like. By default, the caller is sent back to the "opening greeting" call handler created by Unity setup.

This value can be adjusted on the Caller Input page of the directory handler section of the SA.

NOTE   The details of these property values and what they mean are covered in Chapter 21.

TIP   The SA interface shows only a single exit action for all directory handlers, even though four separate exit scenarios are accounted for here. When you select an exit action on the Caller Input page for a directory handler, the SA writes the selection only into the EXIT action described here. The other three exit scenarios are left hard-coded, as described later. In some scenarios sites, users might want to go somewhere other than the built-in operator call handler when they press the 0 key to exit, for instance. If you need this level of granularity, you can use the Audio Text Manager (ATM) application to edit all four exit actions separately.

AVP_NO_SELECTION_OBJECT_ID, AVP_NO_SELECTION_ ACTION, and AVP_NO_SELECTION_CONVERSATION

These three properties work together to determine what Unity does with a call when the user fails to spell the name of a subscriber and simply waits on the line. By default, the caller is sent to the "say goodbye" call handler created by Unity setup.

This value is not exposed on the directory handler page in the SA, although you can change it programmatically or by using the ATM application.

AVP_NO_INPUT_OBJECT_ID, AVP_NO_INPUT_ACTION, and AVP_NO_INPUT_CONVERSATION

These three properties work together to determine what Unity does with a call when the user spells the name of a user but then fails to select someone from the list of names presented for that spelling. By default, the caller is sent to the "say goodbye" call handler created by Unity setup.

This value is not exposed on the directory handler page in the SA, although you can change it programmatically or by using the ATM application.

AVP_ZERO_OBJECT_ID, AVP_ZERO_ACTION, and AVP_ZERO_CONVERSATION

These three properties work together to determine what Unity does with a call when the user presses 0 instead of spelling the name of a subscriber in the system. By default, the caller is sent to the "operator" call handler created by Unity setup.

This value is not adjustable on the directory handler page in the SA, although you can change it programmatically or by using the ATM application.

Primary Domain Accounts

This collection is not really part of the Unity object model. It shows all the accounts that Unity sees in the directory, regardless of whether they are tagged as a subscriber. This is useful for some troubleshooting scenarios. For instance, if you want to import a user from the directory into Unity as a subscriber, but you do not see that user offered for import in the SA, you can verify that the account is visible to Unity by looking at this collection. If the account did show up, it usually was imported as a subscriber onto another Unity system that then was removed from the system, but the user's account still is tagged as a Unity subscriber; as such, it is not allowed to be imported. You can clean off the properties of the user's account with the Global Subscriber Manager tool. We also cover a programming example of how to remove such properties from users in Active Directory in Chapter 21.

Primary Domain Groups

Similar to the domain accounts collection, this is not part of the Unity object model. It shows all the groups defined in the directory. These objects are not referenced directly by objects in the Unity database; this collection is here for troubleshooting purposes.

PW Policies

The password policy object determines how the Unity conversation treats phone passwords. Administrators can dictate that the passwords expire after a specified period of days, that passwords must be of a certain minimum length, how long users are locked out if they exceed the max number of PW retries, and so on. The values for this show up on the Account Policy page in the SA.

Currently, only one password policy is defined for the entire Unity server, so this collection never contains more than the one object created by Unity setup. Down the road, however, multiple policies likely will exist to handle multiple tenant types of configurations.

Restriction Tables

The restriction tables are referenced by the COS objects noted previously. These objects are used to determine which numbers a subscriber is allowed to deliver messages to, transfer callers to, or deliver faxes to. The Unity setup program creates three restriction tables, by default: DefaultFax, DefaultOutdial, and DefaultTransfer. All three of these restriction tables are configured to limit long-distance numbers in the North American dialing plan.

As noted, Unity applies restriction table rules at the time the number is set, *not* when the number is dialed. Users making the change to the number in question use the restriction tables associated with their class of service to determine whether they can set a number to a particular string.

AVP_NUMBER_PATTERNS

This collection contains a series of masks that administrators can configure to allow or disallow a number to be entered into a particular field in the SA or over the phone. The strings consist of numbers, ?, and * symbols used to match any single digit or string of digits. The masks are evaluated from the top of the collection down until a match for the number is found. Only the first match is evaluated. The AVP_BLOCKED property on the number pattern determines whether a number match indicates that it is allowed or disallowed.

The restriction table can contain as many number patterns as you like. However, as noted earlier, the rules are evaluated from the top down until a match is made. Then the process stops.

Trusted Domains

The trusted domains collection is not part of the Unity object model. It is there to show all the domains visible to the Unity server for troubleshooting purposes.

Data Storage

With a basic understanding of how the objects in the Unity system relate to one another, the next obvious question to ask is where is all the configuration information actually stored on the system? Configuration data is located in four different areas for Unity. We cover the important items in each area:

- SQL database
- Windows Registry
- Directory (Exchange 5.5, AD, or Domino)
- Local files on the hard drive

SQL

The majority of the Unity-related information is stored in the SQL database, which runs locally on each Unity server. When conversations in the telephone interface or the SA/PCA pull up information about users, call handlers, interviewers, and so on, they generally pull this from the SQL database. As of the Unity 4.0 release, most of the clients that get at this data still go through the abstracted Data Object Hierarchy (DOH) interface that has been around since Unity 1.0 instead of going directly to SQL. The DOH interface was necessary when the data was strung out in the Exchange 5.5 directory, and getting at it required complex and error-prone LDAP queries. Now that Unity has transitioned to SQL as the primary back end, this abstracted (and slow and somewhat cumbersome) interface is no longer necessary.

Moving forward with releases after Unity 4.0, the DOH interface will be retired and eventually no longer supported. Other interfaces into the Unity database, such as the Simple Object Access Protocol (SOAP), might come online. Currently, however, the only viable alternative to the DOH is to go directly to the SQL database itself. The Customer Applications Team (CAT) within the ECSBU is using SQL exclusively to generate all new tools and utilities that ship with Unity; see http://www.ciscounitytools.com. The details of doing basic administrative functions using SQL directly are covered later in Chapter 21. For now, we just cover the high-level functions of each of the tables in SQL.

Make sure you have read the data object model covered earlier in this chapter to get the most out of this section. It also is a good idea to have the Cisco Unity Data Link Explorer (CUDLE—see Figure 3-4) application in front of you: Many of the details of what specific columns are used for and what valid data can be contained in them is held in its data dictionary tables. When exploring the data object model, you will want to use DOHPropTest; when exploring the database itself, CUDLE is a handy tool.

Figure 3-4   *The Main CUDLE User Interface*

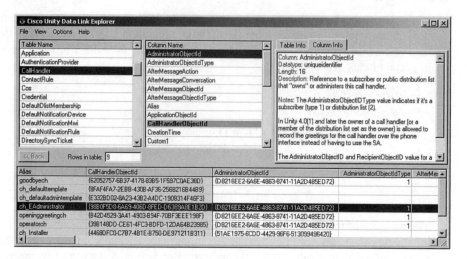

Apart from having basic data dictionary and advanced database-navigation features built in, CUDLE includes information about Unity Registry settings, lets you switch dynamically between views and tables, includes a fully featured query builder, and enables you to explore stored procedure parameters and source code, among other features. You will find the latest version of CUDLE along with a couple of training videos on how to use it at www.ciscounitytools.com.

A quick word about tables versus views is necessary. A view can be thought of as either a virtual table or a stored query. What is stored in the view is not the actual data, but rather a SELECT statement that is used to pull data from the raw tables. The result set of the SELECT statement forms the virtual table returned by the view. Using views provides a number of benefits, such as allowing data from multiple tables to be presented in one spot without requiring complex inner join statements and the like. Views also can be used to restrict access to specific data that you might not want external developers to get at (not a big concern for us here). One of the big benefits that views provide is a mechanism that allows the back-end database tables themselves to be updated, while still providing a consistent interface that is backward compatible across versions. This way, clients that have written applications that use these views do not have to change their code to remain current for each version of Unity that is released.

In Unity 4.0, each of the tables has a corresponding view. However, initially many of them are simply a straight mapping of columns from their corresponding table. As Unity moves forward, the database is reorganized to make it more efficient and faster. As data moves between tables, or as tables are collapsed into each other and the like, any client writing directly to the tables themselves has to update its applications each time a new release of

Unity is introduced. That is not ideal. The views, however, can help prevent this by providing logic underneath to get the data from its new location so that the process is transparent to client applications. Programmers interested in writing applications to interact with the Unity database should use views when querying data and should use stored procedures when writing information into the database. When opening a connection to a database in SQL, you access views in the same way you would a table. More on this comes in Chapter 21.

This section talks generally about what each table is used for. A more complete discussion of what each column in many of the tables is used for, as well as valid value ranges and what they mean, is found in Chapter 21 and in the Data Dictionary built into CUDLE.

NOTE   In each database is a number of tables with lowercase names starting with *sys*, as in syscolumns and syscomments. These are present in every SQL database and are used by the system. They are not relevant to the inner workings of Unity and are not covered here.

UnityDB

The UnityDB database contains all the Unity-specific directory data. The objects that appear in the system administration console and that are available for access over the phone interface are available in this database.

- **AccountLockout**. These first three "Account. . ." tables are used for the new authentication model used for the Unity 4.0 release. These dictate the desktop login-authentication behavior for the clients. The values in these tables are exposed on the SA administration console on the Authentication page.

- **AccountLockoutPolicy**. See *AccountLockout*.

- **AccountLogonPolicy**. See *AccountLockout*.

- **ADMonitorDirObjsList**. This is a "scratch-pad" table used by the Active Directory monitor. It is basically a list of GUIDs for objects in the directory that it is interested in at any given time. See the architecture overview in Chapter 2, "Unity Architecture Overview," and the directory discussion in Chapter 4 for more on what the directory monitor component does.

- **ADMonitorDistributionListMember**. This table, along with the ADMonitorScopeDistributionList, ADMonitorScopeDistributionListMember, and ADMonitorScopeDistributionListPendingChanges, is used as a "scratch-pad" table for the Active Directory monitor to use when pulling in distribution-list members from the directory. Three sets of such scratch-pad tables exist for use when the system is connected to Active Directory (Exchange 2000), Exchange 5.5, or Domino.

None of these 12 "scratch-pad" tables contains static information that is of interest to external developers or administrators. Data in here eventually ends up in one of the four general distribution list tables listed later. Two types of distribution lists are stored in the database: system and scope. A system distribution list is a public distribution list that has been imported into Unity and optionally has been assigned a voice name or extension number. This distribution list is updated in the directory with Unity-specific information (see the schema extensions made to distribution lists in Chapter 4). These distribution lists are used for addressing messages, or as a recipient or administrators for handlers in Unity. Scope lists, on the other hand, can be any public distribution list in the system, even those that have not been imported into Unity. These are used only for limiting user searches for the directory handlers, starting in Unity 4.0. A public distribution list can be both a system distribution list and a scope distribution list, and it appears in both tables.

These four tables contain all the relevant information that Unity knows about distribution lists in the system, regardless of which back end it is hooked up to.

— **DistributionList**. This table contains all the public distribution lists that have been imported into Unity. These are the distribution lists that subscribers can address over the phone by name or ID (if assigned). They can be set as the administrator or recipient of a handler. Yes, this table really should be called SystemDList, but because this existed before the concept of a ScopeDList came into existence, it is not.

— **SystemDListMember**. This table contains all the top-level members of all the distribution lists in the DistributionList table. You find all the members of a specific distribution list by filtering this table's ParentObjectID column against the SystemDListObjectID column in the DistributionList table. You also can filter against the ParentAlias field, but because, strictly speaking, the alias is not guaranteed to be unique and the ObjectID is, this is not a good practice. A member of this list can be a mail user *or* a distribution list. This table does not contain all members of sublists contained in the list; it contains only users and distribution lists at the top level.

— **ScopeDList**. This table contains all the public distribution lists that are used as subscriber lists for directory handlers in Unity. These public distribution lists do not have voice names or extensions added to them, and Unity does not update any extended attributes on it. The big difference here is that the list of members for the scope distribution lists is flattened. In other words, if a distribution list contains other distribution lists, Unity recursively traverses the entire tree of lists and retrieves all mail users in the list. The SystemDList members, on the other hand, include only the top-level members. In other words, distribution lists included in the system distribution list simply are referenced in the SystemDListMember table; users in that list (and sublists) are not referenced explicitly.

— **ScopeDListMember**. This table contains all the members of all the Scope-DList objects. Members of this table can include only mail users because, as noted earlier, Unity recursively traverses the list and all sublists to pull out all users. This is done so that the directory handler conversation can quickly do name lookups across all users in the list. To find all members of a specific scope distribution list, you need to filter this table by its Scope-DListObjectID column with the ScopeDListObjectID column in the Scope-DList table. This table does not follow the normal convention of using a ParentObjectID for this, so be careful.

Be aware that Unity monitors the directory for changes to the distribution lists set up as scope lists. If changes are made to a distribution list in the directory, it might take a while to replicate around the directory to where Unity sees the change and pulls it into the ScopeDListMember table.

• **ADMonitorScopeDistributionList**. See *ADMonitorDistributionListMember*.

• **ADMonitorScopeDistributionListMember**. See *ADMonitorDistributionListMember*.

• **ADMonitorScopeDistributionListPendingChanges**. See *ADMonitorDistributionListMember*.

• **Application**. Currently, the application database contains only one row that does not contain any data of interest to anyone yet. The applications collection in DOHPropTest simply shows this row. This table might get pressed into service when tenant services features are added to Unity in the future, however.

• **AuthenticationProvider**. This table contains a list of all the authentication providers that Unity supports for authenticating desktop users connecting to the SA and PCA web administration consoles. This concept is new to 4.0; earlier versions of Unity supported only NTLM authentication for clients.

• **CallHandler**. All call handlers in the system are stored in this table. This includes primary call handlers for subscribers and templates. The CallHandlers collection in DOHPropTest is simply a list of the rows found in this table. Subcollections, such as contact rules, messaging rules, and user input rules, are stored in separate tables. DOHPropTest queries those tables to populate those subcollections when you click on them. To find all the information for a specific call handler in this table, you need to do the following:

— Find the administrator (or "owner") of the call handler by following the AdministratorObjectID value, which could reference a row in the Subscriber table or the DistributionList table. The AdministratorObjectIDType column tells you which to look for. In this case, a value of 1 means a subscriber and a value of 2 means a distribution list. As always, you can refer to CUDLE for a complete rundown on the legal values for columns in the database.

— Find the message recipient for the call handler by following the RecipientObjectID value, which could reference a row in the Subscriber table or the DistributionList table. The RecipientObjectIDType column tells you which.

— Get its transfer rules. To do this, filter the ContactRule table's ParentObjectID column against the CallHandler's CallHandlerObjectID column.

— Get its user input key mappings. To do this, filter the MenuEntry table's ParentObjectID column against the CallHandlerObjectID column.

— Get the greetings for the handler. To do this, filter the MessagingRule table's ParentObjectID column against the CallHandlerObjectID.

— Get the schedule associated with the handler. To do this, find the Schedule row that has a DisplayName value that matches the call handler's ScheduleObjectName column.

We walk through an example in Chapter 21, which pulls most of the top-level data for a subscriber out of SQL and displays it in human-readable text. This includes the call handler data as well, of course, because the subscriber includes a link to a call handler (called its primary call handler).

- **ContactRule**. All the contact rules (transfer rules on the SA) in the system are stored in this table. To get the contact rules for a particular call handler, you filter the ParentObjectID column in this table against a match for the CallHandlerObjectID in the CallHandler table. This should return three rows from the ContactRule, corresponding to the standard, off-hours, and alternate transfer rules for the selected call handler. Remember, primary call handlers associated with subscribers use only the alternate contact rule.

- **COS**. This stores all the class of service objects in the system. The COS objects determine what subscribers can and cannot do in the web-based administration console, what numbers they are allowed to dial, how long their greetings and messages can be, and which features they are licensed for, among other things. The restriction tables referenced in this table are stored in the RestrictionTable table.

- **Credential**. This table contains a mapping of security identifiers (SIDs) of users to the object IDs of subscribers on the local Unity server. When a user attempts to gain access to the SA or PCA web administration consoles, that user's SID is collected by IIS and passed through to Unity. This ID then is searched for in this table. If a match is found and the object ID corresponds to a subscriber who has a COS reference that allows access to the SA or PCA, that user is allowed to proceed. If no entry is found, or if the subscriber that the ID is associated with does not have rights to access the SA/PCA, the user is denied entry.

Every subscriber on the system has an entry in this table, regardless of whether they have SA/PCA rights. This table is also how administrators can gain SA access to multiple Unity servers without being a subscriber on more than one. Administrators can use the GrantUnityAccess tool found in the Tools Depot to add more DirectoryID mappings to this table. This allows a single account to be associated with a subscriber who has SA access on multiple Unity servers. For large sites that use a central administration staff, this is critical.

In Unity 3.*x*, the table used for this was called SIDHistory. The SIDHistory table still exists in the UnityDB database in 4.*x* versions, but it no longer is used for anything.

- **DefaultDListMembership**. The next four tables that start with *Default* are ones that will go away in 4.0(*x*) releases eventually. The DOH uses them when creating new subscribers. These tables are not needed any longer and are residual stuff left over from older versions of Unity that needed them. All the default information for creating new subscribers should be pulled from the subscriber template selected by the user when creating or importing a subscriber in the system.

- **DefaultNotificationDevice**. See *DefaultDListMembership*.

- **DefaultNotificationMWI**. See *DefaultDListMembership*.

- **DefaultNotificationRule**. See *DefaultDListMembership*.

- **DistributionList**. All the public distribution lists imported into Unity are listed in this table. Currently, any public distribution list that is tagged with a voice name or an extension number by any Unity server on the network shows up in this list. In later versions, each Unity server might see only the public distribution list specifically imported into its database, and every Unity server on the network can use its own, unique extension number and voice name to identify the same shared distribution list. For now, however, all public distribution lists share a single extension number and voice name among all Unity servers on the network.

  The top-level members of these distribution lists are stored in the SystemDList table. See the ADMonitorDistributionListMember discussion, earlier, for more on the distribution list scheme in the database.

- **DominoMonitorDistributionListMember**. See *ADMonitorDistributionListMember*.

- **DominoMonitorScopeDistributionList**. See *ADMonitorDistributionListMember*.

- **DominoMonitorScopeDistributionListMember**. See *ADMonitorDistributionListMember*.

- **DominoMonitorSchopeDistributionListPendingChanges**. See *ADMonitorDistributionListMember*.

- **DTMFAccessID**. The DTMFAccessId table contains all the extension numbers for all subscribers, call handlers, interview handlers, directory handlers, location objects, and public distribution lists in the entire system. Remember that subscribers can have up to nine alternate extension numbers; however, if you look through the call handler table, you will find only one DTMFAccessID column in the view for the table. If you look at the raw table in 4.0(3) and later, you will notice that the column is missing. This is an example of a change to the database structure that is masked by the views. The alternate extensions for all call handlers (which, of course, also includes primary call handlers associated with subscribers) are stored in this table. To find all the extension numbers for a particular call handler, you need to filter this table's ParentObjectID column against the CallHandlerObjectID from the CallHandler table. The resulting rows will be all the extension numbers for the selected call handler.

  This table also contains subscriber and location extensions from other Unity servers on the network. The use of *subscriber* here instead of *call handler* is deliberate. As discussed in Chapter 4, only subscriber and location extensions get pushed into the directory and replicated around so that other Unity servers can pull in that information. Call handlers and interview handlers are local objects only and are not replicated around the directory. The GlobalSubscriber and GlobalLocation tables contain subscriber and location object information from other Unity servers in the directory. These three tables work together to provide the networking functionality discussed in Chapter 21.

  The DTMFAccessID tables serves a couple of very important roles. When you go to add a new subscriber, handler, and so on, you need to make sure that it does not conflict with an ID at the Dialing Domain scope. This table provides an easy way of doing that with a single query instead of having to check several tables individually. In fact, in Unity 4.0(3), a special view has been constructed just for this purpose, reducing the logic to a single request. We talk in Chapter 21 about both the view and other more manual ways to check for conflicting IDs in older versions of Unity. When conversations collect an ID from the caller for addressing a message by ID or for doing an auto-attendant ID lookup or the like, the lookups for a match must be done against this single table instead of using a complex multitable search. In fact, the DTMFAccessID columns found in all the individual tables have been removed in Unity 4.0(3), not just those for call handlers. Some client code is written to expect the DTMFAccessID columns to be there, however, so the views for these tables still have columns represented and pull the data out of the DTMFAccessID table for you to provide backward compatibility when this change is made. This is yet another example of why you want to use views instead of direct table queries.

- **Ex55MonitorDistributionListMember**. See *ADMonitorDistributionListMember*.

- **Ex55MonitorScopeDistributionList**. See *ADMonitorDistributionListMember*.

- **Ex55MonitorScopeDistributionListMember**. See *ADMonitorDistributionListMember*.

- **Ex55MonitorScopeDistributionListPendingChanges**. See *ADMonitorDistributionListMember*.

- **FaxLibraryHandler**. The fax library handler table is not used in the current system.

- **FaxMailHandler**. Like the fax library handler table, this table currently is not used by Unity. It might be used in later versions of Unity to provide "one number fax" functionality.

- **GlobalLocation**. The global location table contains all the location objects for all Unity servers on the network. This is important to the networking functionality for Unity and is discussed in Chapter 12. The monitor watches the directory for any location objects for other Unity servers that might be on the network, and then pulls its information into this table. The architecture overview in Chapter 2 and the directory monitor discussion in Chapter 4 talk more about this process.

- **GlobalSubscriber**. The global subscriber table contains a small amount of information about all subscribers on all Unity servers on the network. This is important to the networking functionality for Unity and is discussed later in Chapter 12. The monitor watches the directory for any mail users who have been tagged as subscribers, and pulls their information into this table. The global subscriber table contains much less information than you will find in the subscriber table for local subscribers, of course, because pushing all the hundreds of pieces of data for each subscriber into the directory is impractical and unnecessary. This information is used only to locate and address messages to users on other Unity servers. The directory discussion in Chapter 4 covers which properties are written through to the directory and replicated for subscribers.

  This table is extremely useful for creating global management tools, such as the Global Subscriber Manager found in the Tools Depot section. Unity does a lot of the heavy lifting for you here. This helps you collect information about remote users, locations, and servers visible on the network that you can leverage to find which server a subscriber in the directory is associated with and, for instance, launch the SA page for that user directly. An example of how to do just this is covered in Chapter 21.

- **Handler**. This table is a bit of a holdover from earlier versions of Unity. It contains a couple of properties for each call handler, interview handler, and directory handler in the local Unity server. In earlier versions of Unity, it was sometimes possible to run across an object ID that referenced a particular kind of handler but to not know which type it was. For instance, the AfterMessageObjectID value could be filled in for a call handler, but there would be no indication of whether it was a call handler, an interview handler, or a directory handler. You would have had to check to see which conversation was being used to handle it before you could tell which object type it was. For instance, the PHTransfer and PHGreeting conversations are used for call handlers, the Active Directory (short for Alpha Directory) conversation is used for directory handlers, and so on. This table allows programmers to find the object ID, figure out its type, and do the lookup in the appropriate table. The object type information is now readily available wherever you need it, without requiring the use of this table. In the earlier AfterMessageObjectID example, another column in the call handler table, called AfterMessageObjectIDType, indicates the type of object referenced by the AfterMessageObjectID.

This table is not really necessary any longer and eventually will be removed. A view for this table (vw_Handler) will be kept around, however, to provide backward compatibility for clients that still might use it.

- **Holiday**. The holiday table contains dates for days that schedules can indicate that they are in holiday mode. When in holiday mode, a schedule simply acts as after-hours for the day, regardless of what time it is or what the schedule normally considers standard time. Administrators can set schedules to respect or ignore holidays on a per-schedule basis.

- **InterviewHandler**. This table contains all the interview handlers on the local system. Like a call handler, an interview handler has an owner and recipient, which are found by following the AdministratorObjectID and RecipientObjectID column values. These can be either a subscriber or a distribution list reference; you use the AdministratorObjectIDType and RecipientObjectIDType columns to determine which it is. The primary pieces of data for an interview handler are the questions that the caller hears when routed this object, which are stored in the InterviewQuestion table.

- **InterviewQuestion**. All questions for all interview handlers on the system are stored in this table. To get all the questions for a specific interview handler, you need to filter this table's ParentObjectID column against the InterviewHandlerObjectID column in the InterviewHandler table. The resulting list of questions is those for the interview handler you are interested in. The conversation plays these questions out in the order of the Alias field, which is a number from 1 to 20 representing up to 20 questions allowed per interview handler. Note that it is possible to have noncontiguous entries in here where you have, say, questions with aliases 1, 2, 3, 6, and 8. The conversation simply sorts these in ascending order and plays them out; it does not cause a problem if there is a missing number in there. The SA, on the other hand, looks a little odd because it includes blank questions for the missing entries. For that reason, this generally should be avoided.

- **Location**. The location table contains all the location objects created on the local Unity server. By default, setup creates one primary location that always must be in this table because all objects created on the local server are associated with this location either directly or indirectly. Additional locations can be created for addressing messages to remote systems via AMIS, SMTP, OctelNet, and VPIM. This is discussed in Chapter 12.

  All location objects created on the local Unity server also are pushed into the directory so that they will replicate around. All other Unity servers using the same directory will see these location objects and pull their information into their local GlobalLocation table, as mentioned earlier.

- **MailboxStore**. The MailboxStore table contains an entry for each mail store that the local Unity server can use when creating a new subscriber. For Exchange 2000/2003, this is all mailbox stores in the forest. For Exchange 5.5, it includes every mail store in the site that Unity is installed in. In the case of Exchange 2000/2003, a single Exchange server can have several separate mail stores that can show up individually in this table. For Exchange 5.5, there is one store per Exchange server. This table is automatically updated by the directory monitors; there should never be any need to edit any values here or remove any rows.

- **MenuEntry**. This table contains all the user input key mappings for each call handler in the system. Of course, this includes primary call handlers associated with subscribers as well. There are 12 key mappings per call handler for all 12 of the keys on the phone pad (0–9, *, and #). To get the menu entries for a particular call handler, you need to filter the ParentObjectID column on this table against the CallHandlerObjectID column in the CallHandler table. The resulting list should contain 12 rows: one for each of the 12 key mapping actions for the call handler you are interested in. The Alias field contains the key the row is for.

- **MessageRule**. This table contains all the message rules (greetings) for all the call handlers in the system. Again, this includes primary call handlers for subscribers. Each call handler has a total of six messaging rules: standard, off-hours, busy, internal, alternate, and error. To get the message rules for a particular call handler, you need to filter this table on its ParentObjectID column using the CallHandlerObjectID column in the CallHandler table.

- **MovedMailbox**. When a mailbox gets moved in Exchange (either between Exchange servers or between mail stores, in the case of Exchange 2000), Unity needs to take some special action. From Chapter 2, you will remember that the notifier component stays logged into every subscriber's mailbox to monitor for message events that might require an MWI update or a notification dialout, or the like. When a mailbox moves, the notifier no longer monitors it. When the directory monitor notices that the mailbox of a subscriber has changed, it throws a row in this table. The notifier then knows to log into this new mailbox and start monitoring it, and that it should remove the row. Technically, this table should not have rows hanging out in it for very long.

- **NameLookupHandler**. This contains all the directory handlers (also call name lookup handlers and alpha directories) in the local Unity server. Before Unity 4.0, there was only one hard-coded directory that contained all subscribers in the local system and that optionally included subscribers on other Unity servers that were a part of the same dialing domain (this term is discussed in Chapter 12). In Unity 4.0 and later, there can be any number of directory handlers per Unity server with custom user lists. This is discussed in Chapter 18.

- **NotificationDevice**. This contains all the notification devices for all subscribers on the local Unity server. In Unity 4.0, 13 notification devices are available per subscriber. Earlier versions of Unity have fewer, going back to the base set of four devices supported in the Unity 2.1 release a few years back. The notification device contains information about the delivery mechanism (pager, e-mail, phone call), such as the phone number to dial, e-mail address to send to, and the like. To find all the notification devices for a particular subscriber, you need to filter this table on its ParentObjectID matching the SubscriberObjectID value from the Subscriber table. The resulting list of rows should be all the notification devices for the subscriber in question. The alias column in this table indicates which notification device you are working with.

Note that you cannot simply add new devices here and expect Unity to start triggering on them (this has been tried, believe me). The notifier is hard-coded to deal with devices that it knows about only, not just any devices added to the collection.

- **NotificationRule**. This table contains all the notification rules for all the subscribers on the local Unity server. Each device is associated with a rule for determining the schedule that the device is active for, what types of messages will cause the device to trigger, and the like. To find all the notification rules for a particular subscriber, you need to filter this table on its ParentObjectID matching the SubscriberObjectID value from the Subscriber table. The resulting list of rows should be all the notification rules for the subscriber in question. The alias column in this table indicates which notification rule you are working with.

  Note that there is no direct link from the notification device to the notification rule or back. You must get the list of devices and rules for a subscriber, and match them using the alias column in the rule and device tables. These tables eventually will merge into one (with separate views for each being maintained for backward compatibility, of course). The need to have the device information and the rule information in separate tables is questionable, at best, because there is a strict one-to-one relationship here. The original idea was to have a single device, such as a cell phone, support multiple rules, and schedules for it. However, this concept proved to be more confusing than helpful and was scrapped.

- **NotificationMWI**. This table contains all the MWI devices for all subscribers on the local Unity server. Remember that each subscriber can have up to 10 MWI numbers associated with a mailbox for handling multiple line appearances or multiple phones. To find all the MWI devices for a particular subscriber, you need to filter this table on its ParentObjectID value matching the SubscriberObjectID from the subscriber table. The alias column in this table indicates which MWI device you are working with. By default, all subscribers get one MWI device with an alias of MWI-1. Subsequent devices added by an administrator through the SA get an alias that is made up of the subscriber alias followed by the MWI extension itself. For instance, if you added a second MWI extension for the Example Administrator that dialed 4321, you would see an MWI device in this table with an alias of Eadmin4321. Because multiple MWI extensions must be unique for a single user, this ensures that the aliases for all MWI devices associated with a single user are always unique.

- **OctelNetObjectQueue**. This table is used as a scratch-pad table for the service that talks to the Unity Bridge server. The Bridge is used to communicate with OctelNet nodes when interoperating with legacy voice-mail systems. One of the features it supports gets user information about subscribers on remote systems, including the voice-mail name. This allows for name confirmation and addressing by name or ID options for subscribers who want to get messages to these remote users. This table temporarily holds that type of information coming from and going to the Unity Bridge. The table does not retain information for long, however. The Bridge functionality is discussed later in Chapter 12.

- **PersonalDList**. This table contains all the personal distribution lists for all subscribers on the local Unity server. Each subscriber can have up to 20 private distribution lists that contain subscribers and public distribution lists. By default, this list is empty; lists are added only when subscribers configure them through the SA or PCA web interfaces or over the subscriber phone conversation. To find all the personal distribution lists associated with a particular subscriber, you need to filter this table by its ParentObjectID column matching the SubscriberObjectID column in the subscriber table.

- **PersonalDListMember**. This table contains all the members of all the personal distribution lists for all subscribers on the local Unity server. A member can be either a mail user or a public distribution list. You cannot include a private list in another private list. Only subscribers (mail users who have been imported into Unity) and public distribution lists that have been imported into Unity can be included in this list. The reference to the subscriber or public distribution lists is done via an object ID (a Unity identifier) instead of a Directory ID (an AD/Ex55 identifier). This means that we need to be able to find these guys in the subscriber or public distribution lists tables in SQL to get messages to them.

  To find all the members of a specific private distribution list, you need to filter this table's ParentObjectID column on the PersonalDListObjectID column from the PersonalDList table. The resulting set of rows is all the members of the personal distribution list in question.

  In earlier versions of Unity, the number of members in a private list was limited to 20 or 25 users per list. This restriction was lifted as Unity moved to SQL. You now can add as many members to a list as you like through the GUI administration applications. However, the phone conversation was not updated to allow this, so adding new users to a private list still limits the total members to no more than 25 at the time of this writing. This is a known issue and will be fixed in later versions of Unity.

  Note that when a subscriber is deleted using the SA or when the mail user is removed entirely from the directory (the monitor picks this up and deletes the subscriber on the fly), a series of SQL triggers make sure that all the references to that subscriber are removed from the system. All contact rules, messaging rules, the primary call handler, and so on are removed. All private distribution lists membership references to that subscriber should be removed as well, but in Unity 3.1(4) and earlier, this is not the case. This does not cause any big problems; just be aware that you might see stranded users referenced in this table, causing the SA to show a blank entry in the list of recipients displayed for that private list.

- **PwPolicy**. Currently, this contains one row that stores the settings for the phone password rules that appear on the Account Policy page in the SA. This is in its own table because, at some point down the road, multiple phone password policies will be supported for multiple tenants on a single Unity server. Currently, however, the phone password policy applies system-wide.

- **RestrictionTable**. This table contains all the restriction table definitions referenced by all the class of service objects on the local Unity server. The COS object references three restriction tables, to limit what numbers can be entered into transfer strings, delivery dialout strings, and fax delivery numbers. There is no ParentObjectID type of filter for this table because multiple COS objects can use a single restriction table. You query the RestrictionTableObjectID column in this table using the FaxRestrictionObjectID, OutcallRestrictionObjectID, and XferRestrictionObjectID columns found in the COS table to find the restriction table you are looking for.

- **RestrictionPattern**. This table contains all the dial-restriction strings contained in all the restriction tables on the local Unity server. A restriction table can have any number of string patterns (such as 91?????????? or 011*), which can be marked for allow or disallow. To find all the number patterns for a specific restriction table, you need to query on the ParentObjectID column in this table against the RestrictionObjectID column in the RestrictionTable table. The strings are evaluated in order of the Index column value in this table, which goes from 0 to the number of patterns associated with the table. Order is important here because the first string pattern that matches the number dictates whether the number is considered blocked or allowed.

- **Rule**. This table contains rows for all the call-routing rules used to route incoming calls to the local Unity server. This is the information that shows up on both the direct and forwarded pages in the SA's Call Routing section. We discuss the use of these rules later in Chapter 18.

   This table showed up in SQL for the release of Unity 3.1(3). It was necessary to move this data into SQL so that it could replicate between two Unity servers for the failover functionality revamped in that release. In earlier versions, this information was stored in a Unicode text file routing.rul found under the \commserver\support\ directory. You will still see this file there for some versions later than 3.1(3), but it is not used for anything.

- **Schedule**. All the schedules defined in Unity that you associate with call handlers and subscribers are stored in this table. For each day, there is a binary string with a series of 0s and 1s representing 96 quarter-hour increments for the day. This indicates whether the schedule is active or inactive for that 15-minute period. This is the same format for schedule information that you find in the earlier notification rules table.

Although the information is stored in quarter-hour increments, the SA exposes only 30-minute chunks in its interface. If you need 15-minute granularity, you can use the Audio Text Manager's Schedule option.

Note that although this table has the usual ScheduleObjectID in it, references to objects in this table are done by name, not by ObjectID, which is normally the case. In the CallHandler table is a column named ScheduleObjectName that contains the string found in the DisplayName column in the Schedule table. This means, of course, that the display name must be unique for all schedules (which the SA enforces). This is a little unusual and is a holdover from the fact that, until Unity 3.1(2), the schedule data was stored locally in the Registry and referenced by its key name. It was moved into SQL to help support the failover feature; to minimize the impact of this move, the existing reference scheme was kept intact.

- **ScopeDListMembers**. See *ADMonitorDistributionListMember*.

- **Servers**. In early versions of Unity, this table contained all the Unity servers found in the directory, but it no longer is used for that. The Servers table now actually contains only one row that stores information about the UnityDB table version. Whenever Unity updates any of the tables as part of an upgrade, this row gets updated to indicate what revision the database is on. Based on this value, the upgrade knows which SQL scripts to apply to a database to get it to the version being installed.

- **SIDHistory**. This table used to store the links between NT/AD SID values and subscriber object ID values for the purposes of authenticating users trying to gain access to the SA and AA web administration consoles. In Unity 4.*x*, this table has been replaced with the Credential table. Even though the table continues to hang around in the UnityDB database, it no longer is used.

- **StreamsToDelete**. When an object that contains a voice name or a set of greetings gets deleted, or when the greeting or voice name is rerecorded, this table gets a list of WAV files (called streams internally) that need to be removed from the \commserver\ StreamFiles\ directory. For instance, if a call handler is removed, its voice name and up to six greeting files are put into this table. A background process eventually checks this table and removes those WAV files from the StreamFiles directory, and then deletes the rows from this table. When rerecording a file such as a voice name, a new file is created until the new name is saved, and the old voice name file is deleted through this same process. You cannot record over a standing voice name, for instance, because then it can be accessed by the conversation while you were busy recording. There should not ever be any static information in here that is of any value.

- **Subscriber**. This table contains all the subscribers on the local Unity server. This table and the CallHandler table are the two most central tables in the directory. This table references the objects in several other tables, and several tables contain items that can be associated with the Subscriber row through their ParentObjectID column. To get all information about a particular subscriber on a row in this table, you need to do the following:

    — Find their primary call handler by filtering the CallHandler table against the CallHandlerObjectID column. The call handler, of course, has several collections with data in other tables (contact rules, message rules, and menu entries, for instance). See the CallHandler table, discussed earlier.

    — Get the class of service for the user. To do this, filter the COS table against the COSObjectID column.

    — Get the notification devices that the user has set up. To do this, filter the NotificationDevice and NotificationRule tables against their ParentObjectID columns matching the SubscriberObjectID column.

    — Get the MWI device information for the user. To do this, filter the NotificationMWI table's ParentObjectID column against the SubscriberObjectID column.

    — Get the private distribution lists that the user might have set up. To do this, filter the PersonalDList table's ParentObjectID column against the SubscriberObjectID column. PersonalDLists, of course, have members stored in the PersonalDListMember table.

    In Chapter 21, we actually walk through an example that uses all these tables and the call handler-related tables to glean most of the basic information about a subscriber and dump it to a CSV file.

- **SubscriberPwDTMFHistory**. This table contains encrypted versions of all the subscriber passwords for all subscribers on the local Unity server. These are kept around as long as is dictated on the password policy page in the SA. This is used to make sure that subscribers do not reuse passwords more often than administrators want them to.

- **SubscriberTemplate**. This table contains all the subscriber templates on the local Unity sever. A subscriber template contains much of the same data and references all the same tables as a subscriber object does. These objects are used to copy in default settings for new subscribers created on the system. See the Subscriber table, earlier, for more details on what to find in this table—they are similar. One thing to be aware of is that the primary call handler associated with a subscriber template is stored in the CallHandler table, along with all other handlers. There is no special CallHandlerTemplate table, and there is no property that you can check for to indicate that the handler is associated with a template instead of a subscriber. As such, determining which handlers are used for templates in the system can be a bit tedious: You need to walk through the SubscriberTemplate table and create the list by seeing which call handlers are referenced.

- **SystemConfiguration**. This table is not used and, in fact, has not been used from day one.

- **SystemDlistMember**. See *ADMonitorDistributionListMember*.

- **SystemState**. This table contains an encrypted binary blob that contains a bunch of licensing information for all Unity servers that the local Unity box can see. The licensing module running on Unity unpacks this table and uses it to determine which features and limits are licensed and how many are used up. This is particularly important for the new pooled licensing features added in Unity 4.0(1) that allow multiple Unity servers to share sets of licenses with one another.

- It is not possible to unpack this information yourself to get at the license data. We offer an example of how to get at the licensing information from off-box using a web page query in Chapter 21.

- **UnitySetupParameters**. This table contains a number of replacement variables that are used by the setup and upgrade routines and other scripts run on the Unity box VPIMObjectQueue. This is another scratch-pad table that keeps a list of subscribers that have changed their display name, extension, or voice name, to know when to include that information with messages to remote systems. No static information sticks around in this table for long. This table is used only if the VPIM feature is enabled.

ReportDB

The ReportDB database contains tables that hold the data used to generate each of the reports found in the SA. Every 30 minutes, the scavenger process pulls information out of the Unity flat data files, from the event log, and from the IIS logs, and pushes it into these tables. The reports engine, in turn, uses this data to generate reports. This is why there can be delays in when information shows up in a report. I have gotten many questions from folks who make a test call, immediately run a call activity report, and do not see their call, yet later that day, the call appears. Currently, the scavenger is hard-coded to do its thing every 30 minutes.

The reports engine in Unity gets a pretty significant overhaul in the next major version of Unity, codenamed Kubrick. The same backward-compatibility requirements imposed on the UnityDB table do not apply here, so expect these tables to change or be removed entirely without notice. As such, I do not recommend modifying these tables much. We have information for folks who want to do their own custom reports for Unity 5.0 after it releases.

Registry

Quite a lot of data is stored in the Unity branch in the Registry—arguably, too much. A healthy portion of it is scratch-pad information for various components that are not intended to be modified by folks in the field. However, much of the data consists of items that folks who are troubleshooting problems in Unity or administrators who want to affect system-wide behavior of various components of Unity are interested in. Unfortunately, little, if any, accurate documentation exists on many of these properties, either internally or externally. Some of the more common properties that administrators and field techs might want to edit are exposed in the Advanced Settings tool found in the Tools Depot on the desktop. The Customer Applications Team (CAT) group tries to keep the Advanced Settings tool up-to-date with the most necessary Registry edits; it is strongly recommended that you stick to this list unless someone in TAC directs you otherwise. You will also find some helpful explanations of what various keys are used for in the CUDLE Registry tree window.

Changing properties in the Registry without knowing the appropriate range of values and what behavior change to expect is asking for trouble. Furthermore, it is easy to screw up your Registry by accidentally making changes by hand. Before doing anything in your Registry, be sure to back it up first.

As Unity moves forward with post-4.0 releases, much of the configuration information currently stored in the Registry will start to move into new tables in SQL. This is necessary to support proper clustering designs in which this information needs to be shared across multiple servers acting in concert to provide more scalable solutions. An effort is being made as part of this process to get decent documentation in place for each component's configuration data and to track changes to it. The careful observer of the current Registry information will also note quite a bit of duplicated data in slightly different formats. This is another issue that should be improved as this configuration information moves into SQL. As a general rule, however, developers currently treat the Registry as their own private spot to stick data necessary for debugging, for not hard-coding some behavior that might change down the road, and the like. Data in the Registry should be treated with caution for administrators, field technicians, and anyone who wants to write applications that use this information. All that being said, we cover the high-level keys here just to give the more eager students of Unity an idea of what type of information can be found down each path.

NOTE Much of the data in the Registry is read-only during the initial Unity startup sequence. As such, changing anything in the Registry can require a restart of Unity before its change takes effect. For keys exposed in the Advanced Settings tool, a note is made of which ones require a reboot, but it is always a good idea to assume that a restart is necessary.

The following branches can be found in the Registry under HKEY_LOCAL_MACHINE\ Software\Active Voice:

- **Arbiter.** The Arbiter component is responsible for handling inbound calls and allocating voice-port resources to incoming and outbound calls. Most of the settings under this branch have to do with what each port on the local Unity server is capable of doing, which is exposed in the SA on the Ports page. Other settings here determine whether Unity allows an incoming call that originated from a Unity port in the first place (by default, this is off), and how many ports Unity allows to be busy before stopping dialouts to handle the incoming call load.

- **AvCsGateway.** The Active Voice Commserver Gateway (AvCsGateway) is the component that talks to all external parties that want to connect to the Unity services. Access to the DOH requires a component first to authenticate through the gateway service before being allowed to connect. By default, no visible keys exist under this branch; hidden keys can be added for debug purposes.

- **AvCsMgr.** The Active Voice Commserver Manager (AvCsMgr) is the primary service for Unity. Most components currently run under this umbrella, although individual items will break out into their own services moving forward, to provide better scalability and multiple-box cluster configurations in the future. The primary piece of data under here is the list of which Unity components to load and in what order. This is the same information that technicians can edit using the MaestroTools.exe application in the \commserver directory. Removing services from the startup list or changing the order is not something to attemp without instruction from TAC, of course.

- **AvCsNodeMgr.** The Node Manager is used for Unity failover configuration data. You will see this key on all Unity 3.1(1) and later systems. However, there is data under here only if the local Unity server was set up as a primary or a failover server in a redundant configuration.

- **AvLic.** This branch contains information used by the License File Installation Wizard and the license viewer applications found in the Tools Depot on the desktop. The default location of the license files and encrypted information about what was read in from the active license file are stored here.

- **AvLogMgr.** All Unity components use the Log Manager to write to data files (used for reports), diagnostic files, and the event log. Under this branch are settings to control how much hard-drive space diagnostics can take up, how low the hard-drive space can get before diagnostics are turned off, which directory the log manager uses for data and diagnostic files, and, most important, the diagnostic levels for each component. When you turn on a diagnostic trace in the SA or use the Unity Diagnostic tool, that value is set in this branch.

- **AvRdbSvr.** The Relational Database Server component provides a wrapper around the database-lookup functions. Currently, nothing is under this branch, but you can add items for debugging purposes.

- **AvRepDir**. The Report Director is responsible for aging data and diagnostic files so that they do not eat up the entire hard drive space. The settings in the SA on the Configuration page under the Files Cleanup section are stored in this branch.

- **AvRepMgr**. The Report Manager, on the other hand, controls which reports are available to run and what directory their output ends up in. Each report offered in the system and subscriber pages in the SA is represented under this branch as a collection of modules (DLLs) that are used to extract the raw data and crunch that information into a report. You will also find settings under this branch to control the file-scavenging behavior of Unity. Every so often (every 30 minutes, by default), the report manager scrapes (or "scavenges") information from the event logs and the IIS activity logs, and pulls them into tables in the UnityReports database.

- **AvSkinny**. Unity uses the Skinny protocol to talk with the CallManager system. Settings for that connection appear under here; most are not visible, by default, but engineers can add them for debugging purposes.

- **AvWM**. The Windows Messaging component is in charge of determining the up or down status of all external Exchange servers that the local Unity server is interested in (that is, all Exchange boxes that home one or more Unity subscribers). This is referred to internally as the MAPI Traffic Cop component. Because MAPI has such long timeouts (more than 15 minutes sometimes), when you attempt to log into a mailbox that is not available, Unity takes preventative measures to ensure that you do not try to do that. Every so often (15 seconds, by default), Unity pings remote Exchange servers to ensure that the necessary message store and directory services are up and running on that box. If those services do not run properly, or if the server does not respond in the specified time (25 seconds, by default), Unity assumes that the Exchange server is offline. Subscribers homed on that server are not allowed to log into their mailboxes over the phone interface while the server is considered offline.

- **CallControl**. The Call Control feature never was completed in Unity, but this Registry branch still contains keys for the partially implemented functionality. It is unclear at this point whether the call control functionality ever will be fully added into Unity; for now, there is nothing of interest in this branch. In later versions of Unity 4.0(*x*), this branch is missing entirely.

- **CDE**. The Conversation Development Environment is the engine on which all telephone conversations are developed in Unity. The idea was to allow the development of several different types of conversations using the same engine so that partners could design and implement their own phone conversations. The dream of having separate subscriber mailbox conversations, for instance, has not yet been fully realized, although a few partners reselling Unity for Active Voice have developed their own custom conversations. The most interesting piece of information under here from an administration standpoint is the soft key configuration file. This file determines whether the subscriber message-retrieval conversation uses the default Unity menu options or the optional conversation menus (which sound more like what an Octel

Aria user might be used to). This key is exposed in the Advanced Settings tool. In Unity 4.0(3), this key is no longer necessary because conversation styles can be selected on a per-subscriber basis. Notice that more of the conversations will appear in the drop-down list for subscribers in the SA as Unity moves forward.

- **Commserver**. This branch holds some general information about the local Unity configuration setup, such as the server name, the Unity install path, and the path to the localized resource files and event log files. You will notice some of this data (in particular, the server name and install path) available in several other branches as well.

- **Commserver Setup**. This branch holds a number of general configuration settings for the local Unity install. Information about the Dialogic and NMS drivers installed (if any), the Unity installation path (in a couple of places in this branch), the version of Unity installed, which type of mail store Unity is connected to, the default languages to use for the SA, TTS and phone conversation, and a number of other items can be found under here.

- **Conversations**. The conversation branch has several settings that can change the phone conversation behavior system-wide. Some of these are visible in the branch by default, and some need to be added for the change to take effect. For instance, the option to characterize return receipts as voice-mail messages is under this branch. The need for that option disappears in 4.0 because receipts of all types will have their own stack in the phone conversation. The options in this branch are exposed in the Advanced Settings tool so that administrators easily can edit them.

- **CUCA**. This branch contains data that the Cisco Unity Configuration Assistant (CUCA) application uses. It includes flags indicating what parts of setup have been completed and what is left to be done.

- **DalDB**. The Directory Access Layer branch indicates the program ID of the monitor that the local Unity server uses to keep the directory and the local SQL database in synch. A separate monitor exists for Exchange 5.5, Exchange 2000 (Active Directory), and Domino. Depending on what back end your Unity server is connected to, the monitor for that back end is noted in this branch.

- **Directory connectors**. The directory connectors branch holds quite a bit of important information for the local Unity server. The subbranches here look somewhat different, depending on whether you are connected to Active Directory (Exchange 2000), Exchange 5.5, or the Domino directories, but the basic idea is the same. All the domains that the local Unity server monitors, the root containers used for searches in each of those domains, and which container objects are created in, by default, are stored under this branch. Information about the Unity Bridge server that the local server is connected to (if you are using that feature) is also found under this branch because the Bridge is considered a connection of sorts to the remote OctelNet directory.

One important piece of information found under this branch if you are using Active Directory (that is, the Unity server is connected to an Exchange 2000 server) is the Global Catalog server reference. This is found under \Directory Connectors\ DirSynchGlobalCatalog\1.00\Directory\DefaultGlobalCatalogServer. It is stored as its fully qualified domain name (as in testbox.mydomain.com). If Unity cannot contact the Global Catalog server using that name, it will not run properly. If a Global Catalog server is taken offline and replaced with another, for instance, it might be necessary to change this reference and restart Unity. The Unity development team is working on a mechanism to dynamically discover and replace this connection on-the-fly for the 4.0(4) release.

- **DOH**. As noted Chapter 2, the Data Object Hierarchy (DOH) is actually a collection of three layers: the Directory Access Layer (DAL), the Message Access Layer (MAL), and the Security Access Layer (SAL). This branch has some general defaults that the DOH component uses when initializing its components. The only item under this branch that field technicians might end up editing is the option to not create domain accounts when subscribers are created in the SA (for example, in Exchange 5.5, create only a mail account—do not create an NT account with it). This option is exposed in the Advanced Settings tool. The Mail Server Name also might be of interest for troubleshooting MAPI logon problems.

- **DPT**. The DOHPropTest branch is visible only if you have run the DOHPropTest.exe application at least once. By default, it has no data under it, but keys can be added for debugging purposes.

- **ExchangeMonitor**. If the Unity server is connected to Exchange 5.5 or 2000/2003, the keys under here determine how often Unity checks the partner Exchange server (the Exchange server that you selected during the configuration setup) to see if its message store is up and running properly. If the partner server is determined to be offline or unresponsive, Unity goes into UMR mode and starts storing messages locally until the mail store comes back up. This sounds a lot like the description of the AvWM component earlier. The Exchange Monitor actually uses the AvWM component to check on the up or down status of remote servers.

- **FailureConv**. Whenever the Unity conversation runs into an error that it canot resolve (for example, it loads a call handler, but the message recipient for that call handler is no longer in the database), it sends the caller to the failsafe conversation. The caller is told, "Sorry, this system is temporarily unable to complete your call. Please call again later. Good-bye." Then an error is logged to the application event log indicating why the call was routed to the failsafe conversation. The FailureConv branch indicates the path and the WAV file to play for the failsafe conversation. The WAV file to play for the shutdown conversation is also listed under here. The Shutdown conversation is played to callers currently in the Unity conversation when an administrator selects to shut down Unity through the status monitor web page and opts not to wait for the conversations to finish on their own first.

- **GAEN**. The General Audio Error Notification (GAEN) utility monitors the event log for errors and then notifies administrators by voice mail, e-mail, or pager access that there is a problem with the local system. This utility is known more commonly by the name Event Notification Utility (ENU). This Registry branch contains some default configuration data for the ENU utility, including the path to the directory that contains the Access database with the list of errors it is monitoring and notification method(s) to use when each error is seen. This information is configurable using the Event Notification Utility administration interface, which is available in the Tools Depot or the Unity program group in the Start menu. By default, the GAEN monitoring service is disabled on new installations as a result of some problems it had in early incarnations. The GAEN tool is being replaced with the newer Event Monitoring Service (EMS) that started shipping with Unity 4.0(3). In Unity 4.0(4), the GAEN tool will not be installed on new systems.

- **Initalization**. This branch used to contain some of the default system-wide settings now found in the Commserver Setup and Commserver branches, discussed earlier. In Unity 3.*x* and later, it is empty. Eventually, this branch will be removed because it is not used for anything at this point.

- **Keypad mapping**. When callers spell the name of a subscriber or a distribution list they are looking for over the phone, the mapping of letters to numbers on the phone keypad is called a keypad map. Three basic keypad mappings are used in the world today, although a few proprietary phone systems use their own, and some countries (such as Japan) do not use any. This branch contains information about the three keypad mappings that Unity supports and which one the local Unity server uses. Unity stores all subscribers' first and last DTMF names in SQL based on the local Unity server's keypad mapping. However, logic was added in Unity 3.0 and later to calculate the DTMF spelled names off the letters of users' names on-the-fly so that names can be looked up quickly based on any of the three keypad mappings. This enables users to easily address to subscribers across multiple Unity servers that are attached to different phone systems with different keypad mappings. Before version 3.0, this was not possible because the directory information was stored in Exchange, not SQL. Such a dynamic conversion of everyone's spelled name was much too slow, and reserving space for storing three versions of everyone's DTMF names was not practical. As a result, callers had to adjust the keys they used to spell a user's name by paying close attention to the message-addressing prompts played to them over the phone; failure rates were high.

- **MALEx/MALDom**. As noted earlier, the Message Access Layer (MAL) is a DOH component that is used to talk to the message store that the Unity server is configured to talk to. In the case of the MALEx branch, an Exchange server is configured as the Unity partner server. This branch contains information about that server and the local message profile used to log into the Unity messaging system account on that server. In addition to the message store connectivity information, there is configuration information for how Unity identifies fax messages in the inbox of subscribers.

Because Unity supports numerous third-party fax servers, the message class(es) and file extensions supported by the fax server software used by a customer can vary quite a bit. This information can be adjusted either in the Advanced Settings tool or by using the Third Party Fax Configuration tool, both found in the Tools Depot interface.

- **MIU**. The Media Interface Unit (MIU) component is responsible for all communication to the switch(es) that Unity is configured to work with. Numerous keys under the initalization branch in here are exposed on the SA pages and in the Unity Telephone Interface Manager (UTIM) application. This branch also contains information about the Automatic Gain Control (AGC) settings for the local system, as well as the recording codec used for new recordings in Unity.

- **MsgStoreMonitor**. This branch just contains the program ID of the mail store monitor used for the message back end that Unity is set up to use. No editable configuration information lives under this branch.

- **Notifier**. The notifier is responsible for all outdials and MWI triggers for the local Unity server. This process logs into each mailbox of every subscriber homed on the local Unity box and watches for message activity that requires a notification or MWI event. This includes the AMIS message delivery functionality. This Registry branch contains default configuration data for the notifier, most of which should not be modified unless the TAC specifically requests it. One value under here that is of interest is the alias of the public distribution list that gets all outside caller messages that could not be delivered. Many times sites in the field do not want to use the unaddressed messages distribution list created by Unity setup, and they delete it without realizing the impact this can have on the system (lost messages from outside callers). It is possible to enter the alias of any distribution list in this key and restart Unity.

  Note that the Unity 4.0 release will reduce but not eliminate the need for this unaddressed messages distribution list. By default Unity 4.0 can be configured to check if a subscriber's mailbox is full before taking a message for that subscriber from an outside caller. There is a small resource impact of making such a check across the network each time a message is taken from an unidentified user so this option is configurable system-wide.

- **PermissionsWizard**. This branch contains information for the Permissions Wizard application. This tool now must be run as part of the setup, so this branch includes flags that indicate whether it has been run yet, as well as keys that note which domain containers and mailstores have been granted what rights on which accounts. This way, if you run it again later, it can remember what you selected the first time and properly default to that data for you.

- **ResourceLoader**. The resource loader is the mechanism that Unity uses for providing localized versions running in several languages at once. Components such as the SA send an ID representing a string to the resource loader, which returns that string in the appropriate language. This branch contains a few global variables used by the resource loader; there is nothing under here that you need to configure.

- **Ruler**. The ruler component is used by the Arbiter when processing incoming calls to determine where the call should be sent in the Unity system. These rules are visible in the SA under the call routing rules pages. In Unity 3.1(3) and later, the rules are stored in an SQL table in the UnityDB database; for earlier versions, they were stored in the ROUTING.RUL file on the hard drive. This branch just stores the path to that file. For some reason, this branch continues to hang around for versions after 3.1(3), even though it contains no usable data.

- **SA**. This branch stores the data for the Contacts section under the configuration pages in the SA. It is just a series of text strings for the contact name and phone numbers for the customer and administrator for the Unity box. This branch is not in the Registry unless you add some information to the contacts page in the SA and save it.

- **SecurityKey**. No data exists in this branch for any version of Unity to date. With the changes for Unity 4.0 in the security key area (the old dongles were replaced with FlexLM software license files), that might change moving forward.

- **SystemParameters**. This branch contains some more general properties for the system as a whole. This information easily could be contained in the Commserver Setup branch noted earlier, but for some reason, another branch of general settings was added by development groups along the way. The primary data under here has to do with the graphical user interface (GUI) and the Telephone User Interface (TUI) languages loaded on the system, and what the default languages are for the GUI, TUI, and Text-To-Speech (TTS) functions. This is also where the number of simultaneous SA sessions can be configured, which is exposed in the Advanced Settings tool.

- **ToolsDepot**. Starting in Unity 3.1(3), the Tools Depot showed up on the desktop by default. However, it can be downloaded from CCO or AnswerMonkey.net, and loaded on any version of Unity 3.1(1) and later. This branch contains information about all the applications and categories visible in that tool. Occasionally, application-specific data, such as recent file lists, window size/position, and the like, is stored under here.

- **TTS**. This branch contains information about which TTS engines are installed on the box, the languages supported by each engine, and characteristics of that engine. Most notably, the pitch, speed, and default speaker for the installed TTS engine are set under here.

- **UMR**. This branch is no longer used. The UnityUMR branch contains the information that was once in this branch. For later Unity 4.0(x) builds, this branch is no longer there.

- **UnityUMR**. The Unity Message Repository (UMR) is used to store messages that need to be sent to the mail store while that mail store is offline or unavailable to Unity. When Unity is in this state, it is referred to as being in UMR mode. Messages are stored as pairs of files (the message itself and a routing file indicating where it needs to go) on the hard drive in a directory specified in this Registry branch (by default, \commserver\UnityMTA). You also can indicate the minimum amount of disk space that can be left on the drive that the UMR is storing messages on before Unity stops allowing messages to be stored here (by default, 5 MB). If that limit is reached and Unity is still in UMR mode, callers simply will not be allowed to leave messages; they instead will get the failsafe conversation noted earlier.

- **VirtualQueue**. Nothing is under this branch, but engineers can add some keys for debugging Unity's internal call-queuing capabilities.

Directory

Just a brief note is needed about information that is in the directory itself. The details on which objects are added to the directory and which objects have additional information added to them are covered in Chapter 4.

In versions of Unity earlier than 3.0, all Unity directory information was stored right in the Exchange 5.5 directory. All lookups from the SA, conversations, and other clients were done to the DOH interface, which did lookups through LDAP right in the directory. This was rather slow and presented serious scalability issues, among other things.

In Unity 3.0 and later, the primary storage location for Unity directory data is the local SQL database. In this model, a small subset of the data stored in the local SQL database is also pushed into the directory that the Unity server is connected to (either Exchange 5.5, AD, or Domino). This is done so that other Unity servers on the network can address messages to one another easily and allow transfers across multiple Unity boxes in a dialing domain (more on this arises in the networking discussion in Chapter 12). Monitors on the local Unity store watch the directory for information about subscribers and location objects from other Unity servers attached to the same directory, and pull that information into the SQL database. More details on this process are found in the architecture overview in Chapter 2 and the directory discussion in Chapter 4.

For the most part, clients do not go straight to the directory to get at this information; they go to SQL and use the data that the monitors have gleaned from the directory for them. This is much faster than accessing the directory itself, and is also much less complicated because the client code remains identical, regardless of which back end Unity is connected to. All the complexity of dealing with the quirks of the various back ends is concentrated in the monitors and change writers.

Two exceptions to this rule exist:

- The Import tools (both in the SA and in the standalone import tools) have to go to the directory to get mail users who can be imported as subscribers.

- The Internet Voice Connector (IVC) does lookups right to the directory when routing inbound messages. This is necessary because a single IVC can service many Unity servers; it normally does not run on a Unity server, so access to SQL on the box can present problems. The IVC handles routing messages that come into Unity from external sources through SMTP, AMIS, VPIM, and the Unity Bridge server. More on this comes in chapter 12.

Local Files

In Unity 4.0, there is very little in the way of configuration information stored in local files on the hard drive itself. As mentioned earlier, moving forward with future releases of Unity there is even less of this as Unity moves toward an architecture that supports clustering multiple boxes together, requiring mechanisms to share all such configuration data across boxes. Most configuration data eventually ends up in a table in SQL that can be configured for remote access or replication to other servers on a network. Currently, however, some data resides on the hard drive itself:

- Telephone switch configuration information is stored in text files on the hard drive. The characteristics of the phone system that the Unity box is connected to and the specifics about its integration data are stored in local files under the commserver\Intlib directory. A switch INI file is referenced in the MIU section of the Registry based on what is selected in the switch configuration pages in the SA and, in Unity 4.0, the Unity Telephone Interface Manager (UTIM) application. Various PBXs are supported with serial, analog, and digital integration mechanisms. This is covered in Chapter 17.

- Before 3.1(3), routing rules exposed in the call routing page in the SA were stored in a Unicode file called routing.rul, stored in the \commserver\support directory. You will still see this file in later versions of 3.x, but it is not used. These rules got moved into SQL so that failover configurations between two Unity servers can share schedule information easily.

- The Event Monitoring Service (which replaces the Event Notification Utility in 4.0(3) and later) has an Access database stored by default under \Commserver\Utilities\ EventMonitoringService\Database. This database stores information about which event log errors the EMS utility should notify administrators about, as well as who to notify and how. This data is exposed in the EMS Administration utility found in the Tools Depot interface under Diagnostic Tools.

- The logs that generate reports are, of course, on the local hard drive as well. By default, these are stored under commserver\logs. These are aged and cleaned up automatically based on settings in the configuration section of the SA.

- The logs that are produced by the Unity setup application itself also are found on the hard drive. The file is called TempuU.LOG and can be found under the Temp folder for the account that did the installation. For instance, if you were logged in as Administrator when you did the Unity install, you would find this under c:\Documents and Settings\Administrator\Local Settings\Temp.

- Greetings and voice names both are stored in the stream files directory, which, by default, is in \commserver\stream files. When the conversation plays a voice name or a greeting, it pulls one off the local hard drive from this directory. Greetings are not pushed around in the directory, but voice names are because they are needed for name confirmation when addressing to a subscriber who might be homed on another Unity server in the network. The monitors push and pull voice name information for subscribers and the public distribution list in and out of the shared directory. As such, if you just copy a voice name WAV file over an existing voice name WAV file in the stream files directory, it eventually gets overwritten with the old version that floats around in the directory. Special consideration is required if you want to change, add, or remove voice names from subscribers in bulk. We cover this in Chapter 21.

- Of course, there has to be an exception to every rule. Although *most* voice names and greetings can be found in the stream files directory noted earlier, there is a big exception to this. For versions of Unity before 4.0(2), all objects created by Unity setup have their voice names and greetings stored in the default configuration directory, which is found under \commserver\localize\defaultconfiguration\enu. The reason for doing this has long since been lost in the fog of history, but it is something you need to be aware of. These default objects created by Unity setup have greetings and voice names stored in this directory:

  — The operator, opening greeting, and "say goodbye" call handlers

  — The default interview handler

  — The example administrator and example subscriber mail users

  — The unaddressed messages, system event messages, and all subscribers public distribution lists

  It is important to note that even if you change or delete and rerecord the greetings and voice names on these objects, they end up being stored in the default configuration directory instead of the stream files directory with everything else.

  This behavior has been modified in Unity 4.0(2) and later. Although you still see the previous WAV files in the DefaultConfiguration folder, they also get copied into the \stream files folder during setup so that everything is consistent.

- As noted earlier, the Unity Message Repository (UMR) stores voice-mail messages as pairs of files on the local hard drive until they can be delivered to the partner Exchange server, which then routes them to the destination mailbox. If Exchange is offline or the network connectivity to that box is interrupted, those messages stay on the Unity server's hard drive until connectivity is restored. By default, the directory where these files reside is under \commserver\UnityMTA. However, you can select a different location during setup or after installation by using the Advanced Settings tool.

Summary

We covered quite a bit of material fairly quickly in this chapter. After one read through, I certainly do not expect you to be an expert in the Unity data object model. The important items to take away from this chapter are a grasp of the basic terminology (primary call handler, contact rule, messaging rule, and so on) and an understanding that what you see in the administration interface and experience over the phone is being drawn from objects in the database that pull from a number of different tables. Knowing the many details of how those tables interact to represent a high-level object, such as a subscriber, is not as important as understanding that data related to that subscriber is located in numerous places in the database. Tools such as DOHPropTest and CUDLE are there to help you navigate the system and fill in those details for you when you need them.

CHAPTER 4

Components and Subsystems: Directory

Chapter 2, "Unity Architecture Overview," discusses the directory monitor and how Unity uses it to synchronize with the directory that it is connected with. This chapter discusses how Unity uses the specific directory objects and properties.

It is important to note that the objects and attributes that Unity uses for version 4.0*x* can change with each new release of the product. Therefore, it is recommended that you use the information found in this chapter to gain a more in-depth understanding of how Unity uses and synchronizes with each of the directories that it supports.

The Unity directory monitor makes use of the directory in a few different ways:

- To unify subscriber data with the user's object in the directory. Subscriber data can be described best as the data that allows subscribers to use the system, to be identified with a system, and to communicate using this data with other subscribers. This includes Unity location objects, distribution lists, and subscribers.

- To carry out proxy changes made by a subscriber through the Telephone User Interface (TUI).

- To gather subscriber and location information from other Unity servers.

The directory monitor facilitates these tasks by providing Unity with a means of synchronizing its data with the data in the directory. The synchronization process is passive, meaning that the monitor primarily queries for changes in the directory as they occur, and it passes the changes on to Unity's change writer service through the Microsoft Messaging Queue (MSMQ). This synchronization process makes Unity efficient in using the directory.

Because of this synchronization, during normal operations, nearly all real-time activity takes place between the Unity application and its database, not between the Unity application and the directory that it is connected to. This helps to minimize the effect of potentially slow response times from the directory during real-time operations. Now, some real-time directory activity does take place, including Unity administrative activity and some proxied changes for subscribers; overall, however, it is not a significant part of the directory monitor's normal activity.

This chapter covers most directory-related topics that describe how and why Unity uses the directory of the given messaging system. The topics are as follows:

- **The message store and the corresponding directory monitor**. An explanation of the message store (or mail store) and its corresponding directory.

- **Protocols, access methods, and interfaces used**. How each directory is accessed, from Unity's perspective.

- **Directory search scope (each version)**. An explanation of what the directory search scope is, how it is used by each version, and why it is important.

- **Synchronization queries**. How Unity uses queries through its directory monitor to synchronize with the directory.

- **Full synchronization**. How full directory synchronization takes place, when it takes place, and why.

- **Extensibility of the directory**. The importance of understanding why extensibility is important to applications that share directory information.

- **Default Unity objects**. How each version of the Unity directory monitor uses default unity objects, their attributes, and why.

- **Exchange 5.5**. The particulars of how the Unity directory monitor accesses and uses the Exchange 5.5 directory.

- **Exchange 2000/2003**. The particulars of how the Unity directory monitors (two, in this case) access and uses Active Directory.

- **Domino R5/R6**. The particulars of how the Unity directory monitor accesses and uses the Domino directory.

Message Store and Directory Monitor Used

For each message store that Unity services, a different directory monitor is used. Regardless of the message store used, the directory monitor essentially performs the same functionality as explained in the beginning of the chapter. The differences depend upon the way in which Unity's directory monitor needs to access the given directory and the way in which it communicates with it and exchanges relevant data. Table 4-1 lists the message store and directory monitor used. It also explains in general what the directory monitor does and why.

For more information, see the Registry key HKLM\software\active voice\directory connector on a Unity server that has been connected to a mail store.

Only one message store–specific monitor can run on a given Unity server. In the case of Exchange 2000, there are two monitors, but they are specific to the Exchange 2000 directory (Active Directory).

Table 4-1   *Unity Directory Monitors and Message Stores*

Message Store	Directory Monitor Name	Explanation
Microsoft Exchange 5.5	AvDsEx55.exe	Monitors the Exchange 5.5 directory for its own subscriber data, including location objects, and subscriber data and location objects from other Unity servers.
Microsoft Exchange 2000	AvDsAD.exe	Monitors the Active Directory domain where Unity is installed. Specifically monitors one domain controller (DC) per domain. Will monitor more than one domain if Unity services subscribers in more than one domain. This service collects (through importing, creating, and synchronizing) subscriber data for subscribers that exist on the server where the directory monitor resides.
Microsoft Exchange 2000	AvDSGlobalCatalog.exe	Monitors all domains in Active Directory through the Global Catalog (GC). Queries the GC to synchronize subscriber data and location objects from other Unity servers.
Lotus Domino	Domino	Monitors the Domino Directory for its own subscriber and location data, and subscriber and location data from other Unity servers.

Protocols Used

When the directory monitor queries a directory, the protocol or programming interface that it uses might vary, depending on the best (or quickest) access method for that directory. Table 4-2 lists the protocols or interfaces used by each specific monitor.

For AvDsAD, CDOExM is made up of both COM classes and interfaces and ADSI classes, to allow for the management of MS Exchange 2000/2003. The specific method that AvDsAD uses allows for the creation of mailboxes.

Table 4-2 *Protocols and Interfaces Used by the Unity Directory Monitors*

Directory Monitor	Protocol or Interface	Unity Connector Used
AvEx55.exe	LDAP	Exchange 5.5
AvDsAD.exe	LDAP through ADSI. Also uses Collaboration Data Objects for Exchange Management (CDOExM) for creating mailboxes.	Exchange 2000
AvDsGlobalCatalog.exe	LDAP through ADSI	Exchange 2000
AvDomino	Notes API	Lotus Domino R5/DUCS

Scope

A search scope is used so that Unity can service subscribers, voice-enabled distribution lists, and Internet subscribers in the directory. The administrator defines this search scope during installation. It also can be reconfigured by using DPT or by changing the Registry. The search scope is used to limit Unity's directory searches by having it search only the parts of the directory that are relevant to its own operations. The search scope has its focus set where the search root is defined. Thus, Unity should search and monitor only the portion of the directory that it services. Expanding the scope—and, thus, changing the search root to something greater than Unity needs—can cause inefficient query response time. For more information about setting and managing the scope, see Chapter 13, "Unity with Microsoft Exchange."

For each message store that Unity connects to, the scope is different. Naturally, this is because the directory for each message store is different. Table 4-3 lists the scope definitions, LDAP ports, and replication periods that Unity uses for each message store.

Exchange 5.5

Exchange 5.5 has its own directory. Unity uses the DSAvEx55 service to access one Exchange 5.5 server in the site it services. Any Exchange 5.5 server in a given site houses a read/write replica of the site it resides in, but Unity needs only to access one server. For Unity, the server it accesses is the partner server (see Chapter 13 for more information).

This server also houses read-only replicas of other sites within the same directory, which Unity uses to gather global directory information, such as subscribers residing on other Unity servers.

Because there is only one service and one directory, the default search scope is much easier to explain. Note, the same parameters have to exist for each directory, although the default setting for each individual directory may be different.

Table 4-3   *The Default Search Scope, LDAP Ports, and Replication Period for Exchange 5.5*

Parameter	Default Setting
DISTLIST_SEARCH_ROOT	Organization (ORG) or Site (OU), depending on the selection made when running the Message Store Configuration Wizard
LOCATION_SEARCH_ROOT	Organization (ORG) or Site (OU), depending on the selection made when running the Message Store Configuration Wizard
MAILOBX_STORE_SEARCH_ROOT	Site (OU)
MAILUSER_SEARCH_ROOT	Organization (ORG) or Site (OU), depending on the selection made when running the Message Store Configuration Wizard
NEWDISTLIST_ROOT	Cn=distributionlists, cn=recipients,ou=sitename,o=orgname
NEWLOCATION_ROOT	Cn=Locations,cn=Cisco Unity,ou=sitename,o=orgname
NEWMAILUSER_ROOT	Cn=recipients,ou=sitename,o=orgname
PORT	389
REPLICATION_PERIOD	10

The search scopes can be controlled by accessing the appropriate directory monitor in DPT. In this case, and as shown in Figure 4-1, this is done by selecting the Exchange 5.5 Monitor button.

Figure 4-1   *DohPropTest Exchange 5.5 Directory Monitor*

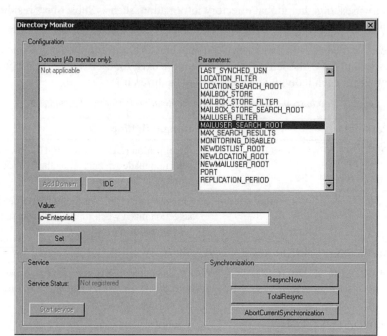

The following further explains each item listed in Table 4-3:

- **DISTLIST_SEARCH_ROOT**. Used to poll for all changes in the subtree, starting with this DN for distribution lists. Used to keep distribution lists in sync. Its default setting can be changed.

- **LOCATION_SEARCH_ROOT**. Used to search for Unity location objects. The default is set at the organizational level to allow a given Unity server to find all location objects in other Exchange 5.5 sites. This setting should not be changed if Unity servers are installed in or reside in more than one Exchange 5.5 site. If this setting is changed, a full resynch is required.

- **MAILBOX_STORE_SEARCH_ROOT**. Finds the mailbox stores or information stores residing on each Exchange 5.5 server. This root is used to synchronize mailbox stores. The default should not be changed.

- **MAILUSER_SEARCH_ROOT**. Set either to the organizational level or site level when using the Message Store Configuration Wizard. It should be set at the organizational level to pull in subscribers who belong to every Unity server. The subscribers who belong to other Unity servers are added to each respective Unity server's global tables in SQL. See Chapter 12, "Unity Networking," for more information on the use of global tables.

- **NEWDISTLIST_ROOT**. Simply acts as the default location for creating new distribution lists if the Unity SA is used to create them. The can be changed if a different custom distribution list location already exists.

- **NEWLOCATION_ROOT**. Where Unity creates new location objects. This is important for Unity's digital networking and VM Interop features.

- **PORT**. LDAP port setting used to access Exchange 5.5 directory.

- **REPLICATION_PERIOD**. For Exchange 5.5, is set to every 10 minutes, by default. This can be changed, depending on the frequency of changes in a given Exchange 5.5 environment. It should never be longer than 10 minutes.

Exchange 2000/2003

With Exchange 2000 and Exchange 2003, the directory is monitored a little differently, as explained at the beginning of the chapter. The service AvDsAd.exe is responsible for synchronization between Unity and a domain controller in the domain where Unity is installed. As Unity administrators import subscribers from other domains, the AvDsAD service also monitors a domain controller in each domain. So, if a Unity administrator imports subscribers from the domain where Unity is installed and then also imports subscribers from two additional domains, the AvDsAD will monitor domain controllers in those domains to synchronize changes to the subscribers it services.

As shown in Figure 4-2, the AvDSAD service can monitor more than one domain. This happens automatically each time a subscriber is imported from a different domain than the one in which Unity resides.

Thus, for the AvDsAD service, an initial set of defaults is used to build domain-specific defaults for each domain that is added as a result of subscriber-importing activity. In Unity version 4.04, these defaults were moved from the Registry to the UnityDB (SQL database). In future versions of Unity, the default settings for Unity's other directory monitors will also be moved from the Registry into the UnityDB.

Within the AvDsAD service, the default search scope is established to point to the DC that Unity monitors to track its subscribers. AvDSAd uses other default search roots, including the default mailbox store that it monitors. The first important default is the mailbox store that houses the Unity system mailbox. As subscribers are added from different mailbox stores, the scope changes to also include these different stores. Other default search roots use the same names as those found in Table 4-3.

Figure 4-2   *The Unity AvDsAD Service Monitors One or More Windows 2000/2003 Domain Controllers*

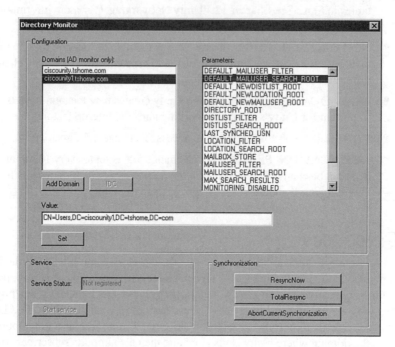

The other Exchange 2000/2003 directory monitor service is the AvDSGlobalcatalog. It monitors the GC in the domain where Unity resides. It monitors only one GC for changes and additions to Unity subscribers, Unity DLs, and Unity location data from other Unity servers. It also monitors the mailbox stores through the GC.

The AvDSGlobalCatalog service performs read-only queries to the GC as its synchronization process. It does not write to the GC. So, the default settings for the GC are created once during installation or when the Unity AvDSGlobalCatalog service reconnects from one GC to another if the GC that it monitored goes offline for any reason. For more information on the GC monitor reconnect, see the Unity 4.04 product documentation.

The default search roots that the GC uses are similar to those in Table 4-3. A complete list of parameters can be found by accessing the tool DohPropTest in read-only mode and selecting the GC Monitor button in the bottom-right corner.

Both the AvDSAD and AvDSGlobalCatalog services have search roots that allow them to expand the scope of the items that they service, such as subscribers, Internet subscribers, Unity locations, and public distribution lists. Any new lists that are created in locations separate from where the search roots are established cause the scope to expand.

In Exchange 2000 and Exchange 2003, Unity also uses the AvDsAd service to monitor the mailbox databases so that it can obtain mailbox quota status for each mailbox owned by a Unity subscriber. Monitoring the mailbox quota status for any Unity subscriber is necessary to ensure that Unity enforces mailbox quota limitations on subscribers when they access their messages through the TUI.

Domino

The Domino directory monitor is similar to the directory monitor used for Exchange 5.5. It uses the same named search roots as those described in Table 4-3.

The Domino directory monitor monitors only a single Domino domain. However, it can monitor one subscriber address book and one contacts address book. In Unity 4.04, this is expanded to support more than one address book and one contacts address book.

Synchronization Queries

Although writing changes to the directory can be a normal part of the directory monitor's activity, Unity spends the majority of its time running periodic queries against the directory to see if any changes have been made to Unity directory objects that it synchronizes with the Unity database.

The actual directory queries might change from version to version, depending on whether they must be revised to improve the behavior of the particular directory monitor. The actual query syntax is stored in the Registry at the following location:

HKEY_LOCAL_MACHINE\Software\Active Voice\Directory Connectors\<MONITOR NAME\1.00>. This is an example for the Exchange 5.5 directory monitor's Registry location:

```
HKEY_LOCAL_MACHINE\Software\Active Voice\Directory Connectors\DirSynchEx55\1.00\
    MailUsers\ChangedFilter:REG_SZ:
(&(|(&(objectclass=organizationalPerson)(MAPI-Recipient=TRUE))(objectclass=Remote-
    Address))(Extension-Attribute-12=01000700300039003A00*)(USN-Changed>=%)(!(Is-
    Deleted=*))).
```

This query is used to find changes to an Exchange mailbox that has the matching entry in its Extension-Attribute-12 (in other words, a Unity subscriber) or a Remote-Address (a custom recipient made a Unity Internet subscriber) with the same matching Extension-Attribute-12. The query also looks for the USN-Changed or Changed ID for the object returned in the query results, and it asks for any objects deleted since the last time it ran the changed query. This might seem overly complex, but it is actually effective for managing changes from the directory. Most queries that the directory monitor uses have hard-coded query strings appended to each query found in the Registry.

The Directory Connectors Registry key also holds other information relative to the monitor, including the query timeouts and search scope information.

The directory monitor runs queries for changes, as listed in Table 4-4. These queries run according to the search scope defined for the monitor. Some of these queries run more than once during a given synch cycle.

Table 4-4   *Unity Objects and Types of Queries Run for Each One*

Object	Type of Query
Subscribers	USN or changedID
Subscribers	Deleted and USN or changedID
Internet subscriber	USN or changedID
Internet subscriber	Deleted or USN
Distribution list or group	USN or changedID
Distribution list or group	Deleted and USN or changedID
Unity location objects	USN changedID
Unity location objects	Deleted and USN Changed

The frequency of each query runs 1, 2, or 10 minutes, depending on the directory monitor used.

Most often, queries to the directory return empty, which means that nothing is changed and, therefore, nothing needs to be synchronized with the Unity database. When data is returned as a result of the query, as shown in Figure 4-3, the monitor takes the data and places it in the Microsoft Messaging Queue (MSMQ) on the Unity server.

The Unity Change Writer service picks up the data from the queue and places it into the UnityDB. The MSMQ currently is used as a one-way repository for data to be synchronized between the directory and the UnityDB. All changes that come from the UnityDB through Unity's administrative interfaces or through proxied subscriber changes are written directly to the directory, and the MSMQ is not used.

As shown in Figure 4-4, the directory monitor writes directly to the directory. Queried results from the Directory Monitor's queries are placed in MSMQ. The Change Writer picks them up and writes the changes to UnityDB.

Figure 4-3   *The avdirchangequeue with Changed Data from the Directory*

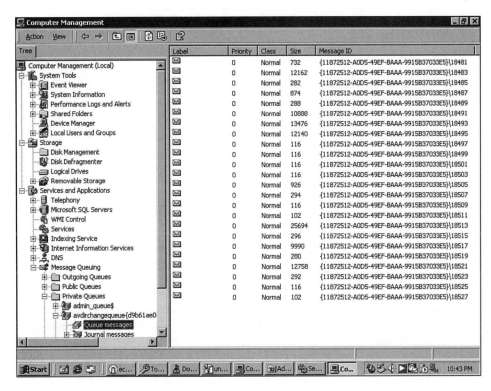

Figure 4-4   *The Flow of Directory Changes to and from the Unity Directory Monitors*

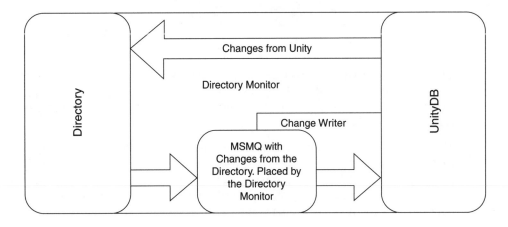

Full Synchronization

In the directory monitor, full synchronization between the UnityDB and the directory takes place at these times:

- When forced by an administrator.
- When Unity first is started. (The first start is a full resynch. Subsequent restarts are incremental.)

When the full synchronization occurs, it queries the entire directory for all Unity objects, subscribers, distribution lists, scope distribution lists, Unity Internet subscribers, and Unity location objects. The queries are the same queries as those used to track changes; in this case. However, they do not consider the last changed value: They resynch all objects that are associated with the Unity server where the resynch occurs.

As shown in Figure 4-4, the synchronization direction is from directory to database.

Full synchronization can take place against the Directory monitors by opening DohPropTest (DPT). You then can run a resynch or a complete refresh. You also can cancel the resynch altogether (see Figure 4-5). Now, running a resynch is not a trivial task. In fact, the Unity subscriber database completely is rebuilt by the information found in the directory. So, if a very large directory exists and, thus, a large number of Unity subscribers belong to the given Unity server from where the resynch is run, there can be a large amount of network traffic as a result. Therefore, if a resynch is necessary, at least be aware of the impact or wait until after hours.

Figure 4-5   *The Synchronization Options for the Unity Directory Monitor*

After you activate a resynch, you can monitor the resynch process by opening the MSMQ and periodically clicking Refresh. You also can check the log file \commserver\logs\diag_ AvDirChangeWriter_*xxxxxxxx_xxxxxx*.txt, where *xxxxxxxx_xxxxxx* is equal to the file ID created by the Unity log manager.

The following extract is an example of the logging performed during the full resynch. In the following example, a full resynch has been run against the Domino directory. The logging is quite verbose. The easiest way to find the right log file is to open the \commserver\ logs folder and order the files by the Modified column. You then can press F5 or allow it to refresh on its own. If you have a lot of objects in the directory, you will see the file build and then stop growing altogether. When it is finished, simply open it using Notepad.exe to view it.

```
01:43:50:220,-1,-1,-1,-1,LogMgr,-1,diagDiag file opened 2004-03-28 01:43:50
01:43:50:220,AvDiagnostics_MC,1129,3768,-1,-1,-1,C:\CommServer\Logs\diag_
   AvDSDomino_20040328_001709.txt,C:\CommServer\Logs\diag_AvDSDomino_20040328_
014350.txt
01:43:50:221,CiscoUnity_LogMgr,1004,3768,-1,-1,-1,AvDSDomino,C:\CommServer\Logs\
   diag_AvDSDomino_20040328_014350.txt
01:43:57:781,AvDiagnostics_MC,1552,3776,-1,DSDomino,16,MsgWaitForMultipleObjects
   returned with 258,e:\views\cs_ue4.0.2.124\un_Doh2\AvDirMonDomino\AvDSDomino\
   DominoSync.cpp,172
01:43:57:782,AvDiagnostics_MC,1552,3776,-1,DSDomino,16,Timed out will do a sync,e:\
   views\cs_ue4.0.2.124\un_Doh2\AvDirMonDomino\AvDSDomino\DominoSync.cpp,178
01:43:57:781,AvDiagnostics_MC,1552,3776,-1,DSDomino,16,m_hSynchReqEvent
   received,e:\views\cs_ue4.0.2.124\un_Doh2\AvDirMonDomino\AvDSDomino\
   DominoSync.cpp,182
01:43:57:782,AvDiagnostics_MC,1555,3776,-1,DSDomino,1,>
   CFailOverData::ActiveStatus()
01:43:57:781,AvDiagnostics_MC,1556,3776,-1,DSDomino,1,<
   CFailOverData::ActiveStatus(),0x00000000,S_OK
01:43:57:782,AvDiagnostics_MC,1555,3776,-1,DSDomino,16,> HandlePendingScopeDlist()
01:43:57:781,AvDiagnostics_MC,1555,3776,-1,DSDomino,15,> GetPendingScopeDLists()
01:43:57:782,AvDiagnostics_MC,1555,3776,-1,DSDomino,15,> CAvDbDLMemList::Logon()
01:43:57:781,AvDiagnostics_MC,1556,3776,-1,DSDomino,15,<
   CAvDbDLMemList::Logon(),0x00000000,S_OK
01:43:57:782,AvDiagnostics_MC,1555,3776,-1,DSDomino,15,>
   CAvDbDLMemList::GetMonitorTable()
01:43:57:781,AvDiagnostics_MC,1556,3776,-1,DSDomino,15,<
   CAvDbDLMemList::GetMonitorTable(),0x00000000,S_OK
01:43:57:791,AvDiagnostics_MC,1552,3776,-1,DSDomino,15,lc =0,e:\views\
   csue4.0.2.124\un_Doh2\AvDirMonDomino\AvDSDomino\AvDbDLMemList.cpp,1545
01:43:57:792,AvDiagnostics_MC,1552,3776,-1,DSDomino,15,rgvarRows.GetNumItems()
   =0,e:\views\cs_ue4.0.2.124\un_Doh2\AvDirMonDomino\AvDSDomino\
   AvDbDLMemList.cpp,1555
01:43:57:791,AvDiagnostics_MC,1555,3776,-1,DSDomino,15,> CAvDbDLMemList::Logoff()
01:43:57:792,AvDiagnostics_MC,1556,3776,-1,DSDomino,15,<
   CAvDbDLMemList::Logoff(),0x00000000,S_OK
01:43:57:791,AvDiagnostics_MC,1556,3776,-1,DSDomino,15,<
   GetPendingScopeDLists(),0x00000000,S_OK
01:43:57:792,AvDiagnostics_MC,1552,3776,-1,DSDomino,11,Notes proxy allocated and
   initialized (d5d9c8),e:\views\cs_ue4.0.2.124\un_Doh2\AvDirMonDomino\AvDSDomino\
   stdafx.h,97
01:43:57:791,AvDiagnostics_MC,1556,3776,-1,DSDomino,16,<
   HandlePendingScopeDlist(),0x00000000,S_OK
01:43:57:792,AvDiagnostics_MC,1552,3776,-1,DSDomino,11,Notes proxy deallocted
   (d5d9c8),e:\views\cs_ue4.0.2.124\un_Doh2\AvDirMonDomino\AvDSDomino\stdafx.h,119
01:43:57:791,AvDiagnostics_MC,1555,3776,-1,DSDomino,15,> CAvDbDLMemList::Logoff()
01:43:57:792,AvDiagnostics_MC,1556,3776,-1,DSDomino,15,<
   CAvDbDLMemList::Logoff(),0x00000001,S_FALSE
01:43:57:791,AvDiagnostics_MC,1555,3776,-1,DSDomino,16,>
   SynchronizeAllAddressBooks()
01:43:57:792,AvDiagnostics_MC,1552,3776,-1,DSDomino,11,Notes proxy allocated and
   initialized (d5d9c8),e:\views\cs_ue4.0.2.124\un_Doh2\AvDirMonDomino\AvDSDomino\
   stdafx.h,97
```

A full synchronization can also occur from Unity to the directory. When this takes place, the Unity database is considered the source database, and the directory is the target. This full synchronization is performed by the Unity SQLSyncer process, which is called through a stored proc in the database. It also has a COM interface that allows some of the Unity components to access it directly. It uses the directory monitor to write the changes from its database into the directory.

The SQLSyncer runs under these circumstances:

- When called by a Unity tool (such as DiRT)
- Upon a service request from an administrative application (for instance, when using the Cisco Unity Bulk Import tool)
- During the connector setup

A good example of the SQLSyncer running through the directory monitor is running Unity configuration setup with the /sync parameter, as shown in Figure 4-6.

Figure 4-6 *The Unity Configuration Setup with the sync Parameter Used*

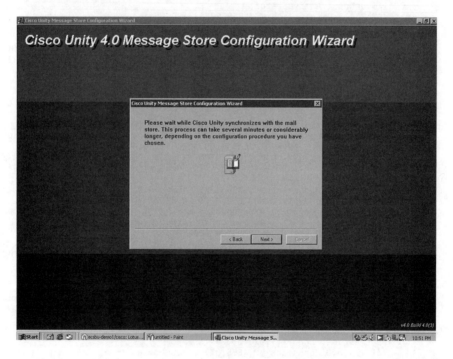

Run the setup by selecting <drive>\commserver\configurationsetup\setup.exe /sync <enter>.

The SQL Sync Log file shows the objects written to the directory from the SQL database.

```
Thu Aug 15 00:32:33.766  Synking Mailuser JPERRY     \DbSync.cpp (line 547)
Thu Aug 15 00:32:33.766  Entering FindDirObject      \ConnectorClientBase.cpp (line 168)
Thu Aug 15 00:32:33.796  Exiting FindDirObject       \ConnectorClientBase.cpp (line 277)
```

```
Thu Aug 15 00:32:33.796  Entering ModifyDirObject \ConnectorClientBase.cpp (line 416)
Thu Aug 15 00:32:34.36  Exiting ModifyDirObject    \ConnectorClientBase.cpp (line 430)
Thu Aug 15 00:32:34.36  Entering AssociateDirObject      \DbSync.cpp (line 1065)
Thu Aug 15 00:32:34.176  Exiting AssociateDirObject, returning 0x0      \DbSync.cpp
  (line 1117)
Thu Aug 15 00:32:34.186  Entering GetOneRow       \ConnectorClientBase.cpp (line 137)
Thu Aug 15 00:32:34.246  Exiting GetOneRow       \ConnectorClientBase.cpp (line 153)
Thu Aug 15 00:32:34.246  Synking Mailuser JHUGHES      \DbSync.cpp (line 547)
Thu Aug 15 00:32:34.246  Entering FindDirObject   \ConnectorClientBase.cpp (line 168)
Thu Aug 15 00:32:34.296  Exiting FindDirObject   \ConnectorClientBase.cpp (line 277)
Thu Aug 15 00:32:34.296  Entering ModifyDirObject\ConnectorClientBase.cpp (line 416)
Thu Aug 15 00:32:34.527  Exiting ModifyDirObject \ConnectorClientBase.cpp (line 430)
Thu Aug 15 00:32:34.537  Entering AssociateDirObject      \DbSync.cpp (line 1065)
Thu Aug 15 00:32:34.657  Exiting AssociateDirObject, returning 0x0      \DbSync.cpp
  (line 1117)
Thu Aug 15 00:32:34.657  Entering GetOneRow       \ConnectorClientBase.cpp (line 137)
Thu Aug 15 00:32:34.657  Exiting GetOneRow       \ConnectorClientBase.cpp (line 153)
```

A portion of text is shown from the Commserver\logs\sqlsync_*xxxxxxxx* file where *xxxxxxxx* is equal to the file ID created by the Unity log manager.

This is a portion of the SqlSyncer log file created when the synch is run on the second part Unity configuration. This essentially writes from the Unity database to the directory. All existing Unity-specific attributes in the directory are overwritten by this process, which calls the Directory monitor directly.

The order of synchronization from the SQL Sync service is as follows:

1 All subscribers first

2 All Internet subscribers

3 All distribution lists

4 All scope distribution lists

5 All members of distribution lists

Extensibility of the Directory

The directory monitor synchronizes each Unity object's subscriber data found in the directory, but this is only a small subset of each Unity object's attributes that reside in UnityDB. To synchronize the objects and attributes, it is necessary to use existing objects and attributes or to originate Unity-specific objects and attributes through a directory schema extension.

When directory-aware applications share and utilize directory information to provide key functionality each in their own products, as with Unity, it is necessary to preserve ownership of important data. Although this same data can be shared, as needed, it is rarely as simple to use common directory schema for unique products such as Unity. Important information can be overwritten, thus increasing the burden of maintaining a more consistent update and identification method; naturally, this takes up more processing time. When less common fields designated for special use are used and written to by more than one unique product, the risk of failure as a result of these changes is much higher. As such, it is always desirable to preserve data used for specific applications, even if they are shared by other applications.

One way to do this in the directory is to allow for some level of extensibility, to create a set of unique and dedicated objects and properties that can be used by the specific application and shared for others to use (as long as that ownership is preserved enough that it does not impair normal operations or prevent the loss of functionality by all applications that use the data). When possible, Unity uses unique, unused schema in the directory, but it is desirable to guarantee uniqueness by creating data elements that it can use as its own. This ensures that multiple applications do not write to those same elements shared by all applications but owned by only one.

A good example of this is Unity's use of existing directory data owned by Exchange to identify a user as the owner of a specific mailbox. Although Unity has the capability to take ownership of this data, this is not its primary objective. In unified messaging, the goal is to use the data as maintained by the owner to provide enhanced functionality to an existing yet functionally limited object, such as an e-mail user.

So, a good rule of sharing and using data owned by other applications is to preserve ownership boundaries as much as possible—that is, to read other owners' data but not write to it just because it is possible. It is acceptable and expected to do this with Unity in a unified messaging configuration. At the same time, it is normal to expect Unity to be the primary owner of all directory data in a voice mail–only configuration, in which the mail stores are dedicated to service Unity alone. These differences in ownership are discussed in Chapter 9, "Planning;" Chapter 10, "Typical Configurations and Deployment Models;" and Chapter 11, "Designing a Unity Solution."

For Exchange 5.5, the schema is not extensible, so it is necessary to use existing objects and attributes. In Exchange 2000, the schema is extensible; this allows Unity to use its own schema, which, in turn, prevents conflicts from multiple sources using the same objects and attributes. The Domino schema is taken care of through the DUCS extensions that are applied to Domino servers prior to or when Unity is introduced into a Domino environment. The Domino schema for DUCS includes extension directory data used by Unity alone in the Domino directory.

As mentioned in Chapter 3, "Components and Subsystems: Object Model," five objects are of importance to Cisco Unity, regardless of the messaging system to which it is connected. Table 4-5 lists these objects.

Table 4-5 *Unity Object Name Matching to the Message Systems Serviced*

Object Name	Exchange 5.5	Exchange 2000/2003	Domino R6
Subscriber	Mailbox (recipient)	User with mailbox	Person
Location	Special	CiscoECSBUUmLocation object	Location
Distribution list	Distribution list	Distribution group	Distribution or mail-only groups
Scope distribution list	Distribution list	Distribution group	Distribution or mail-only groups
Internet subscriber	Custom recipient	Contact	Internet users

- **Subscriber.** To make an existing Exchange 5.5 mailbox a Unity subscriber, it is necessary to first import it into Unity. Then Unity must be allowed to read its existing attributes that are considered necessary for identifying and acting on behalf of the subscriber, and then write to existing hidden attributes. ("Hidden," in this case, means the object attributes that typically are not exposed through a common interface, such as the Exchange 5.5 Admin program or GAL used by Outlook.)

  Default locations for subscribers are as follows:

  — During Unity installation, depending upon the mail store that is serviced by Unity, the installer selects a partner server for Unity to place its system mailbox onto (the exception is Domino, for which no system mailbox exists). This location typically becomes the default location for where subscribers are created if the Unity SA or Unity import is used to create subscribers.

  — The Unity installation for Exchange 2000 uses a default Users container, which an administrator can change to any OU as its default. It does the same for the Unity groups created during installation. The installer has the choice to locate these default locations as needed.

  If it is created administratively through the Unity SA, the following takes place:

  — If Unity is configured for voice messaging, the default locations typically are used for creating subscribers. However, there is quite a bit of flexibility, depending on the mail store used and the size of the installation (how many mail stores and subscribers are serviced).

  — If Unity is configured for unified messaging, the default locations typically are used for the Unity objects created during installation or for special Unity-only related objects used by a given company. In most unified messaging configurations of any size, the Unity SA does not be used to "create" subscribers; an import process is more typical.

If an existing mailbox is imported into Unity, this mailbox's location does not change. Unity simply services it based on its location. If the mailbox being imported is in a different Windows 2000 domain than Unity, the Unity server begins to monitor that domain to track the changes to that mailbox. (It is necessary to make sure that Unity has the proper permissions to do this first. For more information, see the Unity Permissions Wizard and related product documentation.) This means that the scope will change as a result of the import to accommodate the new subscribers that Unity services.

- **Location object**. This is a dedicated object in the directory, strictly for Cisco Unity. No other product or system currently makes use of this object. The location object is a key component of Unity's digital networking functionality.

  — In Domino, a location document is created to represent the Unity-specific location. A new location document exists for each location created by Unity.

  — In Active Directory, the location object resides in the Unity folder by default.

  — In the Exchange 5.5 directory, the location object resides in the Cisco Unity folder underneath the site container.

  Default paths for the location object are as follows:

  — Domino x.500 dn

  — Exchange 2000 ou=Locations, ou=unity, dc=domain name, dc=com

  — Exchange 5.5 /o=organizationname/ou=sitename/cn=Cisco Unity/ cn=Locations

- **Distribution list**. This is simply an existing DL that has a recorded name and a few other Unity-specific attributes affixed to it.

- **Scope distribution list**. This is created and used to support the Unity directory handler feature. The directory handler feature enables you to create a directory handler for a subset of your subscribers, such as those who reside in a branch office. You can create a directory handler that, in turn, creates a scope DL; this is simply a normal DL, but it is specific to the subscribers in a given location or grouping. For more information regarding directory handlers, see Chapter 7, "Components and Subsystems: Features."

- **Internet subscriber**. This is basically an entry in the address book for a contact or remote address. It is used to address voice messages to users who have no mailbox within the existing messaging system.

When Unity is also connected to other voice-messaging systems, there are additional considerations for the directory. Most of these considerations are addressed in Chapter 15, "Upgrades and Migrations," regarding voice mail interoperability and Chapter 12, regarding Unity networking.

Default Unity Objects

During installation (and as shown in Table 4-6), Unity creates the following objects in the directory as part of its default configuration.

Table 4-6 *Unity Default Objects*

Object Name	Role	Comments
Example Administrator	Example administrative account and owner of default call handlers. Also default Unaddressed Messages DL member.	This account is more than an example account: It serves as a default owner of system call handlers.
Example Subscriber[*]	Example subscriber account.	This account can be deleted after installation. It is a good account to use for testing during installation.
Unity_Servername	Unity system mailbox.	In Exchange, this key account delivers messages from outside callers to subscribers.
Unaddressed Messages	A distribution list created to capture messages left by outside callers that were unaddressed to subscribers.	This default DL should not be deleted, but it can be moved to a different container in the directory.
All Subscribers	A distribution list used to place all subscribers in the system in a single global group.	This default DL can be used or not used. It can be deleted after it has been removed from a default subscribers template.
System Event Messages	A distribution list used by the Unity Event Notification utility.	This default DL can be used or not used. It can be deleted after it has been replaced with a different DL in the Event Notification utility.
Default Location Object	A special object created in the directory that links the subscribers and other Unity objects to a specific Unity server. It is used to identify Unity servers for digital networking.	This key object should not be deleted. Doing so renders Unity inoperable.

Note: In Domino, the Example Subscriber and Example Administrator accounts cannot be signed into because they are not created with mailboxes.

Exchange 5.5 Directory Monitor: AvDSEx55

The Exchange 5.5 directory monitor is specific to Unity servicing Exchange 5.5 only. If Exchange 5.5 and Exchange 2000/2003 are installed into a mixed-messaging configuration and it is desired to have Unity service mailboxes on both versions of Exchange at the same time, the directory monitors for Exchange 2000/2003 must be used. For more information, see Chapter 13. Some important details follow:

- When used: Pure Exchange 5.5

- Monitor: Exchange 5.5 Monitor used

- Standard directory permissions: Granted to Unity service account for accessing Exchange 5.5 directory

- Standard messaging permissions: Service account admins role at the site and configuration containers

To use the Exchange 5.5 directory, Cisco Unity uses the existing Exchange 5.5 directory schema. In Service Pack 1 of Exchange 5.5, Microsoft added voice-mail attributes to the Recipient object. Cisco Unity makes use of these attributes in addition to other unused attributes that are available programmatically (meaning that these attributes are included in the common admin tools such as Admin.exe, although all attributes that Unity uses are visible in raw mode, admin /r. As with the other directories, Unity makes use of existing or commonly used attributes as well.

Objects and Their Attributes

In Exchange 5.5, the subscriber is tied to the recipient or mail user. Unity uses the attributes shown in Table 4-7 to make an existing mailbox a subscriber; these attributes also are used when a subscriber is created. Note that these are the LDAP names; the display names might be a little different (for example, with no hyphen separating the names).

Table 4-7   *DoH Names and Corresponding Names in the Exchange 5.5 Directory*

DoH	Recipient or Mail User
AVP_ALIAS	UID
AVP_ALTERNATE_DTMF_IDS	Voice-Mail-Greetings
AVP_AMIS_DISABLE_OUTBOUND	Voice-Mail-Speed
AVP_BUSINESS_TELEPHONE	TelephoneNumber
AVP_CREATION_TIME	CreateTimeStamp

Table 4-7   *DoH Names and Corresponding Names in the Exchange 5.5 Directory (Continued)*

DoH	Recipient or Mail User
AVP_DIRECTORY_ID	DistinguishedName
AVP_DISPLAY_NAME	Cn
AVP_DISTINGUISHED_NAME	DistinguishedName
AVP_DTMF_ACCESS_ID	Voice-Mail-User-ID
AVP_FIRST_NAME	GivenName
AVP_GATEWAY_ADDRESSES	OtherMailbox
AVP_HIDDEN_IN_DIRECTORY	Hide-From-Address-Book
AVP_LAST_NAME	Sn
AVP_LIST_IN_DIRECTORY	Voice-Mail-Flags
AVP_LOCATION_OBJECT_ID	Extension-Attribute-12
AVP_MAIL_DATABASE	Home-Mdb
AVP_MAIL_SERVER	GENERATED(from Home-Mdb)
AVP_MAIL_TRANSFER_AGENT	Home-Mta
AVP_MAILBOX_ID	DistinguishedName
AVP_MAILBOX_SEND_LIMIT	MDB-Over-Quota-Limit
AVP_MAILBOX_SEND_RECEIVE_LIMIT	DXA-Task
AVP_MAILBOX_USE_DEFAULT_LIMITS	MDB-Use-Defaults
AVP_MAILBOX_WARNING_LIMIT	MDB-Storage-quota
AVP_OBJECT_CHANGED_ID	USN-Changed
AVP_OBJECT_TYPE	Generated (from ObjectClass)
AVP_PRIMARY_FAX_NUMBER	FacimileTelephoneNumber
AVP_RELATIVE_DISTINGUISHED_NAME	rdn
AVP_REMOTE_ADDRESS	Target-Address
AVP_SECURITY_DESCRIPTOR	NT-Security-Descriptor
AVP_SID	Assoc-NT-Account
AVP_SMTP_ADDRESS	mail
AVP_XFER_STRING	Extension-Attribute-14
AVP_VOICE_NAME_DATA	Voice-Mail-Recorded-Name

Of these fields, the following are overwritten when an administrator imports the mail user recipient into Unity as a subscriber. However, Unity does not overwrite an existing subscriber with new attributes:

- Field
- Extension-Attribute-12
- Extension-Attribute-14
- Voice-Mail-Flags
- Voice-Mail-Greetings
- Voice-Mail-Password
- Voice-Mail-Recorded-Name
- Voice-Mail-Speed
- Voice-Mail-User-ID

The overwritten fields are important because they are considered the Unity-specific fields used to assign the proper values necessary to identify each recipient as a valid subscriber with specific capabilities. The other Exchange 5.5 recipient attributes uniquely identify the subscriber as a recipient in Exchange. This is essential for message delivery, authentication, and addressing tasks.

TIP   If any of the previous fields are used by other applications, it is important to note this before installing Unity into an existing Exchange 5.5 site. Currently, no options exist for changing the fields from those shown previously for Unity. This means that if any other application makes use of these fields before Unity is installed, Unity overwrites it when that recipient is imported as a Unity subscriber.

As shown in Table 4-8, the following fields are written to when a subscriber is created in the SA and homed on Exchange 5.5.

Table 4-8   *LDAP Names (Objects and Attributes) That Are Written to When a Subscriber Is Created*

Exchange LDAP Names	Examples
objectClass:organizationalPerson;person;Top	This is the actual object type and its object hierarchy.
Rdn	JEllison;
Cn	John Ellison
DistinguishedName	cn=JEllison, cn=Recipients, ou=Corp;o=Enterprise
rfc822Mailbox	JEllison@Corp.Enterprise.com

Table 4-8   *LDAP Names (Objects and Attributes) That Are Written to When a Subscriber Is Created (Continued)*

Exchange LDAP Names	Examples
Mail	JEllison@Corp.Enterprise.com
textEncodedORaddress	c=US;a=;p=Enterprise;o=Corp;s=Ellison;g=John;;
mailPreferenceOption	0 or 1
Extension-Attribute-12*	Directory string representing the default Unity location object.
Extension-Attribute-14*	38338, the transfer string. In this example, it is the same as the subscriber's DTMF ID.
GivenName*	John
Home-MTA	cn=Microsoft MTA, cn=Unity2,cn=Servers,cn=Configuration, ou=Corp,o=Enterprise
Uid	JEllison or the subscriber's alias.
MAPI-Recipient	Set to True or False. Unity looks for those set for True.
Sn*	Ellison, or the last name of the subscriber.
MemberOf*	Group memberships. If imported or created by Unity, the subscriber is added to a default All Subscribers distribution list if using the default Subscribers Template to create subscribers (only Unity voice-enabled groups).
Voice-Mail-Flags*	Used to denote whether it is listed in the Unity alpha directory accessible through the TUI.
Voice-Mail-Password*	The default password from the subscriber's template used to create the subscriber.
Voice-Mail-Recorded-Name*	The recorded name of the subscriber. This is added by either the administrator or, more commonly, by the subscriber.
Voice-Mail-User-ID*	The DTMF ID of the subscriber. This is typically the subscriber's extension.

A * denotes the fields that a Unity Administrator can change through the Unity SA.

When an administrator imports a recipient into Unity as a subscriber, at a minimum, the following attributes already exist:

- Attribute
- Objectclass
- Rdn
- Cn
- DistinguishedName

- Rfc822Mailbox
- Mail
- textEncodedORaddress
- mailPreferenceOption
- GivenName
- Home-MTA
- Uid
- MAPI-Recipient
- Sn

Unity reads most of these attributes and adds their values to the subscriber's object information stored in the Unitydb.

If a Unity administrator removes an existing subscriber by deleting the subscriber account in the SA, the following fields are deleted:

- Attributes
- Custom Attribute 12
- Voice-Mail-Flags
- Voice-Mail-Password
- Voice-Mail-Recorded-Name
- Voice-Mail-User-ID

After subscriber data is removed, the object becomes a normal recipient. Unity identifies this normal recipient as a deleted Unity subscriber by marking the Extension-Attribute-14 as Deleted-Unity-Object. This also tells other Unity servers to remove this subscriber from their global tables.

If the subscriber initially was created by Unity through the SA instead of being imported, the object remains in Exchange 5.5 after its subscriber properties are removed. It then must be deleted from Exchange 5.5 using the Exchange 5.5 Admin utility. If the Unity SA also created a domain account during the subscriber-creation process, that domain account also must be deleted from the Windows domain, using either the NT user manager or the Windows 2000/2003 Active Directory Users and Computers plug-in to fully remove the object.

NOTE   Creating a domain account requires additional permissions than those mentioned. For more information regarding permissions, see the Unity Installation Guide from the Unity product documentation. For more information regarding account management, see Chapter 20, "Subscriber Administration."

Distribution List

The Exchange 5.5 distribution list can be used to allow subscribers to address messages to multiple subscribers through the telephone the same way that an Outlook client can address multiple addresses through a distribution list from the desktop. Table 4-9 shows the Unity object model names for the distribution list and the corresponding LDAP names from the Exchange 5.5 directory.

Table 4-9   *Unity Distribution List and LDAP Names Attributes*

DoH	Distribution List
AVP_ALIAS	Uid
AVP_CREATION_TIME	CreateTimeStamp
AVP_DIRECTORY_ID	DistinguishedName
AVP_DISPLAY_NAME	Cn
AVP_DISTINGUISHED_NAME	DistinguishedName
AVP_DTMF_DLIST_ID	Voice-Mail-User-ID
AVP_GATEWAY_ADDRESSES	OtherMailbox
AVP_LOCATION_OBJECT_ID	Extension-Attribute-12
AVP_OBJECT_TYPE	Generated (from ObjecType)
AVP_RELATIVE_DISTINGUISHED_NAME	rdn
AVP_REMOTE_ADDRESS	TargetAddress
AVP_SID	Assoc-NT-Account
AVP_VOICE_ENABLED	Voice-Mail-Speed
AVP_VOICE_NAME_DATA	Voice-Mail-Recorded-Name

The location object is of type Person ObjectClass. This ObjectClass was used for important reasons. First, it meets all the criteria for serving as a location object; second, it isn't replicated to Active Directory through a Microsoft Active Directory connector connection agreement (CA).

Unity 2.4*x* had specific challenges with its location objects and with its entire collection of objects stored in the Unity folder under the Exchange 5.5 site. The biggest challenge was the alteration of object class properties and types changing when replicating through the Microsoft Active Directory Connector to Active Directory and back, through a two-way connection agreement.

The Unity 3.*x* and 4.0*x* (up to 4.04) location object as used in Exchange 5.5 consists of the Exchange 5.5 properties in Table 4-10.

Table 4-10 *The Unity Location Object and Its Corresponding LDAP Name*

Doh	Exchange
AVP_ADDRESSING_MAX_SCOPE	Voice-Mail-Speed
AVP_ALIAS	Uid
AVP_ALLOW_BLIND_ADDRESSING	Extension-Attribute-1
AVP_AMIS_NODE_ACTIVE	Voice-Mail-Password
AVP_AMIS_NODE_ID	Extension-Attribute-14
AVP_BLIND_ADDRESSING_MAX_SCOPE	Voice-Mail-Recording-Length
AVP_CREATION_TIME	createTimeStamp
AVP_DESTIONATION_TYPE	Extension-Attribute-2
AVP_DIALING_DOMAIN_NAME	Extension-Attribute-5
AVP_DIRECTORY_ID	distinguishedName
AVP_DISPLAY_NAME	Cn
APV_DISTINGUISHED_NAME	distinguishedName
AVP_DTMF_ACCESS_ID	Voice-Mail-User-ID
AVP_HOME_SERVER	Extension-Attribute-6
AVP_LOCATION_OBJECT_ID	Extension-Attribute-12
AVP_OBJECT_CHANGED_ID	USN-Changed
AVP_OBJECT_TYPE	Generated (From ObjectType)
AVP_RELATIVE_DISTINGUISHED_NAME	rdn
AVP_SID	Assoc-NT-Account
AVP_SMTP_DOMAIN	Mail
AVP_SYSTEM_ID	Extension-Attribute-3
AVP_SYSTEM_STATE	Voice-Mail-System-GUID
AVP_TEXT_NAME	Admin-Description
AVP_UNDELETABLE	Extension-Attribute-4
AVP_VOICE_NAME_DATA	Voice-Mail-Recorded-Name

Global Data

Exchange 5.5 global data is subscriber, Internet subscriber, group, and location information about other Unity servers in the enterprise. For Exchange 5.5, this can be Unity information stored in the directory at the site level, at the organization level, or in other Exchange 5.5 sites that are a part of the organization.

The global data is used to allow a Unity server's subscribers to address messages and respond to messages for subscribers on other Unity servers. The location object is key to this process because it is used to identify where the subscribers reside (on which server) and also to provide the necessary information to address those subscribers.

The directory monitor for Exchange 5.5 queries for global data and stores change results in its global tables in SQL. The subscriber data is the same for a local Unity subscriber or one residing on another server. This means that the attributes queried are the same. The difference for Unity is that this data is queried and stored in a read-only manner, and no Unity server writes to the directory to create global data. The queries, described earlier in this chapter, return the necessary results to identify the subscribers as belonging to the server performing the queries or belonging to other Unity servers.

As shown in Table 4-11, each Unity server has a default location object. This object essentially ties a subscriber to a given Unity server.

Table 4-11   *A Subscriber Tied to Its Home Unity Server*

The Default Location Object (AVP_LOCATION_OBJECT_ID) Contains	Subscriber Contains
AVP_HOME_SERVER	AVP_LOCATION_OBJECT_ID

More information can be found in Chapter 12.

Exchange 2000 or Exchange 20003 Directory Monitors: AvDSAD and AvDSGlobalCatalog

The Exchange 2000/2003 directory monitors are specific to Exchange 2000/2003. However, in a mixed-messaging environment, these directory monitors can be used to support Unity servicing both Exchange 5.5 and Exchange 2000/2003 mailboxes. Chapter 13 explains this in detail.

As stated earlier in this chapter, the two Exchange 2000/2003 directory monitors have separate functions for Unity. Some important details are as follows:

- When used: Pure Exchange 2000, or mixed Exchange 5.5 and Exchange 2000.

- Monitor: Exchange 2000 Monitor used.

- Permissions: Set using the Permissions Wizard.

- Standard directory permissions: Implied read access to the entire directory, and some write access to Unity-specific objects or objects being serviced by Unity. Full control is required to manage the Unity location object in Active Directory. More or less access might be required, depending on how Unity is used (as a voice mail–only server or a unified messaging server). The Exchange Full or View-Only Administrator role is used at the organization level in Exchange System Manager.

- Standard messaging permissions: Exchange Domain Servers group membership granted to the Unity Messaging Service account for accessing the Exchange. (Note that after Exchange 2000 SP2, the permissions granted through this group to individual mailboxes were denied. It is now necessary to grant access explicitly to each mailbox for the Unity service account. For more information, see the Cisco Unity Permissions Wizard and accompanying documentation.)

To connect Cisco Unity to Exchange 2000 as its messaging store, it is necessary to extend the Active Directory schema. More information on the Active Directory schema extension can be found in the Cisco Unity product documentation and whitepapers found on the Cisco website.

As shown earlier in this chapter, two monitors exist for Unity for Exchange 2000. One monitor views Unity subscriber information at the domain controller of the domain where Unity resides. This monitor's role is mainly to monitor Unity information that is specific to the Unity server where it resides. The other monitor views Unity subscriber information from other Unity servers through the Global Catalog server.

Objects and Their Attributes

For Unity, the Active Directory mail-enabled user object equals a Unity subscriber. Because the subscriber is the most common and most populated object used by Unity, it is discussed in detail here. Other objects are mentioned throughout this chapter.

In Exchange 2000, the subscriber is tied to the Active Directory user object. Unity detects only user objects that have mailboxes. This is done by using a simple query to filter out users of this type during import operations.

If Unity's administrative interface is used to create a new subscriber, a new user is created in Active Directory and a mailbox is created in Exchange 2000. As shown in Table 4-12, Unity uses the attributes to make an existing mail-enabled user in Active Directory into a Unity subscriber.

Table 4-12 *Doh Names and Corresponding Names in Active Directory*

DOH	Mail-Enabled User
AVP_ALIAS	mailNickname
AVP_ALTERNATE_DTMF_IDS	ciscoEcsbuAlternateDTMFIds
AVP_BUSINESS_TELEPHONE	telephoneNumber
AVP_CREATION_TIME	whenCreated
AVP_DIRECTORY_ID	objectGuid
AVP_DISPLAY_NAME	displayName
AVP_DISTINGUISHED_NAME	objectGuid

Table 4-12   *Doh Names and Corresponding Names in Active Directory (Continued)*

DOH	Mail-Enabled User
AVP_DTMF_ACCESS_ID	CiscoEcsbuDtmfId
AVP_EMAIL_ADDRESSS	legacyExchangeDn
AVP_FIRST_NAME	givenName
AVP_GATEWAY_ADDRESSES	otherMailbox
AVP_HIDDEN_IN_DIRECTORY	msExchHideFromAddressLists
AVP_LAST_NAME	Sn
AVP_LIST_IN_DIRECTORY	ciscoEcsbuListinUMDirectory
AVP_MAIL_DATABASE	homeMdb
AVP_MAIL_SERVER	Generated from HomeMDB
AVP_MAIL_TRANSFER_AGENT	homeMTA
AVP_MAILBOX_ID	legacyExchangeDn
AVP_MAILBOX_SEND_LIMIT	mDBOverQuotaLimit
AVP_MAILBOX_SEND_RECEIVE_LIMIT	mDBOverHardQuotaLimi
AVP_MAILBOX_USE_DEFAULT_LIMITS	mDBuseDefaults
AVP_MAILBOX_WARNING_LIMIT	mDBStorageQuota
AVP_OBJECT_CHANGED_ID	usNChanged
AVP_OBJECT_TYPE	ciscoEcsbuObjectType
AVP_PRIMARY_FAX_NUMBER	facimileTelephoneNumber
AVP_RELATIVE_DISTINGUISHED_NAME	Rdn
AVP_REMOTE_ADDRESS	targetAddress
AVP_SID	objectSid
AVP_SID_HISTORY	sIDHistory
AVP_SMTP_ADDRESS	Mail
AVP_XFER_STRING	ciscoEcsbuTransferId
AVP_VOICE_NAME_DATA	msExchRecordedName

As presented in the Exchange 5.5 directory monitor subsection, nearly all of the non–Unity-specific attributes (those attributes that are a part of the original Active Directory/Exchange 2000 schema) simply are read from during the import process (when a mailbox-enabled user is imported into Unity as a Unity subscriber). Note the Unity-specific attributes (those starting with CiscoEcsbu) that are written to during import. The other Unity-specific attributes are available for more commonly used added functionality, such as when multiple

Unity servers are networked digitally or when Unity servers are connected to legacy voice-messaging systems for interoperability.

When an administrator creates a subscriber, the minimal account settings are created in Active Directory for the user associated with the subscriber. This user is also given an Exchange 2000 mailbox. If the user is created through Active Directory Users and Computers (ADUC) and then is given a mailbox, the same minimal fields are created. So, whether the user is created by the Unity SA or imported, the following fields already exist:

- Active Directory LDAP names
- CN
- homeMDB
- accountExpires
- badPasswordTime
- codePage
- countryCode
- displayName
- mail
- givenName
- instanceType
- lastLogoff
- lastLogon
- legacyExchangeDN
- logonCount
- distinguisheedName
- objectCategory
- objectClass
- objectGUID
- objectSid
- primaryGroupID
- proxyAddresses
- pwdLastSet
- name
- sAMAccountName
- sAMAccountType

- showInAddressBook
- sn
- textEncodedORAddress
- userAccountControl
- userPrincipalName
- uSNChanged
- uSNCreated
- whenChanged
- whenCreated
- homeMTA
- msExchHomeServerName
- mailNickname
- mDBUseDefaults
- msExchMailboxGuid
- msExchMailboxSecurityDescriptor
- msExchALObjectVersion
- msExchPoliciesIncluded
- msExchUserAccountControl

When the import is complete, the user's Unity attributes are written as shown in Table 4-13.

Table 4-13   *Unity-Specific Active Directory Names and Their Use*

Active Directory LDAP Names (for Unity Attributes)	Set To
ciscoEcsbuDtmfId	The extension assigned to the subscriber.
ciscoEcsbuTransferId	Used to perform a release transfer to Unity subscribers on other Unity servers in the same dialing domain.
ciscoEcsbuUMLocationObjectId	The ID of the location that this subscriber is associated with.
ciscoEcsbuUndeletable	Set to False by default. This setting is used so that Unity applications do not delete the object.
ciscoEcsbuListInUMDirectory	Listed in the alpha directory (therefore, searchable by the subscriber's first name or last name, and identifiable by extension).
ciscoEcsbuObjectType	Set to 1, which equals a Unity subscriber.
msExchRecordedName	Is set when the subscriber goes through open enrollment and adds a recorded name.

If a Unity Administrator removes an existing mail-enabled user as a subscriber by deleting the subscriber account in the SA, all of the previous Unity attributes are deleted except the ciscoEcsbuObjectType attribute; it is still set equal to 1.

Domino Directory Monitor: AvDSDomino

Of course, the Domino directory monitor is specific to the Domino directory and used only for a pure Domino environment. This means that Unity cannot also service Exchange mailboxes when connected to Domino. Unity has other requirements to connect to Domino, including the requirement that DUC be installed on each Domino server that Unity services. In fact, DUC has three different components. For a detailed explanation of DUC and each component, see Chapter 14, "Unity with Lotus Domino."

The Domino directory is schemaless, in the sense that Unity does not add a single set of schema elements to the directory (as is done with Active Directory) to expand the directory schema and support the Unity installation. However, Unity-specific attributes are added to the Domino objects when they are made Unity subscribers, or when groups are made public distribution lists for Unity, and so on. The difference here is that, instead of the schema being called from a central schema set in the directory, these Unity-specific attributes simply are added to the Domino person documents and group documents as these objects are made Unity subscribers or distribution lists, or they are added when a Unity location (document) is created. Some important details are as follows:

* When used: Pure Domino R5 and higher.

* Monitor: Domino Monitor used.

* Permissions: Set during installation of Unity. Unity can import Domino users only from the Domino directory. It can create person documents, but it does not create a user ID certificate. Therefore, Unity does not support subscriber creation from the Unity System Administration as it does with Exchange 5.5 or Exchange 2000/2003.

* Standard directory permissions: A single Unity server points to a single Domino directory server in the Domino domain of which the Unity Notes client is a member. The Domino directory server sometimes is called the admin server. The permissions required can be found in Cisco Unity product documentation. In addition, see Chapter 14.

* Standard messaging permissions: A single Unity server connects to and services mailboxes on one or more Domino mail servers in a Domino domain. There are specific deployment requirements for this—see Chapter 10 and Chapter 14.

As mentioned, the Domino directory is schemaless, in the sense that Unity does not require a central or global schema extension before installation. The new Unity-specific attributes simply are added to the various object documents when they are imported into Unity.

With the Domino directory monitor, the primary directory monitored is the names.nsf database. Unity can monitor a secondary "contacts" address book as well use the same directory monitor. The Unity administrator adds this with the Unity System Administrator web-based tool. See Network, Digital Networking Options to administer it. Also see Configuration, Subscriber Address Books to add new address books. Consult Cisco Unity product documentation to determine the total number of address books allowed because that number can increase.

Objects and Their Attributes

To Unity, the Domino Person Document equals a Unity subscriber.

Because all person documents (that is, Domino users) are accessible in the Directory, Unity can import them and then assign the Unity attributes to them. The number of attributes, both non–Unity-related (common) and Unity-related (created by Unity during import), are shown in Table 4-14. The entire set of attributes belonging to the person document is actually quite large compared to those used by Unity.

Table 4-14   *Common and Unity-Specific Subscriber Attributes*

DOH	Person Document
AVP_ALIAS	AVP_ALIAS
AVP_DISPLAY_NAME	AVP-DISPLAY_NAME
AVP_FIRST_NAME	FirstName
AVP_LAST_NAME	LastName
AVP_LOCATION_OBJECT_ID	AVP_LOCATION_OBJECT_ID
AVP_LIST_IN_DIRECTORY	AVP_LIST_IN_DIRECTORY
AVP_DTMF_ACCESS_ID	AVP_DTMF_ACCESS_ID
AVP_OBJECT_TYPE	AVP_OBJECT_TYPE
AVP_XFER_STRING	AVP_XFER_STRING
AVP_SMTP_ADDRESS	InternetAddress
AVP_MAIL_SERVER	MailServer
AVP_MAIL_DATABASE	MailFile
AVP_UNDELETABLE	AVP_UNDELETABLE
AVP_BUSINESS_TELEPHONE	Telephone
AVP_DIRECTORY_ID	Note ID

AVP_DIRECTORY_ID is important because it allows the Unity Domino directory monitor to look up this ID to access the ID's document directly after the directory returns the query.

The Domino Group Document is equal to the Unity Public Distribution List.

Table 4-15   *Common and Unity-Specific Attributes for Groups TS*

DOH	Domino Group Document
AVP_ALIAS	ListName
AVP_CREATION_TIME	From $Revisions
AVP_DIRECTORY_ID	Note ID
AVP_DISPLAY_NAME	AVP_DISPLAY_NAME
AVP_DISTINGUISHED_NAME	Note ID
AVP_LOCATION_OBJECT_ID	AVP_LOCATION_OBJECT_ID
AVP_OBJECT_TYPE	AVP_OBJECT_TYPE
AVP_VOICE_NAME_DATA	Stored in the directory as a WAV file. For example, the AllSubscribers Distribution list is named AllSubscribersVoiceName.wav.

One DOH object attribute that is not listed but that is important for groups is AVP_ MEMBERS. It lists the members of each public distribution list. There is a challenge with the way in which users are found in groups within Domino. A group has the list of users, but there is no relational link to those users in their individual person documents. This means that after the Directory_Object_ID is obtained for each member of the group through the members attribute, the directory monitor must match the found members against the subscribers that it has in the UnityDB. Unity tracks subscribers and their membership in public distribution lists by linking them in the UnityDB.

The Domino Unity Location Document is equal to the Unity Location.

The Domino Unity Location Document is similar to the group document. The Location Document uses a few other attributes that are, of course, similar to the location objects found in the other directories when they are created by Unity (see Table 4-16).

Table 4-16   *Common and Unity-Specific Attributes for Groups*

DOH	Domino Location Document
AVP_ADDRESSING_MAX_SCOPE	AVP_ADDRESSING_MAX_SCOPE
AVP_ALIAS	Name
AVP_DESTINATION_TYPE	AVP_DESTINATION_TYPE
AVP_ALLOW_BLIND_ADDRESSING	AVP_ALLOW_BLIND_ADDRESSING
AVP_AMIS_DIAL_ID	AVP_AMIS_DIAL_ID

Table 4-16   *Common and Unity-Specific Attributes for Groups (Continued)*

DOH	Domino Location Document
AVP_AMIS_DISABLE_OUTBOUND	AVP_AMIS_DISABLE_OUTBOUND
AVP_AMIS_NODE_ACTIVE	AVP_AMIS_NODE_ACTIVE
AVP_AMIS_NODE_ID	AVP_AMIS_NODE_ID
AVP_BLIND_ADDRESSING_MAX_SCOPE	AVP_BLIND_ADDRESSING_MAX_SCOPE
AVP_CREATION_TIME	From $Revisions
AVP_DESTINATION_TYPE	AVP_DESTINATION_TYPE
AVP_DIALING_DOMAIN_NAME	AVP_DIALING_DOMAIN_NAME
AVP_DIRECTORY_ID	Note ID
AVP_DISPLAY_NAME	AVP_ALIAS
AVP_DISTINGUISHED_NAME	Note ID
AVP_DTMF_ACCESS_ID	AVP_DTMF_ACCESS_ID
AVP_LOCATION_OBJECT_ID	AVP_LOCATION_OBJECT_ID
AVP_HOME_SERVER	AVP_HOME_SERVER
AVP_OBJECT_TYPE	Form
AVP_SYSTEM_ID	AVP_SYSTEM_ID
AVP_TEXT_NAME	Field: Full Name
AVP_VOICE_NAME_DATA	Stored as a wav file in the directory
AVP_UNDELETABLE	Field: AVP_UNDELETABLE

The Internet subscriber is similar to the Unity subscriber. Internet subscribers typically do not have mailboxes on the system, however. For more information regarding Internet subscribers, see Chapter 12.

The Unity Domino directory monitor has the same functionality that the other Unity directory monitors do, except that it cannot create subscribers; it can only import them. However, it can write to them along with the other objects that it assigns Unity attributes to in the Domino directory. The exception is the Unity location object, which the DUC csAdmin utility creates when it is installed on the directory server that Unity monitors.

Summary

This chapter discussed all the key facets of the Unity directory monitor, why it is used, and how and why it does what it does. The purpose of the chapter was to provide an in-depth overview of the inner workings of Unity's directory monitors and how they maintain directory synchronization between Unity and the directory/mail store pair that it services.

By examining the various elements specific to each directory monitor, you can understand the items that are uniquely pertinent to each directory monitor. Finally, the primary goal of the Unity directory monitor is to provide an interface into the directory for the Unity application itself and to maintain synchronization between the directory and the Unity database.

CHAPTER 5

Components and Subsystems: Messaging/Unity Message Repository

Messaging is one of the core components of Cisco Unity. From its beginning, Unity was built to use other messaging systems because it does not have its own, proprietary message-storage system. This is an important trait of a true unified messaging system.

Several components make up Unity messaging, and these components allow for the sending and retrieving of voice mail, e-mail, and fax messages to and from the message store that Unity is connected to. Unity's components also allow it to detect when new voice-mail, e-mail, and fax messages have arrived in a given Unity subscriber's mailbox. This chapter discusses messaging actions, messaging components, and MAPI.

Unity's development initially focused on Exchange 5.5 and remained that way until Unity 3.0, when full support for Exchange 2000 was added. Now, with Unity 4.0, Lotus Domino support has been added. It is possible that the next supported messaging system will be IMAP, which will allow Unity to connect to any native IMAP host. But as of this writing, there are no plans to directly support Novell GroupWise.

Messaging Actions in Unity

Unity natively uses each message store it connects to. For Exchange 5.5 and Exchange 2000, it uses MAPI to connect directly to the information store and deliver messages just like a typical Outlook client. The Unity server directly accesses individuals' mailboxes when they are logged into Unity through the telephone and retrieves their messages. For outside callers, Unity uses its own system mailbox to deliver messages on behalf of those callers to subscribers in the system. For Unity with Domino, Unity uses the Domino Unified Communications Service (DUCS) to send and deliver messages.

With the support of two major back-end mail stores, the low-level messaging functions are implemented differently. However, the Unity components that carry these functions out provide basically the same voice-messaging functionality, regardless of the back-end mail store. These Unity components are considered to be messaging components:

- **Messaging Abstraction Layer (MAL)**. This component is responsible for logging into a mailbox to send and retrieve voice-mail messages. Different MALs exist for Exchange and Domino. However, Exchange and Domino cannot be supported simultaneously with one Unity server.

- **Unity Messaging Repository (UMR).** This component is responsible for delivering voice-mail messages left by non-Unity subscribers. Additionally, the UMR enables Unity to take and store messages for Unity subscribers when the message store (Exchange or Domino) is down.

- **MessageStoreMonitor.** This component is responsible for detecting when a new message has arrived in a Unity subscriber's inbox. The functionality between the MessageStoreMonitor for Exchange (ExchangeMonitor) and the MessageStoreMonitor for Domino (DominoMonitor) is the same, but the implementation is completely different. Both of these MessageStoreMonitors live inside the AvMsgStoreMonitorSvr service.

Message Creation, Delivery, and Retrieval

Cisco Unity enables callers to create, send, and retrieve messages over the telephone (this is referred to the Telephone User Interface [TUI]). Because Unity uses a given e-mail system for message storage and submission, when a caller leaves a voice-mail message, that message becomes an e-mail with an attachment that contains the recorded voice. When the caller is finished leaving a message for a Unity subscriber, the voice-mail message is packaged into an e-mail with an attachment and is submitted to the e-mail system for delivery into the subscriber's inbox. This process is analogous to a user creating a new message with an e-mail client (such as Outlook), recording a voice message, and attaching the voice to the e-mail and clicking Send.

When the message submission is completed, the e-mail system delivers the voice-mail message to the recipient's mail store. Again, this is very similar to the e-mail client example; the e-mail client does not deliver the message—it just creates and submits the message. The e-mail system does the brunt of the work in transporting the message from the sender to the recipient. This is an important fact to remember, especially when troubleshooting message delivery in larger enterprise networks.

When a Unity subscriber makes a call to the voice-mail system to retrieve messages, Unity logs into the inbox for that subscriber on the e-mail system. The messages in that inbox are filtered and counted based on message type, quantity, and priority. The e-mail system does not deliver voice-mail messages destined for Unity subscribers to Unity. Instead, it delivers the message to a portion of the e-mail system's database dedicated for that user. Message retrieval for Unity subscribers really involves Unity getting the messages from the user's e-mail database.

If voice-mail messages are awaiting the subscriber, Unity can play back these messages. An important aspect of Unity's capability to perform message playback over the phone is that it can stream the message from the mail store, whether it is installed on or off the Unity server (for more information on placement of mail store configurations, see Part II, "Deployment"). For an e-mail message, the message is opened from the remote mail store and is essentially equivalent to a stream, even though e-mail messages do not take nearly as long to transfer data, such as MP3s or files (such as documents and spreadsheets) to the client.

With the addition of Text-to-Speech (TTS), Unity also can play back e-mail messages over the telephone if TTS is a licensed feature. The subject and body of the message actually are read back to the caller over the phone. TTS has been with Cisco Unity since 2.0, the first widely available version of Unity.

In addition to sending and receiving voice mail messages, Unity supports other messaging functions, such as replying and forwarding of e-mails and fax messages. Table 5-1 shows a quick breakdown of the messaging functionality available in the product.

Table 5-1   *Messaging Functionality*

User Type	TUI (Telephone)	GUI—from Desktop
Outside Caller	Sends messages to a subscriber	—
Subscriber	Addresses messages to one or more subscribers	Addresses messages to one or more subscribers
Subscriber	Receives voice messages from subscribers and outside callers	Receives voice messages from subscribers and outside callers
Subscriber	Replies to voice messages from subscribers	Replies to voice messages from subscribers
Subscriber	Forwards voice messages to subscribers	Forwards voice messages to subscribers
Subscriber	Forwards e-mail messages to subscribers, with a voice introduction	Forwards e-mail messages to subscribers, with a voice introduction
Subscriber	Replies to e-mail messages to subscribers, with a voice response	Replies to e-mail messages to other recipients, with a voice response
Subscriber	Sends messages to public or private lists	Sends messages to public or private lists
Subscriber	Receives message notification	Receives message notification
Subscriber	Sends messages to subscribers on different Unity servers	Sends messages to subscribers on different Unity servers
Subscriber	Sends messages to other voice-mail users on different voice-messaging systems	Sends messages to other voice-mail users on different voice-messaging systems
Subscriber	Sends messages to Internet subscribers	Sends messages to Internet subscribers
Subscriber	Receives messages from Internet subscribers	Receives messages from Internet subscribers

continues

Table 5-1 *Messaging Functionality (Continued)*

User Type	TUI (Telephone)	GUI—from Desktop
Subscriber	Replies to and forwards messages from Internet subscribers	Replies to and forwards messages from Internet subscribers
Subscriber	Sends messages to Internet subscribers by way of blind addressing	Receives messages from Internet subscribers
Subscriber	Plays back e-mail and replies with a voice message	Reads e-mail and replies with a voice message
Subscriber	Plays back e-mail and forwards through voice message	Reads e-mail and forwards through voice message
Subscriber	Receives a fax and sends it to a printer	Receives a fax and reads it or sends it to a printer
Subscriber	Deletes messages or empties Deleted Items folder	Empty Deleted Items folder
Subscriber	Sorts messages using flex stack (performed through CPCA)	Sorts messages through Outlook
Subscriber	Receives mailbox size limit warnings	Receives mailbox size limit warnings

Notification/MWI

Unity also can detect when the e-mail system has delivered a new voice message to a subscriber's inbox. This is necessary to provide for a visual indication that a new voice-mail message has arrived (such as a telephone's message waiting indicator). Along with MWI, the capability to detect these message arrivals enables Unity to use alternate means (such as calling a specified telephone, calling a numeric pager, or sending a message to a text pager) of signaling to the subscriber that a new voice-mail message exists.

Messaging Components

Performing messaging actions in a truly unified messaging environment is a complex task. Instead of having one monolithic component that carries out all messaging actions, Unity has several components to carry out those actions. The next four sections discuss these messaging components.

Messaging Abstraction Layer

The Messaging Abstraction Layer (MAL) handles the low-level work with Unity's connected mail store. The MAL is the component that logs into subscriber mailboxes. It is also the component that handles all interaction with the messages that physically reside for a subscriber on the e-mail system. This includes sending and retrieving messages, and reading any properties off of messages, such as sender, read/unread status, and message type. Because Unity uses the e-mail system for message access and transport, the MAL works directly with the mail system's application programming interfaces to work with messages and the subscriber's inbox.

Conceptually, at the lower level of the MAL, the component handles the semantics of the particular mail system's API. At the high level of the MAL, the component provides support for a consistent, regular interface for MAL clients (such as the conversation) to gain access to voice-mail messages. It should be noted that MAL clients actually do not operate directly on the MAL. Instead, MAL clients invoke functions of the MAL by way of the Data Object Hierarchy (DOH). Any DOH client, such as the conversation or the AvUMRSyncSvr, uses the MAL through the DOH. The idea is that a MAL client can work with the MAL the same way, regardless of the specifics of the mail-store back end.

Windows Monitor

The Windows Monitor (AvWm, or the "wedgie manager," as it is affectionately known in-house) has a couple of jobs. First, it is responsible for determining the status of all Exchange servers that the local Unity system cares about. Second, for Exchange-connected Unity servers, it can act as a wrapper around the Microsoft MAPI API. The wedgie manager exists as a component that other Unity components load up into their own process. For instance, the UMR uses the wedgie manager, so the UMR has its own instance of the wedgie manager; likewise, the MAL uses and has its own instance of the wedgie manager. In essence, a Unity system has multiple wedgie managers running at the same time.

When a process fires up the wedgie manager, the AvWm starts up a thread that regularly pings mail-store servers. The mail-store servers to be pinged are contained in a map, but at the initial onset of the ping, the wedgie manager does not really know which mail-store servers there are. So, it has a process for figuring those servers. The AvWm exposes a simple function that lets clients specifically ask for the status of a given server. When that function is called, the AvWm checks the server name of the mail-store server and looks up that server name in the map. If the name is not there, it is entered into the map, and this server is pinged regularly at the ping interval. Similarly, other methods (especially the MAPI-wrapped methods) take the mail-store server name as a parameter. While processing that function, the AvWm does the map check of the server and pings on behalf of the calling client. Again, if that server name was not previously in the map, it is added and becomes regularly pinged at the ping interval.

For Exchange-connected Unity systems, the ping is not really like an ICMP ping you are all familiar with. It is really a check of one or more services on that Exchange server (MsExchangeIs for E2K/E2K3 servers, and MsExchangeIs and MsExchangeDs for E55 servers). Just as it is possible for an administrator to check the status of a service through the Windows Service Control Manager, a process, a server, or DLL can do the same thing programmatically. The wedgie manager determines whether a given Exchange server is in service or out of service by examining the state of the Exchange Information Store on E2K systems, and both the Exchange Information Store and Exchange Directory Service services on E55 systems.

Another client of the AvWm is the conversation component. When a subscriber signs into the Unity server over the phone to gain access to messages, the conversation checks to see if that Exchange server is up or down before attempting to log into that user's mailbox. If the mail-store server is down, the mailbox logon for that subscriber is not attempted. This is done to avoid potentially lengthy delays in having the logon fail by a network-induced timeout. If this check was not made, the calling thread of the logon could become "wedged" and unresponsive until the failure occurred. That is where the wedgie manager gets its name. On the MAPI-wrapped functions of the AvWm, the server status on these functions' calls is verified for the same reason. So, this is not just a cute name; the wedgie manager is intended to avoid long "stalls" or wedges that might happen when messaging function calls fail (but take a long time to fail) because of network disturbances.

In the case of Domino, the monitoring service cannot assume that the server runs on top of a Windows platform, so things get a little trickier. Because it does not have the luxury of the Service Control Manager, the AvWm simply pings the server by name and checks for a response to make sure it is up. However, it does not know the exact state of the Domino mail services. This ping is a function supplied by the Notes API.

Whenever the AvWm detects that the status of a given mail-store server has changed, an event log message is written through to the application event log.

Unity Messaging Repository

The Unity Messaging Repository (UMR) interface is part of the mechanism that helps insulate Unity from volatility in the external network. Unity uses the Exchange or Domino message stores directly instead of using a proprietary message store and synchronizing, so the availability (or unavailability) of those mail stores affects users' access to messages over the phone interface. The UMR is used to enable callers to continue leaving messages and retrieving some voice-mail messages while access to remote mail-store servers has been interrupted.

Conceptually, the UMR is actually made up of two distinct subcomponents: the Unity Message Transfer Agent (UnityMTA) and the AvUmrSyncSvr. The UnityMTA exposes an API so that clients can create messages destined for the UMR through a simple set of functions. Internal to the UMR, these messages physically exist as a pair of files: the message itself in the form of a WAV file, and a text-routing file indicating where it needs to go. Clients of the UnityMTA create and submit these UMR messages, and these messages reside in a directory until they are processed and sent to the appropriate mail server. Also called the UnityMTA, this directory normally is located in the \CommServer\UnityMTA directory, but it can be specified to reside in another location by the HKLM\Software\ Active Voice\UnityUMR\1.0\MtaStoragePath.

Getting these messages to Exchange is the job of the second subcomponent of the UMR, the AvUmrSyncSvr. This component exists as a Windows service with the same name and fires up its message-delivery functions when a message is present in the UnityMTA directory. The AvUmrSyncSvr grabs the first message that has been waiting in the UnityMTA. It then determines the server that contains the mail store of the recipient by retrieving that recipient information from the DOH. Next, it checks the status of that server to ensure that the mail-store server is ready to accept submitted messages. If the server is up, the message is submitted to the mail store through the DOH. If the DOH submission of that message is successful, the message is removed from the UnityMTA. On the other hand, if the server is down, the message is left in the UnityMTA, and the UMR moves on to the next message and follows the same procedure. This procedure repeats until all messages in the UnityMTA have been processed.

So how does the UMR aid in voice-mail message delivery and retrieval when an Exchange server is down? For starters, the UMR is a fallback delivery location for the conversation component. The conversation first checks the status of a recipient's mail server. If it is down, the message is created and submitted to the UnityMTA. In the pre-UMR days, callers who wanted to leave messages for a subscriber who had a mail store on a down mail server were out of luck. With the UMR, they can leave a message regardless of the mail-server state. Additionally, if the mail server that contains the subscriber's mail store remains down, the subscriber can retrieve the message left in the UMR from the UMR.

The UMR is not used only when the desired mail-store server is down. Outside caller messages also are delivered via the UMR process. When one of the phone conversations records such a message, the phone conversation creates a UMR message and pushes it onto the UnityMTA. A UMR message physically exists as a pair of files: the message itself and a routing file indicating where it needs to go. The UnityMTA is simply a directory on the local Unity server's hard drive.

As previously mentioned, the UnityMTA directory is a subdirectory of the \CommServer directory. The AvUMRSyncSvr service picks up these messages and delivers them to the mail-store back end via the MAL interface of the DOH. If the capability to hand off the message to the Exchange or Domino back ends is interrupted, the messages remain on the local hard drive until they can be delivered. While messages wait on the hard drive for delivery, the subscriber conversation can access them and let users access messages left while connectivity to the mail store is interrupted using a limited UMR conversation.

See the UMR section of Chapter 3, "Components and Subsystems: Object Model," for more details on how the UMR message-delivery mechanism works and how the availability of external Exchange servers affects Unity's message delivery and access behavior.

Message Store Monitor

Whether the mail store is Domino or Exchange, Unity needs to know when changes have occurred to messages of a user's inbox. It monitors these inbox changes so that Unity can perform notification and MWI based on those inbox changes. Although the semantics of how the inbox changes are monitored differ between Exchange- and Domino-connected systems, the Unity architecture is the same. A Windows service contains a component that detects the Unity subscriber inbox changes. Together, the service and the monitoring component make up the Message Store Monitor. The next section discusses these components.

AvMsgStoreMonitorSvr

This Unity service exists as a home for the particular Message Store Monitor that is used by the Unity system. If the Unity message store is Exchange, this process encompasses ExchangeMonitor guts in its process space. If the Unity message store is Lotus Notes, the AvMsgStoreMonitorSvr encompasses the DominoMonitor. On its own, the AvMsgStore-MonitorSvr service is not really all that interesting; it is pretty much a skeletal service. What is interesting is the code that executes inside this process from the respective Message Store Monitor.

It is important to note that the Message Store Monitor itself does not determine if something needs to happen, just that a change has occurred on a mailbox it watches. It knows what type of action happened such as a new message was added, a message was modified (for example, marked read) or deleted; however, it does not know what needs to be done for the subscriber when than action takes place. The notifier running under AvCsMgr must do the work to determine if anything needs to be done, such as lighting an MWI light or initiating a pager dialout or the like.

ExchangeMonitor

The ExchangeMonitor component is responsible for detecting changes in the inbox of Exchange subscribers configured for some type of message notification on the local Unity server. Whenever a change of any kind happens in an inbox that it monitors, Exchange-Monitor pushes the event and the mailbox identifier on the notification queue onto the AvCsMgr process. The notifier, in turn, pulls that information off the queue and filters the inbox to get a message count; it then decides whether a notification action, such as an MWI on/off or an e-mail page, is necessary.

In the case of Exchange 5.5 and Exchange 2000, the Message Store Monitor logs into the mailbox for all subscribers configured for at least one type of message notification on the local Unity server. When this mailbox is off the Unity box (the Exchange server is not installed on the same box), a security warning (more specifically, a success audit) is logged in the application event log because Unity logs in using the account associated with the

AvMsgStoreMonitorSvr (the service that houses ExchangeMonitor). Exchange logs this whenever another account logs into a mailbox that is not its own, even if it has rights to do so; thus, this is not a message to be concerned about:

```
Windows 2000 User LINDBORGLABS\Administrator logged on to
EAdmin@lindborglabs.thinkpad.com mailbox, and is not the primary Windows 2000
account on this mailbox.
```

Another (and perhaps unknown) job of ExchangeMonitor is to detect when an Exchange mailbox of a Unity subscriber has been moved. It is not uncommon for a network administrator to move the mailbox of a give Unity subscriber from one location to another. When this happens, Directory Monitor detects the change on that subscriber object and writes the change into SQL. Writing the change into SQL sets off a special trigger, and information about the subscriber is written into a special Moved Mailbox table. At the same time, the trigger sets off an event that a thread in ExchangeMonitor has been waiting on. When this event is fired, ExchangeMonitor reads the Moved Mailbox table to gather the relevant information on the recently moved subscriber's mailbox. ExchangeMonitor then logs out the old mailbox of that subscriber and logs into the new mailbox while reregistering for change notifications of that new inbox.

DominoMonitor

In the case of Domino, the Message Store Monitor actually registers for changes on any inboxes that it is interested in through the Domino Unified Communications Service (DUCS) interface on each Domino server that houses one or more Unity subscribers. When changes have happened on Unity subscriber inboxes, a message count packet is sent to the Unity server. This contains data wrapped in XML, signifying the user and the type of change that occurred. When any message is added, removed, or modified, the Message Store Monitor is notified of this change and pushes the appropriate event onto the notification queue in the same way the Exchange Message Store Monitor does. At startup, Unity logs into each user's mailbox and synchs. After that, it is simply a matter of adjusting as necessary based on change events for each user's mailbox.

MAPI

Unity uses MAPI to send messages and interact with subscribers homed on MS Exchange. In a lot of ways, Unity behaves as a normal MS Outlook client. In most ways, however, Unity's use of MAPI is truly server-based and more optimized than the normal Outlook client. The optimizations are made to the normal MAPI profile that Unity creates and uses during installation. These optimizations are done so that Unity can log onto many mailboxes at once and register to receive notifications of changes on many inboxes (Exchange-Monitor uses the same MAPI profile as the MAL).

Microsoft Outlook is no longer supported on the Cisco Unity server as of version 3.x. Instead, the Exchange 5.5 Administrator program is required on the Unity server for

Exchange 5.5 support, and the Exchange 2000 System Manager is required on the Unity server for Exchange 2000 support. These programs contain MAPI DLLS and MDAC releases pertinent to Unity's operations.

Unity uses MAPI and DUCS in the following ways:

- To log on to subscribers' mailboxes
- To check for messages (notification)
- To check mailbox size limits for subscribers
- To send voice messages on behalf of subscribers
- To send voice messages on behalf of outside callers
- To play back voice messages for subscribers
- To play back e-mail messages for subscribers
- To play back fax information for redirecting fax for subscribers

The MAL and the AvWm both wrap MAPI and DUCS API functions. This is done so that the MAL provides a common interface to high-level messaging clients, such as the conversation.

Startup and Initialization

While the Directory Abstraction Layer (DAL) component under the DOH is being phased out, the MAL wrapper around the messaging tasks likely lives on—for a while, at least. In of Exchange-connected Unity systems, the MAL uses MAPI client access methods similar to what an Outlook client does to gain access to a mailbox. During configuration setup, a special mailbox named Unity_(server name) is created on the Exchange server selected as the companion server for Unity (which could be on the same box with Unity). This mailbox is referred to as the Unity System Mailbox in the documentation.

At Unity's first mailbox logon, a MAPI profile is created on the local Unity server that points to the Unity System Mailbox. This message profile is necessary for any MAPI client and is similar to a profile created for your Outlook client that points back to the Exchange home server where your mailbox is stored. However, the Unity system mailbox profile is optimized in a couple of ways so that it can support hundreds of simultaneous MAPI connections that are not possible with a standard profile. In short, this profile gains access to all mailboxes for subscribers serviced on the local Unity server.

The configuration information in the profile is not used directly by any Unity code. Instead, it exists as configuration information for the MAPI subsystem, allowing Unity to log onto the Unity System Mailbox and enable ExchangeMonitor to register for notifications of changes to multiple Unity subscriber inboxes. The DOH used to check for the existence of the profile and the Unity System Account at startup, and create them if they did not exist. That is not the case anymore with Unity 4.0. If the profile or the Unity System Account do not exist at startup, they are not be created until the first MAPI logon. This allows Unity to start in case its companion Exchange server is down.

In the case of Domino, the DOH uses the Notes client interface (which must be installed on each Unity server) to access messages for subscribers and send messages of its own. The Domino Server sees Unity as a client, but the user ID that Unity uses to log in has rights to the server's address book and the administrative request database. This allows the Unity system to log into subscribers' mailboxes and access the directory (address book) information.

When subscribers dial into Unity over the telephone, they log in by entering their extension and password. Unity checks Exchange for the mailbox size limitations to determine whether there are any restrictions. Unity walks the subscribers through the conversation. At this point, if the subscribers choose to listen to messages, they can do so by selecting from the touchtone conversation.

Conversation Use of Messaging Components

The Unity conversation component is the major client of the abstraction layer (the MAL) around the mail store. After all, the conversation drives core messaging-related functions such as these:

- Outside caller messages
- Subscriber-to-subscriber messages
- The notification process
- ExchangeMonitor
- DominoMonitor
- TUI message retrieval

Outside Caller Messages

The name *outside caller* suggests that the caller originates outside of the telephone network that Unity is connected to. In one example, the caller calls from a cell phone trying to reach an employee who is a Unity subscriber. That employee has his phone forwarded to voice mail in a "no answer" condition. When Unity answers the call, it checks the ID (provided by caller ID) of the caller to determine whether the caller is a known Unity subscriber. In this case, the caller is not a Unity subscriber. That is where the term *outside caller* originates. This caller also can be thought of a nonsubscriber caller or an unidentified caller. In another example, the caller calls from a phone that is connected to the same telephone system as Unity. The caller is trying to reach an employee who is a Unity subscriber. That employee has his phone forwarded to voice mail in a "no answer" condition. When Unity answers the call, it checks the ID (provided by caller ID) of the caller to determine whether the caller is a known Unity subscriber. Let's assume that the caller ID of the "interna" phone does not match the ID of a Unity subscriber. This caller will also be considered an "outside caller." Whether the caller is outside is determined when the caller's caller ID is recognized as being associated with a Unity subscriber. Technically, it has nothing to do with the origin of the call.

Figure 5-1 provides a simple flowchart that demonstrates when an outside caller message is created. Besides being created for a true unidentified caller, an outside caller message is created in a couple of other instances; we cover these in the "Subscriber-to-Subscriber Messages" section.

Figure 5-1   *Simple Decision Process for Creation of Subscriber-to-Subscriber or Outside Caller Message*

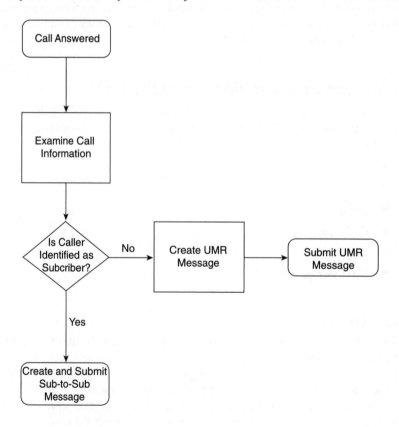

We now walk through an example call in which a message is left for Unity subscriber 1234. The caller is an outside caller.

A call has been forwarded from a Unity subscriber's extension to the Unity server. Unity answers the call and, from the integration information provided, knows that the call was forwarded from extension 1234. Also in that call information is the caller's ID. In this example, the caller is called from a phone outside of the telephone network to which Unity is directly connected.

Unity checks the caller ID to see if it matches the DTMF ID of a Unity subscriber. Because the caller ID does not match a known Unity subscriber, the conversation creates an outside caller message. The conversation checks the mailbox status of the Unity subscriber that matched the called ID, also known as the message recipient. This status check is made to see if the message recipient's inbox can receive messages. In other words, it makes a full mailbox check.

A quick note about full mailboxes and the Unity messaging process is necessary here. In Unity 3.1(5) and later, the PHGreeting conversation, by default, makes a quick check to ensure that the subscriber whom the message will be sent to does not have a full inbox before it takes a message for that user. Checking the status of a mailbox across the network sometimes can be a slow process, so this check can be disabled via a Registry edit (see the Advanced Settings tool for this), although doing so is not a good idea; it is better to fix the source of the network latency.

If Unity takes a message from an outside caller for a subscriber who has a full mailbox, the UMR ends up delivering it to the mail store, which, of course, rejects its delivery to that box and bounces the mail back to the Unity Messaging System account. The message is forwarded to the Unaddressed Messages public distribution list for handling, in that case. The check for a full mailbox is made *only* when an outside caller leaves messages for individual subscribers. Subscriber-to-subscriber messages always are sent through the mail-store back end. For instance, if you log in as a subscriber and send a message to another subscriber who has a full mailbox, it is sent just as if you delivered it through an e-mail client. The mail server sends it back to you nondelivery receipt (NDR), indicating that the user's mailbox is full.

Assuming that the subscriber at extension 1234 has kept the inbox to a reasonable level, the PHGreeting conversation sends the record request to the MIU, and the caller records a message. After the MIU has completed recording the message by timing out on silence or the user enters a DTMF to terminate the record session, the handle to the resulting file is passed back to the conversation. In this case, because the message is from an unidentified caller, the PHGreeting conversation goes through the UMR component to leave the message for the target user. If instead either the caller first signed into Unity as a subscriber and then left a message, or the extension corresponded to a subscriber on the local Unity server, the PHGreeting conversation would have submitted the message to the DOH. Then the DOH would have delivered it from the sender's mailbox directly. In this way, the message is actually from the sender, so the person getting the message, either over the phone or through the inbox client, can simply reply to it directly.

When the UMR process running under AvCsMgr gets the message, it writes two files out to the \Commserver\UnityMTA directory. One file is the WAV file for the recorded message itself. The other is the routing file that indicates to the AvUMRSyncSvr service where it should ask the mail store to deliver the message when it picks it up.

The message is not yet in the mailbox of the target subscriber at this point; it is sitting as a pair of files in the \Commserver\UnityMTA directory. The UMRSyncSvr service notices that there are files in the UnityMTA directory because a programmatic event is set for the UMRSyncSvr when the files are placed in the UnityMTA directory. The UMRSyncSvr picks up these files to deliver to the appropriate mailbox. It uses its own copy of the DOH to deliver the message to the mailbox of the target subscriber using the MAL interface. In the case of Exchange, the message is sent from the Unity Messaging System account that resides on the Exchange server selected during the configuration setup.

You will notice in the architecture diagrams in Chapter 2, "Unity Architecture Overview," that the AvUMRSyncSvr has an instance of the AvWM component running as well. It uses this component specifically to determine whether the Exchange server where the Unity Messaging System account resides and the Exchange server that houses the message recipient's mailbox are currently available. If not, it does not attempt to deliver the message in the UnityMTA directory. Instead, the message is considered to be in UMR mode, and the message recipient subscriber is allowed to access voice-mail messages residing in the UnityMTA directory until connectivity is restored.

To see the outside message-delivery process a little better, it is instructive to look at some diagnostics. For those following along at home, go ahead and open the Unity Diagnostic Tool, found in the Tools Depot or the Unity program group. Select Configure Micro Traces and expand the UMR section. You will see a number of trace options there; in this case, we just want to see when messages are added to the UnityMTA directory and when they are picked up and delivered. Turn on traces 10, "General UMR Sync Thread," and 12, "MTA Walk Through."

Here, MTA stands for Message Transfer Agent. This is technically an Exchange 5.5–specific term, but it applies to all the mail-store back ends that Unity supports. Trace 12 is actually the UMR component that runs under AvCsMgr that the PHGreeting conversation talks to when submitting the outside caller message. Because it runs under the AvCsMgr process, it logs its diagnostic output to the diag_AvCsMgrxxx.txt file. When you finish the Micro Trace Wizard, you might want to select the Start New Log Files option to cycle the diagnostic trace logs and make it easier to see what you were looking for.

After you leave an outside caller message, you can open the diag_AvCsMgrxxx.txt and diag_UMRSyncSvrxxx.txt files in the \Commserver\Logs directory directly and view the output, as shown in Example 5-1. The traces are more readable when they are formatted. To do this, again use the UDT and select the Gather Traces option to collect the files noted previously and save them in formatted output. After formatting, the file is appended with a _fmtd.txt extension. All trace output shown in this document is formatted.

Example 5-1 *AvUmrSyncSvr Trace File Example*

```
08:14:17:375 (AvUMR_MC,152,UMR,12) MTA Directory: =C:\CommServer\unityMta\ on line
330 of e:\views\Unity3.1.3.23\un_Conv3\UnityUMR\UnityMTA\AvMtaSession.cpp

08:14:17:376 (AvUMR_MC,152,UMR,12) New MTA Message file Name=C:\CommServer\
  unityMta\JLindborg_20020728_081417375_cbe96ed3-5245-47d0-b1ea-f67da7279c2c on
  line 101 of e:\views\Unity3.1.3.23\un_Conv3\UnityUMR\UnityMTA\AvMtaSession.cpp

08:14:17:375 (AvUMR_MC,153,UMR,12) CAvMtaMessage::GetAudioStream() : New Message
  Stream on line 343 of e:\views\Unity3.1.3.23\un_Conv3\UnityUMR\UnityMTA\
  AvMtaMessage.cpp
```

We should note a couple of things about trace output in general before moving on. The lines of code noted by components always reference drive letters, as in e:\..., even though the Unity server might not have an E drive. This is actually the drive configuration of the server that stores and builds the Unity code; it has nothing to do with the local Unity install. This information is useful only to development folks who might be tracking down a problem. The first column always contains the time/date stamp; the sixth and seventh columns contain the trace category (UMR, in this case) and the trace number that generated the output (12, in this case). This holds true for all diagnostic trace output and can be handy if you want to extract information for a specific trace from, say, the diag_AvCsMgrxxx.txt file, which can contain a very large amount of output if you have any number of traces turned on.

In this case, you can see that the new message that arrived resulted in a file being created in the C:\Commserver\UnityMTA\ directory named JLindborg_20020710_1819_d702ea8b-5412-4ea2-bc33-9e6c821c51ed. Two files with that name appear in the directory: one with a .WAV file extension, which is the voice message itself, and one with a .TXT extension, which is the routing file that the AvUMRSyncSvr service uses when addressing the message. If you want to see this, you can just stop the AvUMRSyncSvr service and leave an outside caller message. This does not prevent Unity from running normally, other than the fact that outside caller messages are not delivered while it is offline. If you do this and open the .TXT file, it will look something like Example 5-2.

Example 5-2 *Contents of UMR Text File for Addressing Message*

```
RecipientAlias:JLindborg
To:
Subject:Message from an unidentified caller
Priority:1
Sensitivity:0
Date:1026351166
X-AvMailHandlerId:=?unicode?b?AQAHADAAMwA6AHsANgAxAEIAMAA2ADMANwBFAC0AQQAyADQANwA
  tADQAQQBFAEUALQBCADkANQAyAC0ANgAzADAAOABEADkARgA1AEIAQQA1ADUAfQAAAA==?=
```

UMRSyncSvr uses the RecipientAlias field to address the message. If the calling number was collected from the switch and passed on, the subject field would contain that information. In this case, the calling number did not come through in the integration, so the generic, "Message from an unidentified caller," is used by default. Currently, this is not configurable. The priority and sensitivity fields are the same ones that you have access to when sending an e-mail using the desktop client. AvMailHandlerID is the Unicode format for the ObjectID of the primary call handler for the subscriber. When the UMR sends the message, it uses this ID to find the primary call handler and then find the mail user associated with it. The UMR grabs the data from there to fill in the message send information that it passes to Exchange. You can copy and paste this string into DOHPropTest's Find By ObjectID dialog box. DOHPropTest translates this string into a regular object ID and finds the call handler for you, which can be handy for tracking down problems here.

If you fire up the AvUMRSyncSvr service again (or if you left it alone to begin with), it picks up the pair of files and delivers the message to the mail-store back end. It does this by spinning up its own instance of the DOH and delivering the message from the Unity Messaging System Account created by Unity setup. If you take a look at the diag_ AvUMRSyncSvrxxx.txt file, it will look something like Example 5-3.

Example 5-3   *Example Diagnostics of UMR Message Delivery*

```
08:14:26:953 (AvUMR_MC,150,UMR,10) [Thread 0x00000E28] Proceeding to deliver
  messages from UMR on line 413 of e:\views\Unity3.1.3.23\un_Conv3\UnityUMR\
  AvUMRSyncSvr\UMRThread.cpp

08:14:27:031 (AvUMR_MC,150,UMR,10) [Thread 0x00000E28] Message for [JLindborg] in
  the UMR on line 995 of e:\views\Unity3.1.3.23\un_Conv3\UnityUMR\AvUMRSyncSvr\
  UMRThread.cpp

08:14:27:125 (AvUMR_MC,150,UMR,10) [Thread 0x00000E28] Message delivered on line
  514 of e:\views\Unity3.1.3.23\un_Conv3\UnityUMR\AvUMRSyncSvr\UMRThread.cpp

08:14:27:126 (AvUMR_MC,150,UMR,10) [Thread 0x00000E28] No more messages in the UMR
  on line 615 of e:\views\Unity3.1.3.23\un_Conv3\UnityUMR\AvUMRSyncSvr\UMRThread.cpp

08:14:27:125 (AvUMR_MC,150,UMR,10) [Thread 0x00000E28] No messages in the UMR wait
  till we have more messages on line 339 of e:\views\Unity3.1.3.23\un_Conv3\
  UnityUMR\AvUMRSyncSvr\UMRThread.cpp
```

You can see that the AvUMRSyncSvr picked up the message bound for the subscriber with the alias of JLindborg, then noted that it delivered it, and then noted that there are no more messages in the UnityMTA directory to be delivered. The last line is just a note that it will wait until more files arrive in the UnityMTA directory.

If the UMRSyncSvr service gets an error back from the mail server (for instance, the RecipientAlias does not exist in its directory) when it attempts to deliver the message, the pair of files will be moved to the \Commserver\UnityMTA\Failed\ directory. The AvUMRSyncSvr attempts to deliver these failed messages periodically and logs errors to the event log to let you know that there is a problem. In earlier versions of Unity, a failed message delivery backed up the UnityMTA directory, and nothing behind the bad message got through. Starting in 3.1(4), the failed directory was used as a mechanism to get around this.

The first step in troubleshooting such a problem is to open the routing .TXT file. See where it attempts to send the message, and make sure that the destination exists and is accessible. As noted earlier, Exchange does not issue an error if the target mailbox is full; it simply sends the message as an NDR back to the sender. The conversations can be set to check the full mailbox condition for outside callers who want to leave messages to help prevent problems here.

Figure 5-2 shows a simple flow of the UMR's internal process after it has received a message.

In the case of Domino, the full mailbox state actually is not enforced by the messaging back end, as it is in Exchange. As such, Unity does not specifically warn users or prevent the sending or receiving of messages based on specific mailbox size restrictions. With Exchange, we have no choice because the mail store enforces it. Later versions of Domino might include stricter mailbox quota enforcement; at that point, Unity will need to check those limits and act accordingly.

Assuming that the message is handed off to the mail store properly in the last step and that the mail store then delivers the message to the mailbox of the target subscriber, this is where the notifier process kicks in.

Subscriber-to-Subscriber Messages

Subscriber-to-subscriber messages provide more functionality for the message recipient than outside caller messages. First, a message recipient of a subscriber-to-subscriber message can reply to the message sender. The reply is analogous to the reply provided by an e-mail client; it offers a simple way to respond to the original message. This functionality also sometimes is referred to as identified subscriber messaging (ISM).

Another extra feature of subscriber-to-subscriber messages is that the message recipient hears the name of the message sender (if the message sender previously recorded a voice name) upon TUI message retrieval.

So, if subscriber 1234 is Jeff Lindborg, and Jeff has recorded his name, then when the message recipient of Jeff's message listens to the message through the TUI, the recipient hears, "Message from <recorded voice name that Jeff recorded>." If the message recipient checks the message through VMO, the message is from Jeff Lindborg (instead of "Message from an unknown caller") as well.

Figure 5-2   *UMR Message Processing*

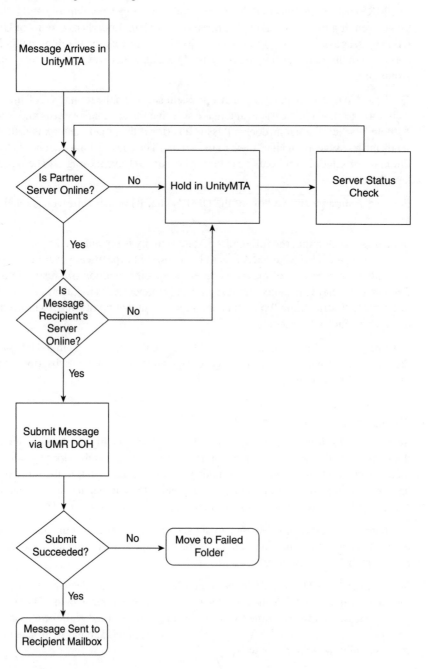

Subscriber-to-subscriber messages also provide extra functionality for the message sender. The vast majority of the time (we later cover a few cases in which this is different), the message sender can mark the sub-to-sub message for future delivery, for private delivery, and can include a return receipt.

Subscriber-to-subscriber messaging can come into effect in a couple of different ways: The caller has called Unity, signed into the voice-mail box, and begins message addressing; or the caller calls another Unity subscriber, that subscriber's phone forwards the call to the Unity server (assuming that the telephone system integration method provides both the caller and called ID in the integration information provided to Unity), and a message for the called subscriber is taken.

Normally, when a subscriber-to-subscriber message is left, the message is sent from the e-mail account that belongs to the caller. This is different than with UMR messages, which are sent from the mailbox owned by the Unity System Account. Unity logs into the mailbox of the messages sender and submits the message to the recipient as if Unity was the message sender. However, there are a couple of different ways in which a message that normally would be sent from the caller's mailbox is sent through the UMR.

This can happen if either the partner Exchange server is down or the message sender's Exchange server is down. (Because sub-to-sub messaging happens by sending from the caller's e-mail box, this is not really possible when that server is down. There is also a dependency on the partner mail server on Exchange-connected Unity systems to be operational even if the message sender's e-mail box resides on an Exchange server that is different than Unity's partner server.) When either one of these servers is down during the subscriber-to-subscriber process, the conversation falls back and submits the message through the UMR. The conversation sets a property on the message that changes the sender so that it is not from the Unity System account, but from the caller instead. From the caller's perspective, ISM functionality, such as future delivery or return receipt, is not available. From the message recipient's perspective, however, it appears that the message was sent from the caller's e-mail box.

Figure 5-3 shows the conversation flow of a subscriber-to-subscriber message. This includes the two instances in which a sub-to-sub message actually traverses the UMR.

Now we take a look at some conversation/MIU traces for the subscriber-to-subscriber message-taking process. Some traces have been removed for clarity, but CDE 0 (High Level, method entry/exit), CDE 16 (Call Progress Diags), Conv PhoneHandler 10 (Call Progress), and MIUGeneral 12 (TAPI events) were set for Example 5-4.

Figure 5-3 *Message Spoofing Algorithm in UMR*

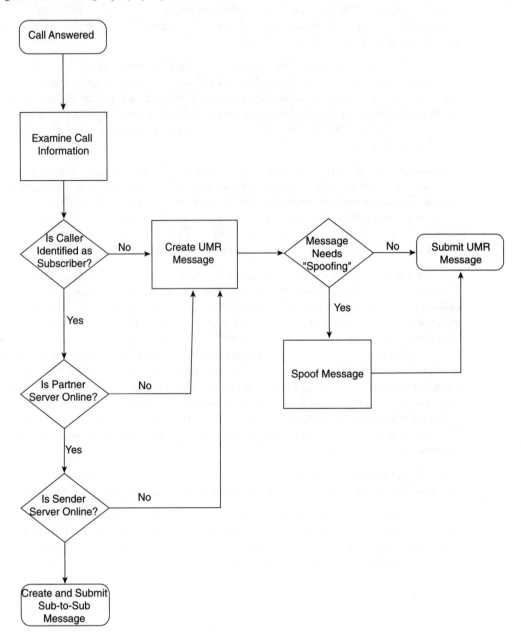

Example 5-4 *Conversation/MIU Traces for Subscriber-to-Subscriber Message Processing*

```
10:55:03:796 (CiscoUnity_Miu,642,MiuGeneral,12) [Thread 3568] [Thread 0x00000DF0]
   [Port 1] TAPI sent Tapi Message LINE_APPNEWCALL on HCALL 0x00010244 with Params
   (0x00000000 | 0x000101BB | 0x00000004).
10:55:03:797 (CiscoUnity_Miu,785,MiuGeneral,12) [Thread 2948] [Thread 0x00000B84]
   [Port 1] INTEGRATION CallInfo received (Origin Internal | Reason FwdUncond |
   CallerID 8102 | CalledID 8103 | RedirectingID 8103).
10:55:03:796 (CiscoUnity_ConvMsg,2001,CDE,0) [Thread 2948] Entering method
   CAvCDEConvBase::Run of conversation [AttemptForward]
10:55:03:797 (CiscoUnity_ConvMsg,2005,CDE,16) [Thread 2948] [Port 1] Entering
   conversation [AttemptForward]
10:55:03:796 (CiscoUnity_ConvPH,116,Conv PhoneHandler,10) [Thread 2948] [Port 1]
   Starting the phone handler conversation - Attempt Forward.
10:55:03:797 (CiscoUnity_ConvPH,122,Conv PhoneHandler,10) [Thread 2948] [Port 1]
   Re-Directing Id for the incoming call is 8103.
10:55:03:828 (CiscoUnity_ConvPH,112,Conv PhoneHandler,10) [Thread 2948] [Port 1]
   Call Handler for extension [8103] found on line 597 in file C:\Views\oliviers_
   402ES\un_Conv2\AvConvPhoneHandler\AvConvPHAttemptForwardSvr\
   AvConvPHAttemptForward.cpp
10:55:03:829 (CiscoUnity_ConvPH,124,Conv PhoneHandler,10) [Thread 2948] [Port 1]
   the re-directing Id matches a subscriber extension. Routing to the subscribers
   primary call handler.
10:55:03:828 (CiscoUnity_ConvMsg,2005,CDE,16) [Thread 2948] [Port 1] Exiting
   conversation [AttemptForward]
10:55:03:829 (CiscoUnity_ConvMsg,2002,CDE,0) [Thread 2948] [Port 1] Exiting method
   CAvCDEConvBase::Run normally for conversation [AttemptForward]
10:55:03:828 (CiscoUnity_ConvMsg,2001,CDE,0) [Thread 2948] Entering method
   CAvCDEConvBase::Run of conversation [PHTransfer]
10:55:03:829 (CiscoUnity_ConvMsg,2005,CDE,16) [Thread 2948] [Port 1] Entering
   conversation [PHTransfer]
10:55:03:828 (CiscoUnity_ConvMsg,2005,CDE,16) [Thread 2948] [Port 1] Conversation
   [PHTransfer]: GetPropObject(CurEnt) returned [0x00000000]
10:55:03:843 (CiscoUnity_ConvMsg,2003,CDE,0) [Thread 2948] [Port 1] Entering method
   OnEntry() of state [PHTransfer LoadInfo]
10:55:03:891 (CiscoUnity_ConvMsg,10001,-1,-1) [Thread 2948] Running conversation
   PHTransfer on Port 1
10:55:03:937 (CiscoUnity_ConvMsg,2005,CDE,16) [Thread 2948] [Port 1] Exiting
   conversation [PHTransfer]
10:55:03:938 (CiscoUnity_ConvMsg,2002,CDE,0) [Thread 2948] [Port 1] Exiting method
   CAvCDEConvBase::Run normally for conversation [PHTransfer]
10:55:03:937 (CiscoUnity_ConvMsg,2001,CDE,0) [Thread 2948] Entering method
   CAvCDEConvBase::Run of conversation [PHGreeting]
10:55:03:938 (CiscoUnity_ConvMsg,2005,CDE,16) [Thread 2948] [Port 1] Entering
   conversation [PHGreeting]
10:55:03:937 (CiscoUnity_ConvMsg,2003,CDE,0) [Thread 2948] [Port 1] Entering method
   OnEntry of state [Play Greeting]
10:55:04:093 (CiscoUnity_PHGreeting,124,ConvPH Greeting,10) [Thread 2948] [Port 1]
   Call answered if needed on line 221 in file C:\Views\oliviers_402ES\un_Conv2\
   AvConvPhoneHandler\AvConvPHGreetingSvr\AvSPlayGreeting.cpp C:\Views\oliviers_
   402ES\un_Conv2\AvConvPhoneHandler\AvConvPHGreetingSvr\AvSPlayGreeting.cpp
10:55:04:125 (CiscoUnity_PHGreeting,119,ConvPH Greeting,10) [Thread 2948] [Port 1]
   [Number of Objects matching extension at the default location level = 1] on line
   4978 in file C:\Views\oliviers_402ES\un_Conv2\AvConvPhoneHandler\
   AvConvPHGreetingSvr\AvSPlayGreeting.cpp (null)
10:55:04:126 (CiscoUnity_PHGreeting,107,ConvPH Greeting,10) [Thread 2948] [Port 1]
   Validating of the caller ID returned [0x00000000] on line 303 of file C:\Views\
   oliviers_402ES\un_Conv2\AvConvPhoneHandler\AvConvPHGreetingSvr\
   AvSPlayGreeting.cpp
```

continues

Example 5-4 *Conversation/MIU Traces for Subscriber-to-Subscriber Message Processing (Continued)*

```
10:55:04:125 (CiscoUnity_PHGreeting,125,ConvPH Greeting,10) [Thread 2948] [Port 1]
 Internal call from extension 8102 on line 351 in file C:\Views\oliviers_402ES\un_
 Conv2\AvConvPhoneHandler\AvConvPHGreetingSvr\AvSPlayGreeting.cpp (null)
10:55:04:312 (CiscoUnity_PHGreeting,131,ConvPH Greeting,10) [Thread 2948] [Port 1]
 [Standard] message rule is actived on line 2208 in file C:\Views\oliviers_402ES\
 un_Conv2\AvConvPhoneHandler\AvConvPHGreetingSvr\AvSPlayGreeting.cpp (null)
10:55:04:328 (CiscoUnity_PHGreeting,149,ConvPH Greeting,10) [Thread 2948] [Port 1]
 'AvConvPhRes'  '2'  'BTestUser 0testB1045'.
10:55:04:343 (CiscoUnity_PHGreeting,149,ConvPH Greeting,10) [Thread 2948] [Port 1]
 (SystemStandard) greeting for call handler id (null) with alias 1045..
10:55:07:734 (CiscoUnity_PHGreeting,133,ConvPH Greeting,10) [Thread 2948] [Port 1]
 Creating subscriber's message on line 4229 in file C:\Views\oliviers_402ES\un_
 Conv2\AvConvPhoneHandler\AvConvPHGreetingSvr\AvSPlayGreeting.cpp C:\Views\
 oliviers_402ES\un_Conv2\AvConvPhoneHandler\AvConvPHGreetingSvr\
 AvSPlayGreeting.cpp
10:55:07:921 (CiscoUnity_PHGreeting,107,ConvPH Greeting,10) [Thread 2948] [Port 1]
 CheckMailServerStatus returned [0x00000000] on line 4503 of file C:\Views\
 oliviers_402ES\un_Conv2\AvConvPhoneHandler\AvConvPHGreetingSvr\AvSPlayGreeting.cpp
10:55:07:921 (CiscoUnity_PHGreeting,107,ConvPH Greeting,10) [Thread 2948] [Port 1]
 IAvDohSession::get_OutsideCaller returned [0x00000000] on line 4524 of file C:\
 Views\oliviers_402ES\un_Conv2\AvConvPhoneHandler\AvConvPHGreetingSvr\
 AvSPlayGreeting.cpp
10:55:07:922 (CiscoUnity_PHGreeting,107,ConvPH Greeting,10) [Thread 2948] [Port 1]
 CheckMailServerStatus returned [0x00000000] on line 4536 of file C:\Views\
 oliviers_402ES\un_Conv2\AvConvPhoneHandler\AvConvPHGreetingSvr\
 AvSPlayGreeting.cpp
10:55:07:921 (CiscoUnity_PHGreeting,107,ConvPH Greeting,10) [Thread 2948] [Port 1]
 ::QueryInterface(IID_IAvDohMailUser) returned [0x00000000] on line 4553 of file
 C:\Views\oliviers_402ES\un_Conv2\AvConvPhoneHandler\AvConvPHGreetingSvr\
 AvSPlayGreeting.cpp
10:55:07:922 (CiscoUnity_PHGreeting,107,ConvPH Greeting,10) [Thread 2948] [Port 1]
 CheckMailServerStatus returned [0x00000000] on line 4558 of file C:\Views\
 oliviers_402ES\un_Conv2\AvConvPhoneHandler\AvConvPHGreetingSvr\
 AvSPlayGreeting.cpp
10:55:07:953 (CiscoUnity_PHGreeting,107,ConvPH Greeting,10) [Thread 2948] [Port 1]
 GetMailBoxStatus returned [0x00000000] on line 4584 of file C:\Views\oliviers_
 402ES\un_Conv2\AvConvPhoneHandler\AvConvPHGreetingSvr\AvSPlayGreeting.cpp
10:55:07:968 (CiscoUnity_PHGreeting,107,ConvPH Greeting,10) [Thread 2948] [Port 1]
 CreateSubscriberMsg returned [0x00000000] on line 4238 of file C:\Views\oliviers_
 402ES\un_Conv2\AvConvPhoneHandler\AvConvPHGreetingSvr\AvSPlayGreeting.cpp
10:55:07:969 (CiscoUnity_PHGreeting,135,ConvPH Greeting,10) [Thread 2948] [Port 1]
 Adding recipient to message on line 4258 in file C:\Views\oliviers_402ES\un_Conv2\
 AvConvPhoneHandler\AvConvPHGreetingSvr\AvSPlayGreeting.cpp C:\Views\oliviers_
 402ES\un_Conv2\AvConvPhoneHandler\AvConvPHGreetingSvr\AvSPlayGreeting.cpp
10:55:08:015 (CiscoUnity_PHGreeting,107,ConvPH Greeting,10) [Thread 2948] [Port 1]
 SendSubscriberMessage returned [0x00000000] on line 3881 of file C:\Views\
 oliviers_402ES\un_Conv2\AvConvPhoneHandler\AvConvPHGreetingSvr\AvSPlayGreeting.cpp
10:55:08:016 (CiscoUnity_ConvMsg,2004,CDE,0) [Thread 2948] [Port 1] Exiting method
 OnEntry normally for state [Play Greeting]
10:55:08:015 (CiscoUnity_ConvMsg,2003,CDE,0) [Thread 2948] [Port 1] Entering method
 OnExit of state [Play Greeting]
10:55:08:016 (CiscoUnity_ConvMsg,2004,CDE,0) [Thread 2948] [Port 1] Exiting method
 OnExit normally for state [Play Greeting]
10:55:08:031 (CiscoUnity_ConvMsg,2003,CDE,0) [Thread 2948] [Port 1] Entering method
 OnEntry of state [Record Message]
```

Example 5-4 *Conversation/MIU Traces for Subscriber-to-Subscriber Message Processing (Continued)*

```
10:55:09:828 (CiscoUnity_ConvMsg,2004,CDE,0) [Thread 2948] [Port 1] Exiting method
  OnEntry normally for state [Record Message]
10:55:09:843 (CiscoUnity_ConvMsg,2003,CDE,0) [Thread 2948] [Port 1] Entering method
  OnEntry of state [Send Message]
10:55:09:844 (CiscoUnity_ConvMsg,2015,CDE,16) [Thread 2948] [Port 1] [Message
  Recipients = 1]
```

The conversation has access to the call information that is present on the call object provided by the MIU. That call information can be seen here:

```
CallInfo received (Origin Internal I Reason FwdUncond I CallerID 8102 I CalledID 8103
  I RedirectingID 8103).
```

In the conversation's AttemptForward state, there is a database lookup to see whether the called party is indeed a Unity subscriber. That is shown here:

```
Call Handler for extension [8103] found
the re-directing Id matches a subscriber extension. Routing to the subscribers
  primary call handler.
```

The conversation checks the caller ID to see if it is also a subscriber. That can be seen here:

```
Validating of the caller ID returned [0x00000000]
Internal call from extension 8102
```

At this point, the conversation continues down the path of creating a subscriber-to-subscriber message:

```
Creating subscriber's message
```

Continuing on, the status of the message sender's exchange server is checked through the AvWm:

```
CheckMailServerStatus returned [0x00000000]
```

Now the partner server (Unity's outside caller always resides on the partner server):

```
IAvDohSession::get_OutsideCaller returned [0x00000000]
CheckMailServerStatus returned [0x00000000]
```

All is well so far, so the conversation continues along. If the check against the sender's server of the partner server had failed, the conversation would have fallen back to creating an outside caller message, but it would have set the sender to the ID of the caller. At this point, the message is recorded and sent:

```
Entering method OnEntry of state [Send Message]
[Message Recipients = 1]
```

As with the sending of an outside caller message, the message is delivered to the inbox of the recipient, and the notification process kicks in.

The Notification Process

The notification process allows Unity to enable or disable MWI and provide dialout or pager notification for letting Unity subscribers know that a message has arrived in the inbox. Whether Unity is connected to Exchange or Domino, the concepts behind the notification process are the same. Here is a basic rundown:

1 A request is made to the mail system to notify Unity of changes in a Unity subscriber's mailbox.

2 When a change occurs in that inbox, Unity is notified and the notification process begins.

3 Components inside Unity act upon the notification events to make a decision about how a Unity subscriber is to be notified.

As mentioned previously, Unity must register with the mail system to receive updates about changes happening in a Unity subscriber's mailbox. The implementation of this registration process is different between Exchange and Domino, but the idea is the same.

First, the Message Store Monitor (ExchangeMonitor or DominoMonitor) that resides in the AvMsgStoreMonitorSvr service is notified as soon as a change occurs in the subscriber inbox.

We take a step back here to demonstrate how both ExchangeMonitor and DominoMonitor implement notifications with the mail server, and we examine some traces.

ExchangeMonitor

ExchangeMonitor uses functionality provided by MAPI to request notifications from the Exchange server when something has changed on a particular inbox. The technical details are pretty hairy, but the process can be visualized like this:

1 When the AvMsgStoreMonitorSvr service starts up, it grabs an instance of the NotifyQ (running in AvCsMgr) through the AvCsGateway.

2 As it starts up, the AvvMsgStoreMonitor pushes a resynch event onto the NotifyQ.

3 The notifier issues a request to ExchangeMonitor for the mailboxes of Unity subscribers configured for at least one type of message notification to be monitored.

4 ExchangeMonitor logs onto the Exchange mailbox of a requested user.

5 ExchangeMonitor loads the contents of the inbox into a table. This table corresponds to a table defined by MAPI and resides in ExchangeMonitor's memory.

6 ExchangeMonitor registers with Exchange to receive changes that occur on that table.

You can think of the table as containing rows (messages of the inbox) and columns (properties on those messages). If the inbox of that subscriber receives a new message, a row is added to the table. If a message has been changed (that is, it has been read), a row is modified. If a message has been deleted, a row is removed from the table. This all really starts to make sense if the MAPI notification diagnostics are enabled for ExchangeMonitor. You can expect to see writes to the diagnostic log that resemble TABLE_ROW_ADDED, TABLE_ROW_MODIFIED, and TABLE_ROW_DELETED for those respective events. Here is a simple example:

```
14:38:28:421 (CiscoUnity_ExchangeMonitor,1031,ExchangeMonitor,13) [Thread 3756]
[Thread 0x00000EAC] Table notification received (TABLE_ROW_ADDED for cn=Otest
cn=Recipients ou=First Administrative Group o=First Organization)
```

This trace shows that a new message has arrived for user Otest. ExchangeMonitor ensures that this notification event from the Exchange sever was destined for a user whom ExchangeMonitor was monitoring (to weed out any possible rogue notifications). If it is for a recognized, monitored user, ExchangeMonitor pushes an event onto the NotifyQ.

From an ExchangeMonitor client's perspective, ExchangeMonitor supplies some core functions for the monitoring of a mailbox: monitor, unmonitor, and resynch.

Note that when Exchange is busy or too many changes take place on an inbox in too short of a time (the user deletes many messages at once, for instance), a table reload message is sent from Exchange, and the Message Store Monitor simply pushes a resynch event onto the notification queue for that mailbox. In this case, the notifier must filter the entire inbox to know what to do. In most cases, however, it is not necessary to filter the entire inbox; the notifier can determine what needs to be done specifically from the change notice that the Message Store Monitor pushes onto the queue. This makes it a little difficult to look at the diagnostics kicked out by the notifier and Message Store Monitor components; there is no hard and fast rule for when Exchange decides that it is too busy to issue a specific change request or a general resynch notice for an inbox.

DominoMonitor

The following traces are pulled from a Unity server hooked to a Domino back end with the DominoMonitor 12(MailboxLogon) diagnostic flag enabled. They show a new message arriving and then being read 10 minutes later:

Example 5-5 *DominoMonitor Traces Showing Inbox Count Change Processing*

```
15:45:50:094 (AvDominoMonitor_MC,1093,DominoMonitor,12) [Thread 1756] [Thread
0x000006DC] Received Notification packet from dna-test1:
<notification><handlerid>unitynotifier</handlerid><applicationdata></
applicationdata><user></user><database>bQBhAGkAbABcAGYAbABkADEALgBuAHMAZgA=</
database><event>NewMessage</event><newmessagedata><type>V</type><priority>N</
priority><sender>ZgAyAF8AbAAyAC8ARABuAGEAZABvAG0AJQBjAG8AbQAlAGMAbwBtAAA=</
sender><subject>TQBlAHMAcwBhAGcAZQAgAEYAcgBvAG0AIABVAG4AaQB0AHkA</
subject><id>2330</id></newmessagedata></notification>
```

continues

Example 5-5 *DominoMonitor Traces Showing Inbox Count Change Processing (Continued)*

```
15:45:50:093 (AvDominoMonitor_MC,1096,DominoMonitor,12) [Thread 1756] [Thread
   0x000006DC] Received NewMessage Notification packet: Type:V; Prio:N; From:f2_12/
   Dnadom%com%com; Subj:Message From Unity; ID:2330

15:45:52:562 (AvDominoMonitor_MC,1093,DominoMonitor,12) [Thread 1756] [Thread
   0x000006DC] Received Notification packet from dna-test1:
   <notification><handlerid>unitynotifier</handlerid><applicationdata></
   applicationdata><user></user><database>bQBhAGkAbABcAGYAbABkADEALgBuAHMAZgA=</
   database><event>CountChange</event><countchangedata><count>2</count></
   countchangedata><id>2330</id><priority>N</priority><type>V</type><eventtype>1</
   eventtype></notification>

15:45:52:563 (AvDominoMonitor_MC,1094,DominoMonitor,12) [Thread 1756] [Thread
   0x000006DC] Received CountChange Notification packet: Cnt:2; ID:2330; Prio:N;
   Type:V; EType:1;

16:10:18:074 (AvDominoMonitor_MC,1093,DominoMonitor,12) [Thread 1756] [Thread
   0x000006DC] Received Notification packet from dna-test1:
   <notification><handlerid>unitynotifier</handlerid><applicationdata></
   applicationdata><user></user><database>bQBhAGkAbABcAGYAbABkADEALgBuAHMAZgA=</
   database><event>CountChange</event><countchangedata><count>1</count></
   countchangedata><id>2330</id><priority>2</priority><type>V</type><eventtype>6</
   eventtype></notification>

16:10:18:075 (AvDominoMonitor_MC,1094,DominoMonitor,12) [Thread 1756] [Thread
   0x000006DC] Received CountChange Notification packet: Cnt:1; ID:2330; Prio:2;
   Type:V; EType:6;
```

Messages come in pairs, with one showing the raw HTML-like message coming in and the second showing what that message means to Unity. You can read through the first four messages there and reasonably easily tell that a new message has arrived for the user f2_l2 (yes, those are bulk-created users' names and are not real creative). You can see the type of V there, which stands for Voice, of course. You can also see F, E, I, R, O, for Fax, E-mail, Invitation, Report, and Other in this field. The message count noted in the third and fourth entries comes after the new arrival and simply notes that there are now two unread voice message counts.

The count returned in the packet indicates the number of unread messages for the specified type. If the type had been E, that would have indicated the number of unread e-mail messages that could be of interest for notification triggers set up to deliver a page (for instance, based on e-mail messages in the inbox). The deletion event (the last two entries) simply is noted as a message count state change. You can see that the count for voice-mail messages is now 1.

The Message Store Monitor pushes this information onto the notification queue running in the AvCsMgr process. This requires that the AvMsgStoreMonitorSvr first authenticate with the gateway to get at the queue. The notifier then picks this information out of the queue and decides what to do with it. In this case, we assume that subscriber 1234's lamp is not on and that no notification devices other than the MWI device itself are active. As such, the notifier adds the MWI upon request to the MWI device manager.

The MWI device manager then asks the resource manager if a port is available to do an MWI request. It makes this same request even if the MWIs are done through the serial port or a voice port. Assuming that a port is available, the resource manager reserves it for the MWI device manager and passes the reserved port ID back. The MWI device manager then sends this port ID to the Arbiter when it requests the actual dialout to turn on the lamp.

The MWI device manager waits until the Arbiter returns success or failure for the MWI request. If it fails, the Arbiter requeues the request to try again 5 minutes later, for five retries. It considers the MWI attempt to have failed only after the total number of retries has been exhausted. When the MWI request either has succeeded or failed, it pushes this result back onto the notification queue to let the notifier know that it has been completed. The MWI device manager also takes care of updating the subscriber's record to indicate that Unity thinks that the MWI lamp is on; this shows up on the messages page in the SA for the subscriber as the current Indicator Lamps status. The DOH is used to write this through to the local SQL record. The lamp status of the subscriber is not written through to the directory, so the directory monitor is not involved here.

This step covers a lot of ground, and some of those steps happen outside of the realm of messaging. Let us again turn on some traces for the components in question and walk through the output you would see from the previous example scenario. In this case, we want to turn on traces for the Message Store Monitor (ExchangeMonitor or DominoMonitor), notifier, and the MWI device manager running under the AvCsMgr service. In the Unity Diagnostic Tool, return to the micro traces section and, in the notifier section, turn on traces 12, "MWI Device," and 21, "NotifyQ." Both of these traces write into the AvCsMgr diagnostic file because these processes run under that service. If you open that diagnostic file, you will see something like the diagnostics in Example 5-6.

Example 5-6 *AvNotifierMgr Diagnostics Showing MWI Processing*

```
08:14:27:937 (AvNotifier_MC,1146,Notifier,21) [Thread 0x00000DA8] NotifyQ popped
  eNOTIFYQ_ACTION_MSG_NEW [2], mailbox='cn=JLindborg cn=Recipients ou=First
  Administrative Group o=E2KDomain', arg1=2, arg2=3, arg3=1, varMessageData=
  (UnexpectedVariantType:8209!!).

08:14:27:938 (AvNotifier_MC,1158,Notifier,12) [Thread 0x00000DA8] Jeff
  Lindborg:MWI-1(1189), 1 messages (message just Added), current status Off, current
  attempt None

08:14:27:937 (AvNotifier_MC,1113,Notifier,12) [Thread 0x00000DA8] Queued MWI task
  for mailuser=Jeff Lindborg, extension=1189, status=On

08:14:27:984 (AvNotifier_MC,1108,Notifier,12) [Thread 0x00000D7C] MWI Device - MWI
  Entry AV_MWI_ON Received: Task Jeff Lindborg 1189 timestamp 1027869267, Port 4

08:14:30:812 (AvNotifier_MC,1146,Notifier,21) [Thread 0x00000DA8] NotifyQ popped
  eNOTIFYQ_ACTION_MWION_COMPLETE [7], mailbox='cn=JLindborg cn=Recipients ou=First
  Administrative Group o=E2KDomain', arg1=4, arg2=0, arg3=0, varMessageData='MWI-
  1' (VT_BSTR).

08:14:30:843 (AvNotifier_MC,1113,Notifier,12) [Thread 0x00000D7C] Completed MWI
  task for mailuser=Jeff Lindborg, extension=1189, status=On
```

The first entry is the notifier process under AvCsMgr picking up the message that the AvMsgStoreMonitor service wrote to the notifier queue when the new voice-mail message arrived in the mailbox. The notifier then takes action on that message by adding an item to the MWI device manager's queue (the second message in the trace). The MWI Device manager issues an MWI ON event, which completes, and then pushes an event back onto the notifier queue to that effect (the eNOTIFYQ_ACTION_MWION_COMPLETE message). What is not shown in the previous traces is the notifier acting on the MWI ON complete message and using the DOH to update the subscriber's record to indicate that the subscriber's lamp is now on (at least, as far as Unity knows).

One thing to note is that you will not always get the specific mail-store event from the Message Store Monitor (the eNOTIFYQ_ACTION_MSG_NEW event in the first line of the diagnostic output). Under normal circumstances, however, the Message Store Monitor gets a specific new\updated\deleted message notification that includes the message type.

TUI Message Retrieval

When a Unity subscriber makes a direct call to Unity, the conversation has access to the call information provided by the switch integration and the MIU. If the caller ID matches a Unity subscriber (either by the primary or an alternate user's extension), the conversation authenticates the caller by prompting for the voice-mail password. After the caller enters the correct password, the conversation offers a few choices of TUI functionality, including message retrieval.

Before messages are played over the TUI, the conversation checks the status of the mail server that contains the subscriber's mailbox. That status check uses the AvWm again. The conversation essentially causes a mailbox logon through the MAL for the mailbox that corresponds to the subscriber. When the mailbox is obtained, filters are placed on the inbox so that the subscriber can be offered messages based on type, priority, and number. The MAL handles the API work for the given connected mail server. Example 5-7 shows the conversation's processing of a TUI sign-in. Although the exact messaging-related functions to accomplish the mail server status check, mailbox logon, and inbox filter might not be clearly seen, the MAL and AvWm messaging components give the conversation this functionality. Diagnostic flags CDE 0 (High Level, method entry/exit), CDE 16 (Call Progress Diags), and Conv PhoneHandler 16 (Call Progress) were enabled for Example 5-7.

Example 5-7 *Conversation Diagnostics Showing Use of Messaging Components for Subscriber Sign-In*

```
10:53:42:125 (CiscoUnity_Miu,785,MiuGeneral,12) [Thread 796] [Thread 0x0000031C]
  [Port 1] INTEGRATION CallInfo received (Origin Internal I Reason Direct I CallerID
  8102 I CalledID 8200 I RedirectingID Unknown).
10:53:42:171 (CiscoUnity_ConvMsg,2001,CDE,0) [Thread 796] Entering method
  CAvCDEConvBase::Run of conversation [AttemptSignIn]
10:53:42:172 (CiscoUnity_ConvMsg,2005,CDE,16) [Thread 796] [Port 1] Entering
  conversation [AttemptSignIn]
```

Example 5-7 *Conversation Diagnostics Showing Use of Messaging Components for Subscriber Sign-In (Continued)*

```
10:53:42:187 (CiscoUnity_ConvPH,116,Conv PhoneHandler,10) [Thread 796] [Port 1]
   Starting the phone handler conversation - Attempt Sign-In.
10:53:42:188 (CiscoUnity_ConvPH,117,Conv PhoneHandler,10) [Thread 796] [Port 1]
   Caller Id for the incoming call is 8102.
10:53:42:328 (CiscoUnity_ConvPH,112,Conv PhoneHandler,10) [Thread 796] [Port 1]
   Call Handler for extension [8102] found on line 441 in file C:\Views\oliviers_
   402ES\un_Conv2\AvConvPhoneHandler\AvConvPHAttemptSignInSvr\
   AvConvPHAttemptSignIn.cpp
10:53:42:329 (CiscoUnity_ConvPH,118,Conv PhoneHandler,10) [Thread 796] [Port 1]
   Caller Id matches a subscriber extensions. Routing to Sign In conversation.
10:53:42:328 (CiscoUnity_ConvMsg,2005,CDE,16) [Thread 796] [Port 1] Exiting
   conversation [AttemptSignIn]
10:53:42:329 (CiscoUnity_ConvMsg,2002,CDE,0) [Thread 796] [Port 1] Exiting method
   CAvCDEConvBase::Run normally for conversation [AttemptSignIn]
10:53:42:328 (CiscoUnity_ConvMsg,2001,CDE,0) [Thread 796] Entering method
   CAvCDEConvBase::Run of conversation [SubSignIn]
10:53:42:329 (CiscoUnity_ConvMsg,2005,CDE,16) [Thread 796] [Port 1] Entering
   conversation [SubSignIn]
10:53:42:359 (CiscoUnity_ConvMsg,2003,CDE,0) [Thread 796] [Port 1] Entering method
   OnEntry of state [SubSignIn Answer Phone State]
10:53:42:546 (CiscoUnity_ConvMsg,2004,CDE,0) [Thread 796] [Port 1] Exiting method
   OnEntry normally for state [SubSignIn Answer Phone State]
10:53:42:547 (CiscoUnity_ConvMsg,2003,CDE,0) [Thread 796] [Port 1] Entering method
   OnEntry of state [SubSignIn Validate ID State]
10:53:42:656 (CiscoUnity_ConvMsg,2004,CDE,0) [Thread 796] [Port 1] Exiting method
   OnEntry normally for state [SubSignIn Validate ID State]
10:53:42:657 (CiscoUnity_ConvMsg,2003,CDE,0) [Thread 796] [Port 1] Entering method
   OnEntry of state [EnhancedSecurity State]
10:53:42:656 (CiscoUnity_ConvMsg,2004,CDE,0) [Thread 796] [Port 1] Exiting method
   OnEntry normally for state [EnhancedSecurity State]
10:53:42:657 (CiscoUnity_ConvMsg,2003,CDE,0) [Thread 796] [Port 1] Entering method
   OnEntry of state [SubSignIn Validate Password State]
10:53:45:703 (CiscoUnity_ConvMsg,2004,CDE,0) [Thread 796] [Port 1] Exiting method
   OnEntry normally for state [SubSignIn Validate Password State]
10:53:45:704 (CiscoUnity_ConvMsg,2003,CDE,0) [Thread 796] [Port 1] Entering method
   OnEntry of state [CheckIfExchangeDown State]
10:53:45:703 (CiscoUnity_ConvMsg,2003,CDE,0) [Thread 796] [Port 1] Entering method
   CheckIfExchangeDown of state [CheckIfExchangeDown State]
10:53:45:718 (CiscoUnity_ConvMsg,2004,CDE,0) [Thread 796] [Port 1] Exiting method
   CheckIfExchangeDown normally for state [CheckIfExchangeDown State]
10:53:45:719 (CiscoUnity_ConvMsg,2004,CDE,0) [Thread 796] [Port 1] Exiting method
   OnEntry normally for state [CheckIfExchangeDown State]
10:53:45:718 (CiscoUnity_ConvMsg,2003,CDE,0) [Thread 796] [Port 1] Entering method
   OnEntry of state [SubSignIn Check if New Mail User State]
10:53:45:719 (CiscoUnity_ConvMsg,2004,CDE,0) [Thread 796] [Port 1] Exiting method
   OnEntry normally for state [SubSignIn Check if New Mail User State]
10:53:45:718 (CiscoUnity_ConvMsg,2003,CDE,0) [Thread 796] [Port 1] Entering method
   OnEntry of state [SubSignIn Check For Leave Msg State]
10:53:45:719 (CiscoUnity_ConvMsg,2004,CDE,0) [Thread 796] [Port 1] Exiting method
   OnEntry normally for state [SubSignIn Check For Leave Msg State]
10:53:45:734 (CiscoUnity_ConvMsg,2003,CDE,0) [Thread 796] [Port 1] Entering method
   OnEntry of state [Send Message Setup State]
10:53:45:735 (CiscoUnity_ConvMsg,2004,CDE,0) [Thread 796] [Port 1] Exiting method
   OnEntry normally for state [Send Message Setup State]
```

continues

Example 5-7 *Conversation Diagnostics Showing Use of Messaging Components for Subscriber Sign-In (Continued)*

```
10:53:45:734 (CiscoUnity_ConvMsg,2003,CDE,0) [Thread 796] [Port 1] Entering method
   OnEntry of state [SubSignIn Run Next Conversation State]
10:53:45:735 (CiscoUnity_ConvMsg,2003,CDE,0) [Thread 796] [Port 1] Entering method
   NextState of state [SubSignIn Run Next Conversation State]
10:53:45:734 (CiscoUnity_ConvMsg,2004,CDE,0) [Thread 796] [Port 1] Exiting method
   NextState normally for state [SubSignIn Run Next Conversation State]
10:53:46:046 (CiscoUnity_ConvMsg,2005,CDE,16) [Thread 796] [Port 1] Exiting
   conversation [SubSignIn]
10:53:46:047 (CiscoUnity_ConvMsg,2002,CDE,0) [Thread 796] [Port 1] Exiting method
   CAvCDEConvBase::Run normally for conversation [SubSignIn]
10:53:46:046 (CiscoUnity_ConvMsg,2001,CDE,0) [Thread 796] Entering method
   CAvCDEConvBase::Run of conversation [SubMenu]
10:53:46:047 (CiscoUnity_ConvMsg,2005,CDE,16) [Thread 796] [Port 1] Entering
   conversation [SubMenu]
10:53:46:093 (CiscoUnity_ConvMsg,2002,CDE,0) [Thread 796] [Port 1] Exiting method
   LogSubActivity normally for conversation [SubMenu]
10:53:46:110 (CiscoUnity_ConvMsg,2003,CDE,0) [Thread 796] [Port 1] Entering method
   CreateSavedFaxFilter of state [Create filter state(root)]
10:53:46:109 (CiscoUnity_ConvMsg,2003,CDE,0) [Thread 796] [Port 1] Entering method
   CreatePersistentFilter of state [Create filter state(root)]
10:53:46:110 (CiscoUnity_ConvMsg,2004,CDE,0) [Thread 796] [Port 1] Exiting method
   CreatePersistentFilter normally for state [Create filter state(root)]
10:53:46:109 (CiscoUnity_ConvMsg,2004,CDE,0) [Thread 796] [Port 1] Exiting method
   CreateSavedFaxFilter normally for state [Create filter state(root)]
10:53:46:110 (CiscoUnity_ConvMsg,2004,CDE,0) [Thread 796] [Port 1] Exiting method
   OnEntry normally for state [Create filter state(root)]
10:53:46:109 (CiscoUnity_ConvMsg,2003,CDE,0) [Thread 796] [Port 1] Entering method
   OnEntry of state [Resume send message state.]
10:53:46:110 (CiscoUnity_ConvMsg,2004,CDE,0) [Thread 796] [Port 1] Exiting method
   OnEntry normally for state [Resume send message state.]
10:53:46:109 (CiscoUnity_ConvMsg,2003,CDE,0) [Thread 796] [Port 1] Entering method
   OnEntry of state [Run message count state]
10:53:46:125 (CiscoUnity_ConvMsg,2001,CDE,0) [Thread 796] Entering method
   CAvCDEConvBase::Run of conversation [SubMsgCount]
10:53:46:126 (CiscoUnity_ConvMsg,2005,CDE,16) [Thread 796] [Port 1] Entering
   conversation [SubMsgCount]
10:53:46:125 (CiscoUnity_ConvMsg,2001,CDE,0) [Thread 796] [Port 1] Entering method
   RunStart of conversation [SubMsgCount]
10:53:46:126 (CiscoUnity_ConvMsg,2002,CDE,0) [Thread 796] [Port 1] Exiting method
   RunStart normally for conversation [SubMsgCount]
10:53:46:125 (CiscoUnity_ConvMsg,2003,CDE,0) [Thread 796] [Port 1] Entering method
   OnEntry of state [GetMailbox status state]
10:53:46:265 (CiscoUnity_ConvMsg,2014,CDE,16) [Thread 796] [Port 1] Subscriber can
   send and receive messages on line 251 of file C:\Views\oliviers_402ES\un_Core2\
   ConversationEng\AvStateSvr\AvSGetMailboxStatus.cpp
10:53:46:266 (CiscoUnity_ConvMsg,2012,CDE,16) [Thread 796] [Port 1]
   IAvEventQueue::PushFrontID(YES_EVENT) returned [0x00000000] on line 137 of file
   C:\Views\oliviers_402ES\un_Core2\ConversationEng\AvStateSvr\
   AvSGetMailboxStatus.cpp
10:53:46:265 (CiscoUnity_ConvMsg,2004,CDE,0) [Thread 796] [Port 1] Exiting method
   OnEntry normally for state [GetMailbox status  state]
10:53:46:266 (CiscoUnity_ConvMsg,2003,CDE,0) [Thread 796] [Port 1] Entering method
   OnEntry of state [Count messages & get sub. properties state]
```

Example 5-7 *Conversation Diagnostics Showing Use of Messaging Components for Subscriber Sign-In (Continued)*

```
10:53:46:343 (CiscoUnity_ConvMsg,2004,CDE,0) [Thread 796] [Port 1] Exiting method
  CheckDominoMailStoreType normally for state [Count messages & get sub. properties
  state]
10:53:46:344 (CiscoUnity_ConvMsg,2004,CDE,0) [Thread 796] [Port 1] Exiting method
  OnEntry normally for state [Count messages & get sub. properties state]
10:53:46:359 (CiscoUnity_ConvMsg,2003,CDE,0) [Thread 796] [Port 1] Entering method
  OnEntry of state [Greet and play message count state]
```

Summary

Because Unity uses a mail system, such as Exchange or Domino, as its mail store, it must be capable of acting as a client of that mail store. Whether submitting new messages or playing messages to a Unity subscriber over the phone, Unity interacts with that mail system. Other Unity features, such as MWI and message notification, also rely on the mail system for updates on changes to user's inboxes.

The Unity messaging components work together to make all of this happen. The MAL provides a simpler common interface while hiding the complex details of mail system operation for DOH clients, including the conversation to create and the capability to send and retrieve voice-mail messages. The AvWm provides a method for Unity components, such as the UMR, to test for mail server availability. The UMR provides a fall-back method of local message storage and retrieval when the mail system is unavailable. The Message Store Monitor handles the details of receiving updates on changes to a subscriber's inbox, while providing a catalyst for the MWI and notification process.

CHAPTER 6

Components and Subsystems: Telephony Services

This chapter examines and discusses Unity's Media Interface Unit (MIU). Along with the roles and responsibilities of the MIU, this chapter outlines the MIU architecture.

The MIU integrates Unity into the phone system. That integration involves linking the rest of Unity to the telephone system by providing call information to other Unity components. Additionally, integration gives other Unity components control over calls that arrive at or originate from the voice-mail system, including the capability to answer, transfer, and disconnect calls that arrive at the voice-mail system. In short, the MIU provides telephony services to other Unity components. Just how the MIU accomplishes this task is discussed in this chapter.

Media Interface Unit

Enabling a PC-based voice-mail system to interface with different types of telephone switching systems (including interfacing with multiple telephone systems simultaneously) is hard work. Computers and telephone systems, especially legacy-based telephone systems (that is, those that employ traditional analog or digital phone lines as a means of connectivity) do not natively speak the same language. With legacy telephone systems, specialized hardware and software are required to connect a computer to a telephone system.

Most of the time, when such a connection is made, the voice-mail system is another connected device (such as a phone) on the phone system. Actually, the voice-mail system is a *series* of connected devices on the phone system. Each line or port of the voice-mail system represents a connection. You can imagine a 40-port voice-mail system as an array of 40 phones connected to the phone system. Additionally, the phone system views the voice-mail system as just that: 40 connected phones.

The MIU uses specialized hardware and software to connect to a telephone system to provide two-way communication between the voice-mail system and the telephone system. The MIU is an abstraction layer, a call state-machine, and an audio system all wrapped up into one.

Unity's MIU provides a mechanism for the voice-mail system to interact with the phone system(s) to which Unity is connected. Think of the MIU as a software component that gives other Unity software components two-way communication with the phone system.

The voice-mail system not only needs to perform simple phonelike operations (such as answering or transferring calls), but it also needs to extract useful data from calls (such as caller/called ID).

In addition to this call information and call control functionality, (that is, the act of performing phonelike operations such as answer, transfer, and drop) the MIU provides a mechanism for audio processing. In both playing prompts and recording messages and greetings, the MIU handles all the complicated tasks of processing audio streams. The MIU abstracts the details from the higher-level Unity components (such as conversation) so that the conversation does not need to know how to extract the calling party ID. Likewise, the conversation does not need to know whether a particular prompt must be transcoded to match the incoming audio stream. (Transcoding is the process of converting audio from one format to another.) Audio streams, such a prompts, messages, or greetings, might be recorded in one particular format but might need to be transcoded to match the format of the audio stream of the caller so that the caller can properly hear the audio.

The technical, low-level details of the MIU's interaction with the phone system build upon each other to provide support for voice-mail features, such as call holding, call screening, message waiting indication, and identified subscriber messaging. Without the intricacies of the MIU, these voice-mail features would not be possible. The MIU even provides some lower-level features, such as speed control, automatic gain control, and codec conversion.

The MIU performs the following tasks:

- Initializes ports and configures the telephony devices offered by the telephony service providers installed in the system.

- Extracts call information from the call. Integration refers to the method used to connect a voice-mail system to a phone system to support both signaling and addressing. Examples are DTMF, serial, and Skinny.

- Responds to client telephony requests. This occurs at the request of a MIU client (such as the conversation or notifier) to provide call control functions, such as answer, transfer, and disconnect.

- Responds to telephony system events. This includes detecting and signaling the event of an incoming ringing call, detecting when the telephone system has provided a disconnect, and detecting and signaling when a caller has pressed DTMF keys.

- Plays, records, and processes audio.

- Handles Text-to-Speech (TTS). TTS is a Unity voice-mail feature that enables a caller to have voice mail read when calling to retrieve messages. The MIU is responsible for interacting with the TTS engine to transfer the text of an e-mail into audio that the caller can hear.

A Few Words About TAPI

TAPI is a Windows standard set of functions that allows a client to operate phonelike operations on phonelike devices. Microsoft's TAPI also provides some infrastructure for client/ TSP (TAPI service provider) communication and managing TSPs, and it also specifies how a TSP should operate. TAPI also allows a TAPI client to perform operations on devices in a device-independent manner. This means that the TAPI client does not need to know the lower-level details of telephony operation because those details vary among phone systems.

A TAPI service provider (TSP) is a software component that handles the implementation of a phone device that supports TAPI. The TSP for a given device translates between TAPI and the native command set of the device. It can be thought of as a Windows hardware driver.

The main purpose of TAPI is to provide an abstraction layer from the TAPI client to the underlying device. This is accomplished through a TAPI service provider that translates between TAPI constructs and the underlying implementation. Unity initially was designed for and implemented around one specific call-control API: TAPI.

The TAPI specification is designed so that a TAPI client can make a function call to answer, transfer, or drop a phone call the same way, regardless of the underlying device. In this model, the TAPI functions that a TAPI client calls (such as answer, transfer, and drop) all take the same parameters, and a client should expect the same returns when dealing with TSP-A or TSP-B. For example, the Dialogic TSP is a TSP designed to control a hardware voice board that is connected to analog lines on a legacy PBX; the Cisco Unity TSP is designed to control a TCP/IP connection to Cisco CallManager. The telephone signaling technologies used in the legacy telephony network are completely different than what is used in the IP telephony network, but the TAPI client need not care. Likewise, the internal work that the Dialogic TSP must do to answer and transfer a call is completely different than with the Cisco Unity TSP, but the client need not care. All the client needs to know is that both the Dialogic and Cisco Unity TSPs are indeed TSPs (and, thus, comply to the TAPI standard) and that the client contains code that makes the same TAPI function calls, regardless of the TSP.

Although the MIU originally was designed around a TAPI-centric model, the writers realized that other telephony devices might not support TAPI. Not every telephony device provides TAPI support for the implementation, so a line server has emerged. The line server model allows the MIU to be decoupled from a TAPI-centric model. Instead of being designed solely around TAPI, the MIU can grow and adapt to future call-control APIs with the use of additional line servers. For legacy and Cisco CallManager integrations, the upper layers of the MIU "talk" to the TAPI line server, and the TAPI line server then "talks" to the TSP. In contrast, for SIP integrations, the SIP line server takes the place of the TAPI line server and interacts with the SIP stack (the SIP stack is a software component written by Cisco that enables the MIU to have SIP-based phone devices). The line server model defines a common interface that the upper layer of the MIU can use without worrying about the lower-level telephony API, whether it be TAPI or some other API.

Figure 6-1 gives a general overview of the TAPI architecture in Unity. It shows the communication flow between example Unity TAPI clients (the MIU) and example TSPs (Dialogic and Cisco Unity-CM).

Figure 6-1 *TAPI Architecture in Unity*

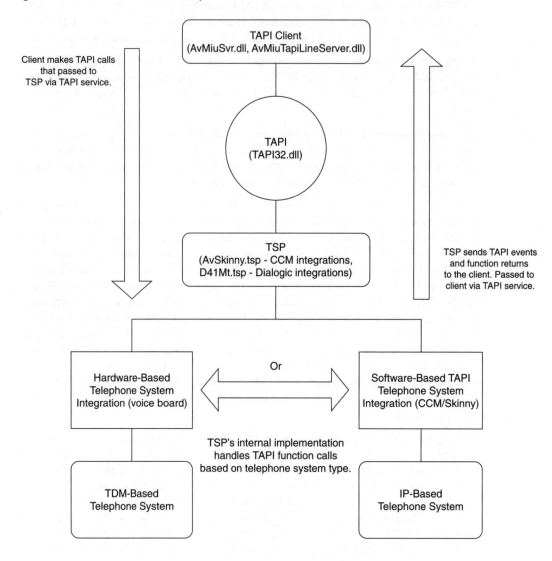

Telephony Subsystem Initialization

Before the MIU can perform any client requests for call control, and before it can respond to events happening on the telephone network, the telephony devices (whether TAPI-based or SIP-based) must be discovered and initialized. The MIU has access to which types of integrations have been installed on the Unity server, based on the information that UTIM wrote into the Windows Registry. If a particular integration's devices are serviced by a TSP (as is the case with Dialogic-based legacy integrations and Cisco CallManager integrations), the MIU enumerates the number of phone devices from the TSP. Because default TSPs are installed by the operating system, the MIU iterates through all TSPs, querying for service provider information and devices. This process can be thought of as a TAPI device-discovery phase for the MIU. If the integration type is not serviced by a TSP (as is the case with SIP integrations), the MIU still gathers device-configuration information from a provider. However, that provider information is not gathered through TAPI function calls.

At this point, the devices have been discovered and are ready for use. In other words, the telephony subsystem has been initialized.

For the majority of Unity installations, the MIU's lower-level telephony functions are provided through TAPI. Although TAPI provides a relatively generic interface for its clients for phone operation, the MIU often needs to configure specific, phone system-dependant parameters. This is usually the case when dealing with TDM phone systems because analog signaling varies from one phone system to another.

No native TAPI support exists for directly configuring such specific parameters for a provider. However, TAPI does provide an indirect way of setting these values that the MIU takes advantage of. TAPI provides a generic function that a TAPI client can call (as long as the provider supports it) to configure device-specific parameters. The TSPs that the MIU supports (such as Dialogic and Cisco Unity-CM TSP) support this specific configuration. For Dialogic, this method is used to configure PBX-specific settings, such as dial tone frequency, hook-flash duration, and ring-back cadence. The MIU configures the given service provider based on settings that the MIU has loaded from the switch file or the Registry.

When the port-discovery process is complete and the has configured and initialized its lines, the MIU is ready to provide its lines to the higher-level Unity components. Configuring the service provider's devices specifically for a given integration type is necessary for extracting call information, responding to MIU client telephony requests, and responding to telephony events that occur on the telephone network.

The event log message examples that follow demonstrate the initialization process on a simple two-port Cisco CallManager integrated Unity server. These were gathered from a typical Unity start-up process. These messages do not necessarily appear in this exact order; other messages not related to the MIU or telephony in the startup process have been removed for clarity.

```
Event Type:     Information
Event Source:     CiscoUnity_Miu
Event Category:     Init
Event ID:     599
Date:          3/17/2004
Time:          9:25:29 PM
User:          N/A
Computer:     UNITY
Description:
Miu CCM Integration discovered 2 Ports.
```

The first message is evidence of the MIU's port-discovery process. A lot of work takes place under the covers to generate this message: The MIU actually iterated through all of the TSPs (Windows has some default TSPs, remember) and discovered which was the Cisco Unity-CM TSP. The MIU queried the TSP to see how many ports (the term *device* is analogous here) the TSP had.

```
Event Type:     Information
Event Source:     CiscoUnity_Miu
Event Category:     Init
Event ID:     618
Date:          3/17/2004
Time:          9:25:29 PM
User:          N/A
Computer:     UNITY
Description:
Cisco Unity is using G.711 (8K Mu-Law) as the record format for all messages and
   greetings.
```

This message shows the MIU continuing its initialization process. This helps to understand what codec conversion might be in effect when recording messages and greetings.

```
Event Type:     Information
Event Source:     CiscoUnity_Miu
Event Category:     Init
Event ID:     504
Date:          3/17/2004
Time:          9:25:29 PM
User:          N/A
Computer:     UNITY
Description:
Media component Miu initialize succeeded.
```

This message is self-explanatory; the MIU's initialization is complete.

```
Event Type:     Information
Event Source:     CiscoUnity_TSP
Event Category:     None
Event ID:     105
Date:          3/17/2004
Time:          9:25:33 PM
User:          N/A
Computer:     UNITY
Description:
Cisco Unity-CM TSP device 6 (Cisco Unity port 2): Created a connection to Cisco
   CallManager 10.0.0.1.  The Cisco Unity-CM TSP version is 7, 0, 3, 1.
```

```
Event Type:     Information
Event Source:      CiscoUnity_TSP
Event Category:     None
Event ID:    103
Date:         3/17/2004
Time:         9:25:33 PM
User:         N/A
Computer:    UNITY
Description:
Cisco Unity-CM TSP device 6 (Cisco Unity port 2): G729a capable with codec version
   2.0.0.6.  This means that Cisco Unity will accept calls in either G.711 or G.729a
   format, depending on the Cisco CallManager region settings.

Event Type:     Information
Event Source:      CiscoUnity_TSP
Event Category:     None
Event ID:    105
Date:         3/17/2004
Time:         9:25:33 PM
User:         N/A
Computer:    UNITY
Description:
Cisco Unity-CM TSP device 5 (Cisco Unity port 1): Created a connection to Cisco
   CallManager 10.0.0.1.  The Cisco Unity-CM TSP version is 7, 0, 3, 1.


Event Type:     Information
Event Source:      CiscoUnity_TSP
Event Category:     None
Event ID:    103
Date:         3/17/2004
Time:         9:25:33 PM
User:         N/A
Computer:    UNITY
Description:
Cisco Unity-CM TSP device 5 (Cisco Unity port 1): G729a capable with codec version
   2.0.0.6.  This means that Cisco Unity will accept calls in either G.711 or G.729a
   format, depending on the Cisco CallManager region settings.
```

The previous two messages were indirectly generated by the MIU's startup process. Because the initialization of the MIU and its ports is complete, the MIU is ready to use these ports. With the Cisco CallManager integration, by asking the TSP to open its lines, the MIU causes the TSP ports to register with CallManager to place and receive calls on the telephone system. Those messages are the Cisco Unity-CM TSP's successful CallManager registration messages (again, codec information is provided).

Extracting Call Information

To provide voice-mail features such as subscriber sign-in during a direct call and the capability to play another subscriber's greeting during a call forward, Unity must know why a call reached Unity and who the called and/or calling parties are. The MIU provides this type of information. By extracting this call information, the MIU supports certain "get" functions that the conversation can call to retrieve such information. The call information extraction methods vary among integrations, but the particular method that the MIU uses is hidden from the MIU clients. Those clients request the call information from the MIU in the same way, regardless of the integration.

Based on configuration settings listed in the chosen switch file, the MIU uses the method to extract call information. The method used is determined by the manner in which the telephone system (or integration device) can send call information to Unity. Certain telephone systems send call information in the form of analog, DTMF sequences, or RS-232 serial packets; some integration devices (such as PBXLink) also send call information in the form of RS-232 serial packets. CallManager and SIP-based integrations send call information in IP packets over the IP network.

Regardless of the method by which the MIU gathers the call information, the MIU places the call information in a consistent call information structure so that it can be retrieved by the conversation and used by other Unity components.

Responding to Client Telephony Requests

The MIU is responsible for handling a client's request to interact with or invoke some function of the telephone system. Examples include a conversation request for call information retrieval, and a notifier request for message waiting indication activation or deactivation. The MIU provides an API of simple interfaces to such clients so that these requests can be serviced.

For instance, a client might call the transfer method. All that the client needs to pass in is the extension number for the transfer, the transfer type (release or supervised), and the switch number (for dual-switch integrations). The MIU performs the remaining tasks, such as determining when a supervised transfer has connected (the transferred-to party answers the call), if any dual-switch functionality is required (if the passed switch ID does not match the switch ID of the transferring port). The MIU also handles several other functions:

- Initiating a transfer (hook-flash, transfer button on an emulated phone)
- Pausing for any configured delays after the transfer is initiated, and dialing the extension of the transferred-to party
- Monitoring/tracking the duration of the digits dialed and the duration of the interdigit delays
- Pausing for any necessary delays after dialing the extension of the transferred-to party (sometimes required on TDM PBX integrations)

The point is that the MIU handles the complicated job of communicating with a given phone system while providing the MIU client with a simple interface to invoke telephony operations such as transfer.

Responding to Telephone System Events

Events that happen on the telephone network must be detected so that the voice-mail system intelligently can communicate with the phone system. The MIU detects, recognizes, and notifies interested parties of such events. When a call forwards to voice mail or a subscriber calls to retrieve messages, the telephone system signals one of Unity's ports that an incoming call is happening. The MIU detects the incoming call and signals to the arbiter that a call has arrived on a given port. Likewise, after the call has been answered and the caller hangs up, the telephone system signals Unity that a disconnect has occurred. The MIU detects the disconnect and signals the event to the conversation.

Playing, Recording, and Processing Audio

The MIU does not actually make the decision to play or record audio; it services the request for each when a client makes a request. The MIU also handles more sophisticated audio-processing features: speed control, codec conversion, and Automatic Gain Control.

MIU Architecture

The majority of the MIU resides in two DLLs: the basic MIU server and a corresponding line server (there is a specific line server for TAPI-based systems and a specific line server for SIP-based systems). Several other DLLs also are involved for audio-processing and integration-parsing systems. Figure 6-2 shows a diagram of the MIU architecture. Not all MIUs look exactly like this because only the components that are needed are loaded. For instance, systems that do not implement SIP do not contain the SIP line server or any of the SIP line server's subcomponents. Likewise, if a system does not implement a TDM PBX-based integration, the TAPI line server does not load any TDM PBX-specific components (such as the telephony service provider and the WAV driver). Figure 6-2 shows the general breakdown of major MIU components (shaded) and the relationship of the MIU to other telephony components.

MIU Server

The MIU server supports client connections to interfaces that allow clients to perform telephony functions or retrieve information about a given telephony system. The MIU server object is the starting point where clients perform telephony operations, such as activating or deactivating the message waiting indicator (MWI), and placing or answering a call to the telephone system.

Figure 6-2   *MIU Architecture*

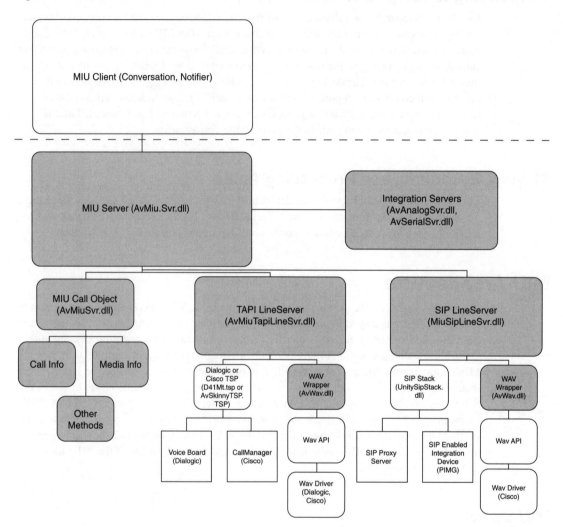

Upon receiving a client request to place or answer a call, the MIU returns a very important object to the calling client: the MIU call object. Implemented inside the MIU server, this call object is exactly what a client needs to retrieve information about the call and perform more sophisticated telephony operations on the call. For instance, the MIU call interface supports methods that grant a client that has retrieved a call object access to PBX-like features, such as transferring, answering, sending and receiving digits, and playing and receiving audio. Additionally, the call object interface supports an advanced set of properties that describe the characteristics of the call, such as call information (also known as integration) and media (audio characteristics).

Whereas some properties are meaningful only to clients external to the MIU, some properties are meaningful to clients internal to the MIU: other MIU components. Only one instance of the MIU server object exists, but there are multiple instances of the MIU call object. As many MIU call objects exist as there are active calls on the system at a given time (with the exception of sometimes more MIU call objects than active calls, as with supervised transfers).

MIU Call (Call Object)

It is important to have an in-depth understanding of the MIU call object because this is where the vast majority of communication between other Unity components and the MIU actually occurs. The MIU call interface is the point of entry for Unity components to engage telephony features and retrieve information from the telephone system. The MIU call object has properties that can be set and retrieved. Most of the properties reside in two structures: the Media IO (input/output) and Call Info structures. MIU clients do not access the structures directly; the MIU supports get and set functions for the properties in the structures.

The Media IO information for the call object is a structure that contains properties used during message/prompt playback and recording. Configuration for digit gathering is contained here. For instance, a MIU client can request that a # digit should terminate a prompt's record (media input) or playback (media output). Numerous Media IO structure elements also relate to the playback of audio. Settings that control the adjustment of audio volume, speed, and position are contained in the Media IO structure.

The term *position* might seem a bit odd at first, but the MIU supports skipping ahead or skipping back while listening to a voice-mail message over the phone. The feature's behavior is similar to the fast-forward or rewind controls of a CD player. In addition to adjusting just how far the jump forward or backward is made, the specific digit that signifies the jump can be assigned. For instance, a MIU client can set properties in the Media IO structure stating that digit 4 signifies an jump ahead request, whereas digit 6 signifies a jump back request. Properties for processing volume or speed change requests during the playback of audio also are supported and follow the same pattern: One setting controls the level of volume or speed to change, and another setting specifies the dialed digit that signifies the request. Along with the volume, the speed of audio playback can be raised or lowered. All of these configuration settings are stored in the Media IO structure.

Properties that signify recording silence timeouts also are stored in the Media IO structure. A recording silence timeout is the duration of silence that occurs after audio recording has begun that signifies the recording should be stopped. Some people hang up or press a digit when finished leaving a message for a Unity subscriber, but other callers do nothing; they wait for the voice-mail system to prompt them for the next step. Following the latter example, configurable silence-recording timeouts help determine when a caller has finished leaving a message and the recording should be terminated.

Three main silence-timeout properties exist. The first is the record leading timeout, which specifies the duration of silence allowed after starting to record but before voice is detected. This duration specifies how long the MIU waits for a caller to start talking during a message recording before it considers the recording to be finished. Additionally, different recording-silence timeouts that can be specified on short messages (that is, messages that have a short duration of detected voice during the recording) and for long messages (that is, messages that have a long duration of detected voice during the recording). Of course, a property also specifies the difference (in time) between a short and a long message.

The other major property structure of the MIU call object is the Call Information structure. As the name suggests, this structure has elements that describe the identification of the called party, the calling party, and the reason for the call. As an example, Bob at extension 1234 calls Shirley at extension 5678, and Shirley's phone forwards to Unity because she does not answer. The Call Information structure in this case contains 1234 as the calling party, 5678 as the called party, and forward no-answer as the call reason. Although the Call Object enables you to set these elements, MIU clients usually just retrieve the elements.

In addition to the functions that allow MIU clients to set and retrieve simple call object properties, the call object has methods for call control. Call-control functions include answer, transfer, and drop exist. The Call Object also has methods for generating DTMF digits (which the notifier needs for numeric pager notification) and gathering digits (which the conversation needs for responding to user input).

Additionally, the call object has a state that is maintained. The states are fairly straightforward: disconnected and not-disconnected. As a call is initiated or answered, the state is connected. The state change of the call is maintained by the line server that is associated with the call object. As the line server receives notification that the phone system has signaled a disconnect, it notifies the call object so that the state transitions to disconnected.

Integration Object

When the Unity system will use an integration type of serial or analog, the integration object is used to initialize and configure either the analog integration-processing mechanism or the serial integration-processing mechanism. It is started up by the MIU, but it is used only if there is an analog or serial integration.

Switch Configuration

These objects are used to configure specialized settings, such as setting up MWI sequences for both analog and serial integrations, and setting up the timing parameters needed with analog and serial integrations. The switch configuration object makes the decision to load either the analog or the serial parsing engine.

MIU Line Servers

The type of MIU line server in existence depends on the type of switch integration being used. If the switch integration uses TAPI (as with TDM PBX integrations or CallManager), the MIU creates a TAPI-centric MIU line manager when it starts up. If the switch integration is SIP, it creates a SIP-centric MIU line manager. Additionally, it is entirely possible for other MIU line managers to be implemented in the future. The MIU line server is self-contained in a DLL, and its main client is actually the MIU server. No Unity components other than the MIU server directly interact with the MIU line server; it separates the MIU server and its call objects from the call-control API employed on a particular line in the system. Certain call-control APIs operate differently that other call-control APIs, and that's the main purpose of the MIU line server: to abstract the subtleties of different APIs from the MIU server.

Even though different TAPI service providers contain different internal implementations, TAPI itself is a defined set of functions for control of phone-like devices. The initialization, usage, and shutdown of the TAPI service providers that Unity uses is pretty much the same, but other call-control APIs operate completely differently. For SIP-based integrations, the MIU creates a SIP line manager and a SIP stack. Although it does not operate with TAPI-based devices, and for general call control functionality, the SIP line manager provides the same basic functionality as the TAPI line manager; likewise, the SIP stack provides the same basic functionality as a TSP.

MIU Line (Line Object)

Both the MIU call object and the MIU line object are important to MIU clients. Clients have indirect access to the MIU line object through the MIU call object. The MIU call object call-control methods are implemented in the MIU line object. Clients have indirect access to the MIU line object because the MIU call object has a pointer to the line object.

The MIU line object is implemented inside a line server, whether that line server is TAPI- or SIP-based. Because the line server is specific to the underlying telephony API or protocol, the line object is representative of a line or a port. A line object exists for every port on the system and is responsible for carrying out telephony operations. Instead of concentrating on setting and retrieving properties, the line object has functions that take a more active role with a call; it handles such telephony operations as call control and media operations.

The MIU line object performs the telephony operations duty of answering and transferring a call. The process of gathering digits dialed by a caller differs greatly between TAPI- and SIP-based systems; the line object handles differences such as these so that the upper layers of the MIU and, more important, MIU clients need not care. More complex telephony operations, such as answering, initiating, transferring, and ending a call, are carried out by the line object.

In addition to call control functions, the line object handles media operations that are specific to a line or port. The most obvious examples are playing and recording audio.

Just as a MIU client requests call-control or media operations for a call, the call object delegates control to its line object (each call object has a pointer back to a line object), and MIU clients do not operate directly on the line object. The implementation of the line object depends on the underlying telephony API, but the job of the line object from system to system is the same.

Media Object

The MIU media object is implemented inside the MIU line server and acts as a wrapper around another MIU audio-processing component called UnityAvWav. The media object is the starting point for media-control methods, such as playing and recording audio, as well as adjusting speed and volume. These calls are handed off to UnityAvWav, and UnityAvWav makes Win32 WAV API calls for processing audio.

TTS Object

The TTS object handles specialized media operations on TTS messages, such as play, stop, set volume, set speed, pause, and resume. It also creates TTS sessions.

UnityAvWav

This object is responsible for handling most of the complicated audio-processing features that Unity supports. It acts as an abstraction layer between the higher levels of the MIU and the Win32 WAV and ACM (Audio Compression Manager) APIs. Dealing with transcoding an audio stream on prompt playback or message recording is complicated work. Additionally, supporting media features, such as jump forward and jump back, becomes quite involved. That is UnityAvWav's job: to simplify the MIU's capability to support and function with audio streams.

In the case of transcoding audio, although the mechanics are complicated, the algorithm remains simple (as long as the appropriate codecs are installed):

- During audio playback (in the form of prompts, messages, voice names, or greetings), an audio stream pointer is passed into UnityAvWav. UnityAvWav compares the audio-compression format of the stream to be played to that of the stream of the incoming caller. If the streams are the same, no audio compression changes on the playback stream happen; the stream simply is played. If the audio-compression format of the playback stream is different than that of the incoming caller's stream, the playback stream is converted (with API calls to the ACM, which, in turn, operate on the installed codec designated for the conversion) to that of the incoming caller.

- During audio recording (in the form of messages, voice names, or greetings), a destination pointer is passed into UnityAvWav. The incoming caller's audio stream is compared to that of the Unity default recording format. If the streams are the same, no conversion takes place. If the audio streams are different, the incoming audio stream is converted to that of the Unity default recording format.

UnityAvWav also handles Automatic Gain Control (AGC). AGC is used to normalize the gain of incoming recordings to Unity. To compensate for the fact that different incoming audio streams to be recorded have different decibel levels, AGC alters the recording stream so that all streams are at the target volume for recording. So, an initial target decibel level is set for recordings. As the audio stream is recorded, but before it is written to disk, AGC raises the level of the audio recording if the decibel level is lower than the target, and lowers the audio recording if the decibel level is higher than the target volume.

Fitting it Together

A strong relationship exists between the call object, the line object, and the media object in the frequently called, day-to-day telephony functions such as answer, transfer, and play. These functions reside in a hierarchy between these objects so that functions start at the high-level and relatively generic interface at the call object, and work their way down to more specialized behavior inside the line object. Figure 6-3 shows how these objects fit together in the MIU.

Consider a simple example that assumes that a MIU client successfully has called the answer function and has a pointer to a call object. Now the client wants to play a voice-mail prompt. Before making the request, however, the client specifies which digits will be termination digits. In other words, the client declares which digits the caller could dial over the phone to stop the audio playback. Next, the client calls the play function and passes the destination to the file containing the prompt as a parameter. The call object's play method does some error checking and diagnostics, and passes the play function to its corresponding line object. The line object does its own level or error checking and diagnostics, makes sure that it has access to its media object, and passes the play call to the media object. The media object performs its own error checking and diagnostics, and passes the call to UnityAvWav. UnityAvWav checks to see whether the codec of the voice-mail prompt matches that of the incoming media stream of the call. Because the incoming media stream in this case is different than that of the prompt (we are pretending here), UnityAvWav converts the codec of the prompt to that of the incoming stream. Finally, the prompt is played to the caller. Assuming that all of this has succeeded, a success code is passed from UnityAvWav to the media object, to the line object, to the call object, and back to the client.

Figure 6-3 *Overall MIU Architecture*

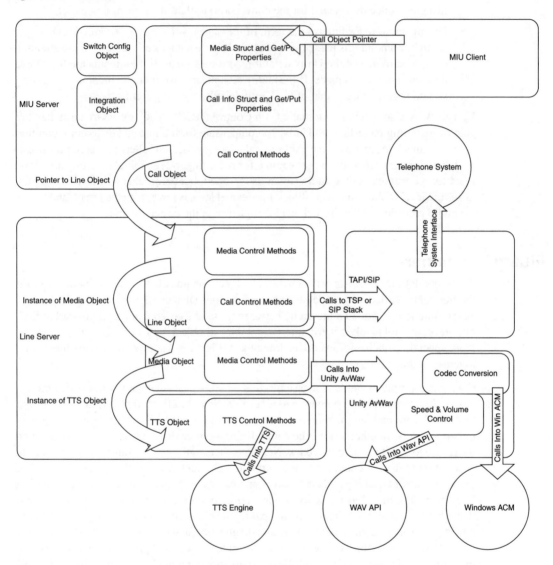

The client wants to receive any subsequent digit key presses that the user dials, so the client calls the gather digits function on the call object's call-control interface method. When this function call is made, a few options are passed in, such as the number of digits that the client wants and just how long the client wants to wait for these digits. The call object does a bit of internal processing on these options, but it also relays the gather digits function call to its corresponding line object. Imagine, for instance, that this integration is TAPI-based. The line object knows that special processing needs to be done in TAPI for proper digit collection (if this was a SIP integration, other special processing would have been done). The line object carries out the request through TAPI to the TSP for digit collection. After some time, the caller dials digits, and these digits are passed back up through the line object to the call object and back to the client.

The MIU diagnostics that follow illustrate this MIU client server activity. In this case, the MIU client is the conversation. Some portions of the diagnostics have been removed for clarity, and comments have been added.

The TSP signals to the MIU that a new call has arrived:

```
11:19:56:218 [Port 1] TAPI sent Tapi Message LINE_APPNEWCALL on HCALL 0x00010244
with Params (0x00000000 | 0x000101AA | 0x00000004).
```

The MIU extracts call information:

```
11:19:56:218 [Port 1] INTEGRATION CallInfo received (Origin Internal | Reason Direct
| CallerID 2065551234 | CalledID 1000 | RedirectingID Unknown).
```

The MIU does some initialization of the call object:

```
11:19:56:218 [Port 1] Trace MiuLine: Method CAvMiuLine::CallInit(IAvMiuCall*) exited
with success (0x00000000).
11:19:56:219 [Port 1] Trace MiuLine: Method
CAvMiuCall::InitMediaIOInfo(StAvMiuCallInitParams*) entered.
11:19:56:218 [Port 1] Trace MiuLine: Method
CAvMiuCall::InitMediaIOInfo(StAvMiuCallInitParams*) exited with success
(0x00000000).
```

The MIU client requests call to be answered:

```
11:19:56:281 [Port 1] Trace MiuCall: COM Method CAvMiuCall::Answer() entered.
11:19:56:282 [Port 1] Trace MiuLine: Method CAvMiuLine::Answer() entered.
11:19:56:281 [Port 1] CallState in CAvMiuLine::Answer() is LINECALLSTATE_OFFERING.
11:19:56:296 [Port 1] TAPI sent Tapi Message LINE_REPLY on HCALL 0x00000000 with
  Params (0x00010199 | 0x00000000 | 0x00000000).
11:19:56:421 [Port 1] TAPI sent Tapi Message LINE_CALLSTATE on HCALL 0x000101AA with
  Params (0x00000100 | 0x00000000 | 0x00000000).
11:19:56:422 [Port 1] TAPI sent Tapi CallState LINECALLSTATE_CONNECTED (Active) on
  HCALL 0x000101AA.
11:19:56:421 [Port 1] Trace MiuLine: Method CAvMiuLine::Answer() exited with success
  (0x00040103).
```

The MIU returns success to the client request to answer:

```
11:19:56:422 [Port 1] Trace MiuCall: COM Method CAvMiuCall::Answer() exited with
  HRESULT 0x00040103 (S_MIU_CONNECTED).
```

The MIU client requests audio to be played:

```
11:19:56:515 [Port 1] Trace MiuCall: COM Method CAvMiuCall::Play(VARIANT* | long |
  long* | long*) entered.
11:19:56:516 [Port 1] Trace MiuLine: Method CAvMiuLine::Play(VARIANT* | long | long*
  | long*) entered.
11:19:56:515 [Port 1] Trace MiuLine: Method CAvMiuLine::IsCallValid() entered.
11:19:56:516 [Port 1] Trace MiuLine: Method CAvMiuLine::IsCallValid() exited with
  success (0x00000000).
```

The MIU validates the media to be played. Although it is not visible in these diagnostics, this is carried out by the AvWav component:

```
11:19:56:515 [Port 1] Trace MiuWave: Method CAvMiuWave::GetLength(IStream* |
CAvString&) entered.
11:19:56:516 [Port 1] Trace MiuWave: Method CAvMiuWave::GetLength(IStream* |
CAvString&) exited with success (0x00003A6F).
11:19:56:515 [Port 1] Trace MiuWave: Method CAvMiuWave::Play(IStream* | CAvString& |
long | StAvMiuMediaIOInfo* | long* | LPDWORD | long*) entered.
11:20:00:234 [Port 1] TAPI sent Tapi Message LINE_MONITORDIGITS on HCALL 0x000101AA
with Params (0x00000038 | 0x00000002 | 0x0083C66F).
```

The TSP notifies the MIU that the caller has dialed a digit:

```
11:20:00:235 [Port 1] Digit 8 received.
```

Audio playback is stopped (due to the termination digit). The MIU notifies the client of the audio playback stop:

```
11:20:00:234 [Port 1] Digit 8 matched DigitString PlayTerminationDigits
(1234567890*#ABCD).
11:20:00:235 [Port 1] Trace MiuLine: Method CAvMiuLine::StopIO(long) entered.
11:20:00:234 [Port 1] StopIO(TermReason TERM_DIGIT | LastTermReason TERM_NONE) is
BEING CALLED.
11:20:00:235 [Port 1] Trace MiuWave: Method CAvMiuWave::Stop(DWORD | DWORD) entered.
11:20:00:234 [Port 1] CAvMiuWave::Stop() requesting WavStop for TermReason 10.
11:20:00:235 [Port 1] Trace MiuWave: Method CAvMiuWave::Stop(DWORD | DWORD) exited
with success (0x00000000).
11:20:00:234 [Port 1] Trace MiuLine: Method CAvMiuLine::StopIO(DWORD) exited with
success (0x00000000).
11:20:00:235 [Port 1] Trace MiuWave: Method CAvMiuWave::Play(IStream* | CAvString& |
long | StAvMiuMediaIOInfo* | long* | LPDWORD | long*) exited with success
(0x00000000).
11:20:00:234 [Port 1] Trace MiuLine: Method CAvMiuLine::Play(VARIANT* | long | long*
| long*) exited with success (0x00040101).
11:20:00:235 [Port 1] Trace MiuCall: COM Method CAvMiuCall::Play(VARIANT* | long |
long* | long*) exited with HRESULT 0x00040101 (S_MIU_TERM_DIGIT).
```

The MIU client requests to receive the digits dialed by the caller:

```
11:20:00:234 [Port 1] Trace MiuCall: COM Method CAvMiuCall::GatherDigits(BSTR* | long
| long* | long) entered.
11:20:00:235 [Port 1] Trace MiuLine: Method CAvMiuLine::GatherDigits(BSTR* | UINT |
UINT | UINT | UINT) entered.
11:20:00:234 [Port 1] GatherDigits (Mode GATHER), Digit 8 found.  This is digit 1
of 1 requested.
11:20:00:235 [Port 1] Trace MiuLine: Method CAvMiuLine::GatherDigits(BSTR* | UINT |
UINT | UINT | UINT) exited with success (0x00000000).
11:20:00:234 [Port 1] GatherDigits (1 digits requested in GATHER Mode) succeeded
with HRESULT S_OK; 1 digits were gathered (8).
11:20:00:235 [Port 1] Trace MiuCall: COM Method CAvMiuCall::GatherDigits(BSTR* | long
| long* | long) exited with HRESULT 0x00000000 (S_OK).
11:20:00:234 [Port 1] Trace MiuCall: COM Method CAvMiuCall::GatherDigits(BSTR* | long
| long* | long) entered.
11:20:00:235 [Port 1] Trace MiuLine: Method CAvMiuLine::GatherDigits(BSTR* | UINT |
UINT | UINT | UINT) entered.
11:20:00:515 [Port 1] TAPI sent Tapi Message LINE_MONITORDIGITS on HCALL 0x000101AA
with Params (0x00000034 | 0x00000002 | 0x0083C788).
11:20:00:516 [Port 1] Digit 4 received.
11:20:00:515 [Port 1] GatherDigits (Mode GATHER), Digit 4 found.  This is digit 1
of 30 requested.
11:20:00:875 [Port 1] TAPI sent Tapi Message LINE_MONITORDIGITS on HCALL 0x000101AA
with Params (0x00000030 | 0x00000002 | 0x0083C8F0).
```

```
11:20:00:876 [Port 1] Digit 0 received.
11:20:00:875 [Port 1] GatherDigits (Mode GATHER), Digit 0 found. This is digit 2 of
   30 requested.
11:20:01:171 [Port 1] TAPI sent Tapi Message LINE_MONITORDIGITS on HCALL 0x000101AA
   with Params (0x00000031 | 0x00000002 | 0x0083CA19).
11:20:01:172 [Port 1] Digit 1 received.
11:20:01:171 [Port 1] GatherDigits (Mode GATHER), Digit 1 found. This is digit 3 of
   30 requested.
11:20:02:671 [Port 1] GatherDigits Timeout. Gathered 3 digits of 30 requested (401).
11:20:02:672 [Port 1] Trace MiuLine: Method CAvMiuLine::GatherDigits(BSTR* | UINT |
   UINT | UINT | UINT) exited with success (0x00040105).
11:20:02:671 [Port 1] GatherDigits (30 digits requested in GATHER Mode) succeeded
   with HRESULT S_MIU_TERM_TIMEOUT; 3 digits were gathered (401).
```

The MIU signals to the client that digit collection is finished (because of a timeout waiting for a subsequent digit) and delivers gathered digits to the client:

```
11:20:02:672 [Port 1] Trace MiuCall: COM Method CAvMiuCall::GatherDigits(BSTR* | long
   | long* | long) exited with HRESULT 0x00040105 (S_MIU_TERM_TIMEOUT).
```

Summary

The MIU handles all the telephony functions for Unity. This includes providing a mechanism for call control and extracting call information. In a sense, the MIU is a server: It provides telephony services to clients. Any component in Unity that wants to answer or place a call uses the MIU to accomplish such a task. The recording and playback of audio also are included in these telephony services, and the MIU handles them as well. The MIU architecture allows the complicated tasks of call control and audio processing to be subdivided across several smaller components. Further subdivision allows different underlying telephony protocols and APIs to be implemented (such as TAPI and SIP). Throughout several DLLs on the Unity server, the MIU facilitates the linkage of Unity to the phone system.

CHAPTER 7

Components and Subsystems: Features

At the core, Unity is designed to provide all the features of a traditional voice-mail system. For the most part, this involves allowing callers to leave a message and allowing subscribers of the system to later retrieve that message. Enterprise customers demand that this functionality work flawlessly, but they also demand that Unity have the capability to retrieve e-mails over the phone. They also demand that Spanish, German, Dutch, Korean, and Australian employees be able to call Unity and hear their native language while they retrieve their voice messages and e-mails. Some enterprise customers even want Unity to send an SMTP message to their cell phone whenever a new voice message arrives in their inbox. Many different customers want to use Unity for many different purposes. As a result, Unity has developed into a robust, feature-rich enterprise messaging and communication system.

The goal of this chapter is to describe the long list of features that are available in Unity. Some of these features are geared toward users, while others are geared toward administrators. Some of these features are system-level features that enable customers to use Unity in a variety of environments, whether integrating with Cisco CallManager and a Nortel Meridian simultaneously or interoperating with an Octel voice-messaging system. Keep in mind that some of the features described here are licensed Unity features so not all Unity systems have these features available for use. For a list of licensed Unity features, see the section entitled "License Pooling and Demo Licenses." In addition, some features are restricted by class of service settings that are controlled by an administrator. See the section "Class of Service" for more information. This discussion is based on Unity 4.0(3); features discussed here might not be available in earlier versions of Unity. This chapter attempts to cover the majority of Unity features, but it should not be considered a comprehensive list. The features discussed in this chapter are organized as follows:

- Subscriber features
- Administrator features
- Maintenance features
- Security features
- System features

Unity Subscriber Features

Unity subscribers can use three main interfaces for messaging and personal account administration:

- Telephone User Interface (TUI), also referred to as the conversation
- Mail client (View Mail for Microsoft Outlook, or Lotus Domino Unified Communication Services [DUCS])
- Cisco Personal Communications Assistant (Cisco PCA), made up of the Unity Inbox and Unity Assistant)

We first look at the features available to Unity subscribers when they use the TUI. This discussion is based on the use of Unity's standard conversation. Unity subscribers can be configured to use Unity's optional conversation 1, which has a different message-retrieval menu structure than Unity's standard conversation. The optional conversation is intended to mimic the menu structure of other voice-mail systems, easing the transition for users when a company migrates from other voice-mail systems to Unity.

Subscriber TUI Features

Unity subscribers have a host of features available to them when they log into Unity over the phone. These features enable subscribers to customize how they send and retrieve messages, as well as to administer personal account settings. We begin by discussing the features available to subscribers when they send and retrieve messages over the phone. Note that Unity can send voice messages only from the TUI interface. However, Unity does allow users to retrieve voice messages, e-mails, and faxes from the TUI interface.

Message Sending over the TUI

When sending a voice message from the phone, subscribers can address the message to a single subscriber, multiple subscribers, a private list, or a public distribution list. In addition, when addressing the message, they can select message recipients either by subscriber ID or by name. Subscribers also have the option to mark a message as urgent, mark a message as private, request return receipt that the message has been read by the recipient, and mark a message for future delivery.

Sending a *private message* lets the recipient know to treat the message confidentially. In addition, a private message cannot be forwarded by the recipient via the TUI or via the Unity Inbox. *Future delivery* allows subscribers to record and address a message when they are logged into Unity, but to have Unity send the message at a later day and time specified by the subscriber. This feature might be useful for a boss who is out of the office on the day a report is due. The boss can address and record a reminder to her employee days in advance, and mark the message to be sent to her employee on the day the report is due.

Message Playback over TUI

Subscribers can listen to both voice messages and e-mail messages over the TUI. E-mail messages are played using text-to-speech, or TTS. When listening to a message from the phone, whether an e-mail or a voice message, subscribers have several features available to make it easier for them to hear the message. Subscribers can use *speed control* to speed up or slow down the playback of a message. During message playback, subscribers can fast-forward or rewind to any part of the message. They can also pause the message and choose to resume playback of the message at any time. Finally, when Unity integrates with a TDM phone system, users have the option to increase or decrease the volume of a message. All of these options are useful when trying to gather information from a detailed message. If a caller talks very fast when leaving a voice message, a subscriber can slow down the playback of the message. If a phone number is missed earlier in the message, a subscriber can go back 30 seconds to the beginning of the message to gather the phone number, and then move forward 30 seconds and resume listening. If a caller talks too softly when recording the message, a subscriber can increase the volume of the message.

In addition, subscribers can choose (from the Unity Assistant) to have the message sender's information played whenever they listen to a message. If the message is sent from a subscriber, they hear the sender's voice name (if recorded), as well as his primary extension. If the message is left from an outside caller, the subscriber hears the phone number of the sender, if Unity gathered this information with the call.

Message Management over TUI

After subscribers listen to a message, they can manage the message in several different ways. They have the usual options to save the message, delete the message, or mark the message as new. In addition, a subscriber can choose Reply to send a voice message to the original sender of the message, or choose Reply All to reply to the sender and all recipients of the message (assuming that they are all Unity subscribers). A message can also be *forwarded* to one or more Unity subscribers. In addition to forwarding a message to another subscriber, users can forward an e-mail to a fax machine, essentially giving them the capability to print their e-mails from the phone. (This capability is available only when Unity is integrated with a third-party fax server, however.) Finally, after listening to a message from a Unity subscriber, a user can choose Live Reply to speak with the subscriber who sent the message. When a subscriber chooses Live Reply to respond to a message, Unity initiates a call to the extension of the message sender. If the call is not answered, the user can leave a voice message. Live Reply allows a subscriber to call another subscriber without hanging up the phone, picking up the phone, and dialing the subscriber's extension.

Subscribers can choose how they want messages presented to them when they retrieve messages over the phone. Subscribers choose these options from the Cisco Unity Assistant. This feature, called Flex Stack, enables subscribers to choose the order in which new and saved messages are presented to them. It gives them the following options when they log into their mailbox:

- They can choose to have different message types presented separately, giving subscribers the option to listen to just voice messages, just e-mails, or just faxes.

- Alternatively, if a subscriber chooses to have all messages presented at once, he can choose the order in which messages are retrieved based on message type—for instance, urgent e-mails first, then urgent voice messages, then normal voice messages, then normal e-mails, and so on.

When listening to both new and saved messages, subscribers can choose to hear either oldest or newest messages first. For example, if a subscriber has five new voice messages, he might want to first hear the first message that arrived. Or, if listening to saved messages, a subscriber might want to first hear the last message that arrived.

Personal Administration over TUI

Aside from listening to messages and sending messages to other subscribers, Unity subscribers can modify a number of personal settings over the phone. All of these settings can also be modified using the Cisco PCA, but the TUI grants subscribers without Cisco PCA access to modify these settings. These include the following:

- **Greeting settings**. Subscribers have access to all five personal greetings—standard, closed, alternate, busy, and internal. From this menu, subscribers can enable or disable a particular greeting, and they can record or rerecord a greeting. This feature is particularly useful for subscribers who leave their office for an extended period of time but who forget to change their greeting to inform callers of their absence. They can call Unity from anywhere, enable their alternate greeting, and record a custom greeting of their choice.

- **Message settings**. From this menu, subscribers can modify the following:

  - **Message notification settings**. Subscribers can enable up to four of their message-notification devices (three phone devices and one pager device), as well as set the number Unity dials for each device.

  - **Menu style**. Subscribers can choose between full menus and brief menus. Brief menus are geared toward frequent users of the system or power users.

  - **Private lists**. Subscribers can create private distribution lists, add other Unity subscribers to these lists, and give the lists a custom voice name. Unity subscribers use private lists to message a group of Unity subscribers. Each Unity subscriber has access to only his own private lists.

- **Personal settings**. From this menu, subscribers can change their account password and the recorded name that Unity uses to identify them to callers. They also can choose whether they want to be listed in Unity's directory.

- **Transfer options**. Subscribers can specify a phone number where Unity should transfer calls, or subscribers can choose to have calls sent directly to their personal greeting. Call transfer is employed when Unity is used as an auto-attendant. For example, a subscriber who is out of the office in the afternoon might expect an important call. He can call Unity and change her transfer extension from his office phone to his cell phone so that he will not miss the call. For more detail on call transfer, refer to Chapter 18, "Audio-Text Applications." This chapter provides much more detail about how call transfer works and how to use it to accomplish desired tasks.

Finally, upon logging into Unity, a subscriber can be notified that an alternate greeting has been set. The subscriber is given the option to leave the greeting enabled, disable the greeting, or listen to the greeting. Often, when a subscriber is away from his phone for an extended time, he will record an alternate greeting informing callers of the duration of his absence and alternate contact information. When he returns to the office, he might forget to turn off this greeting, thus confusing callers about whether he is in the office. This feature reminds subscribers to disable their alternate greeting when they return to the office.

It is worth mentioning here that the Unity conversation enables subscribers to use shortcuts to access certain menus or perform certain actions. Basically, if you know where you are going in the conversation, Unity lets you just enter all the key presses at once, and it will take you to the desired conversation menu. For instance, a subscriber who is often out of the office frequently might enable and disable his alternate greeting. When he logs into his Unity mailbox, he really just wants to do this quickly rather than listen to all the menu options that Unity presents. To do this quickly, he can press 412 right after logging into his account, and he will be presented with the option to turn his alternate greeting on or off.

That summarizes the features available to callers when they interact with the TUI. Now we move on to the features available to Unity subscribers when using mail clients (either ViewMail for Outlook or Lotus Notes DUCS).

Subscriber Features Through Mail Clients

Both ViewMail for Outlook (VMO) and Lotus Notes DUCS give Unity subscribers the capability to compose, retrieve, and manage voice messages, e-mail messages, and faxes all through the same interface. These custom clients transform voice-mail subscribers into Unified Messaging subscribers. VMO and DUCS are simply extensions to a subscriber's everyday mail client (either Microsoft Outlook integrating with Microsoft Exchange, or Lotus Notes integrating with IBM Lotus Domino). This allows subscribers to use a single interface to customize their communications in any way they please. For example, if a Unity subscriber wants to send a voice message to a colleague, she can send it from her desktop PC instead of having to use the phone.

Message Sending from Mail Clients

When creating voice messages from the mail client, subscribers easily can address messages by taking advantage of the same directory they use to address e-mail messages. In addition, all of the delivery options normally available to them when sending an e-mail are also available when sending a voice message. With Microsoft Outlook, for instance, you can mark a message as urgent, customize whom replies should be sent to, and set an expiration date on a message, among many other options. With VMO installed, all of these options can be applied to a voice message as well. Unity voice messages are basically e-mail messages with a WAV attachment. Thus, from the mail client, Unity subscribers can send a voice message to any recipient with an e-mail address in the same way they can send an e-mail to any e-mail address. When the message is received by a non-Unity subscriber, it shows up as an e-mail with a WAV attachment, which can be played in the same way that any audio clip can be played.

When recording a voice message, subscribers use VCR-like controls on the custom mail-client form to record, rerecord, or play back the message they are about to send. To actually record the voice message, subscribers can use a microphone installed on their PC or a telephone, or they can even paste in a wave file from their desktop PC. Recording over the telephone employs Telephone Record and Playback (TRaP). A subscriber specifies a phone number and presses Record on the voice message form, the Unity server initiates a call on a port configured for TRaP, and the specified phone rings. When the user begins speaking, message recording begins. TRaP enables users who do not have a microphone or speakers installed to record and play back voice messages from their mail client. Figure 7-1 shows the voice-message form that a subscriber would use.

Figure 7-1 *Unity VMO Message Form*

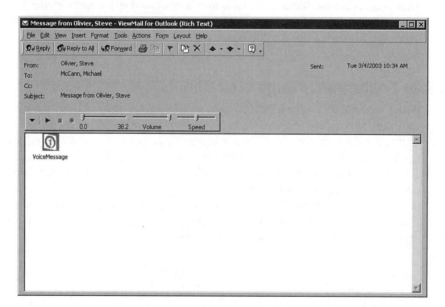

Message Playback from Mail Clients

When using the mail client to play back a voice message, Unity subscribers again use the same form with VCR-like controls to customize how they hear the message. They can listen to the message using either speakers installed with their desktop PC, or by using a phone (again, using TRaP). Whichever they use, the controls on the form allow them to move to any part of the message, increase or decrease the volume of the message, speed up or slow down the playback of the message, and pause and resume playback of the message. In addition, the length of the message is displayed. The controls are extremely intuitive and give subscribers the power to play back a message, or any part of a message, as slow or as fast as they need to. I cannot tell you how many times I have needed to replay the middle 5 seconds of a voice message over and over to get a phone number. The custom mail client forms put this all at your fingertips.

Message Management from Mail Clients

Voice messages and fax messages can be managed in the same way that e-mails are managed through this interface: They can be read (or listened to), deleted, saved, moved to personal folders, replied to, forwarded, and so on. Subscribers also have the option to reply to an e-mail with a voice message, or forward an e-mail with voice attachment. This allows subscribers to customize their communications according to their preferences.

Voice messages and faxes can be sorted by sender, subject, or time stamp in the same way that e-mail messages can be sorted. As Figure 7-2 shows, voice messages also have a custom icon to identify their message type, allowing a subscriber to sort messages by message type as well. When a caller leaves a message for a subscriber, Unity grabs the calling number and puts that information in the subject line of the voice message. If the calling number is a subscriber extension, Unity puts the name of the subscriber in the subject line instead of the phone number, as in shown in Figure 7-2. Note that messages from outside callers are marked as "From: Unity Messaging System," whereas messages from subscribers are marked as "From: {Subscriber Name}." Also, when a voice message has the caller ID in the subject line, subscribers can have the caller ID played back when retrieving messages from the TUI.

The mail client forms enable subscribers with desktop PCs to perform all of their messaging from their desktop. For people who use voice messaging heavily, this can greatly enhance their efficiency by eliminating the need to use the phone to send or retrieve a voice message. Of course, the mail client capabilities are available only for customers who use Microsoft Exchange or IBM Lotus Domino for e-mail as well as voice messaging. So what about customers who use Unity and have a separate e-mail system that Unity does not integrate with? Are they stuck using the telephone interface for all voice-messaging activities? Fortunately, the answer is no. The next section discusses the Cisco Personal Communications Assistant, or Cisco PCA, which consists of the Unity Inbox and the Unity Assistant.

Figure 7-2 *Microsoft Outlook Inbox with Voice Messages and E-mail Messages*

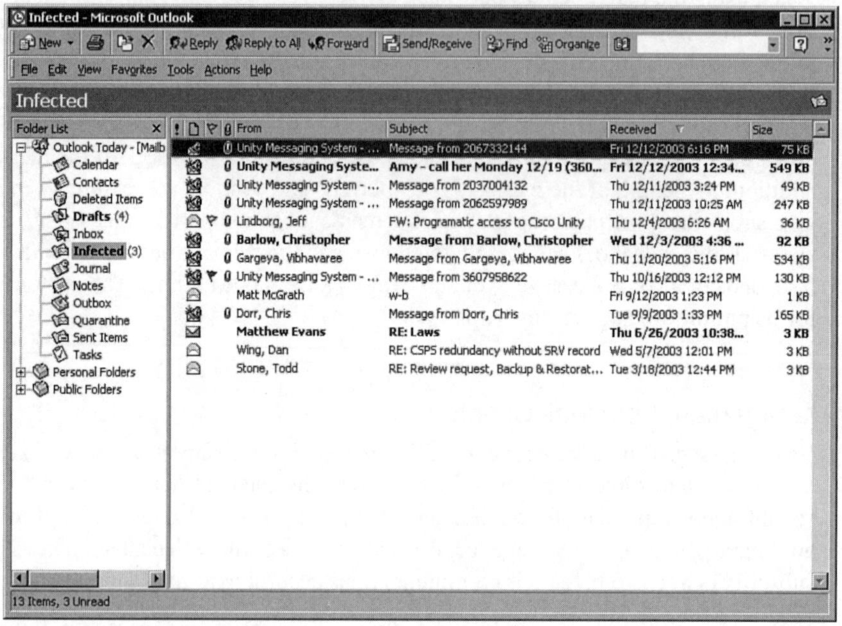

Subscriber Features Through the Cisco PCA

The Cisco Unity Inbox and Cisco Unity Assistant are new and improved versions of the Visual Messaging Interface (VMI) and the Active Assistant (AA) that existed in earlier Unity versions. Beginning in Unity 4.0(1), these two interfaces were rewritten and merged into the Cisco Personal Communications Assistant, or Cisco PCA. The Cisco PCA is a web client that provides a single place to log in and access both the Unity Inbox and the Unity Assistant. The Cisco PCA can be run only under Internet Explorer.

Cisco Unity Inbox

The Unity Inbox offers many of the same advantages that the customized mail clients offer, except that only voice messages can be managed from the Unity Inbox. This feature is useful for customers who do not integrate with existing Exchange or Domino, but who do want to use a GUI to send and listen to voice messages. Subscribers who want a separate interface to manage e-mails and voice messages will also find it useful. The Unity Inbox, shown in Figure 7-3, is a web client that offers similar VCR-like controls to record and play back a message at different volumes and different speeds. Subscribers can record or listen to messages using either multimedia devices (speaker/microphones) installed with their desktop PC or a telephone (using TRaP). As for message options, Mark Urgent, Mark Private, and Request Return Receipt all can be set when messages are composed.

Figure 7-3 *Unity Inbox with Voice Messages*

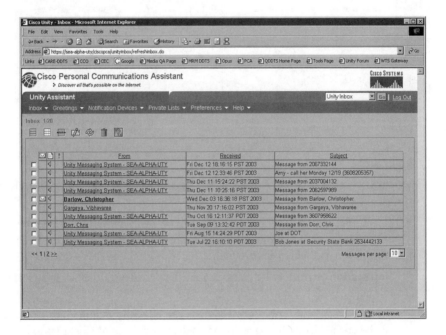

The Unity Inbox also offers an address book, shown in Figure 7-4, which offers the same functionality as the Outlook or Notes address book, with a couple of nice additions. For starters, searches can be performed by extension, in addition to the usual fields, such as first name, last name, and alias. Searches can be done on a subscriber's private lists, in addition to Unity subscribers and Unity public distribution lists. Finally, from the search results, a subscriber name can be played. Say, for instance, that you want to send a message to John Smith, but there are four John Smiths in the directory. You can play the voice name for each one to see which one you recognize as the John Smith you want to send the message to. For Unity systems that are not integrated with existing Exchange or Domino, the address book feature is essential for easy and efficient voice messaging.

Figure 7-4   *Unity Inbox Message Interface and Address Book Interface*

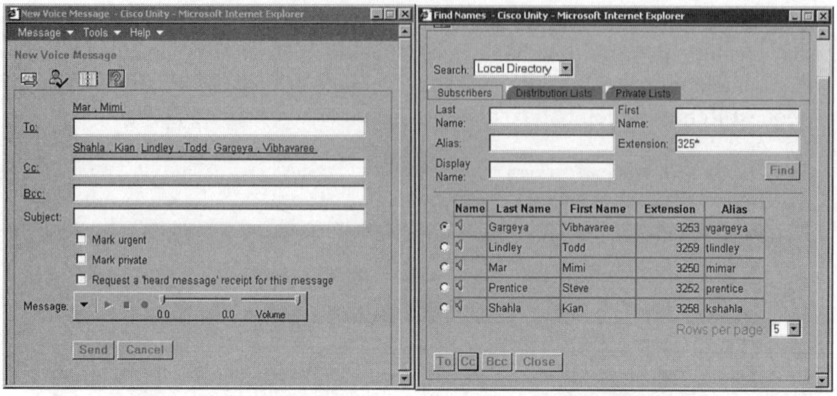

Cisco Unity Assistant

The Unity Assistant offers a GUI for subscribers to manage their personal settings. There are several pages of settings, organized as follows:

- **Greetings**. All five personal greetings can be easily played back, recorded, enabled, or disabled from here. There is also a quick summary view showing which greetings are enabled and which are disabled.

- **Notification devices**. All 13 message-notification devices can be fully managed from this page.

- **Private lists**. A subscriber's private lists can be easily modified, or new private lists can be created from this page. To add subscribers or public distribution lists to a private list, an intuitive interface that is similar to the Unity Inbox address book is used.

- **Preferences**. From this page, a host of subscriber settings can be viewed and modified:

  — Personal settings, such as recorded name, directory listing, and account password.

  — Phone menu options. These include the language a subscriber hears when logged into Unity, menu style, volume, time format (either 12-hour or 24-hour clock), addressing options (by extension, last name first, or first name first), and how message counts are presented to the user (for instance just voice-mail counts can be announced, or total message counts can be announced).

— Message-playback options. These include how messages are sorted and how the message menus are presented (Flex Stack, described in Subscriber TUI features), and what information to play along with the message content (sender's information, time stamp, and message number).

— Call transfer and call-screening options. These include transfer action (send incoming call to greeting or send to phone), options available to callers leaving messages for this account (mark as urgent and listen to and rerecord the message), and call-screening options. Note that the subscriber cannot set transfer type (release transfer or supervised transfer) in the Unity Assistant. Call-screening options are not available if a subscriber is configured to use release transfers.

Other Subscriber Features

A few Unity subscriber features cannot be administered by a subscriber, but must be managed by an administrator. These include alternate extensions and Message Waiting Indicators (MWIs). In addition, message notification should be described in more detail because many settings associated with this feature allow it to be customized in a variety of ways. The following section provides more information on these three subscriber features.

Message Waiting Indicator

The MWI might seem like a simple feature: The little light on your phone is lit when you have new voice messages, and it is extinguished when you have no new voice messages. However simple it might seem, the MWI is perhaps the most scrutinized feature in any voice-messaging system. People really want to know when they have a new message, and if they find out that they have a new message but their MWI lamp is not lit, they get really mad. If they see their MWI lit and call Unity to retrieve messages, and find out they have no new messages, they also get pretty peeved, but maybe a little less so. The MWI is used to notify subscribers of new voice messages only. The MWI cannot be configured to notify them that a new e-mail or fax has arrived. MWIs typically are configured to light the lamp on the phone with the subscriber's primary extension. However, MWIs also can be configured to light lamps at one or more phones by using alternate MWIs. Alternate MWIs are useful in shared-mailbox environments. For example, workers at a help desk might have phones with a personal extension, as well as another phone extension dedicated to the help desk hotline. A help desk account can be created in Unity so that company employees can leave voice messages for the help desk. The help desk account can also be configured with alternate MWIs, one for each help desk worker's hotline extension. With this configured, every time a message is left for the help desk account, the MWI is lit on each worker's help desk hotline extension. Only the system administrator can set MWI extensions; subscribers do not have access to MWI settings from the TUI or the Unity Assistant.

Message Notification

Message notification, sometimes called message delivery, can be performed by up to 13 devices per subscriber. Message notification settings can be managed fully by using the Unity Assistant, as shown in Figure 7-5, and partially through the subscriber TUI. A variety of settings are associated with each notification device:

- Target phone number or e-mail address where notification should be sent.

- Messages that trigger notification. Devices can trigger off of urgent messages (e-mail, voice message, fax, or any combination of these) or normal messages.

- The option to delay initial notification, as well as the option to trigger message notification whenever a new message is received or to trigger a notification only every *x* minutes while new messages exist in a subscriber's account.

- Schedule to determine the hours when notification with that device should and should not occur.

- What to do when the target phone does not answer: Ring how many times? Retry how many times? Retry after how many minutes?

- What to do when the target phone is busy: Retry how many times? Retry after how many minutes?

- Try another device if this device fails? (More on cascading notification comes later in this section.)

Figure 7-5   *Unity Assistant Notification Settings*

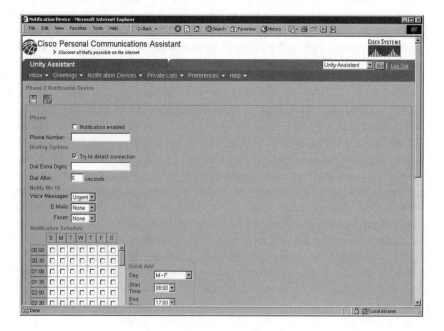

Depending on the device used, Unity performs a different action to notify a subscriber about a message.

- **Phone devices (eight devices).** These devices all have different names, but they do the same thing. A phone device places a call to the destination phone number, either across the street or across the country (availability of long-distance calling depends on the restrictions set up in Unity and the phone system). If someone answers the call, Unity plays "Hello, this is the Unity Messaging System with a message for. . . " It then asks for the subscriber ID and password. If the login is successful, the subscriber has access to his Unity account and can listen to his new messages. If a device mistakenly is configured to dial a wrong number, the notification conversation also allows the called party to turn off message notification for this number, which effectively disables the device. This can prevent Unity from repeatedly calling some poor guy who does not even know what Unity is.

- **Text pager (three devices).** When this device is triggered, Unity makes use of SMTP to send a text message to any e-mail address configured by the subscriber. The message can be configured to include the message counts in a subscriber's account, and it also can contain a short message (for instance, the number to call to retrieve new messages). Subscribers mostly use this device to send a text message to their cell phone whenever they have a new Unity voice message.

- **Pager (two devices).** Pager devices are similar to phone devices in that they dial a destination phone number when the device is triggered. Pager devices often need to take advantage of the option to dial extra digits (sometimes needed to navigate a paging system) after dialing the destination phone number. In addition, Unity allows for the pager device to dial the extra digits after a configurable delay, or to wait for a positive connection before dialing the extra digits. Someone who carries a pager might want Unity to buzz a pager for notification of new messages.

Any combination of notification devices can be enabled for a subscriber, and the devices all can trigger based on different criteria. For instance, a subscriber can set up his pager device to trigger only whenever any urgent messages arrive. He also could have his text pager trigger whenever a new voice message arrives. For subscribers who do not need to be simultaneously notified on six different devices whenever a new message arrives, Unity offers the option to cascade, or chain together, notification devices. Imagine that a subscriber has a notification chain like this: home phone to phone 1 (cell phone) to text pager. When the home phone device is triggered, Unity calls the phone number specified and retries additional calls if the call is not answered. When the retries for that device are complete, the home phone device officially has failed to notify, and the phone 1 device is triggered.
The same process continues for that device; when it fails to notify, the text pager triggers. Because the text pager simply sends a message, it cannot fail, so the chain ends here. It is worth noting here that devices after the first one in the chain do not adhere to their individual trigger criteria—when the first device fails, the next device in the chain automatically is triggered.

Cascading notification can be useful on a Unity mailbox that is monitored by multiple people. For instance, Unity might be used as an audio-text application for a sales support organization. This application guides callers through a series of menu options and also offers callers the opportunity to leave a message. During the week, several members of the team monitor the sales support mailbox. However, on the weekends, no one monitors the mailbox. If an urgent message arrives, someone on the team needs to spring into action to address the emergency. A cascading chain of notification devices, with each device calling a different person in the escalation path, is useful in this situation.

Alternate Extensions

Alternate extensions enable a subscriber to have multiple user IDs in Unity. Only system administrators can administer alternate extensions, so subscribers cannot modify them. This feature is valuable in a couple of different scenarios:

- **Easy message access.** A subscriber can quickly log in to his Unity account using easy message access. If a subscriber calls from his office phone (assuming that the phone extension matches that subscriber's user ID in Unity), he immediately is prompted to enter his password, bypassing the opening greeting and user ID entry. Unity does this based on the caller ID of the call. So what happens if a subscriber calls Unity from his home phone instead? Well, because the caller ID of this call does not match the subscriber's Unity user ID, that person hears the opening greeting and must press * and enter his user ID before hearing, "Please enter you password." However, by adding an alternate extension that matches the subscriber's home phone number, the subscriber can take advantage of easy message access when calling Unity from home.

- **Forward to personal greeting.** When a subscriber receives a call on his office phone (assuming that it is a Direct Inward Dial [DID] line) and he does not answer, the telephone can be set to forward to Unity. When the call is forwarded to Unity, the caller hears the subscriber's personal greeting. Unity does this based on the forwarding station of the call. If the forwarding station matches a subscriber ID, Unity plays the greeting for that subscriber (and perhaps takes a message). So what happens if a subscriber wants to have the cell phone forward to Unity when he does not answer? Because the cell phone number presumably does not match the subscriber's Unity ID, when a call is forwarded from the cell phone to Unity, the caller is sent to the Unity opening greeting instead of the subscriber's greeting. By adding an alternate extension matching the cell phone number, the subscriber can forward calls from his cell phone to Unity and can have those calls sent to his personal greeting.

- **Migration from a different voice-mail system.** Perhaps a company is changing its phone system and has decided to use Unity for voice-mail and auto-attendant instead of the old Octel messaging system. The company is changing its dial plan to use four-digit extensions instead of three-digit extensions, which means that the subscriber IDs will change. This also means that callers into the system need to know the new extension number of the person they want to reach. This can be handled in other ways.

For instance, callers can be instructed to use the directory to find the person they are trying to reach. But there is one way to handle this so that callers do not even need to know that the extension numbers changed. Alternate extensions can be used to allow subscribers to retain their old three-digit extension numbers in addition to their new four-digit number. This way, callers who know the new four-digit number can enter that to reach a given subscriber, and callers who know only the old three-digit extension number can still use that to reach the same subscriber.

It is important to note that alternate extensions must be unique across a given Unity system, in the same way that primary extensions must be unique. This uniqueness requirement applies to call handlers, interview handlers, public distribution lists, and directory handlers, in addition to subscribers. Basically, a Unity entity cannot have a primary extension or alternate extension that matches a primary extension or alternate extension of any other Unity object in that system. Note, however, that the same extension can exist on two Unity systems that are networked together.

That summarizes the list of Unity subscriber features. As you can see, subscribers have the opportunity to use Unity from several different interfaces. These options give users the flexibility to choose the interface that helps them to work most efficiently, as well as choose the interface that might be most appropriate for a particular scenario. The next section deals with features available to Unity administrators.

Unity Administrative Features

A Unity system administrator uses a couple different interfaces to administer and maintain a Unity messaging system. In this section, we assume that Unity already has been deployed and installed; now it is in use. This section does not deal with troubleshooting system problems; that topic is beyond the scope of this book.

Unity administrative activities include creating, modifying, and deleting Unity objects, whether they are subscribers, call handlers, public distribution lists, or interview handlers. Several Unity features give administrators the means to manage Unity in the manner that suits the task that must be performed. This section covers these features and applications, as well as outlines some scenarios in which one application might be used instead of another to perform a specific administrative task.

Cisco Unity Administrator

The Cisco Unity Administrator, or SA, is the main administrative console for Unity. The SA can be used to create, modify, and delete any object in Unity, in addition to modifying a host of other settings. Because the SA is a collection of web pages hosted on the Unity server, it can be accessed either from the Unity server itself or from a remote system. The SA does require Internet Explorer; it is not designed to work with Netscape or any other browser. Instead of going through all the settings available in the SA, we instead cover the administrative features available in the SA that are most useful to someone who administers the Unity system. For a description of all the available settings accessible from the SA, refer to the Unity product documentation.

Subscriber Templates

A Unity administrator can create different subscriber templates for different types of users who are homed on the Unity server. If users are created from customized templates, the administrator does not need to further modify the settings on each subscriber record he creates. For instance, a Unity system might house English-speaking subscribers working from Chicago, French-speaking users working from Montreal, and Spanish-speaking users working from Miami. An administrator can set up a separate subscriber template for each of these user groups. The templates would be set to use the appropriate conversation language and time zone so that when the user is created from the corresponding template, his account is ready for use without further modifications. Subscriber templates can also be used to ensure that subscribers are added to certain distribution lists when the subscriber account is created. Using the previous example, subscriber accounts created from the Montreal subscriber template might be added to the Montreal Office distribution list upon subscriber creation, whereas accounts created off the Miami subscriber template might be added to the Miami Office distribution list automatically.

Class of Service

Class of service (CoS), is used to dictate a subscriber's access to certain Unity features. Several of the personal administration and messaging features described earlier can be restricted based on CoS, including the Unity Inbox, the Unity Administrator, Live Reply, TTS (text-to-speech), and FaxMail (faxing e-mails to a fax machine from the TUI). In addition, CoS can be used to restrict the following:

- The maximum message length a subscriber account can receive
- The maximum length of a subscriber greeting
- The maximum length of a subscriber voice name
- Whether subscribers can change their own voice name
- Whether subscribers can change their directory listing status
- Whether subscribers can send messages to a public distribution list from the TUI
- Whether subscribers can change call-holding and call-screening settings from the Unity Assistant

For a complete list of the features controlled by CoS, refer to the Unity product documentation. As with subscriber templates, multiple classes of service can be set up on a Unity system. CoS can be tied to a subscriber template as well. So, an administrator might set up a Managers CoS that is tied to a Managers template to create subscriber accounts that have access to Unity Assistant and TTS. They also might create a Contractors CoS that is tied to a Contractors template. This template might be used to create subscriber accounts that restrict the use of the Unity Assistant and TTS.

SA access in general is controlled by CoS as well. Using CoS, a head Unity administrator can create several levels of Unity administration. There might be a group of people who are authorized only to change call handlers on the system, and another group that is authorized to modify only subscriber accounts but not create them. Perhaps only the head Unity administrator is authorized to create subscriber accounts. CoS controls all of these access rights.

Media Master Control

The Media Master control (MMC) is the same VCR-like interface that subscribers use in the Unity Inbox, Unity the Assistant, and mail client forms to record and play back wave files. The MMC is especially useful for administrators who need to create greetings, voice names, or questions for system call handlers, distribution lists, and interview handlers. The Media Master is embedded in each SA page that contains settings for greetings and voice names. Using the MMC, an admin can record and play back custom greetings or voice names using both a microphone and speakers, or by using a phone (via TRaP). A company often has professional voice talent record custom greetings or voice names for their Unity system. The MMC can be used to paste in these custom WAV files from the local computer or from anywhere on the network.

Online Help and Field Help

Embedded in each page of the Unity Administrator is both online help and field help pertinent to the page that the administrator uses. The online help provides a link to a general help file about the SA page and also provides access to the entire online help for the Unity Administrator. When field help is enabled, the administrator has access to detailed descriptions and instructions for each setting on a given page. These resources are a big help to administrators using Unity for the first time. Because the information is available with the click of the mouse, it saves time that otherwise might be spent flipping through pages of product documentation.

Cisco Unity Greetings Administrator

The Cisco Unity Greetings Administrator, or CUGA, grants distributed administrative access to call-handler greetings. In earlier versions of Unity, call-handler greetings could be modified using only the SA. This was especially a pain for customers who used Unity for audio-text applications. Often different departments want to manage their own audio-text applications, which usually involves changing custom greetings on the call handlers. CUGA, introduced in Unity 4.0(1), enables customers to use the TUI to change call-handler greetings instead of using the SA. Access to a call handler is based on the owner of the call handler (which can be an individual subscriber or a distribution list providing access to multiple users). The following tasks can be performed using CUGA:

- Rerecord a call handler greeting
- Enable or disable the alternate greeting for a call handler
- Determine which greeting is currently active for a call handler

This feature comes in handy when an unexpected event closes a department, for example. A member of the department can call Unity from anywhere and rerecord the greeting to let callers know that the office will be closed.

Tools Depot Applications

Unfortunately, the SA has some deficiencies that can make administering Unity a tedious and time-consuming task. For instance, there is no way to add a group of subscribers all at once. There is no way to make bulk edit changes to a group of subscribers after they have been created. The SA also makes it difficult to administer a group of Unity servers from a single point of access. Several applications have been developed to fill these gaps and make it easier to administer Unity. The Unity Tools Depot is a collection of administrative, diagnostic, and troubleshooting tools that have been developed to help administrators and system engineers better manage a Unity system. This section discusses some of the administrative tools that are available in the Tools Depot.

Bulk Edit

The Bulk Edit utility enables an administrator to modify one or more settings on either a group of call handlers or a group of subscribers. The SA has no means to modify the same setting on a group of call handlers or subscribers all at once, so the Bulk Edit tool fills a strong administrative need.

The majority of call-handler and subscriber settings can be modified by the Bulk Edit tool. This tool makes it easy to select the objects you want to modify based on extension or class of service, or by selecting certain objects from a list of all objects on the system. What types of scenarios call for using the Bulk Edit tool? Here is one example: A company has a Unity system that integrates with a legacy PBX, so all subscribers are homed on that PBX. The company wants to migrate to IP telephony using Cisco CallManager, and it plans an incremental migration. It wants to start by homing a quarter of its current users on CallManager, keeping the remaining users on the legacy PBX. The administrator can use the Bulk Edit tool to move a quarter of the subscribers to CallManager. As the migration continues, the Bulk Edit tool can be used to move other groups of subscribers off the legacy PBX and onto CallManager.

Here is another example: A Korean company uses Unity 3.1(5), which does not have Korean localization. The subscribers of this system use English as their subscriber language. However, upon upgrading their Unity system to Unity 4.0(3), they have Korean prompts installed. The subscribers on this Unity system obviously would prefer to hear their subscriber conversation in their native language. What is the easiest way to change the subscriber language for all subscribers on the system? By using the Bulk Edit tool, the administrator quickly can change the subscriber language for all subscribers on the system from English to Korean.

These are just a couple examples displaying the usefulness of the Bulk Edit tool. By browsing the settings that can be modified by the Bulk Edit tool, you can come up with some scenarios as well.

Cisco Unity Bulk Import Wizard

The Cisco Unity Bulk Import Wizard, or CUBI (see Figure 7-6), enables administrators to create a group of Unity subscriber accounts at once. Administrators either can import subscriber data from a CSV file or can import data from existing Exchange 5.5, Active Directory, or Domino accounts. CSV import is often useful when migrating from a previous voice-messaging system to Unity. CUBI allows the creation of up to 7,500 Unity subscribers per session. CUBI requires some basic information about each subscriber to be imported, such as subscriber extension, before it can import the information. Beyond the basic information, when using CSV import, a long list of subscriber information can be specified so that each subscriber account is customized when it is added to Unity. In addition, CUBI requires that a subscriber template be selected so that the template settings can be applied to the subscriber accounts that are created. However, only one subscriber template can be specified each time CUBI is run; that template is applied to all users being imported in that batch.

Using CSV import, CUBI also can be run to modify values of subscriber attributes or settings on existing Unity subscriber accounts. This is useful when a setting needs to be modified on a group of subscribers, but the value needs to be different for each subscriber. The Bulk Edit tool enables you to change an attribute to a single value for a group of subscribers. However, it cannot change an attribute to a different value for each subscriber unless you want to run the tool once for each subscriber! Here is an example of when CUBI might be used to modify subscriber accounts: Multiple subscribers on a Unity system have cell-phone numbers that they want to input as alternate extensions. This way, they can have calls forwarded from their cell phone to their Unity mailbox, and they also can benefit from easy message access when calling Unity from their cell phone. Each subscriber has a different cell phone number, so Bulk Edit tool does not quite fit this need. However, an administrator can create a CSV file that includes records for each subscriber to be modified, including the unique alternate extension for each subscriber. The administrator then runs CUBI using the CSV file as the source of import. The administrator easily can add an alternate extension to each subscriber in the list. For this task, using CUBI is much easier than using the SA, especially for a large group of users (more than 10).

Figure 7-6 *Cisco Unity Bulk Import Wizard: Selecting Multiple Subscribers to Import*

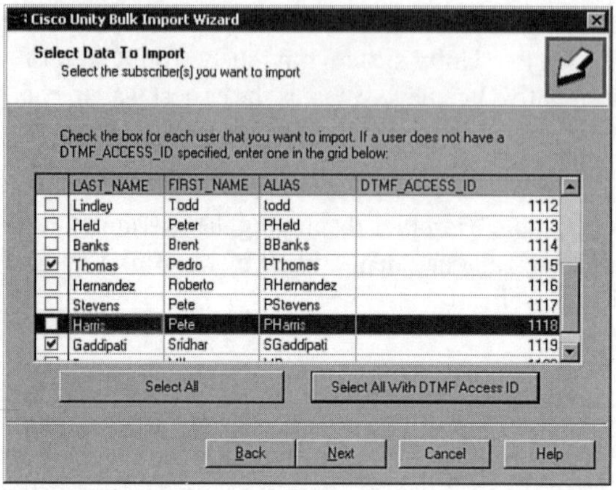

Global Subscriber Manager

The Global Subscriber Manager, or GSM, is useful as a single point of administration for managing networked Unity servers. Using the GSM, administrators can import Unity subscribers, delete Unity subscribers, and move Unity subscribers from one Unity server to another. The GSM enables administrators to view all subscribers within a particular dialing domain, and it also enables administrators to view subscribers according to the Unity server they reside on. This is useful in deployments with multiple Unity servers. In these cases, often an administrator does not know which Unity server a subscriber resides on. Because the SA on each Unity server displays only the subscribers homed on that Unity server, it can take some time to open each SA for each server just to locate a single subscriber. Using the GSM, a subscriber can be located quickly because all subscribers from all the Unity servers in the dialing domain can be listed and sorted in a single list. When the subscriber is located, the admin simply selects the subscriber in question, and the GSM automatically opens the SA to the subscriber page. From there, the admin can modify or read a particular setting. Figure 7-7 shows the GSM.

The GSM also enables administrators to delete Unity subscribers without leaving unresolved references in the system. When deleting an object, the SA does not have the capability to check whether other objects point to the object to be deleted. Unity objects can be connected in many ways, whether by message recipient, after greeting action, after message action, or with one-key dialing options. If a subscriber is deleted and other objects have references to that subscriber, there will be a loss of functionality in the Unity system until that unresolved reference is cleaned up. The GSM can prevent unresolved references from being created when subscribers are deleted. For instance, imagine that Chris Cornell is the message recipient for several call handlers on the Unity system at Somms, Inc. Chris has decided to pursue other opportunities outside the company. When Chris's subscriber account is deleted using the SA, the call handlers that had Chris as a message recipient no longer have a place to send messages. As a result, callers cannot leave messages with those call handlers. If the GSM is used to delete Chris Cornell's account, it asks the administrator for a replacement link for all objects that have references to Chris's account. When prompted by the GSM, the administrator might replace Chris with his manager as the message recipient for the call handlers in question, preventing any loss of functionality because of unresolved references.

Figure 7-7   *Global Subscriber Manager: Managing Subscribers Across Multiple Unity Servers*

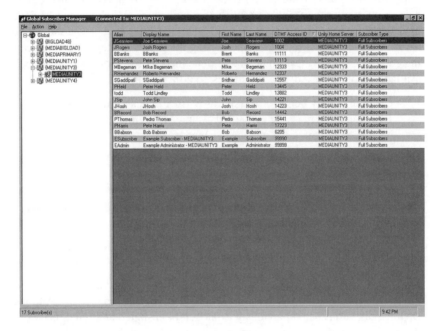

Audio Text Manager

The Audio Text Manager, or ATM, is useful for managing audio-text applications made up of trees of call handlers, interview handlers, and subscriber accounts. As mentioned earlier, Unity objects can be linked in many different ways. Unfortunately, the SA does not provide an interface to easily view a call handler tree, for instance. Using the Audio Text Manager, an administrator can view an audio-text application from the perspective of a caller who enters the call-handler tree. The Audio Text Manager displays a summary view of a call-handler tree and enables an administrator to easily focus in on one object in the tree to view or modify its links to other Unity objects. The ATM is also useful for finding available extension ranges on the Unity system. Chapter 18 provides further detail on using Audio Text Manager to manage audio-text applications in Unity.

Advanced Settings Tool

A handful of settings in Unity cannot be edited using the SA interface. Some of these settings enable hidden features in Unity, whereas other settings provide modifications on existing Unity functionality. For the most part, these settings are not exposed in the SA because they can cause undesirable behavior for the average company using Unity. However, a couple of customers here and there want Unity to behave differently from the default fashion. So, settings to change the default behavior are coded and added to the Registry, and these settings are exposed in the Advanced Settings tool. In most cases, the tool allows a setting to be changed only to supported values. In addition, it allows settings to be edited only on a Unity version that supports the change. The Advanced Settings tool also provides a description of each setting, as well as possible values, which lessens the chance that an undesirable change will be made. In these ways, the Advanced Settings tool gives an administrator access to these settings without using the Windows Registry, which can be a daunting endeavor (and a catastrophic one, if done incorrectly). Some frequently used settings available through the Advanced Settings Tool include these:

- Changing Unity behavior when a subscriber hangs up while listening to a message. By default, the message is marked as unread. Using the tool, the Unity behavior can be changed to mark the message as read.

- Changing how subscribers confirm message addressing. By default, they hear a subscriber's name and extension. A setting can be changed so that they hear just a name, or no confirmation is done before adding the user to the message address list.

- Enabling an end-of-recording warning beep when a caller is nearing the maximum record length. By default, there is no warning beep.

- Disabling Add Subscribers from the SA for administrators of any class of service. Some sites want this capability, to ensure that users are imported only into Unity.

The Tools Depot applications all are installed as part of Unity, and they are accessible from the Tools Deport shortcut on the Unity server desktop. One item to note: Although the Tools Depot applications listed previously cannot all be installed and run directly on remote systems (the GSM is one exception), all of these tools can be run on the Unity system from remote systems by using remote-access software. Windows Terminal Services is the recommended remote-access software to be used with Unity.

Unity Maintenance Features

Maintenance of a Unity system can involve a variety of activities. These can include monitoring subscriber account and voice-mail port usage, backing up system data, monitoring system resources, and identifying and potentially resolving problems on the system. This section covers various applications and features in Unity that help an administrator perform maintenance activities on the Unity server.

Reports

Unity offers several reports that are useful for summarizing system activities and data. In most cases, each report can be customized to display data for a particular time period so that administrators can run reports with any frequency they choose—daily, weekly, or monthly. Reports are launched from the SA, so administrators can generate reports from a remote system. Completed reports are stored on the Unity server, and they can be stored in either HTML format or CSV (comma-delimited) format. The most commonly used reports are listed here:

- **Subscribers report**. This report provides a list of subscribers on the system, including information, such as first and last name, alias, Unity extension, and class of service.

- **Distribution Lists report**. This report provides a list of all public distribution lists on the system, and optionally provides a list of members in each list. The report can be run on a single distribution list or all distribution lists in the system.

- **Administrative Access Activity report**. This report can be used to track which Unity administrators accessed the system and what changes they made.

- **Call Handler Traffic report**. This report can be used to track the call flow through call handlers on the Unity system. It tallies the total calls routed to a call handler in a specified period, and also details the action that the caller took (entered a valid extension, entered a one-key dial option, hung up, and so on). This report can be used to measure the effectiveness of audio-text applications.

- **Billing reports**. Both an Outcall Billing and a Transfer Billing report are offered. These reports list information about out dials from subscriber accounts and transfers from subscriber accounts and call handlers. They can be used to track calls to long-distance numbers for billing purposes.

- **Failed Login report**. This report provides information about failed TUI logons as well as failed Cisco Unity Administrator logons. This information is useful to identify patterns of invalid logons, which can indicate that an individual is trying to gain unauthorized access to Cisco Unity. The report also identifies accounts that have been locked because the maximum number of invalid logons has been exceeded.

Port Usage Analyzer

The Port Usage Analyzer tool (found in the Tools Depot) offers four reports for analyzing call traffic on a Unity system. Report data is displayed in a graphical chart and can also be saved off in a CSV file. For each report, the data can be viewed in a number of ways, making it easy to gather the necessary data. The four reports offered are described here:

- **Port Availability report**. For any given time in the day, this report shows how many ports are in use and how many are available for calls.

- **Call Distribution report**. This report shows what types of calls are coming in or going out of each port on the Unity system.

- **Port Time Use report**. This report shows how long each port is busy with each type of call.

- **Call Traffic report**. This report shows how many of each of the five types of calls came into a port or originated from a port for each minute of the day.

This information is useful to determine whether a Unity system is configured appropriately for the type of load it handles. For instance, the call traffic report might show that the four ports enabled for MWIs are overloaded, while ports set to handle incoming calls are handling a medium load. As a result, an administrator might allot more ports to MWI dialouts to prevent delays in lighting lamps. From the Port Availability report, a Unity administrator might see that a few ports are available for incoming calls throughout the day. As a result, he might choose to purchase more ports for the Unity server, to keep subscribers or outside callers from being denied access to the system. The information in the Port Availability report, shown in Figure 7-8, can also help an administrator decide when to plan downtime for the Unity server.

Figure 7-8 *Port Availability Chart Generated by Port Usage Analyzer*

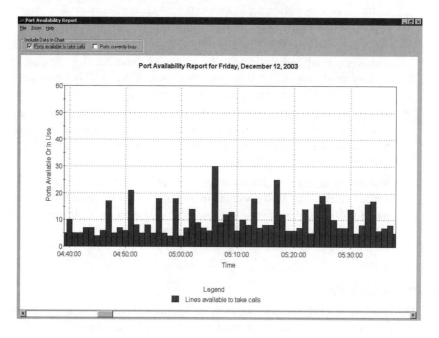

HTML Status Monitor

This tool offers administrators a summary of activities and data on the Unity system. Administrators also can start and stop Unity from the Status Monitor. Because it is web-based, the tool can be run remotely. Class of service controls access to the Status Monitor. The information is displayed on five different pages:

- **System status**. Shows whether Unity is running, and also provides an interface to stop and start Unity. When stopping Unity, administrators can choose to wait until all active calls are finished before shutting down the system. Or, they can choose to interrupt all active calls with a voice message announcing the imminent system shutdown before disconnecting the active ports and shutting down the system.

- **Port status**. Shows real-time activity on all ports.

- **Report status**. Shows the status of all reports that have been generated.

- **License status**. Shows licenses used, licenses purchased, and remaining available licenses for several features.

- **Disk drive status**. Shows the total and available disk space on each disk drive in the Unity server.

For more accurate real-time port status information, the Port Status Monitor tool is available in the Tools Depot. With the Port Status Monitor, activity on voice-mail ports can be logged. Although it is helpful as a maintenance tool, this application is especially useful for troubleshooting.

Unity Performance Counters

Unity has custom performance counters that can be accessed using either Windows 2000 Performance Monitor or Cisco Unified Performance Information and Diagnostics (CUPID). CUPID can be found in the Tools Depot. These custom counters can track a wide variety of Unity-specific data including the following:

- **TTS information**. Total TTS sessions in use and the average duration of TTS sessions can be logged. By tracking this information, an administrator might see that all available TTS sessions are used up at peak times and, therefore, determine that more TTS sessions need to be purchased.

- **Silence counters**. The counters show the average time it takes Unity to perform certain actions, such as log into a subscriber account, delete a message, or play the opening greeting. By monitoring these silence counters across the system, a Unity administrator can determine whether the Unity system is performing well enough to meet user needs.

- **Call statistics**. This is the number of incoming and outgoing calls, the duration of calls, and also includes successful and failed notification calls and MWI requests.

Both the Performance Monitor and CUPID generate CSV files, so any tool that can process CSV files, including Performance Monitor, can be used to analyze the data. Analyzing performance data can help an administrator identify usage trends that might lead to purchasing additional Unity resources (TTS ports), and it also can help identify problems on the system (silence counters). Aside from gathering data from the custom counters, administrators can use Performance Monitor or CUPID to monitor system resource usage, such as memory usage and CPU usage. Analyzing this data also can help an administrator determine how the system performs and perhaps can help identify performance problems that can affect callers and subscribers using the system. CUPID comes with custom configuration files that include recommended performance counters for a given version of Unity. If Performance Monitor is used, the counters need to be added manually.

Tools Depot Applications

A variety of Tools Depot applications are also available for different Unity maintenance tasks. Because maintenance tasks are often specific, having different tools for different types of tasks is suitable. The next section highlights four Tools Depot applications that are used widely for Unity system maintenance.

Message Store Manager

The Message Store Manager enables Unity administrators to schedule routine message store maintenance tasks on Unity subscriber accounts. The MSM also provides detailed usage information on subscriber accounts. This tool is useful for companies that are not familiar with Microsoft Exchange administration but that need to manage the message storage on their Unity server. These are some of the tasks that the MSM can perform:

- Move messages between folders (from Inbox to Deleted Items, from Deleted Items to temporary storage space, from Deleted Items to Inbox, and so on). Messages can be moved based on a number of properties including priority, age, message type, and message status.

- Flush messages from Deleted Items folder, again based on a number of criteria.

- Set mailbox usage limits on Unity subscriber mailboxes in Exchange. This prevents subscribers from storing too many messages on the Exchange server, taking up valuable space. If a subscriber is over the mailbox limit, Unity notifies him when he logs in over the TUI; Unity also will prevent this user from sending new messages from the TUI, if appropriate.

The MSM also provides extremely detailed data on each subscriber mailbox. The report is generated in the CSV file and, therefore, is meant to be analyzed using a tool such as Microsoft Excel. From this report, an administrator can find out just about anything about a subscriber mailbox, from the number of voice messages that arrived three days ago to the number of unread messages in a subscriber's account.

Event Monitoring Service

The Event Monitoring Service, or EMS, monitors the Windows Event Log and alerts administrators when errors or warnings appear on the system. The EMS can be configured to trigger off any event, and it can be configured to notify one or more administrators, or public distribution lists, by way of e-mail or voice message, or both. The EMS can also be configured to send text messages through an SMTP gateway. This functionality is essential when the message store is not available to send messages. This capability is also useful for sending notifications to e-mail addresses external to the company.

The EMS can help minimize downtime when system failures occur, and it can help an administrator be proactive to avoid system failures. For instance, the EMS can be set to trigger off the Windows "disk full" event. If an administrator is notified of this condition in time, she can prevent the problem from affecting voice-messaging services. This tool is also useful for troubleshooting system problems by notifying interested parties when a problem occurs so that diagnostics and other system information can be promptly gathered.

Disaster-Recovery Tools

The Unity Disaster Recovery Backup tool and the Unity Disaster Recovery Restore tool, collectively known as DiRT, back up Unity system data and allow that data to be restored on a freshly installed Unity server of the same software version as the one backed up. DiRT should be used to complement an existing backup strategy. It can be useful in a number of scenarios:

- **Irrecoverable system failure (including hard drive failure).** If a DiRT backup of the Unity system data was made before the failure, a new Unity system can be installed and the failed Unity server data can be restored on the new server. Regular scheduled DiRT backups are recommended so that recovery from a platform failure is possible.

- **Migration to new platform.** As companies grow and add employees, they often must upgrade their infrastructure. In the case of Unity, this involves upgrading to a more powerful server. DiRT provides the means to migrate the Unity server from the older platform to the new, more powerful platform without a loss of data.

- **Server name change or domain change.** In some cases, customers need to change the name of the server where they run Unity. This might be necessary when migrating from voice mail-only (Unity is the domain controller/Global Catalog server in its own domain) to unified messaging (Unity is a member server in an existing domain). DiRT provides the means to migrate system data to a new server with a different name and in a different domain.

Two important items should be noted:

- DiRT must be used to restore data to the same Unity version from which data was backed up. For instance, you cannot use DiRT to back up a Unity 3.1(5) system and then use it to restore to a Unity 4.0(3) system. If possible, the Unity 3.1(5) system should be upgraded to Unity 4.0(3); then DiRT can be used to back up that system, and data can be restored to the Unity 4.0(3) system.

- The latest versions of DiRT offer the option to include subscriber messages as part of the backup. This option can be useful for voice mail-only systems with a small number of users. However, it should not be used on unified messaging systems or any larger Unity systems. For mail store data (messages, and so on), mail store-aware backup tools should be used in correlation with DiRT to restore a Unity system intact with all subscriber messages.

Database Walker

Database Walker, or DBWalker, is a tool that administrators can use to identify—and often fix—problems in the Unity database. DBWalker can be run in report mode or auto-fix mode. In report mode, DBWalker analyzes the Unity database and reports back any problems. From this report, the administrator can use the SA to manually fix broken links or other Unity database problems. In auto-fix mode, DBWalker can be instructed to automatically fix a number of problems. Not all problems with the Unity database can be automatically fixed using DBWalker, but DBWalker can detect and fix these common problems automatically:

- Validate call-handler message recipient
- Validate subscriber and call-handler one-key dialing links
- Validate that the subscriber language is installed on the Unity server

If left unfixed, each of these problems could result in system errors that surely would interrupt subscriber and outside caller voice-messaging services. DBWalker can help identify these problems, in addition to a host of other problems, before subscribers encounter the issue.

Unity Security Features

For many companies, Unity is a business-critical system, and it interfaces with other critical business systems such as e-mail and phone systems. Because of this, administrators must have a means to secure the Unity server against security threats against itself or other interfacing systems. Unity is a messaging system, so it inevitably will access and store private information in the form of recorded messages. Because Unity is a conduit for potentially sensitive information, administrators also must have a means to secure the Unity system data and the Unity subscriber and administrative interfaces. This section discusses the Unity-specific security features available to administrators. Keep in mind that Unity runs on Windows 2000 and requires IE to run its web clients. So, in some cases, Unity leverages the security features of these technologies. In these cases, Unity can be only as secure as the technologies it uses.

Unity TUI Security

At a basic level, Unity secures the TUI access point to subscriber accounts by requiring a password. Using account policies administered through the SA, administrators can set complexity requirements on account passwords to ensure that subscribers do not set trivial phone passwords. The account policy can also specify how often a password expires, requiring subscribers to change their password the next time they log in over the phone. If a subscriber account does come under attack from the TUI, account policy can dictate that an account be locked after a set number of failed login attempts. A locked account cannot be accessed until a Unity administrator unlocks the account. The Failed Login report, described earlier, enables administrators to view the failed logins on the Unity system and perhaps identify that a particular account is under attack. Unity also logs a warning in the event log whenever an account has been locked because the number of failed login attempts set in the account policy has been exceeded.

For additional TUI security, Unity easily can be configured to work with the RSA SecureID system. This enhanced phone security method is known as two-factor user authentication. When subscribers log in, they are required to enter a unique pass code, which is a combination of their Unity account password and an unpredictable token code that the RSA SecureID system generates every 60 seconds. Unity works with the RSA server to determine whether a user should be granted access to the subscriber account. After configuring Unity for use with the RSA SecureID system, class of service determines which subscribers use two-factor authentication to access their Unity accounts.

Administrative Interface Security

To gain access to the Cisco PCA, Status Monitor, or SA, account credentials must be entered and passed to Unity for verification. Unity can be configured to use either integrated Windows authentication or anonymous authentication to validate administrative access to the SA. Depending on a company's security needs or policies, either method might be appropriate. If more advanced security is required, the Secure Sockets Layer (SSL) protocol should be set up on the Unity server to ensure a secure connection between the Unity server and clients, as well as to provide digital certificate authentication. When subscribers log into the Cisco PCA, their credentials are sent across the network in clear text, in the same way that an administrator's credentials are sent in clear text when anonymous authentication is used for SA access. SSL ensures that account credentials, as well as data entered in the SA or Cisco PCA, are encrypted as the data is sent across the network.

Unity System Security

The Cisco Security Agent for Cisco Unity provides intrusion protection, malicious mobile code protection, operating system integrity assurance, and audit log consolidation. This security agent was created using CiscoWorks Management Center for Cisco Security Agents. It makes use of standard Cisco Agent security policies, including Required Windows System Module, Common Security Module, Common Web Server Security Module, Restrictive MS IIS Module, Server Module, User Authentication Auditing Module, and Virus Scanner Module. In addition, the CSA for Cisco Unity includes the Unity Base Group Exceptions policy, which allows normal Cisco Unity operations that the other policies would not allow. The CSA for Cisco Unity enables administrators to closely monitor their Cisco Unity system and helps prevent attacks against the server components that Unity relies upon.

Restriction tables enable Unity administrators to limit the phone numbers that subscribers and administrators can configure for calls made by Unity. Unity can place calls to perform message notification, transfers, to TRaP connections, to deliver faxes to a fax machine, and to send AMIS messages. Restriction tables are designed to prevent toll fraud and other abuses of the phone system through Unity. The default restriction tables restrict domestic long-distance calls and international calls, but the restriction tables can be modified or new restriction tables can be created. The restriction tables can employ number patterns so that one entry can restrict a whole class of numbers to a particular area code, for example. Restriction tables are applied when a change is being made instead of when Unity actually attempts a call. These changes can occur via the Unity SA, the Cisco PCA, or the TUI— restriction tables apply for all of these interfaces. For this reason, restriction table policies should be in place before subscribers and administrators have access to change settings.

In addition, restriction tables are associated with subscribers and administrators through class of service. In this way, administrators can set a subscriber account to transfer to a long-distance number, but a subscriber might not be allowed to configure this same number through the Cisco PCA. To further clarify this point, imagine that a salesperson is traveling away from the home office. He wants to configure his subscriber account so that Unity will transfer calls to his cell phone while he is on the road. However, he is in the Sales class of service, which is associated with the Subscribers restriction table. This restriction table restricts all long-distance calls by restricting the number pattern 91???????* (where ? matches exactly one digit, and * matches zero or more digits). So, when the salesperson uses the Cisco PCA to update transfer settings so that calls will be transferred to his cell-phone number, he is not allowed to save the change. Instead, he is reminded that he needs to contact his local Unity administrator to make this change. The Unity administrator has a subscriber account in the Admin class of service, which is associated with the Admin restriction table. The Admin restriction table does not restrict long-distance calls. Therefore, the local Unity administrator can open the SA, locate the salesperson's account, and successfully change the transfer phone number on the account to the salesperson's cell-phone number.

As you can see, a Unity administrator has a number of tools and features at his disposal to administer, maintain, and secure a Cisco Unity server. It is recommended that each feature be explored in further depth, with hands-on experience, to determine how it might help with the administration of a Unity system. Managing a Unity server can be a complicated task, especially considering all of the different technologies involved. The features and tools described in this section were developed to make this job easier.

Unity System Features

A number of Unity features were mentioned in previous sections, but they need a more detailed description to clearly identify their role. Unity subscribers and administrators indirectly use other features, so these are difficult to describe in the context of a user. This section is devoted to describing Unity features that operate at the system level.

Unity Failover

Unity failover provides customers with a simple redundancy solution so that call processing and voice-messaging services can continue even when one Cisco Unity server fails or is down for maintenance. Failover is a two-server solution, with one Unity server as the primary server and a second Unity server as the secondary server. Only one of the two servers is active at a given time. The active server handles calls, takes messages, and is used to make changes to Unity data. The inactive server is synchronized with any changes made on the active server by means of SQL replication and file replication (file replication does not occur if failover servers are set to manual mode—more on this later).

SQL replication ensures that whenever a Unity object is added, modified, or deleted, the change is mirrored on the inactive server. File replication ensures that greetings, voice names, messages and other data are replicated from the active server to the inactive server, ensuring that this data is not lost. The administrator can configure the frequency of this file replication. Not all Unity data is replicated between servers, so some changes need to be made on both servers (for instance, Registry changes via the Advanced Settings tool). The Failover Configuration Wizard is provided to simplify the process of setting up failover between two Unity servers. However, it should be noted that the voice-mail ports on the phone system need special configuration when failover is used, to ensure that calls and call information properly are delivered to both primary and secondary Unity servers.

Failover can run in either automatic mode or manual mode. When failover is configured for automatic mode, the primary server fails over to the secondary server when a problem occurs on the primary server. Automatic failover occurs without user intervention. Problems that might induce failover include complete Unity system failure, calls not being handled on the primary server, and loss of network connectivity on the primary server. The time that it takes to fail over in any of these situations depends on the settings used for failover and the system configuration, but, on average, it takes less than 1 minute.

When running in automatic mode, failover can be caused by user intervention as well. If a secondary server is active, failback to the primary server can be scheduled or caused by user intervention. Of course, Unity allows failback only if Unity runs on the primary server.

When failover runs in manual mode, a primary server fails over to a secondary server only when an administrator intervenes. If the primary server is not answering calls, the secondary server will not activate and begin handling calls. It is up to the user to manually fail over to the secondary server. When running in manual mode, file replication is disabled. Manual mode specifically was designed for upgrade and install scenarios. In general, failover should not be used for rolling upgrades of Unity servers because of the risk of data loss and lost messages. An example is upgrading the primary server while the secondary server is active, and then activating the primary and upgrading the secondary.

The Failover Monitor runs on both primary and secondary servers. This tool, shown in Figure 7-9, displays the status of each server and enables an administrator to customize the failover configuration.

Figure 7-9 *Failover Monitor Screen*

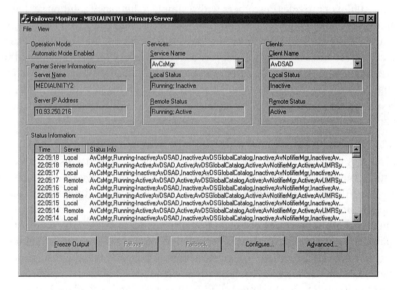

License Pooling and Demo Licenses

Starting with Unity 4.0(1), Unity uses a software-based license scheme. In previous versions, a hardware dongle containing the license information shipped with each Unity server. The new software-based licensing uses FlexLM to manage the software licenses. The license file is tied to the MAC address of the Unity server, so each physical server where Unity is installed needs a separate license file (with the exception of a failover secondary server). A number of Unity features are controlled by this license, including failover, number of TTS sessions, number of languages, number of voice-mail ports, number of Unity subscriber accounts, number of Unity Inbox subscribers, number of Unified Messaging subscribers, and VPIM, Bridge, and AMIS.

License pooling was introduced in Unity 4.0(1) to enable subscriber licenses to be shared across networked Unity servers. For example, imagine that three networked Unity servers are enabled for license pooling, and they each have 1000 Unity subscriber licenses. The administrator is not restricted to having each Unity server with 1000 subscribers; one server could have 2000 subscribers, while the other 2 can have 500 subscribers each. One site where Unity is deployed can grow faster than another site; license pooling gives administrators the flexibility to manage subscriber licenses across an organization instead of on each individual server.

Unity also offers the option to use a default demonstration license, or a time-expiring demo license. The default demo license enables only limited features. However, it is copied to all Unity servers during installation, making Unity readily available for immediate use. A time-expiring license must be ordered separately, but it enables a broader range of features than the default demo license.

The demo license is obviously a very important feature for customers and sales folks who want hands-on experience with Unity without spending the money to purchase a full-blown license. In addition, the demo license enables someone to use a single copy of Unity to install multiple demo systems or test systems. As alluded to earlier, a separate license file must be obtained for each server on which Unity is installed. Upgrading from a demo license to a real license is easy as well; you can install Unity without a real license file and then add it later.

Languages and Multilingual Capabilities

As of Unity 4.0(3), Unity is localized in 22 languages. Unity is designed so that any number of languages can be used on the system simultaneously. A subscriber in one office can use the Cisco PCA in Spanish and have his e-mails read to him in English, while a subscriber in the office next door can use Cisco PCA in Japanese and have e-mails read to her in Japanese. Depending on the language, the localization might include system prompts, Cisco PCA, TTS, VMO, help files, and user documentation, or it might be limited to just some of these. The number of languages allowed to be installed on Cisco Unity system is licensed, and languages are installed during the Unity installation. During installation, a default phone language, default GUI language, and default TTS language are selected. After installation, the languages that will be used are loaded into the system through the SA.

Subscribers can choose their personal phone language through the Cisco PCA. In most cases, this language setting dictates the language that callers hear when they log into their Unity account, as well as the language that will be used to read their e-mails. The default phone language defines what language is used to play system prompts, such as the failsafe message. The default TTS language comes into play when a subscriber has chosen a phone language that has no corresponding TTS language engine, such as Australian English. On systems in which Australian English is the default phone language, U.S. English or U.K. English should be set as the default TTS language because there is no Australian English TTS engine.

Subscribers select the language to use for Cisco PCA and Unity Administrator by setting their browser to the desired language. For the Unity Administrator, if the language chosen is among the loaded languages, the Unity Administrator is localized in the chosen language. For the Cisco PCA, if the language chosen is among the languages that Cisco PCA offers, the Unity Assistant and Unity Inbox are localized in the chosen language. If the language chosen in the browser is not valid in either case, the default GUI language is used.

Unity's multilingual feature can be used to set up audio-text applications that accommodate callers of different native languages. Any call handler, directory handler, subscriber, or interview handler on the system can be configured to use one of the loaded languages so that callers using that handler hear system prompts in the specified language. Unity objects can also be set to inherit their language setting from any referring Unity object. In this way, depending on the phone language of the call handler that routed the call, a single call handler can use Korean or Japanese, for instance, to instruct an outside caller to leave a message. Note that any custom recordings, such as greetings, must be recorded in the desired language. Unity has no way of translating a greeting recorded in English to a Japanese greeting, for instance. The following is the list of Cisco Unity languages as of Unity 4.0(3):

- Australian English
- Brazilian Portuguese
- Cantonese
- Mandarin
- Columbian Spanish
- Czech
- Danish
- Dutch
- European Portuguese
- European Spanish
- French
- German
- Italian
- Japanese
- Korean
- New Zealand English

- Norwegian
- Swedish
- Taiwan Mandarin
- U.K. English
- U.S. English

In addition, Unity supports TTY English for accessibility, which is discussed in the upcoming section "Accessibility Features."

Schedules, Holidays, and Time Zones

Schedules define the open and closed hours throughout Unity. Multiple system schedules can be created to accommodate different working hours for people using Unity. Schedules are one factor that defines how calls flow through Unity, and they also help dictate what type of greeting a subscriber or call handler should play. Virtually every entity in Unity has a schedule associated with it. For a call handler, this means that incoming calls during working hours can be transferred directly to a phone, whereas during closed hours incoming calls can be sent to a call-handler greeting to take a message. Subscribers have Standard and Closed greetings available to them. The Standard greeting plays when the schedule is on, and the Closed greeting plays when the schedule is off. A subscriber might use this functionality to provide different alternate contact information to callers, depending on whether they are working or are off-work.

Schedules are essential to audio text-applications because these applications are usually available every hour and every day. However, during working hours, calls can be routed to phones when a caller chooses a certain options. During closed hours, calls should not be routed to phones because there is no one to man those phones. Each subscriber; notification device also has a schedule that is independent of the subscriber schedule, allowing users to define when each device should send a notification of new messages.

Holidays simply enable administrators to define entire days when all objects on the system use a closed schedule. Holidays override existing schedules, so no schedules need to be edited to accommodate a day in the middle of the week when the office is closed. If an office were closed for an entire week at Christmas, a Unity administrator would simply create a holiday for each day that the office is closed. Of course, the administrator also might want to create some custom holiday greetings for call handlers, and they can do this via the SA or CUGA. Administrators create holidays from the SA.

Each Unity subscriber has a time zone setting. This allows a single Unity server in one time zone to easily service subscribers and incoming callers that are in different time zones. All subscribers on the system might use the same schedule to define their working hours as 9 A.M. to 5 P.M. local time (with local time being in the time zone where Unity is installed). For a Unity server located in New York (EST), subscribers in California (PST) actually would use a schedule of 6 A.M. to 2 P.M., according to their local time. However, the subscribers in California can be set in the PST time zone, effectively telling Unity to shift the schedule forward 3 hours for California subscribers to get their correct working hours. Time zones eliminate the need to create multiple schedules just to accommodate different time zones, greatly simplifying Unity administration, in some cases.

Time zones also ensure that subscribers hear message time stamps in their local time. Again using the previous example, imagine that an administrator leaves a message for a public distribution list at 10:06 A.M. EST. The distribution list contains subscribers from Seattle, Denver, and New York. When subscribers in New York retrieve the message, they will hear the message time stamp as 10:06 A.M. Subscribers in Denver will hear the time stamp as 8:06 A.M., and subscribers in Seattle will hear the time stamp as 7:06 A.M. Knowing when a message was delivered is important information, and time zones ensure that this information is accurate for all users on the system, no matter where in the world they are located.

Accessibility Features

Unity callers or subscribers with hearing disabilities can use Unity thanks to the TTY Angel tool and the TTY prompt set. People interacting with a voice-mail system obviously rely on hearing prompts to navigate the system. This might make a voice-mail system unusable to a hearing-impaired user. However, Unity 4.0(3) introduced a TTY prompt set (ENX) that can be used just like any other system language. The TTY prompt set enables callers to call Unity from a TTY/TDD phone device and interact with the system in the same way that all other subscribers interact with the system. Using a TTY/TDD device, hearing-impaired users have the TTY prompts translated into text that they can read. Note that Unity supports only an English TTY prompt set; TTY prompt sets for other languages are not available at this time. The TTY Angel tool is a Tools Depot tool that translates text into WAV files that Unity can play back to TTY/TDD phones. This tool is designed to create Unity audio-text applications for the hearing-impaired.

Fax

Integrating a fax server with Cisco Unity enables subscribers to manage their fax messages in much the same way that they manage other types of messages on Cisco Unity. Unity can be integrated with a third-party fax server that supports Microsoft Exchange or IBM Lotus Domino. It also can be configured to work with Cisco IOS gateways to provide IP fax services.

Unity supports integration with a variety of third-party fax servers. The third-party Fax Administration tool is used to specify which fax server is in use, as well as which message classes should be denoted as faxes. After this tool is used to configure Unity, faxes sent to subscribers can be retrieved from their mail client or over the Unity TUI. This tool also enables an administrator to restrict what type of attachments a subscriber can forward to a fax machine through the Unity subscriber conversation. Subscribers must be assigned to a CoS that is licensed to use FaxMail and TTS to fax e-mails to a fax machine from the Unity TUI.

When integrating with a Cisco IOS gateway for IP fax services, the gateway is configured to send faxes to a designated mailbox. After running the IP Fax Configuration Wizard, Unity is configured to poll this mailbox for faxes. It then attempts to distribute queued-up faxes to the appropriate recipient. Faxes that Unity receives by IP fax can be accessed via mail client or TUI as well. Unity 4.0(4) includes outbound fax services through Cisco gateways to complement inbound fax support. This provides a low-end complete fax solution for companies using Cisco gateways.

TTS

With text-to-speech (TTS), subscribers can have their e-mails read to them when they are checking messages over the phone. TTS is controlled by CoS, so subscribers that are in a CoS that is not licensed for TTS do not have access to e-mails over the phone. TTS is licensed on a per-session basis. A system with 48 Unity ports might have 12 TTS session licensed. This means that 12 subscribers can listen to e-mails over the phone simultaneously. As of Unity 4.0(4), TTS is localized in the following languages:

- Chinese Mandarin
- Danish
- Dutch
- European Spanish
- French
- German
- Italian
- Japanese
- Norwegian
- Swedish
- U.K. English
- U.S. English
- European Portuguese
- Brazilian Portuguese
- Mainland Mandarin
- Taiwan Mandarin

As noted earlier, not all phone languages have an associated TTS language. In some cases, a similar language is used automatically. For instance, users with Colombian Spanish set for their phone language automatically are configured to use European Spanish TTS to play back e-mails. In other cases, such as Korean, there is no TTS option. It should be noted that TTS does not translate e-mails. If the French TTS engine is used to read an e-mail written in English, you hear the e-mail played back in English, with a heavy French accent.

Hospitality

A hospitality package was released with Unity 4.0(3) so that Unity can be used in hotel environments. The hospitality package consists of a special hospitality conversation as well as the Unity Bellhop Administrator. The hospitality conversation is a scaled-down version of the full Unity subscriber conversation. Hotel guests using voice mail do not need access to certain features, such as message notification and call transfer. Therefore, these options (as well as several others) are not offered in the hospitality conversation. Unity integrates with a third-party Percipia Transient Communications Engine (PTCE) server, which is a standard hotel-management system. Changes made on the Percipia server, such as checking a guest in or out of their room or moving a guest to a new room, are passed to Unity so that a new subscriber account can be created or deleted, or so that the extension can be changed.

The Unity Bellhop Administrator, shown in Figure 7-10, is used to configure Unity for hospitality. This includes setting up the Cisco Unity Bellhop service, which polls the Percipia hospitality server for updates and makes the appropriate changes in Unity. When run for the first time, the Bellhop Administrator also creates a Hotel Guest subscriber template and class of service. These are customized for hotel guests, again disallowing access to certain features or options that are not useful for hotel guests. The Unity Bellhop Administrator provides an interface to view checked-in guests, along with information on guests, such as name, voice-mail extension, and check-in date. Unity also can archive mailboxes for guests that have checked out. This is essential for a hospitality package because guests sometimes mistakenly are checked out or forget to check messages before they check out of their room.

Figure 7-10 *Unity Bellhop Administrator: Guest Interface*

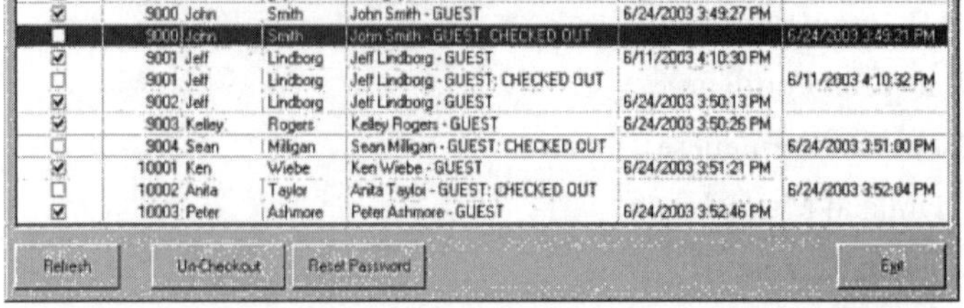

AGC and Message Storage Audio Format

In a Voice over IP (VoIP) solution, audio streams sometimes come from different points on the network and have different levels of gain. When Unity records messages from these different endpoints, subscribers can receive messages of varying volume. At the extremes, messages might be so quiet that they are barely audible, or they might be so loud that distortion occurs. Unity employs Automatic Gain Control (AGC) during recording to ensure that all recordings, whether made over the phone or from the desktop, are stored at the same volume level. Ideally, this volume level matches the same volume level of the Unity system prompts so that when a subscriber calls into Unity to retrieve messages, a consistent volume is used throughout the system.

Unity employs AGC only when deployed in a VoIP solution. For integrations with traditional phone systems, the voice boards in the Unity server perform AGC. By default, Unity AGC normalizes all messages to –26 dB. However, this default can be adjusted through the Advanced Settings tool.

Unity also can be configured to store messages in a variety of audio formats. In reality, Unity can store messages in any audio format, as long as there is an audio codec on the system to perform the conversion. Most commonly, G729a, G711uLaw, and GSM audio formats are used for message storage. Some administrators want to conserve disk space on their Exchange server, so they might use a high-compression audio format such as G729a. Other administrators want superior sound quality when messages are played back from the mail client or Unity inbox, so they might use a low-compression audio format, such as GSM. In general, G711uLaw is used most widely for Unity message storage because it provides good balance between compression (not taking up too much space per message) and sound quality of messages.

A Set Record Format tool in Tools Depot enables administrators to choose the audio format that Unity uses to store recorded messages and greetings. The selected format is used system-wide. On the same Unity system, one subscriber cannot have her messages stored in GSM, while another on the same system has his messages stored in G729a.

When Unity is deployed as part of a VoIP solution, one consideration for choosing the audio format for message storage is the format of the audio streams on calls to and from Unity. Unity supports the sending and receiving of audio in only G711uLaw and G729a formats. Whenever Unity plays a recording (system prompt, greeting, or message) that is stored in a different audio format than the audio format of the call, Unity must perform transcoding to convert the stored audio into the appropriate audio format to be transmitted to the endpoint on the other end of the call. Software transcoding requires extra CPU cycles on the Unity server, so on a very busy system, this extra CPU usage could have an impact on system performance.

To minimize this impact, Unity comes with two prompt sets: one recorded in G711 uLaw and the other recorded in G729a. An administrator should determine the audio format of most calls to Unity. Based on that information, the administrator should choose to use either the G711 uLaw or G729a prompt set to minimize transcoding on the Unity system. Because system prompts are played more frequently than messages or other recordings, administrators who match the system prompt audio format to the most commonly used audio format for calls can minimize the amount of transcoding that needs to be performed on the Unity system.

Networking

In Unity, *networking* is the term used to define messaging between Unity servers, messaging between Unity and other voice-messaging systems, and messaging between Unity and people who might not use a voice-messaging system. Networking is a very important feature in Cisco Unity because it enables users in an organization to message each other as if they are on the same Unity system, even if they are really spread across five Unity servers and two other voice-messaging systems. This section provides an overview of the different types of networking available with Cisco Unity. Networking in both Unity for Exchange and Unity for Domino is described in more detail in chapter 12, "Unity Networking."

Digital Networking

Digital networking refers to messaging among multiple Unity servers that are connected to a single global directory. In certain cases when digital networking is used, a subscriber on Unity 1 can address a message to a subscriber on Unity 2 by entering a five-digit extension in the same way he would address a message to a subscriber on Unity 1 by entering a five-digit extension.

The extension that a subscriber on Unity 1 dials to address messages to a subscriber on Unity 2 depends on whether both Unity servers are serviced by a single networked phone system, as well as whether the two Unity systems are in the same dialing domain. When multiple Unity servers are serviced by a networked phone system and grouped into a single dialing domain, Unity also can transfer calls from the automated attendant or directory assistance on Unity 1 to subscribers on Unity 2.

Addressing messaging across Unity servers and transferring calls in this way is possible because a subset of the data stored in the local directory of each Unity server is replicated to the global directory and then replicated to other Unity servers that share the same global directory. Therefore, certain information about the subscribers on each Unity system is shared among the other Unity servers, enabling the functionality described earlier. With digital networking, the message transport agent (MTA) handles the transport of voice messages between Unity servers.

Note that digital networking does not make multiple Unity systems appear as a single system to subscribers. Each subscriber still has a home Unity system that he specifically must call to log into his account and check messages. A subscriber homed on Unity 1 cannot call Unity 2 to retrieve messages.

SMTP Networking

SMTP networking refers to messaging between Unity servers that do not share the same global directory, or messaging to people who do not reside on any voice-messaging server. The concept of Internet subscribers comes into play when talking about SMTP networking. An Internet subscriber can have local extensions and recorded voice name and greetings, and can be listed in the Unity directory. However, this subscriber does not have a local Exchange mailbox. Instead, it has a reference to an e-mail address.

When a voice message is sent to an Internet subscriber, the message is sent over the Internet or any TCP/IP network using the Simple Mail Transfer Protocol (SMTP). If the destination e-mail address is the Exchange account of another Unity server, the voice message shows up for that subscriber as if it was sent from a subscriber on the local Unity system. If the destination e-mail address is not a Unity mailbox, the recipient receives the voice message as an e-mail with a WAV attachment.

When using SMTP networking between Unity servers, the Cisco Unity Voice Connector should be installed on both sides of the message transport path. The voice connector on the sending side preserves the Unity-specific attributes in outgoing voice messages, and the voice connector on the receiving side restores the Unity-specific attributes for incoming voice messages. By preserving the Unity-specific attributes, the voice message can be recognized as such when it is retrieved from the mail client form or from the Unity TUI. Otherwise, it would just appear as an e-mail with a WAV attachment.

Networking with Other Vendors' Voice-Messaging Systems

Unity's capability to exchange voice messages with another vendor's voice-mail systems is essential for migration from a foreign voice-mail system to Cisco Unity. It is also important for customers who need to have a mix of voice-messaging systems in their organization. Unity supports AMIS networking, bridge networking (specifically for communicating with Octel systems on Octel analog networks), and VPIM networking as a means of exchanging messages with other voice-messaging systems.

The type of networking to be used depends on which protocol the other voice-mail system supports for exchanging messages. In all three cases, a local subscriber account can be created on the Unity system to correspond with an account on the other vendor's voice-mail system. This account has the information that Unity needs to send voice messages left for a subscriber on Unity across to the corresponding subscriber account on the other vendor's voice-mail system. A delivery location also must be created on Unity to correspond to each voice-mail system that Unity will send messages to (this also applies to SMTP networking between Unity servers).

Local Unity accounts associated with users on remote systems are not required for SMTP, AMIS, bridge, and VPIM networking. For some Unity administrators, the overhead of managing these extra accounts outweighs the benefits that they provide to Unity subscribers. If local Unity accounts are not used, these subscribers can be sent messages by using blind addressing on the Unity server. In this case, Unity has the information needed to send messages to other voice-mail systems, but it will not have specific information about each subscriber on the other system.

With blind addressing, subscribers on the Unity server address messages to users on other systems by entering the dial ID of the delivery location that corresponds to the remote systems, as well as the subscriber's extension on the remote system. Some limitations arise when blind addressing is used to address a message. For starters, Unity cannot provide voice name confirmation that the correct addressee was chosen. So, if a mistake is made in addressing the message, Unity might not be capable of sending the message to the correct recipient. In addition, users on the other systems cannot be included on Unity public distribution lists. Spell-by-name addressing also cannot be used; the dial ID of the delivery location plus the subscriber extension on the remote system must be dialed. If local Unity accounts are set up to correspond to remote users, these limitations disappear.

Telephony Features

Unity supports integration with three types of phone systems: traditional phone systems (often referred to as time-division multiplexing, or TDM, systems), CallManager, and Session Initiation Protocol (SIP) phone systems. TDM systems are connected to Unity by plugging analog lines into voice cards installed in the Cisco Unity server. Call information is sent to Unity either inband or out-of-band over a serial link. Unity supports several different serial integrations, including the Simple Message Desk Interface (SMDI), MCI, and MD110. Unity and CallManager communicate using the Skinny Client Control Protocol (SCCP or Skinny for short). Unity and SIP phone systems communicate using the Session Initiation Protocol (SIP).

Integration Features

Although the underlying technology for each of the three main integration types is quite different, basic feature parity exists across all three integration types. This parity across integrations is important because a handful of telephony features are essential for a voice messaging system. Aside from the capability to handle incoming calls, process dialed digits, and generate outgoing calls, these include the following:

- **Rules-based call routing**. Based on information about an incoming call (for example, the calling number, the called number, and the forwarding station), Unity can route the call to any object on the system. This might be useful in the case of audio-text applications that receive calls from several different 1-800 numbers. If customers call 18002223333 for sales support and 18004445555 for tech support, Unity can route incoming calls that dialed 18002223333 to the sales support audio-text application.

- **Call forward to personal greeting**. Unity uses the forwarding station information on a forwarded call to determine whether the call was forwarded from a subscriber phone. If it was, the call is sent to the subscriber's personal greeting.

- **Call forward to busy greeting**. Unity uses the forwarding reason information on a forwarded call to determine whether a call was forwarded to Unity because the phone was busy. If so, Unity routes the call to a subscriber's busy greeting.

- **Identified subscriber messaging**. On forwarded internal calls (calls originating from a subscriber extension), Unity matches the calling number to a subscriber. When the message is retrieved from the phone, the message is announced as being from the subscriber that sent the message. The subscriber appears in the Sent field in messages retrieved from the Unity Inbox or mail clients.

- **Easy message access**. With direct calls to the voice-mail system from a subscriber extension, Unity matches the calling number to a subscriber on the system. This enables subscribers to log into their account without entering their ID. Most phones can be configured with speed dial or a messages button. This means that subscribers can retrieve message simply by pressing one button on the phone and then entering their password.

- **MWI**. Each of the three integration types uses a different mechanism to light lamps on subscriber phones.

Integrating with Multiple Phone Systems

Unity has the capability to integrate with two different flavors of phone system at the same time. For instance, a single Unity server can provide voice-messaging services to subscribers using a TDM system such as a Lucent Definity, while at the same time providing voice-messaging services to subscribers using CallManager. The voice-mail ports can be split between the two integrations in any way.

This feature is often important to customers who are migrating from one phone system to another. If they plan a staged migration, moving subscriber phones to the new phone system in increments, Unity can accommodate this. Each subscriber is associated with one of the switches that Unity is configured to work with. Among other things, this facilitates Unity transfers from one phone system to another. In the same way that callers on one phone system dial a trunk-access code to place calls to phones on the other phone system, Unity can be configured to dial this trunk-access code when transferring calls from one phone system to the other phone system.

When integrating with CallManager, Unity supports CallManager clusters in the same way the Cisco IP phones do. If a cluster consists of three CallManager servers, Unity is configured with the primary, secondary and tertiary server. If the primary server fails, Unity automatically connects to the secondary CallManager server, along with the phones serviced by this cluster. When the primary CallManager server is back in service, Unity reconnects to the primary CallManager server.

Unity also can integrate with up to five CallManager clusters at once. This might be useful in a company that has a CallManager cluster at several different sites. Imagine a case in which Unity is located at a central location with a CallManager cluster. In addition to the central CallManager cluster, this company might have four branch offices, each with a dedicated CallManager cluster. The single Unity server can provide voice-messaging services, including MWIs, to all five CallManager clusters at once. In this case, although Unity is talking to five distinct CallManager phone systems, it still is considered a single integration. So, a Unity server that services five CallManager clusters also could service a TDM phone system. It is also worth noting that multiple Unity servers can integrate with a single CallManager cluster. This is a common deployment scenario.

Unity Telephony Integration Manager

Introduced in Unity 4.0(1), the Unity Telephony Integration Manager (UTIM) is the administrative interface for Unity's phone system integrations. The UTIM, shown in Figure 7-11, provides an intuitive interface to create and delete integrations. It also is used to modify integration settings, such as MWI settings, trunk access codes, IP connectivity information, and Unity port capabilities. UTIM does a good job of conceptually organizing the configuration information, especially when Unity is deployed with two phone systems or multiple CallManager clusters.

Figure 7-11 *Unity Telephony Integration Manager (UTIM) Administrative Interface*

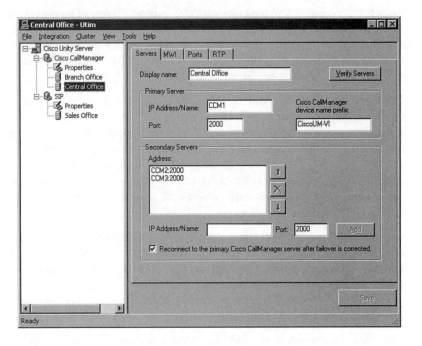

Feature Parity Between Unity for Exchange and Unity for Domino

Most of the features described are available with both Unity for Exchange and Unity for Domino. However, because Unity for Domino was only recently released as part of Unity 4.0(1), some of the Unity features described in this chapter are not available when using Unity with IBM Lotus Domino. The following features are not available with IBM Lotus Domino as of Unity 4.0(3):

- Subscriber features
  - Future delivery from TUI
  - Unity Inbox
- Administrative features
  - Reports (from SA)
  - DiRT tools
  - Message Store Manager
- System features
  - Networking to other voice-messaging systems using Bridge, AMIS, or VPIM
  - Failover
  - Hospitality

Summary

This chapter provided a big picture of the features available with Unity. As you can see, the long list of capabilities means that Unity can be used effectively in virtually any environment. These features not only enable subscribers to communicate in a variety of ways, but they also enable administrators to efficiently manage the system. Keep in mind that, in many cases, this chapter provides only an overview of a given feature. For more details on any feature described here, consult the appropriate chapter in this book or refer to the Unity product documentation. Better yet, see for yourself by checking out a live Unity system.

Deployment

Chapter 8   Deployment Methodology

Chapter 9   Planning

Chapter 10   Typical Configurations and Deployment Models

Chapter 11   Designing a Unity Solution

Chapter 12   Unity Networking

Chapter 13   Unity with Microsoft Exchange

Chapter 14   Unity with Lotus Domino

Chapter 15   Upgrades and Migration

Chapter 16   Installation

Chapter 17   Unity Telephony Integration

CHAPTER 8

Deployment Methodology

This chapter discusses the Cisco Unity deployment methodology. Whether your Unity installation is large or small, it is important to understand this methodology and the methods used to design and deploy a sustainable solution.

The methodology is steeped in the Cisco PDIO deployment process. These primary tasks are associated with the deployment process:

- Presales or decision making
- Planning
- Design
- Implementation
- Installation
- Operations
- Optimization

Following these high-level steps and their accompanying low-level steps gives you a repeatable deployment methodology. As a part of this repeatable methodology, the Unity design process encompasses the first three phases and enables the designer to design a Unity solution that, in turn, provides the data to develop an implementation plan to install Unity.

Presales or Decision Making

The presales phase is also known as the decision-making phase. In this phase, the Unity solution is decided upon and the preliminary design is put in place. In addition, other key decisions are made that enable you to continue into the planning phase for design and deployment. The presales phase is discussed in some detail in Chapter 11, "Designing a Unity Solution."

During the presales/decision-making phase, it is important to make decisions regarding how Unity will be used within a given environment. This includes understanding Unity's features and functionality, as well as understanding Unity's use of and dependencies on the messaging environment that it will service. Another very important aspect of planning is ensuring that Unity can be deployed in your environment.

What would prevent Unity from being deployable in a given environment? First, Unity integrates with a good list of circuit-switched PBXs. If a given environment has specific PBXs that Unity cannot integrate with, this could prevent the deployment from even taking place. Therefore, it is always best to make sure that Unity can integrate with a given legacy PBX. For more on the legacy PBXs that Unity supports, see Cisco Unity product documentation.

What else would prevent Unity from being deployable? What if unified messaging is desired, but one of the three supported messaging stores is not installed in a given environment? How would Unity be capable of providing unified messaging services to a messaging system that it does not currently support? It cannot. However, Unity could provide traditional voice-messaging services to this environment using a dedicated messaging back end (Exchange 2000). This would be very functional, especially if you migrate to Exchange 2000/2003 in the future.

The third issue that would prevent Unity from being deployed is an attempt to use it for something it was not designed for. For instance, Unity is a unified messaging system with traditional voice-messaging capabilities. It does not have ACD functionality (even though the Cisco IPCC does have ACD functionality) for call center support, nor does it have tenant services functionality (but tenant services might be available in future versions of Unity). Unity 4.0 also does not provide an all-in-one-box voice-messaging e-mail solution for a small number of users, as earlier versions of Unity supported.

As shown in Figure 8-1, earlier versions of Unity supported a configuration with fewer than 200 subscribers as a complete solution, including voice messaging, e-mail (unified messaging), and a domain controller for authentication. This solution is not available in Unity 3.1 and higher.

You know that you need to understand Unity's voice-messaging interoperability capabilities (that is, how you can migrate to Unity by using Unity's interoperability features—AMIS, VPIM, or the Unity Bridge for Octel networking). For more information, see Chapter 12, "Unity Networking," and Chapter 15, "Upgrades and Migrations." At this point in the presales/decision-making phase, you must determine whether Unity will be installed as a unified messaging solution or a voice messaging–only solution. The benefits of both are discussed next.

Figure 8-1   *Unity Servicing Both E-mail and Voice Messaging on a Single System*

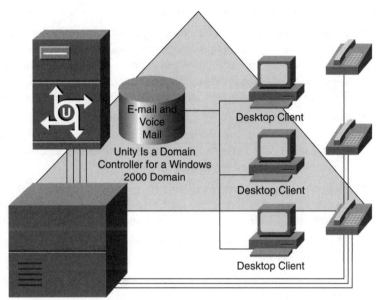

E-mail and
Voice
Mail

Unity Is a Domain
Controller for a Windows
2000 Domain

Desktop Client

Desktop Client

Desktop Client

Legacy Circuit-Switched PBX

Unified Messaging

Unity was designed for unified messaging. It operates best installed into a stable, well-managed messaging environment.

- A unified messaging solution is far easier to deploy than a voice messaging–only solution, even though readiness assessment is still required for unified messaging.

- Client software needs to be deployed to allow subscribers to record or play back voice messages in their client through their telephone (see Chapter 7, "Components and Subsystems: Features," specifically, the discussion on TRaP). Some deployment models are restrictive in the way the VMO client can be used (see Chapter 10, "Typical Configurations and Deployment Models.")

- Unity's unified messaging solution is the easiest solution to manage.

- Voice-messaging interoperability is very effective in a unified messaging configuration, although some planning is necessary. It also is important to conduct a thorough analysis on traffic and usage loads to make sure that your data network is ready for the real-time traffic that is generated by joining your voice-messaging network with your data network.

Voice Messaging-Only

Unity requires a fully dedicated infrastructure.

- Some components of Unity's messaging infrastructure can be shared with an existing environment, depending upon the implementation. This includes the DNS servers, Windows domain infrastructure, and network gear. Unity will need its own dedicated messaging system to provide a voice messaging–only configuration. However, a Unity 4.0 voice messaging–only solution is limited to Unity with Exchange 2000.

- No GUI-based e-mail client (such as Microsoft Outlook, Outlook Express, Eudora, and so on) access is available in a voice messaging–only configuration. This means that the Unity VMO client plug-in into Outlook cannot be utilized—the VMO client is a unified messaging application.

- Web-based client access is available for a voice messaging–only configuration. This includes subscriber access into the Unity Assistant or the Unity Inbox (the complete package is called the CPCA, Unity Personal Communications Assistant).

- Migrating to a unified messaging configuration from a voice messaging–only config- uration is task-intensive.

- Voice-messaging interoperability adds to the complexity of the overall Unity solution in this configuration.

It is important to decide which solution to deploy. The Cisco recommendation is a unified messaging solution. It is the keystone of current and future unified communications capabilities for IP Telephony.

If unified messaging is selected as the solution, the next important step is to perform a thor- ough unified messaging readiness assessment. Readiness is the key to a successful unified messaging deployment. To learn more about unified messaging readiness assessment, see Chapter 11, "Designing a Unity Solution," Chapter 13, "Unity with Microsoft Exchange;" and Chapter 14, "Unity with Lotus Domino."

A readiness assessment also should be performed in a large voice messaging–only configuration, even if it is a dedicated infrastructure.

Finally, if you can answer the questions necessary to determine whether Unity can be deployed in a given environment, and then can determine the configuration you will deploy Unity in (unified messaging or voice messaging), you can proceed to the planning stage. However, as a part of the Unity design process, which can be considered an overlay of the deployment methodology described in this chapter, the decision-making stage of the Unity design process includes some specific tasks; these are covered in more detail in Chapter 11.

Planning

Naturally, the level of planning that you do for any Unity solution is up to you. In some cases, you can get by with minimal planning. In other cases, you must do more planning work, including in-depth analysis and surveys. This is especially true when you migrate from a very large legacy voice-messaging system to unified messaging.

The planning phase is important enough to merit its own chapter. You will find much greater planning-specific detail in Chapter 9, "Planning," and Chapter 11. You must consider some notable items when planning to design a Unity solution. These issues are included in this chapter and are expanded upon in greater detail in the aforementioned chapters.

The main emphasis of planning in this chapter is the end-user analysis. It, too, receives greater coverage in Chapters 9 and 11 (which should indicate how important it is in the process), but it is summarized here.

End-user analysis enables you to effectively evaluate Unity's features and functionality, and to determine how usable it is to your end users. This is an important step, especially if you want to replace a legacy voice messaging system. The end-user analysis is so important that, without understanding how end users use your existing voice-messaging system, you will not be able to determine what is similar and different between the legacy system and Unity. Consider it a fundamental a requirement for large enterprises to perform an end-user feature/functionality analysis by comparing the differences between Unity and the existing legacy voice-messaging system. Performing an end-user usage analysis early when planning the design and deployment of Unity helps you define the root usage requirements for Unity deployment. For more information, read Chapter 9.

Now, if Unity does not replace a legacy voice-messaging system, it is not necessary to determine how a migration might take place. However, it is still important to perform an end-user feature/function usage analysis. For a new installation, this just means that the emphasis should be on end-user training during the cutover to Unity.

As explained in Chapter 9, the results of your end-user analysis will help you determine how Unity should be supported as well as who will support it (or the type of skill set necessary to support it).

To summarize the planning stage, much emphasis is placed on end-user analysis, which is why you will see it mentioned throughout Part II, "Deployment." The planning stage of design and deployment includes many other steps and issues for you to consider, including site surveys. With that in mind, it is suitable to proceed with an overview of the remaining deployment methodology phases in this chapter.

Design

In this phase, a Unity design is put in place. The right decisions made during the planning phase are the key to a sustainable Unity design. As further detailed in Chapter 11, the key purpose of the planning phase is not only to determine how Unity can be deployed and used by your end users, but also to accurately provide the design phase with the necessary data to make your Unity design a sustainable solution.

In the design phase, it is necessary to establish design principles resulting from decisions made and data gathered during the planning phase. This includes understanding the environment that Unity will be installed into. The planning phase also leads you through a readiness assessment. Afterward, if the assessment is successfully completed, the current design of the existing environment should facilitate the placement of the Unity servers.

These factors determine Unity placement:

- Unity configuration (UM or VM), as determined in the presales/decision-making phase and validated in the planning phase

- UM or large VM readiness assessment, as conducted in the planning phase

- Legacy voice-messaging migration priorities and strategy, as conducted in the planning phase

An important point to make is that the design phase depends on specific tasks completed in the earlier phases. If these tasks are not completed or addressed, you will not have much success with your Unity solution.

The design phase is covered along with the entire Unity design process in Chapter 11.

Implementation

Some might argue that implementation and installation are the same. And perhaps too many times, they are. However, in this deployment methodology, the implementation phase involves planning the installation, and the installation phase involves the physical installation and cutover. In the implementation phase, a detailed implementation plan is put together from the design documentation that you should have developed during the design phase (in Unity's case, in the Unity design process).

The implementation plan should include the steps that you will take to perform the installation for each Unity server. This should include three pieces: the steps necessary to prepare for each server installation, the steps necessary to cut over to each Unity server, and the steps necessary to proceed to the next phase when installation is complete.

The implementation plan also should detail the safeguards that you will take to return to your original configuration if you have problems with your installations and cutover of the Unity servers. More detail on both the implementation phase and the installation phase is provided in Chapter 16, "Installation."

The implementation phase uses the Unity design documentation and design principles to develop the installation tasks and implementation plan. The implementation plan also includes defining the way you go about installing Unity, based on your design decisions and the Unity configuration and deployment model(s) selected. For more information on Unity deployment models, see Chapter 10.

To establish an implementation plan, it is necessary to use the design criteria discussed in Chapter 11 and also to use the installation criteria discussed in Chapter 16. Chapter 16 contains the necessary source information and top-level instructions for developing your implementation plan. As with any of the other phases, it is essential to validate the implementation plan by thoroughly testing the solution, either in a lab mock-up configuration or in a small pilot into a production environment. Keep in mind that all the chapters discuss issues or criteria that you will need to understand and address to install Unity.

Installation

The physical work takes place during the installation phase, so it is important to script your installation as much as possible. In essence, your installation should be well planned for, well designed for, and well practiced, especially for a multi-server solution. If you do not know what to expect during your installation, you are simply not prepared. So, although the installation phase should seem like an easy step-by-step script, you can and should write it that way only after you consider the possible issues that you might encounter along the way. Doing so takes out guesswork, which always leads to a support issue and eliminates your chance of having a sustainable solution.

Understanding how your installation should go, documenting how it actually goes, and analyzing the differences and then adjusting them and addressing them ensures that your design is maintainable and is a fully functioning solution. When the installation is complete, the deployment methodology moves into the operations management phase and optimization.

Operations

The operations phase primarily is covered in Part III, "Solutions, Systems Management, and Administration." You will want to take into consideration some key points regarding operations. Operations management requires focus on three main areas:

- Administration
- Systems management
- Performance

Administration

Administration involves administering the system by managing subscribers—or, more broadly, people who use the system. In this case, these are more than just the users who are subscribers to the system: Outside callers are not necessarily subscribers, but they use the system to communicate with subscribers.

Administration also deals with configuring the system for use, including changing configuration parameters to suit subscriber and outside caller needs. This configuration effort also leads to configuring other aspects of the system that administration has a direct dependency with, such as voice ports and system prompts.

Finally, administration deals with subscriber access, whether the users access the system via the phone and Unity's TUI or with their own e-mail client (in the case of unified messaging), or via their web browser (in the case of either unified messaging or voice messaging, if used).

Through the planning phase (and carried on through the design and implementation phases), the administrative aspect of Unity must receive strong consideration. As with knowing that your installation is "practiced" before you perform the actual install, knowing how you will administer the system (or how you *need* to administer the system) is just as important. Waiting until you need to add users and then figuring it out is counterproductive to planning how to administer and could foil your attempts to create a sustainable design. Plan you administration up front. Plan how the system will be administered and by whom. The output from the end-user usage analysis should go a long way in helping you with these two aspects of administration.

Systems Management

Systems management easily can be described as maintaining the system. In reality, the administrator might be very involved and might be primarily responsible for systems management. Systems management of Unity involves managing the following:

- Unity configuration changes
- OS configuration changes and activities
- Events and logs
- Monitoring system access and error detection

During your planning phase, when you pilot Unity, you should have a good idea about what it will take to manage Unity. You will know that it is necessary to regularly check the Event Viewer and investigate errors or warnings from the log. You will know what to look for as far as system activity is involved. Do not just assume that you will figure out how to manage the system when it is fully deployed and in operation. Know what is necessary well before the system is deployed.

Performance

Performance is very important for Unity because subscribers access data in real time from the Unity server. You need to make sure that Unity's response times are acceptable to subscribers. You do this by monitoring and managing the performance of the Unity server, and by understanding Unity's behavior when one of its messaging infrastructure dependencies is offline or otherwise impaired.

Cisco Unity comes with performance-monitoring tools. The most notable is the Cisco Unity Performance Information and Diagnostics (CUPID) utility. You can find more information about CUPID and other performance-monitoring and management techniques for Unity on the voice software link of the www.cisco.com website.

Optimization

During optimization, the system is tuned to maximize its performance. Pure and simple, it is very closely tied to performance, but it also is tied to administration in the sense that some administrative tasks can be automated. Chapter 21, "Administering Unity Programmatically," focuses on automating the administration of Unity and includes a considerable amount of information for all the primary administrative tasks in Unity.

A final aspect of optimization involves considering Unity's operational needs for unrelated system outages and disaster-recovery plans that might affect Unity. Surprisingly, Unity's operational needs often are overlooked when it comes to planning downtimes and system outages on systems that Unity might or might not depend upon. Always remember that things that affect Unity's operations also affect the subscribers who use the system.

Summary

Unity's deployment methodology is a start-to-finish process. Depending upon the complexity of your deployment (complexity can be taken to mean a large number of users on many different systems, or it can be taken to mean many remote locations, or both), you might find that some steps are more cyclical than others.

This chapter focused on the steps in general and discussed how other chapters in Part II discuss them further. The process starts in the presales/decision-making phase and moves on to the planning phase and then the design phase. From the design phase, the implementation plan can be put together and the actual installation of Unity servers can take place. When the installation is finished and a hand-off to operations is established, the post-installation phases of operations and optimization begin. These final phases depend upon work performed in the earlier phases, especially the planning phase.

Also notable is that the Unity design process works on top of this deployment methodology, enabling the designer to focus on the key steps necessary for designing a sustainable Unity solution.

CHAPTER 9

Planning

This chapter focuses on the planning phase of a Unity deployment. It discusses an array of issues that must be addressed before performing a full deployment of Unity, regardless of the Unity configuration used. However, the expectation is that a unified messaging solution is an appropriate end result for any deployment, even if a voice-messaging solution is put in place first.

If your short-term requirements are to deploy Unity in a voice messaging-only configuration, use the guidelines established in this chapter. Remember, though, that a voice-messaging solution—especially a large deployment (with 2500 or more subscribers)—requires a dedicated messaging infrastructure, which is not addressed in this chapter. To build a dedicated messaging infrastructure to support a Unity deployment, see the Cisco website and follow the product page to Unity documentation.

These topics are covered in this chapter:

- Testing Unity's features and functionality
- Planning for the migration
- Determining installation requirements or dependencies
- Preparing for subscriber access
- Performing site surveys
- Gathering design criteria

Testing Unity's Features and Functionality

To plan for a Unity deployment, it is essential to understand Unity's capabilities. This includes understanding Unity's features and how they can be used. Because Unity is rich in features, it is necessary to understand which features your company wants to use. You might end up using only a subset of the Unity features available to you.

It is also essential to understand Unity's functionality. So, what is the difference between Unity functionality and features? With any product, the differences between features and functionality are subject to long philosophical debate, and that is certainly not the scope of this chapter or section. Unity functionality can be explained best as follows: It is the implementation of features or how Unity makes those features usable by end users, administrators, or systems designers.

If you have already read Chapter 7, "Components and Subsystems: Features," you should have a good idea about Unity's features and its functionality. To design a solution, you must understand Unity's features and functionality fully so that you also can understand how Unity can—and *should*—be used in a given deployment. This basically means that you should test Unity in a couple of different ways before deploying it.

Nothing is more frustrating than spending months on planning a full deployment, only to find out that end users do not like or do not know how to use a feature. It is even worse to have executives who are partial to certain functionality within their legacy voice-messaging system be subjected to a new installation of Unity without having a chance to use it or learn about it before rollout. Having unhappy end users and executives does not bode well for anyone who wants to make a living doing this sort of work, whether you work in the information technology department or as consultant or solutions provider.

So, what is the best way to make sure that Unity's feature and functionality are fully understood? You must perform two steps:

Step 1 Test or pilot Unity.

Step 2 Perform an end-user feature/function analysis.

Test or Pilot Unity

Regardless of the size of your company, you must try Unity and see what you do and do not like about it. You should see how its features work and understand whether any of those features can be configured to suit your usage requirements. Is this step necessary? Absolutely! Any voice-messaging product, especially one with unified messaging capabilities (in Unity's case, a unified messaging product with traditional voice-messaging capabilities), has a different set of capabilities than any of its competitors. Naturally, competing products always have some common feature sets, but the differences in those features and how they function set each product apart from the others.

Test Unity. Involve end users of various levels within the company. Many companies start with their IT staff and then simply deploy. This quickly leads to unsatisfied end users. Make sure that your pilot includes users from several different departments, and address their concerns when they participate in the pilot. This includes making sure that executives are involved in the pilot. Now, perhaps your CFO or CEO does not have time to participate in a pilot, or perhaps your CFO or CEO does not even use voice messaging, let alone e-mail. Then find those executives who do use voice messaging and determine whether they have time to participate. Make sure you given them a chance to provide feedback, and address their concerns satisfactorily to all.

What is the best way to perform a pilot? Your goal with a pilot is to determine end-user feedback. However, take the opportunity to understand Unity's behavior on your network. Understand the messaging infrastructure components that Unity depends upon, understand how Unity interacts with your legacy switch or switches, and understand how it interacts with CallManager or a SIP Proxy server. To run a successful pilot of Unity, use the same information found in Part II, "Deployment," so that you understand how to introduce Unity into a production environment. In essence, run your pilot as a minideployment of the product. This gives you a chance to learn everything there is about the product.

Some might ask, why not just attend Unity educational courses and learn how to administer or install the system? The easy answer is that, although these courses are essential and highly recommended, you will not gain the benefit that a real-life deployment into production will give you by attending Unity educational courses only. In fact, although a pilot is important, do both: Attend the educational courses and then begin a pilot of Unity in your production environment.

Can you get away without running a pilot? Yes and no. Yes, you can if you have done your homework. However, unless you know how Unity will interact in your environment and how your end users will respond to Unity in a production environment, you simply should not miss this step; doing so, can be disastrous.

Perform an End-User Feature/Function Analysis

As a part of any pilot, you should evaluate Unity's features/functionality and determine how usable this is to your end users. As with a production pilot, this analysis should be considered a requirement for any successful deployment, especially if you are looking at replacing a legacy voice-messaging system.

As discussed in Chapter 8, "Deployment Methodology," without understanding end-user use of the existing voice-messaging system, you will not be able to determine what is similar and different between the legacy system and Unity. It is considered a design and deployment requirement for any company, large or small, to perform an end-user feature/functionality analysis. Doing so helps you to gain a strong understanding of how and why your end users use their current system and how they might use Unity. This basically becomes an exercise in comparing the differences in the way end users use Unity and the way end users use the existing legacy voice-messaging system.

As a nice benefit of performing an end-user usage analysis early in the deployment of Unity, this analysis enables you to gather and understand a considerable amount of design criteria. In addition, when cutover is complete and the Unity server or servers are in operation, you will understand and can proactively prepare for end-user support.

So, even if you are not migrating from a legacy voice-messaging system, it is necessary to follow these steps to perform an end-user feature/functionality assessment.

Start by using Chapter 7 to determine Unity's capabilities.

- It is important to cover general functionality, such as types of transfers supported, special mailbox usage (such as shared mailboxes or information lines), zero-out to admin capabilities, call restrictions, and TUI key press comparisons. You should place the results in three separate categories:

  — Unity features that can be configured to perform the same functionality as those of the legacy voice-messaging system. Note that not all Unity features can be configured in this way. You must have a good understanding of Unity's features, as well as practical experience using and testing the features by product evaluation.

  — Unity features or functionality that cannot be configured to perform the same functionality as those of the legacy voice-messaging system. Any features or functionality in this category require end-user adaptation or training.

  — New features in Unity that are not currently available on the legacy system. These require end-user training.

- Conduct interviews with various end users and system administrators of the legacy voice-messaging system. It is important to interview executives, managers, administrative assistants, receptionists, operators, and other end users who experience high numbers of calls. Understand how they use the voice-messaging system. Use a focus group of end users to characterize the TUI usage patterns, and compare those usage patterns to Unity's TUI interface.

The system configuration of any legacy voice-messaging system reveals a lot about how end users use the system. It is important to note the system configuration including the integration to the legacy circuit-switched PBX and the voice-port configuration (the way the voice ports are used). Use the following criteria for performing an end-user analysis:

- Determine the TUI key press functionality and its importance to various types of job roles. What is convenient? What key presses or conversational capabilities are most important to end users?

- Determine special use functionality. Do groups of users have their calls forwarded to group administrators or administrative assistants? Do groups of users daisy-chain their calls from one user to another and then roll into a specific mailbox? Both of these and others like these are examples of special use functionality that requires configuration attention.

- Determine how users store their messages. Are the messages saved for just a matter of days, or are they saved forever? Remember, because Unity uses Exchange and Domino as back-end message stores, this type of functionality disappears in a unified messaging configuration.

- Determine how groups of users use distribution lists.

- Determine which groups of users use networking features in the legacy voice-messaging systems if multiple voice-messaging systems are connected. Determine how groups of users use these features, and determine which networking features are most important and which ones end users dislike.

- Do some groups use special audio-text applications in their existing legacy voice-messaging system? If so, refer to Chapter 18, "Audio Text Applications," to understand whether Unity can provide the same or better audio-text services for these groups.

Customization Instructions

After you conduct an end-user analysis, use the data to determine the feature gaps and capabilities with Unity. Unity certainly will have some functionality that differs from the functionality of other legacy systems, especially compared to more common brand names. A feature gap analysis should be a key output of an end-user analysis. Another key component should be customization instructions on how to configure Unity to accommodate usage requirements of end users or groups of end users. These customization instructions can include the following:

- How subscriber templates should be configured
- How CoS should be assigned
- How subscriber call handlers should be configured
- How system schedules should be defined
- How notification devices should be configured
- How special routing rules should be created and managed
- How special call restrictions should be enacted and managed
- How subscribers will be identified in the system (for example, by their DTMF ID)
- Password policies
- Mailbox sizes (typically more important in a voice messaging-only solution, but can be important in a unified messaging solution if the end-user analysis determines that end-user e-mail mailboxes are not large enough to support both e-mail and voice messaging)

For more information, see Chapter 20, "Subscriber Administration."

You also should determine system information, including port usage requirements (how many notification ports will be necessary, how many ports should be used to support TTS, and so on). In addition, you will be able to determine whether end users should know the voice-messaging pilot number and auto-attendant, or whether they will use DIDs only.

Determining Migration Tasks

If you a migrating from a legacy voice-messaging system, you have some standard tasks to perform to make it successful. Typically, you have a couple of options for migrating; these are explored in depth in Chapter 15, "Upgrades and Migrations." However, you need to plan for the migration regardless of which migration option you choose.

To plan your migration, you must determine which legacy voice-messaging servers to migrate first. You can approach this task in a couple of ways. Some organizations find it easier to migrate the largest, most used legacy systems first and move all others afterward. Others consider it easiest to migrate all but the largest systems first and then tackle the big ones last. Whatever approach you take, consider the following tasks:

Step 1 Survey and document the voice port and user density on each legacy voice-messaging system including documenting how the voice ports are used.

Step 2 Survey and document the voice-messaging system's configuration and usage (this can be done during the end-user feature/function analysis period).

Step 3 Survey and document each voice-messaging system's traffic utilization. Specifically, determine the average number of messages left on the system each day, the volume of messages on the entire system (current storage level versus total capacity), the number of subscriber logons, the average size of each message (in minutes), and the average number of messages per subscriber. Determining all traffic utilization on each legacy switch is essential in determining the proper sizing of Unity and the readiness of the supporting messaging infrastructure that Unity will service.

Then you must correlate the user density with the e-mail system that Unity will service. This is also known as finding Unity's correlation point. How is this accomplished? Assuming that you have determined whether you are deploying Unity as a unified messaging solution or a voice-messaging solution with a dedicated infrastructure, you can correlate how to migrate to Unity by evaluating one legacy system at a time.

Take into consideration that, when migrating from a legacy voice-messaging system to Unity, you are importing subscriber data into Unity. The actual location of that subscriber data and messaging store is located natively in one of the messaging stores that Unity supports and its corresponding directory. Thus, to accomplish a migration from a legacy voice-messaging system to Unity, you move the subscriber account data from the legacy voice-messaging system to Unity and the messaging system that it supports.

As shown in Figure 9-1, the migration of subscriber data includes account information and messages from a message store. It is rare and often quite challenging to migrate messages, so this is not readily encouraged. However, it is essential to migrate the subscriber's account information to the messaging store's directory. In addition, the system configuration information is migrated from the legacy voice-messaging system directly to Unity. Thus, you end up moving all data from the legacy voice-messaging system to two different places and also changing the messaging location when you migrate to unified messaging.

Figure 9-1   *Migrating Legacy Data, Accounts, and Message Store Location*

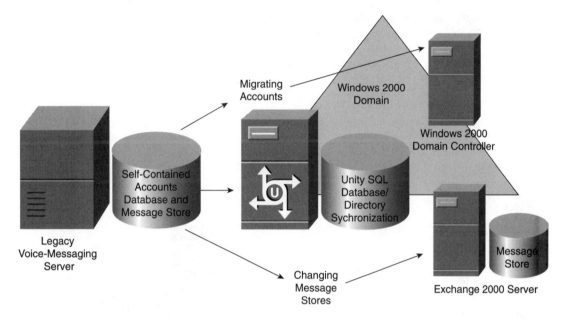

A legacy voice-messaging system has accounts and messages and a system configuration, so a migration to Unity involves all of these. The accounts either migrate to the directory as new accounts, or use the same accounts that exist in the directory and will have Unity data assigned to them. The messages might or might not be migrated from the legacy system. Migrating messages is not a trivial task. Most customers do not even bother with message migration because of the challenges associated with it. Instead, they either require end users to delete their messages or give them a period of time to play them back after Unity has been deployed. Other customers forward messages from legacy accounts to Unity using its voice-messaging interoperability capabilities. The location of the message store changes from a proprietary system to a common repository, such as an Exchange infostore or a Domino mail server.

Migrating to Unified Messaging

If you have decided to deploy Unity as a unified messaging solution, you need to compare the user population on each voice-messaging system with the same user population on the e-mail system that Unity services. Thus, if you have a legacy voice-messaging system with 3000 subscribers and these same subscribers are e-mail clients homed in a single Exchange 2000 routing group, you have found your correlation point. Figure 9-2 shows how mail-enabled mailboxes can span multiple servers even though this account information is stored in the same directory. Note that if the e-mail clients are not homed in the same Exchange 2000 routing group, you still can have Unity service the e-mail clients. However, some considerations arise when connecting Unity to multiple Exchange 2000 routing groups; see Chapter 10, "Typical Configurations and Deployment Models."

Figure 9-2   *Mail-Enabled User Accounts Located in One Directory but Spanning Several Servers*

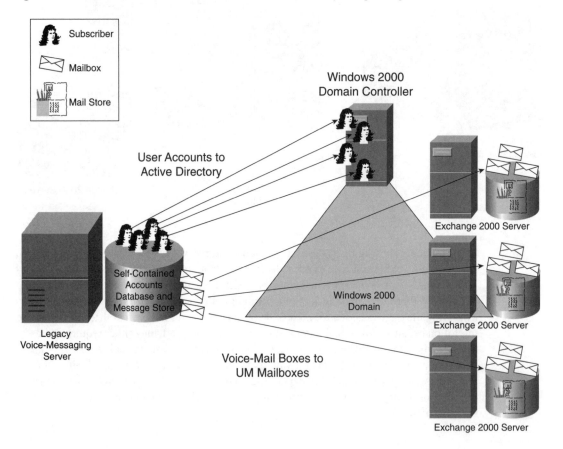

On the other hand, what if these 3000 voice-messaging subscribers' electronic mailboxes are homed on more than one routing group? You have found your correlation point, but it might require more than one Unity server to service them. (See Chapter 10 and Chapter 11, "Designing a Unity Solution," for deployment rules.)

The most important aspect is to determine where the majority of subscribers have their electronic mailboxes homed. This location is the actual correlation point where Unity should be installed. If you are uncertain of where to place Unity, note the number 1 deployment rule for Unity:

> Cisco Unity should be placed as close to the messaging system that it is servicing, including the same network proximity, the same Windows 2000 site (if applicable), the same domain, and even the same subnet and VLAN, if necessary.

Migrating to Voice Messaging Only

If you have decided to install Unity as a voice messaging-only solution with its own dedicated messaging infrastructure, your correlation point is easier: You can design the messaging-system solution around your legacy voice-messaging system user densities.

If you successfully migrate from your legacy voice-messaging system to a Cisco Unity voice messaging-only solution, your next step is to migrate to unified messaging because that should be your ultimate goal. It is best to organize your Unity voice messaging-only infrastructure as a mirror of your existing electronic messaging infrastructure, to ease the next step in the migration from Unity voice messaging-only to Unity unified messaging.

If you organize your dedicated voice-messaging infrastructure for Unity to mirror your existing electronic messaging infrastructure, make sure that you use the same account names and naming conventions. This way, you can use Unity migration tools to match existing Unity voice messaging-only accounts to existing e-mail accounts during the migration.

Extracting User Data from Legacy Voice-Messaging Systems

Another important migration task is determining how to extract user data from the legacy voice-messaging system so that it can be used as source data in creating Unity subscriber accounts. This is important to understand. If Unity will service existing e-mail users in a unified messaging configuration, you will not be creating new e-mail accounts for these users. Instead, you will be preparing their existing e-mail accounts for unified messaging, as explained earlier.

One key point in this process is to gather the subscriber-specific data that will be used during the import process in Unity. This then is written to the existing e-mail accounts, to enable unified messaging for these accounts. This subscriber-specific data includes the unique information that identifies a specific user ID as a subscriber in Unity. This includes the DTMF ID and other pertinent information. It is important to note that when the data is extracted from a legacy voice-messaging system, it must be put in a format that the Unity import facilities can recognize (see the product documentation and www.ciscounitytools.com for more information.)

Dial Plans

You should thoroughly understand how Unity uses the phone system that it is integrated with, including the dialing plan in place with the legacy voice-messaging system and the legacy circuit-switched PBX. Whether you migrate to Unity from a legacy voice-messaging system or from a legacy voice-messaging system and migrate to CallManager from a legacy circuit-switched PBX, the current dial plan supporting your legacy infrastructure most likely will require some modification. Unless you have a perfect, well-planned dial plan in place, you might have overlapping extensions that can cause problems in managing your phone and voice-messaging systems.

Regardless, when you introduce a new voice-messaging system such as Unity, and or a new call processor such as CallManager, you likely will need to modify your dial plan slightly— or even significantly redesign your dial plan to facilitate the new systems that are installed.

This is not actually a bad thing. In fact, the opposite is true. Now is the time to consider how to redesign your dialing plan so that it can support new voice technologies, such as IP telephony.

To understand dialing plans as they pertain to Unity, see Chapter 2, "Unity Architecture Overview," and Chapter 12, "Unity Networking."

Installation Requirements or Dependencies

The Unity installation product documentation and Brian Morgan and Moises Gonzales's book *Unity Fundamentals* (Cisco Press) explain what Unity needs to be installed. In addition, Unity comes with an installation wizard called the Cisco Unity Installation Configuration Assistant (CUICA) that looks for specific components and installs them if they are not present. CUICA is run before the Unity application is installed.

From a planning perspective, it is important to understand what Unity requires to service a given switch, messaging system, and end users.

Determining Unity Installation Dependencies

One way to look at what Unity requires is to consider these dependencies of Unity. It helps in planning and design when you understand what Unity depends upon. So, what does Unity need to be installed? If you have made it this far into the book, you should have a pretty good idea, especially if you read Part I, "Concepts and Architecture." Unity needs the following, both of which involve a considerable number of lower-level dependencies and readiness activities:

- Switch connectivity and readiness
- Messaging system connectivity and readiness

Switch Connectivity

Of course Unity cannot perform voice-messaging tasks without being connected to some type of switch or call-processing facility. It is important to make sure that Unity can support the switch or call-processing facilities in your environment. When you make sure that Unity can support your switch or switches, also make sure that you understand how these need to integrate with that switch. Can Unity integrate the same way that your legacy voice-messaging system does? Would an alternative give Unity additional functionality? Remember that Unity sometimes can support more than one integration type, depending on the switch it integrates with.

PBXs Supported

You must perform four important tasks to plan for a Unity deployment:

Step 1 Verify that Unity can support your switch. This includes verifying the software versions and feature packages that might be required on the switch.

Step 2 Understand the integration to use between Unity and your switch.

Step 3 Make sure that your switch can support Unity.

Step 4 Address any programming necessary to support the Unity server.

Verify That Unity Can Support Your Switch

The list of supported PBXs changes regularly. Rarely are particular switches dropped from the list of supported PBXs. Instead, the list grows. You can find an updated list of supported switches on Cisco Connection online. You also will find required software levels and features sets for the integration method desired between the switch and Unity by accessing the Unity product documentation.

Understand the Integration to Use Between Unity and Your Switch

Unity can support several different integrations, including Simplified Message Desk Interface (SMDI), Skinny Client Control Protocol (SCCP), Session Initiation Protocol

(SIP), in-band DTMF, Rich Feature Set integration using the PBXLink for Nortel, and Lucent switches and analog. Make sure that you understand the type of integration that you will use between Unity and your switch. You have to consider additional requirements and restrictions with a Unity failover configuration. Verify that the Unity failover configuration can support your integration selection.

Cisco also has a program that helps to qualify integration of unsupported switches by following a specific testing process. For more information about this program, see the Cisco website or contact your local Cisco representative.

Ensure That Your Switch Can Support Unity

When you know that your switch or switches are supported by Unity and the type of integration they use, you must make sure that your switch has the capacity to connect to Unity. If you are replacing a legacy voice-messaging system with Unity and plan a phased migration, you must keep both the legacy server and the Unity server connected to the switch at the same time. This means that you must have the correct number of voice ports to connect to a Unity server. Verify that each and every switch has the necessary capacity. Failing to perform this step can slow or halt your project altogether.

Address Any Programming Necessary to Support the Unity Server

Some switch programming is necessary to support Unity's connectivity. Make sure that the integration is properly programmed and that the voice ports property are set up (typically in some type of hunt group or ACD group—see Chapter 17, "Unity Telephony Integration").

CallManager Versions

Unity can integrate with different versions of CallManager. The Cisco website has the latest list of which versions of Unity integrate with which versions of CallManager. In addition, the link between Unity and CallManager is the Telephony Service Provider (TSP). The version of the TSP dictates what version of Unity can support what version of CallManager.

For Unity connecting to CallManager, the same type of planning should take place as that performed between Unity and a legacy PBX. Make sure that you follow the integration requirements as outlined in this book and in other Cisco books on the subject (see Chapter 6, "Components and Subsystems: Telephony Services;" Chapter 17; the Cisco Unity Integration Guides found on the Cisco website; and CallManager product documentation.

SIP Proxy

Cisco Unity 4.0*x* supports SIP Proxy servers. To gain a better understanding of the proxies tested and the RFCs and methods (for dtmf relay, codecs, and so on), see the following web pages:

```
http://www.cisco.com/en/US/products/sw/voicesw/ps2237/prod_technical_
    reference09186a00801181c7.html
```

```
http://www.cisco.com/univercd/cc/td/doc/product/voice/c_unity/integuid/sip/
    itsip.htm
```

Messaging System Connectivity

Messaging system connectivity is the cornerstone of Unity's messaging functionality, so it is important to focus on either planning a messaging infrastructure to support Unity in a voice-messaging deployment, or planning a unified messaging deployment into an existing messaging infrastructure.

For Unity, the most important operational considerations regarding the messaging system involve working within the messaging system's messaging boundaries, readying the messaging system, and identifying the messaging infrastructure dependencies that each Unity installation will have.

Single Messaging System

For unified messaging, a single messaging system is a requirement. In this case, a single messaging system is one autonomous messaging system that resides in its own structured boundary. For Exchange 5.5, this is a single organization with one or more Exchange 5.5 sites (the term *site* is used to describe both Exchange 5.5 sites and Windows 2000 sites; however, although some similarities exist, they are not the same). For Exchange 2000, this is a single organization with one or more admin groups, each containing one or more routing groups. For Domino, this is a single Domino domain in which one address book is used for all systems. Secondary address books might exist, but the single address book makes up the primary directory (NAMES.NSF).

Do not install Unity into its own messaging system and expect it to perform unified messaging functionality for an existing messaging system. Although you can create POP3 or IMAP4 accounts for existing e-mail clients on an existing messaging system to pop their messages from a Unity messaging system, this is not unified messaging; it is a waste of functionality. In addition, this is not supported by Cisco. This solution is more akin to an integrated solution, which is not what Unity is all about.

With Exchange

Unity with Exchange installs and services either a specific Exchange 5.5 site or a specific Exchange 2000 organization (there is no technical restriction that keeps Unity from servicing more than an Exchange 2000 admin group or routing group, although, depending on how your Exchange 2000 organization is structured, you might want to apply this type of restriction yourself). This is Unity's boundary within the given messaging system's boundary.

Why can Unity service not more than one Exchange 5.5 site? Unity's directory monitor connects to only a single server in the site where it is installed. Any Exchange 5.5 server in a given site has a read/write directory partition of its site. It has read-only partitions of all other sites that are in the Exchange 5.5 organization and are connected through site connectors and directory replication. Thus, a given Unity server is limited to a single Exchange 5.5 site. The server can read the read-only directory partitions for other sites when it performs digital networking functionality with other Unity servers in the enterprise, but it does not try to write to those directory partitions outside of the site that it is installed into.

Can Unity service more than one Exchange 2000 admin group? The technical answer is yes. However, when you plan for a Unity deployment, it is rarely practical to plan for a single Unity server to service subscribers in multiple admin groups, let alone routing groups. In most cases, Unity best services a single routing group within a single admin group, and this is by far the easiest way to plan for a Unity deployment. Specific rules govern how Unity can support more than one routing group (see Chapter 10), and these must be followed for a supportable configuration. You can also avoid headaches if you stick as close as possible to all recommendations given for the messaging system where Unity is deployed.

Can Unity work with a mixed-mode messaging environment with both Exchange 5.5 and Exchange 2000? Absolutely. Chapter 13, "Unity with Microsoft Exchange," discusses in depth how Unity can work with a mixed-mode messaging environment.

With Domino

Unity for Domino also must work within a single messaging system. Thus, for unified messaging in Domino (the only supported way that Unity works with Domino is by using DUCS), there simply cannot be a separate messaging system. This constraint exists because of the Domino Unified Communications Services (DUCS) requirement. Regardless of how many different types of Domino servers you have in your environment, Unity services Domino only through DUCS.

The 4.0*x* releases (up to 4.04) of Unity for Domino are limited intentionally in how they support a given messaging infrastructure. Given that a single messaging system is required, also consider that a single physical location is essential to servicing Domino servers through DUCS for unified messaging. Remote clients can be supported for unified messaging in a centralized messaging deployment model, as long as the same considerations are given to minimizing delays that result from streaming messages over low-bandwidth WAN pipes. Again, you should minimize or eliminate the possibilities of delay that result in low bandwidth and unreliable servers.

For more information on Unity for Domino, see Chapter 14, "Unity with Lotus Domino."

Directory Connectivity

Unity's use of the directory often is misunderstood. It is important to understand how Unity uses the directory and why. As explained in several chapters throughout the book (including Chapter 4, "Components and Subsystems: Directory"), you must have a very good understanding of how the directory is used. This section covers important points about Unity's use of the directory.

A single-directory infrastructure is expected for unified messaging (which, of course, is a given, considering that the single messaging system uses this directory). A single-directory infrastructure is an infrastructure in which all directory objects share the same directory structure (administrative and security boundaries) and normally the same namespace. A few examples include a single Active Directory forest and a single Domino domain. For voice messaging-only implementations, a separate directory infrastructure can be used, but is not required. It is possible to deploy Unity using the existing Active Directory forest but to dedicate a domain to voice messaging only. Just remember that if Unity uses Active Directory as its directory, it will service Exchange 2000. This means if an Exchange 2000 or 2003 organization exists, an admin group can be set up to support the voice messaging-only solution, but this means that Unity voice mail-only subscriber names should be hidden in the directory so that they are not visible to normal e-mail clients.

Along with a single-messaging infrastructure, it is necessary to consider how to conduct capacity planning for Unity's use of the directory.

Single Infrastructure

A single-directory infrastructure is another key to a unified messaging solution. This infrastructure contains the common directory data shared between the directory-aware applications. A single-directory infrastructure keeps the data common among a messaging system, Unity, and other directory-aware applications.

If you plan for a voice messaging-only solution for Unity, you can consider a separate directory infrastructure along with a separate messaging solution. However, the directory and messaging solution must be a single messaging system dedicated to Unity. In other words, you cannot have a voice messaging-only solution in which Unity uses the same messaging systems as e-mail clients. However, it is common to have both the messaging system with e-mail–only clients and a new messaging system dedicated for voice messaging only using the same directory. Thus, the directory can be shared between an existing e-mail system and a new messaging infrastructure created for Unity for a voice messaging-only deployment.

Directory Capacity Planning

It is for certain Unity will impact the size of a directory because of the fact that it uses the directory to store common data shared between Unity servers, and between Unity servers and its messaging servers.

The size of the impact varies per messaging solution.

- **Exchange 5.5 directory**. If your dir.edb file and associated directory files are quite large, and if you have limited disk space, you need to consider that adding around 10 new attributes to each recipient object adds up to 128 Kb of data—possibly more, depending on the system codec that you use to record voice names that are stored in the directory. In addition, Cisco Unity creates a special location object in the Cisco Unity folder in the Exchange 5.5 directory. The location object uses an existing schema object as well as the existing voice-mail schema attributes for recipient objects.

- **Active Directory schema**. Cisco Unity extends the Active Directory schema by adding Unity-specific voice attributes to the User, Contact, and Group objects. These attributes become a part of the partial attribute set found in the Global Catalog. The schema extension also includes a new object created as the Cisco Unity location object. This object is used to identify each Unity server and the subscribers that reside there. The location object enables subscribers to address messages to subscribers on other Unity messaging systems. Depending on the system codec that you use for Unity, the size increase per user might be small or large. For more information, refer to the Cisco Unity Active Directory Capacity Planning whitepaper on the Cisco website. This whitepaper discusses Unity's use of each attribute and how large each one is for each object type.

- **Domino directory**. The Domino directory is extended when DUCS is installed. It is discussed in more detail in Chapter 14.

Messaging Infrastructure Readiness

A common mistake that many people make when deploying Unity is failing to ready the messaging infrastructure for unified messaging. It would be a perfect world if this were not necessary, but there is simply no way around it. Whether you use Cisco Unity or any other unified messaging product, you must ready your messaging environment for it.

Why is it necessary to do this? The messaging infrastructure must be readied for unified messaging because a real-time voice interface into that messaging infrastructure is being installed. Without preparing a messaging infrastructure for unified messaging, you most likely will end up with something other than real-time voice messaging. With near–real-time voice messaging, subscribers must wait for long periods of time when performing simple TUI tasks such as signing in, asking the system to retrieve their message counts, checking their messaging limitations, and playing back or sending messages. If subscribers experience significant delay through the TUI right from the start, Unity deployment is not successful.

How can a messaging infrastructure be prepared for unified messaging? You must follow these steps:

Step 1   Survey your messaging servers for capacity and performance.

Step 2   Survey your domain controllers for proximity and performance.

Step 3   Survey your name-resolution hosts for proximity and performance.

Step 4   Survey your domain for proper configuration.

Step 5   Survey your network to make sure the LANs are well connected and consistently have high availability.

Survey Your Messaging Servers for Capacity and Performance

You must perform a survey of each messaging server. Based on optimal unified messaging installations, it is recommended that your messaging servers be at no more than 60 percent capacity. So, during normal and peak periods, the average utilization of the CPU and memory should not be greater than 60 percent (the lower the utilization, the better). You can measure both CPU and memory utilization using Windows Performance Monitor counters. If you use the total CPU and memory usage counters, they should be sufficient for monitoring utilization.

In addition, hard-drive usage (message store and logging) should not be more than 50 to 60 percent of the total recommended maximum for messaging storage for your mailboxes. The recommended maximum depends on the mail system you use. Check the mail system's documentation to verify its maximum setting. Make sure that your mailbox store is not at maximum capacity; otherwise, subscribers cannot leave voice messages.

In addition to making sure that messaging utilization is acceptable, ensure that the messaging servers that Unity will service are highly available. A messaging server that is up and down all the time will not support unified messaging functionality. In fact, the more issues you have with your messaging servers, the more problems you can expect Unity to reveal to you and your end users.

Also monitor your messaging stores' performance, especially their connectivity to their clients. Make sure that the clients do not experience delays or excessive retransmissions of messaging requests. End users might not even realize that they experience delays in accessing their messages. They might even be used to a persistently slow response time and might think that it is the norm. If this is the case, Unity will expose these delays through its TUI conversation. You should be able to monitor server-to-client delays using the Windows Performance monitoring tool. You also might need to check the messaging system's product documentation.

Verify that your messaging servers operate effectively, as described earlier. During your initial pilot phase or implementation, you should monitor the activity between the Unity servers and the messaging servers to make sure that no symptoms are present. Investigate any symptom that appears to be indicative of delay conditions:

- Delays related to general client logons, including Unity logons
- Delays related to messaging access, including opening the inbox, retrieving messages, and sending them
- Delays related to global address list access, lookups, and usage, including address selection

Look for error conditions that might point to persistent response time problems as well, such as message-routing rule errors, event log errors, service interruptions, and connection errors.

Survey Your Domain Controllers for Proximity and Performance

As with messaging readiness, you must make sure that the domain controllers that will service requests from Unity are available and that they do not contribute to response-time issues between Unity and your messaging systems. They can contribute to response-time issues by being unavailable. Unity experiences the same effects as desktop clients if a domain controller goes offline.

Unity uses a Windows NT domain controller (PDC or BDC) when servicing Exchange 5.5. It points to a Windows 2000 DC and GC when servicing Exchange 2000. Unity uses a Windows 2000 DC such as an NT PDC if it services Exchange 5.5 installed in a Windows 2000 domain. Unity requires the use of a Windows 2000 domain controller when servicing Domino servers and Notes clients (however, the Domino servers or Notes clients do not need to be in the same Windows 2000 domain as Unity, but they can be—and vice versa).

Unity uses a domain controller to log on to Exchange messaging servers and to authenticate initial administrative access for Unity for Domino. Unity uses a domain controller to create and manage domain user accounts in voice messaging-only configurations (typically) and uses a domain controller to obtain domain users' information, such as SIDHistory.

Thus, if your domain controllers are not highly available, or if they are constantly under heavy load because of excessive authentication traffic, administrative activity, or other activities, such as replication, Unity will be affected by them, just like any other application that must authenticate user requests or proxy on their behalf. Of course, Unity exposes delays that exist on your domain controllers but that might not necessarily be noticed by normal client activity.

Monitor logon requests and other traffic activities that might place the server under load. Typically, domain controllers can be given the same load-bearing requirements as the messaging systems, such as a 60 percent max utilization during normal and peak periods of operation. You might find it necessary to lower the max utilization to no more than 50 percent, depending on user density and other usage activities on a given domain controller or domain.

A survey should include making sure that Unity can access the same domain controllers used by your messaging systems. This is especially important for Exchange but is not as important with Domino. By adhering to this rule, you are less likely to experience delays in account updates and, therefore, logon requests and the other requests that Unity makes to domain controllers.

Survey Your Name-Resolution Hosts for Proximity and Performance

As with the domain controllers, Unity depends upon name resolution. Unity as an application does not depend upon name resolution directly; it depends upon it indirectly by being a part of the Windows domain, so it depends upon it through the Windows OS.

Also make sure that your name resolution hosts are locally available to Unity, to minimize delays in resolution that result from network hops.

Make sure that the name resolution hosts are highly available. Notice that the term *resolution hosts* is used instead of *DNS server* or *WINS server*. As a rule of thumb, use the name resolution that your messaging servers use. This might not be all that is necessary, depending upon your configuration. Using Host files or LAN Manager Host (LMHost) files is not a substitute for using the Domain Name System (DNS) or the Windows Internet Naming Service (WINS).

Again, just as with your domain controllers, monitor your name resolution hosts for referral delays or simply for slow response times with lookups of server names or service locator records.

The closer a name server is to Unity, the less you will have to worry about Unity being affected by delays due to name resolution.

Survey Your Domain for Proper Configuration

Unity depends on proper domain configuration. You would think this would be a given, but it is not always the case. Unity also depends on consistent availability 100 percent of the time. It can be affected by misconfigurations and service interruptions, such as lost trust relationships. Therefore, your domains must be configured properly and must not be undergoing problems from misconfigurations or service interruptions.

Unity can support Exchange 5.5 in either an NT domain or Windows 2000 domain. If you have an NT domain infrastructure, it is best to make sure that you do not have problems with trust relationships, especially if you plan to install Unity in a resource domain and have its service account created in an accounts domain. Like any other server performing real-time communications for end users, Unity is affected if it is in a resource domain that loses its trust relationship to the accounts domain.

Unity can support Exchange 2000 in a Windows 2000 domain only. However, it is affected directly by a misconfigured or unconfigured Windows 2000 site, or when installed into an IP subnet that is not part of a Windows 2000 site. As stated in Chapter 10, Unity should be installed in the same Windows 2000 site as the Exchange 2000 servers that it services. If you deviate from this rule, expect to have delays with MAPI logins into those Exchange servers.

Unity can support Domino R5 with DUCS, but the Unity server must be installed in a Windows 2000 domain. This domain can be created by promoting the Unity server to a DC in its own domain, or you can have Unity join an existing Windows 2000 domain.

Survey Your Network to Ensure That it Is Well Connected and Is Highly Available

The centralized call-processing model/centralized messaging model (see Chapter 10) supports remotely connected subscribers for voice messaging and unified messaging, as long as there is ample bandwidth. Delays from streaming messages among Unity, its messaging system, and the client also must be minimized.

Unity still can be affected—essentially, the entire telephony solution can be affected—if service interruptions arise on any point in your network among Unity, the call-processing functionality, and remotely connected clients.

Before deploying Unity, you should survey your network to discover any network components, switches, routers, and gateways that have a history of service interruptions, excessive traffic, and hardware problems. Address issues with any of these components, to ensure their availability after Unity and an IP telephony solution are in place.

When you have identified problem network components and have addressed the issues found, remember to monitor these components on a regular basis after Unity, CallManager, and an IP telephony solution are in place.

Mailbox Store for Voice Messaging

If you plan a voice messaging-only deployment of Unity, either as an end solution to replace an existing legacy voice-messaging system or as a stepping stone to unified messaging, you will need to plan for a messaging infrastructure to support Unity. For Unity 4.0, the only supported voice messaging-only configuration is Unity with Exchange 2000. So, you must plan for a dedicated messaging infrastructure as a part of your Unity solution.

How do you design an Exchange 2000 messaging infrastructure to support Unity? You do this the same way you would support a company-wide e-mail solution. Some differences exist, of course: The main one is that, in a dedicated messaging solution for Unity, you do not have to worry about deploying e-mail clients, such as MS Outlook.

For a dedicated messaging infrastructure, Unity is the primary or sole client for all mailboxes, regardless of how many subscribers your total solution will have. This is important because, when sizing Exchange 2000 for thousands of e-mail clients, it is typically necessary to be generous on hardware and conservative on the number of mailboxes that you can place on each mailbox store. With Unity, you do not have to do that as much. In fact, you can expect to place roughly 30 to 40 percent more mailboxes on an Exchange 2000 server, compared to one dedicated to a couple thousand e-mail clients or less. However, having the capability to place more mailboxes on a given Exchange 2000 server is not a liberty to simply jump on and exercise without considering capacity planning for each subscriber mailbox. You also must make sure that the total number of mailboxes on a given server still is supported by Cisco TAC; check the system requirements on Cisco Connection Online.

The Unity hardware guide discusses the maximum number of mailboxes that you can place on a given server. Also see Chapter 16, "Installation," for more information. Make sure that you size your Exchange 2000 servers according to the recommended maximums for the supported hardware.

Now for the bad news: This book does not go into detail on how to design a messaging infrastructure to support Unity. You should contact your nearest Cisco partner for assistance in planning and designing a messaging infrastructure.

Keep in mind these pointers when designing an Exchange 2000 messaging infrastructure for Unity:

- Limit your configuration to one admin group, for ease of administration.
- Limit each routing group to a physical location, LAN, or campus environment.
- You might need one or more dedicated hub routing groups to deliver messages across your messaging backbone, depending upon the messaging traffic and your use of digital networking in Unity.
- Allocate the necessary number of domain controllers for your Exchange 2000 messaging back end.

The Correlation Point: How to Size and Place a Server

For a migration from a legacy voice-messaging system, the point at which you install Unity is called a correlation point. It is called this because this is the point where Unity correlates the subscriber population between the legacy system and the existing e-mail messaging system. Another way to look at it is moving the voice-messaging system closer to a common accounts database shared by many systems, including the e-mail system.

As shown in Figure 9-3, there are differences between the self-contained legacy voice-messaging system with its own accounts database and messaging store and a Unity server with voice connectivity accessing an existing accounts database from the directory and providing voice messaging for the messaging servers.

Figure 9-3   *A Legacy Voice-Messaging System and Unity Using an Existing E-mail Infrastructure*

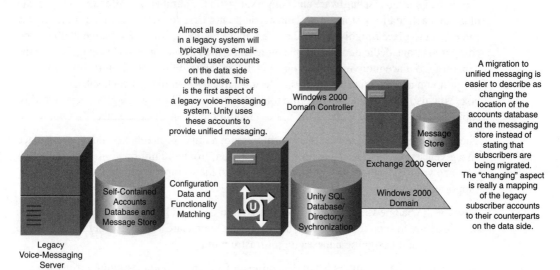

Server Sizing

To size a Unity server, you need to determine the number of subscribers that you are migrating to Unity from your legacy voice-messaging server. The largest server that Unity can be installed onto can support up to 7500 subscribers when the mailbox stores are off-box. Many legacy voice-messaging systems have a larger subscriber density. If they do, you will have to use more than one Unity server to replace the legacy system. A drawback exists to having to use more than one Unity server to replace a single legacy voice-messaging system with a larger subscriber density than Unity: When two or more Unity servers replace a single legacy voice-messaging system, some functionality is lost, as shown in Table 9-1.

Table 9-1   *Functionality Comparison Between a Single Unity Server and Multiple Unity Servers*

	Legacy Voice Messaging Server	Three Unity Servers Replacing the Legacy Voice-Messaging Server
Pilot Number	Single pilot number	One for each Unity server.
Name Confirmation When Addressing Messages (Identified Subscriber Messaging)	Included	Limited between Unity servers. Digital networking must be in place, and all servers should be in the same dialing domain.

Ports or Sessions

The maximum number of ports that a Unity server can support is 72. This maximum does not mean that 72 voice-messaging ports are available. Instead, you need to allocate some ports to support Unity's features. The features that need to use ports are message waiting indicators, multimedia for Telephone Record and Playback (TRaP), and pager notifications through pager, the phone, and so on.

When you plan for a Unity server installation, allocate the necessary number of ports for the features that you plan to use. You typically use the multimedia feature for TRaP. For more information about this feature, see Chapter 7. Note that you need to pay attention to using TTS ports. The more TTS ports you have, the more you must pay attention to the amount of time that a user is logged into voice mail; you also must consider the additional load on the Unity server.

Subscriber Access

Subscribers access Unity in a few different ways. Prepare for their usage the same way that you analyze end-user usage of your existing voice-messaging system. Plan to train subscribers on how to use the Unity TUI; at a minimum, train them on how to use any new features or functionality that they might not be familiar with. Doing so will help make your migration and cutover more successful.

Based on the results of the end-user usage analysis, determine the necessary training for subscribers. This also is the time to plan your policies for subscriber access into the TUI. This includes determining password policies and default settings for each subscriber. In addition, you need to determine the class of service settings and subscriber templates. This is basically when you determine which features you plan for each of your subscribers to use. For more information, see Chapter7, "Components and Subsystems: Features."

- **GUI access from client e-mail applications**. For Outlook, subscribers will use Viewmail for Outlook (VMO), which is an enhanced Outlook form that is used to play back and record voice messages from a subscriber's Outlook client. Consider the default settings for Outlook, and determine how to deploy it in your environment. Again, see Chapter 7.

- **Web access for Unity CPCA and Unity Inbox**. Do you plan to use the Unity Assistant or Unity Inbox? If so, determine who access is going to be granted. Because this is web access, it is very important to make sure that name resolution is fully functional for end users to access the Unity Assistant or Unity Inbox.

- **Server access**. From a security standpoint, subscribers do not need direct access to the Unity server. VMO can be deployed from any server, so you do not need to create a share for it on a Unity server. To perform normal activities, such as accessing the TUI, GUI, or the web, subscribers do not need special privileges to access the server or its resources. Unity provides the necessary authentication facilities for subscribers to access its resources, such as Windows authentication for web access, and CoS for the TUI and CPCA.

Performing Site Surveys

Make sure that your site surveys account for everything necessary to accommodate a Unity deployment. If you have not updated your site survey forms in a while, now is a good time to do so. Unity is a convergence product, so you need to survey both the telephone or voice aspects of a site and the messaging infrastructure aspects.

Your physical site survey should include the physical space, including all the necessary power, network connectivity, security, and air conditioning criteria that you normally would look for with any server deployment.

If Unity is connecting to a physical circuit-switched PBX, inventory this switch to make sure that it can support Unity's voice-connectivity requirements, including integration and voice ports. Verify that it has both physical capacity and system capacity. Determine whether a software upgrade of your switch is required to support a second voice-messaging system. If you must run voice lines for voice ports, make sure that you have rack space and patch panel space available for them.

If Unity is connecting to CallManager, make sure that you have sufficient network connectivity. You can reference the CallManager product documentation to determine exactly how much bandwidth you need between CallManager and Unity (see the information on device weights). However, on a LAN, you should use no less than 100 Mbps full duplex.

Identify all messaging servers, domain controllers, and name resolution hosts. Include their server names, IP addresses, domain names, and physical location. At this point, you can identify Unity's partner messaging server (see Chapter 13, "Unity with Microsoft Exchange," for more information—Unity for Domino does not use a partner server). You also should determine which DC and GC Unity will connect to, and you should know which name resolution host it will use. As a rule of thumb, use the same DC, GC, and name server that your messaging servers use. If you have multiple servers of each type, select one of each type as a target for Unity. You can change your target later when you have a better understanding of capacity.

Survey the total number of desktops if you are doing unified messaging. Make sure that you understand which versions of software the Unity VMO can support. Note also that VMO supports only Windows clients; it does not support Macs or UNIX boxes.

Survey the migration components, including any legacy voice-messaging systems. Determine backup resources and management resources.

When you have the physical survey completed, dig deeper into capacity by interrogating each messaging server that Unity will service:

- **Messaging**. Survey the capacity of each messaging server that Unity will service.
- **Directory**. Survey the directory capacity.
- **Phone system**. Survey the dialing plan for the site, and also pilot numbers and hunt groups slated to be used by Unity.

Your site surveys should be used at two different levels: global and local.

- **Global results**. For all surveys, the directory capacity, messaging capacity, and phone system information should be used to compile a global list. If you understand the capacity of the directory, for instance, you will have a good idea of any prep work necessary to perform before deploying Unity. If any of your directory servers are at capacity, they will need extra hard drive space or extra memory to handle the load. As stated, the load is not significant, but from a readiness standpoint, it is essential to address the capacity requirements of your directory and messaging system.

  From a digital networking standpoint, it is important to understand the dialing plan at each location, along with the DTMF IDs of all subscribers migrated to Unity. Having this information supports the digital networking design for Unity.

- **Local results**. For all surveys, the local results help you to place Unity and will give you the information necessary to install it and support it after it is installed. They also will help you to plan for your migration if you perform a migration, and help you to determine how Unity is managed.

Gathering Design Criteria

From the site survey information, you use the local and global survey data to put together your design criteria for your detailed design. Your design criteria dictates the principles that you follow to install and configure Unity. This criteria is based on operational requirements of the product, which includes administration and management.

To better understand how to turn the design criteria into principles for deployment, read the rest of Part II, especially Chapter 11.

Summary

The purpose of this chapter was to cover in some detail the planning tasks necessary to put together a Unity design. These tasks were presented as special topics, and it can take some time to perform them and analyze their results. Other planning tasks are discussed in Chapter 11. Use the special topics in this chapter to augment the more thorough planning that you need to perform, as outlined in Chapter 11.

The tasks in this chapter discussed ways to prepare your messaging infrastructure for Unity by performing capacity planning on your messaging system and directory for unified messaging. Migration tasks were discussed in some detail, especially when dealing with Unity server placement and how to correlate a Unity installation to an existing legacy voice-messaging system.

Note the references to other chapters to support the planning effort necessary to design and deploy a Unity solution. As previously mentioned, the amount of planning that you need to do depends on the size of your Unity installation and the steps that you take to migrate from an existing legacy voice-messaging system to a unified messaging system using Unity.

Typical Configurations and Deployment Models

This chapter provides an overview of typical Unity configurations and deployment models. All the Unity configurations and deployment models described in this chapter are Cisco supported and comply with design and deployment requirements defined by Cisco Systems.

Before you begin this chapter, you should have an understanding of:

- Windows NT and Windows 2000 domain models
- Domino domain models
- Messaging configuration requirements for one or more of the supported messaging stores: Exchange 5.5, Exchange 2000, and Domino R5
- Chapters 4, 5, 6, 13, 14, 15, and 17 from this book

As stated throughout this book, Unity is first and foremost a unified messaging (UM) product. But, it has all the capabilities of a legacy voice-messaging system and more. Therefore, it is common for Unity to be installed into a voice-messaging configuration for the sole purpose of replacing a legacy voice-messaging system. For some, installing Unity as a voice-messaging system is a stepping stone to migration to unified messaging. There are several reasons why you would do this.

For example, you might need to:

- Immediately replace a legacy-messaging system.
- Deploy voice messaging while preparing the network and messaging (e-mail) system for VoIP and UM, respectively.
- Deploy voice messaging while preparing to migrate from one messaging system to another.

Regardless of the reason, Unity can support a voice messaging-only solution leading to unified messaging, but the size of the installation (ports, subscribers, and so on) can add to the complexity of the voice-messaging configuration. This complexity is created as a need to build a dedicated infrastructure to support the voice-messaging environment. It might be considered a drawback to Unity's voice-messaging functionality to build out a dedicated messaging environment for it, but this is necessary if you want to scale the number of subscribers.

With unified messaging, the complexity diminishes because it is not necessary to build a dedicated infrastructure for Unity to reside. Instead, it is necessary to prepare the existing messaging infrastructure for unified messaging. For more information on preparing an existing environment for unified messaging, see Chapter 9, "Planning."

If unified messaging is desired right from the beginning, each Unity server will be designed and installed using one of the deployment models defined in this chapter.

The first section of this chapter, "Typical Configurations," discusses the standard configurations for Unity 4.0x. It explains how Unity can be configured to run as a single voice-messaging server, a single unified-message server, or as a failover server pair running in either configuration. The "Deployment Models" section of the chapter discusses the supported deployment models for Unity.

Unity is not limited to a single server or failover pair installation. You can install any number of Unity servers in your network. This chapter discusses a Unity server configuration, or how one Unity server can be installed into a given environment. It also has examples of how many Unity servers can be installed into a given environment. Chapter 12, "Unity Networking," examines how you can use multiple digitally-networked Unity servers to enable unified messaging for your enterprise.

This chapter also covers the new installations of Unity 4.0x. It does not, however, cover upgrades. There are some differences in the supported configurations for upgrades verses new installations. Please see Chapter 15, "Upgrades and Migration," for information on supported configurations for upgrades from previous versions of Unity all the way through to Unity 4.0.

Typical Configurations

The typical Unity configuration starts with a single Unity server providing traditional voice messaging-only services where everything Unity needs is self-contained onto a single server. Then the configurations move up to a full unified messaging configuration of one or more Unity servers servicing a very complex messaging configuration.

To simplify, Unity's typical configurations are:

- A voice messaging-only, single-server configuration where everything is self-contained
- A voice messaging-only, multiserver configuration with a dedicated messaging infrastructure
- A unified messaging configuration of one or more Unity servers servicing an existing messaging infrastructure

Each of these configurations has specific criteria that set them apart from one another. Some items can be limiting. For example, having one or more self-contained, single-server configurations installed to provide legacy voice messaging might prevent you from effectively using Unity's networking features. Each configuration described in this section discusses these potential limiting factors and what is necessary to make sure that desired functionality is not lost.

Voice Messaging

Unity can be installed as a voice messaging-only server (no unified messaging), servicing any PBX on the Cisco Unity 4.0 System Requirements and Supported Hardware and Software document on the Cisco website. It can also support Cisco CallManager or a SIP proxy server. Cisco Unity can also support a dual-switch integration between CallManager and a legacy PBX. See the Unity product documentation for more information. For Unity 4.0x, the only acceptable voice messaging-only configuration for Unity is with Unity connected to Exchange 2000.

It is important to pay close attention to the requirements of voice messaging-only for Unity. Because Unity is connected to Exchange 2000 in a voice messaging-only configuration, it is necessary to meet the support requirements for Exchange 2000. In addition, Unity's access into Exchange 2000 is essentially like a glorified client, so this means it is necessary that Unity have the same requirements as Exchange 2000.

For voice messaging-only configurations, Unity with Exchange 2000 needs:

- A Windows 2000 domain with access to a DC and GC (depending upon the implementation, they can be separate servers or one in the same).

- A Windows 2000 domain uses DNS, specifically dynamic DNS, so this is a requirement as well for Unity.

- Windows 2000 site. The Microsoft Management Console (MMC) Windows 2000 sites and services should be used to configure the Windows 2000 site or sites.

- Exchange 2000, which is joined to the Windows 2000 domain.

- Unity is joined to the Windows 2000 domain as a member server in the domain.

Regardless of the voice messaging-only configuration, Unity needs these components in order to function. The components can reside on a single server with Unity installed on it. Larger installations of any complexity require some dedicated servers to support the Unity voice-messaging function. Unity can be configured to run as a single server or installed into a dedicated messaging environment for larger voice mail-only deployments.

Single-Server Configuration

In order to install a single Unity server voice messaging-only configuration, it is necessary to follow the installation instructions as found in the Unity product documentation. For more information, see Chapter 16,"Installation."

Now, for Unity 4.0 a single server can accommodate a subscriber population up to 3000 users. As previously stated, this server can be connected to a legacy PBX or CallManager or both.

Figure 10-1 shows a typical low-end configuration for Cisco Unity. This Unity server is servicing voice messaging-only subscribers in a stand-alone configuration.

Figure 10-1 *A Stand-Alone Voice-Messaging Server Connected to a Legacy Circuit-Switched PBX*

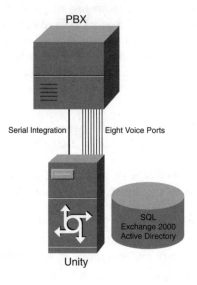

Using Unity's dual integration capabilities, Unity can service both legacy and IP telephony subscribers, as shown in Figure 10-2.

If it becomes necessary to increase the user population, additional Unity servers are needed to support the dual-switch configuration and/or higher capacity hardware might be needed.

Multiserver Configuration

Do not use a single-server configuration if it is certain additional servers are needed from the start either because of a user population greater than 3000, or because the replacement of multiple legacy voice-messaging servers is desired. You do have some flexibility here. It is possible to dedicate a messaging infrastructure (which also includes a domain infrastructure) for your Unity voice messaging-only deployment. As shown in Figure 10-3, this dedicated infrastructure can include dedicated messaging stores on separate servers than the Unity servers, and as shown in Figure 10-14, Unity can be installed on smaller servers containing both Unity and Exchange 2000 for remote sites that might have smaller user populations than a main campus or centralized location.

Figure 10-2 *A Dual-Switch Configuration with a Legacy Circuit-Switched PBX and Cisco CallManager*

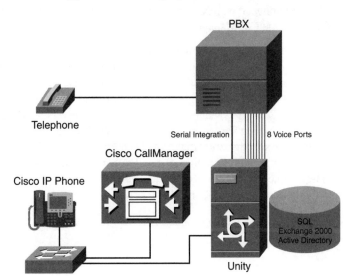

Figure 10-3 *A Typical Voice-Messaging Configuration with Unity and Dedicated Messaging Stores*

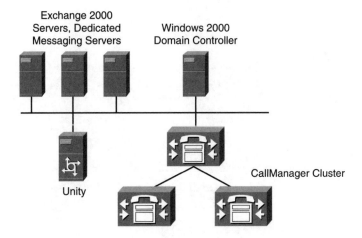

In the example from Figure 10-3, a single Unity server is servicing a CallManager cluster. The single Unity server's dedicated messaging infrastructure includes three Exchange 2000 servers and one Windows 2000 domain controller. Currently, a CallManager cluster can support a larger number of phones than a single Unity server or failover pair can support subscribers. In order to have Unity support a large number of subscribers to correlate to the same number of phones, it is necessary to add Unity servers networked together and registered to the same CallManager cluster.

Figure 10-4 depicts a Unity deployment in a dedicated messaging infrastructure. The environment consists of a distributed call processing, distributed messaging model. Because Unity uses Exchange 2000, it must also use Active Directory. There is a single Active Directory forest with a single tree and single domain structure. Each Unity server is installed into the same Windows 2000 sites where the Exchange 2000 servers reside. There is a Domain Controller/Global Catalog Server (DCGC) in each Windows 2000 site. There is a dedicated messaging hub for Exchange 2000 that provides messaging transfer to all remote locations. The larger Unity deployment contains off-box Exchange 2000 messaging servers dedicated to Unity. The remote locations (only one depicted here) are small enough to use a smaller Unity server with Exchange 2000 installed.

Figure 10-4 *Unity Servers in Two Different Configurations Digitally Networked*

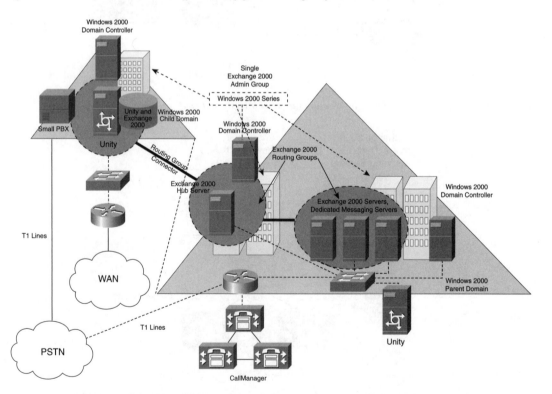

This is just one example of how an Exchange 2000 messaging infrastructure can be used to support multiple Unity servers in a voice messaging-only configuration. Other examples might consist of no hub and instead might use a multi-mesh configuration. In this example, the hub is used to demonstrate how a centralized messaging and distributed messaging infrastructure can be combined to support a Unity voice messaging-only solution.

Allocating the Proper Number of Domain Controllers for Exchange 2000 and Unity 4.0

The standard support requirement for Unity with Exchange 2000 where multiple messaging stores are in place, is that dedicated DCGCs are in place to service the Exchange 2000 servers accessed by Unity.

Although it might be debated as to the number of DCGCs actually required, the recommended standard is one DCGC for every four Exchange 2000 message stores. The expectation is that each Exchange 2000 server will house a max voice-messaging user population of 3000 mailboxes per server. If this is the case, the load on a DCGC might be high and thus the reason for the recommendation. However, depending upon usage, it might be possible to have one DCGC for every six to eight Exchange 2000 servers. Response time is key, however, and it is difficult to determine how much load a given configuration places on a DCGC without understanding the number of Unity systems and subscribers (through the web GUI for example) accessing the messaging infrastructure. For more information, see Chapter 9.

Another important note: A Unity server, with the right hardware, can service up to 7500 subscribers when it has off-box message stores. If this is the case, you can distribute 7500 subscribers across three or more Exchange servers. If you require more than 7500 subscribers, you need to install an additional Unity server and possibly more Exchange servers to service the desired number of subscribers.

An example of this approach is found in Figure 10-5 where Unity is servicing four Exchange servers, one of which is Unity's partner server. In this example, the partner server can also contain subscribers, it is not limited to containing only Unity default objects. Dedicating a single Exchange server as a partner server for such a low number of subscribers (7500 total) is a waste of resources. Note the Exchange 2000 partner server homes the Unity system mailbox and default Unity objects.

In a voice messaging-only configuration, your subscribers might also desire to access their messages or personal settings via the Cisco Unity Personal Communications Assistant (CPCA) which also includes the Unity Inbox. The Unity Inbox is a web-based client that subscribers use to obtain a visual representation of their voice messages left on the Unity server. Depending upon the requirements of the given voice messaging-only implementation, you might need to consider subscriber access to be a factor in sizing and allocating your servers to support the Unity voice messaging-only solution.

Figure 10-5 *Unity Servicing Four Exchange 2000 Servers*

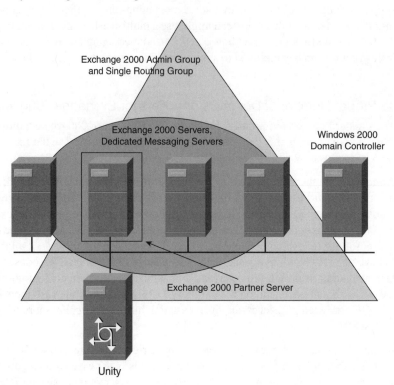

Exchange 2000 Admin Group
and Single Routing Group

Exchange 2000 Servers,
Dedicated Messaging Servers

Windows 2000
Domain Controller

Exchange 2000 Partner Server

Unity

Unified Messaging

For unified messaging, the expectation is that Unity is installed into an existing messaging environment. This sounds easy enough and it can be, but it is essential that the messaging environment be readied for unified messaging first. This means it is necessary to make sure the messaging servers can support unified messaging and also the other messaging infrastructure components, such as domain controllers that can properly handle the added activity that Unity creates. This requirement is really no different than any other server-based application that must service end-user requests and access networked computer resources on their behalf. For more information on preparing an existing environment for unified messaging, see Chapter 9.

With unified messaging, there are no single-server configurations that contain Unity, the message store, and domain controller functionality. In Unity, such unified messaging configurations are unsupported, unlike the single-server voice messaging-only configuration as described previously. But, the same requirements exist for Unity in a unified messaging configuration regardless of the messaging store serviced:

- Unity is installed into a Windows NT domain (For Exchange 5.5 only) or Windows 2000 domain (for Exchange 5.5, Exchange 2000, and Domino R5) as a member server in the domain.

- Unity has access to the same name resolution requirements as the domain and messaging system it services.

With unified messaging, Unity is configured to support the existing subscriber population. If the subscriber population is larger than what can be supported by a single Unity server, additional Unity servers can be added to support them. The way Unity servers are added depends upon the messaging system they service.

During installation of the Unity server, the installer has the option of selecting the specific messaging store they want Unity to join. This is then called the Unity Partner server. When this selection is made, Unity obtains the specific information regarding the message store configuration and version from that message store's primary directory. For more information, see Chapter 4, "Components and Subsystems: Directory."

Partner Server

For Exchange 5.5 and Exchange 2000, Unity uses the concept of a partner server. This is the Exchange server that houses the Unity system mailbox and other Unity objects (see Chapter 1, "Architecture"). In earlier versions of Unity, the partner server was called the Unity bridgehead server, but this was actually a misnomer because only one aspect of Unity messaging originated from the partner server. Unity also logs onto mailboxes on other Exchange servers directly, bypassing its partner server, which makes the term bridgehead inappropriate for such functionality.

The partner server is important to Unity, and connecting Unity to a reliable partner server is a key component of a successful Unity deployment.

For Domino, the notion of a partner server is a little different because Unity does not use a system mailbox to service Notes subscribers. For more information, see Chapter 14, "Unity with Lotus Domino."

Unity with Exchange 5.5

In Chapter 13, "Unity with Microsoft Exchange," you find further detail regarding how Unity should be deployed with Exchange 5.5, Exchange 2000, and Exchange 2003. However, in terms of discussing Unity configurations, the messaging infrastructure components that affect a given Unity configuration merit discussion in this chapter.

Microsoft Exchange, as well as Lotus Domino, can be deployed in seemingly endless ways. In this chapter, we examine some of the ways Unity works and some challenges Unity has.

Aside from the physical constraints of locating Unity as close as possible to the messaging system it services, the messaging boundaries, the domains, and the specifics in which they work are covered here. Use this chapter along with Chapter 13, and the other chapters in Part II, "Deployment," to determine how to design your solution for Unity.

Exchange 5.5 Site Boundaries

With Exchange 5.5, Unity can be installed to service a specific Exchange 5.5 site. All versions of Unity up to version 4.0x do not support servicing subscribers by a single server across multiple Exchange 5.5 sites (this should not be confused with Windows 2000 sites). If multiple sites do exist, at least one Unity server per site is needed.

When Unity 4.0x is installed into an Exchange 5.5 site, a special folder is created under the site container. The folder is named Cisco Unity. The Unity default location object is placed here during the installation process. This object identifies Unity to other Unity servers installed into the same site or other sites if digital networking is used between the Unity servers. For additional information see, Chapter 12, "Unity Networking" and Chapter 13).

Unity can usually service a single Exchange 5.5 site, but there are exceptions. The exceptions are based upon the Exchange 5.5 site configuration. Exchange 5.5 sites that correlate to physical locations or campuses are more easily serviced by Unity than a single site that might span multiple locations separated via WAN connectivity. The main reason for this limitation is that with a single site spanning multiple locations, too many points of failure exist that can cause operational issues with Unity's performance.

Exchange 5.5 Site Where Unity Should Not Be Deployed

If you review Figure 10-6, you can see that this configuration is not suitable to centralized unified messaging or voice-mail messaging deployment if you want Unity to service all subscribers in the same Exchange 5.5 site. It also is not suitable to a distributed unified messaging or voice-mail messaging deployment because there are too many points of failure that impact one or all of the Cisco Unity servers.

No company wants Unity's performance to be affected by slow response time due to congested WAN links or because Exchange 5.5 servers come offline frequently. The more remotely connected Exchange servers in the same site, the worse Unity performance can be, especially if you attempt to have Unity support subscribers on these remote systems. As Unity has to monitor and service these remote servers, it is possible that subscribers colocated on messaging systems with Unity might be affected by the delays caused the access methods available to Unity to access these remote Exchange servers.

Figure 10-6 *Exchange 5.5 Site Spanning Multiple Locations Over a WAN*

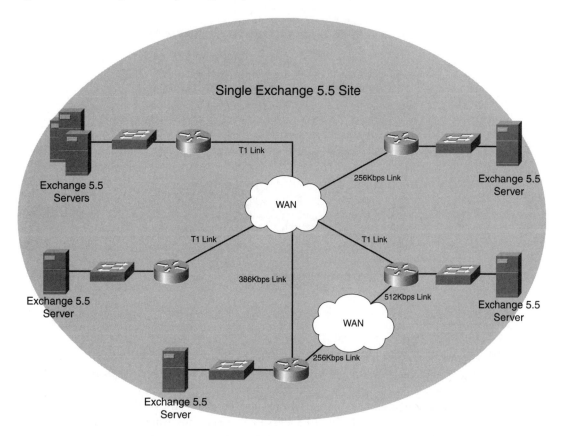

Regardless of the messaging store being serviced by Unity, a remotely-connected server cannot be serviced by Unity because of the possibility of multiple single points of failure, as demonstrated in Figure 10-7. Remote messaging servers should be serviced by a colocated Unity server.

The best Exchange 5.5 site model for Unity is when all servers in the site are in the same physical location or campus. This allows Unity to get the most benefit from LAN connectivity and not be subjected to response time issues due to slow links. Unity can still be affected in this environment by busy Exchange servers or other servers it depends on. In order to manage this type of environment, you must ensure that it is readied for unified messaging and also that the proper capacity planning is performed; see Chapter 9 for more information.

Figure 10-7 *Unity with a Severed WAN Link*

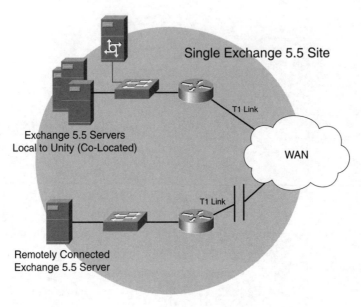

Exchange 5.5 Sites Where Unity Is Deployable

A single Exchange 5.5 site in a campus environment, even where a high-speed backbone connects a metropolitan area, is suitable for a single Unity server to service. A campus environment typically has more resiliency and therefore most single points of failure are eliminated. As shown in Figure 10-8, the single-site campus, while seemingly complex, can easily support a Unity deployment that is both sustainable and manageable.

When multiple Exchange 5.5 sites exist, there needs to be at least one Unity server per site. The Unity servers will then rely on the Exchange 5.5 messaging backbone to deliver messages from one Unity server to another. A good example of this requirement is found in Figure 10-9 where two Exchange 5.5 sites exist. Note the Exchange server at the remote campus location. You might be able to have Unity service this server as long as you verify the readiness requirements for response time, capacity-planning steps, and also manage it after your deployment. Without performing these key steps you will have problems and no sustainable solution.

Figure 10-8 *Exchange 5.5 Site Configuration: Campus*

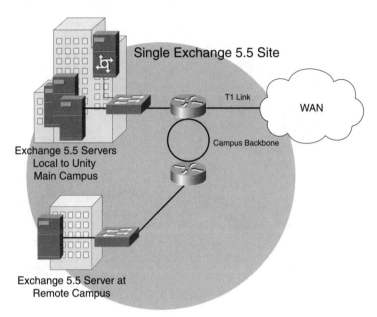

The example shown in Figure 10-10 shows a distributed messaging and distributed call processing deployment model combination. An important note here regarding the Unity servers, they are colocated with each Exchange site where one or more Exchange servers reside within the site. This configuration and deployment scenario is an ideal scenario because Unity services these messaging systems in a more optimal and sustainable fashion. It is also an ideal scenario because they are colocated with the call-processing piece of Unity: CallManager and Legacy PBXs. This diagram is one example where you might take advantage of what is already in place in order to easily fit your Unity solution into it.

Unity makes use of the messaging infrastructure, which has a centralized hub for message delivery to enable Unity networking. Because this allows subscribers on one Unity server to address messages to subscribers on a another Unity server by using this existing messaging infrastructure, the solution becomes a sustainable one as all resources important to subscribers are colocated with them. This might not be economical from a cost and supportability standpoint, but it is practical because single points of failure are significantly reduced. For more information on networking Unity servers in this fashion, see Chapter 12.

Figure 10-9   *Exchange 5.5, Multiple Site Configurations: Campus + WAN*

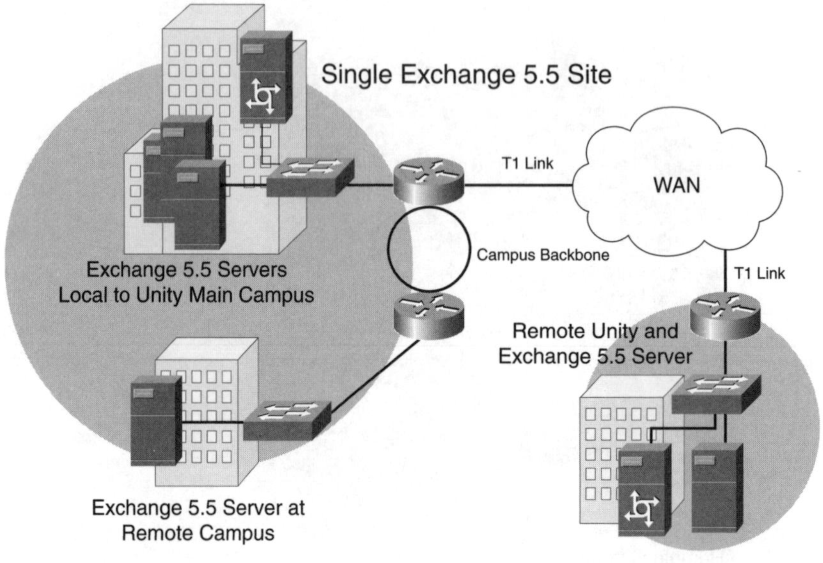

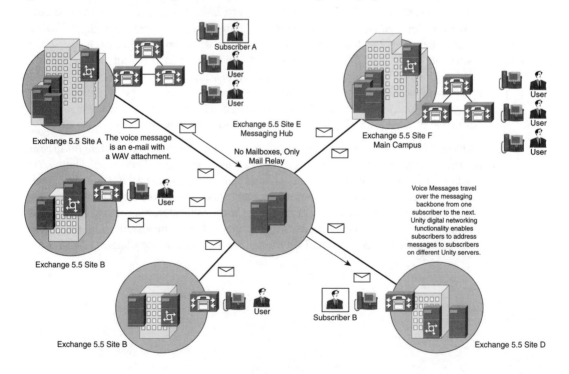

Figure 10-10   *Multisite Exchange with Unity Servers Delivering Messages from One to Another*

Domain Boundaries

For unified messaging (voice messaging-only is a little different as discussed elsewhere in this chapter and throughout this book), Unity 4.0x can reside in either a Windows NT domain, a Windows 2000 domain, or a mixed domain. Regardless, it is necessary to ensure that Unity is installed into an existing domain and that no special domain should be configured for Unity under this model.

If Unity is installed into a resource domain, it should be the same domain as the Exchange 5.5 servers in the site it services, as shown in Figure 10-11.

If Unity is installed into a separate resource domain, it should have access to the Exchange 5.5 servers and there should be no delays as a result of the separation. However, authentication might be affected. If so, Unity response times might be affected if it is located too far away from the domain where Exchange 5.5 servers it services reside.

Figure 10-11 *Master/Resource Domain with Unity and Exchange 5.5 Installed*

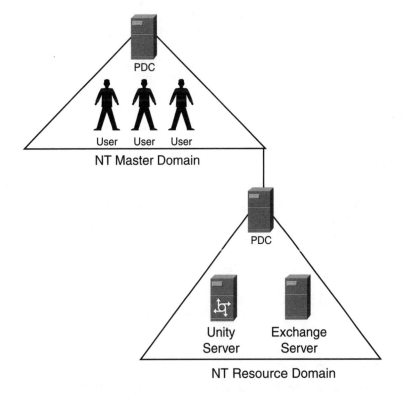

In the diagram in Figure 10-12, a master domain with multiple resource domains is shown; Unity is installed in one, Exchange is installed in another. In this figure, Unity needs access to the Exchange servers. There is no practical reason for Unity not be installed into the same domain as Exchange. However, there is also no technical reason why it cannot be installed into a different domain. It is not recommended but it is not enforced as a limitation in the code. The biggest challenge to locating Unity into a separate resource domain is the permissions required to access the Exchange servers. The further Unity is from the Exchange servers, the more points of failure you will have. In this case, placing Unity into a separate resource domain than Exchange creates another point of failure; this one having to do with account access and permissions. For more information, see Unity product documentation at www.cisco.com.

Figure 10-12 *A Workable Configuration, but Less Desirable Than Figure 10-11*

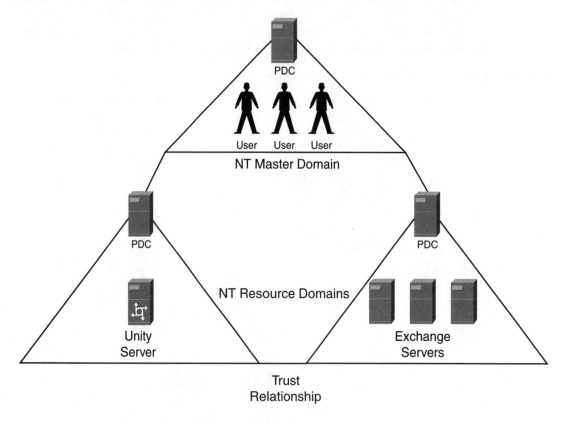

Exchange 5.5 Server Configurations

Unity can service a common Exchange server configuration. It cannot however, support an Exchange 5.5 cluster. Unity can service one or more Exchange 5.5 servers in a given site. The best practice is to limit the total number of Exchange 5.5 servers serviced by Unity to 10, however there is no technical limit. It is impractical to expect a single Unity server to service 15 or 20 servers. The more servers Unity services, the greater the challenge you have managing those servers and Unity's access to them. Unity can coexist with Exchange 5.5 (Outlook Web Access [OWA]), but does not utilize it.

Unity with Exchange 2000/2003

Unity supports unified messaging configurations and voice messaging-only configurations for Exchange 2000. It also supports unified messaging configurations for Exchange 2003. The configuration differences between the two are mentioned as necessary; otherwise, the discussion in this section applies to both unified messaging and voice messaging-only configurations.

Admin Group

Unity has to be installed into the same admin group as the Exchange 2000 servers it services. This means that Unity needs to have the necessary access into the Exchange 2000 admin group. No Unity-specific objects are installed into the Exchange 2000 directory structure to identify Unity as servicing the admin group it is installed into. This is important regardless if the Exchange 2000 server(s) are installed into a single Admin group (as shown in Figure 10-13); running in native-mode messaging; or if there are multiple Admin groups running in mixed-mode messaging with Exchange 5.5.

It is important to note that there is technically no limit on the number of admin groups Unity can service. The more admin groups you have, however, the more you have to be concerned with managing Unity's access into them. Although this should be easy once established, experience has shown less than desirable results. However, like anything, if the proper attention and consideration is given to it then it should not be a serious challenge or administrative overhead. As a recommendation, do not allow multiple admin groups to become a potential problem area for serviceability within Unity.

Figure 10-13 *Unity Servicing Servers in a Same Exchange 2000 Admin Group/with a Single Routing Group*

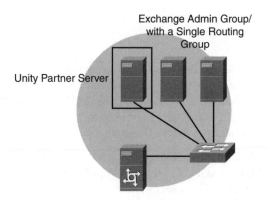

Routing Group

Unity can support more than one routing group. However it can be affected if one routing group is separated from another through a slow WAN link or SMTP connector. In order for Unity to support more than one routing group, the second routing group should be installed into the same Windows 2000 site as the first routing group; naturally, this means Unity should be installed into this same Windows 2000 site as well.

Unity should not be configured to service more than one routing group if it cannot join the same Windows 2000 site as the Exchange servers where that routing group resides. In the case depicted in Figure 10-14, it is suitable because both routing groups are in the same Windows 2000 site. If that were not the case, Unity's support needs to be limited to a single routing group, regardless of how many routing groups reside within an Exchange 2000 admin group.

Figure 10-14   *Unity Servicing More Than One Routing Group within the Same Windows 2000 Site*

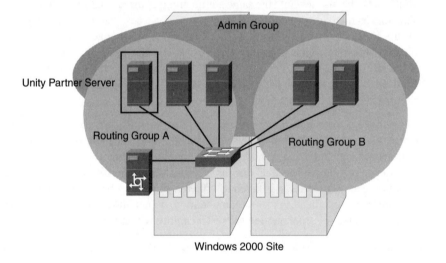

Domain

For Unity with Exchange 2000 in a voice messaging only-configuration, the Windows 2000 domain(s) already exist or be built and dedicated to the Unity installation. A voice messaging-only configuration requires a dedicated Windows 2000 domain. This includes a Windows 2000 domain controller to be used by Unity to authenticate, perform look-ups, and to read and write from Active Directory.

Unity also needs access to a Global Catalog server for MAPI access into Exchange 2000 (it is used for GAL [global address lists] lookups and to read the Global Catalog's directory for changes from other Unity servers).

Figure 10-15 *Unity Accessing a Windows 2000 Domain Controller and Global Catalog*

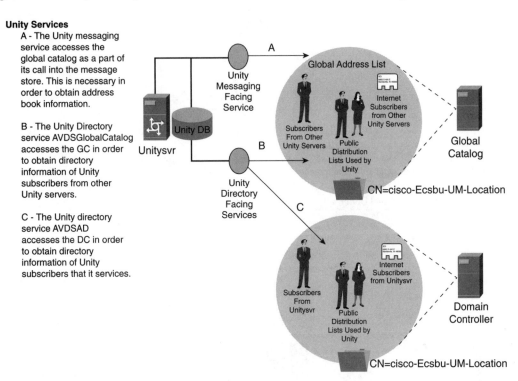

Unity Services
A - The Unity messaging service accesses the global catalog as a part of its call into the message store. This is necessary in order to obtain address book information.

B - The Unity Directory service AVDSGlobalCatalog accesses the GC in order to obtain directory information of Unity subscribers from other Unity servers.

C - The Unity directory service AVDSAD accesses the DC in order to obtain directory information of Unity subscribers that it services.

Although there is no real technical limit to the number of domains a Unity server might be located from Exchange, there is a best practice recommendation that Unity be installed into the same domain as the Exchange servers it services. Earlier Unity documentation has a stated limit of no more than three domains away from Exchange 2000/2003. However, every attempt should be made to install Unity into the same domain where Exchange 2000/2003 exists and where users exist. As mentioned in the Exchange 5.5 section, there is no practical reason to locate Unity in a separate domain from Exchange.

In Figure 10-16, the first example is a child-parent-child domain. The other example is a child-parent-grandparent domain.

Unity should be in the same tree and same forest as the Exchange 2000 servers it services. It should not be installed into a separate tree to service Exchange 2000 subscribers in a different tree. Figure 10-17 shows an incorrect configuration for Unity that should be avoided. This is another example of placing too much of a dependency on access from one tree to another and the overhead involved in managing it. Although it might be argued that there is no technical reason that you cannot do this, it is not practical and, therefore, is not a best practice.

Figure 10-16 *Unity's Domain Limitations*

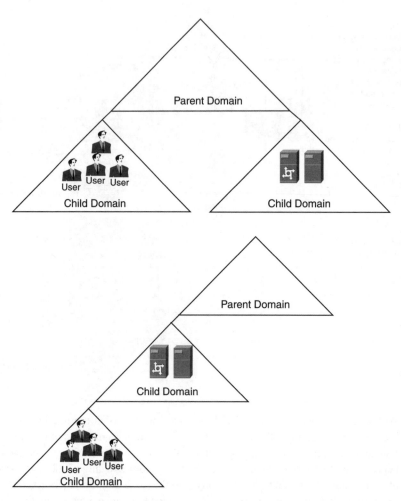

It is important to note that many organizations might create an Active Directory forest that has more than one tree. Unity can coexist with a forest that has more than one tree; it just needs to be installed into the same tree with Exchange.

Figure 10-17 *Two Separate Trees in the Same Forest*

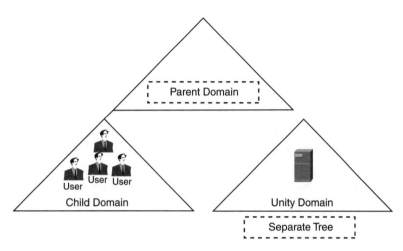

Installing Unity as a separate tree and domain in an Active Directory forest is not suitable for unified messaging. This type of solution would work for a voice messaging-only configuration because the Unity domain is dedicated to Unity and its messaging infrastructure. This means that the dedicated Unity messaging servers would reside in the Unity domain and not the existing tree where the mail-enabled users reside. If unified messaging is desired, there is no avoiding the requirement to install Unity into the same domain and Windows 2000 site as the Exchange servers that it services. This also means that Unity has to have the same access to service the mail-enabled users as Unity subscribers as what Exchange 2000 requires to service e-mail accounts.

Exchange 2000

The following list is provided in order to provide a reference of what Unity can support for Exchange 2000.

- Unity can support a single Exchange 2000 server.
- Unity can support an Exchange 2000 cluster.
- Unity can support a front-end/ back-end configuration of Exchange 2000.

During Unity installation when the Exchange 2000 partner server is selected, Unity essentially joins the Exchange 2000 admin group the partner server resides in. Unity then creates the special Unity default location object in Active Directory and also creates the other Unity objects. It can then service mailboxes in the Administrative group where its partner server is installed. Again, it can also service mailboxes in other admin groups as well.

Earlier Unity documentation stated that each Unity server can support only five mail stores. The reason behind this statement was the expectation that user density on five mail stores would be equal to the total number of subscribers a single Unity server could support, which is 7500. Also, that was the maximum number of mail stores initially specified for qualification.

However, over time, this number has been revised to allow for more flexibility in solutions development for Unity with Exchange. Thus, there is no real limit to the number of Exchange 2000 servers and mailbox databases a single Unity server can support. The trend is to take large user populations and break them up into smaller groups and place them on a separate mailbox database in multiple storage groups in Exchange 2000. This means that a given Exchange 2000 server can support 20 mailbox databases. One mailbox database is typically allocated as the public database, leaving 19 mailbox databases available for subscribers.

If each Exchange server is configured with the maximum number of mail stores on it, then having a single Unity server service a maximum of 10 servers with up 99 mail stores is still a recommended maximum. Depending upon your readiness assessment and capacity planning, you might go higher with more servers and more mail stores. Doubling the total number of servers, however, might be impractical. So although there is no technical limit for the number of mail stores that Unity can connect to, a best practice is to limit the number of mail stores that each Unity server services. In Figure 10-18, a single Unity server is servicing five Exchange 2000 servers.

Figure 10-18 *A Single Unity Server Servicing Five Exchange 2000 Servers*

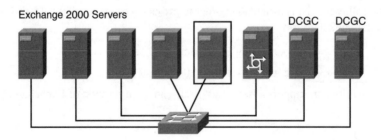

In Figure 10-19, a single Unity failover pair is servicing an Exchange 2000 cluster. It can service active/active or active/passive cluster. See Chapter 13 for more information.

Figure 10-19 *Exchange 2000 Cluster (Active/Passive or Active/Active)*

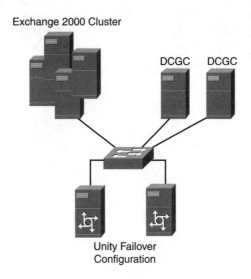

In Figure 10-20, Unity is servicing a front-end/back-end configuration. Now, in this diagram, Unity connects to the back end directly because the front end does not have any mailboxes located on it. The intention of the front-end/back-end configuration is to allow mail-enabled users to use the Microsoft Outlook Web access component for messaging instead of directly connecting mail-enabled users to individual Exchange servers where the URLs are all different.

The front-end/back-end configuration can be supported by Unity in a unified messaging configuration. When dedicating a messaging infrastructure for Unity in a voice messaging-only configuration, the front-end/back-end configuration for Exchange 2000 is not practical because Unity is the only client accessing the mailboxes, and in a voice messaging-only configuration, Outlook Web Access is not used. For more information on requirements for Unity with Exchange 2000, see Chapter 13.

Figure 10-20 *Exchange 2000 Front-End/Back-End Configuration*

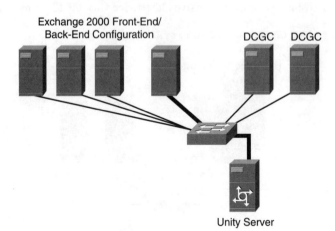

Unity with Domino R5

Just like Unity for Exchange, Unity for Domino has narrow limitations in how it can service Domino servers. First of all, Unity Domino supports only a unified messaging configuration. There is no voice messaging-only offering for Unity for Domino. Unity's primary interface into Domino is through Lotus DUCS (Domino Unified Communications Services), as discussed in the first section of the book. The first release of DUCS worked only with Windows 2000 (a version for AIX is soon to follow), so Unity can service only Notes clients whose mailboxes are homed on Domino servers version R5/Windows 2000. Naturally, newer versions of Domino will be supported with newer versions of DUCS. In the future, Lotus might support DUCS on other versions of Domino aside from just Windows 2000 and AIX.

Unity can service Domino in the following configurations:

- Domino Single Server
- Multiple Domino Servers
- Domino Clusters (restricted to servicing DUCS servers only)

For authentication to work while accessing the Cisco Unity server, it is necessary to install it into a Windows 2000 domain. The example in Figure 10-21 shows a dedicated domain controller. However, it is possible to install the Unity server as its own domain and domain controller if Windows 2000 domains are not used in the Domino environment where Unity is installed. The Domino Address Book (also referred to as the directory) houses the DUCS admin application. Unity needs direct access to this server, whether it is the primary directory server or a replica of it. In a sense, Unity's access to and dependency on this server is equivalent to the partner server Unity connects to when it services Exchange.

Figure 10-21 *Multiple Domino Servers with Unity Servicing Notes Clients*

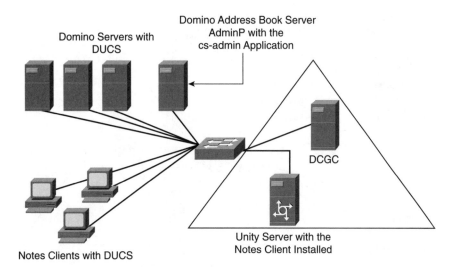

With a Domino cluster, Unity can service mailboxes on servers with DUCS installed (see Figure 10-22). If servers in the cluster do not have DUCS installed, Unity cannot service those mailboxes.

The first release of Unity for Domino had some limiting factors in topology and functionality. Over time, these limiting factors have diminished as Unity for Domino has matured as a product.

The main limiting factor is that Unity can service only Domino servers in a single Domino directory/domain. This is a supported limitation and not one that is based on technical limitations. Unity can service only a single address book or NAMES.NSF. It can, however, service a secondary address book for contacts, known as Internet subscribers in Unity.

With the current releases of Unity for Domino, up to Unity 4.04, there is limited functionality with the offering. And there is currently no failover for Unity for Domino, minimal networking, and no voice-messaging interoperability functionality at all. Future releases of the Unity 4.0x line should include all of these: failover, expanding networking support, and voice messaging interoperability. For more information, see Chapters 12 and 15.

Windows 2000 Domain Requirements

For Unity 4.0, a Windows 2000 domain must exist or be installed for Unity. The Unity server can also be promoted to a DCGC if one does not exist in the Domino environment.

Figure 10-22 *Domino Cluster Servicing Notes Clients*

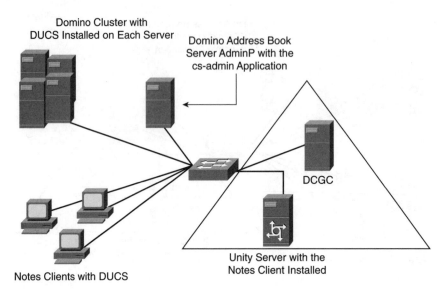

Although Unity can be installed into an existing Windows 2000 domain as a member server in order to support Domino messaging and Notes clients, it is not uncommon for standard Unity configurations to be installed as a domain controller for Domino. As a part of this, all Unity for Domino configurations must use dynamic DNS for name resolution, at least to support the dedicated or existing Windows 2000 domain for Unity.

Failover

Unity enhanced failover has been available in the product since version 3.1. Prior to that, Unity supported what was called "simple" failover. This was a manual setup of failover that allowed for replication of SQL data between Unity servers and also required some Registry changes on each server.

Unity can be configured in failover mode for Exchange. It can be configured in a voice messaging-only configuration or a unified messaging configuration. A failover pair (two Unity servers, one primary and the other secondary) supports Exchange the same way as a single Unity server. This means that for voice messaging, Unity can support a failover configuration that services Exchange 2000 servers only. For unified messaging, it can support either both or only Exchange 5.5 or Exchange 2000 servers.

Unity with Exchange 5.5

The typical configuration for Unity for Exchange 5.5 in a failover configuration is shown in Figure 10-23.

Figure 10-23   *Unity Servicing Exchange 5.5 Servers in an Exchange 5.5 Site*

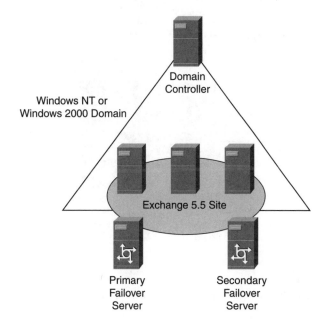

Unity with Exchange 2000

The typical configuration for Unity for Exchange 2000 in a failover configuration is shown in Figure 10-24.

Unity for Exchange 2000 in failover mode can also support any of the Exchange 2000 configurations including clusters or front-end/back-end configurations, as shown in Figure 10-25. Unity can service either an Exchange 2000 active-active or active-passive cluster.

The same applies to failover for a front-end back-end configuration. In Figure 10-26, a failover pair is servicing a front-end/back-end configuration.

Figure 10-24 *Unity Service Exchange 2000 Servers in an Admin Group in a Single Windows 2000 Site*

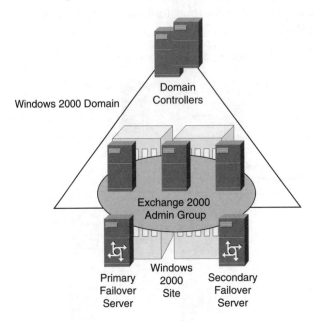

Figure 10-25 *Unity Failover Pair Servicing an Exchange 2000 Cluster*

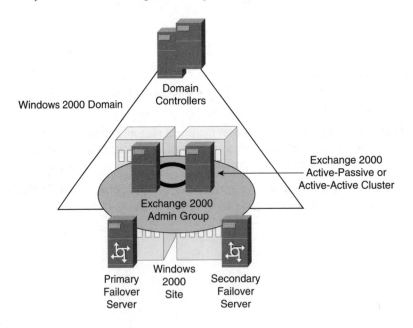

Figure 10-26 *Unity Failover Pair Servicing an Exchange 2000 Front-End /Back-End Configuration*

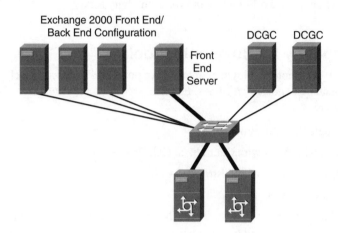

Failover can work in deployment models as well. There are also special considerations necessary depend upon the deployment model used.

All of the typical configurations work with the deployment models. It is necessary to understand these configurations first so that you can then understand how to apply them to the deployment models, as described in the following sections.

Deployment Models

Cisco IP Telephony solutions are delivered using deployment models based on call processing capabilities in Cisco CallManager. Most of these same deployment models for call processing can also apply to legacy PBXs. The voice-messaging TUI interface, voice ports used, and voice-messaging switch integration portions of Unity use the call processing deployment models. However, because Unity is a unified messaging system with traditional voice-messaging capabilities that uses a third-party messaging system to provide this functionality, messaging deployment models are the more prevalent for any Unity deployment. This means they get first consideration for any Unity design.

A benefit of each deployment model is that it provides a list of characteristics that need to be considered when using that model. This list includes defining where users are physically located and how they access the system. Therefore, classifying a given physical site based on these characteristics becomes a key activity in determining a deployment model for a Unity server.

Note that a messaging deployment model is used for a single Unity server or a failover pair. If more Unity servers are used, it is necessary to define the messaging model for each Unity server as they might be different. If you have a large number of Unity servers to deploy, you may end up using a different model for each Unity server.

Cisco IP Telephony Deployment Models

Cisco IP Telephony deployment models are published in Cisco IP Telephony product documentation and design guides. For reference, they are listed here. The deployment models are:

- Single Site Call Processing
- Multisite WAN with Centralized Call Processing
- Multisite WAN with Distributed Call Processing
- Clustering Over IP WAN

Other than the Clustering Over IP WAN, the three remaining deployment models can be used to also describe call processing for legacy phone systems. For more information, refer to the Cisco product documentation and design guides for Cisco CallManager.

Cisco Messaging Deployment Models

As mentioned, the messaging deployment models are most prevalent for Unity. The reason is simple and it is the primary theme throughout this book (especially in Part II): Unity should be installed as close as possible to the messaging systems it services. Voice calls between Unity and CallManager can be QoS'd (or have Quality of Service applied). Voice calls between Unity and a legacy switch are hard-wired and can typically be optimized for best response time. However, aside from preparing the messaging environment through readiness assessment and capacity planning, the connectivity between Unity and the messaging system cannot be QoS'd nor can the connectivity be otherwise guaranteed. Unity can be placed onto the same VLAN as the messaging system in order to improve chances of response time. In many cases, this has proved to also alleviate notification problems resulting from having Unity on a VLAN separate from Exchange. So, the lack of an application level QoS between a messaging system and Unity presents an issue when you are trying to provide real-time data (voice messages and message store information) to callers via a TUI interface. Thus, the best thing you can do is to eliminate the potential risks and dependency issues in order to provide the best possible chance for a sustainable solution.

This is said so that you understand how important it is to associate Unity with the messaging deployment models first and foremost. In each messaging deployment model, Unity is colocated with the messaging system it services. The expectation is that all messaging infrastructure components are colocated with Unity as well. This notion allows you to circle back around from the discussions on this topic in the first part of this chapter. To summarize, these messaging infrastructure components include:

- **Messaging servers**. Servers that have the capacity to support voice messaging, that are highly available, and that are providing the best response time possible to their e-mail clients and ultimately to Unity. Directory access is also important, but Unity does not make use of real-time access into the directory in a great way. However, a directory that is improperly configured or prone to errors can cause problems for any application including Unity.

- **Domain Controllers**. Domain controllers (and Global Catalogs for Exchange 2000/2003) that are not at capacity, but that can provide timely authentication and support for the messaging systems they service.

- **Name Resolution Hosts**. Hosts that provide timely name resolution to support the interactions between domain controllers, directory servers, and the messaging systems and their clients.

- **Network Throughput**. Network throughput that is properly managed and where adequate bandwidth can be provided between all messaging infrastructure components so as to eliminate potential network bottlenecks.

- **Network Access**. Network access that is available to all clients and supporting systems in order to provide direct access into the messaging systems without requiring the use of a firewall to separate messaging systems, their infrastructure components and e-mail clients.

So, these are the characteristics that help to define the messaging deployment models. Deviations from these characteristics can place the design and deployment at risk. This means you must classify a site based on whether it meets all these characteristics and document exceptions that need to be addressed prior to finalizing a design.

The messaging deployment models are:

- **Single Site**. All messaging infrastructure components are located within a single site. The messaging infrastructure does not expand beyond the single site. All clients are located at the single site and access their messages locally. The site classification for a single site might include a single building or a single campus area with more than one building well connected but consisting of no remote campuses.

- **Multisite WAN with Centralized Messaging**. All messaging infrastructure components are located within a single centralized location. The messaging infrastructure might expand beyond the centralized location but this location's primary functionality might include providing messaging routing via a hub and providing message access to remotely located e-mail clients (clients that are separated from the centralized location through a WAN connection). The centralized messaging model might also provide messaging access to e-mail clients colocated at the centralized location. Site classification for a centralized location includes a centralized data center that provides either centralized messaging access for local and remote e-mail clients, messaging hub services to provide message routing to other data centers, or remote messaging systems. The primary characteristic for centralized messaging (aside from all messaging infrastructure components being colocated there) is that the site provides e-mail access for remote and local e-mail clients.

- **Multisite WAN with Distributed Messaging**. All messaging systems are installed at any number of physical locations and they are configured to provide message routing between one another through a messaging backbone either created through a hub spoke configuration or through a multi-mesh configuration or some form thereof. All messaging infrastructure components are located with each messaging system and all e-mail clients accessing that messaging system locally. Site classification includes: physical locations that contain messaging systems and their messaging infrastructure components, and access to the e-mail clients colocated with the messaging systems. The site's messaging systems have message routing to remote locations through a messaging backbone.

- **Disaster Recovery/System Redundancy Sites**. Consists of a portion or all of the primary messaging systems being mirrored or backed up through at least two separate physical locations. The two separate physical locations have highly available bandwidth, typically consisting of a connectivity over a MAN (metropolitan-area network) and on occasion, WAN-level connectivity. From Unity's perspective, Disaster Recovery/System Redundancy Sites can accommodate a Unity failover solution by providing the necessary messaging infrastructure components in a way that both the primary and secondary failover servers can provide unified messaging services to the messaging systems. Because Unity has specific parameters in which it must operate for each failover solution, the emphasis for site classification is based on Unity's requirements and not upon the general messaging characteristics that must be met in order to accommodate this messaging deployment model.

It is important to note that the messaging deployment models used by Unity are based on physical colocation between Unity and the messaging system it services. This is also important when determining how to deploy Unity. It gives light to the two primary deployment rules for any Unity design. They are mentioned here in order to demonstrate how by adhering to these to primary deployment rules, you give yourself the best chance to have a sustainable Unity solution.

1 Unity is installed as close as possible to the messaging system it services. A given Unity server should be installed as close as possible to the messaging servers it services. This includes having access to the same messaging infrastructure resources as the messaging servers (domain controllers if applicable, and name resolution). This is essential. Deviations from this requirement should always be considered

exceptions — and not standard deployment criterion. Also note that deviations from this approach create a risk in the design and deployment. If these risks are managed, you can still provide a sustainable solution.

2 All Unity servers might be limited by physical constraints of connectivity between Unity and a given legacy PBX. Unity's connectivity to CallManager or a SIP Proxy server is far less restrictive. This rule should be given higher priority than the first rule; but, it might also disqualify Unity from being a solution. For example, if Unity is restricted due to cable distance limitations for voice-port connectivity and the messaging system it is expected to service is located across a WAN, then you do not have a supportable design and Unity should be disqualified as a solution. Your only alternatives are to overcome the cable distance limitations, colocate the messaging systems with Unity and the legacy PBX, or replace your legacy PBX with CallManager. If these alternatives are not an option, then you have no solution.

After these primary deployment rules are applied to a given Unity server for design purposes and each site is classified, you can determine the messaging deployment model or models to use for your design. After you have a good understanding of a given Unity configuration, you will be able to use the configurations and fit them with the deployment models described here.

Now, consider that a large roll out of multiple Unity servers might require you to use more than one messaging deployment model, one for each Unity server. This is a completely acceptable approach, and allows for a considerable amount of flexibility in your design, as you are not restricted by a requirement to use only one model for all Unity servers. Use the model you need for each Unity server based on the site classification of the site that it is going to be installed into.

Messaging Boundaries

Aside from the physical requirements, messaging boundaries add an extra dimension to any design for Unity. In fact, the same is true for any unified messaging product. Do not let anyone else tell you it does not. So take the messaging boundaries into consideration once the sites are classified and the two primary deployment rules for Unity are adhered to.

As explained in the first part of this chapter, messaging boundaries are the boundaries that control administrative access, distribution lists, and a shared directory between all e-mail clients. The topmost directory level of nearly any messaging system is the organization, or org for short. MS Exchange 5.5 and Exchange 2000/2003 have the org as their topmost boundary. They can be the same or separate. From Domino, the organization is also the topmost boundary.

Then, each messaging system might have one or more lower level boundaries that control administrative access, distribution lists, and other items, such as e-mail policies for e-mail clients. For Exchange 5.5, a lower-level boundary is the Exchange 5.5 site. For Exchange 2000/2003, it is an admin group. For Domino, it is the Domino domain or address book.

Along with what is described at the beginning of this chapter, each messaging chapter goes into far more detail to describe how Unity uses these messaging systems and how it resides within the given messaging boundaries. Where each Unity server fits within these messaging boundaries is a key step in determining a design for Unity once the site classification and primary deployment rules are considered.

From Unity's perspective, the messaging boundaries also have criteria that must be met in order for Unity to reside in it and service the messaging systems within those boundaries. This criterion is specifically the Windows OS specific boundaries including Windows domain and Windows 2000 sites.

This criterion must be met, and therefore, any Unity design must also account for these aspects of any messaging system(s) serviced by Unity. Once you move from the physical aspect of your design, you then need to address the messaging boundaries for each Unity server.

NOTE   Chapters 13 and 14 have specific requirements for the Windows domain so make sure they are referenced and those requirements are met.

We examine particulars regarding Windows domains and Windows 2000 sites. The Windows domain where you expect to install Unity must be known. A Windows 2000 domain requires service locator records for its servers and client computers, and comes with dynamic DNS so that these service locator records can be dynamically listed in DNS. The servers and clients that have joined the domain then know where to find specific services within the domain. The type of DNS used is important for a Windows 2000 domain. The Windows 2000 site is also important. Make sure that the Windows 2000 site for Unity is identified when it services Exchange 2000 or Exchange 2003.

Combining Deployment Models

For each Unity server design, both sides of Unity must be accounted for. The voice port/ phone system connectivity portion must be accounted for by using one of the IP Telephony Call Processing Deployment Models (or the Legacy PBX Call Processing Deployment Models). The messaging side that touches the end user mailboxes must use one of the messaging deployment models. This is called a Unity deployment model combination.

There are many combinations of deployment models. When you add the messaging boundaries for each messaging system that Unity can service, then the number of possible combinations and deployment scenarios increases drastically. However, for the sake of simplification, five primary combinations can be used as a basis for most designs with consideration for the messaging boundaries following the combinations in order of importance.

The deployment model combinations that can be used by a Unity server are shown in Table 10-1, and are also explained further throughout the rest of the chapter.

Table 10-1   *Deployment Model Combinations*

IP Telephony Deployment Model	Messaging Deployment Model
Single-Site Call Processing	Single-Site Messaging
Multisite IP WAN with Centralized Call Processing	Multisite IP WAN with Centralized Messaging
Multisite IP WAN with Centralized Call Processing	Multisite IP WAN with Distributed Messaging
Multisite IP WAN with Distributed Call Processing	Multisite IP WAN with Centralized Messaging
Multisite IP WAN with Distributed Call Processing	Multisite IP WAN with Distributed Messaging

Single-Site Call Processing/Single-Site Messaging

The single-site messaging deployment model is simple enough to understand. All messaging infrastructure components exist within the site. This site can be one physical location or campus LAN. At the same time, the single-site call processing model means that Cisco CallManager is present in any of the Cisco supported configurations for this deployment model. If a legacy PBX is present, or a Centrex is present instead, the same idea applies.

It is important to note that for the sake of definition, the single-site deployment model does not include connecting Unity to service remote locations. It means that in a single-site deployment model, from Unity's perspective of this model, there are no remote locations being serviced by Unity servers from the single-site. The single-site messaging model can support:

- A single-server voice messaging-only configuration
- A multiserver voice messaging-only
- Unified messaging configuration

The single -server configuration can support up to 3000 subscribers/48 ports. The multiserver configuration can support up to 7500 subscribers/72 ports.

Single-Server Voice Messaging-Only Configuration

The single-server configuration is essentially a stand-alone voice messaging solution. It contains all the components necessary to allow Unity to function as a voice-messaging system. This means it is a self-contained Windows 2000 domain. It has an Exchange 2000 messaging store installed on-box and it also has its own DNS service running on the Unity server.

With a single-server configuration, Unity is isolated from any existing company's domain infrastructure or messaging infrastructure. It can have connectivity to any existing DNS service a company might use. However, because Unity runs as a Windows 2000 domain controller in this configuration, it is necessary that it use dynamic DNS either by installing it on the Unity server or by using existing DNS services deployed by the company.

As shown in Figure 10-27, in a single-server configuration, Unity can service either a legacy circuit-switched PBX, or Cisco CallManager, or both. Alternatively, Unity can also integrate with a SIP proxy server.

Figure 10-27 *Single Unity Server with CCM and PBX*

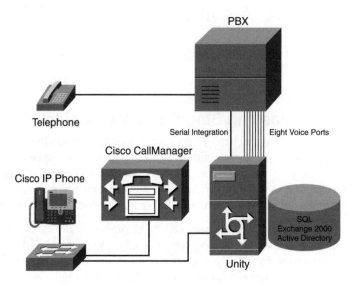

In a single-server configuration, there can be no digital networking between Unity and other Unity servers. In addition, there can be no voice-mail interoperability between Unity and other legacy voice-messaging systems.

Because a single-server configuration means Unity is running as an isolated voice-messaging system, this solution is limited as a low-end solution. There are two reasons for this limitation. First, by installing Unity as a Windows 2000 domain controller and an Exchange 2000 server, there is a limit to the maximum number of subscribers the stand-alone server can support. Second, due to the isolated and self-contained configuration, a lot of functionality, such as the digital-networking and voice-messaging capability, is lost in this implementation.

It is possible that a single-server configuration can be deployed throughout a multisite environment, as shown in Figure 10-28, but it does not change the characteristics of the configuration. In addition, any migration to a more distributed, fully-functional solution will require installing additional servers so a migration can be facilitated from the isolated single-server configuration to a distributed, multiserver configuration. Note how by having single-server configurations installed in multiple locations no interoperability exists between them. In this example, the configurations are isolated from one another.

Figure 10-28 *Single-Server Configurations with Multiple Sites*

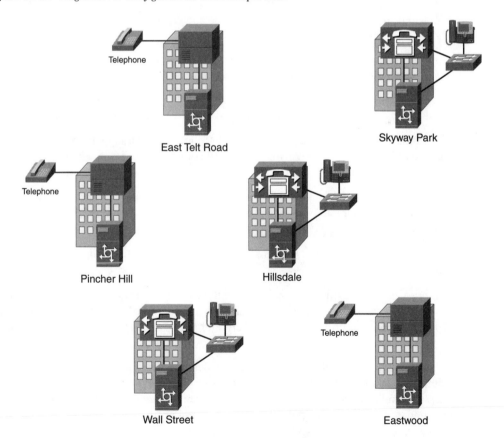

In the single-site deployment model with single servers, all Unity servers are self-contained voice-messaging systems, meaning that they have everything they need to provide voice messaging-only services through its TUI interface. When single servers are used this way, each Unity server houses its own domain controller and message store. They are completely stand-alone, meaning that the domains are not connected to one another through trust relationships, nor are the messaging servers in the same Exchange 2000 organization. There is no digital networking interoperability between the Unity servers.

Use a single-server configuration as a low-end solution where only a few locations need simple, isolated voice messaging with no additional functionality or connectivity requirements to other voice-messaging systems.

Multiserver Voice Messaging-Only

In a single site where a subscriber population of more than 3000 subscribers exists, a multiple server configuration is required for any voice messaging-only solution. For unified messaging, the requirement is the same but the approach is different.

There are scaling requirements for Unity as a voice messaging-only solution in a multiserver configuration. The requirements are necessary to accommodate the additional load on the messaging stores dedicated to this solution.

There are typically two types of voice messaging-only configurations for Unity. There are those with no client GUI or WEB access, and those with client GUI or WEB access.

In a multiserver voice messaging-only configuration, Unity can support populations greater than 3000 subscribers by moving the necessary components off-box. The necessary components as mentioned above are:

- The Windows domain controller functionality, which naturally includes the use of Active Directory and Name Resolution.
- The Exchange 2000 message stores.

A good example of a multiserver voice messaging-only configuration is shown in Figure 10-29.

As shown in Figure 10-30, this single-site, multiserver, voice messaging-only configuration is servicing a campus area of up to 7500 subscribers. Additional Unity servers are necessary to support more subscribers, and most likely additional Exchange 2000 servers are required as well.

In a voice mail-only configuration, as Unity scales, another approach can be to offload one component at a time. Thus, if you have more subscribers than what can reside on a single message store, two stores will be needed. Unity can be supported if the message store functionality is removed first and the domain controller functionality is left intact on the Unity server.

Figure 10-29 *Single-Site, Multiserver Configuration*

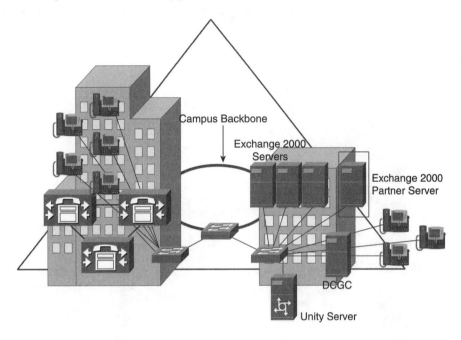

Figure 10-30 *A Single Unity Server Running as a DCGC with Two Off-Box Exchange 2000 Message Stores*

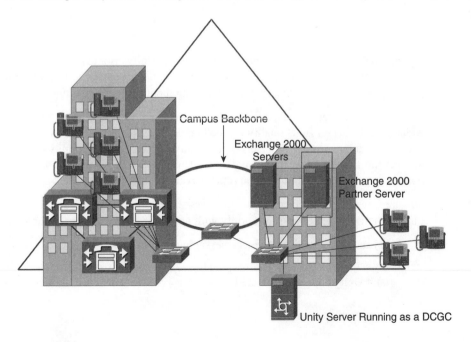

When a third Exchange 2000 server is added to support more mailboxes for subscribers, as shown in Figure 10-31, move the DCGC functionality off of the Unity server as well.

Figure 10-31 *A Single Unity Server Running as a Member Server*

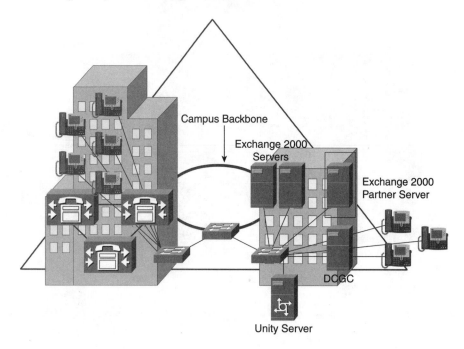

It is important to consider expansion requirements for Unity prior to installing it into a voice mail-only configuration. The main reason for this is that it is easier to start off with the necessary components off-box instead of moving them off-box in the future.

For all Unity configurations, the Windows 2000 domain controller functionality and Exchange 2000 server functionality can be initially installed off-box in a voice messaging-only configuration. The MS SQL server, and Unity web-based functionality provided by IIS (Internet Information Server) will stay on the Unity server. No current 4.0x configuration supports removing SQL and IIS to another server.

Here are some important facts about Unity voice messaging-only in a single site configuration. For voice messaging-only with no GUI/web client access, single site:

- Unity requires a dedicated voice-messaging infrastructure.
- Unity requires a partner server where the system mailbox is homed, and also where default Unity objects are created.

- Unity can service a recommended maximum of 10 Exchange 2000 servers with up to four storage groups per server. Each storage group can have the maximum number of mail stores.

- Unity should service a single Exchange 2000 admin group only.

- The Unity design should have only one Exchange 2000 routing group within the admin group because this is a single-site messaging deployment model.

- All Exchange 2000 servers must reside locally to the Unity server (WAN connections can exist, they just cannot be used by Unity in this configuration).

- Unity uses a Windows 2000 domain only. No NT domains.

- Unity and its supporting messaging infrastructure must be in the same Windows 2000 domain.

- Unity uses Active Directory and must synchronize with the directory.

- Unity must be installed into the same Windows 2000 site as the Exchange 2000 servers.

- Unity must access and connect to the same DC and GC accessed by the Exchange 2000 servers.

- Unity must use dynamic DNS, as it is a part of the Windows 2000 domain. The use of WINS is not required.

Voice Messaging-Only with GUI/Web Client Access, Single Site

Because Unity comes with feature-rich capabilities for GUI and web access, some companies might desire this for their end users, but still use only voice-messaging capabilities instead of unified messaging.

The solution is to provide voice-messaging capabilities in its own dedicated voice-messaging infrastructure and at the same time, integrate Unity's name resolution requirements with those of the existing company's name resolution. It is also necessary to set up accounts so end users can use them to authenticate to the Unity web interfaces. However, the creation of accounts in the Windows 2000 domain occurs once a Unity administrator creates new subscribers through the Unity SA, as explained in the first section of this book. Therefore, the step of creating accounts is not discussed in this chapter. Figure 10-32 shows clients on a different network authenticating and accessing the Unity CPCA where name resolution is in place.

Figure 10-32 *Unity with a Dedicated Voice Messaging-Only Configuration*

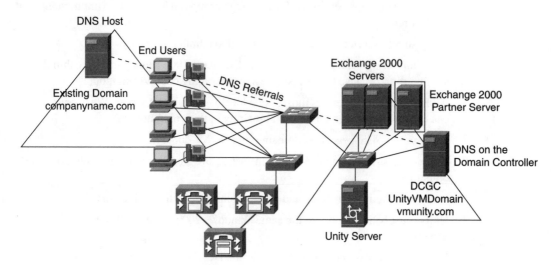

In a voice mail-only configuration, in order to provide web client access into Unity (CPCA or Cisco Unity Inbox) when its messaging infrastructure is separate from the existing infrastructure where the end users reside, it is necessary to use your existing DNS host to provide name resolution for the dedicated Unity configuration. The DNS host must support Windows 2000 and service locator auto-registration. Windows DNS service supports dynamic updates. If your DNS host does not support Windows 2000, you must configure a dedicated DDNS host to support the dedicated Unity infrastructure, then refer end-user URL requests from your DNS host to the dedicated DDNS host servicing Unity.

The following requirements for this configuration are:

- Unity requires a dedicated voice-messaging infrastructure.

- Unity requires a partner server where the system mailbox is homed and also where default Unity objects are created.

- Unity can service a recommended maximum of 10 Exchange 2000 servers with up to four storage groups per server. Each storage group can have the maximum number of mail stores.

- For a voice messaging-only design, Unity should service a single Exchange 2000 admin group only.

- The Unity design should only have one Exchange 2000 routing group within the admin group, because this is a single-site messaging deployment model.

- All Exchange 2000 servers must reside locally to the Unity server (WAN connections can exist, they just cannot be used by Unity in this configuration).

- Unity uses a Windows 2000 domain only. No NT domains.

- Unity and its supporting messaging infrastructure must be in the same Windows 2000 domain.

- Unity uses Active Directory and must synchronize with the directory.

- Unity must be installed into the same Windows 2000 site as the Exchange 2000 servers.

- Unity must access and connect to the same DC and GC accessed by the Exchange 2000 servers.

- Unity must use dynamic DNS, as it is a part of the Windows 2000 domain. The use of WINS is not required.

- The Unity dedicated name resolution can be linked to a company's name resolution (if using DNS) in order to allow client GUI/web access.

Unified Messaging for a Single Site

In general, Unity is expected to install into an existing infrastructure for a unified messaging solution. If the messaging systems are in place, the supporting back end messaging infrastructure components are also in place including domain controllers and name resolution hosts.

Unity with Exchange 2000/2003 Unified Messaging

For Unity with Exchange 2000 in a single site, all the messaging infrastructure components are expected to be local to the Unity server. The Exchange servers, the domain controllers and global catalog servers (This means Active Directory is present) and name resolution hosts, all must be local to the Unity server. All subscribers are also located in the same physical site and have the ability to access their messages through the Unity TUI interface, or through their Outlook client, or both.

The following requirements must be met in order to support Unity with Exchange 2000 in a unified messaging configuration for a single site:

- Unity requires a partner server where the system mailbox is homed and also where default Unity objects are created. The partner server does not have to be solely dedicated to Unity. It can use a highly available server that is used for many other purposes. A very highly utilized server is not practical as a partner server.

- Unity can service a recommended maximum of 10 Exchange 2000 servers with up to four storage groups on each server, each storage group can have a maximum number of mailbox stores.

- A single Unity server can service more than one Exchange 2000 admin group.

- Unity can service more than one Exchange 2000 routing group within the admin group.

- All Exchange 2000 servers being serviced by Unity must reside locally to the Unity server (Unity should not use any WAN connection to access Exchange or any messaging infrastructure components; WAN connections can exist, they just cannot be used by Unity).

- Unity uses a Windows 2000 domain only. No NT domains.

- Unity uses Active Directory and must synchronize with the directory.

- Unity must be installed into the same Windows 2000 site as the Exchange 2000 servers.

- Unity must access and connect to the same DC(s) and GC(s) accessed by the Exchange 2000 servers.

- Unity must use dynamic DNS, as it is a part of the Windows 2000 domain. The use of WINS is not required.

If all these requirements are met, the Unity CallManager configuration is as shown in Figure 10-33.

Figure 10-33 *Components with CallManager*

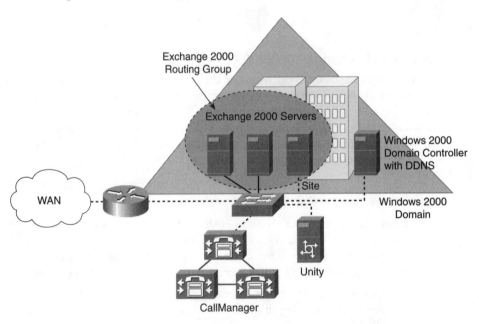

In a single-site deployment model, a WAN connection can exist, but it cannot be used by Unity if Unity's deployment model is to be considered a single-site model. It is simply a matter of definition and understanding how Unity works within each model. The same configuration is also shown in Figure 10-34 with Unity connected to legacy PBX.

Figure 10-34 *Components with Legacy PBX*

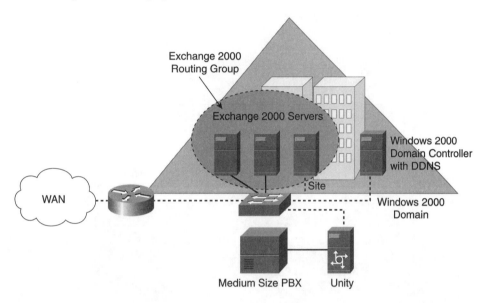

What if there is a larger population than what a single Unity server can handle? In that case, it is necessary to add additional Unity servers. As shown in Figure 10-35, this is typically necessary in a large campus area where a high-speed backbone connects all facilities on the campus to the local area network.

This single-site deployment model depicts multiple Unity servers servicing Exchange 2000 routing groups in a unified messaging configuration. Note, all routing groups are installed into the same administrative group. Each Unity server is installed into the same Windows 2000 site as the Exchange 2000 servers it services. In this example, because it is a campus area network, it is possible to have a single or multiple Window 2000 site(s) depending on the number of users serviced by Unity and CallManager. All Unity servers are connected to the Cisco CallManager cluster. All unified messaging clients access the local Unity servers for web access, and through VMO (Viewmail for Outlook), they record and play back their messages using TRaP (Telephone Record and Playback) over the IP phones. The largest building on the campus houses an Exchange 2000 cluster and a Unity failover configuration to support the large user density and provide redundancy for disaster recovery. The user populations in each Exchange 2000 routing group are nicely accommodated through properly sized Unity servers. This accommodation is provided by Cisco's definition of hardware overlays that can support Unity servers given specific subscriber populations and port densities. For more information on Unity configurations with Exchange, see Chapter 13.

Figure 10-35 *Multiple Unity Servers Servicing Multiple Exchange 2000 Routing Groups*

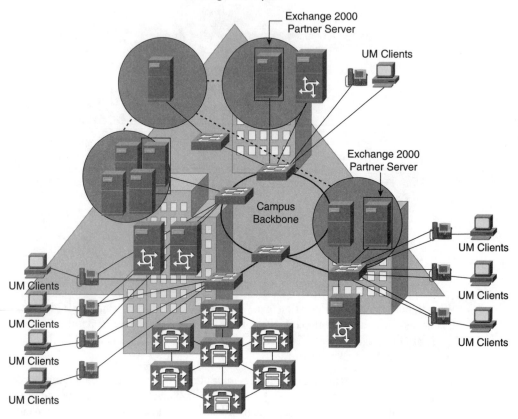

Unity with Exchange 5.5 Unified Messaging

The Unity for Exchange 5.5 configuration is similar to the Exchange 2000 configuration.

In this deployment model, Unity is installed into a single Exchange 5.5 site. The following requirements must be met for each Unity server installed in this model:

- Unity requires a partner server where the system mailbox is homed and also where default Unity objects are created.

- Each Unity server can service a recommended maximum of 10 Exchange 5.5 servers.

- A single Unity server can service a single Exchange 5.5 site only.

- All Exchange 5.5 servers in the site that are being serviced by Unity must reside locally to the Unity server (Unity will use no WAN connection; WAN connections can exist, they just cannot be used by Unity).

- Unity needs access to a domain controller for authentication. An Exchange 5.5 configuration might reside in Windows NT or Windows 2000.

- Unity must be installed into the same domain as the Exchange 5.5 servers it services.

- Unity does not need Active Directory in this configuration.

- Unity needs to use the same name resolution as the Exchange 5.5 servers (either DNS or WINS or both).

In a single-site configuration (see Figure 10-36), more than one Exchange 5.5 site might exist. If this is the case, more than one Unity server is required to service all users in the single site.

In this single-site deployment model, multiple Unity servers service UM clients connected to Exchange 5.5 servers. The largest site has two Unity servers servicing UM clients because the site contains more subscribers than one Unity server can support. In addition, at least one legacy PBX is still in operations at one of the campus locations and is being serviced by a Unity server there. Cisco CallManager provides call processing services for the rest of the Unity servers within the campus. The Windows domain can be either an NT domain or Windows 2000 domain in this case.

For more information on Unity configurations with Exchange, see Chapter 13.

Figure 10-36 *More Than One Exchange 5.5 Site and Multiple Unity Servers*

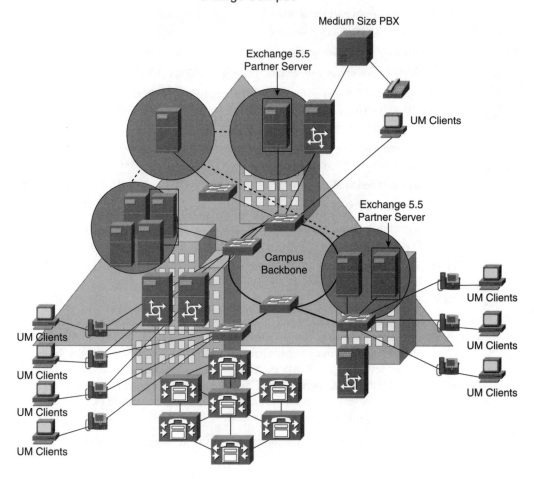

Exchange 5.5 Hub/
Spoke Configuration in
a Large Campus

Medium Size PBX

Exchange 5.5
Partner Server

UM Clients

Exchange 5.5
Partner Server

Campus
Backbone

UM Clients

UM Clients

UM Clients

UM Clients

UM Clients

UM Clients

UM Clients

Exchange 5.5 Sites

- - - - -   Site Connectors

Unity with Domino R5 Unified Messaging Only

As stated, Unity 4.0 with Domino supports a narrower configuration than Unity for Exchange. Thus, the Unity configuration for Domino is rather simple, regardless of the deployment model used.

The following requirements existing for Unity for Domino:

- Unity requires a Windows 2000 domain, either join an existing domain or install Unity in its own domain with it running as a DCGC. The domino servers are not required to be in the domain.

- Unity can service a recommended maximum of 10 Domino servers that are running DUCS. However, there is no known limit to the number of Domino servers that can be supported by a single Unity server.

- Unity can service a single directory/Domino domain.

- Unity requires DUCS on all Domino servers it is going to service.

- Unity can service Domino servers locally. No remote Domino servers can be serviced over a WAN connection. (WAN connections can exist, they just cannot be used by Unity).

- Unity can coexist with other non-DUCS Domino servers, but does not make use of them.

- Unity must use dynamic DNS, as it is part of a Windows 2000 domain. The use of WINS is not required. The Lotus Notes client installed on Unity must use Notes Name Resolution to access the Domino domain.

The example in Figure 10-37 shows Unity servicing a Domino server.

Multisite WAN with Centralized Messaging/Multisite WAN with Centralized Call Processing

In the centralized messaging deployment model, Unity services both local and remote subscribers for voice messaging. Unity is more dependent upon a Cisco IP Telephony (IPT) solution for this model because remote subscribers are accessing voice messaging over the WAN. It is much easier for a voice messaging-only configuration to be supported in this model than it is for a unified messaging configuration, not because of TUI access but because of GUI access. When using the Unity GUI snap-in to Outlook VMO, the amount of bandwidth between the remote location and centralized location can have an impact TRaP. For each VMO TRaP session, approximately 86–128Kbps is needed. Thus, Unity installed in the multisite WAN with centralized messaging can service subscribers through TUI access, but web access using CPCA and VMO or CPCA TRaP sessions should be minimized or disallowed. An alternative is to select Download Before Playback in the VMO form, but subscribers will still have to wait until the message downloads before they can play it back.

Figure 10-37   *Unity for Domino with a Single Domino Server and Notes Clients*

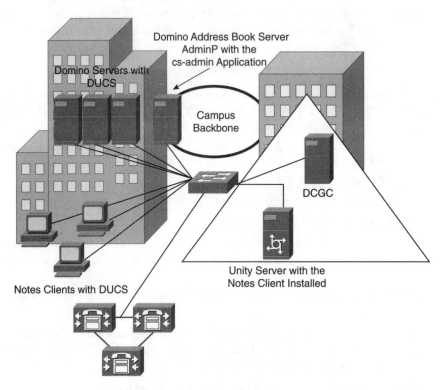

If centralized messaging servers are servicing remote clients, it might be possible to service them through unified messaging as well, but it is necessary to determine if Unity can support the remote clients for unified messaging by performing a readiness assessment of the environment. For more information on conducting an assessment, and ways in which this might be accomplished, see Chapter 9.

A multisite WAN with centralized call processing using a legacy switch might be restrictive in being able to provide call processing to remote locations. Few legacy switches service remote offices through WAN connectivity. Typically, a smaller remote-office switch is in place for each remote location. For IP Telephony, the centralized call processing model removes the requirement to have smaller remote office switches by providing Survivable Remote Site Telephony (SRST) functionality within specific routers for those offices. This means that if the WAN pipe comes unavailable, the router takes control of the call processing (see Figure 10-38) for the remote site until the WAN pipe comes back up.

With SRST, calls can still be routed across the Public Switched Telephone Network (PSTN) to integrate with Unity during a WAN outage. This can be performed using voice-mail integration with analog ports. If Remote Dialed Network Information Service (RDNIS) support is also available from your telco, you can also use it.

The following Cisco Press books provide more information on SRST:

- *Cisco IP Telephony,* by David Lovell
- *Troubleshooting Cisco IP Telephony*, by Paul Giralt, Addis Hallmark, and Anne Smith

As a rule of thumb, you should understand the type of WAN traffic that might be suitable for Unity in order for it to service remote subscribers:

- Unity can support remote subscribers for TUI access if it is integrated with Cisco CallManager.
- Unity can support remote subscribers for web access into CPCA, but there are important considerations that are discussed in the later messaging system-specific sections.
- Unity should not support remote streaming of voice messaging through TRaP.
- All remote VMO client usage should be set to download only (no streaming).
- Unity should not synchronize directory data to a remotely connected directory including Active Directory, Exchange 5.5, or Domino. All Unity directory synchronization should take place locally.

Figure 10-38 *Unity and CallManager Providing IP Telephony Services to Remote Offices Equipped with SRST Routers*

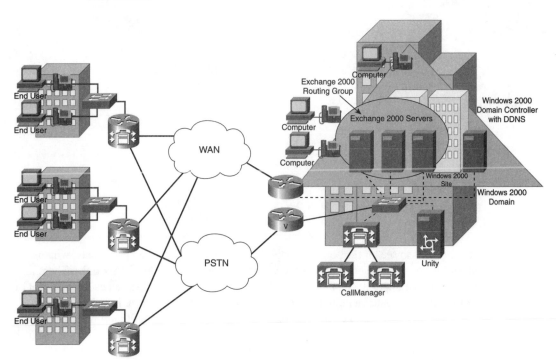

If you are asked why you cannot have a remote messaging system connected to Unity over the WAN, the following diagram as shown in Figure 10-39 demonstrates one reason— all the points of failure. The other reason of course is response time, which is discussed elsewhere.

Figure 10-39 *Remote IPT + Unity Connected to Remote Messaging Store with Potential Points of Failures*

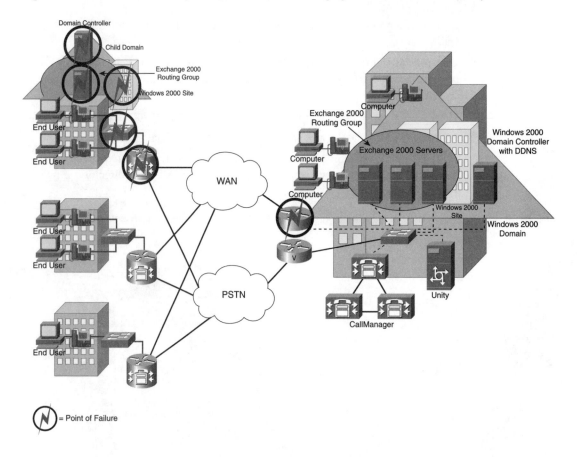

It is obvious to see all the potential points of failures. As explained previously, what is absent is not a failure but a delay that can occur as a result of slow WAN links. There are some items of importance in this example. The routers and switches can each be a point of failure. For the router, a point of failure could also mean any connectivity beyond the demarcation point. For the remote Exchange 2000 server, consider that it is in a separate

Windows 2000 site in a different Windows 2000 domain (a child of the parent domain where Unity resides). Thus, the WAN link can delay access to the Exchange 2000 server or servers at the remote location and that is prime in understanding reasons why Unity cannot service a remote messaging server. Because this remote Exchange 2000 server is in a separate Windows 2000 site in a separate domain, if Unity services this remote server, it has to wait for any directory changes to replicate to the domain where Unity resides before it can update its database with those changes. That can affect Unity's ability to service new subscribers immediately after their creation. In addition, in order for Unity to access each of the remote mailboxes on the remote Exchange 2000 server, it still has to rely on its local Global Catalog to provide the GAL lookups for Unity's system mailbox and MAPI functionality. Again, it is a matter of timeliness, which is not a point of failure as much as it is a potential point of TUI delay. All in all, Figure 10-39 should really bring home the point that having Unity service a remote messaging server in this way is not a good idea and is, therefore, the reason why it is not supported.

A diagram might not be enough to explain all the possible challenges involved with servicing remote messaging servers. The following requirements for each messaging system supported by Unity should help to clarify any concerns about this recommendation.

Unity with Exchange 5.5 Unified Messaging

In a centralized messaging configuration, the following criteria applies:

- The Unity partner server has to be local.

- The Exchange messaging servers being serviced by Unity must be local.

- Unity can service a single Exchange 5.5 site only. However, there are some Exchange 5.5 site deployment models that are less affective from a unified messaging readiness standpoint. For more information, see Chapter 13.

- Unity can service remote subscribers for TUI access.

- Unity can service remote subscribers for web access and VMO access/GUI access, but messages should be downloaded instead of streamed over the WAN. TRaP should not be used over the WAN unless you have ample bandwidth.

- Unity needs access to a domain controller for authentication. An Exchange 5.5 configuration might reside in Windows NT or Windows 2000.

- Unity must be installed into the same domain as Exchange 5.5.

- Unity does not need Active Directory in this configuration. If Windows 2000 domains are present, it will use it just as it uses a Windows NT domain: for authentication.

- Unity needs to use the same name resolution as the Exchange 5.5 servers (either DNS or WINS or both).

Unity with Exchange 2000 Unified Messaging or Voice Messaging-Only with Client Web Access

For Exchange 2000, unified messaging or voice messaging with client web access are almost identical with the exception of ViewMail for Outlook (VMO) not being used in a voice messaging-only configuration. The following requirements should also be adhered to as well:

- Unity requires a local partner server where the system mailbox is homed and also where default Unity objects are created.

- Unity can service a recommended maximum of 10 Exchange 2000 servers with up to four storage groups per server, and each storage group can have the maximum number of mailbox stores.

- Unity should service a single Exchange 2000 admin group, but it is not required

- Unity can service more than one Exchange 2000 routing group within the admin group.

- All Exchange 2000 servers serviced by Unity must reside locally to the Unity server.

- Unity can service remote subscribers for TUI access.

- Unity can service remote subscribers for web access, VMO access/GUI access, but messages should be downloaded instead of streamed over the WAN. TRaP should not be used over the WAN unless there is ample bandwidth.

- Unity uses a Windows 2000 domain only, no NT domains.

- Unity must be installed into the same domain as Exchange 2000/2003.

- Unity uses Active Directory and must synchronize with the directory locally.

- Unity must be installed into the same Windows 2000 site as the Exchange 2000 servers it services.

- Unity must access and connect to the same DC and GC accessed by the Exchange 2000 servers.

- Unity must use dynamic DNS, as it is a part of the Windows 2000 domain. The use of WINS is not required.

Unity with Exchange 2000 Voice Messaging-Only with No Client Web Access

The requirements change somewhat because no client web access is used for this configuration.

- Unity requires a dedicated messaging infrastructure.

- Unity requires a partner server where the system mailbox is homed and also where default Unity objects are created.

- Unity can service a recommended maximum of 10 Exchange 2000 servers with up to four storage groups on each server, each storage group can contain the maximum number of mailbox stores.

- Unity should service a single Exchange 2000 admin group only.

- Unity can service more than one Exchange 2000 routing group within the admin group

- All Exchange 2000 servers serviced by Unity must reside locally to the Unity server.

- Unity can service remote subscribers for TUI access only.

- Unity uses a Windows 2000 domain only, no NT domains.

- Unity must be installed into the same domain as the Exchange servers it services.

- Unity uses Active Directory and must synchronize with the directory.

- Unity must be installed into the same Windows 2000 site as the Exchange 2000 servers.

- Unity must access and connect to the same DC and GC accessed by the Exchange 2000 servers.

- Unity must use dynamic DNS, as it is a part of the Windows 2000 domain. The use of WINS is not required.

Unity with Domino R5 Unified Messaging-Only

With Unity for Domino, the following criteria must be met in order to support this configuration in a centralized messaging deployment model:

- Unity requires a Windows 2000 domain, it must either join an existing domain or Unity must be installed into its own domain with it running as a DCGC.

- Unity can service a recommended maximum of 10 Domino servers with DUCS installed on each mail server it services, although there is no known limit to the number of Domino servers a Unity server can service.

- Unity can service a single Directory/Domino Domain.

- Unity requires DUCS on all Domino servers it services.

- Unity can service Domino servers locally. No remote Domino servers can be serviced by Unity.

- Unity can service remote subscribers for TUI access.

- Unity can service remote subscribers for web access/ GUI access but messages should be downloaded instead of streamed over the WAN. TRaP should not be used over the WAN.

- Unity can coexist with other Domino servers.

- Unity must use dynamic DNS, as it is part of a Windows 2000 domain. The use of WINS is not required. The Lotus Notes client installed on Unity must use Notes name resolution to access the Domino domain.

For more information see Chapters 9 –11.

Multisite IP WAN with Centralized Call Processing/Multisite IP WAN with Distributed Messaging

In this deployment model combination, the call processing is centralized and the messaging is distributed. This means Unity is colocated with the messaging systems and thus, it must connect to CallManager over a WAN connection. This is possible provided that the necessary bandwidth is allocated to support each voice port. Therefore, all issues with this model combination center around Unity's telephony connectivity to CallManager.

Because the messaging servers are distributed, the Unity servers are colocated with them. Thus, from a messaging perspective, Unity's use of this deployment model combination is the same as if it were a distributed call processing/distributed messaging deployment model. Each Unity configuration is due the same considerations for messaging in a distributed messaging deployment model.

Multisite IP WAN with Distributed Call Processing/Multisite IP WAN with Centralized Messaging

In this deployment model combination, the requirements for each Unity configuration are well defined for the centralized messaging deployment model. All issues with this model combination centers around Unity's telephony connectivity to CallManager.

Because the messaging servers are centralized, the Unity servers are colocated with them. Again, this means that Unity is remotely connected to CallManager, except in this case a centralized Unity server might be connected to more than one CallManager cluster.

Multisite WAN with Distributed Messaging/Multisite WAN Model with Distributed Call Processing

A distributed messaging model is like multiple single-site models joined together. The messaging backbone established between all messaging servers located at each remote site supports the voice-messaging capabilities and the shared directory supports the digital networking capabilities in Unity.

In the distributed messaging model, Unity's connectivity to call processing capabilities through CallManager or a legacy PBX is local. This deployment model can support a combination of this model and the centralized call processing model in order to provide remote call-processing and voice-messaging capabilities for smaller sites that can be supported by SRST capabilities in Cisco routers. Another alternative is to install smaller Unity servers at the remote sites using Cisco CallManager Express (for more information about CallManager Express see www.cisco.com).

The ideal solution for Unity is the distributed call-processing, distributed messaging model combination (see Figure 10-40). The reason why is everything used by Unity both on the messaging and telephony site is colocated with Unity. The subscribers are colocated. The messaging backbone connecting to other remote Unity servers and messaging servers is already established and the risk of single points of failure over a WAN are minimized or eliminated altogether.

Figure 10-40 *A Pure Distributed Messaging Model*

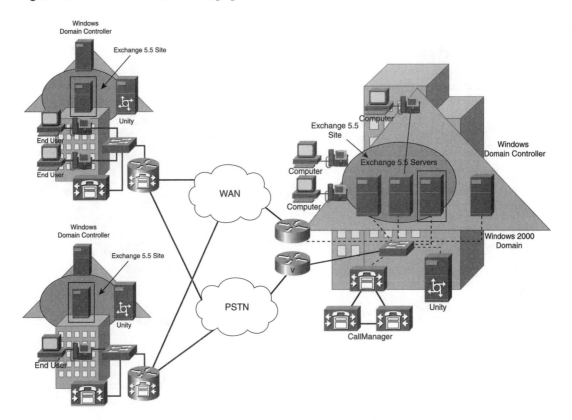

In a pure distributed messaging model and distributed call-processing model all messaging, including voice messaging/unified messaging provided by Unity and all call processing is distributed within each respective location. There is no need for Unity nor CallManager to request services or resources external to the local area network for which it resides. However, with Unity, its digital networking capability is made available to local subscribers and allows them to address messages to subscribers located at remote sites. The messages are delivered over the messaging backbone. The same case holds with CallManager where IP phone users are able to contact remote IP phone users over the PSTN. Or, this same model can also support a private phone network and eliminate the need for PSTN between locations, in which case, each location's connectivity to the PSTN remains local in order for IP phone users to make and receive local outside calls.

Figure 10-41 *Mixed Distributed with a Centralized Deployment Model*

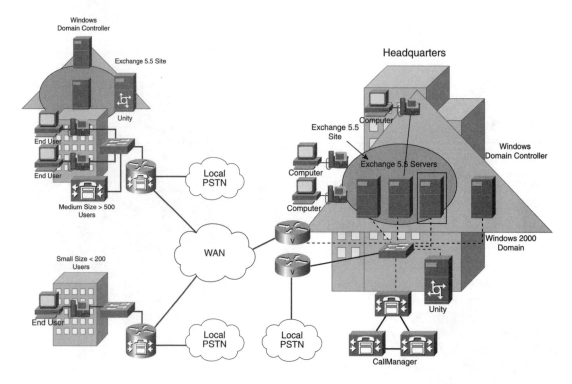

In this configuration, the headquarters Unity server is also providing voice messaging to the small site. The medium site contains its own Unity server to support the larger user density. For the medium site, CallManager call processing is local to the site.

The configuration requirements described in the following sections should be followed closely for this model.

Unity with Exchange 5.5 Unified Messaging

As with the other deployment models, the Unity configurations in this example have the same requirements:

- Unity requires a local partner server where the system mailbox is homed and also where default Unity objects are created. Unity cannot be remotely connected to a partner server.

- Unity can service a recommended maximum of five Exchange 5.5 servers.

- Unity can service a single Exchange 5.5 site only.

- All Exchange 5.5 servers in the site being serviced by Unity should reside locally to the Unity server.

- Unity needs access to a local domain controller for authentication. An Exchange 5.5 configuration might reside in Windows NT or Windows 2000.

- Unity must be installed into the same domain as Exchange 5.5, or must have access to the domain given the required permissions and same name space.

- Unity does not need Active Directory in this configuration

- Unity needs to use the same name resolution as the Exchange 5.5 servers (either DNS or WINS or both).

Unity with Exchange 2000 Unified Messaging or Voice Messaging-Only with Client Web Access

Note that when client web access is included, the list of requirements expands. In all cases, the bandwidth issues associated with remote client web access deserves attention and should be carefully planned for prior to rolling out:

- Unity requires a partner server where the system mailbox is homed and also where default Unity objects are created.

- Unity can service a recommended maximum of 10 Exchange 2000 servers with up to four storage groups per server, each storage group can have the maximum number of mailbox stores.

- Unity should be designed to service a single Exchange 2000 admin group only.

- Unity can service more than one Exchange 2000 routing group within the admin group.

- All Exchange 2000 servers being serviced by Unity should reside locally to the Unity server.

- Unity can service remote subscribers for web access, VMO access/GUI access, and TUI access; bandwidth and the use of TRaP should be carefully planned. If the bandwidth does not exist to accommodate a large population of remote subscribers, then do not use TRaP.

- Unity uses a Windows 2000 domain only, no NT domains.

- Unity uses Active Directory and must synchronize with the directory.

- Unity must be installed into the same Windows 2000 site as the Exchange 2000 servers.

- Unity must access and connect to the same DC and GC accessed by the Exchange 2000 servers.

- Unity must use dynamic DNS, as it is a part of the Windows 2000 domain. The use of WINS is not required.

Unity with Exchange 2000 Voice Messaging-Only with No Client Web Access

The requirements change somewhat when there is no client web access. When only TUI access is required, the primary consideration for remote users is allocating enough bandwidth for the number of calls these users might be making on a regular and peak basis:

- Unity requires a dedicated messaging infrastructure.

- Unity requires a partner server where the system mailbox is homed and also where default Unity objects are created.

- Unity can service a recommended maximum of 10 Exchange 2000 servers with up to four storage groups per server, each storage group can have the maximum number of mailbox stores.

- Unity should be designed to service a single Exchange 2000 admin group only.

- Unity can service more than one Exchange 2000 routing group within the admin group.

- All Exchange 2000 servers being serviced by Unity should reside locally to the Unity server.

- Unity can service remote subscribers for TUI access only.

- Unity uses a Windows 2000 domain only, no NT domains.

- Unity uses Active Directory and must synchronize with the directory.

- Unity must be installed into the same Windows 2000 site as the Exchange 2000 servers.

- Unity must access and connect to the same DC and GC accessed by the Exchange 2000 servers.

- Unity must use dynamic DNS, as it is a part of the Windows 2000 domain. The use of WINS is not required.

Unity with Domino R5 or R6 Unified Messaging Only

For Unity for Domino, the DUCS client is used by both local and remote subscribers. The same considerations for bandwidth and TRaP exist for these clients:

- Unity requires a Windows 2000 domain; it must either join an existing domain or Unity must be installed into its own domain with it running as a DCGC.

- Unity can service a recommended maximum of 10 Domino servers with DUCS, however there is no known limit.

- Unity can service a single directory/Domino domain.

- Unity requires DUCS on all Domino servers it services.

- Unity can service Domino servers locally.

- Unity can service remote subscribers using the DUCS client.

- Unity can coexist with other Domino servers.

- Unity must use dynamic DNS, as it is part of a Windows 2000 domain. The use of WINS is not required. The Lotus Notes client installed on Unity must use Notes Name Resolution to access the Domino domain.

Failover Deployment Models Clustering Over the IP WAN/Disaster Recovery-System Redundancy Sites

Unity failover has specific requirements in order to support the clustering over the IP WAN/ Disaster Recovery deployment model combination. Unity failover can be configured in a local configuration or remote configuration. The local configuration is where both the primary and secondary failover servers are colocated with one another and share the same resources. The remote configuration allows for the primary and secondary failover servers to be remotely located from one another so that the primary can failover to the secondary in the event of an outage or loss of access in the primary's data center.

For Unity, failover support is available for Unity with Exchange 5.5 and Unity with Exchange 2000. There is currently no failover support for Unity with Domino; however, it is slated for an upcoming version of 4.0x. With each configuration, the same requirements exist as with a single server. The challenge is expanding these configuration requirements to include two physical sites for the remote configuration; and of course, the local configuration is simply adding a secondary failover server to the previously stated configuration.

To help explain this further, in a remote failover configuration using the CallManager Clustering Over IP WAN deployment model, Figure 10-42 shows a Unity with Exchange 2000 failover configuration. There are two separate data centers. The first data center houses the primary Unity failover server and the second data center houses the secondary failover server. However, each of these servers still has to reside in the same Windows 2000 site and has to have access to the same messaging systems and messaging infrastructure components including the DCs and GCs. So, both Unity servers have to point to the same DC and the same GC DUCS even though one is remotely connected.

In order to ease the burden a bit, the connectivity between data centers is considered high-speed. In reality, Unity remote failover can exist with a minimal of 45Mbps bandwidth between the two servers. However, this does not account for the bandwidth requirements of your other disaster recovery systems, such as the CallManager servers, domain controllers, Global Catalogs, and messaging servers.

Figure 10-42 *Unity Remote Failover, Where the Call Processing and Messaging Infrastructure Components Span Across Two Physical Locations*

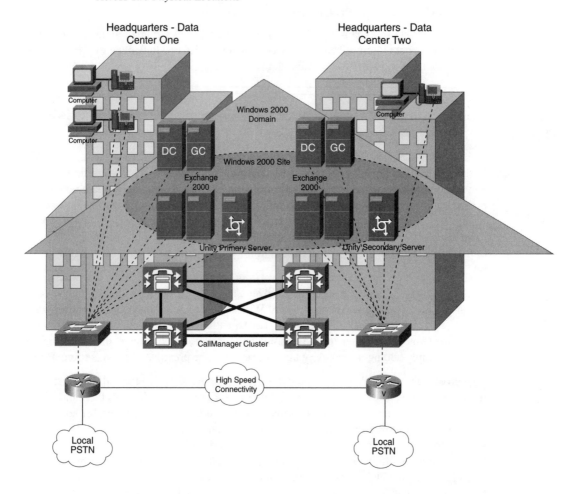

It is important to note that the CallManager Clustering Over IP WAN deployment model becomes quite challenging for two Unity servers (a failover pair) to service when the cluster is spread across more than two locations. Typically, Cisco Unity cannot fully support such a distributed clustering solution within CallManager for Unity failover when both Unity servers are remotely located. Therefore, to make this a successful deployment scenario, the CallManager cluster should be colocated with the Unity servers at both data centers.

Unity with Exchange 5.5 Unified Messaging

When you use Exchange 5.5, all the same dependencies exist for Unity as in any of the previous deployment models. There are additional requirements for both the local failover and remote failover deployment models.

- **Local**. Unity Primary and Secondary are located on the same subnet/VLAN (this can be considered high risk because of the potential loss of access to that subnet). Best Practice: Unity Primary and Secondary should be located on different subnets of the same LAN.

- **Remote**. Unity Primary and Secondary are remotely connected over at least a 45Mbps or greater WAN pipe. Both Unity servers have to have access to same messaging infrastructure components.

Unity with Exchange 2000 Unified Messaging or Voice Messaging Only with Client Web Access

All the same dependencies exist for Unity as in any of the previous deployment models. In addition, the following requirements should be met for each failover model.

- **Local**. Unity Primary and Secondary are located on the same subnet/VLAN (This can be considered high risk because of the potential loss of access to that subnet. Best practice: Unity Primary and Secondary should be located on different subnets of the same LAN.

- **Remote**. Unity Primary and Secondary are remotely connected over at least a 45Mbps WAN pipe. Both Unity servers have to have access to same messaging infrastructure components. This means that both Unity servers must be installed into the same Windows 2000 site and must access the same DCs and GCs at the Exchange servers.

Unity with Exchange 2000 Voice Messaging-Only with No Client Web Access

All the same dependencies exist for Unity as in any of the previous deployment models:

- **Local**. Unity Primary and Secondary are located on the same subnet/VLAN (This can be considered high risk because of the potential loss of access to that subnet). Best practice: Unity Primary and Secondary should be located on different subnets of the same LAN.

- **Remote**. Unity Primary and Secondary are remotely connected over at least a 45Mbps, WAN pipe. Both Unity servers have to have access to same messaging infrastructure components. This means that both Unity servers must be installed into the same Windows 2000 site and must be accessing the same DCs and GCs at the Exchange servers.

Unity with Domino R5

As stated, there is currently no failover support for Unity 4.0x for Domino. However, when the support is available, the same type of requirements will exist for it as what exists for Exchange. Each Unity server will need to be placed into the same infrastructure even though each server is located in its own physical location.

Summary

This chapter covers the typical configurations and deployment models used for most Unity designs. The typical configurations section focused on the three primary Unity configurations for each messaging system it services. The particulars of the messaging system were included to ensure that any design using one of these configurations were complete and sustainable.

The three primary Unity configurations are:

- **Unity Single Server Voice Mail-Only**. All its components are self-contained on the single server as if it were a traditional voice-messaging system.

- **Unity Multiserver Voice Mail-Only**. A dedicated messaging infrastructure is put into place to support the voice-messaging solution. This solution is typically put in place to support an eventual migration to unified messaging. There are slightly different requirements for a multiserver voice mail-only configuration depending upon whether subscribers will also use the client web interface to access the Unity CPCA. In addition, the multiserver voice mail-only configuration is specific as to the messaging system used and how it should be used to support the implementation.

- **Single Server or Failover Server Unified Messaging**. Unity is installed as a single server or failover pair in an existing messaging environment. The particulars of each messaging environment are included along with plenty of diagrams to further illustrate the important aspects of the unified messaging solution.

The second part of this chapter discussed the deployment models used by most Unity deployments. The messaging infrastructure can add an additional dimension when determining how Unity might fit into a given deployment model. The particulars of each configuration were discussed along with the primary challenges that need to be addressed for each model.

Unity uses two deployment models for each deployment: one for the telephony side of Unity, which is typically the Cisco IP Telephony deployment models or more generic legacy PBX models with similar characteristics, the other deployment model is the messaging model, which is based on specific physical characteristics of the given messaging infrastructure. For each deployment model combination, the Unity configurations were then presented with their particular requirements in order to be properly designed for a sustainable solution.

Finally, failover was covered, which included its two primary configurations and deployment models: local and remote. The primary requirements include bandwidth and messaging infrastructure issues.

CHAPTER 11

Designing a Unity Solution

This chapter shows you how to design a Unity solution, starting with navigating the presales period or decision-making period, then gathering significant information during the planning phase, and, finally, putting together the design based on the information accumulated in both the presales and planning phases of your project.

This chapter is not for just solutions providers or computer resellers, however. Any reader should be able to use this chapter to put together a Unity solution. Naturally, you must have the necessary knowledge and product understanding. Therefore, aside from reading this book, you should have direct experience with legacy voice-messaging systems, Unity and or other similar unified messaging systems, and legacy TDM-based switches and IP telephony in general. A good working knowledge of messaging in general and, more specifically, Exchange or Domino is also important when discussing how to design a Unity solution.

Before you begin to plan or design a unified messaging system, you should be familiar with the following:

- Cisco CallManager Design Guides
- Cisco Unity Design Guides
- This entire book and especially Chapter 8, "Deployment Methodology," which covers the design process in more general terms; then Chapter 9, Planning," which covers more specific planning tasks; and Chapter 10, "Typical Configurations and Deployment Models," which gives you the building blocks for putting together a Unity solution

This chapter uses the tasks outlined in Chapters 8 and 9 to develop a repeatable design process by which any Unity solution can be designed. An implementation plan can be developed as a result.

Design Process

When you design a Unity solution, your ultimate goal is to have a functional, highly sustainable deployment of Unity.

A sustainable deployment or sustainable solution can have many different definitions to many people. To narrow the scope somewhat, for the sake of this chapter and for the sake of your ultimate goal in designing a sustainable solution, a sustainable solution meets the following criteria:

- **It minimizes the administrative overhead as much as possible.** Many solutions available with Unity can be applied to a given scenario, but keep in mind that just because a solution is technically doable does not mean that it is administratively feasible. Thus, attempting to minimize administrative overhead is a goal of designing a sustainable solution. The caveat is that some administration is required; to some people, this might be considered more or less than expected. So, to better clarify, administrative overhead should equal normal Unity administration tasks and tasks required to administer and manage the specifics of your Unity solution.

- **It has an upgrade and migration path in place to accommodate future considerations.** For instance, the design should allow for growth (adding significantly more subscribers or systems), reconfiguration (from voice messaging-only to unified messaging), or infrastructure migration (migrating from MS Exchange 5.5 to Lotus Domino).

- **It is included or considered as a part of the ongoing operations effort of your messaging and voice infrastructure.** This means that its dependencies and the components that depend on it are linked; you simply cannot take down your messaging system without affecting Unity, and vice versa. The ones who are affected are your end users. Ensure that if your end users will be affected by an outage that it is a planned outage, not an unplanned one. For instance, if you take down your Exchange servers and do not worry about taking down Unity, or if you do not notify end users that e-mail services as well as voice-messaging services will be unavailable, the end users will not be happy. They will think that they can call into Unity and check messages, only to find that they have limited access. Make sure that the end users know how any outage affects them.

If you follow the design process in this chapter, you can obtain this goal of a sustainable solution. However, there are some caveats. First, do not short-change yourself and bypass any of the steps, unless a step provides instructions for how to skip it. Second, do the footwork and pay attention to the data that you collect to put your design together. If you do not gather the required data, you will feel the effects of it when you put your design in place and start to deploy your solution.

You might ask why it is necessary to pay such close attention to the design process for Unity. Consider all the areas that Unity touches or depends upon. Figure 11-1 shows the different areas that Unity depends on or touches when it is deployed. Because it is a unified messaging solution by design, it uses messaging components and traditional voice-messaging components to make up its total functionality.

Figure 11-1 *Areas of Relevance for a Unity Design*

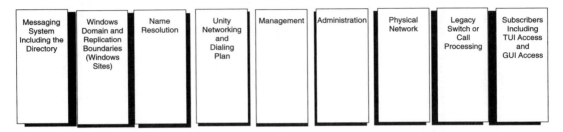

To design your Unity solution, you must gather all the relevant data about each of these areas so that you can successfully deploy Unity in your environment. At the start of your solutions design effort, you must define your primary requirements and make some key decisions. Clearly think over both the requirements definition and the key decision-making tasks in the context of what your end solution might need to be.

For example, the end solution is different if you are designing a Unity solution for your corporation, or if you are a design architect for a computer reseller or solutions provider and design Unity solutions for several organizations. Regardless, this design process is repeatable and focuses on the steps necessary to develop a sustainable solution using Cisco Unity.

At a high level, you can use a flowchart of the Unity design process to give you a good idea of the primary steps involved. However, take into consideration that this design process applies to both a small organization and a large enterprise. If you replace one legacy voice-messaging system with one Unity server, you might find this design process to be a bit of overkill. This is understandable, considering that a single server, in contrast to multiple servers being required for your solution, can be deployed without too much of an issue. So, consider this design process to be for two or more Unity servers; the more Unity servers you have, the more economical this process becomes.

The design process can be shown as a flowchart. However, cycles or iterations might arise as you develop your solution. Therefore, although the intention of this design process is to help you develop a solution using a repeatable process, you can cycle back to an earlier phase, if necessary.

Figure 11-2 depicts the design process as a start-to-finish or top-down process. Along with the possibility that some of these steps might be recycled, some of them can be run simultaneously, depending on your needs and requirements. No mandate states that one step must be completed before the next; however, in some cases, it is necessary to do just that. There is also no mandate that all steps must be completed. In fact—and in a lot of cases—some steps can be skipped. Just make sure that you understand the ramifications of skipping a given step before you skip it. Otherwise, you might find that you have to go back and complete the step before you can complete the project.

Figure 11-2 *A Repeatable and Flexible Design Methodology for Unity*

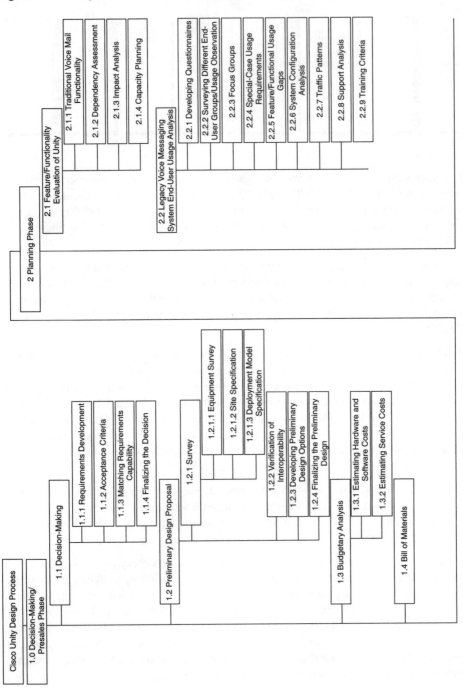

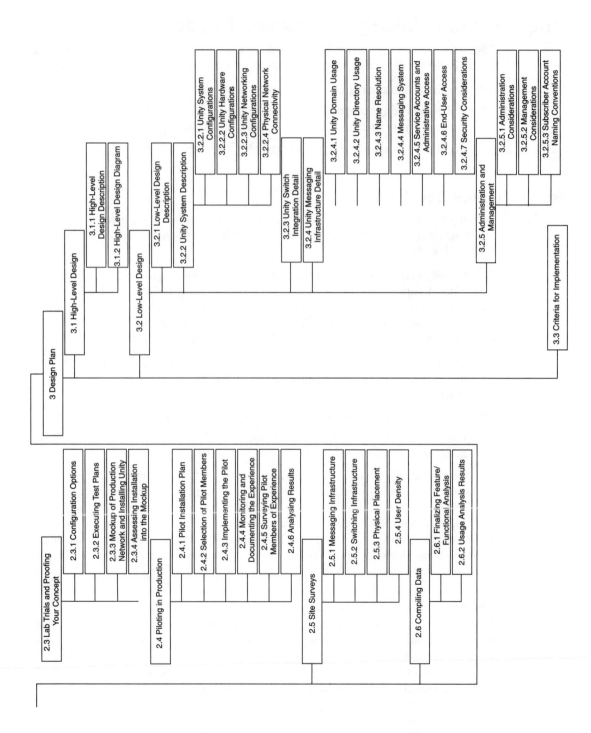

3 Design Plan

3.1 High-Level Design

3.1.1 High-Level Design Description

3.1.2 High-Level Design Diagram

3.2 Low-Level Design

3.2.1 Low-Level Design Description

3.2.2 Unity System Description

3.2.2.1 Unity System Configurations

3.2.2.2 Unity Hardware Configurations

3.2.2.3 Unity Networking Configurations

3.2.2.4 Physical Network Connectivity

3.2.3 Unity Switch Integration Detail

3.2.4 Unity Messaging Infrastructure Detail

3.2.4.1 Unity Domain Usage

3.2.4.2 Unity Directory Usage

3.2.4.3 Name Resolution

3.2.4.4 Messaging System

3.2.4.5 Service Accounts and Administrative Access

3.2.4.6 End-User Access

3.2.4.7 Security Considerations

3.2.5 Administration and Management

3.2.5.1 Administration Considerations

3.2.5.2 Management Considerations

3.2.5.3 Subscriber Account Naming Conventions

3.3 Criteria for Implementation

2.3 Lab Trials and Proofing Your Concept

2.3.1 Configuration Options

2.3.2 Executing Test Plans

2.3.3 Mockup of Production Network and Installing Unity

2.3.4 Assessing Installation into the Mockup

2.4 Piloting in Production

2.4.1 Pilot Installation Plan

2.4.2 Selection of Pilot Members

2.4.3 Implementing the Pilot

2.4.4 Monitoring and Documenting the Experience

2.4.5 Surveying Pilot Members of Experience

2.4.6 Analysing Results

2.5 Site Surveys

2.5.1 Messaging Infrastructure

2.5.2 Switching Infrastructure

2.5.3 Physical Placement

2.5.4 User Density

2.6 Compiling Data

2.6.1 Finalizing Feature/ Functional Analysis

2.6.2 Usage Analysis Results

The Decision-Making or Presales Phase

The initial phase in any Unity solution design is the decision-making phase. Many steps can identified during this phase, but these most notable ones are key to any Unity solution:

- Requirements development. Requirements are defined.

- Preliminary design proposal. The initial high-level design is developed based on both the requirements definition and a preliminary assessment.

- Initial bill of materials made up of hardware, software, and services cost estimates.

Requirements Development

Before you decide on Unity, the first thing you need to do is define the high-level requirements for your ideal solution. Low-level or detailed requirements can be derived from the high-level requirements.

For example, a high-level requirement might be to eliminate a legacy system. The cost of maintaining a legacy voice-messaging system is typically very high, especially if you have more than one legacy voice-messaging system to maintain. The low-level requirements specify how you need to go about eliminating your legacy system and replacing it with Unity. Low-level requirements for this deployment might include the following:

- During replacement of the legacy voice-messaging system, it is essential to minimize the impact on the end-user community. Thus, interoperability during migration is required.

- Unity should support the legacy circuit-switched PBXs that you have in operation.

- Unity subscribers should be able to choose which languages they use after they have migrated from their legacy system.

Another example of a high-level requirement is adapting IP telephony and IP telephony applications such as Unity because of its unified messaging advantage as a strategic direction. Now, to some, this might seem like a lot to bite off, but it is no different than deciding to stick with your legacy voice and messaging systems, and paying the cost to maintain these systems. Adapting IP telephony and Unity for unified messaging capabilities is a very suitable high-level requirement.

Acceptance Criteria

When you have the high-level requirements and low-level/detail requirements defined, you should either base all design decisions on these requirements to maintain consistency with your ultimate goal, or you should measure all design solutions against these requirements as standards for your design. However, if you cannot meet a requirement, do you proceed with the design? In addition to defining and developing your requirements, you must determine which requirements have to be met. You also should determine which requirements would be nice to have but would not impact your solution if they are not met.

So, although defining requirements mainly is a paper exercise, you cannot do the exercise without knowing what the impact of your definitions is if they are not met. This is essentially your acceptance criteria for every requirement. It is recommended that you do the following:

- Target requirements that are acceptable to your end users. What do they need to have, and what can they do without? You might be surprised what users prefer to do without.

- Target requirements that meet your internal guidelines for operations and management. What is acceptable, and what is not? For instance, if your management guidelines support a specific hardware or software solution that Unity cannot support, is it acceptable, or can an exception be made?

- Target requirements that help you obtain your short-term and long-term strategic objectives. For instance, can Unity's support of Exchange 2003 help you obtain your short-term objectives of migrating to Exchange 2003? Do you need Unity to support something specific regarding your migration plans for Exchange 2003? Can Unity help you obtain a long-term objective of being completely converged and migrated off your legacy voice systems in a certain period of time, such as two years?

Matching Requirements to Capability

When you finalize your requirements and determine your acceptance criteria for those requirements, review your requirements. Compare them against Unity's capabilities, and ensure that they can be realistically met. Do not proceed with a Unity design until you understand what requirements can be met, what requirements cannot be met, and whether any requirements that cannot be met might prevent your solution from being acceptable to your end users.

This means that, from a higher level, you need to evaluate Unity's capabilities, and understand what Unity can and cannot do and what it can and cannot support. If a single Unity server must have 288 ports, then you have an unrealistic requirement: Unity's current maximum port limitation is 72 ports. Do you have many switch integrations that Unity cannot support? If your unified messaging solution cannot support your switch types, you will not get very far with Unity. Your evaluation of Unity needs to include assessing all of its capabilities.

Finalizing the Decision

After you define your requirements, you must decide whether you can meet these requirements with Unity. If your ultimate goal is to migrate from a legacy voice-messaging system to unified messaging, be prepared to accept the fact that Unity might not be a perfect fit.

This is not an attempt to bash the product; you will have the same issues with any unified messaging product.

A simple explanation should clarify this issue. As mentioned in Chapter 1, "About Unified Messaging," migrating to a converged network from a legacy environment where voice and data traditionally are kept separate from one another is a serious paradigm shift. Of course, this convergence paradigm does promise that not everything that is separate is the same when converged. This is neither good nor bad; it is the simple reality of the differences between the two. If you look for a perfect fit that addresses every single major and minor issue, you will not find it with any of the leading unified messaging solutions on the market today.

At this point in your project, this paradigm shift becomes an issue of acceptance within the end-user community and the organizations that traditionally maintained voice and data separately. They now must come together and work together to make this solution work. A suitable effort must be made to get all responsible parties on the same page, willing to work toward the end result.

Now you know the necessary "soft skills" required to eliminate potential political obstructions. You should make a decision on whether you can develop a sustainable design based on your requirements and your design decision.

If you decide that you cannot proceed with your design because Unity cannot meet your requirements, do not choose Unity. Or, determine whether you should redefine your requirements so that you can choose Unity as your solution vehicle. Regardless, this is the critical step in your decision. Take your time making this decision: Whether you go with Unity or not, taking your time to make the right decision pays off in the long run.

Preliminary Design Proposal

When you decide on Unity as your unified messaging or voice messaging–only solution, you can begin putting together a preliminary design proposal. This step can be iterative and could take multiple tries before you have an acceptable preliminary design. To save time, complete each of the following steps before you attempt to put together a preliminary design. By completing each of these steps, you should have the building blocks needed to lay the foundation for your preliminary design and your eventual final design.

Survey

Begin by performing high-level surveys to gather general information. No specific detail, such as getting server names, IP addresses, and user densities, is necessary. Instead, determine how many voice-messaging systems you want to replace. Better yet, determine the total number that you have.

Equipment Survey

The equipment survey simply involves the equipment that you will replace and the equipment that Unity will use. You should survey the following:

- Voice-messaging systems
- Circuit-switched PBXs or CallManager clusters
- Messaging systems that Unity will use to service your subscribers
- Messaging infrastructure components, such as DCs, GCs, and name resolution
- Rack space
- Power (if necessary)

You mainly need to know how many of each of these exist and where they are located. You easily can use the names of these systems for identification throughout the project.

Site Specification

It is important to define the type of site you have for each and every site. Is this a data center where centralized resources (such as your phone system and your message systems) are accessed? Is a given site a remote branch office? Is it a large office where resources are located or distributed from the centralized site? It might be easy to identify which sites are which by using the following definitions:

- **Single site**. The site is self-contained. It might have WAN connectivity, but all resources are located to the single site alone.
- **Centralized site**. This site provides services to end users in a centralized location, and also to some or all services to end users in remote sites where little or no resources exist locally.
- **Distributed site**. This site contains resources for end users to use, but is also connected to and shares resource information with other distributed sites or centralized sites. For instance, a distributed site might have some local resources for end users to access, and other resources might be centrally located in a regional data center.
- **Disaster recovery site**. This site is a mirror location for a main data center (centralized site) or distributed site. The disaster recovery site is used for system failover if access to the primary or main data center is lost.

As a part of your site specification, indicate how each site is connected to the others. For instance, if you have several remote sites connected to one data center, and several remote sites connected to a second data center, indicate this on your site specification.

Finally, indicate all types of data and voice circuitry currently in place that establish the connectivity between each site. This information helps to start a preliminary design and also helps ensure that data and voice paths are known and understood early in your project.

Deployment Model Specification

By understanding where your equipment is located and classifying each site, you can determine which deployment model combinations you will employ. You might end up with multiple combinations, depending on the size of your organization and your site classifications.

It is not unusual to have more than one centralized data center that services a regional area, with each remotely connected location having some or no resources for end users to access.

Understanding Unity's deployment rules (see Chapters 10, "Typical Configurations and Deployment Models;" 13, "Unity with Microsoft Exchange;" and 14, "Unity with Lotus Domino") helps you determine how to specify a deployment model combination to use. As mentioned throughout this book, Unity must be located as close as possible to each messaging system that it services. The only overriding factor is whether the telephony resources that it will connect to have a physical constraint, such as cable distance limitations. If this is the case, you might need to address these limitations as part of your solution. Regardless, if Unity replaces a legacy voice-messaging system, and the messaging system that it uses to support this migration is located in the same physical location as the legacy voice-messaging system, Unity must be placed at this location as well.

When you have a site specification for each site (resources are centralized or distributed, or perhaps different for call processing and messaging), you can define how Unity is deployed at that location. For more information, see Chapter 10, which covers site specification and deployment models.

Verification of Interoperability

When you have surveyed your equipment, you need to check two important elements, especially as they pertain to your legacy PBXs:

- Can Unity integrate with each one? If so, how? How is this different than the way in which your legacy voice-messaging system integrates with your legacy switch?

- Does each legacy PBX have the necessary capacity to support a Unity server (integration connectivity, if any, and port density)? Can Unity co-exist with the legacy voice-messaging system? This is simply one of capacity concerning the PBX, and you will be able to answer this question only if you ensure that Unity can connect to the PBX at the same time as your legacy voice-messaging system. If it cannot, you have two options: Either do not deploy Unity at this location, or, better yet, consider how Unity can use the same PBX resources as your legacy voice-messaging system (if Unity is replacing the legacy voice-messaging system).

Verifying interoperability also includes verifying Unity's capability to perform voice messaging between itself and your legacy voice-messaging systems. If this capability is desired, you need to make sure that they can support the interoperability capabilities within

Unity. See Chapter 7, "Components and Subsystems: Features," and Chapter 15, "Upgrades and Migration."

Finally, ensure that Unity's other messaging infrastructure dependencies are available for each location where Unity is installed. The messaging infrastructure dependencies are those that support the messaging systems that Unity services. This includes domain controllers, Global Catalog servers (if Unity is connected to Exchange 2000/2003), and name resolution (Wins/DNS for Exchange 5.5, DNS for Exchange 2000/2003, and Notes Name Resolution for Domino). If these dependencies are not available, you must indicate that when you document your interoperability verification.

Developing Preliminary Design Options

When you have completed your surveys, you can start developing design options. As an example, one option can be to perform a one-to-one swap of your legacy voice-messaging systems (in some cases, depending on the port density, you might need more than one Unity server to replace a legacy voice-messaging system with a high port density). Another option can be to match the subscriber accounts in your legacy voice-messaging systems with the mail-enabled user accounts on your e-mail systems, and determine whether these users would best be served by consolidating your messaging solution at this time. As shown in Figure 11-3 and as mentioned in Chapter 1, Unity is installed into the correlation point between your legacy voice-messaging systems and your e-mail systems.

Figure 11-3 *The Correlation Point*

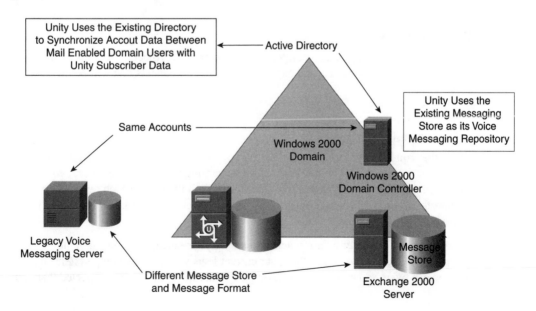

So, your second design option is one of consolidation. This is a change for your subscribers especially if some are split onto different systems. This requires your subscribers to relearn some extensions and possibly also change their private distribution lists and any other personal settings that other subscribers know about them. Take this into consideration if you pursue a consolidated design option.

A third design option is to take a phased approach. You might build out an initial UM solution in one or two areas, then expand to more areas in the second and third phases, and so on. This might mean that you have two or three designs that once overlaid on each other make up your entire Unity solution.

Other options exist, and the best one depends on your situation. What is best for your enterprise and the organization that you design the solution for? The answer depends on what makes the most business sense for your situation. If cost is a factor, that is one reason to adopt a multiphased approach. If you want to stop paying for large service contracts for your legacy voice-messaging systems, that is another reason to include a wholesale equipment swap in your design (a one-to-one replacement across the board).

Finalizing the Preliminary Design

When you finalize which option you will pursue, diagram your high-level design to make sure that it will work for you. Remember, this is a preliminary design: It can change, and you might have to iterate through a few of the steps in this section to finalize the preliminary design.

Budgetary Analysis

When you have a preliminary design, you can determine project costs. This includes hardware/software, services, and any infrastructure components that will be included in your effort.

Estimating Hardware and Software Costs

Now that you have performed high-level surveys and determined your design options, you should have a good idea of how each Unity server might be sized. Therefore, you also should have a pretty good idea of what hardware you will need for each server. Cisco Unity supports certain hardware platforms; see the Cisco website, or talk to your local Cisco partner or Cisco account manager.

You can take two different approaches to sizing your hardware. You can match Unity hardware to the same capacity that your current legacy voice-messaging systems have, or you can overprovision for extra capacity. It is acceptable and often expected that you overprovision because Unity has features and functionality that legacy voice-messaging systems do not have. Over provisioning ports, for instance, ensure that the necessary port density exists for subscribers who want to use TTS to play back their e-mail messages over the phone. Over provisioning ports also help prepare for growth if that is an organizational objective.

When you determine how many servers you need, you must determine the software you need for each server. Will you need any features that are licensed (meaning that you have to pay for them)? If so, determine which servers—perhaps it will be all servers, and you will need software licenses for each one. If you use pooled licenses for subscribers, how many do you need?

Estimating Services Costs

Along with estimating hardware and software costs, you should estimate the cost of services. Do you manage your project or hire someone to do it? Do you install all the servers and perform all the cutovers, or do you hire someone to do it? You should get a general idea of the cost of services when you understand how many servers you must purchase.

Bill of Materials

The output of your hardware/software costs and your service cost estimates is a bill of materials (BOM). You can use this BOM for ordering your equipment, figuring services cost per installation, determining other project-related tasks, and scoping your project in general. You can create your BOM by using a spreadsheet program. List the costs in detail for each of the items discussed in the previous sections "Estimating Hardware and Software Costs" and "Estimating Services Costs."

Planning Phase

When you have your preliminary design and your cost estimates for products and services, you can proceed to the planning phase. In the planning phase, you perform all the analysis and gather all the information that you need to finalize your design. Basically, during the planning phase, your goal is to obtain a design for a functional implementation plan. The planning phase is crucial to the success of any design. In some cases, it might be easy to skip a step or to give it little detail. However, the more attention you pay to each step, the more thorough your design.

The planning phase is important enough to have a chapter dedicated to it; see Chapter 9 for greater detail on some of the more specific tasks. However, this section should give you a more complete idea of which tasks you need to perform to finish the planning phase.

Feature/Functionality Evaluation of Unity

During the planning phase, you want to interrogate Unity, perhaps in several different ways. You must thoroughly understand the feature set available to Unity. You should have a good understanding of all features, even those that you might not plan to use, so that you understand the usage requirements and implications of using each feature.

But do not stop at a feature evaluation. You should also understand the behavior of the system because it touches, uses, and is used by many different components on the network. This section emphasizes understanding the behavior of Unity, which should hint at its importance.

Traditional Voice-Mail Functionality

It is important to understand the more traditional voice-mail functionality that Unity has and does not have. Because Unity is a unified messaging product, it might have some or most traditional voice-mail features, but not all. When you compare it to other legacy voice-mail systems, you can easily see the differences.

A few important areas should be noted: Because Unity is a unified messaging system with traditional voice-mail functionality, it does some things differently. For instance, in traditional or legacy voice-messaging systems, mailbox message retention is important but also taken for granted. In Unity, mailbox message retention is essentially unavailable. You can use the MailStore Manager tool to set it, but this tool should be used only on voice messaging-only installations of Unity, not in a unified messaging configuration. The MailStore Manager is considered too intrusive for unified messaging implementations in which administrators of an existing messaging environment require more hands-on control and less interference from automated tools that they have little control over. So, users have to understand that their messages are not deleted after 10 days and that, if they want to delete these messages, they have to do so manually, either through the Unity TUI or through their own e-mail client.

This is just one example of a feature that works differently in Unity, but there are others; seek out the differences so that you understand them.

Dependency Assessment

You must understand the dependencies that Unity has on the messaging infrastructure. Therefore, a full dependency assessment should be a part of your planning effort, especially if you plan for a large Unity installation. Looking back at Figure 11-1 and all the dependency areas that Unity affects or depends on, you can see how important this exercise is. Consider investigating the dependencies in a lab setting, whether you use Unity with Exchange or Unity with Domino. The dependencies for each are slightly different. Dependencies exist because the messaging environment treats Unity the same as an individual e-mail client. What e-mail clients depend upon, Unity will also depend upon.

Impact Analysis

Another important element of the planning phase involves determining the impact that Unity might have on your messaging environment, as well as the impact your messaging environment might have on Unity.

You have a few options. You can perform focused before-and-after trend periods, or you can evaluate the current and past performance of your messaging systems. This includes understanding how often these systems are unavailable and also how often their dependencies are unavailable (this includes domain controllers, name-resolution hosts, network gear, and so on).

You also must determine UM readiness assessment. See Chapters 13 and 14 for more information on this important task.

Capacity Planning

Capacity planning goes hand in hand with conducting an impact analysis. This important step includes evaluating your messaging infrastructure to determine if it can handle the extra load placed on it as a whole or on separate servers. If you are migrating from a legacy voice-messaging system, you must understand what the expected traffic increase is and also what the increase in the number of messages and message size means to your messaging infrastructure.

An important supporting part of capacity planning is doing a traffic analysis. Use the traffic analysis to determine the increased capacity requirements for your messaging infrastructure.

Legacy Voice-Messaging System End-User Usage Analysis

This task is covered in Chapters 8 and 9. Some of the high-level tasks are included in the following sections. If you gain anything from your migration to unified messaging, you should gain a deeper understanding of how your subscribers use and depend upon the legacy voice-messaging system. Ensure that these steps are followed so that your subscribers' concerns are addressed when you deploy Unity. In fact, unless you perform a usage analysis, you will have less of an idea of how to configure Unity before cutover; as a result, you will have less of an idea of what features and functionality are most important to the end users who are subscribers of the system.

Developing Questionnaires

A good way to get started with usage analysis is to create a simple questionnaire that asks important questions about how subscribers use their existing legacy voice-messaging system. Questions such as, "What features do you find most important when you dial into voice mail?" and "What features do you dislike the most?" go a long way toward helping you understand how your end users use the system.

Surveying Different End-User Groups/Usage Observation

Another way to perform a usage analysis (or as a part of developing questionnaires) is to create a survey for select groups of users. Also observe their activities including the key presses that they use and how they use the system. You might be surprised by what they use and how if you observe their activity. If you already know what they do and how and why, then all the better. However, you should capture the information so that it can support the development of system-configuration issues that need to be addressed for Unity.

Focus Groups

Larger organizations might want to create focus groups with representatives of different areas. These users can carry feedback from their areas to a group of users who can provide consolidated input into the entire usage-analysis effort.

Special-Case Usage Requirements

Through usage analysis, it is important to seek out special-case users who have specific configurations that are unique to the mass population of users on the system. If you ignore these special-case users, you will likely hear about it after you deploy Unity and they no longer can do what they used to be able to do. This can mean a loss of productivity or efficiencies that these users experience with the legacy system. Keep this in mind; make sure that for each voice-messaging system you replace, you account for the special-case users.

Feature/Functional Usage Gaps

Through your questionnaires, surveys, or focus groups, you get a good idea of the features that are important to your end users. Through your evaluation of Unity's features and functionality, you get a good idea of what it can and cannot do. Identify the features that your end users take for granted as subscribers of the legacy voice-messaging system; compare those with Unity's features. Involving your end users ensures that their needs and considerations are addressed and that they are not blindsided by a system that they are not used to.

System Configuration Analysis

As part of comparing features between the legacy voice-messaging systems and Unity, you need to have a thorough understanding of the legacy voice-messaging system configuration, the way subscribers are managed, the way that the switch integration is set up between the voice-messaging system and the legacy circuit-switched PBX, and also the features that are turned on and how they are used in the system.

This step actually tells you how to configure Unity. You can use the Unity configuration worksheets (found on www.cisco.com) to fill in important configuration information, such as schedules, call handlers, and routing rules.

Traffic Patterns

The traffic patterns study helps you to understand the type of traffic on the voice-messaging system, including the volume in size and quantity of messages, and also the number of subscribers using the system each day. When you understand the traffic patterns of your legacy voice-messaging system, you should be able to use this information along with the capacity-planning analysis to understand how Unity and your messaging systems should be configured to support the added capacity. Of course, each legacy voice-messaging system might have different ways to determine traffic patterns. The main emphasis should be placed on call volume into the legacy voice-messaging system, including messages left from outside callers per hour, messages left from subscribers to other subscribers per hour, and also the number of subscriber logon sessions per hour and subscriber messages left and retrieved per hour.

Support Analysis

This is the perfect time to figure out the types of support issues that you might encounter after Unity is deployed. You can do so by understanding the types of support issues you have with your legacy voice-messaging systems and also the types of issues your end users experience in the existing e-mail messaging infrastructure. Both of these should give you a good idea of the types of support issues you might expect to have.

Along with these support issues, you can identify the support issues that you encounter through your pilot, and you might even be able to determine other support-related items through your usage analysis of the legacy voice-messaging system. This should give you a good idea of what your subscribers expect when they use the system.

Knowing your support issues is one thing. The important part of this exercise is knowing what to support and then making sure that your administrators and support personnel are trained to provide this same level of support with Unity.

Training Criteria

The gaps that you end up with in your usage analysis fall into two categories: feature gaps that cannot be reconciled and that can affect the way subscribers operate (especially if specific features or similar features are not available to subscribers when they migrate over to Unity), and gaps that require training. These are features that do not exist in the legacy voice-messaging system or that are similar to features in the legacy voice-messaging system but that require some training so that your subscribers understand them.

If you use new features that are available only in Unity, you also need to address for training.

You might want to take an entire-system approach to training, taking your subscribers through every piece of the TUI conversation and every web page that the subscriber might access. This is fine and is recommended if your subscribers want this type of training. But if you have one or more focus groups, you should get enough input to tell you whether your subscribers need to be trained for Unity. Address training by involving your end users; otherwise, they might not be happy subscribers of the system.

Lab Trials and Proofing Your Concept

A part of your feature evaluation of Unity should include lab trials. These steps can be considered the same, if necessary, but the important part of this effort is to put Unity in a semiproduction environment and test it under load or in different ways.

If you have multiple Unity servers, it is a good idea to proof your preliminary design in your lab. Again, understand the behavior of Unity in the deployment models and messaging infrastructure that suit your environment. Use the evaluation techniques described in this section to finalize your assessment of the Unity installation in your mockup.

Configuration Options

Explore the configuration options that you have with the product until you find the configuration that will support your users. Again, the user usage analysis gives you a lot of configuration information so that you can properly configure Unity. Test different settings and port configurations.

Executing Test Plans

While exploring your configuration options, you can test the configurations using test plans posted on the Cisco website for Unity. You can search Cisco Connection Online or the Cisco Steps-to-Success website for test plans to run.

You will find an application test plan that you can run, as well as others, such as integration test plans and voice-messaging interoperability test plans.

Mockup of Production Network and Installing Unity

As mentioned earlier, if you do a mockup of your production network and install Unity in a simulated production installation as a proof of concept, you can learn quite a bit about Unity's behavior in your environment.

Assessing Installation into the Mockup

Record the installation steps in your production mockup so that you have a good understanding of what to expect. Your goal should be to come up with the exact steps for piloting the product in your production network.

Piloting in Production

When you pilot Unity in your production environment, you should have a very good idea of what your users expect and how the Unity system will behave in your production environment.

Pilot Installation Plan

As with any installation into your production environment, you need to come up with a suitable Pilot installation plan. Consider this a trial for your actual production deployment. In fact, your plan should pay close attention to every aspect of your installation, including any caveats and concerns from your lab trials.

Your installation plan should include go/no go decision-making criteria and a fallback plan for the pilot users whom you will include in your pilot.

Your pilot should include a duration that is suitable for successfully analyzing how successful a Unity deployment is. By all means, make sure that your pilot has a start and stop period, and that all participants (including those who are not included in the pilot but who will communicate with them through their normal means, which is voice-messaging interoperability) understand the purpose of the pilot.

Selection of Pilot Members

During a pilot, a safe approach often includes starting with subscribers who are in your IT department. This is fine and surprisingly common, but it is not as effective as having your core users get involved. Perhaps stage the pilot to include IT team members first, then core users (admins, executives, sales reps, and others targeted from your usage analysis), and then others, such as special-case users, to get a good idea of how a real installation might go.

Perhaps it seems like overkill to go through this type of planning during a pilot, but your subscribers' dependency on your legacy voice-messaging system is often critical to their productivity, and if their use of the legacy voice messaging system is critical then their use of Unity will be the same, therefore include them in your pilot effort as well. When you replace the legacy voice-messaging system, you refocus the emphasis on a very important productivity tool to Unity. The better you are at focusing on this aspect of Unity with your end users, the more success you will have in your deployment.

Implementing the Pilot

Consider every single aspect of the pilot to be an opportunity to study and analyze the behavior of Unity and the effects it has on your environment. Take advantage of this opportunity to fine-tune any specifics from templates used to import subscribers to port settings, and integration issues between Unity and your phone system.

Not only do you want to record and analyze the results of your installation and ongoing pilot, but you also should focus on the fine-tuning aspect so that you can use the experience to prepare for post-deployment, day-two support.

Basically, all aspects of a deployment should be tested against the pilot users, including determining how the users are notified, obtaining end-user evaluations, developing a communications plan, and so on.

Monitoring and Documenting the Experience

As with your lab trials and the impact analysis and capacity planning, your pilot is your first chance to monitor the real-time activity between Unity and the messaging system that it is connected to. You can document useful trends to compare against the real installations after you deploy.

You can capture data by doing the following:

- Using Performance Monitor and Unity counters
- Using Performance Monitor, and monitoring your messaging system and its infrastructure components
- Using the Unity and messaging systems application event viewers for errors and warnings
- Using the Port Usage Analyzer to monitor port usage patterns, especially for maximum port usage for inbound calls, MWI usage, and so on.
- Using other monitoring tools to monitor activity and performance

Surveying Pilot Members of Experience

When the pilot is complete, survey your members to understand their experience. No better feedback is more valuable than when you compare the results of your usage analysis with the experience that these same users have with Unity in a pilot situation.

It is useful to ask the same types of questions of the pilot users that you did the users of the legacy voice-messaging system usage analysis. This way, you can chart the results of the surveys and use them for comparison.

Analyzing Results

With your pilot complete, you can analyze the results of the pilot by reviewing the data captured, the support calls taken, administrative activities, and the feedback from your pilot subscribers. Compare these results with the usage analysis data to ensure that your previous results are accurate.

You now have verified your data and should know what to expect with your Unity rollout.

Site Surveys

During the planning stage, you covered a full usage analysis of your legacy system and noted the characteristics and behavior of Unity by performing throughout impact studies, feature evaluations, and production pilots. The last key piece of your planning stage effort is to survey your infrastructure to ensure that Unity has everything it needs to provide unified messaging services to your end users.

Messaging Infrastructure

If you have correlated the user population on your legacy voice-messaging system to the mail-enabled users on your electronic-messaging system, you should have a good idea of how you will place Unity. You want Unity to utilize the same messaging infrastructure components as your messaging system does; it is best to survey them so that you know which components service which messaging systems.

For each site, inventory your messaging servers and their dependency servers, such as domain controllers and name-resolution hosts. During your survey, verify that each messaging system uses the name-resolution hosts and domain controllers/Global Catalog servers (if you use Exchange 2000 or 2003) that you survey. Unity uses these same servers when deployed.

Note also that you need to include the domain and Windows 2000 site that the messaging servers and other dependency servers are installed into. Even if you have a Domino installation, Unity needs to be installed into a Windows 2000 domain, even if it is for Unity only. So, you still need to either use existing Windows domains or create new ones for Unity, depending on how many locations you have.

You can take an extra step, especially if you have Exchange 2000 or Exchange 2003, and note the organization of the user population for each location and messaging system that Unity will serve. This is actually quite important when you grant permissions to the service accounts that Unity uses to service its subscribers. So, if you note that mail-enabled users on Exchange server A and server B at location X are organized in domain Y in OU containers C and D, you have the information that you need for the Unity server that will install into that same location.

Switching Infrastructure

Before you enter the planning phase of the design process, you should already have ensured that Unity can service all your legacy circuit-switched PBXs. If you deploy Unity with CallManager, this is not a problem. However, if you have legacy PBXs, you should have surveyed them to make sure that they can support Unity and that you can set up the desired port density and integration.

You can use this same inventory to list for each PBX the number of voice ports and the integration. Also include switch settings that are in place or that might need to be in place to support the Unity integration with the switch. Finally, if you have already assessed the capacity, make sure that you know whether Unity can be installed and connected to your PBX with its own resources, or whether it has to be flash-cut from the resources used by your legacy voice-messaging system.

Physical Placement

Surveying each location for physical placement seems like an obvious task. However, it is surprising how often this simple step is missed. Make sure that you have rack space and ample power, a computer monitor, and network resources for each Unity server that you plan to install.

As previously discussed, Unity servers should be installed as close as possible (for the sake of management, it makes good sense to have Unity physically located with the messaging systems that it services). This includes all the other deployment rules that apply to Unity, depending on the messaging system that it services.

User Density

This step might require you do to more than just a user count for each Unity server. Several things must be done to ensure you have an idea of user density, but this is also a good time to clean up your voice-messaging system accounts database. Take the time to clean it up so that when you extract data, it is real, current, valid data.

When your data is cleaned up, determine the user density for each Unity server. You should already have put together a rough estimate from your decision-making period before starting your planning phase. You should have a more accurate idea of the number of subscribers that you will import into each Unity server.

Also note the user data after it is extracted from each legacy voice-messaging system, and verify that Unity can use the naming conventions (typically, Domino or Exchange can use them; Unity can as well). Also start to get a good idea of how you will map the extracted subscriber data to an import CSV for Unity.

Compiling Data

All of your survey data should be compiled and organized, either by site or by any other means that is most suitable to your needs. However, organizing it is the most important goal here. Having the data ready for your detailed design will make your design effort a whole lot easier.

Finalizing Feature/Functional Analysis

In this step, you want to compile the configuration and other important design criteria for use in the design phase. This should include any feature settings that you plan to use in your deployment. Include the lessons learned from your pilot, and note any particulars that affect how your design should be put in place.

Usage Analysis Results

The end-user usage analysis of your legacy voice-messaging system should tell you how to configure Unity, among other things. In your design, indicate how Unity should be configured and note any particular design considerations to accommodate other design-dependent items identified during your usage analysis. For example, if subscribers of a given system use specific names for distribution lists, or if they have special audio-text applications, make sure that you have the details of this information so that you can add them to your low-level design when it is put together.

Design Phase

When you have completed the different aspects of the planning phase, and have collected and compiled all of your data, you enter the design phase. At this point, you determine your final design. With the information in hand, it might seem that the design will just come together, especially if you did the preliminary work before starting the planning phase.

If your preliminary design has held true, use it. If you have had to make changes based on other decisions, such as feature usage or migration approach, or the results of your pilot, take this time to finalize the design.

Your first goal in the design phase is to determine the high-level design. When this is finished and accepted, you can work on the low-level design that enables you to develop a detailed implementation plan. If you cannot develop a useful implementation plan from your low-level design, go back and revisit your design to determine what you need to change or adjust so that you can come up with a suitable implementation plan. Again, this might sound like a no-brainer but you must verify your design before you move to the implementation plan. This does not mean that you need to physically build out your low-level design in a lab mockup of your production environment. However, you need to validate the low-level design criteria that you use for each planned Unity server by making sure that Unity is installed and operates the way you design it to.

High-Level Design

The high-level design should have a summary of everything that you plan to do. This includes your migration strategy and how you expect the design to look after Unity is deployed. If you have a phased-migration strategy, perhaps it is an excellent idea to show how your voice messaging/unified messaging and electronic messaging infrastructure will look at the end of each phase. Providing a design description and diagrams is key in communicating your high-level design to all interested parties.

High-Level Design Description

The high-level design description should revisit all the dependency areas that Unity impacts or is affected by, as explained in Figure 11-1. It should discuss how each site is classified and explain the deployment model that you use for each site. You then should discuss how Unity services your subscribers and how it supports your migration plan. The following is a general outline that you might use. (Naturally, you can come up with your own as well.) You will likely want to include more information than what is covered here, but, at a minimum, you should include these items::

- **Design summary**. Summarize the design and how it might look when finished or at the end of each phase.

- **Approach**. Consider how the Unity solution was designed, denoting the effort involved in planning the solution and how effective it was.

- **Design goals**. Identify the goals of the design—to replace the legacy voice-messaging system through a phased migration or a flash cut, or to provide a greenfield installation of Unity as the organization migrates from one legacy e-mail system to another (from Exchange 5.5 to Exchange 2003, or from Exchange 5.5 to Domino). The term *greenfield* refers to a new installation that does not involve any type of migration from a legacy voice-messaging system.

- **High-level description of the total design that should support your design goals**. Expound upon the design summary and detail the solution, including all areas touched by Unity, as noted in Figure 11-1.

- **High-level description of each Unity installation at each location**. Include the voice-messaging system that Unity will replace, which messaging servers it will service, and where it will be installed (physically). Finally, include how it will integrate with the circuit-switched PBX at this location.

- **Design rationale and supporting documentation**. This should consist of all your planning documentation. You can consider this to be reference documentation so that it is accessible to design reviewers.
- **Approved**. Finally, your high-level design should be approved and should provide instructions for what happens after the design is approved (the low-level design detail and the implementation plan).

High-Level Design Diagram

The high-level design should include one or more diagrams of the high-level design, as well as specific examples of each integration type or connectivity to a PBX. In addition, you might determine to use different sizes of servers, depending on where Unity is installed and how many users it services. This is fine, but if you do, indicate the differences in your diagram so that others understand it as well.

It is suitable to integrate your diagrams into your high-level design document. It is assumed that you will also have diagrams in your low-level documentation, so diagrams should be considered par for the course.

How do you represent Unity in the big picture? Show how Unity fits into the different layers of the solution. For instance, Unity fits into the call-processing side of IP telephony; if IP telephony is not in the picture, it fits into the call-processing side of a legacy circuit-switched PBX. Unity also fits into the messaging environment; this includes messaging boundaries, such as sites and routing groups, and also domains and Windows 2000/2003 sites. Finally, Unity uses name resolution and must be accessible to clients; thus, it is necessary to show how clients access each Unity server, including the DNS entry, if appropriate for the diagram. If you cannot get something into a high-level diagram because of the complexity of the solution or the number of servers, do not worry: You can fit it into your low-level detail design. In other words, consider it a requirement at a minimum for your low-level design.

Low-Level Design

In the low-level design, you add all the detail necessary to give clear direction to all project participants and interested parties. The low-level design should be signed off on after it has been reviewed, which could take a few iterations.

The more detail you add—and, in general, the more thorough your approach is at this stage—the better you can put together an implementation plan that an installation team can use to deploy Unity. If your design is for only a few Unity servers, you still need enough information in the low-level design for the installers to develop a plan to install every Unity server based on important details, such as server name, domain name, account names and passwords, name resolution, location of partner servers and their names, and so on.

As with your high-level design, the low-level design should reflect the high-level documentation and should come in the form of one or more documents. Do you really need more than one document to represent the low-level design? No. In fact, if you are not doing a large install with, say, 10 or more Unity servers, you can probably get all your detail into one document that is suitable to your project participants and interested parties. However, if you install 10 or more Unity servers, you should break your low-level documentation into smaller pieces. This way, specific participants can help develop or write the specific parts of the design that are relevant to their subject areas (messaging system, security, administration, telecom, and so on).

Determine how your documentation is organized at this point, and also determine how everyone will use and identify it. However, this should not be a long, drawn-out process; dragging it out can have a negative effect on your overall design effort.

Low-Level Design Description

Your low-level design is very detailed. With this, you focus on being precise and as thorough as possible. This is more than just a couple of diagrams; the low-level design documentation contains all data necessary to build an implementation plan. From a high-level design perspective, you start by discussing the broader aspects of the design or the overall design. When you start with the low-level design, however, you must become detailed as you integrate each part of your planning stage data into low-level design documentation.

Unity System Description

The Unity system description is the criteria necessary to build each Unity server you install. You develop this system description from the survey data that you gathered about the messaging servers, domains, domain controllers, Global Catalog servers (if applicable), and other survey components.

The system description should be broken into several sections, as follows.

Unity System Configurations

The system configuration is how each Unity server should be configured including how you should set up your subscriber templates, classes of service, distribution lists, naming conventions, extensions, other subscriber data, switch settings, port configuration, and so on. Most of this information can be extracted from the reports that you compiled from the end-user usage analysis (because this is where you should have gathered most of this information).

This section deals mainly with the Unity system configuration detail that is specifically located on each Unity server included in your design. Unity has external dependencies on other components, such as where it stores its directory-specific information in the directory. For this reason, you also must make sure that when you indicate the Unity-specific system configuration data, you also note or cross-reference the external dependencies, such as the folder it uses in a given directory to store and use its own directory objects and default objects.

The same holds true for where all of these objects and data are installed during installation.

Unity Hardware Configurations

The hardware configurations should give you the physical layout of the hardware including how you plan to organize files and applications on the hard drives of each server. See the Unity product documentation for information on this. In addition, by determining which servers you will use and how you will provision them for each set of subscribers that you service, you should be able to determine how to standardize the configurations on each model you use. So, if you use only a single Unity server model, standardization is easy. If you use more than one server, you have to think a little more about how you standardize or organize the OS and applications on each server. That is fine; you probably have your own standards. The bottom line is that you must convey a standard for these servers.

You also want to show how the hardware is connected to your network and how it is connected to your legacy PBXs if Unity will service them. Be specific; show as much detail about the connection, even including which slots to use for voice cards (if they are used), or your SCSI connector for a voice-card chassis (if it is used), and your integration cables and boxes (depending upon the type of integration you are using). If Unity is connected to CallManager, show the network connection and its path to CallManager. Does it use the same VLAN or a different VLAN? Show the actual IP addresses on the cards.

If you will connect any other hardware to Unity to support the server, diagram that and show how it will be connected; discuss how it will be used.

Unity Networking Configuration

If you look ahead to Chapter 12, "Unity Networking," you can see that you must understand the dialing plan that you use with Unity. Is it an existing plan, or is it being modified to accommodate Unity? Use the steps and methods described in that chapter to build out your networking configuration for all Unity servers. Do you create a single Unity dialing domain, or will there be many? Show the networking configuration, perhaps as another layer of the Unity installation.

When you document your Unity network scheme, show how subscribers on each Unity server can be addressed by subscribers on other Unity servers. Document this for each Unity server, and diagram it in detail.

Show a digital networking table depicting how it will be set up for each Unity server (see Chapter 12).

Physical Network Connectivity

As explained in the section "Unity Hardware Configurations," you should show Unity's physical network connectivity. But do not show just the connectivity to and from the network switch that it is connected to. Show also the IP addresses and server/DNS names of each server that it communicates with. You should have this information from the site surveys and messaging infrastructure–specific surveys you conducted. You should be able to use the survey information to show exactly how each Unity server connects to the network and communicates with each and every server that it services or depends upon. This should be a point of reference, so make sure that it is accurate.

Unity Switch Integration Detail

Next, for each server, you should go into considerable detail explaining exactly how Unity will integrate with each switch that each Unity server services. This includes the voice ports and the switch-integration configuration (see Appendix A, "Switch File Settings," if necessary). It is also important to diagram these settings in detail so that an implementation plan can be developed from it.

Unity Messaging Infrastructure Detail

From your site surveys of your messaging infrastructure, and from your impact analysis and trending studies, you should have a very accurate detail of how this infrastructure is laid out. You also should have a good understanding of the specifics of the environment as it pertains to supporting Unity.

Remember, Unity's primary deployment rule is that it must be installed as closely as possible to the messaging systems that it services. This includes the same subnet and the same messaging infrastructure components, such as name resolution, domain controllers, and directory servers or Global Catalog servers.

This section is broken into smaller parts to cover the specifics of the messaging infrastructure. Depending on the size of your deployment, you might need to split out the actual documentation so that core subject experts can take ownership of the documentation and provide it as a part of the low-level design. Regardless, your primary low-level design document should reference this section. If you do have external documents for each subsection, you should reference them in your low-level design document.

Unity Domain Usage

These are the key areas of Unity's use of a Windows domain. Unity uses the domain for account access and permissions verification of subscribers and administrators. It uses the domain for its own service accounts; if Unity services Exchange 2000 or Exchange 2003, it uses the Windows 2000 or Windows 2003 domain for its directory as well. For this reason, it is important to indicate for each Unity server how it will use each domain controller and Global Catalog (for Exchange 2000/2003) at each location where Unity is installed.

As mentioned throughout this book, if Unity services any of the messaging systems it supports, it should be located in the same domain. This is so that it can perform the access and permissions verification for the same subscribers who reside on the messaging systems that it services and so that it can access the same directory components, if applicable.

If your Unity design involves Exchange 5.5 only, list the domain where it resides and the domain where the Exchange 5.5 servers reside, if this is different. Again, it is strongly recommended that these be the same domain; otherwise, you can experience TUI delays because of authentication dependencies with the domain.

If your Unity design involves Exchange 2000/2003 only, you must list not only the domain names and domain controllers that Unity uses, but also the Global Catalog server that Unity uses. Again, Unity must be installed into the same Windows 2000 site as the Exchange 2000/2003 servers that it services and must use the same domain controller and Global Catalog server as these Exchange servers. Finally, you will want to list the directory OUs where all mail-enabled users are located in Active Directory for the same Exchange servers that Unity services.

If your Unity design involves both Exchange 2000/2003 and Exchange 5.5, and if you plan to have a single Unity server service both Exchange 2000/2003 mailboxes and Exchange 5.5 mailboxes from the Windows 2000/2003 domain and Exchange 2000/2003 partner server, you must indicate the locations of each of these Exchange versions in their respective domains, if they are different. If they are the same, indicate that and explain in detail how this setup was established. Also explain how the migration is conducted so that your support staff understands how they need to support Unity in this configuration. How Unity is set up to service both versions of Exchange at the same time is a design consideration. Your site survey information should reveal these particulars about your Exchange messaging environment.

If your Unity design involves Domino only, you must indicate which Windows 2000/2003 domain Unity is installed into. Remember that Unity uses the Windows 2000/2003 domain and that Domino might not; also note that Unity's interaction with Domino primarily depends on DUC and the Domino domain and not the Windows 2000/2003 domain, even though a Windows 2000/2003 domain is required for Unity only. If you dedicate a Windows domain for your Unity installations, note that in your design. Also note how each Unity server accesses and uses the domain controller for the Windows 2000/2003 domain where it is installed.

Unity Directory Usage

As mentioned in section "Unity Domain Usage," Unity's use of the directory is two-fold. It has a location in each directory that it uses for its own location information, typically called the Unity location object. As discussed throughout the book, Unity also uses specific attributes for user, group, and contact objects in the directory (the object names might differ, depending on which directory Unity is servicing, but the emphasis is on these object types).

In your survey effort during the planning phase, you should have accumulated the detail about your directory. You also you should have performed an impact analysis and performed capacity planning for that directory. At some point after your design is finished and before your full rollout of Unity, you must extend the schema of Active Directory if Unity is installed to service Exchange 2000/2003, or you need to install DUCS into the Domino directory (which is essentially the same type of activity). Unity uses an existing schema in Exchange 5.5, so no schema extension is required for it, even though a capacity-planning activity should have been performed before finalizing a design for Unity using Exchange 5.5.

For voice-messaging interoperability, your directory capacity-planning exercise should have helped you determine the impact that legacy voice-messaging objects created in Active Directory have on your directory. Regardless, you will need to indicate location and where these objects will be created at this point.

For Active Directory or Domino, you also might want to include particulars about the detail and activities involved in performing the schema extension or in installing DUCS, in the case of Domino. Doing so helps ensure that this activity is included in an implementation plan and, thus, a project plan after the design is completed.

Name Resolution

Unity uses name resolution indirectly when it accesses a messaging system. It also uses name resolution for clients who need to locate their Unity web pages so that they can access the CPCA application and the Unity inbox.

Consider Unity's indirect dependency on name resolution as just as important to Unity as it is to any other native e-mail client that the messaging system services. For instance, if your system is Exchange 2000 and your e-mail clients are Outlook 2000, you will want to make sure that Unity can use the same name resolution as these clients. This is Windows 2000 DNS or dynamic DNS, or any DNS that allows the service locator structure to be built out as required by Active Directory. See Microsoft's website and product documentation for more details.

In your low-level design, for each Unity server, indicate which name-resolution hosts will service Unity. Note that if name-resolution hosts are not located locally, Unity can be affected with TUI delays while it waits for name resolution during a given TUI-related transaction. Indicate this in both your text and your diagrams.

Messaging System

For each Unity server, indicate which server will be its partner server and which servers Unity will service. Note specific dependencies and any deviations from the recommendations given throughout this book.

Your site survey and impact analysis studies should have revealed the information you need here for each Unity server.

Service Accounts and Administrative Access

For each Unity server, note the service accounts that will be used or created for Unity. You also should have an accurate idea of the permissions that are needed for these service accounts, even though the Unity Permissions Wizard grants the permissions for you. It might be easy enough to indicate the minimal permission areas (locations in the domain structure or directory) where these permissions need to be granted to the service accounts for each Unity server.

You also must consider how the servers will be accessed administratively. Is OS level-access treated differently than the Unity application level? It should be. What about the SQL server access? You should not have to access it, but you need administrative access, just to be safe.

Basically, here is where you indicate how each Unity server will be accessed and how the service accounts will be used, as well as their names, their level of permissions, who will manage them, and what is necessary for management (such as password policies, permissions checks and verification, auditing, and so on). If you plan to use an existing administrative policy or procedure within your organization, indicate that and note how it will be applied to Unity.

Finally, when you indicate the accounts that you will use, you might want to address both the installation of and operations of Unity, which can be considered two different activities.

End-User Access

For each Unity server, indicate which levels of access is to be allowed for your end users. Will it be TUI only? Are only some end users allowed to access the GUI web? What about directly accessing the server? Are any end users allowed or required to access the Unity server directly? Perhaps not for normal users, but you need to address who needs to access the server directly and why it is required so that you can include this in your implementation, project, and administrative plans.

Your usage analysis should have revealed the specifics about end users and what and how they need to access. Use information from that activity in the planning phase to complete this section.

Security Considerations

Security hardly is touched on in this book. However, the Cisco website has quite a bit of information regarding security for Unity. This includes Unity product documentation and whitepapers that cover security-related issues and how to apply specific security policies to Unity.

You also might have your own security considerations that go above and beyond what is published and made available for Unity. Your lab trials and feature/functional evaluations, and your production pilot should have revealed the security issues that you might need to address for any Unity installation.

Securing your systems is important; pay close attention to the design specifics surrounding your security needs for Unity. Make sure that you not only include security considerations in your design, but that you also use the lab trials and production pilot to ensure that whatever you indicate in your design, Unity is capable of supporting.

Administration and Management

If you install multiple Unity servers in multiple locations, a concern certainly arises over how to administer and manage these servers. Indicate the specifics of how these Unity servers should be administered and managed because there are design implications.

Whether your administrative model is centralized to regional data centers, or whether it is distributed so that each location is responsible for its own servers and the services provided by those servers, you should address how Unity should be administered and indicate any design issues associated with your administrative plan. If bandwidth is an issue for remotely accessing the Unity System Administrator, or if you need to run remote administrative clients to access the server, indicate that in this section.

You should have accumulated this information from your site surveys and also by determining your current administrative models.

Administration Considerations

For administration, consider which accounts or which users need to access each Unity server and how. Some organizations divide the responsibility among those who have specific expertise. For instance, you might have a team that is responsible for managing

SQL Server in your organization's enterprise and for managing the Unity messaging-queue activities and the SQL Server installed on the Unity server. You might have your voice-messaging team manage the Unity application itself. You might have the messaging administrative team manage Unity's access (the accounts that Unity uses and the mailboxes used by those accounts) to the messaging system that it services. It all depends on your administrative requirements and what makes the most sense for administering Unity.

Your administrative plan should include how mail-enabled users are imported into Unity and also how those users are managed after they are imported. Is this design specific? It can be if you have administrative needs that require specific attention for administering subscribers. As a part of your design topology, indicate your administrative model and how it will support normal Unity administration, including subscriber management (subscribers, distribution lists, and so on), audio-text applications, and the Unity server system configuration, especially its connectivity to a legacy switch, CallManager, or both.

What tools do you use? Indicate this and set up a policy for how, when, and where these tools are used. Otherwise, you might have a hard time administering multiple Unity servers.

Management Considerations

As with administration, management of Unity includes monitoring the server's resources and performance, as well as also proactively monitoring the server's ongoing, daily activity. This means that you will monitor Unity at different levels: the OS (event logs, SNMP service, Performance Monitor), Unity itself (traces, port status, Unity-specific performance activity, logs, and so on), application event viewer logs (possibly using the event-monitoring service), and other components, such as security, antivirus, and other management tools.

Again, although this might not be design-specific, within your low-level design, you should consider the management requirements and note any specific details related to your Unity design; for instance, the location of Unity servers in comparison to network and system management consoles and other monitoring devices you might use.

Subscriber Account-Naming Conventions

In your design, include the subscriber account-naming conventions, and make sure that your design uses the same naming conventions as your existing user accounts database. Indicate in your design the formats or convention that will be used, and make sure that this is a consideration when an implementation plan is formulated.

Support Considerations

As with administrative and management requirements, you must consider how your Unity design is supported after it is implemented. Your administrative and management plans should define this, but there are other support considerations as well. For instance, if you do a phased migration as a part of your design, indicate any specific support requirements for that design. Who do subscribers call for problems? Who do your tech support engineers contact for operational issues during each phase of the migration? How does moving from legacy voice messaging to unified messaging affect how subscribers are supported? Your usage analysis should indicate a considerable number of support issues and concerns that you need to address in your design, implementation, and operations. Document the expectations and any support or operational standards that each Unity server should adhere to.

Criteria for Implementation

When you have your high-level and low-level design documents finalized and signed off on, you will want to start extracting the low-level information to put together your implementation plan. Your design documentation should provide all the information that you need to devise a sound implementation plan. As stated earlier, if it does not, you probably need to go back and revise your design.

For more information regarding implementation, see Chapter 16, "Installation."

Summary

This chapter discussed the Unity design process from start to finish. It took you step by step through the key steps of the initial stage, the presales stage.

In the planning stage, you really find out about how a Unity pilot might go. In this stage, you gather all your data through capacity planning, site surveys, and usage analysis. The planning stage is essential for putting together a sustainable design for Unity.

The design phase is split in two. The first part involves restating your preliminary design by defining the high-level design. The high-level design also should reference all your source data so that you have a recorded audit trail up to this point in the process. The second part involves the low-level design detail.

Your final goal is to use all the data collected from the planning stage along with your high-level design to develop your low-level design.

Because the low-level design is your goal, it should be detailed. It should cover every important aspect of a Unity server installation, including placement next to the messaging servers that it services and all server-specific details, such as server names, IP addresses, accounts used to access the server, and configuration details. The low-level design should contain all information necessary to develop an implementation plan for any Unity deployment, large or small. This includes both detailed documentation and detailed diagrams for each Unity installation.

This design process is repeatable in the sense that, if you follow the steps outlined, you should be able to come up with a sustainable design for Unity. For smaller deployments (with only a few Unity servers), your low-level design might not be as lengthy, but it should be as thorough. Just remember that smaller deployments have the same design needs as large-scale designs.

CHAPTER 12

Unity Networking

This chapter describes how to design a Unity digital network. The term digital networking refers to a suite of features that can function across two or more Unity nodes. These networking features allow multiple Unity nodes to function together as a larger whole, which is called a Cisco Unity Digital Network or Digital Network for short. At the highest level, Digital Networking can provide an organization with the following networking functionality:

- **Distribution Lists**. Public and private distribution lists that can contain any subscriber in the Digital Network regardless of which Unity node the subscriber is associated with.

- **Message Addressing**. Any subscriber can address a message to another subscriber in the Digital Network by name or extension.

- **Call Transfer**. Outside callers can dial into any Unity node in a dialing domain and transfer, by name or extension, to another subscriber in the dialing domain regardless of the target subscriber's associated Unity node.

- **Pooled Licensing**. Subscriber and Cisco Unity Inbox licensing can be pooled amongst nodes within the Digital Network.

When the choice is made to deploy a Unity solution, it is seldom the first voice-messaging solution in town. More often that not, Unity is replacing an existing solution to set the stage for a migration. When planning a migration, an organization must decide if networking interoperability between their new Cisco Unity Digital Network and their legacy voice messaging network is necessary during the transition. More than half of the organizations that deploy Unity choose to forgo voice messaging interoperability and take what I refer to as a single-phased approach to a migration.

In the pages ahead, we take an in-depth look at Digital Networking from the single-phase migration standpoint. First we focus on the Digital Networking Architecture (DNA) feature set. After the feature set, we move on to the process used to assess a legacy voice-messaging environment and design a new Cisco Unity Digital Network.

Digital Networking Architecture

It goes without saying that a successful Digital Networking architect must have a strong technical understanding of the Digital Networking feature set and its functionality. However, sometimes a strong technological understanding of the feature set is not enough and this is the case with Digital Networking. The features of Digital Networking are extensively documented but are still misunderstood. And although Cisco has spent plenty of time explaining what it *does*, the following sections describe exactly what it *is*.

Protocol Introduction

If you boil it all down, data is the most basic building block of voice-mail networking. Whether the data is a voice message or feature-oriented networking data such as information about a subscriber, a distribution list, and so on—it is all data at the lowest level. To transport this data between voice-mail nodes requires a protocol. A voice-mail networking protocol represents a defined set of rules and procedures used to exchange data between the members of a network.

When most people think about voice-mail networking protocols, popular protocol names, such as Audio Messaging Interchange Specification (AMIS), Voice Profile for Internet Mail (VPIM), and Octel Analog Networking (OctelNet), usually come to mind. Each of these protocols function differently and supports a different feature set. However, they all share a couple of common themes. First, they are each used to transfer data between voice-messaging nodes that would be otherwise isolated. By isolated, we mean that each node is a separate island, if you will, and that they natively transfer zero data among each other. The second thing they have in common is that they are all peer-to-peer protocols. By peer-to-peer, we mean that each communication session is an exclusive conversation between two nodes.

Digital Networking, on the other hand, draws very few similarities to traditional voice-mail networking protocols beyond that fact that it too is used to transfer data. The key differentiator is that Digital Networking is not a peer-to-peer protocol used to transfer data among autonomous nodes. In fact, Digital Networking is more accurately described as a data distribution architecture. As you read ahead, keep in mind that Digital Networking is different than traditional networking protocols. If you try not to force it into the same box it is easier to understand and appreciate.

The Origins of Digital Networking

The design of the Digital Networking Architecture stems from a piece of product history that is not all that well known. It is that Unity was originally designed only to be a unified messaging product. It was never intended to be a traditional voice-messaging product. You see, at the time of development, Active Voice had a more traditional voice-messaging product called Repartee. At Active Voice, Unity was sold to customers that wanted unified messaging and Repartee was sold to customers that wanted a traditional voice-messaging product—or what Cisco now calls voice mail-only.

What this means is that the concept of a voice mail-only Unity solution did not cross the minds of the original product architects. And as such, Unity was designed to be a total departure from the traditional voice-messaging products of the past.

Now admittedly, things have changed quite a bit since Cisco acquired Unity from Active Voice. However, the roots of the product are still in the unified messaging space. The fundamental architecture has not changed much since the acquisition of the product.

Knowing that Unity would be a unified message product, the original product architects at Active Voice could safely assume that an existing electronic-messaging infrastructure would already be in place. With this assumption in mind, one of the underlying themes of Unity became to not duplicate that which already exists. Instead Unity would be just one of several components that combined together would be a complete unified messaging solution. The key point here is that Unity would not be a complete unified messaging solution by itself. This is an important concept to recognize because it provides the rhyme and reason to the unique design of Unity and Digital Networking.

Shared Messaging

When the Unity product architects looked at the components of an electronic messaging infrastructure and the components of a traditional voice-messaging infrastructure, they found them to be very similar. Both had subscribers, distribution lists, directories, databases used to store messages, and so on, and both had a means to transfer those messages and the directory information throughout the infrastructure. With the goal to not duplicate what already exists, the architects designed Unity to be completely different than any previously designed voice-messaging product. Instead, they placed all of their focus on leveraging all that was provided by the electronic messaging infrastructure, namely the directory and message store, which led to a tightly coupled unified messaging solution. The results are what we call the Shared Messaging Architecture.

As it stands today, the nuts and bolts that make up each unified messaging subscriber are split across the various components of the unified messaging infrastructure. For example, the electronic messaging infrastructure provides the subscriber object in the directory and the location to store the messages. Unity provides the component to take a call, play the subscribers greeting, record a message or play back an e-mail message over the phone. Each of these functions is needed for a complete unified messaging solution, and the electronic messaging infrastructure and Unity work in tandem to make this happen.

From a Digital Networking standpoint, the biggest partnership between Unity and the electronic messaging infrastructure is the model used to replicate feature-oriented networking data.

Networking Data Replication Model

For a feature to be extended across multiple nodes requires that data pertaining to it be shared across the Unity nodes as well. At the same time, the demands of real-time call processing make quick and reliable access to the data an absolute requirement. To fulfill both requirements, the architects decided to place a local instance of SQL on each Unity node, which provides quick and reliable data access. They also leveraged the directory component of the electronic message infrastructure (instead of traditional peer-to-peer networking protocols or SQL replication) to provide networking data replication.

The easiest way to think about the Unity data replication model is to picture a bicycle wheel. A bicycle wheel has three main components, the outer wheel, spokes, and a hub. As the wheel spins, the load must be transferred from one spoke to another. But because spokes are not directly connected to each other they cannot directly transfer load from one to another. Instead, each spoke transfers their load to and receives load from the other spokes through the hub.

Now think of a bicycle wheel as a Digital Network. The outer wheel represents the Digital Network boundary, the hub represents the directory, and the spokes are Unity nodes. To support the Digital Networking features, Unity nodes must share networking data (which is only a small subset of their entire SQL database) between one another. Because the databases are not directly connected to each other, they cannot directly transfer networking data to one another. Instead, the Unity nodes transfer their networking data to and from each other through the directory, which is the hub of the Digital Network.

Figure 12-1 shows the physical representation of a Digital Network. The hub of this Digital Network is Directory Replica A and B. These directory replicas can be Active Directory domain controllers, Exchange 5.5 servers, or Domino servers depending on the messaging infrastructure that Unity is integrated with. The spokes are the Unity nodes A, B, and C with their UnityDb SQL database. The outer wheel in this case would be the New York and London sites together.

If we take a look at Directory Replica A, we can see that it contains a copy of the small subset of data required for networking each Unity node in the Digital Network. Moving over to Directory Replica B, we can see that it too has the same data that Replica A has. Now let us focus on Unity Node A and its SQL database UnityDb. The portion of data called Full Node A Data is all of the data needed for Unity to function as a standalone node. The arrow pointing from Full Node A Data to Node A Data Subset on Replica A represents replication of the small subset of data required by other Unity nodes within the Digital Network to network with Unity Node A. The portions of the UnityDb labeled Node B Cache and Node C Cache are the subsets of data required for Unity Node A to network with Unity Nodes B and C.

Figure 12-1 *Physical View of a Digital Network*

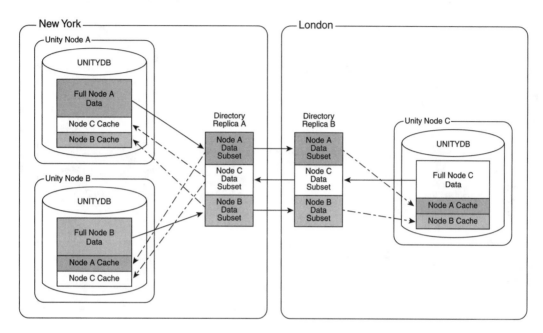

Logical Data Structure

For Digital Networking to function, the networking data needs to be organized in a logical manner. In Unity, the various pieces of networking data are broken down in to three categories. Those categories are Unity node data, subscriber data, and public distribution list data. For the most part, each Unity node, subscriber, and public distribution list is treated as a separate entity with the exception being a logical link between each subscriber and the parent Unity node.

Figure 12-2 is a logical representation of a Digital Network. The Unity nodes, subscribers, and public distribution lists are all recognized as separate entities. However, the subscribers are logically linked to their home Unity node. Each Unity node will have this logical representation of the Digital Network in its UnityDb SQL database.

Each and every Unity node, subscriber, and public distribution list has a corresponding object in the directory. You will see why this is important in just a moment. Subscribers and public distribution lists have a corresponding object by default because they exist within the electronic messaging infrastructure. The Unity nodes, however, do not because they are not native to the electronic messaging infrastructure. They instead create an object in the directory for themselves during installation, which is called a Primary Location Object.

Figure 12-2 *Logical View of a Digital Network*

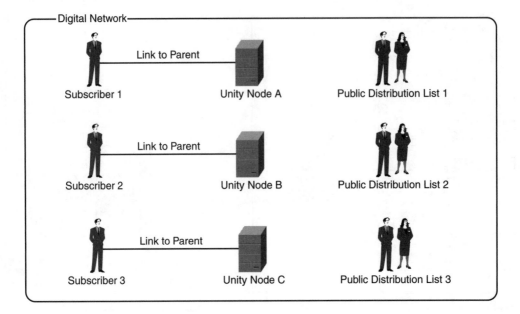

The networking data itself is copied from the SQL database to a specific attribute on the corresponding directory object. Because the directory is shared with the electronic messaging infrastructure and possibly other applications Unity creates custom attributes on the objects, where possible, to avoid conflict. In configurations where Unity cannot create custom attributes, we have limited the possibility of conflicts so they seldom occur.

Knowing which attributes map to what networking data falls outside of the scope of required knowledge for a Digital Networking architect. If you would like to explore this further, you can read Chapter 3, "Components and Subsystems: Object Model," which provides in-depth discussion.

Synchronization Process

Unity incorporates two separate synchronization strategies that are used to keep the data in SQL synched with the data in the directory. There is one strategy for pushing networking data to the directory and one for caching networking data from the directory. Both are needed for proper replication, but they do function independently from one other.

Each Unity node is responsible for the networking data pertaining to itself and the subscribers homed on it. In the case of distribution lists (which are not associated with any one Unity node) the Unity nodeis responsible for any changes made from its administrative interfaces.

All adds, updates, and deletes are written to the directory as they occur. For example, there is no delay from the time you update a subscriber's extension in the System Administration page (SA) to the time it is pushed to the corresponding object property in the directory. It happens immediately.

The process used to cache networking data to SQL starts with the initial build of the cache itself. This is handled at installation by a process called the Syncher. When the Syncher runs for the first time it caches all of the existing Unity networking data in the directory to the local SQL database. Note that this is just the Unity-specific data that gets cached and not all data in the directory.

After the cache is built, synchronization between the SQL database and the directory must be maintained. To do so, each Unity node periodically polls the directory to check for updated data. They do so on a regular interval that ranges from 2 to 15 minutes depending on the electronic messaging backend Unity is integrated with. Any updates found while polling are immediately committed to the SQL cache.

Digital Networking Features

Now that you have a clearer understanding of the Digital Networking architecture and how it functions, we can turn our focus to the actual feature set. The feature set represents the Digital Networking functionality that you, as an architect, will be responsible for designing. As you read through this section, remember that knowledge is the key to designing a successful Digital Network. The stronger your understanding of the features is, the better your chances for success are.

Dial Plans

The feature set of Digital Networking is designed to accommodate organizations with complex dial plans. In this context, a dial plan defines an organization's internal extension ranges, and the combination of numbers known as an access code, which must be dialed to connect each range. Within a dial plan can exist extension overlap, meaning that two different subscribers have the same extension number. Although access codes prevent this from being an issue for normal phone calls, it throws a wrench in a networked voice-mail solution.

Think about how you would address a message by extension when three subscribers all have the same extension. Or how would you transfer a call to a subscriber when the dial string required to reach them varies from phone system to phone system? Clearly the dial plan becomes a big factor in the overall design of the Digital Network.

Unity includes two features that allow it to support dial plans with access codes and extension overlap. They are dialing domains and alternate extensions.

Dialing Domain

A dialing domain is a collection of Unity nodes for which access codes or any other sort of prefixing is not required to dial between the subscribers that are homed on each other. Moving forward, I refer to this as transparent dialing.

A transparent dial plan is required if you have a single Unity node. This basically means that a single Unity node cannot support extension overlap, access codes, or partitioning in the sense that CallManager does. A dialing domain is just a way to create an alliance across multiple nodes that adhere to those same rules. This of course implies that extensions do not overlap within the particular segment of the dial plan and that access codes are not required to dial between the subscribers.

Within a Digital Network, several dialing domains can exist. In fact, there is no limit to the number of dialing domains that can exist. There is no limit to the number of Unity nodes that can be members of a dialing domain either. A dialing domain can contain just a single Unity server or several hundred. It is wide open.

Let us take a look at a few examples to better understand what does and does not constitute a dialing domain.

In Figure 12-3, there are two Unity nodes, A and B, which are members of the same dialing domain. The nodes are connected to different phone switches. Within the dial plan, the extension ranges do not overlap and there are no access codes or special prefixes required to dial between the ranges. This means they have a transparent dial plan that conforms to the rules of a dialing domain. Therefore, someone on Unity node A can, for instance, address a message to a user on Unity node B exactly the same way that they would address it to a user on A.

In Figure 12-4, there are two Unity nodes, A and B, that are not members of the same dialing domain. In this situation, the dial plan does not contain overlap; however, access codes are required (8 in this case) to dial between the two switches. Because access codes are not allowed in a transparent dial plan, the two Unity nodes cannot be bound together into a single dialing domain. If the organization wanted them to be within the same dialing domain, it would need to make modifications to the dial plan to remove the access codes.

An administrator recreates the dialing domain from the Primary Location Object page in the SA of any Unity node within the Digital Network. After a dialing domain is created, Unity writes the name of the dialing domain to the primary location object within the directory. As replication occurs through the directory, and each node learns of the new dialing domain, they add it to their local SQL database. Once written to SQL, the new dialing domain becomes an option in the drop-down box for dialing domains on the Location Object page in the SA for an administrator to choose. When a Unity node is joined to a dialing domain its new membership status it written to its primary location object in the directory. From there, the updated dialing domain status must replicate back to the SQL database of the other Unity node before both Unity nodes will see that they are members of the same dialing domain.

Figure 12-3 *First Dial Plan Example*

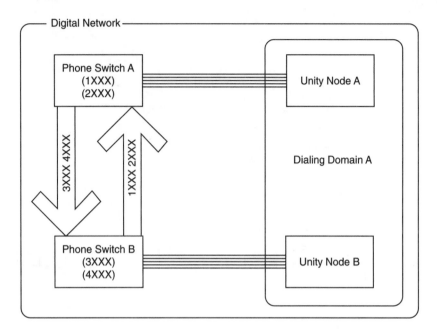

Figure 12-4 *Second Dial Plan Example*

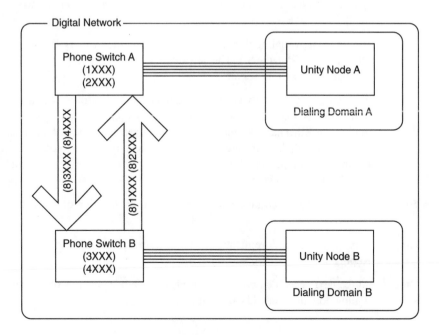

Figure 12-5 *Dialing Domain Creation and Replication*

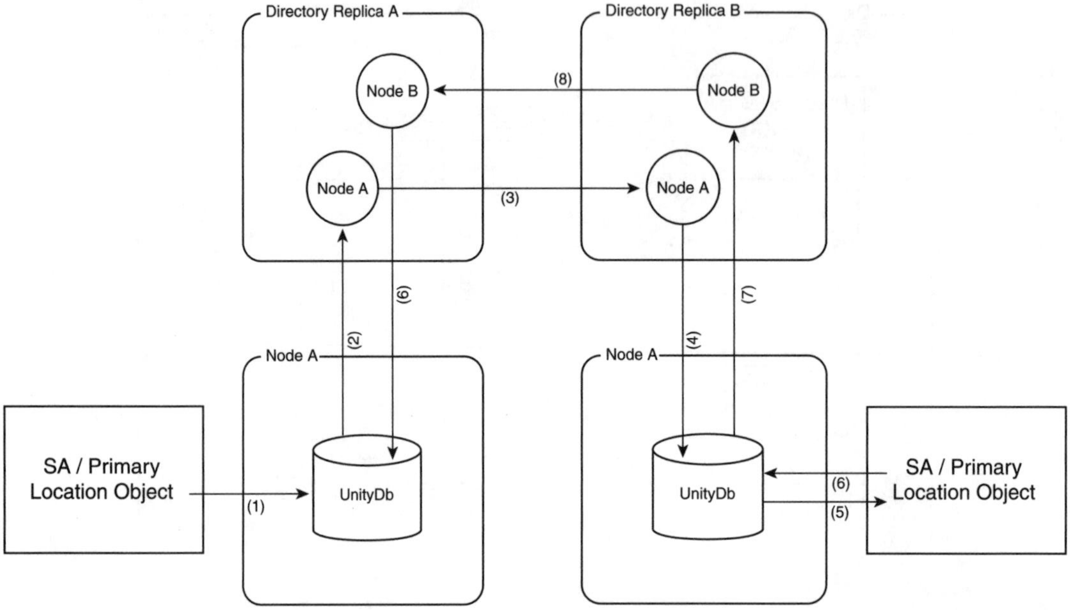

In Figure 12-5, we take a closer look at the process of creating and joining two Unity nodes to the same dialing domain.

Step 1 Create the new dialing domain. This is done on the Primary Location Object page within the SA. The new dialing domain is written to the SQL database of the Unity server.

This name is completely arbitrary and only an administrator with access to the page is able to view it. Generally, it is recommended to give each dialing domain a name that is not based on physical location of the nodes because dialing domains are not dependant on physical topology and dialing domain membership can change over time. Generic names such as DD1, DD2, and so on are recommended.

Step 2 The name of the dialing domain is written to the location object within the directory.

Step 3 Directory Replica A replicates the new dialing domain data to Directory Replica B.

Step 4 At the next scheduled polling interval, Unity Node B learns of the new dialing domain data and caches it to SQL.

Step 5   After the dialing domain is cached to SQL, it is displayed as an existing dialing domain within the Primary Location Object page in the SA.

Step 6   After the new dialing domain is joined through the SA, SQL is updated.

At this point in time, Unity Node B believes that A and B are both in the same dialing domain. However, A still believes that it is the one member. Now the membership information from B must make it back to A.

Step 7   The name of the dialing domain node B joined is written to its location object within the directory.

Step 8   Directory Replica B replicates the dialing domain data to Directory Replica A.

Step 9   At the next scheduled polling interval, Unity Node A learns that Node B has upgraded dialing domain membership data and caches it to SQL.

From the perspective of both Node A and B, they are now both members of the same dialing domain.

As you can see in Figure 12-5, in a Digital Network with lengthy replication times, it can take several days for new and updated data to fully propagate. This type of environment is quite rare because organizations usually try to avoid other types of directory data becoming stale. However, it is possible. If you find yourself in this situation there is a technique you can use to speed up the process.

The name given to the dialing domain is used to represent it within SQL and the directory. This means that adding a dialing domain with the identical name, including case, to each Unity node eliminates the first four steps of the replication process completely. This effectively reduces the replication time to one-half and can be used in a bind.

Unity enforces extension uniqueness across all nodes within a dialing domain. This means that extensions assigned within Unity are checked to ensure that they do not conflict with another subscriber within the same dialing domain. There are a few caveats here that should be noted, which make it possible for duplicate extensions to exist.

- Extension uniqueness is not verified when a node is joined to a dialing domain, only after it joins. This makes it possible for preexisting duplicates to exist.

- Distribution lists are not homed to one specific Unity node and therefore cannot be considered a member of a specific dialing domain. As such, their extension is not verified for uniqueness.

- During the window of time that is takes for replication to complete, duplicate extensions can be added within the dialing domain.

- Extensions given to call handlers, directory handlers, and interview handlers are not replicated to the directory. Therefore, uniqueness is verified only for the handlers of the local node and not the other nodes within the dialing domain.

Alternate Extensions

Prior to Unity 3.0(1), each subscriber in Unity can be associated only with a single extension called the primary extension. This proved to be a big limitation that customers commonly ran up against. Several customers desired a way for a device such as a cell phone to forward unanswered calls to Unity and for Unity to integrate the call to the same mailbox of the subscriber. Tricky routing rules should allow this; however, they really did not scale as a solution. The limitations forced the development of a new solution called alternate extensions.

An alternate extension is just an extensions alias. Each subscriber can be assigned 9 alternate extensions, effectively allowing subscribers to have a total of 10 extensions. Primary and alternate extensions function identically is most every way. And like a subscriber's primary extension, all alternate extensions are replicated throughout the entire Digital Network.

You can create alternate extensions in four different ways. They can be created one at a time through the SA (see Figure 12-6), in bulk using the Add Alternate Extensions utility, through the Cisco Unity Bulk Import (CUBI) utility, or with the Bulk Edit utility. Like primary extensions, each alternate extension must be unique at the dialing domain level and be no more than 30 characters in length.

Figure 12-6 *The Alternate Extension Page in the SA*

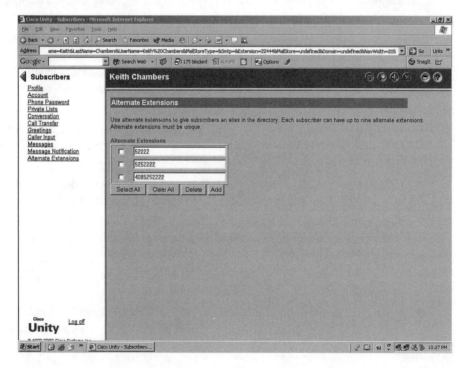

Although alternate extensions can be created in several different ways, they can only really be administered through the SA. Alternate extensions cannot be administered through utilities such as Bulk Edit because they are not stored in a structured order. This is a fairly important limitation to understand. All alternate extensions are stored within the directory in an indeterminate order as opposed to each being a separate and independent property from the others. Long term, this will likely change, however, this is how it works for now. As such, special care should be applied to the design of alternate extensions.

Extension Length

By default, the minimum extension length for a handler within Unity is 3 digits. Several features of Unity were designed around this expected minimum. The most significant is private distribution lists that can consume extensions 1-20. However, it is possible to force the minimum to a lower value through the registry. However, because several features were designed with the expectation of 3 being the minimum, changing it can cause undesired behavior. Therefore changing the minimum length lower than 3 is discouraged and not considered a best practice.

It is possible to change it to a higher value as well. This is a good idea if your extensions are longer than 3 digits because it can prevent an administrator from making an accidental mistake when adding a user to Unity. The advanced settings tool provides an interface to change the minimum length.

Core Digital Networking Features

Now that you have the DNA and the concept of dialing domains and alternate extensions under your belt, we can move into our discussion on each of the core features of Digital Networking.

Distribution Lists

Within Unity there is a concept of a distribution list. A distribution list in Unity functions in much the same way as a distribution list does in any of the supported messaging infrastructures. For Unity, two types of distribution lists are available: public distribution lists and private distribution lists.

Public Distribution Lists

Unity leverages the distribution lists of the messaging infrastructure for its public distribution lists. This means that each public distribution lists has a corresponding distribution list within the Directory. A public distribution list can be created one of three ways. It can be created within the messaging infrastructure and then imported into Unity, it can be created directly from the SA by an administrator or it can be created with the aid of the Public Distribution List Builder utility. Each public distribution list is assigned a name, and optionally can be assigned a spoken name and extension. The spoken name and extension allow them to be addressable through the Unity subscriber conversation.

Members of a public distribution lists can include any subscriber or public distribution list within the entire Digital Network. When a message is sent to a public distribution lists, the messaging infrastructure handles all member expansion. Membership is cached locally to SQL, however, to support directory handler searches. We touch on directory handler searches with Public distribution lists in the pages ahead.

Unlike Unity subscribers, public distribution lists are not homed to any particular Unity node. This allows all of their Unity-specific properties to be edited from any Unity node within the entire Digital Network.

Private Distribution Lists

Private distribution lists differ greatly from public distribution lists. Private distribution lists are designed to be specific to a single subscriber as opposed to being shared like public distribution lists. Due to the design requirements, private distribution lists do not have corresponding distribution lists within the messaging infrastructure. Instead, they are stored in SQL only. This makes Unity responsible for all private distribution list member expansion.

Each private distribution list is created, managed, and owned by a single subscriber. Subscribers can have up to 20 lists and there is no limit to the total number of list members. Private distribution lists can be created and managed through both the subscriber conversation or though the Cisco Unity Personal Communications Assistant (CPCA).

Like public distribution lists, member of a private lists can include any subscriber or public distribution list within the entire Digital Network. Private distribution lists also have a name, and can be assigned a spoken name just like a public distribution list. Each list gets an extension automatically ranging from 1 for the first list to 20 for the last. The extensions are used to address messages through the subscriber conversation.

Message Addressing

The message addressing functionality of Unity allows a subscriber to address a message to other subscribers or to a distribution list by either name or extension. From a technical perspective there are two pieces to the feature. The first piece is what we call the subscriber search; the process and logic used to resolve subscriber input to a name or extension. The second piece is the underlying mechanics of recording, addressing, and submitting the message into the messaging environment for delivery. Of these two parts, only the subscriber searches require design consideration. Unity is designed in such a way that the underlying mechanics function automatically. Here we focus on subscriber searches because it is the only piece of message addressing that requires design consideration.

Before we get too far into the functionality of subscriber searches, we should pause to clarify one point: subscriber searches and directory handlers are two completely different functions of Unity. A lot of organizations are quite concerned that a competitor will try to search for the names of their top brass within a public facing alpha directory. It is important to recognize that subscriber search is not where this is going to happen. The only folks that can get access to the subscriber searches functionality are those who are subscribers of the system themselves. So as long as you do not give the competitions' head-hunter an account on the system, you should be in the clear.

By default, a subscriber can address a message to all public distribution lists within the Digital Network and yet only to other subscribers that reside on their local node. Remember that public distribution lists are not homed to a specific Unity node and therefore must always be treated as if they are local. Most organizations desire to bump the addressing scope up, allowing subscribers to address a message to any other subscriber within the entire Digital Network. Changing the scope requires careful planning because there can be extension overlap to contend with. However, with a little planning, and a good understanding of the logic used for subscriber searches, supporting this functionality is entirely possible in even the most complex of environments.

Subscriber searches can be configured to one of three scopes: local server, dialing domain, or Global Directory. Because setting the value to a level higher than local usually requires planning; the value is set to local server by default. The scope selected for subscriber searches applies to searches by name or by extension. Because the configuration for both types of searches is shared, it is important that functionality of both be considered.

Although the scope selected for subscriber searches applies to searches by name or by extension; the logic Unity uses to do the search differs. Let us take a look at the search logic for each:

- **Subscriber searches by name**. The idea behind subscriber searches by name is simple. When prompted to spell the name of a person or distribution list, the subscriber spells the name from the keypad of their phone. After the subscribers finish entering characters, a single search is preformed at the scope level (local server, dialing domain, or global directory), which has been defined for the Unity node. All possible matches, assuming there are no more than eight, are returned to the subscribers. In the case where more than eight possible matches exist, the subscriber is asked to continue spelling the name.

- **Subscriber searches by extension**. Subscriber searches by extension are handled differently than searches by name. Instead of doing a single search at the scope level, subscriber searches by extension use an expanding scope. The expanding scope is designed to provide a lot of flexibility, most of which is used to support interoperability. This flexibility can cause some extension to not be reachable if configured incorrectly so plan it carefully to ensure this doesn't happen.

With the expanding scope, a search always begins at the local server level. If the subscriber entered 1 or 2 digits, Unity searches for a matching private distribution List. Private distribution lists are numbered from 1 to 20. If a match is found, the search stops.

If a match is not found or if the subscriber entered three or more digits, Unity searches for a matching local subscriber extension on the local node. Remember, alternate extensions function in the same way as primary extensions and can trigger a match. If a match is found, the search stops.

If a match does not exist, Unity will then search for a matching public distribution list. Because public distribution lists are not homed to one particular Unity node, they are all considered to be local. Therefore, all public distribution lists within the Digital Networking are searched for a match. If a match exists, the search stops.

If a match is not found at the local level, the scope expands if the configuration allows. It first expands to the dialing domain level, and if a match is not found to the Global Directory.

If a match is still not found, Unity begins to parse by primary location object dial ID plus extension. For example, if the subscriber entered 5251000, Unity would try to find a combination of a primary location object ID and a subscriber at that primary location object ID that combines to be 5251000. If we had location object 525 and subscriber 1000, then it would match.

If no match is found during that final search, then Unity informs the subscriber that there were no matching names.

Although we talk about this later, I would like to point out that the Global Directory is ultimately the desired value for this setting. Setting the scope to Global Directory allows subscribers to address a message to any other subscriber in the entire Digital Network.

Subscriber Settings

Unity does allow for all addressing by name to be turned off on a per-node basis. This setting is found in the SA on the Setting page in the Configuration section. When turned off, subscribers can address only messages to an extension, at any level. This functionality primarily exists for tenant services applications where multiple organizations share the same Unity node. The only Digital Networking reason for turning addressing by name off is if there were an organization that had such a large subscriber population that massive name overlap resulted. We do not recommend turning it off.

License Pooling

Licensing Pooling is a brand new Digital Networking feature for the 4.0(1) release of Unity. License Pooling allows multiple Unity nodes with a Digital Network to share specific types of licenses among themselves. The types of licenses that can be pooled are subscriber licenses and Cisco Unity Inbox licenses. The licensing for all other features such as Text to Speech (TTS) sessions are handled as usual.

License Pooling is a significant shift from the rigid licensing practices of the past. The idea behind license pooling is if the total utilization of a feature across all Unity nodes participating in the pool does not exceed the total licenses available, then the pool is compliant. In practice, this allows for these features to be licensed on a per Digital Network basis as opposed to the past when they were licensed on a per-node basis.

The example in Figure 12-7 is a logical representation of a typical licensing pool. Two nodes, Unity 1 and Unity 3, contribute to the licensing pool. Unity 2 is not, however, and it is still able to support users because the pool had enough available licenses. In all, this pool's licensing is compliant.

Figure 12-7 *Logical View of a License Pool*

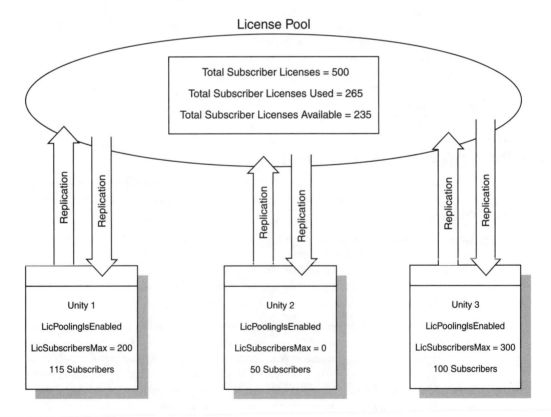

Like all other Digital Networking features, license pooling uses the directory for all data replication. Within the directory there can only be one pool. However, unlike the other Digital Networking features, the data used to support the license-pooling feature is not automatically replicated to the directory. Only when a Unity node becomes a member of the pool does it begin replicating licensing data.

To become a member of the pool, a Unity node must have license pooling enabled in its license key. Once a node becomes a member, it needs to know two things about all Unity nodes in the pool to calculate the total number of licenses and current utilization (or what is known as the system state). Those are the licenses installed on each node and the licenses consumed on each node. This system state data is complied by each Unity node in the pool and replicated to its primary location object in the directory. From there, the other nodes cache the system state data to SQL and factor it into the process of determining total licensing for the pool.

Pooled Licensing has a couple advantages over the traditional method. With license pooling, licenses are tied to a pool rather than to a specific Unity node. Therefore, subscribers can be moved from one Unity node to another within the pool without consideration given to licensing. Licensing pooling can also lower the totally cost of ownership of a Unity solution because licenses are more effectively utilized. This allows an organization to buy one big block of licenses and use them as needed. When more licenses are needed, they can be added to the pool. Couple these advantages with the fact that it is free, and it becomes a desirable feature.

Assessing the Environment

Now that you have a good understanding of the DNA, the supporting functionality, and the features themselves, you are ready to assess the current environment in preparation for the designing phase.

The phrase "assessing the environment" is just a fancy way of saying that we will document it. To help make this section clearer, we will document a fictitious environment along the way. The tool that we use to document the environment in this chapter is Microsoft Excel. It is easy to work with and it gets the job done. Please feel free to substitute whichever tool you prefer.

Now, before we begin to assess the environment, it is important to keep a couple of things in mind. The first is that you need to assess the environment as it is today, not as you plan for it to be in the future. A migration plan is often designed around an organization's future plans and not what actually exists today. This is a sure fire way to shoot yourself in the foot. Rest assured that a reconfiguration of a Digital Network is completely possible. Any changes to the environment made after the migration can be worked into the Digital Network's design. The other thing to keep in mind is that the assessment must be thorough and complete. If you are unsure about an aspect of the current environment, it is critical that you become sure before you begin defining the new Digital Network. If you force ahead without all the facts, there is a good chance you will wind up in trouble. With those points made, we can move on.

Step 1: Assessing the Messaging Environment

The first step is to define the messaging environment. At this point, assessing the messaging infrastructure should be a formality if you have read the preceding pages. What we want to check for here is that each Unity node is integrated within the same directory. This, of course, is the primary requirement of Digital Networking. All Unity nodes must be members of the same Active Directory forest if the organization uses Exchange 2000/2003 or mixed Exchange 5.5 and 2000/2003. If it uses Exchange 5.5 only, then they must all be members of the same organization. If it uses Domino, then they must all be integrated within the same names.nsf database. If you cannot say yes to one of these, then Digital Networking is not a possibility. If you can, you are ready to get started.

Step 2: Define the Physical Structure

The second step is to define the physical structure of the organization. Now, let it be known that the physical structure actually has little to do with the design of a Digital Network. So why do I ask you to define it as one of the first steps of the assessment process? There are a couple of good reasons. For starters, the vast majority of organizations that network multiple Unity nodes also have multiple physical locations. For these organizations, locations serve as an easy way to split an environment into smaller partitions, which makes the design process less complex. Also, the dial plan of an environment has a huge impact on the overall design of its Digital Network. Usually the physical structure of an organization and its dial plan share similar boundaries. By this, I mean that it is common to see access codes used to dial between physical locations and that it is unheard of to see them used to dial within the same physical location. For these reasons, grouping first by physical structure simplifies the entire assessment process.

In Table 12-1, you can see three physical locations. They listed them by city name, but there is nothing that says you have to do the same. If you have internal names that are used for each location, feel free to use them. The idea here is just to break the entire organization down into smaller physical units.

Table 12-1   *Beginning of the Environment Documentation*

Location =	Seattle
Location =	San Jose
Location =	Research Triangle Park

Step 3: Define Each Phone Switch

The third step is to define each phone switch within the organization. When you define each switch, you make the assumption that there is transparent dialing between any extensions within it. Most of the time this is the case, however, it is possible to require an access code within the same switch. In a situation where this is the case, the switch needs to be broken down and documented as virtual switches. Within each virtual switch, there must be transparent dialing.

Each switch should be given a unique name so that you can easily identify it; and it should be placed within the physical location that it resides. In the case where you have a single phone switch that services multiple physical locations, such as Cisco CallManager, treat it as if it exists in both of the locations. Note each switch if you have more than one phone switch within a single location. These entries will be used as the framework for the next section.

As shown in Table 12-2, this environment is straightforward. In this environment, there is a total of four phone switches, which are named Avaya G3 1, CallManager Cluster 1, CallManager Cluster 2, and CallManager Cluster 3. Each has a unique name and each is associated with the physical local in which it resides. In this example, there is not a virtual switch, nor is there one switch that services multiple locations.

Table 12-2 *Environment Documentation with the Introduction of Phone Switches*

Location =	Seattle
Phone Switch =	Avaya G3 1
Location =	San Jose
Phone Switch =	CallManager Cluster 1
	CallManager Cluster 2
Location =	Research Triangle Park
Phone Switch =	CallManager Cluster 3

Step 4: Define the Dial Plan

The fourth step is to define the dial plan. This requires an assessment of the entire environment from the perspective of each phone switch. This might prove tedious in larger environments. Nonetheless, it is required.

When defining the dial plan, the first step is to document the range of extensions that each switch supports. This includes any Direct Inward Dial (DID) prefixes that might exist. After all of the extension ranges and DID prefixes have been documented, the patterns used to dial between each switch in the environment are next.

In Table 12-3, you can see that Seattle uses range 32XX internally and that each internal extension has a DID prefix. The DID range for Seattle is 206 256 32XX. You can also see that the patterns used to dial CallManager Cluster 1, CallManager Cluster 2, and CallManager Cluster 3 each are documented from the perspective of Avaya G3 1. As a reminder, the access code is the portion of the number that the phone switch uses to determine where to route the call.

Table 12-3   *Environment Documentation with the Introduction of Dial Plan*

Location =	Seattle			
Phone Switch =	Avaya G3 1			
Dial Plan =	(DID Prefix) + Extension Range: (206 256) 32XX	(Access Code) + Extension to CallManager Cluster1: (8 525 1) XXX	(Access Code) + Extension to CallManager Cluster2: (8 525 2) XXX	(Access Code) + Extension to CallManager Cluster3: (8 392) 3XXX
Location =	San Jose			
Phone Switch =	CallManager Cluster 1			
Dial Plan =	(DID Prefix) + Extension Range: (408 52) 51XXX	(Access Code) + Extension to Avaya G3 1: (8 256) 32XX	(Access Code) + Extension to CallManager Cluster 2: 52XXX	(Access Code) + Extension to CallManager Cluster 3: (8 392) 3XXX
Phone Switch =	CallManager Cluster 2			
Dial Plan =	(DID Prefix) + Extension Range: (408 52) 52XXX	(Access Code) + Extension to Avaya G3 1: (8 256) 32XX	(Access Code) + Extension to CallManager Cluster 1: 51XXX	(Access Code) + Extension to CallManager Cluster 3: (8 392) 3XXX
Location =	Research Triangle Park			
Phone Switch =	CallManager Cluster 3			
Dial Plan =	(DID Prefix) + Extension Range: (919 392) 3XXX	(Access Code) + Extension to Avaya G3 1: (8 256) 32XX	(Access Code) + Extension to CallManager Cluster 1: (8 525 1) XXX	(Access Code) + Extension to CallManager Cluster 2: (8 525 2) XXX

Step 5: Define Each Legacy Voice-Messaging Node

The fifth step in the process is to define each legacy voice-messaging node that exists within the environment. Each node is documented in relation to the phone switch it is integrated with. In the case where you have a voice-messaging node that services multiple phone switches, it should be treated as if it integrates with each of them. These entries are used as the framework for the next section.

Similar to Table 12-2 for defining each phone switch, Table 12-4 is straightforward. In this environment, you have a total of four legacy voice-messaging nodes named Octel 100 1, Octel 100 2, Octel 250 1, and Octel 250 2. Each legacy voice-messaging node is given a unique name and associated with the phone switch it is integrated with.

Table 12-4   *Environment Documentation with the Introduction of Legacy Voice Mail*

Location =	Seattle			
Phone Switch =	Avaya G3 1			
Dial Plan =	(DID Prefix) + Extension Range: (206 256) 32XX	(Access Code) + Extension to CallManager Cluster 1: (8 525 1) XXX	(Access Code) + Extension to CallManager Cluster 2: (8 525 2) XXX	(Access Code) + Extension to CallManager Cluster 3: (8 392) 3XXX
Legacy Voicemail =	Octel 100 1			
Location =	San Jose			
Phone Switch =	CallManager Cluster 1			
Dial Plan =	(DID Prefix) + Extension Range: (408 52) 51XXX	(Access Code) + Extension to Avaya G3 1: (8 256) 32XX	(Access Code) + Extension to CallManager Cluster 2: 52XXX	(Access Code) + Extension to CallManager Cluster 3: (8 392) 3XXX
Legacy Voicemail =	Octel 250 1			
Phone Switch =	CallManager Cluster 2			
Dial Plan =	(DID Prefix) + Extension Range: (408 52) 52XXX	(Access Code) + Extension to Avaya G3 1: (8 256) 32XX	(Access Code) + Extension to CallManager Cluster 1: 51XXX	(Access Code) + Extension to CallManager Cluster 3: (8 392) 3XXX

Table 12-4   *Environment Documentation with the Introduction of Legacy Voice Mail (Continued)*

Legacy Voicemail =	Octel 250 2			
Location =	Research Triangle Park			
Phone Switch =	CallManager Cluster 3			
Dial Plan =	(DID Prefix) + Extension Range: (919 392) 3XXX	(Access Code) + Extension to Avaya G3 1: (8 256) 32XX	(Access Code) + Extension to CallManager Cluster 1: (8 525 1) XXX	(Access Code) + Extension to CallManager Cluster 2: (8 525 2) XXX
Legacy Voicemail =	Octel 100 2			

Step 6: Define Legacy Voice-Messaging Extension Length

The sixth step is to define the extension length for each of the legacy voice-messaging nodes. In most cases, the extension length used within the voice-messaging node is the same length as the ones used in the phone switch.

Table 12-5   *Environment Documentation with the Introduction of Extension Length*

Location =	Seattle			
Phone Switch =	Avaya G3 1			
Dial Plan =	(DID Prefix) + Extension Range: (206 256) 32XX	(Access Code) + Extension to CallManager Cluster 1: (8 525 1) XXX	(Access Code) + Extension to CallManager Cluster 2: (8 525 2) XXX	(Access Code) + Extension to CallManager Cluster 3: (8 392) 3XXX
Legacy Voicemail =	Octel 100 1			
Extension Length =	4 Digit			
Location =	San Jose			
Phone Switch =	CallManager Cluster 1			
Dial Plan =	(DID Prefix) + Extension Range: (408 52) 51XXX	(Access Code) + Extension to Avaya G3 1: (8 256) 32XX	(Access Code) + Extension to CallManager Cluster 2: 52XXX	(Access Code) + Extension to CallManager Cluster 3: (8 392) 3XXX

continues

Table 12-5 *Environment Documentation with the Introduction of Extension Length (Continued)*

Legacy Voicemail =	Octel 250 1			
Extension Length =	5 Digit			
Phone Switch =	CallManager Cluster 2			
Dial Plan =	(DID Prefix) + Extension Range: (408 52) 52XXX	(Access Code) + Extension to Avaya G3 1: (8 256) 32XX	(Access Code) + Extension to CallManager Cluster 1: 51XXX	(Access Code) + Extension to CallManager Cluster 3: (8 392) 3XXX
Legacy Voicemail =	Octel 250 2			
Extension Length =	5 Digit			
Location =	Research Triangle Park			
Phone Switch =	CallManager Cluster 3			
Dial Plan =	(DID Prefix) + Extension Range: (919 392) 3XXX	(Access Code) + Extension to Avaya G3 1: (8 256) 32XX	(Access Code) + Extension to CallManager Cluster 1: (8 525 1) XXX	(Access Code) + Extension to CallManager Cluster 2: (8 525 2) XXX
Legacy Voicemail =	Octel 100 2			
Extension Length =	4 Digit			

Table 12-5 shows that Octel 100 1 and Octel 100 2 use 4-digit extensions and that Octel 250 1 and Octel 250 2 use 5-digit extensions.

Step 7: Define Legacy Message Addressing Scheme

The seventh step is to document the messaging addressing scheme for the legacy voice-mail network. The documentation process is similar to documenting the dial plan. The difference is that the patterns are used to address messages as opposed to route calls. It should be noted that in some environments, the dial plan and the messaging addressing scheme are the same.

One thing to point out here is that a few voice-mail products on the market allow the prefix and the extension to share digits. For example, when addressing a message to a user, the prefix can be 525 and the extensions can be 51042. If the prefix and the extension shared one digit, then the user would need only to dial 5251042 to address a message because one digit, in this case 5, is known to be shared. This shared digit functionality provides greater flexibility when routing messages among nodes. Unity does not support this functionality. Unity, however, has an alternative method that provides the same net result. We discuss that functionality in the "Alternate Extensions" section, later in this chapter.

In Table 12-6, you can see the patterns used to message from each legacy voice-mail node to the others. Take Octel 100 1, for example. The pattern required to send a message to a user on Octel 250 1 is 5251XXX. You might notice that in the diagram, the pattern to Octel 250 1 from Octel 100 1 is expressed as (52)[51]XXX. The bracket portion, [51], represents the shared digits. Noting the shared digits, if any exist, is important because their existence influences the design process.

Table 12-6   *Environment Documentation with the Introduction of Message Addressing*

Location =	Seattle			
Phone Switch =	Avaya G3 1			
Dial Plan =	(DID Prefix) + Extension Range: (206 256) 32XX	(Access Code) + Extension to CallManager Cluster 1: (8 525 1) XXX	(Access Code) + Extension to CallManager Cluster 2: (8 525 2) XXX	(Access Code) + Extension to CallManager Cluster 3: (8 392) 3XXX
Legacy Voicemail =	Octel 100 1			
Extension Length =	4 Digit			
Message Addressing =	4 Digit Extension within Node	(Prefix) + Extension to Octel 250 1: (52)[51] XXX	(Prefix) + Extension to Octel 250 2: (52)[52] XXX	(Prefix) + Extension to Octel 100 2: (392) 3XXX
Location =	San Jose			
Phone Switch =	CallManager Cluster 1			
Dial Plan =	(DID Prefix) + Extension Range: (408 52) 51XXX	(Access Code) + Extension to Avaya G3 1: (8 256) 32XX	(Access Code) + Extension to CallManager Cluster 2: 52XXX	(Access Code) + Extension to CallManager Cluster 3: (8 392) 3XXX
Legacy Voicemail =	Octel 250 1			
Extension Length =	5 Digit			

continues

Table 12-6 *Environment Documentation with the Introduction of Message Addressing (Continued)*

Message Addressing =	5 Digit Extension within Node	(Prefix) + Extension to Octel 100 1: (256) 32XX	(Prefix) + Extension to Octel 250 2: (5) [2] XXX	(Prefix) + Extension to Octel 100 2: (392) 3XXX
Phone Switch =	CallManager Cluster 2			
Dial Plan =	(DID Prefix) + Extension Range: (408 52) 52XXX	(Access Code) + Extension to Avaya G3 1: (8 256) 32XX	(Access Code) + Extension to CallManager Cluster 1: 51XXX	(Access Code) + Extension to CallManager Cluster 3: (8 392) 3XXX
Legacy Voicemail =	Octel 250 2			
Extension Length =	5 Digit			
Message Addressing =	5 Digit Extension within Node	(Prefix) + Extension to Octel 100 1: (256) 32XX	(Prefix) + Extension to Octel 250 1: (5) [1] XXX	(Prefix) + Extension to Octel 100 2: (392) 3XXX
Location =	Research Triangle Park			
Phone Switch =	CallManager Cluster 3			
Dial Plan =	(DID Prefix) + Extension Range: (919 392) 3XXX	(Access Code) + Extension to Avaya G3 1: (8 256) 32XX	(Access Code) + Extension to CallManager Cluster 1: (8 525 1) XXX	(Access Code) + Extension to CallManager Cluster 2: (8 525 2) XXX
Legacy Voicemail =	Octel 100 2			
Extension Length =	4 Digit			
Message Addressing =	4 Digit Extension within Node	(Prefix) + Extension to Octel 100 1: (256) 32XX	(Prefix) + Extension to Octel 250 1: (52)[51] XXX	(Prefix) + Extension to Octel 100 2: (52)[52] XXX

Step 8: Define Each Unity Node

The eighth step in the process is to define each Unity node that is deployed into the environment. Typically, legacy voice-messaging nodes are exchanged one-for-one with new Unity nodes; however, this is not a requirement. It is fine for multiple legacy nodes to be consolidated into one Unity node, or for a legacy node to be split into multiple Unity nodes.

Each node should be documented in relation to the phone switch that it integrates with. In the case where you have a Unity node that services multiple phone switches, it should be treated as if it integrates with each of them. These Unity node entries are used as the framework for the designing phase.

In Table 12-7, there are four Unity nodes that are introduced into the environment. Their names are UNITY-1, UNITY-2, UNITY-3, and UNITY-4. The legacy Octel nodes are swapped one-for-one with the Unity nodes. For example, Octel 100 1 is swapped for UNITY-1, and so on.

Table 12-7 *Environment Documentation with the Introduction of Unity Nodes*

Location =	Seattle			
Phone Switch =	Avaya G3 1			
Dial Plan =	(DID Prefix) + Extension Range: (206 256) 32XX	(Access Code) + Extension to CallManager Cluster 1: (8 525 1) XXX	(Access Code) + Extension to CallManager Cluster 2: (8 525 2) XXX	(Access Code) + Extension to CallManager Cluster 3: (8 392) 3XXX
Legacy Voicemail =	Octel 100 1			
Extension Length =	4 Digit			
Message Addressing =	4 Digit Extension within Node	(Prefix) + Extension to Octel 250 1: (52)[51] XXX	(Prefix) + Extension to Octel 250 2: (52)[52] XXX	(Prefix) + Extension to Octel 100 2: (392) 3XXX
Unity Voicemail =	UNITY-1			
Location =	San Jose			
Phone Switch =	CallManager Cluster 1			
Dial Plan =	(DID Prefix) + Extension Range: (408 52) 51XXX	(Access Code) + Extension to Avaya G3 1: (8 256) 32XX	(Access Code) + Extension to CallManager Cluster 2: 52XXX	(Access Code) + Extension to CallManager Cluster 3: (8 392) 3XXX
Legacy Voicemail =	Octel 250 1			
Extension Length =	5 Digit			
Message Addressing =	5 Digit Extension within Node	(Prefix) + Extension to Octel 100 1: (256) 32XX	(Prefix) + Extension to Octel 250 2: (5) [2] XXX	(Prefix) + Extension to Octel 100 2: (392) 3XXX

continues

Table 12-7 *Environment Documentation with the Introduction of Unity Nodes (Continued)*

Unity Voicemail =	UNITY-2			
Phone Switch =	CallManager Cluster 2			
Dial Plan =	(DID Prefix) + Extension Range: (408 52) 52XXX	(Access Code) + Extension to Avaya G3 1: (8 256) 32XX	(Access Code) + Extension to CallManager Cluster 1: 51XXX	(Access Code) + Extension to CallManager Cluster 3: (8 392) 3XXX
Legacy Voicemail =	Octel 250 2			
Extension Length =	5 Digit			
Message Addressing =	5 Digit Extension within Node	(Prefix) + Extension to Octel 100 1: (256) 32XX	(Prefix) + Extension to Octel 250 1: (5) [1] XXX	(Prefix) + Extension to Octel 100 2: (392) 3XXX
Unity Voicemail =	UNITY-3			
Location =	Research Triangle Park			
Phone Switch =	CallManager Cluster 3			
Dial Plan =	(DID Prefix) + Extension Range: (919 392) 3XXX	(Access Code) + Extension to Avaya G3 1: (8 256) 32XX	(Access Code) + Extension to CallManager Cluster 1: (8 525 1) XXX	(Access Code) + Extension to CallManager Cluster 2: (8 525 2) XXX
Legacy Voicemail =	Octel 100 2			
Extension Length =	4 Digit			
Message Addressing =	4 Digit Extension within Node	(Prefix) + Extension to Octel 100 1: (256) 32XX	(Prefix) + Extension to Octel 250 1: (52)[51] XXX	(Prefix) + Extension to Octel 100 2: (52)[52] XXX
Unity Voicemail =	UNITY-4			

Step 9: Define Unity Node Extension Length

The ninth step is to define the extension length that each of the Unity nodes assumes. The extension length used within the Unity nodes should be the same length that was used within the legacy voice-messaging node or nodes that it replaces.

Table 12-8 shows that in the fictitious environment, each of the new Unity nodes assumes the role of a previous Octel node. As such, each Unity node uses the same extension length that its predecessor used. For example, UNITY-1 uses a 4-digit extension length because its predecessor Octel 100 1 used a 4-digit extension length.

Table 12-8 *Environment Documentation with the Introduction of Extension Length for Unity Nodes*

Location =	Seattle			
Phone Switch =	Avaya G3 1			
Dial Plan =	(DID Prefix) + Extension Range: (206 256) 32XX	(Access Code) + Extension to CallManager Cluster 1: (8 525 1) XXX	(Access Code) + Extension to CallManager Cluster 2: (8 525 2) XXX	(Access Code) + Extension to CallManager Cluster 3: (8 392) 3XXX
Legacy Voicemail =	Octel 100 1			
Extension Length =	4 Digit			
Message Addressing =	4 Digit Extension within Node	(Prefix) + Extension to Octel 250 1: (52)[51] XXX	(Prefix) + Extension to Octel 250 2: (52)[52] XXX	(Prefix) + Extension to Octel 100 2: (392) 3XXX
Unity Voicemail =	UNITY-1			
Extension Length =	4 Digit			
Location =	San Jose			
Phone Switch =	CallManager Cluster 1			
Dial Plan =	(DID Prefix) + Extension Range: (408 52) 51XXX	(Access Code) + Extension to Avaya G3 1: (8 256) 32XX	(Access Code) + Extension to CallManager Cluster 2: 52XXX	(Access Code) + Extension to CallManager Cluster 3: (8 392) 3XXX
Legacy Voicemail =	Octel 250 1			
Extension Length =	5 Digit			
Message Addressing =	5 Digit Extension within Node	(Prefix) + Extension to Octel 100 1: (256) 32XX	(Prefix) + Extension to Octel 250 2: (5) [2] XXX	(Prefix) + Extension to Octel 100 2: (392) 3XXX

continues

Table 12-8 *Environment Documentation with the Introduction of Extension Length for Unity Nodes (Continued)*

Unity Voicemail =	UNITY-2			
Extension Length =	5 Digit			
Phone Switch =	CallManager Cluster 2			
Dial Plan =	(DID Prefix) + Extension Range: (408 52) 52XXX	(Access Code) + Extension to Avaya G3 1: (8 256) 32XX	(Access Code) + Extension to CallManager Cluster 1: 51XXX	(Access Code) + Extension to CallManager Cluster 3: (8 392) 3XXX
Legacy Voicemail =	Octel 250 2			
Extension Length =	5 Digit			
Message Addressing =	5 Digit Extension within Node	(Prefix) + Extension to Octel 100 1: (256) 32XX	(Prefix) + Extension to Octel 250 1: (5) [1] XXX	(Prefix) + Extension to Octel 100 2: (392) 3XXX
Unity Voicemail =	UNITY-3			
Extension Length =	5 Digit			
Location =	Research Triangle Park			
Phone Switch =	CallManager Cluster 3			
Dial Plan =	(DID Prefix) + Extension Range: (919 392) 3XXX	(Access Code) + Extension to Avaya G3 1: (8 256) 32XX	(Access Code) + Extension to CallManager Cluster 1: (8 525 1) XXX	(Access Code) + Extension to CallManager Cluster 2: (8 525 2) XXX
Legacy Voicemail =	Octel 100 2			
Extension Length =	4 Digit			
Message Addressing =	4 Digit Extension within Node	(Prefix) + Extension to Octel 100 1: (256) 32XX	(Prefix) + Extension to Octel 250 1: (52)[51] XXX	(Prefix) + Extension to Octel 100 2: (52)[52] XXX
Unity Voicemail =	UNITY-4			
Extension Length =	4 Digit			

Step 10: Define Legacy Distribution Lists

The last step is to document the legacy distribution lists and membership. Now this could prove to be somewhat of a challenge for a large environment. It is not a reasonable expectation for an architect to write down the names of 500 members of a distribution list. Especially when you consider that there could be several distribution lists of this size, or larger, in an organization. For now, you should get a rough idea of how many distribution lists exist, their names, extensions, what their purpose is, and how vital they are to the organization.

You might find yourself in a position where you have a large number of distribution lists, of which each has a significant number of members, which must be migrated over. If you do, you will be happy to know that there is an option available to assist in porting them over. The option is a tool called the Public Distribution List Builder. In the "Designing the Digital Network" section we discuss its use.

In Table 12-9, you see that the fictitious environment has nine distribution lists. Out of these nine lists, the departmental list, Sales, Marketing, Support, Engineering, and HR are not considered required. All others are required.

Table 12-9   *Table of Environment Distribution Lists*

Distribution Lists	Purpose	Extension	Required
All Employees	Company Wide Announcements	8000	Yes
Sales	Sales Announcements	8005	No
Marketing	Marketing Announcements	8010	No
Support	Support Announcements	8015	No
Engineering	Engineering Announcements	8020	No
HR	HR Announcements	8025	No
Seattle	Regional Announcements	8030	Yes
San Jose	Regional Announcements	8035	Yes
Research Triangle Park	Regional Announcements	8040	Yes

Designing the Digital Network

Finally, we have reached the point where the rubber meets the road, the design phase. After reading through the previous mind-numbing pages of techno babble, it is probably a good idea for us to pause to remember the true purpose of Unity. Unity is a communication tool and nothing more. We often find ourselves forgetting this when we get too deep into the technical side of Digital Networking. Try not to fall into the same trap.

Now that you are thinking of Unity as a communication tool again, we can discuss what makes a Digital Network successful. The success of a Digital Network is ultimately measured by the quality of the end user experience. Therefore, as you design a Digital Network, your goal should be for its features to be easy to use and intuitive. Doing so ensures that you get the most out of Unity as a communication tool. As such, the approach taken to design is focused around optimal end user experience as opposed to documenting every possible way to skin a cat.

Documenting the Design

The features of Digital Networking are configured through a series of properties. With the exception of public distribution lists, the feature properties are all set on a per-node basis. Therefore, as we go through the features and their properties, the values that we determine to be appropriate must be documented on a per-node basis. The same spreadsheet used to document the environment is the most logical place to document the design of the new Digital Network. This keeps all of the data in one place.

Define Extension Length

The rule of thumb is that the minimum extension length should remain at the default of 3 or above. Using less than three has the potential to cause conflicts with the dial keys assigned to private distribution lists. Those dial keys can range from 1 to 20.

Check your spreadsheet to see if there are any legacy voice-messaging nodes that support 2-digit extensions in the environment. If there are, verify that there are not extensions in the 1 to 20 range. If extensions do exist within that range, they must be changed to something else to avoid overlap. If you find that the default value of 3 digits is lower than your actual minimum, you can opt to bump it up. This is not a requirement, but doing so prevents an administrator from accidentally adding a user with a lower value.

After you have determined the minimum extension length for each Unity node, you can document it.

Table 12-10   *Environment Documentation with Introduction of Minimum Extension Length*

Unity Voice Mail =	UNITY-1	UNITY-2	UNITY-3	UNITY-4
Extension Length =	4 Digit	5 Digit	5 Digit	4 Digit
Min. Extension Length =	4	5	5	4

I chose to set the minimum extension length parameter for each node to the actual minimum. Although I did not need to bump the minimum extension length up to the actual minimum, I did because it is never a bad idea to prevent accidental mistakes. The minimum extension can be set with the Advanced Settings tools.

Define the Dialing Domains

When designing dialing domains, the best practice is to include all possible nodes into the same one. Including all possible nodes into the same dialing domain opens the door to the best possible functionality. Occasionally, I find organizations trying to use dialing domains as a way to segment their directory. This really is not what they are intended for and they do not do a very good job at it as a result.

Defining dialing domains is straightforward once you have the dial plan documented. Remember, the two requirements are that extensions cannot overlap within a dialing domain and access codes must not be required to dial between extensions within a dialing domain. Again, we call this transparent dialing. All Unity nodes that adhere to these two rules should be joined to the same dialing domain.

If you have some Unity nodes that do not match up with any others, it is not a bad idea to go ahead and put them in their own dialing domain. Doing so does not change any functionality; however, it is advised in case the environment changes down the line. By assigning each node to a dialing domain from the beginning, you can join Unity nodes together down the road and the dialing domain will already be available in the directory. This avoids having to wait for replication to occur.

The actual name given to a dialing domain is arbitrary and is seen only by administrators. When picking a name, keep in mind that dialing domains are not bound to physical locations or specific phone switches. Therefore, a dialing domain name should not include references to either because each Unity nodes' relation to a physical location or phone switch can change over time. The recommendation is to keep the name simple. I use the naming convention DD followed by a number. For example, I useDD1, DD2, DD3, and so on. It gets the job done, it is simple, and it does not have to change over time.

We have extension overlap and access codes to deal with. The only nodes that can be combined into the same dialing domain are UNITY-2 and UNITY-3 because there is no overlap and access codes are not required to dial between extensions on each. They are both members of DD2. The other nodes, UNITY-1 and UNITY-4, will be added to their own dialing domains. They are added to DD1 and DD3, respectively (see Table 12-11).

Table 12-11   *Environment Documentation with the Introduction of Dialing Domains*

Unity Voice Mail =	UNITY-1	UNITY-2	UNITY-3	UNITY-4
Extension Length =	4 Digit	5 Digit	5 Digit	4 Digit
Min. Extension Length =	4	5	5	4
Dialing Domain =	DD1	DD2	DD2	DD3

Message Addressing

There are four pieces to the message addressing design puzzle that must be defined: the address scope, addressing by extension, addressing by name, and the preferred addressing method.

Addressing Scope

The first step in designing the message address scheme for a Digital Network is to determine the search scope (see Table 12-12). This value should always be set to Global Directory on all Unity nodes. Setting the Search Scope to Global allows any subscriber to address a message to another other subscriber in the entire Digital Network. Setting it to anything lower prevents communication between subscribers of different nodes or dialing domains. Plus, setting it lower and forcing a user to call on the phone or send an e-mail contradicts the whole idea of networking. So again, the value should be set to Global on all nodes.

Table 12-12   *Environment Documentation with the Introduction of Search Scope*

Unity Voice Mail =	UNITY-1	UNITY-2	UNITY-3	UNITY-4
Extension Length =	4 Digit	5 Digit	5 Digit	4 Digit
Min. Extension Length =	4	5	5	4
Dialing Domain =	DD1	DD2	DD2	DD3
Search Scope =	Global	Global	Global	Global

The search scope itself is set from the addressing portion of the primary location object in the SA.

Addressing by Extension

In the spirit of focusing on the end-user experience, it usually is best to preserve the legacy method of message addressing. Doing so helps to avoid costly end-user retraining and overall confusion. This is the approach we take to designing message addressing by extension.

There are essentially two different ways to address a message by extension. The first is for the digits entered to explicitly match either a primary or alternate extension. If an explicit match cannot be found, then the second method is called. The second method takes the digits entered and tries to match them to a subscriber's primary or alternate extension at a location's extension.

Using the first method to explicitly match entered digits is preferred because it provides the most flexibility while reducing the possibility of addressing overlap. The idea behind explicit addressing is simple. Everybody gets at least one globally unique extension, which others can use to address messages to them. Since everybody has a unique extension, primary location objects are not required at all for addressing. Because of these advantages, this is the method we will run with and it is considered a best practice.

Even though we have determined that we will not use primary delivery locations for addressing, we still need to give them a little attention. As you may recall, primary location objects are required to have a 3-digit extension by default. Because the extension can cause overlap, we need to set the minimum extension length for location objects to 0 and not assign an extension to any. These choices should be documented as well (see Table 12-13).

Table 12-13   *Environment Documentation with the Introduction of Location Object DN*

Unity Voice Mail =	UNITY-1	UNITY-2	UNITY-3	UNITY-4
Extension Length =	4 Digit	5 Digit	5 Digit	4 Digit
Min. Extension Length =	4	5	5	4
Dialing Domain =	DD1	DD2	DD2	DD3
Search Scope =	Global	Global	Global	Global
Min Location Object DN Length =	0	0	0	0
Location Object DN =	Null	Null	Null	Null

The minimum extension length for primary location objects can be set with the Advanced Settings tool.

To preserve the legacy method of message addressing, most organizations need to leverage alternate extensions, which provide globally unique extensions to each user. If you find yourself in the lucky position where you will not need to use alternate extensions to maintain the legacy method of message addressing, you can skip ahead to the "Addressing by Name" section. For all others, please continue on.

When we define alternate extensions for addressing, we do not do so on a per-subscriber basis. That approach is far too tedious. Instead, we summarize the extra digits that subscribers on different nodes must dial to send them a message. We like to call the results of the summary an alternate extension prefix. We use this name because each subscriber needs an alternate extension comprised of the prefix and their primary extension for this model to work. For example, Seattle has an extension range of 32XX and subscribers in San Jose and the Research Triangle Park address messages to them using 2563XXX. In this example, 256 would be the alternate extension prefix and each subscriber would need an alternate extension of 25632XX.

To determine the alternate extension prefix needed for each Unity node, you must examine how messages are addressed to its subscribers in the legacy environment. Anything a subscriber has to dial on top of the primary extension becomes the alternate extension prefix. In most cases, there is only one alternate extension prefix required to preserve the legacy method of message addressing. If you find that different nodes use different addressing methods to send a message to the same destination, you should not sweat it. You just need to add multiple alternate extension prefixes to each node and then double-check to make sure the alternate extensions are not going to overlap. In the rare event that they overlap, something needs to give.

One other thing that you might want to consider when you design your alternate extension strategy is your ideal messaging address situation. Remember that each user can have a total of nine alternate extensions. If you were to use a method in your legacy environment that does not follow any particular logic, you can keep that legacy method and define a more logical one at the same time. Perhaps one based on 10-digit globally unique extensions. This way, users still get the functionality they are accustomed to while they are introduced to the new, more logical method. See Table 12-14.

Table 12-14   *Environment Documentation with the Introduction of Alternate Extension Prefixes*

Unity Voice Mail =	UNITY-1	UNITY-2	UNITY-3	UNITY-4
Extension Length =	4 Digit	5 Digit	5 Digit	4 Digit
Min. Extension Length =	4	5	5	4
Dialing domain =	DD1	DD2	DD2	DD3
Search Scope =	Global	Global	Global	Global
Min Location Object DN Length =	0	0	0	0
Location Object DN =	Null	Null	Null	Null
Alternate Extension Prefix =	256XXXX	51XXXXX	52XXXXX	392XXXX

In our demonstration environment, the prefix used to address messages to a node is consistent across all other nodes in the environment. For example, the pattern 256XXXX is used to address a message from Octel 250 1, Octel 250 2, and Octel 100 2 to Octel 100 1 in Seattle. Therefore, all users on UNITY-1, which replaces Octel 100 1, will have their primary 4-digit extension and a 7-digit extension begin with 256 and end with their primary extension. Using 7-digit alternate extensions that are the same as the users' phone numbers is a logical addressing scheme. As such, no other alternate extensions are required at this time.

Bulk Edit has powerful options that can be used to assist with adding and removing alternate extensions. You can download the latest copy and complete documentation from http://www.ciscounitytools.com.

Addressing by Name

Addressing by name is relatively simple from a design standpoint. Either you want to allow it or you do not. Most organizations want to allow it because it is a simple way for subscribers to address messages. The only exception is when there is an excessive number of users with the same name. This is a rare situation reserved for only the largest organizations.

If you find yourself in the majority and would like to allow addressing by name, it is a good idea to force users to be available in the directory. This can be achieved by turning on List in Phone Directory for each subscriber template (it is on by default), and Subscribers Cannot Change this Setting for Themselves for the Directory Listing setting on the corresponding class of service (CoS). Setting these forces new subscribers to be present in the directory once they have a recorded name and it prevents them from removing themselves. In the event that somebody does need to be removed from the directory, you are covered. An administrator can go in and manually remove a single user if the need arises.

If you find yourself in the extremely rare situation where you need to disable addressing by name, you can do so. Again, this is not recommended. Turning off Addressing By Name also prevents subscribers from adding other subscribers to a private distribution list by name over the phone. If you still feel that you need to turn it off, you need to turn off Enable Spelled Name Search from the System Configuration page. The setting is on a per-server basis so you will need to set it on all nodes within the Digital Network.

From Table 12-15, you can see that for the demonstration environment we want subscribers to be able to address each other by name and we don't want to allow subscribers to remove themselves from the directory.

Table 12-15   *Environment Documentation with Introduction of Address by Name Allowed and for Subscribers into Directory*

Unity Voice Mail =	UNITY-1	UNITY-2	UNITY-3	UNITY-4
Extension Length =	4 Digit	5 Digit	5 Digit	4 Digit
Min. Extension Length =	4	5	5	4
Dialing Domain =	DD1	DD2	DD2	DD3
Search Scope =	Global	Global	Global	Global
Min Location Object DN Length =	0	0	0	0
Location Object DN =	Null	Null	Null	Null
Alternate Extension Prefix =	256XXXX	51XXXX	52XXXX	392XXXX
Address By Name Allowed =	Yes	Yes	Yes	Yes
Force Subscribers into Directory =	Yes	Yes	Yes	Yes

Preferred Addressing Method

After you have developed a plan for addressing by extensions and addressing by name, you should choose which you prefer users to use. You see, when addressing a message, the addressing conversation instructs the user to spell by name to enter an extension. Addressing by name can be configured as last name first, or as first name last. The default is to address by name, last name first. Also, users can always hit ## to change between name and extension address modes. However, users usually choose to address using the method that is automatically presented.

This, of course, is assuming that you are going to allow both name and extension address. If you chose not to allow addressing by name, then they are stuck with addressing by extension as their only choice.

Choosing the preferred method is a matter of preference. Some organizations prefer addressing by extensions and others by name. However, it should be pointed out that the larger an organization gets, the more difficult addressing by name gets. Further more, choosing to address by first name last is rarely a good idea. You will almost certainly run into issues so it should be avoided completely.

After eliminating first name then last as a possibility, you have last name first and by extension as your only viable options. Either could work for most organizations. However, as an organization gets larger, last name conflict becomes more prevalent. The rule of thumb is to set the default addressing method to extension if the organization has more than 2500 subscribers. But this is just a suggested threshold. There is no hard and fast rule to determine when addressing by name becomes too cumbersome.

To change the preferred addressing method from the default of last name first to extension requires an update to each subscriber template. After the change is made, all new subscribers that are created will have the preferred method set. Because only new subscribers get this setting, take care to configure the templates before adding users to the new Unity nodes.

It should be noted that a subscriber with access to the UPCA will be able to change the addressing mode to his individual preference. There is no way to prevent this other than disallowing UPCA access. This really should not be a problem. If he begins to have issues with addressing he already knows where to change it back.

Table 12-16 is pretty simple. We will say that there are 5000 subscribers in the demonstration environment, and for that size organization, addressing by extension is usually best.

Table 12-16   *Environment Documentation with the Introduction of Preferred Addressing Type*

Unity Voice Mail =	UNITY-1	UNITY-2	UNITY-3	UNITY-4
Extension Length =	4 Digit	5 Digit	5 Digit	4 Digit
Min. Extension Length =	4	5	5	4
Dialing Domain =	DD1	DD2	DD2	DD3

Table 12-16 *Environment Documentation with the Introduction of Preferred Addressing Type (Continued)*

Search Scope =	Global	Global	Global	Global
Min Location Object DN Length =	0	0	0	0
Location Object DN =	Null	Null	Null	Null
Alternate Extension Prefix =	256XXXX	51XXXXX	52XXXXX	392XXXX
Address By Name Allowed =	Yes	Yes	Yes	Yes
Force Subscribers into Directory =	Yes	Yes	Yes	Yes
Preferred Addressing Type =	Extension	Extension	Extension	Extension

Automated Attendant

The automated attendant functionality is a combination of two different features that together allow outside callers to contact a subscriber by extension or name. Each of the features function independently from the other; however, they both share a common set of caveats. After a quick refresher on the functionality, we look how to design the features.

Transfer by Extension

During the greeting portion of any call or subscriber handler, a caller can enter the extension of the subscriber they want to contact. This, of course, assumes that the handler is configured to allow the caller to do so. The scope used to match the caller input to a subscriber can be set to either the local node or to the dialing domain.

Setting the scope to the dialing domain allows a caller to dial into any Unity node within the domain and release to switch transfer to any subscriber within the domain, regardless of the node that they are associated with. Setting the scope to the dialing domain also opens the opportunity for other functionality. For example, if an organization has a particular site with thousands of users, it might be desirable to have a large 72-port Unity node that handles only automated attendant functionality.

The down side to setting the scope to the dialing domain is that functionality is lost. With the scope set at the dialing domain, only release to switch transfers are possible if the destination subscriber is not local. This means that call screening, call holding, and so on are not available if the target subscriber is homed on a different Unity node.

Choosing which is more important is left to the needs of the organization. Most organizations choose to set the scope to the dialing domain. Regardless of which you choose, consistency must be maintained to prevent end-user confusion. Remember that most subscribers are not familiar with the ins and outs of Unity. If a subscriber were to configure

Unity to send callers directly to their mailbox, they would likely be confused when they find that callers are still getting transferred to their phone. If you are going to set the scope to the dialing domain, there are a few settings that should be in place to maintain consistency.

The first thing you need to ensure is that each subscriber's transfer extension gets populated to the directory. By default, the value is not populated to the directory until call transfer has been enabled. To ensure that it is enabled for all subscribers, you want to set the Call Transfer option for each subscriber template. The templates should have Yes, Ring Subscriber's Extension enabled. After this is set, subscribers created with this template will automatically have their transfer extension populated into the directory. You also want confirm that the transfer type is set to release to switch transfer and not supervised transfer on each template. This is the default setting for the templates and it should not be changed if the scope is set to the dialing domain.

The other thing that you want to do for consistency is remove the "please wait while I transfer your call" prompt. This prompt is played only if the call is transferred to a subscriber that is homed on the node. If the transfer is going to a subscriber on another node, Unity transfers the call immediately and the caller will hear ring back only, no prompt. It is not the end of the world if you do not remove it, but it is good for do for consistency. Details on how to remove the prompt are covered in Chapter 18, "Audio-Text Applications."

The auto attendant search scope itself can be set using the Advanced Settings utility.

Directory Handler

A directory handler is an alpha directory that outside callers can use to contact subscribers. A directory handler can be configured to search for matching subscribers using a variety of different methods. Two of these search methods allow callers to search for subscribers homed on another Unity node in the dialing domain. Those search options are dialing domain and public distribution list. All of the other search options look for subscriber homed on the Unity node only. When designing the search options, it is important to be clear that even though the members of a public distribution list can be subscribers for any dialing domain in the Digital Network, the directory handler checks to ensure that the subscriber requested is homed on a node within the same dialing domain.

Some organizations choose to avoid directory handlers all together because it provides a way for outsiders to get the name of their staff. This is a completely reasonable concern. If your organization does not feel comfortable providing an alpha directory to outside callers, then you do not have to. If you do want to provide one, then you need to consider the scope that it should search at.

If you chose to set the Transfer by Extension scope to dialing domain, the most logical choice is to provide a directory handler to outside callers that use the same search scope. If you chose to keep the Transfer by Extension scope at the local server level, then you will want to do the same for the directory handler provided to outside callers. There is nothing that says you can set only the directory handler scope to dialing domain if the Transfer by Extension is also set to dialing domain. Mismatching like this does not make a sense, and would not be a best practice, but it is not an illegal configuration. If you decide that you want to do this, make sure to add the same consistency settings that were introduced in the "Transfer by Extension" section.

Table 12-17 shows that callers should be able to transfer to any subscriber in the dialing domain by name or extension. Now this works across UNITY-2 and UNITY-3 only because they are the only ones that share the same dialing domain. We still set UNITY-1 and UNITY-4 to dialing domain in case their membership changes down the line. Also, we aim for consistency so we remove the transfer prompt and set the transfer type to Release to Switch.

Table 12-17   *Environment Documentation with the Introduction of Transfer and Auto Attendant Search Scope*

Unity Voice Mail =	UNITY-1	UNITY-2	UNITY-3	UNITY-4
Extension Length =	4 Digit	5 Digit	5 Digit	4 Digit
Min. Extension Length =	4	5	5	4
Dialing Domain =	DD1	DD2	DD2	DD3
Search Scope =	Global	Global	Global	Global
Min Location Object DN Length =	0	0	0	0
Location Object DN =	Null	Null	Null	Null
Alternate Extension Prefix =	256XXXX	51XXXX	52XXXX	392XXXX
Address By Name Allowed =	Yes	Yes	Yes	Yes
Force Subscribers into Directory =	Yes	Yes	Yes	Yes
Preferred Addressing Type =	Extension	Extension	Extension	Extension
Directory Handler Scope =	Dialing Domain	Dialing Domain	Dialing Domain	Dialing Domain
Call Transfer Turned On =	Yes	Yes	Yes	Yes
Call Transfer Type =	Release to Switch	Release to Switch	Release to Switch	Release to Switch
Remove Transfer Prompt =	Yes	Yes	Yes	Yes
Auto Attendant Scope =	Dialing Domain	Dialing Domain	Dialing Domain	Dialing Domain

Pooled Licensing

There are not too many factors to consider when it comes to pooled licensing. Each Digital Network can have one and only one license pool and the Unity nodes within the Digital Network can either be a member of the pool or not. It is that simple.

Most organizations want to use pooled licensing because it is more flexible than the traditional method. The added flexibility allows licenses to be allocated more efficiently, which ultimately drives down the total cost of ownership. Because saving money is always a good idea, pooled licensing is a practical choice.

The downside to pooled licensing is that there is only a single pool. If an organization has several departments or units and each is responsible for licensing, pooled licensing might not be good option. There is no way to segment out who does and does not get to use the licenses. Like it or not, licenses end up getting shared across internal boundaries, which can cause conflict. If an organization is divided in such a way, pooled licensing should be avoided.

In Table 12-18, you can see that our organization likes to save money as much as the next and there is no internal divisions to contend with. Therefore, pooled licensing is a good fit.

Table 12-18   *Environment Documentation with the Introduction of Pooled Licensing*

Unity Voice Mail =	UNITY-1	UNITY-2	UNITY-3	UNITY-4
Extension Length =	4 Digit	5 Digit	5 Digit	4 Digit
Min. Extension Length =	4	5	5	4
Dialing Domain =	DD1	DD2	DD2	DD3
Search Scope =	Global	Global	Global	Global
Min Location Object DN Length =	0	0	0	0
Location Object DN =	Null	Null	Null	Null
Alternate Extension Prefix =	256XXXX	51XXXX	52XXXX	392XXXX
Address By Name Allowed =	Yes	Yes	Yes	Yes
Force Subscribers into Directory =	Yes	Yes	Yes	Yes
Preferred Addressing Type =	Extension	Extension	Extension	Extension
Directory Handler Scope =	Dialing Domain	Dialing Domain	Dialing Domain	Dialing Domain
Call Transfer Turned On =	Yes	Yes	Yes	Yes
Call Transfer Type =	Release to Switch	Release to Switch	Release to Switch	Release to Switch
Remove Transfer Prompt =	Yes	Yes	Yes	Yes
Auto Attendant Scope =	Dialing Domain	Dialing Domain	Dialing Domain	Dialing Domain
Pooled Licensing =	Yes	Yes	Yes	Yes

Public Distribution Lists

Public distribution lists present some unique design challenges. Determining which public distribution lists are needed is the easy part. Designing them in such a way that they do not cause conflict in the dial plan, populating the members, and controlling who can and cannot send messages to them is a little more difficult. Let us break these designing challenges down one by one and design a new public distribution lists.

Public Distribution List Extensions

You may recall that public distribution lists are not homed to one particular Unity node like subscribers are. This means that they are always treated as if they are local for administrative and addressing purposes. Public distribution lists are not required to have an extension like subscribers are. However, if the organization requires that they do, it can open the door to possible conflict within the dial plan. Because public distribution lists are not homed to one node, their extensions are not forced to be unique. So if a subscriber and a public distribution list are given the same extension, they will be in conflict with each other. Therefore, public distribution lists must be carefully designed to avoid this situation.

The best practice for assigning extension to public distribution lists is to set aside a range of extensions that do not conflict with the dial plan for their exclusive use. A recommended range is 00XXX. This range is recommended because there is a low probability of an organization using or adding a new extension range that conflicts.

There is some legacy functionality they can force an organization to go down a path other than the best practice. If you find yourself in a position where you cannot set a new range aside for public distribution lists, you need to determine if there will be a conflict within the dial plan. You can do so by comparing the extension ranges used within the dial plan with the extension assigned to each legacy distribution list. If the extension for a legacy distribution list is part of any range, there is a high possibility of conflict. In this situation, the new public distribution list should really be assigned an extension, which is not part of any range in the dial plan, even if the exact extension is not in use. This is the safest way to avoid conflict down the line. If you still have your heart set on using the same extension, you need to see if the extension is in use. If it is, the current owner needs to be assigned a new extension. After you have determined that the extension is not in use, it can be assigned.

You might have read between the lines during this section and noticed another issue that can possibly arise. The issue is that by default, any administrator on any Unity node in the Digital Network can assign an extension to a public distribution list. Because the extension is not checked for overlap, the door is left wide-open for an administrator to cause overlap. The potential for error can be mitigated by controlling administrative access to public distribution lists. The best practice is to give the least amount of administrators possible edit rights for public distribution lists. This is controlled through the CoS. For the administrators that are assigned these rights, it is important that they understand the implications of public distribution list extensions.

Populating Public Distribution Lists

The more members a public distribution list has, the more difficult it is to get them populated. Other than manually doing the job, there are few ways that you can populate public distribution lists in bulk. Those ways are to import an existing distribution list through the use of subscriber templates or with the aid of the Public Distribution List Builder utility.

Import an Existing Distribution List

There is no doubt that the easiest way to populate a public distribution list is to not do it at all. If you integrate Unity with an existing messaging infrastructure, there will already be several e-mail distribution lists present. Many organizations find that their e-mail distribution lists and their legacy voice-messaging distribution lists are essentially the same. In this situation, it makes sense to import the e-mail distribution lists into Unity rather than duplicating them.

This is by far the most simplistic way to handle the population of public distribution lists. Unfortunately, the existing e-mail distribution lists do not always match up nicely with the legacy voice messaging distribution lists that must be ported over. If you find this to be the case, you will want to leverage those that do match up and then use subscriber templates and/or the Public Distribution List Builder utility for the remaining.

Subscriber Templates

Among other things, a subscriber template includes a list of public distribution lists. When a subscriber is created, they are automatically added to each public distribution list defined within the template. This presents an opportunity for organizations that have a simple distribution list structure to automatically assign subscribers to the appropriate public distribution lists. For example, you can create a template for each department or unit within the organization and assign the corresponding public distribution list to it. Also, because a Unity node usually services only a single location, all templates on that node can have a location-oriented public distribution list defined, such as San Jose, if that is a requirement.

What you want to avoid here is the urge to get subscriber-template happy. Although you are not limited in the number of subscriber templates that you can create, remember that you must define, add, and maintain each of them. If the distribution list needs of the organization do not fit into a subscriber template strategy, then do not force it. Instead, use them where they do fit and leverage the Public Distribution List Builder for where they don't.

Public Distribution List Builder

The Public Distribution List Builder is a utility that can help with the task of populating subscribers into public distribution lists. With the Public Distribution List Builder, subscribers can be added to a public distribution list through a variety of methods including by CoS membership, switch assignment, extension range information, imported by extension or alias from a CSV file, or picked manually from a list. The public distribution list that subscribers are added to can either be an existing list or the utility can create a new list on the fly. In all, the Public Distribution List Builder is a flexible tool. But of all the different methods available, one is by far the most powerful for porting legacy distribution lists with a large number of subscribers over to public distribution lists. That method is importing by extension from a CSV file.

The idea behind importing by extension from a CSV file is not anything too spectacular. Basically, if you can dump the extensions of the legacy distribution list members to a file, then you can use it to add them to the new public distribution list. Unfortunately, you might need to get the vendor or a reseller involved to help get this done, but it will save you a lot of time and man-hours.

One limitation to note is that the Public Distribution List Builder works only with Exchange as the messaging backend. This can be with Exchange 5.5, 2000, or mixed mode. If you are using Lotus Domino for your messaging backend, you cannot use the Public Distribution List Builder.

You can obtain the latest version of the Public Distribution List Builder and documentation on its use from http://www.ciscounitytools.com.

Controlling Access

Controlling who can and cannot send messages to public distribution lists is important for medium-to large-sized organizations. Often times, organizations have several public distribution lists that have hundreds or even thousands of subscribers. Now imagine what it would be like if every disgruntled employee at an organization of 25,000 could send a message to all of them. Or imagine if a message that is sensitive in nature could be sent to all by accident. Neither of these situations is desirable. Luckily, there are a couple different techniques that you can use to avoid this type of situation.

There are two different levels for which you can apply restrictions to who can and cannot send messages to a public distribution list. At the highest level, you can control which subscribers can and cannot send messages to a public distribution list using the TUI. This is controlled by users through CoS and it is an all or nothing setting. Either subscribers can address messages to public distribution lists or they cannot. And if it is allowed, which it is by default, the subscriber can address a message to any public distribution list within the entire Digital Network. At this level there is no concept of granularity. Now, once the message has been addressed to a public distribution list, Unity submits it to the messaging infrastructure for delivery, which is where the lower-level access comes into place.

Exchange and Domain both allow you to control who can and cannot send messages to an e-mail distribution list in a much more granular manner. Because public distribution lists are e-mail distribution lists, the rights are transparent across both. The process used by Unity to submit a message for delivery to a public distribution list allows these rights to be respected. So if a user tries to address a message to a blocked public distribution list, the message is returned as undeliverable. Also, for sites that use Unified Messaging, setting the rights at this level prevents subscribers from sending to the public distribution list through an e-mail client. For these reasons, setting the rights from within the messaging infrastructure is the best practice.

Summary

From here you should have the knowledge required to design a successful Digital Network. As you go through these steps, make sure to take your time, and be as diligent as possible with documenting the environment you are migrating from and the environment you are migrating to. If you need any assistance or clarification, please feel free to post your questions to the Networking Professionals (NetPro) forum for Unified Communications. NetPro is available at:

http://www.cisco.com/go/netpro

Please keep in mind that as Unity evolves, there will be new networking features to consider. It is wise to review the latest Digital Networking guide at www.cisco.com before beginning your design. It is also critical that you validate your design in a lab prior to deployment to avoid any surprises. Best of luck!

CHAPTER **13**

Unity with Microsoft Exchange

This chapter discusses how to plan for, design, and deploy a solution using Unity with Microsoft Exchange. Topics covered in this chapter are:

- The characteristics of Exchange
- Unity's perspective of Exchange and what it needs
- Planning a Unity installation
- Planning to administer Unity with Exchange
- Designing for sustainable operations
- How to deploy Unity with Exchange

The chapter also discusses some important operational aspects of Unity with Exchange. After reading this chapter you will be able to:

- Identify the key components that Unity uses for each version of Exchange.
- Identify how Unity sees Exchange.
- Identify ways to plan for a Unity installation with Exchange.
- Identify how to design a solution with Unity for Exchange.
- Identify how Unity is deployed to service Exchange mailboxes.

Before you read this chapter, it is strongly recommended that you have an understanding of how MS Exchange messaging solutions are designed and how each version of MS Exchange works with its intended directory. You also need to understand how the Outlook messaging client interacts with Exchange.

The Characteristics of MS Exchange

Naturally, because Unity is a Cisco product, you will want to hear about Unity from Cisco as the authority on its own product. The same holds for Microsoft Exchange and everything its use entails: Windows domains, Active Directory, and Exchange 5.5 directory. You should hear it from Microsoft as they are the authority on their products. However, for the sake of convenience and in an attempt to simplify the concepts surrounding MS Exchange as a widely deployed and heavily used messaging system, the important characteristics of

Exchange are included in this chapter. The main purpose is to give you a general under-standing of the messaging boundaries and terms used to describe how each version of Exchange is deployed and managed.

You do not learn how to design or deploy Exchange by reading about it here, but you do learn important aspects of Exchange as they pertain to Unity and its unified messaging capabilities. Regardless, it is also necessary to demonstrate a few ways that each specific Exchange version might be deployed. After you have an understanding of Exchange's characteristics and how it is deployed, you can then proceed on through the rest of the chapter.

Exchange 5.5

MS Exchange 5.5 comes in two separate editions, Standard and Enterprise. Unity works with both editions. Exchange 5.5 can run in a single-server configuration or in a cluster configuration. All versions of Unity support a single-server Exchange 5.5 configuration but none support an Exchange 5.5 cluster.

Exchange 5.5 servers have a few important components, including:

- Directory
- Information Store
- Public Store
- MTA (Message Transfer Agent)

In order for Exchange 5.5 servers to be administratively organized, it is necessary to set up a single organization. This organization is supposed to represent a large or small company. Sometimes, a larger company might have more than one Exchange 5.5 organization. This can be considered good and bad, depending on the way you look at it. Separate organiza-tions mean that mail-enabled domain users in one organization do not share the same global address list as the other organization. It is possible to have each organization share their own global address lists through some form of replication or LDAP operation, but that is outside the scope of this book.

The Exchange 5.5 organization is represented as O=Companyname or Org=Companyname. For Exchange 5.5, underneath the organization are Exchange 5.5 sites. An Exchange 5.5 site is also equivalent to an Organizational Unit or OU. Underneath each site is where Exchange 5.5 servers reside.

The Exchange 5.5 Site can be considered an administrative boundary and an Exchange administrator can grant various administrative roles at the Exchange 5.5 site level. These same roles can also be granted at the org level, but this typically implies greater permissions than necessary to perform normal administrative tasks within an Exchange 5.5 site. If an administrator is granted an Exchange administrative role in an Exchange 5.5 site, they typically do not have access to administer other Exchange 5.5 sites.

All servers within a site can message one another without any configuration effort on an administrator's part. However, in order for messages to travel from one site to another, it is necessary to set up a connector between the two sites. It is necessary to designate one Exchange 5.5 server in each site to act as a bridgehead server that will connect to other bridgehead servers through this connector. These are the only servers that move messages from one site to another. More than one bridgehead can be used, and message routing comes into play. However, message routing is outside the scope of this book.

Figure 13-1 shows an example of an Exchange 5.5 organization with three sites. Each site is linked using the Exchange 5.5 site connector and also a directory replication connector for replication of the Exchange 5.5 directory. Each site contains a bridgehead server designated for site-to-site message routing and directory replication between each site. Organizations and sites can be named according to a given company's need. In the example in Figure 13-1, the Exchange sites are simply named A, B, and C, but they can as easily be named Payroll, Manufacturing, and Human Resources.

Figure 13-1 *Exchange 5.5 Organization with Three Sites*

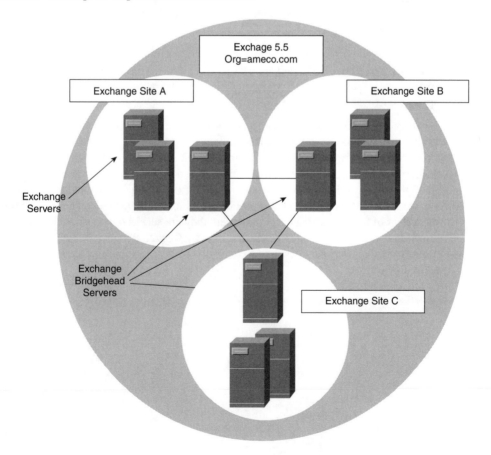

There are a few different connectors that can be used to message between sites. An Internet or SMTP connector, an X.400 connector, or an Exchange 5.5 site connector are the most common. There are different reasons for using each connector. It is more common to see Exchange 5.5 Site connectors for small- and medium-size organizations. It is more common to see X.400 connectors for large organizations, but it is not the rule. The Internet or SMTP connector generally provides connectivity to an SMTP-based Internet host. This can be a remotely connected Exchange 5.5 site accessible through the Internet. Another connector called the Directory Replication connector is also commonly used depending upon the type of messaging connector used. For more information, see the MS Exchange 5.5 product documentation.

An organization that has multiple Exchange 5.5 sites typically have all messaging and directory connectors in place and larger ones even have more elaborate configurations, such as dedicated Address Book servers and dedicated mail relay hosts (dedicated mail relay hosts are Exchange servers without mailboxes installed and are configured to be dedicated to relaying mail). Figure 13-2 shows that the Exchange 5.5 sites are connected in a hub and spoke configuration where each bridgehead server is connected to a bridgehead in a centralized hub site. In any Exchange configuration, it is possible to also set up an Internet connector to the Internet.

Exchange 5.5 servers can also connect to other messaging systems. This is typically performed by installing a dedicated connector to the given messaging system; for example, Novell GroupWise or Lotus Domino, and allowing messaging and directory information to replicate between the two.

Exchange 5.5 mailboxes or recipients can be organized into one or more containers. By default, there is one container called Recipients for All Mailboxes, Custom Recipients (which are basically Internet addresses accessible through the global address list), and distribution lists (which is a collection of recipients and custom recipients or other distribution lists [DLs]). Some organizations separate these different objects out into their own containers, which are certainly reasonable, especially the more of them that you have to administer. Regardless of how these objects are grouped, they are serviced by a single Exchange 5.5 information store where the mailboxes (Recipients), Custom Recipients, and DLs are created. Figure 13-3 shows nested OUs used to logically group users to allow for easier management of these users.

Figure 13-2 *Exchange 5.5 Hub and Spoke Configuration*

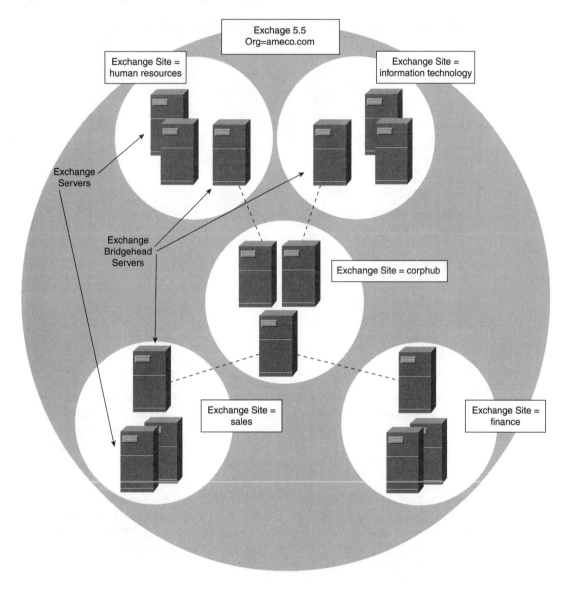

Figure 13-3 *Microsoft's Active Directory Users and Computers Utility*

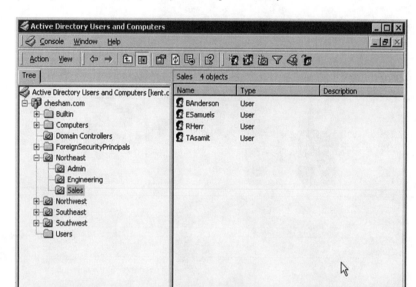

In Figure 13-4, nested OUs are used to administratively group mailboxes.

It is possible to give recipients more than one address or address type, such as an X.400 address, fax address, Internet address, and so on. This way the actual Exchange client, Outlook, can resolve the name to the address as necessary. A mail-enabled domain user has access to and uses his own Outlook client, and he has the ability to use the global address list, which contains the addresses of all recipients, custom recipients, and DLs. He can also create a contact list, which will contain personal addresses and DLs.

For any Outlook client, if a specific address type is desired, it is necessary to use the proper format to address the message. For Exchange, this typically means embedding the address within square brackets and using a message type designator, such as FAX: or SMTP: or some other designator. Microsoft Exchange uses these addresses if they exist for a recipient. This functionality allows Unity to support sending faxes to fax machines, printers, or e-mail addresses.

Figure 13-4 *The User Mailboxes in the Exchange 5.5 Admin Utility*

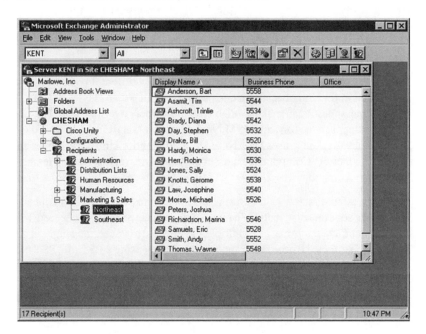

The Exchange 5.5 directory is accessed through the Exchange 5.5 Administrator. It is also accessed programmatically through Directory Access Programming Interface (DAPI) or most commonly through LDAP. Because the Exchange 5.5 directory complies with LDAP, it is easiest to understand access into the directory in the context of LDAP. In order to query the directory for subscriber information; which in this case is information about mail-enabled domain users or recipients who have Unity data assigned to less commonly used attributes, it is necessary to bind to the directory using a service account with the necessary access into the directory. Normal queries and read- and write-operations to the directory are allowed once the Unity service account is granted the proper role within Exchange. For more information, please review Chapter 4, "Components and Subsystems: Directory".

For every Exchange 5.5 server, a directory replica is kept on the server. In fact, depending upon the number of Exchange 5.5 sites, it is possible that multiple replicas exist on a given Exchange 5.5 server. For Exchange 5.5, all servers in a given site house a read/write replica of the directory entries for that site. It houses a read-only replica for every other site that it replicates. The replication is facilitated through the establishment of the Exchange 5.5 connector and/or its associated directory replication connector to all other sites.

Therefore, for an administrator to administer a given Exchange 5.5 site, it is necessary to connect to one of the servers in the site. In order to administer another site, the administrator has to connect to a server in the other site; otherwise real administration cannot take place. This is typically the reason why administrators in one site are not able to administer other sites.

Exchange uses the idea of a message class to identify different types of messages. This is a key attraction for Unity because it can make use of message classes to identify the different types of messages it can make available to subscribers over the TUI. The Outlook client sends messages in the format of IPM.Note. Other message classes are used to identify other message classes. Unity uses IPM.Note.Unity to identify Unity voice messages. Please review Chapter 5, "Components and Subsystems: Messaging/Unity Message Repository," for more information.

Exchange 5.5 uses the notion of a single instance message store. This means that when a message is sent to a distribution list, only one message is sent per server. This works quite well to minimize the impact of multiple messages. However, the single instance message store can be affected by the restoration of mailboxes using a PST file. PST files are used for mail-enabled users to store their e-mail messages on their local computer instead of keeping them stored on the Exchange 5.5 server. This works for mail-enabled users, but does not work for Unity as it then has no way to validate or provide message notification because the message is removed off the information store and onto the end user's local PST file.

To summarize, Exchange 5.5 has the following characteristics:

- Its messaging boundaries consist of an Exchange 5.5 organization and Exchange 5.5 sites.

- Exchange 5.5 servers reside in sites.

- Message delivery between servers in the same site does not require any additional configuration work; but message delivery between servers in other sites or to the Internet requires the establishment of "connectors" in order to deliver messages and also to replicate directory information. Typically, bridgehead servers are designated to be a central point of focus for message delivery for each site. Some organizations create hub and spoke configurations where they have a one or more sites dedicated to routing messages only.

- Recipients, custom recipients, and distribution lists can be grouped or organized into different containers, which can be created within a given site. Regardless how they are grouped, the recipients all use the same Exchange 5.5 information store, which is typically the store of the server they were created on. The default container for recipients is called recipients.

- Different address types can be given to the same recipient so they can receive messages from different messaging systems or components. Do not confuse this with message class or message type.

- In order for Outlook clients to address messages to certain message address types, it is necessary to use specific formats contained with in square brackets.

- Access to the Exchange 5.5 directory is provided through either the Exchange 5.5 administrator, or programmatically through the DAPI, or through LDAP. Through LDAP is the most common way to provide access.

- Unity subscribers are mail-enabled domain users who have Unity-specific information stored about them within less commonly used attributes.

- All Exchange servers house a read/write replica of the directory within the site in which they reside and they house read-only replicas of all other sites in the organization.

- Exchange 5.5 servers use single-instance message stores to house all messages from recipients who reside on a given messaging server; typically, one message per server.

- Messages can be left on the information store or end users can move their messages to a PST file on their local computer.

Exchange 5.5 servers can reside in a Windows NT 4.0 domain or a Windows 2000/2003 domain. Common configurations, especially for larger installations, include Exchange servers installed into Windows NT resource domains servicing mail-enabled end users (MAPI recipients) typically housed in master accounts domains. For those Exchange 5.5 deployments running on Windows 2000/2003, the same thing can take place; however, it is easier to group end users by directory entries, such as organizational units, in Active Directory in the same domain where the Exchange servers reside.

Exchange 2000/2003

Exchange 2000 was introduced shortly after the introduction of Windows 2000. It was different from Exchange 5.5 in several ways. First of all, the Exchange 2000 offering came without its own directory. Instead, it uses Active Directory, which is a key part of Windows 2000. Second, Exchange 2000 is organized differently with its message storage and its messaging boundaries, both administrative and routing.

Exchange 2000 comes in two separate editions: Standard and Enterprise. Unity works with both editions. Exchange 2000 can run in a single-server configuration or in a cluster configuration. All versions of Unity including, 3.0 and higher, support a single Exchange 2000 server, or an Exchange 2000 cluster. With the release of Unity 4.03, Exchange 2003 is also supported.

Exchange 2000 servers have a few important components. They are as follows:

- Directory access through Active Directory. Exchange 2000 does cache the directory locally for faster access times.

- Information stores. Actually, these are called storage groups. It is possible to have more than one storage group per Exchange 2000 server (Enterprise Edition) and each storage group can have up to five mailbox stores/databases.

- Exchange 2000 supports a more robust public store.

- MTA (Messaging Transfer Agent). The MTA transfers messages from e-mail clients connected to the Exchange server to other Exchange servers. An Exchange server can also be configured to act as an MTA only. An example of this is an Exchange server acting as a bridgehead for all other Exchange servers.

- Exchange 2000 also supports the idea of a front-end/back-end configuration where the front-end is mainly a web interface that accesses mail-enabled end users' mailboxes on the back-end systems. The web interface is Outlook Web Access.

Some enhancements were added to Exchange 2003 and information about them can be found in the Exchange 2003 product documentation or on Microsoft's web site.

Exchange 2000/2003 servers are administered by being a part of an administrative group. The whole idea behind an administrative group is to allow an organization to segment how their messaging servers are administered. Some organizations create a single administrative group. Others create multiple administrative groups. It simply depends upon the organization's ongoing operational requirements.

Exchange 2000/2003 servers are grouped into routing groups, which are essentially well-connected or should be well-connected server sets. Groups of Exchange 2000/2003 servers make up separate routing groups. The routing groups are then connected through a routing group connector.

Exchange 2000/2003 servers use the same notion of an organization in order to denote an entire set of Exchange servers operating as part of the same collective. The designators for the other Exchange 2000/2003 components, such as storage groups and servers themselves, are somewhat different than those found in Exchange 5.5. But it is important to note that all components of Exchange 2000/2003 are represented in Active Directory under the configuration naming context.

Figure 13-5 shows that the Exchange container for the MS Exchange Organization is located in the configuration naming context in Active Directory. The utility, Microsoft Active Directory Users and Computers, does not expose this naming context. However, the lower-level utility MS ADSI Edit does. It is not the only utility that does, but it is useful for finding how the objects really look and are organized compared to how they are presented in their native utility. Of course, because this is a low-level utility and it does provide access to the schema and configuration of the directory, typical administrative policies for many companies do not permit using these low-level utilities to view the directory. You can, however, view them in your own lab configuration.

Figure 13-5 *ADSI Edit with Exchange Location*

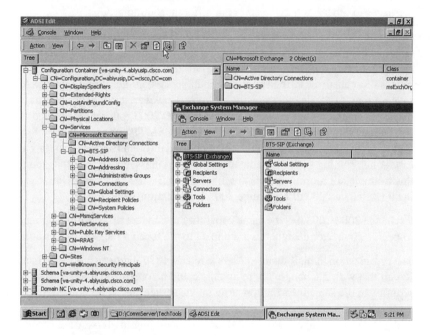

Exchange 2000/2003 can be installed into one of two different messaging modes: mixed mode or native mode. Mixed-mode messaging allows Exchange 2000/2003 to become a part of an existing Exchange 5.5 organization and site structure. Native-mode messaging is how Exchange 2000/2003 should be installed if Exchange 5.5 is not present. After Exchange 2000/2003 is installed in native-mode messaging, you cannot switch to mixed-mode messaging.

Exchange 2000/2003 servers are installed into a given administrative group (there is a default administrative group; if more administrative groups are desired they have to be created using the system manager). By default, all Exchange 2000/2003 servers will be able to message one another, but it is best to configure one or more routing groups and move the servers into these routing groups so they can message each other according to well-connected boundaries. Microsoft has criteria and recommendations about when and how to set up administrative groups and routing groups. If you are not familiar with when or how you should set them up, please read Microsoft Exchange 2000/2003 documentation or attend a class on MS Exchange 2000/2003.

In a native-mode messaging configuration, routing groups are similar to Exchange 5.5 sites. Each routing group can message another routing group by the establishment of routing group connectors. This is similar to the Exchange 5.5 site connector. Therefore, one or more servers in the routing group must be designated as a bridgehead server so it can route messages to other Exchange servers in different routing groups.

Other connectors exist for Exchange 2000/2003 servers, as they exist in Exchange 5.5. For larger enterprises, the message routing topology can become complex and might require the establishment of multiple hub routing groups that are dedicated solely for message routing. This is most easily described as a multi-hub/spoke configuration. As in Exchange 5.5, message routing is outside the scope of this book. However, it is a good idea to understand how messages can be routed between Exchange 2000/2003 routing groups and how messages can be routed to other message systems through SMTP connectors or other connectors. In Figure 13-6, all the routing groups are connected through Exchange routing groups connectors. A hub routing group is dedicated to routing messages to the other routing groups. In this example, all routing groups are in the same Exchange administrative group, which is in an Exchange 2000 or Exchange 2003 organization.

Exchange 2000/2003 has the same capability to connect to other messaging systems using a specific connector designated to connect to the foreign messaging system.

The organization of mail-enabled users is relatively straightforward in Exchange 2000/2003. Recall that with Exchange 5.5, recipients could be organized into separate containers, all pointing to the same information store on the server they were homed. In Exchange 2000/2003, all mail-enabled users can be organized in Active Directory through organizational units, and in Exchange 2000/2003 their corresponding mailboxes are typically organized into specific mailbox databases located on a specific storage group on a specific Exchange 2000/2003 server. Therefore, it is more manageable in the sense that groups of users can be segmented according to their needs, and often grouping smaller numbers of users is a best practice for managing mailboxes in a given store. This type of flexibility allows an administrator to group end users by mail store size so that the mailbox size policies can be placed against all users on a given mailstore.

For Exchange 2000/2003 and Active Directory, there are three object classes of importance to messaging and addressing. They are user, contact, and distribution group. In Active Directory, a user might not be mail-enabled. The phrases "mail-enabled user" or "mail-enabled end user" refer to those users who are created of the user object class in Active Directory and who are mail-enabled. Mail-enabled, in this case, means a user who has an Exchange 2000/2003 mailbox homed on an Exchange 2000/2003 server. In Active Directory, a user can have only one Exchange 2000/2003 mailbox. Users typically cannot share mailboxes. It is, however, possible to grant privileges for one user to send or receive messages on behalf of another.

Figure 13-6 *Exchange 2000/2003 Bridgehead Servers Through Several Different Routing Groups*

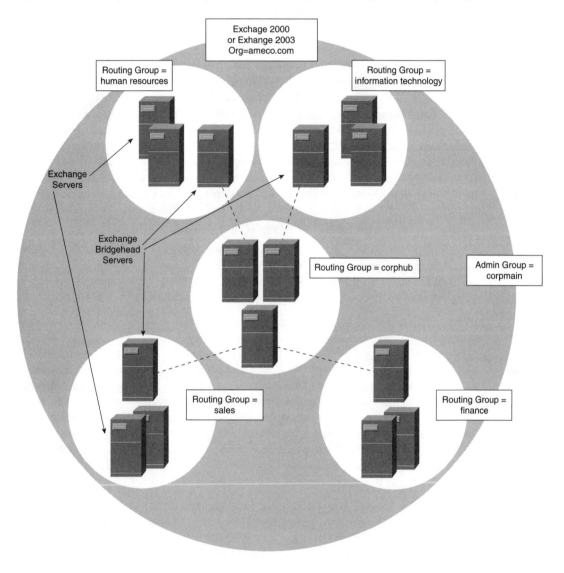

The contact is a user who has no privileges in Active Directory, but who does have an e-mail address, so that mail-enabled users can send messages by finding such contacts listed in Active Directory through the global address list. It is an easy way for the mail-enabled community at large to find commonly mailed non-Exchange 2000/2003 addresses and to be able to address messages to them.

In Active Directory, there are several different types of groups. It is important to note the differences between them. A distribution group is created to assemble mail-enabled users and contacts for addressing messages. It is easiest to understand a distribution group in Active Directory is the same as a distribution list in any messaging system.

With Exchange 2000/2003, another component in addressing becomes very important. It is the Recipient Update Service or RUS. RUS helps create the proper e-mail addresses for each mail-enabled end user. The RUS is established on the server in the Windows 2000 domain that has the Exchange 2000/2003 Setup.exe DomainPrep run on it. DomainPrep is run prior to the first Exchange 2000/2003 server installed into the domain. When mail-enabled users are created or when changes are made to user addresses, it is important for the RUS to run in order to update any addresses that might have changed. This is an important consideration, and a necessary process that must be completed prior to having addressable access to these mailboxes. It is also necessary for RUS to be complete on a given mailbox prior to being able to see a given user as mail-enabled in the directory. More information about RUS can be found in Microsoft documentation.

From a client perspective, the Outlook client connected to Exchange 2000/2003 has the same functionality as the Outlook client connected to Exchange 5.5. With Exchange 2003, some additional functionality is included, such as performing more specific LDAP searches, but this functionality is not crucial to Unity functionality.

Exchange 2000/2003 uses Active Directory, as it does not have its own directory like its predecessor, Exchange 5.5. The Exchange 2000/2003 portions of Active Directory are accessed through the Exchange 2000 System Manager. Managing and mail-enabling users takes place using the Active Directory Users and Computers MMC Microsoft Management Console (MMC). On a server that has Exchange installed, on Unity and on computers that administer Exchange 2000, the administrator has the ability to mail-enable users by selecting one or more users in a container or OU and right-clicking and selecting Exchange Tasks. This will allow for the creation of mailboxes, moving mailboxes, deleting mailboxes, and enabling other Exchange-related services. There are other ways to access the Exchange 2000/2003 information in Active Directory, such as using ADSIEdit, LDAP, or programmatically using ADSI.

Just as with Exchange 5.5, in order to query the directory for subscriber information, it is necessary to bind to the directory using a service account with the necessary access into the directory. Granting the Unity service account the proper access into Active Directory allows normal queries and read and write operations to the directory.

For Exchange 2000/2003, its use of Active Directory means that Unity has to focus on Active Directory whenever it services Exchange 2000/2003 or whenever Unity services both Exchange 2000/2003 and Exchange 5.5 in a mixed-mode configuration. Exchange uses both a domain controller and Global Catalog server. Outlook clients do so as well.

To administer an Exchange 2000/2003 server or subscribers, the administrator must have the proper permissions granted to access the necessary applications. It is necessary to understand Active Directory account permissions to administer users. It is also necessary to understand Exchange administrator roles to administer Exchange servers through the System Manager.

With these versions of Exchange, the message class scheme is still used to identify different types of messages. Unity uses it the same way in Exchange 2000/2003 as it does in Exchange 5.5.

Exchange 2000/2003 uses the idea of storage groups, which is a way to group mail stores in order to make it easier to manage smaller groups of user mailboxes. Up to four storage groups can be set up on Exchange 2000/2003 server with each storage group capable of housing up to five mail stores. This arrangement of storage groups and mail stores allow administrators to have more control over subscriber mailboxes so they can perform backups and restores and perform other mailbox administration tasks. Just as in Exchange 5.5, mail-enabled users can use PSTs to archive their own messages out of the mail store. Unity still has the same issues with PSTs in Exchange 2000/2003 as it did with Exchange 5.5.

To summarize, Exchange 2000/2003 has the following characteristics:

- Their messaging boundaries consist of an Exchange 2000 org and admin groups. For message routing, routing groups can be set up and this is typical.

- Exchange 2000/2003 servers reside in only one administrative group, and most certainly exist in an Exchange routing group.

- Message delivery between Exchange 2000/2003 servers in the same routing group does not require any configuration work. However, in order to route messages to other routing groups, it is necessary to set up routing group connectors. These connectors are typically set up using bridgehead servers as they are in Exchange 5.5.

- It supports two messaging modes: mixed mode and native mode. Mixed-mode messaging implies that Exchange 2000/2003 servers are joined to an Exchange 5.5 site and native-mode messaging implies that Exchange 5.5 or the Active Directory Connector (ADC) is not present and that only Exchange 2000/2003 servers are configured to run in native-mode messaging.

- Mail-enabled users, contacts, and distribution groups can be grouped and organized into different containers in Active Directory and placed in different Exchange 2000/2003 servers, storage groups, and mail stores. Unlike Exchange 5.5, mail-enabled users in Exchange 2000/2003 might not necessarily use the same mail stores in the same storage groups on the same Exchange 2000/2003 servers.

- Different address types can be given to the same mail-enabled user so they can receive messages from different messaging systems or components. Message types and message classes are different.

- Exchange 2000/2003 uses the Exchange Recipients Update Services (RUS) to update subscriber information, such as addresses.

- One or more Address policies might be used in order to dictate how mail-enabled users are addressed.

- In order for Outlook clients to address messages to certain message address types, it is necessary to use specific formats contained within square brackets.

- Access to Active Directory is provided by a few different administrative applications, most importantly, Exchange System Manager and Active Directory Users and Computers. There are other ways to access Exchange 2000/2003 information in Active Directory, including programmatically using ADSI.

- Unity subscribers are mail-enabled domain users who have a Unity-specific information store and Unity-specific attributes in Active Directory.

- Exchange 2000/2003 servers typically do not house Active Directory. They do, however, cache the directory locally for faster access.

- Exchange 2000/2003 servers have one or more storage groups, each with one to 5 mail stores per storage group and no more than four storage groups per server.

- For Outlook clients, messages are left in their own mailboxes residing on the Exchange 2000/2003 servers or they might be archived using PST files on their local computers.

Exchange 2000/2003 servers can reside only in a Window 2000/2003 domain. Windows 2000/2003 domains contain Windows 2000/2003 sites, which are typically based on a physically well connected group of computers. Each site contains at least one Windows Global Catalog server, which acts as a directory replication bridgehead (not to be confused with a messaging bridgehead) for the site. Exchange 2000/2003 servers reside within Windows 2000/2003 sites.

Exchange in a Mixed-Messaging Configuration: Mixed-Mode Messaging and Native-Mode Messaging

There is a difference in the treatment of administrative groups and routing groups between mixed-mode messaging and native-mode messaging. In a mixed-mode messaging environment, an administrative group is created when the first Exchange 2000 server is joined to a specific Exchange 5.5 site. The whole purpose behind this activity is to facilitate the interoperability between Exchange 5.5 and Exchange 2000/2003. The most important aspect of this facility is to allow for a migration from Exchange 5.5 to Exchange 2000/2003.

In a native-mode messaging environment, only Exchange 2000/2003 is present. Native- mode messaging can be obtained through a new installation or through the completed migration and removal of Exchange 5.5 and the ADC (which synchronizes the Exchange 5.5 directory with Active Directory). More information can be found on the importance of distinguishing the differences between mixed messaging and native-mode messaging and the requirements for Unity to support each configuration in the sub-section below.

It is important to understand the characteristics that make up an Exchange mixed-messaging environment. Unless all characteristics are met, Unity cannot service both Exchange 5.5 and Exchange 2000/2003 mailboxes at the same time. Remember that a mixed-messaging environment is established to facilitate the migration from Exchange 5.5 to Exchange 2000/2003.

A mixed-messaging environment consists of:

- One or more Exchange 5.5 sites in a single Exchange 5.5 organization.

- Existing Exchange 5.5 servers that can be installed into a Windows NT or Windows 2000 domain. However, it is best to upgrade the domains to Windows 2000 prior to introducing the other components of a mixed-messaging environment.

- Either an existing NT domain that has been migrated to a Windows 2000 domain, which means Active Directory is present or a new Windows 2000 domain has been installed to accommodate the migration from NT to Windows 2000 and from Exchange 5.5 to Exchange 2000/2003. Exchange 2000/2003 can run only in a Windows 2000/2003 domain on Windows 2000/2003 servers.

- A Microsoft Active Directory Connector is installed.

- One or more connection agreements are in place between the Active Directory and Exchange 5.5 directory. The connection agreements must be replicating Exchange 5.5 object information from the directory to Active Directory. The specific objects replicated depend upon the Connection Agreement (CA) established. A company can set up a recipient's CA or a public folders CA. The recipients CA is relevant to Unity. The public folders CA does not apply. The way in which a given CA is replicated is typically dependent upon the need of a given organization. Often, it is desired to preserve the existing Exchange 5.5 directory as it is the primary corporate directory. As many companies migrate to Exchange 2000 or 2003, however, the emphasis is placed on making Active Directory available to most organizations. In this case, it might be desirable to replicate directory information both ways or from Exchange 5.5 to Active Directory only. See Microsoft documentation for more information.

- A recipient's CA can:
  - Replicate Exchange 5.5 recipient directory information to an Active Directory user object.
  - Replicate Exchange 5.5 custom recipient directory information to an Active Directory contact object.
  - Replicate Exchange 5.5 distribution lists information to an Active Directory distribution group.

— The recipient's CA can one-way replicate from Exchange 5.5 directory to Active Directory. It can two-way replicate from Exchange 5.5 to Active Directory and back. Or it can one-way from Active Directory to Exchange 5.5 directory.

• A CA can be established at any container level in Exchange 5.5 and Active Directory. A company should follow Microsoft's guidelines to set up CAs and container levels in the directories. Setting up CAs at different levels in the Exchange 5.5 directory than the same equivalent level in Windows 2000 Active Directory can affect how objects are replicated back into the Exchange 5.5 directory in a two-way CA configuration.

The Active Directory schema is extended with Exchange 2000 schema. This is done by running ForestPrep from the Exchange 2000 setup program. DomainPrep is run in each domain where Exchange 2000 resides.

This is important: When ForestPrep is run, it looks for the ADC and any connection agreements established between Active Directory and the Exchange 5.5 directory. The installer is prompted to either create a new Exchange 2000 org or join an Existing Exchange 5.5 site.

If the installer joins the Exchange 5.5 site, the first Exchange 2000 server establishes a special CA between its directory configuration container and the Exchange 5.5 directory configuration container. This connection agreement is called the ConfigCA. This is an automated process and one which should be best left alone from a Unity standpoint. With the ConfigCA in place, the first Exchange 2000 server joined to the Exchange 5.5 server becomes the Site Replication server. This server typically does not house mailboxes, although it is possible to place mailboxes on this server.

If the installer chooses to create a new organization for Exchange 2000, it is not possible for Unity to then service both Exchange 5.5 and Exchange 2000 mailboxes in this configuration because a single Unity server cannot service more than one Exchange organization.

If any of the characteristics are not met, the way in which Unity can be deployed to service mailboxes is different in that it is necessary to have different Unity servers service the two different Exchange organizations. This means connectivity between the Unity servers is still one where SMTP networking is required, but it is not possible to have one Unity server service mailboxes on both Exchange versions because the company chose to use a different method to migrate mailboxes then the one described above. Figure 13-7 shows SMTP networking occurs between the servers.

If all of the mixed-mode messaging characteristics are not met, a mixed-messaging environment does not exist.

Figure 13-7 *Unity Servers Servicing Each of Their Respective Organizations*

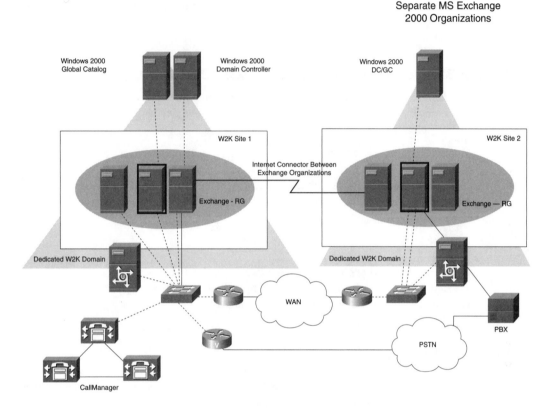

This means there will be one organization and site configuration structure for the Exchange 5.5 servers and a separate organization structure with one or more administrative groups for the Exchange 2000 servers. For Unity, this means that a single Unity server cannot service mailboxes on both versions of Exchange at the same time. One or more Unity servers is required to service the Exchange 5.5 organization and one or more Unity servers is required to service the Exchange 2000 organization and administrative group(s). Instead of treating this configuration as a mixed-messaging environment, it is considered two separate messaging organizations.

Without the ADC and connection agreements in place, Exchange 5.5 sees Active Directory as another accounts domain, just the same way it sees an NT domain. This means, in Active Directory, a user account is associated with an Exchange 5.5 mailbox, but the msExchange attributes in Active Directory are not utilized or known about by the Exchange 5.5 directory because directory replication between the two directories is not taking place. This also means the user object in Active Directory appears as if it is not mail-enabled in Active Directory.

Unity's Perspective and Requirements

In order to deploy Unity with MS Exchange, it is important to pay close attention to the way Unity sees Exchange. Understanding the way Unity sees Exchange is the key to designing a Unity solution.

A note of caution: How Unity sees Exchange is important, but it is more important to understand that Unity's viewpoint is not the limit of Exchange, nor is it the limit of Unity interoperating or coexisting with Exchange and its features. Therefore, it is best to consider the following perspective as a guide to ensuring a successful and accurate design.

Exchange 5.5

As mentioned in earlier chapters, Exchange 5.5 was the first version of Exchange that Unity serviced. You can gain a good understanding of how Unity uses any version of Exchange by understanding how it sees and uses Exchange 5.5.

How Unity Sees Exchange 5.5

When Exchange 5.5 is the only version of Exchange present and when it is not replicating with Active Directory through the ADC functionality, then it can be considered a native Exchange 5.5 solution or "pure" Exchange 5.5.

Therefore, the way Unity views Exchange 5.5 is pure. This means that it takes advantage and uses what Exchange 5.5 has to offer. When Unity is configured to service Exchange 5.5, it is configured to access and use the Exchange 5.5 directory and the Exchange 5.5 message store. Unity does not look outside (at another directory) of Exchange 5.5 in order to provide unified messaging services for the mailboxes homed on Exchange 5.5 servers when servicing Exchange 5.5 only.

So, in this regard, Unity behaves the same as Exchange 5.5 does when it comes to the Windows domain that Exchange 5.5 resides in, whether that is a Windows NT 4.0 or a 2000/2003 domain. Exchange 5.5 uses any Windows domain (through the domain controllers in the domain where it resides), to provide account authentication and account access. While this might seem obvious, it is a important concept to understand.

To Exchange 5.5, Windows NT 4.0 or 2000/2003 domain controllers have domain user accounts that have an Exchange 5.5 mailbox tied to it or associated with it. The mailbox to user relationship can be severed through the Exchange Admin program or through the

NT 4.0 User Manager for Domains Exchange snap-in. While this mailbox to user relation-ship changed in future versions of Exchange, the fact that it exists in Exchange 5.5 is a unique quality and must be understood when planning a Unity design around Exchange 5.5.

NOTE   Familiarize yourself with the Exchange Admin program and how mailboxes are associated to domain accounts, regardless of whether the domain account for a given mailbox is a Windows NT or a Windows 2000 domain. Note that to Exchange 5.5, the version of the domain does not matter; it treats each the same way.

As shown in Figure 13-8, Exchange 5.5 considers all mailbox associations with domain accounts to be based on the NT domain. Even if the domain is an Active Directory domain (Windows 2000/2003 domain), to Exchange 5.5 it still considers the mailboxes to be associated with the domain account. This is because Exchange 5.5 mailboxes can exist with or without a domain account. This is different than how Exchange 2000 or Exchange 2003 views the domain. In fact, it is the opposite. To Exchange 2000 or Exchange 2003, a user must exist before a mailbox can be created for it. The only alternative you have in Exchange 2000 or Exchange 2003 to is to create e-mail addresses (not mailboxes), which are called contacts. A contact has no permissions or rights and cannot be used as an account to access a Windows 2000 or Windows 2003 domain.

Figure 13-8   *Exchange 5.5 Admin Depicting an Exchange 5.5 Mailbox and its Association with a Windows Domain Account*

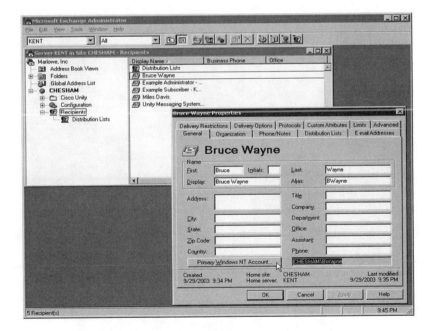

It is possible to use the Exchange 5.5 Admin program to create a mailbox and domain user account at the same time. All that is needed is permission to create users in the domain and the Account Admin role in Exchange 5.5.

If Unity is going to service Exchange 5.5, it takes the same viewpoint as Exchange 5.5 when it comes to Windows domains and domain controllers. So, what about Active Directory in this situation? To Unity it does not matter if it is present or not, and of course, it is present if a Windows 2000/2003 domain exists. If Active Directory is present (Exchange and Unity is installed into a Windows 2000/2003 domain), Unity's viewpoint of Exchange 5.5 does not need to change until it is time to migrate Unity subscribers from Exchange 5.5 to Exchange 2000/2003. For more information on migration, please refer to Chapter 15, "Upgrades and Migrations."

As shown in Figure 13-9, when Unity services Exchange 5.5 only, the domain type does not matter to Unity. Unity treats the domain the same way that Exchange 5.5 does, as an NT accounts domain. So, even if Active Directory exists, Unity does not use it as a directory when it services Exchange 5.5. Figure 13-9 shows how Unity sees Exchange 5.5. In each of the domains (one NT and one Windows 2000 or Windows 2003), Unity's focus is on the Exchange 5.5 partner server and the Exchange 5.5 directory. Figure 13-9 shows Unity's directory connector pointing to the site. This is representative of the directory and in reality, Unity will use the Exchange 5.5 directory replica located on the Exchange 5.5 partner server. However, the Exchange 5.5 directory replica has a read/write replica of the site where the Exchange 5.5 server resides (permission is required to write to it) and it has a read-only replica of all other sites in the Exchange 5.5 organization.

Figure 13-9 *Unity Servicing Exchange 5.5*

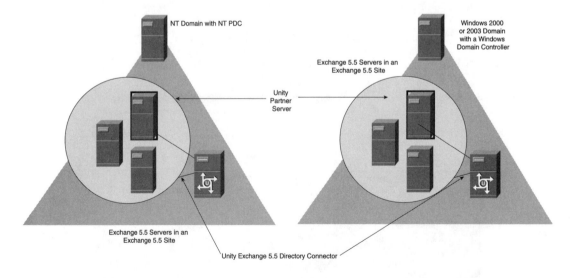

Other Exchange 5.5 objects, such as custom recipients and distribution lists, reside solely in the Exchange 5.5 directory as long as Exchange 5.5 is the only version of Exchange in existence in a given organization. There are no domain users and groups associated with the custom recipients and distribution lists between a Windows NT 4.0 domain and Exchange 5.5, respectively. There can be an association between Windows 2000 domain contacts, groups, and Exchange 5.5 custom recipients, and distribution lists if the ADC is properly set up to allow for directory replication between the two directories (Active Directory and the Exchange 5.5 directory). For more information on the MS ADC, please see later section "Exchange in a Mixed-Messaging Configuration."

When Unity is set up to service mailboxes in Exchange 5.5, it uses the directory to access the subscriber information, and the information store to access those same mailboxes.

Unity's perceived boundaries of Exchange 5.5 are as follows:

- **Directory**. A Unity server is installed into an Exchange 5.5 site. When this takes place, it means that Unity might be able to read directory information above the site level, but it will not be able to service subscribers above the site level where it is installed. If multiple sites exist, multiple Unity servers are needed.

- **Cisco Unity Folder**. The first Unity server installed into an Exchange 5.5 site creates a special folder under the site container. The special folder is called Cisco Unity and it houses the Unity location object for the first and subsequent servers installed to service that site. All subsequent Unity server installations into the same site use this same Cisco Unity folder in order to store their own Unity location object. In order for any Unity server to create the special folder or to create its own Unity location object, the domain account used to install Unity must have the Exchange 5.5 Service Account Admin role granted to it at the site level and configuration container level in the site Unity is installed into.

- **Recipients Container**. Unity expects to service subscribers at the recipient container level or at the site container level. The default is the recipient's container, but this can be changed to point Unity to the site level. Doing so means that Unity will look at all containers under the site container to find subscribers.

How Unity Uses Exchange 5.5

Unity accesses the Exchange 5.5 directory through LDAP. It accesses the Exchange 5.5 information store through MAPI.

Unity does not use the public store at all and only uses the Exchange 5.5 information store (AKA Priv.edb). Unity uses the information store to provide UM services to the mailboxes that reside it in. Within Exchange 5.5, mailboxes can be organized in the Exchange 5.5 directory by setting up containers in the Exchange 5.5 directory. During a standard Exchange 5.5 installation, two containers are created by default, a recipients and public folders container. Then, mailboxes can be created in the recipients container and new public folders can be created in the public folders container. An Exchange 5.5 administrator can create new recipient containers and this is common. In fact, some organizations will create nested containers made up of Exchange 5.5 mailboxes, custom recipients, and distribution lists all separated into some organizational structure. This is perfectly valid and supportable to Unity. Be aware that the more nested containers a given Exchange 5.5 directory has, the more work that is required to maintain mailboxes and other objects. This is compounded when Unity is now servicing these mailboxes.

NOTE
To learn more about how Unity works with components of Exchange, refer to Chapters 4 and 5.

Unity's view of the directory or scope is set at for the mailbox store is set at the OU or Exchange 5.5 site. This view will allow it to see any recipient container below the site. So, if there are nested containers, Unity will be able to see all mailboxes in the structure.

In Figure 13-10, Unity's scope of the directory is at the site level—it can see all the nested containers under the site container. The scope can be limited to the recipient's container as well. If this is done, Unity will see only mailboxes in the recipient's container and its nested or sub containers. If you use the Unity SA, viewing the same recipients appears as displayed in Figure 13-10.

Figure 13-10 *Directory Scope of Unity*

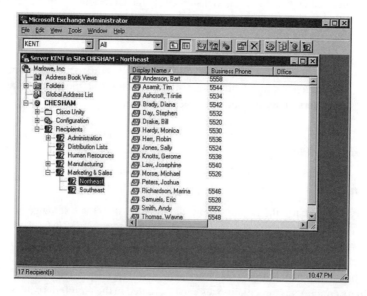

After the recipients are imported as subscribers, they appear as displayed in Figure 13-11.

Figure 13-11 *How Unity Sees Recipients When Importing Them.*

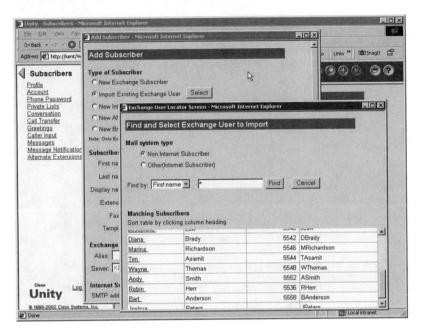

After a recipient is imported as a subscriber, the subscriber's individual information is readily available for administration using the Subscriber Search page, as shown in Figure 13-12.

When Unity makes an existing Exchange 5.5 recipient a subscriber, it does so by tying the subscriber-specific directory data to the location object it creates in the Cisco Unity folder in the site container of the Exchange 5.5 directory.

When Unity services Exchange 5.5 mailboxes, it uses a domain controller to provide authentication for subscribers when they access the Unity web and VMO interfaces. Unity also obtains the domain user SID during initial creation of the subscriber.

Exchange 2000/2003

Unity accesses Active Directory using the ADSI programming interface. It accesses the Exchange 2000/2003 mail stores through the MAPI protocol.

Figure 13-12 *Subscriber Search Page: How Unity Sees a Recipient Once it Is Imported as a Subscriber.*

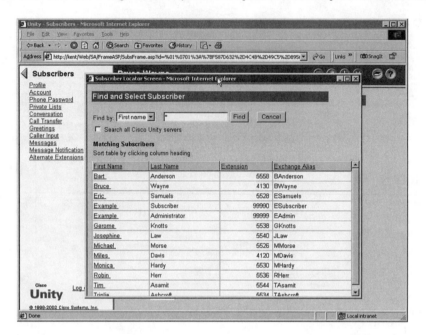

Unity uses only the Exchange 2000/2003 mail stores. It does not use the public folders. It uses only the Exchange 2000/2003 storage groups/mail stores to provide UM services to the mailboxes that reside there. Within Exchange 2000/2003, mailboxes are organized in a linear fashion, but can be organized into smaller groups called mail stores. Each storage group can contain up to five mail stores, which can contain any number of mailboxes. The actual number of mailboxes each mail store can contain depends upon the hardware used and other factors. See Microsoft documentation in order to determine the acceptable number of mail boxes for each mail store in a given storage group. Typically the number is small in order to have the ability to back up and restore groups of users.

During an Exchange 2000/2003 installation, a default storage group is created and a single default mail store is created in that storage group. If more mail stores or storage groups are desired, they must be administratively created. Unity can service multiple mail stores in multiple storage groups on a given Exchange 2000/2003 server.

Unity's view of the directory or scope is set at the OU and corresponding Exchange 2000/2003 storage groups/mail stores. As new subscribers are added from different OUs, storage groups, or Exchange servers, the scope is expanded to view the subscribers in these locations as well.

An example of having different OUs is shown in Figure 13-13. It is not uncommon for a nested OU structure to be set up so that users might be grouped according to the administrative needs of the organization.

Figure 13-13 *Nested Containers (Organizational Units or OUs) in the Active Directory*

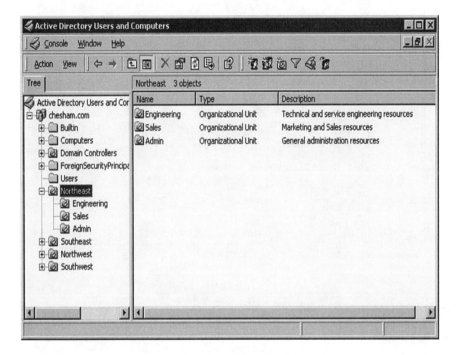

If an administrator were to search this OU structure, they would search at the domain level of the directory, as shown in Figure 13-14.

Again, after the users are imported into Unity as subscribers, you can search for a subscriber to perform administrative tasks (see Figure 13-15).

When Unity makes an existing mail user a subscriber, it ties the subscriber to the location object it creates in the Unity folder in the Active Directory.

When Unity services Exchange 2000/2003 mailboxes, it uses a domain controller to provide authentication for subscribers when they access the Unity web and VMO interfaces. Unity also obtains the domain user Security Identification (SID) during initial creation of the subscriber.

Figure 13-14 *Importing Users from Active Directory*

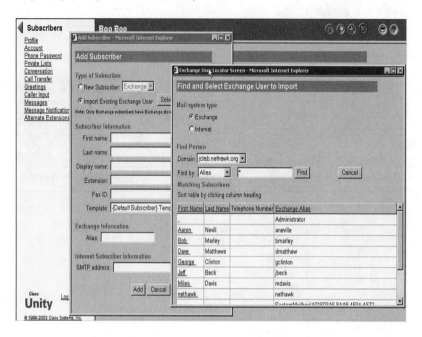

Figure 13-15 *Active Directory Users After They Are Subscribers*

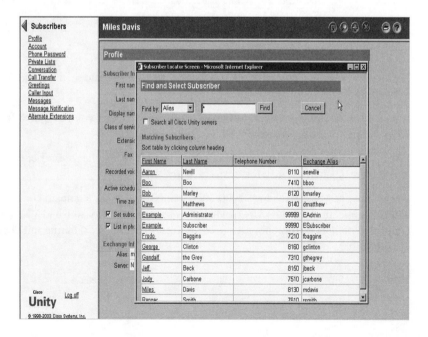

Exchange in a Mixed-Messaging Configuration

Unity servicing Exchange in a mixed-messaging configuration can be confusing. Here are some important facts to consider. If the characteristics of a mixed-mode messaging configuration are met, then Unity can service subscribers in two ways. It can service subscribers in both Exchange versions separately, or it can service them jointly. In order for Unity to service subscribers in both Exchange 2000/2003 and Exchange 5.5 at the same time, Unity must point to Active Directory (using the Active Directory Monitor) and must recognize both Exchange 5.5 users and Exchange 2000/2003 users in the Active Directory. If these characteristics are not met, then you have to have one or more Unity servers installed into an Exchange 5.5 site in order for Unity to service subscribers in both Exchange 2000/2003 and Exchange 5.5. You need at least one Unity server per site, and you can add more servers per site to service larger user densities. You need one or more Unity servers installed into Exchange 2000/2003 administrative groups. You also need one or more Unity servers installed into individual routing groups that make up an administrative group.

As mentioned, in a mixed-messaging configuration Unity can operate in two different ways. Both ways are unified messaging-specific. Table 13-1 describes the two different ways that the Unity Directory Monitor is used.

Table 13-1   *How Unity Services Different Versions of Exchange*

Directory Monitor	Use
Unity Exchange 5.5	Connects to the Exchange 5.5 directory and the Exchange 5.5 information store. It makes Unity aware of the Exchange 5.5 directory. This means Unity is not concerned with Active Directory even if Active Directory is present in the same environment. Because Exchange 5.5 directory is the primary directory in Unity's point of view during this configuration, Unity sees and services only Exchange 5.5 mailboxes.
Unity Exchange 2000/2003	Connects to Active Directory and the Exchange 2000/2003 mail store. Using this connector, Unity can service Exchange 2000/2003 mailboxes and Exchange 5.5 mailboxes that are a part of the mixed-messaging configuration (see the previous description).

The Unity Exchange 5.5 Directory Monitor-Exchange 5.5 Mailboxes Only

Because Unity can service Exchange 5.5 mailboxes using only the Unity Exchange 5.5 Directory Monitor, in this configuration, Unity can continue to service Exchange 5.5 mailboxes regardless of whether or not Exchange 2000 servers are in place.

In this configuration, Unity uses the Exchange 5.5 directory as its primary directory. Therefore, it is dependent upon maintaining reliable data in the directory.

Figure 13-16 shows an Exchange 5.5 site that has been joined by Exchange 2000/2003. The Exchange 2000/2003 site replication server is the first Exchange 2000/2003 server that joins the Exchange 5.5 site. It does this through the MS ADC. The ADC is installed on a Windows 2000/2003 server, typically a Global Catalog server. Then, connection agreements are established between Exchange 5.5 and Active Directory for directory synchronization. The order of installation is Exchange 5.5, Windows 2000/2003 domain, MS ADC, connection agreements, and the Exchange 2000/2003 Site Replication server. Then you end up with a mixed-mode messaging environment. To Unity, if it is servicing Exchange 5.5 (only in this case), it will continue to do so and will not care about the Exchange 2000/2003 servers or Active Directory. Figure 13-16 includes a one-way CA or one-way CAs from Exchange 5.5 to Active Directory. This does not affect Unity. A two-way CA has the potential to affect Unity if the objects and attribute mappings are administratively altered between Active Directory and the Exchange 5.5 directory.

Figure 13-16 *Unity Servicing Exchange 5.5 in a Mixed-Messaging Configuration*

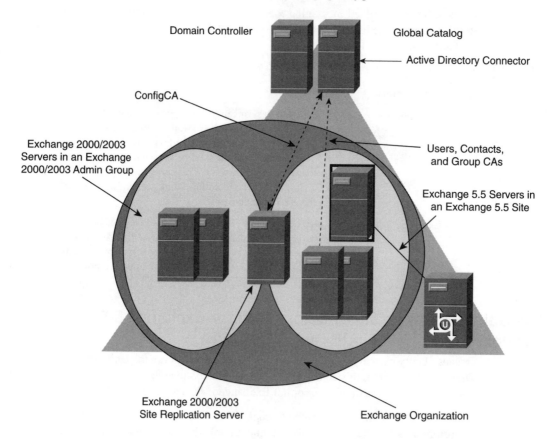

The Unity Exchange 2000/2003 Directory Monitor-Exchange 5.5 Mailboxes and Exchange 2000/2003

After Unity is connected to Active Directory and services Exchange 2000 mailboxes, it can also service Exchange 5.5 mailboxes as long as the characteristics of the mixed-mode messaging environment are met as listed previously. The best way to tell is if the Exchange 2000 server's administrative group is joined to the Exchange 5.5 site.

In this case, Unity can only service the Exchange 5.5 mailboxes in the specific site in which the Exchange 2000 servers are joined.

In this configuration, Unity will be able to service Exchange 2000 mailboxes and Exchange 5.5 mailboxes. However, how Unity services these mailboxes does depend upon the way the CAs are configured between Exchange 5.5 and Windows 2000.

- For a two-way CA between the recipients residing in Exchange 5.5 and Windows 2000, Unity does not have any difficulty accessing the Exchange 5.5 mailboxes provided the proper permissions are granted.

- For a one-way CA from Exchange 5.5 to Windows, Unity does not service Exchange 5.5 mailboxes unless the Unity system mailbox is created in Exchange 5.5 and moved to Exchange 2000/2003. This step is necessary because of the limitations of directory visibility resulting from the CA. This is not a Unity limitation but an Exchange limitation. In order to create the Unity system mailbox in the Exchange 5.5 directory, follow the steps found in the Unity 4.0 Installation Guide. These steps include the tasks necessary to create the new system mailbox and to delete the system mailbox originally created by Unity during installation.

With Unity connected to Exchange 2000/2003 and Active Directory and servicing both Exchange 5.5 and Exchange 2000 mailboxes, Unity looks at Active Directory as its source of information about both Exchange 5.5 and Exchange 2000/2003 mailboxes. This means it simply uses the Active Directory information for all identification of users regardless of where their mailboxes are homed.

Typically, changes made to recipients in the Exchange 5.5 directory do not affect Unity's normal operations. Unity's use of the Active Directory schema includes using nonUnity-specific attributes, such as display name, first name, and also Unity-specific attributes that are added as a result of the Unity Active Directory schema extension. With the ADC in place, changes to a user's attributes can be made in the Exchange 5.5 directory, which will be replicated to Active Directory. However, it is not possible for an administrator to make changes to Unity- specific Active Directory attributes in the Exchange 5.5 directory. Any changes made to Unity-specific Active Directory attributes do not replicate through the ADC to the Exchange 5.5 directory.

NOTE   It is important to recognize that in a mixed-messaging environment, setting the proper permissions for Unity are essential. The best way to look at permissions is that both sets of permissions are required to connect Unity to Exchange 5.5 and Exchange 2000 mailboxes. For more information about setting up permissions, refer to the Cisco Unity installation guide or the Permissions Wizard documentation. As a rule of thumb, remember the following: For Unity to also communicate with Exchange 5.5 mailboxes, it is necessary to establish the permissions necessary for Unity to access the Exchange 5.5 information stores. This means the account running the Unity-messaging facing services (AvCsMgr, AvCsGateway, AvCsGaenSvr, AvExMonitor, and AvUMRSyncSvr) must have the role of service account admins granted to it in the Site and Configuration container in the Exchange 5.5 directory. This can be explicitly or implicitly granted through its membership in the Exchange Domain Servers group in Active Directory. This group is typically used to allow Exchange 2000 to obtain replication information through the configCA used by the Exchange 2000 Site Replication server.

Planning a Unity Installation

When planning to install Unity to service Exchange mailboxes, there are several considerations. Naturally, the first set of questions asked is all about impact. How does Unity impact Exchange? Does Unity cause an increase in storage space on the Exchange servers? Does Unity require more bandwidth on the network? Is it a bandwidth hog? Does Unity cause Exchange to slow down to a crawl? There are a lot of questions like this, and there is one way to find out the answers—trending.

To understand the impact that Unity has on an Exchange installation, it is necessary to trend Exchange prior to installing Unity. To understand the impact of Unity on the Exchange servers, it is necessary to also perform the same trending after Unity is installed. Naturally, Unity has an impact on Exchange. Once Unity is installed, it essentially takes all the voice-messaging traffic that was previously separated and puts it onto the Exchange infrastructure. Thus, Unity becomes a main source of messages for subscribers in an Exchange installation.

Unity does not take Exchange down or cripple an Exchange installation however, so there is no worry that Unity will do so much damage that you have to uninstall the installed Unity software, but it is also unrealistic to expect that Unity will not have an impact.

For Exchange or its messaging infrastructure, bottlenecks such as slow servers or excessive traffic might exist and can also directly affect Unity. In fact, Unity is excellent in exposing these bottlenecks.

Installing Unity to Service Exchange

In order to better understand how Unity affects Exchange and is affected by Exchange, it is important to understand how to properly install Unity with Exchange. Once you understand how Unity installs with Exchange, you will then have a good idea of how to proceed.

Regardless of how you deploy Exchange, whether you have a distributed messaging deployment or a centralized deployment, Unity should be installed directly with Exchange and not separated through a WAN connection. This means Unity should be installed as close to Exchange as possible. Does this mean physically? No, of course not, but your goal should be to install Unity onto the same subnet. It goes further. Install Unity into the same Windows 2000/2003 domain and most importantly into the same Windows 2000/2003 site. In fact, as a best practice, Unity should connect to the same domain controller and Global Catalog servers as the Exchange servers it services.

Why do you need to install Unity this way? Because you need a means to eliminate potential response time issues related to locating Unity further away. Installing Unity as close to Exchange as possible does not eliminate all potential response time issues, however. You also have to ensure that the Exchange messaging infrastructure is optimal. So, the best way to install Unity with Exchange is after you ensure that Exchange is running optimally, and you ensure that Unity is installed as close as possible to Exchange.

Assessing Exchange For UM Readiness

Chapter 9 teaches you how to assess your messaging system for UM Readiness. Because this chapter is dedicated to Exchange, a few specifics are included here.

For unified messaging readiness, response time is the most important aspect when adding true unified messaging to Exchange or any other messaging system for that matter. Why is response time so important? Because, although passive activity might be suitable for the GUI client, and the way a user interacts with their own messages and mailbox objects, it is not suitable to TUI interaction. A user is often willing to wait for a response from the server when logging in or when clicking on a message to view it, even if the response is only a second or two. However, when the same user has to hear silence (resulting from the same delays they experience with their GUI clients) between prompts or between a prompt and activity (message retrieval, for example), even a couple of seconds is unacceptable.

Trying to manage response time might seem like a challenge. Generally, however, it is not as much of an issue. However, it is important to know how to manage or prepare for it in the event one or more of your Exchange servers become symptomatic of slow responses.

In order to assess Exchange for UM readiness, you need to not only look at Exchange but also the entire messaging infrastructure. The quickest response is, "Well, Exchange is the messaging infrastructure." However, you have to take into consideration that to Unity, the Exchange messaging infrastructure is not only the servers themselves, but also those components that the Exchange messaging infrastructure depends on, such as Windows domain controllers, Windows Global Catalog servers, name servers, and e-mail clients. In other words, you need to view the messaging infrastructure from the Unity perspective and not just at Exchange.

As mentioned in the previous section, the best way to install Unity is to do so as closely as possible to Exchange. Ideally, this also means that the other messaging infrastructure components are installed into the same logical proximity (Windows 2000/2003 site, Windows 2000 domain, Windows domain controllers, and name resolution hosts). This of course is not always possible. Even though it is not possible, it should be a goal and is ideal for Unity.

All of the messaging infrastructure components might have an effect on unified messaging readiness, however the effect might be different depending upon the component. The effects you want to minimize or eliminate are those that cause delays in the subscriber TUI experience or while they are dialed into the system.

In order to eliminate or minimize these delays, check the following and measure the average response time for each of these items:

- MAPI logons to each mailbox serviced by Unity
- Message retrieval times from Exchange to Outlook
- Mailbox limits

You can use Microsoft Windows Performance Monitor or a packet analyzer to measure these settings. There are other items you can and probably should monitor; client-to-server interactions are the important items. Mailbox access and message retrieval are the main areas, but you will also want to check logon times to the domain controller and address book lookup times to the Global Catalog.

In general, the types of measurements you will want to make are all based on Outlook client access to Exchange. Because Unity uses MAPI, the types of MAPI calls made to Exchange are similar between Outlook and Unity. There are some differences, and they are discussed later.

Aside from measuring response times from your servers to your clients, you should have an indicator of how response time differs compared to the time it takes for an MS Outlook client to load and retrieve messages from the Exchange mail store. Another area to check is response time during name resolution. This should not be an issue but, surprisingly, name resolution can sometimes be a factor with slow response time.

As shown in Figure 13-17, different dependencies affect response times. In this example, Unity is installed at one location and should only use the messaging infrastructure components located there. Any dependencies on remotely located resources, such as name resolution, Windows domain controllers, or Global Catalog servers cause unacceptable delays—up to 5 seconds or greater between prompts. If Unity is installed to service the Exchange server in the Eastside Windows 2000 site, it should be installed into that site as well. You must ensure that Unity is installed into the correct site. For example, the Exchange server in the Windows Westside site should not be serviced by the Unity server in this diagram, as it is separated by one or more WAN connections (router hops), which is considered an unsupported configuration. Having a configuration where the dependencies can cause unacceptable TUI delays should be avoided. Install Unity as close to Exchange as possible, including the same data VLAN that Exchange is located. Because MAPI is not manageable by regular IP prioritization and QoS techniques, any components that can cause MAPI delays should be readily accessible to Unity.

Figure 13-17 *Different Messaging Infrastructure Dependencies*

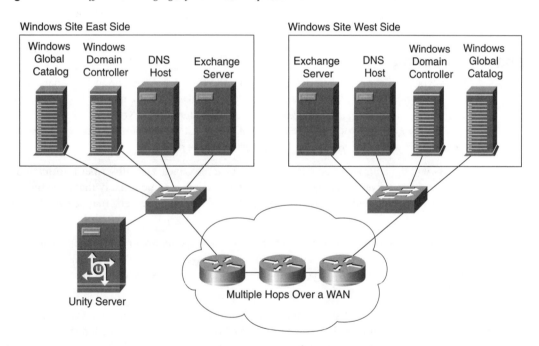

For Exchange, not only do client interactions matter, but the actual behavior and performance of the Exchange servers matters. Here are a few questions you can ask about each and every Exchange server you plan to have serviced by Unity:

- Are the Exchange servers optimized?
- Are they at capacity or do they have ample utilization for the user density on each server?

- Are there issues with memory utilization, CPU utilization, or hard-drive access and/or write times?

- Are Exchange transaction logs recorded quickly enough to prevent MAPI delays?

- Do the Exchange servers have other activities on them besides mailbox access and message retrieval? If so, these other activities can impair response time.

- Is there anti-virus software or other third-party management software that can affect the IO of the server?

If any of the answers to the previous questions are yes, then you might want to investigate that area in order to ensure it does not affect response time.

Although you might not have any issues with TUI delays as a result of slow responses between Unity and Exchange, it is always useful to understand how to monitor for and manage response time in order to ensure satisfactory subscriber experiences with unified messaging.

Capacity Planning

What type of capacity planning do you need to do for Exchange in order to prepare for Unity? There are a couple of ways to plan. You can take a holistic approach, especially if you are migrating from a legacy voice-messaging system. When you take a holistic approach, you simply look at the capacity of your existing voice-messaging system and determine if you can move it over to your Exchange servers.

Rarely will the entire user population, their voice messages, and subscriber information move in a one-server to one-server correlation. Instead, it is more likely that one voice-messaging system will migrate over to a couple of Exchange servers, maybe even several of them.

Regardless, you should be able to determine the average number of messages a voice-messaging subscriber has and even determine their average size. You will want to know both pieces of information if you want to get an idea of how each one of your Exchange mailboxes will be affected.

An alternative to the holistic approach is to perform a more technical or scientific analysis of the capacity requirements for Unity. To do this, you must go into the lab and create a mockup of some of your Exchange servers including their physical and logical layout and user density. This includes creating a sample set of Exchange recipient information. Then once you install Unity into this simulation, you should be able to determine the effect Unity has or will have on your Exchange server. Of course, you might have a strong need to simulate this under normal load, especially if you have a large user density or some other special circumstance. The closer your mockup gets to your production environment, the better you can understand the capacity requirements for Unity.

So, the areas you want to check regardless of whether or not you use a holistic approach or a scientific approach are:

- Response time between the Exchange servers and Outlook clients (or between Unity and Exchange if you are in a simulation).
- Bottlenecks including memory, CPU, and hard-drive, read and write times.
- Storage space (see trending).

In general, message size is easily considered to be an issue. Unity can support a couple of different voice coders/decoders (CODECS). The two most prevalent CODECS are G.711 or G.729a. Each of these CODECS are used to encode and decode your voice messages, greetings, and recorded names.

The G.711 CODEC encodes a voice message at about 8KB per second. So, a 60-second message would be roughly 480KB.

The G.729a CODEC encodes a voice message at about 1KB per second. So, a 60-second message would be roughly 60KB.

Immediately, the G.729a CODEC seems like a no-brainer, but if voice quality is important, it is also a no-brainer that the G.711 CODEC will sound much better because the voice sampling time is so much greater, thus better voice quality. So you have a choice to make depending upon what your users will accept and what works best for your messaging environment.

To some it might not matter, and there are efficiencies with the G.729a CODEC over the G.711 CODEC when WAN links come in to play. However, aside from bandwidth concerns, storage space concerns for voice messages are the most prevalent. The space that a voice message takes up in an Exchange mailbox might seem alarming, and that is where trending comes into play. You might also be surprised that your average size is not as small as what you think. However, you will not know until you trend or take some samples of message sizes, both from the e-mail system and voice-mail system you migrate from.

In order to help you know whether to be concerned about which CODEC you use, it is a good idea to see what your average voice message recording length is. If you find that the average recorded message length is 30 seconds, then to use the G.711 CODEC would mean average message sizes of roughly 240KB. At G.729A, the same message would be roughly 30KB. It helps to know what your average recorded voice message length is in order to properly plan capacity. Once you know what the average length is, you can add growth overhead of 20 to 40 percent, or higher. This should be your target capacity for storage space for introducing unified messaging to your Exchange infrastructure.

Trending

Trending your messaging servers gives you a good idea of what the before and after effects of Unity are going to be. It helps you establish an operational baseline. Measuring the after effects of your messaging system once Unity is installed will tell you what has changed and what you need to monitor. Do you need to trend? No. Should you trend? Yes, especially if you are concerned about the impact that Unity and unified messaging might have on your existing messaging environment.

What is the best way to trend if you want to deploy Unity? Depending upon the size of your messaging environment, you will want to trend the most active messaging systems. You should also trend the systems you might have in any type of monitor mode because of previous operational issues you might have encountered. If you have Exchange servers that you are concerned about, select and monitor some or all of them.

For monitoring, any messaging administrator wants to make sure that message delivery is working optimally. This means that the messaging systems' message transfer agents are delivering messages as rapidly as necessary, getting delivered to mail client inboxes rapidly without any alarming delays, being managed as efficiently as possible, and that disk storage integrity is being preserved.

To monitor Exchange, there is an abundant array of Windows Performance Monitor counters for all aspects of Exchange. Refer to Exchange documentation or the Microsoft Exchange web site. In addition, you can find white papers on monitoring Unity's performance on the Cisco website, which has a large amount of counters you can use to monitor Exchange. The Cisco Unity installation CD also has a performance Visual Basic Script (VBS) file you can run to monitor Exchange.

Here are some recommendations for trending:

- Determine where data is going to be collected and then determine what you are going to do with it once you collect it. If you are planning on graphing categories of data, consider how you are going to organize the data once it's captured.

- If you have never trended for baselines, establish a period between one and two weeks for an initial trending cycle. During this period, attempt to minimize making drastic changes that could skew the trend results. These drastic changes include offloading a large number of mailboxes from one server to another, taking your target servers down for maintenance during the trending period, and flooding your subscribers with test broadcast messages that they might not otherwise receive. Remember, you want to start your trending to establish a baseline. Over time, you might see variance and the drastic changes mentioned previously might be included in that variance, but initially your goal should be able to establish a normal operational baseline.

- During the initial trending cycle:
  - Note both normal and peak periods. You might find that both these periods change over time. This is neither good nor bad, but should be used as indicators of your end users' activities to help you better manage your Exchange servers. Naturally this applies to any messaging system, not just Exchange.

- As with all cycles, keep your sampling intervals to a manageable level. Sampling every 5 seconds or even every 60 seconds is a lot of data. You will find through some trial and error that a 15-minute sampling cycle is as accurate as a 2-minute cycle.

- For subsequent trending cycles:

  - Maintain the same sampling intervals as the initial cycle.

  - Do not add new categories to sample. If you think you might be interested in certain aspects of your messaging system before you start your initial cycle, then collect that data and review it from the beginning. Do this, even if you do not think you need it now. You never know how important it will become over time.

  - Do not delete sampling categories unless you know you are not going to use the data any longer. In some cases this might be the true, in other cases it might not. So, if there is any doubt, keep sampling the data.

When you measure the before and after effects of Unity and unified messaging, you will benefit the most from repeating everything you do in the before period during the after period. If you deviate too much, you run the risk of skewing your trending and thus your results might be invalid. If you trend before Unity is installed and your duration is two weeks, then do the same afterward.

Make sure you know what the Unity configuration is supposed to look like and that all installation is complete and the server has been successfully deployed without any ongoing operational issues prior to starting your trend. Again, if Unity is taken offline or having features turned on and reconfigured during the after period, your data will be skewed. For example, if you deploy Unity without adding TTS to any CoS and the after the installation you decide to add TTS so subscribers can play their e-mail over the phone, you will change the trending variables and you will skew the data. Make sure your configuration is established before you start the after period.

How Unity Can Affect Exchange

During the after trending period, you should notice a change in the following areas of your messaging system:

- Mailbox sizes will most likely increase.

- The average message size might increase.

- The number of messages passing through your messaging servers from server-to-server and from client-to-client will increase.

- The number of logon sessions will increase.

- The amount of messaging activity from Unity to Exchange mainly flows one way; from Unity to Exchange. However, if you use TTS, you might see the messaging activity differently, even more equal both ways.

It is a given if an Exchange recipient becomes a Unity subscriber as well, the mailbox size will increase because of adding voice messages to the mailbox. If there were none in the mailbox before, and you migrate the voice-messaging functionality to Exchange through Unity, your average mailbox size increases. How much? An estimate cannot be given because every implementation and usage of Exchange is different. Some companies might notice only slight changes. Other companies might notice drastic changes. Some users might be heavy e-mail and voice-mail users. If they are, you will most likely see the habits of these heavy users manifest in an increase in mailbox size. Heavy users have a tendency to keep messages longer as well, so the fact that messages stick around longer might prove that the mailbox size is an issue.

Because mailbox size increases, how should it best be handled and planned for? That is up to you. Some companies simply do nothing, meaning they do not change any mailbox size limitation settings and expect the end-users to manage their own messages by archiving them to local PSTs or through other methods. Some companies change their mailbox size limitation policies so that the mailboxes are allowed to grow to larger sizes. This is fine, of course, but it means that it becomes necessary to manage storage space or add larger disks into your Exchange servers.

The average message size might increase once Unity is installed and operational. Is it a given the size will increase? No, if your users are used to sending large e-mail messages around to one another, Unity might not affect the average message size at all. Remember a 60-second voice message using the G.711 CODEC is roughly 480KB in size. Check your average message size during the before trending cycle and see what the average size is. Also, if you use only the G.729 CODEC, you should not see much of an average message size increase.

The average number of messages traveling through your messaging system might increase. This is especially the case if you are performing a wholesale migration from a legacy voice-messaging system to Unity. The number of voice messages you had in the legacy system ends up in Exchange. Depending upon the legacy voice-messaging system you were using prior to deploying Unity, you might notice that Unity has more features in specific areas or that unified messaging makes using some features more attractive to subscribers. If this is the case, you can actually experience a turnpike effect where the number of total messages becomes greater than the total number of voice messages and total number of e-mail messages combined.

The number of logon sessions increases on each Exchange server serviced by Unity. Unity's message store monitor server logs onto each mailbox that is also a Unity subscriber to monitor the messages submitted to the inbox. It then lights the lamp of the telephone when any voice message appears in the inbox. Unity also logs onto a subscriber's mailbox in real time when a subscriber calls into the system and checks their messages. However, depending upon the port density you have installed on each Unity server, the total number of real-time subscriber logons will never be greater than the total number of ports you have dedicated to in-bound voice messaging at any given time.

If you are not using TTS so subscribers can play back their e-mail messages over the phone, then you should see that Unity sends more messages to Exchange than it receives. If TTS is enabled for some or all of your subscribers, your total number of sent messages could be higher.

You might ask the question, "Is Unity load bearing on Exchange?" It can, if you have a large user density on each Exchange server being serviced by Unity and if you have a high volume of messages being submitted to the subscribers on that server from Unity. However, you need to determine if your Exchange servers have large user densities. Some companies have a policy dictating the maximum number of mailboxes they can have on a given Exchange server. Does this mean that if the maximum number of mailboxes is reached on a server applied to it that Unity is load-bearing? No, but if you have any servers you consider to be at capacity, then you might find that Unity's interaction with that server creates an undesirable load on that server.

How Unity Is Affected by Exchange

Because Unity provides true unified messaging, it will certainly tell you if Exchange is not healthy. If you have two thousand Outlook clients connected to a given Exchange server, they might tell you the same thing that Unity does. The difference is that for Unity, all the delays and timeouts that occur with those two thousand Outlook clients occur on Unity as if it were two thousand clients all on the same server; this is essentially the case.

So, if Exchange is not running in an optimized or healthy fashion, Unity will tell you, even if you know it already. If your Exchange server is slow because of performance reasons, Unity is affected by it. If your Exchange server is slow because of some type of hardware constraint, such as low-memory usage, Exchange will have a hard time committing its transactions to its transaction logs. This type of condition causes MAPI IO to be suspended and thus keeps all clients, not just Unity, from being able to access the mailbox store for a short period of time. If these delays or stalls happen, Unity subscribers are affected by long delays during the TUI conversation especially with any prompt that requires an off-box call to Exchange, such as a log on to the mailbox, message retrieval, or message submittal. To test for this condition, you can monitor Exchange log record stalls using the Exchange database performance monitor counters.

Planning to Administer Unity with Exchange

Section 3 of this book covers administration in detail. In order to plan for administering subscribers, which are Exchange mailboxes, you should consider your current administrative tasks surrounding the management of and administration of those Exchange mailboxes.

When planning a Unity installation, regardless of size, it is a good idea to compare administrative tasks between both Unity and Exchange and determine the implications of any routine administrative tasks. This is not to say that starting out you have complete incompatibility. Instead, the objective here is to make sure you understand the administrative tasks associated with Unity and integrate those tasks into your Exchange administrative mantra.

The following tasks require consideration for subscriber accounts in Unity:

- **Moving an Exchange mailbox**. This requires time to replicate and for the change to be written to Unity. During the replication and until the change is replicated to Unity (such as the Exchange homeMDB and homeMTA change), the subscriber might not be able to access their messages.

- **Changing mailbox settings**. This includes settings, such as mailbox size limitation settings. Unity needs to synchronize these changes in order for the subscriber to have TUI access without any type of anomalous behavior. If Unity cannot check the mailbox size and limitation settings, it cannot determine whether your mailbox is full and whether you are allowed to send messages.

- **Changing mailbox addresses**. This includes SMTP addresses or Exchange addresses. Naturally, Unity is not able to properly address a message if its copy says the address is one thing but the directory says it is something else. The Unity database needs to have time to synchronize the change before it can be effective. This is typically between 2 and 15 minutes once the change is written to the directory. It can be longer depending on the time it takes to replicate to the domain controller and/or the Global Catalog Unity is connected to.

It is simply a good idea to consider how Unity sees the Exchange mailbox information and make sure you give Unity time to update prior to considering the change action completed.

Designing for Sustainable Operations

Outside of administration, any type of management action that can affect Unity's operations should be made to include the impact on Unity as a dependency factor—for example, taking an Exchange server down for scheduled maintenance. If you do and Unity is servicing the mailboxes on that server, it will affect Unity's ability to access messages from both Exchange and Unity. So, make sure that Unity is included in the maintenance plans.

The same holds for domain controllers, Global Catalog servers, and name resolution hosts. Consider that Unity is dependent upon these components just the same way as it is on Exchange. If you schedule one of these components for down time, simply make sure you consider the impact on Unity and understand that subscribers will be affected.

One area that deserves attention is the service accounts used to run Unity. Because Unity needs different service accounts with different needs depending upon what role that service account has, it is a good idea to set up a workable policy for managing these service accounts.

Making sure that password changes are managed on a regular basis is one good example. Make sure that group policies applied to these service accounts do not have a negative impact on the resources they need access to. For example, when you grant a service account permissions in the directory, that account then has no control over when those permissions might be taken away from it. Some companies might have security bots roaming the directory trying to find permissions out-of-place. Or an administrator, who is simply unaware of the Unity service account and its needed permissions, removes them without understanding the impact to the Unity server itself or the subscribers who access it. If possible, make sure that service account permissions and access are managed in such a way that their permissions are not needlessly revoked for any reason. Doing so impacts the subscribers who use the system by one or all of the following symptoms:

- The server becomes completely unavailable.
- Subscribers are not able to sign in; they get the failsafe conversation.
- Subscribers can sign in and check messages but are not able to send messages.
- Subscribers might experience excessive delays and timeouts.

Once these considerations are in place and are included in the operations management practices of your server administration and management team, you are ready to install Unity.

How to Deploy Unity with Exchange

For each version of Exchange, there are some differences in how Unity can be deployed. It is recommended that you read through every section even if you are concerned only about one specific version of Exchange.

Exchange 5.5

With Exchange 5.5, the way that Unity can service any number of Exchange servers within a single Exchange 5.5 site fits nicely with the Exchange 5.5 organization and site model. Because of the deployment rule of installing Unity as close to Exchange as possible, if you have an Exchange 5.5 site in location A, then install Unity in location A and try to follow the deployment rule as closely as possible.

In Figure 13-18, two Unity servers are installed to service Exchange 5.5 servers. The diagram depicts a Windows domain and an Exchange 5.5 site. The Unity servers are installed into the domain and servicing the Exchange 5.5 servers. Note that all servers are connected to the same physical switch. In reality, this switch can represent the local area network that might consist of multiple subnets.

Figure 13-18 *Unity Installed into the Same Physical Location as Exchange Servers in a Given Exchange 5.5 Site*

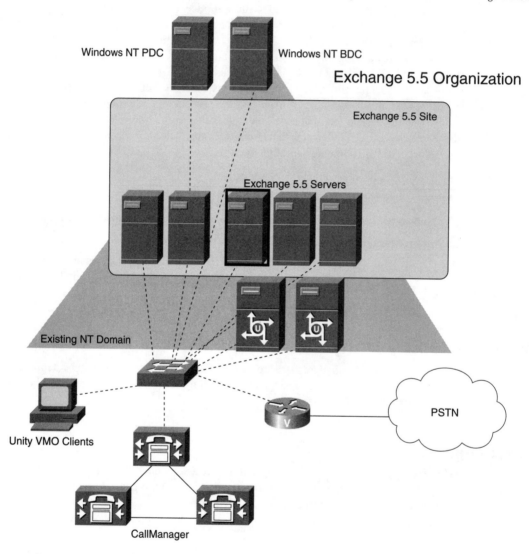

However, if your Exchange 5.5 site spans multiple locations, consider how this might affect Unity's capability to service these servers when they are separated by a WAN connection. Unity cannot be remotely connected to Exchange. The chance of latency is too high and the quality of service cannot be easily guaranteed. Thus, if your Exchange 5.5 site spans multiple locations, colocate Unity with each group of Exchange 5.5 servers.

The diagram in Figure 13-19 shows two Unity servers: one installed at location A and the other installed at location B. Note, even though this is a single Exchange 5.5 site, the Exchange 5.5 servers are distributed. This is a challenging Exchange-messaging topology to manage; however, many organizations employ this topology for their messaging solution. For Unity, it can effectively support this solution if the deployment rules for Unity are adhered to. Unity is located with the messaging servers it services and all messaging infrastructure components are colocated as well, such as accounts, domain controllers, and name resolution hosts. In this example, Unity is deployed in a distributed messaging and distributed call processing deployment model combination.

Figure 13-19 *Two Unity Servers Servicing Their Own Separate Physical Locations*

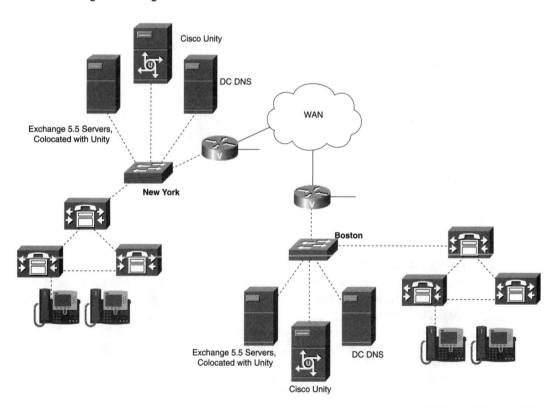

Server Placement

As stated, place the server as close as possible to Exchange servers. Do not take this to mean you can install Unity close to any Exchange servers. Instead, install Unity as close to the Exchange servers it is going to service. Following are some examples of why installing Unity as close to the Exchange servers can be problematic.

Example 1: Unity on a Different VLAN

As shown in Figure 13-20, a common drawback to installing Unity into a voice VLAN with CallManager and IP phones is that notification delays and TUI prompts can occur when the Exchange servers are on a different VLAN. However, notification delays do not have a tendency to occur when Unity is located on the same VLAN as Exchange.

Figure 13-20 *Unity on a Different VLAN than Exchange*

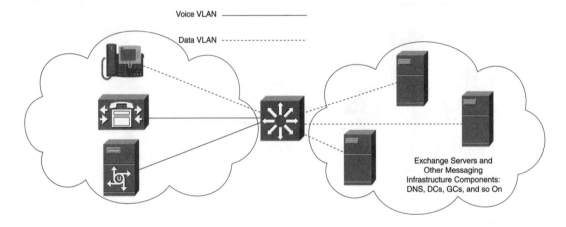

Example 2: Unity in a Separate Building in a Campus LAN

It is easy to install Unity, as shown in the example in Figure 13-21, and have no issues with response time. However, if Unity is going to service Exchange 5.5 and especially Exchange 2000 or 2003, the need for it to be in the same Windows 2000/2003 site and accessing the same GC as Exchange is key to acceptable service levels. Exchange 5.5 has its own directory and when Unity is servicing it, Unity's access to the Exchange 5.5 directory and its dependency on a Windows 2000 site is minimized. If these requirements can be met, then it is certainly a valid solution to place Unity in a completely separate physical location from

Exchange. However, not too many networks and Windows infrastructures are so accommo-dating. If yours is and latency can be managed and measured, then you should not expect to experience problems with TUI delays.

Figure 13-21   *Unity Connected to Exchange Over a Campus LAN*

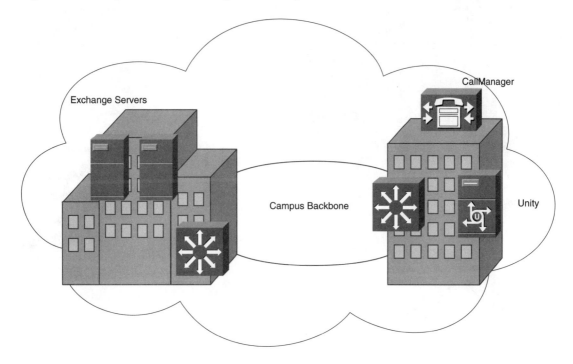

Example 3: Unity Across the WAN

As shown in Figure 13-22, Unity cannot service Exchange remotely. It does not matter if it is Exchange 5.5 or Exchange 2000/2003. In the following example, Unity is deployed in an unmanageable configuration because the Exchange servers it services are separated through a WAN connection. In this example, there are too many points of failure.

If you examine the reasons why server placement is so important, you will see that in addition to eliminating points of failure, you also reduce your chances of loss of dependencies.

Figure 13-22 *Unity Separated from Exchange Through a WAN Connection*

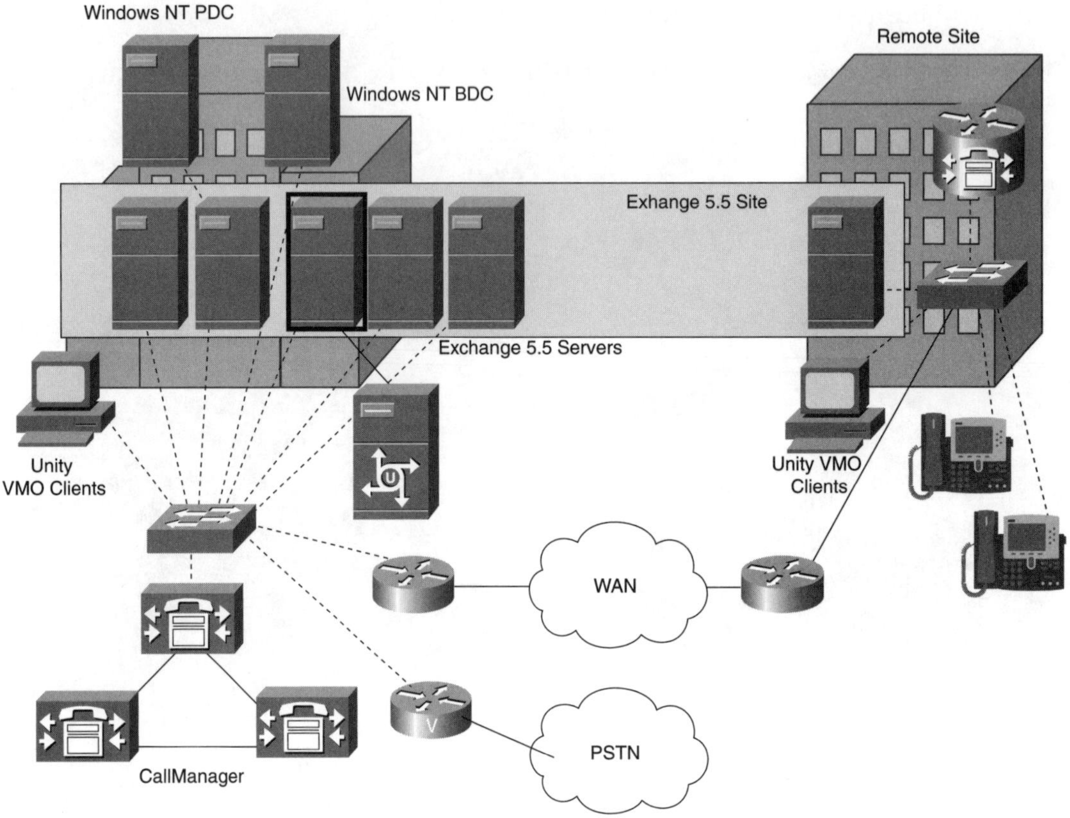

Figure 13-23 depicts the ideal Unity installation—Unity colocated together with its messaging infrastructure dependencies on the same subnet. In this example, CallManager might be on a separate VLAN.

Figure 13-24 depicts a more common Unity installation. In this example, Unity is still colocated with Exchange. Other messaging infrastructure components, however, are on different subnets. This is typical but comes with higher latency risk.

Figure 13-23 *Unity's Ideal Installation*

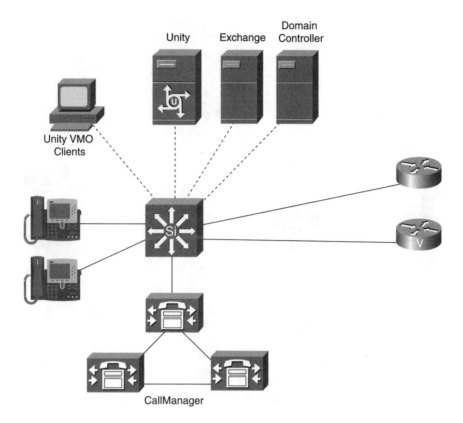

Are there other ways that Unity can be deployed? Actually, no. It is that simple. Keep Unity close to Exchange and you will maximize the unified messaging capabilities of the application and minimize the risks of TUI latency.

Figure 13-24 *Unity's Typical Installation*

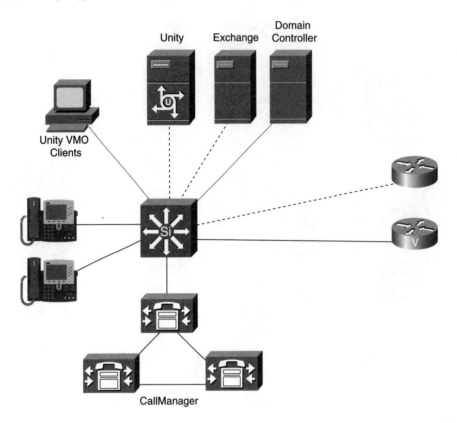

Unity Networking

With one or more Unity servers installed to service one or more Exchange 5.5 sites, you will want to allow the subscribers on different Unity servers to address messages to one another. Most of the issues surrounding setup of digital networking in Unity are included in Chapter 12, "Unity Networking." However, there is one thing to take into consideration is the search scope setting for each Unity server. If you want subscribers to address messages to other subscribers in your Exchange organization, then you need to set the search scope to global on every Unity server.

In Figure 13-25, all Unity servers are in an Exchange 5.5 organization where the search scope is set to global, and each Unity server services its own Exchange 5.5 site. Unity sees the objects in its site and looks only in the site to import mail recipients of that site as Unity subscribers. However, its search scope is set to the organizational level like all the other Unity servers. This allows subscribers in one site to address messages to subscribers in another.

Figure 13-25   *Unity Networking*

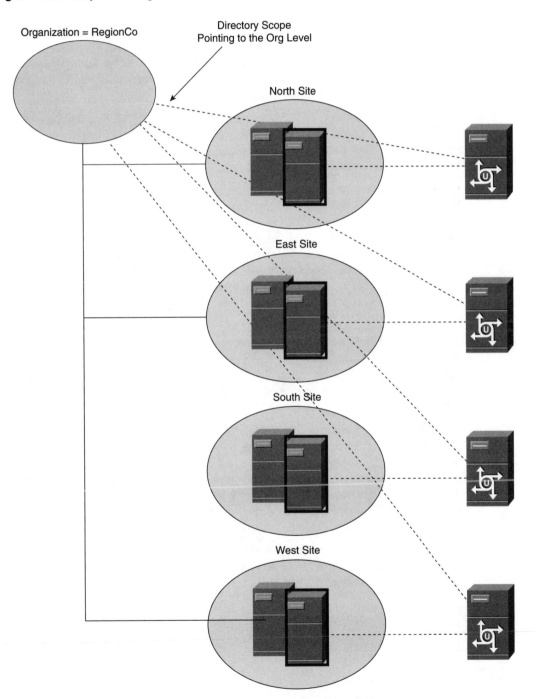

Selecting a Partner Server

An important aspect of deploying Unity is selecting the partner server for it to connect to. The partner server is simply an Exchange 5.5 server that is dedicated to house the Unity system mailbox and other default objects created during installation. The Unity system mailbox is used to deliver messages to subscribers from outside callers. The system mailbox is also used to logon to subscriber mailboxes in order to perform notifications (light message waiting indicators on the subscriber's phone).

The main considerations for selecting a partner are the volume of calls and messages you receive from outside callers and the availability of the server housing the mailbox. In Figure 13-26, a Unity failover pair is connected to a partner server and it services other Exchange 5.5 servers in the Exchange 5.5 site.

If you have a high volume of calls from outside callers with a lot of messages submitted to your subscribers, you need to ensure that you use a partner server that typically has a lighter load. When you trend your messaging servers, make sure you get a good idea of how active each server is including how many messages are submitted to and from the MTA. Also, if you trend uptime or have another means to track your server availability, then select an Exchange server that has less activity and is always available. This helps to ensure that Unity can always deliver messages to subscribers from outside callers. As far as Unity is concerned, if its system mailbox delivers the message to the MTA, then the message is delivered.

The question might be asked: Should you set up a new partner server for Unity? The answer is no. It is not necessary unless you do not have any servers that are up all the time. After you trend your Exchange servers and have a good idea of the volume of messages on your current voice-messaging server, you should be able to easily determine which Exchange server to make a Unity partner server.

For deployment, you might decide that a larger Exchange 5.5 site needs more than one Unity server to service the user population in the site. If that is the case, then you might point each Unity server to the same Exchange 5.5 server as the partner server. Or, you can point each Unity server to a separate Exchange server. Again, it all depends on the estimated volume of messages and availability. There is no hard number for the number of Unity servers that can be serviced by a single partner server. Note also that the partner server is assigned when you install Unity. It is where you create the default objects.

As shown in Figure 13-27, three Unity servers use the same partner server. The maximum number of Unity servers that can be serviced by one Exchange server is limited to the maximum physical capacity plus any other usage on that Exchange server.

Figure 13-26 *A Unity Failover Pair Connected to a Partner Server and Servicing Other Exchange Servers*

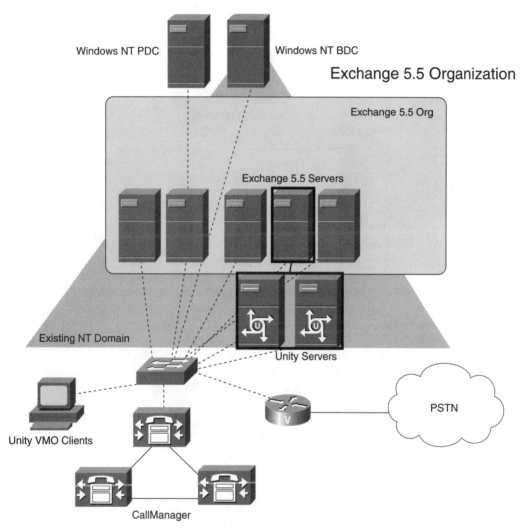

After the partner server is established and the Unity System Mailbox is created, make sure that the system mailbox does not get deleted. If it is deleted, Unity attempts to recreate it on startup. If it cannot recreate the mailbox, it starts up in Unity Messaging Repository (UMR) mode.

Figure 13-27 *Three Unity Servers Using the Same Partner Server*

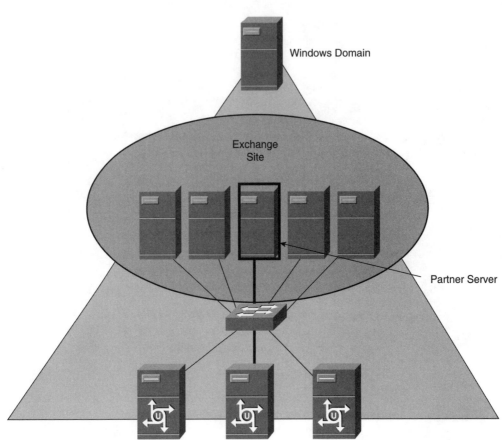

Exchange 2000/2003

With Exchange 2000/2003, the way that Unity can service any number of Exchange servers is similar to the way it services Exchange 5.5 servers. There are some differences however, although the strict rule of deploying Unity close to Exchange still applies, there are a couple more levels of restrictions that should be closely followed. The Exchange 2000/2003 model for deployment uses an administrative group and a routing group. As mentioned in the "Exchange 2000/2003 Characteristics" section, the fact that there are both administrative groups and routing groups immediately tells you that Unity's placement restrictions should reside within these group borders and not throughout. Again, this is a recommendation for ease of administration and a reduction in the risk potential of latency in the case of routing groups. Sometimes it not always is practical to have a separate solution for each administrative group.

An Exchange 2000/2003 administrative group should be considered the upper-most boundary for deploying Unity, just for ease of administration. There is no technical limitation here, however. If you have more than one administrative group, you need to consider one Unity server per administrative group at a minimum. To narrow it down even further, any administrative group can have one or more routing groups. This adds an additional level of restriction because routing groups can be made up of one or more physical sites where Exchange 2000/2003 servers reside. Unity documentation might even state that Unity can service only one routing group and no more than that. However, the main reason this is stated is because a routing group might span beyond a single location. If this is the case, then you will want to restrict Unity's servicing ability to only those servers that are local to it.

The example in Figure 13-28 depicts Unity installed into the same physical location as Exchange servers in an Exchange 2000 administrative group and routing group. Note the larger administrative group with a few routing groups, and how Unity services Exchange 2000 servers in a single physical location and the routing group there. The trend is to have only one routing group in a single organization or as few as possible, but there is no restriction on the number of routing groups. Therefore, it is possible to see any number of routing groups within an Exchange 2000/2003 organization.

Figure 13-28 *Unity Installed into an Administrative Group with Multiple Routing Groups, Each Separated by a WAN Connection*

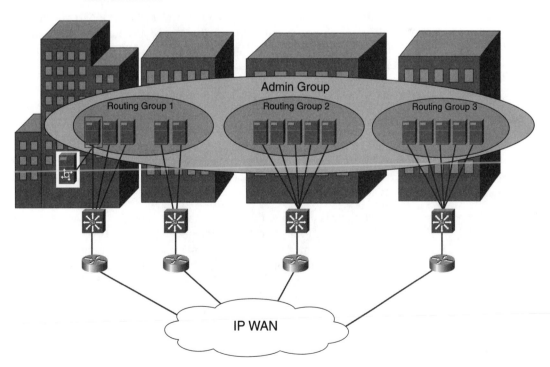

Of course, there is another piece to this puzzle. If you evaluate Unity or use it for some time, you will note a rule that states, "Unity should be installed into the same Windows 2000 site as the Exchange 2000 servers it services." This is exactly true. In fact, it is key. As you narrow the scope of which Exchange servers Unity should service, it becomes simple. Can you install Unity to service Exchange 2000/2003 servers in more than one Windows 2000/2003 site? The answer is no; that it is unlikely your subscribers located in the site that Unity was not located might be left with response time issues. Many more potential issues exist and it is best not to expose Unity to them. So, place the Unity server in the same Windows 2000/2003 site as the Exchange 2000/2003 servers that it servicees. Unity might, however, be able to service subscribers and Exchange servers across a Windows site boundary in a campus network. It is not, however, considered optimal or best practice because response time is less likely to be controlled. Again, the issue is response time. If your network has sufficient bandwidth and your Exchange servers are optimized, then it is probably safe to deploy Unity this way. It is recommended, however, that you thoroughly test this type of configuration and make sure it provides normal operations to subscribers prior to a full cutover.

Let us delve further. Point the Unity server to the same Windows 2000/2003 DC and GC being serviced by the Exchange 2000/2003 servers in single site. This also includes the DNS server that should reside there. What happens if you do not do this? One thing that can happen is that Unity does not get timely updates on changes made to other Unity servers and subscribers. Therefore, if Unity is servicing subscribers in two different Windows 2003 sites, Unity has to wait for directory replication to complete prior to trying to service a subscriber that has its mailbox moved so Unity can record that change too. If you do not allow Unity to wait for the change to come through directory replication, then the results of trying to reach that subscriber from the TUI might end up with Unity playing back the failsafe conversation.

This entire issue might seem like a minor issue unless your environment has a large user population and administrative changes take place with roughly 10 to 20 percent of your population on a daily basis. You want to minimize the possibility of errors resulting in these types of configurations.

As shown in Figure 13-29, Unity is installed into the same physical location as Exchange servers in an Exchange 2000/2003 administrative and routing group pointing to the same DC and GC Windows 2000 site and domain.

For server placement, there is one more rule you want to use to determine where to install Unity. That is making sure that Unity is installed onto the same data VLAN as Exchange. This is more important as your messaging environment's messaging volume increases, including an increase in the number of messages left from outside callers or subscribers. The larger the activity the more outdial ports you need in order to light the MWIs. If you install Unity onto a separate VLAN than Exchange you might have operational issues such as not being able to light the MWIs in a reasonable period of time (a few seconds).

Figure 13-29 *Unity Accessing the Same DC and GC as the Exchange Servers it Services*

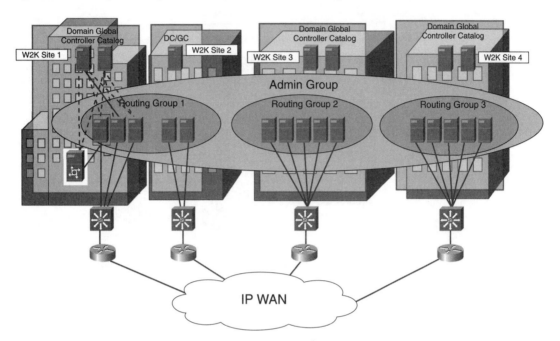

In Figure 13-30, Unity is in a more constrained, but ideal, configuration. This example shows Unity in the same configuration as in Figure 13-29, but in this case it is installed into the same VLAN as Exchange.

While this seems restrictive, it is important to note that in order to optimize Unity's service-ability, it is necessary to take away the possibilities that it might be subjected to response time or error conditions beyond its control. Because it uses the Exchange messaging infra-structure, it has to play by the rules, which means it can be subjected to the same dependen-cies as Exchange. That said, by reducing or eliminating these dependencies (by getting Unity as close as possible to Exchange), you maximize the likelihood that Unity is best able to service its subscribers.

So, should you deploy Unity to service multiple Exchange 2000/2003 routing groups? The answer is not if they are not in the same Windows 2000/2003 site. Can you have remote Exchange servers in a given routing group even if Unity services only the local Exchange servers in that routing group? The answer is yes, however, Unity should not service any sub-scribers on any remotely located Exchange 2000/2003 servers. The response time delays cannot easily be accounted for. So, minimize or eliminate deviations from these server placement rules of Unity, and you should be able to ensure that Unity services its subscrib-ers with less chance of any delay.

Figure 13-30 *Unity Installed into the Same VLAN and Windows 2000 Site as Exchange*

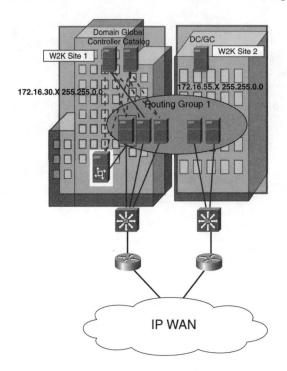

In the example shown in Figure 13-31, the routing group spans to more than one location. Unity services only the Exchange servers it is colocated with. If Unity were to service the remotely located servers as well, higher latency between the Unity and Exchange servers would result in TUI delays for all subscribers regardless of whether or not they are local or remote to Unity. If Unity was expected to service all the servers in this routing group, you would have a good example of what not to do when deploying Unity with Exchange. However, it is possible to deploy Unity in a single routing group and have Unity service only the Exchange servers that were colocated with it and not those located across the WAN, even though they are in the same routing group.

As with Exchange 5.5, subscribers in Exchange 2000/2003 might want to address each other regardless of which Unity server they installed. It is necessary to set the service scope.

It is necessary to select a partner server for each Unity server servicing mailboxes on Exchange 2000/2003 servers. The same rules apply for selecting a partner server as listed in the Exchange 5.5 section. Again, messaging activity and availability are the two key areas that you will want to concentrate on for partner server selection. Following are a few examples of partner server selections for Exchange 2000/2003.

Figure 13-31 *Unity Servicing Exchange Servers in a Given Routing Group*

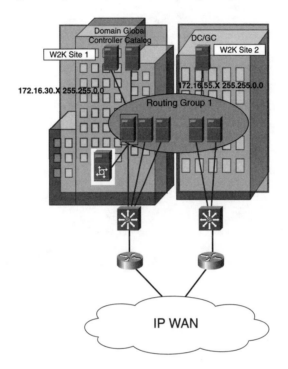

In Figure 13-32, a single Unity server is connected to a partner server and services multiple, Exchange servers.

In Figure 13-33, more than one Unity server uses the same Exchange server as its partner server. The Exchange partner server would be primarily dedicated to the Unity servers. This is typically set up this way when the Exchange routing group has a large user density and when you need multiple Unity servers to service them.

Figure 13-32 *A Single Unity Server Servicing Multiple Exchange Servers*

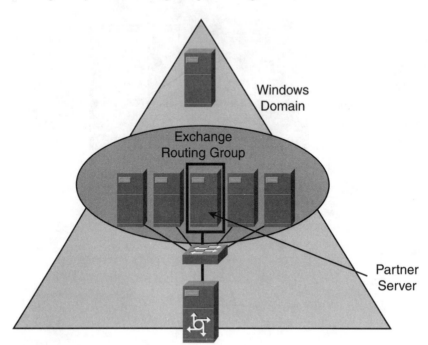

In the example shown in Figure 13-34, each Unity server has its own partner server in its own routing group. This is the scalable solution for Unity. If its correlation between Unity server and routing group is one-to-one. Naturally, any routing group that has a larger user density than what a single Unity server can handle can support more than one Unity server.

One important item to know about selecting the Exchange 2000/2003 partner server for Unity: Your partner server needs to have a mailbox store; otherwise, it cannot be used by Unity.

Exchange in a Mixed-Messaging Configuration

If your goal is to have Unity service Exchange 5.5 and Exchange 2000/2003 mailboxes while you migrate to Exchange 2000/2003, then you need to make sure that each Unity server is placed according to the server placement rules established in the Exchange 2000/2003 section. The only difference is that, in order for Unity to also service the Exchange 5.5 mailboxes, it is important to make sure that it has the proper permissions in the Exchange 5.5 site.

Figure 13-33 *Multiple Unity Servers Servicing Multiple Exchange Servers*

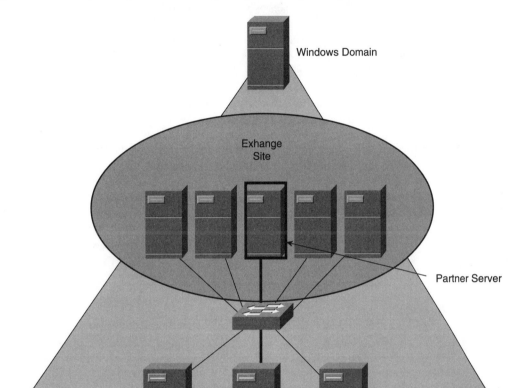

Figure 13-34 *A One-to-One Correlation Between Unity Servers and Routing Groups*

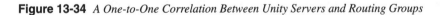
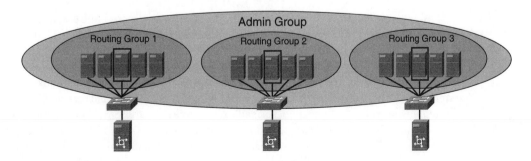

The example shown in Figure 13-35 shows Unity installed to service both Exchange 5.5 and Exchange 2000/2003 mailboxes using an Exchange 2000/2003 partner server and joining Unity to the same Windows 2000 site as the Exchange 2000/2003 servers it services. In order for Unity to service the mailboxes located on the Exchange 5.5 servers, it is necessary to make sure that Unity has the necessary permissions and also that the characteristics of a mixed-messaging environment are met. In this case, those characteristics of a mixed-messaging environment are in place and Unity can service mailboxes in both versions of Exchange. Note that in this example Unity uses Active Directory to identify all subscribers whether their mailboxes are located on Exchange 5.5 or Exchange 2000/2003.

Figure 13-35 *Unity Servicing Both Exchange 5.5 Mailboxes and Exchange 2000/2003 Mailboxes*

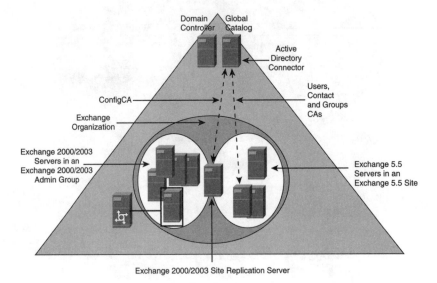

An alternative is to have Unity installed to service the Exchange 2000/2003 mailboxes only and not allow Exchange 5.5 mailboxes the use of unified messaging through Unity. This is not practical if Unity is already servicing Exchange 5.5 mailboxes.

So, if you review the example shown in Figure 13-35, Unity is servicing Exchange 2000/2003 mailboxes only. This same diagram can also be used to demonstrate how Unity can be installed not to service Exchange 5.5 mailboxes, but reside in the same configuration. The difference in this example is that Unity has no permissions to service mailboxes in Exchange 5.5. In order to allow Unity to service only Exchange 2000/2003 mailboxes, it is simply a matter of making sure it has no permissions to Exchange 5.5, and then making sure that administratively, the Exchange 5.5 mailboxes directory entries are kept separate from the Exchange 2000/2003 directory entries. For Active Directory, this is typically done by keeping the mail-enabled users in separate OUs in the directory. Thus, administratively, only Exchange 2000/2003 mail-enabled users can become subscribers, and Exchange 5.5

mailboxes remain e-mail users only. The characteristics of a mixed-mode messaging environment are still met as this is a requirement for migrating mailboxes from Exchange 5.5 to Exchange 2000/2003.

In a mixed-messaging environment, Unity can provide only digital networking between all subscribers if all Unity servers are installed on the Exchange 2000/2003 side of the messaging environment. Because Unity uses different directory data in Exchange 2000/2003 than it does in Exchange 5.5, and the data is not shared between Unity servers. For instance, subscribers who are still homed on a Unity server installed into and exclusively servicing Exchange 5.5 mailboxes cannot address messages to subscribers who have been migrated to an Exchange 2000/2003 server that is serviced by a different Unity server.

In Figure 13-36, two separate Unity servers service their own version of Exchange. In this example, subscribers of the Unity server in the Exchange 5.5 site cannot perform message addressing to the subscribers of the Unity server in the Exchange 2000/2003 administrative group. In order to enable message addressing, SMTP networking has to be performed. This requires undue administrative overhead in that custom recipients, such as Unity Internet subscribers must exist in Exchange 5.5 to represent the subscribers in Exchange 2000/2003, and contacts, such as Unity Internet subscribers in Exchange 2000/2003 must exist to represent the Exchange 5.5 subscribers. And, these subscribers should not be replicated through the ADC because they already exist as mail-enabled users in their respective directories. Therefore, if they are replicated, then you end up with two records for each user. Having such an administrative overhead is simply not manageable and should not be a reason to require digital networking (message addressing and searching) between the two Unity servers that service different versions of Exchange.

Figure 13-36 *Two Separate Unity Servers Servicing Different Versions of Exchange in the Same Organization*

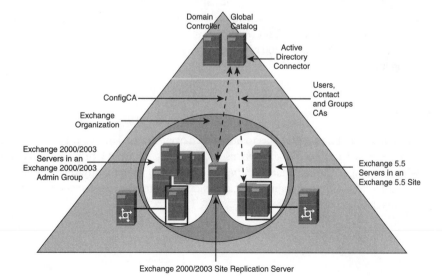

As a part of the migration of Unity from Exchange 5.5 to Exchange 2000/2003, follow the same rules for selecting a partner server as what are found in the Exchange 2000/2003 section.

Maximizing Unity's Servicing Capabilities

The best way to get the most out of Unity is to maximize its servicing capabilities. There are a few ways to do this. One way to do this is to use Unity in a streamline fashion. This means use only the features and functionality you need in order to allow Unity to focus on providing unified messaging services to your users. So, if you have subscribers who do not need to access the Unity inbox, then do not give them access or put them into a CoS that gives them the ability to access it on their own. If you do not intend to use the auto attendant and instead plan on using DIDs for all your subscribers, then you do not need to spend too much time worrying about configuring the auto attendant. However, consider all hours of your operation, not just during the day when most businesses are in operation. You might have after-hours considerations for your auto attendant.

Another way to maximize Unity's servicing capabilities is to make sure that you focus on keeping the server optimized. Periodically you need to trend the activity of the server, and make sure that the proper number of voice ports are dedicated to inbound calls and outbound calls (for notification). A part of your trending exercise should include monitoring the CPU, memory, and network adapter usage (use the CUPID tool). Monitor storage space and disk activity, of course. By keeping the server optimized and minimizing opportunities for bottlenecks, you should be able to get the most out of Unity.

Yet another way to maximize Unity's servicing capabilities is by keeping all Unity servers configured the same way and using the same configuration steps or standards for each and everyone. It is without fail that the more Unity servers you have, the more likely you might end up with misconfigured Unity servers. However, this has been mostly because of lack of attention on administrative and management tasks that should be given to the server during its operations.

Summary

The purpose of this chapter was to provide an overview of Microsoft Exchange and explain in detail how Unity sees Exchange, uses Exchange, and what Unity needs in order to work with Exchange. The next chapter emphasizes how to plan a Unity installation. Several examples are used to explain the concepts involved in planning, designing, and deploying a Unity solution using Exchange.

CHAPTER 14

Unity with Lotus Domino

This chapter discusses how to plan for, design, and deploy a solution using Unity with Lotus Domino. It discusses the key components of Domino and Notes that are most relevant to Unity, and it explains how Unity sees Domino and Notes. These topics are covered in this chapter:

- The characteristics of Lotus Domino and Notes
- Unity's perspective of Lotus Domino
- How to plan a Unity installation

Before you read this chapter, it is strongly recommended that you read the following chapters from this book:

- Chapter 1, "About Unified Messaging"
- Chapter 5, "Components and Subsystems: Messaging/Unity Messaging Repository"
- Chapter 8, "Deployment Methodology"
- Chapter 9, "Planning"
- Chapter 10, "Typical Configurations and Deployment Models"
- Chapter 15, "Upgrades and Migration"
- Chapter 19, "Administering Multiple Unity Servers"
- Chapter 20, "Subscriber Administration"

In addition, you can read any books on Lotus Domino administration.

The Characteristics of Lotus Domino and Notes

You do not learn to design and deploy Lotus Domino and Notes here. But you do learn the relevant aspects of both as they pertain to Unity and its unified messaging capabilities. To successfully deploy Unity for Domino, you must be familiar with the architectural framework of Domino and Notes, and their messaging and directory components. Having sufficient knowledge of the directory and messaging foundation that Unity depends upon for operation is the key to a successful deployment.

The release of Unity 4.0(1) marked the first time that Cisco Unity supported connectivity to a mail store other than Microsoft Exchange—in this case, IBM Lotus Domino. Lotus Software produces a cadre of products in the genre of groupware. Regarding Unity, the only products of concern currently are Lotus Domino and Lotus Notes. These two products comprise both a messaging platform and a framework for building applications that require collaboration within a team.

Cisco Unity for Domino is a unified messaging (UM) solution only. It cannot be used as part of a plain old voice-mail (POV) solution. Moreover, most UM deployments of Unity occur in a pre-existing Lotus Domino infrastructure; unified messaging is add-on functionality to Lotus Domino.

Lotus Domino is sold as a server product to handle, among other tasks, messaging needs and applications built using the Domino/Notes framework. Notes is the end-user interface to Domino. The relationship between Domino and Notes is analogous to the relationship between Exchange and Outlook: Exchange runs on servers, and Outlook resides on the end user's desktop. The same relationship holds true for Domino and Notes.

Server Component: Lotus Domino

The last major release of Lotus Domino was release 6, or R6, for short. The previous release, R5, is forward compatible with R6, and R6 is backward compatible with R5. As such, there still exists a significant install base of R5, and it is not uncommon to find a mixed-version deployment as a customer rolls out R6 to the infrastructure. Unity for Domino functions fine with both R5 and R6 versions. Although you must know whether Unity is pointed to an R5 or an R6 Domino server (setup asks for this information), the process is identical when installing Unity to an R5 and an R6 server.

From the beginning, Domino and Notes were designed to be independent of operating systems. Domino runs on a variety of operating systems, including OS/400, AIX, Sun Solaris, certain flavors of Linux, and Microsoft Windows NT, 2000, and Advanced Server. Operating system independence was accomplished by writing the product using portable C and C++ code and not building the product upon the proprietary technology of a third party.

Although Domino functions on a variety of operating systems, the server(s) that Unity communicates with must be installed upon a Windows 2000 Server platform because this is the only currently supported platform for Lotus Domino Unified Communication (DUC). DUC is software written by Lotus and branded for Cisco that allows for unified messaging functionality within a Domino/Notes deployment.

DUC consists of several components, each providing different functionality. One component is installed onto each Domino server that contains at least one mail file that receives voice messages. These mail files are termed DUC-enabled. The server component installs additional server tasks for processing message notifications sent to Unity and for DUC-enabling users. Additional mail templates that contain design elements for unified messaging also are installed. Another portion of DUC modifies the Domino directory database. The last portion is installed by the end user at the workstation and further modifies the user's mail file. In addition, DUC provides an extra API designed specifically for handling voice messages.

Lotus Domino exists in both Standard and Enterprise versions. The principal difference is support for clustering in the Enterprise version. Clustering offered by Domino can be used for both failover and load-balancing purposes. Unity for Domino takes advantage of clustering functionality when available, and this is a powerful means of offering redundant access to subscribers' mailboxes. Of course, Domino clustering does not provide failover capability for Unity functionality.

Domino clustering exists at the application level, meaning that its implementation is for the Domino server processes only. In addition, clustering does not replace the need for periodic backups in case of catastrophic failures. Lotus Software provides extensive documentation on disaster recovery of the product.

Client Component: Notes, Administrator, Designer

When you install Notes, three choices of clients are offered: Lotus Notes, Lotus Administrator, and Lotus Designer. Each of these can be installed upon the same physical machine as Domino, although Lotus does not recommend doing so. As client software, Notes, Administrator, and Designer are meant for installation upon a workstation machine.

As already mentioned, Notes is the end-user GUI. An example of a Notes client is shown in Figure 14-1. In the context of Unity, Notes is used to send and retrieve e-mail and voice messages from mail files, whether by individuals from their own desktop or by Unity when callers access their inbox over the telephone. Lotus Notes can be installed upon the physical machine that Unity is installed on. Unity utilizes the Lotus Notes API to interact programmatically with the Domino server.

Lotus Administrator greatly simplifies the tasks associated with administering a Domino deployment. Figure 14-2 shows an example of the Domino Administrator. This GUI provides a simplified means of creating users, monitoring servers, and moving mail files to other servers, among other things. The Lotus Administrator is not installed on the server containing Unity; in fact, Unity does not need it for its functionality. However, you will be well served to familiarize yourself with the Administrator's interface and functionality because you need to use them as part of the Unity installation. For example, the Administrator is used to register the person (that is, the account) that Unity uses to access the Domino server(s).

Figure 14-1 *Screen Image of a Lotus Notes 6 Client*

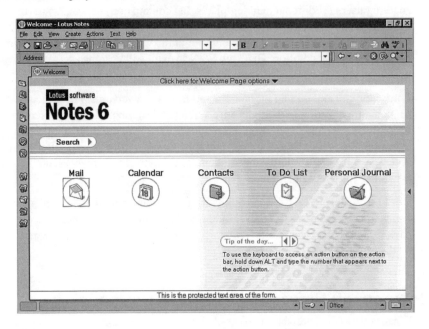

Figure 14-2 *Domino Administrator*

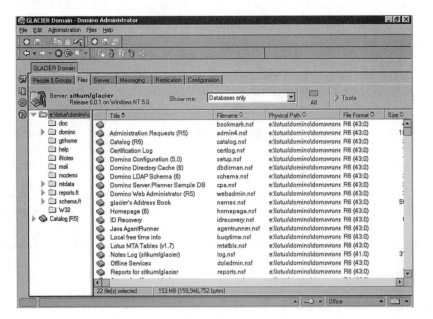

Finally, Lotus Designer is an integrated development environment (IDE) for building applications for use within the Domino/Notes environment. Although the capability to use this IDE to "dissect" a Domino/Notes application provides you with a much deeper understanding of how Domino applications are built, it is not necessary when installing and maintaining a Unity for Domino deployment. Unity does not require any access to Lotus Designer during either the installation or administration.

The release numbering of the clients follows that of Domino. That is, R6 is the latest and has a significant number of Notes R5 clients installed. At a minimum, Unity requires Notes R5 (specifically, 5.0.10) on the machine hosting Unity. Notes R6 also is supported.

Databases and Database Design

All information that is created and stored in Domino and Notes is stored in databases. A Domino/Notes database is the common storage unit for information and is shared readily among other Domino servers and Notes clients. A database is a single file and contains an extension of the Notes Storage Facility (NSF).

Information within a database is stored in individual documents (also called notes). The documents contain fields that represent the actual data. A mail database, for example, contains e-mail and fax messages and even voice messages. Each message is one document. Each document contains fields to represent the data in the message. Examples of the data in such a message and the fields that represent that data are the To and From items that are common to a mail message. A field also exists to contain the actual message body (or audio file, if this is a voice message).

That said, Domino databases generally contain documents that are related in some manner. Often the use or purpose of the document is the common thread. For example, a mail database would contain many mail documents, but you likely would not find a document representing, say, an invoice for a customer's product purchase (although there is no restriction on that occurring). Domino makes no distinction among documents; they simply contain data. As an analogy, you might have a dresser at home that contains clothing. One drawer might have socks, and another might have shirts. There is no restriction against placing socks in the shirt drawer, but that is not very logical or, more important, functional. The same logic holds true for Domino databases.

For the most part, placement of documents in a Domino/Notes database is unstructured. The database is an electronic bucket of bits. This is true at least compared to a relational database, which, by its very nature, places constraints on where data is stored. In a Domino/Notes database, the presentation of the documents and the data on a document is the responsibility of the database design.

The design of a database contains numerous elements. First, the design can dictate the way(s) in which documents are organized for viewing when the database is opened in one of the clients described previously. This viewing of documents is done either by placing documents in folders (analogous to folders in a Windows file system) or, more commonly, by using a mechanism termed *views*. To display the contents of a document, the database design supplies *forms*. Forms are basically templates meant to display specific data on a document in a specific manner in a GUI.

All databases have the same design elements available. Whether they are used depends on the application of the database. For the most part, every database contains views, forms, and folders. The design elements of any database can be viewed through the Designer client. Figure 14-3 shows an example of this for one particular database. Some of the design elements that are common to all Domino databases are shown in the left window. The right window displays instances of each design element present. Figure 14-3 shows some of the views that are present in this particular database. The views shown in the right window of the Designer client are examples of some views found in any domain directory database.

Figure 14-3 *Screen Image of the Domino Designer*

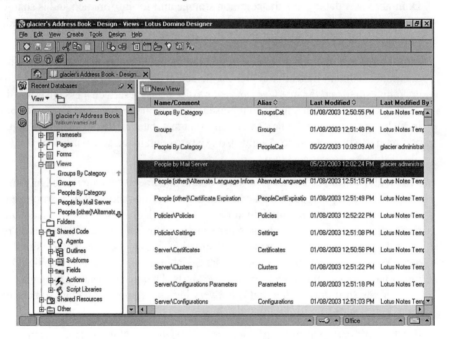

Views

Views are used more extensively than folders for most databases. In fact, Unity relies upon the presence of two specific views, $UnityNameLookup and $UnityLocLookup, for much of its unified messaging functionality. A view displays a collection of documents that are present in the database based on some selection criteria. There is a way to display documents containing some common data. For example, the R6 directory database contains a view called Groups that displays all groups (distribution lists) in the directory. Another view displays all users (or person) in the directory; this view is called, not strangely enough, People.

Views can be seen in a client GUI or can be hidden and not meant for use by a person. Generally, applications programmatically use hidden views. For example, Unity retrieves voice messages from a mail file through a view titled ($UCInbox) (the "UC" stands for Unified Communications). This hidden view is created automatically after importing the user into Unity and occurs as part of the DUC-enabling process.

Forms

Forms visually display the data within a document. The only data that is displayed is what the form is programmed to display. This is another reason why a given database should contain only documents that are related in some manner. If a form does not exist to display the document's data, it is of little use in the database. Almost always a document will contain a field listing the name of the form meant to display that document. If the form does not exist, the document generally will not display.

Database Templates

A database must be created from *something*. Lotus documentation states that a database of a given design is generated from a template that copies the design elements into a new database. In reality, a database template is a database with no data. Templates contain design elements (views, forms, and so on) only. A database template generally is given the extension NTF (for Notes Template Facility), to distinguish it from a database version of itself (which would contain an extension of NSF). To confuse matters more, a database actually can create a template: Notes makes a copy of the database but copies only the design elements, not any of the documents.

The take-home message is this: A database and the template that created the database are essentially the same species. The template simply contains none of the documents (data), but it is identical in design. In practice, though, databases and templates are treated differently and used differently.

One of these practical differences is that the database design often is altered after creation. This generally occurs when it inherits new design elements from the template that created it. However, it is possible to specify different templates to inherit from for specific design elements. The capability of a database to inherit future changes to a template is a very powerful design functionality and a convenient deployment methodology.

For example, when a user is imported into Unity for Domino, that user's mail file is modified to contain a view for displaying voice messages only, as well as buttons for creating, replying to, and forwarding voice messages. These design elements are created from a DUCS mail template. If later DUCS is upgraded to a newer version, the DUCS mail template first is updated. All mail files that contain design elements from that template automatically pull the new design elements to themselves and update the database design.

Updating a database design from a template is a function of the Domino server and, by default, occurs every night at 1 A.M. Obviously, updates occur only if the template itself has been modified since the previous update.

Database Replicas

A vital concept to understand and a powerful tool in practice is Domino's capability to create copies of a given database, place those copies on different Domino servers within a deployment, and, most important, keep the documents in those database copies synchronized. Copies of an active database are termed *replicas*.

A number of reasons exist for creating replicas. Some reasons arise from fundamental aspects of the Domino/Notes architecture. Other reasons are to make efficient use of available resources, such as network bandwidth. The most common replica in a Domino deployment is the directory database (known now as the Domino Directory). This database is analogous to Active Directory.

A replica of the Domino Directory is present on every Domino server within a Domino domain (more on domains later) and is placed there automatically when a server is installed into a domain. These replicas are kept synchronized automatically so that clients connecting to that server will have an up-to-date directory of information to access. The Domino Directory is one example of a database that requires replicas of itself for Domino servers to function. Other databases that are essential to the operation of a Domino server fall into this category, but the directory is the most prevalent and the one that is most important to Unity.

For databases created to support specific applications, replicas are distributed across servers to prevent bottlenecks that result from network bandwidth availability between, say, central and remote offices. If bandwidth is not an issue, an administrator might place replicas on other servers for end users to access, to ensure that resources on any one server are not overly consumed. This is particularly true of individual mail files for users. It is not uncommon for a user to keep a replica of the mail database on the desktop machine and perform work using that replica. Synchronization between replicas on the desktop machine and the server occur periodically (as determined by the user).

Finally, utilization of Domino's proprietary clustering functionality also relies upon database replicas. If a user has a replica of the mail database on two separated and clustered servers, access to either replica occurs automatically and seamlessly if one of the servers becomes unavailable.

Server Tasks

In a Domino server, most requests/actions are executed by what is termed a task. Some tasks are run by almost every Domino server, and some are present only if certain functionality is installed. To see which tasks a given server runs, type **show tasks** at the Domino server console window. At an operating system level, most tasks also execute as a separate process. These tasks are most relevant to Unity functions:

- **Router**. Exists on every Domino server that routes mail messages. The router task delivers messages locally to mail databases on that server and forwards mail to other servers when the intended recipient's mail file does not exist on the local server. When the router task is not running, mail messages entering that server are not processed.

- **Administration Process (AdminP)**. Performs administration type requests in the background of the server. These requests can cover a wide range, such as user creation, user deletion, name change, and movement of databases to other servers. When a user is imported into Unity, a request is carried out by the AdminP tasks both to modify the user's Person document in the directory to indicate that the user is now a Unity subscriber, and to modify the user's mail file of UM operation. Requests to AdminP are placed in the database admin4.nsf and are processed periodically.

- **Replica**. Keeps documents between database replica synchronized. How often synchronization occurs between replicas and how it should occur (for instance, whether over a dial-up modem and using which network protocol) is dictated by a document kept in the Domino Directory database. Replication is efficient: Only the precise fields modified since the last replication are transferred. Many steps are involved in replication. Fortunately, users are completely abstracted from the underlying details of how it occurs and can leave it to Domino.

The Domino Domain

The previous section laid out the individual pieces of a Domino server and the functionality of each piece. This section covers how those pieces come together to form a Domino domain and, primarily, a domain consisting of two or more servers. Later, this will extend to a discussion of how Unity views a Domino domain and uses its functionality for unified messaging.

A Domino domain is a group of Domino servers that share the same Domino Directory. Put another way, a Domino directory defines a domain. A Domino domain has no relationship to a Microsoft Windows domain. A Domino server has no requirement that it reside on a host that is a member of a Windows domain, whether NT or Active Directory. In fact, all Domino servers within a Domino domain can reside on machines in individual workgroups.

As the control and administration center for Domino servers in a domain, the Domino Directory contains a Server document for each server and a Person document for each Notes user. In addition, when two or more servers exist in the domain, additional documents must be created to control database replication between the servers. This includes replication of the directory database. If mail is to be routed between the servers, additional documents exist to control how and when mail should be routed.

Four general scenarios should be considered when establishing a Domino domain. The first scenario, and the easiest to manage, involves creating a single Domino domain and registering all servers and users in one Domino Directory. The second scenario involves spreading an organization across two or more domains. Then all servers and users are members of the same organization, and each entity administers its own Domino Directory. A third scenario is the converse: one domain and multiple organizations. Finally, the fourth scenario involves maintaining multiple domains and multiple organizations. This scenario often occurs when one company acquires another.

As of the 4.0(3) release, Unity for Domino can function within only a single Domino domain. Thus, only the first and third scenarios apply in this chapter. Future releases of Unity will likely support multiple domains and, thus, multiple Domino directory databases, but not at the current moment.

Within a single domain, the operation of Unity depends little on the number of Domino servers present. However, the proper functioning of Domino depends heavily on the number of servers present. As a system grows, the number of documents required to route mail between the servers and ensure proper replication between database replicas grows. This chapter is not meant to deal with scaling Domino servers, so it focuses on several smaller, simple designs that are most relevant to Unity. As the numbers of servers grows within a domain, the principle concerns to Unity are network bandwidth and latency.

The Directory

The Domino Directory, which previous releases referred to as the Public Address Book or Name and Address Book, is a database that a Domino server automatically creates. A replica of this database exists on every server in the domain.

The Domino Directory serves two purposes. It is a directory of information about users, servers, groups, and other things that might be of interest to an organization. The directory is also a tool that administrators use to manage the Domino domain. For example, administrators create documents in the Domino Directory to connect servers for replication and mail routing, to register users and servers, to schedule server tasks, and so on. When registering users and servers in a domain, Person documents and Server documents are created in the Domino Directory. These documents contain detailed information about each user and server. When setting up the first server in a Domino domain, Domino automatically creates the Domino Directory database and gives it the filename names.nsf. This name can be altered and often is, to better reflect the domain that it covers. However, the directory database often is referred to simply as names.nsf or even, more briefly, names.

When a new server is added to a domain, Domino automatically creates a replica of the Domino Directory on the new server. This is an important point to remember and cannot be overstated: Every server within a domain contains a replica of the directory database. The replicas are kept consistent through Domino replication. A key architectural fact of Domino is that databases of identical information are distributed across multiple Domino servers and that these distributed databases are kept synchronized through Domino replication.

The directory database is the only database that Unity regularly monitors for changes. The Directory Change Monitor (listed in the services.msc as AvDsDomino) has this responsibility. Unity monitors the database for changes to any documents that previously were imported into any other Unity server also monitoring the same Domino Directory or that Unity wrote to the Directory. Documents that fall into this category are person records, groups, and location objects. For example, the Directory Change Monitor will notice a change to a subscriber's name, and a corresponding update will occur in the Unity database in SQL Server 2000 or MSDE.

As stated earlier, names.nsf Unity regularly scans for changes since the last synchronization to persons, groups, and location objects. It is vitally important that Unity monitor a replica of names.nsf on a server that is close and accessible to it. First and foremost, this means not forcing Unity to use a WAN connection or a slow LAN link. This issue is discussed more thoroughly in the section "Planning a Unity for Domino Installation."

Naming in Domino Is Hierarchical

Users and servers within a Domino domain are named with a hierarchical naming scheme. A hierarchical name reflects a user or server's place in the hierarchy and controls whether users and servers in different organizations and Organizational Units can communicate with each another. Regarding Unity, the hierarchical name given to the person record that Unity utilizes for database access is largely irrelevant. Unity cares only about having access to all the databases that it needs.

A hierarchical name in Domino can include these components:

- **Common name (CN)**. Corresponds to a user's name or a server's name. All names must include a common name component.

- **Organizational Unit (OU)**. Identifies the location of the user or server in the organization. Domino allows for a maximum of four Organizational Units in a hierarchical name. Organizational Units are optional.

- **Organization (O)**. Identifies the organization to which a user or server belongs. Every name must include an organization component.

- **Country (C)**. Identifies the country in which the organization exists. The country is optional.

An example of a hierarchical name using all of the components follows:

Bob Smith/Engineering/Acme/US

Generally, a user or server's name is entered and displayed in the previous abbreviated format. Internally, however, a canonical format containing the name and its associated components is used:

CN=Bob Smith/OU=Engineering/O=Acme/C=US.

Likewise, before installing Unity into a Domino domain, a person (that is, an account) will have been registered in the directory. Unity uses this person or account to authenticate into any server within the domain and to obtain access to any database on a server. This record also has a canonical name. At this point, it is useful to provide an example of why it is important to understand where in the hierarchy the Unity person record exists before installing.

Imagine that a Unity server is deployed to the Engineering department of the Acme company to satisfy its growing unified messaging needs. A person from Acme's Informational Technology (IT) department is assigned the task of deploying the system. Because only users within Engineering use this Unity server, a person record is created for Unity with this name:

Unity Person/Engineering/Acme

Thus, Unity is part of the Engineering Organizational Unit within the Acme organization. During installation, the installer is asked which server Unity should use as its partner server; this is the server for obtaining directory information (that is, which names.nsf replica) and for accessing the Administration Process database (needed when importing a subscriber). Acme is a fairly large organization, so it maintains a master replica of its directory on a server at the hub of its organization. By policy, all changes to the directory database are made to the replica on this server and then are pushed out to other replicas through Domino replication. This master replica resides on a server with this name:

Master Directory Server/Information Technology/Acme

Unbeknownst to the installer of Unity, however, the server document for the server Master Directory Server explicitly denies access to all users and servers that are not within the Information Technology OU. After all, the data on this server is vital, and access to it should be restricted to those with a need to access it. Such a restriction is accomplished by listing ***/Information Technology/Acme** in the Access Server portion of the Security tab of the server document. With the person record, Unity operates as within the Engineering OU and not the Information Technology OU, so Unity cannot access the directory database on that server or submit requests to the Administration Process to DUC to enable a user upon importation.

The solution is to either explicitly allow in the server document Unity Person/Engineering/Acme access to the server or have Unity access a server within the Engineering/Acme hierarchy. All other things being equal (namely, network bandwidth), either solution is acceptable. Whatever the solution is, it should be decided during the Unity planning phase, not the Unity installation phase.

Scaling Servers Within a Domain

As servers are added to a Domino domain, the degree of complexity can rise rapidly. With the addition of each server, several issues generally must be addressed. Chief among these are mail routing between servers and replication of databases. Of course, if no database on a particular server will receive mail, this is not an issue. But then such a server would not likely be of interest to Unity.

This section in no way attempts to detail all the issues and considerations involved in scaling a Domino domain, or the steps involved in carrying out that task. This section merely mentions and briefly describes the relevant pieces of a Domino domain that are necessary for Unity to function when multiple servers are present and accessed.

To assist with this discussion, imagine a fictional Domino deployment for the Acme Corporation, as illustrated in Figure 14-4. As shown in the figure, all servers live within the Acme organization, but each is within a separate Organizational Unit.

Figure 14-4 *Domino Domain Diagram for Acme Corporation*

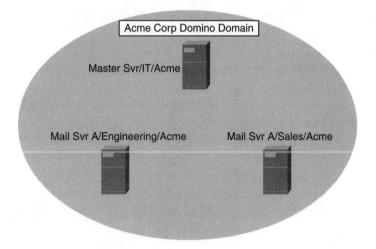

In this deployment, the Domino domain consists of three servers that are arranged in a typical hub and spoke style. At the hub is Master Svr, which resides in the Organizational Unit of IT in the organization of Acme. Its canonical name as represented internally within the directory is CN=Master Svr/OU=IT/O=Acme (Acme has chosen to not use the optional country designator, C, which would be appended to the right of the organization portion). To users, the server appears in the shortened format of Master Svr/IT/Acme. The domain currently contains two additional servers for housing users' mail files. These servers are distributed between the Engineering and Sales departments and are named MailSvrA/Engineering/Acme and MailSvrA/Sales/Acme, respectively.

The following sections discuss what documents must exist within the directory database for each server to talk to, to accomplish mail routing and database replication. These two bits of functionality are of primary interest to Unity.

Server Documents

Every server within a Domino domain has a document in the directory database associated with it. Such a document is called, not surprisingly, a Server document. An example of a Server document is shown in the Figure 14-5.

Figure 14-5 *Server Document for MasterSvr in the IT Organizational Unit Within the Acme Domain*

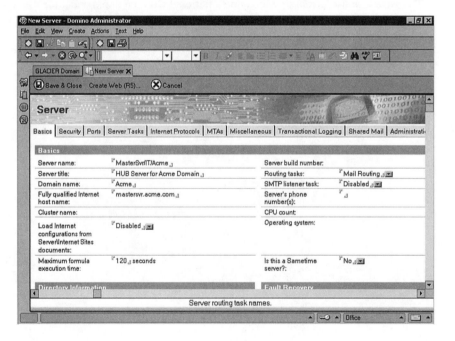

For Acme's deployment, three Server documents would exist, one for each server. These types of documents are established when the server is registered. The document contains many of the settings that define how the server functions. This includes who may (or may not) access the server, who may (or may not) create new databases and database replicas, and what network protocols can operate on that server. A lot of information is stored in this document. None of it, however, dictates mail routing or database replication. A Server document is about the server it was created for, not so much how it interacts with other servers.

Mail Routing

Mail routing between servers within a single Domino domain is achieved in one of two ways. The first is to create connection documents dictating how and when mail should be transferred from one server to another server or multiple servers. A second option is to establish a Notes Named Network (NNN). The advantage of an NNN is that each server automatically knows how to route mail directly to all other servers within the same NNN. To create an NNN, several criteria must be met, as spelled out clearly in Lotus Domino documentation. Most important is that each server must have an always-on network connection and that all servers must communicate on a common protocol (such as TCP/IP). The disadvantage of an NNN is that much less control exists over how and when mail is routed.

The option chosen within an existing Domino deployment is of little concern to Unity. The main concern is that all voice messages submitted by Unity must be routed to their intended recipient promptly, regardless of which server the mail file database exists upon. Long before Unity is installed, all mail-routing issues within a Domino domain should be resolved. As an academic exercise, however, let us see how the Acme domain can arrange mail routing.

Figure 14-6 illustrates one possible method of installing Unity into the Acme domain. Unity uses MailSvrA/Engineering/Acme as its partner server for obtaining directory information. In addition, the person record created for use by Unity, Unity Person/Engineering/Acme, has its mail file on this server. This means that all voice messages submitted by Unity first enter the Acme domain at MailSvrA server. More exactly, messages are submitted to the special database mail.box on MailSvrA. The database mail.box exists on every Domino server that is capable of routing mail messages. The router task periodically queries this database for messages waiting for delivery.

If the message is intended for a recipient whose mail file exists on that server (Bob Smith, for example), the router places the message directly into the recipient's mail file. If the recipient's mail file exists on a different server (Jon Stewart, for example), the router must obtain information on how to reach that other server. For Jon Stewart, this server would be MailSvrA/Sales/Acme. When the router knows how to reach the other server, the message is placed in the mail.box database of that server. The router task on that server places the message in Jon Stewart's mail file. As Figure 14-6 shows, if the person record that Unity uses has its mail file on MailSvr A/Engineering/Acme, all voice messages submitted by Unity first enter the Domino domain at this server. Domino mail routing then delivers the message to the recipeint's mail file or forwards it to another server for delivery.

Figure 14-6 *Unity Submits Messages to the mail.box Database on the Partner Server*

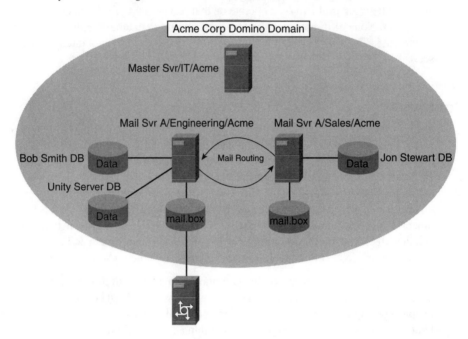

The information that the router needs resides within a mail connection document. Figure 14-7 shows an example of a mail-routing document. The document indicates the starting and ending servers for mail routing, the method to use (network protocol, dialup, and so on), and what schedule applies. Mail-routing documents are one-way. For mail to route from MailSvrA/Engineering/Acme to MailSvrA/Sales/Acme and vice versa, two documents must exist, one for each direction.

Figure 14-7 shows one part of a mail-routing document between MailSvrA/Engineering/ Acme and MailSvrA/Sales/Acme. For a voice message left for Jon Stewart to arrive in his mail file, there must exist a mail-routing document for routing mail from MailSvrA/ Engineering/Acme to MailSvrA/Sales/Acme (or an NNN must be established).

Another option for mail routing is to route all mail through the Master Svr/IT/Acme server. Perhaps this server also functions as a bridge-head, and the administrator wants all mail to pass through it. In this case, four mail-routing documents need to exist. Two documents would control mail routing between MailSvrA/Engineering/Acme and MasterSvr/IT/ Acme, and the other two would control mail routing between MailSvrA/Sales/Acme and MasterSvr/IT/Acme.

Figure 14-7 *Server Connection Document for Routing Mail Between MasterSvrA/Engineering/Acme and MasterSvrA/Sales/Acme*

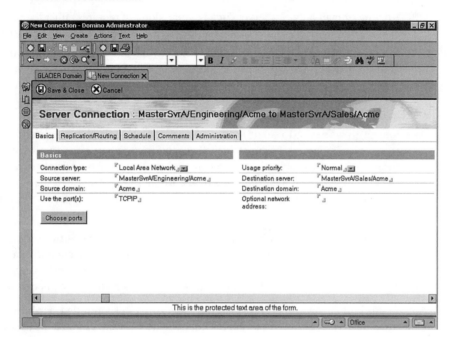

Regardless of the mail-routing mechanism used within a domain (NNN or connection documents), the effect upon Unity is trivial. When submitting messages, Unity sees only the partner server. The routing of messages to intended recipients is strictly under the control of the Domino mail-routing infrastructure. These, then, are the main points to consider with respect to Unity and mail routing within a Domino domain:

- Unity submits messages to the Domino server functioning as the partner server. This is generally the same server containing the mail file for the person (account) that Unity uses.

- When submitting messages, Unity places them in the database mail.box on the partner server.

- If Unity cannot access the partner server to deposit messages in mail.box, Unity enters UMR mode (assuming that the message is from an outside caller) and stores the messages locally until they can be delivered.

- If a voice message is submitted from a subscriber and the partner server becomes unavailable after logging into their mailbox, the caller will hear the failsafe conversation and the message will not be submitted. Subscriber-to-subscriber messages do not pass through the UMR messaging-handling mechanism.

- When a message is placed in mail.box, delivery of that message completely depends on Domino mail routing.

- Routing of mail between servers in a Domino domain requires either the presence of explicit routing documents or the establishment of a Notes Named Network (NNN).

- Routing mail messages over a slow or periodic (that is, dialup) connection delays the delivery of voice messages and the generation of MWI notifications.

Database Replication

As a domain grows beyond a single server, the need to initiate database replication between servers becomes important. Fortunately, just as mail routing between servers within a domain should be well established before Unity is installed, so should database replication. Normal database replication is controlled by the Replica server task. Clustered databases are kept synchronized through an entirely separate mechanism, so they are not discussed in this section.

Database replication can occur between replicas of any databases that two servers have in common. With respect to Unity, the primary databases that need replication within a domain are the directory (names.nsf) and the Administration Process (admin4.nsf) databases. For carrying out functionality of a Domino domain, these are also the most important.

An example best illustrates how replication is established and controlled, and brings to light replication issues that are most relevant to Unity. Figure 14-8 shows the Acme domain again with its three servers. Also shown is the replica of the directory database, names.nsf. For the sake of simplicity, this example focuses strictly on replication of this database as it is most relevant to Unity. Replication of other database replicas follows the same logic.

Figure 14-8 *Each Server Within the Acme Domain Contains a Replica of the Directory Database names.nsf*

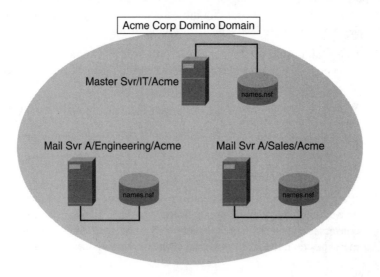

When MailSvrA/Engineering/Acme and MailSvr/Sales/Acme were installed, a replica of names.nsf was placed on the server. That replica was a snapshot of the directory at the point in time that it was created. To keep all replicas synchronized, replication documents must be created. This is analogous to mail-routing documents being created to handle the movement of mail messages between servers. Figures 14-9 and 14-10 illustrate two portions of a replication document.

Figure 14-9 *Source and Destination Server Information for Replication of Databases Between Two Servers*

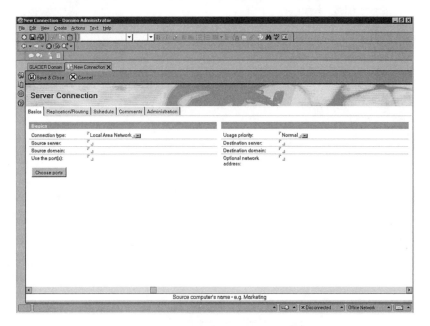

Replication documents are actually quite simple, given the complicated task that they control. First and foremost, a replication document indicates which two servers replication should occur between (see Figure 14-9) and on what schedule. Next, the database replicas to synchronize are listed (see Figure 14-10). A blank value (the default) in this field implies that all replicas in common are to be synchronized. Also of importance is whether the replication is to be a pull, push, or pull and push type of replication. Unlike mail-routing documents that are strictly one-way, a replication document can be two-way; this means that a single replication document can be used to keep replica databases on two separate servers fully synchronized.

In the Acme domain illustrated, the three replicas of names.nsf can be kept synchronized through a couple of arrangements. Perhaps the most common, especially for domains with few servers, is to create replication documents to handle the task between each pair of servers. In this situation, a minimum of three replication documents is required. This assumes that each document performs push/pull replication, as shown in Figure 14-11.

Figure 14-10 *Database Replication Information Portion of a Connection Document*

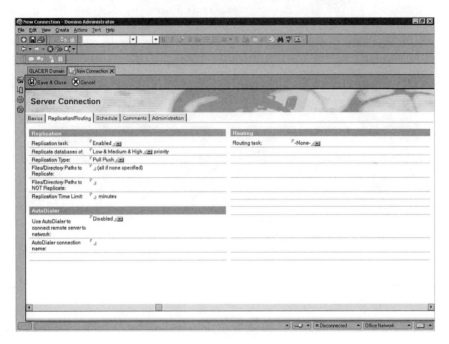

Figure 14-11 *Push/Pull Replication Between Servers*

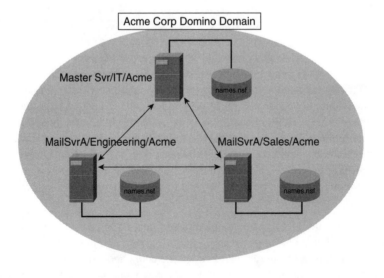

In this scenario, each replication document has one of the server pairs listed as the source and the other as the destination server. Because push/pull replication is used, the source server performs all the work of pushing the changes to documents over to the destination and then pulling changes to documents on the destination server over to it. This is the most efficient scheme for replicating changes because each server directly is connected to every other server. However, as the number of servers in a domain grows, this scheme quickly becomes unworkable. For n servers in a domain, each server must make n-1 connections. And although Domino database replication is efficient (only the individual fields within a document that have changed are transferred), the time that each server spends performing replication grows quickly as servers are added.

As a domain grows in servers, an administrator likely will turn to the common hub-and-spoke design for maintaining database replication. For Acme, the top-level server MasterSvr/IT/ Acme is identified as the hub. The remaining two servers are the spokes. In this scenario, the hub server is used to push changes to the spoke servers and pull changes from the spoke server to the hub. This leaves the spoke servers free to focus on other tasks (see Figure 14-12). One advantage of the hub-and-spoke arrangement is that it can provide better control over where changes to the directory database can occur. For example, an administrator can deny anyone (except a few select administrators and servers, perhaps) from modifying any documents in the replicas on the spoke servers. Instead, changes to documents in the directory database must occur on the hub server. Changes then are pushed out directly to each spoke server.

With respect to Unity, the replication scheme in use is nearly irrelevant, as long as Unity can open, read, and write to a directory replica. What is of concern is the issue raised in the last example: access control list (ACL) settings preventing modification to documents on specific replicas. If modifications to documents are prevented on spoke server replicas, Unity cannot use one of those servers as its partner server. Unity cannot modify Person documents when needed, create groups, and create location objects. Instead, Unity needs to use the hub server as its partner server.

With respect to Unity, the following points should be kept in mind when planning a Unity deployment:

- Database replication does not occur automatically between servers within a domain.
- Database replication occurs through the creation of replication documents. Replication documents are between two specific servers.
- Replication is done to keep database replicas on different servers synchronized.
- The most important database replica to keep synchronized within a domain is the directory database, names.nsf.
- Unity needs to monitor one replica of names.nsf in a single domain.
- The directory database that replica Unity monitors must allow changes to be made to it, and those changes must be replicated to all other replicas within the domain.

Figure 14-12 *Database Replication Using a Hub Server to Push/Pull Changes to Other Servers in the Domain*

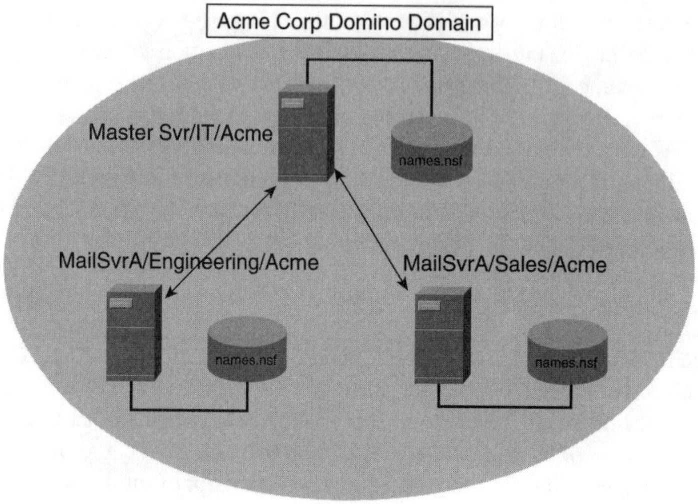

Security and Domino/Notes

Domino and Notes provide a comprehensive array of mechanisms for securing access to Domino and Notes and the data on each. Domino and Notes provide privacy of data, authenticity of users, and integrity of data, and they can control who can access data. Each of these works to satisfy user requirements. Notes has a long history of providing mechanisms right out of the box for securing data—in fact, Notes was among the first commercially available software packages natively to support encryption of data.

Regarding Unity, only authenticity of users and access to data are of concern and are discussed here. Authenticity is guaranteed through the Note ID file. Controlling access to databases is done through access control lists (ACL), which exist for every database. For a discussion of the other layers of security that are available in Domino/Notes, consult any good text on Domino administration.

The Note ID file and ACLs answer different questions. A Note ID file answers the question "Who are you?" An ACL on a database answers the question, "What are you allowed to do?"

Note ID File

Registered users and servers in a Domino domain have an ID file created when their record in the directory is created. This ID file uniquely identifies them to others; this is the identification card in the Domino world. If an ID file is stolen, an electronic version of identity theft has occurred, and the thief can gain access to databases and commit acts as that person. This issue is of particular concern to Unity because Unity has Manager-level rights to the mail files of users that it has imported. It is vitally important to harden the physical machine where Unity resides, to prevent theft of its ID file.

Generation of an ID file is the job of the certifier. A certifier itself has a Note ID file. Stealing a certifier ID is equivalent to stealing a plate to print currency. When you have this, you can make all the valid ID files you want. These fraudulent IDs can be put to little use because of adequate restrictions in database ACLs, however. ACLs are discussed more in the section "Access Control Lists."

A Note ID file contains quite a bit of information. At its heart is a private key. A copy of the public key is kept attached to the person record in the directory. This private-public key pair is used for user authentication. When it attempts to connect to a server, Domino passes back a random number. The person or server attempting to connect encrypts this random number with its public key and passes it back to the server. The server then uses the public key attached to the person record of the person who supposedly attempts access to decrypt the number. If the decrypted value matches the original random number, authentication is valid. A similar exchange occurs so that the user attempting access can verify that it actually is connecting to the correct server. This challenge/authentication process is talkative; the actual packets of information sent back and forth are small, but there are quite a few. If this conversation occurs over a slow or narrow bandwidth connection, it directly translates into additional silence heard by a caller into Unity.

An additional layer of security can be placed on an ID file in the form of a password. This is done when the ID file is created. In this case, any attempt to use the ID file is met with a prompt first to enter the correct password. If an ID file is stolen, the thief also must know the password for the file to make use of it. Understand that the password is to allow or prevent use of the ID, not access to any server or database. The ID file is the password to server access.

The ID file for Unity most certainly should have a password that is as strong as possible. Best practices dictate that the password should be at least eight characters in length. However, when Unity is functioning, the password is passed to Notes programmatically without requiring human intervention. As such, there is little reason not to place an even stronger password on the Unity ID file, particularly given the scope of access to user mail files.

Access Control Lists

If a Note ID answers the question of, "Who are you?" an access control list (ACL) answers the question of, "What are you allowed to do?" Every database has an ACL. It specifies the activities that users and servers may do to a database and the documents in it. ACLs are a powerful method for controlling access to database.

Access and the capability to perform various tasks on a database are categorized in seven levels. From highest level of access to lowest, these levels are Manager, Designer, Editor, Author, Readers, Depositor, and No Access. Each level contains certain default actions that users can perform and optional rights that may be granted. If a person or server that has authenticated into a server attempts to perform an action that is not explicitly allowed in the ACL, Domino prevents that action from occurring. To learn more about each of the seven levels of access, consult the Domino online help or any text on Domino administration.

Unity requires specific levels of access to the Domino Directory and Administration Process databases. In addition, DUCS grants Unity (through the UnityServers group) Manager-level rights to any mail file imported into Unity. These levels are discussed in further detail in the next section, "Unity's Perspective of Lotus Domino." Figure 14-13 shows the database ACL. The check boxes on the right side indicate the rights allowed for a given person, group, or server.

Figure 14-13 *Database Access Control List*

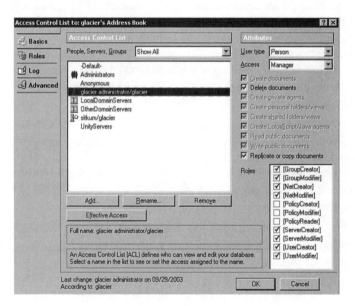

Unity's Perspective of Lotus Domino

Perhaps a better title for this section is "How Domino Sees Unity" because answering that provides greater insight to potential problem issues. To Domino, Unity functions as any other registered Notes user does. Within the Domino Directory is a Person document that represents Unity. In addition, a Note ID file is created along with the Person document to identify this person uniquely (also known as Unity). Finally, a mail file associated with Unity is created on a server in the domain. This mail file is listed in the person record created for Unity. All three of these steps are carried out before installing Unity. When Unity accesses anything on a Domino server, it does so in the context of the user listed in the person record created for Unity. It is vital to commit that concept to memory.

In addition, an instance of Notes is installed on the machine hosting Unity. This Notes instance is configured to use the person record or account created for Unity when authenticating for access to a Domino server. Obviously, Unity is not a physical person and has no use for the Notes GUI. However, it does have use for the binary files installed with Notes. Unity uses the Domino/Notes API programmatically to access Domino servers and the databases on the servers. From the Domino viewpoint, this is no different than a physical person opening Notes and using the mouse to point to and click buttons for access to the server.

Although Unity is "just another user," it requires a higher level of access to several of the domain databases than most users. For Unity to function, it needs access to the following:

- A replica of the Domino Directory
- A replica of the AdminP database
- The mail databases of users imported into Unity
- A Domino server to hand off voice messages for delivery

Access is granted to Unity through proper settings in database ACLs. The first three types of access are granted to Unity before the Unity installation. The fourth, access to a Domino server, occurs automatically as part of the DUCS-enabling process upon importation into Unity.

Database Permissions

The person record representing Unity can be granted access to the databases that it needs through explicit addition to the ACL or through group membership. The latter is preferable; in fact, Unity expects this for access to individual mail files. Cisco Unity documentation states to create a group named UnityServers and grant this group the necessary permissions. The person record for Unity is then made a member of the UnityServers group. The minimum required access levels to different databases required by Unity are discussed next.

Domino Directory: Editor + Delete Documents Rights

In the ACL of the Domino Directory, Unity requires Editor-level access. This is needed to modify fields on Person documents, create new fields on Person documents, create groups in the directory, modify group memberships, and create location objects. Delete permissions are needed only to delete location objects from the directory if you have created additional delivery location objects.

Granting the Delete Documents option does not limit Unity to deleting location object documents, however. Having this right to the database can allow Unity (technically, anyone authenticating with Unity's Note ID file) to delete any document in the directory database, including groups, person records, and server documents. Obviously, granting Delete Document permissions opens a wide door, and an administrator might not feel comfortable with this. Not granting the Delete Documents right does not lessen any Unity messaging functionality. If this level of permissions is needed at some point, it can be granted simply by modifying the database ACL again.

Administration Process: Editor Rights

Upon importing a subscriber into Unity or deleting a subscriber, Unity submits a request to the database (admin4.nsf) used by the Administration Process (AdminP). These requests relate to DUCS either enabling or disabling a user. However, DUCS will not execute the request unless Unity electronically signs it. Unique electronic signatures for user and server accounts are provided through the private key in an ID file.

Electronically signing requests submitted to admin4.nsf requires Editor-level rights. By signing the DUCS requests, the Administration Process can determine whether a third party has altered or tampered with the request between the time it was placed in the database and the time the Administration Process acts upon it. This guarantees authenticity.

Why is this desirable? A DUCS enable/disable request includes modifying a user's personal mail database, including modifying the ACL. If the request were not signed to guarantee authenticity, anyone with adequate permissions to the admin4.nsf database can modify the request, for example, to be added to the ACL of a user's mail file. By signing DUCS enable/disable requests, the Domino server knows whether the request has been tampered with and, if so, does not execute the request. This level of security is highly desirable.

Mail Files

Upon DUCS enabling a user, Unity is granted (through membership in the UnityServers group) Manager-level rights to that user's mail file. Unity loses all access to the mail file upon deleting the user from Unity. Although the user might have been imported into Unity, Unity cannot access that user's mail file until the DUCS-enabling process has been completed. This generally takes a few minutes, although it might take longer if users are being imported in bulk and there are many DUCS enable requests to process.

Manager-level access is very high, and the security implications of this cannot be overstated. Security of Unity's Note ID is vital. This is another reason to severely limit both physical and network access to the machine hosting Unity. Placing a strong password (at least eight characters in length) on the Note ID file for Unity is also prudent.

Delivery and Retrieval of Voice Messages

Delivery of messages in Unity for Domino is quite a simple affair. Unity submits the message to be delivered to the mail.box database on the same server as the mail file for the Unity account. From this point forward, delivery of the message to its ultimate recipient depends completely upon Domino mail routing. The most vital point to remember is that all messages that Unity submits use the same single point of entry. Remembering this point proves helpful if you are troubleshooting a message-delivery problem. If a recorded voice message makes it into the mail.box database, Unity's handling of the voice message ceases. Further routing is the responsibility of the Domino Router task. The Notes Log database contains logging information about all messages submitted to it.

Retrieval of voice messages is a more straightforward affair. The Unity database kept on SQL Server 2000 or MSDE contains information about each subscriber, including the server containing the mail file and the name of the mail file itself. The Unity person account has Manager-level access to the mail file. When a subscriber logs into Unity from the telephone, Unity programmatically opens the mail file through Notes and determines the appropriate message counts. When a voice message is listened to, Unity opens the document in the mail file and streams the contents of the wave-file attachment to itself and eventually through the telephone line to your ear.

Because message retrieval requires Unity explicitly to open mail-file databases on the servers where they reside, latency can become an issue. Network latency directly translates to a caller hearing silence. If Unity is required to travel a lengthy distance over a network to access mail files, unacceptable levels of silence can result. This issue is examined in more detail in the upcoming section "Planning a Unity for Domino Installation."

Message Waiting Indicator Light

The Message Waiting Indicator (MWI) light of a phone seems like such a simple device. When a new or unread voice message awaits, the light is active. When the message is read or deleted, the light extinguishes. When the light does not correlate to the reality of a voice message inbox, users are incensed.

But to make this simple on/off binary state function, a lot of communication occurs between Unity and the back-end mail server. In Unity for Domino, DUC is responsible for passing notifications on message states (new, read, deleted) to Unity. This section describes how DUC informs Unity of message state changes to light and extinguish MWI lights.

This section also discusses how the Domino server and the DUC software function to inform Unity of changes in message counts (new, read, deleted) for any type of message—voice, e-mail, or fax. The process is the same for all types. The actual lighting or extinguishing of an MWI lamp is controlled by Unity and is the same as in the Unity for Exchange version. Perhaps the simplest approach to describing the entire process is to walk through it step by step, starting with the arrival of a new voice message.

New Message Arrival

Figure 14-14 illustrates the various steps in creating a message notification and handing it to Unity. A voice message (or any other type of message, for that matter) sent from the telephone or Notes to a user on a Domino server first enters the Domino domain at the mail.box database of the server that the sender is connected to (Steps 1a and 1b). With respect to Unity, this is the partner server. From here, the Router task (Step 2) routes the message to mail.box of the server containing the recipient's mail file, perhaps passing through additional servers along the way. This is the same for all message types. In this example, the recipient's mail file happens to reside on the same server as the mail.box database where the message was deposited. The first step that is different for DUC-enabled users occurs when the message arrives in mail.box of the server containing the intended recipient's mail file database. This is Step 2 for this example.

Part of the DUC csServer installation includes code to extend the Router task to determine whether a user is DUC-enabled. This determination is made by looking for a specific profile document in the recipient's mail file that exists only after the user is imported as a subscriber into Unity. More is said on profile documents later: For now, suffice it to say that the profile document in question is created as part of the DUC-enabling process. If a recipient has been DUC-enabled, the router places another field on the message document called UCInbox and assigns it a value of 1.

As a side note, you might remember from earlier in this chapter that Unity looks in the view called ($UCInbox) in each DUC-enabled mail file to obtain message counts and other information. If you opened a DUC-enabled mail file in the Domino Designer, you would see that the selection criteria for the ($UCInbox) view is for a document to have the field UCInbox and to be set to a value of 1. If a message does not have the field UCInbox present and set to 1, Unity will not know that the message exists. As such, a useful troubleshooting tip if Unity reports incorrect voice message counts or if MWI lamps do not activate as expected is to look in the ($UCInbox) and see the number of messages appearing. If a message appears in the regular Inbox but not the ($UCInbox), that message likely does not have the UCInbox field present. Moreover, the Router task likely concludes that the recipient is not DUC-enabled.

At this point, the message is placed in the recipient's mail-file database, where it can be accessed from Notes or the telephone. Because the recipient was determined to be DUC-enabled, a notification is generated and passed to the UCEvent (Step 3) server task, also installed with csServer. This notification contains specific information (type of message, priority, and so on) regarding the message and is structured as XML. The UCEvent task passes the notification to the CSUMHlr server task (Step 4), also installed as part of csServer. This server task handles the communication between the Domino server and Unity.

When Unity starts, the Domino Monitor resides within the AvMsgStoreMonitorSvr process. It is not a separate process on its own and diagnostic information is *written* to the AvMsgStoreMonitorSvr log. The Domino Monitor creates a socket connection to port 2284 of each DUC-enabled Domino server containing a mail file for an imported subscriber. The CSUMHlr task uses this socket connection to push the XML data that constitutes the notification to Unity's Domino Monitor (Step 5). When the Domino Monitor has the XML data for a single notification (a single notification is demarcated by the tags <notification> and </notification>), the XML is parsed and the data is passed up to the Notifier for appropriate handling (Step 6). The Notifier in both Unity for Exchange and for Domino tracks current message counts and determines when an MWI light should be activated or deactivated.

Figure 14-14 *Generating a DUC Notification*

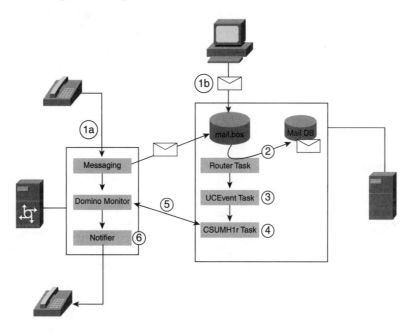

This is a summary of the steps shown in Figure 14-14:

1   A new message is submitted to mail.box. The message can be a voice message, an e-mail, or a fax.

2   The Router task determines whether the recipient is DUC-enabled by looking at a profile document in its mail-file database. If it is, the field UCInbox is written to the message document and placed in the mail file.

3   Because the recipient is DUC-enabled, a notification with the data structured as XML is generated and passed it to the UCEvent task.

4   The UCEvent task passes the notification to CSUMHlr.

5   The CSUMHlr task sends the notification from port 2284 to the Domino Monitor over a previously created socket.

6   The Domino Monitor parses the XML for the data in the notification and passes it to the Notifier.

Steps 3 through 6 also apply whenever a message already in a DUC-enabled mail file changes state (is deleted or is read). In other words, the notification process is independent of the state change of a message. The only aspect of a notification that changes with the message type (voice, e-mail, fax) or state change is the data in the notification. If the notification results from an urgent e-mail, for example, the data in the XML indicates that the notification is from an e-mail message and that its priority is High.

If you want or need to see the actual XML data received by the Domino Monitor, simply activate the Domino Monitor diagnostics in the Unity Diagnostic Tool and then perform some action to trigger a DUC notification (such as leaving a new voice message). Then view the diagnostic file generated by AvMsgStoreMonitorSvr. You can also monitor port 2284 on the Domino server generating the notification using a network packet analyzer. Note, however, that some of the data in the XML packet is Base-64 encoded and is not immediately readable. Both the Unity diagnostics and a packet analyzer can be educational in better understanding what information goes into a DUC notification message.

Profile Documents

Mail-file databases can contain profile documents. These documents are strictly data and are not visible by opening the database through Notes, the Administrator, or Designer. The simplest way to view a profile document is through NotesPeek, a low-level, read-only utility available for download for free from the Lotus Software website (www.Lotus.com). NotesPeek must be used on a machine with Notes or the Administrator installed, and a user Note ID is required. NotesPeek connects to servers and opens databases in the context of the ID used. Thus, ACL settings are honored. I highly encourage you to download NotesPeek and use it to examine the raw nature of Notes documents.

Regarding Unity and DUC, two profile documents are of interest; both are created when a user is imported into Unity and the DUC enable request is executed by Domino. These profiles are named ucprofile and ucprofilecountchange. Figure 14-15 illustrates the attributes of each of these profiles for a DUC-enabled user.

The Router server task examines the ucprofile profile to determine whether a user is DUC-enabled. When this profile is present, messages have UCInbox written to them and, thus, appear in the ($UCInbox) view. As such, Unity sees the message and knows that they are accessible from the telephone interface. Without this profile, Unity believes that the mail file database contains no messages. This profile is deleted when a subscriber is deleted from Unity.

Figure 14-15 *Viewing DUC-Related Profile Documents in a Mail File with NotesPeek*

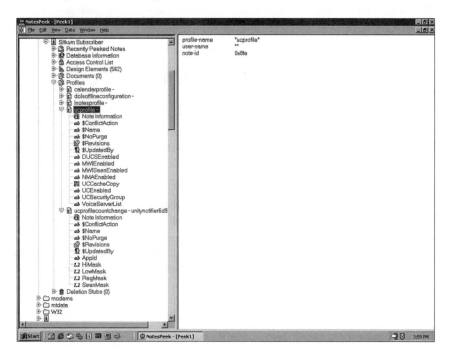

The ucprofilecountchange profile dictates the types of messages that generate notifications. Specifically, the value in the HiMask, LowMask, and RegMask fields corresponds to the high-, low-, and regular-priority messages. The value written to each is a bit mask, and the value written controls the types of messages (voice, e-mail, fax) that cause a notification to be generated.

A voice message has a value of 1, a fax has a value of 2, and an e-mail has a value of 4. The sum of these values in a particular field tells DUC when to generate a notification for a particular message event. For example, if the HiMask has a value of 5, the RegMask has a value of 1, and the LowMask has a value of 1, DUC generates notifications for high-priority voice and e-mail messages and for low- and regular-priority voice messages. No notifications are generated for fax messages in this example. If a subscriber wants to have DUC notifications generated for all message types, a particular field would have a value of 7.

The initial values written to the ucprofilecountchange document upon the creation of a subscriber are based on the message notification settings in the subscriber template used. There is one exception: Voice messages always generate a notification for all message priorities. Thus, the minimum value for any one of the masks is 1. Moreover, the only allowed values are 1 (voice only), 3 (voice + fax), 5 (voice + e-mail), and 7 (voice + fax + e-mail). If a subscriber enables or disables a particular notification device (say, a pager) or modifies the settings of an enabled device, the values in the fields are updated automatically.

Planning a Unity for Domino Installation

Before installing Unity to utilize Domino mail files, you should consider several issues. Just as when installing Unity for Exchange, the question of how Unity will impact the Domino servers arises. Many areas potentially are affected by Unity's presence, including storage space on the servers, network bandwidth availability, CPU utilization, and increase in the size of certain Domino databases (namely, names.nsf and admin4.nsf). As with Unity for Exchange, there is one way to inspect these areas: trending.

To fully understand the impact of Unity on a Lotus Domino domain, "before" and "after" snapshots are needed. All other things being equal, the difference between the two reasonably can be attributed to Unity. Of course, Unity has some impact on the Domino servers within the domain because all voice-messaging traffic is placed on to the data network. Likewise, Unity can be affected by the deployment of Domino servers and its messaging and directory infrastructure. Bottlenecks in the system, particularly in the messaging infrastructure, will be revealed—often quickly.

Trending

Trending messaging servers gives a good picture of the before and after affects of Unity. The "before" snapshot provides an operational baseline. Trending is not required but is prudent, especially if there is a concern about the impact that Unity and unified messaging will have on your existing messaging environment. Trending a Domino server is similar to trending an Exchange server. For recommendations on gathering trending information, see Chapter 13, "Unity with Microsoft Exchange." The recommendations there are as applicable to Unity for Domino as they are to Unity for Exchange; the tools are simply different. The tools available for collecting trending information on a Lotus Domino server are listed shortly.

Domino can generate statistics on server and platform use and activity. Together, these statistics provide information on the processes, networks, and use of the Domino system. From the Domino Administrator, specific statistics can be selected for monitoring and can be viewed in real time, if desired, or logged for later analysis; from the server console, you can view a representation that uses your predefined colors and text attributes to illustrate the status of a process. The following system-monitoring tools are used to track and view the Domino system and are configured through the Domino Administrator:

- The Monitoring Configuration database (events4.nsf) stores the documents created for monitoring. These documents define and configure the events to monitor and define how the event is handled.

- The Monitoring Results database (statrep.nsf) stores the gathered statistics.
- The log file (LOG.NSF) stores the server's log documents.

Prudent use of these tools provides an accurate picture of the load on a server, including the load from mail routing and database replication. You can find appropriate implementation of these tools and a detailed explanation of the many events that can be monitored in the Help documentation of Lotus Domino.

Another tool that is available for monitoring and analyzing a Domino server is the IBM Tivoli Analyzer. This tool is purchased separately from Lotus Domino and functions separately. Two integrated system-management tools come with Tivoli, the Server Health Monitor and Activity Trends. The former provides real-time assessment of server performance; Activity Trends provides data collection, data analysis, and resource balancing. Using these tools, you can manage servers and databases, ensure better server performance, and plan for current and future needs. If data from a Tivoli Analyzer is available, it can provide a very accurate "before" snapshot of the servers within a Domino domain.

Finally, for Domino servers running on a Windows 2000 Server platform, Windows Performance Monitor counters are available. These counters can record information on each of the Lotus Domino processes, including CPU and memory usage.

Regarding Unity, these are the most relevant statistics to gather in the "before" and "after" snapshots:

- Number of logon sessions on servers hosting UM-enabled mail files and the server containing the directory replica Unity monitors
- Network bandwidth usage throughout a day
- Disk I/O activity
- CPU and memory utilization
- Volume of message routing on servers hosting UM-enabled mail files
- Mail database size

The number of logon sessions increases on each Domino server being serviced by Unity and each server containing a directory database that Unity monitors. Each time a subscriber logs into a mailbox, Unity opens that mail file on the server. It is possible to limit the number of allowed users connected to a server at any one time. This is done through the Notes.ini setting of Server_MaxUsers=<number of users>. If a server reaches the number specified for this setting, it refuses any new Database Open requests. This can result in Unity giving the failsafe conversation to a caller if its Database Open request is denied. Collecting the average number of open connections on a server throughout a day before Unity is installed is prudent. An unlimited number of users can be allowed to access a server at any given moment by giving the Server_MaxUsers setting a value of 0.

One factor that is unique to Unity for Domino that is not of concern to the Exchange version is the impact of Domino database replication upon Unity. The impact manifests itself in the amount of network bandwidth utilization, disk I/O activity, and machine CPU and memory availability. All of these can affect Unity's performance and the real-time nature of a voice-messaging system. Database replication, whether normal scheduled replication or cluster replication, generally creates a spike in the use of all of these areas. However, if a server hosts both mail files and Domino applications distributed across multiple servers, the volume of database replication can increase significantly.

With respect to not creating bottlenecks in disk I/O activity and CPU and memory utilization, the best and perhaps easiest solution is to have dedicated servers for hosting mail files. Let mail servers manage mail files and application servers manage applications. If this is not possible, Lotus provides numerous best practices for maximizing server performance. Even if dedicated mail servers are used, following best practices will maximize performance of those servers. Documentation published by Lotus is the best source for those best practices. A few of the primary suggestions are listed here:

- Use PCI-based systems, not EISA.
- Use faster disk drives.
- Use hardware-based RAID (assuming that RAID is being used).
- Increase the number of Replicator server tasks (although this will cause an increase in CPU usage).
- Use faster CPUs.
- Increase the amount of available memory.
- On Windows 2000 Server platforms, use a separate pagefile disk.
- On Windows 2000 Server platforms, use the NTFS file system.
- Remove Domino server tasks that are not appropriate for the purpose of the server. (For example, do the mail servers need to run an LDAP or HTTP service? If not disable these tasks.)

Regarding potential network bandwidth bottlenecks that arise from database replication, one common approach is to place replication traffic on a separate network line or a VLAN. This is especially true for replication in a clustered environment. It is not possible to determine whether network traffic from database replication is an issue for Unity's performance unless the appropriate data is collected through trending.

Placement of Unity Within a Domino Domain

The decision that most can affect the performance of Unity is where in a Domino domain to place Unity. This refers to how close on the network Unity resides to the server(s) containing the directory replica(s) monitored and the server(s) containing UM-enabled mail files. Each time Unity opens a database, whether the directory or a mail file, Unity (through the Notes client) must make a connection to the server and authenticate with the server before opening the desired database and retrieving the desired information.

Notes and Domino communications are chatty. Because of this, network latency or simply slow network throughput can create noticeable delays to a caller on the telephone. Adequate trending of the Domino servers before installation can help in determining whether delays might arise because of inadequate bandwidth. Response time in Unity for Domino is important for the same reasons that it is in Unity for Exchange. A user hearing silence for more than a couple seconds between prompts or between a prompt and an activity, such as message retrieval, is perceived as unacceptable. This is true even if the length of the silence is the same duration as experienced in a GUI for same activity.

Several examples illustrate the issues to consider most when deploying Unity for Domino. All examples assume a single Domino domain because Unity for Domino functions only within a single domain.

Figure 14-16 shows a rather simple Domino domain of three servers connected on high-bandwidth LAN segments. All Notes users reside in the same physical location and utilize one or more of the three Domino servers for their needs. The placement of Unity in the network in this case is obvious: on the same network switch as the Domino servers. For message retrieval, Unity will access any of the servers that contain the mail file of a subscriber. For directory information, Unity has a choice of one of the three servers. As you will remember, each Domino server within a domain contains a replica of the domain directory, names.nsf.

Figure 14-16 *Single Domino Domain of Highly Available Servers*

Single Domino Domain with all Servers
on the Same Subnet

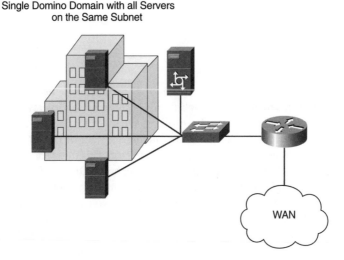

If all servers are equally available in the network, the decision tree can exclude that issue. If the domain servers are arranged in a hub-and-spoke style and the administrator has decided that all modifications to person records should occur on the hub server replica, Unity must use the hub as its partner server. Likewise, the administrator might have chosen to severely restrict access to the hub server directory replica. In this case, Unity must use one of the remaining servers as it partner server. In addition, the changes made to the directory replica on that server should be allowed to replicate back to the replica on the hub, to keep all person records synchronized. This last point is especially relevant when two or more Unity servers are present in the same Domino domain and use different partner servers.

Figure 14-17 extends Figure 14-16 slightly. In this case, another Domino server resides in another physical location, although all servers are within the same Domino domain. The lone server might be on a different network, but the networks are connected by a highly available campus backbone.

Figure 14-17 *Single Domino Domain of Servers That Are Physically Separated but Connected by a Highly Available LAN*

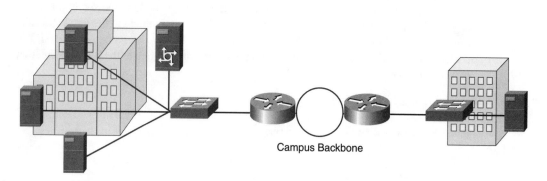

Campus Backbone

In this situation, Unity still would want to obtain directory information from a replica on a server connected to the same switch simply because those servers are closer on the network. If mail files of imported users also reside on the lone Domino server, careful attention must be given to the amount of bandwidth available. Remember that a 60-second voice message recorded using the G.711 codec is 480KB in size. This message must be streamed across the backbone when it is retrieved over the telephone. On top of this is the normal network traffic of opening mail file databases and retrieving, say, message counts. Multiply this by the number of voice ports available to Unity, and you begin to obtain a reasonable picture of Unity's bandwidth needs. If only Unity were allowed to utilize the campus backbone, there is no doubt that enough bandwidth would be available in a modern network. However, because Unity must share the pipe with other applications, and, more important, because Unity is a real-time system, delays in data retrieval manifest themselves directly as a caller hearing silence.

If trending data indicates that Unity might experience unacceptable network latency, one solution is to install a second Unity server at the same physical location as the lone Domino server and have subscribers utilize that Unity server. Another option is to relocate the mail files of UM-enabled users to a server closer to Unity. This might transfer the delay experienced from the telephone to the Notes client. However, users are generally more accepting of a several-second delay in a GUI application than in a real-time voice-processing application. If the mail files are relocated to a different server across the campus backbone, users also can create a replica of their mail file locally to their desktop and work from that replica. Domino database replication is used to keep the local and server replicas synchronized periodically (say, every 2 or 3 minutes). This is a common practice for Notes users. Finally, another option is to expand the bandwidth available across the campus backbone. This is not an inexpensive option, of course, and might not be viable for every installation facing these issues.

The last example is shown in Figure 14-18. Again, all Domino servers reside within the same Domino domain, but one of the servers resides in a remote office site connected to the campus through T1 WAN links. For UM-enabled mail files on the Domino server connected over the WAN links, there is only one choice: A separate Unity server must be installed at that physical site and must use the single Domino server present for both directory monitoring and mail file access. The latency involved in Unity accessing mail files across a WAN link is significant and translates directly into silence heard by the caller. The latency comes from authenticating into a server (through Notes), opening a mail database, and gathering message count information.

Deployment of Domino Unified Communications Services (DUCS)

To enable Notes users for unified messaging, the Domino Unified Communications Services software must be installed. This is purchased separately from IBM Lotus Software and is required. The installation of DUCS is actually quite straightforward when you understand the purpose of DUCS. This book does not provide information on the installation of DUCS; it offers an explanation of the purpose of DUCS and where it needs to be installed. Consult the documentation accompanying the DUCS software for installation steps.

DUCS actually consists of three pieces, named csServer, csAdmin, and csClient. The csServer installation installs additional server tasks to a Domino server and the code necessary to enable a user's mail file for unified messaging after it is imported into Unity. Additional UM-related mail templates also are installed. The csAdmin installation alters the domain directory for UM capability. This is similar to extending the Active Directory schema when installing Unity for Exchange 2000. Finally, csClient further modifies individual end-user mail files for UM functionality.

Figure 14-18 *Remote Domino Server Connected Domino Domain Over Highly Available WAN Links*

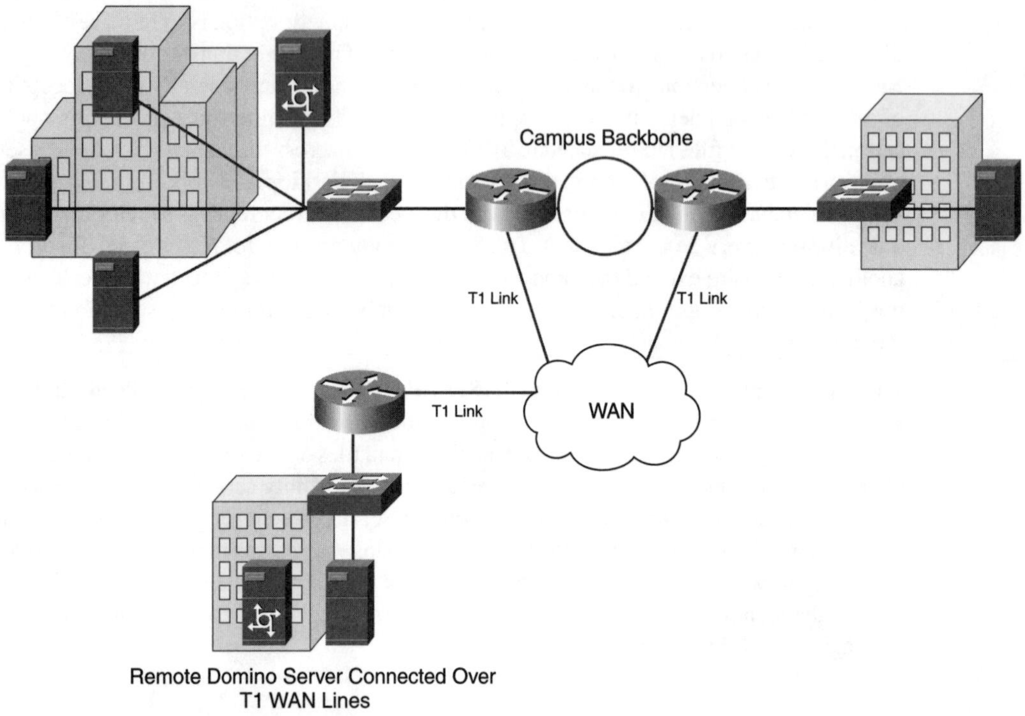

Remote Domino Server Connected Over
T1 WAN Lines

Every mail server in a domain that will contain a UM-enabled mail file must have csServer installed on it. This is because the installation installs server tasks that cannot be distributed through any replication scheme. On the other hand, csAdmin generally requires only a single installation per domain. csAdmin modifies the design of the directory database, and because every Domino server in the domain contains a replica of this database, the changes made by csAdmin should be replicated out to other database replicas.

What must be considered, however, is that the first replica to receive the modified design can have the design changed and then can push those changes out to other replicas. Remember the hub-and-spoke design issue? An administrator might allow changes to the directory only from a centralized hub server and will not accept changes pushed back from a spoke server. If this is the case, the directory database modifications done by csAdmin must be applied to the replica on the hub server. In fact, this is a wise choice because the changes generally are replicated throughout the domain more quickly in a hub and spoke type of deployment.

The csClient installation technically is not required for Unity to function. CsClient installs additional forms and views for use by the end user in the Notes client. For example, a form is installed so that the opening of a voice message in Notes displays VCR-like controls for the playback of the voice message, either over speakers attached to the computer or over the telephone. Likewise, a user might record a voice message using the form and send it to another subscriber in a manner identical to sending an e-mail message.

Summary

When planning, installing, and administering a Unity with Domino installation, the most important database replica to keep synchronized within a domain is the directory database, names.nsf. Unity needs to monitor one replica of names.nsf in a single domain.

The directory database that replica Unity monitors must allow changes to be made to it, and those changes muse be replicated to all other replicas within the domain.

Unity requires a minimum of Editor-level rights in the ACL of the Domino domain directory database and the Administration Process database. Adding Delete Documents rights to the domain directory is optional.

Unity obtains Manager-level rights to individual mail files after they are imported into Unity. This is part of the DUC-enabling process.

To adequately plan, install, and tune a Unity installation, "before" and "after" snapshots of the Domino infrastructure are needed. Trending messaging servers provides a good picture of the before and after affects of Unity. The "before" snapshot provides a baseline measurement. Domino servers can generate a wealth of statistics on server and platform use and activity.

With respect to Unity, these are the most relevant statistics to gather:

- Number of logon sessions on servers hosting UM-enabled mail files and the server containing the directory replica Unity monitors
- Network bandwidth usage throughout a day
- Disk I/O activity
- CPU and memory utilization
- Volume of message routing on servers hosting UM-enabled mail files
- Mail database size

Where Unity is placed in a Domino domain can affect the user experience most (in response time and dead air heard, for example). Forcing Unity to communicate over a WAN link to retrieve voice messages usually produces extensive dead air to callers.

CHAPTER 15

Upgrades and Migrations

This chapter provides guidance for managing your Unity upgrades and Unity infrastructure migrations. It explains the high-level steps necessary to plan, practice, and refine any Unity reconfiguration or upgrade. In addition, ways to manage Unity and apply best practices are provided to support a legacy voice-messaging infrastructure migration to Unity, or from one Unity configuration to another.

This chapter is a high-level reference for best practices on upgrades and migrations. Thus, you will need to access the following resources to help you perform important migration or upgrade steps:

- Unity product documentation
- Unity whitepapers
- Third-party messaging product documentation
- Legacy voice-messaging system documentation
- Information about Unity integration with CallManager, SIP proxies, and legacy PBXs (see Chapter 17, "Unity Telephony Integration")
- Information about subscribers and system administration (see Chapter 19, "Administering Multiple Unity Servers," and Chapter 20, "Subscriber Administration")

Upgrades

With the Unity application, the term *upgrade* implies moving your existing version to a more recent one. Upgrades are used not only to fix identified issues, but also to enhance the application with newer features or functionality.

Managing Unity Upgrades

Because Unity provides voice-messaging services for your voice messaging-only installation or your unified messaging installation, you naturally will want to minimize any downtime associated with upgrade activity. It is not possible to upgrade Unity without any downtime. Even with Unity failover, both the primary and secondary must be taken offline temporarily while you perform an upgrade. To keep downtime to a minimum, you will want to focus on two important items: timeliness and the preservation of your configuration settings and data.

NOTE With Unity 4.03, upgrade instructions vary, depending upon the version you upgrade from. Check the product documentation and thoroughly understand the upgrade steps before you start any upgrade process.

Because you must take Unity offline to upgrade the software, you need to make sure that you upgrade after hours, when the system is least used. It might be a good idea to route inbound calls to a recording that states voice messaging is unavailable from a given period of time for system maintenance. If you have a Unity server in your lab, you can create a greeting specifically for this purpose and route all calls to it during the upgrade period. Do not try to get the lab server to take messages; just send all calls to the opening greeting, and then gracefully end the call. Regardless of what you do or how you do your upgrade, you do not want to just have your system offline without some type of message for inbound callers, even if you tell all your subscribers that the system is offline for a while. In fact, it is advisable to make sure that your subscribers are aware of the planned upgrade period.

If you trend the activity on your system, you should have a good idea of when the best time is to perform an upgrade. Unfortunately, if your business hours are nine to five, that time most likely is after hours and during weekend periods.

When you have several Unity servers, it is best to manage one upgrade at a time. When you perform your upgrade, you should upgrade each server only. Sometimes it is easy to get caught up in a big project and try to upgrade, reconfigure, and physically relocate all at the same time. This type of approach might seem necessary, but consider this: If your upgrade does not go as planned, you should not proceed with any other project steps, such as reconfiguration work or administrative work, until the issues or obstacles are cleared.

Planning Upgrades

The high-level upgrade plan should include the following tasks:

- Evaluating the Unity version you plan to upgrade to
- Performing an upgrade lab trial
- Performing a fallback lab trial
- Cleaning up and preparing your production servers
- Performing a project walkthrough and fallback readiness evaluation

- Conducting a site survey of each Unity server to be upgraded
- Handling scheduling and notification of downtime messages
- Performing the upgrade
- Verifying the upgrade
- Falling back

Evaluating the Unity Version You Plan to Upgrade To

Without a doubt, this is one of the most important upgrade tasks you can perform. First, you must understand the differences between the version you evaluate and the version you use. Reading the system requirements is not enough. Reading the upgrade steps defined in the product documentation is much better, but it still is not enough. You must understand the differences as they pertain to your specific configuration. Your evaluation should include a full application assessment, which means that you should install the new version in your lab and perform a full comparison between the new version and the version you upgrade from. Can you get away with not performing a full comparison? Maybe, but it is well worth the time to perform the comparison. Your users will appreciate knowing what is different about the new version—is something new or taken away?

When you have a comparison and you understand what affects your subscribers, you also need to understand whether the differences require you to perform additional upgrade tasks. Is new hardware required? New OS service packs? Are there changes in the service accounts? Licensing differences? See the product documentation for a checklist of items to consider when you plan an upgrade.

Performing an Upgrade Lab Trial

After the version evaluation, the upgrade lab trial is probably most important. An upgrade lab trial should include a mockup of your production server. If you have different hardware or software configurations of Unity, you will want to make sure that you perform an upgrade trial on each specific configuration. The assumption is that you have mockups of your production installs. You should have production server mockups in your lab, especially if you have many subscribers and systems. (Even if you do not, this is strongly recommended.)

With each upgrade trial, do the following before running the trial:

- **Perform a database and configuration cleanup of your production system**. You should do this same step for your mockup servers and perform identical steps. In fact, these steps can or should be developed from instructions provided by the Cisco Unity database cleanup tools (dbWalker) and other steps that you might include. Database cleanup is just one example.

- **Perform a full application test before and after your upgrade**. Doing a full application test before your upgrade ensures that you capture any errors or conditions that can be identified as pre-existing to your upgrade. Without performing a full application test before your upgrade, you will not be able to accurately identify or address those pre-existing conditions.

The post-upgrade application test should prove whether your upgrade was successful. In addition, you can read the logs created during the upgrade and those found in the Application Event Viewer. If issues do arise, you should determine whether they are severe enough to be considered showstoppers or whether they can be resolved and allow normal operations to continue at the same time. You might have to repeat an upgrade trial. Your goal should be to have a successful and smooth trial; achieving your goal should be validated by success measurements.

Performing a Fallback Lab Trial

Even if every single upgrade lab trial is smooth and successful, you should make sure that you can fall back to the original Unity version. Make sure that you have good backups of your lab servers before performing an upgrade. This way, if you need to fall back, you can ensure that the same configuration is available. Refer to the Cisco Unity product documentation, and make sure you know how to use the Unity tools that can back up and preserve your data. The Cisco Unity product documentation also lists supported backup software.

If possible, your lab fallback trial should include steps associated with changes to your call-processing and switch-integration configurations. For instance, if before performing your database cleanup and version upgrade you want to point your switch to a different server with a "system unavailable" recording, include that step in your upgrade and fallback trial so that it is not missed if you really do have to fall back.

Hopefully, you will not have to perform fallback operations. If you are prepared for it, though, you can ensure minimal operational downtime and also ensure that falling back to the original configuration is no more difficult than upgrading your Unity application.

Cleaning Up and Preparing Your Production Servers

Evaluate your Unity servers and determine whether the accounts database and system configuration should be cleaned up. Use the Cisco Unity database tool dbWalker to report inconsistencies with each Unity database. Make sure that all accounts are known and that rights and permissions assigned to Unity service accounts are recorded.

The goal of your cleanup is to make sure that you do not migrate unwanted data. A good example of unwanted data is subscriber accounts for users who no longer use the system. Or, perhaps you created temporary audio text applications that are no longer in use. These are good items to check for.

You also should prepare your production servers for the upgrade by making sure that they do not have ongoing notable problems that could prevent your upgrade from being successful. With hardware or server preparations, ensure that the server or involved hardware can perform the tasks required of it and is up-to-date with current BIOS revisions, service packs, and so on. Naturally, you might have an ongoing problem that can be solved by performing an upgrade. That need might simply override the thoroughness that is recommended to perform a well-planned upgrade of your Unity servers. If the upgrade is unsuccessful, care still should be taken to ensure that a fallback plan is in place to restore existing services until the upgrade issue can be resolved.

Check the application log for errors, and use the Event Monitoring Service (EMS) to find any errors. The Unity Event Log Error lookup site is useful in identifying the cause and potential error corrections for Unity-specific errors; see http://www.ciscounitysupport.com/find.php.

Isolate all errors, and determine whether they might prevent a successful upgrade. If necessary, open a case with Cisco TAC to address any problems. To ensure that the Unity server runs as cleanly as possible, use the Directory Walker, the Subscriber Information Dump, and Gather Unity System Information (GUSI) utility. These tools help to make sure the Unity database is clear of errors, ensure that the subscribers in use are active user accounts, and supply Unity server version information, respectively.

Performing a Project Walkthrough and Fallback Readiness Evaluation

As with the initial installation of Unity, it is necessary to pay attention to detail. Determine the project timeline, and perform a walkthrough of the tasks associated with the project. Identify all tasks before performing your upgrade, and make sure that you have identified the criteria that you will use to determine whether you should fall back.

As mentioned earlier, you should perform the upgrade process in a lab to ratify the fallback process as well. Having a fallback strategy can be the difference between restoring previous functionality and having to reinstall from scratch—not to mention potentially saving your employment.

After you create a task list, craft a realistic timeline associated with the tasks needed. Then develop a walkthrough of tasks to make sure that no steps are missing. Some test cases should be developed to ensure that the system works. Test cases should be used for either an upgrade or a fallback.

"Go/no go" decision-making criteria should be established to determine whether the upgrade should be performed. If the criteria cannot be met, a "no go" decision should be made. List all tasks that need to be performed to have acceptable go-based criteria for the upgrade.

Conducting a Site Survey of Each Unity Server to Be Upgraded

Perform a site survey of each Unity server to capture unique tasks associated with the specific Unity server. Make sure that each Unity server can be taken down as planned and that all project resources are available for each server taken offline.

In addition to ensuring the Unity servers can comply with the upgrade schedule, you should record and save information that is unique to each location. Use the same criteria for performing a site survey, found in Chapter 13, "Designing a Unity Solution."

The following information should be recorded:

- Server name
- IP address of the server
- Unity version
- Service pack levels of Windows, SQL, and Exchange
- Exchange partner server name
- Switch integration type
- Port configuration

This information and more can be collected with the Gather Unity System Information (GUSI) utility, available in the Tools Depot on the Unity server or from the Cisco Unity Tools website. Other information to keep in mind for upgrades includes custom settings made in the Registry, prompts, or system files that are outside of the normal upgrade process. As a part of any upgrade process, the need to ensure proper licensing cannot be stressed enough, especially when an upgrade can move across several versions at one time, or if the configuration changes.

Handling Scheduling and Notification of Downtime Messages

When you are ready to perform your upgrade and you have finished your site surveys, lab trials, fallback readiness, and project walkthrough, schedule your downtime and make sure that all users and interested parties are notified properly. Ensure that all interested parties approve your downtime schedule before the day of the upgrade, and make certain that proper personnel are on hand or available.

It seems that no matter how hard you try, some people will not get the outage notification. To help ensure that everyone is aware of the upcoming outage, I recommend using several delivery methods. These methods can include e-mails, voice mails, written memos, or a posting to the company's intranet home page. Another recommendation is to begin the notification about two to three weeks in advance and repeat them at least once a week.

Another precautionary method involves giving your desktop services group the outage timeframe and informing it of expected results from the upgrade.

Performing the Upgrade

Earlier, in the section "Performing a Project Walkthrough and Fallback Readiness Evaluation," we talked about using a task list to assign a timeline to. Developing the task list is most important to ensure that the proper steps are taken at the right time for a successful upgrade.

The Cisco Unity product documentation includes steps for upgrading your Unity servers. The instructions to perform an upgrade depend upon which version of Unity you upgrade from to the version of Unity you plan on upgrading to. For instance, the Unity 4.03 product documentation—namely, the Installation Guide—provides the necessary steps and information that should be used for upgrading from 4.01, 4.02, 3.X, and 2.X versions.

After the task list has been created, tested, and documented, all that is left to do is the actual upgrade. Deviations from what previously was documented and tested during the upgrade are strongly discouraged. Sticking to the plan that has been tested and documented greatly reduces the chances of an abnormal upgrade.

Verifying Operations After the Upgrade

With most upgrades having to take place after hours or on the weekend, a lack of due diligence can impact an otherwise clean upgrade. Due diligence refers to testing the functionality of Unity and any new features that might have been introduced as a result of the upgrade.

Testing the upgrade implies that there are test procedures and a means of determining a pass or fail mark for each test case. In testing the upgrade, two types of tests are used. Functionality tests are fundamental and really do not change that much, if at all, among versions or vendors. Feature tests are typically unique to the version in which the feature or features were released.

Functionality tests include the following:

- MWI on and off
- Telephone User Interface (TUI)
- The capability to add, delete, or modify subscriber accounts
- Phone system integration

Feature tests include the following:

- Pager notification
- Identified Subscriber Messaging (ISM) for networked Unity servers
- A prompt when the mailbox is full
- Automatic Number Identification (ANI) playback on message retrieval

Some method should be devised for recording the results. Documenting the test cases should follow a similar structure as that shown in Table 15-1.

Table 15-1 *Example Test Case and Results*

Test Case Name	Test Criteria	Expected Result	Pass or Fail Designation
MWI ON	Call into the Unity server and leave a message for Extension 12345.	After the message has been left, the MWI lamp on the phone should turn on.	Pass

Falling Back

We discussed preparing for and performing an upgrade, as well as preparing for the chance of an unsuccessful upgrade. As part of the preparation for the upgrade, a task list and fallback strategy should have been developed and tested to ensure that functionality can be restored to its previous state.

The fallback strategy should have included the steps and utilities needed to restore the Unity server. The utilities mentioned can be found on the Unity server itself in the Tools Depot container, or at the Cisco Unity Tools website (www.ciscounitytools.com). Besides having the steps and tools to fall back, you should have test cases to ensure that the Unity server works after it has been restored.

Reconfiguring Unity

The 4.03 release includes a reconfiguration document that provides direction on how to reconfigure several aspects of Unity.

Not unlike an upgrade, planning and testing should take precedence over merely trying to run through what seems to be the logical motions and then reading the directions later. With that approach, potentially irreversible damage can take place, causing a reinstallation to be required. It can also lead to a very dissatisfied enduser population.

Reconfiguring a Unity server can include, but is not limited to, the following tasks:

- Changing the IP address
- Moving Exchange off the box
- Changing the Exchange Partner Server
- Changing the Global Catalog Server
- Moving from Exchange 5.5 to 2000
- Renaming the Unity server

- Upgrading or downgrading SQL/MSDE
- Upgrading the Exchange version from 5.5 to 2000

These areas of change and more are covered in the Reconfiguration Guide. The Reconfiguration Guide details the steps needed to accomplish the identified change needed.

Migrations

The dictionary defines *migration* as moving from one place to another. Keeping that mindset, installing Unity in a customer's site does not always involve a brand new business or site, or "Green Field," the term associated with these types of deployments.

More often than not, Unity is replacing an existing voice-mail solution. It might be necessary to move subscribers from the incumbent voice-mail system to the new Unity solution in a way that causes the least amount of pain to the end user population.

This section discusses migration types and strategies for accomplishing the move.

Migrating from a Legacy Voice-Messaging System to Unity

The high-level steps for migrating from a single legacy voice-messaging system to Unity are as follows:

- Perform an end-user usage analysis. See Chapter 9, "Planning." Output from the usage analysis should be a feature/function gap analysis.

- Gather system configuration information on how to configure Unity. This can include information, such as pager notification and class of service.

- Monitor traffic patterns to understand how to size Unity and to understand the impact of the voice-messaging traffic on your messaging system. Trend your existing messaging system if you are migrating from legacy voice messaging to unified messaging.

- Determine whether you will perform a flash cut migration or an interoperability migration.

If you plan to perform a flash cut migration, your migration will be easy. If your migration requires you to migrate users over a period of time, it will require a bit more work: You will have to set up the voice-messaging interoperability features in Unity so that you can support the migration.

For a flash cut migration, simply set up a Unity server according to your needs. Make sure that it is configured as required, and then import all your subscribers into the Unity server. Make sure that the application functions as desired, and then simply point your voice port pilot or extension number from the legacy voice-messaging system to Unity. When you are sure that the cutover is successful, you can remove the legacy voice-messaging system from your network.

If you use Cisco Unity's voice-messaging interoperability features to support your migration, you must familiarize yourself with the pros and cons of each interoperability method available with Unity. With interoperability between voice-mail systems on a new installation, the new voice-mail system can move subscribers over at a slow pace. These types of migrations are referred to as *phased migrations*. Phased migrations are the typical choice of enterprise customers largely because of their geographical makeup.

The current methods of interoperability are Audio Messaging Interchange Specification (AMIS), Voice Profile for Internet Messaging (VPIM), and Unity Bridge. To learn more about interoperability, see Chapter 12, "Unity Networking." For more on the capabilities of Unity's interoperability, design and deployment documents, such as the Networking Guide, Design Guide, and Installation Guide, are required reading. However, understanding how Unity can leverage AMIS, VPIM, and Bridge for a migration is important; this will be discussed at a functionality level.

AMIS

Audio Messaging Interchange Specification (AMIS) is the oldest of the interoperability methods and is the least robust in capability. AMIS basically performs the task that its name implies. The voice-messaging products of the past did not have a means of communicating with each other: What we take for granted today with digital networking in Unity was unheard of in the not-so-distant history of voice messaging platforms. When companies formed alliances or partnerships, mergers or replacement AMIS fulfilled a gap that otherwise left the voice-mail server an island of its own.

To deliver an AMIS message, the sending voice-mail system dials the receiving voice-mail system and then plays back DTMF codes from the message header that identifies the target mailbox. This is followed by analog playback of the voice-mail message itself. The analog playback of the message is the biggest drawback. If the message is 5 minutes long, then it takes 5 minutes to play back the message. In this manner, however, any two AMIS-compliant voice-mail systems can exchange messages. The received message is recorded and stored in the format native to the receiving system. The issue of incompatible message file formats between different voice-mail systems thus is avoided.

Unity does not deviate from the AMIS standard communication stack, with the exception of how it addresses a message to the receiving voice-mail system. Unity supports two ways of addressing a message: creating an AMIS subscriber or using blind addressing. With Unity leveraging AMIS, replacing the existing voice-messaging system negates the need for a flash cut and provides for a phased move to Unity. At the same time, it allows message processing for subscribers on both systems as well as between them. The benefit of AMIS is that it is well established and adopted by most voice-mail manufacturers, ensuring a larger base of compatibility.

Migrating to Unity using AMIS requires the AMIS licensing option on both Unity and the existing voice-mail system. Configure both Unity and the existing voice-messaging system to accept and process AMIS calls. Test the functionality between the two. Determine whether to use blind addressing or to create AMIS subscribers. Because this is a phased migration approach, the subscriber accounts are created in Unity one at a time or a few at a time while other subscribers still exist on the old voice-mail server. This gives administrators control over what subscribers are moved and when. An additional benefit is realized by creating AMIS subscribers and utilizing the Migrate Subscriber tool to create a full Unity subscriber account from the AMIS subscriber account used for message delivery to the existing voice-mail server.

VPIM

Voice Profile for Internet Mail (VPIM) is a relatively new means of interoperability. It is not unlike AMIS in that it enables VPIM-compliant voice-mail systems to send and receive messages between themselves.

VPIM differs in how the message is delivered to the receiving messaging system. Traditionally, messages sent from one voice-messaging system to another were transported using analog networking protocols based on DTMF signaling and analog voice playback, as discussed with AMIS earlier. As the demand for networking disparate voice-messaging systems increased, there was a need for a standard protocol to connect these machines in a much more efficient way. VPIM addressed this need by utilizing SMTP and MIME protocols for message delivery.

Because VPIM is relatively new, older voice-mail systems do not have the capability to take advantage of VPIM. With this slight handicap, VPIM would be the weapon of choice for a migration if it were supported because it is more efficient and faster than AMIS. Here again, the flash cut means of replacement can be alleviated by supporting a phased migration while maintaining communication between subscribers of Unity and the voice-messaging system or systems being replaced.

Migrating to Unity using VPIM requires configurable VPIM on both Unity and the existing voice-mail system. The Unity server enables this functionality through licensing, so an update to the licensing profile might be necessary if it was not a part of the original installation. Configure both Unity and the existing voice-messaging system to accept and process VPIM messages. Test the functionality between the two. Because this is a phased migration approach, the subscriber accounts are created in Unity one at a time or a few at a time while other subscribers still exist on the old voice-mail server. This gives administrators control over what subscribers are moved and when. An additional benefit is realized by creating VPIM subscribers and utilizing the Migrate Subscriber tool to create a full Unity subscriber account from the VPIM subscriber account used for message delivery to the existing voice-mail server when it is time for that subscriber to be migrated.

Unity Bridge

With Unity Bridge, interoperability is less focused on a wide means of interoperability, as with AMIS and VPIM. Instead, it is focused on communicating with Octel using analog Octel networking. Unity Bridge enables Unity subscribers to send and receive messages to Octel systems by representing itself as an actual node or several nodes.

Unity Bridge is more robust in its feature and functionality, positioning itself well for migrations off of Octel to Unity. Functionalities, such as directory replication and account aging, are among the many benefits that make it such an attractive means of migration. This functionality, coupled with Unity's Octel-like TUI conversation, makes the move to Unity easier for businesses, as well as easier for the end user to adopt the new Unity voice-messaging server. Like that of VPIM and AMIS, the subscriber account created can be migrated to a full subscriber account, or the administrator can simply create the new subscriber accounts using the system administrator or import utilities.

An additional and final key step after migration of the subscriber account for all methods of interoperability involves ensuring that the subscriber's phone is forwarded to the appropriate pilot number of the new Unity voice-messaging server.

With all methods of migrating through interoperability, Unity's flexibility makes AMIS, VPIM, and Unity Bridge the catalyst for moving from an older voice-messaging system or becoming a mainstay and continuing communications with voice-mail systems outside of the organization that Unity supports. Another key benefit is that Unity takes advantage of its own digital networking in conjunction with the different types of interoperability.

A single Unity server can house interoperability functionality along with Unity's normal messaging capabilities. For a larger deployment and multiple Unity servers, an AMIS, VPIM, or Unity Bridge bridgehead server can be used for interoperability functions. This enables the other Unity servers to perform their respective tasks without additional overhead. This is accomplished through Unity's digital networking powers; for more on digital networking, see Chapter 12.

Migrating from a Unity Voice Messaging-Only Configuration to a Unity Unified Messaging Configuration

A migration from a Unity voice messaging-only configuration to a unified messaging configuration is not as tedious as it might seem. Some high-level tasks must be met to perform the migration. The best way to perform this type of migration is to do a flash cut between Unity servers. If you have more than one Unity voice messaging-only configuration, you can decide whether to migrate all voice messaging-only servers to unified messaging-only servers at once or over a short span of time.

The high level tasks are listed here:

- Clean up the data and configuration on the existing Cisco Unity voice messaging-only server.

- Build out the new Cisco Unity unified messaging server in the new Active Directory environment.

- Ensure that the Unity server is updated with the latest service packs.

- Test and monitor the system for impact management.

- Make sure that the alias names for the voice messaging-only configuration are the same as the alias names in the UM environment. If not, you might need to perform this task manually. If the aliases match, run a DiRT backup on the voice messaging-only configuration and run DiRT restore on the new unified messaging configuration.

Cisco Unity voice messaging typically is installed into its own Active Directory structure (recommended). However, Unity also can be deployed using the customer's existing corporate directory and Exchange organization. This is accomplished by creating duplicate accounts for the voice-mail accounts. The obvious downside to this type of installation is the need for a duplicate account because of licensing, as well as the sizing requirements that are introduced into the environment. However, the upside is that the Unity server is already a part of the domain structure and the Exchange organization; moving subscriber information does not entail a new install of Unity.

With this type of deployment, Unity can take advantage of the Move Subscriber Information utility, which associates the information from the VM account with the user's corporate account. This capability arises because the VM and Corporate accounts share the same directory. More information on this tool can be located at www.ciscounitytools.com.

Migrating the Messaging System That Unity Services

Cisco Unity currently supports Exchange 5.5, 2000, and 2003, as well as Domino as its message store. Migrating a Unity server from one messaging server to another can be the result of a need to upgrade the messaging organization to a more recent version, a hardware update, or a plethora of other reasons.

This section discusses the high-level steps. For more detail, consult the Unity Reconfiguration Guide, as well as IBM or Microsoft's documentation.

Exchange 5.5 to Exchange 2000 or 2003

Begin the migration by making sure that the Unity database is clean:

Step 1 Download and install the latest version of the Cisco Unity Directory Walker utility.

Step 2 Run Directory Walker, and correct all errors that the utility finds before continuing.

Step 3 Perform a full backup of the Unity server.

After these steps, basically two options exist for moving the Unity server to the new messaging server environment. These largely depend upon the methods used by the customer. The first method is to create an entirely new messaging infrastructure from scratch. With this method, new accounts are created in Active Directory that are mail-enabled in the new Exchange 2000 or 2003 messaging organization.

This methodology is relatively simple for Unity because a reinstall of the Unity server is necessary to integrate with Active Directory. The existing Unity server and its subscriber accounts must make sure that the mail aliases for each user match the new Exchange 2000/2003 accounts. This is a consideration so that the DiRT utility can back up the existing Unity configuration and restore it to the new Unity server. It is highly recommended that you read up on the DiRT utility before attempting this on the production servers. You can find information about DiRT at www.ciscounitytools.com.

The second choice of migrating the servers from Exchange 5.5 to Exchange 2000/2003 involves setting up a mixed-mode environment. In this environment, you are currently on Exchange 5.5, and you introduce an Exchange 2000 server into the existing environment. Again, you should adhere to Microsoft's documentation and best practices and follow the steps detailed next for Unity to function in a mixed-mode Exchange environment.

Mixed-Mode Exchange

Verify configuration in these areas to ensure that you can work in a mixed Exchange environment:

* The Exchange 2000 or Exchange 2003 servers must be installed into one of the existing Exchange 5.5 sites.

* The Exchange version of the Active Directory connector must be installed.

* A recipient connection agreement must be set up to replicate data between the Exchange 5.5 directory and Active Directory.

* Install the current Exchange service pack and updates recommended for use with Cisco Unity.

- Extend the Active Directory Schema.

- Install Exchange 2003 System Manager or Exchange 2000 System Manager on the Cisco Unity Server.

- Install the current Exchange service pack and updates recommended for use with Cisco Unity.

- Configure Cisco Unity for Exchange 2003 or Exchange 2000 by running the Configuration Wizard.

- Move users' mailboxes from Exchange 5.5 to Exchange 2003 or Exchange 2000. Refer to Microsoft documentation for more information.

- Remove Exchange 5.5 from the environment when the migration is complete.

Migrating Unity Between Different Active Directory Forests

In today's world, we constantly hear about companies merging or being bought out. The architecture of two such companies might have similarities—they might both use Exchange, for instance, or they might both use Active Directory.

Another reason for moving Unity between Active Directory forests can be the need to move from voice messaging to unified messaging.

With Unity relying on Active Directory for connection and replication services, Unity can service only one Active Directory forest. So, for two companies to merge, or for a change from voice messaging to unified messaging, Unity might have to move to another Active Directory forest.

This change is unlike that of migrating from VM to UM, discussed earlier. The big challenge might be that accounts exist in Unity that do not exist in the new environment, and vice versa. With this type of scenario, thought should be given to what types of issues can be introduced by this migration. A few are listed here:

- Security differences
- Account-creation policies
- Active Directory OU structure

Going through the differences between the organizations, a recommended means might be to deploy Unity as voice messaging, merge the Active Directory structures, stabilize both the Active Directory and Exchange environments, and then migrate to unified messaging.

By taking this approach, you allow for an easier migration in Active Directory/Exchange, and you also provide an opportunity for architectural differences to subside. Also, the mail alias issue can be fixed before the migration for those that require correction. The migration steps from the VM to UM mentioned earlier can be reused here:

Step 1   Clean up the data and configuration on the existing Cisco Unity voice messaging-only server.

Step 2   Build out the new Cisco Unity unified messaging server in the new Active Directory environment.

Step 3   Ensure that the Unity server is updated with the latest service packs.

Step 4   Test and monitor the system for impact management.

Step 5   Make sure that the alias names for the voice messaging-only configuration are the same as the alias names in the UM environment. If not, you might need to perform this task manually. If the aliases match, run a DiRT backup on the voice messaging-only configuration and run DiRT restore on the new unified messaging configuration.

Migrations with Unity and Domino

Cisco Unity supports Exchange and Domino as the back-end mail store. However, a big difference between Unity Exchange and Unity Domino is that with Domino the only supported configuration is unified messaging.

With UM being the only option for the Domino message store, the migration strategy narrows quite a bit. If a site has Domino for e-mail services but wants Unity for voice messaging only, the Unity server has no other option than to be in its own standalone configuration.

Another bit of information is that when Unity migrates from voice messaging to unified messaging with Domino, the Unity server must be reinstalled from scratch. User information also must be re-created.

Summary

Throughout this chapter, we discussed processes for upgrading and migrating a Unity server. The key to ensuring a successful upgrade or migration is to begin with a thorough understanding of the tasks necessary and then document the tasks and execution plan. To minimize the downtime and impact to subscribers, make sure that you do the following:

- Understand the products that you are moving from and moving to so that expectations can be properly set.

- Schedule the event so that all parties concerned are informed of when it takes place.

- Plan the methodology to be used so that the documented tasks flow properly and give the desired result in the migration or upgrade.

- Test the plan to ensure accuracy of the tasks necessary and to confirm that the planned steps accomplish the goal of the migration or upgrade.

The final—and, arguably, most important—piece of the pie is to ensure that, in the case of failure to accomplish the upgrade or migration, there is a means of falling back or restoring the system to a previously known working state. The moral of the story is to know, schedule, plan, and test to achieve success.

CHAPTER 16

Installation

This chapter describes how to put together an implementation plan to install one or more Unity servers. This chapter is a continuation of the planning, design, and implementation and operations (PDIO) deployment methodology described throughout this book. You use content from your low-level design documentation to put together your implementation. The detailed design shows you how your solution looks, the implementation plan tells you the steps necessary to build your solution as it is designed. Because this chapter is a part of the PDIO methodology, you should have a strong understanding and practical application of the following chapters:

- Chapter 8, "Deployment Methodology"
- Chapter 9, "Planning"
- Chapter 11, "Designing a Unity Solution"

In addition, all remaining chapters in Part II, "Deployment," help you to understand the criteria necessary to design a Unity solution before you develop an implementation plan.

It is also helpful to understand the operational aspects of Unity. This means having a strong understanding of Unity's architecture and features from Part I, "Concepts and Architecture," as well as the administrative capabilities of Unity detailed in Part III, "Solutions, Systems Management, and Administration." In addition, you should read Unity product documentation, tech notes, release notes, and whitepapers on specific topics relevant to your requirements.

A disclaimer is probably important at this point: No solutions-design methodology is a guarantee for success. Instead, the methodology (such as the one conveyed in this book) is a guide. You can be successful using this process, but the process cannot guarantee that you will do everything that you need to do to be successful. That is up to you. Your situation might be completely different than what is typified throughout this methodology; some particulars of your deployment requirements might be left out of this process. Make sure that those particulars are covered in your plans. The best way to ensure that you have done everything right is to test Unity after it has been deployed and make sure that you are satisfied with the results of the tests. This includes making sure that your end users are happy with its behavior and performance, and that the Unity server or servers can be administered and maintained without significant resource or financial overhead.

Implementation Plan Development

The best way to develop your implementation plan is to address it as outlined in this chapter and to also use the low-level design documentation as the source-level content.

Within the implementation plan, you have the following high-level tasks:

- Preinstallation tasks
- Installation
- Cutover
- Fallback readiness
- Operations acceptance

You source your implementation plan from your low-level design documentation. Basically, the information contained in each section of your low-level design maps to the subtasks found under each high-level task in this chapter. Instructions are provided on how to use the low-level design content to complete the subtasks.

You should be able to use your low-level design data to build your implementation plan. If you cannot, you should rethink the level of detail that you put into your design during the design phase and make the necessary adjustments before proceeding to the implementation stage.

Preinstallation Tasks

Working your way backward from your design, some of your operational requirements should be set up first, to support the installation. The output of your site surveys should tell you whether you need new equipment or configuration changes to the different components of your environment. Project-related tasks also must be performed. These include making sure that your legacy call-processing resources are in place and ready for integration with Unity, as well as ordering non-Unity equipment to support the Unity installations or configuration/reconfiguration of that equipment to be used for the same purpose. Those project-related tasks are not included here. The guidelines provided in this chapter assume that they have been completed. If they are not, it is probably a good idea to go back and address them before you start your implementation planning of Unity. These subtasks are outlined in the following sections:

- Setting up administrative consoles
- Creating accounts and verifying permissions
- Extending the schema

Administrative Console

To set up and manage multiple Unity servers, it is essential that you set up one or more administrative consoles, which are simply workstations or low-end servers. You already might have administrative consoles that you use to support your messaging infrastructure or voice-related products. Nothing prevents you from using existing consoles to support your Unity installation.

Your administrative consoles should have the following applications:

- Unity-related tools installed or ready to be installed (some tools must be installed directly onto each Unity server—some do not need to be). See http://www.ciscounity tools.com for more information regarding tools that can be used to administer Unity. Each tool lists how it is supported and how it can be used.

- Unity product documentation, which includes installation guides, administrative guides, and so on.

- Links and specific URLs used to manage and maintain Unity servers. This includes Unity support links, such as http://www.ciscounitysupport.com and the Cisco Unity NetPro public forum at http://forum.cisco.com/eforum/servlet/NetProf?page=main.

- Along with maintaining links for support, you should also have contract number information and TAC contact information in order to obtain support from Cisco TAC.

- Monitoring tools, such as Windows performance monitor, third-party management consoles, antivirus consoles, and back-up monitoring software (if applicable).

- Microsoft Office or some other office suite that includes a word-processing application, a spreadsheet application, and possibly a database application if you maintain a separate database of users and subscriber information.

- Disk storage for storing logs and trace files.

- Some type of activity log for tracking administrative activities.

- Remote access tools, such as Windows Terminal Services or VNC.

The following low-level design information supports the administrative and management requirements for your admin console:

- Service accounts and administrative access
- End-user access
- Security considerations
- Administration considerations
- Management considerations
- Support considerations

See the "Low-Level Design" section in Chapter 11 for more information.

Monitoring Facility

The monitoring facility is separate from the administrative console, but it does not have to be physically separated. It is separate with the expectation that ongoing continuous monitoring of your Unity servers will require a dedicated system or two, especially if you will trend your systems after you install Unity. Of course, if you want to manage Unity performance or monitor for TUI delays, you also will want to monitor your Unity servers in a consistent and dedicated fashion.

This source information should be included in the following sections of your low-level design:

- Management considerations
- Support considerations

See the "Low-Level Design" section in Chapter 11 for more information.

Account Creation and Permissions Verification

To prepare for your Unity installations, for each set of service accounts that you plan to use for your Unity services, use the Unity Permissions Wizard to grant the necessary permissions to those accounts. Also make sure that the service accounts have group policies applied to them (if applicable) to treat them specifically as service accounts and not user accounts.

This source information should be included in service accounts and administrative access section of your low-level design. See the "Low-Level Design" section in Chapter 11 for more information.

Schema Extension

If Unity is servicing Exchange 2000 or Exchange 2003, extend the Active Directory schema at this time if it has not been extended already. Note that if you pilot Unity in a production environment, you must extend the schema at that time.

If Unity is servicing Domino, you will want to install DUCS on the servers that will house subscribers.

This source information should be included in the Unity directory usage section of your low-level design. See the "Low-Level Design" section in Chapter 11 for more information.

Installation

Your installation of Unity can be broken into four parts:

- The physical installation of the server hardware and cables. This information is found in the following sections of your low-level design:
  - Physical placement
  - Unity hardware configurations
- The installation of software, including the OS, third-party components, and the Unity application itself. This information is found in the following sections of your low-level design:
  - Unity hardware configurations
  - Unity system configurations
  - Physical network connectivity
- The installation of the VMO client on subscribers who use Outlook, or DUC clients on subscribers who use Notes.
- The configuration and importing of subscribers. This information is found in the following sections of your low-level design:
  - Unity system configurations
  - Subscriber account naming conventions

You should reference Unity product documentation for step-by-step installation procedures. Some organizations might use their own instructions written from the Unity product documentation. This is often more desirable because it is specific to a given organization's standards for installation, especially for installation of the operating system and supported third-party tools running on top of them.

Installation is complete when all hardware and software is installed and considered functional. This does not include configuration work that essentially customizes the hardware and software for your environment.

When installation of the Unity server is complete, it is necessary to configure each Unity server. This includes the following tasks:

- Configuring the integration and voice ports
- Verifying the connectivity to the message store
- Configuring subscriber data (templates, COS, schedules, and other settings)
- Importing or creating subscribers
- Importing or creating distribution lists
- Configuring system management for administrators
- Documenting the configuration

You can use Cisco Unity configuration worksheets to document your configuration for each server. The worksheets can be found at Cisco.com.

For each of these items, see the Unity system description in the low-level design.

Precutover Tasks

When you get to this point in your plan, you have a good list of tasks that should be conducted and listed in your implementation plan.

After you install and configure Unity, you will want to determine when you can cut over. Typically, this is a timing issue. You might choose to cut over a group of users at a time or entire legacy voice-messaging systems at a time. Either way, you basically can have Unity set up and running before you perform your cutover. Note that nothing prevents your subscribers from finding the VMO application in Outlook or from using DUCS and sending messages to one another, especially if they have microphones. However, no harm is done if messages are sent from the client; Unity is not needed to use the client unless you have TRaP configured, so you might consider installing the client application before cutover.

The main event that causes the cutover to take place is redirecting or repointing calls from your legacy voice-messaging system to Unity. This is one question that you might want to ask when you devise the plan. If you have surveyed your legacy voice-messaging system connectivity to your legacy PBXs or to CallManager, you should have a good idea of how it is connected and what is necessary to redirect your calls to Unity. For more information, see your low-level design documentation and Chapter 17, "Unity Telephony Integration."

Before performing cutover, however, you must make sure that Unity operates according to your configuration requirements. It is always best to test and validate your configuration before cutover. These other precutover tasks should be performed:

- Configuration testing
- Conversation test planning
- Integration test planning
- Simulated load testing
- Go/no go decision making
- Precutover subscriber enrollment

Configuration Testing

Configuration testing simply means making sure that all your configuration functions work as they should. This testing should include making sure that you can copy files and import subscribers into your system. Can you make changes to subscriber properties? Can you verify that you have no unforeseen restrictions that a group policy might have applied to your installation?

Develop a script that tests the server at several levels: the OS, the third-party components, and the Unity application itself.

Specifically, include in your script tests that verify your data. Refer to the Unity tools, including dbWalker and Subscriber Information Dump, to verify that your data is consistent and has no errors. As another part of configuration testing, make sure that you validate Unity's connectivity to the network and to your legacy switch or CallManager. Make sure that you can access the server with your management tools, that it is completely ready to be managed, and that no special nonUnity-related work is still pending, such as setting up schedules for backups or setting up third-party agents for management (antivirus, intruder detection, and so on).

Conversations Test Plan

Through your usage analysis, you should have become quite intimate with the TUI conversation of Unity and your legacy voice-messaging system. Thus, you probably developed test plans to test the conversation and any customizations that you might have made. If so, for each Unity server installed, you should dial into the server, test the conversation, and make sure that it functions as intended. Do not assume that it is okay. Chances are, you have nothing to worry about, but you will be happier if you test.

If you have special audio-text applications built for specific groups or departments, make sure that you have their setup validated by the groups or departments requesting them. This means that you will want to have them run through the conversations of their application and make sure that they are satisfied with it. Be prepared to make adjustments to their applications before and after cutover.

Integration Test Plan

Of course, you should include a test plan that validates your integration with legacy PBX or with CallManager. If Unity is connected to a legacy PBX, you need to ensure that all the voice ports are in the correct order physically and logically, and also that your integration operates as expected. Make sure that your subscriber's message waiting indicators (MWI) are lit and that they turn off when the last unheard message is played back.

When you test the order of your voice ports, do not just do a physical or visual test. Call them and monitor the port using Status Monitor, and make sure that the correct port answers. This is the best way to validate that the ports are in order. If they are not in order, you most likely will have issues with your switch integration. Make sure that you correct the order of the physical ports into Unity before finishing your integration testing.

Simulated Load Testing

The simulated load test is probably the single most important precutover test that you can run on each Unity server installed, especially your larger Unity servers. You do this simply by having enough callers call into the system for a short period of time—say, a half hour or so—and leave messages, listen to messages, log in, log out, change greetings, and do anything else they can do to put the Unity server under load. Now, you do not need to max out your ports. If you have 72 port systems and use four or six ports for outbound, you have 68 or 66 voice ports total. You can effectively test your servers by getting about 30 to 34 callers to call into the system and test it. If you are concerned about affecting existing mailboxes, do not use them. Create and use dummy mailboxes and dummy extensions.

The amount of time that it takes to set up this simulated load test is well worth it and will give you an excellent idea of the types of problems you might encounter.

Performing the Simulated Test

This load test can be accomplished as follows:

Step 1 Create test mailboxes and import them as test subscribers on each Unity server.

Step 2 Schedule a test period from 30 minutes to an hour in duration. It might even be possible to test in a shorter time span, such as 15 minutes.

For each test subscriber, the testing should include the following activities:

— Unity user activity generation

— Performance monitoring

— Post-testing assessment

The goal of this stress test is to ensure that the server can maintain acceptable response time during peak load (roughly 60 percent).

Step 3 Generate Unity user activity by completing the following:

— Assign a test DTMFID to a caller who dials into the server from the outside.

— Provide a list of other DTMFIDs to each participant to be used for the test session.

— To make the testing easy, note the password used for the assigned DTMFID of the test participant (LAST_NAME, FIRST_NAME, DTMF_ACCESS_ID, ALIAS).

— Make sure that each participant is ready at a particular time and that they understand the instructions.

Step 4   Begin the testing. Table 16-1 outlines a test procedure.

Table 16-1   *Simulated Load Test*

Step	Action	System Response or Next Step
1	Dial the Unity Pilot: <insert number>.	"Please enter your ID, followed by #."
2	Log into the Unity server with the selected DTMF_ACCESS_ID and the assigned password.	Unity reads the number and type of messages available.
		You might hear Unity respond with "Do you want to erase your deleted messages? For Yes, press 1, for No press 2." Press 2 to save the deleted messages.
		Note: Do not erase any deleted messages.
3	If messages exist for the subscriber, press 1 from the subscriber menu to listen to them and proceed to step 4. If no messages exist, proceed to step 8.	After you log in as a subscriber, Unity tells you if you have any messages and how many.
4	During the message menu conversation, attempt the following activities:	Any of these options can be selected from the main menu.
	a. Choose a voice message to repeat. (Press 1.)	After completing this, perform another activity from step 4 or go to step 5.
	b. Choose a voice message to save. (Press 2.)	
	c. Choose a voice message to delete. (Press 3.)	
	d. Choose a voice message to skip. (Press #.)	
	e. Choose a voice message to forward. (Press 5.)	
	f. Select message menu help (by pressing 0) if you are confused.	
5	Document any response-time issues or other concerns.	Notes:
6	At the subscriber menu, press 2 to leave a message for a subscriber. Select a DTMFID at random.	"Enter the extension, followed by #."
7	Document any response-time issues or other concerns.	Notes:
8	Send a minute-long message for two subscribers from the DTMFID list. (The extensions are the same as the DTMFIDs previously provided.)	After completing this, note any issues and go to step 9.
	Document any response-time issues or other concerns.	Notes:

continues

Table 16-1 *Simulated Load Test (Continued)*

Step	Action	System Response or Next Step
9	After the messages have been sent, hang up and return to step 1.	Attempt as many consecutive login sessions as possible within the allotted timeframe.
10	Document any response-time issues or other concerns.	Notes:

When the testing period is complete, the test can be considered "passed" if all of the following criteria are met:

- No failsafe conversations (heard as "I am sorry, this system is currently unable to take your call").
- No TUI delays longer than 3 to 5 seconds between prompts. (This can be measured by hearing the delay and also by the performance monitor counters.)
- No severe error events in the application or system event logs.
- No unusual logging behavior on the Unity server itself. This includes Unity logging and SQL logging.

This test should be considered the primary acceptance test before going to the next stage of this installation process.

Go/No Go Decision Making

A go/no go decision should be mutually determined by all responsible parties before the scheduled cutover. The decision should be based on the satisfaction of Unity performance during the various tests run on a given Unity server. At this point, the severity of any unexplained errors should be known and identified. If any such errors or problems still exist, it should directly influence a no go decision for cutover.

If all testing is satisfactory and any or all error conditions are satisfactorily explained, these should influence a go decision to cut over the server at the scheduled time.

Now, this is an important point: If you have taken a scientific approach to piloting Unity in your production environment during the planning phase, you should have a very good idea of the issues and items that affect a go/no go decision. Another benefit of performing a production pilot is that you should know many of the particulars of Unity's behavior in your environment. You should know what to check and what needs to be addressed. This should make your go/no go decision-making process that much easier and effective as well.

Precutover Subscriber Enrollment

It is necessary to ensure that the end-user experience is satisfactory by providing a period of availability when subscribers can go through the open enrollment process without waiting for an available port to sign into Unity. This sounds funny, but it is important nevertheless.

An "open enrollment only" period should be established before doing a full cutover. The end-user population should be provided with a schedule of when users can enroll and instructions, including a notice similar to: "Do not leave any voice messages at this time because you will not be able to retrieve them until after the Unity voice-messaging system is live."

The open enrollment period should be able to accommodate the majority of the subscribers in a given period of time, based on subscriber population and port density on the Unity server.

Each open enrollment session takes about 1 minute to complete. It can take longer while the subscribers familiarize themselves with the system.

The Unity tool Subscriber Information Dump provides a list of subscribers who currently have completed the open enrollment process. You can run it throughout the open enrollment period and ensure that subscribers actually enroll as instructed.

An open enrollment period is more important to larger Unity installations than smaller ones in which open enrollment can be managed. However, for large locations with thousands of subscribers, an open enrollment period before cutover alleviates the possibility that your subscribers get a busy system when they attempt to first log into your Unity servers. Any Unity server can handle the load of enrollment; however, under no circumstances should cutover begin with a notice to inform all subscribers to enroll at the same time. This action results in an unacceptable end-user experience because any number of subscribers greater than the number of ports available for a given Unity server will receive busy signals. This means that the wait period to log into the server might be very high while subscribers try to gain access to go through the enrollment process. Just think what your end users would say if you tell 3000 of them to enroll into the system first thing on a Monday morning. If you create a period of pre-cutover enrollment, you should not have to worry about this issue.

Cutover

During the appointed time for cutover, each server should be monitored carefully through continuous repeated checks of the Unity TUI and also through performance monitoring and port activity monitoring using the Unity status monitor. In addition, Unity tools are available for monitoring integration issues associated with message notification and transfers.

These tools should be set up and readied before cutover, and support personnel should be available to assist the helpdesk with any incidents opened by end users.

Any severe performance issues might require a fallback to your existing legacy voice-messaging systems until the issues can be resolved. Remember, the goal is to minimize or eliminate any downtime or unsatisfactory user experience during the cutover period.

Intermittent issues with any of the following should be monitored closely and most likely can be resolved after hours on the first or second day of the cutover:

- Sporadic MWI issues being experienced by individuals (not the entire user population)

- Isolated, rare, or unexpected delays in the TUI conversation, especially during peak periods experienced by individuals (not the entire user population)

- Any unusual activity on the Unity or the messaging server that it services, such as logs filling up too quickly

- Unexpected response-time issues resulting from secondary outages, such as a router failure or a messaging infrastructure dependency going offline

Severe issues with any of the following should be considered candidates to fall back to the existing legacy voice-messaging systems. However, they should be considered candidates for fallback only if the problem cannot be remedied in a timely fashion (such as through a reboot or configuration change).

- Continuous failsafe conversations that indicate a serious corruption or configuration issue that cannot be resolved in a timely fashion or through a reboot

- Unexpected integration problems, such as failure to transfer to a greeting or MWIs not working for any subscriber

- Ports constantly timing out because of connectivity issues with the PBX

- Hardware failures, such as voice-board failures or intermittent cabling problems affecting greater than 10% of the ports

- Software failures, such as Unity services terminating because of unexpected or unknown software conflicts or defects

- Infrastructure failures, such as Ethernet switches or routers coming offline, preventing Unity from communicating with CallManager or the legacy PBX, the messaging system Unity is servicing, and messaging infrastructure components such as domain controllers or name-resolution hosts

- Other unknown or unexpected failures or events beyond your control

The cutover should be considered complete when all open tickets resulting from the cutover are resolved and when Unity system and operational performance is considered satisfactorily equal to or better than existing legacy voice-messaging systems. This is not intended to be a contractual guarantee; it is intended to be a measurement criteria for cutover success or failure.

Fallback Readiness

It is essential to document and prepare for the possibility of falling back to the original configuration before performing the cutover. If you decide to fall back because any of the previously stated criteria, the exact steps to recover to the original configuration should be documented and understood.

It is important to ensure that the Unity systems can be taken out of available service and that your legacy voice-messaging systems can be placed back in service. As always, a dry run to verify fallback readiness is strongly recommended if there is any doubt about being able to fall back.

Performing Fallback

If you have to fall back from a failed cutover attempt, remember that you will have to switch the pilot number back over to your legacy voice-messaging system. However, remain in fallback readiness only until your cutover period is complete and you have handed off to operations. Waiting longer than this prevents you from being able to decommission your legacy voice-messaging system(s). Some organizations want to keep their systems running offline for a month or so after cutover. That is fine if it is necessary. However, through your lab trials and lab testing, you should have been able to validate the steps necessary to fall back to your legacy system.

Operations Acceptance Criteria

Achieving normal operations is the primary goal of deployment. Your implementation plan is incomplete without establishing operational acceptance criteria that can be measured for each Unity installation.

This criteria should include acceptance of Unity's performance by verifying the following:

- No unexpected or un-remedied errors or erratic behavior is observed or reported.
- Unity answers calls, and all voice ports are persistently operational.
- Unity responds normally to subscriber key presses during TUI sessions, especially during peak periods.

If all criteria is met, or if some percentage of the criteria is met, you can determine that the given installation is operationally acceptable and that it can be handed over to an operations team. At this point, all installation activity should be considered complete.

You might choose to tune the server after the cutover and before turning over the server to operations. This is fine. It also might be useful for the installation team and the operations team to jointly tune the server as a handover step.

Post-Installation Server Tuning

When the cutover is complete, it is necessary to determine any adjustments that must be made to the Unity server, the legacy PBX or CallManager, or messaging servers, and then make those on a scheduled basis.

It should be determined whether any or all such adjustments can be made after hours and the amount of work required making them. Any downtime resulting from the adjustments should be noted and performed during the most acceptable period, based on your trends.

Adjustments can include any or all of the following:

- Changing Unity port configurations
- Changing Unity system settings
- Changing messaging system configuration settings, such as Registry entries and system settings
- Changing integration settings or physical cabling between Unity and the legacy PBX

Post-Cutover Hand-Off to Operations

After post-cutover adjustments (if any) have been made, the hand-off to operations can take place.

Per your low-level design documentation and, specifically, the criteria you established through the results of your usage analysis (see Chapter 11) to properly administer the Unity servers and their supporting infrastructure, you can hand off support of the implementation to your operations team.

When hand-off is complete, the data accumulated through the usage analysis should allow your operations personnel to establish all processes necessary to completely administer the system, perform system backup/recovery, and maintain documentation and logging information on a consistent basis.

Your operations team then can contact Cisco TAC for support in the event of system outages that cannot be remedied by your team.

Post-Implementation Assessment

When the Unity implementation is complete, conducting a full project assessment is strongly recommended to determine the level of satisfaction with the project. This includes assessing the performance of your Unity servers.

The post-implementation assessment should include documenting the project's efficiencies and inefficiencies, including what went right and what went wrong, as well as what could have been performed better and what should be included in any future projects.

Summary

For each Unity server, be sure to address each section noted in this chapter. Thus, your implementation plan might seem to be repetitive, but at the same time, if you have selected more than one server platform for Unity and have more than one type of legacy PBX, you might have different criteria for each section in your implementation plan for each server. Whether you group your servers based on the switch they are connected to or group them based on location, make sure that you account for the specifics of each Unity server as it pertains to the subscribers you migrate to it. In this case, the specifics simply mean the main tasks and steps found throughout this chapter.

If you have only a handful of Unity servers to install—say, three or four—your implementation plan is short and to the point. If you install 30 or 40 Unity servers, however, you might end up needing to put together a primary implementation plan with site-specific detail for each physical location/site where Unity is installed. This is fine. Your low-level design and the high-level steps conveyed in this chapter easily should accommodate that requirement.

Transfer your low-level design specifics, such as server names, physical rack locations, and everything else, to your implementation plan so that the installer needs only to follow the information listed in the plan to install the server software and configure it.

It might take you more than one draft—and maybe even more than one attempt—to get your implementation right. Using the low-level design data, however, is the key to feeding your implementation plan and making sure that you cover all your bases. As previously mentioned, the best chance your plan has at succeeding is totally up to you and your team. The deployment methodology is simply a guide for helping you get there.

CHAPTER 17

Unity Telephony Integration

This chapter focuses on exactly what switch integration is. We isolate and explore the key elements of switch integration. We also discuss the configuration of Unity's switch integrations and exactly how Unity implements the key elements of switch integration.

Beyond the specific technologies, hardware devices, telephony signaling protocols, and connectivity methods, integrating a voice-mail system to a phone system includes two major concepts. These concepts are call control and call information. Call control is the set of operations that a device connected to a phone system (such as a telephone) must perform to maneuver calls throughout the switch network. Examples of call control are answering, transferring, or initiating a phone call on the phone system. The exact mechanics of how a phone call is answered, transferred, or initiated varies from PBX to PBX, but the concept of call control is the same. Call information is data sent from the phone system to a device connected to the phone system. This data might include identification of the calling and or calling parties and why a call was directed to the device receiving this call information.

The simplest example of call control and call information can be found in regular household phones. Most homes have a device (the phone set) that is connected to a phone system (the switch provided by the phone company). Most people do not think about it, but call control is absolutely necessary to answer an incoming call or place an outbound call. The phone rings and somebody lifts the handset off of the receiver to answer that call, and now we have an example of call control. The person sitting next to the phone had to respond and invoke some action to answer the call. The simple act of picking up the receiver closed a circuit between the phone and the phone system, thus enabling the connection of the calling and called parties.

Now let us imagine that our phone has one of those caller ID displays on it. Our phone rings once again, but before simply answering the call, we take a look at the caller ID display to see who is calling. We see a phone number, and even in some cases a name of the calling party, and now we have call information.

The home phone example might seem trivial, but these simple examples provide insight into just how Unity implements, understands, and supports call control and call information when connected to a phone system. It is amazingly simple for someone to take a peek at the caller ID display and answer that phone. However, it is unbelievably difficult to have a PC-based voice-mail system intelligently do the same thing. It takes a mountain of software, and in a lot of cases, specialized hardware (it can even take special hardware that is not even on the voice-mail system). For the most part, phone devices are pretty dumb. They do not do a lot without a person (or in Unity's case, a computer) on the other end. It is Unity's job to handle both its hardware and software to act on call control and call information to successfully be a connected and intelligent phone device.

That is the basic phone system integration for Unity: intelligently handling call control and call information. We will dive deeper into the mechanics of integrations as we look at specific methods and technologies of implementing call control and call information. We will also examine exactly how Unity processes the call information that is passed to it. Additionally, we will take a higher-level view of integrations and discover how integrations are closely related to many voice-mail features one can see in Unity.

Unity can connect to both IP-based phone systems and traditional, TDM (also known as legacy) phone systems, and Unity can even connect to both at the same time. Since the methods of call control and call information of these two types of phone systems differ greatly, we will draw an imaginary line between IP-based phone systems and legacy PBX phone systems. From within the legacy phone system group, many of the different phone systems employ similar mechanics and technologies for Unity, so it makes sense to lump the PBXs together. Since IP-based phone systems do not use the traditional mechanics and technologies, we will take a separate view of that group.

As mentioned previously, phone system integration is call control and call information. How each PBX implements these concepts can and will be different. Additionally, call control and call information can be broken down even further into more specific concepts and technologies. For example, call control relies upon certain types of signaling to have devices and the phone system maneuver calls throughout the switch network. Signaling can and will vary depending upon the connectivity type. Signaling can also vary depending on what device is talking to what. For example, the connection between a phone system and a phone might use one type of signaling, whereas the connection between two separate phone systems might employ a completely different type of signaling. Likewise, the way call information is sent between the two aforementioned connections can and will vary.

The TDM World of PBXs and Unity

With Unity's support of legacy switch integrations, special hardware called voice boards are used. The voice boards take care of the physical requirements of representing the phone sets and have the ability to support the same signaling and addressing available to single-line telephone sets. With this type of integration, the end point connected to the phone system is limited to the telephony functions that can be done with a single-line set. It is a fairly limited functionality but generally sufficient to carry out most voice-mail needs.

Switch Files and Integration Files

For the configuration of an integration, Unity employs switch files and integration files. These files are simple text files that contain settings to configure Unity to exercise call control and receive call information. The particular switch file that will be used depends upon what has been configured through UTIM (Unity Telephony Integration Manager) (4.0) or Unity's SA (System Administration) Switch page (3.X). If the integration is a legacy integration, the switch file contains a reference to another configuration file. This is the integration file and configures either the serial or analog-parsing engine.

All of the switch files for the PBXs that Unity supports can be found in the \Commserver\ Intlib directory. The integration files reside in the same directory as well. The switch files are *.ini files, whereas the integration files are *.avd files.

We will go into a quick breakdown of a portion of a switch file to show the relationship between the switch file and integration file (in-depth coverage of the switch file will be covered in the switch file settings appendix). This section of the switch file tells Unity not only what type of integration is being used, but how to configure the parsing engine for that integration:

```
[Identity]
SwitchManufacturer=Generic
SwitchModel=Centrex
SwitchSoftwareVersion=All w/ SMDI
IntegrationType=Serial

[Configuration]
Integration=SMDI
```

For now, we are only interested in the IntegrationType and Integration settings. As you might have guessed, the IntegrationType specifies the integration type (i.e. serial or analog). The Integration setting points to the specific integration file to be used. If the IntegrationType is serial, the value is used in the following manner:

```
Integration file name = Av + <value for "Integration"> + .Avd
```

For our first example, the corresponding integration file would be AvSMDI.Avd.

For the next example switch file, the IntegrationType is analog, so the Integration value points to a specific location in the AvAnalog.Avd integration file:

```
[Identity]
SwitchManufacturer=DEFAULTS
SwitchModel=Default Parameters
SwitchSoftwareVersion=All
IntegrationType=Analog

[Configuration]
DelayBeforeOpening=0
Integration=DEFAULT
```

For this example, there is a section in the AvAnalog.Avd file named DEFAULT, which contains specific configuration settings.

To view which switch file is currently being used by Unity, select the properties tab for the given integration in the UTIM utility for 4.0 systems.

Call Information Extraction (Analog DTMF Integration)

Perhaps the simplest Unity call information extraction method can be found in what Unity considers to be Analog DTMF integrations. The concept is simple: Unity's voice boards emulate an array of simple, single-line telephone sets. The single-line telephone is analogous to the phone set one can find in one's own home. Since this integration method is based on regular telephone sets, call addressing is limited to the set of digits that can be dialed from a phone.

NOTE In addition to the set of digits dialed from a phone, call addressing also includes 4th column tones. The 4th column tones are A, B, C, and D. The 4th column tones would reside on the rightmost column of a phone set, right next to 3, 6, 9, and # which is why they were named 4th column.

Typically, a phone system will send DTMF digit sequences in regular patterns to a voice-mail system to signify this call information. When a call forwards to voice mail, and after the voice-mail system has answered that forwarded call, the phone system dials out these digits. When this happens, the speech path from the caller to the voice-mail system has not yet opened, so that caller does not hear the DTMF sequences. If you were monitoring the particular line, you would hear the DTMF digits just as you would on a call with another person if they dialed the digits. Likewise, if a the telephone line running into the Unity voice board was run into a single-line phone instead, the DTMF digits used for call information could be heard on the single-line telephone.

It should be noted that the call information for an analog DTMF integration is in-band. That is to say that the call information is sent on the same media and channel as the audio (voice, prompt, or recording) for the call. If we were to take a look at an extremely simple two-port Unity voice-mail system, the first port (or telephone line) provides the media for audio record (taking messages) and playback (listening to message) in addition to the call information. Likewise, the second port provides media for audio and call information. This is a sharp contrast to serial integrations where call information is carried on a different channel than what is used for the audio stream. Figure 17-1 shows the telephone line connection between Unity and a PBX and how call information digits are sent in-band.

Figure 17-1 *Information Digits Sent In-band*

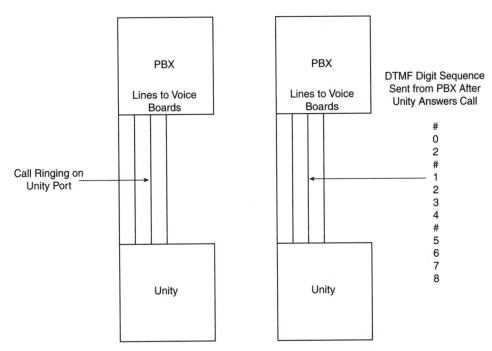

Each PBX might define its own flavor of DTMF packets to send; there is no standard set for the contents of these packets. Unity has to be able to connect to PBXs that implement different sets of DTMF integration packets. As long as the packets are sent in a similar fashion from call to call (a call forward busy on two different calls forwarding from two different extensions differs only by the extension that forwarded), Unity will parse the packet based on its own customizable configuration. A voice-mail system can typically expect that these packets consist of smaller sub-packets that represent the individual pieces of call information. These sub-packets are the blocks of data that make up call information, and they might take the form of something like call reason + caller + called. Figure 17-2 shows an example packet.

The main idea is the packet sent from the PBX contains several pieces of call information. Our example packet needs to be broken apart so that its individual call information elements are represented correctly for integration. Let us say, for example, that the 02 in our example packet signifies that the forwarding phone forwarded because of a busy condition. It does not really matter if 02, #1, or **3898 means busy; as long as this code always means busy, the packet parsing will work. In a moment, we will go into detail as to the mechanics of breaking this packet into its individual call information elements.

Figure 17-2 *Sample DTMF Packet*

When a PBX's call information is handled by sequences of DTMF packets, Unity must decode these packets into useful information. As the voice boards detect DTMF digits being sent from the switch, it signals these DTMF events to its client, the Media Interface Unity (MIU) (which is discussed in more detail in Chapter 6, "Components and Subsystems: Telephony Services"). The MIU has a specialized sub-component, a DTMF digit-processing engine, designed for parsing the analog packets sent from the phone system. The main purpose the sub-component serves is to separate the entire DTMF packet into specific call information pieces such as called party, calling party, and reason. If the DTMF packet from the phone system was successfully parsed, those digits are never presented directly to any other Unity components as user-dialed digits because they are integration digits. There has to be a distinction between integration digits and digits that were dialed by a caller on the other end. There is no support for distinction between each type of digit other than the time of reception and pattern of reception.

Figure 17-3 shows the flow of integration digits from the phone system, to the voice board, and to the MIU for processing. The call object shown in this figure represents a programmatic object that is used by different Unity components throughout the lifetime of the call. The call object is discussed in more detail in Chapter 6.

Unity's DTMF digit parser is tremendously configurable via a text file with regards to timing and defining packet definitions. The text file that the digit processing engine uses is called AvAnalog.Avd, and this file can be located in the \Commserver\Intlib directory. The configuration settings in this file enable the analog parsing engine to complete the following tasks:

1 Defines a maximum, valid duration after answering a call and receiving the first DTMF digit of a DTMF packet (this is known as the first digit delay).

2 Defines a maximum, valid duration after receiving a DTMF digit that matches a portion of a valid DTMF packet, and a subsequent DTMF digit (this is known as next digit delay).

3 Building a configurable set of packet definitions. The digits that make up these definitions are what Unity expects to get for a given call.

Figure 17-3 *Flow of Integration Digits*

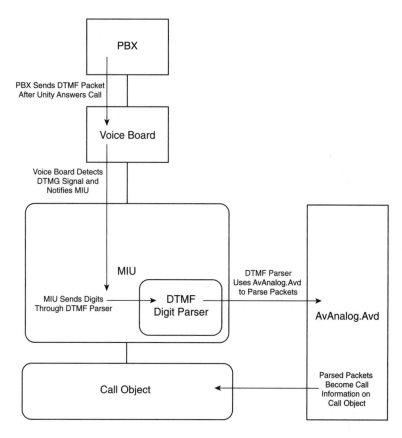

The AvAnalog.Avd configuration file contains sections for different types of known DTMF integrations, and each section has its own settings and packet definitions. The section used depends upon the configuration setting in the switch file. Example 17-1 shows a portion of the header for the file that describes timing settings and variables used in packet definitions.

Example 17-1 *Example of AvAnalog.Avd Integration File*

```
Name            Text name of integration (e.g. Definity Mode Code)
MinExtSize      Minimum allowed extension size (default 1)
MaxExtSize      Maximum allowed extension size (default 10)
DefaultExtSize  Default exact extension size. (Must be between MinExtSize and
  MaxExtsize)
TrunkSize       Number of digits in trunk id (default 2)
```

continues

Example 17-1 *Example of AvAnalog.Avd Integration File (Continued)*

```
MaxDelayFirstDigitMs # Milliseconds allowed before receiving first digit (default
    2000)
MaxDelayNextDigitMs  # Milliseconds allowed before second digit (default 250)
DataN                 Pattern/Action pair (N is >= 1)

PATTERNS:

0-9 Actual DTMF digit
A-D Actual DTMF digit
#,* Actual DTMF digit

I - Incoming extension ID
F - Forwarding extension ID
S - DNIS Information ID
U - Unused extension id
T - Trunk ID
X - Any single TT (0-9 only)
N - ANI digits

ACTIONS:

OPENING         Restart Intro prompt.
DIRECT          Direct message retrieval.
NOANSWER        Handle with message box not available greeting.
BUSY            Handle with message box busy greeting.
HANGUP          Disconnect immediately.
TRUNK           Tie Trunk mapping integration.

[Example]
Name=Example PBX
MinExtSize=3
MaxExtSize=10
DefaultExtSize=3
MaxDelayFirstDigitMs=3000
MaxDelayNextDigitMs=500
Data1=  #00#I(3-10)##        DIRECT
Data2=  00#I(3-10)##         DIRECT
Data3=  #00#I(3-10)#F(3-10)#    NOANSWER
Data4=  00#I(3-10)#F(3-10)#     NOANSWER
```

When we talk about the MaxDelayFirstDigitMs, we are referring to how long Unity will wait between answering a call and receiving an integration digit. If a digit does not come during this time period (for example, no integration digits are sent from the PBX), the MIU considers the call not to have any incoming call information. It aborts the digit parsing process (an exception is the detection of hangup integration packets discussed later in this section) and moves along with the rest of the call. If there was a delay in the reception of these digits (for example, the PBX delayed sending the integration digits), and that delay exceeded the timing parameter for this first digit delay, those digits would not be processed as integration digits. Instead, those digits would be processed as if a caller had actually dialed them.

The MaxDelayNextDigitMs is the duration the parser will wait for a subsequent integration digit after having received an integration digit. If another digit does not come within this timeframe, the existing digit sequence is considered complete.

The DataN entries are the packet definitions the parser is configured to recognize. Additionally, the patterns specified here determine which portions of the packet sequence correspond to which portions of the call information. The packet definitions can be thought of in terms of digit substrings of variables and literals. A literal in a DTMF packet definition specified in the AvAnalog file is literally, digit for digit, what Unity expects to receive. If a literal substring in a packet definition was "0#2", then Unity is expecting to receive exactly that substring. Literals often correspond to special codes in the DTMF packet; in other words, the reason why the call arrived. For example "#02" might represent a call that forwarded on a busy condition, whereas "#03" represents a forward on no-answer. Variables are digit sub-sequences that Unity does not know the exact contents of, but the contents often represent called or calling parties on the call.

Let us dissect the Data1 packet sequence pattern in Example 17-1:

```
Data1=    #00#I(3-10)##          DIRECT
```

Just as the header mentioned, the substring "#00#" are literal DTMF digits. Likewise, the "##" at the end of the sequence are also literal DTMF digits. "I" is a variable that signifies "Incoming extension ID" (digits must be 0-9) and will be considered the calling party. We know that "I" signifies "Incoming extension ID" by reviewing the "Patterns" section of AvAnalog.avd in Example 17-1. Notice there is "(3-10)" after the "I" variable. This actually means that the digits that will represent the incoming variable can be a string 3 to 10 digits long. The numbers contained within the parenthesis specify the length; they are not literally expected digits. A variable in a packet definition defined like "I(3-10)" is considered to be a variable-length variable. That is, "I" can be a length of 3 to 10 characters long. Finally, the "DIRECT" specification simply means that the call reason for the calls is "direct"—that is a call that was placed to voice mail directly (that is, the call did not reach voice mail because of another phone forwarding). Considering the packet definition for Data1, if the integration packet from the PBX matches the defined pattern of "#00#I(3-10)##", the reason for the call is "DIRECT".

Let us assume that Unity receives a DTMF integration packet from the PBX with the following contents:

```
                #00#12345##
```

This packet does match the packet definition for Data1, and as such, the calling party is parsed as "12345" and the call reason is marked as "DIRECT".

Now let us assume that Unity receives a DTMF integration packet from the PBX with the following contents:

```
#12345##
```

This packet does not match the packet definition for Data1 or any other packet definition in Example 17-1. Because of the lack of a packet match, the digits are not considered integration digits. Instead, the digits are treated as if the caller dialed them.

A couple of things need to be considered when using variable lengths:

1   Two variable-length variables cannot be adjacent to each other in a packet definition. The following example packet sequence is invalid:

```
Data1=    #00#I(3-10)F(3-10)##           NOANSWER
```

The I and F variable-length variables are adjacent to each other. Since the digits contained within I and F are the same (0-9), there is no way to determine when I ends and F begins. The following example packet is valid:

```
Data1=    #00#I(3-10)#F(3-10)##          NOANSWER
```

The "#" in between the I and F variables delimits the two variables; the parser now knows where I stops and F begins.

2   Variable lengths can be applied to literals as well as variables. The following example packet illustrates this:

```
Data1=    #(0-3)00#I(3-10)    DIRECT
```

The substring "#(0-3)" allows this packet sequence to begin with any number of #s from zero to three. All of the following packets would find a match with the preceding example packet definition (we use 1234 as an example "I"):

```
00#1234
#00#1234
##00#1234
###00#1234
```

If a variable such as I or F is not configured for variable length, the parser expects the length of that variable to be the same as DefaultExtSize.

At times, the first digit of a packet sent from the PBX is not properly detected by Unity. Even though the digit was sent by the PBX which can be verified with a digit grabber (a special device that connects inline on a single-line phone circuit to display digits that have been sent on that circuit), the digit is not processed. This might happen because the digit was sent right before or during the time the voice board physically answered the call. If the phone system does not support a packet sending delay, this problem might be compounded. As long as the packet sequences from the phone system are configurable, there is a workaround. By adding a prefix of a few #s or *s in the packet that the PBX sends, we can take advantage of the variable length functionality of the parser. If the first "#" is missed, the remaining packet still finds a match.

Considering, once again, the "Data1" packet definition in Example 17-1:

```
Data1=   #(0-3)00#I(3-10)   DIRECT
```

All of these packets would match our example Data1 packet definition:

```
###00#1234
##00#1234
#00#1234
00#1234
```

If multiple packet definitions in the configuration file match the same incoming packet, the fist definition listed sequentially is the matching definition. Consider the following packet definitions:

```
Data1=   #(0-3)00#I(3-10)        DIRECT
Data2=   #00#F(3-10)         NOANSWER
```

A DTMF packet of "#00#1234" could actually match either definition. Two completely separate results will occur upon matching one of these definitions, but the Data1 definition will be a match since it was listed sequentially first in the configuration file.

Some phone systems send a DTMF packet to the voice-mail system completely separate from the packet that signifies call information. A hangup packet is such an example. When a caller hangs up on the voice-mail system, the phone system might send a DTMF packet signifying to the voice-mail system that the caller has hung up and the voice-mail system should do the same. Because of this potential behavior, incoming digits from the phone system throughout the entire call are checked against any packet definition matches for Hangup. On a side note, the hangup packet is actually recorded into a message if the caller disconnects in the middle of recording a message. The MIU uses a set of timers and the packet is actually deleted off of the end of the message.

Putting all of this together, here is how the DTMF digits are processed for an incoming call when the integration method is DTMF:

1   After the call has been answered, the MaxDelayFirstDigitMs timer starts and waits for the first digit.

2   If a digit arrives before the timer expires, the digit is placed into a packet queue. The contents of the queue (one digit at this point) are compared to the packet definitions residing in the configuration file. If the digit is a potential match for any of the packet definitions, further digit integration processing occurs, and the MaxDelayNextDigitMs is started. If there is not a match, integration processing stops and the digits are returned as dialed digits.

3   If a subsequent digit arrives before the MaxDelayNextDigitMs timer expires, the digit is placed into the packet queue. The packet queue is once again compared to the

packet definitions residing in the configuration file. If the digits are a potential match for any of the packet definitions, further digit integration processing occurs and the MaxDelayNextDigitMs is started. If there is not a match, integration processing stops and the digits are returned as dialed digits. If the subsequent digit arrives after the MaxDelayNextDigitMs timer expires, integration processing stops and the digits are returned as dialed digits.

4 The previous step repeats until either the MaxDelayNextDigitMs expires without receiving a digit (a natural occurrence when the phone system is simply done sending digits of a packet) or the contents of the packet queue do not match any packet definitions in the configuration file.

5 If the packet queue does match a packet definition at this point, that packet is parsed and the defined variables in that packet definition become the pieces of call information that fill the MIU's call object.

A utility in Unity for viewing integration digits is the IntegrationMonitor.exe. IntegrationMonitor.exe shows what digits Unity recognized that were sent from the PBX, along with the parsed out variables such as calling party, called party, and call reason from an analog, DTMF packet.

Figure 17-4 demonstrates the digit parser algorithm with respect to the timing of arriving digits and packet definition matches.

Call Information Extraction (Serial Integrations)

Unity's other call information extraction method for TDM PBXs is serial integration. The term *serial* is used because the call information is carried over an RS-232 serial link to a COM port on the Unity server.

Unity's notion of serial integration consists only of extracting call information and sending message-waiting indicators to the PBX. When Unity is configured to use serial integration, the call control is still handled by the voice board. There is no direct connection between the voice boards and the serial link to the PBX; neither knows the other even exists. It is Unity's responsibility to use both pieces together.

Serial integration information is out-of-band. The call information is passed on a completely separate connection from the path that handles the audio. This is in direct contrast to analog DTMF integrations. Because of this, a way to link the call information on the serial link to the actual call on the voice board has to exist. How else would Unity know which serial packet belonged to which call?

Figure 17-4 *The Digit Parser Algorithm*

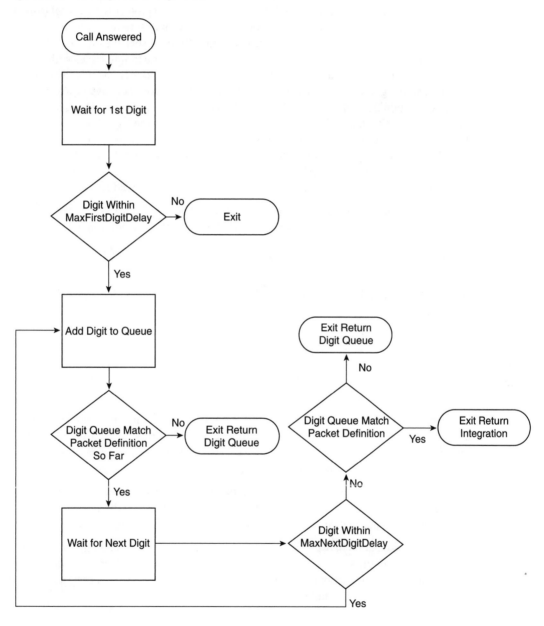

One can find a few different flavors of serial integration protocols, and the main differences stem from the contents of the packets. Examples of these serial protocols are SMDI (Simple Message Desk Interface), Ericsson, and MCI (Message Center Interface, which is NEC-proprietary). Although a bit more sophisticated than DTMF packets, the information inside the serial packet is still relatively simple to pick apart. There are timing issues with regards to serial integrations, but they are not the same type of timing issues one would encounter with DTMF integrations. Unlike DTMF integrations, Unity does not have to worry about the time duration from digit to digit (technically, character to character). The characters of a packet arrive essentially all at once. Unity also knows when the packet begins and ends the second it is received (once again, there is no waiting for more contents of the packet like DTMF integrations). Additionally, the content of a serial packet is not limited to digits that can be dialed; it might be any ASCII character. Similar to DTMF packets, serial packets might contain information about call reason and calling and/or called parties.

Figure 17-5 is an example of a serial packet that would be sent from a PBX (the characters encapsulated in <> are representative of ASCII characters that are not printable).

Figure 17-5 *Sample Serial Packet*

With any serial integration, there is one physical serial link for any given number of voice ports or lines. So, all call information data for every voice port is carried over one serial link. Because of that fact, for an incoming call, the call information packet must be associated to a particular line or port.

Figure 17-6 demonstrates the out-of-band nature of a Unity serial integration where call information is carried on a separate link than the audio. Not only is the call information carried on a separate channel, it is carried on completely different media.

To make the association between the incoming serial packets to the incoming calls, there is one expectation of the serial packet; it must contain information to identify to which voice line the call information belongs. Without that information, Unity would not be able to take serial integration calls in parallel.

Figure 17-6 *Out-of-band Call Information*

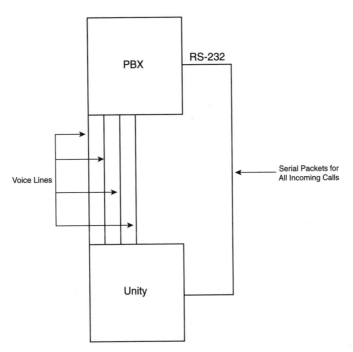

So, the voice-mail system expects to get a serial packet with every incoming call. Does the serial packet arrive simultaneously as the signaling of a new call on the corresponding voice line? There is no guarantee exactly when the serial packet will arrive. The packet might be before the signaling of a new call, or it might be after. In some instances, a serial packet might arrive without the signaling of a new call. Or, the signaling of a new call might occur without the arrival of a serial packet. The aforementioned situations do not happen often, but nevertheless, Unity has mechanisms to accommodate each abnormal condition.

With Unity's support of serial integration, on each new incoming call, the serial packets are matched to the corresponding voice lines. The raw information inside the serial packet is parsed so that individual elements of call information such as call reason and calling party can be extracted and used elsewhere.

Figure 17-7 shows the logical configuration of a serial integration. The integration device shown in the diagram might not exist. Some PBXs support serial voice-mail integration natively. That is, the PBX supports a direct RS-232 connection for voice-mail system integration. In other cases an integration device (such as a PBXLink) relays call information (usually by emulating a PBX proprietary telephone set) from the PBX to voice mail by way of a serial packet.

Figure 17-7 *Configuration of a Serial Integration*

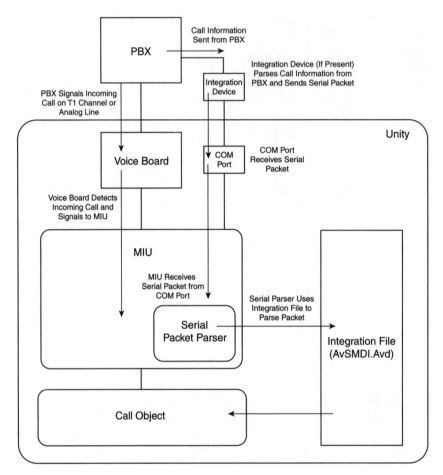

The serial integration parser is similar to the analog parser; however, there are some differences because of the fact that call information arriving over a serial link is typically more complex. The notion of literals and variables are in the serial parsing engine logic. The variables typically represent call information including called and calling parties; call reason; and, most importantly, port or channel number. We pick apart some of Unity's serial integration configuration files and examine exactly how the serial parser operates.

Let us begin by taking a closer look at the separate pieces of the integration file.

The integration file can be broken down into the following components:

- **Keywords**. The keywords are the variables spoken of earlier. They are the fields or containers that hold data from a packet; the keywords by themselves are not data. By stringing keywords together in different patterns, one can form multiple serial-packet definitions. When an incoming serial packet is parsed, or an outgoing packet is generated, data (ASCII characters in our case) fill these keywords to produce the major contents of a packet. The parser recognizes a default set of keywords, and these keywords can be defined with keyword switches.

- **Keyword switches**. Keyword switches can define characteristics of the keyword. Examples of characteristics might include the length, or variable length, of the keyword or whether data that fills the keyword is right- or left-justified.

- **Literals**. Literals are portions of packet definitions that are literally matched. Literals can be used in conjunction with keywords to form packet definitions.

- **Delimiters**. While one type of delimiter signifies a keyword, others separate the different portions (keywords and literals) in a packet definition.

- **Packet definitions**. Packet definitions are built to represent different incoming serial packets sent by the PBX. They are also used to represent any outbound serial packets sent to the PBX from Unity. The integration file contains packet definitions that represent all of the different types of serial packets Unity might receive for different call conditions. By way of keywords, a single packet definition can be used to parse call information such as called and calling parties, and call reason, when a serial packet for a call has arrived at Unity.

- **Protocol settings**. Protocol settings define detailed characteristics of the serial protocol. This includes the serial packet headers and trailers. Most of the protocol settings are legacy and no longer used.

- **General configuration settings**. These settings define extension length defaults (used for SMDI integrations discussed later in this section) and COM port characteristics such as COM port number, baud rate, and so on.

Example 17-2 is an excerpt from an integration file.

Example 17-2 *Example Set of Default "Keywords" in Serial Integration File*

```
VMEXT          - Voice mail extension
CHANNEL        - voice board channel number
TRUNK          - trunk ( Trunk or Internal Extension )
CALLER         - caller id
CALLED         - called id
DNIS           - DNIS information
LAMPEXT        - message lamp extension
IGNORE1        - ignore 1 byte
IGNORE12       - ignore 1 byte
IGNORE13       - ignore 1 byte
IGNORE73       - ignore 7 byte
```

Used for incoming packet definitions, both the VMEXT and CHANNEL keywords correspond to a portion of an incoming serial packet that signifies to which telephone port the integration packet belongs. In order to link a serial packet to a call, Unity receives the extension number (as in 101, 102, or 103) of the corresponding telephone port in the serial packet. For such integrations, the VMEXT keyword is used in packet definitions. For other serial integrations, the channel number (as in 1, 2, or 3) is sent. For these integrations, the CHANNEL keyword would be found in the incoming packet definitions instead.

The next keywords are self-explanatory. TRUNK, CALLER, CALLED, and DNIS map to their respective pieces of call information. However, LAMPEXT is a keyword used in outbound packets that maps to an extension for which Unity requests message waiting indication. If Unity wants to enable the message-waiting indicator for 1234, "1234" is placed into the position where the LAMPEXT keyword resides in a packet definition and used in an outgoing packet to the switch. The IGNORE keywords might appear strange, but their function is straightforward: They simply ignore a given number of characters in a portion of a serial packet definition. IGNORE4 means that four characters will be discarded and not used in building any call information elements. Likewise, IGNORE41 also means that four characters will be discarded (later in this section, we discuss why there are multiple IGNOREs for a given number of characters). As you might have guessed, IGNORE5 and IGNORE51 both mean that five characters will be discarded. Keywords are not logical, but once we take a look at some packet definitions, their use comes to light.

Keywords are defined in the integration file in the following sequence:

1 **Keyword name**. The name of the keyword must be prefaced by the "$" character (the "$" character signifies a keyword interestingly enough).

2 **Length of keyword**. This is the number of characters in the keyword.

3 **Keyword switches**. Switches are optional.

4 **Mapping**. Maps to the default keyword used by the parser.

Keyword definitions basically look like this:

```
$CHANNEL=            4,       CHANNEL
$CALLER=            10,       CALLER
$CALLED=            10,       CALLED
$IGNORE3=            3,       IGNORE3
```

So, the $CHANNEL keyword name is a four-character string that maps to the parser's internal CHANNEL keyword. If one had the desire, the $CHANNEL could be renamed to $PORTNUM and placed into packet definitions just the same. However, if the CHANNEL keyword were to be renamed, the declaration would be broken; the parser only recognizes its own keywords and associates them to the keyword names. The $CALLER keyword name is a ten-character string that maps to the parser's CALLER variable and its place in the Unity call object is obvious.

As previously mentioned, keywords might also be defined with keyword switches which provide extra manipulation on the data that fills the keyword. Although the many keyword switches are implemented by the serial parsing engine, we only cover the ones that are used with Unity's supported serial integrations (there are other, old and unused switches in this section, too). These are the "R", "Z", and "V" keyword switches.

Example 17-3 *Example Set of Keyword Switches in Serial Integration File*

```
R   - Flush field to the right  (default: flush left)
Z   - ASCII zero character fill (default: blank, ' ')
V   - Variable length field. Size is the maximum size the field can be.
```

If you have been paying attention, or you have looked at the integration file notes before, you might have noticed that the default justification is left. That is to say in an example where the data placed into the keyword is less than the length of the keyword definition, a left-justification of the data takes place, followed by the padding. This can be changed to right-justification by the "R" switch.

Example:

```
$LAMPEXT=                10 ZR,  LAMPEXT
```

With our same example data of "1234", the formatted data placed into the keyword field would look like this:

```
"0000001234"
```

The "Z" keyword switch is an odd bird, and it is only used for keywords in outbound packets. If the keyword's length is defined as 10, but the data placed in the keyword field has a length less than 10, by default the parser pads the field with blanks. This keyword overrides the default blank pad character with a 0.

Example:

```
$LAMPEXT=                10 Z,  LAMPEXT
```

Let us say that the data placed into $LAMPEXT was 1234. Since the data is certainly not ten characters long, it is padded. With the "Z" switch it would be padded like this:

```
"1234000000"
```

Without the "Z" switch it would have looked like this:

```
"1234      "
```

The "V" keyword switch signifies that the keyword is of variable length size. Data filling the keyword is variable length up to the length that is specified in the rest of the keyword definition.

Example:

```
$ANI=                40 V,  ANI
```

In this definition, the data contained in $ANI might be any length up to 40 characters and fills the parser's ANI variable. One important rule to remember is that if a keyword is defined with the "V" switch and is present in a packet definition, the packet definition must contain a literal directly after the placement of the variable-length keyword. If there were another keyword placed after the variable-length keyword, the parser would not know when one keyword ended and the other began.

These keyword names (we consider them variables) are used in conjunction with literals and delimiters to make a packet definition. The packet definitions correlate to the packets that arrive for a given call type. In simple terms, they match up. Here is an example of a packet definition (the $SMDIER and $VCALLER keyword variables are discussed in more detail later in this chapter):

```
RingDirect1=  D,$IGNORE3,$CHANNEL,D ,$SMDIER,$VCALLER,$IGNORE2
```

The RingDirect1 signifies that the Unity call-object reason will be of type direct. It is possible from call to call, that Unity might receive different packet formations for any given call type. This may occur if the serial integration protocol allows for multiple packet formations for the same call type. In the event the serial integration protocol allows for two types of direct call packet formations (direct call types, for example), another packet definition intended for direct calls that matches the alternate direct call packet formation could be defined under "RingDirect2". The integration parser is hard-coded to look for defined sets of strings on the left side of the = character in the packet definition (RingDirect1 in our example). There can be a total of 21 different types of packet definitions for any given call-reason type. That is, one could define 21 different packet definitions that all parse call information for a call-reason type of direct. If all 21 definitions were to be used, the strings on the left side of the = character in the packet definitions would take the form of RingDirect, RingDirect1, RingDirect2, RingDirect19, and RingDirect20.

The first character in our example packet definition, the D, is a literal; the parser is literally expecting a D character in that position of the incoming packet. The comma that follows the D serves as a delimiter signifying that the literal string (in this case, a single character) has ended. The $ preceding the "IGNORE3" signifies a keyword variable. In this case, the keyword represents a variable to hold three characters that will not map to any portion of Unity's call object. Those characters are ignored. The rest of the packet definition is self-explanatory; more keywords are used (separated by the comma delimiters, the parser does not expect the commas that are in the packet definition to actually be in the packet sent from the switch) to extract meaningful call information into Unity's call object.

Let us assume the switch sends a serial packet with the contents of

```
<CR><LF>MD0010001D 0001234<CR><LF><EOT>
```

In this example, the portions of the packet like <CR> represent non-printable ASCII control characters. These control characters are common to all serial integrations that Unity supports and are represented in the <CR> format. <CR> for example, is a carriage-return.

Figure 17-8 shows how the packet from the switch is parsed by Unity's serial integration engine based on our example packet definition:

```
RingDirect1=  D,$IGNORE3,$CHANNEL,D ,$SMDIER,$VCALLER,$IGNORE2
```

Figure 17-8 *Packet Parsed by Unity's Serial Integration Engine*

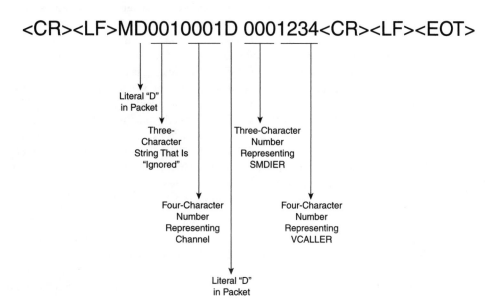

There are a few other characters in the actual packet that do not seem to line up to our example packet definition (the control characters, for example), but do not worry; they line up as soon as we cover that. For now, let us dive a bit deeper into the SMDIER and VCALLER since I mentioned these keywords' lengths were to be overridden. The settings that override the length of those keywords are contained in the [Configuration] section of the integration file.

The following example is the [Configuration] section of the serial integration AvSmdi.avd file:

```
[Configuration]

Name=        SMDI
Integration= SMDI
Version=     SMDI 1.0
DefaultExtLen=4
SwsDefaultExtLen=10
```

The DefaultExtLen and SwsDefaultExtLen settings are the ones that set the expected length of those keywords. It helps to understand a bit about Centrex SMDI and Unity's implementation of Centrex SMDI before diving into these settings. By Centrex SMDI, we simply mean a SMDI integration provided within a Centrex environment. A true Centrex environment is the phone company providing PBX-like services to an office or company. Instead of connecting to a local PBX, the phones and voice-mail system's lines run back to the switch operated by the phone company. With Centrex SMDI, in addition to the phone lines running back to the phone company's switch, there is a data link designed to send serial packets that also run back to the phone company's PBX. When Centrex callers call voice mail (or call another voice-mail user that forwards to voice mail), Unity is provided with a serial packet as the line rings on the voice board. The fact that the lines are coming from the phone company is not all that interesting to Unity. In fact, Unity cannot tell the difference between a PBX and the phone company. What is interesting is the numbering plan typically used by Centrex in comparison to the numbering plan you would expect to see with a PBX. In a Centrex environment, the lines have extension numbers that are similar to your home phone number. The phone users behind a PBX typically are 3, 4, or 5 digits long, whereas the phone users in a Centrex environment have extensions that are typically 7 (or more commonly, 10) digits long. Normally these extension numbers would map to DTMF Access IDs for Unity subscribers. Because it is a pain to enter in a 7- or 10-digit number for retrieving or sending voice mails, one can make the DTMF Access IDs for these users shorter by using only a subset of the digits contained in the number.

Behind a PBX, my extension is 1234, but as a Centrex user, it is 111-123-1234. However, you want my DTMF Access ID in Unity to only be the 1234 of 111-123-1234. With Unity's implementation of SMDI, you set the DefaultExtensionLength to 4 (since 4 digits are in 1234), and you set the SwsDefaultExtLen to the total length of my Centrex phone number (in this case 10, since 10 digits are in 111-123-1234). It is simple. Just use the last 4 digits.

Using the Centrex example that we discussed earlier, and with the same parameters for extension lengths (DefaultExtLen=4, SwsDefaultExtLen=10), I am dialing from 111-123-1234 to Unity and the Centrex switch is going to send an SMDI packet as Unity is offered the call. The actual packet from the switch looks like Figure 17-11. Figure 17-9 shows an example packet sent to Unity with a Centrex integration when the calling party is 111-123-1234.

We are still using the same packet definition as earlier examples even though the length of the calling party (as well as the entire packet) is longer.

```
RingDirect1=  D,$IGNORE3,$CHANNEL,D ,$SMDIER,$VCALLER,$IGNORE2
```

The 1111231234 of the calling number is going to get split up between these two variables in this fashion:

- The last N digits, where N = DefaultExtLen, is mapped to $VCALLER (which is actually the same as $CALLER in other serial integration file packet definitions).

- The left-over digits, which is the difference between DefaultExtLen and SwsDefaultExtLen (the difference is 6), is mapped to $SMDIER (the length of $SMDIER = SwsDefaultExtLen − DefaultExtLen).

Figure 17-9 *Packet Sent to Unity with a Centrex Integration*

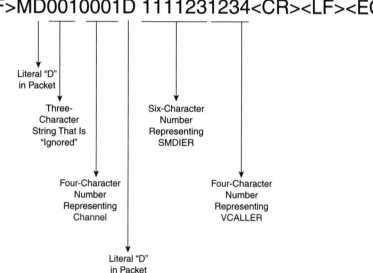

Our Centrex SMDI integration using 4-digit dialing inside Unity might seem great, but what if there is a call from 222-789-1234? Will I be integrated as the same Centrex user calling from 123-555-1234? Well, the answer is no. That is the point in emphasizing the $SMDIER portion of the packet and its value. Roughly speaking, it is the prefix of the Centrex caller. By configuring prefixes that belong to Unity subscribers in the switch configuration file, Unity will not integrate the caller from 222-789-1234 as Unity subscriber 1234. Under the [Integration] section of the switch file, you would add:

```
SMDIPrefix1=111123
```

You can add any other prefixes as well by using SMDIPrefix2, SMDIPrefix3, and so on.

When the caller's prefix does match a configured prefix, Unity actually throws away the prefix and the caller's number becomes the number that filled the $VCALLER keyword. Figure 17-10 demonstrates what characters fill the caller portion of call information with the identified SMDIPrefix of 111123 in a serial packet sent from the switch.

When the caller's prefix does not match a configured prefix, the values in $SMDIER and $VCALLER are used together to form the caller.

Figure 17-11 demonstrates what characters fill the caller portion of call information with the unidentified SMDIPrefix of 222789 in a serial packet sent from the switch.

Figure 17-10 *Calling Party Information in a Serial Packet with Prefix Match*

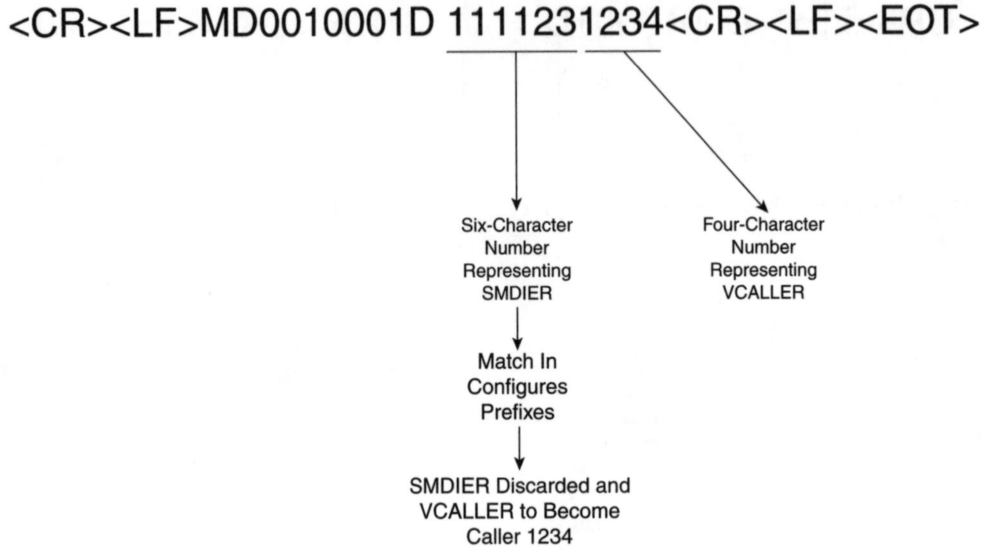

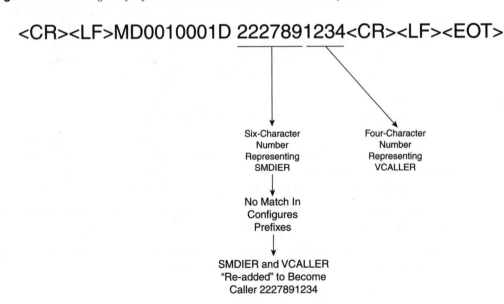

Figure 17-11 *Calling Party Information in an Aerial Packet Without Prefix Match*

For non-Centrex SMDI integrations, there really is not a true prefix. Instead, that data area is usually padded with zeroes. However, the exact same prefix match happens on callers with zeroes as their prefix, but there is a default-configured prefix of all zeroes so the zeroes are essentially discarded. Figure 17-12 shows an example calling-party information in a serial packet for a non-Centrex SMDI integration.

Figure 17-12 *Calling Party Information in a Serial Packet with Zero-Padded Prefix*

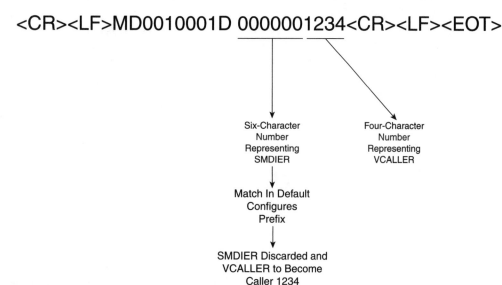

Under normal circumstances, a packet from the PBX is matched; that is, the parser is able to determine the packet matched one of its packet definitions. The keywords inside that packet definition will go on to fill the corresponding properties in the Unity call object. When there is a configuration mismatch between the PBX and Unity, or if the PBX sends Unity a packet that does not match a packet definition, the parser returns nothing that will go on to fill the Unity call object. It is as if there were no packets sent at all.

We have seen a few packet examples, and they all have special control characters appended and post-pended to the contents of the packet. Similarly to IP packets, the packets in serial integrations have headers and trailers. Their purpose is simple; they signify when one packet begins and the same packet ends. The actual characters that are to be used vary from one serial voice-mail integration protocol to another, and it is left to the discretion of the PBX designer to decide what to send. For a packet to even be a candidate for parsing, it must be properly delineated. Unity determines if the packet has the correct headers and trailers by the parser's configuration for packet delineation. Both incoming and outgoing packet delineation can be defined independently if needed. The configuration is contained in the [Protocol] section of the integration file. The majority of the configuration settings in that section are unused, and we will only be discussing the "StartOfData", "EndOfData", "TxStartOfData", and "TxEndOfData" settings.

NOTE   For you voice-mail history buffs out there, Unity's serial parsing engine originated from an older product that supported integration with many Property Management Systems (PMS). PMS was frequently found in hotel environments, and the basic idea was that the system would send a serial packet to the voice-mail system when a guest checked in. The voice-mail system would automatically create a voice-mail account for that user. When the guest checked out, another packet was sent, and the voice-mail system removed or disabled the account. An entire other set of needs and features arose from this integration, hence all the extra, unused settings for Unity.

Below is an example of the [Protocol] section of a serial integration file:

```
[Protocol]
StartOfData=                    M
TxStartOfData=
EndOfData=
TxEndOfData=
```

Some strange-looking characters are displayed when viewing the configuration file with a text editor. Those characters are actually non-printable ASCII control characters. All of these settings listed here correspond to a single character, and for the vast majority, these characters are ASCII control characters. Unfortunately, to know what these control characters really are, one needs a binary file editor. The StartOfData and EndOfData settings refer to what Unity uses to recognize incoming packets. Any data between these two control characters is parsed for potential packet matches. Data that is not contained within the limits of these control characters is considered to be garbage. Likewise, the TxStartOfData and TxEndOfData are the packet delimiters Unity places on outbound packets.

TIP   There is an easier way of configuring these settings and why it is not used is beyond me. The control characters might be set in the format of "\x0d or \x0a", where the "0d" or "0a" corresponds to the hex value of the control character.

Based on this information, let us revisit our earlier packet examples to look at the headers and trailers. We will once again be using SMDI, and we discover something interesting (the author did not even know of this fact until writing this book). Included here is our packet definition and we make the protocol settings a little easier to read.

Below is an example packet definition and [Protocol] section of an integration file to aid in illustrating the serial integration parse's handling of control characters in a serial packet:

```
RingDirect1=  D,$IGNORE3,$CHANNEL,D ,$SMDIER,$VCALLER,$IGNORE2

[Protocol]
StartOfData=              M
TxStartOfData=
EndOfData=                \x0d (Carriage-return)
TxEndOfData=              \x0d (Carriage-return)
```

Figure 17-13 shows control character handling with a serial packet.

Figure 17-13 *Control Character Handling*

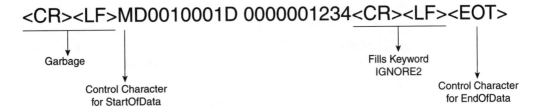

That interesting thing is that the first portion of an SMDI packet is considered by the parser to be garbage. The parser does not accept having the same control characters in both the header and the trailer. With this SMDI packet example, both the header and trailer contain the control characters <CR> and <LF>. To work around that, the parser is configured to use M as the StartOfData, even though with the real packet, M is not the start of data.

Since Unity is dealing with COM-port communication, it needs to configure the COM port with the same communication settings that the remote serial port on the PBX is using. In the [Configuration] section of the integration file, the following settings are present:

```
Port=             1
baud=             1200
parity=           even
dataBits=         7
stopBits=         1
```

If you are familiar with configuring serial ports, these settings will look familiar. Additionally, for any given serial integration, it does not matter what flavor of COM-port communication is used, as long as it matches the COM-port settings on the PBX.

Unity needs to send serial packets to the switch as well. That is how Message Waiting Indicators generally work with serial integrations. The packet definitions for outbound packets follow the same set of rules as inbound packets. Example 17-4 shows of the MWI (Message Waiting Indicator) on and off packets for SMDI:

Example 17-4 *OutputMessages*

```
LampOn=      =0ü,:0ü,OP:MWI ,$LAMPEXT,!
LampOff=     =0ü,:0ü,RMV:MWI ,$LAMPEXT,!
```

Here is where things get weird, especially with the "=0ü,:0ü" portion of the packet. That is is actually Unity's representation of <CR><LF>. Here is how it works:

1 The ü character is an escape character signifying that the preceding two characters in the packet definition are to be used to construct the hex value of an ASCII control character (<CR> and <LF> are control characters).

2 The hex values of those two characters preceding the ü in the packet definition are reversed and the lower nibbles of these characters construct the control character.

Let us examine the first instance of a control character in the "LampOn" packet definition: =0ü. The hex value is read from the first character 0 preceding the ü, which is simply 30. The hex value of the second character =is 3D. Reverse the order of these two characters and we have 30 (used to be the 0) 3D (used to be the =). Now use the lower nibble of these two values to come up with a single control character 0D. That is the hex value of a carriage-return <CR> control character. By examining the :0ü in the same manner, we find this equates to a line-feed <LF> control character. I told you it was weird. Why it is implemented this way is beyond me. If you ever need to place ASCII control characters in an incoming or outgoing packet definition, follow that bizarre method.

Use the same [Protocol] section that was used earlier, and with $LAMPEXT defined as:

```
$LAMPEXT=              10 ZR,  LAMPEXT
```

Unity sends a "LampOn" request for the extension 1234, and the "LampOn" packet looks like this:

```
<CR><LF>OP:MWI 0000001234!<EOT>
```

Now if that is not confusing enough, there is one more monkey wrench to throw into the machine. The SwsDefaultExtLen setting overrides the length definition of the $LAMPEXT keyword. Under the same configuration settings used before, with the exception that the SwsDefaultExtLen is set to 7, now the MWI packet would look like this (even though the $LAMPEXT length was originally defined as 10):

```
<CR><LF>OP:MWI 0001234!<EOT>
```

From these examples, you can see the following general rules of the parser:

1 The definition of a packet header (StartOfData, TxStartOfData) must be different than the definition of the packet trailer (EndOfData, TxEndOfData).

2 When building a packet definition in the integration file, a keyword might be used only once in that packet definition. For example, if there was the need to ignore 2 bytes multiple times in the same packet definition, the keyword $IGNORE2 cannot be used twice. Instead, the parser allows for a $IGNORE2 and $IGNORE21. An example from the MCI integration file illustrates this:

```
RingForwardNoAns1=    0!,$IGNORE4,$VMEXT,
402,$IGNORE2,$IGNORE6,0,$IGNORE21,$CALLED
```

3 If using a variable length keyword in a packet definition, the keyword must be followed by a literal in the packet definition. An example from the MCI integration file illustrates this (ANI is defined as $ANI= 40 V, ANI):

```
$ANI=               40 V, ANI
RingTrunk2=     0!,$IGNORE4,$VMEXT,
432,$IGNORE2,$TRUNK,$IGNORE31,$IGNORE61,A,$IGNORE10,$ANI,Z
```

4 If an incoming packet matches multiple packet definitions, the parser decides the best match by the packet definition that has the highest amount of literals in a packet definition. No matter how many characters are present in a literal, it is only one literal.

Figure 17-14 demonstrates serial packet definition literal handling.

Figure 17-14 *Serial Packet Definition Literal Handling*

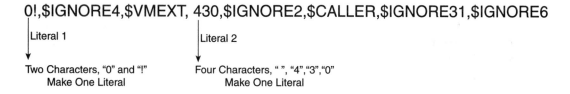

5 If an incoming packet matches multiple packet definitions, and those packet definitions contain the same amount of literals, the first, sequential packet definition in the file is used.

Let us go back and reexamine the parsing of a packet on an incoming call. Here are the steps that take place:

1 The serial data considered a packet to be processed must be contained with a serial header and trailer that match the configured StartOfData and EndOfData in the integration file.

2 The contents of the packet are compared against the packet definitions in the integration file (as in RingDirect, RingForwardBusy, and so on).

   3 If a match is found, the MIU uses the data in the call information keywords to fill the call object.

   4 The IntegrationMonitor.exe utility in Unity can show serial data that is sent from the switch. It has the ability to show parsed and unparsed serial information.

Call Control

Regardless of the call information extraction method, call control with Unity's legacy integrations is much the same. The signaling of call control with a legacy integration on analog connectivity can be essentially broken down into two forms: 1) electronic stimuli and 2) audible stimuli. The electronic stimuli comes in the form of voltage and current changes on the line that connect the voice-board port to the PBX. That line is essentially an electronic circuit and lends support to basic characteristics of any electronic circuit including electric fundamentals like voltage and current. The second signaling form comes in the form of tones or sets of tones that are sent from the PBX to the voice-board port. These tones typically signify different call control states (proceeding, busy, disconnected).

One important electronic stimuli of legacy call control is ring voltage. Ring voltage is voltage that is applied on an analog line from the switch to an end device in a cadenced pattern to signal a new call has arrived. The cadenced pattern is usually a pattern of a short time period of ring voltage (ring-on), followed by a longer time period with the absence of ring voltage (ring-off). The duration of a single ring-on and ring-off can be referred to as a ring cycle. The voice board on Unity detects this ring voltage to let Unity know that a new call has arrived. Figure 17-15 gives a visual representation of ring voltage over a period of time at the onset of a new call.

Figure 17-15 *Ring Voltage During a New Call*

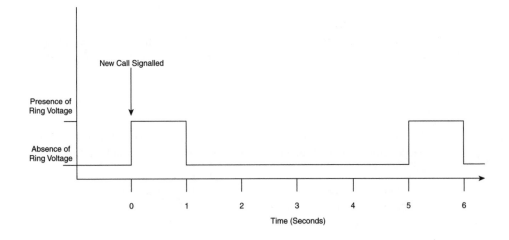

There are configuration parameters to configure the voice board to expect a certain pattern of ring voltage of a new call. This ability to configure these parameters is needed because there are really no standard timings for ring voltage. Although most PBXs use the same timing patterns, they can be and are often different.

Call Control Settings: Incoming Ring Voltage

The following section discusses the configurable call control settings to recognize incoming calls for legacy integrations. These parameters can be found in the switch files (located in the \Commserver\Intlib directory) that unity uses for legacy integrations:

- **MinimunRingOn**. This setting is the duration in milliseconds that defines a burst of ring voltage to be considered a valid one. Figure 17-16 demonstrates the RingOn duration as the switch applies cadenced ring voltage to signal an incoming call.

Figure 17-16 *RingOn Duration*

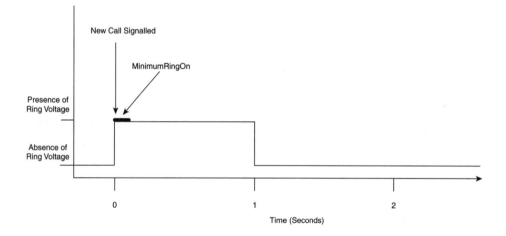

- **MinimumRingOff**. This setting defines the minimum time in which ring voltage is absent after first validating a ring-on to be considered a valid ring-off. Figure 17-17 demonstrates the "RingOff" duration as the switch applies cadenced ring voltage to signal an incoming call.

- **MaxWaitBetweenRings**. This setting defines the time that must elapse in between two ring-ons so the first ring-on is considered to be one call and the second ring-on is to be considered a second call. This setting comes into play if a call arrives at voice mail but Unity does not immediately answer the call. It is a way to separate ring-ons into two different calls. Figure 17-18 demonstrates the relationship between incoming ring voltage from one call to another over time.

Figure 17-17 *RingOff Duration*

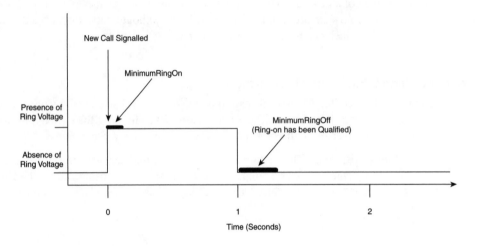

Figure 17-18 *Incoming Ring Voltage*

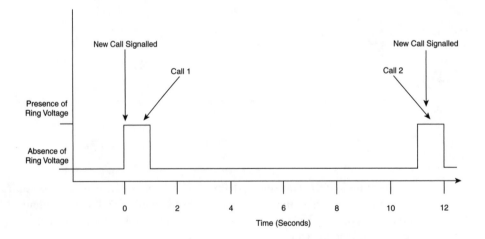

You could expect to run into a situation where MaxWaitBetweenRings comes into play if someone calls into voice mail, but before Unity answers the call, that caller hangs up. Now a second person calls in on that same port. With the type of analog signaling that is used (analog loop-start), the only way to tell the difference between these two calls (because the first call was never answered) is the time duration between the two ring-ons.

- **IncomingCallRings**. This setting defines approximately how many rings must pass before Unity is notified of a new incoming call.

  With IncomingCallRings=1, the call flow would look like that shown in Figure 17-19.

Figure 17-19 *IncomingCallRings Set to 1*

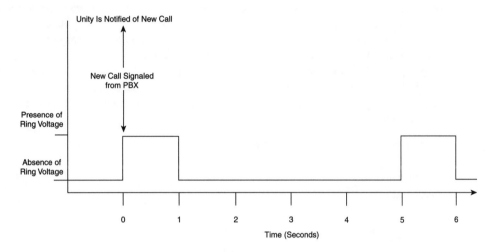

With IncomingCallRings= 2, the call flow would look like that shown in Figure 17-20.

Figure 17-20 *IncomingCallRings Set to 2*

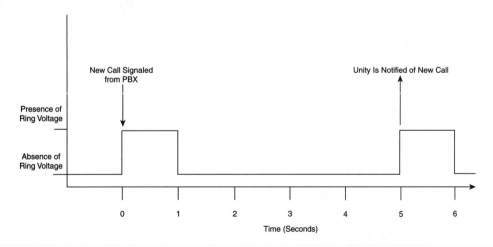

Tone Definitions

Unity configures the voice board for tone settings to detect what tones sound like ringing and what tones sound like busy to determine the state of a called extension. Unity also configures the voice board to recognize the PBX's dial tone, to know that it is fine to dial out for a call, and the different types of disconnect tones that a PBX might send. All of these tones are configured from a tone template. Some of these tones are actually dual-tones, a tone consisting of two different frequencies, and some of these tones are cadenced similarly to the ring voltage. Once again, because there is no standard for these types of tones and the call states that they represent, the ability to define these tones is important. The tone templates and the ability for the voice board to detect the defined tones accommodates for dual-tones, cadenced tones, and variations of the tones and cadence. The tones Unity intends to recognize are the exact same tones a human hears when placing a call from the home telephone (as in, dial-tone, ringing, busy, and so on).

Below is a skeletal example of a tone template:

```
[Tone Name]
Frequency1=
FrequencyDeviation1=
Frequency2=
FrequencyDeviation2=
TimeOn1=
TimeOnDeviation1=
TimeOff1=
TimeOffDeviation1=
TimeOn2=
TimeOnDeviation2=
TimeOff2=
TimeOffDeviation2=
Cycles=
```

The Tone Name is populated with one of the valid tones that the voice board would expect to see:

- Switch Busy Tone
- Switch Reorder Tone
- Switch Dial Tone
- Switch Ringback Tone
- Switch DND Tone
- CO Dial Tone
- Switch Disconnect Tone
- CO Disconnect Tone
- Fax CNG Tone
- Fax CED Tone

The fact that the deviations come into play is important. One has to remember that we are dealing with the analog world here. The tones, for the most part, are consistently represented by the switch. But tones have slight deviations in their frequency and/or cadence at times. These tolerances are accounted for. Table 17-1 lists the definitions of the tone template settings.

Table 17-1   *Tone Template Settings*

Setting	Definition
Frequency1	The frequency in Hz of Tone1.
FrequencyDeviation1	The frequency deviation in Hz of Tone1. As the name suggests, the deviation is ± the Frequency1.
Frequency2	The frequency in Hz of Tone2.
FrequencyDeviation2	The frequency deviation in Hz of Tone1. As the name suggests, the deviation is ± the Frequency1.
TimeOn1	The time in milliseconds in which Frequency1 is present in a cadenced tone.
TimeOnDeviation1	The deviation in milliseconds of TimeOn1. As the name suggests, the deviation is ± the TimeOn1.
TimeOff1	The time in milliseconds in which Frequency1 is absent in a cadenced tone.
TimeOffDeviation1	The deviation in milliseconds of TimeOff1. As the name suggests, the deviation is ± the TimeOff1.
TimeOn2	The time in milliseconds in which Frequency2 is present in a cadenced tone.
TimeOnDeviation2	The deviation in milliseconds of TimeOn2. As the name suggests, the deviation is ± the TimeOn2.
TimeOff2	The time in milliseconds in which Frequency2 is absent in a cadenced tone.
TimeOffDeviation2	The deviation in milliseconds of TimeOff2. As the name suggests, the deviation is ± the TimeOff2.
Cycles	In a cadenced tone, the number of times the tones must iterate before the tone is considered valid.

Viewing a tone template graphically makes a lot more sense. We will use a tone template for busy and graph that tone. In the real world, this tone would have slight deviations and for a tone to be recognized as busy it must fall into this tone template.

```
[Busy]
    Frequency1=480
FrequencyDeviation1=50
Frequency2=620
FrequencyDeviation2=50
TimeOn1=500
TimeOnDeviation1=50
TimeOff1=500
TimeOffDeviation1=50
Cycles=4
```

Figure 17-21 Graphs the range of frequencies that could qualify as busy as determined by the tone template listed previously.

Figure 17-21 *Range of Frequencies for Busy*

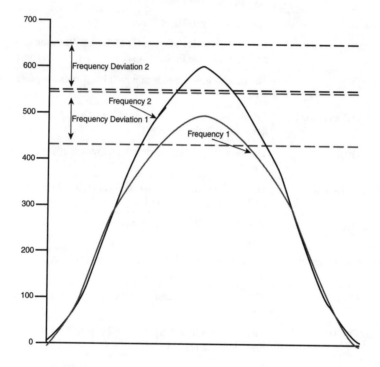

Figure 17-22 graphs the range of tone-on and tone-off cadence that could qualify as busy as determined by the tone template listed previously.

For a tone to fall into our tone template here for [Busy], it does not need to match the frequencies and cadence exactly; it's cadence and frequencies would just need to fall into our graphed dotted lines for the deviations.

Figure 17-22 *Range of Cadences for Busy*

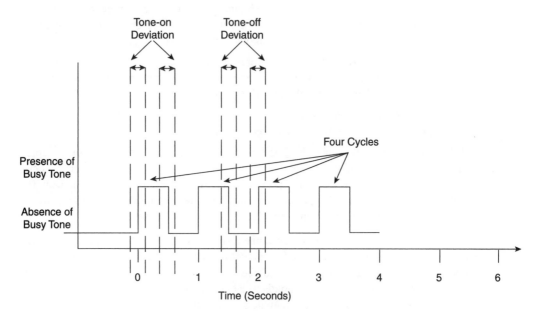

Disconnect Supervision

Disconnect supervision is so important to Unity on legacy integrations that it deserves a bit of discussion. Disconnect supervision is a fancy way of saying "when a caller hangs up on Unity, what method does the PBX use to notify Unity that this has happened?" There are a few ways of doing this, and they include:

- **Disconnect tones**. Examples of disconnect tones include re-order, busy, and dial tone. As long as the tone that is sent from the PBX matches a tone definition specified by the integration, Unity places the port on-hook after recognizing the tone.

- **Loop-current drop**. A loop-current drop is a brief moment of time (usually somewhere between 250 and 500ms) when the circuit connecting the Unity port to the PBX is interrupted by the PBX. It would be analogous to quickly unplugging the line cord from the Unity port and plugging it back in. Loop-current drop is also referred to as "power denial."

- **Loop-current reversal**. Loop-current reversal is similar to loop-current drop in that there is a brief moment of time in which the PBX signals to Unity. However, the signal is a polarity reversal in the current applied to the line as opposed to a break in the current. Loop-current reversal is also referred to as "battery reversal."

- **Serial packet**. The PBX may send a serial packet that signifies a disconnect event. Included in this serial packet would be the port or channel number corresponding to the disconnect event. Unity's serial integration parsing configuration would contain a packet definition to match the serial disconnect packet.

- **DTMF packet**. A digit sequence representing a disconnect event may be sent from the PBX to Unity. Unity's analog integration parsing configuration would contain a packet definition to match the DTMF disconnect packet.

- **DTMF tone (4th column)**. The PBX may send a single DTMF 4th column tone (A, B, C, or D) that signifies a disconnect event.

If the integration method supports disconnect supervision or does not support reliable disconnect supervision, the voice-mail system will not know when to hang up. Voice-mail ports would be tied up as that Unity port remains off-hook after the caller hangs up. If that caller hangs up in the middle of recording a message, then the message recording would not terminate; Unity would simply record silence as that port remained off-hook.

If the integration method supports disconnect supervision in the form of a serial packet, the serial integration configuration file includes a packet definition to parse out a serial disconnect packet. Such a packet would contain an enumerated value of the analog line to which the disconnect event corresponds (the enumerated value would be either the extension or channel number of that analog line). Below is an example:

```
Disconnect=              89,$CHANNEL,=0ü,
```

If the integration method supports disconnect supervision in the form of a DTMF packet, a configuration entry in AvAnalog.Avd will be present. Below is an example:

```
Data20= B9            HANGUP
```

If the integration method supports disconnect supervision in the form of a single 4th column DTMF tone, a configuration entry in the switch file will be present under the [Configuration] section. Below is an example:

```
HangUpTone=D
```

Cisco Unity CallManager Telephone Service Provider

The AvSkinny.TSP emulates an array of IP phones that communicate with Cisco CallManager by way of the Skinny Client Control Protocol. The TSP (Telephony Service Provider) registers with Cisco CallManager and receives the same Skinny messages as an IP phone. It is the TSP's job to act as protocol-translator between Unity's call control component, the MIU, and Cisco CallManager. Simply put, it converts Skinny to TAPI (Telephony Application Programming Interface) and TAPI to Skinny. The TSP also serves as broker between the RTP (Real-Time Protocol) streams of voice audio on the IP network to Unity's WAV devices for audio record and playback.

Figure 17-23 *Cisco Unity-CallManager TSP Model*

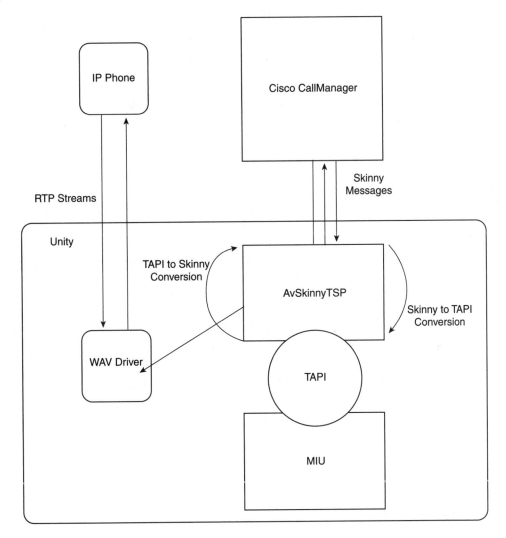

The IP Telephony–based model enables Unity to provide some features that are merely impossible with the legacy PBX integrations that Unity supports. First of all, the TSP supports Cisco CM fail-over. The TSP has defined primary Cisco CM to serve as its switch. If this server encounters a failure, the TSP can reconnect to another secondary Cisco CM server.

The Skinny protocol, for the most part, is a stateless protocol consisting of simple telephony messages to end devices and a simple set of requests sent from end devices to CM. Some messages include instructions for the end device including "play this tone", "enable this light (for an IP phone), or "change the display on the phone". TAPI, in contrast, is a state-based API where states include connected, idle, and offering. Additionally, TAPI calls for specific, high-level telephony functions including answer, transfer, and drop. There is no direct translation or one-to-one relationship between Skinny messages and TAPI call states or functions, so it is the responsibility of the Cisco Unity-CallManager TSP to bridge Skinny and TAPI.

It can take several Skinny messages to make a TAPI call state transition from one state to another, and there generally is much more Skinny activity on a call than TAPI activity. For example, it takes several Skinny messages to enable the transition from TAPI call state idle (just as it sounds, the port is idle; nothing is happening) to offering (an incoming call is ringing on that port) and finally to connected (the port is off-hook and talking to the incoming caller).

Since the Cisco Unity-CallManager TSP is simply emulating an IP phone (an old 12SP+ to be exact), the Skinny messages it receives are the same as any other IP phone would receive. There will be messages from CallManager to tell the phone (the TSP, really) that a certain light on the phone is flashing or a certain DTMF tone has arrived. It really helps to remember that each port of the Cisco Unity-CallManager TSP is a virtual phone. It can expect to receive the same Skinny messages as a phone. When it wants to perform telephony operations such as answering, transferring, or placing a call, it needs to send the same Skinny requests to CallManager as an IP phone.

Since the TSP acts like an actual IP phone, the TSP also follows the same registration process that the phones use. However, it does not download any configuration file or any settings (such as to which Cisco CallManager server it should register). Instead, the SA configures these settings on the Unity server.

Call Control

With the Cisco Unity-CallManager TSP as a virtual CallManager phone that translates Skinny message to TAPI for the MIU, an incoming call that is answered can be illustrated in the following example:

1 CCM (Cisco CallManager) sends Skinny message of "line appearance light is flashing".

2 TSP sends TAPI the call state of offering to MIU.

3 MIU calls TAPI function "answer".

4 TSP goes off-hook (sends Skinny message StationOffHookMessage).

5 TSP waits for Skinny message of connected (StationCallStateMessage of connected).

6 TSP sends TAPI call state connected to MIU.

Figure 17-24 illustrates the message transfer from CCM to the TSP and from the TSP to the MIU for an incoming call.

Figure 17-24 *Message Transfer from CCM*

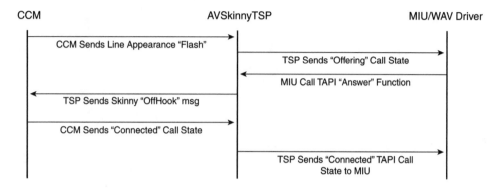

For the most part, that is how call control is implemented by the Cisco Unity-CallManager TSP. It supports the TAPI functions that the MIU needs to invoke for answering, transferring, and placing calls. We build on the previous example to demonstrate a transfer within the same call sequence:

1 MIU calls TAPI function "blind transfer" (a parameter to that function is the extension of the destination address, or the extension to transfer the caller to).

2 TSP presses the transfer key (sends StationStimulusMessage with the stimulus as the transfer key).

3 TSP waits for dial tone (StationStartToneMessage of type dial tone) and flash for the transfer light.

4 TSP dials digits of transfer string (sends StationKeyPadButton Skinny message for each digit in the transfer string).

5 TSP waits for ringout call state (StationCallStateMessage of ringout) or opening of send portion of audio path (StationStartMediaTransmissionID).

6 TSP presses the transfer key again (StationStimulusMessage with the stimulus as the transfer key).

7 TSP sends TAPI call state of disconnected to MIU.

Figure 17-25 illustrates the message transfer from CCM to the TSP and from the TSP to the MIU for a transfer request.

Figure 17-25 *Transfer Request*

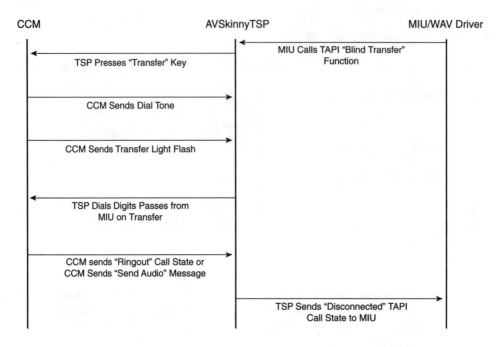

Things become more complicated when doing more sophisticated call control functions such as transfer, and this is an example when everything works correctly. There is also logic in the TSP to handle conditions including it received busy or reorder tone after dialing the digits of the transfer.

There is a lot more call control going on, but it would be impossible to document every single case. These two illustrations are provided to show the interaction between the MIU, Cisco Unity-CallManager TSP, and CCM.

Call Information

One thing that has not been mentioned is call information. At the onset of an incoming call, CCM sends a Skinny message called StationCallInfoMessage. Depending upon the version of CM, this message can contain slightly different pieces of information, but for the most part, it contains calling and called (in the case of a forwarded call) and the reason for the call. Since the message is defined by the Skinny protocol, there is no parsing that needs to be done as there is with analog or serial integrations. The Cisco Unity-CallManager TSP simply looks for defined fields for called party, calling party, and reason and stores the information. Whenever the MIU asks for the call information (via a TAPI function), it simply returns what it received from that Skinny message.

There is logic inside the TSP that decides which pieces of the StationCallInfoMessage will be used, and it is not that complicated. In CCM 3.1 and up, a new field was added to StationCallInfoMessage, and it was intended as a voice-mail box value. For example, there is an IP phone with a DN of 1234, but the user at this phone has a Unity subscriber account with a DTMF ID of 5678 (one can expect to see an instance where a user has two different phone extensions, but they want to forward to and call into the same voice-mail account from both phones). The CCM administrator can enter 5678 as the voice-mail box number for this user. So, when this caller calls or forwards to Unity, Unity will consider that user to be 5678 instead of 1234. The fields of interest to the Cisco Unity-CallManager TSP in StationCallInfoMessage can be thought of as these:

- Calling party DN
- Calling party voice-mail box DN
- Original called party DN
- Original called party voice-mail box DN
- Call reason

If there is a value present in the calling party voice-mail box DN, the Cisco Unity-CallManager TSP will use that field as the calling party for its call information. Otherwise, it uses calling party DN. Similarly, the Cisco Unity-CallManager TSP uses the original called party voice-mail box DN for the called party if there is a value present, or if there is no value, it uses the original called party DN.

The call reason (as in direct, call forward busy, and call forward no answer) is directly used with one following exception. If the DN that has filled the called party portion of the Cisco Unity-CallManager TSP's call information is the same DN as one of the AvSkinny TSP ports, the call reason is considered direct by the Cisco Unity-CallManager TSP. This is because if there is a current call on the first port of voice mail, and another caller calls the first port of voice mail (by simply hitting the messages button on their phone), the call is going to forward from that first port to another free port. Inside StationCallInfoMessage, the call reason is a forwarded reason, but Unity is accustomed to seeing forwarded calls when one extension calls another, not when one voice-mail port has forwarded to another. So, the call type is changed to direct since the original intent of the caller was to simply call voice mail. How does the Cisco Unity-CallManager TSP know what its DNs are? When the TSP registers with CM, it asks CallManager what its DNs are and saves them.

Audio Control

Beyond call control and call information, the Cisco Unity-CallManager TSP acts as a broker for the audio streams sent to and from Unity. The setup and tear-down of the audio path happens via Skinny messages, but the actual audio path itself is RTP and has nothing to do with Skinny. There will be two separate audio streams for any given conversation: one stream for Unity to receive audio and one stream for Unity to send audio. After a call has been answered by the Cisco Unity-CallManager TSP, CallManager sends a Skinny message stating to open a receive channel. Included in that Skinny message is the compression type and packet size for the stream. After receiving this message, the Cisco Unity-CallManager TSP sends an acknowledgement that it received the message. In that acknowledgement, it tells CCM what IP address and port number that it will be listening on. CCM relays this information to the other end device—gateway, phone, or whatever—so that device knows where to transmit the audio. The other message sent is a message to start a send channel. Included in this message is the IP address and port number of the remote device to where Unity should send the stream. This information is gathered with the equivalent open receive channel sent to the remote device by CCM.

The TSP gets the initial information for setting up the audio stream and simply hands that information off to the WAV driver. It is actually the WAV driver that opens the UDP (User Datagram Protocol) ports and sends and receives the real RTP data. The TSP just tells it which origination and destination ports to use.

Putting the call control, call information, and audio stream setup together, we can provide a more detailed call example:

1 CCM sends Skinny message that the line appearance light is flashing.

2 TSP sends TAPI call state offering to MIU.

3 MIU calls TAPI function "answer."

4 TSP goes off-hook (sends Skinny message StationOffHookMessage).

5 TSP waits for Skinny message of connected (StationCallStateMessage of connected).

6 TSP waits for opening of send portion of audio path (StationStartMediaTransmissionID).

7 TSP tells WAV driver to open a channel for sending and passes in the remote IP address and port number.

8 CCM sends message to open a listen channel (StationOpenReceiveChannelMessageID).

9 TSP tells WAV driver to open a channel for listening.

10 TSP sends ack (acknowledgement) to CCM and passes along the IP address and port number of the WAV device it just previously told to listen.

11 TSP sends TAPI call state connected to MIU.

Figure 17-26 illustrates the message transfer from CCM to the TSP and from the TSP to the MIU and WAV driver for an incoming call and audio channel setup.

Figure 17-26 *Message Transfer for an Incoming Call and Audio Channel Setup*

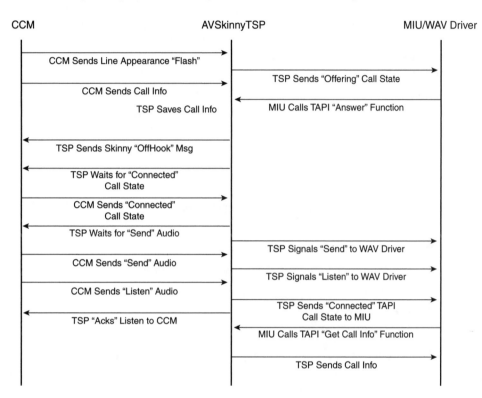

Startup and Initialization

When Unity starts up, the MIU will open up the Cisco Unity-CallManager TSP ports (it does the same with legacy/Dialogic ports). Each Cisco Unity-CallManager TSP port has its own configuration information that is used when it is opened. When a port is opened, several things happen. First of all, the port gathers the MWI on- and off-DNs for its configuration. Then it starts creating its internal guts of components. This includes the WAV device from the WAV driver that is associated with this Cisco Unity-CallManager TSP port. There is a one-to-one relationship between Cisco Unity-CallManager TSP ports and the WAV devices. When the WAV device is associated, the source UDP ports for RTP data are set for the WAV device, and the base address for these devices is also configurable through UTIM. The next step is for the Cisco Unity-CallManager TSP port to register with CM. A network connection is first attempted and, upon success, the registration request is sent to CM. This network connection and registration request is directed to the particular CallManager that is associated with the Cisco Unity-CallManager TSP port (it is possible to have the TSP register with multiple CallManagers). The registration message that it sends to CallManager includes its device name, IP address, and device type. After registration, the Cisco Unity-CallManager TSP port sets up the keepalive interval to send periodic heartbeats back to CallManager (IP phones do the same). Finally, the Cisco Unity-CallManager TSP port returns a success code back to the MIU. The Cisco Unity-CallManager TSP port is now ready to receive TAPI function calls from the MIU and Skinny events from CM.

The Cisco Unity-CallManager TSP has the notion of CallManager Cluster objects that it uses for the initialization. Through UTIM, the administrator configures each cluster. The configuration information is straightforward. It consists of the following configuration parameters:

- IP address of the CallManager
- IP address of and failover CallManager servers
- The destination port number for Skinny connections
- CallManager device ID prefix
- The starting range for the UDP ports that the WAV devices use
- The MWI DNs that enable and disable MWIs
- Number of ports
- Port capabilities

There is nothing fancy about the configuration parameters; however, the fact that the TSP can be configured on a CallManager cluster object basis easily allows the TSP to connect to multiple CallManager clusters simultaneously.

MWI Functionality

It is easy to enable and disable the MWI on an IP phone if you are sitting right in front of the phone. All you have to do is dial the appropriate MWI DN and the MWI status changes. But how does Unity do it? Would Unity enable the MWI for its own port if it simply dialed the MWI on- or off- DN? Well yes, but that obviously will not work well for Unity subscribers that need their phone's MWI status to change. Unity will go off-hook as the DN of the phone that it wants to change the MWI status. Then it dials the appropriate MWI DN. It is not rocket science, but it is quite different than how legacy integration MWIs work. Just try going off-hook as the DN of another phone from an analog port; it is just not possible.

Multiple CallManager Cluster Support

One Unity server can service multiple CallManager clusters. This is possible because of the CallManager cluster objects that the TSP keeps track of. Each cluster object can have its own, unique configuration parameters. With multiple clusters, the administrator can aim the

TSP at these clusters a couple of different ways. One option is to direct TSP ports that are configured to answer calls to only one cluster and direct at least one MWI port to the other CallManager clusters. Figure 17-27 illustrates the Cisco Unity-CallManager TSP connected to a dedicated CCM cluster for incoming calls with MWI-only ports to other CCM clusters.

Figure 17-27 *Unity-CallManager TSP Connected to a Dedicated CCM Cluster*

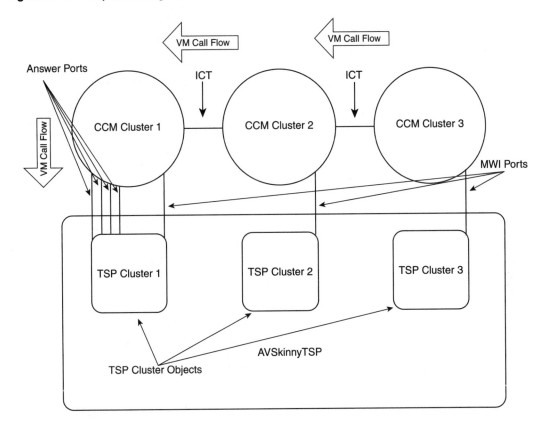

With this configuration, Unity subscribers calling into or forwarding phones to voice mail would traverse CM inter-cluster trunks to reach Unity. When calling voice mail, a Unity subscriber on CCM Cluster3 calls a Skinny device (the Cisco Unity-CallManager TSP port) that is connected to CCM Cluster1 rather than CCM Cluster3. The TSP ports that are going to answer calls regardless of the origination are centralized to one CallManager cluster. The actual network connections are not relevant (a single network link might be supporting the MWI connections to all clusters); the connections in this illustration are purely logical.

Alternatively, all of the Cisco Unity-CallManager TSP cluster objects could contain ports that answer calls as well as enable/disable MWI. Calls placed to and forwarded to Unity from a cluster would arrive at a Skinny connection to Unity directly on the respective CCM cluster. Figure 17-28 illustrates the Cisco Unity-CallManager TSP connected to multiple CCM clusters for incoming calls and MWI.

Figure 17-28 *Unity-CallManager TSP Connected to Multiple CCM Clusters*

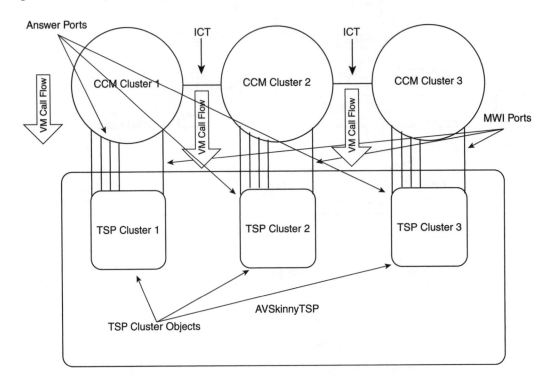

With this configuration, the ports that answer incoming calls are decentralized from one particular cluster. Conceptually, this configuration is the same as three separate, small voice-mail systems as opposed to one larger voice-mail system in the centralized connection method (given the same number of total Cisco Unity-CallManager TSP ports are distributed in both models).

Any number of ports can be distributed to the cluster objects as desired. There is only one strict requirement that exists: Each cluster object must have at least one Cisco Unity-CallManager TSP port that can enable/disable MWI. This requirement is because of the fact that Unity does not have any knowledge of which CallManager cluster a Unity subscriber's phone resides on. When enabling/disabling MWI, Unity must go off-hook as the subscriber's IP phone, and it must do this on a Cisco Unity-CallManager TSP port that is in the same cluster as the IP phone. In essence, Unity uses the shotgun approach and sends MWI requests out to each Cisco Unity-CallManager TSP cluster object that contains an MWI-enabled port.

SIP

Session Initiation Protocol (SIP) is an emerging standard currently used for telephony, presence, and instant messaging, among other services. SIP makes use of an Internet-like distributed architecture and reuses several existing Internet Engineering Task Force (IETF) standards such as RTP for media streaming, URLs and DNS for naming and locating, HTTP/text for message formatting, and Session Definition Protocol (SDP) for media capabilities negotiation. As a telephony call control protocol, SIP pushes much of the call-control intelligence to the endpoints (as in a phone or Unity), called SIP User Agents (UAs), rather than centralizing it in a PBX-type system. This is obviously quite a shift from TDM-PBX systems, as well as from non-SIP IP-PBX systems such as Cisco CM. In telephony terms SIP is new, and as such it does not yet offer the same level of features provided by many TDM-PBX telephony services. However, because of its structure, SIP also offers flexibility and extensibility that allows SIP-based telephony systems to offer an entire new level of services previously not offered by TDM-PBX systems. SIP is currently defined by RFC 3261. However, the protocols and technologies used by SIP, several of which were mentioned previously, are defined in different RFCs. Furthermore, essential voice-mail functions like call transfer, MWI, and digit transmission are defined in other RFCs and Internet drafts. The documents that define these essential voice-mail functions are listed below, current as of Unity 4.0(4):

- **RFC 2833**. RTP Payload for DTMF Digits, Telephony Tones and Telephony Signals
- **RFC 3515**. The Session Initiation Protocol (SIP) Refer Method
- **Draft**. Diversion Indication in SIP
- **Draft**. Extensions for Message Waiting Indication

Unity 4.0(1) was the first version of Unity to support SIP. With the Unity SIP integration, TAPI is no longer used. This removes a layer of abstraction that has previously always existed with Unity's call-control solution. Unity has its own SIP stack that allows it to communicate natively with other SIP devices. Although TAPI is no longer used with the SIP integration, many of the media-related Unity functions (as in play, record, speed control, and silence detection) are implemented in much the same way for the SIP integration as they are for the Cisco CallManager (Skinny) integration.

Overview of Unity SIP Component

Like the TAPI-based Unity legacy PBX and Unity CCM integrations, the Unity SIP integration takes care of initiating and ending a call, call-control functionality during that call, and media operations over that call. So what is new in Unity with the implementation of SIP?

The Unity SIP component consists of three main pieces: the media component, the MIU SIP component, and the SIPStack. The media component for SIP functions is much the same as the media component for CCM integrations although it was newly designed as a media plug-in for Unity 4.0(1). Future call-control plug-ins can use this new media component rather than reimplement media handling. The MIU SIP component interfaces with the media component and SIPStack on one side and MIU clients on the other side. The component abstracts call control and media events for MIU clients, such as the Conversation and Arbiter. The SIPStack handles all SIP-specific tasks, such as generating outgoing SIP messages, as well as parsing incoming SIP messages and determining to which Unity port they should be sent. This brings us to an important distinction between the Unity SIP integration and other Unity integrations.

With legacy and CCM integrations, each Unity port has its own unique identifier, or extension, that can usually be dialed individually. With the Unity SIP integration, a contact-line name is established, behind which multiple Unity ports exist. Contact-line names can be alphanumeric strings (as in 4000 or Unity). Calls to Unity are all destined for this contact-line name and are first handled by the SIPStack. The SIPStack then distributes calls among free Unity ports in the same fashion as a circular hunt group. Because of this, there is no way to dial a particular Unity port. Multiple contact-line names can be established on a single Unity server, with each contact-line name having distinct Unity ports associated with it. Multiple contact-line names might be configured in order to separate ports that handle incoming calls from ports that make outgoing calls for MWI, message notification, and Telephone Record and Playback (TRaP). Since incoming calls have priority over outgoing calls, this separation can ensure that outgoing calls can be made on Unity systems with heavy traffic. You could have a 48-port Unity system, with 40 ports dedicated to incoming calls, existing behind one contact-line name. The remaining 8 ports could be responsible for outdials and would exist behind a second contact-line name.

SIP Methods Unity Uses

So how does a SIP phone contact Unity? First, Unity must make its presence known on the network by registering its contact-line name with a SIP registrar upon Unity startup. Below is an example of a REGISTER request sent from Unity to a SIP registrar:

```
REGISTER sip:farm.ecsbu-lab-sea.cisco.com:5060 SIP/2.0
From: sip:Unity@farm.ecsbu-lab-sea.cisco.com;tag=1DA40540E0EF4438B741B9AD40B60587
To: sip:Unity@farm.ecsbu-lab-sea.cisco.com
Via: SIP/2.0/UDP 10.93.250.230:5060;branch=z9hG4bK7EF48555D3B341E78B803E81E684B4D4
Max-Forwards: 70
Contact: sip:Unity@10.93.250.230:5060
```

```
Expires: 1800
Call-ID: 6FB2A83F9EB44ED297F1E188EB49A26A@farm.ecsbu-lab-sea.cisco.com
CSeq: 100 REGISTER
Content-Length: 0
```

Notice the following line in the REGISTER request:

```
Contact: sip:Unity@10.93.250.230:5060
```

This tells the SIP registrar the Unity contact-line name and the IP address of the Unity server (10.93.250.230). Upon accepting the REGISTER request, the registrar responds to Unity acknowledging that REGISTER was accepted, and records the contact-line name and IP address in a local database.

Once registered, Unity can easily be reached by a SIP UA that uses the same SIP proxy server and registrar as Unity. A SIP proxy server processes SIP messages and passes them to the appropriate destination, whether it be another SIP proxy server or a SIP endpoint. A SIP proxy server and a SIP registrar are logical entities, so they might reside on a single server or on separate servers. So when a SIP phone dials "Unity" (assuming that is Unity's contact-line name), it sends a call initiation request to the SIP proxy server, which refers to the SIP registrar to determine Unity's IP address. Once the SIP proxy obtains this information, it can pass the call initiation request along to Unity. Once Unity receives this new call request, it responds in order to establish the SIP session, and the call is set up on a free Unity port, assuming Unity answers the call. Although this example is valid, SIP networks will not always have a single SIP proxy server handling SIP requests and a single registrar where all SIP devices register. Often SIP UAs that need to communicate with each other will register with different SIP registrars and will send SIP requests to different SIP proxy servers. If a SIP UA sends a call initiation request destined for Unity to a SIP proxy server that cannot determine Unity's IP address from the local registrar, the SIP proxy needs to find another SIP proxy that can determine Unity's IP address. SIP proxy servers might make use of a number of methods, including DNS or static database lookups, to find another SIP proxy server that is able to determine Unity's IP address. SIP requests might be passed through multiple SIP proxy servers before finally reaching one that can determine the destination IP address. Once the destination IP address is determined, the call initiation can continue.

Before we go further, a description of the SIP methods employed by Unity should be presented. Following are the main SIP methods used by Unity and the functions they are used for:

- **REGISTER (outgoing only)**. The method used to register Unity with a SIP registrar to make its presence known on the network. This first occurs during Unity startup, and thereafter periodically while Unity is running. REGISTERs expire after a given period defined in the REGISTER method (30 minutes in Unity 4.0(4)). Unity attempts to renew its registration before the existing REGISTER expires to ensure continuity of service (register renewal occurs every 15 minutes in Unity 4.0(4)). Unity also supports HTTP-digest authentication with the REGISTER request. If authentication is required, a challenge is received in response to the first REGISTER request. Unity then resends the REGISTER request, this time providing a username and password that presumably matches credentials stored on the SIP registrar. The username and password for each contact-line name is configured in Unity during integration setup.

- **INVITE**. The SIP call initiation request. An incoming INVITE signals a new incoming call to Unity. An outgoing INVITE signals a Unity outdial (message notification, pager notification, or TRaP call). An INVITE can also be used to modify an existing SIP session (as in put a call on hold). Unity also supports HTTP-digest authentication with outgoing INVITE requests. If authentication is required, Unity resends the INVITE with a username and password in order to authenticate with the SIP proxy server and proceed with the call.

- **REFER**. The method is used for call transfers.

- **NOTIFY (outgoing only)**. The method used for MWI. Unity uses unsolicited NOTIFY rather than SUBSCRIBE/NOTIFY.

- **CANCEL**. The method used to cancel a pending request. For example, imagine Unity performs a message notification outdial to an unattended phone. Unity is configured to ring four times before hanging up. If the phone rings four times without being answered, Unity will send CANCEL to end the pending INVITE request.

- **BYE**. The method used to terminate an existing call.

- **ACK**. The method used to acknowledge receipt of a final response to an INVITE request.

In addition to SIP methods, a slew of SIP responses indicate different conditions such as success, failure, and information. The Unity SIP component is periodically updated to comply with the latest SIP specifications. The latest Unity SIP compliance information can be obtained from www.cisco.com.

SIP sessions are best described by call flows that show the order and origin of SIP methods, SIP responses, and other events in the lifetime of a call. The simplest call flow is that between two SIP endpoints that establish a call, exchange media, and then disconnect the call. This simple call flow, from RFC 3665, can be seen in Example 17-5.

Example 17-5 *Sample Call Flow*

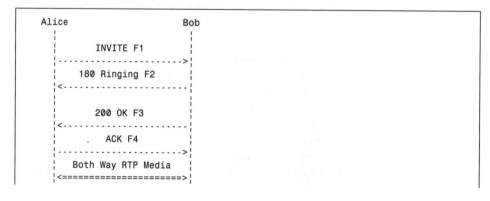

```
   Alice                           Bob
     |                               |
     |          INVITE F1            |
     |------------------------------>|
     |        180 Ringing F2         |
     |<------------------------------|
     |                               |
     |           200 OK F3           |
     |<------------------------------|
     |          .  ACK F4            |
     |------------------------------>|
     |      Both Way RTP Media       |
     |<=============================>|
```

Example 17-5 *Sample Call Flow (Continued)*

```
   :              BYE F5            :
   :<----------------------:
   :            200 OK F6           :
   :---------------------->:
   :                               :
```

In this scenario, Alice completes a call to Bob directly:

```
F1 INVITE Alice -> Bob

INVITE sip:bob@biloxi.example.com SIP/2.0
Via: SIP/2.0/TCP client.atlanta.example.com:5060;branch=z9hG4bK74bf9
Max-Forwards: 70
From: Alice <sip:alice@atlanta.example.com>;tag=9fxced76sl
To: Bob <sip:bob@biloxi.example.com>
Call-ID: 3848276298220188511@atlanta.example.com
CSeq: 1 INVITE
Contact: <sip:alice@client.atlanta.example.com;transport=tcp>
Content-Type: application/sdp
Content-Length: 151
v=0
o=alice 2890844526 2890844526 IN IP4 client.atlanta.example.com
s=-
c=IN IP4 192.0.2.101
t=0 0
m=audio 49172 RTP/AVP 0
a=rtpmap:0 PCMU/8000


F2 180 Ringing Bob -> Alice

SIP/2.0 180 Ringing
Via: SIP/2.0/TCP client.atlanta.example.com:5060;branch=z9hG4bK74bf9
 ;received=192.0.2.101
From: Alice <sip:alice@atlanta.example.com>;tag=9fxced76sl
To: Bob <sip:bob@biloxi.example.com>;tag=8321234356
Call-ID: 3848276298220188511@atlanta.example.com
CSeq: 1 INVITE
Contact: <sip:bob@client.biloxi.example.com;transport=tcp>
Content-Length: 0


F3 200 OK Bob -> Alice

SIP/2.0 200 OK
Via: SIP/2.0/TCP client.atlanta.example.com:5060;branch=z9hG4bK74bf9
 ;received=192.0.2.101
From: Alice <sip:alice@atlanta.example.com>;tag=9fxced76sl
To: Bob <sip:bob@biloxi.example.com>;tag=8321234356
Call-ID: 3848276298220188511@atlanta.example.com
CSeq: 1 INVITE
Contact: <sip:bob@client.biloxi.example.com;transport=tcp>
Content-Type: application/sdp
Content-Length: 147
v=0
o=bob 2890844527 2890844527 IN IP4 client.biloxi.example.com
s=-
c=IN IP4 192.0.2.201
```

```
t=0 0
m=audio 3456 RTP/AVP 0
a=rtpmap:0 PCMU/8000


F4 ACK Alice -> Bob

ACK sip:bob@client.biloxi.example.com SIP/2.0
Via: SIP/2.0/TCP client.atlanta.example.com:5060;branch=z9hG4bK74bd5
Max-Forwards: 70
From: Alice <sip:alice@atlanta.example.com>;tag=9fxced76sl
To: Bob <sip:bob@biloxi.example.com>;tag=8321234356
Call-ID: 3848276298220188511@atlanta.example.com
CSeq: 1 ACK
Content-Length: 0

/* RTP streams are established between Alice and Bob */

/* Bob Hangs Up with Alice. Note that the CSeq is NOT 2, since
   Alice and Bob maintain their own independent CSeq counts.
   (The INVITE was request 1 generated by Alice, and the BYE is
   request 1 generated by Bob) */


F5 BYE Bob -> Alice

BYE sip:alice@client.atlanta.example.com SIP/2.0
Via: SIP/2.0/TCP client.biloxi.example.com:5060;branch=z9hG4bKnashds7
Max-Forwards: 70
From: Bob <sip:bob@biloxi.example.com>;tag=8321234356
To: Alice <sip:alice@atlanta.example.com>;tag=9fxced76sl
Call-ID: 3848276298220188511@atlanta.example.com
CSeq: 1 BYE
Content-Length: 0


F6 200 OK Alice -> Bob

SIP/2.0 200 OK
Via: SIP/2.0/TCP client.biloxi.example.com:5060;branch=z9hG4bKnashds7
 ;received=192.0.2.201
From: Bob <sip:bob@biloxi.example.com>;tag=8321234356
To: Alice <sip:alice@atlanta.example.com>;tag=9fxced76sl
Call-ID: 3848276298220188511@atlanta.example.com
CSeq: 1 BYE
Content-Length: 0
```

Any SIP call can be mapped by a call flow, and understanding these call flows greatly enhances your understanding of how SIP works. In addition, SIP messages can easily be gathered and analyzed with a network sniffer that has a SIP parser. Unity also has SIP call-control diagnostic traces that dump incoming and outgoing SIP messages to the standard Unity trace files. By gathering SIP messages that are sent to or from a SIP UA or passed through a SIP proxy server during a call, one can reconstruct or debug the call flow.

For more interesting SIP call flows that go beyond the most basic phone call, refer to www.cisco.com or several of the IETF documents available online at http://www.ietf.org.

Call Information with SIP Integration

Just as with legacy and CCM integrations, Unity gathers call information upon receiving an incoming SIP call. This information is gathered from the INVITE request that Unity receives, and the information populates the call object. From there, Unity uses the call object to handle the call in the same way as for other Unity integrations. Here is the pertinent piece of an incoming INVITE for a call that was forwarded busy from a phone to Unity. In this example, SIP UA 6205 called SIP UA 6101, but 6101 was busy. So the call was forwarded to Unity (6700):

```
INVITE sip:6700@10.93.249.11:5060 SIP/2.0
Via: SIP/2.0/UDP 10.93.248.67:5060;branch=3f47f9ca-687e03fc-9e081c8a-5f65d41b-1
Via: SIP/2.0/UDP 10.93.248.67:5060;received=10.93.248.67;branch=93a24d00-f22c9cf7-
    df7b8424-dcb1936b-2
Via: SIP/2.0/UDP 10.93.249.28:5060;received=10.93.249.28
CC-Diversion: <sip:6101@farm.ecsbu-lab-sea.cisco.com>;reason=user-busy
From: 'User ID' <sip:6205@farm.ecsbu-lab-
sea.cisco.com>;tag=0003e363121d000259575c7a-417fff48
To: <sip:6101@farm.ecsbu-lab-sea.cisco.com>
Call-ID: 0003e363-121d005c-1769a6d8-071657ba@10.93.249.28
Date: Sat  15 Mar 2003 01:18:06 GMT
CSeq: 102 INVITE
User-Agent: CSCO/4
Contact: <sip:6205@10.93.249.28:5060>
```

Here is the key call information gathered from the INVITE:

- Calling party ID is gathered by reading the From: header.
- Called party ID (forwarding station) is gathered by reading the CC-Diversion header.
- Call-forward reason is gathered by reading the CC-Diversion header.

Assume x6205 and x6101 are associated with Unity subscribers. In this case, x6205 is forwarded to Unity and hears x6101's busy greeting (assuming x6101 has a busy greeting recorded). Then, the message received by x6101 identifies the voice message sender as x6205.

Media Format Negotiation

With SIP, media format negotiation is performed on a per-call basis using the SDP section of the INVITE and subsequent 200 OK. Just as with the Unity CCM integration, Unity 4.0(4) only supports sending and receiving media in either G711uLaw or G729a audio formats.

Example 17-6 is the SDP portion of an INVITE to Unity from a SIP phone configured with G711aLaw as the preferred audio format, and Example 17-7 is the SDP of the subsequent 200 OK sent from Unity back to the phone.

Example 17-6 *SDP Portion of INVITE from Phone to Unity*

```
v=0
o=Cisco-SIPUA 14068 24809 IN IP4 10.93.250.224
s=SIP Call
c=IN IP4 10.93.250.224
t=0 0
m=audio 21372 RTP/AVP 8 0 18 101
a=rtpmap:8 PCMA/8000
a=rtpmap:0 PCMU/8000
a=rtpmap:18 G729/8000
a=rtpmap:101 telephone-event/8000
a=fmtp:101 0-15
```

The m= header shows the RTP port on which the phone expects to send and receive media, and it also lists its supported audio formats in priority order. So this phone prefers to communicate using G711aLaw, G711uLaw, and G729a, in that order.

Example 17-7 *SDP Portion of 200 OK from Unity to Phone*

```
v=0
o=10.93.249.11 104998094 104998094 IN IP4 10.93.249.11
s=No Subject
c=IN IP4 10.93.249.11
t=0 0
m=audio 22806 RTP/AVP 0 18 101
a=rtpmap:0 PCMU/8000
a=rtpmap:18 G729/8000
a=rtpmap:101 telephone-event/8000
a=fmtp:101 0-15
```

From the m= field, we can see that Unity expects to send and receive media on RTP port 22806, and it supports G711uLaw first, then G729a. As a result, this call uses G711uLaw for audio transmission.

When responding to an INVITE, Unity looks at the media list in the SDP of the incoming INVITE. It chooses the first audio format in the list that it supports (either G711uLaw or G729) and responds with that audio format in the m= header of its 200 OK response. So in the previous example, if Unity supported G711aLaw it would have put that first in the list of supported audio formats in its m=header, and the call would have proceeded using G711aLaw. If Unity does not find either of its supported audio formats in an incoming INVITE, it responds with the appropriate SIP response (415 Unsupported Media) and ends the pending call. For outgoing calls, each contact-line name is configured for either G711uLaw or G729a during integration setup. Unity lists the configured audio format first in its m= header for any outgoing INVITEs it sends. The destination SIP UA might use that information to decide which audio format it wants to use and sends that information to Unity in the subsequent 200 OK. The audio path then is set up using the agreed upon audio format.

Digit Detection and Generation

Unity's capability to detect and generate digits during an existing call is essential to its telephone user interface, as well as such features as pager notification and AMIS. With Unity SIP, digits dialed during a call are transmitted over the existing RTP stream. This contrasts with the CCM integration, where digits are transmitted on the call-control path rather than the audio path. Unity SIP uses the AVT-Tone mechanism for digit transmission described in RFC 2833.

Unity SIP generates digits as follows: An MIU client requests a digit string be dialed, and the MIU SIP component passes the request to the Unity media component. The Unity media component converts each digit in the dial string into an AVT-Tone digit event, inserts each AVT-Tone digit event into an RTP packet, and sends the RTP packets along the existing RTP stream.

Unity detects digits by the reverse mechanism: The Unity media component analyzes the incoming audio stream for RTP packets that contain AVT-Tone digit events. When it finds one, it converts it into a DTMF event and passes that to the MIU SIP component. The MIU SIP component, based on instructions from an MIU client, passes that digit along to the interested MIU client or compiles the received digits into a string before passing them along to the MIU client. A SIP UA advertises its support for AVT-Tone digit events in the SDP portion of an INVITE or subsequent 200 OK. So in the previous SDP examples, the line a=rtpmap:101 telephone-event/8000 in both the SIP phone's INVITE and Unity's 200 OK response indicates they both support AVT-Tones. Furthermore, the line a=fmtp:101 0-15 indicates they both support AVT-Tone digit events 0-15.

Unity SIP Failover

Unity failover using the SIP integration takes advantage of the forking feature of a stateful SIP proxy server. Forking is when a SIP proxy server receives an INVITE for a particular SIP address and sends an INVITE out to multiple SIP UAs that are associated with that address. When one of those SIP UAs responds to the INVITE and initiates a SIP session, the proxy server sends CANCEL to all the other SIP devices to which it originally sent an INVITE. Forking would allow a person to receive the same call on multiple devices (as in work phone, home phone, and cell phone) simultaneously. As soon as one device answered, the other devices would stop ringing. Unity SIP takes advantage of forking to implement failover in a much simpler way than is possible with either legacy or CCM integrations.

With Unity SIP failover, both active and inactive servers are configured with the same contact-line name. They both register this contact-line name with a SIP proxy registrar. The inactive Unity server is automatically set to wait a certain period of time without receiving a CANCEL before responding to an incoming INVITE. So when a call is made to Unity, the SIP proxy server forks the call so the same INVITE is sent to both the active and inactive Unity servers. If the active Unity server answers the incoming call, the inactive Unity server receives a CANCEL from the SIP proxy server promptly and therefore doesn't handle the call. But if the active server does not answer the incoming call, the inactive server answers the call after the configured period of time has passed and the non-answering active server receives the CANCEL. If automatic failover is configured, the inactive Unity server then becomes the active Unity server and the previously active Unity server becomes inactive. The newly inactive Unity server now enacts the wait timer before responding to any incoming INVITEs.

PIMG Integration

Unity 4.0(4) introduces support for a new device called PIMG (PBX/IP Media Gateway) that takes advantage of the Unity SIP interface. PIMG replaces the voice board as the means for Unity to integrate with legacy PBX systems. Rather than connecting lines from the legacy PBX system to a voice board installed in the Unity server, lines from the legacy PBX system are connected to the PIMG and Unity communicates with the PIMG over the network using SIP. With the PIMG integration, a voice board is no longer installed in the Unity server. Many of the PBX-specific parameters that were previously configured on the Unity server (mostly in the switch file) are now configured on the PIMG, albeit under different headings. As of Unity 4.0(4), one PIMG can support up to eight Unity voice ports. Multiple PIMGs can be configured with Unity to scale to a higher number of voice ports.

PIMG translates call-control commands from the PBX into SIP and sends these SIP messages to Unity. Likewise, PIMG translates SIP messages from Unity into call-control commands that the PBX can understand. Because the PIMG integration relies on Unity's SIP interface, much of the discussion in the previous section about SIP methods, digit generation and detection, and media-format negotiation apply to the PIMG integration as well. One SIP method that is not used with the PIMG integration is REGISTER. PIMG is configured with the IP address of the Unity server, so it knows where to send SIP messages destined for Unity. Because of this, there is no need for Unity to advertise its IP address using REGISTER. Figure 17-29 is an example call flow for a call setup between a phone on the legacy PBX system and Unity, via PIMG.

Figure 17-29 *PIMG Call Flow for a Call Setup*

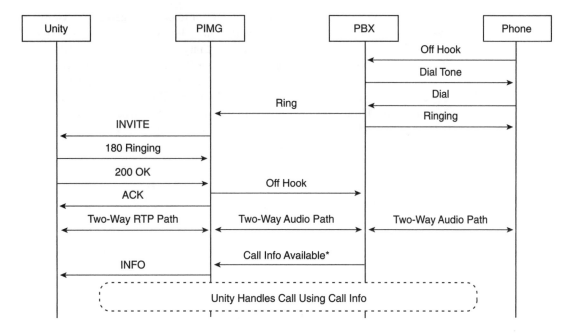

Notice that the SIP call flow between Unity and PIMG is the same as the call flow shown in the previous section, "SIP Methods used by Unity." Because the PIMG integration is new with Unity 4.0(4), Unity using PIMG does not yet support all of the legacy PBXs that Unity using a voice board can support. However, it is expected that the PIMG integration eventually will allow Unity to communicate with the entire currently supported legacy PBXs. In addition, PIMG opens the door to digital integrations with legacy PBXs that were previously not possible. In general, digital integrations to PBXs are considered more efficient and feature-rich than analog integrations to the same PBX. With PIMG, Unity will eventually support digital integrations to widely deployed PBXs like Nortel Meridian, Avaya Definity, and Siemens HiCom 300, among others. Another benefit of using PIMG with Unity instead of using voice boards is that Unity no longer needs to be collocated with the PBX. This allows for more easily managed systems, where several Unity servers could potentially be located at a central site, and each of these Unity servers could service a different legacy PBX at a remote site.

Summary

The integration with the phone system is one of the most important interfaces in Unity. Managing call control and call information properly and reliably is essential to basic voice-mail functionality. As you can see from this chapter, Unity can integrate with several different kinds of phone systems, whether it is a legacy PBX, a Cisco CallManager cluster, or a SIP phone system. Comprehending how Unity works with each different phone system requires understanding the various technologies. After reading this chapter you should have a strong grasp of how Unity integrates with different phone systems, as well as a better understanding of the technologies employed to make these integrations work.

PART III

Solutions, Systems Management, and Administration

Chapter 18   Audio-Text Applications

Chapter 19   Administering Multiple Unity Servers

Chapter 20   Subscriber Administration

Chapter 21   Administering Unity Programmatically

Chapter 22   Third-Party Tools and Applications

Chapter 23   The Future of Unity

Audio-Text Applications

This chapter explores the audio-text capabilities found in Unity. The term *audio text* is used quite a lot, but its meaning changes, depending on whom you are talking to. As we use it here, *audio text* encompasses everything that you can do with a phone call in Unity other than leaving and retrieving messages. According to this definition, routing calls to other subscribers, ringing phones, finding subscribers in the directory by name, and navigating trees of prerecorded greetings and options all fall into the category of audio text.

We also lump in the more common auto-attendant capabilities here. This simply means that Unity can act as the primary entry point for callers into a company instead of requiring a human operator to field all calls or requiring DID integrations only. We consider auto-attendant functionality to be a strict subset of the larger audio-text definition.

Unity has a much more full-featured set of audio-text capabilities than many people realize. This is because documentation and training tend more to the installation, integration, and support end of things than to detailed investigation into audio-text matters. You can make trees of menus and options as deep as you like, and then either allow users to exit those trees or try extensions, or trap them in the tree until they submit to your wishes. Unity can also provide call screening and call holding for subscribers, and interviewing capabilities. With the release of 4.0(1), it can also handle any number of name-lookup handlers for search capabilities across the entire corporate directory or cross-sections of it.

However, Unity cannot handle full Integrated Voice Response (IVR) type applications. Unity is restricted to using a set of objects (discussed later) with prerecorded greetings and options that you decide on; it cannot dynamically retrieve information from external sources or push data to external systems based on user response or the like. If you need to provide a system that gives users their bank balance, for instance, you must use a proper IVR application.

This chapter describes the objects in the SA interface, such as call handlers, directory handlers, and interview handlers. It also examines routing rules and examples of audio-text applications as well troubleshooting information. In addition, it takes a quick look at the Audio Text Manager interface.

Call Handlers

The primary object that you use in most audio-text applications is the call handler. This object can ring phones, play prerecorded messages (greetings) to callers, act on caller input, take messages for one or many subscribers, and transfer callers to other handlers or subscribers in the system. No licensing restrictions govern the use of call handlers, so you can create as many of them as you like. We have created more than 10,000 handlers on test systems; because they are not represented in the directory (they are stored only in the local SQL database on the Unity server where they are created), no performance problems arose.

The SA interface for finding and editing call handlers is a little clumsy for databases of that size, admittedly, but the Audio Text Manager (ATM) tool that ships with Unity 3.1(3) and later makes creating and editing large numbers of handlers much easier. We do not cover the ATM tool in detail here; you can visit its home page to get the tool, detailed help, and training videos on how to use it. You can find the latest ATM version (and all other Unity tools created and maintained by the Customer Applications Team) at http://www.ciscounitytools.com.

The fact that handlers are not replicated in the directory is important. This means that, unlike subscriber information, audio-text information is not shared between Unity servers on the same network. As such, if multiple Unity servers work together to handle calls for an installation, you must replicate your audio-text information between those servers on your own. Currently, no tool can copy call-handler data or audio-text trees and duplicate them on other servers (although the customer applications team has this on the list of items to tackle as part of updated versions of the Audio Text Manager).

Dealing with all the inbound and outbound links for call handlers in such a move is complex, as you will see in Chapter 21, "Administering Unity Programmatically," when we cover some of these issues. This is something to keep in mind when deciding how to deploy multiple Unity servers in a site. It is a good idea to have a single box dedicated to audio-text applications and spread the subscriber load across other servers in the network. This greatly reduces the overhead in creating and maintaining complex audio-text applications.

The next section covers the high-level, call-handler properties visible in the SA, starting with the profile page.

Profile

The Profile page, shown in Figure 18-1, shows the basic top-level information about a call handler.

Figure 18-1 *Profile Page for a Call Handler in the SA*

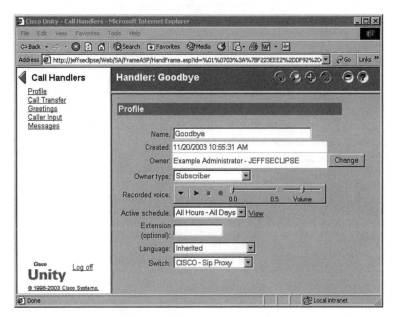

The Name field, of course, shows up in the administration interface and enables you to search for a handler by name. However, this is also its unique alias in the CallHandler table in the UnityDB SQL database. When you first create a call handler, the display name that you give it is used to construct its alias. This alias does not change later if you update the display name. For this reason, the names of all call handlers on a local Unity box must be unique. Primary call handlers (those handlers associated with subscribers) use ch_ followed by the alias of the subscriber that they are tied to. So, ch_lindborg would be the alias for Jeff Lindborg's primary call handler. Primary call handlers do not show up in the call-handler search pages in the SA on their own; their information is shown on the subscriber pages in the SA.

The Created field is the time and date when the handler was created; it is a read-only property.

The Owner field is an interesting one. The owner can be set to either a subscriber or a public distribution list that has been imported into the local Unity server's SQL database. Although this field has been around since the first version of Unity, it was completely meaningless until the release of 4.0(1). The original intent behind the owner concept was to enable users to update call-handler properties over the phone if they were owners or members of the distribution list that was the owner. Eventually, this would provide a class of service (CoS) flag that would give users access to objects (such as call handlers) in the SA that they owned.

This was one item that did not get done in the first few rounds of development and then got put on the back burner. Unfortunately, the owner properties were enforced by the conversations in Unity, even if they had no useful purpose. As such, if you deleted a subscriber who was listed as the owner of a call handler, when a caller accessed that handler over the phone, the call was terminated with the failsafe conversation ("I am sorry, I cannot talk to you now. . ."). The wisdom of this aggressive enforcement of a field with no utility is left as an exercise for the reader.

As of 4.0(1), however, the Owner field *does* have some meaning, at least for call handlers. If you are listed as the owner or are a member of the public distribution list that is listed as the owner of a call handler, you are allowed to change the greetings for that call handler from over the phone. Finally! Before this, there was no way to edit call-handler greeting other than via the SA interface—for instance, companies could not change the opening greeting's message unless they had SA access. For this very reason, many sites resorted to using subscribers in place of call handlers for the opening greeting duties, burning a user license to do it. We cover the use of this special Greetings Administrator conversation used to record handler greetings in the Changing Greetings for Call Handlers over the Phone example section later in this chapter.

The Voice Name field primarily is used to identify which call handler a message was routed to a subscriber through. For instance, if a company had a dozen call handlers set up and all left their messages in a subscriber's box, the messages would be identified as being "from" the voice name of the call handler each was left for. The voice name is also used to construct the system greeting for a handler. If the system greeting option is selected on an active greeting, the voice name is used to construct a prompt that says, "Sorry, (handler voice name) is not available." Call handlers are not used for much else because outside callers or subscribers cannot search for call handlers by name.

The Active Schedule field indicates what times this call handler considers standard (business hours) and what times are considered closed (after business hours). Back in the old days, these were referred to as day and night schedules, but in this 24×7×365 world, night is not necessarily closed time for businesses. The schedule comes into play when deciding which transfer rule or greeting rule to trigger when callers reach the call handler.

The Extension field is an optional 3- to 30-digit extension that can be assigned to the handler. Subscribers allow up to 30 digits in their extensions to accommodate SIP-based addresses; application call handlers are limited to 10 digits, assuming that they are dialable extensions only. In most cases, sites that use many call handlers to create complex audio-text trees do not want to clutter the numbering space in their system by assigning extension numbers to these handlers. The only time that you would want to have an extension number here is if you wanted callers to be able to dial the ID of a handler directly from the opening greeting, or if you wanted to have a call handler dealing with calls forwarded from a specific phone extension into Unity.

The Language field indicates the language in which the system prompts are played to callers who reach this handler. It is important to note that this affects *only* the system prompts that make up the conversation ("I will transfer you now," "Please hold on while I transfer your call," and so on). The bulk of what callers hear are the custom-recorded greetings by the customer, and there is only one set of those for each call handler. This means that you need separate sets of handlers to deal with each language that you want to support.

Also of note here is that, by default, the language is set to Inherited, as shown in Figure 18-1. Whatever language the call has been set to is the language that the call handler uses. Unity employs a "tag, you are it" language model in which a call can be tagged with a language when it enters the system. That language follows the call until it hits an object (such as a call handler) that is set to a specific language. Then the call is tagged with that language until it runs into another object set for a specific language. This is important when designing multiple-language audio-text applications; we cover the details of this process in the "Scenario Examples" section later in this chapter.

The Switch field is visible on your system only if you have two switch integrations installed. This field indicates which phone switch the call handler is associated with, in case Unity is configured for dual-switch support. Unity knows which switch an inbound call is associated with. If the call handler is associated with the other switch, it knows that it needs to use the prefix (if defined) for sending calls from one switch to the other, or vice versa. This is necessary if a call comes in on a CallManager line, for instance, and the call handler is set up to ring the phone on an analog PBX extension (see the "Call Transfer" section, next). This value defaults to the first switch (switch 0) defined in the system.

Call Transfer

Figure 18-2 shows the call-transfer page for the "say goodbye" application call handler in the SA interface.

We talk a little about when and how the transfer rules are processed for call handlers and subscribers in the "Call Handler Flow" section, later in this chapter. For now, we just define the options here.

Figure 18-2 *Call Transfer Page for Call Handlers in the SA*

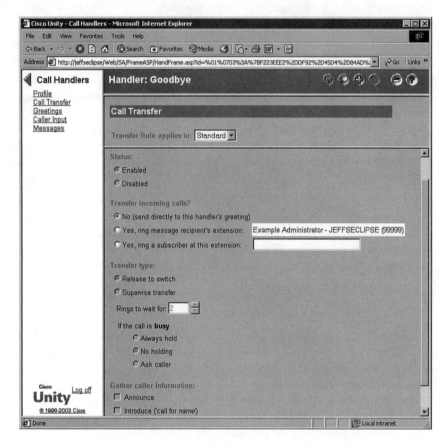

The status is either enabled or disabled. However, notice in Figure 18-2 that the buttons are disabled and Enabled is set. This is because the selected transfer rule is Standard, which never can be disabled. For call handlers, there are three transfer rules: standard, off-hours (called closed on the SA), and alternate. Both the off-hours and alternate rules can be enabled and disabled as desired, but at least one transfer rule always must be active, to tell Unity what to do with the call if it enters the transfer conversation for this call handler. The standard rule, then, is treated as the "backstop" transfer rule and always is enabled. A similar principal applies to greeting rules, which we cover in the "Call Handler Flow" section later.

Note that on the subscriber page in the SA, the transfers do not show a drop-down list for selecting one of the three. This is because subscribers are limited to one transfer rule that is either on or off; they do not have a selection of three as application call handlers have. This was done originally to simplify the subscriber options conversation, and it needs to be updated. This is the only thing that you can do with call handlers that you cannot do with subscribers, and it sometimes is an annoying limitation to have to work around. We cover such a scenario in the examples section later.

The Transfer incoming calls section lets you decide whether Unity will attempt to ring a phone, which number to dial, or whether you want to skip the transfer attempt entirely and proceed to the greeting rules. Note that you can use any number that you want in the transfer string, including long-distance or international numbers, as long as the Transfers restriction table associated with your class of service (CoS) allows it. This is an important concept and is probably one of the most commonly misunderstood parts of the Unity administration design. The restriction tables are enforced *only* when the number is changed; Unity uses the restriction tables of the person *making the change* to test this. When a number is in a notification delivery dialout, transfer, or fax delivery number field, Unity uses it. This is not checked again at dialout time or any other time.

In this way, individual subscribers can be restricted from making any changes, if desired, and administrators (who presumably have highly flexible restriction table settings) can adjust various dialout numbers in the SA as desired. If you trust your users, you can give them options to change their own numbers, but this model is built around the idea that sites normally restrict end users from such things and expect administrators to be trustworthy people.

The Transfer type field tells Unity to either dial the number and hang up (Release), or stay on the line to see if the called number answers (Supervised). Supervised transfers are useful because they offer some nice features, including call screening and call holding; however, they also tie up voice ports longer. Many sites prefer to have Unity release the call to the switch as quickly as possible. If the transfer type is set to Release, the remainder of the options on this page are disabled because they do not apply.

The Rings to wait for supervised transfers setting indicates how long Unity waits before deciding that a phone is not answering and pulls back the call. This value must be at least 2, but it is advisable to have more rings than that. If you have your phone system set to forward to voice mail on a Ring No Answer condition, you need to make sure that Unity is set to ring fewer times than the phone system is set to forward on—otherwise, Unity might end up talking to itself. You also want to remember not to set the phones to forward on busy when using supervised transfers because, again, you can end up forwarding the phone right back to Unity.

The If the call is busy option allows Unity to hang on to the call and play a series of hold music prompts (recorded classical music). After each hold music prompt is played (roughly 30 seconds a shot), Unity checks the line to see if the phone is still busy. If not, the call goes through; if so, Unity asks the user whether it should continue to hold. There is no way to turn off the option for Unity to prompt the user to stay on the line. This is designed to make sure that someone does not tie up a voice line for too long. In general, if your phone system can handle queuing calls, it is highly recommended that you make use of this option and not use voice-mail ports for call holding. This option is generally there for smaller phone systems that do not offer holding services.

It should be noted that you cannot use Unity's call-holding feature if your phones are set to forward on busy. Again, for Unity to know that the phone is busy, you must get a busy signal back from the switch; if the phone is set to forward somewhere, you might not get that.

The Gather caller information section consists of four options:

- **Announce**. If this is checked, Unity plays a short beep tone when the subscriber answers the phone. This is to warn the subscriber that it an external caller is coming through the auto-attendant, not Bob down the hall who wants to hear you scream "Whatsuuuuup!" into the phone.

- **Introduce**. If this is checked, Unity plays the voice name of the subscriber the call is for ("call for <voice name>") before releasing the call to the subscriber's extension. This is used when more than one subscriber shares the same phone extension.

- **Confirm**. If this is checked, the subscriber is asked whether to take the call or send it to voice mail before the call is released to the extension. This normally is used in conjunction with the Ask caller's name option so that you know who is calling and can decide whether you want to talk to that person. If the call is rejected, Unity smoothly lies to the caller and says that you are busy or away from your phone.

- **Ask caller's name**. With this checked, Unity asks the caller to speak his name before ringing the subscriber's phone. This recorded name is played to the subscriber before the call is released to the extension. Normally, this is used in conjunction with Confirm so that the subscriber can accept or reject the call.

Subscribers cannot change their own transfer type through the Personal Communications Assistant (PCA) web interface, so the Holding and Gather caller information options are not enabled on their individual interfaces unless the administrator has set their transfer type to Supervised. This is done because admins usually want to control features that can tie up voice-mail ports on their system, and restrict who can use them.

NOTE   A little-known and undocumented feature on the transfer page enables you to insert replacement variables into the transfer string itself. You can include the forwarding station number, the calling number, the dialed number, the trunk, or the voice-mail port number into the dial string itself. Say, for instance, that you want to have Unity send the caller to a different extension based on the number dialed to reach Unity. You might have ports 1 through 8 set up for different languages and want to be able to transfer to different operators based on the port called. You can have the transfer go to extension 1001 through 1008 by tacking on the port number to the right and using that as your transfer string. You can create eight different call handlers and do this manually with routing rules, but using this method you can use just a single call handler. To do this, you can make the dial string look like this:

```
"100%Port%"
```

Assuming that the call came in on port 7, the resulting dial string Unity that actually would send when transferring the call would be "1007". Here is a list of all the valid replacement variables that you can use (these are case sensitive and must be bounded on either side by %, as shown previously):

```
"Forwarding_Station"
"Calling_Number"
"Dialed_Number"
"Trunk"
"Port"
"Extension"
```

This also can be used when forwarding a call to an IVR system, for instance, as follows on DTMF digits for routing a call to a specific location in the IVR.

If you want to get only the leftmost or rightmost *X* digits, insert a number after the left or before the right % character respectively. For instance, if you want to include the rightmost four digits from the dialed number, include this in your dial string: `%Dialed_Number4%`. Only a single digit is allowed on either side, and you can get only left or right—you cannot get, say, the leftmost two digits and the rightmost two digits from the same number. The SA complains if you try to enter that.

If the value for the variable that you include is not provided by the switch integration or is blank for that particular call, Unity just inserts nothing and dials the remaining digits defined in the string. If there are no other digits in the string, the transfer simply is not attempted and Unity proceeds as if the call were RNA. This can cause problems with busy features and the like, so use this feature with caution. Definitely test what the switch sends in all cases to be sure that you know how it will behave.

Some of you probably are thinking, "Cool! I can stuff these same variables in my tone or text pager notification devices." Yeah, that would be cool, but, no, you cannot do this. These variables are active only on live calls and are not stored with the message, which is what activates the notification dialout. The calling number is included in the subject line of the message; it would be possible to dig that out and offer it as an option in the information included in pages, but that is not available today. Even cooler would be the option to have a conversation *ask* the caller what number he can be reached at if the subscriber wants that, and include that in the page. These type of "find me, follow me" features are all on wish lists, but I cannot say when they will hit the streets. As usual, ping your account team and let it know which types of such features are important to you so that these are prioritized appropriately.

Another important limitation can be noted about this: The SA still enforces the 30-character limit for transfer strings, which includes all the characters in the variable name. As such, if your transfer string includes `%Forwarding_Station%`, you use up 20 of your 30 characters right off the bat. You can insert more than one variable into the string, if you like, but you quickly run out of available digits allowed in the string, so this is not very practical; we have a hard time coming up with a scenario in which this would be necessary.

Greetings

Figure 18-3 shows the greeting page for the "say goodbye" application call handler in the SA interface.

Figure 18-3 *The Greetings Page for Call Handlers in the SA*

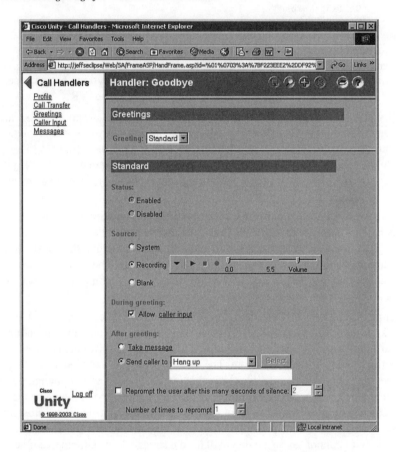

When a transfer attempt fails, Unity proceeds to the greeting rules. A caller can also be routed directly to the greeting rules in some cases and can skip the transfer attempt altogether. We talk about this in a bit when we discuss call flow through the handlers.

Six greetings exist for each call handler in the system, although, by default, only five show up in the SA. The usual list of greetings includes alternate, standard, off-hours (closed), internal, and busy greetings. The error greeting is the sixth and is hidden by default because it tends to be a confusing concept and rarely needs to be edited in most cases. You can expose it in the SA by using the Advanced Settings Tool, if you want to see it. The error greeting is exposed in the Audio Text Manager all the time. You can also access it in the

Bulk Edit utility, which offers some options for changing its behavior across groups of subscribers and call handlers.

The status can be enabled or disabled. Notice again in Figure 18-3 that the buttons are disabled and that the Enabled option is set. Similar to the transfer rule behavior discussed earlier, this is because the selected greeting rule is standard, which can never be disabled. One greeting always must be active to serve as the "backstop," and that is the standard greeting here. Error greetings cannot be disabled, either, but that is because they serve a special purpose and are not included in the normal hierarchy of greeting rules precedence that the other five greetings are in. We cover the order precedence of the greetings and the function of the error greeting in the "Greeting Rules" section later.

The Source section indicates what Unity should play to the caller when this greeting rule is invoked. The System option governs Unity's act of constructing a prompt using the voice name of the subscriber or call handler (if present); the extension number, if it is not there; or, failing both of those, the voice name or extension of the message recipient for the call handler. It is a generic sounding "Jeff Lindborg is busy or not available." The Recording option is just what it sounds like: a custom-recorded greeting that is played to callers. Blank means just that: No greeting is played, and the system skips right to the after-greeting action. This is useful for various call-flow scenarios in which you use call handlers to route calls around the system. We cover a couple of these scenarios in the example sections later.

The Allow Caller Input option is a short way of turning off all user-input keys while this greeting is active. This option affects only the current greeting, so you can, say, have a standard greeting that allows user input but have the closed greeting not accept any input. Remember that all greetings share the same set of user input keys; there are no separate sets of user input mappings. Turning off this option also restricts users from dialing other extension numbers while listening to the greeting.

After Greeting Action determines what Unity will do with the call after the greeting defined in the Source section completes. Normally, this is set to Take Message, by default, but you have full routing options here: You can do anything from simply hanging up to sending the call to a call handler of your choice, to going to the subscriber sign-in conversation.

The Reprompt section at the very bottom confuses some people; I have gotten a number of "bug" reports with Unity playing the greeting multiple times. Part of the problem is that this option is at the bottom of the greetings page, which often does not show up unless you scroll down to see it. This option is here if you are expecting input from a caller and nothing is entered. By default, this value is 0, meaning that the greeting is played only one time and then the after-greeting action is executed. You can wait a set number of seconds and then replay the greeting, giving callers another chance to enter a selection provided in the greeting. You can set it to reprompt many times, but once or twice is normally as many as you want. If someone cannot figure out what to do after three times through the greeting, it is probably time to send the caller to a human operator for assistance.

Caller Input

Figure 18-4 shows the caller-input page for the "say goodbye" application call handler in the SA interface.

Figure 18-4   *Caller-Input Page for Call Handlers in the SA*

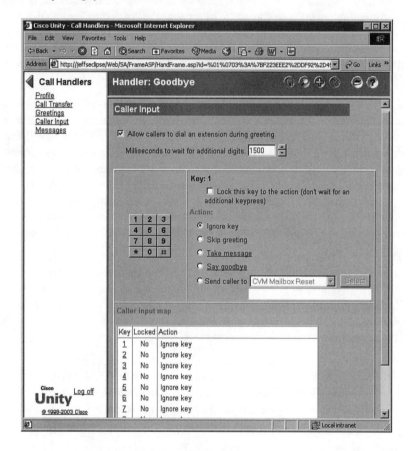

The caller-input page is probably the source of the most confusion and configuration errors that I have seen in the field. From a high level, the concept of the user input page is very simple. You can define actions that Unity takes when users enter digits 0 through 9, *, or # while listening to a greeting for this call handler or subscriber. The same set of key-action mappings in this user-input page is active for all greetings for the call handler (we cover one way to work around this limitation in the Separate Caller-Input Options for Day and Off-Hours Schedules section later). The difficulty for most people, however, is understanding how the user-input keys interact with the capability to dial extensions from a greeting.

Typically, the one-key rules (as they are called internally) are used to construct trees of call handlers that users can navigate through to get to the information they want, leave a message for a group of people, find someone in the directory, or the like. Of course, these are at the heart of any robust audio-text application. Beyond just linking to other handlers, you can have a one-key action take a message, skip to the end of the greeting, send the caller to the sign-in conversation, go to the new greetings administration conversation, and so on—you have a lot of control over what you can do here.

Things get tricky when you allow the callers to either enter one-key options mapped to specific actions, or free-dial extensions of other objects in the database during the greeting. This is where the concepts of locking down a key and tweaking the interdigit delay come into play and confuse some people. Here is the short version:

> If user input is allowed during a greeting (see the greetings page, discussed earlier), the greeting plays through until the caller presses a key. At this point (with one exception noted later), the greeting stops playing and Unity waits for the interdigit timeout period; this is the Milliseconds to Wait for Additional Digits field at the top of the form. If no further digits are entered, the action associated with that key is taken. If the action is Ignore, Unity considers this an error and sends the call to the error greeting. By default, this greeting says, "I am sorry—I did not hear that entry," and then sends the caller to the opening greeting call handler created by setup (this can be changed, as noted later in the "Scenario Examples" section).

> If the user enters more digits, Unity continues to collect digits until the user stops for the timeout period or presses # to terminate the input process. Unity then looks up that string of digits in the database to see if any extension number for a call handler, interview handler, subscriber, or name-lookup handler matches. If a match is found, the call is sent off to that object. If no match is found, Unity again considers this an error and sends the call to the error greeting.

When a key is locked, if that is the first digit that the user enters to interrupt the greeting, the action associated with the key takes place immediately, without waiting for the inter digit timeout for more digits to be entered. If the key's action is set to Locked *and* Ignore, however, the key is thrown away and the greeting is not interrupted. This is a handy way to not allow outside callers to dial extensions that begin with a particular number. For instance, if your engineers all have extensions that start with 7 and you do not want outside callers being able to dial them directly, you can set key 7 for Locked and Ignore for all call handlers in your audio-text application; they then cannot reach these extensions directly. Bugs in earlier versions of Unity up through 3.1 allowed the locked keys to be acted on immediately, even if they were not the first digit that the user entered; this caused all kinds of interesting issues. Those problems have been resolved in 4.0.

The concept really is not that complex; it is just a matter of understanding that the user-input page affects both one-key actions and the capability to dial extensions freely while the active greeting is plays.

One final note on this page is necessary: unchecking allow callers to dial an extension during the greeting is simply shorthand for locking all the keys. When a user enters a digit, it is acted on immediately and there is never any period during which Unity waits to see if the caller enters more digits. This is different than unchecking the Allow caller input box on the greeting page. If you do that, it is the same as locking all the keys *and* setting them to Ignore. No input is allowed, and the greeting never interrupts.

Messages

Figure 18-5 shows the messages page for the goodbye call handler in the SA.

Figure 18-5 *Messages Page for Call Handlers in the SA*

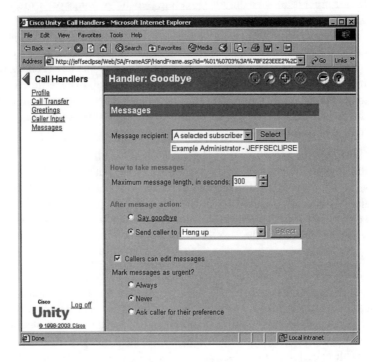

The messages page is pretty straightforward. The primary input here involves designating which subscriber or public distribution list should get messages if the call handler has an after-greeting or one-key option set to take a message. Even if no option in the handler is configured to let callers leave a message, you still must have a valid subscriber or distribution list designated here.

The first thing Unity does when it loads a call handler is fetch the recipient. If no recipient exists (if you deleted the subscriber that you had set as the recipient), Unity sends the call to the ever-popular failsafe greeting, and the caller is sent to the opening greeting call handler (in 3.*x* and earlier, the caller simply was hung up on), with some helpful information written into the application event log concerning what happened. DbWalker is designed to help you locate and fix such broken links; deleting subscribers and handlers through the updated Global Subscriber Manager tool prevents such broken links in the first place.

Maximum message length does exactly what it says: You can limit the number of seconds that a caller can record for. Note that this does not affect subscribers leaving messages for other subscribers. This value affects only outside callers leaving messages for subscribers. You can dictate how long of a message any given subscriber can leave in the subscriber's class of service on the messages page. By default, all subscribers can leave 300-second (5-minute) messages for other subscribers. If you want to extend this or, more likely, trim it back, you can do that in the CoS settings.

TIP   By default, Unity does not warn callers when they near the end of their recording session. However, you can turn on three settings in the Advanced Settings Tool to help: All three start with "Record Termination Warning." Using them, you can instruct Unity to play a beep or a WAV file that you dictate to callers when they approach the end of their recording leash. This works only with CallManager switch integrations. Dialogic board drivers do not support this functionality.

The after-message action section dictates what Unity does with the caller after the message is left. By default, this is set to go to the "say goodbye" call handler. Notice that this section looks similar but not identical to the after-greeting and user-input action sections. Fewer options exist here because, after leaving a message, for instance, it does not make sense to select Take Message. That would be pretty obnoxious, so we removed the option.

You can also decide whether users can rerecord or append to their message with the Callers can edit message check box, and whether they can mark the message as urgent. The option to always mark messages as urgent can be handy if you have a high-priority, after-hours, problem line. You can configure the handler so that all messages taken through it are marked as urgent and, for instance, trigger a pager dialout in the notification devices for the subscriber(s) who get messages from that handler.

Call Handler Flow

We have run through the basic call-handling elements that make up a call handler and subscriber object in the database. The key to grasping how call handlers work is understanding how calls flow into, through, and out of them. Call handlers were built to process calls in a sequential way, which is not apparent by just looking at the administration interfaces provided by the SA and the Audio Text Manager applications.

Call handlers are the grandson of a transaction box provided in an earlier DOS-based voicemail product. The old ASCII-based interface actually showed this very intuitively, with the transfer rules on the left, the greeting rules in the middle, and the after-greeting actions on the right. You can see at a glance that calls flowed from left to right and then exited. (Of course, there were not nearly as many options to deal with then, and everything fit on a couple of text-based pages that were 80 characters wide. Still, the clunky old interface was much more effective at conveying how these objects worked.)

A call handler flows through four separate "stages" in its life cycle. Transfer rules (contact rules, in the SQL database) are executed first; then, if necessary, the greeting rules (messaging rules in the database) are evaluated, followed by the after-greeting action and then, if necessary, the after-message action. Figure 18-6 is a rather ungainly graphical representation of that flow.

The first thing to notice is that there are exactly two entry points into a call handler. You can jump in at the top and start with the transfer rules, or you can jump in right at the greeting rules. The idea here is that many times you want to send a caller directly to the greeting for a subscriber or a call handler without ringing the phone; sometimes you want to ring the phone. The default when you choose to send a call to either a call handler or a subscriber is to go directly to the greetings and skip the transfer rules. This throws a lot of people off the trail. We have probably answered the question of, "Why is the phone not ringing?" as a result of this more than 200 times in the last three years or so. This option is selected in the Conversation drop-down list when you choose which handler or subscriber you want to send the call to, as shown in Figure 18-7.

Leaving the default Send to greeting for skips the transfer rules. Selecting Attempt transfer for starts at the top of the flow with the transfer rules. The choice of the term *conversation* here is questionable, at best, because it requires administrators to understand that these are separate conversations that are invoked, with the ID of the call handler being passed into it. This concept is not evident anywhere else in the administration interfaces and is not discussed in the documentation. Just remember that the PHTransfer is the "attempt transfer for" conversation and PHGreeting is the "send to greeting for" conversation. As you will remember from the data object model discussion in Chapter 3, "Components and Subsystems: Object Model," the PH stands for Phone Handler, the original term for call handlers before we changed it before the release of 1.0.

The next sections start at the top and work down through Figure 18-7.

Figure 18-6 *Call Flow Through a Call Handler*

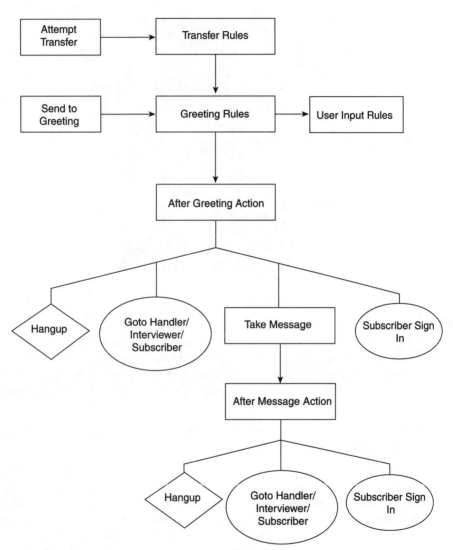

Figure 18-7 *Call Handler Selection Dialog Box in the SA*

Transfer Rules

In Figure 18-7, the top of the flowchart is the transfer entry point. In the SA, this is characterized with the Attempt transfer for selection. In the database, this is characterized using the PHTransfer conversation to get to the call handler. Remember that even when sending a call to a subscriber, you go to a call handler; it is the primary call handler that is associated with that subscriber record.

In the database itself, the transfer rules are referenced as contact rules. In the SA, they are shown as transfer rules. We use both terms interchangeably here because they mean the same thing.

If the call handler is an application handler (a "normal" call handler instead of a primary call handler associated with a subscriber), three rules can be active here. The order of precedence is simple, in this case. If the alternate transfer rule is enabled, it is evoked no matter what. It overrides the other rules, which are never called until the alternate rule is disabled. After that, if the schedule that the call handler is associated with indicates that it is after hours and the after-hours contact rule is enabled, the off-hours transfer rule is triggered. In all other cases, the standard contact rule is the one used. Remember that you cannot disable the standard greeting, so you always can count on it to be there.

Remember, however, that if the call handler is a primary handler tied to a subscriber, the alternate transfer rule is hard-coded as active and cannot be disabled. For subscribers, transfers are very basic indeed: They are either on or off.

It is common for people to fiddle endlessly with the standard contact rule and not realize that the alternate rule is active. They end up calling for help when trying to figure out why Unity is so obstinate and is not transferring to the phone that they want for this call handler. We normally recommend using the alternate transfer rule when testing call flows for this reason. That way, you do not have to worry about what time of day it is (frazzled field techs testing late at night often miss the fact that it is not day anymore) or which rules are enabled. With the alternate rule active, you know what you are working with.

It should be noted here that it is perfectly okay for a contact rule to do nothing but send the call to the greetings. We often are asked if people should send calls to the greetings directly in all cases or to transfer rules. We always advise them to send to the Attempt transfer for if they think that they might want to ring the phone. Then simply change the contact rules on the call handler in question to turn it on or off. If you have 100 call handlers sending calls to a handler's greeting, and you then decide that you want to have that phone ring during the day, for instance, you have a much bigger cleanup job on your hands. There is no performance hit for entering a call handler at the contact rule entry point and then falling through to the greeting rules.

One scenario skips the transfer rules. When a call forwards from an extension into Unity, by default, Unity searches for the original forwarding extension among all call handlers and subscribers. If it is found, the call is sent directly to the greetings for that call handler; no attempt is made to go to the transfer rules, even if they are active. This is done so that Unity does not get caught in a transfer loop, with a call forwarding into Unity and then being forwarded to the extension, which, of course, forwards back to Unity and so on. This quickly uses all your available ports and causes all kinds of problems.

In some special scenarios, however, you want Unity to dial an extension in this case. We cover a tricky way to get around this issue in the "Scenario Examples" section later.

Greeting Rules

The greeting rules have a much more complex order of precedence. The five greetings used for handling incoming calls are processed in order from the top down. The first enabled rule in this list that matches the call criteria is used to handle the call.

- **Alternate**. At the top of the heap, of course, is the alternate greeting. Again, if it is active, all other greetings are ignored; this greeting then always plays, no matter where the call came from or what schedule the call handler is associated with.

- **Busy**. This handles the call if the call forwards into Unity from a busy extension, the phone switch integration passes along this information accurately, and the busy greeting is enabled.

- **Internal**. If the calling number is reported and corresponds to the extension (either primary or alternate) of a subscriber homed on the local Unity server, it is considered an internal call. If the internal greeting is active, it is used to handle the call. The internal definition is important: It does not mean that the caller is on the local phone switch to which Unity is hooked up; it means that the caller is a known subscriber. It also has nothing to do with the Origin property on an inbound call, which shows up in the Call Viewer as Internal or External. It is based solely on the calling number that matches the extension of a known local subscriber. The idea here is that employees might want to give other employees different information in their greetings that they do not want nonemployees getting (for instance, indicating where they *really* are that week).

- **Off-hours**. If the schedule a call handler indicates that it is off-hours and this greeting is enabled, the off-hours greeting handles the call.

- **Standard**. If all other rules are disabled or fail to match the call data, the standard rule is invoked. Remember that you never can disable the standard greeting); Unity can count on this rule always being enabled.

The error greeting also exists, but it is not included in the flow of precedence here. The error greeting is invoked only when the user enters an invalid selection or dials an extension number that does not exist; it never is used to handling incoming calls directly. This is an important greeting for dealing with routing calls around your audio-text applications, however. Modifying the behavior of this greeting rule is discussed later in the "Example Scenarios" section.

After-Greeting Action

As the name implies, Unity takes this action after the greeting is played. Each greeting has its own action field, of course, so you can do different things, depending on which greeting is active for a given call. By default, this is set to Take Message because, most of the time, that is what you want to do. However, you can do what you want with it, such as send the call to another handler, hang up, or even go to the subscriber sign-in conversation, if you like. This becomes especially important when using a call handler as a router with a blank greeting, which is handy for several scenarios.

After-Message Action

After taking a message, the default action is to go to the "say goodbye" call handler and hang up on the user politely. You can pick other actions, but the list is a little smaller here because you are not allowed to select Take a Message as the after-message action—that would be pretty annoying for callers.

Subscribers

This is a very short section because subscribers and call handlers are almost identical with respect to their call-handling characteristics. As was discussed in the "Data Object Model" section in Chapter 3, subscribers are really two separate objects that work together. There is a mail user object and its corresponding primary call handler. This is just a call handler that is assigned to a subscriber; it does not appear in the call handler search dialog boxes. In all respects except one, subscribers have the same call-handling characteristics and capabilities as regular application call handlers do. A quick look at the SA interfaces for subscribers and call handlers quickly shows that their call-handling features are nearly identical, with one exception.

That one difference, however, can be a real nuisance. Subscribers have only one transfer rule instead of the full three that regular call handlers have. This is accomplished by forcing primary call handlers to always have their alternate contact rule enabled. This is the rule that is visible on the SA interface for subscribers. It is not possible to disable this or use the other two rules, even if you hack the database on your own.

Reaching back through the fog of history, the reasoning for this course of action is a little murky. The conversation people wanted to keep the subscriber options as limited as possible; having to deal with three transfer rules instead of one that is either on or off all the time simplified things a great deal. Backed up against a whole series of rather brutal "hard" schedule requirements, lots of little things like this got hacked out along the way.

This is one of those things that was going to be addressed in the ever-present "later version" and just never got picked up. Some years later, we still find ourselves with this state of affairs, which is a bit frustrating because often a subscriber wants one phone to ring during the day and another to ring off-hours. This requires the use of an extra call handler now.

This is on deck to finally get addressed in a later version, although I do not know which one.

Interview Handlers

An interview handler is a specialized handler that is designed to interrogate a user for specific information so they do not forget to provide, for instance, their product serial number, return phone number or whatever else you need callers to provide. An interviewer is considerably less complex than a call handler or subscriber because there is no user input options, call transfer options or the like. This handler is, as they say, a one trick pony. Figures 18-8 and 18-9 show the only two screens you will see in the SA for these objects.

Figure 18-8 *Profile Page for Interview Handler in the SA.*

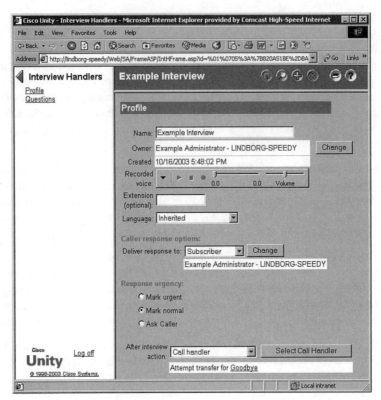

Most of the options shown on the profile page in Figure 18-8 are identical to those found on the call handler or subscriber profile pages, and they mean the same thing. As with call handlers, owners and message recipients exist for interview handlers. However, the owner does not have special meaning in Unity for interviewers as it does for call handlers in 4.0(1) and later. Of course, responses can be delivered to a specific subscriber or a public distribution list just like call handlers can. Extensions are optional and typically are left blank. Normally, interview handlers are reached through one-key dial options or as after-greeting action links or the like because it would be pretty unusual to expect outside callers to dial an extension to reach an interviewer.

The only call-routing option you have for call handlers is shown at the very bottom of the profile page. You can decide where callers are sent when they finish leaving their message for the interviewer. By default, this sends them to the Say Goodbye call handler created by Unity setup, which is the same as the after-message action defaults for call handlers and subscribers as well.

The heart of the interviewer, however, is the list of questions played to callers and the time limit for their responses (see Figure 18-9). You can construct up to 20 separate questions that can be asked of callers in a interview handler, although expecting callers to sit through a grueling interrogation like that is probably a little on the optimistic side.

Figure 18-9 *Questions Page for Interview Handlers in the SA*

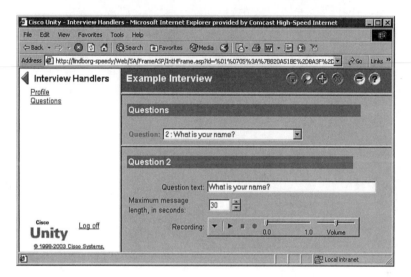

Callers hear each question that you record and are given the number of seconds that you dictate to record a response. If the user hits * or # (all other keys are ignored) during a response portion, it advances to the next question; it does not skip all the questions and advance to the after-message action. Essentially, callers are trapped in the interview handler until they give some response to each question. This is one of the reasons you probably want to keep the number of questions to a reasonable limit. The questions are asked in the order that they are listed in the drop-down list in Figure 18-9.

In the SA, unfortunately, there is no easy way to delete a question from the middle of the list or rearrange the questions. The Audio Text Manager tool, however, allows this. You can find this tool in the Tools Depot on your desktop in the Administration Tools section. As with most tools, you can also find the latest version at www.ciscounitytools.com.

The message is left as a series of WAV file attachments, one for each question. Even if the user is silent or presses # immediately, a WAV file attachment is included for that question. The one exception to this is the last question asked: If the user presses * or # right away, the last question is not included. Figure 18-10 shows what you would see in Outlook with VMO installed if a message for an interviewer were delivered to your inbox.

Figure 18-10 *E-Mail with WAV Attachments from an Interview Handler*

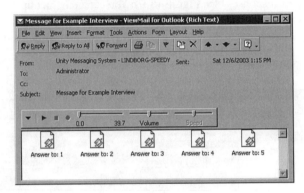

The media master control in the VMO form automatically appends all the WAV files into one file, so the 39.7 seconds shown in Figure 18-10 is the cumulative total for all five answers attached to the message. When you call in over the phone to listen to your messages, the answers are played with a beep tone inserted between each answer, to help distinguish responses and more easily identify blank responses. When playing back using the VMO form or the PCA web-based inbox view, these beeps are not inserted.

Directory Handlers

A directory handler is a mechanism by which callers can find subscribers in the directory by spelling their name, starting with either the last name or the first name. These also sometimes are referred to as alpha directories; they are referenced internally as name-lookup handlers in the SQL database.

Versions of Unity before 4.0(1) had only a single, hard-coded directory handler. You could select to enter first name or last name first when searching for a subscriber; in 3.0(1) and later, you could choose to limit subscribers included in the search to those on the local Unity server or all subscribers on all Unity servers in the same dialing domain. You could tweak some list-presentation options, but that is as much customization as you had at your disposal. You also could not create additional directory handlers.

Big changes in the 4.0(1) release came to the directory handlers, however. You now can create as many directory handlers as you want, and you have numerous options for limiting the subscribers included in the search for each handler. For instance, you can create directory handlers for each department in your company or for each physical location. You even can present lists of subscribers without requiring callers to enter anything.

For each directory handler, there are four pages in the SA:

- Profile, shown in Figure 18-11
- Search options, shown in Figure 18-12
- Match list options, shown in Figure 18-13
- Caller input, shown in Figure 18-14

Figure 18-11 *Directory Handler Profile Page in the SA*

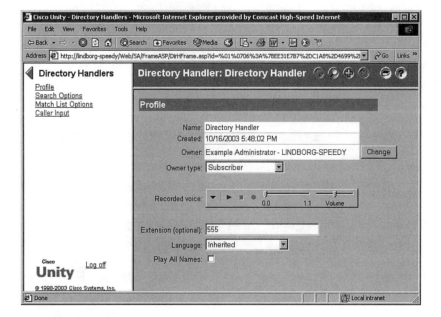

The profile page shown in Figure 18-11 looks identical to the directory handler profile pages in older versions of Unity, with the exception of the Play All Names check box option at the bottom. With this option checked, Unity does not ask users to spell the name of the subscriber. Instead, all the subscribers associated with that directory handler are listed in their entirety. This option is intended to help in areas where letters on the keypad used for spelling names are not the norm (such as in Japan).

Administrators can create numerous directory handlers that span all the users in a company and then provide a call-handler tree, enabling callers to narrow their search. For instance, you can have a directory handler for all subscribers whose last name begins with *A* or *B*, one for *C* or *D* or *E*, and so on, covering the entire alphabet (or character set of choice for the language in question). As long as the list of subscribers at the leaves of this tree are reasonably small, you can work through the problem. Clearly, a large company would have difficulty implementing such a plan, or callers would have to be patient and persistent to find the user they are looking for.

Again, the extension here is optional, and the owner means nothing at this point, similar to the interview handlers. However, the owner does need to be filled in with a valid subscriber or distribution list, or it will be considered an error. One question that we are asked periodically is what the recorded voice name on the directory handler is used for. The short answer is that it currently is used for nothing. It never is played over the phone, and because you cannot edit directory handlers over the phone interface, the only time you ever see or hear it is on the SA interface itself. You can record one, if you want, but it serves no direct purpose at this point.

The search options page shown in Figure 18-12 is considerably different in 4.x than in previous versions.

Figure 18-12 *Search Options Page for Directory Handlers in the SA*

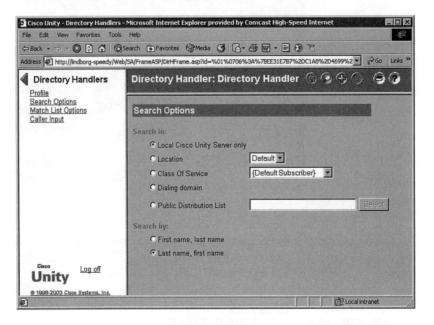

This page enables administrators to decide which subscribers are included in the search list when users spell the name of a user they are searching for in the directory. Remember, subscribers here include both full subscribers and remote subscribers (AMIS, Bridge, VPIM, and SMTP subscribers). Here is how the options break down:

- **Local Cisco Unity Server only**. All subscribers (both full and remote) who were created on the local Unity server are included. This does not mean that their mailboxes need to be stored on the local Unity server; this means that they are associated with the local Unity server. This an important distinction that confuses some people. If multiple Unity servers are on your network, users in the other Unity servers are not included in this search.

- **Location**. This enables you to select a delivery location created on the local Unity server or the default primary location that all full subscribers are associated with. You cannot select a location object from another Unity server on the network; this is simply a way to limit subscriber searches to subsets of the subscribers on the local Unity box. Specifically, it is a way to limit searches to just full subscribers (select the primary location created by setup) or to a group of remote subscribers (VPIM, AMIS, SMTP, or Bridge subscribers). Remember, unlike in earlier versions of Unity, all remote subscribers other than SMTP (Internet) subscribers must be associated with a delivery location. This option provides a way to screen remote subscribers if you do not want callers to find them in the directory.

- **Class Of Service**. This option limits the search to subscribers associated with a class of service on the local Unity server.

- **Dialing domain**. This limits searches to all subscribers on all Unity servers in the directory who are associated with the same dialing domain that the local Unity server is in. If the local Unity server is not in a dialing domain, this has the same effect as selecting the Local Unity Server only option. See the networking discussion in Chapter 12, "Unity Networking," for more information on dialing domains and how they work.

- **Public Distribution List**. This was the toughest option to add and the most powerful. This enables you to select any public distribution list in the directory and limit subscribers searches to that list. The public distribution list can contain nonsubscribers, of course, because the lists actually reside in Exchange 5.5, Active Directory, or Domino. Nonsubscribers in the list simply are ignored.

A couple of notes about the Public Distribution List option need to be mentioned here. When a member is added or removed from a public distribution list that is used as a scope filter for a name-lookup handler, Unity must traverse the entire distribution list membership, including all subdistribution lists. It constructs a full, flattened list of subscribers in that list, which is stored in SQL. There is simply no way for Unity to go to the directory dynamically and do a lookup of a user by name in a list that is stored externally in the directory fast enough to be acceptable over the phone interface—the list must be flattened and stored locally. As such, if you make a change to the list and then immediately test it over the phone, the list might not have been updated locally in SQL yet.

Unity checks for changes to all objects it cares about, including these distribution lists, every 1 to 10 minutes, by default. For Exchange 5.5 it is every 10 minutes, for Active Directory (Exchange 2000 or 2003) it is every 2 minutes, and for Domino it is every

1 minute. This is the synch time for the directory monitor; this can be adjusted in the Registry, but it really should be left alone because each directory has its own characteristics that mandate the different default synchronization times. See Chapter 2, "Unity Architecture Overview," for more details on how the directory monitor itself works.

The distribution lists used for scope restrictions on directory handlers (called scope lists internally) and distribution lists used as owners and recipients for handlers in Unity (called system lists internally) are represented separately in the local SQL database. In fact, if you use the same distribution list as a scope list and as, say, a message recipient for a call handler, that same distribution list shows up twice in the local SQL database: once in the ScopeDList table and once in the DistributionList table. Their respective members also are stored in separate tables (ScopeDListMembers and SystemDlistMembers, respectively). Membership information for scope lists is complete, which means that all sublists (and subsublists, and so on) are walked to get a full accounting of members in the list.

System lists, on the other hand, get only the top-level members of the list, meaning that subdistribution lists are not traversed, only noted as members. This does not have any real impact on administrators, but it could be of interest to people pulling information out of the local UnityDB database in SQL. We touch on this a bit further in the programmatic administration discussion in chapter 21.

The match list options page shown in Figure 18-13 has not changed since early versions of Unity 2.*x*.

Figure 18-13   *The Match List Options Page for Directory Handlers in the SA*

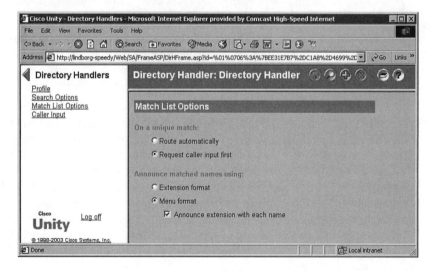

The On a unique match option lets you decide what the directory handler does with the caller when there is only one match to the name spelled. By default, it confirms the match with the user and asks the user to decide whether to transfer to the extension. You can change the behavior to not ask and send the user right to the subscriber's transfer rules instead.

The Announce matched names using option lets you determine how the list of matches is presented to the user. By default, it lists the subscribers by voice name and gives the user the option of selecting the subscriber by position in the list ("for John Smith, press 1; for Tim Smith, press 2"). You can change this to require the user to enter the extension of the subscriber instead. You might want to do this if you want callers to remember the subscriber's extensions the next time, but there is no good reason to force this option.

The caller input page, shown in Figure 18-14, has been the same for some time as well. This is where administrators can decide how long Unity waits when users do not respond, how many times to present the list of matching subscribers, as well as where to go when exiting the directory handler.

Figure 18-14 *The Caller Input Page for Name-Lookup Handlers in the SA*

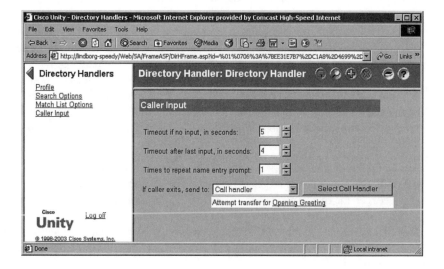

One thing to note here, however, is that the curious Unity aficionado poking around in SQL or DOHPropTest will notice that there are several exit events defined for a directory handler in the database: exit, no input, no selection, and zero. Currently, however only the exit events are exposed by the SA; as shown in Figure 18-14, this defaults to the opening greeting call handler created by setup. The SA sets all four exit actions to match what is selected, but the Audio Text Manager (ATM) application exposes all four exit options separately. If you need to have that level of control over the call exit points for your name-lookup handlers, you can use the ATM application found in the Tools Depot.

One of the most common problems that I see in the field with directory handlers in general is people getting frustrated that some subscribers are not included in the search when they spell their name. This is a bigger problem now that you have scope options on the Search Options page, but most of the time, there is a simple explanation for this.

Subscribers must have a recorded voice name *and* have the List in Phone Directory option set on their profile page. Otherwise, they automatically are excluded from any searches. The recorded voice name confuses a lot of people because it is not immediately obvious why that limitation would be in place. Cisco put that restriction in place because outside callers who spelled a user's name and got back a list of matches that did not include the voice names of everyone would not know which user to select.

Even if their extensions are included in the list, this still would not be of help: If the user knew the subscriber's extension in the first place, he simply would have dialed it directly instead of going through the directory handler. Yes, it would be handy if Unity would run the user's name through a TTS engine and generate the name on-the-fly for subscribers who have not recorded a name. However, TTS licensing issues come into play here (not every system ships with TTS enabled). In general, TTS engines are really bad at proper names unless they are spelled phonetically, which is not usually the case. This option might become available in later versions of Unity as we include alternate and improved TTS engines. If you need to find out which subscribers have recorded voice names and which do not, you can use the Subscriber Information Dump utility that ships with Unity 3.1(2) and later, and is also available on www.ciscounitytools.com.

Another point of confusion here is the relationship between the name-lookup handlers and subscribers addressing messages to one another. The short story is that there is no relationship between the two. We are often asked why a subscriber can find a user by name but that user does not appear in the name-lookup handler search using the same spelling. Again, if the voice name is not recorded, outside callers will not find that user. Subscribers, on the other hand, always get all matches, whether the user is listed in the directory or has a voice name recorded.

The changes to directory handlers take Unity 4.*x* one step closer to a proper tenant services capability. The big missing piece now is strict directory-segmentation capabilities. Directory-segmentation features that allow multiple companies to share a single Unity without bumping into each other's subscribers and audio-text applications over the phone interface are reasonably tough to crack well. If you add separate administration interfaces to that mix, it gets even more difficult. This is on the radar for Unity in the next major development cycle. We discuss some tenant services options and pitfalls in Unity 4.*x* later in the "Scenario Examples" section.

Routing Rules

Routing rules figure very prominently into handling inbound calls and can be critical for getting your auto-attendant applications working properly, particularly if you want to route callers to specific audio-text trees automatically based on the number they dialed or the like. Every call that comes into Unity goes through the call-routing rules, no matter what. Even if you never touch or look at the routing rules, they are critical to the proper functioning of the Unity server.

The routing rules are actually straightforward, from a high level. Unity gets information about a call coming in from the switch, which can include the calling number, the number it forwarded from, the dialed number, and so on. Unity then starts at the top of the list of routing rules and looks for the first rule that matches the information that it got from the switch. If that rule succeeds, the routing rules are done and the call is then in the hands of the Unity conversation as it passes around in the collection of call handlers, subscribers, interviewers, and name-lookup handlers in the database. If not, it proceeds to the next rule in the list until it finds a rule that succeeds.

A rule *always* succeeds here: A special rule at the bottom of the table is hard-coded to catch all calls and send them to the opening greeting call handler created by Unity setup, which cannot be deleted. Of course you can add your own rules to this list by going to the SA's routing rules page and adding new rules for forwarded or direct calls into the list. However, you cannot delete or move that hard-coded "send to opening greeting" rule in either list. It is there as a backstop, ensuring that Unity always can do something with an inbound call.

The key to understanding and using routing rules is knowing what information you get from the switch on an inbound call and realizing that the order in which the rules are processed is crucial to how calls are handled. If you put a perfectly valid new routing rule in the wrong place in the list, you can break all inbound call handling in a hurry. New rules become live on-the-fly, so, in general, you want to do your tinkering off-hours, when call volumes are lower. The "Troubleshooting" section at the end of this chapter covers how to restore the default routing rules in case you mess up your system so badly that you cannot get it back easily.

Checking Your Sources

Before you start making many custom routing rules, take the time to determine if information is coming into Unity from the phone switch (or switches, in the case of a dual integration). Many administrators repeatedly have changed their Unity routing rules and call-handler configurations in an attempt to make them work the way they want them to, only to discover that the source of the problem has nothing to do with Unity. Their switch configuration needed their attention because it passed some unexpected information to Unity on the inbound call.

The first step in customizing your routing rules should *always* be to launch the Call Viewer application and run some test calls from or to the numbers that you want to create routing rules for. You can find the Call Viewer in the Switch Integration Tools section of the Tools Depot (see Figure 18-15).

Figure 18-15 *Call Viewer Application*

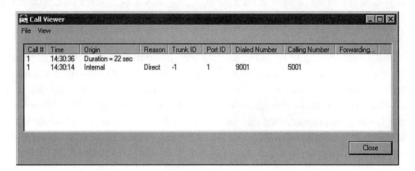

In fact, this application was designed specifically for use in creating and editing routing rules. The columns in Figure 18-15 correspond directly to the values that you can include in your custom routing rules. The call-routing rules pull their information from the exact same place that the Call Viewer does, so there can be no question of the data being manipulated between what you see and what the rules use. There is even an Always on Top option under the View menu so that you can see what comes in from the switch and look at your routing rules data on the SA at the same time. (We think of everything.) Note that the Call Viewer shows only incoming call information. Outdials for notification, MWI, or TRaP sessions do not show up in the Call Viewer.

Here is a quick rundown on what data shows up in the columns:

- **Call #**. This column is simply a counter of the number of calls that have come in since you opened the Call Viewer. When you start the Call Viewer, the first call to come in is call #1, the next is 2, and so on. This has nothing to do with the call information from the switch; it is just there to help you with troubleshooting (especially if you dump it to a file for later review). Notice that when a call terminates, another row is added with the same call number value and an indication of how long the call lasted.

- **Time**. This is the time that the call started or ended, depending on which row you look at.

- **Origin**. This can be internal or external. As noted later, you probably should not rely on this value coming from the switch because most do not provide an accurate flag here. If Unity is hooked up to CallManager, this value *always* is Internal.

- **Reason**. This can be either direct or one of three forwarding reasons: Busy, RNA (Ring No Answer), or Unconditional. As noted later in this section, you cannot make routing rules use the specific types of forwarding reasons.

- **Trunk ID**. This is the switch trunk that the call came in on, if provided. A value of 0 means that Unity knows there is no trunk information provided. A value of –1 means that Unity cannot tell what the trunk number is—or even if there is one. This is a subtle but important difference.

- **Port ID**. This is the Unity port that the call came in on. This can be useful if you have a dual-switch integration and you want to have different routing rules, depending on which switch the call came in on, for instance.

- **Dialed Number**. This is the original number that the caller dialed when coming into the system. This can be useful for creating multiple audio-text applications that callers are sent to based on the phone number they dialed. For instance, you could have one number published in a Spanish periodical and a different number published in a German periodical; callers using those two different numbers would get different audio-text trees in the appropriate language. It should be noted that, in some cases, this value does not correspond to the original dialed number. If the switch is set up with virtual extensions for mapping calls into the voice-mail ports, for instance, this value can be switched behind the scenes. However, this is what the switch reports as the dialed number. See Chapter 17, "Unity Telephony Integration," for more details on this type of thing.

- **Calling Number**. This is the calling number, if provided. Unity includes the ANI information of external callers in the subject line of the message left, if it is provided by the switch integration.

- **Forwarding Station**. This is the number of the station that forwarded to the Unity ports. Note that if a call forwards from one Unity port to the next until a free line is found, the forwarding number reported is the original forwarding station, not the last redirecting number. The last redirecting number is not exposed anywhere in Unity.

As noted, as a general rule, the origin should not be trusted because very few switches actually send information specifically about the call being internal or external; when in doubt, Unity defaults to internal. This does not affect whether Unity plays the internal greeting on call handlers or subscribers, however. Unity determines whether a caller is internal for the purposes of playing that greeting (if it is active) by checking to see if the calling number matches an extension of a subscriber on the local Unity server. In this way, a subscriber calling from home who has his home phone set up as an alternate extension for his subscriber mailbox still is considered an internal caller when dialing another subscriber's extension, even though, from the switch's perspective, this is an external caller. People often confuse these concepts. It is a good idea to always choose Both for the origin on your custom routing rules, or you can run into problems with call routing that are difficult to debug.

Notice in Figure 18-15 that a couple of different types of forwarding are shown in the Reason column (busy and unconditional). In fact, you can get three separate types of forwarding codes from the switch: busy, ring no answer, and forward all. However, the keen observer also will notice that, on the forwarded calls routing rules page in the SA, you do not have the opportunity to specify these types. Early versions of Unity allowed users to specify which types of forwarding conditions a rule would trigger on, but this was prone to error given the varying degrees of integration information across the different phone systems that it caused more problems than it was worth. As such, all rules in the forwarded calls section assume that *any* forwarded call is valid. You see more of this in the next section.

Understanding Rule Order

The routing rules are shown in the SA as separate tables: one for direct calls and one for forwarded calls. This is purely a user interface convention. They are stored in a single table in SQL and are evaluated from the top down using the RuleIndex column until a matching rule is found. To see this, you can open the Rule table in the UnityDB database using the Cisco Unity Data Link Explorer (CUDLE) in the Tools Depot, or you can open the AVRulerEditor found under \Commserver\techtools. Figure 18-16 shows the AvRulerEditor application after the routing rules have been selected.

Figure 18-16 *AvRulerEditor Application*

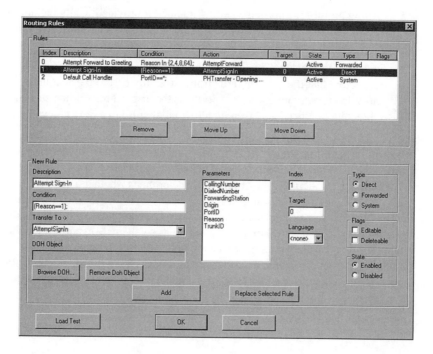

This shows all the default rules created by Unity setup. The Type column on the right dictates which rules show up in the forwarded calls and which rules show up in the direct calls tables in the SA. The system type shows up in both tables, which is why you have a total of four rules in the SA on a default install but, in reality, only three actual rules. This is the backstop rule that we talked about earlier; it ensures that an active rule succeeds in all cases. The Type column just indicates which table the rule appears in on the SA; it has nothing to do with processing the inbound calls.

As a side note here, when you open the RulerEditor application, you have the option of viewing either the routing or rejection rules. The rejection rules are not used in Unity and serve no purpose. The idea is to provide a way to have Unity deflect inbound calls based on the information Unity received on it from the switch without answering the call first. Unfortunately, many switch integrations do not send information about a call until after it is answered. Furthermore, deflecting a ringing call is not done easily with most switches using the integration options provided by the switch vendors. The feature was dropped, but the RulerEditor was not modified to remove it from its interface.

When a call comes in, Unity starts at the first rule and checks the Condition column to see if the call information matches the conditions for this rule. A condition can be any number of items, such as the Port ID being 1 through 4, the forwarding number being 1234, or the like. Any of the conditions that you can set on the SA when creating or editing a routing rule are included in the Condition column.

The first two default rules in Figure 18-16 have Reason=xxx as their sole condition. As you might remember, the reason is if it is direct or forwarded. A reason of 1 means that it is a direct call. A reason of 2, 4, or 8 means that it is call-forwarded RNA, busy, or unconditional, respectively. All routing rules that you create in the direct calls table in the SA include the {reason == 1} condition; all rules created on the forwarded calls table include the {reason == 2,4,8} condition. The 64 type value that you see on the earlier default forwarding rule is a forwarding type that no longer is used. New forwarded call rules that you create do not have that value on them. Additional conditions that you apply, such as limits on which ports you are interested in and which forwarding numbers to use, are additional constraints added to the Condition column. Notice that the last row has a simple condition of PortID==*. This means that the rule takes effect if the port ID is anything; this means that it *always* takes effect.

When a row in the table has a set of conditions that pass based on the call information, the Action column is executed. The Action column is the name of a conversation and sometimes the name of a target object. For instance, in the last row, the conversation is PHTransfer and the target is the opening greeting call handler. This means that the call is sent to the call transfer rules entry point for the opening greeting call handler. The other rules have just the names of some special conversation that do not appear anywhere in Unity other than in the call-routing rules:

- **ConvUtilsLiveRecord**. This conversation does not get used much currently in Unity because it's hard-wired to work only with certain switch integrations that are not supported by TAC. A modified version of this live record conversation DLL that works with any switch integration is available on www.ciscounitytools.com. If you download the DLL and register it on your Unity 4.0(1) or later system you can evoke a live record session if you manually set up a conference that includes a Unity port and configure a routing rule to launch the live record option. This conversation uses the calling number and does a lookup in the database to see if a subscriber with that extension exists. If so, it simply records silently, with no prompts playing. When the call terminates, the resulting message is left in the inbox of that subscriber. If no subscriber is found with that extension, the rule fails and the routing rules continue processing with the next rule in the table.

- **AttemptForward**. This shows up in the database as AttemptForwardToGreeting. This conversation uses the forwarding number and does a lookup in the database to see if a local subscriber or call handler with that extension number exists. If so, the call is sent to the greeting rules for that call handler. If not, the rule fails and the routing rules continue processing with the next rule in the table.

- **AttemptSignIn**. This conversation uses the calling number and does a lookup in the database to see if a local subscriber exists with an extension that matches. It checks primary and alternate extensions for this operation. If a match is found, the caller is sent to the subscriber sign-in conversation; the next thing heard is a request to enter the password, if one is set. If no subscriber is found, this rule fails and the routing rules proceed to the next rule in the table.

You do not find these conversations as options in the drop-down lists in the SA for user-input keys, after-message actions, after-greeting actions, and the like. These conversations can be applied only when the call first enters the system through the routing rules—they include database-searching options that return a failed or succeeded return code to its caller that must be specifically accommodated.

Because the rules are evaluated in order, the order in which you have them in the tables is important. For instance, if you create a rule stating that all calls that hit ports 1 through 4 should go to a specific call handler, and you have this it at the very top of your direct call rules, then all subscribers calling in to check messages that happened to hit ports 1 through 4 would not get automatically logged in as they should. You would want to move that rule below the "attempt sign in" rule, to make sure that internal subscribers calling in were logged in first. External callers would fail the "attempt sign in" conversation and proceed to your new rule as they should. Whenever you make changes to your routing rules, test your system to make sure that forwarding to greeting and subscriber sign-in functions are working as you expect. This is the most common routing rules problem in the field.

You will notice that the forwarding and direct calls are mixed in the list of rules shown earlier. Unity preserves the order only among the direct call rules and the forwarded call rules. Because a call never can be both forwarded and direct, this is a safe assumption. When you reorder your forwarding routing rules in the SA, for instance, and if you look at the AvRulerEditor, you might notice direct call rules interspersed. This is okay as long as the order of the forwarded call rules is preserved. If you are looking at the Rule table in SQL, the RuleIndex column dictates the order in which the rules are evaluated.

Do not edit rules using the AvRulerEditor. It is fine to use it to help you understand what is going on, but it is very difficult to use on a live system. Using the AvRulerEditor, it is extremely easy to damage your routing rules, including the ever-important system default rules that are crucial to the proper functioning of your system. When making changes, it is best to go through the SA. If you do damage your routing rules beyond repair, you can easily restore the system default rules. This is covered later in the "Troubleshooting" and "Damage Control" sections.

Extension Remapping

There is a way to change the calling and forwarding numbers before Unity actually gets them and processes the routing rules. This is done through a mechanism called extension remapping. Extension remapping has been around in Unity for a while, but it has not been used often since the introduction of alternate extension support for subscribers. Occasionally, however, a scenario warrants its use.

Under \Commserver\IntLib\ExtensionMapping, you will find two directories: Calling and Forwarding. In each of these directories is a sample.txt file that covers the basics for how to construct a mapping file. We do not cover the details in depth here; you can read them there for yourself. You can create .EXM files in either or both of these directories that instruct Unity to replace a forwarding or calling number coming from the switch with another number *before* it is processed by the routing rules.

For instance, imagine that you have the file test.exm (the filename does not matter—only the extension is significant) in the Forwarding directory that contains the following rules:

    1000, 2000
    5???, 62???

If a call forwards into Unity from extension 1000, when Unity processes it, it uses 2000 as the forwarding number. This is because the first line in the remapping file dictates that all forwarding extensions that match 1000 will be replaced with 2000. Even the information in the Call Viewer will show 2000. If you want to see the original forwarding number, you must look in the Media Interface Unity (MIU) diagnostic logs.

The 5???, 62??? rules take any four-digit number that starts with 5 and changes it so that it starts with 62 instead. For instance, 5432 would be translated to 62432. You can also use * as a wildcard to match zero or more digits, if you like. The extension-mapping files are flexible enough to enable you to dictate that only calls coming in on certain ports should be manipulated; this can be handy in a dual-switch integration scenario. You can also have multiple mapping files in each of the Calling and Forwarding directories with their own set of port mappings and extension maps. In this way, you can provide different extension-remapping rules for different sets of ports that correspond to the different switches Unity can be hooked up to.

The extension-remapping files can be extremely powerful, but they also can cause you a lot of headaches. If you have multiple, large, and complex remapping files for both direct and forwarded calls, your system can be very difficult to troubleshoot when calls are not going where you expect them to. If you need to use a remapping rule, keep it as simple and straightforward as possible. The need to use a remapping file should be very rare indeed; use these files sparingly, if at all. In most cases, alternate extensions will do what you need here. If you need to, you can check out the very cleverly named Alternate Extension Adder tool on www.ciscounitytools.com to help you add alternate extensions to large numbers of users based on CSV file input.

Languages, Prompts, and Greetings

Unity is built on a "tag, you are it" model of language assignment. A call is tagged with a language when it enters the system. It retains that language as it passes through various call handlers, subscribers, interviewers, and name-lookup handlers in the system until it encounters an object that changes its language. On all language options in the SA, except for the language that subscribers hear when they call in to check messages, Inherited is an option. This leaves the language of the call as is; it is the default option for all newly created objects in the database.

What people find confusing is *what* is played in the language of the call. The Unity phone conversation plays four types of WAV files to callers: messages, prompts, greetings, and voice names. Greetings are custom-recorded greetings for subscribers and call handlers that an administrator or subscriber records. Voice names are administrator- or subscriber-recorded files that are played in various parts of the conversation. Messages, of course, are recorded by callers or other subscribers. Prompts are the collection of around 2400 individually recorded system WAV files per language that Unity uses to construct the conversation that the callers hear.

Only *prompts* are played in the language specified. Each call handler or subscriber has only one set of greetings and a single voice name. Those greetings always play, no matter what language is selected for the call. This might seem obvious, but you would be surprised by how many times people have e-mailed to complain that they selected a different language for their opening greeting, yet it is still saying, "Hello, this is the Unity messaging system," in U.S. English. Even though that greeting is recorded in the same voice that the prompts are, it is still a custom greeting; it does not change when you change languages on the call handler. You must record your own greetings in the language that you want callers to hear for any call handler in the system, including the default handlers created by Unity setup. The default handlers get a set of greetings during the initial installation based on the default language installed. After they are created, these greetings do not ever change automatically based on language selection.

If you want to offer a multilingual audio-text application for callers, you must create duplicate sets of call handlers that have greetings recorded in the languages you want. You cannot support more than one language with the same set of call handlers. We cover this a little more later in the "Scenario Examples" section, but because it comes up often enough, we wanted to mention it separately here.

One last note is in order before leaving this subject: Localizing the prompts into other languages is not a simple matter of recording each individual prompt WAV file in the desired language. Different languages say things in different orders and patterns. If you just strung the set of WAV files together in the same order that you do in, say, U.S. English, it would sound decidedly bad. Unity employs a series of files called phrase servers that act as the agent to assemble the collection of individual prompt files into a syntactically correct phrase in the language desired. Each language has not only a set of prompt files recorded in the appropriate language, but a full suite of phrase servers for that language as well. So, you cannot just record your own language if Unity currently does not offer the language that you or your customer wants. Code work and a lot of professional voice time and testing are required before a new language can be added to the list that Unity supports.

Default Configuration of Unity

It is important to understand the default configuration of Unity out of the box. Customers who do not understand the default configuration can end up routing callers to the example interview handler at night and leaving those messages for the Example Administrator. Months later, they discover hundreds of messages sitting in the Example Administrator's mailbox.

Out of the box, Unity has (among others) the following default objects that it adds to the database and, in the case of subscribers and distribution lists, to your directory:

- **Opening greeting call handler**. By default, this is set up to play a generic greeting between 8 A.M. and 5 P.M., and send calls to the operator call handler if the user enters no digits during the greeting. During the day, the operator call handler attempts to ring extension 0 and then takes a message that is left, by default, for the Example Interviewer account. At night, it plays a generic after-hours greeting and, again, sends calls to the operator mailbox, which forwards them to the Example Interviewer at night. This is the default destination for all incoming calls that are not forwarded from a subscriber's extension or that are not direct incoming calls from subscriber extensions. It is also the default destination when subscribers exit their conversation or when users enter an invalid digit sequence during a call handler/subscriber greeting. It is *also* the default destination when someone presses # during the subscriber sign-in conversation. It is marked undeletable, so you cannot remove it in the SA. However, if you access SQL directly, you can delete it and cause yourself all kinds of grief. Do *not* do this. If you do not want to use the opening greeting call handler, make a routing rule that sends callers to different call handler(s) for inbound calls—but leave this call handler there. Trust me, you will save yourself all kinds of trouble.

- **Operator call handler**. Also an undeletable call handler, this is mapped to extension 0. This is unusual because you are not allowed to enter extensions of less than three digits in length when you create new handlers in the system. By default, every single call handler in the system has its 0 key mapped to this call handler. No hard-coded references to this object exist, but it is still a reasonably bad idea to delete it unless you have a *very* good reason to do so. You can change the extension on it and everything else, so there is no compelling reason to remove it entirely. Also be aware that the after-hours behavior on the operator call handler is set up by default to send callers to the Example Interviewer, which is configured to take a message for the Example Administrator account. You will very likely want to change this on new installs.

- **Say Goodbye call handler**. The last of the undeletable call handlers created, this is one that you definitely want to leave alone. In many spots in the SA, you can select "say goodbye" as a call destination, and that is a hard coded reference to this call handler. If you delete this, you break everything. Do not do that. You might not want to use this handy option in the SA, unless you are trying to do multiple tenant–type scenarios. This is covered in the "Tenant Services" section, later in this chapter.

- **Example Interviewer**. Although this interviewer handler is marked undeletable, you can remove it relatively easily if you feel the need to do so; but it is not doing any harm. By default, the operator call handler sends calls to this handler after hours and leaves its messages in the Example Administrator's account. If you decide to remove it, be sure to change the behavior of the operator call handler accordingly.

- **Example Subscriber**. This is just what the name implies: an example subscriber account, nothing more. No references to this call handler exist from other objects in the database; it can—and probably should—be deleted from your system because it parks on a subscriber license in your system and provides no direct value. You will not see this account in Unity 4.0(3) and later installations.

- **Example Administrator**. Not quite as straightforward as Example Subscriber, this is marked undeletable for a reason. However, you *can* remove it if you follow all the appropriate steps. This subscriber is set up as the owner and recipient for all new handlers created in the system. It is also the only member of the Unaddressed Messages public distribution list, among other things. If you just delete this subscriber, you risk losing messages from outside callers destined for subscribers with full mailboxes and the like. It *does* chew up a license and can present a security hole unless you change its default password. A tech tip on the Cisco website details the steps necessary for removing this subscriber; see http://www.cisco.com/en/US/partner/products/sw/voicesw/ps2237/products_tech_note09186a00800e25f2.shtml.

- **All Subscribers public distribution list**. This is the default distribution list added to the two default subscriber templates created by setup. Any additional templates that you create, by default, also reference this. It is generally a good idea to leave this as is: The need commonly arises to have a mechanism to leave all subscribers a message, and this is the easiest way to do that. If you do decide to remove it, update your subscriber templates to no longer reference it.

- **Unaddressed Messages public distribution list**. This distribution list is critical. Do *not* remove it. This is referenced in the Registry as the place where all voice-mail messages Unity cannot deliver from outside callers (that is, not subscriber-to-subscriber messages) get sent. If this list is gone or it contains no members, you lose these messages. Some sites just arbitrarily delete this distribution list from the directory and do not find out for months that they seriously have damaged their system, even though many event log errors were getting logged. This is a very bad thing—please do not do it.

- **System Event Messages public distribution list**. This is the default list used by the Error Notification Utility (also called General Audio Error Notification, or GAEN). You can delete it if you are not using it in the ENU utility. In Unity 4.0(4) and later, the ENU utility is replaced with the updated Event Monitoring Service (EMS), which no longer uses this default distribution list.

Common Problems

Calling into systems in the field, I see a few often-repeated problems related to the default objects noted earlier:

- The site has removed a default object in the database. For instance, someone has managed to delete the "say goodbye" call handler directly in SQL or DOHPropTest. The hard-coded references to these objects noted earlier are done so by the alias of the handler. If you accidentally delete one of these objects and want to put it back, use the same alias that the default script does when creating a new one to replace it. You might be better off using the FixDefaultObjects.sql script to have Unity re-create all the default objects. We cover the use of this script in the "Troubleshooting" section later in this chapter.

- The installer has not changed the default behavior of the opening greeting and operator call handlers. You would be amazed by how many sites do not even realize that callers are being sent to the example interview handler after hours and that messages are being deposited in the Example Administrator's e-mail account. This is the most common problem experienced in the field. Make sure that you either have someone monitoring the Example Admin's mailbox or, better, have a real admin type of account set up as the recipient for those objects.

- The installer did not make sure that a real, live administrator is a member of the unaddressed distribution list. This is a *very* important concept. You need to remember to have an administrator type on the local site added to this DL to handle messages that get sent to it.

- A customer IT–type person removed an object, such as the Example Administrator account or the unaddressed messages DL, in the directory without realizing that it would cause problems. Even though these are marked undeletable in Unity's database, nothing stops a user from removing them in the directory. As noted earlier, it is fine to remove the Example Admin account, as long as you carefully follow the steps necessary to do it right. Removing the unaddressed messages DL is never a good idea. In Unity 4.0(3) and later, whenever an object is removed in the directory that was marked undeletable in Unity's database, an event log warning should be written by the directory change writer to indicate a potential problem. For instance, if an IT type deleted the Example Administrator from AD directly, you would see a message similar to this:

```
Event Type:Warning
Event Source:CiscoUnity_DirChangeWriter
Event Category:Warning
Event ID:1050
Date:     6/7/2003
Time:     3:36:41 PM
User:     N/A
Computer:LABSystem8
Description:
The EAdmin directory object was deleted. The corresponding Cisco Unity account
   is undeletable.
Some functionality will be unavailable, and Cisco Unity may fail to function
   properly until the directory object is restored.
To restore the directory object, run the Message Store Configuration Wizard
   with the sync flag: "C:\CommServer\ConfigurationSetup\setup.exe" /sync
For more information, click: http://www.CiscoUnitySupport.com/find.php
```

Scenario Examples

Now that you understand the mechanics of how Unity handles calls, it is helpful to look at some scenarios that users commonly encounter in the field. Before discussing these applications, we briefly discuss the Audio Text Manager. The ATM is an alternative to using the SA for managing audio-text applications that makes much quicker work of constructing complex trees than using the SA.

Audio Text Manager

First, a quick word about the Audio Text Manager (ATM) application, which started shipping with Unity in 3.1(4), is in order. This is a TAC-supported tool designed to help you quickly and easily design and support complex audio-text applications. This chapter is targeted at the concepts involved in audio-text applications, not the mechanics of creating and associating objects in question. Although we touch on its use and show a few related figures, we do not spend significant time here discussing the details of the ATM tool itself. You can view the training videos and read the extensive help for this application online at http://www.ciscounitytools.com. The training videos on its home page walk through the creation of a simple audio-text application from start to finish, which should be helpful to new users of the system.

If you will be creating audio-text applications of any size or complexity, we highly recommend that you take the time to familiarize yourself with this tool. Although it is not necessary that you use it for handling any of these scenarios, you will find that you can move through them considerably quicker and with fewer mistakes than doing it using the standard web-based SA interface.

Basic Audio-Text Application

We start with the most basic example: the classic handler tree that gives callers options to access different types of information through call handlers. In this example, we create a simple application that enables users to get production information, obtain technical support, or search for a subscriber by name in one of two cities.

First, we create the entry point into the audio-text application. We use a call handler named Tiny Audio Text Application for this example. The first decision that you need to make is how callers access this call handler to get to your little audio-text application in the first place. You have a few basic options to choose from:

- Use a DID number dedicated to this application. You create a direct call routing rule that triggers on this dialed number and routes the call directly to the call handler acting as the root node of your audio-text tree. For applications offered in multiple languages, or for a multitenant environment, this method is ideal, as discussed in the "Tenant Services" section. Although this is certainly a slick mechanism, it might be a little heavy for the typical company just doing some light audio-text work.

- Use a virtual extension that forwards into Unity. This is a little more approachable then using a dedicated DID line for most people. If you assign the root call handler (in this case, the Tiny Audio Text Application call handler) an extension and then have calls forwarded from that same extension into Unity, they automatically are routed to the handler for you. Of course, you also can create a custom routing rule to do the same thing and avoid assigning the handler an ID.

- Set up a link to the root handler from the opening greeting call handler, and allow callers to choose to enter the audio-text application manually. This is fine for typical lightweight applications that do not get much traffic or that are used by internal users. For instance, this works if you want to have a simple tree of call handlers available for your internal users to find and ring a conference room in the office.

- Similar to the one key link off the opening greeting, you can assign the root handler an extension and have users dial it from the opening greeting (or any other greeting, for that matter). This is not a typical method that you would want outside callers using, but for power users who do not want to navigate through a layer of links, this method can be handy: It enables them to get right where they want to go in a hurry. Be sensitive to users who need to use these applications repeatedly, and keep such shortcuts for them in mind.

When you have decided how callers will get to the audio-text application, you can put it together. In this case, we keep it simple and create three call handlers and two name-lookup handlers.

Tiny Audio Text Application Call Handler

This is the root node, or entry point, into the audio-text application. You can have its alternate transfer rule enabled and set to not transfer. It is a good idea to use the alternate rules for both transfers and greetings, unless you have a good reason not to, such as if you want it to ring a phone during the day but not after hours. In this case, the handler never rings a phone, so it makes sense to do it this way. It is also a good idea to use the alternate greeting because, in this case, you want callers to always hear the same greeting, no matter what time of day it is. The greeting gives the callers the option of selecting 1 for product information, 2 for technical support, 4 to find an employee in Seattle, 5 to find an employee in Chicago, or 0 to reach the operator.

It is always a good idea to leave the 0 linked to the operator. You can choose area operators depending on which handler you are in and the like, but you should always give callers the option of exiting your application and talking to a human. In fact, the ISO standard conversation specification for voice mail lists this as a requirement for all parts of a conversation. If you, like me, pattern your life after ISO proclamations, you will want to follow its lead here.

This handler is a routing handler only and will not be used for taking messages, so the user is expected to input one of the options here. As such, we have the greeting set up to repeat twice with a 2-second pause (if you do not remember how to do this, revisit the greetings page information earlier in this chapter). This means that the greeting plays three times, giving the caller more than enough time to make one of these five choices. The after-greeting action is set to go to the operator call handler. If the user did not input an option, that user clearly is having trouble or is dialing from a rotary phone and cannot input anything.

With this setup, calls flow through this handler in a very predictable manner. They always hit the alternate greeting, which plays up to three times if the user does not input anything; then users are sent to the operator. If you are concerned about users being able to dial extensions, you can lock down the handler here as well. This is covered in the appropriately named section "Locking Down Handlers and Subscribers," later in this chapter. Now you need to create the product information and technical support handlers.

Product Information Call Handler

This handler can play a greeting that simply lists all the products available, with short descriptions. If you want to get fancy, this handler can have links off of it to additional call handlers for each product, with longer descriptions. The setup for this handler is basically the same as for the root handler discussed previously, but the after-greeting action should be set to return to the Tiny Audio Text Application call handler. In general, it is a good idea for any audio-text application to have a no input action that returns one level up in the tree. The top of the tree should go to the operator or to the "say goodbye" call handler for exiting purposes.

Keep in mind *all* your exit routes from a call handler here. As a refresher, a caller can exit from a call handler in six ways:

- A transfer rule can ring a phone and release the call.

- The user can dial an extension during the greeting. If you do not want to allow this, you can lock down the handler , which is covered in the later section "Locking Down Handlers and Subscribers."

- The user can dial a user-input key that is mapped to an action to send users somewhere.

- The after-greeting action can be configured to send the user somewhere.

- The after-message action can be configured to send the user somewhere.

- The error greeting can kick in if the user enters an invalid option and can send the user somewhere.

We have covered items 1 through 5 because the transfer rule is not ringing a phone, the handler is not taking a message, and the after-greeting action is configured to go to the Tiny Audio Text Application. Item 6 causes confusion because, by default, this greeting is not visible in the SA and people do not know it is there. We cover how to deal with this in the section "Locking Down Handlers and Subscribers," a little later; just keep this in mind when creating any type of application.

Technical Support Call Handler

You can configure this call handler to send calls to a call queue during the day or go to an interview handler after hours to collect the caller's details so that you can return the call in the morning. To do this, you configure its standard transfer rule to be active and do a release transfer to the call queue (it is a good idea to have calls that are stacking up handled by the switch, not using ports on your Unity server, if you can help it). Set up the off-hours transfer rule to go right to the greeting.

Because only calls after hours will reach the greetings, you again can use the alternate greeting and avoid confusion here. In this case, you want to use the blank greeting option and have an after-greeting action configured to go to an interview handler that is set up the way you want it. The training videos available for the Audio Text Manager noted earlier cover the steps of setting up this type of application, if you need more details.

All Seattle Employees Name-Lookup Handler

This name-lookup handler would be associated with a public distribution list containing all the employees at the Seattle office. Of course, you also can use a location object if multiple Unity servers are involved and you use a networking or a class of service object, if you have set up your system that way. Select the name entry order (first or last name first) and the list presentation style, and you are good to go.

Again, you need to decide where callers who do not successfully find a name in the directory go when exiting this name-lookup handler. If this handler is used only in this audio-text application, it is good style to return these callers to the root handler (in this case, the Tiny Audio Text Application call handler).

All Chicago Employees Name-Lookup Handler

This works the same as the Seattle employees name-lookup handler, but, of course, with a different distribution list, location, or CoS selected to get only Chicago employees.

When you have created your objects, you need to go back to the root handler and establish the links to the user-input keys. Figure 18-17 shows this simple application's root handler in the tree view of the Audio Text Manager tool.

Figure 18-17 *Audio Text Manager Tool's Tree View*

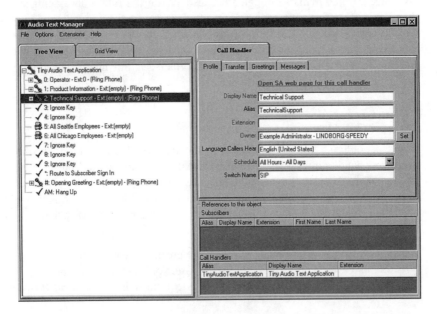

This type of view makes it easier to see how the calls flow through the system. Also note that if you created this application in the ATM, you simply can right-click on the 1, 2, 4, and 5 keys there; create the call handler or name-lookup handler in question; *and* make the link active in one step. You can see how generating a large and complex audio-text application goes much quicker this way than through the SA.

You can keep drilling down and creating new levels under the product information and technical support handlers as deep as you want. Just remember that callers navigate this over the phone and probably do not appreciate traversing a 20-level-deep audio-text application. This is a pretty simple example, but it covers the basic framework of what a typical audio-text application is. We have a few rules of the road for creating audio-text applications in Unity that you should keep in mind regardless of the scale or type of application you are constructing:

- Watch your exit points. Callers can exit from every call handler and subscriber in six ways callers. Make sure that you have accounted for all of them, to keep callers from ending up somewhere unexpected. The error greeting is the most common oversight you will see here—see the later section "Locking Down Handlers and Subscribers" for more on this.

- Assign owners and recipients appropriately. Even if a handler is not taking a message, all handlers need to have a valid owner and recipient at all times. If you assign a subscriber or a distribution list to serve as the owner or recipient and then you later remove it, you have to go back and clean up all those broken links. Also remember that owners of a call handler are allowed to record greetings for it over the phone in Unity 4.0(1) and later. Another thing to consider about owners is that they are handy mechanisms for selecting call handlers using the Bulk Edit utility if you want to make changes across an entire audio-text application but not for all call handlers in the database. The Bulk Edit utility lets you select call handlers based on switch association, extension range, owner, or recipient. If you do not assign extensions to your handlers (which, in general, you should not) and all handlers in your system are owned by the same user, selecting specific groups of call handlers for bulk-edit purposes will be difficult, at best.

- Make sure that your "no input" paths are set appropriately. Do not allow users to navigate 10 levels deep into an audio-text application and then send them back up to the root node if they make a mistake. In general, it is best to jump them up one level at a time, unless you have a good reason not to (for example, if your switch does not provide supervised disconnect and you want to terminate "dead" calls as quickly as possible). It is also good style to offer an explicit menu option to jump back up a level (such as "Press 9 to return to the previous menu").

- Always give callers the "0 out" option. The purpose of many audio-text applications is to prevent callers from reaching live people as much as possible, but trapping callers in audio-text trees that they cannot get out of is just evil. People have a bad image of voice mail in general precisely because of such poorly designed applications.

- Watch your tree depth. A good test to perform after you get your application built is to call in yourself and reach each leaf node in your application, watching how much time it takes. Do not cheat and dial ahead; listen to all the options first and then select your option—this is what callers do. If it takes you 10 minutes to get to what you want, you can flatten your application or perhaps break it up into multiple applications that are more specific.

- Always use alternate greetings and transfer rules, unless you have a good reason to do otherwise. "Bugs" in Unity turn out to be the wrong greeting or transfer rule triggering based on the time of day or the way in which the call reached the handler. There are times to use schedules, of course, but not unless you need to.

- Explicitly set the Send to Greeting and the Attempt Transfer settings when sending a call to another handler or subscriber through a user-input key or an after-greeting/ after-message action. This is the most commonly misconfigured setting in the field. You can get a quick view of all the Ring Phone For and Send to Greeting For settings for all your user-input, after-greeting, and after-message actions by using the Export Tree Information to File option in the Audio Text Manager application's File menu. This shows "(greeting)" or "(ring phone)" after each action in the tree, to give you a quick way to find possible problems.

- Give your callers a chance to input something. Remember, callers do not take action on the first menu option that they hear that is close to what they want. People almost always listen to all the options the first time they hear a greeting and then make a decision. If your call handler is expecting input, repeat it at least once, with a small delay in between.

- Remember your repeat users. It is easy to design an audio-text application with first-time users in mind. However, do not forget people who have to navigate this application often. Give them the option of jumping right to a specific handler in the application by direct ID, and avoid situations in which callers are forced to listen to an entire greeting without accepting input unless it is absolutely necessary.

Transferring to External Numbers in Unity 4.0(4) and Later

Unity 4.0(4) introduced a new concept that allows administrators to grant the ability for callers to dial any number they want either on the local switch or external numbers if they choose. Prior to 4.0(4), administrators had to create call handlers for each and every number they wished to dial on or off the local switch that did not have a subscriber associated with it.

In Unity 4.0(4), this transfer functionality is provided using two new conversations: Caller System Transfer and Subscriber System Transfer. You will find both of these conversations as options for user input keys on call handlers or subscribers or in the call routing rules. The differences between the two conversations are as follows:

- **Caller System Transfer**. This conversation is intended to be used by outside callers and it does not require the user to provide a login or password when the conversation is accessed. The caller can simply enter any number they wish and if it passes a check against the system-wide Default System Transfer restriction table, Unity does a release transfer to that number. In general this would be used to allow access to local numbers off the switch, such as conference room phones or the like. Out of the box, the Default System Transfer restriction table allows no numbers to be dialed, so to use this conversation, you need to go to the Restriction Tables page in the SA and configure the rule to allow the appropriate numbers.

- **Subscriber System Transfer**. This conversation is used by subscribers on the local system and the user is required to provide their Unity subscriber ID and phone password to gain access to the conversation. Once in the conversation, they can enter any number they wish and if it passes the Transfer Restriction table associated with their Class of Service, Unity does a release transfer to that number. This allows users to dial any number allowed by their COS, such that admins and other trusted user can dial offsite numbers while other users can be restricted from doing so.

Both the Subscriber System Transfer and the Caller System Transfer conversation will dial the exact number entered by the user. So if you have the system configured to allow calls to offsite numbers, the user will need to enter the trunk access code necessary for this, such as "9."

Transferring to External Numbers in Unity 4.0(3) and Earlier

In Unity 4.0(3) and earlier, to transfer to external numbers or ring internal phones that were not associated with subscribers you have to create call handlers for each number you want to dial. Prior to the release of Unity 4.0(4), there were no "free dial" capabilities offered in the Caller System Transfer and Subscriber System Transfer options noted in the previous section.

For instance, if you want callers trying to reach a particular subscriber to be able to optionally ring their home phone number, this can be done easily. First, create a call handler called, say, Dial Jim At Home, or use some appropriately scalable naming convention. Set its alternate transfer rule to be active, and set the transfer string to be Jim's home phone number, preceded by the appropriate trunk access code (for instance, 9,5551212).

You must add any long-distance code or area code or trunk-access codes necessary for Unity to dial out on the switch(es) it is connected to. Unity does not automatically prepend digits for you on dialout; it dials exactly what is in the transfer string—nothing more, nothing less. Keep this in mind particularly for dual-switch integrations that might have different trunk-access codes, depending on which switch you configured the call handler to be associated with. When you have the call handler configured properly, set a user-input key on Jim's subscriber account to attempt transfer for the new call handler that you just created. Finally, Jim can record his greeting that includes "To reach me at home, press 3 now." Callers then will be transferred to his home phone.

You should think about a couple of things for such scenarios:

- What transfer type should you use for the call handler? Whenever possible, I always recommend using release transfers to any external number, particularly cell phones. Call progress to external numbers is tricky business, and doing supervised transfer reliably is a roll of the dice. This can be a problem, however, if the cell phone is forwarded to its own voice-mail system instead of back to Unity. In most cases, phones can be programmed to forward to a custom number, and the cell phone number can be added as an alternate extension for Jim's subscriber account. Forwarding the cell phone on busy/RNA to Jim's Unity server would make the release transfer scenario work smoothly here.

- If Jim does not want to be getting calls at 3 A.M., you will want to configure the call handler to be associated with an appropriate schedule. Also use the standard and closed transfer rules, with the closed transfer rule falling through to a greeting for the handler. The greeting could say, for instance, "Jim is not available now," with an after-greeting action of Send to Greeting For Jim's subscriber account. The caller can keep trying, but it will just loop around to his subscriber greeting every time. If this is not a consideration, use the alternate transfer rule so that you do not have to concern yourself with schedules.

- Remember that restriction tables limiting which numbers can be dialed are enforced only at the time the number is edited, not when it is dialed. Because an administrator must do this through the SA (Jim cannot do this over the phone or through the PCA), this does not come into play for this scenario. Administrators typically are associated with restriction tables that are open.

If you need to create a lot of call handlers because you have many internal extensions that you want callers who are not subscribers to access (such as conference rooms and lobby phones), you can use the Bulk Handler Create tool. This tool can create handlers by ranges of extensions or by importing from CSV files to make short work of such a request. You can find this tool at www.ciscounitytools.com.

One last thing should be noted here: Some PBXs have ports that are defined for voice-mail restricted from getting an outside line under any circumstances, to keep users from ripping off the company for long-distance charges. The transfer attempt simply fails outright. This can cause some weird situations when using release transfers (callers get "turkey tone" in their ear, which is not pleasant). Take this into consideration when setting up handlers to do external dials.

Locking Down Handlers and Subscribers

One of the issues that audio-text designers must take into account is how restrictive they want to be with callers navigating around their system. For some sites, it might be perfectly acceptable to let users jump around between audio-text trees, try subscriber extensions directly, or the like. However, many times this is undesirable. For instance, you probably do not want headhunters randomly dialing your engineers to make them a better offer (if this is a big problem, you should consider paying your hard-working engineers more), and you do not want your 800 lines provided for specific audio-text applications being abused. If your application falls into the later category, pay attention to all the exit points from a call handler, and fully understand the use of Ignore and Locked flags on user-input keys.

As noted in the first basic example, there are six exit points off a call handler or subscriber. The transfer rules, user-input keys, and after-greeting and after-message destinations are pretty straightforward and easily are managed using either the web-based SA or Audio Text Manager interfaces. People typically have difficulty with preventing users from dialing extensions directly and managing the error greeting destinations.

Error Greetings

Error greetings are easily the most misunderstood and overlooked items by Unity administrators. The first problem is that, by default, this greeting does not even show up in the SA interface; people do not even know it is there. If they do, people often do not understand what it does.

As you remember from earlier in this chapter, the error greeting is evoked when the user dials digits that Unity does not know what to do with. For instance, the user might dial an extension that does not exist in the database, or selects a one-key user-input option that is mapped to Ignore. By default, the error greeting plays, "I am sorry, I did not hear your entry," and then sends the caller to the opening greeting call handler. Of course, this not always what you want it to do when a user makes a mistake in your applications.

The first step is to expose it in the SA. This can be done using the Advanced Settings tool found in the Administration Tools section of the Tools Depot. The option that you want is Expose the Error Greeting for Subscribers on the SA; set its value to 1. The Error greeting option appears in the greetings drop-down list for all subscribers and call handlers in the SA. Frankly, this should be on by default, but in early versions of Unity, we got so many calls from people wanting to know what this error in the SA was about that the decision was made to hide it in the interface (at that time, the need to customize the greeting's behavior was limited).

The easiest way to handle the error greetings for handlers and subscribers that already are created in your system is to simply change the default behavior for the error greeting across the entire system using the Bulk Edit utility. By default, the error greeting plays a system-generated prompt that says, "I am sorry, I did not hear that entry." Then it sends the caller to the opening greeting call handler created by Unity setup.

This can be maddening for people creating large audio-text applications that are many levels deep. Using the opening greeting when people enter something invalid is really harsh on callers. This can also be a problem for people trying to created limited tenant services scenarios because there is only one opening greeting, and sending all callers who make a mistake here is less than ideal.

Instead, you can set the behavior to loop the caller back to the same handler or subscriber that the caller is currently in. The caller hears the same system-generated prompt saying that the input was not received. Then the greeting for that handler is played again so that the user has another chance. Figure 18-18 shows the Error Greetings tab found on both subscribers and call handlers in the Bulk Edit utility.

Figure 18-18 *Greeting Options for Call Handlers in the Bulk Edit Utility*

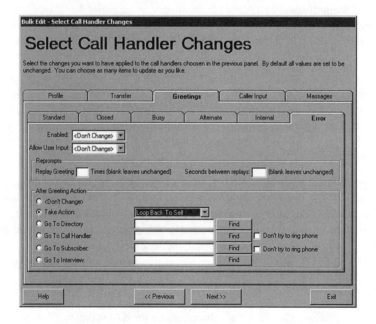

The Loop Back To Self option for the action in the After-Greeting Action section specifically was added to accommodate this scenario. You will want to do this for all subscribers and then again for all call handlers in Bulk Edit, to make sure you get everything.

Unfortunately, you cannot change the subscriber templates so that the behavior is Loop Back To Self; this not an option in the SA. When a subscriber or call handler is created off of a template, all the exit destinations are copied in from the template onto the new object; there is no logic setting the destination to be the new object just created.

Another problem here is that call handlers do not have their own templates like subscribers do. Unless you manually select a call handler to copy from, the default behavior is to use the primary call-handler settings off the default subscriber template when creating a new call handler. This is annoying because you cannot create a separate call-handler template for each audio-text application that is configured with appropriate exit destinations, owners, and recipients (which would be ideal). As near as you can get to this is to select the Base on Existing Call Handler radio button and choose a call handler to act as a template when you create new call handlers in the SA. Unfortunately, the SA does not remember your choice, and you have to select it manually each time.

The Audio Text Manager, on the other hand, remembers your last template selection here. If you create a bunch of handlers for an application, you can create the first handler, configure it as you want, and then use it as your template for the rest of the handlers in that application. Again, however, there is no Loop Back to Self option for the template here. All destinations, including the error greeting destination, are copied over exactly as is. So, if the call handler that you use as a template is set to point back to itself as the error greeting's after-greeting action, other handlers created using that handler for its default settings will point to the template handler, not back to themselves. Be sure to keep this in mind.

Restricting Dial Options

Depending on how restrictive you want to be, you can prevent users from dialing extensions directly while a greeting is playing:

- You can disallow all input for a particular greeting in a call handler. This is done by unchecking the Allow User Input box on the greeting page for the handler and greeting that you want to do this for. This forces Unity to ignore completely all digits entered while that greeting plays; the greeting will not be interrupted as would normally be the case when a touch tone is entered. This option should be used only in extreme circumstances when you have good reason to force the user to hear the entire greeting before moving on (for instance, if some important change has taken place in the application recently, and you want to bring callers' attention to it before they go tearing off). This option should be used *very* sparingly and on greetings that are reasonably short. Expecting users to sit through a couple of minutes of mandatory listening material is both evil and highly optimistic. Expect to see a lot of "hang up" termination reasons in your call-handler traffic report if you try that.

- You cannot allow users to dial any extensions during any greeting for a particular call handler or all handlers in your audio-text application. This is done by unchecking the Allow Callers to Dial an Extension During Greeting option on the caller input page for the call handler or subscriber in question. This option still allows user input of one-key options, such as dialing 0 to get an operator or other actions that you decide on. However, multiple-digit input is not allowed, so callers have no opportunity to dial the extension of a subscriber or call handler in the database. It should be noted that setting this option on the caller input page affects callers regardless of which greeting is active; this is not a per-greeting option. With this option, all the keys are marked for Locked, so whatever action they are mapped to, including Ignore, is taken immediately when the caller enters it. Remember that, in the case of keys mapped to Ignore and Locked, the greeting does not interrupt and the key is not acted on.

- You can get a little more granular and lock down specific keys so that users cannot dial extensions that start with those numbers. For instance, if you have all your employees on phones with extensions that start with 4 or 5, you can lock all 4 and 5 user input keys for all call handlers in your audio-text application. This prevents callers from dialing extensions starting with 4 or 5. Other extensions that can be mapped to other call handlers still would be reachable.

Again, if you have many handlers or subscribers created and you want to selectively change the one-key behavior, including which keys are locked, you can use Bulk Edit to do this quickly.

Although this was discussed earlier in the chapter, it should be mentioned again simply because most people do not understand the distinction. A key mapped to Ignore behaves very differently than a key mapped to Ignore *and* set to Locked. For instance, if you have key 7 set to Ignore but not Locked, a caller can enter 7114 during the greeting. If there is a handler or subscriber in the database that has extension 7114, the caller is sent there. If there is no extension found, the error greeting for that handler is acted on instead. The same thing happens if the user presses 7 and nothing else. The greeting stops, and Unity waits the number of milliseconds configured for the interdigit delay (1500 milliseconds, by default). Then Unity sends the caller to the error greeting. On the other hand, if the 7 key is marked Ignore *and* Locked, then if the user presses 7, the greeting does not stop and the key is thrown away.

It should be noted that if the user enters 7114 and the keys 1 and 4 are not also set to Ignore and Locked, Unity interrupts the greeting and attempts to find 114 in the directory. This is another reason to make sure your error greeting is set up for something more intelligent than dumping the caller back to the opening greeting.

With a properly laid-out numbering plan on your phone system, you can protect your subscribers from outside callers without being overly restrictive about letting them dial call handlers that have IDs directly for power users who want to jump to a particular spot in your application. It takes a little more work to do the individual locked keys, but, in general, you recommend this. If your numbering plan is all over the boards, then you might consider simply not allowing users to dial extensions and locking them into user-input keys that you have mapped for the audio-text application itself only. Just remember that, for power users who are return callers, it can be extremely annoying to have to navigate through a series of handlers to get to where they want, instead of being given the option of a direct-dial "jump" option.

It should be noted that the Lock and Ignore combination had a bug in versions of Unity 3.1(5) and earlier that caused problems with the selective locking option here. The key should be ignored and thrown away only if it is the first digit entered that would have interrupted the greeting. When the greeting has been interrupted and Unity is accepting digits for an extension lookup, all keys should be accepted, regardless of what their settings in the user-input page are. For instance, if the 7 key is locked and the 1 key is not, then if the user enters 1774, this extension should be allowed. In previous versions of Unity, the 7s were being thrown out and Unity would attempt to find 14 in the database—which, of course, failed to find a match. For administrators building applications on Unity 4.0(1) and later, this will not be a problem. If you find yourself working on an older system, this is something to keep in mind.

Changing Greetings for Call Handlers over the Phone

One of the new features in Unity 4.0(1) is the capability (finally) to edit greetings for call handlers over the phone interface. In earlier versions of Unity, users were forced to press a subscriber object into service as an opening greeting, for instance, if they wanted to change the greeting for it over the phone in the event of a snow day or the like. This chewed up a subscriber license and was generally pretty annoying.

With this feature, you must map a user-input key, after-message action, or after-greeting action to go to the greetings administration conversation in the SA or the ATM. This option is not part of the subscriber conversation itself; it is a standalone routable conversation (remember from earlier in this chapter that routable conversations that appear as options in the after-message, after-greeting, and user-input pages). After callers are sent to the greetings administration conversation, they must sign in by providing their extension and password (if set). In the conversation, they can select call handlers for which you are listed as the owner edit their greetings, if you want. It is not necessary, for instance, to use a one-key link on every call handler that you want to edit that maps to the greetings administration conversation.

Keep in mind a couple of important things when you want to use the greetings administration conversation for editing greetings on call handlers over the phone:

- Be careful where you configure your entry point into the greetings administration conversation. It is not a good idea to place this as a one-key option off the opening greeting, for instance: Callers who accidentally are sent here will be very confused. A much better option is to hide this in an unconnected call handler specifically set up to grant access to callers who should be editing greetings like this. For instance, set up a call handler that has no connections to it with a long 10-digit (you can go up to 30 digits, but that is pretty brutal) extension that callers will not likely stumble on. This call handler's alternate greeting could be enabled, the greeting would be blank, and the after-greeting action would be set to go to greetings administrator. This way, callers who need to change greetings could just call in, dial the 10-digit number, and sign in.

- The call handlers that have greetings that you want to edit over the phone must have an extension assigned to them. The only way that you can select call handlers in the greetings administration conversation currently is by ID. This is unfortunate because assigning IDs to call handlers generally should be avoided unless it is necessary. In this case, it is necessary for the handlers that you want to edit greetings for over the phone. In future versions of Unity, you will be allowed to find call handlers by spelling their names instead or by using a list of all the handlers that the logged-in caller owns.

- The selection of greetings offered in the greetings administration conversation is different than those you will find in the standard subscriber conversation when you go to edit your own greetings. Specifically, the subscriber conversation grants you access to only the standard, off-hours, and alternate greetings. The greetings administration conversation, however, enables you to get at the alternate, standard, closed, internal, and busy greetings. However, you cannot specifically enable or disable the internal and busy greetings; you can only record greetings for them. Furthermore, the conversation does not inform you if the greeting currently is enabled or disabled, which can be a real problem. The expectation is that you are changing a greeting that is currently in use on the call handler, which could be a bad assumption. If you plan to use the busy or internal greetings on a call handler, do not expect to be able to enable or disable them over the phone; you still have to do this through the SA or the ATM interfaces.

But even with those limitations in the current implementation, this is considerably better than having to use subscribers as a vehicle for providing an interface over the phone for changing greetings in an emergency situation.

Multiple-Language Applications

As we discussed earlier in this chapter, Unity handles multiple-language configurations in a fairly simple "tag, you are it" model. When a call touches a handler or subscriber that is marked for a specific language, the call is considered to be that language until another handler or subscriber is touched that says otherwise. By default, objects are configured for Inherited, which means that the language the caller already is tagged as is used. When a call comes into the system, it is tagged with the default phone language that is configured in the SA under the System Configuration section on the phone languages page.

One important issue seems to confuse people in the field often. The greetings on call handlers and subscribers are not affected by the language selection. Each handler or subscriber has one set of greetings, and that is all; there is no way to record three or four sets of greetings in each language that you want to support and have a single audio-text application that serves all these languages. You must construct a separate audio-text application for each language that you want to support.

People in the field get thrown off because Unity ships with some default greetings for the opening greeting, operator, and "say goodbye" call handlers that are done in the same voice that does the prompt sets. We are often asked why the opening greeting is still in English, even though the language for the opening greeting is set to another language. This is expected. The greetings are up to you to record in whatever language you want to support. If you installed Unity with a default language of Spanish, for instance, the set of greetings for the opening greeting, operator, and "say goodbye" call handlers would be in Spanish, not English. However, the same rule applies: If you want to change the opening greeting call handler to play French, you need to set it to French as the language that callers hear so that prompts for that handler are played in French. You also need to record the greetings in French yourself; they do not change automatically for you. The same applies, of course, to voice names and questions for interview handlers.

The greetings are actually the majority of what outside callers hear. The prompts are just the system-generated phrases, such as "Please hold while I try that extension," and "Spell the last and first name, and then press pound," and the like. The majority of the more than 2400 prompts in the Unity conversation are used for subscribers when they call into their mailboxes, retrieve messages, and configure their mailbox options over the phone. As such, the major burden for creating multiple-language applications falls on the administrator.

As noted earlier, you must construct identical audio-text trees for each language that you want to support. Currently, no handy tool exists for duplicating entire trees quickly; however, I do have this on my list of things to take on. This is much trickier than it looks at first glance, as we discuss in Chapter 21. Furthermore, not every audio-text application is a nicely segmented tree of call handlers that simply can be duplicated. Often shared objects exist that do not need to be localized separately; one example of these is directory handlers that do not have greetings associated with them. For now, you must construct your audio-text applications in their entirety for every language that you want to support. You definitely want to look into using the Audio Text Manager tool for this because it reduces the time to do this over using the SA tenfold.

The big thing that you have to decide is how callers are routed to the root of the appropriate audio-text tree, based on the language they want to hear. You can approach this problem in a few ways:

- The slickest method here is to create routing rules and use separate DID numbers for each language that you want to support. In this way, for instance, a company can advertise different 1-800 numbers in different language publications so that callers dialing those numbers automatically would be routed to the appropriate language interface in the database, without having to do anything.

- You can set up routing rules that do the same thing as the DID lines, except that they trigger forwarding numbers for virtual extensions in the switch instead of dialed numbers. This might be a somewhat lower bar for people to get over than using dedicated DID lines.

- You can dedicate particular ports for particular languages, and have the routing rules tag the port range for deciding which entry point the caller is sent to. This is a lot tougher to get right because it requires you to nicely load-balance your ports based on how many callers using which language will be hitting your system. Generally, segmenting your ports in this way is a pretty bad idea, but the option is there if you need it.

- You can route all calls to a single call handler that is configured to play a greeting that says something like, "For English, press 1; for Spanish, press 2," and let the callers manually select which language they want to hear. Of course, each option would be presented in the appropriate language, and the user-input key would be mapped to route the caller to the root of the appropriate audio-text tree. This is how a lot of large organizations and government agencies handle this issue; it is easy to set up, it does not require fancy switch work, and it works no matter which integration you use with Unity. However, the caller experience is less than optimal, and having to select this every time you call can get annoying for repeat callers.

Group Mailboxes

Sometimes you need to accommodate multiple subscribers who share a single phone line. For instance, in a shared-office environment or a dorm room setting, multiple users might need their own mailboxes but do not each have their own phone line for callers to reach them.

The easiest way to handle this is to create subscriber mailboxes for everyone as normal, but use IDs for the subscribers who do not overlap with the phone extension numbering plan on the switch(es) that Unity is connected to. For instance, if four-digit extensions are used on the switch, use seven-digit IDs for the subscribers to use. This might be the subscriber's student number, or it can be a employee ID number or something similar. For example, if John, Jack, and Jim Smith share a single phone line in an office, you would set up subscribers for all three and then construct a call handler that is assigned an extension matching the one phone line they use. In the ATM tree view, it would look something like Figure 18-19.

Figure 18-19 *Group Mailbox as Shown in Audio Text Manager*

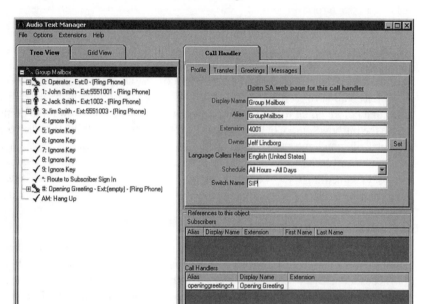

The Group Mailbox Ext 4001 call handler would have its alternate greeting enabled. This would use a greeting that sounded something like, "To leave a message for John, press 1; to leave a message for Jack, press 2; to leave a message for Jim, press 3; to reach the operator press 0." Of course, you would want to repeat the greeting at least once to give callers a chance to enter the option they want. In this way, each of the Smiths could get messages in his own box. Each of the Smiths would sign into the system using his seven-digit ID and his own password to get at his mailbox. Of course, they all would have to log in manually if they were calling in from the same phone: Automatic login works only if the calling extension matches the ID of a subscriber—in this scenario, this obviously is not the case.

Message Waiting Indicators (MWIs) are a little tricky in this scenario. You cannot have three separate subscribers turning lamps on and off on the same phone; the phone does not stay synchronized properly. If separate line appearances or multiple message indicators on the phone are used, each subscriber can have his MWI extension string set up to light a specific indicator. With a single shared line; however, the MWI typically does not work very smoothly as a mechanism to indicate that users have messages waiting.

You can get a little fancier with this model and create a distribution list that contains all the subscribers at a shared extension. You set the after-greeting action for the call handler to be to take a message and have the message left for the distribution list. In this way, you can add a note to the greeting that says, ". . .or stay on the line to leave a message for all the

Smiths," in case the caller is not sure which one he wants to talk to or if the caller wants to leave a message for everyone.

Because each of the Smiths has his own ID associated with his mailbox, people who call the Smiths regularly can dial the desired extension directly from the auto-attendant instead of dialing, say, 4001 or forwarding in from the 4001 extension. For instance, if a caller reached the opening greeting and dialed 5551001, he would get John's mailbox directly. You even could have each of the Smiths' phones set up to ring extension 4001 in the transfer rules first before going to the respective personal greetings. If you want to do this, be sure to use the Introduce and Confirm options on the transfer page; this plays the voice name of the subscriber and gives the person the option to take the call. In this way, if a call comes in for John and Jack picks up, Jack can send the call directly to John's greeting without talking to the caller, or he can accept the call and hand the phone to John, if he is there.

Find First Available Extension (Simple Hunt Group)

In some scenarios, it is handy to try a series of extensions until you find one that is not busy (for instance, a group of extensions for handling incoming sales or support calls). Normally, this is best done by the phone switch itself, which most often has more sophisticated and cost-effective methods of handling large numbers of calls waiting to find an open extension than Unity has at its disposal. However, when Unity runs behind a switch without such capabilities, or for small-scale needs in which the call does not end up parking on a port in Unity if a line is not available, it might make sense to have Unity do the hunting for you.

To do this in Unity, you take advantage of the blank greeting option, which is provided for fast call-routing scenarios just like this. Imagine that you want to have Unity try to find an open extension between 4001 and 4009 and, if none of the extensions is available, send the caller to an interview handler and collect the caller's information for later callback. To do that, follow these steps:

Step 1   First, create 10 call handlers. Configure their alternate transfer rules to be active, and have them configured to do a supervised transfer to extensions 4000 through 4009. You do not need to assign extensions to these call handlers if you do not want to; it is necessary only to configure the transfer rules properly to get Unity to try the phones that you want here. Depending on how you route callers to this hunt group, it is probably a good idea not to assign extensions to these handlers. Note that this scenario assumes that if an extension is not busy, someone is there to answer it. If you have agents in this group, have them be sure to take their extension out of service with a DND setting so that the switch returns busy when Unity tries the extension. If Unity spends time ringing the phone four times or more on these extensions, the caller could wait quite a while.

Step 2   Configure the alternate greetings for all 10 of the handlers to be active, and have the greeting source selected as blank. Using blank here instead of using a custom-recorded greeting that is blank means that Unity will take the after-greeting action instantaneously. Using a custom-recorded greeting that you simply leave empty results in a second or two of delay, even though there is no greeting recorded. This might not sound like much, but when strung over 10 or 20 call handlers, it makes a big difference. The blank option is there specifically for cases when you want to skip the greeting and move directly to the after-greeting action as quickly as possible.

Step 3   Configure the after-greeting action for each of the first nine call handlers to Attempt Transfer For the next call handler in the chain. Be sure not to use Send to Greeting For here because Unity does not actually try any of the extensions in the chain.

Step 4   On the last call handler (4009, in this case), you must decide what to do because this means that none of the extensions is open. In this example, you would have the after-greeting action set to go to an interview handler that is configured to take the caller's information and leave the message for a subscriber or public distribution list where someone can call them back when an agent frees up.

Of course, you have the last call handler play a greeting stating that no one is available now, followed by hold music that lasts 30 or 60 seconds, and then have an after-greeting action of sending the caller to the "attempt transfer" point on the first call handler at extension 4001. This queues calls until an extension becomes available.

Although this works, it also uses a port on your Unity system for each call holding in the queue. There is no easy way to limit how many calls Unity allows to pile up here, so with any kind of heavy call traffic, you run the risk of using all your ports with this application. In general, this is a bad idea unless you somehow have limited how many callers can reach this application. For instance, you can have calls that come in on particular ports on Unity go to the application, and provide no other mechanism for reaching the hunt group head. In this way, you can limit how many callers are in the queue at any given time. However, this is a pretty awkward mechanism; we definitely recommend using your switch to handle such queuing capabilities, to avoid problems with limited port resources on the Unity server.

You also can have the last call handler loop back to the first call handler and just keep trying until an extension opens up. Do *not* do this. Not only will you use port resources on the Unity server to do this, but in the case of a CallManager integration, you might overload the switch. Because the busy state comes back immediately in a CallManager integration, this would whip through all the handlers hundreds of times a second, which can overload the system. If you really want to queue the calls, be sure to have a 30- to 60-second greeting in the last handler before going back to the head of the hunt group.

One last note to keep in mind here: Different switches take different amounts of time to determine whether an extension is busy. As such, you might decide to include an actual recorded greeting that says, "Please stay on the line—your call is important to us," every three or four handlers in the chain. In the case of a CallManager integration, this is not necessary because the busy state is reported immediately. However, for analog switches, this can take a little while because the Dialogic card actually has to listen to the tone patterns being played back to determine whether it is a busy signal or a ring tone before reporting the state to Unity. This can take a couple of cycles, which can take a few seconds. Be sure to test how long of a delay callers will hear in your system for this scenario. Remember that they will not hear anything, in most cases. If callers hear more than 5 seconds or so of dead air, they might assume that the call has been dropped and hang up on you.

Holiday Greetings

Unity does not have a designated greeting that plays during holidays. Unity does have the concept of a holiday, but this simply forces the schedule to report back that it is off-hours, no matter what time of the day it is for the days that are marked for holidays. As such, during holidays, all the call handlers, subscribers, routing rules, and so on that check the schedule act on their off-hours schedule actions. This is not ideal for many companies because they want special greetings to play to callers when the company is closed for a holiday, distinct from the general "we are closed now" greetings.

You can provide this functionality with a little extra work. By leveraging the fact that during holidays the schedules *always* are returned as off-hours, you can chain together three call handlers to provide standard, off-hours, and holiday greetings for your company. As long as you provide this only for your "entry point" call handlers for outside callers, this is a reasonably practical solution to the problem. Let us say, for instance, that you want to configure your system so that the opening greeting provides a special holiday greeting that you record for each new holiday coming up. To do this, follow these steps:

Step 1   Create a business hours schedule and an off-hours schedule. The business hours schedule would be active, for instance, between 8 A.M. and 5 P.M. The off-hours schedule would be active between 5 P.M. and 8 A.M. In other words, these schedules are exact opposites of one another. Make sure that both schedules have the Observe Holidays option checked. This option ensures that the schedules return off-hours no matter what time of day it is during a holiday.

Step 2   Assuming that you use the opening greeting call handler for the business hours handler here, go ahead and create two new call handlers, named opening greeting—off hours and opening greeting—holiday, so that they appear next to each other when the list of handlers is presented in the SA or in the ATM interfaces.

Step 3   Associate the opening greeting call handler with the business hours schedule and the opening greeting—off-hours handler with the off-hours schedule. It does not matter which schedule the opening greeting—holiday call handler is configured for because you will be using its alternate greeting, which plays regardless of schedule.

Step 4   Record your normal day greeting in the opening greeting call handler's standard greeting. Record your normal off-hours greeting in the opening greeting—off-hours call handlers' standard greeting (do not get confused here and use the off-hours greeting—that will not work here). Record the greeting that you want to play for the next upcoming holiday in the opening greeting—holiday handler's alternate greeting, and make sure that its alternate greeting is active.

Step 5   Set the off-hours greetings for both the opening greeting and opening greeting—set off hours call handlers to be active and to have the source selected as blank. Make sure that the alternate, internal, and busy greetings are disabled.

Step 6   Set the after-greeting action for the opening greeting call handler's off-hours greeting to be Send to Greeting For the opening greeting—off-hours call handler. Set the after-greeting action for the opening greeting—off hours handler's off-hours greeting to Send to Greeting For the opening greeting—holiday call handler.

You are finished. The holiday call handler is reached only when it is a holiday. All other times, only the day or off-hours opening greeting call handlers will be accessed, depending on what time of day it is. So, what is happening here, and why does this work? Because you selected observe holidays on your schedules, they always return off-hours during the day that you have designated as a holiday. As such, on holidays, the call will hit the opening greeting call handler and be sent to the off-hours greeting, which is configured to hand the call to the opening greeting—off-hours call handlers. It always gets sent to the off-hours greeting for that handler as well, which is configured to pass the call through to the opening greeting—holiday call handler. Because that handler's alternate greeting is active and recorded, it plays and then takes whatever after-greeting action you choose.

In this setup, all that is necessary is to record the custom greeting for the next upcoming holiday ahead of time. It is okay to record it well ahead of time because no calls ever can reach that holiday call handler until it is actually a designated holiday. You can change greetings for call handlers over the phone in Unity 4.0(1), so it is reasonably easy to edit the holiday greeting, as long as you assign an extension to the opening greeting—holiday call handler. See the earlier section, "Changing Greetings for Call Handlers over the Phone," for more on that.

Separate Caller-Input Options for Day and Off-Hours Schedules

Remember from earlier in this chapter that Unity uses the same set of user-input key mappings for all greetings on a particular call handler. No way exists to have separate sets of user inputs for each greeting on the same call handler. In some situations, this can pose problems. For instance, during the day you want callers to be able to reach the sales support group by pressing 1, but after-hours you do not want that opening available. You certainly cannot voice the option of pressing 1 in the after-hours greeting for the call handler. Nothing would stop users from dialing it anyway, if they knew the option was there. You also cannot allow input during the after-hours greeting. However, this would shut down all user-input options entirely, which is not really a good solution.

Using a simplified version of the holiday greeting method, you can use two call handlers to provide separate caller-input options during the day and after-hours. Follow these steps:

Step 1 Create a business hours schedule and an off-hours. The business hours schedule would be active, for instance, between 8 A.M. and 5 P.M. The off-hours schedule would be active between 5 P.M. and 8 A.M. In other words, these schedules are exact opposites of one another.

Step 2 Assuming that you use the opening greeting call handler for the business hours handler here, go ahead and create a new call handler named opening greeting—off-hours.

Step 3 Associate the opening greeting call handler with the business hours schedule, and the opening greeting—off-hours handler with the off-hours schedule.

Step 4 Record your normal day greeting in the opening greeting call handler's standard greeting. Record your normal off-hours greeting in the opening greeting—off-hours call handlers' standard greeting (do not get confused here and use the off-hours greeting—that do not work here). Include the respective one-key options that you want to provide to callers for day versus off-hours schedule here.

Step 5 Set the off-hours greetings for the opening greeting handler to be active, and have the source selected as blank. Make sure that the alternate, internal, and busy greetings are disabled. Set its after-greeting action to be Send to Greeting For the opening greeting—off-hours call handler.

Step 6 Configure the user-input key mappings for each handler as you like.

Now you can have separate user input key options available during the day and during off hours times. Remember that during holidays the schedules will always return "off hours" all day if the schedules are set to "observe holidays." Make sure you account for this in your setup here.

Separate Transfer Rules for Subscribers

As noted earlier in this chapter, the only real difference between the call-handling characteristics of a subscriber and those of a call handler is that subscribers have only one transfer
rule that is always active. No separate standard, off-hours, and alternate transfer rules exist
as they do for call handlers. For subscribers, the transfer rule is always active. If you have
it set to ring a phone, it will ring that phone 24 hours a day 7 days a week if a caller dials
the subscriber's extension through the auto-attendant.

When the extension being dialed is at the workplace, this might not present a problem
because it will just ring a set number of times and then forward to the subscriber's greeting,
as it should. However, when the subscriber works from home, for instance, and wants to be
called only until a reasonable hour in the evening, this is not an ideal state of affairs.

Unfortunately, there is no clean way to work around this that does not involve some amount
of administrative overhead. When people ask about such scenarios, normally we recommend that they use a call handler that is associated with the subscriber in question to get
around this limitation.

Step 1   Set the subscriber to not transfer anywhere, but instead to go right to the
greeting.

Step 2   Enable the alternate greeting, set its source to blank, and have it attempt
transfer for a new call handler created just for this subscriber.

Step 3   For the call handler, associate it with a schedule that is appropriate, such
as standard hours between 8 A.M. and 5 P.M. Configure the standard and
off-hours transfer rules as appropriate. Presumably, the standard transfer
rule is set up to ring the home phone (see the earlier "Transferring to
External Numbers" section for more on this), and the off-hours transfer
rule is set to not transfer, but go right to the greeting. You want to use
supervised transfers in this scenario, so call progress to an external number can be an issue. You definitely want to test a few calls to make sure
that this goes smoothly.

Step 4   Record the appropriate greetings for the call handler. You can elect to
have a generic greeting that you record in the alternate greeting play
all the time, or you can use separate standard and off-hours greetings.
Whichever you choose, have the after-greeting action set up to take a
message.

Step 5   Configure both the owner and the message recipient to be the subscriber
for which you are building this call handler. This way, the messages taken
for this call handler show up in the mailbox as normal, and the subscriber
can change the greetings for the call handler over the phone using the
greetings administration conversation option (see the earlier section,
"Changing Greetings for Call Handlers over the Phone," for more on

that). Remember that for the subscriber to change the greetings for the call handler over the phone, the call handler must have an extension associated with it. You can opt to use a numbering convention, such as 9, followed by the subscriber's extension or the like so that it is easy for subscribers to remember.

Callers will not know that they are being transferred to a call handler behind the scenes, but for both the administrator and the owner of the mailbox, this entails some extra work. For large numbers of subscribers who need this type of functionality, you might want to check out the Bulk Handler Create tool on http://www.ciscounitytools.com.

The call progress to the home phone in this scenario can be an issue. If the home phone can be configured to forward back to Unity on busy or RNA issues, you can use release transfers here, which helps. Make sure that the call handler is assigned an extension that corresponds to the forwarding number here; do not associate it with the subscriber. When a call forwards into Unity, it looks up the extension in the database, and then goes right to the greeting for that handler or subscriber and overrides the transfer rules for it so that you do not get stuck in a transfer loop. However, if you do this for the subscriber in this case, the greeting rule then sends the call to the call handler's transfer rule and you *will* be caught in a transfer loop. If the call handler's extension matches, however, Unity automatically overrides the transfer rules for the call handler and sends the caller to the appropriate greeting for that handler instead, which is what you want.

This is more work than it really should be, I know. Including all three transfer rules for subscribers is on the radar for future versions of Unity. Hopefully, it will be there soon and people will not have to jump through this hoop.

Working Around Forwarding Transfer Rule Override

As noted in the last example, when a call forwards into Unity, the extension reported as the forwarding station is searched for in the database. If it matches a call handler or subscriber, the transfer rules for that object are deliberately skipped and the greeting rules are evaluated instead. This is done to prevent callers from getting stuck in a never-ending loop of transfers and forwards back to Unity, which then transfers back to the number, and so on.

However, in some rare cases you might want Unity to ring another phone if a call forwards into Unity from a particular extension. Normally, it is best to do this with switch programming and not use Unity for this type of thing, but sometimes that is not an option.

Suppose that you want calls that come forwarded busy from extension 7001 to be redirected to call extension 7002 all the time. If you just set up a call handler with an extension of 7001, and set up its alternate transfer rule to be active and to do a release transfer to 7002, it would never do what you want it to. Unity would find 7001 in the database when the call forwarded in from 7001, but it would not execute the transfer rules; it would go to the greeting rules directly instead.

To get around this, the blank greeting source is again your friend. The simplest method is to set the busy greeting to active, set its source to blank, and have its after-greeting action configured to Attempt Transfer For itself. Set its destination to be the call handler with extension 7001. This seems odd, but this is what happens: Unity clears the transfer override flag when it hits the busy greeting. When you loop the call back to the same call handler, it evaluates the transfer rules and does a release transfer to 7002, as you want.

Keep in mind that this can be dangerous. We put the transfer override flag in there for a good reason. For instance, if you made a mistake while entering the transfer destination in the SA and used 7001 instead of 7002, you create a bad transfer loop that can crash your Call-Manager and certainly chew up CPU resources on the Unity box (not to mention stranding your caller in limbo hearing nothing but dead air for who knows how long). Do not do this.

The only time that it is appropriate to use call deflection like this is if you are sending the caller to a *different* extension than the one that forwarded in—and the need to do even that should be very rare. If at all possible, you should provide such functionality with switch programming.

Send Directly to Greeting from the Operator Console

Many people are under the incorrect impression that doing such transfer overrides from the operator console should be a function of the voice-mail system, which is just not the case. The voice-mail system does only what the telephone switch tells it to.

In most situations, this is handled through a transfer override function in the switch itself. Just about every PBX has such a function; in recent versions, so does CallManager. This works in a very straightforward manner. A code that the receptionist can dial tells the switch not to ring the phone for that extension, but instead to act on the phone's RNA action programmed for that extension; this normally is set to go to voice mail. For instance, if the receptionist had someone on the line who wanted to leave a message for the person at extension 1234, she can put the caller on soft hold, dial something like 1234#7, and then complete the transfer. The switch then forwards the caller to the voice-mail system just as if it rang the subscriber's phone and forwarded in RNA. The voice mail does not know the difference between this operation and one that normally forwards from an extension after ringing a number of times. That is the idea; it should not have to.

We do not go into detail about how to do this in CallManager or any other PBX; you need to refer to your switch vendor's documentation for more on that. In the case of CallManager, you can find a tech tip on the versions that support this function and how to set it up at http://www.cisco.com/warp/customer/788/AVVID/transfer_voicemail.html.

If you are stuck in a situation in which your switch does not support a transfer override capability, this gets a whole lot less smooth. Unity does support a transfer override function from within the auto-attendant that you can use here. From the opening greeting, if you dial 1234#2 all as one number (do not pause after the 4 here—people make that mistake often),

Unity skips the transfer rules for the subscriber at extension 1234 and goes right to the greeting.

A couple of issues arise with this. First, the receptionist must dial into Unity's auto-attendant and then dial the extension followed by #2 for this to work. This is considerably more time-consuming than just dialing the extension with a transfer override function and releasing the call. Also, if the receptionist's phone corresponds to a subscriber in the voice-mail system, this user automatically is logged in as a subscriber. The subscriber must back out of the sign-in conversation first and *then* dial the extension followed by #2, which is even more cumbersome.

One way to ease this problem is to have the receptionist access the voice-mail system using a separate number when wanting to do such a transfer. This separate number routes to a call handler that just plays a greeting so that the receptionist can dial the extension followed by #2. You create a routing rule stating that any call forwarding from this virtual extension you create goes to your special handler setup for this. You put this at the top of your routing rules so that it does not attempt to forward to a greeting or do an attempt sign-in or the like. This at least ensures that the steps for the receptionist are limited to dialing into Unity, dialing the extension desired followed by #2, and then releasing the call. This is still not as smooth as using the switch to do this, but it is not as bad as having to back out of the subscriber mailbox every time the receptionist calls in, either.

Tenant Services

Before going further here, it needs to be said that Unity does not yet properly support true tenant-services configurations. You can get reasonably close for low-end applications, but there is no proper directory or administration segmentation that is necessary in a full tenant-services application. These things are on deck for future versions of Unity but are not there today. However, if you want to provide voice-mail services for a couple of small companies, and they can handle their subscribers finding other subscribers outside of their company in the address book, you can get most of the way there with Unity 4.0(1).

The main goal for a typical tenant-services application on the low end here is to route external callers to different sets of call handlers and make sure that they cannot jump out to another company's set of handlers or subscribers. As much as possible, the subscribers also should be unaware that other companies use the same voice-mail server they are, although this cannot be achieved completely in Unity today. Here is a short list of the steps you can take to create a new tenant on your Unity server:

Step 1 Create an opening greeting call handler for the new tenant. Of course, you can create entire audio-text applications, if you want, but at a minimum, you need a call handler to play a greeting that gives callers the chance to enter a subscriber's extension. Even if you do not allow outside callers access through auto-attendant features, you still need to do this: Subscribers need some place to go when they exit their conversations and also need some way to log into their mailboxes from outside the company.

Step 2 Next, create a routing rule that sends callers to this new opening greeting call handler that you created for the tenant. Typically, this is done through a dialed number routing so that each company can have its own dial-in number for external callers and subscribers to use when outside the company.

Step 3 Make sure that all the call handlers created for this tenant have their exit destinations set up properly. We have discussed this topic in detail earlier in this chapter, so the details are not repeated here. Make sure that you watch the error greeting destination and the user-input key mappings, in particular. A quick checklist of the database objects and their exit points to worry about appears at the end of this section.

Step 4 Create an all subscribers public distribution list for this tenant, named appropriately, of course. This comes in handy for several things down the road, including offering name-lookup handlers that limit the searches to subscribers in this tenant. You can apply Bulk Edit changes to all subscribers in a tenant quickly and easily using this distribution list as a filter.

Step 5 Create an operator call handler for that tenant. Presumably, each tenant will want the 0 out keys going to his own receptionist.

Step 6 Create a "say goodbye" call handler for that tenant. You need to be sure to use this call handler as the after-message destination and the like for all subscribers and call handlers created for this tenant.

Step 7 Create subscriber templates for this tenant, and use them when creating subscribers for them. This is the easiest way to keep the exit destinations and default distribution list membership stuff straight. Make sure that you associate the all subscribers public distribution list with the template(s) for this tenant so that it stays properly populated as you add subscribers to your tenants. Also make sure that you set the subscriber exit destination to be the opening greeting call handler for this tenant. You will find this on the conversation page for the subscriber template. By default, it goes to the opening greeting call handler that created the Unity setup, which is not where you want subscribers to go when they exit the subscriber conversation (by pressing *, in this scenario). Do not forget your error greeting and after message actions because, by default, those both take callers out of this tenant's set of handlers, which is not what you want.

Step 8   Create a name-lookup handler specifically for the subscribers associated with this tenant. The easiest way to do this is to have the name-lookup handler configured to use the all subscribers distribution list created in the last step as a filter. If you do not have outside callers find users by name, this step is not strictly necessary.

At this point, you are ready to add subscribers for that tenant. Just for a quick review, here is a short checklist of exit points from each database object that you have to worry about in a multiple-tenant environment:

- **Call handlers.** The user-input keys all can map to external objects that are outside the objects for a particular tenant. In particular, check the 0 key for operator access. The after-greeting actions for all greetings, particularly the error greeting, need to be checked. If you have not already done so, you should expose the error greeting in the SA using the Advanced Settings Tool. The after-message action needs to be watched as well. The default "say goodbye" sends the caller to a single call handler created by setup. If users opt to dial another extension from that greeting, they easily could end up in the wrong set of objects, particularly if you have locked down keys for user input.

- **Subscribers.** All the same exit points that exist for call handlers exit for subscribers, of course. One additional exit point for subscribers is found in the conversation page that was introduced for Unity 4.0(1). This is the exit destination where subscribers are sent when they use * to exit their message-retrieval conversation. By default, this is the opening greeting call handler created by setup, which is not likely what you want here.

- **Interview handlers.** Only one exit destination for interview handlers is taken after the caller responses are recorded. Again, the default here is to send the caller to the "say goodbye" call handler created by setup. You want to change this to be the "say goodbye" call handler that you add for the tenant in question.

- **Name-lookup handlers.** Only one exit destination is exposed for name-lookup handlers, and it defaults to the opening greeting call handler created by setup. You want to change this to the opening greeting created for this tenant.

If you can plan ahead and have each tenant's phone extension numbering plan nicely segmented so that tenant 1 has extensions that start with 1, tenant 2 has extensions that start with 2, and so on, you can get fancy and lock down those keys in the other tenant's audio-text applications. Outside callers would be unable to accidentally direct-dial a subscriber associated with another tenant. Of course, this limits you to nine tenants, but it is a nice way to segment your directory cheaply. It is less work and safer to simply not allow direct-dials and to force callers to go through the name-lookup handlers for each tenant if they want to reach a subscriber through the auto-attendant. This might be a little harsh if you do not set up DID lines for users to get right to the subscribers they want, however.

Be aware that you can do nothing to keep subscribers from addressing messages to other subscribers, even those associated with other tenants. Because subscriber lookups by name or ID automatically include all subscribers on the box (and, optionally, subscribers on other Unity servers on the network), you cannot do anything to prevent this presently. There is also no way to allow each tenant administrative access for his own users and handlers in the database through the SA without seeing the other tenant's objects. Both of these items are on deck for development work soon but will not be here for a while yet.

You cannot control two hard-coded references to the opening greeting in Unity 4.0(1). From the subscriber sign-in conversation, if users press # instead of entering their ID, Unity sends them to the opening greeting call handler. This is not a common scenario, but it can happen and puts subscribers outside their tenant objects, which can be confusing. The other hard-coded reference is that, if the Unity conversation invokes the failsafe conversation because of a database error, it sends the caller to the opening greeting call handler in most cases. This is also not adjustable, but it should be a reasonably rare occurrence; you can further limit it if you regularly check your system's health with the latest dbWalker version. Recent versions include the option to run automatically on a scheduled basis and e-mail the results to one or more administrators. This is a handy feature for staying on top of common broken link problems that might result in failsafe conversation events.

Customizing Unity Prompts

I often am asked how to get rid of a couple specific prompts (noted later) in the Unity conversation in the forums and through e-mail. Yes, you can replace these prompts with a silent prompt and effectively remove them from your system. Although I list the steps to do that here, you need to understand that TAC does not support this. In addition, any Unity upgrade, even between minor versions, replaces the modified prompt with its default version again. If you elect to modify these or any other prompts, TAC does not help you with this, and you have to redo the procedure again after you upgrade your system.

With that said, this is not terribly difficult. If Unity setup did not wipe out such changes on upgrades, we would have a prompt editing tool to help users do this type of thing properly. However, with the upgrade situation being what it is, providing a tool to do this seems pointless. The setup is being redesigned for Unity moving forward, and this is one of the issues on the plate for the people doing that work. Hopefully, we can get a proper prompt editing tool in place to help with these items in the future.

Finding Your Prompt

The first thing you need to do is find the prompt in question. Between Unity 4.0(1) and 4.0(2), the paths to the prompt files themselves changed a bit. Before 4.0(2), all prompts could be found under \Commserver\localize\prompts\ENU\ (on a U.S. English system). After 4.0(2), the codec of the prompt (either G711 or G729) was inserted into the path. As such, you would look under \Commserver\localize\prompts\enu\G711\. Throughout, we use the pre–4.0(2) path; just take this into account, depending on the version of Unity you look at.

If you poke around under \Commserver\localize\Prompts\ENU\ on a U.S. English system, you can see several subdirectories. These are all the various phrase groups that Unity uses. A phrase group is a logical portion of the phone conversation that makes it easier to find what you looking for here. Depending on the version of Unity you look at, there will be 25 to 30 phrase directories here. For instance, you will see AvCommon, which is a collection of prompts used by a number of different conversations, such as numbers and dates. AvPHGreet is the collection of prompts used to play the call handler greeting conversation, which is one of the most important ones in the system. You also find the AvSubSignIn directory, with prompts used, surprisingly enough, to construct the subscriber sign-in conversation; AvSubAddrMsg, which has prompts for subscribers addressing messages; and so on.

Under each of these conversation area directories, you find a file called PROMPTS.INI. This file contains the full text of all the prompts and the filename they are recorded in. These files are actually used to generate the scripts that the professional voices work off of when updating prompts for the system. They are kept up-to-date with the specific wording of the prompts for each release of Unity. If you search for a prompt this way, be sure that you search them all; several similar (sometimes identical) prompts are recorded in different groups, and you can end up changing the wrong one. It is also a really good idea to make a backup of any prompt that you change so that you can undo it easily without having to restore the entire prompt set off the install CDs.

Note that we cover a way to have the Port Status Monitor show you all the prompt names that play on a particular port as you call into Unity (see the "Troubleshooting" section at the end of this chapter). If you are not sure what phrase group a prompt falls into, but you know the part of the conversation it is in, this is another way to find the prompt you are looking for.

"Please Hold While I Transfer Your Call"

When Unity goes to perform any transfer, either supervised or release, it plays this prompt to callers before "hook flashing" to put them on soft hold and trying the number. In some cases, sites really hate this, particularly if a call goes through several handlers looking for an available extension.

The very sharp observer will note that on the contact rules table in SQL, there is a column called StreamPath that usually points to a WAV file for playing voice names and greetings. This value is not used, but it originally was intended to allow administrators to customize this very message played to callers on a per-handler or per-subscriber basis. As such, if you wanted to play a message to callers here, you could; if not, you simply select blank, as you do for greeting rules. Unfortunately, this work never was done, so the system defaults to playing the hard-coded prompt for all transfers on all handlers and subscribers.

In this case, the prompt that you want to replace can be found under \Commserver\Localize\ Prompts\ENU\AvPHGreet\AvPhGreetENU005.WAV. However, you cannot just delete the prompt and go. If the Unity conversation goes to grab a prompt to construct a phrase and it is missing, the conversation gets annoying, logs an error to the event log, and sends the caller to the failsafe conversation. You do not want this. To get rid of a prompt, you need to replace it with an empty prompt that is just a fraction of a second of silence. You can use several blank prompts, but we normally suggest using the one found here:

```
\Commserver\Localize\Prompts\ENU\AvAddrSearch\AvAddrSearchENU003.WAV.
```

You then copy the AvAddrSearchENU003.WAV file over the AvPhGreetENU005.WAV file, and the prompt no longer would play. No reboot is necessary; the next time Unity tries to play that prompt, it fetches the empty file and play nothing.

If you accidentally delete the wrong greeting or the like, all the greetings for all languages can be found on the Unity install CDs. They are uncompressed and are stored in the exact same directory structure as in your Unity installation on the hard drive. It is a simple matter of fetching the one you want, or doing an XCOPY to reset the entire set of prompts, if necessary.

"You May Record Your Message After the Tone; Stay on the Line for More Options"

This is the most requested prompt to remove by far. People who have custom-recorded greetings (that would be most people) typically do not want this to play because they record in their greetings to wait for the tone, and they might not have additional options configured for the after-message menus. Yes, this does beg the question of why this prompt is there at all and, more to the point, why it is set to play by default. To remove it, again copy a blank prompt over the offending prompt (or prompts, in this case). So, the first step is to find a blank prompt—again, we suggest using this:

```
\Commserver\Localize\Prompts\ENU\AvAddrSearch\AvAddrSearchENU003.WAV.
```

Unity actually uses two identical prompts to play this message, in two different spots in the conversation. One is used for subscribers leaving messages for other subscribers, and one is used for outside callers leaving messages. People who want this prompt removed typically do not make such fine distinctions and want them both out of there. These are the two prompts:

```
\Commserver\Localize\Prompts\ENU\AvPHGreet\AvPhGreet016.WAV
\Commserver\Localize\Prompts\ENU\AvPHGreet\AvPhGreet037.WAV
```

Copy AvAddrSearchENU003.WAV over both of these, and the prompt is no longer played.

It should be noted that the requests specifically for this prompt to be removed have been frequent enough to get attention here. Subsequent releases of 4.0(x) should include a systemwide configuration option enabling you to skip these prompts instead of copy blank prompts over them. These configuration settings are also preserved over upgrades, which is much nicer than having to repeat these steps after every update.

Directory Handler Name-Spelling Options

Unity offers the option of asking callers to spell the first name and then the last name, or the last name and then the first name when outside callers look for subscribers in the directory handler. However, everyone seems to want these prompts to sound slightly different, it seems. Smaller sites want the specific number of letters to be voiced; larger sites want more letters asked for or to go with a generic "spell the first few letters" option. Because there is no way we can come up with one prompt that will do what everyone wants, we recorded a set of 12 alternative prompts for the directory handler spelling conversation with the same voice that does the rest of the system prompts. You can download all the prompts from the Documents page on www.ciscounitytools.com. You find them under the Alternative Directory Handler Prompts section. Just follow the instructions for unpacking and installing the ones that you want off its home page.

Note, however, that the Unity upgrade replaces these prompts with the defaults, so you need to reapply the changes after upgrading. Also note that these prompts affect only the conversation that outside callers access when finding subscribers by name through a name-lookup handler. The conversation that subscribers use to address messages to one another by name or by ID is not affected.

Building Applications for TTY/TDD Users

Versions of Unity 4.0(3) and later include the U.S. English TTY prompt set (with a language code of ENX) as an optional phone language set that you can install. This provides a simple mechanism for administrators to add subscribers who use TTY/TDD devices, and also provides a mechanism to construct audio-text applications for callers using TTY/TDD devices.

Because the TTY prompt set is treated as any other language, such as French or Spanish, administrators can use the language-selection options on call handlers, subscribers, interviewers, and name-lookup handlers to have Unity generate the conversation presented to callers using TTY tones that will display as text on TTY/TDD devices. As with other languages, it is up to the administrator to record greetings for these handlers that provide the audio-text experience to the caller.

It is certainly possible to simply use Telephone Record and Playback (TRaP) and use a TDD phone to manually record greetings for audio-text applications, voice names, and the like. However, the TTY Angel utility makes this considerably quicker and easier by enabling administrators to type in text and producing a WAV file that contains the TTY tones that represent those characters. The TTY Angel application is shown in Figure 18-20.

Figure 18-20 *TTY Angel*

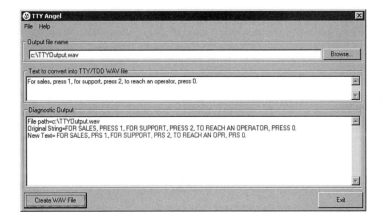

TTY Angel ships with Unity 4.0(3) and later, but it is not tied to a specific version of Unity and can run on- or off-box. You can download the latest version off www.ciscounitytools.com. Apart from making it easier and faster to create clean greeting files for use in TTY audio-text applications, it can apply a custom abbreviation dictionary of word replacements for you. Because in North America the Baudot protocol is used at 45.45 baud, the text transmission is rather slow; shortening up the text sent is important. For instance, *telephone* can be replaced with just *ph*, *thank you* can be replaced with *thnx*, and so on. There is no generally agreed upon dictionary, so TTY Angel lets you define your own replacements, if you like, and automatically applies them to provide consistency across your applications.

One last thing to note about TTY Angel is that it can be used to convert any standing U.S. English–based prompt set into TTY tones automatically. For instance, if you use an older version of Unity that does not offer the ENX prompt set, you can install, say, U.K. English or Australian English and then convert that prompt set into TTY tones using TTY Angel. It takes roughly 5 minutes to convert the more than 2000 prompts; afterward, you can use that language to be your designated U.S. English TTY prompt set in Unity. Obviously, upgrading to 4.0(3) or later is your best move, but that is not always a possibility for sites. See the TTY Angel help file for more details on how to go about this.

While you are at www.ciscounitytools.com, you should also take a look at the TTY WAV Reader tool. This tool started shipping with Unity 4.0(4) and later. It parses any WAV file and, if TTY tones are found in it, displays the text on the form and copies it to the Clipboard. It is sophisticated enough that it can be your default WAV file reader, but if it does not find TTY tones in the file that you select, it passes the file to the next registered WAV reader in your system.

For instance, if you have a receptionist who is going through a general inbox of outside caller messages that contains messages from both voice and TTY callers, she can install TTY WAV Reader and simply click on each WAV file in the inbox. If it is a TTY message, the text is displayed instantly; if not, the standard WAV player (such as Windows Media Player) comes up playing the voice message automatically. This can be very handy for sites that use Unified messaging and also support TTY users. See the help file for the TTY WAV Reader application for more details on how to install it and set it up. Like TTY Angel, it is not Unity version–specific and is designed to install on any Windows 98 or later desktop.

You can treat audio-text applications created for TTY/TDD users just as you do an application created for different-language callers. However, you must keep one thing in mind: Unity does not yet recognize TTY tones for call-routing purposes. Users are still required to use DTMF tones to navigate menus. Most voice-mail and IVR systems require this, so it is not completely unexpected by callers. Still, you should keep it in mind as you construct the greetings that your audio-text application uses.

The other concern for handling TTY callers is routing the initial call into the appropriate audio-text tree. One way to handle this is the same mechanism discussed earlier for handling different-language calls by using separate DID lines for each language. In this way, French callers are greeted immediately with a French opening greeting, and TTY users get TTY prompts right away. This is the higher-end solution, and it obviously involves more overhead and expense in setting up the different inbound numbers. For smaller companies, it might not be practical to advertise different inbound 1-800 numbers for all different languages. Another solution here is to have the caller manual select the language at the opening greeting. With TTY, this is a little tricky because the tones played to TTY devices are rather piercing to the human ear. Simply inserting the selection into the opening greeting can alarm users, or they can think that they got a fax machine and hang up.

One way to get around this is to front-load the greeting with your language selection and then default to the TTY application. For instance, you record your opening greeting to say (in English) "To continue in English, press 1"; (in French) "To continue in French, press 2"; and (in Spanish) "To continue in Spanish, press 3." Then you pause for a second and route the call to your TTY call-handler tree. In this instance, callers select the first option they hear that is appropriate, unlike with other audio-text menus, in which they typically wait to hear all the options first. As such, it is not necessary to repeat the menu here, although you can. TTY callers see the voice energy light on the phone flicker for 8 or 10 seconds and see text coming across, welcoming them to the TTY audio-text entry point. For repeat callers, you can have a one-key option off the opening greeting (such as 4, in this case) set to go immediately to the TTY entry point so that experienced callers simply can press the 4 DTMF (remember, Unity does not route calls based on TTY tones at this point) to skip the initial wait for language selection.

Also note that you must use the G711 codec for recordings if you use TTY/TDD devices. G729a compresses based on human voice sound limits, and the tones used by TTY devices get garbled and do not play back reliably. G711 records and plays back TTY tones reliably. You can check out the help file for TTY Angel for a quick overview on how the TTY/TDD tone sets works and a little history behind the Baudot protocol used in North America today. At the time of this writing, the codec selection for recordings in Unity is a systemwide setting, not a per-subscriber/per-handler one; you must default all recordings to G711.

Call Traffic Reports

Two reports provided in the SA are designed to help you track activity in the Unity auto-attendant:

- The Transfer Call Billing report in the SA Subscriber Reports section is designed to provide a complete accounting of all calls transferred internally and externally for call handlers and subscribers. This provides an easy mechanism for getting a list of all numbers that callers have been transferred to over a set period of time. You should be able to tell at a glance if you have a system administrator, for instance, that uses Unity to dial long-distance numbers or the like.

- A Call Handler Traffic report in the SA System Reports section can provide an accounting of how many calls hit each call handler in the system and how the callers exited them (selecting a one-key option, hanging up, and so on). This can also be helpful, depending how callers use your system, particularly if they are getting impatient and bailing out of your call-handler trees by hanging up in frustration. This is a good indication that you need to flatten your trees or break up your audio-text applications so that they are not so large and complex.

For more general information about how much call traffic your Unity system experiences or generates, you can use the Port Usage Analyzer tool. This tool generates a set of four reports that can be viewed in table or graphical format to show the following:

- **Port availability**. This view shows how many ports are busy and, more important, how many are available to take calls over the course of the day you select. If you experience call spikes or think that you might require more ports, this is the report to look at.

- **Call distribution**. This shows what type of call activity each port in your Unity system experience or generate. This is handy for finding ports that are not utilized to their maximum extent, or spotting trouble with outbound dials that possibly are conflicting with inbound call traffic and the like.

- **Port time use**. This is similar to the call distribution view, but instead of showing the number of calls, it shows how much time is spent on the various types of outbound and inbound calls on a per-port basis. Again, it can help spot port underutilization and unexpected call patterns in your system.

- **Call traffic**. This shows how many calls of each type came in and went out of the Unity system for each minute of the day. This is useful for analyzing port spikes and periods of the day when there is low port availability.

You will find the Port Usage Analyzer in the Tools Depot on the Unity desktop. It can be installed and run off the server—and, of course, you can get the latest version off its home page at www.ciscounitytools.com.

Damage Control

Before you do much of anything with your system, you should understand how to get it back into a running state quickly. The following sections help you recover from such problems as accidentally deleting default objects or removing rules, or fixing damaged or corrupted templates.

Backups

There is no excuse to not back up your Unity system information any longer; we have been shipping the Disaster Recover Tools (DiRT) since 3.1(4). When you get your system the way you want it, you should back up with DiRT immediately. Without messages, this takes just a minute or two. It includes all the SQL data, of course, but also the switch-integration files, Registry branches of interest, greetings and voice names, and so on.

TIP   Restoring with DiRT is supposed to happen on a clean system, but we put this check there to protect people from themselves, not because DiRT needs a clean system to restore onto. If you have a system that you just fouled up by corrupting the database (for instance, you deleted a bunch of call handlers that you did not mean to directly in SQL), you can restore from your DiRT backup without reinstalling first by calling it with the **/DirtyRestore** command-line option. This forces the DiRT restore to skip the checks to be sure that the system is clean and replaces your entire database with the one that was backed up. Be *sure* that this is what you want to do, however, because there is no Undo option here.

Of course, you can do entire system backups with tape-backup packages, such as Backup Exec, but these cost money and are designed to back up and restore entire systems, not just the Unity-specific data. As such, they are quite a bit slower at getting your system back up and flying right. DiRT specifically is designed to snag and restore just the Unity-related data; it is the perfect tool for covering your back if you are experimenting in your database and have a messy accident.

As a side note, it is always a very good idea to check http://www.ciscounitytools.com for updated versions of DiRT backup and restore tools. This is a good idea for all tools, but DiRT, in particular, is one of those failure-sensitive items that you really do not want to run into problems with. I update it aggressively, even for minor problems encountered in the field. Starting with the release of 4.0(3), most tools automatically check back to their home pages for updated versions and warn you when they start that a newer version is available. However, if you run on systems that do not have access to the Internet, make such checks on your own.

Reconstruct Default Objects

If you have deleted one or more default objects and you just want to get them back to their default state, you can do this easily using the ConfigMgr.exe application, found in the \Commserver directory where you installed Unity. This application does not show up in the Tools Depot because it is considered too low level for the typical administrator. But because you are reading this right now, clearly you have distinguished yourself from the unwashed masses and can handle it.

That said, this *is* a dangerous tool, and you *can* wipe our your system configuration information in a flash. Proceed with caution. Furthermore, using the Configuration Manager incorrectly actually can wipe out your entire Unity database in one shot. There is an option to replace the existing database with the default database instead of applying the default objects to your database. The wording on the form is clear, but accidents can happen. Make sure that you back up your system first and proceed with extreme caution.

When you open the Config Manager application in 4.0(3) and later, you get an initial dialog box that presents you with options to create the AMIS or bridge accounts. It also includes an Advanced button. Pressing the Advanced button shows the main ConfigMgr form after issuing a warning to be careful. The main form is shown in Figure 18-21; it presents a list of radio buttons. When one of these buttons is selected, it automatically picks scripts to run from the list of SQL scripts that the Unity setup process uses to construct the default database tables during install. In this case, you want to select the Reset All Default Configuration Settings While Preserving All Existing Objects radio button. This automatically selects the FixDefaultObjects.sql script at the top, which is the script that you want to run here.

If you run an older version of Unity, the configuration manager interface is not as helpful, and you have to choose that script name manually. Be sure to get the FixDefaultObjects.sql script and not another one; other scripts can easily damage your system. If you run 4.0(3) or later, the ConfigMgr application dialog box should look like Figure 18-21.

Figure 18-21 *The Configuration Manager Interface*

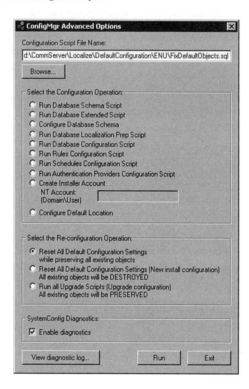

After you have double- and triple-checked that the proper script is selected, press the Run button at the bottom to apply the script. This script re-creates most of the default objects in the database, if they are not there:

- The default restriction tables, including DefaultTransfer, DefaultOutdial, and DefaultFax

- The DefaultAdministrator and DefaultSubscriber COS objects

- The SayGoodbye, OpeningGreeting, and Operator call handlers

- The Example Subscriber and (in versions of Unity before 4.0(3)) the Example Administrator subscriber objects

- The DefaultTemplate and DefaultAdminTemplate subscriber template objects

For instance, it does not reconstruct your schedules and routing rules, or rebuild the default public distribution lists. It is important to note that this script adds an object to the database only if there is not already one there with a matching alias. If there is an object with that alias, it is skipped. As such, if you want to have, for instance, the opening greeting call handler reconstructed from scratch, but it is still in your system in a damaged state, you must delete it before running the script. You will want to do this directly in SQL using Enterprise Manager (yes, it is okay to install Enterprise Manager even if you are using the MSDE version of SQL).

Go to the UnityDB database, open the CallHandler table, find the call handler with an alias of OpeningGreetingch, and delete that row. The triggers built into the database take care of removing its contact, greeting, and user input rules automatically. You also can do this through the SQL Query Analyzer, if you have it installed, or by using the Query Builder window in CUDLE that ships with Unity 4.0(1) and later. You would enter **DELETE FROM CallHandler WHERE Alias='openinggreetingch'**. This does the same thing as deleting the opening greeting call handler in the enterprise manager. Either way, after you remove it, you can run the script; the handler is re-created.

If you do not have Enterprise Manager installed and using the Query Builder window is not to your liking, you can perform the necessary delete operation using DOHPropTest, found in the diagnostic section of the Tools Depot. You must enter the password, discussed earlier (remember, it is [100-month][month+day]), to edit or delete objects.

To delete the opening greeting call handler, open DOHPropTest, enter the appropriate password, and then select Call Handlers in the far left list. Select the opening greeting alias in the middle column; this is the opening greeting call handler's alias. Because it is marked as undeletable in the Unity interface, DOHPropTest will not let you remove it until you clear the flag. To do this, select the AVP_UNDELETABLE value in the far-right columns, enter 0 as the value at the bottom, and press the Set button. Now you can delete the call handler itself by pressing the Remove button in the middle of the form. This removes the handler and all its contact rules, menu entries, and messaging rules. You then can run the FixDefaultObjects.sql script to re0-create it.

Reconstructing the Default Routing Rules

If you foul up your routing rules and Unity is no longer processing inbound calls properly, you might want to rebuild the default call-routing rules and start over. Again, using the ConfigMgr application noted previously, select the Run Rules Configuration Script radio button; the script that you want is automatically selected. Press the Run button and restart Unity. Because the routing rules are loaded into a table in memory at startup, the new rules are not visible or acted on until you restart the system.

It should be noted that this script wipes out all routing rules in your system and replaces them with the defaults. It is not like the fixDefaultObjects.slq script mentioned earlier; it does not care what is in the database already.

Reconstructing the Default Schedules

If you foul up your schedules or remove the default rules by accident, you might want to rebuild the default schedules. Again, using the ConfigMgr application noted earlier, press the Run Schedules Configuration Script radio button; the script that you want automatically is selected. Press the Run button and restart Unity. Like the routing rules, the schedules are loaded into a table in memory at startup. The new schedules are not visible or acted on until you restart the system.

Again, this script wipes out all schedule information in your system and replaces the schedules with the defaults. It is not like the fixDefaultObjects.slq script mentioned earlier; it does not care what is in the database already.

Rebuilding the Default Subscriber Templates

If you accidentally damage your default subscriber template objects or they have been corrupted by a bug in the SA or the like, you might want to just construct the default templates and not touch any of the rest of the default objects. You can use dbWalker to do this on any Unity 3.1(2) or later system. Under the File menu is a Re-create Default Templates option. This option blows away the default template and default admin template objects added by Unity setup and rebuilds them from scratch. This does not touch any of the other default objects or anything else in the database.

Because the default templates are used when constructing new subscriber templates and all call handlers in the system, problems with the templates can be especially troublesome. A series of problems with the SA also caused the templates to become corrupted if a user creation or import failed because of an account permissions problem in the directory. As such, replacing the templates is much more common in the field, and the option was added to the dbWalker tool to make this more accessible and less intrusive for users.

Troubleshooting

Certainly, a lot of diagnostic traces and tools can be used to troubleshoot problems that you encounter while processing calls in Unity. However, the scope of this book does not extend to detailed troubleshooting steps, by any means. That said, you can use a few tools to get a handle on where calls are going in your system and why.

Event Log

Whenever you try to run down a problem in Unity, you should always check the application event log for errors. Many times, the problem reveals itself there; Unity is designed so that the event log is the entry point into the troubleshooting process. For instance, if you create a routing rule that points to a call handler that then is subsequently deleted, callers will hear the failsafe conversation stating that an error has occurred. You will see this entry in the application event log:

```
Event Type:      Error
Event Source:    CiscoUnity_Arbiter
Event Category:    Run
Event ID:      1017
Date:          12/1/2002
Time:          3:02:20 PM
User:          N/A
Computer:      LLTHINKPAD
Description:
[Port 2] Failed attempting to load database object for application [PHGreeting],
    specified in routing table rule [0].  Use the RulerEditor to find the rule and
    check that the database object exists.  For more information, click: http://
    www.CiscoUnitySupport.com/find.php
```

This indicates that the first rule in the routing rules list failed. It does not indicate which rule specifically (it could be a forwarding rule or a direct-call rule), but you should be able to narrow it fairly quickly. Note that the advice in the event log message shown earlier to use the ruler editor to check this is bad advice—it should be more than sufficient to use the rules editor in the SA to find what the problem is (and it is a whole lot less dangerous).

Another thing to note here is that the failsafe conversation behaves a little differently in 4.0(1) than in previous versions of Unity. The users hear, "Sorry, a system error has occurred; please report this error to your system administrator." Then the call is routed to the opening greeting. In earlier versions of Unity, the failsafe greeting was played and then the caller was hung up on. If the error is catastrophic enough (the opening greeting call handler is removed from the system), callers still get hung up on, but generally this will not happen. In the case of a missing message recipient on a call handler, for instance, the failsafe message plays and the call is sent to the opening greeting instead of just hanging up on the caller, as was done in previous versions. This still lets admins know that there is a problem without unduly terminating calls on a common problem.

Call Viewer

As was discussed earlier in this chapter, the Call Viewer application is ideal for seeing what information Unity actually gets from the switch on inbound calls. It is a very good idea to look here first to make sure that calls come in with the data that you assume they are before running down the "what is wrong with Unity?" path too far. See the "Routing Rules" section, earlier in this chapter, for more specifics on the Call Viewer application. If the information that you see in the Call Viewer does not match what you expect, and you use a serial or analog integration to your switch, you sometimes can get additional information using the Integration Monitor (see Chapter 17).

Also remember that if you use extension-remapping files in your system, the Call Viewer displays the remapped extension information, not the original "raw" information received from the switch. See the "Extension Remapping" section, earlier in this chapter, for more on this.

Port Status Monitor

With the release of Unity 4.0(3), a new and much improved version of the Port Status Monitor (PSM) was released. This version works on all versions of Unity back to 3.1(1), so if you run an older version of Unity, feel free to download this updated tool from www.ciscounitytools.com and use it.

The Port Status Monitor tool is found in the Tools Depot under the Switch Integration Tools section on Unity 4.0(3) and later systems. Do not confuse this tool with the status monitor website that is the companion to the SA; they are not the same thing. The PSM tool shows a lot of detailed information about what is happening on calls on each port, and this can be very useful for determining where calls are going in the system and why. Figure 18-22 shows what the monitor looks like when a call comes into the opening greeting and the user dials 5551001 to reach a subscriber's mailbox and records a message.

Figure 18-22 *Port Status Monitor*

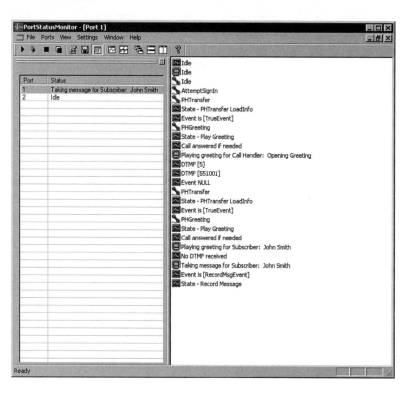

Figure 18-22 shows just a single port being monitored. You can view all ports on the system at once, if you want, but the screen gets cluttered. It is much easier to monitor a single port and make your test calls to that line, if you can. Three types of output show by default in the port-monitoring pane. You can choose to turn off one or two of them off under the Settings menu option, but, in general, it is a good idea to leave them all on:

- **Display**. This shows high-level information and is, in fact, the text that shows up in the web-based status monitor. Not a lot of detail shows here, but it helps you keep straight the context of what is going on in the other windows as you navigate the system. The display output is prefaced with the icon that looks like a computer screen. In Figure 18-22, it includes the line "Playing greeting for call handler: Opening greeting."

- **Conversation**. This shows a lot more detail, some of which does not make a lot of sense to the casual observer (or even the not-so-casual observer). For instance, we cannot tell you what the "Event is [TrueEvent]" lines in that pane in Figure 18-22 actually mean. The conversation output is prefaced by the icon that looks like a sine wave form on a screen. A conversation developer likely could glean some use from much of this output, but that is probably about it. The most interesting thing for the conversation output for nondevelopers using this tool is the DTMF events that show every key press made. Note that, for this test, we dialed 5551001 all as one string during the opening greeting. However, the conversation output in Figure 18-22 shows the first 5 by itself, followed by the 551001 remainder on the next line. This is because the first 5 pressed interrupted the greeting and is its own event. The other digits were part of the "gather digits" event, which gathers as many digits as the user enters (up to 30) and does a lookup in the database. It looks a little odd at first glace, but it is supposed to look that way.

- **Application**. The application output is prefaced by a small phone hand set icon and shows which conversation names are spawned. In this case, the attempt sign-in conversation is spawned on the direct inbound call by the routing rules. The PHTransfer and PHGreeting conversations are spawned when the call is sent to the opening greeting. You will notice that the default routing rules send the calls to the Attempt Transfer For entry point for the opening greeting call handler, which calls the PHTransfer conversation. However, the transfer rule is disabled on the opening greeting, so the PHTransfer conversation exits and spawns the PHGreeting conversation.

With a little bit of practice, you will find that the status monitor is a very powerful tool for troubleshooting your audio-text applications. Numerous options exist for altering the output and appearance of the tool, including showing real-time port status information on the left of the tool, dumping the output to a CSV file, running it with command-line options to capture call traffic information over time, and so on. Refer to the help file and the training video on its home page on www.ciscounitytools.com for more details on what you can do with this tool.

TIP	One thing that you can do with the Port Status Monitor is not mentioned in its help file: You can have it output the specific filenames of all the prompts being played out to the caller on the phone. This can be very useful if you are trying to run down a specific prompt that you want to edit or remove, but you do not know what phrase group it goes under, or you cannot find it in the PROMPT.INI files. Refer to the "Customizing Unity Prompts" section, earlier in this chapter, for details on how to do that.
	To turn on the prompt filename output, you need to turn on a special conversation trace. To do this, open the Unity Diagnostic Tool (UDT), in the Tools Depot or in the Unity Program Group on your Unity server. Go to the Configure Micro Traces Wizard and, on the list of micro traces, scroll down to the PhraseServer to Monitor branch. Check trace #11, "Phrase IDs, Prompt Filenames, and Audio Stream Info." Click Next and then Finish to activate the trace.
	After you have turned on that trace, the conversation output includes a list of all prompt names (complete with the path to the specific WAV file being referenced) used to construct each phrase being played to the caller. Obviously, this will generate a lot more output and is not something that you want to have turned on all the time. However, if you are trying to run down a specific prompt and you want to make sure that you get the right one, this is one way to go about that.

Call-Routing Rules Diagnostic Traces

For sites that use a lot of routing rules to do specialized audio-text application entry points for DID routing and the like, it is not uncommon for administrators to run into trouble figuring out why their calls are going places they do not expect them to. Using the Call Viewer and looking at your routing rules configuration is normally sufficient. However, every so often it is difficult to see why a particular rule is selected or passed over on for incoming call with just the naked eye.

For the purposes of this discussion, we add a couple of new direct call-routing rules to the system and make a test call that triggers one of those new rules. We then walk through the diagnostic output that shows how the ruler component (discussed back in the architecture overview in Chapter 2) evaluates the rules and selecting the one we want.

We added a rule called Route Calls from 5002 and a rule called Route Calls from 5001 to the list of direct call-routing rules. These two new rules are configured to route calls from 5001 directly to the All Seattle Employees name-lookup handler, and calls from 5002 to the All Chicago Employees name-lookup handler. We arranged them so that they are evaluated after the attempt sign-in rule and before the default call handler rule, as shown in Figure 18-23.

Figure 18-23 *Call-Routing Rules with Two New Direct Call Rules Added to the Defaults*

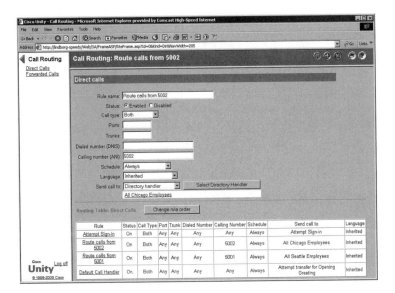

To see what the ruler is doing as new calls are processed through the routing rules, you need to turn on a trace output option in the Unity Diagnostic Tool (UDT). You find the UDT in the Tools Depot on the desktop, or in the Unity program group off your Start menu on the local Unity server. Run it and select Configure Micro Traces. On the list of traces, scroll down to the RulerDomain branch and turn on trace #11, "Rules Creation/Deletion/Evaluation." Select Next and Finish to activate the trace. I normally select the Start New Log Files option after turning on a new trace, to make it easier to find the output I am looking for after making a test call.

When the trace has been set up and the log files have been cycled, I make a test call into the system, calling from extension 5001. I hear the directory handler for Seattle employees start playing its conversation and then hang up. I then use the UDT's Gather Logs Files function to get the log information converted into a more human-readable format. Remember from the architecture overview discussion in Chapter 2 that the ruler component lives under the AvCsMgr. When gathering log files, you can get the AvCsMgr diagnostic logs and ignore all the others. I have numbered the lines in the trace output here so that you can refer to them easily. Outside of that bit of editing, the formatted trace output for that call looks like this:

```
10:51:17:735 (AvDiagnostics_MC,643,RulerDomain,11) [Thread 4104] [Port 1]
   CRulerDomain::FindFirstTrueRule: StartIndex=[0]
10:51:17:734 (AvDiagnostics_MC,1292,RulerDomain,11) [Thread 4104] [Port 1]
   Evaluating Rule 'Attempt Forward to Greeting' in Domain 'Routing'.
10:51:17:735 (AvDiagnostics_MC,1296,RulerDomain,11) [Thread 4104] [Port 1]
   Expression 'Reason IN 2 4 8 64' evaluates to false: Rule Parameter 'Reason'
   evaluates to 1.
```

```
10:51:17:734 (AvDiagnostics_MC,1293,RulerDomain,11) [Thread 4104] [Port 1] Rule
   'Attempt Forward to Greeting' in Domain 'Routing' evaluated to FALSE.
10:51:17:735 (AvDiagnostics_MC,1292,RulerDomain,11) [Thread 4104] [Port 1]
   Evaluating Rule 'Attempt Sign-In' in Domain 'Routing'.
10:51:17:734 (AvDiagnostics_MC,1295,RulerDomain,11) [Thread 4104] [Port 1]
   Expression 'Reason == 1' evaluates to true.
10:51:17:735 (AvDiagnostics_MC,1293,RulerDomain,11) [Thread 4104] [Port 1] Rule
   'Attempt Sign-In' in Domain 'Routing' evaluated to TRUE.
10:51:17:734 (AvDiagnostics_MC,643,RulerDomain,11) [Thread 4104] [Port 1]
   CRulerDomain::FindFirstTrueRule: Rule evaluates to TRUE; Index=[1]
10:51:17:735 (AvDiagnostics_MC,1301,RulerDomain,11) [Thread 4104] [Port 1] First
   Rule to evaluate to TRUE in Domain 'Routing' is 'Attempt Sign-In':
   Action='AttemptSignIn'.
10:51:17:734 (AvDiagnostics_MC,643,RulerDomain,11) [Thread 4104] [Port 1]
   CRulerDomain::FindFirstTrueRule: StartIndex=[0]
10:51:17:735 (AvDiagnostics_MC,643,RulerDomain,11) [Thread 4104] [Port 1]
   CRulerDomain::FindFirstTrueRule: No Rule evaluates to TRUE; Index=[-1]
10:51:17:734 (AvDiagnostics_MC,1302,RulerDomain,11) [Thread 4104] [Port 1] No Rule
   evaluated to TRUE in Domain 'REJECTION'.
10:51:17:765 (AvDiagnostics_MC,643,RulerDomain,11) [Thread 4104] [Port 1]
   CRulerDomain::FindFirstTrueRule: StartIndex=[2]
10:51:17:766 (AvDiagnostics_MC,1292,RulerDomain,11) [Thread 4104] [Port 1]
   Evaluating Rule 'Route calls from 5002' in Domain 'Routing'.
10:51:17:765 (AvDiagnostics_MC,1296,RulerDomain,11) [Thread 4104] [Port 1]
   Expression 'CallingNumber == 5002' evaluates to false: Rule Parameter
   'CallingNumber' evaluates to 5001.
10:51:17:766 (AvDiagnostics_MC,1293,RulerDomain,11) [Thread 4104] [Port 1] Rule
   'Route calls from 5002' in Domain 'Routing' evaluated to FALSE.
10:51:17:765 (AvDiagnostics_MC,1292,RulerDomain,11) [Thread 4104] [Port 1]
   Evaluating Rule 'Route calls from 5001' in Domain 'Routing'.
10:51:17:766 (AvDiagnostics_MC,1295,RulerDomain,11) [Thread 4104] [Port 1]
   Expression 'CallingNumber == 5001' evaluates to true.
10:51:17:765 (AvDiagnostics_MC,1295,RulerDomain,11) [Thread 4104] [Port 1]
   Expression 'Reason IN 1' evaluates to true.
10:51:17:766 (AvDiagnostics_MC,1293,RulerDomain,11) [Thread 4104] [Port 1] Rule
   'Route calls from 5001' in Domain 'Routing' evaluated to TRUE.
10:51:17:765 (AvDiagnostics_MC,643,RulerDomain,11) [Thread 4104] [Port 1]
   CRulerDomain::FindFirstTrueRule: Rule evaluates to TRUE; Index=[3]
10:51:17:766 (AvDiagnostics_MC,1301,RulerDomain,11) [Thread 4104] [Port 1] First
   Rule to evaluate to TRUE in Domain 'Routing' is 'Route calls from 5001':
   Action='AD'.
```

This looks a little long at first, but if you break it down into sections, it is actually simple to read. The first four lines show it starting at the top of the routing rules list and rejecting the attempt forward to greeting rule because the reason value is 1 (direct call) and the attempt forward to greeting rule applies only to forwarded calls (reasons 2, 4, 8, 64). Remember that the ruler evaluates all rules on all calls, so even though this is a direct call, you see it evaluating rules found in the forwarded calls list as well.

Lines 5 through 9 in the output show the ruler evaluating the second rule that it encounters, which is the attempt sign-in rule. You notice that the rule itself evaluates to True because we have a calling number and the call is direct, which are the two criteria for that rule to be activated. Notice that it writes out the fact that the rule evaluated to True as index [1]. This means that it is the second rule found in the list of routing rules—the first item is index [0].

On Lines 10, 11, and 12, you see it evaluate the REJECTION rules. On the first routing rule that evaluates to True, the ruler checks for rejection rules that override it. This feature never was implemented in Unity, so the rejection rules never evaluate to True. This check is made only on the first routing rule to evaluate to True; it is not done on subsequent True matches.

On Lines 13 through 16, you see it jumping back to the routing rules and starting the search for another routing rule that matches, starting with an index of 2 (the third item in the list of routing rules). What happened here? The attempt sign-in conversation was executed, but it did a lookup of 5001 in the subscriber database and did not find a match. As such, it failed the rule and told the ruler to find the next rule that evaluates to True. The same thing happens on a forwarded call if the attempt forward to greeting conversation looks up the forwarding number and does not match the extension of a call handler or subscriber. The attempt sign-in and attempt forward to greeting conversations are specialized conversations that are designed to be used only by the routing rules because they have this unique behavior. This is why you do not see these conversations offered elsewhere in the SA interface. In any case, you will notice in the output that the next rule it evaluates is the call from 5002 rule, which fails because the call is from 5001.

Finally, on Lines 17 through 22, you see the call from 5001 rule evaluating to True, and the call being sent to the AD conversation. AD stands for Alpha Directory in this case, which is a name-lookup handler. This happens to be the All Seattle employees name-lookup handler, but the diagnostic output does not indicate which specific object the call is sent to—it gives only the name of the conversation used.

The key information to take out of the diagnostic output is the failure and success reasons noted as each rule is evaluated. This can help you pinpoint why a particular rule is rejected; this might not be immediately obvious to you when just looking at the Call Viewer output.

Summary

This long chapter covered a lot of varied material, much of which is relevant to sites with specific call-processing needs. The main thing to take away from this chapter is that Unity has a fully featured set of call-processing capabilities that allow it to do most audio-text application design. The basic set of call-processing objects in Unity is much more flexible than most administrators realize because the basic documentation for Unity does not go into too much detail on how to use them. The only time that it should be necessary to employ a separate IVR system with Unity is if specialized services, such as reading bank balances over the phone or doing a similar type of integration with external systems, is needed.

CHAPTER 19

Administering Multiple Unity Servers

This chapter focuses on how to administer a network of multiple Unity servers. You can use many tools and several optimizations to greatly reduce the complexity of managing subscribers globally. The following sections discuss administrator accounts, access, and global subscriber management.

Unity Administrator Accounts and Access

This section covers how to grant administrative access to users. Depending on the company, there can be a single administrator with one Unity server or many administrators with varying levels of access administering many servers.

Using Class of Service for Administrative Access

By default, two Windows accounts have Administrative access to Unity. One is the account specified as the Admin account during installation. The other is the Example Administrator account that Unity creates during setup. The Example Administrator should be left untouched. This means that, by default, you must log into the Unity SA using the Admin account to do any administrative tasks. Any person logging in using this account has full admin access and can make any desired change.

Figure 19-1 shows a very simple network consisting of a single Unity server integrated with CallManager. This type of scenario is commonly seen in small and medium businesses.

In the figure, the Unity Admin account specified during install was VNT\unityadmin, where VNT is the Windows domain name and unityadmin is the username. VNT Inc. has a small network administration staff consisting of three people. Each is allowed to administer the server, but two have limited administrative access.

Figure 19-1 *Typical Topology, Small and Medium Businesses*

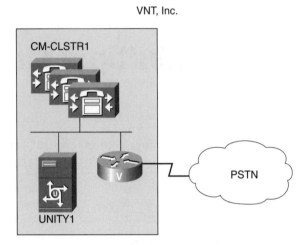

In a simple network like this, you can solve this problem by using a class of service (CoS). A CoS enables you to detail exactly what level of access users will have. By default, Unity is already configured with two CoSs: Default Subscriber and Default Administrator. The Default Administrator CoS is granted all permissions, by default. So, for the one user who is granted full administrative access, you can use the Default Administrator CoS. For the other two users, you must create a new CoS.

Figure 19-2 shows the CoS configuration page on the Unity server.

Figure 19-2 *CoS Configuration Page*

In Figure 19-2, a new CoS called HelpDesk has been created. Users with this CoS can add and edit user accounts. The Edit permission enables the user to do common tasks, such as resetting PINs or unlocking accounts. This CoS will be assigned to the other two administrators.

Administering Multiple Unity Servers with a Single Account

In a network consisting of multiple Unity servers, using a CoS will not work for some types of administrators. Because a single Windows user account can be a subscriber on only one Unity server, it is not possible to import a particular user into multiple Unity servers and specify a CoS for that user on each server.

NOTE   Using CoS is a problem only when a single user account needs access to multiple servers in the same domain. CoS works properly in an environment with multiple Unity servers, as long as the user does not meet this condition.

This type of user is a Global Administrator: That is, the user has administrative access to multiple Unity servers. This means that either you must specify the same Admin account on all Unity servers in your network, or you must maintain a list of usernames/passwords for each Unity server that you need to administer.

It is easy to see the shortcomings of both of these options. If you use a single account, the information about this account might need to be shared with multiple people within your organization, which greatly reduces your visibility and span of control. However, maintaining a list of usernames/passwords is just plain tedious.

One more option exists; however, it enables you to have a unique account for each Unity server *and* to use a single account to administer any number of Unity servers that you want. This method enables you to be very granular; you can specify exactly which servers certain user accounts have administrative access to.

The tool that facilitates this is called GrantUnityAccess, located in C:\Commserver, where you have installed the Unity software. If the folder does not exist, you can also pull the utility off the Unity installation CD/DVD in the Apps folder in the root of the CD/DVD.

Consider the topology in Figure 19-3, which shows two sites, each with two Unity servers.

For an Administrator in RTP to have access to a Unity server in San Jose, that person needs to know the username/password for the administrative account on the Unity server in San Jose. One way of defeating this problem is to use the same administrative account for all of the servers in each site. This works but is not optimal because it lacks granularity and leaves the servers exposed to the folly of other administrators in the organization.

Figure 19-3 *Multisite Unity Topology*

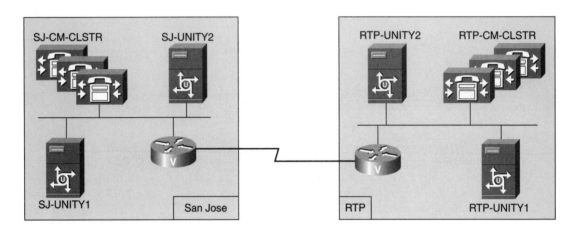

VNT, Inc.

You decide instead that you will use a unique Admin account for each Unity server and that you also will allow the administrators in RTP access to the Unity servers in San Jose (not vice versa).

GrantUnityAccess enables you to associate Windows user accounts with Unity subscriber accounts. This is done by mapping the Windows security ID to the subscriber account. This mapping is stored in the Credentials table in SQL. Figure 19-4 shows the mappings before any modifications are made.

Figure 19-4 *Output of GrantUnityAccess Before Modification*

Now you add an association between a Windows user and a subscriber in Unity. Assume that the user in RTP that you need to grant access has the user ID of marschne. The Windows domain is VNTINC, so the command that you use is shown in Figure 19-5.

Figure 19-5 *Example Usage of GrantUnityAccess*

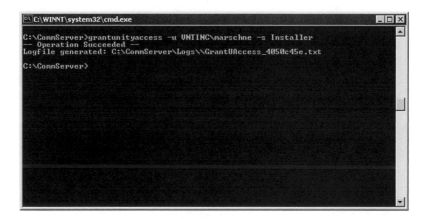

The Installer alias is a subscriber alias that exists only in the Unity user database, and it is given the default administrator CoS, by default.

Figure 19-6 shows the new output of the same command used in Figure 19-4. You can see that the marschne Windows account is now associated with the Installer alias in Unity.

Figure 19-6 *Output of GrantUnityAccess After Modification*

The GrantUnityAccess Tool

The GrantUnityAccess tool can be very helpful in many different scenarios. We now take a deeper look at what this tool actually does, to help you understand what problems this tool can solve for you.

All Windows user accounts are identified uniquely by a security identifier, or SID. Unity looks at this SID when it determines what subscriber your Windows account is associated with. This mapping of SID to subscriber is kept in the SQL database on the Unity server. With a simple SQL query, you can see what SIDs are associated with a subscriber.

Figure 19-7 shows that currently two SIDs are associated with the Installer account. Depending on the version of Unity and the configuration, you might have several different SIDs associated with the Installer account. These can include the Message Store service account, the Directory Service account, the Administrator account used to install Unity, and the account used to administer unity.

Figure 19-7 *SQL Query Showing the SIDs Associated with the Installer Account*

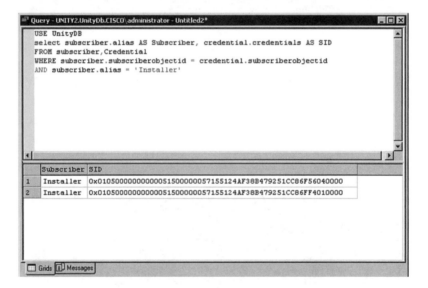

You can verify that the SID in the SQL database is actually the SID of a particular account by using ADSI Edit. ADSI Edit can be found as part of the Windows 2000 Support Tools package found in the SUPPORT folder of the Windows 2000 Server CD-ROM, as well as in the C:\Commserver\Techtools directory, where C:\commserver is the directory you installed Unity in.

NOTE   You might have to enter the command **regsvr32 adsiedit.dll** for the ADSI Edit utility to work properly.

Figure 19-8 shows what the value of the objectSid is for the user account named unitystore. The account unitystore (sometimes called UnityMsgStoreSvc) is the account that the Message Store Service uses to log on. Comparing this with the value found in the Credential table in SQL, you can see that they are the same.

Figure 19-8 *Windows ADSI Edit*

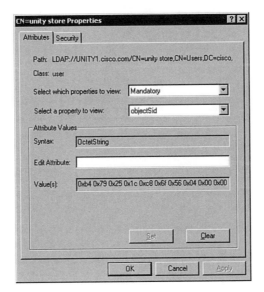

NOTE   Figure 19-8 shows only the last part of the SID because of the constraints of the field in the dialog box. Scrolling to the left would reveal the entire SID.

Figure 19-9 shows the result of the same SQL query pictured in Figure 19-7. The only difference is that the query is executed after running the GrantUnityAccess tool associating marschne with the Installer account.

Figure 19-9 *SQL Query Showing the SIDs Associated with the Installer Account*

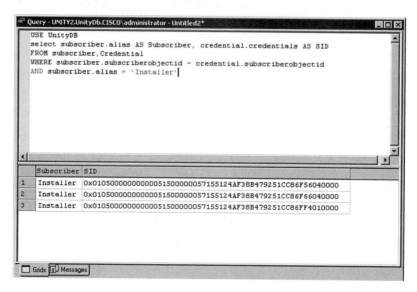

As you can see, the GrantUnityAccess tool simply associates the SID of the Windows user account that you specify with a subscriber of the Unity system. When the Windows user logs into the Unity SA, Unity treats the newly associated user exactly the same as the original subscriber.

During the writing of this book, a new tool was released that functions in the same way as GrantUnityAccess, but is GUI-based. The tool is called Unity Credentials Map and is available from www.ciscounitytools.com. Figure 19-10 shows what the GUI of the new tool looks like.

Figure 19-10 *Unity Credentials Map*

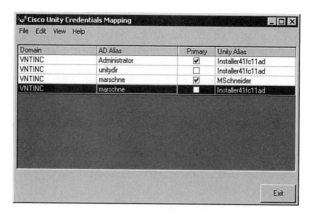

So now you have a solution for giving a single user account full access to multiple Unity servers. However, handing out full access to any personnel who need access to multiple servers is undesirable. Consider a more complex scenario using the topology in Figure 19-11.

Figure 19-11 *VNT, Inc., Topology*

VNT, Inc.

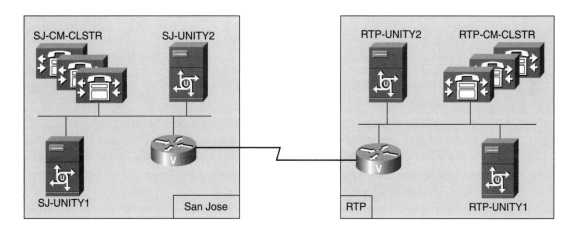

This scenario has the following requirements:

- Administrators in San Jose and RTP will have full access to all Unity servers.

- Help-desk personnel will have subscriber Add and Edit access to all Unity servers.

- Users will use their own Windows user account to log into the Unity SA.

To solve this problem, you can do the following:

Step 1   Create an XX-helpdeskY subscriber on each Unity server, where XX is the site code (SJ or RTP) and Y is the server number.

Step 2   Create a CoS on each server that allows Add and Edit access to subscriber properties, and assign the CoS to the XX-helpdeskY users.

Step 3   Use the GrantUnityAccess tool to associate the help-desk personnel Windows user accounts to the XX-helpdeskY subscriber.

Step 4   Use the GrantUnityAccess tool to associate the administrator's user accounts with the Installer subscriber.

By now, you should understand what the GrantUnityAccess tool does and begin to see how this tool can come in handy in many different scenarios.

Global Subscriber Management

Although the GrantUnityAccess tool grants a single user administrative access to multiple Unity servers, managing users globally still can become very tedious. The user must find out what server a particular subscriber is homed to, log into the SA of the server, and navigate to the subscriber properties page. For any user who does this several times a day, this quickly gets old.

The Global Subscriber Manager (GSM) greatly simplifies administration of users across any Unity server through a single GUI interface. The requirements for Global Subscriber Manager are as follows:

- Unity 3.1(2) or greater is required.

- The user account that you run this tool under must have rights to access the SA on all the home servers of the users to administer. Use the GrantUnityAccess tool as outlined previously to do this.

- The user account also must have public and db_datareader rights to the UnityDB SQL server database on the Unity server you connect to. You can check these permissions by using Enterprise Manager and viewing the User configuration under the UnityDB.

The GSM GUI looks similar to that of Active Directory Users & Computers, with a navigation pane on the left side and users listed on the right side. There you can search for users in your network in several ways, and when you find the user, you simply can double-click to automatically open the SA configuration page for that user.

Figure 19-12 *Global Subscriber Manager*

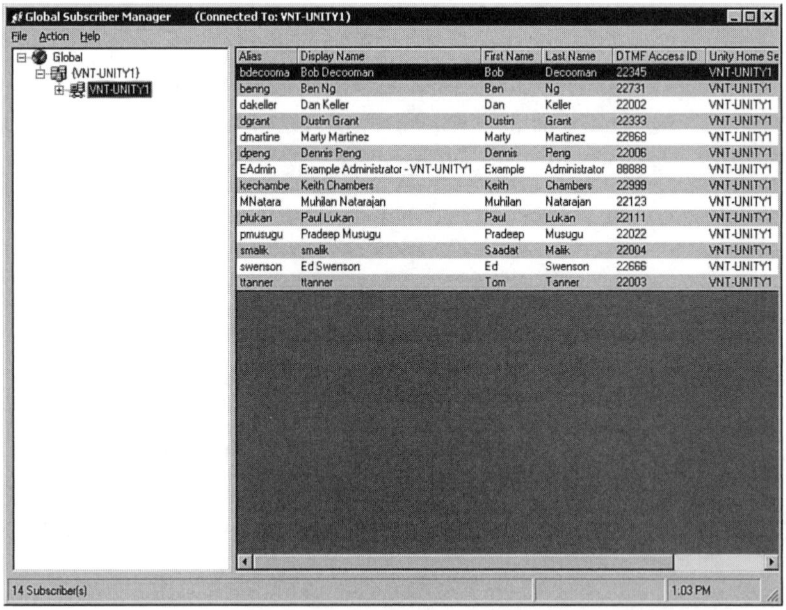

Start a search by selecting Action, Search or by simply pressing F2 on your keyboard. A search dialog box appears and presents you with several attributes that you can use to search for your subscriber. Fill in one or more textboxes, and also check the check box next to the search fields that you want to use. Pressing OK returns a list of subscribers that match your search criteria.

Figure 19-13 *Search Screen for Global Subscriber Manager*

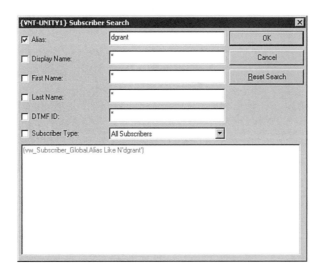

Using the GSM to Import Users from Active Directory

If you use Unity 3.1(5) or greater in an Active Directory environment, the GSM has the capability to import users. In the GSM, right-click the Unity server that you run the GSM from and select Import User. This brings up a dialog box that enables you to navigate your Active Directory tree. Browse to the container that holds the user, right-click the user, and select Import User.

Using the GSM to Delete Subscribers

Another useful feature in the GSM is the capability to "cleanly" delete subscribers from Unity. The Unity SA does not prevent you from deleting subscribers that are referenced by other objects, so if you do this, it causes some problems. The GSM helps avoid this problem by finding the objects that are linked to the subscriber, prompting you with each object, and allowing you to specify where the object should link to instead. If you have any doubt about whether deleting a subscriber causes problems, we highly suggest using this tool.

Figure 19-14 shows the last screen of the Delete Subscriber Wizard in the GSM. Notice all of the attributes that must be updated to cleanly delete the subscriber.

Figure 19-14 *Delete Subscriber Wizard*

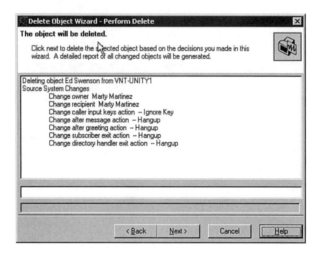

Using the GSM to Move Subscribers Between Unity Servers

You can use the GSM to move Unity subscribers between Unity servers in the same dialing domain. If you right-click on a subscriber, you are presented with a menu that includes the option to move the subscriber. If you select this option, you start the Move Object Wizard, which guides you through the process of moving the subscriber. You are asked a series of questions regarding both the source system (the Unity server you move the subscriber from) and the destination system (the Unity server you move the subscriber to).

The source system questions deal with changes that must be made to the remaining Unity objects (subscribers, call handlers, interview handlers, and so on), with these objects referencing the soon-to-be-moved subscriber. The destination system questions deal with changes that must be made to the object you move so that it fits into the design of the destination system (class of service, schedule, caller-input key destinations, and so on).

Using the GSM Off-Box

You can run the GSM from machines other than a Unity server (known as running it off-box), as long as some requirements are met:

- The machine should be in the same domain as the Unity box with which you want to connect.

- Your user account also must have public and db_datareader rights to the UnityDB SQL server database on the Unity server that you connect to. You can check these permissions by using Enterprise Manager and viewing the User configuration under the UnityDB.

- This account also should be a Unity administrator.

The Unity server that you connect to is not that important because the GSM works off the GlobalSubscriber and GlobalLocation tables. Connecting to the closest Unity server is probably best because the query results will have fewer network hops over which to travel.

When you first launch the GSM, it detects whether it is running on-box or off-box. In the case of off-box, a dialog box appears in which you select the Unity server to connect to. The dialog box shows all SQL servers in the current domain; it is your responsibility to choose a Unity server. Select a Unity server and press the Attempt Connection button. If the connection succeeds, the Attempt Connection button turns into an OK button. To use the new server, press OK. If the connection fails, you should see the reason in the status box at the bottom of this dialog box.

After you have selected a server, that server name is stored and used for subsequent launches of the GSM. If you want to change the server later, you can do so by selecting Connect to Another Unity Server from the File menu.

Summary

This chapter introduced some tools to help you administer multiple Unity servers and manage subscribers globally. New and updated tools are constantly becoming available on www.ciscounitytools.com; it is good practice to check the website regularly.

CHAPTER 20

Subscriber Administration

This chapter addresses various aspects of subscriber administration. We look at some common administration scenarios and the different methods of performing common tasks and also introduce tools that allow you to import, delete, edit, and migrate subscribers easily. Most of these tools, which are useful when administering your server, are available from http://www.ciscounitytools.com.

Subscriber Templates

The subscriber template is a basic feature, but it significantly reduces the amount of manual work needed when adding a subscriber. In fact, you cannot add a user without the use of a subscriber template. A fresh installation of Unity has a preconfigured Default Subscriber template that you can customize to suit your needs. The subscriber template contains all of the properties that a normal subscriber has; therefore you can create users with the same properties easily. You can add/change a subscriber template by going to the SA page and selecting Subscriber Template as shown in Figure 20-1.

Once you have a subscriber template defined, all you need is the subscriber's first and last name and their extension. When you add the user, you are prompted to enter the template to be used. This is where the subscriber template will be copied into the new user's configuration. Based on this information, a username is automatically generated; you can optionally change this to any unique user ID.

But what if you need to add hundreds or thousands of users? Creating users one at a time is obviously inefficient. In order to tackle this problem, we turn to one of the many tools available for Unity.

Figure 20-1 *Subscriber Template*

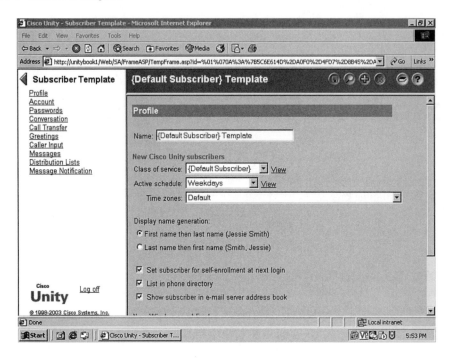

Bulk Import Utility

The Cisco Unity Bulk Import wizard allows you to create multiple subscriber accounts at once by either importing user data directly from the Exchange 5.5 directory or Active Directory, or by importing user data from a comma-separated value (CSV) file. You can create either regular, AMIS, Bridge, Internet, or VPIM subscriber accounts when you run the Bulk Import wizard.

Importing User Data from a CSV File

CSV is a common text file format for moving data from one data store to another. As long as the user data contained in the CSV file is formatted correctly, you can use it to create subscriber accounts for users with or without existing Windows domain accounts and Exchange mailboxes. As a best practice, do not include more than 7,500 records in a single CSV file, as you might encounter unexpected results when the Cisco Unity Bulk Import wizard imports the data. You can only create one type of subscriber account each time that you run the Cisco Unity Bulk Import wizard. For example, if you need to import both regular subscribers as well as Unity Bridge subscribers, you must run the Cisco Unity Bulk Import wizard two times, with separate CSV files for each type of subscriber.

The first row in your CSV file must contain column headers that identify the type of data in each column; information in the subsequent rows must contain the data you want to import. Column headers must be in uppercase, separated by commas, and spelled as shown in the tables in the following sections:

- Required Column Headers for a CSV File
- Optional Column Headers for a CSV File

NOTE   In addition, make sure that for each row in your CSV file, commas separate the data, including the column headers in the first row. Do not use a tab, spaces, or a semicolon to separate values in the file. Finally, if any data includes a space, quotes, or commas, contain it within quotes.

See Table 20-1 for more information on the options presented in each dialog box that appears as the Cisco Unity Bulk Import wizard proceeds. The left column lists the title of each dialog box in their display order.

Table 20-1   *Cisco Unity Bulk Import Wizard Dialog Boxes*

Dialog Box	Considerations
Save Log Files	Enter a name and location where the Cisco Unity Bulk Import wizard will save the error log file (the default is C:\Error.log). This file contains data that the Bulk Import wizard could not import because of errors in the records of the CSV file.
	Then, enter a name and location where the Cisco Unity Bulk Import wizard will save the output log file (the default is C:\Output.log). This file contains the records that were not imported when the subscriber accounts were created.
Choose Subscriber Type	Select either:
	Unified Messaging. Click this option if you want to import data for traditional Exchange mail users. Unified messaging subscribers can access voice messages in their Outlook Inboxes by using ViewMail.
	Voice mail-only. Click this option if you want to import data for traditional Exchange mail users to create voice mail-only subscriber accounts.

continues

Table 20-1 *Cisco Unity Bulk Import Wizard Dialog Boxes (Continued)*

Dialog Box	Considerations
Choose Subscriber Type (*Continued*)	**Internet**. Click this option if you want to import data for custom recipients (known as mail-enabled contacts in Exchange 2000/2003/Active Directory) to create Internet subscriber accounts.
	Bridge. Click this option if you want to import data for mail-enabled contacts in Exchange 2000/2003/Active Directory to create Bridge subscriber accounts.
	AMIS. Click this option if you want to import data for custom recipients (known as mail-enabled contacts in Exchange 2000/2003/Active Directory) to create AMIS subscriber accounts.
	VPIM. Click this option if you want to import data for mail-enabled contacts in Exchange 2000/2003/Active Directory to create VPIM subscriber accounts.
Select Subscriber Data Import Option	Select either:
	Create New Cisco Unity Subscriber Accounts. Click this option to create new Exchange mailboxes and Windows domain accounts at the same time that you create subscriber accounts.
	Use Existing Mailboxes and Windows Accounts. Click this option to use existing mailbox and Windows domain account information when you create subscriber accounts. If you choose to use existing mailbox and Windows account data to create AMIS, Bridge, or VPIM subscriber accounts, consider that when you import existing Active Directory contacts or Exchange 5.5 custom-recipients, the imported objects can no longer be used for outbound message addressing to remote e-mail addresses. However, they can be used for addressing voice messages to remote voice-messaging systems.
	Modify Existing Cisco Unity Subscribers. Click this option if you want to edit multiple subscriber accounts that already exist in Cisco Unity.
Select Subscriber Template	Select the Cisco Unity subscriber template that you want to associate with the subscriber accounts. Subscriber templates contain settings that are appropriate for subscribers of a particular type, such as a department.
	Most optional column headers correspond to the subscriber settings defined in the subscriber template, including class of service (CoS), call transfer, and message notification settings. The template settings are applied to subscriber accounts as the individual accounts are created. However, when data for a particular subscriber setting is not included in the CSV file, the Cisco Unity Bulk Import wizard uses the subscriber template that you select here to define the subscriber accounts that you create.

Table 20-1   *Cisco Unity Bulk Import Wizard Dialog Boxes (Continued)*

Dialog Box	Considerations
Select Exchange 5.5 Server	If you opted to have the Cisco Unity Bulk Import wizard create new mailboxes and Windows accounts when it creates the Cisco Unity subscriber accounts, the Exchange 5.5 mailbox is created in the Recipients container that you specify on this page. Otherwise, indicate where the mailbox data associated with the users in your CSV file currently exists. Note that the Cisco Unity Bulk Import wizard does not create any additional mailbox or Windows accounts when you import existing user data from the Exchange 5.5 directory.
Select Domain and Container	If you opted to have the Cisco Unity Bulk Import wizard create new mailboxes and Windows accounts when it creates the Cisco Unity subscriber accounts, the Active Directory account is created in the domain and container that you specify on this page. Otherwise, indicate where the mailbox data that is associated with the users in your CSV file currently exists. Note that the Cisco Unity Bulk Import wizard does not create any additional mailbox or Windows accounts when you import existing user data from Active Directory. Similarly, Cisco Unity also does not enable Active Directory accounts if they are disabled at the time that you import mailbox data from Exchange 2000/2003.
Select the CSV File	Click Browse to locate the CSV file that contains the user data that you want to import from your CSV file.

Required Column Headers for a CSV File

There are at least three column headers that you must include in your CSV file, and you might need to include more—depending on the type of subscriber account that you plan to create.

The required column headers for all subscriber types are indicated in Table 20-2. The headers are listed in the recommended order that they should be included in your CSV file. For an example of what your file would look like, see Table 20-3.

Table 20-2   *Required CSV Headers for All Subscriber Types*

Column Header	Required for	Description
LAST_NAME	All subscriber types	Subscriber last name. Enter any combination of letters, digits, spaces, apostrophes, and dashes, up to a maximum of 32 characters.
FIRST_NAME	All subscriber types	Subscriber first name. Enter any combination of letters, digits, spaces, apostrophes, and dashes, up to a maximum of 32 characters.

continues

Table 20-2 *Required CSV Headers for All Subscriber Types (Continued)*

Column Header	Required for	Description
DTMF_ACCESS_ID	Regular, AMIS, Bridge, VPIM	The number that callers dial to reach a subscriber. This is also the extension that subscribers on the local Cisco Unity server use to address messages to AMIS, Bridge, Internet, or VPIM subscribers. Note, however, that this column is optional for Internet subscribers.
		This value corresponds to the Extension field on the Subscribers > Subscribers > Profile Page in the Cisco Unity Administrator.
		Enter any combination of digits from 0 to 9, up to a maximum of 40 digits. Do not include any spaces. Note that the value must be unique among all extensions on the local Cisco Unity server and within the dialing domain, if there is one.
REMOTE_ADDRESS	Internet subscribers	If the remote message recipient that the Internet subscriber corresponds to uses Cisco Unity, then enter the remote address in the following format:
		VOICE:<Delivery Location Dial ID>_<Remote Primary Extension> (e.g. VOICE:123_5678)
		If the remote message recipient does not use Cisco Unity, specify the e-mail (SMTP) address to which messages to the Internet subscriber will be sent:
		SMTP:alias@domain.com (for example, plukan@cisco.com)
		For more information on Internet subscribers, refer to the *Networking in Cisco Unity Guide*.
		Enter any combination of letters, digits, colons, ampersands, dashes, periods, or underscores, up to a maximum of 128 characters.
REMOTE_USER_ID	AMIS, Bridge, or VPIM subscribers	The number that the remote voice-messaging system uses to route messages to the subscriber.
		Enter any combination of digits, up to a maximum of 128 characters.

Table 20-2   *Required CSV Headers for All Subscriber Types (Continued)*

Column Header	Required for	Description
ALIAS* Note	All subscriber types	The Cisco Unity Bulk Import wizard searches for the Exchange mailbox that matches the alias entered here. The matching Exchange mailbox will be associated with the subscriber account.
		If you do not specify an alias here, the Exchange alias for the created account will be derived from a rule specified in the subscriber template, using a combination of first and last name. Typically, you enter an alias here in order to override the alias generation rule (for example, when there are users who need to have aliases that do not follow the convention, such as when there is a naming conflict).
		Enter any combination of letters and digits, up to a maximum of 64 characters.

*   This column header is only required when you create subscriber accounts with existing mailbox and
Windows account data. If you choose to create subscriber accounts and create new mailboxes and Windows
accounts at the same time, the column header is optional.

For example, using the sample data, a CSV file would look like the results outlined in
Table 20-3.

Table 20-3   *CSV File Example with Required Column Headers*

Subscriber Type	Example
Regular *(including voice mail-only and unified messaging subscribers)*	LAST_NAME,FIRST_NAME,DTMF_ACCESS_ID,ALIAS Lukan,Paul,2001,plukan Giralt,Paul,2002,pgiralt Goodwin,Dave,2003,dgoodwin Brinsfield,Sean,2004,sbrinsfi
Internet *(when using the VOICE format for remote address)*	LAST_NAME,FIRST_NAME,REMOTE_ADDRESS,ALIAS Lukan,Paul,VOICE:123_5678,plukan Giralt,Paul,VOICE:123_4789,pgiralt Goodwin,Dave,VOICE:123_8521,dgoodwin Brinsfield,Sean,VOICE:123_3214,sbrinsfi

continues

Table 20-3   *CSV File Example with Required Column Headers (Continued)*

Subscriber Type	Example
Internet *(when using the SMTP format for remote address)*	LAST_NAME,FIRST_NAME,REMOTE_ADDRESS,ALIAS Lukan,Paul,SMTP:plukan@cisco.com,plukan Giralt,Paul,SMTP:pgiralt@cisco.com,pgiralt Goodwin,Dave,SMTP:dgoodwin@cisco.com,dgoodwin Brinsfield,Sean,SMTP:sbrinsfi@cisco.com,sbrinsfi
AMIS, Bridge, and VPIM	LAST_NAME,FIRST_NAME,DTMF_ACCESS_ ID,REMOTE_USER_ID,ALIAS Lukan,Paul,2001,3000,plukan Giralt,Paul,2002,3100,pgiralt Goodwin,Dave,2003,3200,dgoodwin Brinsfield,Sean,2004,3300,sbrinsfi

Optional Column Headers for a CSV File

There are several optional column headers that you can include in your CSV file. Most optional column headers correspond to the subscriber settings defined in the subscriber template, including class of service (CoS), call transfer, and message notification settings. When data for a particular subscriber setting is not included in the CSV file, the Cisco Unity Bulk Import wizard uses the subscriber template that you choose when you run the Cisco Unity Bulk Import wizard to define the subscriber accounts that you create. For this reason, you should review the settings in the subscriber template that you will use to create the accounts before adding any of the optional column headers to your CSV file. For details on the optional column headers, please refer to the Help file included with the Cisco Unity Bulk Import wizard.

Importing User Data Directly from a Message Store Directory

When importing user data directly from Exchange, it is not recommended that you use the Cisco Unity Bulk Import wizard to create more than 7,500 Cisco Unity subscriber accounts at once. If you have more than 7,500 Exchange users for whom you want to create Cisco Unity subscriber accounts, you will need to run the wizard multiple times. Once the wizard has created a subscriber account for an Exchange user, it will not process the data for that user when it is run again. Although you can import user data for both Exchange 5.5 and Exchange 2000/2003 users, the Cisco Unity Bulk Import wizard can only import data from one server at a time. In addition, you can only create one type of subscriber account each time that you run the wizard.

When you are creating regular, AMIS, Bridge, or VPIM subscribers, the Cisco Unity Bulk Import wizard requires that each user have a DTMF_ACCESS_ID that callers can use to reach a subscriber. Typically, the DTMF_ACCESS_ID is the same as the subscriber extension. Before running the wizard, print out a list of the usernames that you plan to import and specify a DTMF_ACCESS_ID for each user. The ID must be unique among all extensions on the local Cisco Unity server and within the dialing domain, if there is one. Save this list to use when you enter any missing DTMF_ACCESS_IDs during the import process.

See Table 20-4 for more information on the options presented in each dialog box that appears as the Cisco Unity Bulk Import wizard proceeds. The left column lists the title of each dialog box in the order that they are displayed in the wizard.

Table 20-4   *Cisco Unity Bulk Import Wizard Dialog Boxes*

Dialog Box	Considerations
Save Log Files	Enter a name and location where the Cisco Unity Bulk Import wizard will save the error log file (the default is C:\Error.log). This file contains data that the Bulk Import wizard could not import because of errors that occurred when importing data from the Exchange 5.5 directory or Active Directory.
Select Subscriber Data Import Option	Select either: **Unified Messaging**. Click this option if you want to import data for traditional Exchange mail users to create unified messaging subscriber accounts. Unified messaging subscribers can access voice messages in their Outlook Inboxes by using ViewMail. **Internet**. Click this option if you want to import data for custom recipients (known as mail-enabled contacts in Exchange 2000/2003/Active Directory) to create Internet subscriber accounts.
Select Subscriber Template	Select the Cisco Unity subscriber template that you want to associate with the subscriber accounts. Subscriber templates contain settings that are appropriate for subscribers of a particular type, such as a department. The template settings are applied to subscriber accounts as the individual accounts are created.
Select User Domain and Container	Select the domain from which to import user data. Then, for Exchange 2000/2003, select the user container where the new user accounts will be created.

Correcting Import Errors

The error log file contains data that the Cisco Unity Bulk Import wizard could not import. The Cisco Unity Bulk Import wizard reports the first error it detects in any Exchange mailbox or row in a CSV file. Once you correct that error, the Cisco Unity Bulk Import wizard might detect additional errors in the same mailbox or row when the data is imported again. Thus, you may need to repeat the correction process, running the Cisco Unity Bulk Import wizard and correcting an error several times to find and correct all errors.

The output log file contains all the records that were not imported. You can save it as a CSV file and use it when you run the Cisco Unity Bulk Import wizard again. Note that each time that you run the Cisco Unity Bulk Import wizard, the error and output log files are overwritten unless you specify a new name for the files each time you run it.

To correct import errors, use one of the two procedures below.

Correct Errors That Occurred When Importing Data from the Message Store

Step 1   Go to the directory location of the error log file you specified during the import. (The default location and filename is C:\Error.log.)

Step 2   Use a text editor to open the error log file. You will use the error codes in the file to make corrections.

Step 3   When importing data from Exchange 5.5, open the **Microsoft Exchange Administrator**. When importing data from Exchange 2000/2003, open **Active Directory Users and Computers**.

Step 4   Double-click an Exchange mailbox that contains an error to see the properties.

Step 5   Enter corrections in the appropriate boxes in the Exchange mailbox.

Step 6   Click **OK**.

Step 7   **Repeat Step 4 through Step 6** for each Exchange mailbox listed in the error log file.

Step 8   Run the **Cisco Unity Bulk Import wizard** again.

Step 9   Repeat this procedure until all subscriber accounts are created without error.

Correct Errors That Occurred When Importing Data from a CSV File

Step 1   Go to the directory location of the error log file you specified during the import. (The default location and filename is C:\Error.log.)

Step 2   Use a text editor to open the error log file. You will use the error codes in the file to make corrections.

Step 3   Go to the directory location of the output log file you specified during the import. (The default location and filename is C:\Output.log.) This file contains all the records that were not imported.

Step 4   Use a text editor to open the output log file.

Step 5 Correct any records in the output file that are listed as errors in the error log file.

Step 6 When you have finished editing the output log file, save it as a CSV file with a new name.

Step 7 Run the Cisco Unity Bulk Import wizard again with the CSV file that you saved in Step 6.

Step 8 Repeat this procedure until all subscriber accounts are created without error, and then proceed to the "After Creating Subscriber Accounts" section in the appropriate guide, as indicated in the Additional Documentation section.

Modifying Existing Cisco Unity Subscriber Accounts

You can run the Cisco Unity Bulk Import wizard when you want to modify unique subscriber settings, such as primary or alternate extensions, for multiple subscribers at once.

NOTE If you want to modify a subscriber setting shared by multiple subscriber accounts, use the Bulk Edit utility that is discussed later in this chapter. Bulk Edit is appropriate when you want to associate a group of regular subscribers with a particular class of service or remove a group of regular subscribers from directory assistance. Bulk Edit cannot be used to modify AMIS, Bridge, Internet, or VPIM subscriber settings.

To use the Cisco Unity Bulk Import wizard to modify Cisco Unity subscriber accounts:

Step 1 Create a CSV file with the modified subscriber data. Your CSV file must include the ALIAS column, and the following columns cannot be modified with the Bulk Import wizard:

— LAST_NAME

— FIRST_NAME

— REMOTE_ADDRESS

— REMOTE_USER_ID

— DELIVERY_LOCATION_ID

— ALIAS

— SUBSCRIBER_TEMPLATE

Step 2 On the Cisco Unity server, on the Windows Start menu, click Programs > Cisco Unity > Cisco Unity Bulk Import.

Step 3 Follow the instructions to use a CSV file to create subscribers.

Step 4 When prompted to choose how you want to use the imported data, click Modify Existing Cisco Unity Subscribers.

Step 5 Click Next, and proceed through the wizard. If the wizard reports any errors, you can:

— Click OK to continue with the import, and fix the errors later.

— Fix the errors. See the previous step list, "Correcting Import Errors" for details.

Step 6 Once the subscriber accounts are modified, click Finish.

Step 7 If you had import errors, but in Step 5 you chose to correct them later, see the previous step list, "Correcting Import Errors," for details.

Now that we have learned all about how to add users in bulk, let us take a look at how we can delete users in bulk with the Bulk Subscriber Delete tool.

Bulk Subscriber Delete

From time to time you might need to delete large numbers of subscribers from Unity without removing their Exchange account information. The Bulk Subscriber Delete tool is designed for that need. It allows you to select subscribers based on an extension range, distribution list membership, CoS membership, or switch assignment or load them from a CSV file. Figure 20-2 shows the Bulk Subscriber Delete GUI.

Once you have selected a group of subscribers to work with you can individually select/ unselect users by toggling the checkbox in the far left column. The grid (shown previously) can be sorted by any of its columns to quickly find the user or users you want to remove.

With the Bulk Subscriber Delete utility, you can select the subscriber mailboxes that you want to remove Unity information from.

NOTE The Bulk Subscriber Delete utility does NOT remove the Exchange and/or the NT/AD account itself. Only the Unity data added when the mail user was made a subscriber is removed. You will need to manually remove these users from Exchange or AD/NT directly if you want their accounts deleted.

Figure 20-2 *Bulk Subscriber Delete*

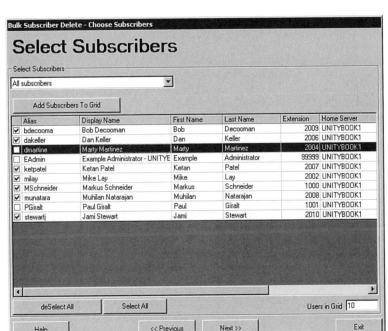

The first step is to populate the grid with subscribers you want to remove. You can add multiple groups of users to the grid; duplicates will automatically be filtered out. You can add users to the grid using one or more of the following:

- All subscriber mailboxes.

- A group of subscriber mailboxes based on an extension range, membership in a public distribution list, an association with a class of service (CoS), or an assigned switch (in dual-switch environments).

- You can also use a comma-separated value (CSV) file to select subscribers based on their Exchange aliases. CSV is a common text file format for moving data from one data store to another. You can edit CSV files in a text editor or in a spreadsheet application. If you choose to select subscribers from a CSV file, format your file by using the following guidelines to ensure that it parses correctly:

    — Separate values by commas. Do not use a tab, spaces, or a semicolon to separate values in the file.

    — Include a column header titled "alias" in the first line. Column headers are not case sensitive and can be formatted with spaces on the left, right, or on both sides.

For example:

first name, last name, home server, alias

Ketan, Patel, EXServer1, ketpatel

Mike, Lay, EXServer1, milay

Once you have the grid populated with the subscribers you want, you can pick individual users and select/unselect them using the checkbox column on the far left of the grid. All subscribers that have their box checked will be removed; those that have a cleared box will be skipped. You can clear or check all boxes in the grid using the Select All and Unselect All buttons in the lower left of the form.

Once you have the subscribers selected the way you want them, just click the Remove Subscribers button in the lower left. The progress bar will move along until it is is complete. An error count will be provided when the utility is complete. Review the log if there are any errors, and refer to the Help file included for more information.

Bulk Edit

The Bulk Edit utility is designed to allow you to select large numbers of call handlers or subscribers and make changes to them in bulk quickly and easily. Nearly every value you can see and edit via the SA is available to change using Bulk Edit as well as a few items not visible in the SA. Figure 20-3 shows the Bulk Edit GUI.

The tool is designed as a wizard that walks you through four steps:

Step 1   Choose to edit call handlers or subscribers. Whereas the properties available on each are so different, the selection made on the main form here will take you down a different path with different options. This latest version allows you to select the various subscriber types including AMIS, SMTP (Internet), Bridge, or VPIM subscribers as well as full subscribers.

Step 2   Select which subscribers or call handlers you want to edit. You can select to edit all of them or filter them based on extension number, CoS membership, DL membership, pull from a CSV file, and so on. The details of which options are available and how they work are covered next.

Step 3   Select which changes you want to make. There are tabs for each of the pages available on the subscribers or call handlers page in the SA that contains a list of fields that you can force a value for. You can change as many items in one shot as you like.

Step 4   Apply the changes. A progress bar will show you how far along the process is and a dialog will come up telling you when it is complete.

Figure 20-3 *Bulk Edit*

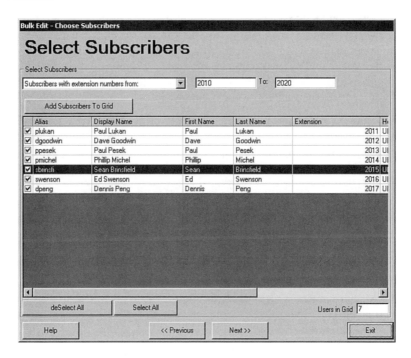

When you are done you can review the output log automatically and look for errors that were reported. A new log file is created in the \logs folder under the Bulk Edit installation directory each time you run the tool.

CAUTION   There is no undo option for Bulk Edit. Any changes you make using this tool are permanent. Please make sure you understand the options you are selecting and try it first on a test subscriber or call handler before applying the changes to large numbers of objects!

Main Form

The opening dialog of the Bulk Edit utility allows you to choose if you want to edit call handlers or subscribers. Because the options/values for handlers versus subscribers are so different, the resulting pages of the wizard will present different options to you based on this selection.

Select Subscribers

In this step you need to populate the grid with a list of subscribers you want to edit. You can add as many subscribers to this grid as you want; however, you can only use one selection criteria per run. For example, when you select to add all subscribers from a class of service it will clear the grid before adding the new users. This is a change from previous versions that allowed you to merge multiple searches into the grid. For large databases, this proved to be a big performance drag so it was removed.

Once you have users in the grid you can sort the grid columns or move the columns around any way you like. You can individually select/unselect users using the checkbox in the far left column. Only users that have the check mark on will be edited with the changes you select in the next step. You can use the Deselect All button to uncheck all the users in the grid and the Select All button to check all the users in the grid. If you opt to add a large number of users to the grid, be patient. The updates on the grid are turned off to speed the process up; it might take a minute or two to populate the grid and then updates are turned back on and you can see your users.

You can add subscribers to the grid using the options at the top of the form in the drop-down list box:

- **All subscribers**. This adds all the subscribers associated with the local Unity server into the grid. If you have a lot of users on your system, this might take a minute or two to populate the grid.

- **Subscribers with extension numbers**. Enter a lower and an upper extension range and all subscribers that have primary extensions in that range will be added to the grid. This includes both primary and alternate extensions in the search.

- **All subscribers in this public distribution list**. Hit the Browse button and select a public distribution list in the resulting dialog. All subscribers associated with the local Unity server that are members of that distribution list will be added to the grid.

- **All subscribers in this class of service**. Hit the Browse button and select a class of service in the resulting dialog. All subscribers associated with that class of service will be added to the grid.

- **All subscribers associated with this switch**. In a multiple switch configuration you can select a switch in the drop-down list and all subscribers associated with that switch will be added to the grid. The switches offered in the drop-down are pulled from the Registry so if you've already removed the 2nd switch configuration via the SA, the old switch name will still appear in the drop-down list. This can be handy if you forgot to assign all your subscribers/handlers over to your new primary switch if you are going from a multiple switch to a single switch configuration. Note: The drop-down list is populated with the switch filename (as in CISCO002.INI) not the display name you see in the SA.

- **All subscribers referenced in this CSV file**. You can load subscribers into the grid using a CSV file that is populated with the Alias and/or the extension numbers of the subscribers you want to edit. The details of the CSV file format requirements are covered in the next section.

- **All subscribers homed on this mail server**. The drop-down list to the right of this option allows you to select one of the message stores Unity sees that has at least one subscriber homed on it. Selecting this will include all subscribers homed on that mailstore in the grid.

- **All subscribers associated with this remote node ID**. The drop-down list to the right of this option shows all the remote node ID values seen in the database if your Unity server is connected to a Cisco Unity Bridge server talking to an Octel network. You can select a node ID from the list and include all subscribers on the local server that were moved over from that node in Octel to the local Unity server.

- **All subscribers associated with this delivery location**. If you have selected Bridge, AMIS, or VPIM subscribers, this option will be available and will allow you to select all subscribers associated with a particular delivery location object. A drop-down list will be provided that contains only local delivery locations of the type you selected on the main form (AMIS, VPIM, or Bridge).

CSV Format

One of the methods of populating the grid with subscribers you want to edit is browsing to a CSV file and loading those users based on their aliases or extension numbers. The format of the CSV file only needs to follow two rules:

- The values need to be separated by commas. Tab or CrLf (Carriage return Line feed) or semicolon-separated files will not be parsed correctly.

- It needs to include a column header in the first line of the extension and/or alias. This is not case sensitive and can be padded on the left or right (or both) with spaces.

For instance, a file that starts like this will be parsed without a problem:

```
first name, last name, home server, alias, fax number, extension, department, domain
Paul, Lukan, EXServer1, plukan,,2199, Engineering, ENG_MAIN
Sean, Brinsfield, Exserver7, sbrinsfi,,,ENG_LAB
```

If the CSV file contains a column for both extension and alias, the extension column is used to search first. If a match is not found, then the alias column value will be used.

Each row of the CSV file will be read in and the corresponding column that contains extension (column #6 above) or alias in the first line (column #4 above) will be used to search for the subscriber. If a match is found, that user will be added to the grid. If more than one match is found for that extension (which should never happen) or alias, that row will be skipped and no duplicate users will ever be added to the grid. When the import is complete, a dialog will pop up which will show the total number of rows read in from the file and how many of those users were added to the grid.

In the preceding example, the first row tells the parser that column #6 contains the user's extensions and column #4 contains the alias. This will cause the parser to search for "2199" among all extensions for subscribers on the local box. If no match is found, then it would fall back and look for "plukan" among all aliases for subscribers on the local box. The 2nd row does not contain an extension, so only a search for "sbrinsfi" will be done among aliases for all subscribers on the local box.

Again, only subscribers associated with the local Unity server will be loaded. If you have multiple Unity servers in the same Exchange site, only those users associated with the local Unity server the Bulk Edit tool is being run on will be loaded into the grid.

Select Subscriber Changes

The Select Subscriber Changes page is for just what it sounds like: selecting changes you want on the subscribers you added to the grid in the previous step. You can select as few or as many changes as you want, without limit. You can change every property on every tab on this page if you want.

By default, all settings are configured so that no changes will take place. You need to actively select an item to change for any edits to be made. Older versions of Bulk Edit used to always force the standard greeting and transfer rules to be enabled due to bugs in previous versions of Unity. This version of Bulk Edit no longer does that as it is not necessary any more, and dbWalker will perform this same task should it be necessary.

Each tab on this page corresponds to a page on the subscriber section of the SA. Details of the properties on each tab follow.

Profile

- **Set Subscriber for Self Enrollment at Next Login**. With this drop-down set to true, all users will be asked at the next logon to record a name and a standard greeting, to set a password, and to choose whether to be listed in directory assistance. Once the subscriber has enrolled, the option is cleared automatically.

- **List in Phone Directory**. With this drop-down set to true, all subscribers will be listed in directory assistance, which callers can use to reach subscribers. When allowed by the class of service, subscribers can change this setting over the phone or by using the ActiveAssistant.

- **Change Switch Assignment to**. In a dual-switch integration you can select the phone system in this drop-down that all selected subscribers will be assigned to. This setting changes which switch Unity assumes it needs to use when transferring calls to subscribers, MWI on/off functionality, and which switch is used when Unity dials the subscriber when they use the Media Master to record/play back by phone.

- **Change Subscriber's Schedule**. You can change which schedule the subscriber is associated with. This effects which greetings rule triggers based on the time of day (play the off-hours greeting when the subscriber is out of the office, for example).

- **Change Default Language Subscriber Hears to**. You can select the language in which instructions are played for the subscriber in this drop-down list. Only the languages currently installed and active on Unity are offered in the list. Note: This value is set in the SA on the Conversation page, not the Profile page.

- **Change Default Language Callers Hear to**. You can select the language that Unity uses when playing the system-supplied greeting and system prompts to outside callers when they hit these subscribers' mailboxes. Callers hear the system-supplied greeting when the subscriber has not recorded a greeting. Select Inherited to use the language currently associated with the call. Only languages currently installed and active on Unity will be offered here. Note: This value is set in the SA on the Messages page, not the Profile page.

- **Change Time Zone for Subscriber**. You can select the desired time zone for the subscribers in this drop-down. If you select <Default to Time Zone on Unity Server, all users will have their time zone set to whatever the Unity server's time zone is set to. When a subscriber listens to messages over the phone, Unity announces the time that messages were received according to the time zone set here. This time zone value is also used to determine when notification dialouts happen for each subscriber.

Account

- **Set Billing ID**. You can enter any number or string in this box you want and it will be applied to the Billing ID value for each subscriber you selected. This value is only used for reporting purposes (it shows up in a couple of the Unity reports).

- **Force Billing ID to Be Blank**. If you select this option, the edit box for the Billing ID will be set to blank and Bulk Edit will force a blank string into the billing ID property for each user selected.

- **Unlock Account**. If you check this box, all subscribers will have their accounts unlocked. If users have locked themselves out after too many failed attempts to log in over the phone, this might be a quick mechanism to unlock them all at once. If you leave this field blank, it will not be touched.

Passwords

The Passwords tab changes values for the Phone password only. These settings have no bearing on the Windows password behavior:

- **User Cannot Change Password**. Set this drop-down to true to prevent the subscriber from changing the phone password via the phone interface (they can still change it by accessing the AA if you have them configured to allow it).

- **User Must Change Password at Next Login**. Set this drop-down to true to force the selected subscribers to change their phone password the first time they log into their mailbox over the phone.

- **Password Never Expires**. Set this value to true to allow subscribers to use the same phone password indefinitely regardless of what the system-wide password policy dictates for password expiration time. If this value is set to false instead, the password expiration time set on the password policy page in the SA will dictate how often the subscribers have to change their phone password.

- **Force Phone Password to Be**. Check this box and provide a number (up to 10 digits) that will be applied to all the selected subscribers as their new phone password. If you check the box and leave the value blank, all the phone passwords for the selected subscribers will be disabled. USE WITH CAUTION.

Conversation

The Conversation tab allows you to modify the conversation that the user hears while checking voicemail via the TUI:

- **Greet Subscriber by Name**. Set this value to true to have all subscribers hear their voice name when they call in to check messages over the phone. Set to false to have subscribers go directly to the subscriber menu when they sign in.

- **Conversation Type**. You can choose Full Prompts or Brief Prompts in this drop-down. The Full Prompts conversation is a detailed conversation targeted at newer users not familiar with the phone conversation. The Brief Prompts conversation is a more abbreviated menu structure for subscribers who are familiar with the phone conversation.

- **Address Messages to Other Subscribers by**. You can choose First Name, Last Name, or ID in this drop-down list. Subscribers address messages over the phone by entering recipients' extensions, by spelling their first names, or by spelling their last names; this sets the default mode. In the subscriber conversation, subscribers can switch between addressing by name or ID by pressing ##, but they cannot change between spelling by last name first or by first name first. That must be set via the SA/AA or using Bulk Edit.

- **Announce Total Number of New Messages**. Choose true from this drop-down list to have Unity announce the total number of unopened messages for all selected subscribers when they call in to check messages. This number includes unread voice, e-mail (if the user has TTS enabled), fax (if the user has fax mail enabled), and return receipt messages.

- **Announce Total Number of Saved Messages**. Choose true from this drop-down list to have Unity announce the total number of messages that have been opened but not deleted. This number includes voice, e-mail (if the user has TTS enabled), fax (if the user has fax mail enabled), and return receipt messages.

- **Announce Total Number of New Voice Messages**. Choose true from this drop-down list to have Unity announce the total number of unread voice-mail messages to users when they call in to check message.

- **Announce Total Number of New Fax Messages**. Choose true from this drop-down list to have Unity announce the total number of unread fax messages for users when they call in. This only applies to users that have fax mail enabled in the class of service they are associated with.

- **Announce Total Number of New E-mail Messages**. Choose true from this drop-down list to have Unity announce the total number of unread e-mail messages for users when they call in. This only applies to users that have TTS enabled in the class of service they are associated with.

- **Announce Sender**. Choose true from this drop-down list to have Unity say the name of the subscriber that sent the message (if known) when users are listening to messages over the phone.

- **Say Message Number**. Choose true from this drop-down list to have Unity announce the sequential number of a message ("Message one is...") when users are listening to messages over the phone. This can be used with the Announce Total Number of New Messages check box to help subscribers keep track of the number of unheard messages as they go through the list.

- **Announce Timestamp**. You can choose Before Message or After Message in this drop-down to dictate if the timestamps are played before subscribers hear the message or after when they are listening to messages over the phone.

- **Playback Volume**. You can choose quieter, medium, or louder. Medium is the default and means messages play back at normal volume (that is, no change). Quieter means they play back about 25 percent quieter than normal and louder means they play about 25 percent louder than normal.

Transfer

The Transfer tab allows you to modify how callers are transferred to the subscriber's phone or voice-mail box:

- **Enable Transfer.** Choose true to enable transfers for all selected subscribers and false to disable it. If you disable transfer here, Unity will not try to ring the subscriber's phone when a user dials their extension from the opening greeting, for example. If you enable transfer and the subscriber doesn't have a custom transfer string set on the Call Transfer page in the SA, their extension number will be used (that is, the value on the Profile page will be dialed directly).

- **Transfer Type.** You can choose Release or Supervised in the drop-down list here. Use this setting with caution and only if you understand call transfer and its implications on the phone and voice messaging systems:

  — **Release.** Unity puts the caller on hold, dials the extension, and releases the call to the phone system. Unity does not monitor the call. When the line is busy or is not answered, the phone system forwards the call to the sub-scriber's greeting. This transfer type allows Unity to handle calls more quickly. Use only when call forwarding is enabled on the phone system.

  — **Supervised.** Unity acts as a receptionist, monitoring the transfer. If the line is busy or the call is not answered within the number of rings you set in Rings to Wait for, Unity does not complete the transfer and plays the subscriber's greeting. You can use supervised transfer whether or not the phone system forwards calls. These options are unavailable if transfer has been disabled. Bulk Edit will allow you to set them, but they will mean nothing for the subscribers if transfer has been disabled.

- **Rings to Wait.** You can enter any number between 2 and 19 here. This dictates the number of rings Unity will wait before pulling a call back and assuming no one is going to answer it. This option is only used if the subscriber is set to Supervised transfer. Release transfers will simply ignore this value. Again, Bulk Edit will still let you set the value even if it is not going to be used.

- **Edit Transfer Number.** There are three options for adjusting the transfer string for subscribers:

  — **Set Transfer Number to Be Subscriber's Extension.** Check this box to force the Bulk Edit utility to replace any transfer string that might be in the selected subscriber's transfer field with their extension number. This can be useful if you've changed numbering plans and want to be sure all users are dialing the correct extensions. Use with caution! If you have custom dial strings configured for users, they will be wiped out with this option.

  — **Append Digits to the Left.** You can append any dialable character to the left of the existing transfer string. Dialable characters include "0123456789*#,". If you opted to set the transfer string to the subscriber's extension previously, this will be the value that is modified. If not, the existing transfer string will be added to. One common use of this feature would be to stick a 9 on front of an existing extension to create the transfer string.

— **Append Digits to the Right**. You can append any dialable character to the right of the existing transfer string. Dialable characters include "0123456789*#,". If you opted to set the transfer string to the subscriber's extension, this will be the value that is modified. If not, the existing transfer string will be appended to.

- **If Call Is Busy**. You can choose Always Hold, No Holding, or Ask caller in this drop-down list. This dictates what action Unity performs for external calls when the subscriber's phone is busy. An external call is defined as a call from someone that is not a Unity subscriber. You might want to use holding options sparingly as having calls on hold can tie up ports:

  — **Always Hold**. Unity plays a prompt indicating that the extension is busy. The caller is put on hold and will periodically be asked if they would like to continue holding or leave a message until the line frees up.

  — **No Holding**. Unity plays the subscriber's greeting (if recorded) and prompts the caller to leave a message.

  — **Ask Caller**. Unity gives the caller the options of holding for the subscriber, leaving a message, or dialing another extension. Note: These options only come into play when the subscriber is configured for supervised transfers. Again, though, Bulk Edit will let you set the values even if they are not going to be used.

- **Announce**. Choose true in this drop-down list to have Unity say "transferring call" to subscribers before releasing a call to their extension. This indicates an incoming call is external and not an internal caller (that is, they should answer the call in their professional voice). This option only comes into play when the subscriber is configured for supervised transfers. Again, though, Bulk Edit will let you set the values even if they are not going to be used

- **Introduce**. Choose true in this drop-down list to have subscribers hear Unity say "call for <subscriber's recorded name>" or "call for <dialed extension number>" when they answer an incoming external call from the automated attendant. Use this setting when subscribers share a phone or a subscriber takes calls for more than one dialed extension. This option only comes into play when the subscriber is configured for supervised transfers. Again, though, Bulk Edit will let you set the values even if they are not going to be used

- **Confirm**. Choose true in this drop-down list to have Unity prompt the subscriber to accept or refuse an external call. The caller waits a few extra seconds during the confirmation. If the call is accepted, it is transferred to the subscriber's phone. If the call is refused, Unity plays the appropriate subscriber greeting. This is normally used in conjunction with the Ask Callers Name option. This option only comes into play when the subscriber is configured for supervised transfers. Again, though, Bulk Edit will let you set the values even if they are not going to be used.

- **Ask Callers Name**. Choose true in this drop-down list to have Unity prompt external callers to say their names. Before a call is transferred, the subscriber hears, "Call from." This is normally used in conjunction with the Confirm option. This option only comes into play when the subscriber is configured for supervised transfers. Again, though, Bulk Edit will let you set the values even if they are not going to be used.

Greetings

This tab has six tabs on it for each of the greetings associated with each subscriber:

- **Standard**. This greeting is active when the subscriber's schedule is on and indicates they are in the office. This greeting cannot be disabled and is the backstop greeting that will play if all others are disabled or not active at the time for a call.

- **Closed**. This greeting is active when the subscriber's schedule is off and indicates that they are out of the office. This greeting can be disabled, in which case the call will be handled by the standard greeting.

- **Busy**. If the call reached this subscriber's mailbox because their extension was busy, this greeting will be played. This allows subscribers to have a special greeting asking the caller to hold and the like. If this greeting is not enabled, the closed or standard greeting will be used to handle the call as appropriate.

- **Internal**. If the calling extension is another subscriber on the Unity server, the internal greeting will play. This allows subscribers to tell co-workers information they would not want external callers to hear (that is, where they really are that day). If this greeting is not enabled, the busy, closed, or standard greetings kick in as appropriate.

- **Alternate**. If this greeting is enabled, it overrules all other greetings and will play no matter what time of day it is or how the call got to this subscriber or who the calling extension is. If it is not enabled, the internal, busy, closed, or standard rules kick in as appropriate.

- **Error**. This is a special greeting that is not visible in Unity 2.4.6 and earlier, although it is used. This greeting rule dictates where callers should be sent if they enter an illegal option when listening to this subscriber's greeting. By default this plays an "I am sorry, I did not hear your entry" prompt and sends the caller to the opening greeting. In cases where you want callers to go to a different handler on an error condition, you can edit this greeting. You should never disable this greeting, and edit its behavior carefully.

On each greeting tab you can set the following values:

- **Enabled**. Choose true in this drop-down list to enable the greeting or false to disable it. Note that the standard greeting cannot be disabled and the error greeting should only be disabled in special circumstances.

- **Allow User Input**. Choose true in this drop-down list to allow callers to dial extensions of other users when listening to a subscriber's greetings. Set this value to false if you want users to be locked in and only allow them to select one key routing rule available for this subscriber and nothing else.

- **Reprompts**. By default Unity plays the greeting one time and then executes the after greeting action. However, you can change that to have Unity replay the greeting multiple times (that is, if you expect the user to actively select an option rather than simply fall through to the after greeting action). In this box you can select how many times to replay the greeting by entering a value of 0 (only play greeting once) to 99 (Unity will play the greeting a total of 100 times) in the replay greeting edit box. You can dictate how many seconds to wait after the end of the greeting before starting the next play of the greeting by entering a value (in seconds) of 0 – 99 in the seconds between replays edit box. If you leave these boxes blank, the current values in the database will be preserved.

- **After Greeting Action**. After the greeting is played normally you would want to take a message from the caller. If, however, you want to do something different you can configure it here:

  — **Take Action**. Select this radio button and choose the action from the drop-down list:

    Take Message. The caller will be allowed to leave a message for the subscriber after the greeting completes playing.

    Hang Up. Unity will hang up on the caller immediately after the greeting is finished. This is a little abrupt. Typically you would want to send someone to the "say goodbye" call handler and hang up nicely.

    Sign In. The caller will be sent to the subscriber sign in conversation after the greeting completes.

    Loop Back to Self. This option will have the caller sent back to the beginning of the greeting for the current subscriber. It will not attempt the transfer sequence for the subscriber; it will go directly to the greeting. This option is a popular choice for changing the error greeting's behavior. Some people find this preferable to dumping the caller back to the opening greeting.

    Greetings Administrator. This option will send the caller to the greetings administration conversation. This will allow them to select a call handler they own by name or ID and record the greetings for it over the phone.

- — **Go to Directory**. Select this radio button to send the caller to a selected directory handler after the greeting completes. A directory handler allows callers to find subscribers in the system by spelling their names using the phone dial pad.

- — **Go to Call Handler**. Select this radio button if you want to send the caller to a call handler after the greeting completes. Hit the Browse button and select a call handler from the resulting dialog. The display name of the call handler will appear in the edit box to the right of the radio button. If you check the Don't Try to Ring Phone box, Unity will send the caller directly to the greeting of the selected call handler without trying a transfer rule, even if one is enabled and active.

- — **Go to Subscriber**. Select this radio button if you want to send the caller to a subscriber's mailbox after the greeting completes. Hit the Browse button and select a subscriber from the resulting dialog. The display name of the user will appear in the edit box to the right of the radio button. If you check the Don't Try to Ring Phone box, Unity will send the caller directly to the greeting of the selected subscriber without trying the transfer rule, even if it is enabled.

- — **Go to interview**. Select this radio button if you want to send the caller to an interview handler after the greeting completes. Hit the Browse button and select an interview handler from the resulting dialog. The display name of the interview handler will appear in the edit box to the right of the radio button.

Caller Input

Each subscriber and call handler in the system has a set of caller input rules that allow you to dictate what action Unity takes when a caller presses a digit while a greeting is playing. There is one set of caller input rules that apply to all the greetings; there are not separate rules for each greeting.

You can configure a total of 12 keys: the 0-9, *, and # keys. The 4th column tones (A, B, C, and D) are not available to be mapped as part of the caller input rules:

- • **Milliseconds to Wait**. You can set this value from 0 to 2000/2003. It indicates how many milliseconds Unity will wait for another digit before determining that a user has completed entering a string of numbers (or a single digit) before taking action. If you set this value too low, people will not be able to dial extensions from a greeting and, if you set it too high, people will have to wait before Unity takes action on their key presses that will be perceived as slowness. Fiddle with this with extreme caution. Be sure to try it out on a test user/handler first before applying it to large numbers of users/handlers. Note: If you do not want users to be able to try extensions at all while listening to greetings, you can set the allow user input value for the greeting(s) on the handler or subscriber to false to accomplish this. It is not a good idea to set the Milliseconds to Wait value to 0 to do this.

- **Rule Options**. For each of the keys you have the following options for what action Unity will take when that key is entered while the greeting is played:

  — **Apply Change Only if Key Is Set to Ignore**. If you check this value, the changes you indicate for each key will only be applied if the existing key on the subscriber is set to ignore. If custom action set already exists for the existing key, it is skipped. This can be useful if you have a user who has custom settings set up you do not want to write over.

  — **Take Action**. Select this radio button and choose the action from the drop-down list:

  Skip Greeting. If the user hits this key; the greeting is skipped and Unity advances right to the after greeting action configured for this greeting.

  Take Message. If the user hits this key; they are taken right to the recorded message asking the caller to leave a message, regardless of what the after greeting action is set to.

  Hang Up. If the user hits this key, Unity hangs up on them immediately.

  Sign In. If the user hits this key they are taken to the subscriber sign in conversation.

  Loop Back to Self. If the user hits this key, they start over at the beginning of the greeting for this subscriber.

  Greetings Administrator. This option sends the caller to the greetings administration conversation. This allows them to select a call handler they own by name or ID and record the greetings for it over the phone.

  — **Go to Directory**. Select this radio button to send the caller to a selected directory handler when they hit this key. A directory handler allows callers to find subscribers in the system by spelling their names using the phone dial pad.

  — **Go to Call Handler**. Select this radio button if you want to send the caller to a call handler when a user hits this key. Hit the Browse button and select a call handler from the resulting dialog. The display name of the call handler appears in the edit box to the right of the radio button. If you check the Don't Try to Ring Phone box, Unity will send the caller directly to the greeting of the selected call handler without trying a transfer rule, even if one is enabled and active.

— **Go to Subscriber**. Select this radio button if you want to send the caller to a subscriber's mailbox when they hit this key. Hit the Browse button and select a subscriber from the resulting dialog. The display name of the user appears in the edit box to the right of the radio button. If you check the Don't Try to Ring Phone box, Unity sends the caller directly to the greeting of the selected subscriber without trying the transfer rule, even if it is enabled.

— **Go to interview**. Select this radio button if you want to send the caller to an interview handler when they hit this key. Hit the Browse button and select an interview handler from the resulting dialog. The display name of the interview handler will appear in the edit box to the right of the radio button.

— **Lock Key**. If you lock the key, Unity takes action on that key immediately without waiting to see if the caller is going to enter more digits (that is, they are dialing an extension number and possibly not selecting a one key option). As soon as the user hits this key, Unity immediatly executes the action indicated.

Messages

The Messages tab allows you to modify MWI properties for the subscriber, as well as options that define the caller's experience when leaving messages for the subscriber:

- **MWI Code**. You can enter any number string in here or X. X will automatically be replaced with the user's extension number; this is the most common use of this field. You might need to do this if you are changing numbering plans and want to make sure everyone is using the updated values for their lamps. It would be very unusual to stick a static number in here and have a large number of subscribers. Note: For Unity 3.0 and later where up to 10 lamp codes can be assigned per user, this value touches only the first MWI in the list.

- **Disable MWI Functionality for User**. If you check this box, all MWI codes for the selected subscribers will be removed and no MWI strings will be set up for them. Checking this box clears and disables the MWI Code edit box as well. For Unity 3.0 and later, this means ALL MWI codes for the user will be removed (up to 10 are supported).

- **Maximum Message Length**. This sets the number of seconds for the maximum message length outside callers will be limited to when leaving this subscriber a message. This can be a number between 0 and 1200 (20 minutes). Note: Subscribers leaving messages for this user are not limited by this value; they are limited by their class of service setting for the maximum message record time they are allowed.

- **Callers Can Edit Messages**. Set this drop-down to true to allow callers to review, rerecord, or append to messages they have just recorded for this subscriber.

- **Callers Can Mark Messages as Urgent**. Set this drop-down to true to allow outside callers to mark messages for this subscriber as urgent.

- **After Message Action**. After the user leaves a message, normally you would want to send them to the "say goodbye" call handler. If, however, you want to do something different you can configure it here.

  — **Take Action**. Select this radio button and choose one of the following actions from the drop-down list:

  Hang Up. Unity will hang up on the caller immediately after they finish recording their message. This is a little abrupt. Typically you would want to send someone to the "say goodbye" call handler and hang up nicely instead.

  Sign In. The caller will be sent to the subscriber sign in conversation after they finish recording their message.

  Loop Back to Self. This option will have the caller sent back to the beginning of the greeting for the current subscriber after they finish recording their message. It will not attempt the transfer sequence for the subscriber; it will go directly to the active greeting.

  Greetings Administrator. This option will send the caller to the greetings administration conversation. This will allow them to select a call handler they own by name or ID and record the greetings for it over the phone.

  — **Go to Directory**. Select this radio button to send the caller to a selected directory handler after the caller finishes recording their message. A directory handler allows callers to find subscribers in the system by spelling their names using the phone dial pad.

  — **Go to Call Handler**. Select this radio button if you want to send the caller to a call handler after the caller finishes recording their message. Hit the Browse button and select a call handler from the resulting dialog. The display name of the call handler will appear in the edit box to the right of the radio button. If you check the Don't Try to Ring Phone box, Unity sends the caller directly to the greeting of the selected call handler without trying a transfer rule, even if one is enabled and active.

  — **Go to Subscriber**. Select this radio button if you want to send the caller to a subscriber's mailbox after the caller finishes recording their message. Hit the Browse button and select a subscriber from the resulting dialog. The display name of the user will appear in the edit box to the right of the radio button. If you check the Don't Try to Ring Phone box, Unity sends the caller directly to the greeting of the selected subscriber without trying the transfer rule, even if it is enabled.

> — **Go to interview**. Select this radio button if you want to send the caller to an interview handler after the caller finishes recording their message. Hit the Browse button and select an interview handler from the resulting dialog. The display name of the interview handler appears in the edit box to the right of the radio button.

Notification

Depending on which version of Unity you are running, you will see anywhere from 4 to 13 different notification devices. For each you can indicate if the device is enabled or disabled and which switch it is associated with (if it is a phone delivery device).

It might be necessary to change switch assignment for notification devices if you are moving from a single-switch to a multiple-switch environment, or vice versa. It is possible to individually assign each notification device to a different switch on a per-device basis. For example, this is necessary if a site wants all pager devices going out the legacy PBX and all other devices to go out the IP phone.

Each user is able to edit their own notification devices via the phone (the first four devices) or via the Cisco Unity Personal Communications Assistant (CPCA). It is not possible to change dialout numbers, e-mail addresses, schedules, and so on via the Bulk Edit utility.

Extension

The Extension page lets you change a selected subscriber's primary extension number based on a set of rules listed here. You can select one or all the rules to apply depending on what changes you want to make. These rules are applied from the top down so, if you select more than one, keep that in mind. If a particular rule you selected does not apply to an extension (that is, you indicate you want to strip all but the leftmost four digits off and the extension being processed is already only four digits long), that rule is simply skipped and the next selected rule is applied. Once the new extension is calculated, it is checked against other extensions in the system to make sure it is unique. If it is not, an error is logged and the original extension is left alone.

This can be handy if a site is changing their numbering plan to a different length of digits or the like. It can also be useful if you have used a full 10-digit number set (which you can pull from the Business Phone field in Exchange during Unity import) and you want to reduce it to the rightmost or leftmost 4 digits.

Before proceeding off this page, be sure to test the changes you have laid out by entering a test extension and pressing the test button. The resulting value after processing that number through your proposed changes will show up in the new value edit box. Once you are sure you have the changes you want in place, proceed.

NOTE   Unity 3.0 and later versions allow up to nine alternate extensions along with the primary extension. The changes applied on this page do not touch any of the alternate extensions. Only the primary extension (found on the subscriber's Profile page in the SA) is modified.

Alternate Extensions

The Alternate Extensions tab allows you to remove all alternate extensions for selected subscribers. There is no way to remove specific or only some alternate extensions; this will remove all alternate extensions so be careful when using this.

Exit Destination

The Exit Destination tab allows you to set an exit destination for all selected subscribers on this tab:

- **Take Action**. Select this radio button and choose the action from the drop-down list:
  - **Hang Up**. Unity hangs up on the caller immediately after they exit the subscriber conversation. This is a little abrupt. Typically you would want to send someone to the "say goodbye" call handler and hang up nicely instead.
  - **Sign In**. The caller is sent to the subscriber sign in conversation after they exit the subscriber conversation. This is a little odd but is allowed.
  - **Loop Back to Self**. This option has the caller sent to the greeting of their own subscriber when they exit the subscriber conversation. Again, this is a little odd but legal. It does not attempt the transfer sequence for the subscriber; it will go directly to the active greeting.
  - **Greetings Administrator**. This option sends the caller to the greetings administration conversation. This allows them to select a call handler they own by name or ID and record the greetings for it over the phone.
- **Go to Directory**. Select this radio button to send the caller to a selected directory handler after they exit the subscriber conversation. A directory handler allows callers to find subscribers in the system by spelling their names using the phone dial pad.
- **Go to Call Handler**. Select this radio button if you want to send the caller to a call handler after they exit the subscriber conversation. Hit the Browse button and select a call handler from the resulting dialog. The display name of the call handler appears in the edit box to the right of the radio button. If you check the Don't Try to Ring Phone box, Unity sends the caller directly to the greeting of the selected call handler without trying a transfer rule, even if one is enabled and active.

- **Go to Subscriber**. Select this radio button if you want to send the caller to a subscriber's mailbox after they exit the subscriber conversation. Hit the Browse button and select a subscriber from the resulting dialog. The display name of the user appears in the edit box to the right of the radio button. If you check the Don't Try to Ring Phone box, Unity sends the caller directly to the greeting of the selected subscriber without trying the transfer rule, even if it is enabled.

- **Go to interview**. Select this radio button if you want to send the caller to an interview handler after they exit the subscriber conversation. Hit the Browse button and select an interview handler from the resulting dialog. The display name of the interview handler appears in the edit box to the right of the radio button.

Apply Subscriber Changes

When you have the subscribers you want selected and the changes you want applied to those subscribers, press the Update Subscribers button here and those changes will be applied. The progress bar will indicate how far along the process is, and when it is complete a dialog will pop up indicating we're done and how many errors were encountered in the process.

You'll be given the opportunity to view the output log automatically when the process is complete. If there are any errors noted, I strongly recommend you search the log for "(error)" to find the problem. Remember, a new output log is generated in the \logs folder under the Bulk Edit installation directory each time you run the tool.

Select Call Handlers

In this step you need to populate the grid with a list of call handlers you want to edit. You can add as many handlers to this grid as you want, and you can do it using different criteria. If, for example, you want to add all handlers with extension numbers 100–200 and all handlers with a message recipient of "Example Administrator", you can do that. Duplicate handlers (that is, if some handlers with Example Administrator as the message recipient are also in the 100–200 extension range) will automatically be corrected in the grid such that only one instance of each handler will appear in the grid.

Once you have handlers in the grid you can sort the grid columns or move the columns around any way you like. You can individually select/unselect handlers using the checkbox in the far left column. Only handlers that have the check mark on them will be edited with the changes you select in the next step. You can use the Deselect All button to uncheck all the handlers in the grid and the Select All button to check all the handlers in the grid.

If you opt to add a large number of handlers to the grid, be patient. The updates on the grid are turned off to speed the process up, so it might take a minute or two to populate the grid and then updates are turned back on and you can see your handlers.

NOTE   Only normal call handlers are added to the grid here. Primary call handlers (associated with subscribers) are not included here. Use the subscriber path to edit subscribers and their corresponding primary call handlers.

You can add call handlers to the grid using the options at the top of the form:

- **All Call Handlers**. All call handlers on the local Unity server will be loaded into the grid. If there are a large number of handlers, be patient; this might take a minute or two.

- **All Call Handlers Associated with This Switch**. If you have a multiple-switch configuration setup you will want to add all call handlers that are configured to be associated with one switch or the other.

- **Call Handlers with Extension Numbers from**. Enter a lower and an upper extension range and all call handlers that have extensions in that range are be added to the grid. Remember that extensions are optional for call handlers so not all handlers will have an extension.

- **Call Handlers Owned by This Distribution List**. Every call handler has an owner and a message recipient. Owners and message recipients can be either subscribers or public distribution lists. You can add all handlers owned by a specific distribution list to the grid by hitting the Browse button and selecting a distribution list in the resulting dialog.

- **Call Handlers Owned by This Subscriber**. Every call handler has an owner and a message recipient. Owners and message recipients can be either subscribers or public distribution lists. You can add all handlers owned by a specific subscriber to the grid by hitting the Browse button and selecting a subscriber in the resulting dialog.

- **Call Handlers with This Distribution List as the Message Recipient**. Every call handler has an owner and a message recipient. Owners and message recipients can be either subscribers or public distribution lists. You can add all handlers set up to deliver their messages to a specific distribution list to the grid by hitting the Browse button and selecting a distribution list in the resulting dialog.

- **Call Handlers with This Subscriber as the Message Recipient**. Every call handler has an owner and a message recipient. Owners and message recipients can be either subscribers or public distribution lists. You can add all handlers set up to deliver messages to a specific subscriber to the grid by hitting the Browse button and selecting a subscriber in the resulting dialog.

- **All Call Handlers Referenced in This CSV File**. You can add call handlers to the grid by using a CSV file and looking them up by alias and/or extension number. The details of the CSV file format requirements are in the following section "CSV Format."

CSV Format

One of the methods of populating the grid with call handlers you want to add to edit is browsing to a CSV file and loading those handlers based on their aliases or extension numbers. The format of the CSV file only needs to follow two rules:

- The values need to be separated by commas. Tab or CrLf or semicolon-separated files will not be parsed correctly.

- It needs to include a column header in the first line of the extension and/or alias. This is not case sensitive and can be padded on the left or right (or both) with spaces.

For instance, a file that starts like this will be parsed without a problem:

```
display name, alias, extension, recipient
Opening greeting, openinggreetingch,,Eadministrator
Sales Info Line,ch_salesinfoline,1174,Eadministrator
. . .
```

If the CSV file contains a column for both extension and alias, the extension column is used to search first. If a match is not found, then the alias column value will be used.

Each row of the CSV file will be read in and the corresponding column that contains extension (column #3 above) or alias in the first line (column #2 above) will be used to search for the call handler. If a match is found, that handler is added to the grid. If more than one match is found for that extension (which should never happen) or alias, an error dialog will pop up alerting you to that fact and that row will be skipped in the file.

In the preceding example, the first row tells the parser that column #3 contains the handler's extensions and column #2 contains the alias. The next row would cause the parser to search for an alias of "openinggreetinch" among all call handlers on the local box for a match because no extension value is provided. The third row does have an extension number of 1174 that will be searched for first. If no match is found, then the alias of "ch_salsinfoline" will be searched for.

Again, only call handlers associated with the local Unity server are loaded. If you have multiple Unity servers in the same Exchange site, only those handlers associated with the local Unity server the Bulk Edit tool is being run on are loaded into the grid.

Select Call Handler Changes

If, at the beginning of the wizard you chose to edit call handlers, you will be presented with these options.

Profile

The Profile tab allows you to modify properties of the call handler such as owner, schedule, or switch ID:

- **Owner Option**. Every call handler has an owner and a message recipient. These can be either a specific subscriber or a public distribution list. You can dictate that all listed call handlers be owned by a specific subscriber or distribution list here by selecting a radio button and hitting the corresponding Browse to select an object in the resulting dialog box. The display name of the selected subscriber/distribution list appears in the edit box to the right of the radio button.

- **Change Switch Assignment to**. In a dual-switch integration you can choose the phone system in this drop-down that all selected call handlers will be assigned to. This setting changes which switch Unity assumes it needs to use when transferring calls.

- **Change Default Language to**. You can choose the language that Unity uses when playing the system-supplied greeting and system prompts to outside callers when they hit these call handlers. Callers hear the system-supplied greeting when the call handler has no recorded greeting. Choose Inherited to use the language currently associated with the call. Only languages currently installed and active on Unity will be offered here.

- **Change Handler Schedule to**. You can force the selected handlers to be associated with a specific schedule configured on the local Unity server. This effects which greeting and/or transfer rule triggers for the call handler based on the time of day (that is, if the Standard or the Off Hours greeting/transfer rule is used).

Transfer

Unlike subscribers that only have one transfer option, call handlers have three transfer rules that can be configured:

- **Standard**. This transfer rule is active when the call handler's schedule is on. The standard transfer rule cannot be disabled and is the backstop transfer rule. You can make it not transfer, but you cannot disable the rule.

- **Closed**. This transfer rule is active when the call handler's schedule is off. The rule can be disabled, in which case control passes to the standard transfer rule instead.

- **Alternate**. If this transfer rule is enabled, it overrides the other two rules and is active all the time regardless of what the call handler's schedule indicates.

For each of these transfer rules you can apply the following changes:

- **Enable Transfer**. Select true to enable transfers for all selected call transfers and false to disable it. If you disable transfer here, Unity will not try to ring the subscriber's phone when a user dials this extension from the opening greeting, for example. If you enable transfer and the call handler does not have a custom transfer string set on the

Call Transfer page in the SA, the extensions number is used (that is, the value on the Profile page is dialed directly). Because extension numbers are optional for call handlers, if an extension is not provided the transfer is automatically set to no.

- **Transfer Type.** You can choose release or supervised in the drop-down list here. Use this setting with caution and only if you understand call transfer and its implications on the phone and voice messaging systems:

  — **Release.** Unity puts the caller on hold, dials the extension, and releases the call to the phone system. Unity does not monitor the call. When the line is busy or is not answered, the phone system forwards the call to the call handler's greeting. This transfer type allows Unity to handle calls more quickly. Use only when call forwarding is enabled on the phone system.

  — **Supervised.** Unity acts as a receptionist, monitoring the transfer. If the line is busy or the call is not answered within the number of rings you set in Rings to Wait for, Unity does not complete the transfer and plays the call handler's greeting. You can use supervised transfer whether or not the phone system forwards calls. These options are unavailable if transfer has been disabled. Bulk Edit allows you to set them, but they will mean nothing for the call handlers if transfer has been disabled.

- **Rings to Wait.** You can enter any number between 2 and 19 here. This dictates the number of rings Unity waits for before pulling a call back and assuming no one is going to answer it. This option is only used if the call handler is set to Supervised transfer. Release transfers simply ignore this value. Again, Bulk Edit still allows you set the value even if it is not going to be used.

- **Set Transfer Number to Be Subscriber's Extension.** Check this box to force the Bulk Edit utility to replace any transfer string that might be in the selected call handler's transfer field with their extension number. This can be useful if you've changed numbering plans and want to be sure all call handlers are dialing the correct extensions. Use with caution! If you have custom dial strings configured for handlers, they will be wiped out with this option.

- **If Call is Busy.** You can choose Always Hold, No Holding, or Ask Caller in this drop-down list. This dictates what action Unity performs for external calls when the call handler's phone is busy. You might want to use holding options sparingly as having calls on hold can tie up ports:

  — **Always Hold.** Unity plays a prompt indicating that the extension is busy. The caller is put on hold and is asked periodically if they would like to continue holding until the line frees up or leave a message.

  — **No Holding.** Unity plays the call handler's greeting (if recorded) and prompts the caller to leave a message.

— **Ask Caller**. Unity gives the caller the options of holding, leaving a message, or dialing another extension. Note: These options only come into play when the call handler is configured for Supervised Transfers. Again, though, Bulk Edit lets you set the values even if they are not going to be used.

- **Announce**. Choose true in this drop-down list to have Unity say, "transferring call" before releasing a call to the extension. This indicates an incoming call is external and not an internal caller (that is, they should answer the call in their professional voice). This option only comes into play when the call handler is configured for Supervised Transfers. Again, though, Bulk Edit lets you set the values even if they are not going to be used.

- **Introduce**. Choose true in this drop-down list to have Unity say, "call for <message recipient's recorded name>" or "call for <dialed extension number>" when they answer an incoming external call from the automated attendant. Use this setting when subscribers share a phone or a subscriber takes calls for more than one dialed extension. This option only comes into play when the call handler is configured for Supervised Transfers. Again, though, Bulk Edit lets you set the values even if they are not going to be used.

- **Confirm**. Choose true in this drop-down list to have Unity prompt to accept or refuse an external call. The caller waits a few extra seconds during the confirmation. If the call is accepted, it is transferred to the call handler's transfer string. If the call is refused, Unity plays the appropriate greeting. This is normally used in conjunction with the Ask Callers Name option. This option only comes into play when the call handler is configured for Supervised Transfers. Again, though, Bulk Edit lets you set the values even if they are not going to be used.

- **Ask Callers Name**. Choose true in this drop-down list to have Unity prompt external callers to say their names. Before a call is transferred, the subscriber hears, "Call from." This is normally used in conjunction with the Confirm option. This option only comes into play when the call handler is configured for Supervised Transfers. Again, though, Bulk Edit lets you set the values even if they are not going to be used.

Greetings

This tab has six tabs on it for each of the greetings associated with each call handler:

- **Standard**. This greeting is active when the call handler's schedule is on. This greeting cannot be disabled and is the backstop greeting that plays if all others are disabled or not active at the time for a call.

- **Closed**. This greeting is active when the call handler's schedule is off. This greeting can be disabled, in which case the call is handled by the standard greeting.

- **Busy**. If the call reached this handler because the extension was busy, this greeting is played. This allows handlers to have a special greeting asking the caller to hold and the like. If this greeting is not enabled, the closed or standard greeting is used to handle the call as appropriate.

- **Internal**. If the calling extension is another subscriber on the Unity server, the internal greeting plays. This allows subscribers to tell co-workers information they would not want external callers to hear (that is, where they really are that day). If this greeting is not enabled, the busy, closed, or standard greeting kicks in as appropriate.

- **Alternate**. If this greeting is enabled, it overrules all other greetings and plays no matter what time of day it is or how the call got to this handler or who the calling extension is. If it is not enabled, the internal, busy, closed, or standard rule kicks in as appropriate.

- **Error**. This is a special greeting that is not visible in Unity 2.4.6 and earlier, although it is used. This greeting rule dictates where callers should be sent if they enter an illegal option when listening to this handler's greeting. By default, this plays an "I'm sorry, I didn't hear your entry" prompt and sends the caller to the opening greeting. In cases where you want callers to go to a different handler on an error condition you can edit this greeting. You should never disable this greeting and edit its behavior carefully.

On each greeting tab you can set the following values:

- **Enabled**. Choose true in this drop-down list to enable the greeting or false to disable it. Note that the standard greeting cannot be disabled and the error greeting should only be disabled in special circumstances.

- **Allow User Input**. Choose true in this drop-down list to allow callers to dial extensions of other users when listening to a handler's greetings. Set this value to false if you want users to be locked in and only allow them to select one key routing rules available for this call handler and nothing else.

- **Reprompts**. By default Unity plays the greeting one time and then executes the after greeting action. However, you can change that to have Unity replay the greeting multiple times (that is, if you are expecting the user to actively select an option rather than simply fall through to the after greeting action). In this box you can select how many times to replay the greeting by entering a value of 0 (only play the greeting once) to 99 (Unity will play the greeting a total of 100 times) in the Replay Greeting edit box. You can dictate how many seconds to wait after the end of the greeting before starting the next play of the greeting by entering a value (in seconds) of 0–99 in the Seconds Between Replays edit box. If you leave these boxes blank, the current values in the database are preserved.

- **After Greeting Action**. Normally, after the greeting is played you would want to take a message from the caller. If, however, you want to do something different, you can configure it here.

— **Take Action**. Select this radio button and choose the action from the drop-down list:

Take Message. The caller is allowed to leave a message for the call handler's message recipient after the greeting completes playing.

Hang Up. Unity hangs up on the caller immediately after the greeting is finished. This is a little abrupt. Typically you would want to send someone to the "say goodbye" call handler and hang up nicely.

Sign In. The caller is sent to the subscriber sign in conversation after the greeting completes.

Loop Back to Self. This option has the caller sent back to the beginning of the greeting for the current call handler. The transfer sequence for the handler is not attempted; the caller will go right to the active greeting. This option is a popular choice for changing the error greeting's behavior. Some people find this preferable to dumping the caller back to the opening greeting.

Greetings Administrator. This option sends the caller to the greetings administration conversation. This allows them to select a call handler they own by name or ID and record the greetings for it over the phone.

— **Go to Directory**. Select this radio button to send the caller to a selected directory handler after the greeting completes. A directory handler allows callers to find subscribers in the system by spelling their names using the phone dial pad.

— **Go to Call Handler**. Select this radio button if you want to send the caller to a call handler after the greeting completes. Hit the Browse button and select a call handler from the resulting dialog. The display name of the call handler appears in the edit box to the right of the radio button. If you check the Don't Try to Ring Phone box, Unity sends the caller directly to the greeting of the selected call handler without trying a transfer rule, even if one is enabled and active.

— **Go to Subscriber**. Select this radio button if you want to send the caller to a subscriber's mailbox after the greeting completes. Hit the Browse button and select a subscriber from the resulting dialog. The display name of the user appears in the edit box to the right of the radio button. If you check the Don't Try to Ring Phone box, Unity sends the caller directly to the greeting of the selected subscriber without trying the transfer rule, even if it is enabled.

— **Go to interview**. Select this radio button if you want to send the caller to an interview handler after the greeting completes. Hit the Browse button and select an interview handler from the resulting dialog. The display name of the interview handler appears in the edit box to the right of the radio button.

Caller Input

Each subscriber and call handler in the system has a set of caller input rules that allow them to dictate what action Unity takes when a caller presses a digit while a greeting is playing. There is one set of caller input rules that apply to all the greetings; there are not separate rules for each greeting.

You can configure a total of 12 keys: the 0-9, *, and # keys. The 4th column tones (A, B, C, and D) are not available to be mapped as part of the caller input rules:

- **Milliseconds to Wait**. You can set this value from 0 to 2000/2003. It indicates how many milliseconds Unity waits for another digit before determining that a user has completed entering a string of numbers (or a single digit) before taking action. If you set this value too low, people will not be able to dial extensions from a greeting and, if you set it too high, people have to wait before Unity takes action on their key presses, which will be perceived as slowness. Fiddle with this with extreme caution. Be sure to try it out on a test user/handler first before applying it to large numbers of users/handlers. Note: If you don't want users to be able to try extensions at all while listening to greetings, you can set the allow user input value for the greeting(s) on the handler or subscriber to false to accomplish this. It is not a good idea to set the Milliseconds to Wait value to 0 to do this.

- **Rule Options**. For each of the keys you have the following options for what action Unity takes when that key is entered while the greeting is played.

  — **Apply Change Only if Key Is Set to Ignore**. If you check this value, the changes you indicate for each key are only applied if the existing key on the subscriber is set to ignore. If a custom action set already exists for the existing key, it is skipped. This can be useful if you have some users that have custom settings set up you do not want to write over.

  — **Take Action**. Select this radio button and choose the action from the drop-down list:

    Skip Greeting. If the user hits this key, the greeting is skipped and Unity advances right to the after greeting action configured for this greeting.

    Take Message. If the user hits this key, they are taken right to the message recording conversation, regardless of what the after greeting action is set to.

    Hang Up. If the user hits this key, Unity hangs up on them immediately.

    Sign In. If the user hits this key, they are taken to the subscriber sign in conversation.

    Loop Back to Self. If the user hits this key, they start over at the beginning of the greeting for this call handler.

Greetings Administrator. This option sends the caller to the greetings administration conversation. This allows them to select a call handler they own by name or ID and record the greetings for it over the phone.

— **Go to Directory**. Select this radio button to send the caller to a selected directory handler when they hit this key. A directory handler allows callers to find subscribers in the system by spelling their names using the phone dial pad.

— **Go to Call Handler**. Select this radio button if you want to send the caller to a call handler when a user hits this key. Hit the Browse button and select a call handler from the resulting dialog. The display name of the call handler appears in the edit box to the right of the radio button. If you check the Don't Try to Ring Phone box, Unity sends the caller directly to the greeting of the selected call handler without trying a transfer rule, even if one is enabled and active.

— **Go to Subscriber**. Select this radio button if you want to send the caller to a subscriber's mailbox when they hit this key. Hit the Browse button and select a subscriber from the resulting dialog. The display name of the user appears in the edit box to the right of the radio button. If you check the "Don't try to ring phone box, Unity sends the caller directly to the greeting of the selected subscriber without trying the transfer rule, even if it is enabled.

— **Go to interview**. Select this radio button if you want to send the caller to an interview handler when they hit this key. Hit the Browse button and select an interview handler from the resulting dialog. The display name of the interview handler appears in the edit box to the right of the radio button.

— **Lock Key**. If you lock the key, Unity takes action on that key immediately without waiting to see if the caller is going to enter more digits (that is, they are dialing an extension number and possibly not selecting a one key option). As soon as the user hits this key, Unity immediately executes the action indicated.

Messages

- **Maximum Message Length**. This sets the number of seconds for the maximum message length outside callers are limited to when leaving this subscriber a message. This can be a number between 0 and 1200 (20 minutes). Note: Subscribers leaving messages for this user are not limited by this value; they are limited by their class of service setting for the maximum message record time they are allowed.

- **Callers Can Edit Messages**. Set this drop-down to true to allow callers to review, rerecord, or append to messages they've just recorded for this subscriber.

- **Callers Can Mark Messages as Urgent**. Set this drop-down to true to allow outside callers to mark messages for this subscriber as urgent.

- **Message Recipient**. Every call handler has an owner and a message recipient. These can be either a specific subscriber or a public distribution list. You can dictate that all listed call handlers be configured to deliver their messages to a specific subscriber or distribution list here by selecting a radio button and hitting the corresponding Browse button to select an object in the resulting dialog box. The display name of the selected subscriber/distribution list appears in the edit box to the right of the radio button.

- **After Message Action**. After the user leaves a message, normally you would want to send them to the "say goodbye" call handler. If, however, you want to do something different you can configure it here:

  — **Take Action**. Select this radio button and choose the action from the drop-down list.

    Hang Up. Unity hangs up on the caller immediate after they finish recording their message. This is a little abrupt. Typically you would want to send someone to the "say goodbye" call handler and hang up nicely instead.

    Sign In. The caller is sent to the subscriber sign in conversation after they finish recording their message.

    Loop Back to Self. This option has the caller sent back to the beginning of the greeting for the current call handler after they finish recording their message. This will not attempt the transfer sequence for the handler; the caller will be sent directly to the active greeting for the handler.

    Greetings Administrator. This option will send the caller to the greetings administration conversation. This will allow them to select a call handler they own by name or ID and record the greetings for it over the phone.

  — **Go to Directory**. Select this radio button to send the caller to a selected directory handler after the caller finishes recording their message. A directory handler allows callers to find subscribers in the system by spelling their names using the phone dial pad.

  — **Go to Call Handler**. Select this radio button if you want to send the caller to a call handler after the caller finishes recording their message. Hit the Browse button and select a call handler from the resulting dialog. The display name of the call handler will appear in the edit box to the right of the radio button. If you check the Don't Try to Ring Phone box, Unity will send the caller directly to the greeting of the selected call handler without trying a transfer rule, even if one is enabled and active.

— **Go to Subscriber**. Select this radio button if you want to send the caller to a subscriber's mailbox after the caller finishes recording their message. Hit the Browse button and select a subscriber from the resulting dialog. The display name of the user will appear in the edit box to the right of the radio button. If you check the Don't Try to Ring Phone box, Unity will send the caller directly to the greeting of the selected subscriber without trying the transfer rule, even if it is enabled.

— **Go to Interview**. Select this radio button if you want to send the caller to an interview handler after the caller finishes recording their message. Hit the Browse button and select an interview handler from the resulting dialog. The display name of the interview handler will appear in the edit box to the right of the radio button.

Alternate Extensions

The Alternate Extensions tab allows you to remove all alternate extensions for selected call handlers. There is no way to remove specific or only some alternate extensions; this will remove ALL alternate extensions so be very careful when using this.

This option will NOT remove the primary extension if one is set for the call handler.

Apply Call Handler Changes

When you have the call handlers you want selected and the changes you want applied to those handlers, press the Update Call Handlers button here and those changes will be applied. The progress bar will indicate how far along the process is and, when it is complete, a dialog will pop up indicating we are done and how many errors were encountered in the process.

You will be given the opportunity to view the output log automatically when the process is complete. If there are any errors noted, I strongly recommend you do so and search the log for "(error)" to find the problem. Remember, each run of Bulk Edit generates its own output log in the \logs folder off the Bulk Edit installation directory.

Migrate Subscriber Data Tool

The Migrate Subscriber Data tool allows the Cisco Unity administrator to migrate subscriber settings from a Cisco Unity subscriber account to a mail user account. Use of this tool allows you to preserve all of the subscriber settings such as voice name, greetings, private distribution lists, and so on because these Cisco Unity-specific attributes are added to the mail user account attributes.

The tool is useful for moving from a voice mail-only installation to unified messaging or for migrating users from another voice-mail system to Cisco Unity (for example, migrating Octel users who have been set up as Bridge subscribers).

How to Migrate Subscriber Data

The Migrate Subscriber Data tool is available from within the Tools Depot. When the Migrate Subscriber Data tool launches, it determines the type of mail store Cisco Unity uses and presents a list of e-mail servers it finds on your network. See the steps in the following procedure for details on how to use the tool:

Step 1   Choose the server or domain/server you want to migrate subscriber data to. The tool presents two lists of users:

— On the left, a list of all Cisco Unity subscribers

— On the right, a list of all mail users that are not subscribers

Step 2   Choose a Cisco Unity subscriber from the list on the left.

Step 3   Choose a mail user from the list on the right.

Step 4   Click the Migrate Subscriber Data button.

The Cisco Unity subscriber data is pointed to the mail user account, and the existing Cisco Unity subscriber account attributes are removed from the subscriber directory account.

Step 5   Repeat Step 3 and Step 4 as needed.

Note that the Migrate Subscriber Data tool removes the accounts from both lists as you work, so that you do not accidentally select the same account again.

Step 6   Optionally, if you are migrating AMIS, Internet, or Bridge subscribers, click Options > Delete Contacts from Directory.

Clicking this option will delete the applicable contacts from the directory after you have migrated the subscriber settings to another account. This is usually a safe option because these types of subscribers do not have mail stores.

Step 7   Optionally, you can copy messages from the Unity subscriber to the mail user; click Options > Merge Messages.

See the following Notes section below for detail about this option.

Step 8   To refresh the lists, click File > Synch Directory and Refresh.

As soon as the database is synchronized with the directory, new messages for the migrated subscribers will be delivered to the mail users' mail stores.

Requirements/Special Notes

- The Migrate Subscriber Data tool can by used only with Cisco Unity version 3.1(2) or later.

- The Migrate Subscriber Data tool must be run from a Cisco Unity system.

- The Migrate Subscriber Data tool will delete directory contacts for Internet subscribers only if the Delete Contacts from Directory option is enabled. Migrate Subscriber Data will always delete directory contacts for AMIS, Bridge, and VPIM subscribers.

- The Migrate Subscriber Data tool can be used to move messages from the Unity subscriber account to the new account. This is done using Microsoft's ExMerge. You can use this feature by selecting Merge Messages from the Options menu. Only messages in the subscriber's inbox are merged; no messages in any other folders, even those folders under the inbox, will be merged. Duplicate copies of messages are not created; if a message exists in both inboxes only one copy of it ends up in the destination mailbox. If ExMerge encounters an error, you will be given the option to examine ExMerge's log file. Even if the ExMerge fails, you will be given the option to continue with the migration of subscriber settings. You should refer to Microsoft's documentation on ExMerge for troubleshooting found in Microsoft Knowledge Base articles KB265441 and KB174197.

- In using, Exchange 2000/2003, ExMerge will fail if the mailbox is hidden. Consider temporarily un-hiding the user's mailbox before attempting the migration and then re-hiding the mailbox once the migration is complete. In using Exchange 5.5, ExMerge will not fail because a mailbox is hidden. That does not mean there will not be other reasons why ExMerge might fail.

Configuring Permissions for MSD

The account you run MSD under has to have specific rights to the local system and, optionally, to Exchange to do a complete migration. In short it needs complete access to SQL in all cases and access to all mailboxes if you have selected to merge messages. The tool will notify you upon startup if it is missing any permissions.

The account must be a member of the local administrators group to gain full read/write access to SQL. Without this subscriber, migration will fail. If the Unity system is its own domain controller, add the account to the Administrators group in the Built-in folder. If the Unity system is a member server, you need to add the account to the Administrators group from the Local Users and Groups section in the Computer Management applet.

NOTE	Being a member of the Domain Administrators group is NOT sufficient for this; you MUST be a member of the local administrators group.
	If you are not merging subscriber messages, this is all you need to worry about. If you want to merge subscriber messages using MSD, follow the procedures for the messaging back end you are using.

Exchange 5.5

For Exchange 5.5, the account must have Service Account Admin privileges at the organization, site, and configuration levels.

Exchange 2000/2003 or Mixed 2000/2003/55

On Exchange 2000/2003, the account needs to have Full Control rights for each mailbox you are migrating.

Summary

Cisco Unity has an entire host of tools that help you with common, and not-so-common, tasks that you need to do. This chapter covered some of the more common tools used by administrators. Make sure that you explore the Unity Tools Depot as well as www.ciscounitytools.com to find more tools that can help you administer Cisco Unity.

CHAPTER 21

Administering Unity Programmatically

In this chapter, we find and connect to remote Unity servers and retrieve necessary information for report applications. We also create, import, modify, and delete subscribers as well as create and add new members to public distribution lists. This chapter assumes at least a beginner's level of familiarity with SQL concepts.

The vast majority of what people ask me about is how to plug Unity into existing provisioning systems. This involves the creation, deletion, and modification of subscribers in the Unity database. Surprisingly enough, we do not get many requests about how to automate the construction of interview handlers. Some stored procedures have been created for doing just that, however, and over time there will be more sample applications added to www.ciscounitytools.com that show how to use them. If you have items you want covered, be sure to ping me at the address on the website and we try to accommodate you. However, in this chapter, we stay focused mostly on subscribers.

This chapter assumes you have a good understanding of the basic architecture and data object model for Unity. If you have not already done so, we strongly encourage you to read Chapter 2, "Unity Architecture Overview," and Chapter 3, "Components and Subsystems: Object Model," before proceeding. It is also a good idea to cover the topics in Chapter 18, "Audio Text Applications," because the chapter provides in-depth coverage of how call handlers and subscribers are related and interact in the system, which is important if you want to do anything beyond simply creating and deleting subscribers.

Complete working versions of all the examples we will cover in this chapter are available for download from the Code Samples page at www.ciscounitytools.com. These are all done in Visual Basic 6.0; however, if you do not have Visual Basic you can still open the forms and modules with a text editor and review them. We will be reproducing only small chunks of source in this chapter, so we recommend you review the entire sample applications. The mechanisms used here are not language specific because they concentrate almost entirely on accessing SQL databases and using stored procedures and views which almost any language is capable of.

While you are on the http://www.ciscounitytools.com site, get the latest version of the Cisco Unity Data Link Explorer (CUDLE) application (see Figure 21-1). This tool started shipping with 4.0(1). However, you will want to get the latest version and frequently check back for updates. This tool is specifically designed for use by those developing applications against Unity's SQL database.

Figure 21-1 *Cisco Unity Data Link Explorer (CUDLE) Application*

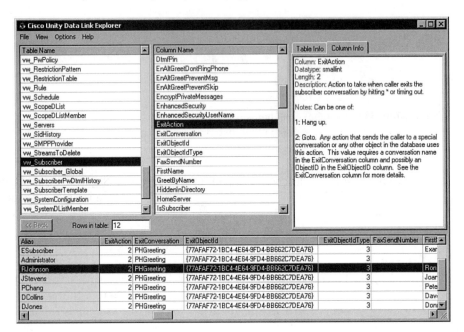

Information about what data is stored in the SQL database tables and columns and what is in the Registry and details on the stored procedures used for programmatic administration (including the full source for all stored procedures) is frequently updated and added in this tool. The built-in data dictionary for SQL is useful for beginning Unity developers. Throughout this chapter, we assume you have access to this for looking up what values for a particular column mean. For example, in the screen shot shown in Figure 21-1 the After-MessageAction values are enumerated and explained in the Column Info tab. CUDLE also has its own Query Builder in it for those who are not using the full SQL 2000 install and do not have the SQL Query Builder at their disposal. You will definitely want to have one or the other handy to pull data from the UnityDB as you work out the queries you need. One last plug for CUDLE: All the columns in all the tables are listed alphabetically, which makes it easy to find what you are looking for. The SQL Enterprise Manager shows columns in the order in which the creation scripts add them, which makes navigation difficult at times for large table. You will also need a running copy of Unity 4.0(1) or later. Ideally you will want to have 4.0(3) or later as some functions discussed in this chapter were not active in 4.0(1) or 4.0(2). You can download versions of Unity 4.0 off of the Cisco Software Center site. All versions of Unity include a limited demonstration license that allows you to install it and test against 2 ports and up to 10 users. The limited license also restricts record time for messages to be sure it is not used in production environments and features such as AMIS or VPIM are not active. If you need more users and a full production test environment, you can apply for a free temporary license that will time out in 30, 60, or 90 days. Information and links for these licenses can be found on the Links page of www.ciscounitytools.com.

APIs and Support

For Unity 4.0(x), the only mechanisms available for administering Unity programmatically are the direct connections to the SQL database on the Unity server. We use views for reads and queries and stored procedures for updates so that those using them will be isolated from changes to the actual data structures behind the scenes. If you do not know what a view or a stored procedure is, you should get an introductory book on Sequential Query Language (SQL) before going further. For you to get the most out of this, it is a real good idea to get some of the basics under your belt.

For the examples in this chapter, we use Visual Basic 6 with service pack 5 using ADO to connect to SQL. You can, however, pick whatever set of tools you prefer. All the code samples and projects in this chapter and on the http://www.ciscounitytools.com website are in VB 6. You should be able to apply the concepts laid out here to whatever tools you prefer to use.

We want to make clear that *nothing* in this chapter is supported directly by the Cisco Technical Assistance Center (TAC). There will be no official support for remote programmatic administration of Unity in 4.0(x) either from TAC or the engineering group responsible for Unity, the Enterprise Communications Software Business Unit (ECSBU). With the next major release of Unity in 2005, there will be support for the provisioning API(s). It is impossible for me to set a date as to when the support will be available, but we can tell you it is being worked on. We also cannot tell you what form those provisioning API(s) will be in, but they will very likely include a Simple Object Access Protocol (SOAP) type interface that essentially thinly wraps the SQL functionality. There is not going to be a custom, proprietary interface provided as an API; the work will revolve around what we cover here and the logic will remain largely the same. The primary difference will be in providing additional mechanisms that allow you to attach and execute queries and procedures remotely.

That said, what is discussed here will continue to work regardless of what other APIs and connectivity methods are provided to the public. If you are like me, we like to get down to the real data rather than have a high-level wrapper abstract it. Wrappers make things easier and are ideal for many types of operations you need to do remotely. However, they can also be a performance impediment and will many times lack the functionality needed for a particular application. The Customer Applications Team will continue working directly with SQL for their applications and will ensure the functionality remains backwards compatible as much as possible. As long as you stick to using views when reading from the tables and use only stored procedures when adding/updating/deleting objects, any changes in the actual table structures in subsequent versions of Unity should be largely transparent.

Rights Needed in SQL

To connect to a Unity server from off box, the account you are logged in as needs to have read access. If you are doing updates in your application, you also need write access to the UnityDB database. By default, the SQL database installs with NT authentication only and this is what we recommend. You can set up SQL to also do its own authentication that allows you to pass in a login and password via your connection string. However, we do not recommend this as it is not very secure. Relying on NT to do this for you is a safer and cleaner approach.

The Unity server's SQL installation is typically configured so that any account that is a member of the local administrators group (or the built-in administrators group if it is a domain controller) has full read/write access to the two Unity databases in SQL: UnityDB and ReportsDB. One easy way to deal with authentication is to create a security group in AD/NT that is added to the local administrators' group on all Unity servers you want to connect to. You can then add those who should be allowed to run your application(s) into that security group. You can also add individual users to the local administrators group or, if you like, take care of adding additional users or groups that have read and/or write access to UnityDB directly in the SQL administration interface.

The easiest way to use the direct add mechanism is through the SQL Enterprise Manager application. Remember that it is OK to install Microsoft's SQL Enterprise Manager and attach to systems running the MSDE version of SQL as well as the full SQL 2000 server version. The same is not true for the SQL Query Analyzer tool that requires the full SQL 2000 server to be installed. For example, on my box we created a security group called "Jeff's Unity Access Group" and added a few accounts to it. The next step is to open the Enterprise Manager and drill down to the Security node on the server in question. Figure 21-2 shows what this looks like.

Figure 21-2 *Direct Add Mechanism via SQL Enterprise Manager*

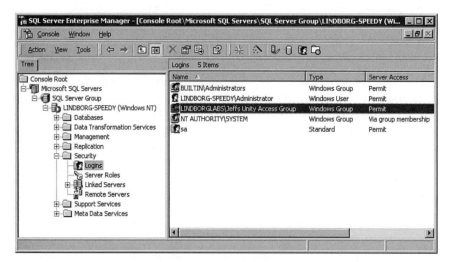

You can add as many individual accounts or groups as you want. In this case we want to grant full read/write access to the UnityDB database only. On the properties page for my group's entry, we select the Database Access tab and click only the UnityDB database and assign appropriate roles to the group. For this example, we assign public, db_datareader, and db_datawriter roles to that group as shown in Figure 21-3.

Figure 21-3 *Granting Full Read/Write Access to the UnityDB Database Only*

CAUTION   Please note that you should NOT give any rights found on the Server Roles tab for this! That gives accounts the right to create databases and edit properties in SQL Server itself, which are absolutely not necessary for anything we will be doing with Unity.

This same task can be performed using SQL directly using the GRANT command. This allows you to get more specific about which rights are applied to which tables within the UnityDB database and even get down to the column level. For instance, this command gives my account read/write/add/delete capabilities on just the CallHandler table within UnityDB:

```
GRANT SELECT, INSERT, UPDATE, DELETE
ON CallHandler
TO Jlindborg
```

However, this is dangerous because many of the tables reference other tables and you have to be certain you gave all necessary rights to all tables that were involved in the types of transactions you wanted to allow. This can be tricky at best and a neverending pit of pain at worst. we do not recommend this method unless you know what you are doing and have a good reason for getting so specific.

The method you use is up to you, but one way or another the account you are running these applications under should be granted read and, if necessary, write access on UnityDB on the Unity server(s) you need to attach to.

SQL Rules of the Road

You only need to remember two basic rules when dealing with the UnityDB SQL database.

First, *all* read queries must use views. Do not query directly on the raw tables in SQL. Currently there are views for all the tables and as of 4.0(2), they are a 1-to-1 mapping to the raw tables. However, in 4.0(3) there was a major revision in the back end that involved moving the DTMFAccessID (extension) columns out of all the tables and consolidating them into the DTMFAccessID table. The views for all the tables affected continued to expose the DTMFAccessID by referencing the DTMFAccessID table in the background. Those who were going directly to the raw tables had to go back and alter their code to account for this. If you are going directly to the raw tables, your applications might break with every new release of Unity, and you will become annoyed in a hurry, so do not do that.

A quick note to all you new CUDLE users: You can switch back and forth between looking at the raw tables and views under the options menu using the Use Views and the Use Tables options. we highly recommend leaving it in views mode for most of what you do.

Second, *all* adds and updates *must* go through stored procedures. While it is tempting to write values directly onto the raw table and hit the update method, do not do this. Again, backwards compatibility as well as some basic value checking will be done within stored procedures to prevent problems with future versions of Unity breaking client applications. As you will see in the examples, the stored procedures are also designed to make your life easier and offer you some options that would otherwise be tedious and error prone. In most cases, if you are deleting an entire record you also want to go through a stored procedure for that. The only exception to that rule is for updating the MessagingRule (greeting) table. You can edit information directly on the table because there is not a stored procedure available for that table prior to Unity 4.0(4). The release of Unity 4.0(4) should include that stored procedure.

Exercises

Before you begin the examples in this section, read Chapter 2 and Chapter 3. All the examples here assume you know what is meant by having to synchronize data between SQL and the directory, how all the collections and sub-collections in the database are used, how objects are linked together, and so on. You will have difficulty gleaning useful information here if you do not understand those basics.

We start with the simple connection basics; then we progress to some fairly easy read-only exercises. Finally, we end with more advanced subscriber creation, import, modification, and deletion scenarios.

Finding and Connecting to a Unity Server on the Network

The first thing we need to do is learn how to find and connect to remote Unity servers on your network. If you know the domain and server name of the Unity server you want to connect to, it is just a matter of constructing the SQL connection string properly. You can jump ahead a few sections to the section "Getting Version and License Information." If, instead, you want to make your applications capable of browsing the network and finding Unity servers to connect to dynamically, please keep reading.

Download a sample application that has a full listing of this code and includes reusable modules for populating domain and server lists. Choose the Attaching to Unity Remotely Code download on http://www.ciscounitytools.com/CodeSamples.htm. We will cover the high points here.

Retrieve a List of All Servers Running SQL on a Domain

The easiest way to find Unity servers in a domain is to first start with the list of all servers running SQL on them. Microsoft provides a WinAPI call to do just exactly that. This function pulls all the servers that are running MS SQL server (full SQL 2000, SQL 7, MSDE, and so on) and returns them as a collection. The calling function will have to determine if Unity is installed on that box by attempting to open the UnityDB database on that server. This particular function is a bit more advanced than most other items we will be covering because it involves dancing with the Windows API, moving chunks of memory around, and dealing with pointers in VB. Do not worry, the rest of the code samples in this chapter are not nearly so obscure. A collection is a simple VB object that is a fancy way of bundling up a list of items you want to iterate over without having to create an array of objects. You need to pass in the name of the domain you want to look for servers in. The full code sample in Example 21-1 also shows you how to get a list of the domains you can see from the server running the application.

Example 21-1 *Finding SQL Servers in a Windows Domain*

```
Public Function getServers(vDomain As Variant) As Collection

Dim pszTemp As String, pszServer As String, pszDomain As String
Dim nLevel As Long, i As Long, BufPtr As Long, TempBufPtr As Long
Dim nPrefMaxLen As Long, nEntriesRead As Long, nTotalEntries As Long
Dim nServerType As Long, nResumeHandle As Long, nRes As Long

! The SERVER_INFO_101 structure is defined in the full code listing -
it is an object that contains a number of pieces of information about
a server including, of course, its name.
Dim ServerInfo As SERVER_INFO_101
Dim collServers As New Collection

    pszTemp = vDomain

! The WinAPI calls to go fetch the servers we want to look at needs unicode
strings to be passed in. We have to manually construct that here.  VB provides
a snappy little function to do just this type of thing called "StrConv".  The
resulting Unicode string will be stored in the pszDomain string.

    If Len(pszTemp) = 0 Then
        pszDomain = vbNullString
    Else
        pszDomain = StrConv(pszTemp, vbUnicode)
    End If

! The nLevel value here is used to tell the API call if we want to get
SERVER_INFO_100 or SERVER_INFO_101 structures back.  It is not  really important
to understand the differences between these structures.  We want the 101structures
    for what we are doing here because it includes the name of the computer as a
string, among other things, and it is easier to deal with in VB.
    nLevel = 101
    BufPtr = 0
    nPrefMaxLen = &HFFFFFFFF
    nEntriesRead = 0
    nTotalEntries = 0

! The nServerType flag tells the API call that we want to find all servers in the
selected domain that are running SQL server on it.  All the flags you can
pass in are defined at the top of this module in the full program listing.  You
can also use this to find all Exchange servers, domain servers, and so on.
    nServerType = SV_TYPE_SQLSERVER
    nResumeHandle = 0
    pszServer = vbNullString

! Loop through all the list of servers returned and add them to the collection of
  server names to be returned from this function.  The trick is the nEntriesRead
```

Example 21-1 *Finding SQL Servers in a Windows Domain (Continued)*

```
value we pass in gets incremented each time we call it - keep looping through
until the number of entries read equals the total number of entries found.
Do
        nRes = NetServerEnum(pszServer, nLevel, BufPtr, nPrefMaxLen, nEntriesRead,
        nTotalEntries, nServerType, pszDomain, nResumeHandle)


        If ((nRes = ERROR_SUCCESS) Or (nRes = ERROR_MORE_DATA)) And (nEntriesRead > 0)
Then

!The function actually returns the server info as a pointer to a block of memory
parked somewhere.  VB does not deal with pointers natively so you need to use
the RtlMoveMemory function to move the info from memory into the ServerInfo
structure.
        TempBufPtr = BufPtr
        For i = 1 To nEntriesRead
            RtlMoveMemory ServerInfo, TempBufPtr, SIZE_SI_101

! Now the server info structure contains an address in memory where a string that
contains the name of the server is stored.  Use the PointertoString function to
go fetch the string and stick it in our collection.
            collServers.Add PointerToString(ServerInfo.lpszServerName)
            TempBufPtr = TempBufPtr + SIZE_SI_101
        Next i
Else
        MsgBox "Error reading SQL servers from the domain"
        Exit Do
End If

! Free up the memory we allocated to read the SQL server info into.
NetApiBufferFree (BufPtr)
Loop While nEntriesRead < nTotalEntries

    Set getServers = collServers

    Exit Function
```

The calling party will get a nice collection of server name strings they can iterate to populate list boxes, drop downs, grids, or whatever here. With the server name string in hand, it is just a matter of constructing the appropriate connection string and attempting to bind to the UnityDB SQL database, if it exists, on that server.

Deciding on a Connection Method

In all my examples here, we use ActiveX Data Objects (ADO) to connect to SQL. The ins and outs of using Dynamic versus Keysets versus ForwardOnly versus Static recordsets and choosing between client-side and server-side cursors used by ADO is a chapter unto itself.

A number of good ADO books are out there that would benefit you if you want to take your knowledge to the next level. We will cover the basics in this section.

When you open a database with ADO you are creating a cursor which is a temporary database structure stored on the local box your application is running on. When you read from your data, it goes through this local cursor which either caches the data locally or retrieves it from the server as necessary, depending on the type of cursor you are using. When your application changes or deletes rows this is done on the cursor structure locally and is transmitted back to the Unity server's database for you through the drivers under the ADO libraries on the client side. RDO (Remote Data Objects), DAO (Data Access Objects), and other database connection libraries use similar mechanisms. ADO is the most mature, most widely supported, and nicest to use in my opinion. You will catch me using DAO on rare occasions when we pull in lots of data from external text files (when parsing a log file for reports, for example). DAO has a noticeably faster add record capability than ADO does and this speeds things up a bit. However, DAO and ADO are just different enough that you can get yourself in trouble mixing and matching. If you are going that route, definitely get a good book and understand the differences.

A client-side cursor does what it sounds like; the cursor is maintained on the local machine your client is running on and makes requests back to the server as necessary. This cursor scales well, especially for large numbers of clients doing a lot of queries, because the minimum overhead is added back to the main server database. This is what we want because Unity's real-time call processing capabilities are paramount here. Administrative functions are in the back seat so we want to add as little overhead to the server as possible.

A server-side cursor sends all your queries back to the server and the temporary results are generated in the server, which can be a big performance boost for your applications but adds overhead on the server itself. We will talk about indexing tricks you can do on your client-side cursor to help speed things up. Because most of the types of operations you will need to do on Unity are quick, client-side cursors are ideal. These quick operations include adding, updating, or deleting individual users. And because all our updates go through stored procedures and not through recordsets, we can get acceptable performance for reads on recordsets using the indexing and by being careful to only pull over the data we need for the operation to keep the sizes of the cursors reasonable.

The four recordset types are designed for different types of client-server applications:

- When reading in a large number of records into a bound data control such as a grid for display/lookup functions, use **adOpenForwardOnly** with an **adLockReadOnly** flag. This is known as a "firehose" cursor because it is fast at reading in data and passing it off. You cannot move around in this cursor, do searches or filters, or anything of the kind. However, if you are passing the information into another structure, such as a bound grid or list control, with its own table handling capabilities or an array then this cursor is lightning fast and the one to use.

- Using the **adOpenKeyset** flag actually populates the local cursor with pointers back to the rows in the server-side database using unique identifiers, or keys, for the tables in question. Only a subset of the actual data for some rows are returned, and it will retrieve the information it needs if you reference rows not in its local cache. When other clients make changes to the information back on the server, a keyset recordset will pick that up when you reference it. It will not, however, pick up new rows added by other clients and when you reference a deleted row it throws an error you need to trap and handle. If you open a keyset recordset as a client-side cursor, however, it behaves like an updatable static recordset. Keyset and static cursors are also the only ones that support the RecordCount property that can be handy in many situations. For example, if you search on an alias in a table, you expect to get only one row back and it is nice to be able to check the number of rows returned up front to verify that.

- Using the **adOpenStatic** flag opens a static cursor which, as the name implies, is a static snapshot of the data that matches your query. It pulls all the data over in one shot and you can do all the things you would expect such as filtering, searching, moving forward and backwards, getting record counts, and so on. It does not pick up changes made by other clients on the data in your result set, and this cursor is traditionally read-only, although you can force it to do updates. As noted before using the keyset cursor on the client side behaves similarly but is more appropriate for making updates back to the server. Because we will not be making updates to the database through recordset structure, but rather through stored procedures, that is not an important characteristic to take into account here.

- The **adOpenDynamic** flag is similar to a keyset recordset except that it picks up adds and deletes on the fly and simply adjusts the recordset as necessary. Rather than only updating the rows in the cursor based on keys, it reissues the query back to the server and pulls over deltas. we have never had a need to use a dynamic cursor in the applications we write for Unity. You can perform filters, searches, sorts, and so on just as you can with keyset recordsets. However, the dynamic cursor does not provide a snappy count of the records in the set.

Because most of your applications use client-side keyset recordsets, it is up to you to check for updated information on the server or new and deleted rows in the results of your query. You can use the **resync** command from the recordset object which will refresh all the rows currently in your recordset with updated information. Or you can use the requery method which will reexecute your original query that produced the recordset and bring over the differences (which includes removing deleted rows and adding new rows that match the query). The requery method is by far the more useful of the two. Any changes you make to your local cursor will not be written back to the server database automatically as they would be with a server-side cursor. It is up to you to execute the update property on the recordset. The local cursor engine will translate your changes into action queries (neat term for generating Transact Sequential Query Language, or TSQL, looking command strings) back to the server. In this way you can make a number of changes locally and issue one large update back to the server, which can be helpful. As noted, this helps keep the overhead on the server itself to a minimum. That said, you only make changes directly in your recordsets in rare cases where there is no stored procedure that meets your needs. In 4.0(3) and earlier, there is only one valid reason for making changes in your recordsets and we will cover it in this chapter's examples section. All other updates should be done through calls to stored procedures. Unity 4.0(4) includes the stored procedure that is missing in 4.0(3) and earlier so updates shuld be done through procedures in 4.0(4) and later.

Any recordset type can be opened with any of the read flag options (adLockReadOnly, adLockOptimistic, adLockBatchOptimistic, or adLockPessimistic). The Audio Text Manager did initially use LockBatchOptimistic for dealing with rolling back changes until a user had committed them. This allowed for nicer logging of updates and letting users undo mistakes, which can be very handy. However, the overhead involved with keeping this model flying was too great; we simplified it to make changes to the back end immediately. Again, we will not update data through recordsets here but rather through the use of stored procedures. Therefore, only the adLockReadOnly flag is necessary outside of rare instances where a stored procedure is not available to make a change we need.

A quick word about client- versus server-side recordsets and indexing. As noted before you always want to force recordsets to run on the client side when dealing with Unity to preserve as many server-side CPU cycles for handling calls and other important voice server activity. You can easily force client-side cursors to build a keyed index that will dramatically improve lookup performance if your application is going to be doing a lot of lookups in the result set. For instance, if you are reading in a large text file and then doing reports processing on the results, indexing your lookup keys is essential for performance. If you are adding and reading data to tables in, say, an Access databases, you can mark keys for indexing in the database itself. This is what we have done with some of the report generation applications such as the Bridge Traffic Analyzer. If you are constructing cursors from SQL, however, you have to explicitly tell it to index one or more columns if you want. There is a small hit when constructing the cursor, but the increase in performance when reading will more than make up for it if you are going to be doing any kind of repeated lookups in the result set.

To force a particular column or columns to be indexed in your cursor, you need to use the fields type and flag each column for indexing. The following sample shows how to open some cursors in the Port Usage Analyzer tool:

Example 21-2 *Indexing Columns in a Recordset*

```
Dim rsRawData as ADODB.Recordset
Dim f as ADODB.Field

Set rsRawData = New ADODB.Recordset
rsRawData.CursorLocation = adUseClient
rsRawData.Open "Select * from RawPortData" ORDER BY Port", strConnectionString,
adOpenKeyset, adLockReadOnly
```

Example 21-2 *Indexing Columns in a Recordset (Continued)*

```
Set f = rsRawData("Port")
f.Properties("Optimize") = True
Set f = rsRawData("CallType")
f.Properties("Optimize") = True
```

Force the cursor type to be on the client side before opening the database. The default is for server-side cursors so be sure to do this in your applications as well. Setting the Optimize property on the fields collection forces the cursor to create a local index table for all columns you flag that for. The difference in performance on the port data crunching is in the neighborhood of a 40 to 50 percent increase because it looks for rows based on their port number and the call type often in the process of creating its reports.

A parting word about opening recordsets in your applications. Always make an effort to keep the number of columns you ask for to a minimum. Always using "SELECT * …" may be easy, but in the case of tables with a large number of columns and rows it will put a real hitch in your performance. All that information needs to be carted over from the Unity server onto your local cursor. Be sure to keep your queries tightly bound and pull over only what you need.

Learning to Share

One important thing to remember when making connections to the Unity database by using older versions of ADO libraries or other DB connection libraries is that they can, by default, make multiple connections for you if you open multiple recordsets. This can chew through available connections which are precious, particularly in the case of systems running MSDE instead of full SQL 2000, because the number of simultaneous connections are restricted by its license. This also hurts the performance of your applications.

When you use recent ADO libraries, such as those found in Microsoft Data Access Components (MDAC) 2.6 or later, much of this logic is handled smoothly for you in the background. It will automatically create connections to the database only when necessary and cache open connections for you instead of tearing them down right away to increase performance and reduce overhead. That said, not everyone will be using ADO to connect to SQL and it is a good idea to know what is going on behind the scenes. While the newer ADO libraries do the connection management for you, we normally explicitly handle the sharing of connections back to the UnityDB database as discussed in this section. It is only a little more code and gives you the comfort of knowing how the system is behaving regardless of the connection libraries being used.

Most of the examples in this section only open a single recordset and then close it when they are done and, as such, do not present a problem here. However if you are writing a more robust application that has a need to open multiple recordsets and keep them open for an extended period of time, it is a good idea to force your recordsets to all share a single connection to the database. You can go about this in a couple of ways and they both work the same way behind the scenes.

The first method is to explicitly use a connection object in ADO when opening your recordsets. This means opening your database would look like this:

```
Set cnConnection = New ADODB.Connection
cnConnection.CursorLocation = adUseClient
cnConnection.Open strConnectionString
```

You can, of course, pass in an explicit username and password in the open connection, but we do not normally do that. We rely on NT-based authentication because it is more secure. Now that the database connection is opened, you can use that same connection for every recordset you open. Opening a new recordset looks like this:

```
Set rsDB1 = New ADODB.Recordset
rsDB1.Open strSQL1, cnConnection, adOpenKeyset, adLockReadOnly

Set rsDB2 = New ADODB.Recordset
rsDB2.Open strSQL2, cnConnection, adOpenKeyset, adLockReadOnly
```

All the recordsets you open this way will share a single connection back to the database. Be careful, however, because the default behavior of older versions of ADO is to tear down the connection when you close a recordset. For instance, if you closed out the rsDB1 recordset, it could tear down the connection in the background and the next time you went to access rsDB2, it would have to reestablish the connection again. As noted, with recent ADO library versions this is not the case, but it does not hurt to explicitly control this behavior regardless. You would not notice any specific problem in your application, but it could be doing a lot of thrashing in the background that you do not want. To avoid this, you can explicitly detach the recordset from the connection before closing it, like this:

```
Set rsDB1.ActiveConnection = Nothing
rsDB1.Close
```

You need to worry about this any time you close out a recordset in such an application, including when you declare a recordset in a procedure that then goes out of scope. The recordset will automatically be closed and destroyed for you and if you did not explicitly set the ActiveConnection to nothing, it can tear down the connection as well. This is one of the perils of getting too comfortable with the built-in VB garbage collection which will automatically destroy objects when they go out of scope and so on. While it is nice to not worry about such things which plague our C++ brethren, you need to be aware of this activity in the background or the performance of your application and the overhead you add will be higher than you want.

Creating a global connection object that is shared across all recordsets that you can open in all forms and modules is a good move. For large applications needing to make several connections to the database and leave them open, this is a good technique. For smaller applications that need to open a couple recordsets for a brief time, you can use the connection made by one recordset open command as a parameter in another recordset's open command. The code for that looks like this:

```
Set rsDB1 = New ADODB.Recordset
rsDB1.Open strSQL1, strConnectionString, adOpenKeyset, adLockReadOnly

Set rsDB2 = New ADODB.Recordset
rsDB2.Open strSQL2, rsDB1.ActiveConnection, adOpenKeyset, adLockReadonly
```

This achieves the same thing as creating an explicit connection object and sharing it around; it is just a little less code. Again, if you are going to be closing one of your recordsets out before the others, be sure to disconnect the recordset first as we did before. This works well for small applications.

Making the Connection

Once you have decided on your cursor style and you have the name of a server in the domain that is running SQL, determining if Unity is on that box is pretty straightforward. Simply try to open the UnityDB database on that server and if it succeeds you know it is running Unity 3.0(1) or later. If it fails, either it is not running Unity or the account you are running your application against does not have rights to connect to that box.

To actually connect (or attempt to connect) to the remote Unity server is just a matter of constructing the proper connection string and opening a recordset directly or a connection object. You have several options in a connection string and some handy tools out there for helping you construct them to meet your needs. For my purposes, we use two types of connection strings in my applications when connecting with SQL databases. we use this simplified string when an application is running on the local Unity server:

Example 21-3 *Opening a Recordset on a Local Unity Server*

```
strConnectionString = "Driver={SQL Server};server=;database=UnityDb"

! Then I can open databases directly through recordsets, such as this:

Dim rsSubscribers As New ADODB.Recordset

On Error GoTo Connection_Error

rsSubscribers.Open "SELECT Alias, DisplayName FROM vw_Subscriber WHERE
Alias='Eadmin',strConnectionString, adOpenKeyset, adLockReadOnly
<...>
```

For simply checking to see if we can establish a connection to a remote server, it is necessary to use a more robust connection string than the one on box we are using above. This code chunk is from the remote connection example shown in Figure 21-4.

Example 21-4 *Opening a Recordset on a Remote Unity Server*

```
Dim cnAttempt As New ADODB.Connection

strConnectionString = "Provider=SQLOLEDB.1;Integrated Security=SSPI;Persist
Security Info=False;Initial Catalog=UnityDb;Data Source=" + strServerName

On Error GoTo Connection_Error
cnAttempt.Open strConnectionString
! If we're here, the connection must have completed ok.
>
Exit Sub

Connection_Error:
    Select Case Err.Number
! Cannot open database requested in login 'UnityDb'.
        Case -2147467259
            MsgBox strServerName & " does not appear to be a Unity server or you do
              not have rights to log into UnityDB on that server"
            Set cnAttempt = Nothing
            Exit Sub
    Case Else
        MsgBox "Error in cmdConnect: " + Err.Description + " code="+str(Err.Number)
            Debug.Assert False
            Resume Next
    End Select
```

The error handling is the trick there. When attempting to connect to a database remotely, there could be any number of reasons the connection fails. We are specifically interested in the most common reason which is the logon fails error, which is error reason 0x80004005 (-2147467259 decimal). This means simply the DB is not there or you do not have rights to connect to it. Any other failure is just treated as a generic failure and reported as such.

A quick word about security here. You will notice that the connection string does not contain a login name or password as you might have seen in other samples. Without them the connection uses the credentials of the currently logged-in user account which, as we discussed earlier in this chapter, needs to be a member of a security group that has rights to UnityDB (such as the Local Administrators group on the box) or be explicitly granted rights to the database. Using SQL authentication instead of Windows authentication and passing in a hard coded login/PW string in your connection here is not a good idea. The connection attempt should go quickly here, so if you wanted to hit a bunch of servers in a row and create a list you can do that. It would be better to find one Unity server and do a query on that box to find all other servers it found in the directory for you, particularly with several Unity servers on the network. Unity is already gathering such information in the background through the directory monitors anyway and you might as well leverage that work rather than repeating it yourself. We will cover an example of how to do that in the "Find All Unity Servers in the Enterprise" example later in this chapter.

Getting Version and License Information

The short story is there is some information you want about a Unity server that is simply not available in the SQL database. Yes, this is annoying and it is something that is going to be addressed in later versions of Unity. If you have looked over the Data Object chapter earlier, you know quite a lot of data resides in the Registry on the local Unity server. Getting at the Registry on a remote box is possible but the rights issues are pretty painful. If you want to go that route, feel free. There is, however, also licensing information which is not available in SQL or in the Registry and if you are going to be adding or updating users, you definitely need to have access to this. The licensing information is especially tricky because you have to deal not only with single Unity servers that have their own set of license limits, but also with the new pooled licensing available in 4.0(1) and later where multiple Unity servers contribute and pull from a common set of license data.

Fortunately, there is a mechanism that allows you to hit a URL on the Unity box in question and get an XML page back that has the most critical information about the Unity server. This information includes selected data from the Registry and a full accounting of the licensing information on that box that will take pooled licenses into account as well. If you run a production 4.0(1) server, this function will not work for you. If you have Unity 4.0(2) installed you will need to apply the same files before this will work. This was a last-minute thing for 4.0(2) and it was not quite out of the oven by the time it shipped to production so you will have to run the Cisco Unity Access Library (CUAL) setup provided on the code samples page of www.ciscounitytools.com on the Unity servers itself and restart the TomCat service in the service control manager. Shut down the TomCat service, run the setup, restart the TomCat service, and you are done. Unity never has to go offline and this is a safe patch because it is just adding an additional web page you can address, it is not touching any core functionality in Unity. If you run 4.0(3) or later, you are golden because these files are there and work after you complete the standard installation. Short story, if you are running 4.0(2) and cannot upgrade to 4.0(3) or later, we recommend you run and apply the setup on all your Unity servers that you want to create or import users on or you want to connect to remotely.

The Remote Connection source sample provides modules that use the server name to construct the URL to hit for both licensing and server information pages provided by the CUAL setup and then shows how to parse them out. If you are familiar with XML, this is not complicated. To retrieve the licensing information on a particular server, you construct a URL that looks like this:

> http://MyUnityServer:8080/cual/
> CiscoUnitySystemInformation.jws?method=GetLicenseInformation

Where, of course, MyUnityServer is the name of the Unity server you want licensing information for. You would need this if you were going to create or import a subscriber onto that box to be sure the class of service (CoS) you are adding the user to can take another subscriber against it. The 8080 address is necessary for this to work and this can be a bit of a headache because of firewalls, but at the moment there is no workaround for this. When you hit that page in your browser, it spits back a little SOAP wrapped XML text that looks like this:

Example 21-5 *XML Output for Unity Licensing Information*

```
<?xml version="1.0" encoding="UTF-8" ?>
- <soapenv:Envelope
      xmlns:soapenv="http://schemas.xmlsoap.org/soap/envelope/"
    xmlns:xsd="http://www.w3.org/2001/XMLSchema"
    xmlns:xsi="http://www.w3.org/2001/XMLSchema-instance">
  - <soapenv:Body>
    - <GetLicenseInformationResponse
          soapenv:encodingStyle="http://schemas.xmlsoap.org/soap/encoding/">
        <GetLicenseInformationReturn xsi:type="xsd:string"><?xml version="1.0"
          standalone="yes"?><AvXmlLicData> <Licenses>
          <LicLanguagesMax>6</LicLanguagesMax>
          <LicRealspeakSessionsMax>2</LicRealspeakSessionsMax>
          <LicSubscribersMax>100</LicSubscribersMax>
          <LicUMSubscribersMax>100</LicUMSubscribersMax>
          <LicVMISubscribersMax>100</LicVMISubscribersMax>
          <LicVoicePortsMax>4</LicVoicePortsMax> </Licenses> <Utilization>
          <AvLicUtilizationSecondaryServer>0</AvLicUtilizationSecondaryServer>
          <AvLicUtilizationSubscribers>51</AvLicUtilizationSubscribers>
          <AvLicUtilizationVMISubscribers>0</AvLicUtilizationVMISubscribers>
          </Utilization> <ErrorAlerts>0</ErrorAlerts>
          <WarningAlerts>1</WarningAlerts></AvXmlLicData>
        </GetLicenseInformationReturn>
      </GetLicenseInformationResponse>
    </soapenv:Body>
  </soapenv:Envelope>
```

In short this shows you the total counts available to that Unity server and how many it is using for each licensed feature. If the Unity server in question is part of a pool of licenses, the total counts will reflect that for you. When going to add a user to that box, you need to check if the subscriber count can take one more and if the CoS you are associating the user with has available seats. On the CoS, if Visual Messaging Interface (VMI) is enabled you have to check that there are available seats for that license and if the CoS has text-to-speech (TTS) enabled you have to make sure there are TTS sessions enabled. Technically, the CoS should not be able to have TTS enabled if no TTS sessions are defined. However, you can do this programmatically by accident so it is proper to check.

In the previous dump you can review it real quick and see that it is a 4-port system with 2 sessions of TTS, and 100 subscribers with 51 used up so far. However, you might (as many do) puzzle over "**<LicSubscribersMax>100</LicSubscribersMax>**" and "**<LicUMSubscribersMax>100</LicUMSubscribersMax>**" both being in the same dump. What does this mean? Currently in Unity, the licensing scheme does not allow for mixing UM and VM seats; it is an all-or-nothing deal. Yes, we know this is annoying, you are preaching to the choir. However, in the license dump that is a UM configuration because all 100 seats are UM-enabled, which is what the two counts mean. If this had been a VM-only configuration, you would see 100 LicSubscribersMax and 0 for LicUMSubscribersMax. Someday they might allow mixing licenses on the same box and you will see a total subscriber count and a UM count that is a subset.

To pull out the license information is an exercise in XML parsing which is fairly easy using the MSXLM 3.0 libraries. We walk through the libraries for the system information section below if you want to go through the details. There is a checkForAvailableLicense routine in the Remote Connection sample project that wraps things up nicely for you. All you have to pass in is the AccessTTS and AccessVMI flags on the CoS you want to add the user to, and it will return TRUE or FALSE to tell you if you can add a user to the box with that CoS or not. Here is a chunk of code showing how to use that routine.

Example 21-6 *Checking License Information*

```
! First, you need to get the AccessVMI and AccessTTS columns from the row in the
COS table for the class of service you will be adding the user to.  You can pull the
COSObjectID off the subscriber template you are using to create the subscriber
using this query.
    Set rsCOS = New ADODB.Recordset
    rsCOS.Open "SELECT AccessTTS, AccessVMI FROM vw_COS INNER JOIN vw_
      SubscriberTemplate ON vw_SubscriberTemplate.COSObjectID=vw_COS.CosObjectID
      WHERE vw_SubscriberTemplate.Alias='" + strTemplateAlias+ "'",
      strConnectionString, adOpenKeyset, adLockReadOnly
    If checkForAvailableLicense(strUnityServerName, rsCOS("AccessTTS"),
      rsCOS("AccessVMI")) = False Then
        Msgbox "No licenses available for that COS, you cannot add a new user to it"
    Else
!       <…code to add subscriber…>
    End If
```

If the INNER JOIN used in the query there is new to you, it is a good idea to retrieve the "SQL Sample Queries" code example from www.ciscounitytools.com and spend some time working through it. A decent book on introductory SQL queries (this is not Microsoft SQL specific by any means) is also a good idea. Getting comfortable with both INNER and OUTER JOINs is critical to doing much of anything useful in a database where information about a particular object is strung across multiple tables (which describes just about any database of even medium complexity out there).

A quick note about making your applications secure when constructing such SQL queries as we used here. Even though we opened the rsCOS recordset for read-only, you can insert strings into the select query that executes applications on the server running SQL. If the server has not been locked down, strings such as "xp_cmdshell (do something bad)" can be inserted to run applications under the context of the account you are using to attach to the database. In most of the sample applications provided, you will notice that users are not given the opportunity to just randomly enter strings such as aliases or display names which are then inserted directly into the queries. Users are forced to select users or CoS aliases or the like from a static list presented to them. If you find yourself in a situation where you need to allow a user to enter some text you need to search the database for, be sure you take precautions to prevent malicious user input.

There are other pieces of information you want about a Unity server, other than licensing, are not available in SQL at this point. As noted before, these items will find their way into SQL at some point. However, for now, you have to ping the GetSystemInformation method from the same web page we get the licensing information from to get at such things as the Unity version, what back-end messaging system is being used, which messaging server we are connected to for our "partner" server, and so on. To see this information, you can ping the following web address where, again, TestBox is the name of your Unity server:

http://TestBox:8080/cual/
CiscoUnitySystemInformation.jws?method=GetSystemInformation

The browser will show the following data when you hit that site:

Example 21-7 *XML Output for Unity System Information*

```
 <?xml version="1.0" encoding="UTF-8" ?>
- <soapenv:Envelope
   xmlns:soapenv="http://schemas.xmlsoap.org/soap/envelope/"
   xmlns:xsd="http://www.w3.org/2001/XMLSchema"
   xmlns:xsi="http://www.w3.org/2001/XMLSchema-instance">
 - <soapenv:Body>
   - <GetSystemInformationResponse
       soapenv:encodingStyle="http://schemas.xmlsoap.org/soap/encoding/">
       <GetSystemInformationReturn xsi:type="xsd:string"><?xml version="1.0"
         encoding="UTF-8"?>
         <CiscoUnitySystemInformation><Version>4.00.01.54</Version><DirectoryType>Av
         DsAD.AvDsAD.1</DirectoryType><MailServer>LINDBORG-
         SPEEDY</MailServer><Integrations><Integration name="Cisco CallManager"
         number="1"/></Integrations></CiscoUnitySystemInformation></GetSystemInforma
         tionReturn>
     </GetSystemInformationResponse>
   </soapenv:Body>
 </soapenv:Envelope>
```

This is very similar to the previous licensing data in that it has a SOAP envelope around some XML text. To parse out the information using the Microsoft MSXML 3.0 libraries in VB it looks like this:

Example 21-8 *Parsed Information*

```
! Trim off the extra text that comes at the beginning and end of the page. Sometimes
the XML libraries do not appreciate it even though IE does not seem to have a
problem with it.
    strXML = removeLeadingWhitespace(GetURL(strURL, INTERNET_OPEN_TYPE_DIRECT))
```

Example 21-8 *Parsed Information (Continued)*

```
! Because the information comes in wrapped in a SOAP envelope, you actually need
to open the xmlDOC against it and then open another xmlDOC from that to get the
data within the SOAP wrapper.  I did not want to require folks to have the SOAP
libraries on their client machines here so I am digging the info out of it "XML
Old School" style.  If you want to use SOAP libraries directly, feel free.
    xmlDoc.loadXML strXML
    If xmlDoc.parseError.errorCode <> 0 Then
      MsgBox "There was a problem with the system information data from the server.
          This is likely caused because you have not applied the CUAL patch to your
          Unity 4.0(2) Unity server that you're querying here."
      Exit Function
    End If

! Snag the actual XML meat out of the SOAP sandwich currently in the xmlDOC
object.
    xmlDoc.loadXML xmlDoc.documentElement.Text
    If xmlDoc.parseError.errorCode <> 0 Then
      MsgBox "There was a problem with the system information data from the server.
          This is likely caused because you have not applied the CUAL patch to your
          Unity 4.0(2) Unity server that you're querying here."
      Exit Function
    End If

!Get at the information in the XML string and dump it out.  In the Remote
Connection code example this info is added to a dictionary and passed back to
the calling routine for processing.
    MsgBox "Version: " + xmlDoc.getElementsByTagName("Version").Item(0).Text

! The directory type can be "AvDsAD.AvDsAD.1" for Active Directory (Exchange
2000/2003), or "AvDsEx55.AvDsEx55.1" for Exchange 5.5 or
 "AvDsDOM.AvDsDOM.1" for Domino.
    MsgBox"DirectoryType: "
       xmlDoc.getElementsByTagName("DirectoryType").Item(0).Text

! The mail server name is the partner server Unity is connected to that you
  selected during the setup.
     MsgBox "MailServer: ", xmlDoc.getElementsByTagName("MailServer").Item(0).Text

!There can be more than one switch integration, as such it is a collection under
the Integrations node. This output method used here is rather silly and
just throws up a message box for each switch found as Switch0, Switch1,
Switch2, and so on. Currently there are only two integrations allowed on a
particular Unity but that will likely change soon.
    Set nodesInfo = xmlDoc.getElementsByTagName("Integrations").Item(0).childNodes

    iCounter = 0
    For Each nodeCurrent In nodesInfo
      MsgBox "Switch: " + Trim(Str(iCounter)), nodesInfo.Item(0).Attributes(0).Text
        iCounter = iCounter + 1
    Next
```

The licensing URL will remain indefinitely but in later versions of Unity, data now stored in the Registry will migrate into tables in SQL and the need to hit the Unity information URL will go away. However at the time of this writing, Unity 4.0(4) still stores much of the previous information in the Registry.

Find All Unity Servers in the Enterprise

The nice thing about the design of Unity is that you only need to connect to one Unity server in the directory and it will have all the information about other Unity servers and subscribers you need to find and connect to them. The directory monitors have done all the heavy lifting for you here and you can easily exploit it.

As discussed in Chapter 2 and Chapter 3, information about remote Unity servers and remote subscribers stored on those servers can be found in the global location and global subscriber tables in UnityDB. If the other Unity server is in the same directory, information about it and its subscribers will be available to you.

In this case we just want to get a full list of all visible Unity servers on the network. Once you have your connection string constructed as described earlier, you simply need to open a recordset using this query:

```
rsUnityServers.Open  "SELECT HomeServer FROM vw_Location_Global GROUP BY
    HomeServer", strConnectionString, adOpenKeyset, adLockReadOnly
```

The rsUnityServers recordset now includes a complete list of all Unity server names visible on the network. Yes, there is another HomeServer column in the subscriber table that throws some folks off. The HomeServer value in the subscriber table is the server name of the mail store server the subscriber's mailbox is stored on, not their home Unity server. The wisdom of using the same column name for two different concepts is left as an exercise for the reader.

Listing and Finding Subscribers Anywhere in the Enterprise

In much the same way information about remote Unity servers can be found in the global location table, information about remote Unity subscribers can be found in the global subscriber table. As we discussed extensively during the discussion of the data object model in Chapter 3, there is a lot of information about a subscriber that does not get replicated around the directory, such as most of the data associated with their primary call handler. For a complete rundown on what data we have on remote subscribers, whip open your copy of CUDLE and look through the columns for the GlobalSubscriber table.

For the first part of this example we are going to generate one table that includes the alias, first name, last name, display name, primary extension, and home Unity server for each subscriber in the directory.

Example 21-9 *SQL Query to Get All Subscribers in the Directory*

```
SELECT vw_Subscriber_Global.Alias, vw_Subscriber_Global.DisplayName, vw_
   Subscriber_Global.FirstName, vw_Subscriber_Global.LastName, vw_Subscriber_
   Global.DTMFAccessID AS 'Primary Extension', vw_Location_Global.HomeServer
FROM vw_Subscriber_Global INNER JOIN vw_Location_Global
ON vw_Subscriber_Global.LocationObjectID=vw_Location_Global.LocationObjectID
WHERE vw_Subscriber_Global.SubscriberType NOT IN (0,6)
```

Because the home Unity server name is stored in the global location table we need to do an inner join here to get at it. The subscriberType filter in the WHERE clause specifically excludes the special built-in installer account (type 6) and the Unity Messaging System account (type 0), which are not Unity subscribers but special objects used internally. As such, the resulting recordset contains information about all subscribers including full Exchange and Domino subscribers as well as remote subscribers (AMIS, SMTP, Bridge, and VPIM users). If you want to filter out all but full subscribers, you could replace that with "WHERE vw_Subscriber_Global.SubscriberType IN (1,3)" for example. Again, check CUDLE for the SubscriberType column and you will get a full run down on what all the legal values for this column are and what they mean.

If you want to find all the subscribers in the directory that are on Unity servers in the same dialing domain, this is easily done by adding another simple JOIN clause into the query. Dialing domains are defined as all primary location objects that have a matching DialingDomainName string associated with them. As such, adjust the query to look like this:

Example 21-10 *SQL Query to Get All Subscribers in the Dialing Domain*

```
SELECT vw_Subscriber_Global.Alias, vw_Subscriber_Global.DisplayName, vw_
   Subscriber_Global.FirstName, vw_Subscriber_Global.LastName, vw_Subscriber_
   Global.DTMFAccessID AS 'Primary Extension', vw_Location_Global.HomeServer
FROM vw_Subscriber_Global INNER JOIN vw_Location_Global
ON vw_Subscriber_Global.LocationObjectID=vw_Location_Global.LocationObjectID
INNER JOIN vw_Location
ON vw_Location.DialingDomainName=vw_Location_Global.DialingDomainName
WHERE vw_Subscriber_Global.SubscriberType NOT IN (0,6) and vw_
   Location.Alias='default'
```

The location alias of 'default' is a handy way of grabbing the local primary location where the dialing domain name is stored. This query will grab all the Unity subscribers stored on any Unity server that is in the same dialing domain as the Unity server you are attached to when running the query. Remember that if the Unity server you are attached to is not part of a dialing domain, the resulting recordset will contain no members because the DialingDomainName column for the local location is NULL and in SQL land NULL <> NULL and so there will not be any matching rows. To deal with this you can explicitly check for "IsNull(vw_Location.DialingDomainName)" and execute an appropriate query.

To get a list of all the dialing domains in the directory is similar to getting all the server names:

```
SELECT DialingDomainName FROM vw_Location_Global GROUP BY DialingDomainName
```

Take this subscriber recordset you created above and bind it to a grid control and you have a decent subscriber browser for little effort. You can easily throw a tree control on there to adjust the query to include users only stored on specific Unity servers or servers within a dialing domain. Combine this with the ability to directly open a subscriber's SA page off their home Unity server discussed in the next section and you are on your way to making your own Global Subscriber Manager.

While we are rummaging around in the global subscriber and global location tables to find information about remote users, there are a couple common problems that come up when dealing with the enterprise-level directory that we can easily solve. First, if you have a user in your directory, it is good to know which Unity server they live on so that you can launch their SA page directory. You then also know which Unity server you need to attach to so you can update the user's information or delete them. Assuming you have their mail alias from the directory to start with, this is easily solved with a simple query on the global tables:

Example 21-11 *SQL Query to Find a Specific Subscriber by Their Alias*

```
SELECT vw_Subscriber_Global.DisplayName, vw_Location_Global.HomeServer
FROM vw_Subscriber_Global INNER JOIN vw_Location_Global
ON vw_Subscriber_Global.LocationObjectID=vw_Location_Global.LocationObjectID
WHERE vw_Subscriber_Global.Alias='jlindborg'
```

It gets a little trickier to find someone from their extension number. The primary extension number of a subscriber is stored in the global subscriber table that is easy enough to deal with when using the view (remember this column was removed in 4.0(3) in the raw table). However, subscribers can have up to nine alternate extensions and you cannot be certain which one the user is looking for. For this, you have to add a join to the DTMFAccessID table itself. As information about remote Unity subscribers is pulled into the database, the directory monitor unpacks the alternate extension number "blob" that is added to the subscriber's directory object and puts the resulting values into the DTMFAccessID table.

If the extension of the user you were looking for was "4321", the query would look like this:

Example 21-12 *SQL Query to Find a Subscriber by an Extension Number*

```
SELECT vw_Subscriber_Global.DisplayName, vw_Location_Global.HomeServer
FROM vw_Subscriber_Global INNER JOIN vw_Location_Global
ON vw_Subscriber_Global.LocationObjectID=vw_Location_Global.LocationObjectID
INNER JOIN vw_DTMFAccessID
ON vw_DTMFAccessID.ParentObjectID=vw_Subscriber_Global.SubscriberObjectID
WHERE vw_DTMFAccessID.DTMFAccessID='4321'
```

Be aware that it is perfectly legal for the previous query to return more than one match. The global subscriber table will include users from all over the directory, not just those in a dialing domain. As such, it is possible for there to be overlapping numbering plans in the corporate directory. You can include restrictions in your query for only getting users in a particular dialing domain, or you can just present a list of display names and aliases and let the user running your application make a smart decision.

Find an Extension Anywhere in the Dialing Domain with Unity 4.0(3) or Later Versions

In the previous section, we learned how to find the extension of a subscriber anywhere in the directory. However, sometimes you just want to find any and all objects using a particular extension number in the dialing domain. This can include local objects such as call handlers, interview handlers, and name lookup handlers. It can include global objects like distribution lists, location objects and, of course, subscribers in the dialing domain.

You need to check any time you want to add a new object with an extension defined or edit a standing object's extension to be sure you do not introduce a conflict in the dialing domain. The Unity conversation assumes that all extensions across all objects are unique in the dialing domain, and you will get "undefined behavior" if you do not take care to avoid conflicts.

For Unity 4.0(3), a new view was added that greatly simplifies this process and that is why we include two separate sections for how to do this. The following code chunk grabs a new extension number off the txtNewExtension text control on the form and checks to ensure the extension in there does not conflict with anything in the dialing domain. Checks on the validity of the text in the edit box have already been performed; this just shows the mechanism for reporting conflicts to the user in a reasonable way.

Example 21-13 *Checking for Extension Conflicts in the Dialing Domain in 4.0(3)*

```
rsTemp.Open "SELECT * FROM vw_DTMFaccessID_DialingDomain WHERE DTMFAccessID='"
    + txtNewExtension.Text + "'", strConnectionString, adOpenKeyset,
    adLockReadOnly

If rsTemp.RecordCount > 0 Then
' Conflict found in the dialing domain - report this to the user.  Technically
there should only be one but, it is possible the site has other conflicts
that already exist so iterate through the recordset and produce a message box
that lists all conflicts found, what object.
    strTemp = "That extension cannot be used since it conflicts with the following
        objects in the dialing domain: "
    rsTemp.MoveFirst
    Do While rsTemp.EOF = False
        strTemp = strTemp + "Extension= " + rsTemp("DTMFAccessID") + " is owned
            by " + strGetObjectTypeDescription(rsTemp("ObjectType")) + " with a
            Display Name= " + rsTemp("DisplayName") + ".  "
```

continues

Example 21-13 *Checking for Extension Conflicts in the Dialing Domain in 4.0(3) (Continued)*

```
            rsTemp.MoveNext
        Loop

        MsgBox strTemp
    End If
```

The strGetObjectTypeDescription function used there is a simple case statement that translates the ObjectType number into a human readable string. As always, a quick trip to CUDLE shows the list of values possible here, but here is the listing for that function so you know what is occurring.

Example 21-14 *Routine to Convert Object Type Number into Human Readable String*

```
Public Function strGetObjectTypeDescription(iObjectType As Integer) As String
Dim strTemp As String

    Select Case iObjectType
    Case 1
        strTemp = "Subscriber"
    Case 2
        strTemp = "Distribution List"
    Case 3
        strTemp = "Call Handler"
    Case 5
        strTemp = "Inteview Handler"
    Case 6
        strTemp = "Directory Handler"
    Case 9
        strTemp = "Location Object"
    Case Else
        strTemp = "Unknown"
    End Select

    strGetObjectTypeDescription = strTemp

    Exit Function
End Function
```

Find an Extension Anywhere in the Dialing Domain with Unity 4.0(1) or 4.0(2)

If you run 4.0(1) or 4.0(2) and you cannot upgrade to 4.0(3) or later, you need to check for conflicting extensions in the dialing domain. Finding the ID you want and getting the information about that object can be a little tricky because you have to check multiple places by using a difficult query. It also requires you know what all the ParentObjectIDType values in the DTMFAccessID table actually mean. A quick trip to CUDLE will get you a list of all six values we need in this situation (the same ones we used in the CASE statement in the previous section):

1 = Subscribers
2 = Public Distribution Lists
3 = Call Handlers
5 = Interview Handlers
6 = Directory Handlers (name lookup handlers)
9 = Location Objects

Call handlers, interview handlers, and directory handlers are local to the Unity server they are created on so finding them is simple. Locations can span dialing domains and, as such, their IDs need to be unique across all Unity servers that are in their dialing domain. Subscribers also span dialing domains but include alternate extensions and require special consideration. Distribution lists are always global and this can introduce special problems in a directory that spans dial plans.

Fortunately all you have to worry about is checking the DTMFAccessID table that consolidates all the extensions, both local and global, in one place to make such checks easy. However, if you want to construct a list of display names and basic object information to show the user should a conflict arise, there is a little more work involved.

The first check we will do here is against all subscribers in the dialing domain. We need to be careful here. If the Unity server we are connected to is not part of any dialing domain, the DialingDomainName value will be NULL. If the value is NULL, then you can just check against the local subscriber table instead of doing an inner join against the global subscriber and global locations table as you would normally.

Example 21-15 *Finding Subscribers with Conflicting Extensions in the Dialing Domain in 4.0(1) or 4.0(2)*

```
! First, get the dialing domain name the local box is in, if any.
Rstemp.open "SELECT DialingDomainName FROM vw_Location WHERE vw_
   Location.Alias='default'",strConnectionString, adOpenKeyset, adLockReadOnly
If IsNull(rsTemp("DialingDomainName")) then
           StrDialingDomainName=vbNullString
Else
           StrDialingDomainName=rsTemp("DialingDomainName")
EndIf

RsTemp.Close

! If the local server is not in a dialing domain then we only need to check local
  subscribers for possible conflicts.  Otherwise we have to include all
  subscribers and location objects in the dialing domain as well.
If len(strDialingDomainName)=0 Then
```

continues

Example 21-15 *Finding Subscribers with Conflicting Extensions in the Dialing Domain in 4.0(1) or 4.0(2) (Continued)*

```
        strSQL = "SELECT vw_DTMFAccessID.DTMFAccessID, vw_Subscriber.Alias, vw_
    Subscriber.DisplayName FROM vw_DTMFAccessID INNER JOIN vw_Subscriber ON vw_
    DTMFAccessID.ParentObjectID=vw_Subscriber.SubscriberObjectID WHERE vw_
    Subscriber.SubscriberType NOT IN (0,6) AND vw_DTMFAccessID.DTMFAccessid='" +
    strDTMFID + "'"

    Else

        strSQL = "SELECT vw_DTMFAccessID.DTMFAccessID, vw_Subscriber_Global.Alias,
        vw_Subscriber_Global.DisplayName, vw_Location_Global.HomeServer FROM vw_
        DTMFAccessID INNER JOIN vw_Subscriber_Global ON vw_
        DTMFAccessID.ParentObjectId=vw_Subscriber_Global.SubscriberObjectId
        INNER JOIN vw_Location_Global ON vw_Location_Global.LocationObjectId=vw_
        Subscriber_Global.LocationObjectId WHERE vw_Subscriber_
        Global.SubscriberType NOT IN (0,6) AND vw_Location_
        Global.DialingDomainName='" + strDialingDomain + "' AND vw_
        DTMFAccessID.DTMFAccessid='" + strDTMFID + "'"
    End If

    rsTemp.Open strSQL, strConnectionString, adOpenKeyset, adLockReadOnly

    If rsTemp.RecordCount > 1 Then
!           <…code to report conflicting subscribers to user…>
    End If
```

The rsTemp recordset would contain all subscribers in the dialing domain that had a primary or alternate ID that conflicted with the ID you passed into the routine. If the server was not a member of any dialing domain, the result set would just contain local subscribers. If there was one or more matches then you would have to present an error to the user indicating they cannot use the ID they have selected for a new object or for updating the extension of an existing object. You can do this by constructing a dictionary or an array of structures. The structure would contain the information so that you could display a decent error message indicating which subscriber on what server was causing the conflict.

Next, the routine checks location objects which optionally have IDs as well.

Example 21-16 *Finding Locations with Conflicting Extensions in 4.0(1) or 4.0(2)*

```
If Len (strDialingDomainName)=0 then

    StrSQL="SELECT vw_Location_Global.TextName, vw_Location_Global.Alias, vw_
        DTMFAccessID.DTMFAccessID
FROM vw_Location_Global INNER JOIN vw_DTMFAccessID
ON vw_Location_Global.LocationObjectID=vw_DTMFAccessID.ParentObjectId
WHERE vw_DTMFAccessID.DTMFAccessid='" + strDTMFID + "'"

Else

    StrSQL="SELECT vw_Location_Global.TextName, vw_Location_Global.Alias, vw_
        DTMFAccessID.DTMFAccessID
```

Example 21-16 *Finding Locations with Conflicting Extensions in 4.0(1) or 4.0(2) (Continued)*

```
FROM vw_Location_Global INNER JOIN vw_DTMFAccessID
ON vw_Location_Global.LocationObjectID=vw_DTMFAccessID.ParentObjectID
WHERE vw_Location_Global.DialingDomainName='"+strDialingDomainName+"' AND vw_
   DTMFAccessID.DTMFAccessID='"+strDTMFID+"'"

EndIf

    rsTemp.Open strSQL, strConnectionString, adOpenKeyset, adLockReadOnly

    If rsTemp.RecordCount > 1 Then
<…code to report conflicting subscribers to user…>
    End If

    RsTemp.Close
```

Now the structure that you are adding to for all potential conflicts will contain all subscribers and location objects in the dialing domain (if any) the local Unity server is a part of. The last thing you need to do is check all objects that remain. Public distribution lists are shared objects and can as such be considered local to all Unity servers. This concept is tricky. If you assign an ID to a public distribution list, that ID is used by ALL Unity servers in the entire corporate directory. This is a common source of ID conflicts. As a general rule, do not assign IDs to public distribution lists unless you are sure you have a coordinated dialing plan across your network.

To do this, grab all objects referenced in the DTMFAccessID table that are not subscribers or location objects that are using the ID in question. By definition these are all the local objects, and any ID to be used by any other object on this server should not conflict with these IDs. Iterate over the list of objects found (if any) and add descriptive information about each object (as in its type, its display name, and alias at a minimum) into the structure you are using to pass this data back to the calling party. The following code chunk is a simplified version of what you find in the Add Subscriber example:

Example 21-17 *Find Conflicting Extensions for All Local Objects in 4.0(1) or 4.0(2)*

```
strSQL = "SELECT * from vw_DTMFAccessID WHERE DTMFAccessID='" + strDTMFID + "' AND
ParentObjectIDType NOT IN (1,9)

    rsTemp.Open strSQL, strConnectionString, adOpenKeyset, adLockReadOnly

    If rsTemp.RecordCount > 0 Then
        Do While rsTemp.EOF = False
                Select Case rsTemp("ParentObjectIDTYpe")
                    Case 2
                    rsFind.Open "Select Alias, DisplayName from vw_DistributionList
                        WHERE SystemDListObjectID='" + rsTemp("ParentObjectID")
                        + "'", strConnectionString, adOpenKeyset, adLockReadOnly
```

continues

Example 21-17 *Find Conflicting Extensions for All Local Objects in 4.0(1) or 4.0(2) (Continued)*

```
! <…insert code for reporting distribution list conflict…>
                    rsFind.Close
                Case 3
! Yes, subscribers have their DTMFAccessID for their primary extension stored in
their primary call handler and you would think that perhaps this would pick that up
and do a "double-check." However, in the DTMFAccessID table, the parent of an
extension associated with a subscriber is a subscriber, not a call handler.  As
such, this check is only going to pick up local application call handlers as we
want.  This is a little confusing because in other places such as calls to the
PHGreeting and PHTransfer conversations, and references to subscribers are done
through their primary call handler.
                    rsFind.Open "Select Alias, TextName from CallHandler WHERE
                        CallHandlerObjectID='" + rsTemp("ParentObjectID") + "'",
                        strConnectionString, adOpenKeyset, adLockReadOnly
!<…insert code for reporting call handler conflict…>
rsFind.Close
                Case 5
                    rsFind.Open "Select Alias, TextName from vw_InterviewHandler
                        WHERE InterviewHandlerObjectID='" +
                        rsTemp("ParentObjectID") + "'", strConnectionString,
                        adOpenKeyset, adLockReadOnly
!<…insert code for reporting interview handler conflict…>
                    rsFind.Close
                Case 6
                    rsFind.Open "Select Alias, TextName, NameLookupHandlerObjectID
                        from vw_NameLookupHandler WHERE
                        NameLookupHandlerObjectID='" + rsTemp("ParentObjectID")
                        + "'", strConnectionString, adOpenKeyset, adLockReadOnly
            !<…insert code for reporting name lookup handler conflict…>
                    rsFind.Close
                Case 9
                    rsFind.Open "Select Alias, TextName, LocationObjectID from
                        vw_Location_Global WHERE LocationObjectID='" +
                        rsTemp("ParentObjectID") + "'",
                        strConnectionString, adOpenKeyset, adLockReadOnly
                    rsFind.Close
                Case Else
                MsgBox "Error! Invalid ParentObjectID type in DTMFAccessID table!"
                End Select
            End With
            rsTemp.MoveNext
        Loop
    End If
```

After performing all three checks, whatever you selected as your mechanism for reporting conflicts back to the calling routine will contain ALL conflicts with the selected ID within the dialing domain. This is a prevalent need for those doing subscribers adds, imports, and updates so it is a good idea to get this routine in place early in the development cycle.

After reviewing the above it should be obvious that you will want to upgrade to Unity 4.0(3) or later if you can.

Open an SA Web Page Directly to Any Object

Once you find an object in the database such as a subscriber or a call handler, you might just want to fall back and punt to the Unity web-based SA interface to allow your users to update the properties. This is a good technique to use because it absolves you from having to do all the business logic legwork and having to handle licensing issues and other headaches that the SA console already has in place. We use this technique in a number of applications such as the Global Subscriber Manager, Audio Text Manager, and dbWalker among others.

The idea is simple; the Unity SA web pages are designed so that you can open them up directly to the object you want without having to go through search dialogs, deal with frames, or any of the things that can trip you up with other web interfaces. Once you are armed with a unique ID for the object, the Unity home server name it lives on, and the formula for constructing the URLs, you can jump directly to almost any object in the database.

The unique ID in most cases is the "ObjectID" value for the table. For example, the Call-Handler table would use the CallHandlerObjectID column as its unique identifier. The exception to this is subscribers which use the DirectoryID column instead of its SubscriberObjectID column as you would expect. The reason for this is because the original concept was to allow you to grab the DirectoryID value out of the directory (AD, Exchange 55, or Domino) and be able to jump to the web page for that user without having to access the database to find their ObjectID value. On paper this looks nifty. In reality you are missing one important piece of information: the home Unity server name. You have to open the web page for the object you want to edit, including subscribers, on the Unity server that object is homed on. This server name is not stored in the directory on the subscriber itself; it is on the location object the user is associated with. The subscriber's directory object has a reference to the location object by ID and technically you could rummage through the directory, get all location objects, find the one you are looking for, and pull the home server name off of it. While this is possible, it is far from easy. It is easier to connect to a Unity server and get what you need out of SQL rather than doing things right out of the directory.

The "Generating SA Links" example on the sample page of www.ciscounitytools.com runs through how to create links to all object types, but here is the quick version. Assuming you have the home Unity server name stored in the variable strServerName and the CallHandlerObjectID stored in the strObjectID variable, you can construct the URL that jumps right to that call handler using this code:

```
strURL = "http://" & strServerName & "/Web/SA/FrameASP/
  handFrame.asp?id=%01%0703%3A" & transformObjectID(strObjectID)
```

The transormObjectID function is used to replace characters that the web server has problems with that are found in the ObjectID value. Being a GUID it contains { , } and - characters, all which throw things off and, as such, need to be replaced with their escape code equivalents. This is very simple in VB; the function looks like this:

Example 21-18 *Replacing GUID Characters with Their Escape Code Equivalents*

```
Public Function transformObjectID(strObjectID As String) As String
    transformObjectID = strObjectID
    transformObjectID = Replace(transformObjectID, "{", "%7B")
    transformObjectID = Replace(transformObjectID, "}", "%7D")
    transformObjectID = Replace(transformObjectID, "-", "%2D")
End Function
```

This same technique applies to all objects except subscribers. The only thing that changes from object to object is the .asp page name and the preamble to the object ID. For example, the interview handler link code would look similar to the call handler code above but look carefully and you will spot the differences:

```
strURL = "http://" & strServerName & "/Web/SA/FrameASP/
    IntHFrame.asp?id=%01%0705%3A" & transformObjectID(strObjectID)
```

For subscribers, however, it is a little simpler because the directory ID has no characters that need to be replaced with escape codes and there is no preamble to deal with. The code to construct the URL for a subscriber would look like this:

```
strURL = "http://" & strServerName & "/Web/SA/FrameASP/SubsFrame.asp?DirID=" &
    strDirectoryID
```

Even if you are planning on doing all your own administration interfaces down the road, you should consider this technique to bridge the gap and provide users of your applications with fast, easy access to administration interfaces you have not yet developed.

Call Handler Information Dump

This example walks you through the process of dumping out the basic information about any call handler in the Unity server you are connected to. We discuss the application call handlers here; however, this same technique also works with primary call handlers associated with subscribers. You only need to modify the logic to take into account that subscribers can have alternate extensions, subscribers always have their alternate contact rule enabled, and the standard and off hours rules are never used.

This type of application is largely an exercise of knowing which tables contain what information related to call handlers. As much of this was covered in the discussion of the data object model in Chapter 3, we are not going to spend too much time on this here. You would do well to cover a couple of important points if you are building a reporting or database "dump" type application in general.

Many places in the Unity database have a trilogy of properties that indicate where a caller should be sent. The properties are an Action, Conversation Name, and Destination Object ID set that can be found in varying forms in dozens of places throughout the database. Pop open UnityDB and you will find these for user input keys, messaging rules, on call handlers for after message actions, on subscribers for exit actions, name lookup handler exits, interview handler exits, and so on. If you are building a reporting type application, you will definitely want to construct a generic routine that can convert these values into a human readable text you can reference in your output. The following routine is one used in the Call Handler Information Dump sample code for this purpose:

Example 21-19 *General Routine for Converting Action, Conversation, and DestinationObjectID Sets into Human Readable Text*

```
Public Function strConstructActionString(iAction As Integer, strConversationName As
String, strObjectID As String) As String
Dim strAction As String
Dim strSQL As String
Dim rs As New ADODB.Recordset

    Select Case iAction
        Case 0
!           an ignore action is only found for user input keys
            strAction = "Ignore"
        Case 1
            strAction = "Hangup"
        Case 2
!An action of 2 is the generic "go to" action, which is by far and away the most
common action value you will encounter.  This is used for sending callers to any
other object in the system which is, of course, something that happens
frequently.  The conversation name dictates what type of object it is we will be
sending the caller to next.
            If (StrComp(strConversationName, "chInterview", vbTextCompare) = 0) Then
! The chInterview conversation means the conversation is going to send the caller
to an interview handler here so there should be the ObjectID of an interviewer
in the ObjectId parameter here.
                strSQL = "SELECT TextName FROM vw_InterviewHandler WHERE
                    InterviewHandlerObjectID='" + strObjectID + "'"
                rs.Open strSQL, strConnectionString, adOpenKeyset, adLockReadOnly
                If rs.RecordCount = 0 Then
                    strAction = "(error) Send caller to missing interview handler.
                        ObjectId=" + strObjectID
                Else
                    rs.MoveFirst
                    strAction = "Send caller to interview handler: " + rs("TextName")
                End If
            ElseIf ((StrComp(strConversationName, "PHGreeting", vbTextCompare) = 0)
                Or (StrComp(strConversationName, "PHTransfer", vbTextCompare)
                = 0)) Then
!The PHGreeting or PHTransfer conversation means the conversation is sending the
caller to another call handler - either to the transfer rules entry point
(PHTransfer) or skipping the transfer rules and going right to the greetings
(PHGreeting).  Remember that a call handler can also be marked primary, which
```

continues

Example 21-19 *General Routine for Converting Action, Conversation, and DestinationObjectID Sets into Human Readable Text (Continued)*

```
means it is part of a subscriber so we need to take that into account here.
                If StrComp(strConversationName, "PHGreeting", vbTextCompare = 0) Then
                    strAction = "Send caller to greeting for "
                Else
                    strAction = "Send caller to transfer for "
                End If
                strSQL = "SELECT TextName, CallHandlerObjectID, IsPrimary FROM vw_
                    CallHandler WHERE CallHandlerObjectID='" + strObjectID + "'"
                rs.Open strSQL, strConnectionString, adOpenKeyset, adLockReadOnly
                If rs.RecordCount = 0 Then
                    strAction = "(error) Send caller to missing call handler.
                        ObjectId=" + strObjectID
                Else
                    rs.MoveFirst
                    If rs("IsPrimary") = 1 Then
!It is a primary call handler, which means it is a subscriber we are sending the
  caller to.  Adjust the action string accordingly.
                        strSQL = "SELECT DisplayName FROM vw_Subscriber WHERE
                            CallHandlerObjectID='" + rs("CallHandlerOjectID") + "'"
                        rs.Close
                        rs.Open strSQL, strConnectionString, adOpenKeyset,
                            adLockReadOnly
                        If rs.RecordCount = 0 Then
                            strAction = strAction + " subscriber - (error) could
                                not find subscriber that owns this primary call
                                handler."
                        Else
                            strAction = strAction + " subscriber with display name
= " + rs("DisplayName")
                        End If
                    Else
!                     it is just an ordinary application call handler
                        strAction = strAction + " call handler: " + rs("TextName")
                    End If
                End If

            ElseIf StrComp(strConversationName, "AD", vbTextCompare) = 0 Then
! Send the caller to a name lookup handler (or alpha directory, hence the "AD"
conversation name there) - there should be an ObjectID of a name lookup handler
in the ObjectID parameter.
                strSQL = "SELECT TextName FROM vw_NameLookupHandler WHERE
                    NameLookupHandlerObjectID='" + strObjectID + "'"
                rs.Open strSQL, strConnectionString, adOpenKeyset, adLockReadOnly
                If rs.RecordCount = 0 Then
                  strAction = "(error) Send caller to missing name lookup handler.
                     ObjectId=" + strObjectID
                Else
                    rs.MoveFirst
                  strAction = "Send caller to name lookup handler: " + rs("TextName")
                End If
            ElseIf StrComp(strConversationName, "SubSignIn", vbTextCompare) = 0 Then
! The subscriber sign in conversation does not take a destination object ID, it is
```

Example 21-19 *General Routine for Converting Action, Conversation, and DestinationObjectID Sets into Human Readable Text (Continued)*

```
a stand-alone "routable" conversation that you can just launch directly.
                strAction = "Subscriber sign in"
            ElseIf StrComp(strConversationName, "GreetingsAdministrator",
                vbTextCompare) = 0 Then
!The greetings administration conversation also does not take a destination object
ID, you just send the call to the conversation directly.
                strAction = "Greetings administration"
            Else
                MsgBox "Error! Unknown conversation string passed to
                    strConstructActionString: " + strConversationName
                Exit Function
            End If
        Case 4
! The take message option is available only in the user input table
            strAction = "Take Message"
        Case 5
! The skip greeting action is also available only in the user input table.
            strAction = "Skip Greeting"
        Case Else
            ! bad action value
            strAction = "Error in strConstructActionString - Invalid action value
                passed in:"+str(iAction)
    End Select
    StrConstructActionString = strAction
End Sub
```

With your action string routine in place, the rest of the call handler information dump work is not difficult. You can look in CUDLE and decide which high-level information you want off your call handler object itself and then walk through the related collections. The following code chunks assume you already have the rsCallHandler recordset open and pointing to the row with the call handler you are interested in.

To get all the transfer rules associated with a call handler, use this query:

```
RsTemp.Open "SELECT * FROM vw_ContactRule WHERE vw_
    ContactRule.ParentObjectID='"+rsCallHandlers("CallHandlerObjectID")+"'",
    strConnectionString, adOpenKeyset, adLockReadOnly
```

This should result in a recordset with three rows in it: the standard, off hours, and alternate transfer rules for the call handler. You can decide what information you want to gather and report on for each contact rule. Remember that like messaging rules, contact rules are enabled and disabled by using the TimeExpires column. A time in the future or set to NULL means the rule is active; a time in the past means it is disabled. The standard contact rule should *never* be disabled, even for primary call handlers where it is not used because the alternate is always enabled and overriding it. Other important information on a contact rule is if it is going to try and ring a phone or not which is determined by its action column: 0 means no transfer will take place and a 1 means the transfer will be attempted. If a transfer is enabled, you will need to report which transfer string, which is stored in the "Extension" column, is going to be used. There is also information about the number of rings, the transfer type, what we do when it is busy, and which switch (in the case of a dual switch integration) the contact rule is associated with. Again, a trip through the ContactRule table in CUDLE will help you decide which items you want to include in your report output.

To get all the greetings associated with a call handler, use this query:

```
RsTemp.Open "SELECT * FROM vw_MessagingRule WHERE vw_
    MessagingRule.ParentObjectID='"+rsCallHandlers("CallHandlerObjectID")+"'",
    strConnectionString, adOpenKeyset, adLockReadOnly
```

This should result in a recordset with six rows in it: the standard, off hours, alternate, busy, internal, and error greetings associated with the call handler. Items of interest in the greeting rows will be the Action, ConversationName, and DestinationObjectID set that determines what will happen with the call after the greeting plays as described previously. You also need to know the "PlayWhat" value that determines if Unity will play the canned system greeting (0), a custom recorded greeting (1), or a blank greeting (2). There is a number of other settings such as how many times the greeting will replay before taking the after greeting action, the path to the WAV file for a custom recorded greeting, if digits are being ignored during this greeting, and so on. Again, you can look through the table itself in CUDLE and decide which properties you want to report on. The only tricky bit is checking to see if the greeting rule is enabled or not using the TimeExpires column as described with the contact rules above.

To get all user input keys defined for a call handler, use this query:

```
RsTemp.Open "SELECT * FROM vw_MenuEntry WHERE vw_
    MenuEntry.ParentObjectID='"+rsCallHandlers("CallHandlerObjectID")+"'",
    strConnectionString, adOpenKeyset, adLockReadOnly
```

This should result in a recordset with 12 rows in it: one each for the keys 0-9, *, and, #. The primary information about a one-key rule is what its action values indicate will happen when the user presses that key while a greeting is playing for its parent call handler. The action string routine we built above will glean this information nicely for you using the Action, ConversationName, and DestinationObjectID columns. The only other piece of information on a user input key row that would be of interest is if the key is locked or not.

There are a number of other references in the call handler table to other tables that you should be able to figure out how to deal with fairly easily. The LocationObjectID references a row in the Location table, the ScheduleObjectName references a row in the Schedule table, and there's a set of action values for the After Message action as discussed previously. The AdministatorObjectID and RecipientObjectID, however, can reference either a subscriber or a public distribution list. You have to check the AdministratorObjectIDType and RecipientObjectIDType values to know which table to go look the ObjectID value up in. A value of 1 means it is a subscriber and a value of 2 means it is a public distribution list.

The only other piece of information on a call handler that needs special attention is the language it is assigned to. These are stored as four-digit Windows language codes. For example, the US English is language ID 1033. To convert them into human readable strings, you use a WinAPI call to do this. In VB you have to jump through a couple hoops to make this work because the language does not have pointers like C and C++ do, so you need to wrap the function to make it usable. The following code chunk can be found in the Call Handler Information Dump example as well:

Example 21-20 *Converting a Windows Language ID into a Human Readable String*

```
! WinAPI call as defined in VB to convert a language code into a language name
 string
Private Declare Function VerLanguageName& Lib "version.dll" Alias
  "VerLanguageNameA" (ByVal wLang As Long, ByVal szLang As String, ByVal nSize As
  Long)

! VB function that calls the above WinAPI function and passes back a usable string
to the calling routine. The string returned from the strLanguageIDToFullName
should be a full language description string that looks like "English (United
States)".
Public Function strLanguageIDToFullName(lLanguageID As Long) As String
Dim strBuffer As String
Dim rt As Long
! You need to preallocate space into the string and pass the string variable into
the WinAPI call to get the language name - this is how VB "simulates" pointers
for the purpose of dealing with the Win32 interface here.
    strBuffer = String$(256, vbNullChar)
    ! rt gets the number of characters read into the buffer
    rt = VerLanguageName(lLanguageID, strBuffer, Len(strBuffer))
    If rt > 0 Then
        strLanguageIDToFullName = Left(strBuffer, rt)
    Else
        strLanguageIDToFullName = "(error) No language found for ID=" +
            Str(lLanguageID)
    End If
End Function
```

We examine how to get at subscriber information for similar reporting type needs in the next section, "Subscriber Information Dump."

Subscriber Information Dump

Similar to the call handler information dump in the previous section, this example walks through the process of dumping out the basic information about any subscriber in the Unity server you are connected to. Of course, a healthy portion of the information about a subscriber is stored in their primary call handler, and you can use the previous example to mine that information. You just have to keep in mind that the alternate contact rule is always enabled for primary call handlers and you are good to go. We will be sticking to subscriber-specific data here.

As with the call handler information dump, I'm not going to go into too much detail here as this is mostly a process of knowing what tables the subscriber information you are interested in is stored and what the values mean. You need to make sure you have familiarized yourself with the object model and spend some time wandering around in CUDLE. You can get a full code listing for the Subscriber Information Dump on the code samples page of www.ciscounitytools.com. Here are some of the highlights for subscriber-related data.

You can use the same routine discussed in the previous section for constructing action strings for the exit destination that will take effect when the subscriber uses * to exit out of their subscriber conversation. By default, this goes to the opening greeting but as of 4.0(1) it can be customized on a per-user basis.

To retrieve the primary and alternate extensions for this subscriber, you need to make a simple query against the DTMFAccessID table:

```
"SELECT * FROM vw_DTMFAccessID WHERE ParentObjectID=SubscriberObjectID"
```

This will get both primary and alternate IDs. If you want to filter against just the primary or just the alternates, you can add a WHERE clause condition against the IsPrimaryID column being 0 or not.

To get the MWI devices for a subscriber is a similar affair:

```
SELECT * FROM vw_NotificationMWI WHERE ParentObjectID=SubscriberObjectID
```

A subscriber can have up to 10 MWI devices defined for their mailbox.

To get your notification devices and rules is a little trickier because the devices and rules are stored in separate tables and do not explicitly reference one another. They are associated only by their alias matching. As we discussed in Chapter 3, the device table contains the notification device information. The rules table contains the schedule and the triggering criteria that will activate its device counterpart.

To get information about, say, the Home Phone delivery for a subscriber you would need to get information from both tables using a query like this:

```
SELECT vw_NotificationRule.*, vw_NotificationDevice.* FROM vw_NotificationRule
   INNER JOIN vw_NotificationDevice ON vw_NotificationRule.DlvRuleDevice=vw_
   NotificationDevice.Alias WHERE vw_NotificationDevice.Alias='Home Phone Rule'
```

Most of the information associated with devices is straightforward. CUDLE includes the logic for how the schedules for notification rules are stored. This is an arrangement that is a result of the rules being included in Exchange 5.5's directory back in the 2.x days.

The language value found on the Subscriber table indicates which language callers hear when they call into the system to check messages. The language is set on the subscriber's primary call handler. The same language code handling discussed in the call handler dump example applies here.

As of Unity 4.0(1), each subscriber can dictate the order in which messages are presented to them in the subscriber message retrieval conversation for both the new message stack and the old (read) message stack. This is a feature called FlexStack and the settings for it are stored in the StackOrder column of the subscriber table. By default this column is NULL, which means the default stack order is used. Here is a chunk of code from the Subscriber Information Dump example that hows how to parse this string out for your users:

Example 21-21 *Displaying Message Stack Information for a Subscriber*

```
AddText "Active Stack message order for new messages"
If IsNull(rsSubscribers("StackOrder")) Then
     !The default for new the new message stack is FIFO
     AddText "    Stack Order= FIFO"
! The default order for new the new message stack items 1 through 7 in the order
laid out in this Choose function (which is just a short hand case statement in
VB by the way).  If the user has specified a specific order, the StackOrder
column will not be NULL and we will parse it out in the Else statement next.
     For iCounter = 1 To 7
          AddText "    " + Choose(iCounter, "Urgent Voice Mail", "Voice Mail",
               "Urgent Fax", "Fax", "Urgent Email", "Email", "Receipts")
     Next iCounter
  Else
!The user has customized the stack order, we need to pull out the string for new
messages.  The string looks something like this "NN:F1532467:0:L1234567".  In
this case we want the 7 characters after the "N:" which stands for new messages.
Check the description of this field in CUDLE for more details.  The string is
always the same length if it is not null so we can simply do this with a MID and
Choose function here in just a few lines of code.
The first character indicates if we're going to play messages for the stack in
question (new messages here) in LIFO or FIFO order - L or F respectively.
     If StrComp(Mid(rsSubscribers("StackOrder"), 4, 1), "L", vbTextCompare) = 0
       Then
          AddText "    Stack Order= LIFO"
     Else
          AddText "    Stack Order= FIFO"
     End If

!Now snag the 7 digits after the first character (position 5 in the string) and
we will parse it out to determine the order the user is palying messages for this
stack.
     strTemp = Mid(rsSubscribers("StackOrder"), 5, 7)
     For iCounter = 1 To 7

! Pull the numbers out of the string of 7 characters, one after another and print
the human readable representation of which message type plays in that spot.
          AddText "    " + Choose(Val(Mid(strTemp, iCounter, 1)), "Urgent Voice
               Mail", "Voice Mail", "Urgent Fax", "Fax", "Urgent Email", "Email",
               "Receipts")
     Next iCounter
  End If
```

continues

Example 21-21 *Displaying Message Stack Information for a Subscriber (Continued)*

```
! The read message stack info is stored in the same string as the new message
stack order, just after the "O:" near the end.  We will  run through the same
process here.
      AddText "Active Stack message order for read messages"
      If IsNull(rsSubscribers("StackOrder")) Then
! The default for read messages is LIFO
          AddText "      Stack Order= LIFO"
! The default order is message items 1 through 7 laid out in the "choose"
function below
          For iCounter = 1 To 7
              AddText "      " + Choose(iCounter, "Urgent Voice Mail", "Voice Mail",
                  "Urgent Fax", "Fax", "Urgent Email", "Email", "Receipts")
          Next iCounter
      Else
! The user has customized the stack order, we need to pull out the string for new
messages.  The string looks something like this "NN:F1532467:0:L1234567."  In
this case, we want the 7 characters after the "O:" which stands for old messages.
The string is always the same length if it is not null, so we can simply do this
with a MID function
          If StrComp(Mid(rsSubscribers("StackOrder"), 15, 1), "L", vbTextCompare) =
0 Then
              AddText "      Stack Order= LIFO"
          Else
              AddText "      Stack Order= FIFO"
          End If

          ! Grab the next 7 digits starting at string position 16.
          strTemp = Mid(rsSubscribers("StackOrder"), 16, 7)
          For iCounter = 1 To 7
! Pull the numbers out of the string of 7 characters one after another and print
the human readable representation of which message type plays in that spot.
              AddText "      " + Choose(Val(Mid(strTemp, iCounter, 1)), "Urgent Voice
                  Mail", "Voice Mail", "Urgent Fax", "Fax", "Urgent Email", "Email",
                  "Receipts")
          Next iCounter
      End If
```

Armed with the information here, you can generate a robust call handler and/or subscriber report and, with a little generalized application, you can apply that to other objects in the directory as well.

Create New Subscribers

Creating new subscribers requires you to work with the Unity server (Exchange 5.5, Active Directory, or Domino) to create objects and mailboxes external to Unity. In the case of Domino, this is not currently possible. The DUC interface provided by the Domino team does not allow for the ability to dynamically create accounts on the fly as we can in Exchange 5.5 and Active Directory. As such, this section only applies if your Unity servers are connected to Exchange 5.5, 2000, or 2003.

With the release of Unity 4.0(1), much of the ugly legwork for adding directory and mail accounts has now been nicely wrapped up in the SQLSyncSvr functionality, which is a huge win for folks wanting to do their own administration interfaces to Unity. The functionality is the primary reason we have waited until the release of 4.0 before documenting any external administration work. Prior to this, the work to deal with this from off box was nothing short of a nightmare. Now it is all handled for you on the back end through stored procedures.

The key to understanding adding, importing, editing, and deleting subscribers in Unity is understanding how this synchronization process works. Now is a good time to review the synchronization concept as covered in Chapter 2. Let us review the interaction with the directory process as it pertains to creating new users.

The first step is to ensure you have licenses to accommodate a new user or the group of users you want to add on the Unity server you want to create the subscriber on. Getting the license information from the Unity box is covered in the "Getting Version and Licensing Information" section earlier in this chapter. A couple of routines are defined in the Create Subscriber and Import Subscriber examples on the code samples page of www.ciscounitytools.com. These routines allow you to pass in if the CoS associated with the subscriber template is using TTS and/or VMI licenses, and it will return to you if you can or cannot create a new subscriber using that CoS on the box. In this case, you need to find the CoS referenced by the subscriber template you are using to create the subscriber. This is easy enough to do if you have the alias or ObjectID of the subscriber template using this code:

Example 21-22 *Finding if the CoS Referenced by a Subscriber Template Uses TTS or VMI Licenses*

```
StrSQL="SELECT AccessTTS, AccessVMI FROM vw_COS INNER JOIN vw_SubscriberTemplate ON
    vw_SubscriberTemplate.COSOBjectID=vw_COS.CosObjectID WHERE vw_
    SubscriberTemplate.Alias='" + strAlias + "'"

RsCOS.Open strSQL, strConnectionString, adOpenKeyset, adLockReadOnly

!You can check out the source for this routine in either the Create Subscriber or
    Import Subscriber code samples.
If checkForAvailableLicense(strUnityServerName, rsCOS("AccessTTS"),
    rsCOS("AccessVMI")) = False Then
        ! <no licenses available to add new user to that COS>
Else
        ! <code to create subscriber>
EndIf
```

If you decide to exceed your license limits, the SA will no longer allow you to add/import users directly. Errors will be logged daily to the application event log warning you that you are out of compliance and you need to either purchase more licenses or delete users. Eventually, Unity will shut itself down entirely. In short, you want to be careful not to exceed your license counts and, if you do, remedy the situation post haste. Once you know your licensing is OK, the next step is adding the information about the subscriber into the local SQL database in the Subscriber table using the sp_CreateSubscriber stored procedure. The stored procedure requires you to pass in a primary extension number; a reference for a subscriber template to use when creating the subscriber, and the new subscriber's alias, first, and last names. You can optionally pass a number of other items in, such as the display name, SMTP Address, AddressByExtension value, language, and so on. Not all properties associated with a subscriber can be customized in this call to create the subscriber; if you want to fiddle with things such as alternate extensions, greeting rules, contact rule configuration, and the like you will have to do that after the user has been created. This stored procedure will use the subscriber template you pass in and create the subscriber's primary call handler and all the associated objects such as contact rules, messaging rules, user input keys, notification devices, and so on. The subscriber will be complete in the database with one big exception; they will not have a mailbox or a directory account.

The next step is to create the aforementioned directory and mailbox accounts. You can do this by setting the DirectorySync and DirectorySyncFlags values into the stored procedure such that Unity will attempt to create these accounts for you automatically when you add the subscriber to SQL. This process is asynchronous, which means the stored procedure is going to return to you right away. If you want to see if the user was successfully added to the directory, you need to pass in a DirectorySyncTicket, watch the DirectorySyncTicket table, and wait for your ticket to show up there with a pass or fail grade. You definitely do not want to assume the user has been added to the directory because this can fail for any number of reasons, all of which are external to Unity and out of your control. If the user failed to get a directory and mailstore object created, you need to report that error back to the user somehow and back that user out of SQL by deleting their subscriber record. Triggers in SQL will automatically remove all their associated information in other tables as needed.

You can also do this by adding a bunch of subscribers to SQL using the same sp_CreateSubscriber stored procedure and not passing in any DirectorySync flags. When you are done adding users to the database, you can call the sp_DirectorySync stored procedure and have it synchronize all users in the Subscriber table that do not have a DirectoryID value. The lack of a DirectoryID value indicates the user does not have an object in the directory associated with them and, as such, they are not a valid subscriber. We cover this method of adding and importing users in bulk in the "Batch Subscriber Operations" section later in this chapter.

The directory creation function is done using the rights of the domain account you have associated with your directory facing accounts in Unity—specifically, the account associated with the directory facing account such as AvDSAD service in the case of Exchange 2000/2003 or AvDSEx55 in the case of Exchange 5.5. If the permissions on that account do not have rights to create new user objects in the container specified (which defaults to the container you selected during Unity configuration setup if you do not override it when calling the sp_CreateSubscriber stored procedure) then the create will fail.

You need to be sure that account has all the permissions you need for creating users where you want.

The high-level details here are clear-cut. Let us work through the code needed to do this and discuss some of the options you have along the way. This is part of the code you find in the Create Subscriber example found on the source code samples page of www.ciscounitytools.com:

Example 21-23 *Creating a New Subscriber*

```
! This function returns true if the subscriber has their directory object and
mailbox created OK and false otherwise.  This function is specifically set up to
add only a new user to the directory, it will not allow the synchronization
process to bind to an existing user in the directory.  It is a good idea
for you to follow the same convention to avoid accidents in your
directory.  For binding to existing users, you should use a separate import
function as discussed in the next section.

!This function returns true of the subscriber was properly created and false
otherwise.
Public Function CreateSubscriber() As Boolean
Dim rsCreate As ADODB.Recordset
Dim oCommand As ADODB.Command
Dim strSyncTicket As String
Dim iCounter As Integer
Dim strTemp As String

    Set rsCreate = New ADODB.Recordset
    Set oCommand = New ADODB.Command

    oCommand.ActiveConnection = strConnectionString
    oCommand.CommandType = adCmdStoredProc

!I assume at this point that you have already gathered the alias, extension number,
the alias of the subscriber template you want to use for creating this user and
their first and last names.  If you are getting this from the user directly or
slurping it in from a CSV file or whatever is not really important to the
creation process here.
    oCommand.CommandText = "sp_CreateSubscriber"

! It is a good idea to use the CreateParameter function provided off the Command
object in ADO here to add parameters to your stored procedure as it takes
care of expunging stray single quotes and the like automatically to protect yourself
from malicious people slipping in ugly stuff into your SQL commands.  You
can build a straight string with the parameters yourself but all my code uses
this method.
```

continues

Example 21-23 *Creating a New Subscriber (Continued)*

In this example, the alias, extension number (DTMFAccessID), first name, last name, and display name are being pulled off of text controls on the main form that the user has populated manually. You can, of course, snag this information any way you like.

```
oCommand.Parameters.Item("@Alias") = oCommand.CreateParameter("Alias",
    adVarChar, adParamInput, , txtAlias.Text)
oCommand.Parameters.Item("@DtmfAccessId") =
    oCommand.CreateParameter("DtmfAccessId", adVarChar, adParamInput, ,
    txtExtension.Text)
oCommand.Parameters.Item("@FirstName") = oCommand.CreateParameter("FirstName",
    adVarChar, adParamInput, , txtFirstName.Text)
oCommand.Parameters.Item("@LastName") = oCommand.CreateParameter("LastName",
    adVarChar, adParamInput, , txtLastName.Text)
oCommand.Parameters.Item("@DisplayName") =
    oCommand.CreateParameter("DisplayName", adVarChar, adParamInput, ,
    txtDisplayName.Text)
```

! For this example, I assume we're creating a full Exchange subscriber here, not an internet subscriber so we hard code the SubscriberType parameter to "1". You can, as always, check CUDLE for the different subscriber type values allowed here; however, creating remote users is a bit of a different bag than creating full subscribers so be sure you know what you are doing.

```
oCommand.Parameters.Item("@SubscriberType") =
    oCommand.CreateParameter("SubscriberType", adInteger, adParamInput, , 1)
```

! Only the default Example Administrator account should be marked undeletable. However, in special cases, you might want to add your own accounts that cannot be deleted from the SA interface as well. Here I assume the normal case of deletable.

```
oCommand.Parameters.Item("@Undeletable") =
    oCommand.CreateParameter("Undeletable", adInteger, adParamInput, , 0)
```

! You can pass either the alias of a subscriber template here as I do or, perhaps better style, the SubscriberTemplateObjectID value into the @templateOid parameter instead. Either way will work fine, I use the alias here because it was easier to list it in a combo box and have the user select one.

```
oCommand.Parameters.Item("@templateAlias") =
    oCommand.CreateParameter("templateAlias", adVarChar, adParamInput, ,
    cmbTemplates.Text)
```

! The UID and the alias should almost always match - the UID is actually what maps to the mail alias in the directory - the alias field above is used internally by Unity - if you do not pass a UID value it'll use the Alias string but it is a good idea to always pass it explicitly to avoid any confusion.

```
oCommand.Parameters.Item("@Uid") = oCommand.CreateParameter("Uid", ,
    adParamInput, adVarChar, txtAlias.Text)
```

! The phone password is passed in as clear text here —and it gets crunched and encrypted into MD5 by the stored procedure during the subscriber create process. This parameter is optional, the subscriber template has a default phone password that will be applied if this is not included.

```
oCommand.Parameters.Item("@PWDTMF") = oCommand.CreateParameter("PWDTMF",
    adVarChar, adParamInput, , txtPhonePassword.Text)
```

Example 21-23 *Creating a New Subscriber (Continued)*

```
! Another optional value is to list the user in the directory based on a checkbox
value on the main form.  Again, the subscriber template will fill in a default
value for this if it is not passed in.
    oCommand.Parameters.Item("@ListInDirectory") =
        oCommand.CreateParameter("ListInDirectory", adBoolean, adParamInput, ,
        chkListUsersInDirectory.Value = vbChecked)

! The mail store you create the user on can be left up to the back end if you like;
it will create the user in the Organization Unit (E2K) or user container (E55) you
selected during the mail store configuration setup portion of the Unity install.
If you would like to dictate a particular mail store you need to include the
MailboxStoreObjectID value from the MailboxStore table for the store you want.
We have this information stored on the form in two drop- down controls on the
main form in my example here.  The MailboxStore table will include ALL
mail stores visible in the forest or organization.  Remember, it is up to you to
make sure the domain account you have associated with the Unity directory
services has rights to create users in this container.  The Permissions Wizard
will check only the one container you selected during initial setup.
On my form I have a readable list of mail store names in the cmbMailstores combo
box and a list of MailstoreObjectID values in the hidden cmbMailstoreObjectIDs
combo box.  The two are tied together using the list ID values such that when a
user selects a readable mail store name we can fish out it is objectID easily.
! With a decent third-party grid control at your disposal this would be a little
better but we are trying to keep the sample code generic.
    oCommand.Parameters.Item("@MailboxStoreObjectID") =
        oCommand.CreateParameter("MailboxStoreObjectID", adGUID, adParamInput, ,
        cmbMailstoreObjectIDs.List(cmbMailStores.ListIndex))

! You usually want to tell the stored procedure to synchronize SQL to the
directory for this subscriber after adding them so you should pass a 1 for the
DirectorySync flag here.  In rare cases, you might want to add users without
synching and then do it "all at once" after, say, a big batch operation.  We will
deal with that scenario in the Batch Subscriber Operations section later.
    oCommand.Parameters.Item("@DirectorySync") =
        oCommand.CreateParameter("DirectorySync", adInteger, adParamInput, , 1)

! We want to pass in a resynch mask that synchs the subscriber, the DLs they were
added to and to only try create a new object in AD, not to bind to an existing
one if the mail alias happens to match something already there. The
synchronization process accepts a number of flags to control what it is going to
write to the directory from the SQL database.  Here's a list of the flags of
interest to us:

! 0x00000001 - synch subscribers
0x00000002 - synch distribution lists
0x00000008 - synch locations.  For synching new users this flag does not apply.
                     You would only use this if you were creating or editing
                     delivery location objects.
0x0000FFFF - synch all types
0x01000000 - only synch new guys without directory ID values - used for batch
                     processing.  In this case where we are synching an
                     individual user this flag does not apply.
```

continues

Example 21-23 *Creating a New Subscriber (Continued)*

```
0x02000000 - do not create anything, just try to associate to existing object.
                        This prevents accidental object creation in AD.
0x04000000 - only try to create new, do not attempt to associate
0x08000000 - Create NT account - for use with Ex55 systems.  You have the
                        option of only creating a mailbox in Exchange 5.5 and not
                        an NT account to go with it.  This would prevent the user
                        from getting access to the SA or PCA interfaces but might
                        be desirable in some scenarios.  This example is written
                        against Exchange 2000 so I do not pass this in.

! The values we're interested in for this operation are to create only new
subscribers and to sync distribution lists that user might have been added via
their subscriber template definition.  These flags are 0x04000000 + 0x00000001 +
0x00000002 = 67108867 decimal.  With this flag if there is a conflicting alias
in the directory in the domain the user is being added to, the sync will be
considered a failure and the user will not be added.
    oCommand.Parameters.Item("@DirectorySyncFlags") =
    oCommand.CreateParameter("DirectorySyncFlags", adInteger, adParamInput, ,
    67108867)

! We need to create a GUID that we can pass into the stored procedure such that we
can look for it in the DirectorySyncTicket table in SQL which is used to pass
back the results of this sync - we have to use an asynchronous process here
Because the synch with AD can take a while and doing a blocking call for such
things is not a good idea.  See below where we wait for the ticket to get
inserted into the table and let us know how things went.  If you do not pass a
synch ticket here, no record is created in the DirectorySyncTicket table.  We
show another method of dealing with this issue in the Subscriber Batch
Operations section later.  The generateDirectorySyncTicket is routine that calls
the "GUID" function in the Scriptlet.TypeLib library.  This just generates a
random GUID we can use as a unique identifier to watch for - you can get the
code behind this in the full listing for this example on
www.ciscounitytools.com.
    strSyncTicket = generateDirectorySyncTicket
    oCommand.Parameters.Item("@DirectorySyncTicket") =
    oCommand.CreateParameter("DirectorySyncTicket", adGUID, adParamInput, ,
    strSyncTicket)

! Execute the stored procedure.  Remember, this will return right away even
if you have asked it to sync the user to the directory.
    rsCreate.CursorLocation = adUseClient
    rsCreate.Open oCommand, , adOpenDynamic, adLockOptimistic

! The SP will return a recordset populated with one row for the subscriber you
added.  The row returned is from the subscriber table in UnityDb so if you want
to customize your users' properties with items that are not included in the
stored procedure's parameters, now is your chance.  If something went wrong, the
recordset will be empty.
    If rsCreate.RecordCount = 0 Then
        MsgBox "SubscriberCreate stored procedure failed: " + Err.Description
        CreateSubscriber = False
! Because the subscriber creation stored procedure failed to create anything,
```

Example 21-23 *Creating a New Subscriber (Continued)*

```
        there is nothing to clean up here.  We can just exit out after cleaning up the
        local recordsets
          GoTo BailOut
          End If


    ! The stored procedure itself kicked off the synchronization process with the
    directory using the flags we used above. You need to wait for the synch to
    complete here and check for errors before moving on unless you are doing some
    batch operation or you have a note from your mother stating otherwise.  The
    WaitForSyncToFinish function will wait for the syncher to finish and will also
    take care of cleaning up the synch ticket row for you as well as rolling back
    the subscriber add if it fails for whatever reason.  The code listing for this
    function follows shortly.

          If WaitforSyncToFinish (strSyncTicket) = False Then
    ! We remove the subscriber using the sp_DeleteSubscriber stored procedure here,
    because leaving a subscriber that has not properly been tied to a directory object
    in SQL is a bad idea all around.  The only required parameter for this stored
    procedure is the SubscriberObjectId value which we have off the rsCreate
    recordset returned from the subscriber creation stored procuedure earlier.
                oCommand.CommandText = "sp_DeleteSubscriber"

                oCommand.Parameters.Item("@SubscriberObjectID") =
                  oCommand.CreateParameter("SubscriberObjectID", adGUID, adParamInput,
                  , rsCreate("SubscriberObjectID")
    ! There is no reason to pass in any flags to force a directory synch here because
    this guy was not tied to a directory object to begin with.  As such, just
    execute the stored procedure here.  Triggers in SQL will take care of getting
    rid of all the related objects in the database associated with this subscriber
    such as it is primary call handler, MWI entries, notification devices and so on.
                oCommand.Execute

                CreateSubscriber=False
                MsgBox "The syncronization to the directory failed for this subscriber
                  add.  Subscriber removed from SQL.  You can check the SQLSyncSvr
                  logs in the \commserver\logs directory for more details."

          Else
                CreateSubscriber=True
                MsgBox "Subscriber Added"
          End If
    BailOut:
    ! clean up after ourselves - not strictly necessary with the VB garbage collection
    stuff but not a bad thing to do in general
    On Error Resume Next
          rsCreate.Close
          Set rsCreate = Nothing
          Set oCommand = Nothing
    End Function
```

If the sync process went through then the subscriber is ready to roll. The licensing service will automatically update the used license counts and, if you are in a pooled license scenario, push that information out to the directory for the other Unity servers to know about. You should not need to do anything other than checking for available license counts up front before adding a new user.

We have consolidated the logic for waiting for a synchronization operation to complete and cleaning up after myself into one function because it is something that needs to be done so often. Whenever you add, delete, or edit a subscriber or add, delete, or edit a distribution list, you have to synchronize that information to the directory. It is a good idea to get such a function in place in your own applications early on because you need to use it often.

Example 21-24 *Routine to Wait for Directory Synchronization to Finish*

```
! The WaitForSyncToFinish function returns TRUE of the synchronization succeeds
  and FALSE if it fails.  In either case, it will clean up the SyncTicket table
  when it is done.
Public Function WaitForSyncToFinish(strSyncTicket As String) As Boolean
Dim rsSyncTicket As ADODB.Recordset
Dim iCounter As Integer
Dim oCommand As ADODB.Command

    Set rsSyncTicket = New ADODB.Recordset
    Set oCommand = New ADODB.Command
    oCommand.ActiveConnection = strConnectionString
    oCommand.CommandType = adCmdStoredProc

! I have this hard coded to check every 2 seconds up to 20 times (40 seconds).
You can change this or make it a parameter you pass in or whatever.  If it takes
more than 40 seconds to sync something to the directory, however, you have some
latency issues outside of Unity that you need to take a close look at.
    For iCounter = 1 To 20
        Sleep 2000
        rsSyncTicket.Open "SELECT * FROM vw_DirectorySyncTicket WHERE Ticket='" +
            strSyncTicket + "'", strConnectionString, adOpenKeyset, adLockReadOnly
        If rsSyncTicket.RecordCount > 0 Then
! The record is created and then the result value is populated in it, the timing
can bite you here, so after we open the recordset and find a match on the
DirectorySyncTicket check the result value. It should never be NULL so if it
is, fall through and close/reopen the record set in another 2 seconds.
            If IsNull(rsSyncTicket("result")) = False Then
                GoTo TicketFound
            End If
        End If
        rsSyncTicket.Close
    Next iCounter

! We timed out waiting for the synchronization to complete.  There is no row to
remove so we can just pull the rip cord here.
    WaitForSyncToFinish = False
    GoTo BailOut
```

Example 21-24 *Routine to Wait for Directory Synchronization to Finish (Continued)*

```
TicketFound:
    rsSyncTicket.MoveFirst
    If rsSyncTicket("result") = 0 Then
        ! You are golden, everything finished OK.
        WaitForSyncToFinish = True
    Else
        ! You have not been living right and the synch failed for some reason.
        WaitForSyncToFinish = False
    End If

! Because we explicitly requested a synch ticket we need to clean up that row
in the DirectorySyncTicket table
    oCommand.CommandText = "sp_DeleteDirectorySyncTicket"
    oCommand.Parameters.Item("@Ticket") = oCommand.CreateParameter("Ticket",
        adGUID, adParamInput, , rsSyncTicket("Ticket"))
    oCommand.Execute

BailOut:
    On Error Resume Next
    Set oCommand = Nothing
    rsSyncTicket.Close
    Set rsSyncTicket = Nothing
End Function
```

We reference the WaitForSyncToFinish function in other routines that require synchronization to the directory later in this chapter.

Import Subscriber

You can import subscribers from Active Directory (Exchange 2000/20003), Exchange 5.5, or Domino. This example uses the alias of the subscriber to find the user in the directory and, assuming that value is unique (it really should be for Exchange), this will work fine across all back ends Unity can be connected to. If you have a situation where the alias is not unique in Active Directory or Domino, then you need to also pass in the DirectoryID value which is discussed at the end of this section. In the case of Domino, the alias maps to the short name for the user, which might not be unique, so it is a good idea to pass in the Unique ID (UID) of the user as the DirectoryID to ensure we match up with the right user. The full code listing for this example on www.ciscounitytools.com is specific to importing users from Active Directory because it shows how to navigate the directory using a tree control; however, the base code for importing users via SQL stored procedures is a valid for all back ends.

Importing a subscriber is similar to creating a new one except you are expecting the SQLSyncer to bind to an existing object in the directory instead of creating a new one. The chances of failure here are much less than in creating a new user; however, it is not a slam dunk so you need to check for success or failure here.

You use the same sp_CreateSubscriber stored procedure that you do for creating a new user. Yes, there is a sp_ImportSubscriber stored procedure but that is specifically for use by the dbImport tool as it is pulling 2.x data into a 3.x and 4.x system. You definitely do *not* want to use that one for importing users from your directory. In fact, you will not even find it in Unity 4.0(3) and later versions because the FullDBImport application was depreciated and it was no longer necessary. You need to follow the same procedure for importing a user as for creating a new user outlined before. First check for available licenses, then fill in the required values for the sp_CreateSubscriber stored procedure, then synchronize with the directory and check the results. There are a couple of differences for the import scenario, however.

The first and most important difference is in the flags passed in for the synchronization option. We want to pass in a resynch mask that synchs the subscriber and the DLs they were added to. We only want to bind to an existing Active Directory object, not create a new one if a match in Active Directory is not found for the alias (and directory ID if you choose to pass that in). Remember, from the list of flags in the last section, that 0x02000000 means to not create anything and to only look for an existing directory object to bind with, and if none is found to fail. The values for these flags are 0x02000000 + 0x00000001 (sync subscribers) + 0x00000002 (sync distribution list changes) = 33554435 decimal. So the DirectorySyncFlags parameter looks like this for import:

```
oCommand.Parameters.Item("@DirectorySyncFlags") =
  oCommand.CreateParameter("DirectorySyncFlags", adInteger, adParamInput, , 33554435)
```

Yes, you could not pass any specific flag in and tell it to synch the subscriber and distribution list and not specifically limit it to creating a new user or importing an existing user only. If you do not pass in the 0x02000000 or the 0x04000000 values then the syncher will simply try to find the user, and if no one is found, then create a user on the fly. We do not recommend this, however, as it is easy to get into situations where you accidentally create a directory account you did not mean to or bind to an existing account you did not intend to. It is best to have explicit imports and create functions to prevent problems like this.

The second difference is you can pass in the DirectoryID of a user in the directory and the SQLSyncSvr will use that value for searching for the user before then searching for the alias. You must still pass in the alias value here as well, but if you are concerned about mail aliases not being unique in your directory you might want to go this route. Technically, you can have the same alias in multiple domains in Active Directory. However, the practice is a bad idea in most cases. The SQLSyncSvr will first try to find the directory ID if it is passed in. If no match is found or it is not passed in, it will search for a user by alias in the domain. If that fails to find a match, we will consider it a failure because we are passing in synchronization flags that force it to only bind to an existing user and not to create one. You could, of course, have it quickly create a new account (for Active Directory and Exchange 5.5) but, as a rule, we do not recommend that practice.

To add the directory ID you would include this extra line in the stored procedure construction code:

```
oCommand.Parameters.Item("@DirectoryId") =
    oCommand.CreateParameter("DirectoryId", adVarChar, adParamInput, ,
strDirectoryId
```

The full code listing for the Import Subscriber example on the website also shows how to navigate around Active Directory and retrieve the directory ID of the user you want to import. What we refer to as the DirectoryID value is actually the ObjectGUID value in Active Directory. We convert this into a string before stuffing it into SQL or using it in a stored procedure. The same conversion needs to take place if you are importing a subscriber by DirectoryID or a public distribution list (discussed later). The logic for converting the GUID in Active Directory into a string looks like this:

Example 21-25 *Converting a GUID into a String*

```
!This function converts the ObjectGUID value in Active Directory into a
DirectoryID string that we store in SQL and that the stored procedures can use
to find the user in the directory.  The ObjectGUID property on the user is
stored as an array of 16 byes - to convert it to a usable DirectoryID string we
need to convert each of those bytes to a zero padded hex value (i.e. 7=0x07,
18=0x12 etc...) and link the values into one 32 character long string
which is what is stored in SQL and passed into the stored procedures.  If you have
used ADSI to search by this value you also know you have to do a similar
conversion to get it to work properly there as well.
Function strConvertObjectGUIDToString(unityUser As IADsUser) As String
Dim iCounter As Integer
Dim strTemp As String
Dim strDirectoryID As String

! Walk through each of the 16 bytes in the array off the ObjectGUID property for
the user.  For the record, the ObjectGUID off a distribution list needs to be
converted in the same way.
    For iCounter = 0 To 15
        strTemp = vbNullString
        strTemp = Trim(Hex(unityUser.Get("OBjectGUID")(iCounter)))

        !if the value is only one character, force it to be zero padded on the left
        If Len(strTemp) = 1 Then
            strTemp = "0" + strTemp
        End If
        strDirectoryID = strDirectoryID + strTemp
    Next iCounter

    strConvertObjectGUIDToString = strDirectoryID

    Exit Function
```

In Domino, the DirectoryID value corresponds to the UID of the user in the directory. Again, you can pass just the alias of the user or both the alias and the DirectoryID (UID) to bind to an existing user in Domino. This is the only method for adding new subscribers to Domino programmatically because creating new users is not supported.

Other than those differences, the procedure is identical to that outlined for creating new subscribers including the synchronization ticket handling. In the "Batch Subscriber Operations" section later, we discuss how to import in bulk which is also similar to bulk create operations.

Edit Subscriber

Editing properties on subscribers is straightforward. However, you need to keep in mind that when you change some properties on a subscriber, if you do not force those values to write through to the directory, they will not stick. As soon as another change happens on the subscriber or their user object in the directory, the local value you stuffed into SQL will get stomped on. For example, if you add an alternate extension for a subscriber in SQL but do not initiate a directory synchronization to force that value into the directory, it will appear to be fine for a while. Being the careful engineer that you are, you do test calls and SA lookups to be sure it is working and then go home. Days later your extension is suddenly gone! Unity has a heinous bug and is dropping data randomly! Yes, we have gotten several such escalations. This is an easy trap to fall in, one I've tripped up on myself from time to time. Eventually SQL triggers will take care of knowing which changed values require a synch with the directory, but for now it is up to you to ask for the synch when you edit the user.

So, which properties do you need to worry about? The easiest way to approach this is to look at what all Unity will synch with in the directory. For Active Directory, you can turn on AvDSAD traces to see what the directory monitor writes through when you make a change to a subscriber in the SA. This was demonstrated in the "Architectural Overview" discussion in Chapter 2. For review, 27 values are pushed into and/or pulled from the directory when you make a change to a subscriber. All properties are pushed and fetched regardless of what you have changed; the SA is not smart enough to know which property you have changed so it asks the directory writer to push or get them all regardless. Some of these properties are read-only from Unity's perspective so we will only get updated values from the directory and pull them in.

The following is a quick rundown on the 27 properties we keep synched with in the directory; a good chunk of them are things you will not (or should not) be changing in the local SQL database:

- **AddrType**. This indicates what type of mailstore the subscriber is connected to. Currently this can be "55" for Exchange 55, "2K" for Exchange 2000, or "DO" for Domino. This is one of those read-only properties you should never be changing in SQL, or you will wreak all kinds of havoc.

- **Alias**. Once a user is created in the directory you should not be changing this value in SQL and then synching it through. You should only set this value in SQL when creating or importing a new user. Once created, this value should not be changed in SQL again.

- **AMISDisableOutbound**. This only applies for Analog Messaging Interface System (AMIS) remote subscribers. It is used to indicate that someone received an AMIS delivery attempt through an Internet subscriber and requested their number not be called by pressing the indicated DTMF keys in the conversation. This property does not exist for full subscribers.

- **AlternateDTMFIDs**. If you add, remove, or update any alternate DTMF IDs in the DTMFAccessID table, you need to synch those changes through to the directory or they will be lost.

- **DirectoryID**. This is the unique identifier for the user in the directory and once it is set you should never change it in SQL. You can set it when importing a new subscriber from the directory, but once it is filled in you should never touch it. It is a read-only property from Unity's perspective.

- **DisplayName**. If you change the display name on a subscriber, you need to synch that change to the directory or it will be lost.

- **DTMFAccessID**. If you change the primary extension number of a subscriber, you need to synch that change through to the directory or it will be lost. In versions prior to Unity 4.0(3), this value was actually stored in the DTMFAccessID column of the primary call handler associated with the subscriber. In 4.0(3) and later, that column is removed (though preserved through the views to remain backwards compatible) and is instead stored in the DTMFaccessID table.

- **FirstName**. If you change the first name of a subscriber, you need to synch it through to the directory or it will be lost.

- **LastName**. If you change the last name of a subscriber, you need to synch it through to the directory or it will be lost.

- **ListInDirectory**. If you change the list in directory status of a subscriber, you need to synch it through to the directory or it will be lost. This allows or restricts the subscriber from appearing in any name lookup handler (directory handler) in the system.

- **LocationObjectID**. For full subscribers you would never change their location object ID assignment because all full subscribers are associated with the one primary location object on the Unity server they are created on. You cannot change location assignments on the fly.

- **MailDatabase**. This points to the message store in the mail database that the subscriber's inbox is stored on. You should never touch this value; it is read- only from Unity's perspective. If the user is actually moved between mail servers in the back end, the directory monitors will pick up on this change and update this value for you. You never need to change this value on your own.

- **MailboxID**. This points to the specific mailbox in the mail database this subscriber is associated with. You should never touch this value; it is read-only from Unity's perspective.

- **MailboxSendLimit**. This value is only pulled from the directory in; it is not pushed out. You should never change it in SQL; it is read-only from Unity's perspective. If you need to change this value for an Exchange back end, you can use the Message Store Manager to accomplish that as well as the receive and warning limits below. The MSM utility uses Collaborative Data Objects (CDO) interfaces to make this change. The Unity directory monitors do not have the ability to fiddle with these values in the mailstore at this point.

- **MailboxRecieveLimit**. This value is only pulled from the directory in and its value is not pushed out. You should never change it; it is read-only from Unity's perspective.

- **MailboxWarningLimit**. This value is only pulled from the directory in and its value is not pushed out. You should never never change it; it is read-only from Unity's perspective.

- **ObjectChangedID**. This value is used to keep track of who has the newer version of the user's information: the directory or the local SQL database. The only time you should touch this value is if you are trying to force the synch to pull in data from the directory into SQL for this user. You could set the value to 0 in SQL, which would force the directory monitor to take the information in the directory and pull it in for that record because obviously 0 is going to be less than any change ID found in the directory. The reasons for doing this are rare but include disaster recovery scenarios. Outside of that, you should never be fiddling with this value in the database.

- **PrimaryFaxNumber**. This is the value stored in the Fax Number field in Exchange and it shows up as the Fax ID value in the SA. If you change it in the database, you need to synch it through to the directory or the change will be lost.

- **RecipientEmailAddress**. This maps through to the AddressId in SQL and is read-only from Unity's perspective.

- **RemoteAddress**. The only time you edit this value in SQL would be for Internet subscribers (AMIS, Bridge, VPIM, and SMTP subscribers), and even then only if you know what you are doing. You should never touch this for full subscribers.

- **SID**. You should never alter this value in SQL at all. This is what is passed through to Unity from IIS when a user attempts to gain access to the web-based system administration console or the Cisco Unity Personal Communications Assistant (CPCA) or the like. This is read-only from Unity's perspective.

- **SIDHistory**. This value is read-only and should not be changed. If you need to map an alternate directory SID to a Unity subscriber account, you can do this in the Credentials table in SQL using the GrantUnityAccess command-line tool.

- **SMTPAddress**. The full SMTP address associated with the subscriber. Typically, the mail server automatically generates this upon user creation. You should not be changing this value in SQL; it's read-only from Unity's perspective.

- **VoiceName**. If you change the recorded voice name of a subscriber (or remove it), you need to synch that change through to the directory or it will be lost.

XferString. If you change the Extension value on the Alternate Contact rule associated with the subscriber's primary call handler, that change should write through to the "Xfer-String" column on the subscriber through a trigger. If you are going to change the subscriber's transfer string, you need to do it on the alternate contact rule. Then, let the trigger do the copy, and then synch the change through to the directory. If you just change the Xfer-String directly, it will not have the desired effect. This value is used for cross-box transfers when servers are in the same dialing domain.

There are nine properties you might change on subscribers that require you to request the SQLSyncSvr to push the information into the directory for you:

- Alternate extensions
- Primary extension
- Display name
- First name
- Last name
- List in directory
- Primary fax number
- Voice name
- Transfer string

Keep this list handy somewhere because you need to be careful to force a synch only when necessary. Doing a synchronization to the directory is time-consuming and if you are editing properties on users that do not need to be updated in the directory, you do not want to ask for the synch.

The next thing you should be concerned about is how you go about editing properties associated with subscribers. As we have noted throughout, whenever doing adds and updates, you should always use stored procedures if you can. Information about subscribers is, of course, stored in several tables. Because Chapter 3 goes in-depth on the topic of tables, we will be brief here. We do want to note the list of stored procedures necessary to edit values in all the tables you need for subscriber information:

- Sp_ModifyCallHandler
- Sp_ModifyContactRule
- Sp_ModifyMenuEntry
- Sp_ModifyNotificationDevice
- Sp_ModifyNotificationMWI
- Sp_ModifySubscriber
- Sp_AddAltDTMFID 4.0(3)
- Csp_MessagingRuleModify 4.0(4) and later

- Sp_RemoveAltDTMFIDsByOID (4.0(3))
- Csp_DTMFAccessIDAlternateExtensionCreate (4.0(4) and later)
- Csp_DTMFAccessIDAlternateExtensionDelete (4.0(4) and later)
- Csp_DTMFAccessIDAlternateExtensionModify (4.0(4) and later)

The Alternate DTMFAccessID values do not require you to edit the table as much as add and remove rows. In Unity 4.0(3) and earlier versions, there is a pair of stored procedures necessary for that: sp_AddAltDTMFID and sp_RemoveAltDEMFIDsByOID. Be aware, however, that the sp_RemoveAltDTMFIDsByOID will remove *all* alternate IDs for the subscriber you identify by their ObjectID. In Unity 4.0(4) there are three new stored procedures for dealing with alternate extensions noted above.

In 4.0(3) and earlier there is no stored procedure to remove or edit a standing alternate ID. In versions of Unity prior to 4.0(3), you change the primary extension of the subscriber on the DTMFAccessID column of the primary call handler associated with that subscriber. SQL triggers then take care of pushing the updated value into the DTMFAccessID table as necessary. For Unity 4.0(3) that column only exists in the view for backwards compatibility. Regardless, the sp_ModifySubscriber stored procedure allows you to update the primary extension, and it will take care of doing the dirty work on the back end for you.

The keen observer will notice that there is no sp_ModifyMessagingRule to update greetings for subscribers. There is an sp_SetMessagingRule but we dislike that stored procedure because if it does not find the rule you asked it to find; it creates one on the fly! This is a bad practice because you do not want to create new messaging rules unless you are writing the setup scripts for Unity. Also, it does not contain all the properties for messaging rules that you might need to edit. This is an unfortunate state of affairs, but unavoidable unless you use the release of 4.0(4) or later. For Unity 4.0(3) and earlier, we will have to edit the messaging rule tables directly through raw table access. If you are using 4.0(4) or later, you will definitely want to change over to using the stored procedure because, as we mentioned earlier, changes in the database architecture will be phased in over the next few 4.0(x) releases.

We are not going to exhaustively cover every possible property on subscribers that you can change; you should be able to extrapolate what you need here and use the Data Object Model information to run down which table has the information you want to change. we will cover a couple examples here and you can check out the "Edit Subscriber" sample project on the code samples page of www.ciscounitytools.com for more.

Add an Alternate Extension to a Subscriber, Unity 4.0(4) and Earlier

This section covers the process of adding an alternate extension for a subscriber on Unity 4.0(3) and earlier systems. In Unity 4.0(4), the concept of reserved ordering of alternate extensions was added that requires you take into account which alternate extension you want to add. Prior to 4.0(4) all the alternate extensions were simply stored in an unordered bucket, so it did not matter. Be sure to use the appropriate technique for the version of Unity you are working with.

The process of adding an alternate extension is easy. You just need the SubscriberObjectID value of the user you want to add and the DTMFID you want to add, and then you call the sp_AddAltDTMFIDByOID stored procedure. However, you need to be aware of a few pitfalls here.

First, it is up to you to limit the number of alternate extensions to nine. If you add more than nine, the SA pages that show this information will not load properly because they are designed to show a maximum of nine alternate extensions.

Second, and more importantly, in 4.0(3) and earlier, there are no defined slots for alternate extensions to live in. They are all carted around in an unsorted blob of data that is unpacked by the directory monitor and stuffed into the DTMFAccessID table. As such you cannot, for example, make a company-wide policy that alternate extension "4" is going to be used for cell phones and alternate extension "7" is everyone's fully qualified 10-digit North American Dialing Plan ID. In Unity 4.0(3) and earlier, once you add an ID for a large number of users in bulk, for example, there is no easy way to change that ID for everyone because it is difficult to identify it as opposed to IDs users might have for their home phone or cell phone. Unity 4.0(4) delivered this by introducing named alternate extensions that can be edited by name. We cover an example that shows how to use this functionality in the "Add an Alternate Extension to a Subscriber, Unity 4.0(4) and Later" section. Just keep this in mind before heading down a path where you start slamming alternate extensions in left and right. You might create a mess if you are not careful.

Finally, it is up to you to make sure the alternate extension does not conflict with any ID in the dialing domain. Earlier in this chapter, we covered a couple ways to do this depending on which version of Unity you are running. Just be aware the stored procedure for adding alternate extensions does not make such checks.

Adding the alternate extension is easy. In this example, we assume you have the SubscriberObjectID of the subscriber you want to add the ID to and, of course, the DTMFID. we also assume you have checked that the DTMFID meets the requirements: It is all digits, less than 30 characters long, and does not conflict with any other ID in the dialing domain. See the earlier section on subscriber creation for details on how to check for ID uniqueness.

Example 21-26 *Adding an Alternate Extension in Unity 4.0(3)*

```
Dim oCommand As ADODB.Command

    Set oCommand = New ADODB.Command

    oCommand.ActiveConnection = strConnectionString
    oCommand.CommandType = adCmdStoredProc
```

continues

Example 21-26 *Adding an Alternate Extension in Unity 4.0(3) (Continued)*

```
oCommand.CommandText = "sp_AddAltDTMFID"

! yes, strGUID is not a very descriptive parameter name.  This is the
SubscriberObjectID of the subscriber you want to add the alternate extension
for.
    oCommand.Parameters.Item("@strGUID") = oCommand.CreateParameter("strGUID",
        adGUID, adParamInput, , strSubscriberObjectID)

! ParentObjectIDType for subscriber is 1.  Refer to CUDLE.
    oCommand.Parameters.Item("@nParentObjType") =
        oCommand.CreateParameter("nParentObjType", adInteger, adParamInput, , 1)

! The actual ID you want to associate with this user
    oCommand.Parameters.Item("@strAltID") = oCommand.CreateParameter("strAltID",
        adVarChar, adParamInput, , Trim(txtNewExtension.Text))

        oCommand.Execute
```

There are no synchronization options for this stored procedure. However, as noted before, this is one of the values you need to make sure is written through to the directory. You can call the sp_SqlDirectorySync stored procedure directly. Or you can call the sp_ModifySubscriber stored procedure, which takes a set of synchronization flags just as the sp_CreateSubscriber stored procedure does. sp_ModifySubscriber is a better choice for this because it will only synchronize information about the user you are updating, whereas the sp_SqlDirectorySync is targeted more at batch operations where it will synch groups of users. If you are making other changes to the subscriber, the sp_ModifySubscriber stored procedure is an ideal choice but we recommend using it regardless. If you just want to kick off a synchronization to the directory for the user, the code looks like this:

Example 21-27 *Force a Directory Syncronization for a Subscriber*

```
oCommand.CommandText = "sp_ModifySubscriber"

oCommand.Parameters.Item("@SubscriberObjectID") =
    oCommand.CreateParameter("SubscriberObjectID", adGUID, adParamInput, ,
    strSubscriberObjectID)

    oCommand.Parameters.Item("@DirectorySync") =
        oCommand.CreateParameter("DirectorySync", adInteger, adParamInput, , 1)

!We want to pass in a synch mask that synchs the just the subscriber here.  That is
a value of 1 which is the default, but it is always good to pass it in explicitly
anyway.
        oCommand.Parameters.Item("@DirectorySyncFlags") =
            oCommand.CreateParameter("DirectorySyncFlags", adInteger, adParamInput,
            , 1)
```

Example 21-27 *Force a Directory Syncronization for a Subscriber (Continued)*

```
! We need to create a GUID that we can pass into the stored procedure such that we can
look for it in the DirectorySyncTicket table in SQL, which is used to pass back
the results of this sync.We have to use an asynchronous process here because the
synch with AD can take a while and doing a blocking call for such things is not
a good idea.  See below where we wait for the ticket to get inserted into the
table and let us know how things went.  If you do not pass a synch ticket here,
no record is created in the DirectorySyncTicket table.
        strSyncTicket = generateDirectorySyncTicket()
        oCommand.Parameters.Item("@DirectorySyncTicket") =
          oCommand.CreateParameter("DirectorySyncTicket", adGUID, adParamInput, ,
          strSyncTicket)

    !Execute the stored procedure
    oCommand.Execute
```

You can then wait for the ticket to be inserted into the DirectorySyncTicket table just as we did in the Create Subscriber section previously by using the WaitforSyncToFinish. The chances of a synch failure here are much less likely than in creating or importing subscribers. However, if problems exist with the directory connection or the rights of the directory-facing account for the Unity services, this *can* fail on you so it is always a smart move to ensure your directory write went through.

Add an Alternate Extension to a Subscriber, Unity 4.0(4) and Later

As noted in the previous section, Unity 4.0(4) added a new concept to alternate extensions that allows administrators to reserve specific alternate extensions for a designated use. For example, you can decide that you will use alternate extension #7 to represent the fully qualified 10-digit North American Dialing Plan (NADP) number for users and extension 9 for the users' mobile phone. Prior to 4.0(4), all the alternate extensions were stored in an ordered bag and, as such, it was not possible to edit specific extensions for groups of users. The only option available in Bulk Edit was to clear all alternate extensions for users and add a new alternate extension to the bag of extensions for users. This was less than ideal for large sites using alternate extensions heavily, as you might imagine.

If you install Unity 4.0(4) or later, and go to the Alternate Extensions page for a subscriber, you will notice a couple of significant changes there. First, you will see a full table of 9 alternate extensions defined and numbered from 1 through 9 instead of an expanding list you can add numbers to. You will also see a table of user-defined extensions at the bottom that you are not able to edit as an administrator. If the user's CoS allows for it, subscribers can define up to 5 of their own extensions via the CPCA web interface, which is what is displayed in that table.

Taking a quick look at the vw_DTMFAccessID view; three new columns are added to the table:

- **Alias.** This is used to determine which slot the alternate extension is for. They can be named SYSTEM_DEFINED_ALT_EXT_1 through SYSTEM_DEFINED_ALT_EXT_9 or USER_DEFINED_ALT_EXT_1 through USER_DEFINED_ALT_EXT_5. It is important that when editing or adding alternate extensions that you use this format because the conversations and administration clients are looking for the aliases to be in this format. Note that primary extensions for all objects have a NULL value for the alias field.

- **Description.** This is a text description that can be associated with an alternate extension if desired. It is only used for display purposes.

- **DTMFAccessIDType.** This can be 0 for primary, 1 for system alternate extension, or 2 for user alternate extension.

Three new stored procedures are also added that you should use instead of the method discussed in the previous section: csp_DTMFAccessIDAlternateExtensionCreate, csp_DTMFAccessIDAlternateExtensionDelete, and csp_DTMFAccessIDAlteranteMofidify.

The names on these stored procedures are self-explanatory and most of the information you pass in is identical to what was described in the previous section. Specifically, you pass in the SubscriberObjectID value into the ParentOID column for all three of these routines to identify which subscriber you are dealing with. There are two big differences here:

The alias parameter needs to be filled in when adding and editing an alternate extension. Follow the format noted previously for all system- and user-defined alternate extensions. Other than that, they work the same way, including the directory synchronization flags.

The DTMFAccessIDType needs to be filled in with 1 or 2 depending on the type of alternate extension you add. As a rule you should not be programmatically editing/creating/deleting user-defined extensions; those are reserved for end user's use. However, in some rare cases, it might be necessary.

The last thing to take note of here is that it should never be necessary to delete all alternate extensions for a user and rebuild for Unity 4.0(4) or later as was described in the previous section for earlier versions.

Updating One Key Rules to Go Directly to the Opening Greeting

Let us walk through a simple example here.

Say, for example, your company has decided that they want the 7 user input key on all subscribers (not application call handlers) configured to go to the opening greeting. You could, of course, apply this same process to setting subscribers' 0 keys to map to local area operators for groups of users or similar types of user input settings. We grab the CallHandlerObjectID for the opening greeting and use that value to update the Action,

Conversation, and Destination settings for the 7 user input key on each subscriber in the system. The code for this follows:

Example 21-28 *Update the Action for a User Input Key on a Call Handler*

```
Dim rsMenuEntries As New ADODB.Recordset
Dim rsTemp As New ADODB.Recordset
Dim strSQL As String
Dim strOpeningGreetingObjectID As String
Dim oCommand As ADODB.Command

! First, try to find the opening greeting call handler by its alias.  This call
  handler should always be there; if it is not, the system will likely have all
  kinds of interesting problems.
strSQL = "SELECT CallHandlerObjectID FROM vw_CallHandler WHERE
  Alias='OpeningGreetingch'"

!If the opening greeting call handler cannot be found, exit out of the function
rsTemp.Open strSQL, strConnectionString, adOpenKeyset, adLockReadOnly
If rsTemp.RecordCount <> 1 Then
    MsgBox "Error could not find opening greeting call handler by alias"
    Exit Sub
End If

!Grab the CallHandlerObjectID off the opening greeting call handler - we will be
  using this value to update the menu entry values for all the subscribers later.
strOpeningGreetingObjectID = rsMenuEntries("CallHandlerObjectID")

! This query will snag all the subscriber's user input keys for the 7 key.
  Remember to be a good SQL citizen, and get only the columns we need for this
  operation.
StrSQL=" SELECT vw_MenuEntry.MenuEntryObjectID
FROM vw_MenuEntry INNER JOIN vw_CallHandler
ON vw_CallHandler.CallHandlerObjectID=vw_MenuEntry.ParentObjectID
INNER JOIN vw_Subscriber
ON vw_Subscriber.CallHandlerObjectID=vw_CallHandler.CallHandlerObjectID
WHERE vw_MenuEntry.Alias='7'"

! We will be using stored a stored procedure for updating the values on the user
  input table so we will be opening this recordset as read-only.
rsMenuEntries.CursorLocation = adUseClient
rsMenuEntries.Open strSQL, strConnectionString, adOpenKeyset, adLockReadOnly

'Setup the command connection for the stored procedure we will be using to update
the menu entry rows.
Set oCommand = New ADODB.Command
oCommand.ActiveConnection = strConnectionString
oCommand.CommandType = adCmdStoredProc
oCommand.CommandText = "sp_ModifyMenuEntry"

! Now iterate through all the rows in the table and update the Menu Entry value
  as needed.
```

continues

Example 21-28 *Update the Action for a User Input Key on a Call Handler (Continued)*

```
rsMenuEntries.MoveFirst
Do While rsMenuEntries.EOF = False

    'Pass in the ObjectID of the menu entry row we want to update
    oCommand.Parameters.Item("@MenuEntryObjectID") =
        oCommand.CreateParameter("MenuEntryObjectID", adGUID, adParamInput, ,
            rsMenuEntries("MenuEntryObjectID"))

    'The "goto" action is 2 - check CUDLE for other options
    oCommand.Parameters.Item("@Action") = oCommand.CreateParameter("Action",
adInteger, adParamInput, , 2)
    ! Setting the conversation name to PHTransfer here sends the caller to contact
    rules (transfer rules) for the opening greeting call handlers.  By default, the
    opening greeting does not have any transfer rules enabled but if you decided
    later to do that you could.
    oCommand.Parameters.Item("@ConversationName") =
oCommand.CreateParameter("ConversationName", adVarChar, adParamInput, ,
"PHTransfer")
    oCommand.Parameters.Item("@DestinationObjectID") =
oCommand.CreateParameter("DestinationObjectID", adGUID, adParamInput, ,
strOpeningGreetingObjectID)

    ! The Object type for a call handler is 3.  Check CUDLE for more details.
    oCommand.Parameters.Item("@DestinationObjectIDType") =
oCommand.CreateParameter("Action", adInteger, adParamInput, , 3)

    ! Let the stored procedure fly.  There is no synch required for this and no need to
    check to see if it "worked", just move right on to the next item.
    oCommand.Execute
    rsMenuEntries.MoveNext
Loop
```

Of course in a production application you want some sort of logging function and a nice progress indicator for your always-stressed-out users. However, what you are looking at here is the basic engine behind applications such as Bulk Edit.

Updating Passwords

Setting the password is easy going through the stored procedure. The stored procedure takes care of hashing your raw phone password into an Message Digest Algorithm #5 (MD5) string for you on the back end. MD5 strings should always be exactly 32 characters here. Because phone passwords can only be 20 digits in length, the stored procedure assumes that if the string is 32 characters long it has already been hashed into an MD5 string and will pass it through directly. Otherwise, it will hash it for you on the back end so you can pass through the raw digits for the phone password you want to set and it will take care of it for you. If you are paranoid, you can also hash the phone password into its MD5 string and then pass that into the stored procedure instead.

When setting the password for a subscriber, it is up to you to be sure it complies with the password policy for the site. If you pass in a blank string for the password, for example, the phone password will be cleared. You can check the phone password policies in the PwPolicy table in UnityDB. The stored procedure does not do any enforcement of the site's policy, so make sure you are careful here.

Example 21-29 *Updating the Phone Password for a Subscriber*

```
oCommand.CommandText = "sp_ModifySubscriber"

oCommand.Parameters.Item("@SubscriberObjectID") =
   oCommand.CreateParameter("SubscriberObjectID", adGUID, adParamInput, ,
   strSubscriberObjectID)

!'The phone password is passed in as clear text in this example - it gets crunched
and encrypted by the SP during the subscriber update process.  You can pass in
a "pre-hashed" MD5 string yourself - if the string is exactly 32 characters long,
the stored proc will pass it through "as is".
   oCommand.Parameters.Item("@PWDTMF") = oCommand.CreateParameter("PWDTMF",
      adVarChar, adParamInput, , txtPhonePassword.Text)

! Passwords are not written through to the directory, no need to synch.
      oCommand.Parameters.Item("@DirectorySync") =
         oCommand.CreateParameter("DirectorySync", adInteger, adParamInput, , 0)
   oCommand.Execute
```

Because phone passwords are not pushed into the directory there is no need to issue a synchronization request for this.

Updating the Behavior of an Error Greeting in Unity 4.0(3) and Earlier

Because it is the ugly duckling here without a stored procedure to work with in Unity 4.0(3) and earlier, we cover editing the greeting for a subscriber so that the error greeting is configured to loop back to itself instead of going to the opening greeting which is the default behavior. In Unity 4.0(4) and later, you will want to use the CSP-Messaging Rule Modify stored procedure to do this work. This means that if a user is listening to a greeting for that subscriber and accidentally hits the wrong entry, they will hear the usual, "I'm sorry, we did not hear that entry" system greeting, but will then hear the subscriber's greeting start over instead of being tossed to the "opening greeting" call handler.

Say, for example, we wanted to change the error greeting here for the Example Subscriber account. We would construct an SQL Query that snagged the items we needed to update from their error messaging rule along with the CallHandlerObjectID for the primary call handler associated with that subscriber. The messaging rules reference the primary call handler of a subscriber as their parent, not the subscriber itself.

Example 21-30 *Updating the Behavior of the Error Greeting for a Subscriber*

```
StrSQL="SELECT vw_CallHandler.CallHandlerObjectID, vw_MessagingRule.Action, vw_
   MessagingRule.ConversationName, vw_MessagingRule.DestinationObjectID, vw_
   MessagingRule.DestinationObjectIDType
FROM vw_CallHandler INNER JOIN vw_Subscriber
ON vw_Subscriber.CallHandlerObjectID=vw_CallHandler.CallHandlerObjectID
INNER JOIN vw_MessagingRule
ON vw_MessagingRule.ParentObjectId=vw_CallHandler.CallHandlerObjectID
WHERE vw_Subscriber.Alias='esubscriber' AND vw_MessagingRule.Alias='Error'"

Set rsGreetings  New ADODB.Recordset
rsGreetings.CursorLocation = adUseClient
rsGreetings.Open strSQL, strConnectionString, adOpenKeyset, adLockOptimistic

! In this case, we were looking for one specific user and if we did not get that,
bail out.
If rsGreetings.RecordCount <> 1 Then
    MsgBox "Could not find subscriber by alias"
    Exit Sub
End If

! You can check CUDLE for explanations for all 4 columns here. We are going to use
the GoTo action of 2 and send the call to the PHGreeting entry point for the
primary call handler of this subscriber.  The ObjectIDType for a call handler
is 3.
rsGreetings("Action") = 2
rsGreetings("ConversationName") = "PHGreeting"
rsGreetings("DestinationObjectID") = rsGreetings("CallHandlerObjectID")
rsGreetings("DestinationObjectIDType") = 3
rsGreetings.Update
```

If you wanted to make this change for all subscribers and call handlers in your system instead of for an individual user, you could just take out the "vw_Subscriber.Alias= 'esubscriber'" from the WHERE clause and get a full list of all Error greetings and then just iterate through them making the same change as above:

Example 21-31 *Updating the Behavior of the Error Greeting for All Subscribers*

```
rsGreetings.MoveFirst
Do While rsGreetings.EOF = False
    rsGreetings("Action") = 2
    rsGreetings("ConversationName") = "PHGreeting"
    rsGreetings("DestinationObjectID") = rsGreetings("CallHandlerObjectID")
    rsGreetings("DestinationObjectIDType") = 3
    rsGreetings.Update
    rsGreetings.MoveNext
Loop
```

Because synchronization issues do not exist with the directory for messaging rules, you are in and out quickly. Just remember, with Unity 4.0(4) and later you should use stored procedures for updating the messaging rules.

Batch Subscriber Operations

There is nothing complicated about doing bulk subscriber imports, creates, or edits. You can, in fact, do large numbers of all three operations using the techniques outlined before. If you call for individual user synchs to the directory on each subscriber you create, for example, the operation will not take any longer than if you save up your synch until the end and synch everyone all at once, assuming you are moving on to the next user after creating/ importing them and not waiting for their sync to complete. If you are importing hundreds of users at once, you might notice a small increase in performance by doing it in batch, but not enough to justify using a different method just for that.

The one exception here is synchronizing public distribution lists. Unity currently does not provide a way to synch a single user into a specific distribution list or set of lists in the directory. When you select to synchronize public distribution lists when adding a subscriber to that list, it does all members for the list. Worse, if you select to include distribution lists in the synch flags when adding a new subscriber to the system, it will synch all users for all lists. This can be time-consuming and if you issue such a request for each user you import in a large set, it can take many hours to complete. This is not a good idea. If you can, you should issue a single synch request for distribution lists after you complete the import or creation of all subscribers in a batch.

For adding or importing large numbers of users, doing it in batch mode does make a couple things, other than the distribution list, go smoother. For example, you can easily provide an overall synchronization progress indicator for your users. If you synch each individual user as you add or import them, it is up to you to maintain the table of synch tickets and know when they are all complete. Providing progress on this is tricky at best because you have to assume other folks might be requesting synch tickets for their various tasks as well.

Let us say you are adding a number of new users as Unity subscribers from a CSV file and having them created in the directory as well. One way to do this would be to add them to SQL, but not request a synch for each user as we did in the previous create subscriber example. Simply do not pass the DirecotrySync, DirecotrySyncFlags, or DirectorySyncTicket flags into the stored procedure. Then, when you are all done adding users, issue a command to synchronize new subscribers and public distribution lists using the sp_SqlDirectorySync stored procedure. This stored procedure is nice because it provides explicit flags for indicating if you want to synch subscribers, distribution lists, new users only, and so on instead of having to construct the flags manually as we do in the sp_CreateSubscriber stored procedure. The code for constructing this procedure looks like this:

Example 21-32 *Requesting a Synchronization of All Objects at Once*

```
oCommand.CommandText = "sp_SqlDirectorySync"

oCommand.Parameters.Item("@SyncSubscriber") =
  oCommand.CreateParameter("SyncSubscriber", adInteger, adParamInput, , 1)

oCommand.Parameters.Item("@SyncDistributionList") =
  oCommand.CreateParameter("SyncDistributionList", adInteger, adParamInput,
  , 1)

! This will tell the synch process to only look at rows in the subscriber table
that have a NULL DirectoryId column which indicates they do not have an object
associated with them in the directory.  We assume these are new users waiting
to be created.
oCommand.Parameters.Item("@SyncNewOnly") =
  oCommand.CreateParameter("SyncNewOnly", adInteger, adParamInput, , 1)

! Again, we force it to only attempt to create new users in this process.  If a
user with the same mail alias is encountered in the directory already, the sync
of that user will fail.
oCommand.Parameters.Item("@SyncCreateOnly") =
  oCommand.CreateParameter("SyncCreateOnly", adInteger, adParamInput, , 1)

! As we did in the individual create example we generate a GUID and pass it in
such that we know what ticket to look for in the DirecotyrSyncTicket table so
we know when the synchronization process is complete.
strSyncTicket = generateDirectorySyncTicket
oCommand.Parameters.Item("@DirectorySyncTicket") =
  oCommand.CreateParameter("DirectorySyncTicket", adGUID, adParamInput, ,
  strSyncTicket)
```

You then execute the stored procedure and wait for the synch ticket to arrive in the DirectorySyncTicket table just as we did in the individual create example earlier in this chapter. You can check less aggressively because every 2 seconds is probably too often for a large synch. Perhaps checking every 30 seconds is more appropriate.

So, how do you go about showing progress here while you are waiting for the synch process to complete? You cannot check the progress of the distribution list synch, unfortunately, but you can easily see how many users have been added and how many are left to be added. You can do this by querying the subscriber table to see if the DirectoryID column is NULL or not. If a value is NULL, that user has not been synched to the directory yet or the synch has failed for some reason. Assuming you do not have a significant number of users that fail the synch process, you can check for how many rows have a NULL DirectoryID column and update a progress bar as you go. For example, before starting the subscriber add process, execute this query:

```
SELECT Count(*) FROM vw_Subscriber WHERE DirectoryID IS NULL AND SubscriberType NOT
  IN (0,6)
```

And save this number as your base count. There really should not be any subscribers in the table that have NULL DirectoryIDs other than the installer account (type 0) and you should investigate if you get anything other than 0. After you finish adding users to your subscriber table, issue the same query and the difference of the two values will be how many subscribers you have added to the table that are waiting to be synched. We assume that your process is the only one doing such adds on the server; if that is incorrect, you need to use a different technique.

Once you issue the synchronization process outlined previously, you can periodically issue the same query and update a progress bar or a rolling counter to show basic subscriber synchronization progress. If a user fails to synch, however, they are left at NULL so your progress can never get to 100 percent. Also, there is no way to check for progress on the distribution list synchronization; however, the synch ticket will not show up until that is complete so you might have to wait. One way to get around this is to issue two separate synch requests—one for just subscribers where you pass in a synch ticket and wait while showing progress, and another one for distribution lists only where you do not bother to pass a synch ticket and just let it run in the background until complete.

Once the synchronization ticket for the subscriber synch shows up, you can issue another query against the subscriber table and get a full list of all the users that did not get synched properly. This can generate a report for the user and also for deleting those rows out of the subscriber table because you do not want to leave users not in sync in the table because they are not valid subscribers. For example, you can use this query:

```
StrSQL="SELECT Alias, DisplayName, FirstName, LastName, SubscriberObjectID FROM vw_
   Subscriber WHERE DirectoryID IS NULL"
RsTemp.Open strSQL, strConnectionString, adOpenKeyset, adLockReadOnly
```

You can then iterate through the rsTemp recordset, dump user-readable information about which users failed to synch properly, and then use the sp_DeleteSubscriber stored procedure shown in the Add Subscriber example to remove these rows from the table.

When importing versus creating new users, you might be passing in the DirectoryID value to find users in the directory. If so, you cannot use the NULL value in that column as we did for the previous create example. Another technique is to use the ObjectChangedID value, which for objects not synchronized with the directory will be 0. If the value is greater than 0, you can assume the sync has taken place for that user.

For batch updates, as opposed to adds, there is no easy way to make a bunch of changes in SQL. For batch updates, as opposed to adds, there is no easy way to make a bunch of changes in SQL; issue a synchronization request and then check for progress. You just have to wait until it is complete. If you do not have to synchronize to the directory, do not. Keep track of what values are being edited and be smart about sending the synch flag in. If you have to synchronize public distribution lists, do it once at the end of your update process. Issuing a bunch of DL sync requests over a batch operation will result in long delays for the sync completion.

Delete Subscriber

Compared to the complexity of creating or importing a subscriber into Unity, deleting a subscriber properly without introducing any database corruption in the form of broken links is significantly more difficult. It demands you understand all the ways objects in Unity can reference a subscriber and how to accommodate the fact the subscriber is going away. The really tricky part is collecting information about what to do with these references. For example, if a subscriber is the owner and message recipient on a number of call handlers, you have to replace that with another valid subscriber or distribution list or you introduce corruption.

Even the casual observer will note that the current Unity web-based SA interface happily deletes subscribers, call handlers, and other objects without making sure references to those objects are properly cleaned up. This creates numerous broken link issues in the database. Although Unity delivered some relief here by allowing administrators to configure default behavior for cleaning broken links subscribers deleted in the SA, there are still some holes.

This has kept me churning out updated versions of dbWalker to help find and patch up these links. The Global Subscriber Manger does provide for deleting users from Unity without potentially breaking such links. However, those in the field do not tend to use that capability either because they prefer the web interface or because they do not realize the capability is there. There are several reasons why the SA is in the condition it is now, but mostly it is because it was built on top of Unity 2.x which did not have a relational database under it at the time and so the job of rummaging through the database and finding all references to an object was slow and painful. The SA was not redesigned when the Unity back end went to SQL and now looks silly around the edges. The administration interface is undergoing a major rebuilding to remove its dependency on the DOH and provide an improved interface that will support user-extensible plug-in pages so people can do their own thing.

What is involved in this process? First and foremost, it is gathering from the user what to do with all possible references to the subscriber being removed. This extends to the removal of any object, of course, but for subscribers it is particularly important because they can be referenced as message recipients. Unity will not load a call handler or interview handler that does not have a valid message recipient assigned to it, even if that handler is not configured to take a message. You will receive the ever-popular failsafe message that tells you to try your call again later and then dumps you to the opening greeting. Callers do not appreciate this and you want to avoid this in your Unity adventures. A subscriber can be referenced by another object in several ways:

1 They can be a message recipient on a call handler or interview handler.

2 They can be an administrator (owner) on a call handler, an interview handler, a public distribution list, or a name lookup handler.

3 The after greeting action on a messaging rule can send the caller to the removed subscriber.

4 The after message action on a call handler can send the caller to the removed subscriber.

5 A menu entry key associated with a call handler or a subscriber's primary call handler can be set to go to the greeting or transfer rule entry point for the removed subscriber.

6 The exit action from the subscriber conversation (introduced in 4.0(1)) could send the caller to the removed subscriber.

7 The four exit actions from a name lookup handler can each reference the removed subscriber.

8 A call routing rule might reference the removed subscriber.

9 They could be referenced by subscriber templates for the subscriber exit destination, after message destination, after greeting destination, or a caller input destination.

Dealing with all these possibilities when removing a user from the system is a daunting task. Fortunately, for items 2–8, there is a stored procedure that simplifies the process. For item #1 on the list there are two separate stored procedures to help you replace all owners and recipient references in the system. As for item #9, we do not deal with it in my deletion example because it is an extremely rare case that sites will have specific subscribers referenced as destination points in their subscriber templates. You can deal with this possibility in your applications, but the stored procedure mentioned does not include templates in its sweep of the database.

The hard part is collecting information about what to replace links for items 1–8 with when removing the user. Take a quick look at the SA, and you see many possibilities for setting a user input key, after message options, and so on. The Global Subscriber Manager has an example of one way to approach this, which is a full wizard interface that interrogates the user making the deletion about what they want to do with each and every possible link that will break. While this is robust, it is also a lot of work and administrators are less than thrilled with having to walk through this wizard each time they delete a subscriber. You can take it a step further and remember the previous set of values and let the user skip the wizard. However, you need to be careful that references selected and saved by the user are valid. For example, if they have selected a public distribution list as a replacement for the message recipient link on removed subscribers and that distribution list is removed, you need to note that and force them to select another object. Another approach is to hard code as many of the replacements as you can and ask only for a subscriber or distribution list as the owner and recipient replacement. For example, all one-key actions that referenced the deleted subscriber could be set to Ignore and after message actions could be set to Hang Up. This is easier to code and involves less collaboration with the administrator, but can produce undesirable phone behavior. Callers frown on getting dial tone right after leaving a message when they want to try another user in the system.

How you approach the replacement information collection issue depends on the type of application you are providing. An automated provisioning application that runs off scripts does not have the option of asking a human questions so you will end up having to go with some predefined hard-coded values. Other types of tools have other options. we did not spend a lot of time in the example application here gathering information from the user. we took a middle-of-the-road approach where some items were hard coded and a few items were adjustable, but with a limited set of options. For example, the after message action can only be sent to go to a selected call handler. We did not give the full range of options available for this in an effort to keep the application as simple as possible. Given the information covered in Chapter 3, and the data available in CUDLE, you should be able to apply the full range of options to your application.

Example 21-33 shows part of the code found in the Delete Subscriber example application.

Example 21-33 *Deleting a Subscriber Without Corrupting the Database*

```
Private Sub DeleteSubscriber()
Dim rsCreate As ADODB.Recordset
Dim rsTemp As ADODB.Recordset
Dim oCommand As ADODB.Command
Dim strSyncTicket As String
Dim iCounter As Integer
Dim strDeletedSubscriberObjectID As String
Dim strNewOwnerRecipientObjectID As String

    Set rsTemp = New ADODB.Recordset


! First, we need to retrieve the SubscriberobjectId of the subscriber we want to
delete which will get used later.  The alias of the subscriber we are about to
remove is stored in the txtAlias text box on the form here.
    rsTemp.Open "SELECT Alias, SubscriberObjectID from vw_Subscriber where Alias='"
        + txtAlias.Text + "'", strConnectionString, adOpenKeyset, adLockReadOnly

    If rsTemp.RecordCount <> 1 Then
        MsgBox "Error pulling the ObjectID for the subscriber to be deleted...
aborting removal"
        rsTemp.Close
        Exit Sub
    End If

    rsTemp.MoveFirst
    strDeletedSubscriberObjectID = rsTemp("SubscriberObjectID")
    rsTemp.Close


! Next, we want to make sure we can get the SubscriberobjectId of the subscriber
that will replace this guy as the owner and/or recipient which we will be updating
later.  We do this now because it would be disappointing to find out we cannot find
this replacement user after we cleaned up other links to this user with the
spPreDeleteObject stored procedure.  In this sample, I allow only the selection
of another subscriber to replace the removed user as both owner and recipient
and the alias for this replacement user is stored in the
txtOwnerRecipientSubscriberAlias text box on the form.
    rsTemp.Open "SELECT Alias, SubscriberObjectID FROM vw_Subscriber WHERE Alias='"
        + txtOwnerRecipientSubscriberAlias.Text + "'", strConnectionString,
        adOpenKeyset, adLockReadOnly
```

Example 21-33 *Deleting a Subscriber Without Corrupting the Database (Continued)*

```
If rsTemp.RecordCount <> 1 Then
    MsgBox "Error pulling the ObjectID for the subscriber that will be the
        replacement as the owner/recipient... aborting removal"
    rsTemp.Close
    Exit Sub
End If

rsTemp.MoveFirst
strNewOwnerRecipientObjectID = rsTemp("SubscriberObjectID")
rsTemp.Close

! Now we are ready to start the pre-deletion activities.
Set rsCreate = New ADODB.Recordset
Set oCommand = New ADODB.Command
oCommand.ActiveConnection = strConnectionString
oCommand.CommandType = adCmdStoredProc

! First, do the pre-delete actions and clean up references to this subscriber in
other objects in the database before removing them such that we do not corrupt
the database.  Note that this stored procedure can also be used when removing
other objects such as a call handler.  This stored procedure handles fixing up
all the links to the removed user except the owner and recipient links, which
we will deal with shortly.
oCommand.CommandText = "sp_PreDeleteObject"

! Pass in the SubscriberObjectID of the user to be removed.
oCommand.Parameters.Item("@ObjectID") = oCommand.CreateParameter("ObjectID",
    adGUID, adParamInput, , strDeletedSubscriberObjectID)

! The object type is a subscriber which is "1", you can check CUDLE for this if
you forget in the future.
oCommand.Parameters.Item("@ObjectType") =
    oCommand.CreateParameter("ObjectType", adInteger, adParamInput, , 1)

! In this case we are going to set the user input keys mapped to this subscriber
to "ignore".  I do not give the user a choice on the form here but, of course,
you can do what you like here.  I am simply hard-coding the action to ignore
which maps to a value of "0".  Again, check CUDLE under the MenuEntry table to
see what your options are here.  With a value of 0 for the action the
conversation name, destination object ID and the destination object ID type
values are meaningless and do not get used, however the stored procedure is still
expecting them to be passed in regardless.  As such we pass in some dummy values
here to make it happy.
oCommand.Parameters.Item("@CallerInputAction") =
    oCommand.CreateParameter("CallerInputAction", adInteger, adParamInput, , 0)

! This value is not used in this case.
oCommand.Parameters.Item("@CallerInputConversationName") =
    oCommand.CreateParameter("CallerInputConversationName", adBSTR,
    adParamInput, , "PHTransfer")
```

continues

Example 21-33 *Deleting a Subscriber Without Corrupting the Database (Continued)*

```
! Because a blank GUID is not considered valid and the stored procedure requires this
parameter, I am just passing in the ObjectID of the guy we are deleting to the
procedure here - this is not used by anything - this parameter should really be
optional.
    oCommand.Parameters.Item("@CallerInputDestObjectID") =
        oCommand.CreateParameter("CallerInputDestObjectID", adGUID, adParamInput, ,
        strDeletedSubscriberObjectID)

! Arbitrarily pass in the type for call handler here (2) - again the stored proc
demands a value here but it is not used in this case
    oCommand.Parameters.Item("@CallerInputDestObjectIDType") =
        oCommand.CreateParameter("CallerInputDestObjectIDType", adInteger,
        adParamInput, , 2)

! For the after message action I allow the user to select a call handler .
I do not offer a lot of options here but you can do what you like.  We need to
retrieve the ObjectID for the destination call handler which the user selected
and has it is alias stored in the txtCallHandlerAfterMessageAlias text box on
the form.
    rsTemp.Open "SELECT Alias, CallHandlerObjectID FROM vw_CallHandler WHERE
        alias='" + txtCallHandlerAfterMessageAlias.Text + "'", strConnectionString,
        adOpenKeyset, adLockReadOnly

    If rsTemp.RecordCount <> 1 Then
        MsgBox "Error pulling the ObjectID for the call handler destination for
            after message destinations... aborting removal"
        rsTemp.Close
        Exit Sub
    End If

    rsTemp.MoveFirst

! Pass in the destination object ID for the after message replacement which is the
call handler we just looked up.
    oCommand.Parameters.Item("@AfterMessageDestObjectID") =
        oCommand.CreateParameter("AfterMessageDestObjectID", adGUID, adParamInput,
        , rsTemp("CallHandlerObjectID"))
    rsTemp.Close

!The AfterMessageDestObjectIDType needs to be a "2" for a call handler in this
case.
    oCommand.Parameters.Item("@AfterMessageDestObjectIDType") =
        oCommand.CreateParameter("AfterMessageDestObjectIDType", adInteger,
        adParamInput, , 2)

! The conversation name is "PHTransfer" here - to do this right you would give them
the option of attempting the transfer or going right to the greeting for the call
handler in question.  Defaulting to PHTransfer is generally pretty safe because
the handler itself will be configured to do a transfer or not the way you want
them to regardless.  If you do not know what I mean by PHTransfer versus.
PHGreeting you need to review the Object Model and Audio Text Applications
chapters.
```

Example 21-33 *Deleting a Subscriber Without Corrupting the Database (Continued)*

```
      oCommand.Parameters.Item("@AfterMessageConversationName") =
        oCommand.CreateParameter("AfterMessageConversationName", adBSTR,
        adParamInput, , "PHTransfer")

!The action for this needs to be 2 for "goto" - refer to CUDLE for more details
      oCommand.Parameters.Item("@AfterMessageAction") =
        oCommand.CreateParameter("AfterMessageAction", adInteger, adParamInput, , 2)

! Again, I do not give any options for the after greeting action - it is hard coded
to take a message if it happened to have been set to go to the subscriber being
deleted.  You can, of course, go wild here.  The Action for "take a message"
corresponds to a value of 4.  Check CUDLE under the MessagingRule table to
find out what all your options for the after greeting action are.  With an action
of "take message" it is not necessary to fill in the AfterGreetingConversationName,
AfterGreetingDestObjectID or the AfterGreetingDestObjectIDType values, however
you need to pass the parameters anyway because the stored procedure expects to
see them even though they do not get used.
      oCommand.Parameters.Item("@AfterGreetingAction") =
        oCommand.CreateParameter("AfterGreetingAction", adInteger, adParamInput, , 4)

! This value is not used in this case since an action of 4 does not use a
conversation
      oCommand.Parameters.Item("@AfterGreetingConversationName") =
        oCommand.CreateParameter("AfterGreetingConversationName", adBSTR,
        adParamInput, , "PHTransfer")

! Because a blank GUID is not considered valid and the stored proc requires this
parameter, I am just passing in the ObjectID of the guy we're deleting to the
procedure here - this is not used by anything - this parameter should really be
optional.
      oCommand.Parameters.Item("@AfterGreetingDestObjectID") =
        oCommand.CreateParameter("AfterGreetingDestObjectID", adGUID, adParamInput,
        , strDeletedSubscriberObjectID)

! Arbitrarily pass in the type for call handler here (2) - again the stored proc
demands a value here but it is not used in this case
      oCommand.Parameters.Item("@AfterGreetingDestObjectIDType") =
        oCommand.CreateParameter("AfterGreetingDestObjectIDType", adInteger,
        adParamInput, , 2)

! I lumped the subscriber exit destination and the name lookup handler exit
destinations into one option and it is forced to go to a call handler to simplify
things here.  First we need to get the objectId of the call handler the user
has selected as the alternative destination.  It is alias is stored in the
txtCallHandlerAfterMessageAlias text box on the form.
      rsTemp.Open "SELECT Alias, CallHandlerObjectID FROM vw_CallHandler WHERE
        alias='" + txtCallHandlerAfterMessageAlias.Text + "'", strConnectionString,
        adOpenKeyset, adLockReadOnly

      If rsTemp.RecordCount <> 1 Then
        MsgBox "Error pulling the ObjectID for the call handler target for the exit
          destinations on subscribers and name lookup handlers... aborting removal"
```

continues

Example 21-33 *Deleting a Subscriber Without Corrupting the Database (Continued)*

```
            rsTemp.Close
            Exit Sub
      End If


      rsTemp.MoveFirst

! Pass the CallHandlerObjectID we just grabbed into the stored procedure as both
the name lookup handler exit destination and the subscriber exit destination
object IDs.
      oCommand.Parameters.Item("@SubExitObjectID") =
         oCommand.CreateParameter("SubExitObjectID", adGUID, adParamInput, ,
         rsTemp("CallHandlerObjectID"))

      oCommand.Parameters.Item("@NameLookupHandlerExitObjectID") =
         oCommand.CreateParameter("NameLookupHandlerExitObjectID", adGUID,
         adParamInput, , rsTemp("CallHandlerObjectID"))
      rsTemp.Close

!Again ,we are forcing a call handler here and the objectType for that is 2.
      oCommand.Parameters.Item("@SubExitObjectIDType") =
         oCommand.CreateParameter("SubExitObjectIDType", adInteger, adParamInput, , 2)

      oCommand.Parameters.Item("@NameLookupHandlerExitObjectIDType") =
         oCommand.CreateParameter("NameLookupHandlerExitObjectIDType", adInteger,
         adParamInput, , 2)

!Again, we will assume the PHTransfer entry point here instead of the PHGreeting.
      oCommand.Parameters.Item("@SubExitConversationName") =
         oCommand.CreateParameter("SubExitConversationName", adBSTR, adParamInput, ,
         "PHTransfer")

      oCommand.Parameters.Item("@NameLookupHandlerExitConversationName") =
         oCommand.CreateParameter("NameLookupHandlerExitConversationName", adBSTR,
         adParamInput, , "PHTransfer")

!The action for all transfers is 2 for goto - again, refer to CUDLE for help
here.
      oCommand.Parameters.Item("@SubExitAction") =
         oCommand.CreateParameter("SubExitAction", adInteger, adParamInput, , 2)

      oCommand.Parameters.Item("@NameLookupHandlerExitAction") =
         oCommand.CreateParameter("NameLookupHandlerExitAction", adInteger,
         adParamInput, , 2)

!OK, let us execute the Predelete procedure.
      rsCreate.CursorLocation = adUseClient
      rsCreate.Open oCommand, , adOpenDynamic, adLockOptimistic

!The rsCreate recordset now contains a list of all the objects that were changed
as part of this procedure.  If you want to get fancy you can generate a report
based on this information.
      rsCreate.Close
```

Example 21-33 *Deleting a Subscriber Without Corrupting the Database (Continued)*

```
!We now need to make sure we change any call handler, interview handler or
distribution list that's setup with their owner and/or recipient properties
pointing at the subscriber we're going to remove. We'll replace references to
this subscriber with the subscriber selected on the form that we looked up
earlier in this routine.  We need to use the sp_ChangeOwner and
sp_ChangeRecipient stored procedures for this.
    oCommand.CommandText = "sp_ChangeOwner"

    oCommand.Parameters.Item("@PrevOwnerObjectID") =
      oCommand.CreateParameter("PrevOwnerObjectID", adGUID, adParamInput, ,
      strDeletedSubscriberObjectID)

    oCommand.Parameters.Item("@NewOwnerObjectID") =
      oCommand.CreateParameter("NewOwnerObjectID", adGUID, adParamInput, ,
      strNewOwnerRecipientObjectID)

!Because we're hard coding this to only allow a subscriber to be the replacement we
pass in a 1 as the type here.  If you were allowing a public distribution list
as a replacement you would use a value of 2 here.
    oCommand.Parameters.Item("@NewOwnerObjectIDType") =
      oCommand.CreateParameter("NewOwnerObjectIDType", adInteger, adParamInput, , 1)

!Execute the stored procedure
    rsCreate.CursorLocation = adUseClient
    rsCreate.Open oCommand, , adOpenDynamic, adLockOptimistic

!The rsCreate recordset now contains a list of all the handlers updated by the
stored proc.  You can include this in a reporting option for your tools if you
like.  We are keeping this simple so I'm not going to go that route, we will just
move on.
    rsCreate.Close

    'Now change the recipient in the same way we did the owner.
    oCommand.CommandText = "sp_ChangeRecipient"

    oCommand.Parameters.Item("@PrevRecipientObjectID") =
      oCommand.CreateParameter("PrevRecipientObjectID", adGUID, adParamInput, ,
      strDeletedSubscriberObjectID)

    oCommand.Parameters.Item("@NewRecipientObjectID") =
      oCommand.CreateParameter("NewRecipientObjectID", adGUID, adParamInput, ,
      strNewOwnerRecipientObjectID)

! Because we are hard coding this to only allow a subscriber to be the replacement
we pass in a 1 as the type here
    oCommand.Parameters.Item("@NewRecipientObjectIDType") =
      oCommand.CreateParameter("NewRecipientObjectIDType", adInteger,
      adParamInput, , 1)

    'Execute the stored proc.
    rsCreate.CursorLocation = adUseClient
    rsCreate.Open oCommand, , adOpenDynamic, adLockOptimistic
```

continues

Example 21-33 *Deleting a Subscriber Without Corrupting the Database (Continued)*

```
!Again, the rsCreate recordset contains a list of all the handlers updated by
this stored proc which you can use for a reporting function here if you like.
    rsCreate.Close

! Now that we have the pre-delete activity complete we can delete the subscriber
themselves without worrying about causing any kind of broken links or other
problems in the database unless the site is weird and has referenced
this subscriber in their subscriber templates for whatever reason.
    oCommand.CommandText = "sp_DeleteSubscriber"

    oCommand.Parameters.Item("@SubscriberObjectID") =
      oCommand.CreateParameter("SubscriberObjectID", adGUID, adParamInput, ,
      strDeletedSubscriberObjectID)

!You definitely want to tell the stored procedure to synchronize SQL to the
directory for this subscriber after deleting them so you should pass a 1 in here.
There is really no valid reason not to pass this in, frankly, but it is an optional
parameter nonetheless.  If you do not pass this flag in the user will be removed
from Unity's database but will still be "stamped" as a subscriber in the
directory and you will not be able to import them as a subscriber on any Unity
server in the directory.
    oCommand.Parameters.Item("@DirectorySync") =
      oCommand.CreateParameter("DirectorySync", adInteger, adParamInput, , 1)

!We want to pass in a sync mask that syncs the subscriber info back to the
directory.  You have the option of removing the subscriber from the directory if
your back end is Exchange 55 or Exchange 2000 here.  If the user has checked that
option on the form you want to pass in 0x50000000 + 0x00000001 = 1342177281
decimal.  If this option is not checked, just you need to pass in 0x20000000 +
0x00000001 = 536870913.  You can also simply pass the "ForceRemove" flag into
the stored procedure which will simply "or" in the 0x50000000 for you rather than
making you do all that complicated math on your own.  You must be extremely
careful with this option!  The SA does not offer this option for a very good
reason.  Folks get real annoyed if you blow away their directory and messaging
accounts by accident so make sure you know what you are doing with this.
    If Me.chkRemoveMailbox.Value = vbChecked Then
!Pass the synch flags to remove the user from the directory and blow away their
mailstore account as well.
        oCommand.Parameters.Item("@DirectorySyncFlags") =
          oCommand.CreateParameter("DirectorySyncFlags", adInteger,
          adParamInput, , 1342177281)
    Else
! Pass the sync flags to remove just the subscriber properties from the user in
the directory.  This should definitely be the default option.
        oCommand.Parameters.Item("@DirectorySyncFlags") =
          oCommand.CreateParameter("DirectorySyncFlags", adInteger,
          adParamInput, , 268435457)
    End If

!We need to create a GUID that we can pass into the stored proc such that we can
look for it in the DirectorySyncTicket table in SQL which is used to pass back
the results of this sync - we have to use an asynchronous process here because the
synch with AD can take a while and doing a blocking call for such things is not
```

Example 21-33 *Deleting a Subscriber Without Corrupting the Database (Continued)*

```
a good idea.  See below where we wait for the ticket to get inserted into the
table and let us know how things went.  If you do not pass a synch ticket here,
no record is created in the DirectorySyncTicket table.
    strSyncTicket = generateDirectorySyncTicket
    oCommand.Parameters.Item("@DirectorySyncTicket") =
        oCommand.CreateParameter("DirectorySyncTicket", adGUID, adParamInput, ,
        strSyncTicket)

    rsCreate.CursorLocation = adUseClient
    rsCreate.Open oCommand, , adOpenDynamic, adLockOptimistic

!As we have done earlier, we need to wait for the sync to complete and check the
results.  You can check the code for the WaitForsyncToFinish in the
Add Subscribers example.
If WaitForSyncToFinish (strSyncTicket) = False Then
    MsgBox "Synch to directory failed during subscriber removal.  Check the
        SQLSyncSvr logs in \commserver\Logs for more details"
Else
    MsgBox "Subscriber removed"
End If

BailOut:

    !Clean up a little on the way out.
    Set rsCreate = Nothing
    Set oCommand = Nothing
End Sub
```

Remove Unity Properties from an Active Directory Object

Several people have asked how they can automate the cleaning process for users in Active Directory when, for example, a Unity server was removed from the network without uninstalling it properly first. This strands users in the directory because they are stamped as Unity subscribers and other Unity servers will not allow you to import them. We should note here that using the sp_CreateSubscriber to import these users will let you do that. The stored procedure does not check to see if the user you identified is already a subscriber. This is why DiRT restores work when you reinstall a Unity server that has crashed into a network with subscribers in the directory still.

However, you can easily clean the user of Unity properties by using code that looks like navigating around databases. You can bind Active Directory services using ADO in the same way you can bind to SQL. You can find your way around Active Directory and update objects other ways; however, this is the easiest we have encountered. For this to work, it requires you include the Active DS Type Library in your VB project that will give you the ADSI interface plumbing you need.

We first need to connect to the "root" of the Active Directory domain so that we can then find folders/users in that container and move down through the tree. The root container can be retrieved using the "RootDSE" keyword in your query. You could go out and find your domain controller and build this yourself, but it is easy to just ask Active Directory to tell you what default domain you are running in.

Example 21-34 *Getting Handle to "Root" Container in Active Directory*

```
Dim sContext As String
Dim rootDSE As IADs

!Get the rootDSE. This is basically the default container for the domain.  It'll
  look something like this: "LDAP://DC=AnswerMonkey,DC=net".
    Set rootDSE = GetObject("LDAP://RootDSE")
    sNamingContext = "LDAP://" & rootDSE.Get("defaultNamingContext")
```

The sContext string will now contain a string you can use to retrieve users in containers of your choice. Now that you have the path to the root container, you can build a recordset of all the users and/or containers in that container.

Example 21-35 *Get All User Objects in an Active Directory Container*

```
Dim con As New Connection
Dim rs As New Recordset
Dim sFilter As String
Dim sLdapQuery As String

    !Open the connection using the special Active Directory connection string.
    con.Provider = "ADsDSOObject"
    con.Open "Active Directory Provider"

! Build the query.  In this case we're only interested in seeing users in the
  container in question, not all the other stuff that you find hanging out in an
  Active Directory container.
    sFilter = "(objectCategory=User)"

! If the user has opted to only see subscribers, include a filter that will only
  show users that have the ciscoECSBUUMLocationOBjectID value on them.  Otherwise
  leave the filter off and all user objects will be returned.  If a user in the
  directory does not have a location object ID associated with them, we assume
  they are non-Unity subscribers.
    If bShowAllUsers = False Then
        sFilter = "(&" & sFilter & "(ciscoEcsbuUMLocationObjectId=*)" & ")"
    End If

! Remember the sContext string constructed from the RootDSE above looks
  something like "LDAP://DC=AnswerMonkey,DC=net"
    sLdapQuery = "<" & sContext & ">;" & sFilter & ";AdsPath,cn;onelevel"

    ! Get the users from the query into a nice recordset
    Set rs = con.Execute(sLdapQuery)
```

At this point, you have a list of all users in the container. However, you probably do not have users in the root container, so the recordset is empty. You adjust this by adding to the sContext string on your own if you know the container you want to see. Or, you can build it dynamically and do the tree control navigation thing by getting all the containers in the current container and letting the user navigate down to where they want to go. The query to get containers is similar to the one to get users; you only have to provide a different filter.

Example 21-36 *Obtaining a List of Organizational Unit Containers in Active Directory*

```
!Build the query.  We are only interested in seeing OUs and containers here so
 filter everything else out or else it'll show a huge clutter of stuff we do not
 want to see.
    sFilter = "(¦(objectCategory=organizationalUnit)(objectClass=container))"
    sLdapQuery = "<" & sContext & ">;" & sFilter & ";AdsPath,cn;onelevel"

!Get the result record set which contains all the containers and OUs in the
 passed in container
    Set rs = con.Execute(sLdapQuery)
```

The recordset now contains all the containers found in the container path you passed it using the sContext string. To navigate to a sub-container you just need to adjust the sContext string and reload the users and sub-containers in that container and so on. To do this, you need to iterate through the recordset returned and assign the "ADSPath" column value as desired. You can assign this to an adsContainer object and get at the GUID, class, path, name, parent, and schema values on that node in Active Directory if you want. For example, if you had the previous container recordset positioned on the Users container from the root, you could do this:

```
Dim adsContainer As IADs
    Set adsContainer = GetObject(rs.("ADSPath"))
    MsgBox adsContainer.ADSPath
    MsgBox adsContainer.Name
```

The first message box would spit out something like this:

```
"LDAP://OU=Users,OU=Unity,DC=AnswerMonkey,DC=com"
```

and the second message box would show simply

```
"CN=Users".
```

Using this mechanism you can easily build a tree control to let users navigate around the directory, which is exactly what the Remove Subscriber Properties example project does.

Once you have found the user you want to clean, you need to remove the ciscoEcsbuUMLocationObjectId and ciscoEcsbuObjectType properties from that object so that they can be imported into another Unity server. The sAdsPath used here is an LDAP string that identifies the user in the directory similar to what we used before. It looks something like this:

```
LDAP://CN=JLindborg,CN=Users,DC=AnswerMonkey,DC=net
```

You can get it the same way we got the ADSPath on the previous container: by iterating through the recordset created with the users filter and populating a list for users to choose from, or constructing it manually.

Example 21-37 *Clearing Unity Properties from a User Object in Active Directory*

```
Dim unityUser As IADs
    Set unityUser = GetObject(sAdsPath)
    unityUser.PutEx ADS_PROPERTY_CLEAR, "ciscoEcsbuUMLocationObjectId", vbNull
    unityUser.PutEx ADS_PROPERTY_CLEAR, "ciscoEcsbuObjectType", vbNull
    unityUser.SetInfo
```

At this point, the Active Directory user is now clean and can be imported into any Unity server in the directory.

Adding a New Public Distribution List

A couple of important notes about working with distribution lists here before we dive into the code example. First, the stored procedures for dealing with public distribution lists were not added and working properly until the release of Unity 4.0(3). If you are running 4.0(2) or earlier, you will not be able to create or remove distribution lists or add members to lists using SQL.

When we refer to "public distribution lists" we are referring to "system distribution lists" that were discussed in Chapter 3 and not to the "scope distribution lists" that are used to bound user lists for the name lookup handlers. The csp_DistributionListCreate stored procedure discussed here can be used to either create a brand-new distribution list or to import an existing distribution list from the directory.

The distribution lists stored procedures will all work with Exchange 5.5, 2000, 2003, and Domino; however, there are a few things to keep in mind:

In Active Directory (Exchange 2000 and 2003) new lists are created in the container you selected as new universal distribution lists during the Unity installation. The account associated with the directory-facing services must have rights to create distribution lists. Therefore, if you restricted such rights during the installation of Unity you need to rerun the permissions wizard and grant such rights or these scripts will fail. When importing lists in Active Directory, you can include universal (distribution) or security groups; both will work just fine. When importing lists in Active Directory, use the directory ID value from the object which corresponds to the ObjectGUID field. You need to convert this into a usable string, which we covered earlier in the Importing a Subscriber example.

In the case of Domino, new lists are created as multipurpose groups. When importing with Domino, only import either Multipurpose or Mail groups. If you import an Access Control, Deny Access, or Servers type group, strange things will happen because you cannot send mail to those types of groups. Do not do that. When importing a list from Domino, pass in the value from the Unique Identifier (UUID) field into the DirectoryID parameter and you are good to go.

There are stored procedures for creating scope distribution lists and adding members to them as well, but you will also notice they lack many of the features found in the system distribution list procedures, most notably the directory syncronization flags. These scope distribution lists are, at the time of this writing, intended only for internal use by the directory monitors and should be avoided until they are cleaned up and ready.

The creation of a new distribution list here is easy. You only need to provide a display name, alias, and the ObjectID of a subscriber or distribution list to act as the owner for the list. You also have the option to pass in an extension as well, but it is not required. If you are importing an existing distribution list from the directory, then you only need to pass in the DirectoryID and alias of that list, as well as providing the ObjectID of the owner. You can refer to the importing subscribers example to see how to pull directory ID values from objects in the directory. We will only cover the creation of a new list here.

Example 21-38 *Creating a New Distribution List*

```
Private Sub cmdCreateList_Click()
Dim strDLAlias As String
Dim strDLDisplayName As String
Dim strAdministratorObjectID As String
Dim oCommand As ADODB.Command
Dim strSyncTicket As String
Dim rsTemp As ADODB.Recordset
Dim strText as String

!Collect the display name of the distribution list to be added.  Because this is the
string used to identify distribution lists in the SA interface you need to make
sure it is unique.  While not necessary from a database perspective, presenting
the user with multiple lists named the same thing and expecting them to select
the right one is not terribly friendly.
    strDLDisplayName = InputBox("Enter display name for new public distribution
        list", "Enter distribution list display name")

! If the display name is empty, bail out.  We will limit the display name here to 40
characters because the SA limits the input of the display name for DLs to 40
characters as well,this should be sufficient for our purposes here.
    If Len(strDLDisplayName) = 0 Then
        Exit Sub
    ElseIf Len(strDLDisplayName) > 40 Then
        MsgBox "Easy there Tex.  Keep the display name under 40 characters please."
        Exit Sub
    End If

! Check to see if the display name is unique, technically the display name
does not have to be unique, but the SA only shows the display name as a selection
criteria and there is no way to distinguish the lists apart , so we will
enforce uniqueness here.
```

continues

Example 21-38 *Creating a New Distribution List (Continued)*

```
Set rsTemp = New ADODB.Recordset
rsTemp.CursorLocation = adUseClient
rsTemp.Open "SELECT Alias, DisplayName FROM vw_DistributionList WHERE
  DisplayName='" + strDLDisplayName + "'", strConnectionString, adOpenKeyset,
  adLockReadOnly
If rsTemp.RecordCount > 0 Then
    MsgBox "That display name conflicts with one or more public distribution
      lists already in the database.  Please select a unique display name."
    rsTemp.Close
    GoTo CleanUp
End If

rsTemp.Close
```

```
! Generate an alias from the display name. The SQL Syncher will tack on the
system ID of the local Unity install for this so as long as the alias is unique
within the set of public DLs we know about in SQL you can be sure the
alias is unique in the directory. If you want to be extra sure you can tack on
the number of seconds since midnight on 1/1/2000 or something but it should not
be necessary.  Regardless, if the alias is not unique, the stored procedure will
fail and return to you a description to that effect so it wont be the end of the
world.
    strDLAlias = Replace(strDLDisplayName, " ", "_")
```

```
!We could get sophisticated and check for illegal characters in
the display name, however I am going to be draconian and only allow
characters, letters, spaces, and underscores.  If you want to get fancy and let
your users add various special characters (making sure you account for the
differences in Exchange 5.5 and AD and Domino here) you can go wild.  I leverage
the handy "Like" operator here to evaluate the string quickly in one shot.  I
first remove the underscores from the alias to make this easier, and because
the spaces were removed when constructing the alias we only need to check that
all characters are letters or numbers here.
    strText=Replace(strDLAlias,"_","")

    If strText Like "*[!0-9,!a-z,!A-z]*" Then
        MsgBox "The display name can contain only spaces, letters, numbers and
          underscores.  No other characters are allowed"
        Goto CleanUp
    End If
```

```
!Finally, force the user to select a subscriber to act as the owner/administrator
for this list. At this time this value is not actually used for anything other
than display purposes in the SA. Eventually, however, it will be and it is
considered a database inconsistency if it is not set properly.  You could also
allow the user to select a distribution list for this, of course, but for our
purposes here we will just use a subscriber.  The frmSubscriberSearch form exposes
3 public variables that include the ObjectId of the subscriber selected, their
display name and a bCancelHit Boolean that indicates the user exited out of the
form without selecting a user.
    frmSubscriberSearch.Show vbModal
```

Example 21-38 *Creating a New Distribution List (Continued)*

```
! This is not  the greatest user interface in the world and for a
production application I would put this on a separate form so the
display name and administrator and possibly an optional extension could be
entered and checked separately .For our purposes here, however, the user is
just going to take it in the shorts if they screw up here and they will have to
start again.
    If frmSubscriberSearch.bCancelHit or Len(frmSubscriberSearch.strObjectID) = 0
      Then Then
        MsgBox "You must select a subscriber to act as the administrator for the
          new list... please try again."
        GoTo CleanUp
    Else
        strAdministratorObjectID = frmSubscriberSearch.strObjectID
    End If

! Force a redraw of the main form and then put the mouse into "I'm working on it"
mode.  For a production application I would float a splash screen to the
top indicating the DL was being created or the like, but for our purposes here
this is fine.
    frmMain.Refresh
    frmMain.MousePointer = vbHourglass
    DoEvents

    Set oCommand = New ADODB.Command
    oCommand.ActiveConnection = strConnectionString
    oCommand.CommandType = adCmdStoredProc

!OK, we have everything we need — the alias and display name of the DL to create
and the ObjectId of the subscriber that will act as the administrator - let us
create the new DL.
    oCommand.CommandText = "csp_DistributionListCreate"

    oCommand.Parameters.Item("@Alias") = oCommand.CreateParameter("Alias",
      adVarChar, adParamInput, , strDLAlias)
    oCommand.Parameters.Item("@DisplayName") =
      oCommand.CreateParameter("DisplayName", adVarChar, adParamInput, ,
      strDLDisplayName)
    oCommand.Parameters.Item("@AdministratorObjectID") =
      oCommand.CreateParameter("AdministratorObjectID", adGUID, adParamInput, ,
      strAdministratorObjectID)

!Tell the SQLSyncher to push this new DL into the directory.  The synch Flag of 2
means just distribution lists here, of course.  It is the default value and it is
not strictly necessary to pass it in here but whenever forcing a synch I like to
be explicit about the flags regardless.
    oCommand.Parameters.Item("@DirectorySync") =
      oCommand.CreateParameter("DirectorySync", adInteger, adParamInput, , 1)
    oCommand.Parameters.Item("@DirectorySyncFlags") =
      oCommand.CreateParameter("DirectorySyncFlags", adInteger, adParamInput, , 2)
```

continues

Example 21-38 *Creating a New Distribution List (Continued)*

```
! We need to create a GUID that we can pass into the stored procedure so we can
look for it in the DirectorySyncTicket table in SQL which is used to pass back
the results of this sync
    strSyncTicket = generateDirectorySyncTicket
    oCommand.Parameters.Item("@DirectorySyncTicket") =
      oCommand.CreateParameter("DirectorySyncTicket", adGUID, adParamInput, ,
      strSyncTicket)

    oCommand.Execute

! Wait for sync process to complete.  This is the same generic synch ticket wait
routine used in the subscriber add routine, you can check the code details there
if you like.
    If WaitForSyncToFinish(strSyncTicket) = False Then
        MsgBox "SQL Sync to directory failed when adding new distributionlist" +
            vbCrLf + "You can check the SQLSyncSvr logs in the \commserver\logs
            directory for more details"
    Else
        MsgBox "The directory sync is complete for new distribution list"
    End If

    frmMain.MousePointer = vbDefault

CleanUp:
    ! Close out the recordsets and exit
    On Error Resume Next
    rsTemp.Close
    Set rsTemp = Nothing
    Set oCommand = Nothing
End Sub
```

Removing an Existing Public Distribution List

Removing a public distribution list is similar to removing a subscriber, however the potential for creating broken links in the database as a result of its removal is considerably more limited. You do still need to worry about removing a list that is set as an owner or a message recipient of a handler, and replacing the list you are removing with another user or list, but that is it. No other references to a public distribution list are allowed.

You have the option of either removing just the Unity properties from a distribution list and leaving it in the directory or using the force remove flag on the directory syncronization options to delete the object in the directory entirely. This is similar to removing subscribers, however there is an important difference for public distribution lists that should be noted. Unlike subscribers, distribution lists can be shared across multiple Unity servers that are installed into the same directory. Therefore, if you remove a distribution list from the directory, or just remove the Unity properties, you can actually yank it out of other Unity servers. After a distribution lists has its Unity properties removed, all Unity servers will drop that list out of its local database of system distribution lists. As noted earlier, this is not the case for scope distribution list references. There is not an easy way to determine what other Unity servers in the directory might be affected by this (that is, which servers might have used that distribution list as an owner/recipient on a handler object) other than connecting to each one remotely and checking. This is not ideal. It is unusual to delete distribution lists programmatically, but just in case you find yourself in such a situation we will cover the high points here.

The first thing to do is to go through the predelete steps to see if any objects on the local Unity server are using this distribution list as an owner and/or message recipient and to provide a suitable replacement object. You can use the sp_ChangeOwner and sp_ChangeRecipient stored procedures to do this as was discussed earlier in the delete subscriber example. Once you have taken care of any potential reference issues there, the process of removing the distribution list is straightforward.

Example 21-39 *Delete a Public Distribution List*

```
!Delete the distribution list currently selected in the listDLs list box on the
  form.
Private Sub cmdDeleteList_Click()
Dim oCommand As ADODB.Command
Dim strSyncTicket As String
Dim rsTemp As ADODB.Recordset

! Verify that the user wishes to delete this distribution list.
    If MsgBox("Are you sure you want to delete the selected distribution list?",
        vbYesNo) = vbNo Then
        Exit Sub
    End If


    Set rsTemp = New ADODB.Recordset
    rsTemp.CursorLocation = adUseClient

! We need to pass the SystemDListObjectId of the selected distribution list into
  the stored procedure for deletion - as such we will need to find this record in
  SQL to fetch that data.
    rsTemp.Open "SELECT SystemDListObjectID, Alias FROM vw_DistributionList WHERE
        Alias='" + listDLs.Text + "'", strConnectionString, adOpenKeyset,
        adLockReadOnly

! Really none of the 3 error conditions would happen in a typical system, but
  you cannot be too careful.
    If rsTemp.RecordCount = 0 Then
        MsgBox "Unable to find distribution list by the selected alias."
        GoTo CleanUp
    ElseIf rsTemp.RecordCount > 1 Then
        MsgBox "More than one match for in the distribution list table for the
selected alias."
        GoTo CleanUp
    End If
```

continues

Example 21-39 *Delete a Public Distribution List (Continued)*

```
        If IsNull(rsTemp("SystemDListObjectID")) Then
            MsgBox "The SystemDListObjectId property for the selected distribution list
                is NULL."
            GoTo CleanUp
        End If

        Set oCommand = New ADODB.Command
        oCommand.ActiveConnection = strConnectionString
        oCommand.CommandType = adCmdStoredProc

! OK, we have the ObjectID of the distribution list to delete which is all we need.
        oCommand.CommandText = "csp_DistributionListDelete"

        oCommand.Parameters.Item("@SystemDListObjectID") =
            oCommand.CreateParameter("SystemDlistObjectID", adGUID, adParamInput, ,
            rsTemp("SystemDListObjectID"))

! Tell the SQLSyncher to push this change into the directory.  The "2"
for the synch flags here tells the syncher to only work with the DL — which in
this case is really the only flag that makes sense.  It is the default if you
do not pass anything in but it is good to be explicit anyway.
        oCommand.Parameters.Item("@DirectorySync") =
            oCommand.CreateParameter("DirectorySync", adInteger, adParamInput, , 1)
        oCommand.Parameters.Item("@DirectorySyncFlags") =
            oCommand.CreateParameter("DirectorySyncFlags", adInteger, adParamInput, , 2)

! NOTE: We COULD pass in a ForceRemove flag set to 1 here to make the directory
monitor remove the distribution list from the directory as well, but for this
example I just remove it from Unity which will also clean the Unity properties
from the list in the directory. You can import it again later.

! We need to create a GUID that we can pass into the stored procedure so we can
look for it in the DirectorySyncTicket table in SQL which is used to pass back
the results of this sync.
        strSyncTicket = generateDirectorySyncTicket
        oCommand.Parameters.Item("@DirectorySyncTicket") =
            oCommand.CreateParameter("DirectorySyncTicket", adGUID, adParamInput, ,
            strSyncTicket)

        'Let the stored proc fly.
        oCommand.Execute

        !Wait for sync process to complete.
        If WaitForSyncToFinish(strSyncTicket) = False Then
            MsgBox "(error)SQL Sync to directory failed when deleting the
                distributionlist" + vbCrLf + "You can check the SQLSyncSvr logs in the \
                commserver\logs directory for more details"
        Else
            MsgBox "The directory sync is complete for the distribution list removal"
        End If

CleanUp:
    !Close out the recordsets and exit.
```

Example 21-39 *Delete a Public Distribution List (Continued)*

```
        On Error Resume Next
        rsTemp.Close
        Set rsTemp = Nothing
        Set oCommand = Nothing
End Sub
```

Adding a Member to a Public Distribution List

Before adding users to a system distribution list, you must first create a new one or import an existing one from the directory. The distribution list you want to add the subscriber to must be in the DistributionList table in SQL. This will only be the case if you have created them through Unity or imported them.

Example 21-40 *Adding a Member to a Public Distribution List*

```
! Select a subscriber to add to a distribution list.  The distribution list is
referenced by an alias string in the listDLs list box on the form.  The user to
add to the list is selected in a subscriber search dialog that returns the
ObjectID of the selected subscriber.
Private Sub cmdAddUser_Click()
Dim strSubscriberObjectID As String
Dim strSubscriberDirectoryID As String
Dim strSystemDlistObjectID As String
Dim strDLDirectoryID As String
Dim rsTemp As ADODB.Recordset
Dim strSQL As String
Dim oCommand As ADODB.Command
Dim strSyncTicket As String

    !Make sure a distribution list is selected in the list box.
    If Me.listDLs.ListIndex < 0 Then
        MsgBox "You must first select a distribution list to add users to"
        Exit Sub
    End If

! Get the user to select a subscriber on the local Unity server.  This form allows
the user to select a subscriber in a simple grid and then exposed the selection
via public variables.  If the user hits cancel without selecting a subscriber
the public bCancel Boolean will be set to true.  Showing this using the vbModal
option means it will require input before the user is allowed to do anything
else which simplifies things a great deal.
    frmSubscriberSearch.Show vbModal

    If frmSubscriberSearch.bCancelHit = True Then
!The user opted to cancel out of the dialog without selecting a user -—exit out.
        Exit Sub
    End If
```

continues

Example 21-40   *Adding a Member to a Public Distribution List (Continued)*

```
!Snag the directoryID and objectID of the subscriber to add.  This stored
procedure is a little extra fussy in that it wants both the objectID and
DirectoryID of both the subscriber being added and the distribution list they
are being added to.  The reasons for this are a bit mysterious but my role is
not to ask why.
    strSubscriberObjectID = frmSubscriberSearch.strObjectID

    Set rsTemp = New ADODB.Recordset
    rsTemp.CursorLocation = adUseClient

! Retrieve the subscriber's directoryID which is required for this SP to work
properly.
    strSQL = "SELSECT DirectoryID FROM vw_Subscriber WHERE SubscriberObjectID='" +
        strSubscriberObjectID + "'"
    rsTemp.Open strSQL, strConnectionString, adOpenKeyset, adLockReadOnly

    If rsTemp.RecordCount = 0 Then
       MsgBox "Error!  Subscriber could not be found by SubscriberObjectID=" +
          strSubscriberObjectID
       GoTo CleanUp
    ElseIf rsTemp.RecordCount > 1 Then
       MsgBox "Error!  More than one subscriber found by SubscriberObjectID=" +
          strSubscriberObjectID
       GoTo CleanUp
    End If

! Check to see if the DirectoryID for the selected subscriber is NULL —this
usually means there was a problem synching them to the directory when they were
first entered. Either way it spells bad news for us so we will have to bail out.
    If IsNull(rsTemp("DirectoryID")) Then
       MsgBox "Error! The selected subscriber has a NULL directory ID - this usually
          means they did not synch to the directory properly when created."
       GoTo CleanUp
    End If

    strSubscriberDirectoryID = rsTemp("DirectoryID")

    rsTemp.Close

! Check to see if this subscriber is already a top level member of the
distribution list.
    strSQL = "SELECT vw_Subscriber.Alias FROM vw_Subscriber INNER JOIN vw_
        SystemDListMember ON vw_systemDListMember.DirectoryID=vw_
        Subscriber.DirectoryID WHERE ParentAlias='" + listDLs.Text + "' and vw_
        Subscriber.Alias='" + strSubscriberAlias + "'"
    rsTemp.Open strSQL, strConnectionString, adOpenKeyset, adLockReadOnly

    If rsTemp.RecordCount > 0 Then
      MsgBox "This subscriber is already a member of the selected distribution list"
       GoTo CleanUp
    End If

    rsTemp.Close
```

Example 21-40 *Adding a Member to a Public Distribution List (Continued)*

```
! Retrieve the SystemDListObjectID and DirectoryID of the currently selected
distribution list that the user wants to add this subscriber to.  We will need
both for the stored procedure to work properly.
    strSQL = "SELECT Alias, SystemDListObjectID, DirectoryID from vw_
        DistributionList WHERE Alias='" + listDLs.Text + "'"

    rsTemp.Open strSQL, strConnectionString, adOpenKeyset, adLockReadOnly

    If rsTemp.RecordCount = 0 Then
        MsgBox "Error!  Could not find distribution list by selected alias."
        GoTo CleanUp
    ElseIf rsTemp.RecordCount > 1 Then
        MsgBox "Error!  Found more than one match in the distribution list table
            for selected alias."
        GoTo CleanUp
    End If

! Check to see if the DirectoryID is NULL as above -— again this usually indicates
there was a problem synching the object to the directory when it was created
originally.
    If IsNull(rsTemp("DirectoryID")) Then
        MsgBox "Error! The DirectoryID of the selected distribution list is NULL -
            this usually means there was a problem synching the list to the directory
            when it was created."
        GoTo CleanUp
    End If

    strDLDirectoryID = rsTemp("DirectoryID")
    strSystemDlistObjectID = rsTemp("SystemDListObjectID")

    rsTemp.Close

! OK, we have the ObjectID and DirectoryID of both the subscriber to be added and
the distribution list to add them to so we are   ready to roll with the stored
procedure here.
    Set oCommand = New ADODB.Command
    oCommand.ActiveConnection = strConnectionString
    oCommand.CommandType = adCmdStoredProc

    oCommand.CommandText = "csp_SystemDListMemberCreate"

    oCommand.Parameters.Item("@SystemDListObjectID") =
        oCommand.CreateParameter("SystemDListObjectID", adGUID, adParamInput, ,
        strSystemDlistObjectID)
    oCommand.Parameters.Item("@SystemDListDirectoryID") =
        oCommand.CreateParameter("SystemDListDirectoryID", adVarChar,
        adParamInput, , strDLDirectoryID)

    oCommand.Parameters.Item("@SubscriberObjectID") =
        oCommand.CreateParameter("SubscriberObjectID", adGUID, adParamInput, ,
        strSubscriberObjectID)
```

continues

Example 21-40 *Adding a Member to a Public Distribution List (Continued)*

```
        oCommand.Parameters.Item("@SubscriberDirectoryID") =
          oCommand.CreateParameter("SubscriberDirectoryID", adVarChar,
          adParamInput, , strSubscriberDirectoryID)

! Tell the stored proc to force this change into the directory for us, of course.
The 1 for the directory synch flag here indicates to only synch the user
information.
        oCommand.Parameters.Item("@DirectorySync") =
          oCommand.CreateParameter("DirectorySync", adInteger, adParamInput, , 1)
        oCommand.Parameters.Item("@DirectorySyncFlags") =
          oCommand.CreateParameter("DirectorySyncFlags", adInteger, adParamInput, , 1)

! We need to create a GUID that we can pass into the stored proc such that we can
look for it in the DirectorySyncTicket table in SQL which is used to pass back
the results of this sync.
        strSyncTicket = generateDirectorySyncTicket
        oCommand.Parameters.Item("@DirectorySyncTicket") =
          oCommand.CreateParameter("DirectorySyncTicket", adGUID, adParamInput, ,
          strSyncTicket)

        frmMain.Refresh
        frmMain.MousePointer = vbHourglass
        DoEvents

        oCommand.Execute

        frmMain.MousePointer = vbDefault

! Wait for sync process to complete.
        If WaitForSyncToFinish(strSyncTicket) = False Then
            MsgBox "(error)SQL Sync to directory failed when adding subscriber to DL"
              + vbCrLf + "You can check the SQLSyncSvr logs in the \commserver\logs
              directory for more details"
        Else
            MsgBox "    Directory sync complete for subscriber add"
        End If

CleanUp:
    ! Close out the recordsets and exit.
    On Error Resume Next
    rsTemp.Close
    Set rsTemp = Nothing
    Set oCommand = Nothing
End Sub
```

Summary

We have covered only a relatively small number of functions you can do using stored procedures and views against the UnityDB database on your Unity server. A quick glance through the UnityDB tables and stored procedures will reveal we have only discussed a rather small percentage of what is in there. However, for most people in the field, the basic provisioning of subscribers and public distribution lists is sufficient for their needs.

The main thing we want you to take away from this chapter is that regardless of the type of connection to the system we provide in the future, the basic use of stored procedures and views will remain. Nothing you to today will be "throw away" work that needs to be scrapped entirely in the future. For example, an XML/SOAP wrapper around this functionality will still simply pass through remote calls to these same stored procedures and views that we have discussed. Do not be afraid to jump in now because you are worried everything will change in the next version. Nearly all the tools found today on www.ciscounitytools.com, as well as the Unity conversations in later 4.x versions, use these same interfaces and rebuilding them all from scratch is not going to happen, we assure you! As long as you avoid editing tables directly wherever possible, your code should continue to work with few, if any, modifications moving forward.

Also, check for updated versions of the Cisco Unity Data Link Explorer (CUDLE) tool on www.ciscounitytools.com. The data dictionary is constantly being updated and improved to provide more and better details on the values found in the various database tables as well as the use of the stored procedures themselves. This will be you best resource as a developer working with Unity.

CHAPTER **22**

Third-Party Tools and Applications

In addition to Cisco Unity, there are other software components that are needed to successfully run a stable voice-messaging environment. This mainly includes virus-detection software and backup software. This chapter covers Cisco's support policy for third-party software and lists the third-party software that has been tested in a Cisco lab and is qualified to run in a Unity voice-messaging environment.

Supported Backup Software

- VERITAS Backup Exec for Microsoft Windows NT and Windows 2000, version 8.5 and later
- NetBackup, version 4.5 and later

Supported Fax Server Software

The following fax servers installed with an Exchange gateway are supported for use with Cisco Unity 4.0(*x*):

- Biscom FAXCOM for Microsoft Exchange, version 6.19 and later
- Captaris RightFax, version 6 and later
- Esker Faxgate, version 7 and later
- Fenestrae Faxination, version 4 and later
- Interstar Technologies LightningFax, version 5.5 and later
- Omtool Fax Sr., version 3 and later
- Optus FACSys, version 4.5 and later
- TOPCALL, all versions

The following fax servers are supported for use with Cisco Unity 4.0(*x*) with VPIM. They are installed with an Exchange gateway and use the TIFF-F file format with images encoded so that there is only one image strip per facsimile page.

- Biscom FAXCOM for Microsoft Exchange, version 6.19 and later
- Captaris RightFax (version 6 and later for Exchange, version 8.0.0120 and later for Domino)
- Esker Faxgate, version 7 and later
- Fenestrae Faxination, version 4 and later
- Interstar Technologies LightningFax, version 5.5 and later
- Omtool Fax Sr., version 3 and later
- Optus FACSys, version 4.5 and later
- TOPCALL, all versions

Install the fax cards, fax server software, and dedicated fax lines on the fax server. Installing fax software on the Cisco Unity server is not supported. Refer to the fax server documentation for a list of supported cards and integration methods.

Supported Monitoring Software

The following monitoring software has been qualified by Cisco for use with Cisco Unity 4.0(*x*):

- Adiscon EventReporter.
- Concord SystemEDGE, version 4.1.
- Hewlett-Packard OpenView. Supported for IP monitoring of Cisco Unity, SQL Server, and Exchange services, on all supported Cisco Unity hardware platforms.
- Microsoft:
  - Management Console (MMC)
  - Network Provider Monitor
- NetIQ VoIP Manager, version 2.0 for Cisco Unity. Install only the agent on the Cisco Unity server.

Supported Virus-Scanning Software

The following virus-scanning software has been qualified by Cisco for use with Cisco Unity 4.0(*x*):

- Computer Associates InoculateIT for Microsoft Windows NT and Windows 2000, version 4.53, build 627 and later

- McAfee:
  - GroupShield Domino, version 5.0 and later
  - NetShield for Microsoft Windows NT and Windows 2000, version 4.5 and later
- Symantec:
  - Norton AntiVirus for Lotus Notes/Domino, version 2.5 and later
  - Norton AntiVirus for Microsoft Exchange, version 2.13 and later
  - Norton AntiVirus for Microsoft Windows NT and Windows 2000, version 5.02 and later
- Trend Micro:
  - ScanMail for Lotus Notes, version 2.5 and later
  - ScanMail for Microsoft Exchange 2000, version 5 and later
  - ScanMail for Microsoft Exchange 5.5, version 3.x and later
  - ServerProtect for Microsoft Windows, version 5.5

Additional Supported Software

The following optional software has been qualified by Cisco for use with Cisco Unity 4.0(x):

- Adobe Acrobat Reader, version 4.0 and later.
- American Power Conversion (APC) PowerChute Plus for Windows 2000 and Windows NT, version 5.2.1 and later.
- Cisco IDS Host Sensor Agent, version 9/26/2001 and later.
- Dell OpenManage. Supported when used in conjunction with the Dell Remote Assistant Card.
- Hewlett-Packard Insight Manager. Supported when used in conjunction with the Hewlett-Packard Remote Insight Lights-Out Edition card.
- IBM Director. Supported when used in conjunction with the IBM Remote Supervisor Adapter.
- RSA SecureID ACE/Agent for Microsoft Windows 2000, version 5.0.
- WinZip, version 7.0 and later.
- Cisco Secure Agent for Unity.

Unsupported Third-Party Software

Third-party software that has not been qualified for use with Cisco Unity is not supported. Cisco TAC might ask that it be removed during troubleshooting. The products below should not be installed on the Unity server.

- Command Anti-Virus for Windows on subscriber workstations
- Fax software on the Cisco Unity server
- Microsoft Outlook on the Cisco Unity server

In addition to the aforementioned products, always check the documentation for the current version of Unity for new and updated compatibility information.

CHAPTER 23

The Future of Unity

Cisco Unity is reaching maturation in the unified messaging industry. However, it has not yet reached its peak. This means that several more years or longer of life are expected for the product. Competition might come and go, but the Unity product offering will continue to be innovative and a strong and viable alternative to legacy voice messaging and other competing UM products.

Continuing with Unity 4.04 and Unity 4.05, you will see the Unity for Domino offering expand its VM interoperability capabilities. Unity's Bridge networking capabilities will also improve and will provide a stronger migration solution for those who want to replace their Octel networks.

The next major release of Unity (5.0) will support migrations from the 4.x line of Unity, but will be a new breed of voice messaging and unified messaging. The specific improvements in the next major release of Unity will come in two areas: minimal or no dependencies on existing messaging infrastructures to provide standard voice-messaging services, and the capability to scale to large user and port densities.

Unity's focus continues to expand into the enterprise space and beyond. A strong focus is placed on developing a high-capacity, enterprise-class solution for UM, VM, and possibly even integrated messaging, to support the managed service space that is developing in the convergence industry. The product should grow into the tenant services market as a high-scale and highly resilient offering.

Unity's UM capabilities are expected to become more precise, with far less impact or dependence on an existing third-party messaging infrastructure than the 4.x line. At the same time, Unity's UM capabilities are expected to become less affected by existing messaging infrastructures, whether MS Exchange, Lotus Domino, or more open IMAP-based solutions.

As for features, Unity's product solution set will include a stronger emphasis on customized TUI conversations, administrative, and even subscriber interfaces. Of course, this potential future of Unity is subject to change and could be altered in many ways beyond the control of this author. Regardless, it is sure to be an interesting ride watching the product grow and expand in the market.

Switch File Settings

A *switch file* is a text file that contains a number of settings that configure Unity to integrate to a particular private branch exchange (PBX). Basic settings determine which type of integration is used (analog serial or Telephony Application Programming Interface [TAPI]), whereas other settings refer to dial-tone templates. A Unity installation copies the switch files for all supported switch integrations to the \Commserver\Intlib directory. The integration files also reside in this directory.

The Unity switch file (along with any possible corresponding integration files) contains all of the switch-specific configuration information necessary to operate with that particular switch. For instance, the dial-tone frequencies on one PBX might be quite different than the dial-tone frequencies on another PBX. Different switch files for these two hypothetical PBXs will have different dial tone–recognition information for those two PBXs.

Throughout a given switch file, the characters & and , frequently are used in values for settings. The & represents a hook-flash, and the , represents a pause with a duration specified by PauseDuration. These characters are used to make up what often is referred to as a *dial string* (because it can be dialed from a phone).

Not all settings are relevant to every type of integration. For instance, tones sent from the switch for conveying call progress or disconnect are not applicable to Unity's Cisco Call-Manager integration. Therefore, no tone-specific settings are relevant to that type of integration. The following tables contain a note if the switch file setting is applicable to only a certain type of integration (for example, legacy only, for only serial and analog integrations; serial only, for only serial integrations; or CCM only, for only CallManager integrations,)

The values of the [Identity] section of the switch file generate a unique identifier for an integration selection. No two switch files should contain the same combination of values for the [Identity] section.

Table A-1   *Identity Values*

Setting	Description
SwitchManufacturer	(Text string) Used by the SA or UTIM to select the switch manufacturer. This describes the manufacturer of the switch (for example, Cisco).
SwitchModel	(Text string) Used by the SA or UTIM to select the switch manufacturer. This describes the manufacturer of the switch (for example, CallManager).
SwitchSoftwareVersion	(Text string) Used by the SA or UTIM to select the switch manufacturer. This describes the version of the switch software for the given switch (for example, 3.0 (1) or later).
IntegrationType	(Text string) Value used by the SA or UTIM to select the switch manufacturer. Also used by the MIU to determine which type of integration parser to load on PBX integrations, serial, or analog.

The [Configuration] section of the switch file contains information for call-control functions, such as transfer and recall, along with many timing parameters for ring cadence. The vast majority of the settings in the [Configuration] section are supported only for legacy integrations.

Table A-2   *Configuration Values*

Setting	Description
AllowZeroLeadingExtensions	Value that controls how a leading zero will be treated in a digit string representing a called or calling party. When set to 0, a called or calling party with the digit string of 0123 is considered 123.
DelayBeforeOpening	(Integer value, in seconds) Unity application setting that allows for a delay to be introduced after integration digits have been parsed and a particular greeting is played. The PBX sends integration digits to the voice-mail system after it has answered the call, so most PBXs do not open the voice path to the calling party (otherwise, that party would hear the digits rudely dialed). The PBX opens the voice path to the calling party after all the integration digits have been dialed. Some PBXs delay opening that voice path until after integration digits have been dialed. This setting allows Unity to accommodate the delay. Otherwise, Unity might start playing a greeting when the voice path has not been fully opened to the calling party, resulting in the first portion of the greeting being clipped.

Table A-2   *Configuration Values (Continued)*

Setting	Description
Integration	(Text string/legacy only) Pointer to section in AvAnalog.Avd file for switch files containing an IntegrationType of analog. Pointer to integration file for switch files containing an IntegrationType of serial. For serial, the Integration value is used to construct a particular integration filename in the following manner: `Av + <value for "Integration"> + .avd`
ConfirmReturn	(Text string/legacy only) The dial string that Unity must dial to return to a party on hold after placing that party on hold and connecting to another party. If nothing is specified, the value for the Recall setting is used. This is used in Unity's call-screening feature. For instance, a caller reaches Unity, and Unity places this caller on hold and dials another caller. That caller answers, but Unity wants to return to the original caller. The ConfirmReturn dial string is used for this.
DropDialtoneConsult	(Text string/legacy only) The dial string that Unity must dial to return to a party on hold after placing that party on hold and receiving a dial tone when attempting to connect to another party. If nothing is specified, the value for the Recall setting is used. This is used in Unity's call-screening feature. For instance, a caller reaches Unity, and then Unity places this caller on hold and dials another caller. Instead of the caller answering, Unity receives dial-tone and then wants to return to the original caller. The DropDialtoneConsult dial string is used for this.
DropDisconnectedConsult	(Text string/legacy only) The dial string that Unity must dial to return to a party on hold after placing that party on hold and receiving a dial tone when attempting to connect to another party. If nothing is specified, the value for the Recall setting is used. This is used in Unity's call-screening feature. For instance, a caller reaches Unity, and Unity places this caller on hold and dials another caller. Instead of the caller answering, Unity receives a disconnect and wants to return to the original caller. The DropDisconnectedConsult dial string is used for this.

continues

Table A-2   *Configuration Values (Continued)*

Setting	Description
TransferInitiate	(Text string/legacy only) The dial string that Unity must dial to start the transfer sequence on the PBX. The dial string usually places the incoming caller on hold and returns a dial tone to Unity.
BusyRecall	(Text string/legacy only) The dial string that Unity must return to the original caller when supervised-transferring to a phone that returns a busy condition. If nothing is specified, the value for the Recall setting is used.
Recall	(Text string/legacy only) The dial string that Unity must return to the original caller when supervised-transferring to a phone that returns a no-answer condition.
PauseDuration	(Integer value in milliseconds/legacy only) Duration of pause time represented by a , (comma) in a dial string.
ToneDialInterDigitDelay	(Integer value in milliseconds/legacy only) Duration of pause between dialing DTMF digits in a dial string.
DigitToneDuration	(Integer value in milliseconds/legacy only) Duration of DTMF digit in a dial string.
DTMFDebounce	(Integer value, in milliseconds/legacy only) The time between receiving DTMF tones during which the tone is considered to be two tone events instead of one.
MinimumRingOnInterval	(Integer value in milliseconds/legacy only) As incoming ring voltage arrives at the voice board, the ring voltage must be present for this duration before the voice board considers the ring voltage a valid ring. The setting is only for incoming ring voltage. This setting does not affect call progress (ring cadence that the voice board hears after dialing a number).
MinimumRingOffInterval	(Integer value in milliseconds/legacy only) The minimum amount of time that must persist after a qualified ring signal (specified by MinimumRingOnInterval).
MinimumRingOnInterval	(Integer value in milliseconds/legacy only) The minimum amount of time before a subsequent ring signal can be a candidate for qualification. The setting is only for incoming ring cadence. This setting does not affect call progress (ring cadence that the voice board hears after dialing a number).

Table A-2 *Configuration Values (Continued)*

Setting	Description
WaitAnswerRings	(Integer value in approximate ring cycles/legacy only) Number of rings Unity waits before answering an incoming call when receiving an incoming call. Unity uses this number to calculate a delay to configure the Dialogic TSP to delay incoming call notification.
MaxWaitBetweenRings	(Integer value in milliseconds/legacy only) The maximum duration of absence of ring voltage in between two ring signals before the two ring signals are considered two different calls.
MinLoopCurrentOff	(Integer value in milliseconds/legacy only) The minimum duration of absence of the loop current to qualify for a valid disconnect signal.
IncomingCallRings	(Integer value/legacy only) Value that enforces a delay after the voice board detects a ring signal before the voice board software signals to Unity that a new call has arrived. During the delay, ring signal happens at the voice board, but Unity is unaware of the incoming call until after the delay.
MinimumMWIRequestInterval	(Integer value in milliseconds) The duration that Unity waits between dialing MWIs. Unity waits this duration after completing one MWI request and starting another. This setting affects both analog and serial MWI requests.
TrimDisconnectTonesOnRecordings	(Integer value, Boolean/legacy only) Value that determines whether Unity will trim off the tail end of a recorded message. The duration of the trimming is specified in the [Switch Disconnect Tone] section of the switch file. It has the following tone template: ```[Switch Disconnect Tone]\nFrequency1=480\nFrequencyDeviation1=50\nFrequency2=620\nFrequencyDeviation2=50\nTimeOn1=250\nTimeOnDeviation1=50\nTimeOff1=250\nTimeOffDeviation1=50\nCycles=8``` The formula is as follows: $(\text{TimeOn1} + \text{TimeOff1}) \times \text{Duration}$ or $(250 + 250) \times 8 = 4000$ (4 seconds)

continues

Table A-2 *Configuration Values (Continued)*

Setting	Description
HangUpTone	(Character/legacy only) Fourth-column DTMF tone that a PBX sends for a disconnect signal.
HookFlashDuration	(Integer value in milliseconds/legacy only) The time in which a "hook flash" is to be carried out when specified by & in a dial string.
RestrictDialing	(Text string) Schedule used to prevent dialed MWIs and notifications from happening. This often is used when a PBX conducts routine maintenance during which the PBX would place those ports out of service if dial-out activity happened. This string is generated by the RestrictDial.exe utility.
OutgoingGuardTime	(Integer value in milliseconds) Delay after call activity has ceased on a particular port and subsequent dialout activity can begin on that same port.
OutgoingPreDialDelayMs	(Integer value in milliseconds) Delay prepended to out-bound dial strings, such as transfer, MWI, and notification dialouts.
OutgoingPostDialDelayMs	(Integer value in milliseconds) Delay post-pended to out-bound dial strings, such as transfer, MWI, and notification dialouts.
WaitIfBufferedPacketPresent	(Integer value, Boolean/serial only) If there is already a serial packet in the packet buffer upon receiving a ring event, Unity waits for another serial packet (specified by MsToWaitForCallInfo in the integration file) if this setting is enabled. This might be necessary because the serial packet that is in the buffer was due a previously abandoned call.
SerialAutoAnswer	(Integer value, Boolean/serial only) When enabled, Unity answers a call immediately and then waits for a subsequent serial packet (specified by MsToWaitForCallInfo in the integration file), instead of waiting for a serial packet and then answering the call.
MaximumConcurrentMWIRequests	(Integer value) A "ceiling" for the total number of concurrent MWIs operating at one given time.
RingbackTimeout	(Integer value, milliseconds/legacy only) The duration of time with no ringback in a ringback cycle that must pass to consider the ring events two separate calls instead of one.

The following settings are applicable for MWI sections of a given switch file. In the case of alternate MWIs, more than one MWI section might exist for a given switch file. Requirements for the naming of MWI switch file sections are as follows:

- If multiple MWI sections exist, each section must have a unique name.

- MWI sections must contain the string "MWI."

Example MWI section:

```
[MWI Default]
Active=Yes
MWIType=Serial
SerialConfiguration=SMDI
UpdateDisplay=No
CodesChangeable=No
RetryCount=0
RetryInterval=0
```

Table A-3 *MWI Section Settings*

Setting	Description
Active	(Text string) Value that specifies whether a given MWI method in a switch file is enabled. A value of Yes signifies active.
MWIType	(Text string) Value used for specifying the MWI method type for a given MWI method. Serial and Analog are examples. It is possible to have one integration type specified for incoming call information and another for MWI.
SerialConfiguration	(Text string/serial only) Value that specifies a particular serial protocol to be used if the MWIType is Serial. Different serial protocols require different MWI packet formations. The serial MWI protocol settings are loaded from the following file: Av + <SerialConfiguraition value> + .Avd (for example, if the SerialConfiguration=SMDI, AvSmdi.Avd is used for MWI configuration).
UpdateDisplay	(Integer value, Boolean) If a subscriber receives a new message, by default, Unity does not attempt to light a MWI if it believes that the MWI is currently lit. By enabling this setting, Unity attempts to light the MWI, regardless of its current state.
CodesChangeable	(Text string/legacy only) Value that controls SA-editable MWI codes.

continues

Table A-3 *MWI Section Settings (Continued)*

Setting	Description
RetryCount	(Integer value) Number of subsequent MWI attempts made after making a normal successful MWI attempt (for instance, MessageWaitingRetryCount=2 actually sends three requests). This setting is used for both on and off attempts. If the initial MWI request is determined to be unsuccessful, the retry for that failure is not considered a MessageWaitingRetry. Retries are not uncommon for analog MWI methods; analog MWI methods do not support PBX confirmation of receiving the voice-mail server's MWI request. Retries generally are not needed for Serial and Skinny MWI types.
RetryInterval	(Integer value in minutes) Interval between subsequent MWI retry attempts.
PortMemory	(Integer value, Boolean) Value that requires that whichever port that lit MWI is also the same port to extinguish MWI. This is a requirement of some PBXs. This is applicable to analog MWI methods only. PortMemory also is used for MWI resyncs and retries. If enabled, the only time that PortMemory is not followed is when MWI status for a given subscriber transitions from off to on.
SeekMWIPort	(Integer value, Boolean/CCM only) Value that is applicable to Unity's multi-CCM cluster support. Unity sends MWI requests for a given subscriber to all connected CCM clusters (for instance, MWI requests are sent to all MWI-enabled ports).
Digit	(Character value) Value used to specify an alternate MWI type in the MWI section of a given switch file. The value for Digit is usually a character.
LampOn	(Text string/analog only) Feature access code used to light a MWI. It is used only for analog integrations (for serial integration, the MWI is configured in the corresponding integration file).
LampOff	(Text string/analog only) Feature access code used to extinguish an MWI. It is used only for analog integrations (for serial integration, the MWI is configured in the corresponding integration file).

A switch file for legacy integrations often contains a series of configuration settings that configure Unity to recognize different types of tones sent from the switch. The switch sends those tones to represent some sort of signaling for a call. These tone templates are discussed in more detail in Chapter 17, "Unity Telephony Integration."

INDEX

A

access
  hearing impairments, 260
  message, 267
  server administration
    COS (class of service), 755, 757
    GrantUnityAccess tool, 760–763
    single accounts, 757–759
  subscribers, planning, 305–306
  voice messages, 20–22
AccountLockout, UnityDB database, 107
accounts, Select Subscriber Changes page, 787
ACK method, SIP (Session Initiation Protocol), 652
ACLs (Domino), 549–550
Active Directory
  capacity planning, 298
  migration between two forests, 581–582
  property removal, 893–896
  switch file setting, 923
  user export, 765
Active Fax, 23
Active Voice CommServer Gateway (AvCsGateway)
  component, Registry, 123
Active Voice CommServer Manager. *See* AVCsMgr
Active Voice Media Master Proxy Server
  (AVMMProxyServer), 55–56
ActiveX Data Objects (ADO), Unity server
  connection, 825
activity reports, 741–742
AD conversation, 39
addressing digital networks, 449
AddrType property, directory synchronization, 868
adLockReadOnly flag, 826
admin group, Exchange, unified messaging
  configuration, 327
administration
  authentication, 253
  CUGA (Cisco Unity Greetings Administrator),
    241–242
  deployment methodology operations, 280
  multiple servers
    COS (class of service), 755–757
    GrantUnityAccess tool, 760–763

GSM (Global Subscriber Manager),
    764–767
  single account admin access, 757–759
programmatic administration
  adding public distribution lists, 896–900
  APIs support, 819
  call handler information retrieval,
    848–853
  creating subscribers, 856–865
  deleting subscribers, 884–893
  editing subscribers, 868–883
  importing subscribers, 865–868
  locating extension in dialing domain,
    841–846
  locating subscribers, 838–841
  locating Unity server, 838
  member addition to public distribution
    list, 903–906
  property removal in Active Directory,
    893–896
  removing public distribution list, 900–903
  SQL rights, 820–822
  subscriber information retrieval, 853–856
  Unity server connection, 823–838
  Unity web based SA interface, 847–848
  UnityDB SQL database rules, 822
SA, 239–240
  COS (class of service), 240–241
  field help, 241
  MMC (Media Master control), 241
  online help, 241
  subscriber templates, 240
Tools Depot, 242
  Advanced Settings tool, 246
  ATM (Audio Text Manager), 245
  CUBI (Cisco Unity Bulk Import Wizard),
    243
  GSM (Global Subscriber Manager),
    244–245
TUI features
  alternate extensions, 238–239
  message notification, 236–238
  MWI (message waiting indicator), 235
  subscribers, 228–229
Unity with Exchange, 501–502

Administration Process (Domino), 552

Administrative Access Activity report, 247

administrative consoles, configuring for Unity server installation, 587

Administrator

    Domino, 529–531

        object ID, call handler, 89–90

ADMonitorDirObjsList, UnityDB database, 107

ADMonitorDistributionListMember, UnityDB database, 107–108

ADO (ActiveX Data Objects), Unity server connection, 825

adOpenDynamic flag, 827

adOpenForwardOnly flag, 826

adOpenKeyset flag, 827

adOpenStatic flag, 827

ADSI, AvDsAD.exe directory monitor, 138

Advanced Settings tool, Tools Depot, 246

After Message Actions, call handler, 92

after-hours greeting, call handling, 88

AGC (Automatic Gain Control), 263–264

Alias property, directory synchronization, 868

All Subscribers object

    directory default, 153

    public distribution list, 705

AllowZeroLeadingExtensions switch file setting, 918

Alpha Directory Conversation, 39

alternate extensions

    Bulk Edit Utility, 811

    call handler, 93

    digital networks, 424–425

    editing subscribers, 872–876

    mail users collection, 100

    Select Subscriber Changes page, 799

    TUI administrator management, 238–239

alternate greeting, call handling, 88

AlternateDTMFIDs property, directory synchronization, 869

AMIS (Audio Messaging Interchange Specification), 576–577

AMISDisableOutbound property, directory synchronization, 869

analog DTMF integrations, 604–612

analysis, design costs

    hardware and software, 388–389

    services, 389

APIs (application programming interfaces), 6, 819

Application, Unity DB database, 109

application programming interfaces (APIs), 6, 819

applications

    audio-text

        activity reports, 741–742

        ATM (Audio Text Manager), 706–707

        call handlers, 666–684

        classic handler tree, 707–712

        directory handler, 688–694

        extension remapping, 701–702

        external number transfers, 713–715

        first available extension hunt, 724–726

        forwarding transfer rule override, 730–731

        greeting edit over phone interface, 719–720

        group mailboxes, 722–724

        holiday greetings, 726–727

        interview handler, 685–688

        language options, 702–703

        lock down call handlers, 715–719

        multiple languages, 720–722

        problem recovery, 742–746

        prompts, 735–738

        routing rules, 695–701

        scheduled off-hour caller-input options, 728

        subscriber transfer rules, 729–730

        subscribers, 685

        tenant services, 732–735

        troubleshooting, 746–753

        TTY/TDD users, 738–741

        Unity default configuration, 703–706

        voice mail greeting from operator console, 731–732

    object model, 85

Arbiter, 36–37

Arbiter component

    new call processing, 61

    Registry, 123

architectures, 32

    AVCsGateway, 34

    AVCsMgr component, 34

        Arbiter, 36–37

        AVWM (Windows Monitor), 45–46

        DOH (Data Object Hierarchy), 35–36

        DOHMMSvr, 45

integration, 43
log manager, 40–42
MIU, 42
RDBSvr, 44
resource manager, 36
ruler component, 37
SIP (Session Initiation Protocol), 43–44
TAPI interface, 42–43
TRaP connection server, 44–45
TUI applications, 38–40
UMR (Unity Messaging Repository), 37
UnityAVWAVE, 44
virtual queue, 44
AVCsNodgeMgr service, 57–58
AVDirChangeWriter service, 52
AVLic service, 53–54
AVMMProxyServer service, 55–56
AVMsgStoreMonitorSvr component, 47–48
AVNotificationMgr component, 46–47
AVRepDirSvrSvc service, 54–55
AVSQLSynchSvr service, 53
AVTTSSvc service, 56
CSBridgeConnector service, 56–57
CSEMSSvc service, 55
digital networks, 414
    data replication model, 416
    logical data structure, 417–418
    origins, 414–415
    protocols, 414
    shared messaging, 415
    synchronization, 418–419
directory monitor, 49–50
    Domino, 52
    Exchange 2000, 51–52
    Exchange 2003, 51–52
    Exchange 5.5, 50
MIU, 213, 216
    call object, 215–216
    integration object, 216
    line object, 217–218
    line servers, 217
    media object, 218
    object relationships, 219–223
    server, 213–215
    TTS object, 218
    UnityAvWav object, 218–219

TAPI, 208
TomCat service, 58
assessing post-implementation plans, 599
ATM (Audio Text Manager), 93, 102, 245, 706–707
Attempt Forward to Greeting conversation, 39
Attempt Sign In conversation, 39
AttemptForward conversation, 700
AttemptForwardToGreeting conversation, 39
AttemptSignIn conversation, 39, 700
attributes
    Domino directory monitor, 167–169
    Exchange 2000 directory monitor, 162–166
    Exchange 2003 directory monitor, 162–166
    Exchange 5.5 directory monitor, 154–158
audio
    control, CallManager TSP, 643–644
    MIU, 213
Audio Messaging Interchange Specification (AMIS), 576–577
Audio Text Manager (ATM), 93, 102, 245, 666, 706–707
audio-text applications
    activity reports, 741–742
    ATM (Audio Text Manager), 706–707
    call handlers, 666
        after-greeting action, 684
        after-message action, 684
        call flows, 679–680
        call transfer, 669–673
        caller-input, 676–678
        greetings, 674–675, 683–684
        messages, 678–679
        profile, 666–669
        transfer rules, 682–683
    classic handler tree, 707–708
        name lookup call handler, 710–712
        Product Information call handler, 709
        Technical Support call handler, 709–710
        Tiny Audio Text Application call handler, 708
    default subscriber template objects, 746
    directory handler, 688–694
    extension remapping, 701–702
    external number transfers, 713–715
    first available extension hunt, 724–726
    forwarding transfer rule override, 730–731
    greeting edit over phone interface, 719–720

group mailboxes, 722–724
holiday greetings, 726–727
interview handler, 685–688
language options, 702–703
lock down call handlers, 715–719
multiple languages, 720–722
problem recovery
    backups, 742–743
    default routing rules, 745
    resetting defaults, 743–745
    schedule reconstruction, 746
prompts, 735
    directory handler name-spelling, 738
    holding for transfer, 736–737
    locating, 736
    recording message after tone, 737–738
routing rules, 695
    checking phone switch information,
        695–698
    rule order, 698–701
schedule off-hour caller-input options, 728
subscribers, 685, 729–730
tenant services, 732–735
troubleshooting
    Call Viewer application, 747
    call-routing rules diagnostics, 750–753
    event log, 746–747
    PSM (Port Status Monitor), 748–750
TTY/TDD users, 738–741
Unity default configuration, 703–706
voice-mail transfer from operator console,
    731–732
authentication, administrative security, 253
AuthenticationProvider, Unity DB database, 109
automated attendants, digital networks, 451
    directory handler, 452–453
    transfer by extension, 451–452
Automatic Gain Control (AGC), 263–264
AvAnalog.Avd, integration file, 607–608
AvCsGateway (Active Voice CommServer Gateway)
    component, Registry, 123
AVCsGateway service, 34
AvCsMgr (Active Voice CommServer Manager)
    component, 34
    Arbiter, 36–37
    AVWM (Windows Monitor), 45–46
    DOH (Data Object Hierarchy), 35–36

DOHMMSvr, 45
integration, 43
log manager, 40–42
MIU, 42
RDBSvr, 44
Registry, 123
resource manager, 36
ruler component, 37
SIP (Session Initiation Protocol), 43–44
TAPI interface, 42–43
TRaP connection server, 44–45
TUI applications, 38–40
UMR (Unity Messaging Repository), 37
UnityAVWAVE, 44
virtual queue, 44
AvCsNodeMgr component, Registry, 123
AVCsNodgeMgr service, 57–58
AVDirChangeWriter service, 52
AvDomino, directory monitor, 138
AvDsAD.exe, directory monitor, 137–138
AvDSDomino, directory monitor, 166–169
AvDSEx55, directory monitor, 137, 154
    attributes, 154–158
    distribution list, 159–160
    global data, 160–161
AvDSGlobalCatalog.exe, directory monitor,
    137–138
AvEx55.exe, directory monitor, 138
AvLic component, Registry, 123
AVLic service, 53–54
AvLogMgr component, Registry, 123
AVMMProxyServer (Active Voice Media Master
    Proxy Server), 55–56
AvMsgStoreMonitorSvr component, 47–48
AvMsgStoreMonitorSvr service, 180
    DominoMonitor, 181, 197–200
    ExchangeMonitor
        component, 180–181
        notification, 196–197
AVNotificationMgr component, 46–47
AvNotifierMgr, diagnostics, 199
AVP_ADD_TO_DLS, mail users templates, 100
AVP_ADMINISTRATOR_OBJECT_ID, call
    handler, 89–90
AVP_AFTER_MESSAGE_ACTION, call
    handler, 92

AVP_AFTER_MESSAGE_OBJECT_ID, call handler, 92

AVP_AFTERMESSAGE_CONVERSATION, call handler, 92

AVP_ALTERNATE_DTMF_IDS, call handler, 93

AVP_CONTACT_RULES, call handlers, 87

AVP_COS_OBJECT_ID, mail users collection, 99

AVP_DEFAULT_PW_XXX, mail users templates, 101

AVP_EXIT_ACTION, Name Lookup Handler, 102

AVP_EXIT_CONVERSATION, Name Lookup Handler, 102

AVP_EXIT_OBJECT_ID, Name Lookup Handler, 102

AVP_FAX_RESTRICTION_OBJECT_ID, COS object, 93

AVP_LOCATION_OBJECT_ID
    call handler, 91
    mail users collection, 100

AVP_MENU_ENTRIES, call handlers, 87

AVP_MESSAGING_RULES, call handlers, 87–88

AVP_NO_INPUT_ACTION, Name Lookup Handler, 103

AVP_NO_INPUT_CONVERSATION, Name Lookup Handler, 103

AVP_NO_INPUT_OBJECT_ID, Name Lookup Handler, 103

AVP_NO_SELECTION_ACTION, Name Lookup Handler, 102

AVP_NO_SELECTION_CONVERSATION, Name Lookup Handler, 102

AVP_NO_SELECTION_OBJECT_ID, Name Lookup Handler, 102

AVP_NOTIFICATION_DEVICE, mail users collection, 97–98

AVP_NOTIFICATION_MWI, mail users collection, 98–99

AVP_NOTIFICATION_RULE, mail users collection, 98

AVP_NUMBER_PATTERNS, restriction tables, 104

AVP_OUTCALL_RESTRICTION_OBJECT_ID, COS object, 93

AVP_PDL_ADD_ACCESS, COS object, 94

AVP_PDL_DELETE_ACCESS, COS object, 94

AVP_PDL_MODIFY_ACCESS, COS object, 94

AVP_PDL_READ_ACCESS, COS object, 94

AVP_PERSONAL_DLS, mail users collection, 99

AVP_RECIPIENT_OBJECT_ID, call handler, 90–91

AVP_SCHEDULE_OBJECT_NAME, call handler, 92–93

AVP_XFER_RESTRICTION_OBJECT_ID, COS object, 93

AVP_ZERO_ACTION, Name Lookup Handler, 103

AVP_ZERO_CONVERSATION, Name Lookup Handler, 103

AVP_ZERO_OBJECT_ID, Name Lookup Handler, 103

AvRdBSvr component, Registry, 123

AvRepDir component, Registry, 124

AVRepDirSvrSvc service, 54–55

AvRepMgr component, Registry, 124

AvSkinny component, Registry, 124

AVSQLSynchSvr service, 53

AVTTSSvc service, 56

AvUmrSyncSvr, trace file example, 187

AVUMRSyncSvr service, subscriber call delivery, 64

AvWm (Windows Monitor), 45–46, 124, 177–178

B

backups
    problem recovery, 742–743
    software, 909–910

batch operations, editing subscribers, 881–883

Bellhop Administrator, 262

bill of materials (BOM), 389

Billing reports, 247

BOM (bill of materials), 389

budgets, design costs
    hardware and software, 388–389
    services, 389

Bulk Edit Utility, 782–783
    applying changes, 800, 811
    call handlers, 800–801
        changes, 803–811
        CSV file, 802
    main form, 783
    Select Subscriber Changes page, 786
        account, 787
        alternate extension, 799

caller input, 794–796
conversation, 788–789
exit destination, 799–800
extension, 798–799
greetings, 792–794
messages, 796–798
notification, 798
passwords, 788
profile, 786–787
transfer, 790–792
selecting subscribers, 784–786
Tools Depot, 242–243
Bulk Import
correcting errors, 777–779
data from message store directory, 776–777
modify existing accounts, 779–780
subscribers, CSV files, 770–776
Wizard dialog boxes, 771–773
Bulk Subscriber Delete tool, 780–782
busy greeting, call handling, 88
BusyRecall switch file setting, 920
BYE method, SIP (Session Initiation Protocol), 652

C

Call Distribution report, 247
call distribution report, Port Usage Analyzer tool, 741
call forward, 266
Call Handler Traffic report, 247, 741
call handlers
audio-text applications, 666, 707–708
after-greeting action, 684
after-message action, 684
call flows, 679–680
call transfer, 669–673
caller-input, 676–678
greeting rules, 683–684
greetings, 674–675
messages, 678–679
name lookup call handler, 710–712
Product Information call handler, 709
profile, 666–669
Technical Support call handler, 709–710
Tiny Audio Text Application call handler, 708

transfer rules, 682–683
Bulk Edit Utility, 800–801
alternate extensions, 811
caller input, 808–809
CSV file, 802
greetings, 805–807
messages, 809–811
profile, 803
transfer, 803–805
edit over phone interface, 719–720
information retrieval, 848–853
lock downs, 715
dial option restrictions, 717–719
error greetings, 715–717
mail users collection, 99
object model, 85–86
Administrator object ID, 89–90
After Message Actions, 92
alternate extensions, 93
contact rules, 87
location object ID, 91
menu entries, 87
messaging rules, 87–88
Recipient object ID, 90–91
schedules, 92–93
CallManager, 266, 638–640
audio control, 643–644
call control, 640–642
call information, 642–643
CallManager clusters, 646, 649
clusters, 646, 649
features, 266–267
MWI, 646
startup, 645–646
switch connectivity, 294
call objects, MIU, 215–216
call processing
IP WAN multisite processing, 366–371
WAN multisite processing, 359–363
Domino, 365
Exchange 2000, 364–365
Exchange 5.5, 363
call statistics, performance counters, 249
Call Traffic report, 248
call traffic report, Port Usage Analyzer tool, 742
Call Viewer application, troubleshooting audio-text applications, 747

CallControl component, Registry, 124
Caller input
    audio-text applications, 676–678
    Bulk Edit Utility, 808–809
    off-hours, 728
    Select Subscriber Changes page, 794–796
CallHandler, Unity DB database, 109
calls
    control, 630–631
        CallManager TSP, 640–642
        disconnect supervision, 637–638
        incoming ring voltage, 631–633
        tone definitions, 634–636
    flow through call handlers, 679–680
    information
        CallManager TSP, 642–643
        extraction, MIU, 211–212
        SIP (Session Initiation Protocol), 655
    routing rules, diagnostics, 750–753
    transfer
        audio-text applications, 669–673
        digital networking, 413
CANCEL method, SIP (Session Initiation
    Protocol), 652
capacity
    design planning evaluation, 391
    Exchange, 496–497
CDE component, Registry, 124–125
CDOExM (Collaboration Data Objects for
    Exchange Management), AvDsAD.exe directory
    monitor, 138
centralized messaging, deployment model, 359–363
    Domino, 365
    Exchange 2000, 364–365
    Exchange 5.5, 363
    multisite IP WAN, 366–371
    teams, 13
centralized sites, design planning surveys, 385
Choose Subscriber Type dialog box, 771
Cisco IP Telephony, 361
Cisco IP Telephony deployment models, 340
Cisco Messaging deployment models, 340–343
Cisco PCA (CPCA), 226
    phone settings, 21
    TUI features, 232
        Unity Assistant, 234–235
        Unity Inbox, 232–233

Cisco Personal Communications Assistant. *See*
    Cisco PCA (CPCA)
Cisco Security Agent, 254–255
Cisco Unified Performance Information (CUPID),
    249–250
Cisco Unity Assistant, Cisco PCA, 234–235
Cisco Unity Bulk Import Wizard (CUBI), 243
Cisco Unity Configuration Assistant (CUCA),
    Registry, 125
Cisco Unity Data Link Explorer (CUDLE), 817
Cisco Unity Greetings Administrator (CUGA),
    241–242
Cisco Unity Inbox, Cisco PCA, 232–233
Cisco Unity Installation Configuration Assistant
    (CUICA), 292
Cisco Unity Personal Communication Assistant
    (CUPCA), TomCat service, 58
class of service. *See* COS
clients, telephony services, 212
Clustering Over IP WAN, Cisco IP Telephony
    deployment model, 340
CodesChangeable switch file setting, 923
Collaboration Data Objects for Exchange
    Management (CDOExM), AvDsAD.exe directory
    monitor, 138
comma-separated value files. *See* CSV files
CommServer component, Registry, 125
companies, unified messaging (UM) challenges,
    11–12
    e-mail perception issues, 14–17
    messaging topology management, 12–14
    security issues, 17–19
    solution and deployment, 23–24
    user adaptation, 24–25
    user support, 26–27
    voice message storage, 19–23
components
    AVCsMgr, 34
        Arbiter, 36–37
        AVWM (Windows Monitor), 45–46
        DOH (Data Object Hierarchy), 35–36
        DOHMMSvr, 45
        integration, 43
        log manager, 40–42
        MIU, 42
        RDBSvr, 44
        resource manager, 36

ruler component, 37
SIP (Session Initiation Protocol), 43–44
TAPI interface, 42–43
TRaP connection server, 44–45
TUI applications, 38–40
UMR (Unity Messaging Repository), 37
UnityAVWAVE, 44
virtual queue, 44
AVMsgStoreMonitorSvr, 47–48
AVNotificationMgr
    notification queue, 47
    notifier, 46–47
conversation, 183
    notification process, 196–200
    outside caller messages, 183–189
    subscriber-to-subscriber messages,
        189–195
    TUI (Telephone User Interface), 200–203
mail user change in directory, 72–77
messaging
    mail store monitor, 180–181
    MAL (Messaging Abstraction Layer),
        176–177
    UMR (Unity Messaging Repository),
        178–179
    Windows Monitor (AvWm), 177–178
scenarios, outside call leaves message, 59–72
SIP (Session Initiation Protocol), 650
subscriber update in SA, 77–80
confidentiality, organization security issues, 17–18
configurations, 312–313
    failovers, 336
        Exchange 2000, 337–339
        Exchange 5.5, 337
    general settings, integration file, 617
    MAPI, 182–183
    testing, 590
    unified messaging, 318–319
        domain boundaries, 325–326
        Domino, 334–335
        Exchange, 319–326
        Exchange 2000, 327–333
        Exchange 2003, 327–331
        partner server, 319

voice messaging, 313
    DCGCs for Exchange 2000, 317
    multi server, 314–317
    single server, 313–314
    Windows 2000 domain, 335–336
ConfirmReturn switch file setting, 919
contact rules, call handlers, 87
ContactRule table, Unity DB database, 110
Conversation Development Environment
    component, Registry, 124–125
conversations, 38–40
    components, MAPI, 183
        notification process, 196–200
        outside caller messages, 183–189
        subscriber-to-subscriber messages,
            189–195
        TUI (Telephone User Interface), 200–203
    Select Subscriber Changes page, 788–789
    test plan, 591
ConvUtilsLiveRecord conversation, 700
correlation point, installation planning, 303–304
    port allocation, 305
    server sizing, 304
COS (class of service), 240–241
    admin access, 755–757
    mail users collection, 99
    object model, 93–94
    table, UnityDB database, 110
costs, design
    hardware and software, 388–389
    services, 389
Credential table, UnityDB database, 110
criteria, design planning requirements, 382–383
CSBridgeConnector service, 56–57
CSEMSSvc service, 55
CSV files (comma-separated value files), 770
    Bulk Import, correcting errors, 778–779
    call handlers, 802
    importing subscribers, 770–776
    subscriber edits, 785–786
CUBI (Cisco Unity Bulk Import Wizard), 243
CUCA (Cisco Unity Configuration Assistant),
    Registry, 125
CUDLE (Cisco Unity Data Link Explorer), 817
CUGA (Cisco Unity Greeting Administrator),
    241–242
CUICA (Cisco Unity Installation Configuration
    Assistant), 292

CPCA (Cisco Personal Communications Assistant), 317
    phone settings, 21
    TomCat service, 58
CUPID (Cisco Unified Performance Information), 249–250
cutover, post-cutover hand-off to operations, 598
cutover tasks, 595–596
CVM Mailbox reset conversation, 40

D

DAL (Directory Access Layer), DOH subcomponent, 35
DalDB (Directory Access Layer branch), Registry, 125
damage control
    backups, 742–743
    default routing rules, 745
    resetting defaults, 743–745
    schedule reconstruction, 746
data
    digital networks, 416–418
    site surveys, 399
    storage, object model, 105
        directory, 130–131
        local files, 131–133
        Registry, 122–130
        SQL database, 105–121
Data Object Hierarchy (DOH), 35–36, 126
Data*.txt files, time stamps, 41
Database Walker (DBWalker), 252
databases
    Domino, 531–532
        forms, 533
        permissions, 551–552
        replicas, 534
        server tasks, 535
        templates, 533–534
        views, 532–533
    replication (Domino), 544–547
DBWalker (Database Walker), 252
DCGCs (Domain Controllers/Global Catalog Servers), 317

decision-making
    deployment methodology, 273–274
        unified messaging, 275
        voice messaging, 276
    Unity solution design
        bill of materials (BOM), 389
        cost analysis, 388–389
        develop design options, 387–388
        preliminary design proposal, 384–387
        requirements, 382–384
Default Location object, directory default, 153
defaults
    configurations
        audio-text applications, 703–706
        resetting, 743–745
    objects, directories, 153
    routing rules, resetting, 745
    subscriber template objects, rebuilding, 746
DefaultDListMembership table, UnityDB database, 111
DelayBeforeOpening switch file setting, 918
deleting subscribers, 780–782, 884–893
delimiters, integration file, 617
delivery messages, 174–176
demo licenses, 256–257
deployment models, 339–340
    centralized messaging, 359–363
        Domino, 365
        Exchange 2000, 364–365
        Exchange 5.5, 363
        multisite IP WAN, 366–371
    Cisco IP Telephony, 340
    Cisco Messaging, 340–343
    combining, 344–345
    failover, 371–373
        Domino, 374
        Exchange 2000, 373–374
        Exchange 5.5, 373
    messaging boundaries, 343–344
    single-site messaging, 345
        GUI and web access, 351–353
        multiserver configuration, 348–351
        single-server configuration, 346–348
        unified messaging, 353–359
    specifications, 386

Unity with Exchange
 Exchange 2000, 514–520
 Exchange 2003, 514–520
 Exchange 5.5, 503–512
 mixed-messaging configuration, 520–524
design
 deployment methodology, 278
 digital networks, 443–444
  automated attendant, 451–453
  dialing domains, 445
  documentation, 444
  extension length, 444
  messaging addressing, 446–450
  pooled licensing, 454
  public distribution lists, 455–458
 planning, 307
 Unity solution, 377–379, 399–400
  decision-making phase, 382–389
  high-level design, 400–401
  implementation plan, 410
  low-level design, 401–408
  planning, 389–399
  presales, 382–389
Designer (Domino), 529–531
devices, 237
Diag*.txt files, 41
diagnostic files, viewing, 42
dial option restrictions, lock down call handlers,
 717–719
dial plans
 digital environment, 432–433
 digital networks, 419
  alternate extension, 424–425
  dialing domain, 420–423
  extension length, 425
 migration planning tasks, 292
 site surveys, 307
dialing domains
 digital networks, 420–423, 445
 extension conflicts, 841–842
 local objects extension conflicts, 845–846
 locating extensions, 841–846
 location extension conflicts, 844–845
 subscriber extension conflicts, 843–844
dialog boxes
 Bulk Import Wizard, 771–773
 Choose Subscriber Type, 771

 ObjectID jump, 89
 Save Log Files, 771, 777
 Select Domain and Container, 773
 Select Exchange 5.5 Server, 773
 Select Subscriber Data Import Option, 772, 777
 Select Subscriber Template, 772, 777
 Select the CSV File, 773
 Select User Domain and Container, 777
Digit switch file setting, 924
digital networks, 264, 413
 architecture, 414
  data replication model, 416
  logical data structure, 417–418
  origins, 414–415
  protocols, 414
  shared messaging, 415
  synchronization, 418–419
 design, 443–444
  automated attendant, 451–453
  dialing domains, 445
  documentation, 444
  extension length, 444
  messaging addressing, 446–450
  pooled licensing, 454
  public distribution lists, 455–458
 environment assessment, 430–431
  dial plan, 432–433
  extension length, 435–436
  legacy distribution lists, 443
  legacy voice-messaging node, 434–435
  messaging addressing scheme, 436–438
  messaging environment, 431
  phone switch, 432
  physical structure, 431
  Unity node, 438–442
 feature set, 419
  dial plans, 419–425
  distribution lists, 425–426
  Licensing Pooling, 428, 430
  message addressing, 426–428
  subscriber settings, 428
DigitToneDuration switch file setting, 920
directories
 capacity survey, 307
 data storage, 130–131
 default objects, 153
 digital networks, 452–453

mail user changes, 72–77
messaging infrastructure, 406
messaging system connectivity, 297–298
monitor
    extensibility, 149–152
    full synchronization, 146–149
    message store, 136–137
    protocol use, 137
    search scope, 138–143
    synchronization queries, 143–144
subscriber synchronization, 874
Directory (Domino), 536–537, 551–552
Directory Access Layer (DAL), DOH
  subcomponent, 35
Directory Access Layer branch, Registry, 125
directory connectors branch, Registry, 125–126
directory handlers
    audio-text applications, 688–694
    name-spelling option, 738
directory monitor, 49–50
    Domino, 52, 166–169
    Exchange 2000, 51–52, 161–166, 491–492
    Exchange 2003, 51–52, 161–166, 491–492
    Exchange 5.5, 50, 154, 489–490
        attributes, 154–158
        distribution list, 159–160
        global data, 160–161
    extensibility, 149–152
    full synchronization, 146–149
    message store, 136–137
    protocol use, 137
    replicated information, 72
    search scope, 138
        Domino, 143
        Exchange 2000, 141–143
        Exchange 2003, 141–143
        Exchange 5.5, 138–141
    synchronization queries, 143–144
DirectoryID property, directory synchronization, 869
DiRT (Disaster Recovery Tools), 251–252, 742
Disaster Recovery Backup tool, 251
Disaster Recovery Restore tool, 251
disaster recovery sites, design planning surveys, 385
disconnect supervision, call control, 637–638
disconnect tones, hang up notification, 637
disk drive status page, Status Monitor, 249
DisplayName property, directory synchronization, 869

DISTLIST_SEARCH_ROOT parameter, Exchange
  5.5 default search scope, 139–140
distributed call processing, WAN, 366–368
    Domino, 370–371
    Exchange 2000, 369–370
    Exchange 5.5, 368–369
distributed sites, design planning surveys, 385
distribution groups, directory monitor
  synchronization queries, 144
distribution lists (DLs)
    adding member, 903–906
    creating new, 897–900
    deleting, 901–903
    digital networking, 413, 425–426
    directory monitor synchronization queries, 144
    Exchange 5.5 directory monitor, 159–160
    legacy, digital networks, 443
    object extensibility, 152
    object model, 94–95
    public
        adding, 896–900
        digital networks, 455–458
        member addition, 903–906
        removing, 900–903
Distribution Lists report, 247
Distribution List table
    distribution lists, 108
    UnityDB database, 111
DLs. *See* distribution lists
documentation
    design planning pilot, 396
    digital network design, 444
DOH (Data Object Hierarchy), 35–36, 126
DOH Media Master Server (DOHMMSvr), 45
DOH Property Tester tool. *See* DPT tool
DOHMMSvr, 45
DOHPropTest branch, Registry, 126
domain controllers, messaging infrastructure,
  300–301
Domain Controllers/Global Catalog Servers
  (DCGCs), 317
domains
    dialing
        digital networks, 420–423, 445
        locating extensions, 841–846
    DiRT, 251
    Domino, 535–536, 560–563

Exchange, unified messaging configuration, 328–331

scaling (Domino), 539–540

unified messaging configuration, boundaries, 325–326

Windows, finding SQL servers, 824–825

Domino

characteristics, 527–528

client component, 529–531

database replication, 544–547

databases, 531–535

Directory, 536–537

domain, 535–536

hierarchical naming, 537–539

mail routing, 541–544

scaling domain, 539–540

server component, 528–529

server documents, 540–541

directory

capacity planning, 298

directory monitor, 52, 137, 143, 166–169

mail storage monitor, 181, 197–200

messaging system connectivity, 296–297

migration, 582

planning Unity installation, 558

domain, 560–563

DUCS (Domino Unified Communications Services), 563–565

trending, 558–560

security, 548

ACLs, 549–550

ID file, 548–549

unified messaging, 359

centralized messaging, 365

configuration, 334–335

failover, 374

multisite IP WAN, 370–371

Unity perspective, 550–551

database permissions, 551–552

MWI light, 553–558

voice message actions, 553

Unity unavailable features, 269

Domino Unified Communications Service (DUCS), 181–182

DPT branch, Registry, 126

DPT tool (DOH Property Tester tool), 83

applications object, 85

call handlers, 85–86

Administrator object ID, 89–90

After Message Actions, 92

alternate extensions, 93

contact rules, 87

location object ID, 91

menu entries, 87

messaging rules, 87–88

Recipient object ID, 90–91

schedules, 92–93

class of service (COS) object, 93–94

data storage, 105

directory, 130–131

local files, 131–133

Registry, 122–130

SQL database, 105–121

distribution lists (DLs), 94–95

FaxLibrary handlers, 95

FaxMail handlers, 95–96

interview handlers, 96

location objects, 96–97

mail users collection, 97–101

Name Lookup Handler, 101

exiting handlers, 102

input handlers, 103

operator call handler, 103

selection handlers, 102

password policy (PW) object, 104

primary domain accounts collection, 103

primary domain groups collection, 103

restriction tables, 104

trusted domains collection, 104

DropDialtoneConsult switch file setting, 919

DropDisconnectedConsult switch file setting, 919

DTMF packets, hang up notification, 638

DTMF tones, hang up notification, 638

DTMFAccessID property, directory synchronization, 869

DTMFAccessID table, UnityDB database, 112

DTMFDebounce switch file setting, 920

DUCS (Domino Unified Communications Service), 181–182, 563–565

E

edits
    subscribers, 782–783
        alternate extensions, 872–876
        batch operations, 881–883
        error greetings, 879–881
        password updates, 878–879
        Select Subscriber Changes page, 786–800
        selecting, 784–786
        user-input key settings, 876–878
        utility main form, 783
    Tools Depot
        Bulk Edit utility, 242–243
        CUBI (Cisco Unity Bulk Import Wizard), 243
e-mail
    GUI access, 305
    messaging actions, 174–176
    organizations perceptions, 14–17
    TUI, playback, 227
EMS (Event Monitoring Service), 251
encryption, security issues, 19
environments, digital networks, 430–431
    dial plan, 432–433
    extension length, 435–436
    legacy distribution lists, 443
    legacy voice-messaging node, 434–435
    messaging addressing scheme, 436–438
    messaging environment, 431
    phone switch, 432
    physical structure, 431
    Unity node, 438–442
equipment, design planning proposal, 385
error greetings
    call handling, 88
    editing subscribers, 879–881
    lock down call handlers, 715–717
Event Monitoring Service (EMS), 55, 131, 251
events
    logs, troubleshooting audio-text applications, 746–747
    telephony services, 213
Example Administrator account, 704
Example Administrator object, directory default, 153
Example Interview handler, 704

Example subscriber account, 704
Example Subscriber object, directory default, 153
Exchange
    characteristics, 461–462
        mixed-messaging configuration, 476–480
        version 2000, 469–476
        version 2003, 469–476
        version 5.5, 462–469
    deploying with Unity
        Exchange 2000, 514–520
        Exchange 2003, 514–520
        Exchange 5.5, 503–506, 510–512
        mixed-messaging configuration, 520–524
    directory, capacity planning, 298
    MAPI, 181–182
        conversation component, 183–203
        startup, 182–183
    messaging system connectivity, 295–296
    planning Unity installation, 492
        administration planning, 501–502
        capacity planning, 496–497
        designing operation management, 502–503
        Exchange affect on Unity, 501
        servicing Exchange, 493
        trending, 497–499
        UM Readiness assessment, 493–496
        Unity affect on Exchange, 499–501
    subscribers, importing from, 776–777
    unified messaging configuration, 319–320
        deployment sites, 322–323
        server configurations, 326
        site boundaries, 320
        site deployment limitations, 320–321
    Unity perspective, 480
        Exchange 2000, 485–487
        Exchange 2003, 485–487, 491–492
        Exchange 5.5, 480–485, 489–490
        mixed-messaging configuration, 489
    Unity servicing capabilities, 524
Exchange 2000
    characteristics, 469–476
    deployment with Unity, 514–520
    directory monitor, 51–52, 161–166
    directory monitor search scope, 141–143
    failover configuration, 337–339

unified messaging, 353–355
  centralized messaging, 364–365
  failover, 373–374
  multisite IP WAN, 369–370
unified messaging configuration, 331–333
  admin group, 327
  domain, 328–331
  partner server, 319
  routing group, 328
Unity perspective, 485–487, 491–492
voice messaging configurations, 313, 317
Exchange 2003
  characteristics, 469–476
  deployment with Unity, 514–520
  directory monitor, 51–52, 161–166
  directory monitor search scope, 141–143
  unified messaging, 353–355
  unified messaging configuration
    admin group, 327
    domain, 328–331
    routing group, 328
  Unity perspective, 485–487, 491–492
Exchange 5.5
  characteristics, 462–469
  deployment with Unity, 503–506, 510–512
  directory monitor, 50, 154
    attributes, 154–158
    distribution list, 159–160
    global data, 160–161
    search scope, 138–141
  failover configuration, 337
  server components, 462
  unified messaging, 357
    centralized messaging, 363
    failover, 373
    multisite IP WAN, 368–369
  unified messaging configuration, 319–320
    deployment sites, 322–323
    partner server, 319
    server configurations, 326
    site boundaries, 320
    site deployment limitations, 320–321
  Unity implementation, 7–8
    Unity Messaging Repository (UMR), 9
    versus integrated messaging, 10–11
  Unity perspective, 480–483
    accessing, 483–485
    Directory monitor, 489–490

ExchangeMonitor, 180–181
  MAPI notification, 196–197
  Registry, 126
exit destinations, Select Subscriber Changes page, 799–800
exit objects, Name Lookup Handler, 102
extensibility, directory monitor, 149–152
extensions
  alternate
    editing subscribers, 872–876
    mail users collection, 100
  call handler, 93
  conflicts in dialing domain, 841–842
  digital networks
    addressing by extension, 446–448
    alternates, 424–425
    lengths, 425, 435–436, 444
    public distribution lists, 455–457
    Unity node, 440–442
  local objects, dialing domain conflicts, 845–846
  locations, dialing domain conflicts, 844–845
  remapping, audio-text applications, 701–702
  Select Subscriber Changes page, 798–799
  subscribers, dialing domain conflicts, 843–844
external numbers, transfer call handler, 713–715

F

facsimiles, 260–261
Failed Login report, 247
failovers, 255–256
  configuration, 336
    Exchange 2000, 337–339
    Exchange 5.5, 337
  deployment models, 371–373
    Domino, 374
    Exchange 2000, 373–374
    Exchange 5.5, 373
  SIP (Session Initiation Protocol), 657–658
FailureConv component, Registry, 126
failures, DiRT, 251
fallback
  lab trials, upgrade planning, 570
  performing, 597
  preparing for, 597
  upgrades, 574

Fax Administration tool, 260–261
faxes, 260–261
    server software, 909
    voicemail integration, 23
FaxLibrary handlers, object model, 95
FaxLibraryHandler table, UnityDB database, 113
FaxMail handlers, object model, 95–96
FaxMailHandler table, UnityDB database, 113
field help, 241
FirstName property, directory synchronization, 869
FlexLM, license management, 256–257
focus groups, legacy voice-message system
    analysis, 392
forms (Domino database), 533
forwarding transfer rule override, 730–731
functions
    planning evaluation, 390
        capacity, 391
        dependency assessment, 390
        impact analysis, 391
        traditional voice-mail, 390
    testing, 283–284
        end-user analysis, 285–287
        pilot, 284–285
future delivery, TUI features, 226
future of Cisco Unity, 915

G

GAEN (General Audio Error Notification) utility,
    Registry, 127
gateway services, 34
General Audio Error Notification (GAEN) utility,
    Registry, 127
Global Administrators, 757
global data, Exchange 5.5 directory monitor,
    160–161
global site surveys, 307
Global Subscriber Manager (GSM), 244–245,
    764–765
    moving subscribers between servers, 766
    off-box use, 766–767
    subscriber deletion, 765
    user import from Active Directory, 765
GlobalLocation table, UnityDB database, 113

GlobalSubscriber table, UnityDB database, 113
go/no go decision-making, as installation precutover
    task, 594–595
Gonzales, Moises, *Unity Fundamentals,* 292
GrantUnityAccess
    output, 758
    tool, 760–763
    usage example, 759
greetings
    after-greeting actions, 684
    audio-text applications, 674–675
    Bulk Edit Utility, 805–807
    Cisco Unity Assistant, 234
    CUGA (Cisco Unity Greetings Administrator),
        241–242
    edit call handlers over phone, 719–720
    error
        editing subscribers, 879–881
        lock down call handlers, 715–717
    holiday, 726–727
    language options, 702–703
    rules, audio-text applications, 683–684
    Select Subscriber Changes page, 792–794
    TUI features, 228
GreetingsAdministrator conversation, 39
groups, mailboxes, audio-text applications, 722–724
GSM (Global Subscriber Manager), 244–245,
    764–765
    moving subscribers between servers, 766
    off-box use, 766–767
    subscriber deletion, 765
    user import from Active Directory, 765

H

Handler table, UnityDB database, 113–114
handlers
    call, 85–86
        Administrator object ID, 89–90
        After Message Actions, 92
        alternate extensions, 93
        contact rules, 87
        location object ID, 91
        mail users collection, 99
        menu entries, 87

messaging rules, 87–88
Recipient object ID, 90–91
schedules, 92–93
FaxLibrary, 95
FaxMail, 95–96
interview, 96
Name Lookup Handler, 101
exiting handlers, 102
input handlers, 103
operator call handler, 103
selection handlers, 102
HangUpTone switch file setting, 922
hardware, cost analysis, 388–389
hearing impairments, 260
help
field, 241
online, 241
hierarchical naming (Domino), 537–539
high-level designs, 400–401
high-level requirements, Unity solution design, 382
acceptance criteria, 382–383
capability matching, 383
decision finalizing, 383–384
history
digital networks, 414–415
UM (unified messaging), 5–7
holiday greetings, 259–260, 726–727
Holiday table, UnityDB database, 114
HookFlashDuration switch file setting, 922
Hospitality Checked Out conversation, 40
hospitality packages, 262
HTML Status monitor, 248–249
hunt groups, audio-text applications, 724–726

I

IBM Lotus Domino, Unity unavailable features, 269
ID files (Domino), 548–549
IDC (Import Directory Connector), 49
implementation
deployment methodology, 278–279
design planning, 410
planning for Unity server installation, 586
Import Directory Connector (IDC), 49

Import tools, 131
importing subscribers, 865–868
inbound calls, component scenarios, 59–72
IncomingCallRings
parameter, legacy integrations, 633
switch file setting, 921
indexing columns, 828
initialization
CallManager TSP, 645–646
MAPI, 182–183
telephony services, 209–211
Initialization branch, Registry, 127
input handlers, Name Lookup Handler, 103
installation
dependency determination, 292
messaging infrastructure, 298–302
messaging system connectivity, 295–298
switch connectivity, 293–295
deployment methodology, 279
implementation plan, developing, 586
operational acceptance criteria, 597–598
planning
with Domino, 558–565
with Exchange, 492–503
post-cutover hand-off to operations, 598
post-installation server tuning, 598
pre-cutover tasks, 590
configuration testing, 590
conversations test plan, 591
go/no go decision making, 594–595
integration testing, 591
simulated load testing, 592–594
subscriber enrollment, 595
pre-installation tasks, 586
administrative console configuration, 587
monitoring facility, 588
schema extension, 588
verifying account permissions, 588
Unity servers, 589
cutover, 595–596
fallback, performing, 597
readiness, 597
integrated messaging, 6, 10–11
integration, 43
files, legacy PBXs, 603–604
object, MIU, 216

phone systems, 266
   multiple systems, 267–268
   technology features, 266–267
   UTIM (Unity Telephony Integration
      Manager), 268
   switch file setting, 919
   technologies, Telephony Application
      Programming Interface (TAPI), 27–28
   testing, 591
IntegrationType switch file setting, 918
internal greetings, call handling, 88
Internet subscribers
   directory monitor synchronization queries, 144
   object extensibility, 152
Internet Voice Connector (IVC), 131
interoperability
   AMIS (Audio Messaging Interchange
      Specification), 576–577
   preliminary design proposal, 386–387
   Unity Bridge, 578
   VPIM (Voice Profile for Internet Mail), 577
interview handlers
   audio-text applications, 685–688
   object model, 96
InterviewHandler table, UnityDB database, 114
InterviewQuestion table, UnityDB database, 114
INVITE method, SIP (Session Initiation Protocol),
   652
IVC (Internet Voice Connector), 131

J-K

keypad mapping, Registry, 127
keywords, integration file, 617–618

L

lab trials
   design planning, 394
      configuration options, 394
      mockup installation analysis, 395
      production network mockup, 394
      test plans, 394
   upgrade planning, 569–570

LampOff switch file setting, 924
LampOn switch file setting, 924
languages
   audio-text applications, 702–703, 720–722
   multilingual capabilities, 257–259
LastName property, directory synchronization, 869
LDAP, 138
legacy distribution lists, digital networks, 443
legacy PBXs, integration, 602
   analog DTMF, 604–612
   call control, 630–638
   integration files, 603–604
   serial, 612–630
   switch files, 603–604
legacy voice-message systems
   digital environment, 434–435
   migrating to Unity, 575–576
      AMIS (Audio Messaging Interchange
         Specification), 576–577
      extracting user data, 291–292
      Unity Bridge, 578
      VPIM (Voice Profile for Internet Mail), 577
   user analysis, 391
      configuration analysis, 392
      end-user group analysis, 392
      focus groups, 392
      identifying user needs, 392
      questionnaire, 391
      special-case users, 392
      support issues, 393
      traffic patterns, 393
      training criteria, 393–394
licenses
   AVLic service, 53–54
   checking information, 835
   FlexLM management, 256–257
   pooling, 256–257
   status page, Status Monitor, 249
   XML information output, 834
Licensing Pooling, digital networks, 428–430
line objects, MIU, 217–218
line servers, MIU, 217
ListInDirectory property, directory
   synchronization, 869
literals, integration file, 617
local files, data storage, 131–133

local objects, extensions, conflicts in dialing
    domain, 845–846
local site surveys, 307
location object
    directory monitor synchronization queries, 144
    ID, call handler, 91
    mail users collection, 100
    object extensibility, 152
    object model, 96–97
Location table, UnityDB database, 114
LOCATION_SEARCH_ROOT parameter,
    Exchange 5.5 default search scope, 139–140
LocationObjectID property, directory
    synchronization, 869
locations, extensions, conflicts in dialing domain,
    844–845
lock down call handlers, 715
    dial option restrictions, 717–719
    error greetings, 715–717
log manager, 40–42
Log Manager component
    Registry, 123
logs, events, troubleshooting audio-text applications,
    746–747
loop current drop, hang up notification, 637
loop current reversal, hang up notification, 637
Lotus Administrator. *See* Administrator
Lotus Designer, 529–531
Lotus Domino. *See* Domino
Lotus Notes, 529–531
low-level designs, 401–402, 408
    description, 402
    messaging infrastructure, 404–408
    switch integration, 404
    Unity system description, 402–404
low-level requirements, Unity solution design, 382
    acceptance criteria, 382–383
    capability matching, 383
    decision finalizing, 383–384

M

mail clients, TUI features, 229
mail users
    object model, 97
        alternate extensions, 100
        call handler, 99

        COS object, 99
        location object, 100
        notification device, 97–98
        notification MWI, 98–99
        notification rule, 98
        personal distribution list, 99
    templates, object model, 100–101
mailboxes, groups, audio-text applications, 722–724
MailboxID property, directory synchronization, 869
MailboxReceiveLimit property, directory
    synchronization, 870
MailboxSendLimit property, directory
    synchronization, 870
MailboxStore table, UnityDB database, 115
MailboxWarningLimit property, directory
    synchronization, 870
MailDatabase property, directory synchronization,
    869
MAILOBX_STORE_SEARCH_ROOT parameter,
    Exchange 5.5 default search scope, 139–140
MAILUSER_SEARCH_ROOT parameter,
    Exchange 5.5 default search scope, 139–140
maintenance
    HTML Status Monitor, 248–249
    performance counters, 249–250
    Port Usage Analyzer tool, 247–248
    reports, 247
    Tools Depot
        DBWalker (Database Walker), 252
        Disaster Recovery tools, 251–252
        EMS (Event Monitoring Service), 251
        MSM (Message Store Manager), 250
MAL (Messaging Abstraction Layer), 173–177
MAL (Message Access Layer), DOH
    subcomponent, 35
MALDom component, Registry, 127
MALEx component, Registry, 127
management
    Unity administrator
        CUGA (Cisco Unity Greetings
            Administrator), 241–242
        SA, 239–241
        Tools Depot, 242–246
    upgrades, 567–568
MAPI (Messaging Application Programming
    Interface), 27, 181–182

conversation component, 183
    notification process, 196–200
    outside caller messages, 183–189
    subscriber-to-subscriber messages,
        189–195
    TUI (Telephone User Interface), 200–203
    startup, 182–183
MaximumConcurrentMWIRequests switch file
    setting, 922
MaxWaitBetweenRings parameter
    legacy integrations, 631
    switch file setting, 921
media, format negotiation, SIP (Session Initiation
    Protocol), 655–657
Media Interface Unit. *See* MIU
Media Master control (MMC), 241
media objects, MIU, 218
menu entries, call handlers, 87
MenuEntry table, UnityDB database, 115
menus, TUI personal settings, 228
Message Access Layer (MAL), DOH
    subcomponent, 35
message monitor, 47–48
Message Store Manager (MSM), 63, 250
message stores
    directory monitor, 136–137
    importing subscribers, 776–777
Message Waiting Indicator (MWI) light (Domino),
    553
    new message arrival, 554–556
    profile documents, 556–558
MessageRule table, UnityDB database, 115
messages
    access, 267
    addressing
        digital networking, 413
        digital networks, 426–428
    after-message actions, 684
    audio-text applications, 678–679
    Bulk Edit Utility, 809–811
    digital networks, addressing scheme, 436–438
    management, 231
    notification, 228, 236–238
    playback, 231
    Select Subscriber Changes page, 796–798
    sending, 230
        files (Domino), 552

routing (Domino), 541–544
storage monitor, 180–181
stores, directory monitor, 136–137
storage, audio formats, 263–264
subscriber identification, 267
TUI feature
    mail clients, 230–231
    management, 227–228
    modifying personal settings, 228
    playback, 227
    sending, 226
MessageStoreMonitor, 174
messaging
    actions, 173–176
    addressing
        extension, 446–449
        method selection, 450
        search scope, 446
    boundaries, deployment models, 343–344
    components
        mail store monitor, 180–181
        MAL (Messaging Abstraction Layer),
            176–177
        UMR (Unity Messaging Repository),
            178–179
        Windows Monitor (AvWm), 177–178
    digital networks, assessing environment, 431
    infrastructure, 298–299, 397
        domain configuration, 301–302
        domain controllers, 300–301
        name-resolution hosts, 301
        network connectivity, 302
        server capacity, 299–300
    infrastructure components, 341–342
    infrastructure planning, 302–303
    MAPI, 181–182
        conversation component, 183–203
        startup, 182–183
    rules, call handlers, 87–88
    server survey, 307
    servers, migration, 580–581
    shared digital networks, 415
    system connectivity, 295
        directory capacity, 298
        directory use, 297
        Domino, 296–297

Exchange, 295–296
single messaging system, 295
single-directory infrastructure, 297
technologies, Messaging Application
Programming Interface (MAPI), 27
unified. *See also* unified messages
deployment methodology, 275
migration planning, 290–291
Messaging Abstraction Layer (MAL), 173–177
Messaging Application Programming Interface
(MAPI), 27
methodologies (deployment)
design, 278, 377–379
decision-making phase, 382–389
final design, 399–410
planning, 389–399
presales, 382–389
implementation, 278–279
installation, 279
operations management, 280–281
optimization, 281
planning, 277
correlation point, 303–305
design criteria, 307
installation dependencies, 292–302
messaging infrastructure, 302–303
migration tasks, 288–292
site surveys, 306–307
subscriber access, 305–306
testing capabilities, 283–287
presales, 273–276
methods, SIP (Session Initiation Protocol), 650–654
Microsoft Messaging Queue (MSMQ), 135
Migrate Subscriber Data tool, 811–812
basics, 812
MSD permission configuration, 813–814
requirements, 813
migration
between Active Directory forests, 581–582
DiRT, 251
Domino unified messaging, 582
legacy voice-messaging system, 575–576
AMIS (Audio Messaging Interchange
Specification), 576–577
Unity Bridge, 578
VPIM (Voice Profile for Internet Mail), 577

messaging servers, 580–581
planning tasks, 288–292
voice messaging-only to unified messaging,
578–579
MinimumMWIRequestInterval switch file
setting, 921
MinimumRingOff parameter, legacy integrations, 631
MinimumRingOffInterval switch file setting, 920
MinimumRingOnInterval switch file setting, 920
MinimunRingOn parameter, legacy integrations, 631
MinLoopCurrentOff switch file setting, 921
MIU (Media Interface Unit), 42, 205–206
architecture, 213, 216
call object, 215–216
integration object, 216
line object, 217–218
line servers, 217
media object, 218
object relationships, 219–223
server, 213–215
TTS object, 218
UnityAvWav object, 218–219
audio, 213
call information extraction, 211–212
client request responses, 212
events, 213
Registry, 128
subsystem initialization, 209–211
TAPI, 207–208
mixed-messaging configuration
deployment with Unity, 520–524
Unity perspective, 489
versus native-mode messaging, 476–480
MMC (Media Master control), 241
monitoring
design planning pilot, 396
facility, configuring for Unity server
installation, 588
mail storage, 180
AvMsgStoreMonitorSvr service, 180–181
DominoMonitor, 197–200
ExchangeMonitor, 196–197
software, 910
Morgan, Brian, *Unity Fundamentals,* 292
MovedMailbox table, UnityDB database, 115

MsgStoreMonitor branch, Registry, 128
MSM (Message Store Manager), 250
MSMQ (Microsoft Messaging Queue), 135
multilingual capabilities, 257–259
multiple languages, audio-text applications, 720–722
multiple servers
    COS (class of service), 755, 757
    GrantUnityAccess tool, 760–763
    GSM (Global Subscriber Manager), 764–765
        moving subscribers between servers, 766
        off-box use, 766–767
        subscriber deletion, 765
        user import from Active Directory, 765
    single account admin access, 757–759
    voice messaging configuration, 314, 317
multisite WANz, centralized messaging, 359–363
    with Centralized Call Processing, 340
    with Distributed Call Processing, 340
    Domino, 365
    Exchange 2000, 364–365
    Exchange 5.5, 363
    IP WAN, 366, 368–371
MWI, 267
    CallManager TSP, 646
    light (Domino), 553
        new message arrival, 554–556
        profile documents, 556–558
    message notification, 176
    section, switch files, 923–924
    TUI administrator management, 235
MWIType switch file setting, 923

N

Name Lookup Handler, object model, 101–103
name matching, 151
NameLookupHandler table, UnityDB database, 115
name-resolution hosts, messaging infrastructure, 301
names
    digital networks, addressing, 449
    Domino, 537–539
    lookup call handler, 710–712

native-mode messaging, *versus* mixed-messaging, 476–480
networking, 264–266
networks
    connectivity, 302
    digital, 413
        architecture, 414–419
        design, 443–458
        environment assessment, 430–443
        feature set, 419–430
NEWDISTLIST_ROOT parameter, Exchange 5.5
    default search scope, 139–141
NEWLOCATION_ROOT parameter, Exchange 5.5
    default search scope, 139–141
NEWMAILUSER_ROOT parameter, Exchange 5.5
    default search scope, 139
Node Manager component, Registry, 123
Node Manager service, 57–58
Notes (Domino), 529–531
notification, 46–47
    Cisco Unity Assistant, 234
    device, mail users collection, 97–98
    MAPI conversation component, 196
        DominoMonitor, 197–200
        ExchangeMonitor, 196–197
    messages
        actions, 176
        TUI administrator management, 236–238
    MWI, mail users collection, 98–99
    queue, 47
    rule, mail users collection, 98
    Select Subscriber Changes page, 798
    TUI message settings, 228
NotificationDevice table, 115–116
NotificationMWI table, 116
NotificationRule table, 116
notifier component
    MWI light turn on, 69
    Registry, 128
NOTIFY method, SIP (Session Initiation Protocol), 652

O

object model
    applications, 85

call handlers, 85–86
    Administrator object ID, 89–90
    After Message Actions, 92
    alternate extensions, 93
    contact rules, 87
    location object ID, 91
    menu entries, 87
    messaging rules, 87–88
    Recipient object ID, 90–91
    schedules, 92–93
class of service (COS) object, 93–94
data storage, 105
    directory, 130–131
    local files, 131–133
    Registry, 122–130
    SQL database, 105–121
distribution lists (DLs), 94–95
FaxLibrary handlers, 95
FaxMail handlers, 95–96
interview handlers, 96
location objects, 96–97
mail users collection, 97
    alternate extensions, 100
    call handler, 99
    COS object, 99
    location object, 100
    notification device, 97–98
    notification MWI, 98–99
    notification rule, 98
    personal distribution list, 99
mail users templates, 100–101
Name Lookup Handler, 101
    exiting handlers, 102
    input handlers, 103
    operator call handler, 103
    selection handlers, 102
password policy (PW) object, 104
primary domain accounts collection, 103
primary domain groups collection, 103
restriction tables, 104
trusted domains collection, 104
ObjectChangedID property, directory
    synchronization, 870
ObjectID jump dialog box, 89
objects
    converting type number to string, 842
    default directory objects, 153

OctelNetObjectQueue table, UnityDB database, 117
off-box, GSM (Global Subscriber Manager),
    766–767
online help, 241
Opening Greeting call handler, 703
operations management, deployment methodology,
    280–281
Operator call handler, 103, 704
operator console, transfer to voice-mail, 731–732
optimization, deployment methodology, 281
organizations, unified message (UM) challenges,
    11–12
    e-mail perception issues, 14–17
    messaging topology management, 12–14
    security issues, 17–19
    solution and deployment, 23–24
    user adaptation, 24–25
    user support, 26–27
    voice message storage, 19–23
OutgoingGuardTime switch file setting, 922
OutgoingPostDialDelayMs switch file setting, 922
OutgoingPreDialDelayMs switch file setting, 922
outside caller messages, conversation components,
    183–189

P

packet definitions, integration file, 617
pagers, message notification, 237
parsed information, 836–837
partner servers, unified messaging configuration, 319
password policy (PW) object, object model, 104
passwords
    Select Subscriber Changes page, 788
    subscriber editing, 878–879
    TUI security, 253
PauseDuration switch file setting, 920
PBX/IP Media Gateway (PIMG), SIP (Session
    Initiation Protocol), 658–659
PBXs, connectivity determination, 293
PDIO deployment methodoloy, 585–586
performance
    counters, 249–250
    deployment methodology operations, 281

permissions
    database (Domino), 551–552
    verifying before server installation, 588
PermissionsWizard branch, Registry, 128
personal distribution list, mail users collection, 99
personal settings, TUI administration, 228–229
PersonalDList table, UnityDB database, 117
PersonalDListMember table, UnityDB database, 117–118
phased migrations, 576
phGreeting (Phone Handler Greeting), 92
PHGreeting conversation, 38, 62
PHInterview conversation, 39
phone devices, message notification, 237
Phone Handler Greeting (phGreeting), 38, 92
Phone Handler Interview conversation, 39
Phone Handler Transfer conversation, 38
phone switches, digital environments, 432
phone systems, integration, 266
    multiple systems, 267–268
    technology features, 266–267
    UTIM (Unity Telephony Integration Manager), 268
PHTransfer conversation, 38
physical structures, digital environment, 431
pilots
    design planning, 395–396
    test planning, 284–285
PIMG (PBX/IP Media Gateway), SIP (Session Initiation Protocol), 658–659
planning
    correlation point, 303–305
    deployment methodology, 277
    design criteria, 307
    installation dependencies, 292
        messaging infrastructure, 298–302
        messaging system connectivity, 295–298
        switch connectivity, 293–295
    installation with Domino, 558
        domain, 560–563
        DUCS (Domino Unified Communications Services), 563–565
        trending, 558–560
    messaging infrastructure, 302–303
    migration tasks, 288–292
    site surveys, 306–307

subscriber access, 305–306
testing capabilities, 283–287
Unity installation with Exchange, 492
    administration planning, 501–502
    capacity planning, 496–497
    designing operation management, 502–503
    serving Exchange, 493
    trending, 497–499
    UM Readiness assessment, 493–496
    Unity affect on Exchange, 501
    Unity effect on Exchange, 499–501
Unity solution design, 389
    feature evaluation, 390–391
    lab trials, 394–395
    legacy voice-message system user analysis, 391–394
    pilot, 395–397
    site surveys, 397–398
    survey data organization, 399
upgrades
    downtime scheduling, 572
    evaluate version upgrading to, 569
    fallback, 574
    fallback lab trial, 570
    lab trial, 569–570
    operation verification, 573–574
    performing upgrade, 573
    server cleanup, 570–571
    server site survey, 572
    walkthrough tasks, 571
playing audio, MIU, 213
pooled licensing, 413, 454
Port Availability report, 247, 741
PORT parameter, Exchange 5.5 default search scope, 139, 141
Port Status Monitor (PSM), troubleshooting audio-text applications, 748–750
Port Time Use report, 248, 742
Port Usage Analyzer tool, 247–248
    indexing columns, 828
    reports, 741–742
PortMemory switch file setting, 924
ports, server installation planning, 305
post-implementation assessment, performing, 599
post-installation server tuning, 598

pre-cutover tasks, 590
 configuration testing, 590
 conversations test plan, 591
 go/no go decision making, 594–595
 integration testing, 591
 simulated load testing, 592–594
 subscriber enrollment, 595
pre-installation tasks for Unity server installation,
 586
 administrative console configuration, 587
 monitoring facility, 588
 schema extension, 588
 verifying account permissions, 588
preferences, Cisco Unity Assistant, 234
preliminary design proposals, 384
 development, 387–388
 interoperability verification, 386–387
 surveys, 384–386
presales
 deployment methodology, 273–276
 Unity solution design
  bill of materials (BOM), 389
  cost analysis, 388–389
  develop design options, 387–388
  preliminary design proposal, 384–387
  requirements, 382–384
primary domain accounts collection, 103
primary domain groups collection, 103
PrimaryFaxNumber property, 870
private distribution lists, 426
private lists
 Cisco Unity Assistant, 234
 TUI personal settings, 228
private messages, 226
Product Information call handler, 709
profiles
 audio-text applications, 666–669
 Bulk Edit Utility, 803
 documents (Domino), 556–558
 Select Subscriber Changes page, 786–787
programmatic administration
 adding public distribution list, 896–900
 APIs support, 819
 call handler information retrieval, 848–853
 creating subscribers, 856–865
 deleting subscribers, 884–893

 editing subscribers, 868–872
  alternate extensions, 872–876
  batch operations, 881–883
  error greetings, 879–881
  password updates, 878–879
  user-input key settings, 876–878
 importing subscribers, 865–868
 locating extensions in dialing domain, 841–846
 locating subscribers, 838–841
 locating Unity servers, 838
 member addition to public distribution list,
  903–906
 property removal in Active Directory, 893–896
 removing public distribution list, 900–903
 SQL rights, 820–822
 subscriber information retrieval, 853–856
 Unity server connection, 823
  connection method, 825–829
  list servers running SQL, 823–825
  making connection, 831–832
  multiple connections, 829–831
  server version and license information,
   833–838
 Unity web-based SA interface, 847–848
 UnityDB SQL database rules, 822
prompts
 audio-text applications, 735
  directory handler name-spelling, 738
  holding for transfer, 736–737
  locating, 736
  recording message after tone, 737–738
 language options, 702–703
properties
 COS objects, 94
 removal using Active Directory, 893–896
proposals, preliminary design, 384
 interoperability verification, 386–387
 surveys, 384–386
protocols
 digital networks, 414
 directory monitor, 137
 setting, integration file, 617
PSM (Port Status Monitor), troubleshooting audio-
 text applications, 748–750
public distribution lists
 adding, 896–900

digital networks, 425–426, 455
    controlling access, 457–458
    extensions, 455
    importing, 456
    list builder, 456–457
    subscriber template, 456
    member addition, 903–906
    removing, 900–903
PW (password policy) object, 104
PwPolicy table, 118

Q-R

questionnaires, legacy voice-message system
    analysis, 391

RDBSvr component (Relational Database Server
    component), 44
Recall switch file setting, 920
Recipient object ID, call handler, 90–91
RecipientEmailAddress property, directory
    synchronization, 870
reconfiguration, 574–575
recording audio, MIU, 213
recording message after tone prompt, 737–738
REFER method, SIP (Session Initiation Protocol),
    652
REGISTER method, SIP (Session Initiation
    Protocol), 651–652
Registry, 122–130
Regsvr32 adsiedit.dll command, ADSI Edit
    utility, 761
Relational Database Server component (RDBSvr
    component), 44
release 5.0, 915
remote subscribers, locating, 838–841
remote users, voice message accessibility, 20–22
RemoteAddress property, directory synchronization,
    870
replicas (Domino database), 534
REPLICATION_PERIOD parameter, Exchange 5.5
    default search scope, 139–141
Report Director component, Registry, 124
Report Director Server service, 54–55
Report Manager component, Registry, 124
report status page, Status Monitor, 249
ReportDB database, 121

reports, 247
    activity, 741–742
    Port Usage Analyzer tool, 247–248
requirements, Unity solution design, 382
    acceptance criteria, 382–383
    capability matching, 383
    decision finalizing, 383–384
resource manager, 36
ResourceLoader component, Registry, 129
RestrictDialing switch file setting, 922
restriction tables, object model, 104
RestrictionPattern table, UnityDB database, 118
RestrictionTable table, UnityDB database, 118
retrieving messages, 174–176, 200–203
RetryCount switch file setting, 924
RetryInterval switch file setting, 924
ring voltage, 630–633
RingbackTimeout switch file setting, 922
routing
    group Exchange, unified messaging
        configuration, 328
    mail (Domino), 541–544
    ruler component, 37
routing rules, 266
    audio-text applications, 695
        checking phone switch information,
            695–698
        rule order, 698–701
    resetting defaults, 745
    troubleshooting audio-text applications,
        750–753
Rule table, UnityDB database, 118
RuleIndex column, 698–701
ruler component, 37, 129
rules. *See* routing rules

S

SA, 239–240
    activity reports, 741–742
    call transfer page, 669–673
    caller-input page, 676–678
    COS (class of service), 240–241
    directory handlers, 688–694
    field help, 241
    greetings page, 674–675

interview handlers, 685–688

messages page, 678–679

MMC (Media Master control), 241

online help, 241

profile page, 666–669

subscriber templates, 240

subscriber updates, 77–80

Unity web-based interface, 847–848

web interface administrator access, 77

SA branch, Registry, 129

Save Log Files dialog box, 771, 777

Say Goodbye call handler, 704

scaling domain (Domino), 539–540

SCCP (Skinny Client Control Protocol), 293

Schedule table, 118–119

schedules, 259–260

    call handler, 92–93

    reconstructing, 746

scope distribution lists, object extensibility, 152

ScopeDList table, distribution lists, 108

ScopeDListMember table, distribution lists, 109

search scopes, directory monitor, 138

    Domino, 143

    Exchange 2000, 141–143

    Exchange 2003, 141–143

    Exchange 5.5, 138–141

sections, 917–922

Secure Sockets Layer protocol (SSL protocol), 253

security, 252–253

    administrative authentication, 253

    Domino, 548

        ACLs, 549–550

        ID file, 548–549

    organization challenges, 17

        confidentiality, 17–18

        encryption, 19

        text-to-speech (TTS) technology, 18–19

    Security Agent, 254–255

    TUI, 253

Security Agent, 254–255

SeekMWIPort switch file setting, 924

Select Domain and Container dialog box, 773

Select Exchange 5.5 Server dialog box, 773

Select Subscriber Changes page (Bulk Edit Utility), 786

    account, 787

    alternate extension, 799

    caller input, 794–796

    conversation, 788–789

    exit destination, 799–800

    extension, 798–799

    greetings, 792–794

    messages, 796–798

    notification, 798

    passwords, 788

    profile, 786–787

    transfer, 790–792

Select Subscriber Data Import Option dialog box, 772, 777

Select Subscriber Template dialog box, 772, 777

Select the CSV File dialog box, 773

Select User Domain and Container dialog box, 777

selection handlers, Name Lookup Handler, 102

Sequential Query Language. *See* SQL

serial integrations, 612–630

serial packets, hang up notification, 638

SerialAutoAnswer switch file setting, 922

SerialConfiguration switch file setting, 923

servers

    access, 305

    CSBridgeConnector service, 56–57

    database replication (Domino), 544–547

    documents (Domino), 540–541

    Domino

        characteristics, 528–529

        database, tasks, 535

    failover, 255–256

    locating, 838

    messaging

        capacity, 299–300

        migration to another, 580–581

    MIU, 213–215

    moving subscribers, 766

    multi–voice messaging configuration, 314–317

    multiple

        COS (class of service), 755–757

        GrantUnityAccess tool, 760–763

        GSM (Global Subscriber Manager), 764–767

        single account admin access, 757–759

    name changes, DiRT, 251

    network connection, 823

        connection method, 825–829

        list servers running SQL, 823–825

making connection, 831–832
multiple connections, 829–831
server version and license information,
    833–838
opening recordset, 831–832
scaling Domino domain, 539–540
single voice messaging configuration, 313–314
sizing, 304
unified messaging configuration, 326
upgrade planning, 570–572
Servers table, UnityDB database, 119
services
    AVCsGateway, 34
    AVCsNodgeMgr, 57–58
    AVDirChangeWriter, 52
    AVLic, 53–54
    AVMMProxyServer, 55–56
    AVRepDirSvrSvc, 54–55
    AVSQLSynchSvr, 53
    AVTTSSvc, 56
    cost analysis, 389
    CSBridgeConnector, 56–57
    CSEMSSvc, 55
    TomCat, 58
servicing capabilities, Exchange, 524
Session Initiation Protocol. *See* SIP
shared messaging, digital networks, 415
SID property, directory synchronization, 870
SIDHistory property, directory synchronization, 870
SIDHistory table, UnityDB database, 119
silence counters, 249
Simplified Message Desk Interface (SMDI), 293
simulated load testing, 592–594
single messaging systems, 295
single servers, voice messaging configuration,
    313–314
Single Site Call Processing, Cisco IP Telephony
    deployment model, 340
single-site messaging, deployment model, 345
    GUI and web access, 351–353
    multiserver configuration, 348–351
    single-server configuration, 346–348
    unified messaging, 353–359
single sites, design planning surveys, 385
single user accounts, admin access, 757–759
single-directory infrastructure, 297

SIP (Session Initiation Protocol), 43–44, 266, 294
    features, 266–267
    switch integration, 649
        call information, 655
        components, 650
        digit detection and generation, 657
        failover, 657–658
        media format negotiation, 655–657
        methods, 650–654
        PIMG (PBX/IP Media Gateway), 658–659
SIP Proxy servers, 295
site surveys
    design planning
        data organization, 399
        messaging infrastructure, 397
        physical placement, 398
        switch infrastructure, 398
        user density, 398
    installation planning, 306–307
Skinny Client Control Protocol (SCCP), 293
Skinny protocol, Registry, 124
SMDI (Simplified Message Desk Interface), 293
SMTP, networking, 265
SMTPAddress property, directory synchronization,
    870
software, cost analysis, 388–389
special-case users, legacy voice-message system
    analysis, 392
speed control, TUI message playback, 227
SQL (Sequential Query Language), 819
    AVSQLSynchSvr service, 53
    databases, 105–107
        ReportDB, 121
        UnityDB, 107–121
    rights, 820–822
    servers, finding in Windows domain, 824–825
SQLSyncer process, directory monitor full
    synchronization, 147
SRST (Survivable Remote Site Telephony), 360
SSL protocol (Secure Sockets Layer protocol), 253
standard greeting, call handling, 88
startup
    CallManager TSP, 645–646
    MAPI, 182–183
Status Monitor, 248–249

storage
    data, 105
        directory, 130–131
        local files, 131–133
        Registry, 122–130
        SQL database, 105–121
    inbox monitor, 180–181
    messages, audio format, 263–264
    voice messages, 19–20
        end user accessibility, 20–22
        fax integration, 23
        unified message (UM) coexistence, 22–23
StreamsToDelete table, UnityDB database, 119
subscriber enrollment (pre-cutover), 595
Subscriber Sign In conversation, 39
Subscriber table, UnityDB database, 120
SubscriberPwDTMFHistory table, UnityDB
  database, 120
subscribers
    access planning, 305–306
    audio-text applications, 685
    Bulk Edit Utility, 782–783
        applying call handler changes, 811
        applying changes, 800
        call handlers, 800–811
        main form, 783
        Select Subscriber Changes page, 786–800
        selecting subscribers, 784–786
    Bulk Import
        correcting errors, 777–779
        CSV files, 770–776
        data from message store directory,
          776–777
        modify existing accounts, 779–780
    Bulk Subscriber Delete tool, 780–782
    call handlers, lock down, 715–719
    COS (class of service), 240–241
    creating, 856–865
    default template objects, rebuilding, 746
    deleting, 765, 884–893
    digital networks, 428
    directory monitor synchronization queries, 144
    directory synchronization, 874
    editing, 868–872
        alternate extensions, 872–876
        batch operations, 881–883
        error greetings, 879–881
        password updates, 878–879
        user-input key settings, 876–878
    extensions, conflicts in dialing domain,
      843–844
    importing, 243, 865–868
    information retrieval, 853–856
    legacy voice-message system, analysis,
      391–394
    locating, 838–846
    mail users collection, 97
        alternate extensions, 100
        call handler, 99
        COS object, 99
        location object, 100
        notification device, 97–98
        notification MWI, 98–99
        notification rule, 98
        personal distribution list, 99
    mail users templates, 100–101
    message identification, 267
    Migrate Subscriber Data tool, 811–814
    moving between servers, 766
    object extensibility, 151
    primary domain accounts collection, 103
    primary domain groups collection, 103
    report, 247
    SA update, 77–80
    SQL alias query, 840
    SQL dialing domain query, 839
    SQL directory query, 839
    SQL extension query, 840
    templates, 240, 769
    transfer rules, 729–730
    TUI features, 226
        administrator management, 235–239
        Cisco PCA, 232–235
        mail clients, 229–231
        message management, 227–228
        message playback, 227
        message sending, 226
        personal settings, 228–229
SubscriberTemplate table, UnityDB database, 120
subscriber-to-subscriber messages, 189–195
    conversation/MIU traces, 193–195
SubSignIn conversation, 39
support
    legacy voice-message system analysis, 393

organization challenges, 26–27
supported third-party tools
    backup software, 909–910
    fax server software, 909
    monitoring software, 910
    virus-scanning software, 910–911
surveys
    design planning
        data organization, 399
        messaging infrastructure, 397
        physical placement, 398
        switch infrastructure, 398
        user density, 398
    design planning proposals, 384
        deployment model specification, 386
        equipment, 385
        site specifications, 385
Survivable Remote Site Telephony (SRST), 360
switch files
    legacy PBXs, 603–604
    settings, 917, 923–924
switches
    checking information, 695–698
    connectivity dependency, 293
        CallManager version, 294
        connection capacity, 294
        integration type, 293–294
        PBXs support, 293
        programming requirements, 294
        SIP Proxy servers, 295
        Unity switch support, 293
    infrastructure, 398
    integration
        CallManager TSP, 638–649
        legacy PBXs, 602–638
        SIP (Session Initiation Protocol), 649–659
    TAPI interface, 42–43
SwitchManufacturer switch file setting, 918
SwitchModel switch file setting, 918
SwitchSoftwareVersion switch file setting, 918
synchronization
    digital networks, 418–419
    directory monitor
        full, 146–149
        queries, 143–144
    subscribers, batch operations, 882
System Event Messages public distribution list, 705

System Event Messages object, directory default, 153
system information, 836–837
System status page, Status Monitor, 249
SystemDListMember table, distribution lists, 108
SystemParameters branch, Registry, 129
systems management, deployment methodology operations, 280
SystemState table, UnityDB database, 121

T

TAPI (Telephony Application Programming Interface), 27–28, 42–43, 207–208
TDM (time-division multiplexing), 266
    features, 266–267
    phone systems integration, 602
        analog DTMF, 604–612
        call control, 630–638
        integration files, 603–604
        serial, 612–630
        switch files, 603–604
Technical Support call handler, 709–710
Telephone Application Programming Interface (TAPI), 27–28, 42–43, 207–208
Telephone Record and Playback (TRaP), voice message response, 21
telephone systems, integration, 266
    multiple systems, 267–268
    technology features, 266–267
    UTIM (Unity Telephony Integration Manager), 268
Telephone User Interface. *See* TUI
telephony services, MIU, 205–206
    architecture, 213–223
    audio, 213
    call information extraction, 211–212
    client request responses, 212
    events, 213
    subsystem initialization, 209–211
    TAPI, 207–208
telephony switch integration
    CallManager TSP, 638–646, 649
    legacy PBXs, 602–638
    SIP (Session Initiation Protocol), 649–659

templates
    Domino database, 533–534
    mail users, 100–101
    subscriber, 769
    subscribers, 240, 746
tenant services, 732–735
testing
    design planning lab trials, 394
    planning deployment, 283–284
        end-user analysis, 285–287
        pilot test, 284–285
text
    pagers, message notification, 237
    voice message response, 20
Text-to-Speech (TTS), 261–262
    message playback, 175
    organization security, 18–19
third-party tools
    backup software, 909–910
    fax server software, 909
    monitoring software, 910
    unsupported, 912
    virus-scanning software, 910–911
time stamps, 41
time zones, 259–260
time-division multiplexing (TDM), 266–267
Tiny Audio Text Application call handler, 708
TomCat service, 58
ToneDialInterDigitDelay switch file setting, 920
tones
    definitions, call control, 634–636
    template settings, 635
Tools Depot, 242
    Advanced Settings tool, 246
    ATM (Audio Text Manager), 245
    CUBI (Cisco Unity Bulk Import Wizard), 243
    CUPID (Cisco Unified Performance
        Information), 249–250
    GSM (Global Subscriber Manager), 244–245
    maintenance
        DBWalker (Database Walker), 252
        Disaster Recovery tools, 251–252
        EMS (Event Monitoring Service), 251
        MSM (Message Store Manager), 250
    Port Usage Analyzer tool, 247–248
ToolsDepot branch, Registry, 129

topology
    messages, management, 12–14
    multiple servers, 757
traffic, legacy voice-message system analysis, 393
training
    legacy voice-message system analysis, 393–394
    users, unified messaging (UM), 24
Transfer Call Billing report, 741
TransferInitiate switch file setting, 920
transfers
    Bulk Edit Utility, 803–805
    external number call handler, 713–715
    forwarding rule override, 730–731
    operator console to voice-mail, 731–732
    rules, audio-text applications, 682–683
    Select Subscriber Changes page, 790–792
    subscriber rules, 729–730
    TUI features, 229
TRaP (Telephone Record and Playback)
    connection server, 44–45
    voice message response, 21
trending
    Domino, 558–560
    Exchange, 497–499
trials
    design planning, 394
        configuration options, 394
        mockup installation analysis, 395
        production network mockup, 394
        test plans, 394
    upgrade planning, 569–570
TrimDisconnectTonesOnRecordings switch file
    setting, 921
troubleshooting audio-text applications
    Call Viewer application, 747
    call-routing rules diagnostics, 750–753
    event log, 746–747
    PSM (Port Status Monitor), 748–750
Troubleshooting Cisco IP Telephony, 361
trusted domains collection, object model, 104
TSP (TAPI service provider), CallManager, 207,
    638, 640
    audio control, 643–644
    call control, 640–642
    call information, 642–643
    CallManager clusters, 646–649

MWI, 646
startup, 645–646
TTS (Text-to-Speech)), 261–262
message playback, 175
objects, MIU, 218
organization security, 18–19
performance counters, 249
Registry, 129
TTY Angel tool, 260
TTY prompt set, hearing impairments, 260
TTY/TDD devices, user applications, 738–741
TUI (Telephone User Interface), 135, 226
administrator management
alternate extensions, 238–239
message notification, 236–238
MWI (message waiting indicator), 235
applications, 38–40
Cisco PCA, 232
Unity Assistant, 234–235
Unity Inbox, 232–233
mail clients, 229
message management, 231
message playback, 231
message sending, 230
messages
actions, 174
management, 227–228
playback, 227
retrieval, 200–203
sending, 226
personal settings, 228–229
security, 253
turnpike affect, 25

U

UMs (unified messages), 5
configurations, 318–319
domain boundaries, 325–326
Domino, 334–335
Exchange, 319–323, 326
Exchange 2000, 327–333
Exchange 2003, 327–331
partner server, 319
Windows 2000 domain, 335–336
deployment methodology, 275

history, 5–7
messaging infrastructure, 298–299
domain configuration, 301–302
domain controllers, 300–301
name-resolution hosts, 301
network connectivity, 302
server capacity, 299–300
migration planning, 290–291
organization challenges, 11–12
e-mail perception issues, 14–17
messaging topology management, 12–14
security issues, 17–19
solution and deployment, 23–24
user adaptation, 24–25
user support, 26–27
voice message storage, 19–23
Readiness, Exchange, 493–496
single site messaging deployment model, 353
Domino, 359
Exchange 2000, 353–355
Exchange 2003, 353–355
Exchange 5.5, 357
Unity, 7–8
Unity Messaging Repository (UMR), 9
versus integrated messaging, 10–11
UMR (Unity Messaging Repository), 9, 37, 174
addressing message text file contents, 187
branch, Registry, 129
message delivery diagnostics, 188
message processing, 190
message spoofing algorithm, 192
messaging component, 178–179
Registry, 130
voice message storage, 19
Unaddressed Messages object
directory default, 153
public distribution list, 705
unified messages (UMs), 5
configurations, 318–319
domain boundaries, 325–326
Domino, 334–335
Exchange, 319–326
Exchange 2000, 327–333
Exchange 2003, 327–331
partner server, 319
Windows 2000 domain, 335–336
deployment methodology, 275

history, 5–7
messaging infrastructure, 298–299
domain configuration, 301–302
domain controllers, 300–301
name-resolution hosts, 301
network connectivity, 302
server capacity, 299–300
migration planning, 290–291
organization challenges, 11–12
e-mail perception issues, 14–17
messaging topology management, 12–14
security issues, 17–19
solution and deployment, 23–24
user adaptation, 24–25
user support, 26–27
voice message storage, 19–23
Readiness, Exchange, 493–496
single site messaging deployment model, 353
Domino, 359
Exchange 2000, 353–355
Exchange 2003, 353–355
Exchange 5.5, 357
Unity, 7–9
Unity Assistant
access, 305
Bridge, 578
Cisco PCA, 234–235
Diagnostic Tool, 42
pure unified messaging product, 7–8
Unity Messaging Repository (UMR), 9
versus integrated messaging, 10–11
Unity Fundamentals, 292
Unity Inbox
access, 305
Cisco PCA, 232–233
Unity Messaging Repository (UMR), 9, 37
Registry, 130
voice message storage, 19
Unity System Administration Guide, 31
Unity Telephony Integration Manager (UTIM), 268
Unity User Guides, 31
Unity_Servername object, directory default, 153
UnityAvWav object, MIU, 218–219
UnityAVWAVE component, 44
UnityDB database, 107–121, 821–822
UnitySetupParameters table, UnityDB database, 121
unsupported third-party tools, 912

UpdateDisplay switch file setting, 923
upgrades
management, 567–568
planning
downtime scheduling, 572
evaluate version upgrading to, 569
fallback, 574
fallback lab trial, 570
lab trial, 569–570
operation verification, 573–574
performing upgrades, 573
server cleanup, 570–571
server site survey, 572
walkthrough tasks, 571
user-input, key settings, 876–878
users
admin access, 755–757
GrantUnityAccess tool, 760–763
single accounts, 757–759
change in directory, 72–77
density determination, 398
groups, legacy voice-message system analysis,
392
importing from Active Directory, 765
legacy voice-message system, analysis,
391–394
mail collection, object model, 97–100
mail templates, object model, 100–101
migration, extracting data, 291–292
subscriber templates, 240
support, challenges, 26–27
testing analysis, 285–287
unified messaging (UM) adaptation, 24
features, 24–25
training, 24
turnpike affect, 25
voice message, accessibility, 20–22
UTIM (Unity Telephony Integration Manager), 268

V

verifying user account permissions, 588
ViewMail for Outlook (VMO), TUI features, 229
Viewmail for Outlook (VMO), 305
views (Domino database), 532–533
virtual queue, 44

VirtualQueue branch, Registry, 130
virus-scanning software, 910–911
VMO (ViewMail for Outlook), 229, 305
voice messages
    Cisco PCA
        Unity Assistant, 234–235
        Unity Inbox, 232–233
    configuration, 313
        DCGCs for Exchange 2000, 317
        multiserver, 314–317
        single-server, 313–314
    deployment methodology, 276
    Domino, 553
    mail-clients, 230-231
    migration planning, 291
    planning messaging, infrastructure, 302–303
    storage, 19–20
        end user accessibility, 20–22
        fax integration, 23
        unified message (UM) coexistence, 22–23
    TUI playback, 227
voice messaging-only configuration, migration to unified messaging configuration, 578–579
Voice Profile for Internet Mail (VPIM), 577

voice-mail, design planning evaluation, 390
VoiceName property, directory synchronization, 870
VoIP (Voice over IP), AGC (Automatic Gain Control), 263–264
VPIM (Voice Profile for Internet Mail), 577

W-Z

WaitAnswerRings switch file setting, 921
WaitIfBufferedPacketPresent switch file setting, 922
WANs, centralized messaging, 359–363
    Domino, 365
    Exchange 2000, 364–365
    Exchange 5.5, 363
    multisite, 366–371
Windows 2000, domain, 335–336
Windows Messaging component, Registry, 124
Windows Monitor (AvWm)m 45–46, 177–178

XferString property, directory synchronization, 871

SEARCH THOUSANDS OF BOOKS FROM LEADING PUBLISHERS

Safari® Bookshelf is a searchable electronic reference library for IT professionals that features more than 2,000 titles from technical publishers, including Cisco Press.

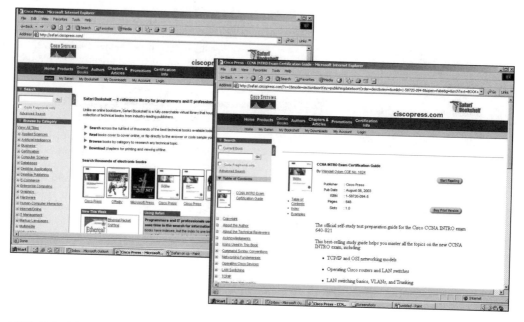

With Safari Bookshelf you can

- **Search** the full text of thousands of technical books, including more than 70 Cisco Press titles from authors such as Wendell Odom, Jeff Doyle, Bill Parkhurst, Sam Halabi, and Karl Solie.

- **Read** the books on My Bookshelf from cover to cover, or just flip to the information you need.

- **Browse** books by category to research any technical topic.

- **Download** chapters for printing and viewing offline.

With a customized library, you'll have access to your books when and where you need them—and all you need is a user name and password.

TRY SAFARI BOOKSHELF FREE FOR 14 DAYS!

You can sign up to get a 10-slot Bookshelf free for the first 14 days. Visit **http://safari.ciscopress.com** to register.

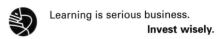

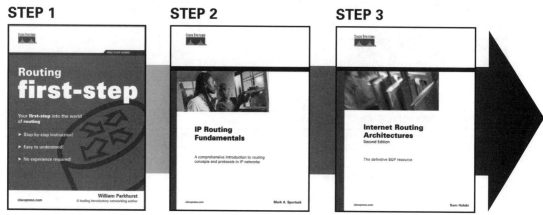

CISCO SYSTEMS

Cisco Press

Your **first-step** to networking starts here

Are you new to the world of networking? Whether you are beginning your networking career or simply need a better understanding of technology to gain more meaningful discussions with networking experts, Cisco Press First-Step books are right for you.

➤ **No experience required**

➤ **Includes clear and easily understood explanations**

➤ **Makes learning easy**

Check out each of these First-Step books that cover key networking topics:

- **Computer Networking First-Step**
  ISBN: 1-58720-101-1

- **LAN Switching First-Step**
  ISBN: 1-58720-100-3

- **Network Security First-Step**
  ISBN: 1-58720-099-6

- **Routing First-Step**
  ISBN: 1-58720-122-4

- **TCP/IP First-Step**
  ISBN: 1-58720-108-9

- **Wireless Networks First-Step**
  ISBN: 1-58720-111-9

Visit **www.ciscopress.com/firststep** to learn more.

What's your next step?

Eager to dig deeper into networking technology? Cisco Press has the books that will help you move to the next level. Learn more at **www.ciscopress.com/series**.

ciscopress.com   **Learning begins with a first step.**

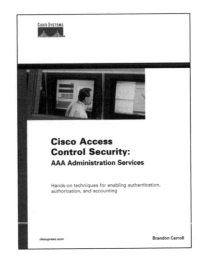

CISCO SYSTEMS

Cisco Press

DISCUSS

NETWORKING PRODUCTS AND TECHNOLOGIES WITH CISCO EXPERTS AND NETWORKING PROFESSIONALS WORLDWIDE

VISIT NETWORKING PROFESSIONALS
A CISCO ONLINE COMMUNITY
WWW.CISCO.COM/GO/DISCUSS

THIS IS THE POWER OF THE NETWORK. now.

CISCO SYSTEMS

☐ **YES!** I'm requesting a **free** subscription to *Packet*™ magazine.

☐ No. I'm not interested at this time.

☐ Mr.
☐ Ms.

_____
First Name (Please Print)   Last Name

_____
Title/Position (Required)

_____
Company (Required)

_____
Address

_____
City   State/Province

_____
Zip/Postal Code   Country

_____
Telephone (Include country and area codes) Fax

_____
E-mail

_____
Signature (Required)   Date

☐ I would like to receive additional information on Cisco's services and products by e-mail.

1. Do you or your company:
A ☐ Use Cisco products   C ☐ Both
B ☐ Resell Cisco products   D ☐ Neither

2. Your organization's relationship to Cisco Systems:
A ☐ Customer/End User   E ☐ Integrator   J ☐ Consultant
B ☐ Prospective Customer   F ☐ Non-Authorized Reseller   K ☐ Other (specify):
C ☐ Cisco Reseller   G ☐ Cisco Training Partner
D ☐ Cisco Distributor   I ☐ Cisco OEM   _____

3. How many people does your entire company employ?
A ☐ More than 10,000   D ☐ 500 to 999   G ☐ Fewer than 100
B ☐ 5,000 to 9,999   E ☐ 250 to 499
c ☐ 1,000 to 4,999   f ☐ 100 to 249

4. Is your company a Service Provider?
A ☐ Yes   B ☐ No

5. Your involvement in network equipment purchases:
A ☐ Recommend   B ☐ Approve   C ☐ Neither

6. Your personal involvement in networking:
A ☐ Entire enterprise at all sites   F ☐ Public network
B ☐ Departments or network segments at more than one site   D ☐ No involvement
C ☐ Single department or network segment   E ☐ Other (specify):
                                                              _____

7. Your Industry:
A ☐ Aerospace   G ☐ Education (K–12)   K ☐ Health Care
B ☐ Agriculture/Mining/Construction U ☐ Education (College/Univ.) L ☐ Telecommunications
C ☐ Banking/Finance   H ☐ Government—Federal   M ☐ Utilities/Transportation
D ☐ Chemical/Pharmaceutical   I ☐ Government—State   N ☐ Other (specify):
E ☐ Consultant   J ☐ Government—Local   _____
F ☐ Computer/Systems/Electronics

CPRESS

PACKET

Packet magazine serves as the premier publication linking customers to Cisco Systems, Inc. Delivering complete coverage of cutting-edge networking trends and innovations, *Packet* is a magazine for technical, hands-on users. It delivers industry-specific information for enterprise, service provider, and small and midsized business market segments. A toolchest for planners and decision makers, *Packet* contains a vast array of practical information, boasting sample configurations, real-life customer examples, and tips on getting the most from your Cisco Systems' investments. Simply put, *Packet* magazine is straight-talk straight from the worldwide leader in networking for the Internet, Cisco Systems, Inc.

We hope you'll take advantage of this useful resource. I look forward to hearing from you!

Cecelia Glover
Packet Circulation Manager
packet@external.cisco.com
www.cisco.com/go/packet

PACKET